HLT 2002

Human Language Technology Conference

Proceedings of the Second International Conference on Human Language Technology Research

March 24-27, 2002

San Diego, California

Edited by Mitchell Marcus

Sponsored in part by

Defense Advanced Research Project Agency

National Science Foundation

Association for Computational Linguistics

in cooperation with

International Speech Communication Association

Production and Manufacturing by
Omnipress, Inc.
Post Office Box 7214
Madison, WI 53707-7214

Order copies of this and other DARPA publications from:

Morgan Kaufmann Publishers
San Francisco

http://www.mkp.com
orders@mkp.com
800-745-7323 (407-345-3800 for international calls)
(fax) 800-874-6418 (407-345-4060 for international calls)

HLT 2002, Second Conference on Human Language Technology Research
ISBN: 0-12-470870-6

Preface from the Conference and Program Chair

Human language technology (HLT) incorporates a broad spectrum of disciplines working towards two closely related goals: to enable computers to interact with humans using natural language capabilities, and to serve as useful adjuncts to humans in language understanding by providing services such as automatic translation, information retrieval and information extraction. Human Language Technology 2002 provided a single unified forum for researchers across this entire spectrum of disciplines to present very recent high-quality, cutting-edge work, to exchange ideas and to explore emerging new research directions.

The conference received 171 submissions of very high quality from across all areas of Human Language Technologies. The program committee worked quite hard to select the very best papers and demonstration proposals from this group, while maintaining reasonable balance across the various subfields of HLT, and insuring that accepted papers were widely accessible. Essentially all submissions received two full reviews, plus a "breadth" review from outside the topic area of the submission to insure accessibility. Of the 30 proposals for demonstrations, 20 were chosen for presentation, five of these at a plenary session. Of the remaining 141 submissions for papers and posters, 28 were chosen for presentation at the conference as papers (20 %), and 21 as posters (15 %). The conference was kicked off to a wonderful start by a keynote speech by Bill Swartout of the Institute for Creative Technologies.

HLT 2002 included a special focus on Language Processing of Biological Data, sponsored by the National Science, intended to bring to the attention of a wide audience the research opportunities and recent breakthroughs in these newly emerging areas. A subcommittee consisting of Aravind Joshi and Lynette Hirschman organized these focus sessions, which included tutorial sessions presented by J. Tsujii of the University of Tokyo and Richard Hughey of UC Santa Cruz, an invited talk by Russ Altman of Stanford, and a special paper session.

I would like to thank all those who played a role in organizing this conference and in making it a success, but especially the Executive Committee who guided the review and paper selection process through a set of very demanding deadlines, and the Program Committee for a very thorough job of reviewing. James Allan, the chair of HLT 2001 and the driving force behind reviving the HLT conferences, was a constant source of good advise when needed. The team at SPAWAR of Bob Younger, Sally Parker, Sue Ellen Moore, Matt Tran and Candy Kwiatkowski did a wonderful job of providing web support to for electronic submission and reviewing, and of handling networking and computer support during the conference itself. The financial and logistic support of the conference sponsors, DARPA, NSF, and ACL is very much appreciated.

Finally, I would like to offer very special thanks to Priscilla Rasmussen of ARCS, who did a remarkable job of organizing the myriad logistics of the conference, and who provided wonderful support during the conference itself. Thanks to Christine Metz for helping with support during the conference. Also, very special thanks to David Yarowsky, the conference co-Chair, for providing back-up whenever it was needed without fail, and for the onerous job of helping to assemble these final proceedings.

Mitchell Marcus
HLT 2002 Conference and Program Chair
Department of Computer and Information Science
University of Pennsylvania

HLT 2002 Conference Committee

General chair: Mitch Marcus, University of Pennsylvania (USA)
Co-chair: David Yarowsky, Johns Hopkins University (USA)

Special Focus Committee:
Chair: Aravind Joshi, University of Pennsylvania (USA)
Co-chair: Lynette Hirschman, MITRE (USA)

Demonstration Co-chairs:
Clifford Weinstein, MIT Lincoln Laboratory (USA)
Bob Younger, SPAWAR Systems Center (USA)

HLT 2002 Conference Coordinator: Priscilla Rasmussen, ARCS/ACL/IJCAII (USA)

Local Arrangements:
- Candy Kwiatkowski, SPAWAR
- Sally Parker, SPAWAR
- Sue Ellen Moore, SPAWAR
- Matt Tran, SPAWAR
- Bob Younger, SPAWAR

Conference Administration:
- Christine Metz, University of Pennsylvania
- Dan Bikel, University of Pennsylvania

Executive Program Committee:

- James Allan, University of Massachusetts (USA)
- Sadaoki Furui, Tokyo Institute of Technology (Japan)
- Ralph Grishman, New York University (USA)
- Donna Harman, NIST (USA)
- Lynette Hirschman, MITRE (USA)
- Eduard Hovy, ISI (USA)
- Kevin Knight, ISI (USA)
- Joseph Mariani, LIMSI-CNRS (France)
- John Makhoul, BBN Technologies (USA)
- Nelson Morgan, University of California at Berkeley (USA)
- Mari Ostendorf, University of Washington (USA)
- Hans Uszkoreit, Saarland University and DKFI (Germany)

Program Committee:

- Salah Ait-Mokhtar, Xerox Research Centre Europe (France)
- Alex Acero, Microsoft (USA)
- Tim Anderson, WPAFB (USA)
- Doug Appelt, SRI (USA)
- Breck Baldwin, Baldwin Language Technologies (USA)
- Srinivas Bangalore, AT&T Research (USA)
- Jerome Bellegarda, Apple Computer (USA)
- Ole Bernsen, NIS (Denmark)
- Christian Blaschke, CNB (National Center for Biotechnology) (Spain)
- Thorsten Brants, Xerox PARC (USA)
- Michael Brent, Washington University (USA)
- Eric Brill, Microsoft Research (USA)
- John Carroll, University of Sussex (UK)

- Khalid Choukri, ELRA/ELDA (Luxembourg and France)
- Renato de Mori, LIA (France)
- Gregor Erbach, Saarland University (Germany)
- Eric Fosler-Lussier, Bell Laboratories (USA)
- Horacio Franco, SRI International (USA)
- Jean-Luc Gauvain, LIMSI (France)
- Edouard Geoffrois, DGA (France)
- Bjorn Granstrom, CTT/KTH (Sweden)
- John Grieco, Air Force Research Lab (USA)
- David Grossman, Illinois Institute of Technology (USA)
- Sanda Harabagiu, University of Texas Dallas (USA)
- Ulf Hermjakob, ISI (USA)
- Julia Hirschberg, AT&T (USA)
- Pierre Isabelle, Xerox Research Centre Europe (France)
- Douglas Jones, Lincoln Labs (USA)
- Tatsuya Kawahara, Kyoto University (Japan)
- Sanjeev Khudanpur, Johns Hopkins University (USA)
- Katrin Kirchhoff, University of Washington (USA)
- Kevin Knight, ISI (USA)
- Satoshi Kobayashi, University of Electro-Communications (Japan)
- Wessel Kraaij, TNO TPD (Netherlands)
- Francis Kubala, BBN (USA)
- Roland Kuhn, Panasonic Lab (USA)
- John Lafferty, Carnegie Mellon University (USA)
- Young-Suk Lee, IBM Research (USA)
- Anton Leuski, University of Massachusetts Amherst (USA)
- Liz Liddy, Syracuse University (USA)
- Dekang Lin, University of Alberta (Canada)
- Inderjeet Mani, MITRE (USA)
- Jim Mayfield, Johns Hopkins University (USA)
- Dan Melamed, New York University (USA)
- Helen Meng, Chinese Univ. Hong Kong (Hong Kong)
- Scott Miller, BBN (USA)
- Masaaki Nagata, NTT (Japan)
- Hermann Ney, RWTH Aachen (Germany)
- Corinna Ng, Canon Research Centre Europe (UK)
- Steve Nunn, SPAWAR (USA)
- Paul Over, NIST (USA)
- Ted Pedersen, University of Minnesota (USA)
- Barbara Peskin, ICSI (USA)
- Thilo Pfau, ICSI (USA)
- John Prager, IBM (USA)
- Steve Pullman, Oxford University (UK)
- James Pustejovsky, Brandeis University (USA)
- Dragomir Radev, University of Michigan (USA)
- Steve Renals, Sheffield University (UK)
- Phil Resnik, University of Maryland (USA)
- Ellen Riloff, University of Utah (USA)
- Roni Rosenfeld, Carnegie Mellon University (USA)
- Salim Roukos, IBM (USA)
- Mark Sanderson, Sheffield University (UK)
- Satoshi Sekine, New York University (USA)
- Stephanie Seneff, MIT (USA)
- Amit Singhal, Google (USA)
- Karen Sparck Jones, Cambridge University (UK)
- Beth Sundheim, SPAWAR (USA)
- Kentaro Torisawa, JAIST (Japan)
- Hwee Tou Ng, DSO Singapore (Singapore)
- Alfonso Valencia, CNB (National Center for Biotechnology) (Spain)
- Ellen Voorhees, NIST (USA)
- Wayne Ward, University of Colorado (USA)
- Ralph Weischedel, BBN (USA)
- Janyce Wiebe, University of Pittsburgh (USA)
- Limsoon Wong, Kent Ridge Digital Laboratories (Singapore)
- Alex Yeh (MITRE)

Table of Contents

Plenary Demonstrations (in alphabetical order)

HLT 2002 Conference Program

Sunday, March 24, 2002

11:00 Registration Opens
1:30 Conference Convenes

1:30 SPECIAL FOCUS TUTORIALS: Language Processing of Biological Data
1:30 Special Focus Tutorial 1

NLP Techniques for Information Extraction from Biological Documents
– Resource building and our experience

Professor J. Tsujii, University of Tokyo (Japan)

Demands for Information Extraction (IE) and text mining have been increasing rapidly in the biological and medical sciences. Most of the on-going projects treat medline abstracts since this is the largest collection of papers in these fields. Compared with newspaper articles, reports, etc., the abstracts in these fields have peculiar characteristics, which make the IE task harder than those we have treated so far. In particular, complex term formations, systematic metaphor, numerous semantic classes and various types of co-ordinations and parenthetical expressions pose serious challenges for existing NLP techniques. In this tutorial, I will talk about our experience of IE in these fields together with resource building attempts.

2:50 Break
3:10 Special Focus Tutorial 2

Profile HMMs and other grammatical models of sequences

Professor Richard Hughey, University of California at Santa Cruz (USA)

Since their introduction to biological sequence analysis a decade ago, hidden Markov models (HMMs) have become a standard tool for sequence alignment and remote homology detection. This tutorial examines the effective use of profile HMMs and provides a taste of other modeling techniques such as generalized HMMs and stochastic context-free grammars.

4:30 Break
4:50 Welcome

5:00 KEYNOTE, "Technology Meets the Entertainment Industry: Building Virtual Humans for Immersive Training"

William Swartout, Institute for Creative Technologies, USC

6:00 PAPERS: Across Human Language Technologies

- "Asynchrony Modeling for Audio-visual Speech Recognition"
  Guillaume Gravier, Gerasimos Potamianos and Chalapathy Neti (IBM Thomas J. Watson Research Center)
- "Arabic Speech and Text in TIDES OnTAP"
  Jayadev Billa, Mohamed Noamany, Amit Srivastava, John Makhoul and Francis Kubala (BBN Technologies)
- "Automatic Learning of Dialogue Strategy using Dialogue Simulation and Reinforcement Learning"
  Konrad Scheffler and Steve Young (Cambridge University)

7:20 Reception ("light" hors d'eouvres)
8:45 Adjourn

Monday, March 25, 2002

7:30 Breakfast (provided)
8:30 PAPERS: Speech Recognition

- "Selective Sampling of Training Data for Speech Recognition"
  Teresa Kamm and Gerald G.L. Meyer (Johns Hopkins University)
- "DynaSpeak: SRI's Scalable Speech Recognizer for Embedded and Mobile Systems"
  Horacio Franco, Jing Zheng, John Butzberger, Federico Cesari, Michael Frandsen, Jim Arnold, Venkata Ramana Rao Gadde, Andreas Stolcke and Victor Abrash (SRI International)
- "Word and Sub-word Indexing Approaches for Reducing the Effects of OOV Queries on Spoken Audio"
  Beth Logan, Pedro Moreno and Om Deshmukh (Compaq Computer Corporation)
- "Beyond the Phoneme: A Juncture-accent Model of Spoken Language"
  Steven Greenberg, Hannah Carvery, Leah Hitchcock and Shuangyu Chang (International Computer Science Institute)

10:15 Break
10:45 PAPERS: Summarization

- "The DUC Summarization Evaluations"
  Donna Harman and Paul Over (National Institute of Standards and Technology)
- "Experiments in Multi-document Summarization"
  Barry Schiffman, Ani Nenkova and Kathleen McKeown (Columbia University)
- "Automated Multi-document Summarization in NeATS"
  Chin-Yew Lin and Eduard Hovy (USC/ISI)

12:05 Lunch (provided)

SPECIAL SESSION: LANGUAGE PROCESSING OF BIOLOGICAL DATA

1:30 Intro to special session
1:45 INVITED TALK: Statistical NLP approaches for annotating genes and gene clusters

Dr. Russ Altman,
President, International Society for Computational Biology,
Director, Biomedical Informatics Training Program
Stanford University Medical Center, Stanford University (USA)

Bioinformatics has been driven by a series of data explosions: sequence data, structure data, and functional data (most recently from microarray expression experiments). Another data explosion is the availability of text describing major biological results. Most important biomedical literature since 1966 has been indexed in Medline and is available on the web at PubMed (http://www.ncbi.nlm.nih.gov/entrez/query.fcgi?db=PubMed). The literature is an important source of information to help make sense of the other data explosions. In this talk, I will review some of the challenges for natural language processing in biology, and discuss statistical techniques that my laboratory has used for adding knowledge derived from text to the tasks of 1) improving sequence homology searches, 2) assigning controlled terminologies to free text discussions, 3) evaluating the biological coherence of a group of genes, and 4) creating a lexicon of abbreviations.

2:50 PAPER: Biology and Natural Language Processing

- "Formal Grammars for Estimating Partition Functions of Double-stranded Chain Molecules"
  David Chiang and Aravind Joshi (University of Pennsylvania)

3:15 Break POSTER SETUP DURING THIS BREAK
3:45 PAPERS: Biology and Natural Language Processing

- "Massive Bio-ontology Engineering for NLP"
  Udo Hahn and Stefan Schulz (Freiburg University)
- "Comparative n-gram Analysis of Whole-genome Protein Sequences"
  M. Ganapathiraju, D. Weisser, R. Rosenfeld, J. Carbonell, R. Reddy and J. Klein-Seetharaman (Carnegie Mellon University)
- "The GENIA Corpus: An Annotated Research Abstract Corpus in Molecular Biology Domain"
  Tomoko Ohta, Yuka Tateisi and Jin-Dong Kim (University of Tokyo and CREST, JST)

5:00 Discussion

5:30 Boaster session for poster session
6:15 POSTER SESSION ("heavy" hours d'eouvres)
9:30 Adjourn

Tuesday, March 26, 2002

7:30 Breakfast (provided)
8:50 PAPERS: Text Understanding

- "A Knowledge-rich Approach to Understanding Text About Aircraft Systems"
  Peter Clark, Lisbeth Duncan, Heather Holmback, Tom Jenkins, John Thompson (Boeing)
- "Can we Derive General World Knowledge from Texts?"
  Lenhart Schubert (University of Rochester)

9:45 Boaster session for demonstrations
10:30 DEMONSTRATIONS ("Science Fair")

12:30 Lunch (provided)

2:00 PAPERS: Information Retrieval & Text Tracking and Detection

- "A Formal Approach to Score Normalization for Metasearch"
  R. Manmatha and H. Sever (University of Massachusetts, Amherst)
- "Quantifying Query Ambiguity"
  Steve Cronen-Townsend and W. Bruce Croft (University of Massachusetts, Amherst)
- "An Algorithm for Unsupervised Topic Discovery from Broadcast News Stories"
  Sreenivasa Sista, Richard Schwartz, Timothy R. Leek and John Makhoul (Northeastern University and BBN Technologies)
- "Relevance Models for Topic Detection and Tracking"
  Victor Lavrenko, James Allan, Edward DeGuzman, Daniel LaFlamme, Veera Pollard and Stephen Thomas (University of Massachusetts, Amherst)

3:45 Break
4:15 PAPERS: Machine Translation and Multilingual Systems

- "Named Entity Translation"
  Yaser Al-Onaizan and Kevin Knight (USC/ISI)
- "Speaker, Accent and Language Identification using Multilingual Phone Strings"
  Tanja Schultz, Qin Jin, Kornel Laskowski, Alicia Tribble and Alex Waibel (Carnegie Mellon University)
- "Corpus-based Comprehension and Diagnostic MT Evaluation: Initial Arabic, Chinese, French and Spanish Results"
  Kishore Papineni, Salim Roukos, Todd Ward, John Henderson and Florence Reeder (IBM and MITRE)
- "Automatic Evaluation of Machine Translation Quality using N-gram co-occurrence Statistics"
  George Doddington (NIST)

6:00 Banquet (provided)
8:00 Plenary Demonstration Session

- "A Statistical Mixed-initiative Dialog System for 401k Management"
  Rajesh Balchandran, Linda Boyer, Mark Epstein, Robert Krewson, Margaret Marler, Howard Page, Thomas Kazmierczak and Edward Kemp (IBM T.J. Watson Research Center and T. Rowe Price)
- "OnTAP: Mixed-media Multi-lingual Language Processing"
  Sean Colbath, Scott Shepard, Daben Liu, Amit Srivastava, Jay Billa, James Gugerty, Daniel Kiecza, Mohamed Noamany, Kathleen Egan, Francis Kubala (BBN Technologies and DoD)
- "An Automatic Speech Translation System for Travel Conversation"
  Akitoshi Okumura, Ken-ichi Iso, Shin-ichi Doi, Kiyoshi Yamabana, Ken Hanazawa and Takao Watanabe (NEC Corporation)
- "Medstract: Natural Language Tools for Mining the Biobibliome"
  James Pustejovsky, Brent Cochran and Jose Castaño (Brandeis University and Tufts University)

9:30 Adjourn

Wednesday, March 27, 2002

7:30 Breakfast (provided)
8:30 Panel of Government Sponsors

James Bass, DARPA
John Prange, ARDA
Gary Strong, National Science Foundation
Charles Wayne, DARPA
(another speaker to be arranged)

9:45 Break
10:15 PAPERS: Across Human Language Technologies

- "Does Confidence Annotation Meet the Dialog Goal? A Quantitative Analysis"
  Kadri Hacioglu and Wayne Ward (University of Colorado at Boulder)
- "Statistical Answer-type Identification in Open-domain Question Answering"
  John Prager, Jennifer Chu-Carroll and Krzsztof Czuba (IBM T.J. Watson Research Ctr. and Carnegie Mellon University)
- "Japanese Spoken Document Retrieval Considering OOV Keywords using LVCSR System With OOV Detection Processing"
  Hiromitsu Nishizaki and Seiichi Nakagawa (Toyohashi University of Technology)
- "An Adaptive Approach to Named Entity Extraction for Meeting Applications"
  Fei Huang and Alex Waibel (Carnegie Mellon University)

12:00 Wrap-up session
12:30 Conference ends

PLENARY PAPERS
(in order of presentation)

Asynchrony modeling for audio-visual speech recognition

Guillaume Gravier* Gerasimos Potamianos Chalapathy Neti

IBM Thomas J. Watson Research Center
Yorktown Heights, NY 10598, USA
(—,gpotam,cneti)@us.ibm.com

ABSTRACT

We investigate the use of multi-stream HMMs in the automatic recognition of audio-visual speech. Multi-stream HMMs allow the modeling of asynchrony between the audio and visual state sequences at a variety of levels (phone, syllable, word, etc.) and are equivalent to product, or composite, HMMs. In this paper, we consider such models synchronized at the phone boundary level, allowing various degrees of audio and visual state-sequence asynchrony. Furthermore, we investigate joint training of all product HMM parameters, instead of just composing the model from separately trained audio- and visual-only HMMs. We report experiments on a multi-subject connected digit recognition task, as well as on a more complex, speaker-independent large-vocabulary dictation task. Our results demonstrate that in both cases, joint multi-stream HMM training is superior to separate training of single-stream HMMs. In addition, we observe that allowing state-sequence asynchrony between the HMM audio and visual components improves connected digit recognition significantly, however it degrades performance on the dictation task. The resulting multi-stream models dramatically improve speech recognition robustness to noise, by successfully exploiting the visual modality speech information: For example, at 11 dB SNR, they reduce connected digit word error rate from the audio-only 2.3% to 0.77% audio-visual, and, for the large-vocabulary task, from 28.3% to 19.5%. Compared to the audio-only performance at 10 dB SNR, the use of multi-stream HMMs achieves an effective SNR gain of up to 9 dB and 7 dB respectively, for the two recognition tasks considered.

1. INTRODUCTION

We have made significant progress in *automatic speech recognition* (ASR) for well-defined applications like dictation and medium vocabulary transaction processing tasks in relatively controlled environments. However, ASR performance has yet to reach the level required for speech to become a truly *pervasive user interface*. Indeed, even in "clean" acoustic environments, and for a variety of tasks, state of the art ASR system performance lags human speech perception by up to an order of magnitude [1]. In addition, current systems are quite sensitive to channel, environment, and style of speech variations, as a number of techniques for improving ASR *robustness* have met limited success in severely degraded environments, mismatched to system training [2–4]. Clearly, novel, non-traditional approaches, that use orthogonal sources of information to the acoustic input, are needed to achieve ASR performance closer to the human speech perception level, and robust enough to be deployable in field applications. *Visual speech* constitutes a promising such source, obviously not affected by the acoustic environment and noise.

Both human speech production and perception are bimodal in nature [5, 6]. This fact has recently motivated significant interest in automatic recognition of visual speech, formally known as *automatic lipreading*, or *speechreading*. Work in this field aims at improving ASR by exploring the visual modality of the speaker's mouth region, in addition to the traditional audio modality, thus giving rise to *audio-visual automatic speech recognition* (AVASR) systems [6–14]. There are two main problems in achieving this goal [6]: First, the design of the visual front end, i.e. how to obtain informative visual features given the video of the speaker's face, and, second, the combination of such features with the traditional audio features. In this paper, we concentrate on the latter issue.

A number of audio-visual integration strategies appear in the literature that can be grouped into two broad categories (see Fig. 1): *Feature fusion* methods and *decision fusion* techniques. The first category consists of algorithms that combine the single modality features, by projecting them onto an audio-visual feature space, and subsequently use traditional classifiers to model the generation of the joined audio-visual observations [7–9]. In contrast, decision fusion methods combine single-modality (audio-only and visual-only) classifier outputs (decisions), such as the scores (likelihoods) of the classes of interest on basis of single-modality features.

A popular method within the decision fusion framework employs the *multi-stream hidden Markov model* (MSHMM). Such a model, originally proposed for multi-band (audio-only) speech recognition [15], has been successfully used in the AVASR literature to improve speech recognition performance [9–13]. The MSHMM linearly combines the class log-likelihoods based on the audio- and visual-only observations at a number of possible stages, thus allowing a limited *asynchrony* between the state sequences of its audio and visual HMM components. In most cases, the log-likelihoods are combined at the HMM state level, thus forcing a complete *synchrony* between the two streams. However, it is well known that, although the visual activity and the audio signal are correlated, they are not synchronous. As a matter of fact, the visual activity often precedes the audio signal by as much as 120 ms [14]. To take this asynchrony into account, the MSHMM approach can be used

*Dr. Gravier is currently at IRISA/INRIA Rennes, 35042 Rennes Cedex, France. He can be contacted at ggravier@irisa.fr

Proceedings of HLT 2002, Second International Conference on Human Language Technology Research, M. Marcus, ed., Morgan Kaufmann, San Francisco, 2002.

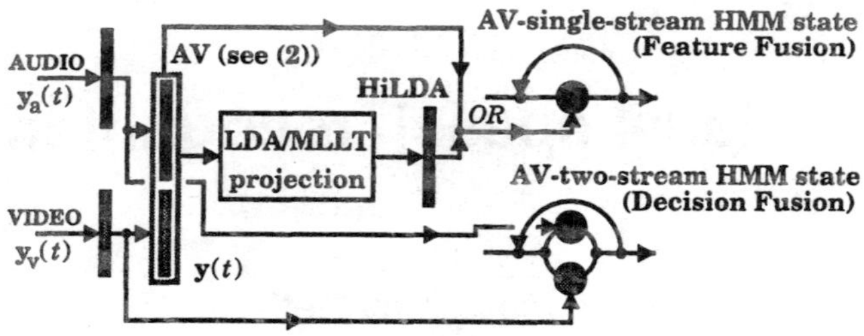

Figure 1: Two feature fusion methods versus multi-stream HMM based decision fusion (see also Figs. 2 and 4).

to combine log-likelihoods at a coarser level than the HMM state, such as the phone, syllable, or word level. Asynchronous multi-stream models are based on the use of *composite* HMMs [16], built as the "*product*" of the audio and visual HMMs (see also Fig. 2). Such product HMMs have already been proposed for AVASR [9–12], however, in these works, they have either been composed by audio-only and visual-only HMMs, which have been *independently* trained for each stream [10–12], or they have been jointly trained without the appropriate stream observation probability tying [9]. As a result, to date, comparisons between state-synchronous and state-asynchronous MSHMMs have been inconclusive and incomplete.

In this paper, we proceed to *jointly* estimate all the product HMM parameters in a single step, using the appropriate stream density tying across states, by employing the standard *expectation-maximization* (EM) HMM parameter estimation algorithm. Such a scheme ensures that the audio-visual state asynchrony within each phone is *modeled at training*, whereas stream tying guarantees that the new model has the *same number* of HMM density parameters as the state-synchronous MSHMM. In addition, in this paper, we investigate whether state-asynchrony modeling is beneficial to AVASR by considering both a small- and a large-vocabulary recognition task, namely, *connected digit* (DIGIT) ASR, and *large-vocabulary continuous speech recognition* (LVCSR) of read, dictation-like, speech. To the extent of the authors' knowledge, such models have seldom been studied on large-vocabulary tasks.

The rest of the paper is organized as follows: In Section 2, we present in detail the MSHMM approach, discuss its implementation as a product HMM, and consider possible maximum likelihood based estimation techniques of MSHMM parameters. Section 3 describes the DIGIT and LVCSR tasks, the audio-visual feature extraction method employed, and some specifics of the recognition algorithm (decoder) and HMMs used. Experimental results are reported in Section 4, followed by our conclusions in Section 5.

2. THE MULTI-STREAM HMM

In this section, we briefly review the multi-stream hidden Markov model in the framework of audio-visual speech recognition, and we discuss strategies for estimating its parameters.

2.1 Preliminaries

Given an audio-visual utterance, we denote the extracted audio and visual features at time t by $\mathbf{y}_s(t)$, where $s = \mathrm{a}, \mathrm{v}$ denotes the audio or visual modality (stream), respectively. Such features are obtained as described in Section 3.2, below, and it is assumed that they are extracted at a common rate (frequency), i.e., that $\mathbf{y}_\mathrm{a}(t)$ and $\mathbf{y}_\mathrm{v}(t)$ are time-synchronous.

Classical single-stream HMMs are used to model sequences of audio- or visual-only features, where the state-conditional density

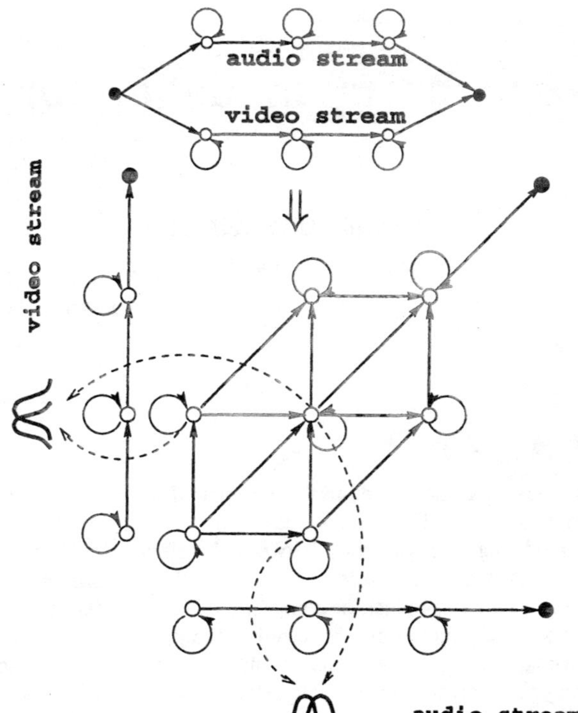

Figure 2: ***Upper:*** **Multi-stream HMM consisting of three audio and three video HMM states.** ***Lower:*** **The corresponding product (composite) HMM that limits the possible asynchrony between the audio and visual state sequences to one state. The class-conditional observation probabilities of its composite audio-visual states are given by (4), with their audio and video component densities tied along states lying on the same column, or row, respectively.**

function (emission probability) is a Gaussian mixture defined as

$$Pr(\mathbf{y}_s(t) \mid i_s) = \sum_{k=1}^{K_{s i_s}} c_{s i_s k} \mathcal{N}_{d_s}(\mathbf{y}_s(t); \mathbf{m}_{s i_s k}, \Sigma_{s i_s k}), \quad (1)$$

where $s = \mathrm{a}, \mathrm{v}$, respectively. In (1), i_s denotes a class (state) of the single-stream HMM used in modality s, and d_s is the dimensionality of observation vector $\mathbf{y}_s(t)$. Typically, the audio and visual HMMs are considered to have an identical set of states $\{i_\mathrm{a}\} = \{i_\mathrm{v}\}$.

Single-stream HMMs are also used in audio-visual feature fusion to model sequences of concatenated audio-visual features

$$\mathbf{y}(t) = [\mathbf{y}_\mathrm{a}(t)^\top, \mathbf{y}_\mathrm{v}(t)^\top]^\top \in \mathrm{R}^d \quad (2)$$

of dimension $d = d_\mathrm{a} + d_\mathrm{v}$ (concatenative feature fusion), or of any transformation of (2), such as the hierarchical discriminant feature fusion [8] (see also Fig. 1 and Section 3.2).

2.2 MSHMMs for audio-visual modeling

The principle of the multi-stream HMM is to model independently each stream between two pre-determined synchronization points, using a number (here, two) of single-stream HMMs of form (1). In this study, the synchronization points are taken to be the *phone boundaries*. At every phone boundary, the log-likelihoods of each stream are linearly combined to get the phone posterior. Such a model can be implemented as a product, or composite, HMM, as illustrated in Fig. 2. In this model, the observation log-likelihood conditioned on an audio-visual state i, that has been composed

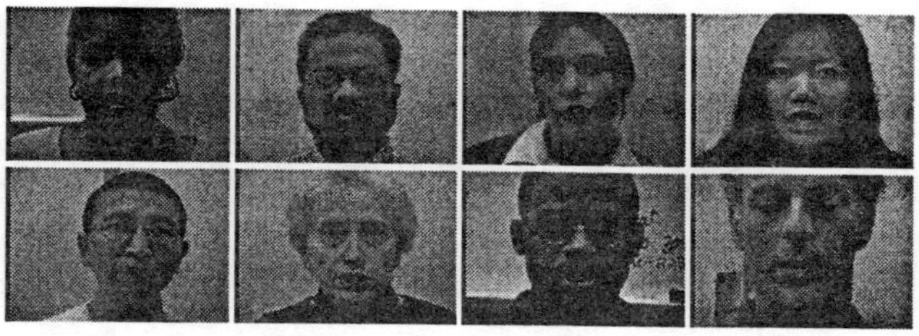

Figure 3: Eight audio-visual database example subjects.

from the audio and visual stream states i_{a} and i_{v}, respectively, is given by

$$\ln \mathcal{L}\,(\mathbf{y}(t)|i) = \lambda_{\mathrm{a}} \ln Pr(\mathbf{y}_{\mathrm{a}}(t)|i_{\mathrm{a}}) + \lambda_{\mathrm{v}} \ln Pr(\mathbf{y}_{\mathrm{v}}(t)|i_{\mathrm{v}})\,. \quad (3)$$

Equivalently, the product HMM emission "score" (or, state-conditional likelihood) is given by (see also (1))

$$\mathcal{L}(\mathbf{y}(t)|i) = \prod_{s\in\{\mathrm{a},\mathrm{v}\}} \Big[\sum_{k=1}^{K_{si_s}} c_{si_sk}\, \mathcal{N}_{d_s}(\mathbf{y}_s(t)\,;\, \mathbf{m}_{si_sk}, \Sigma_{si_sk})\Big]^{\lambda_s}. \quad (4)$$

In (3) and (4), λ_s, where $s = \mathrm{a}, \mathrm{v}$, denote the stream likelihood combination weights (exponents). These determine the contribution of each modality to the joint audio-visual conditional log-likelihood, and they can be used to model the reliability of each stream in deciding about the hidden class i. In general, such weights can also be a function of class i and the time instant t. In this paper, however, we consider them to be constant within each stream, and, in addition, to satisfy $\lambda_{\mathrm{a}}+\lambda_{\mathrm{v}}=1$.

It is not hard to observe that the number of states per phone in the composite HMM (3) is equal to the product of the number of audio and visual phone states (assuming left-to-right single-stream HMMs). Typically, such single-stream phone HMMs consist of 3 states, therefore the resulting MSHMM has 9 states per phone, allowing a within-phone maximum asynchrony of 2 states between its audio and visual state sequences. One can choose to reduce the maximum tolerated within-phone asynchrony of the two streams, by restricting the product model states to appropriate subsets of the Cartesian product $\{i_{\mathrm{a}}\} \times \{i_{\mathrm{v}}\}$. A MSHMM with a one-state maximum asynchrony is illustrated in Fig. 2, where two states are missing w.r.t. the full 9-state product model. In the extreme case of zero maximum asynchrony, and assuming that $\{i_{\mathrm{a}}\} = \{i_{\mathrm{v}}\}$, the product model is equivalent to the state-synchronous MSHMM, and $i = i_{\mathrm{a}} = i_{\mathrm{v}}$ holds.

Note that, although the number of states in the state-asynchronous MSHMM increases compared to the state-synchronous MSHMM, the number of emission density parameters *remains the same*, due to the *stream parameter tying*, inherent in (3). This is also true for the HMM *transition probabilities*, if they are set to the product of the transition probabilities of the single-stream HMMs, for example (transition probability tying).

2.3 Parameter estimation

With the exception of exponents λ_s, maximum-likelihood estimates of all other HMM parameters in (4) can be obtained using the EM algorithm. This can be achieved either separately per-stream (*independent* stream training), or all at once, using *joint* training. The first strategy consists in estimating the stream HMM parameters independently for each stream before composing the product HMM. In this case, the synchrony, or asynchrony, constraints between the two stream models are not considered during training, but only used at recognition, thus creating a mismatch between the training and testing assumptions. In contrast, the second strategy utilizes the product HMM representation of the MSHMM to directly estimate all its parameters using the standard EM procedure. In this scenario, (a)synchrony constraints between the two streams are used for both parameter estimation and decoding. The difference between these two approaches lies on the E-step of the estimation algorithm.

In the AVASR literature, both independent [9,11], and joint training schemes [9,13] have been considered in the case of state-synchronous MSHMMs. However, for state-asynchronous MSHMMs, only independent training has been considered [9–12], whereas in the joint training algorithm of [9], stream tying has not been employed, thus resulting to trained HMMs with significanlty more density parameters than the MSHMM of (4). Proper joint training of the product HMM parameters is employed for the first time in this paper.

Note that exponent values λ_s cannot be obtained using maximum-likelihood approaches. Instead, they can be estimated using discriminative training [12, 13], or by minimizing the *word error rate* (WER) on a held-out set [9, 11], as in this paper.

Table 1: The training and test sets of the two audio-visual databases used in this paper. The number of utterances, words, duration (in hours), and number of subjects are depicted for each set. Two recognition tasks are considered: Connected digits (DIGIT) and continuous, read speech (LVCSR).

Recog. task	Training set				Test set			
	Utter.	Wds.	Dur.	Sub.	Utter.	Wds.	Dur.	Sub.
DIGIT	5490	46638	8:01	50	529	4513	0:46	50
LVCSR	17111	219470	34:55	239	207	3176	0:30	26

3. EXPERIMENTAL FRAMEWORK

In this section, we describe the two audio-visual recognition tasks (databases) considered, the audio-visual feature extraction algorithm employed, and specifics on MSHMM training and decoding.

3.1 Audio-visual databases

As already mentioned, in this paper we report AVASR experiments on two recognition tasks, namely connected digits recognition and LVCSR. For this purpose, two suitable audio-visual databases have been recently collected at the IBM T.J. Watson Research Center, under similar recording conditions. The data consist of full-face frontal video and audio of a large number of subjects (see also Fig. 3), uttering connected digit strings (7- or 10-tuples) with an 11-word vocabulary, or ViaVoice^{TM} scripts (continuous read speech with mostly verbalized punctuation) with a 10,400 word vocabulary [9]. In both cases, the database video is of size 704 × 480 pixels, interlaced, captured in color at a rate of 30 Hz (60 fields per second are available at a resolution of 240 lines), and is MPEG2 encoded at the relatively high compression ratio of about 50:1. High quality wideband audio is synchronously collected with the video at a rate of 16 kHz in an office environment at a 20 dB *signal-to-noise ratio* (SNR).

The duration and other specifics of the two datasets are depicted in Table 1. Each is partitioned into a training, test, and held-out set. The latter is only used for estimating MSHMM exponents in (4), and it is not shown in Table 1. Notice that the DIGIT task corresponds to a multi-speaker training/testing scenario, as the same 50 subjects are used for both training and testing. On the contrary, the LVCSR task is speaker-independent, as the 26 test subjects are disjoint to the 239 training set ones. It is worth mentioning that the second database is the largest audio-visual corpus collected to date, and the only one suitable for LVCSR [6, 7].

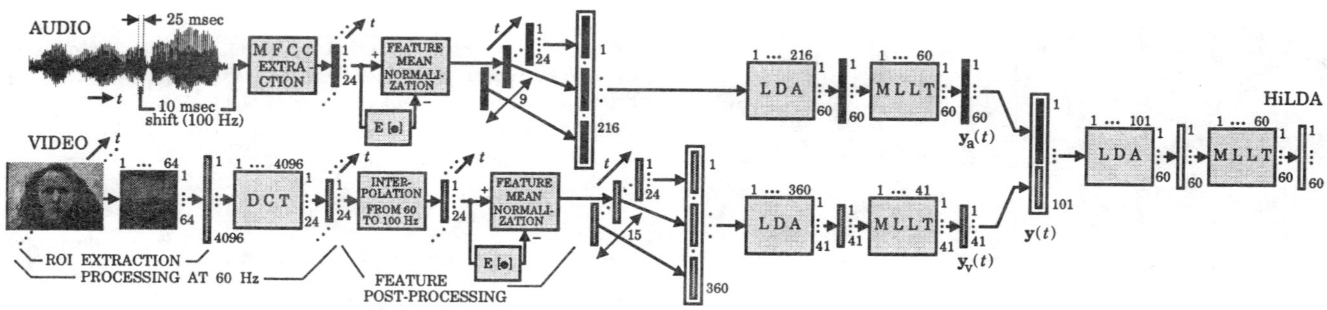

Figure 4: Feature extraction for audio-visual ASR [8] (see also Fig. 1).

To investigate the benefit of the visual modality to ASR noise-robustness, *speech "babble"* (i.e., non-stationary) noise is artificially added to the audio data at various SNRs, ranging from 20 dB (corpus original audio) to approximately -3 dB. In the experiments reported in Section 4, a matched to the noise training/testing scenario is considered, i.e., HMMs are trained at each noise level and tested on the data at the same noise condition.

3.2 Audio-visual feature extraction

We now briefly describe the audio and visual feature extraction algorithms (front ends) employed in our AVASR system, as well as a baseline technique, proposed in [8], for automatic recognition of audio-visual speech, based on feature fusion. The whole AVASR system is schematically depicted in Fig. 4.

From the audio signal, 24 mel-frequency cepstral coefficients are retained as "static" audio features, after feature mean normalization. At every frame, 9 consecutive audio features are concatenated, subsequently projected to a lower dimensional space using linear discriminant analysis (LDA), and rotated by a maximum likelihood linear transform (MLLT). The final audio features $\mathbf{y}_a(t)$ have a dimension of $d_a = 60$, and they are extracted at a 100 Hz rate.

Given the video of the speaker's face, sampled at 60 Hz, a normalized mouth region-of-interest (ROI) is first extracted, and subsequently compressed using a discrete cosine transform (DCT). The 24 highest energy DCT coefficients are retained, and after linear interpolation (up-sampling from 60 to 100 Hz) and mean normalization, they result to "static" visual features. Similarly to the audio features, dynamic information is obtained by concatenating consecutive "static" features over 15 frames, and by applying the LDA and MLLT transforms. The final visual feature $\mathbf{y}_v(t)$ dimension is $d_v = 41$.

Notice that the audio and visual features are time-synchronous, extracted at 100 Hz. Therefore, a joint audio-visual feature vector $\mathbf{y}(t)$, of dimension $d = 101$, can easily be obtained by concatenating them, as in (2). Sequences of the resulting vectors can then be modeled using the MSHMM framework of Section 2.2. For completeness, the performance of these MSHMMs will also be gauged against an altrenative method for AVASR, namely a feature fusion technique that applies a second stage of LDA and MLLT data transforms on the audio-visual vector $\mathbf{y}(t)$, and uses a single-stream HMM to model the resulting 60-dimensional features (see also Figs. 1 and 4). This feature fusion algorithm is known as *hierarchical LDA* (HiLDA), and it has been demonstrated to perform better than feature fusion using single-stream HMMs to directly model $\mathbf{y}(t)$ [8].

3.3 HMM training and decoding

For both recognition tasks considered (DIGIT and LVCSR), we use 3-state, left-to-right phone HMMs, with context-dependent sub-phonetic HMM classes (states). These classes are obtained by means of decision trees that cluster phonetic contexts spanning up to 5 phones to each side of the current phone, in order to better model co-articulation and improve ASR performance. The DIGIT and LVCSR decision trees are estimated using the clean audio of the corresponding database training sets, by bootstrapping on a previously developed audio HMM (and its corresponding front end) that provides data class labels by forced alignment. Subsequently, K-means clustering is used to estimate the single-stream audio HMMs, that correspond to the newly developed trees. It is by bootstrapping on these models, that the parameters of all HMMs considered in this paper are estimated (on their required front ends). The total number of the resulting context-dependent HMM states are 159 for the DIGIT task and approximately 2.8k for LVCSR, whereas all single-stream HMMs considered in the experiments (i.e., for audio-only, visual-only, or audio-visual HiLDA feature modeling) have identical number of Gaussian mixture components, namely about 3.2k and 47k for the DIGIT and LVCSR tasks, respectively.

Once decision trees and initial DIGIT and LVCSR audio HMMs are developed, we proceed to estimate the parameters of single-stream HMMs that model visual-only, as well as audio-only and audio-visual HiLDA feature sequences at the required SNR levels. We use three EM algorithm iterations for this task, with the E-step of the first iteration employing the initial audio HMM (for bootstrapping). Subsequently, we proceed to estimate MSHMMs using the audio-only and visual-only single-stream HMMs, as outlined in Section 2.3. In particular the following schemes are used:

(i): In the first method, we consider independent MSHMM training, by composing the required MSHMMs from the two single-stream HMMs as in (4) (note that $\{i_a\} = \{i_v\}$). We denote this scheme by n=3, to indicate the three EM iterations used to separately train each single-stream HMM. We then choose exponents λ_a and λ_v that minimize the WER using the resulting MSHMM on the held-out set.

(ii): The second scheme jointly estimates MSHMM parameters. It first composes the required MSHMM from the audio- and visual-only single-stream HMMs, which have been independently obtained after the first iteration of the EM algorithm (note that the same model has been used at the E-step for bootstrapping both). Subsequently, two more EM iterations are performed using the MSHMM with exponents set to the ones estimated in the previous scheme. We denote this scheme by n=12.

(iii): Finally, a third scheme considers independent training of the MSHMM parameters, followed by their joint re-estimation. It is similar to the previous scheme, with the main difference being the use of audio- and visual-only single-stream HMMs obtained at the third (instead of the first) EM iteration, in order to compose the initial MSHMM (identical to the one of the first scheme). Two additional joint MSHMM estimation iterations of the EM algorithm are used. The method is denoted by n=32.

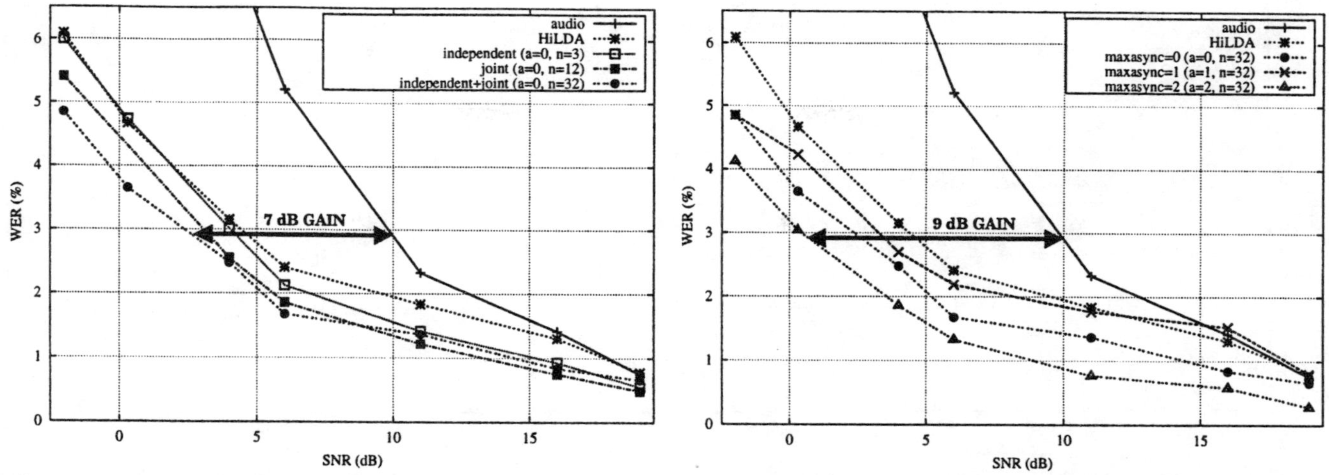

Figure 5: Results on the DIGIT recognition task. Test set audio-only and audio-visual WERs using HiLDA feature fusion and MSHMM based decision fusion are depicted against the audio channel SNR. ***Left:*** **WER for different training strategies with state-synchronous MSHMMs.** ***Right:*** **WER for different levels of asynchrony for jointly trained MSHMMs.**

All three schemes are used for various levels of maximum allowed within-phone state asynchrony between the audio and visual state sequences of the MSHMM. Since the single-stream HMMs are 3-state phone models, there can be a maximum allowed asynchrony (denoted by "a") of 0 (state-synchronous MSHMM), 1, or 2 states. Notice that in the state-asynchronous MSHMM cases a=1,2, the transition probabilities in the product model can be tied to the transition probabilities in the stream models in the same way the state conditional densities are tied. However, unless otherwise stated, transition probability tying is not used in the experiments reported in this paper.

Finally, recognition of matched test data (same SNR as in training) is carried out. For the DIGIT task, decoding is based on a simple digit-word loop grammar (with unknown string length), whereas for LVCSR, a trigram language model is used. In both cases, a two-stage stack decoding algorithm is employed, that uses a fast match followed by a detailed match [17]. Preliminary experiments on state-asynchronous MSHMMs have shown that the best results are obtained with a fast-match selection of candidate words based on state-synchronous MSHMMs rather than on asynchronous product models. The latter are solely used in the subsequent detailed match. Apart from the fact that different models are used, the fast and detailed matches are carried out as described in [17].

4. EXPERIMENTAL RESULTS

We now present a number of ASR results that employ the experimental framework discussed of Section 3. We first describe ASR on the DIGIT task, followed by LVCSR.

4.1 Results on the DIGIT task

A first experiment aims at comparing the independent and joint parameter estimation strategies discussed in Sections 2.3 and 3.3. WERs as a function of the SNR are reported in Fig. 5 (left graph) for state-synchronous MSHMMs using the three different parameter estimation schemes of Section 3.3: Independent (n=3), joint (n=12) and independent followed by a joint re-estimation (n=32). Results for the feature fusion (HiLDA) and for audio-only HMMs are also depicted. Not surprisingly, AVASR exhibits dramatically improved noise-robustness w.r.t. audio-only ASR. In addition, state-synchronous MSHMMs outperform HiLDA based feature fusion. Notice that, below 7 dB SNR, the best results are obtained by scheme n=32, i.e., independent parameter estimation followed by a joint re-estimation. The resulting MSHMM provides a 7 dB *effective SNR gain* in ASR, compared to the audio-only performance at 10 dB SNR (see Fig. 5). For less degraded audio (above 7 dB SNR), all three parameter estimation schemes perform similarly well.

Next, we study the influence of allowing MSHMM within-phone asynchrony. Results are depicted in Fig. 5 (right graph) for maximum allowed asynchrony of a=0,1,2. In view of our previous results, the MSHMMs are obtained using the combined parameter estimation scheme, n=32. Results clearly demonstrate that increasing the allowed asynchrony to a=2 improves AVASR performance. It is worth noticing, that even at 20 dB (original database clean audio), the state-asynchronous MSHMM (a=2) reduces WER from the audio-only 0.75% to an audio-visual 0.28% (if the n=3, independent training scheme is used, the WER becomes 0.40%). Overall, the state-asynchronous MSHMM provides a 9 dB effective SNR gain (see Fig. 5).

4.2 Results on the LVCSR task

The experiments described in the previous section are repeated on the LVCSR task and results are reported in Fig. 6. As for the DIGIT task, state-synchronous MSHMMs demonstrate increased robustness to noise over the audio-only and HiLDA based feature fusion, yielding a 7 dB effective SNR gain, compared to the audio-only performance at 10 dB SNR. Also, similarly to Section 4.1, joint estimation (n=12) of MSHMM parameters outperforms their independent estimation (n=3). In contrast to the DIGIT task however, joint re-estimation following independent training (n=32) significantly hurts performance. Similar observations hold for the state-asynchronous MSHMMs, as well. A possible explanation for this discrepancy between the DIGIT and LVCSR tasks is that for the latter, when the audio and visual HMMs are independently trained, they may converge to very different state alignments of the data, due to the much higher confusability present in the visual stream, compared to the DIGIT task. Forcing the alignments to be synchronous at the phone boundary level when jointly re-estimating the parameters may yield a sub-optimal solution because the initial (stream) models are not suited for this resynchronization. We have not verified this hypothesis so far.

A second observation is that for LVCSR, allowing MSHMM state-asynchrony degrades audio-visual speech recognition. This is

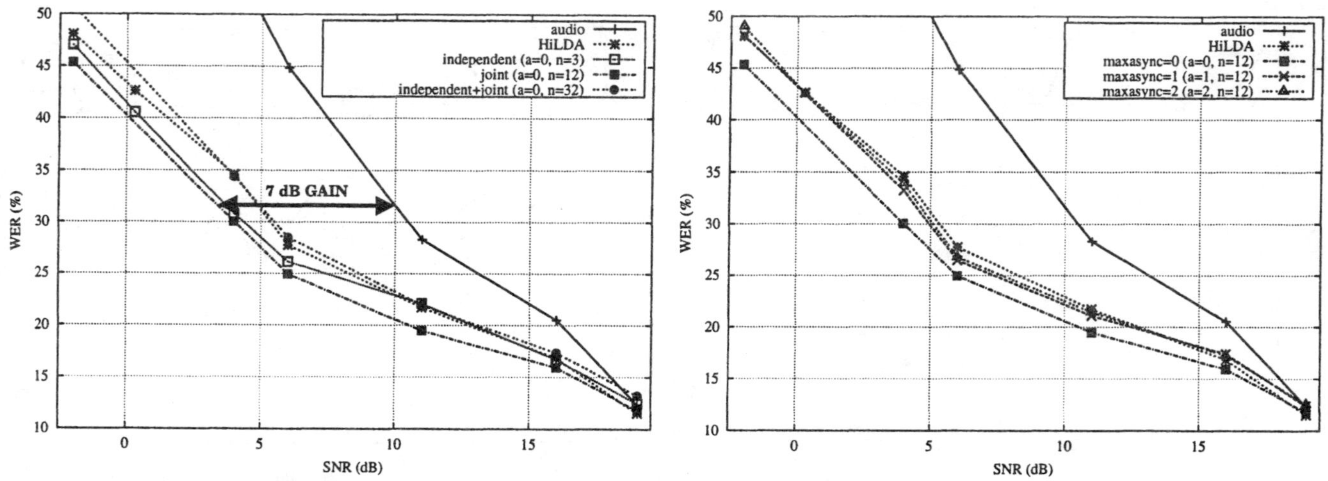

Figure 6: Results on the LVCSR task. *Left:* WER for different training strategies with state-synchronous MSHMMs. *Right:* WER for different levels of asynchrony for jointly trained MSHMMs.

clearly demonstrated in Fig. 6 (right graph), where, in view of the previous remarks, all MSHMMs depicted (for a=0,1,2) are jointly trained (n=12). Together with our earlier observations, this performance degradation indicates that the phone boundary may not be an appropriate resynchronization point for a visually confusable task such as LVCSR.

Finally, we briefly visit the issue of tying transition probabilities when jointly training (n=12) MSHMMs with a=1, or 2. Such tying affects performance only slightly: For a=2, and at 20 dB SNR, transition probability tying degrades WER from 12.6% (when no tying is present) to 12.9%, and from 33.0% to 33.9% at 4 dB SNR.

5. SUMMARY

In this paper, we considered audio-visual speech recognition by means of multi-stream hidden Markov models. We investigated various degrees of allowed audio-visual state asynchrony of these models, as well as a number of schemes for estimating their parameters. We reported experiments on both a small-vocabulary (connected digits) recognition task and on a more complex, large-vocabulary continuous speech recognition task. On both tasks, we demonstrated a significant advantage of the state-synchronous multi-stream approach over a baseline feature fusion approach, and observed that joint training of multi-stream HMM parameters outperforms their independent estimation. Allowing state asynchrony further improved connected digit recognition, however it degraded performance on the large-vocabulary continuous speech recognition task. For this more complex task with a highly confusable vocabulary, it is possible that the audio and visual alignments differ in more than a phone length, illustrating the fact that phone boundaries may not constitute a proper synchronization point.

6. REFERENCES

[1] R.P. Lippmann, "Speech recognition by machines and humans," *Speech Comm.*, *22*(1):1–15, 1997.

[2] H. Hermansky and N. Morgan, "RASTA processing of speech," *IEEE Trans. Speech Audio Process.*, *2*(4):578–589, 1994.

[3] C.J. Leggetter and P.C. Woodland, "Maximum likelihood linear regression for speaker adaptation of continuous density hidden Markov models," *Comp. Speech Lang.*, *9*:171–185, 1995.

[4] R. Stern, A. Acero, F.-H. Liu, and Y. Ohshima, "Signal processing for robust speech recognition," In C.-H. Lee, F.K. Soong, and K.K. Paliwal, Eds., *Automatic Speech and Speaker Recognition. Advanced Topics*. Kluwer Academic Pub., pp. 357–384, 1997.

[5] R. Campbell, B. Dodd, and D. Burnham, Eds., *Hearing by Eye II*. Psychology Press Ltd. Pub., 1998.

[6] D.G. Stork and M.E. Hennecke, Eds., *Speechreading by Humans and Machines*. Springer, 1996.

[7] T. Chen, "Audiovisual speech processing. Lip reading and lip synchronization," *IEEE Sig. Process. Mag.*, *18*:9–21, 2001.

[8] G. Potamianos, J. Luettin, and C. Neti, "Hierarchical discriminant features for audio-visual LVCSR," *Proc. Int. Conf. Acous. Speech Sig. Process.*, pp. 165–168, 2001.

[9] C. Neti, G. Potamianos, J. Luettin, I. Matthews, H. Glotin, D. Vergyri, J. Sison, A. Mashari, and J. Zhou, "Audio-visual speech recognition," *Final Workshop 2000 Report*, Center for Language and Speech Processing, The Johns Hopkins University, 2000.

[10] M.J. Tomlinson, M.J. Russell, and N.M. Brooke, "Integrating audio and visual information to provide highly robust speech recognition," *Proc. IEEE Int. Conf. Acous. Speech Sig. Process.*, pp. 821–824, 1996.

[11] S. Dupont and J. Luettin, "Audio-visual speech modeling for continuous speech recognition," *IEEE Trans. Multimedia*, *2*:141–151, 2000.

[12] S. Nakamura, "Fusion of audio-visual information for integrated speech processing," In J. Bigun and F. Smeraldi, Eds., *Audio-and Video-Based Biometric Person Authentication*. Springer-Verlag, pp. 127–143, 2001.

[13] G. Gravier, S. Axelrod, G. Potamianos, and C. Neti, "Maximum entropy and MCE based HMM stream weight estimation for audio-visual ASR," *Proc. Int. Conf. Acous. Speech Sig. Process.*, pp. 853–856, 2002.

[14] C. Bregler and Y. Konig, "'Eigenlips' for robust speech recognition," *Proc. IEEE Int. Conf. Acous. Speech Sig. Process.*, pp. 669–672, 1994.

[15] H. Bourlard and S. Dupont, "A new ASR approach based on independent processing and recombination of partial frequency bands," *Proc. Int. Conf. Spoken Lang. Process.*, pp. 426–429, 1996.

[16] P. Varga and R.K. Moore, "Hidden Markov model decomposition of speech and noise," *Proc. Int. Conf. Acous. Speech Sig. Process.*, pp. 845–848, 1990.

[17] L. Bahl, S. De Gennaro, P. Gopalakrishnan, and R. Mercer, "A fast approximate acoustic match for large vocabulary speech recognition," *IEEE Trans. Speech Audio Process.*, *1*(1):59–67, 1993.

Arabic Speech and Text in TIDES OnTAP*

Jayadev Billa, Mohamed Noamany, Amit Srivastava, John Makhoul and Francis Kubala
BBN Technologies, Cambridge MA 02138.
jbilla@bbn.com

ABSTRACT

This paper describes the introduction of Arabic speech and text into the TIDES OnTAP system. This includes the development of the BBN Audio Indexing System for broadcast news in Arabic, development and the introduction of an Arabic event tracker and Arabic querying into the TIDES OnTAP system. Key issues addressed in this work revolve around the three major components of the audio indexing system: automatic speech recognition, speaker identification, named entity identification and Arabic document tracking. The system deals with several challenges introduced by the Arabic language, including the absence of short vowels in written text and the presence of compound words that are formed by the concatenation of certain conjunctions, prepositions, articles, and pronouns, as prefixes and suffixes to the word stem. The absence of short vowels in the transcripts was addressed with a novel solution that leverages the strengths of Hidden Markov models. Another challenge was the acquisition of appropriate language modeling data, given the absence of broadcast news data for that purpose. We present performance results for all three components of the Audio Indexing System.

1. INTRODUCTION

TIDES OnTAP, "Online Text and Audio Processing", is a fully automatic language processing demonstration system for processing human-language data in mixed media and multiple languages. Created under the DARPA TIDES program, OnTAP acts as a technology test bed for the program. In addition to processing human-language data, TIDES OnTAP provides the user with facilities to query the database for relevant documents as well as track documents of interest to the user in the incoming speech and text data stream.

Within TIDES OnTAP audio data is passed through the BBN Audio Indexing system based on the *Rough'n'Ready* [4, 6] system developed at BBN for the real-time indexing and browsing of broadcast news in English. The system includes the following technologies: speech recognition, speaker identification, named-entity extraction, topic classification, and story segmentation. The system runs in streaming mode, recording broadcast news data off the air, performing recognition and indexing in real-time, and storing the results in a database. In TIDES OnTAP, text data is typically passed through the named-entity identification, topic classification, and story segmentation components and stored in the same database. This normalization of speech and text provides a powerful mechanism for accessing mixed-media documents.

In this paper, we report on extending the capabilities of the TIDES OnTAP system to include the real-time audio indexing of Arabic broadcast news, processing of Arabic newspaper articles and Arabic document tracking. The Arabic capability currently includes the following four components: automatic speech recognition (ASR), speaker identification, named entity extraction and tracking. In the case of raw broadcast speech, the audio is passed first into the speech recognition component where the audio stream is analyzed for speaker changes and pauses and each speaker "turn" is converted into a word sequence. The speaker identification component then takes in the speaker-turn information, identifies known speakers by name, and clusters unknown speakers and identifies their gender. Finally, named entities representing the names of people, places, and locations, are extracted and highlighted. Newspaper articles enter at the named-entity component processing stage. The end result of both speech and text processing is an enriched textual document of the spoken audio stream. Incoming data, in the form of this enriched textual document, can be tracked based on a user defined tracking profile.

First, we provide a brief primer on the Arabic language and the challenges it represents for speech recognition, followed by an overview of the the Arabic resources used in the development of the Audio Indexer components. In order, we then detail the development of each system component, starting with the Arabic ASR component, moving to speaker identification, and the named entity extraction component. Following the description of the processing technologies we end with a brief description of the tracking process and underlying technologies.

2. ARABIC LANGUAGE

The various colloquial dialects that are spoken across the Arab World are very different from each other in pronunciation, vocabulary, and grammar; they are typically not written at all; and they all differ markedly from the only written language, known as Modern Standard Arabic (MSA). In addition to being the only written language, MSA is also used as the dominant language for broadcast news and for formal speeches. So, except for some pronunciation differences, the MSA spoken in Saudi Arabia, for example, is the same as that spoken in Syria, Egypt, and Morocco. Below, we use

*This work was supported in part by The Office of Advanced Information Technology under Contract 1999-S0189000-000 and by DARPA under Contract N66001-00-C-8008.

Proceedings of HLT 2002, Second International Conference on Human Language Technology Research, M. Marcus, ed., Morgan Kaufmann, San Francisco, 2002.

the term Arabic to refer to MSA only.

Arabic has a system of 25 consonants, three quasi-consonants (w, y, and glottal stop or *hamza*), and three vowels (a, u, i). Duration is phonemic in Arabic (i.e., a difference in the duration of a vowel or a consonant can change the meaning of a word), so vowels can be either short or long, and the consonants can be doubled. Arabic does not have regular letters to represent short vowels and the doubling of consonants; these, when written, appear as marks, or diacritics, above or below the consonants. The long vowels are always written, but the symbols used for the long vowels are also used to write /w/, /y/, and the hamza, so that creates an ambiguity between what is written and how those letters are pronounced. (The hamza takes on several forms, one of which is placed above or below the *alif*, the character used to represent the long vowel /aa/.) In ordinary Arabic text, like newspapers and most books, diacritics, including the short vowels and the doubling of consonants, are almost never written, except sometimes to disambiguate a word. Morphologically, Arabic words consist of CV and CVC syllables and the language has a basic verb-subject-object structure.

As an example of the ambiguities that are inherent in the writing system, the word that appears as "ktb" can be either "katab" (he wrote), "kattab" (he dictated), "kutib" (it was written), "kuttib" (it was dictated), or "kutub" (books). Which of the words is meant has to be inferred by the reader from the context.

Arabic is a highly inflected language, with gender, number, person, tense, mood, and case, are all indicated as prefixes, infixes, or suffixes to a basic root. The resulting *word stem* can then be "enlarged" by other prefixes and suffixes. All single-letter conjunctions and prepositions that precede a word stem, as well as the definite article, are attached to the word stem as prefixes, and any following pronoun is attached to the word as a suffix. So, what is considered as a single word in Arabic can actually represent a whole phrase. For example, the phrase "and he will write it" is written as a single word in Arabic "wsyktbh": "w" = and, "s" = will, "y" is a marker for 3rd person singular masculine, "ktb" = write, and "h" = it.

When reading, an Arabic reader has the freedom to pronounce or delete any vowel case marker at the end of a word. There are cross-word assimilation phenomena which are also optional. These effects complicate correspondences between the written form and what is spoken.

The ambiguities mentioned above, as well as the optional pronunciations exercised by each speaker, introduce difficulties for Arabic ASR, both for acoustic modeling and training, as well as language modeling.

3. ARABIC DATA RESOURCES

Acoustic data for the ASR models consisted of approximately 42 hours of spoken Arabic, transcribed without diacritic markings, from Egyptian and Syrian broadcast radio and TV. The 42 hours of acoustic data were split into a training set and a test set. The test set of approximately 4.5 hours was chosen to be temporally disjoint from and later than training. Following the initial work, an additional 20 hours of broadcast news, from the Al-Jazeera TV network, was added to the acoustic training.

Language-modeling (LM) data was acquired from two Lebanese newspapers, Al-Hayat and An-Nahar, and one newswire source, the Arabic service of Agence France Presse (AFP) newswire service. Al-Hayat data consisted of four years of newspaper text spanning 1997-2000, whereas the An-Nahar data consisted of four years spanning 1996-1999. The AFP newswire data consisted of seven years of newswire text spanning 1994-2000 and was obtained from the Linguistic Data Consortium (LDC).

Recently, we have acquired additional data from both An-Nahar (year 2000) and Al-Hayat (years 1994-1996). Al-Hayat is also now part of the daily feed into the TIDES OnTAP system. This daily feed is collected and added to the language modeling data at appropriate intervals to give a very close-in-time language model – the current system uses data as recent as Jan-Nov 2001.

Table 1 shows the sizes of the acoustic training and test sets and the three-language modeling sources as measured by total number of word tokens and number of unique words.

Source	Total Words	Unique Words
Al Hayat	156M	1.2M
An-Nahar	74M	800k
AFP	65M	540k
Acoustic Training	330k	38k
All Training	290M	1.6M
Test	25k	8k

Table 1: Arabic Data Resources.

4. ARABIC ASR

4.1 Initial ASR System

The speech recognition component of TIDES OnTAP is derived from the BBN Byblos system [8] and has been further engineered for real-time speech recognition. But before we could start developing the Arabic system, we had to make a number of modeling decisions that were affected by the peculiarities of the language and the data.

First of all, since the transcriptions of the audio data did not include the short vowels and consonant doubling, and did not resolve the various pronunciation ambiguities mentioned above, we had to decide whether to produce accurate phonetic transcriptions that corresponded to the audio or not. We decided *not* to produce accurate phonetic transcriptions and to use the given transcriptions as is. One reason for this decision was that all the language modeling data from newspaper text was not diacritized either, so we thought it would be easier to be consistent throughout. (Diacritizing the language modeling data would have been extraordinarily costly and impractical. Furthermore, commercially available diacritizing software was not accurate enough to be usable for our purposes.) Another reason was that, even if accurate phonetic transcriptions were available, speaker optionality in pronouncing word endings would make it difficult to provide a consistent phonetic dictionary.

So, we simply assigned one phoneme model to each character. In this manner, a model for a consonant would actually be modeling that consonant alone, as well as that consonant followed by each of the three vowels, or whatever actually occurred in the data. This assignment would also work well for word endings where the vowels were optional anyway. No allowance was made for pronunciation differences across different countries. Although Arabic is a particularly good language for making such modeling assignments because of the phonetic regularity of its writing system, we believe it could work well for other languages as well.

Another major decision had to do with compound words – words with multiple affixes attached to the stem. Because many of those words are essentially phrases, treating each of those words as a unique word results in a very strong language model (we use a statistical trigram model), thus improving recognition accuracy. However, simultaneously, we were concerned that the resulting out-of-vocabulary (OOV) word rate would be too high. With a 65,000-

word lexicon, we measured the OOV rate in the test set at 4%, which is certainly on the high side. In comparison, for English broadcast news, the same size lexicon results in an OOV rate of less than 1%. One choice we had was to perform automatic stemming of the compound words to separate the various affixes from the word stem. Unfortunately, we were unable to find automatic stemming software that was accurate enough for our purposes. Therefore, we decided on keeping each compound word as a single word and eventually increased our vocabulary size to reduce the OOV rate. For example, with a 128,000-word vocabulary, the OOV rate went down to 2.4%.

Our first ASR system, based on this approach of considering each Arabic character as a phoneme, ignoring the need to stem, and allowing the acoustic models to model short vowels implicitly, performed surprisingly well. This initial ASR system, running sub-real-time, using a 65,000-word lexicon and the acoustic transcripts of the acoustic training data as the sole language modeling data (only 230k words without the Al-Jazeera data), gave a baseline word error rate (WER) of 31.2%, which was very encouraging.

4.2 Language Modeling

Following our initial results, we focused on potential improvements with better language modeling using language data obtained from Al-Hayat and AFP. First, the text was stripped of all formatting information and punctuation. In Arabic, digits can be spoken in a number of ways depending on the kind of number (date, monetary amount, quantity, etc.) and context. The multiplicity of possible pronunciations preempted any rational attempt to convert digits to words. We therefore mapped all digits to an unknown-word marker. In all, approximately 145 million words were added to the initial 290k words of language modeling data and the models were retrained. There was a substantial improvement in system performance with WER dropping from 31.2% to 26.6%. Results are summarized in Table 2.

4.3 System Improvements

To build on the initial results, we first attempted to improve the core acoustic models with a combination of better description of Arabic acoustic categories for clustering, and larger, more complex acoustic models.

To further improve performance, two new capabilities were added to the BBN Audio Indexer ASR component: Maximum Likelihood Linear Regression (MLLR) and the ability to use lexicons greater than 65,000 words.

MLLR [2] is a common technique used to adapt speech recognition system models to an incoming speaker. However, MLLR has hitherto been used chiefly in research systems where system speed was a tangential distraction. BBN has now implemented MLLR within the core speech recognition system with essentially no penalty in speed. The current system still runs faster than real-time with up to a 10% reduction in word error rate.

To consolidate our improvements we tuned and optimized our real-time system for best possible performance. We found a very large improvement (10% reduction in WER) for tuning and optimizing the ASR component, indicating a sub-optimal starting point. The result of all the above improvements was a reduction in the WER from 26.6% to 21.0%.

We then augmented our system with the capability to run with lexicon sizes greater than 65,000 words, again in faster than real-time. We created a 128,000 word lexicon based on the most frequent words in the three language modeling datasets (Al-Hayat, An-Nahar and AFP) and all the words in our acoustic training set. The larger lexicon contributed to a further reduction in the WER to 20.4%.

Later in our work, we received about twenty hours of transcribed broadcast news from the Al-Jazeera TV network which were added to the acoustic training corpus. This additional data provided another incremental improvement in performance to a WER of 19.1%.

The recent availability of additional LM data has allowed us double the language model from a 145M word- to a 300M word language model. Furthermore, we took the opportunity to refine the dictionary and data by normalizing and correcting orthographic variations. The current WER is 17.3%, as shown in Table 2 on a system that runs in real-time. The system is currently operational as part of TIDES OnTAP at BBN, and receives streaming audio from Al-Jazeera Arabic broadcast news as well as a daily text feed (via ftp) from the Al-Hayat newspaper.

System	WER
Baseline	31.2
+ 145M word LM	26.6
+ System Improvements	21.0
+ 128k Lexicon	20.4
+ Additional data	19.1
+ 300M word LM + improved lexicon	17.3
+ New scoring	15.3

Table 2: Improvements to ASR component performance with refinements. Each row indicates incremental improvements over the component in the preceding row.

4.4 Scoring Issues

One of the liberties that writers of Arabic allow themselves is in the placement of the hamza when it occurs above or below the alif character. In all, there are three variations of hamza placement, plus the alif alone. Writers often strip the hamza and leave the alif alone, but they are not consistent in doing that. Since each of the four forms is treated as a separate character in our system, the resulting lexicon and the transcribed data are not always consistent, therefore resulting in recognition errors that generally are of little consequence to the Arabic reader.

So, we performed an experiment where the reference and hypothesized word sequences were changed to remove orthographic variations due to hamza/alif forms. The resulting WER of 17.1% in the second row of Table 3 is to be compared with the error rate of 19.1% in Table 2, showing the prevalence of hamza/alif inconsistencies in Arabic writing. We then performed another experiment where we changed the actual training data by removing all hamza/alif orthographic variations and retrained the ASR system. The WER was reduced further to 16.5%.

System	WER
Most conservative system	19.1
Change reference and hypothesis only	17.1
Change transcripts and retrain ASR system	16.5

Table 3: Effect of changes in scoring methodology for Arabic ASR.

We have had opportunity to consult with native Arabic speakers on the suitability of each of these methods. We found that native speakers consistently preferred errorful hamza/alif variants over a complete absence of hamza/alif form even though the transcripts were readable in both cases. We therefore decided to retain the hamza/alif forms throughout the core system while removing them for scoring purposes. This approach on the current "best"system yields a WER of 15.3% as noted in the last row of Table 2.

5. SPEAKER IDENTIFICATION

The Speaker Identification component in the Arabic Audio Indexer was modeled on the English version of the system [3, 5]. For our initial experiment, a total of eighteen speakers, eight female and ten male, were selected by picking the speakers with the most training data in the acoustic data. For consistency, the training and test set was kept identical to the one used in the ASR component.

On evaluation, the speaker identification component was able to identify all segments correctly without any false accepts or false rejects.

This result, while satisfying, has its caveats; the test set was unrealistically small with high quality audio and we had no cross-validation test so the speaker identification component was optimized on the same data it was tested on. It is prudent to expect the system to degrade when presented with more speakers and poorer acoustics.

To test this idea further, a total of two hundred and twenty nine speakers (189 male, 41 female) were selected, by picking the speakers that had at least three minutes of training data. The selected speakers were distributed over Cairo Radio, Cairo TV, Arabic VOA, Damascus Radio and Al-Jazeera TV network. Again, for consistency, the training and test sets were kept identical to the ones used in the ASR component.

On evaluation, the speaker identification component gave a segment error rate of 12.2%, i.e., the speaker was identified correctly in 87.8% of all test segments. This is an unoptimized result and should improve with tuning.

6. NAMED ENTITY EXTRACTION

The Name Entity Extraction component was also modeled on the English version of the Audio Indexer [1]. However, since various assumptions the tools make for the English version were no longer applicable, we had to modify the system for use on Arabic. The training and test sets were again kept identical to the ones used for ASR component development.

The training set consisted of approximately 3700 named entities and about 800 named entities in test. In Arabic, named entities are often combined with prefixes, typically "w" (and), "b" (with) and "l" (for), and are normally written as single words. Since this is quite different from English, the transcribers were asked to separate the prefix from each named entity. We found that, for the most part, the prefixes were accurately separated from the named entity, but, inconsistencies remain. The final breakdown of named entities is given in Table 4.

Named Entity Type	Training	Test
Persons	1899	307
Locations	1224	378
Organizations	630	118
Total	3753	803

Table 4: Distribution of named entities by type over training and test set.

The named-entity extraction component gave an F-measure (harmonic mean of precision and recall) of 90.26, measured on the original text, i.e., without any speech recognition errors. This translates to a slot-error-rate (SER) [7] of 17.0%. These results are quite impressive when one considers the fact that both the F-measure and slot-error-rate numbers are close to the best-reported results on English broadcast news text.

To further investigate the effect of the inconsistent prefix separation, we reran the system on data where we manually re-attached the separated prefix to each named entity and also where we manually and consistently separated the three most common prefixes (w, b and l) from each named entity. Table 5 summarizes the results of the three experiments. The first experiment is the baseline system with all the inconsistencies in prefix separation kept as-is during training and testing. In the second experiment, we manually re-attached all separated prefixes to its corresponding named entity, and retrained and tested the system. This increased the errors somewhat to an F-measure of 89.59 or SER of 18.0%. The last experiment was the reverse of the second experiment in that we manually separated the three common prefixes (w,b and l) in the transcripts to ensure consistent prefix separation and repeated the experiment. This final experiment gave the best results, with an F-measure of 91.25 and SER of 15.2%. The results are expected since

System	F-measure	%SER
Baseline w/ inconsistent prefix separation	90.26	17.0
with no prefix separation	89.59	18.0
with consistent prefix separation	91.25	15.2

Table 5: Named Entity component performance with variations on the treatment of named entity prefixes in Arabic.

each compound name (prefix + named entity) results in a "new" named entity within our system causing both an increase in named entities as well as a reduction in training data per named entity. However, in real life, such separation of prefix from named entity is highly improbable and the results of the second experiment, i.e., with no prefix separation, is closest to what one might expect in normal usage.

7. ARABIC DOCUMENT TRACKING

Event tracking [10] attempts to track user designated events in a stream of news articles. The event tracking component builds a statistical language model from the documents the user specifies for an event of interest and uses this model to estimate the relevance of future news documents to the user event. The user is then alerted when relevant documents are detected by the system.

We adapted the TDT tracking research system[9] for the task of event tracking on Arabic documents. About 500k Arabic news articles were used to create a background language model on 121 million words taken from the language-modeling data. A few modifications were made to the research system to adapt it to Arabic. Stop word removal and stemming of Arabic tokens were turned off in the tracking system. The research system was then integrated into an online event tracking service that tracks Arabic news documents based on user-defined events.

8. CONCLUSIONS

This work focused on the extending TIDES OnTAP to include Arabic speech and text processing. Major challenges introduced by the Arabic language, such as the absence of short vowels in written text and the presence of compound words were addressed. Our solutions to these language issues yielded what we believe to be a state-of-the-art Arabic speech and text processing capability. This system currently runs in streaming mode, processing both Arabic broadcast news sessions and Arabic newspaper text, and makes it available to the user to both query and track via a web-interface.

9. REFERENCES

[1] D. M. Bikel, R. Schwartz, and R. Weischedel. An algorithm that learns what's in a name. In *Machine Learning*, volume 34, pages 211–231, 1999.

[2] M. J. Gales. Maximum likelihood linear transformations for HMM-based speech recognition. Technical Report CUED/F-INFENG/TR. 291, Cambridge University, Engineering Department, Cambridge, England, 1997.

[3] H. Gish and M. Schmidt. Text-independent speaker identification. In *IEEE Signal Processing Magazine*, pages 18–32. IEEE, October 1994.

[4] F. Kubala, S. Colbath, D. Liu, A. Srivastava, and J. Makhoul. Integrated technologies for indexing spoken language. In *Communications of the ACM*, volume 43, pages 48–56. ACM, February 2000.

[5] D. Liu and F. Kubala. Fast speaker change detection for broadcast news transcription and indexing. In *Proceedings of Eurospeech99*, pages 1031–1034, Budapest, September 1999.

[6] J. Makhoul, F. Kubala, T. Leek, D. Liu, L. Nguyen, R. Schwartz, and A. Srivastava. Speech and language technologies for audio indexing. In *Proceedings of the IEEE*, volume 88, pages 1338–1353. IEEE, August 2000.

[7] J. Makhoul, F. Kubala, R. Schwartz, and R. Weischedel. Performance measures for information extraction. In *Proceedings of the DARPA Workshop on Broadcast News Understanding*, pages 37–40. Morgan Kaufmann, March 1999.

[8] L. Nguyen, S. Matsoukas, J. Davenport, J. Billa, R. Schwartz, and J. Makhoul. The 1999 BBN Byblos 10xRT broadcast news transcription system. In *Proceedings of the 2000 NIST Speech Transcription Workshop*, Maryland, May 2000. NIST.

[9] F. Walls, H. Jin, S. Sista, and R. Schwartz. Probabilistic models for topic classification. In *ICASSP*. IEEE, March 1999.

[10] C. Wayne. Topic detection and tracking (TDT) overview and perspective. In *Proceedings of the DARPA Workshop on Broadcast News Understanding*, Febuary 1998.

Automatic learning of dialogue strategy using dialogue simulation and reinforcement learning

Konrad Scheffler
Department of Engineering
Cambridge University, Cambridge, UK
khs22@cam.ac.uk

Steve Young
Department of Engineering
Cambridge University, Cambridge, UK
sjy@cam.ac.uk

ABSTRACT

This paper describes a method for automatic design of human-computer dialogue strategies by means of reinforcement learning, using a dialogue simulation tool to model the user behaviour and system recognition performance. To the authors' knowledge this is the first application of a detailed simulation tool to this problem. The simulation tool is trained on a corpus of real user data. Compared to direct state transition modelling, it has the major advantage that different state space representations can be studied without collecting more training data.

We applied Q-learning with eligibility traces to obtain policies for a telephone-based cinema information system, comparing the effect of different state space representations and evaluation functions. The policies outperformed handcrafted policies that operated in the same restricted state space, and gave performance similar to the original design that had been through several iterations of manual refinement.

1. INTRODUCTION

In automatic design of dialogue strategy, a finite state representation of the dialogue is used so that the dialogue manager can be specified as an agent to be trained using machine learning techniques. We follow the approach [2, 17] of describing dialogue as a Markov decision process (MDP).[1] The dialogue strategy to be designed is then an MDP policy, which can be optimised by means of reinforcement learning algorithms [12].

[1]The presence of imperfect recognition means that the dialogue state is not fully observable and the dialogue would be better described as a partially observable Markov decision process (POMDP) [6, 18]. However, the computational complexity involved in learning policies for POMDPs makes this approach problematic. We argue that the benefits of having a tractable computational framework outweigh the slightly inferior modelling accuracy of MDPs.

Proceedings of HLT 2002, Second International Conference on Human Language Technology Research, M. Marcus, ed., Morgan Kaufmann, San Francisco, 2002.

There are two types of dialogue model that can be used for this purpose. The first [15, 14, 9, 10, 4, 11, 6] is a model of dialogue state transitions, which can be estimated directly from a corpus in which these transitions have been logged. The model is then used with a model-based reinforcement learning algorithm such as dynamic programming to find the optimal policy.

An alternative approach is to generate training episodes by simulation so that the optimal policy can be found using a simulation-based reinforcement learning algorithm such as Q-learning [3, 1]. An advantage of this approach is that the system state representation need not be fixed: if the chosen state space proves problematic during training, it can be changed and the system retrained without having to change the data set, data transcriptions or user model. However, the lack of detailed user models meant that this method could so far only be applied to very simple dialogues.

This paper describes how a quantitative, data driven model[8] of the user behaviour and system recognition performance can be used to enable complex strategies to be learnt in a real dialogue system.

2. APPLICATION TO A REAL DIALOGUE SYSTEM

The proposed approach to dialogue design was evaluated using an application which was originally developed by a team of dialogue design engineers and refined via user trials. The application provides cinema information via the telephone and it was used to collect a data corpus on which the user and error models were trained. Evaluation of the simulation system has been reported previously in [8].

2.1 User and error models

In the cinema information application, the user is able to access information via four transaction types: *film listings, film distribution, film times* and *cinema address*. It can be treated as a form-filling dialogue, with a transaction being described by filling in a subset of the fields *type, day, film* and *cinema*. Recognition rates and user response patterns, both of which are modelled by the dialogue simulation system, differ for the different fields.

The user model is based on the assumption that the user acts in a consistent and goal directed fashion, while varying his/her actions in a probabilistic way. The internal user state is modelled around a goal structure such as that in Table 1, and comprises the following variables

Goal field	Value	Status
Type:	FILMLIST	specified
Film:	NA	NA
Cinema:	CINEMANAME	urgent
Day:	DAYVALUE	pending

Table 1: Example of a user goal and associated status variables in the cinema application.

that are updated throughout the course of the dialogue:

- The current contents of the user goal
- Status variables associated with the goal fields.
- Secondary goal structures representing the user's beliefs on the current system goal and the newly completed goal (if any).
- Application specific variables describing items such as the type (eg. direct question) of the previous prompt.

The user and error models also use parameters estimated from the training data which quantify the frequencies of different user goal initialisations, how often particular types of details will be specified in mixed initiative situations, how likely each possible insertion, deletion and substitution error is to occur during recognition, and what the distribution of confidence levels is for both correct and incorrect recognitions. Training of these parameters is described in [8, 7].

The models are generated automatically from a dialogue task specification and the tagged syntaxes used by the recognition / understanding subsystem. They can then be used to generate intention level versions of responses to system utterances, governed by the model probabilities as well as the current user state. By interfacing them with an implementation of the system, complete dialogues can be simulated.

2.2 Action set

Some decisions that need to be taken in the course of the dialogue, such as deciding which slot should be in focus at a given moment, or which syntax to use after deciding to do a system initiative query on the current slot, are easy to design and can be implemented by hand. It is therefore only necessary to define a restricted set of actions to make available to the learning system. These actions determine the extent of the strategy learning problem, and the amount of freedom available in choosing between different policies. The action set chosen for the cinema application is summarised in Table 2. It allows for automatic design of the choice between mixed and system initiative and the confirmation strategy (a choice between explicit confirmation, implicit confirmation, and delaying confirmation until later).

2.3 Cost functions

Rather than enter the debate on which factors are important in dialogue system evaluation, we choose two easily measurable objective quantities: average transaction length in number of turns and average transaction success rate. These are then used as the basis for the cost function on which the dialogue strategy is optimised. Of course, the approach can be used with any function of objectively measurable quantities, and the choice of cost function will usually depend on the nature of the application. We report results for 4 cost functions of the form

$$Cost = NumTurns + FailCost \times NumFailures \tag{1}$$

where *NumTurns* is the average number of turns per transaction, *NumFailures* is the average number of failures per transaction, and *FailCost* is a weighting factor to which we assign the values 20, 10, 5 and 2.

2.4 State space representations

The choice of state space representation is a difficult and critical part of automatic strategy learning. Knowledge of the current state should provide sufficient information not only for selecting an optimal action, but also to enable the learning algorithm to estimate the expected future reward from that state. In addition, it should contain enough history information for the Markov assumption to be reasonable. On the other hand, the size of the state space (which increases exponentially with the number of state variables) should be kept small enough for the problem to remain tractable.

Since these requirements are not easy to satisfy, it is useful to be able to experiment with different state space representations. We used the variables summarised in Table 3 to construct a number of different state spaces. These are listed in Table 4, along with the corresponding state-action space sizes. The latter are equal to the number of Q values that need to be stored after impossible states and state-action combinations have been pruned out.

All of the representations rely on the idea of restricting the state space size by retaining detailed information only for the slot that is currently in focus. Information about other slots is hidden from the reinforcement learning algorithm, while the algorithm for deciding which slot should be in focus at any given moment (based on this hidden information) is simple enough to be handcrafted.

The simplest state space representation (*Small*) does not store any knowledge related to the reliability of the information in the current slot. Such knowledge is added in the other representations, at the cost of enlarging the size of the state space. The *ConfLevel* variable used in *Small Confidence* and *SmallConf + InfoSource* was designed after studying the policies learned for the *Large Confidence* state space, where it was observed that these policies tended to base their actions on a single confidence threshold. In this way it is possible to keep the state space size down without degrading performance.

2.5 Learning algorithm

2.5.1 *Description of algorithm*

Since we are trying to find a memoryless policy by describing dialogue as an MDP in an environment that is in reality only partially observable (POMDP) [6], there are arguments in favour of using eligibility trace based methods rather than standard Q-learning [5]. These provide a means of combining Q-learning, where state-action values are updated based on the current estimate of the value for the next state, with Monte Carlo learning where

Action	Description
Mixed Initiative	Mixed initiative query for more information (available if current slot is empty).
System Initiative	Query for information on the current slot (available if current slot is empty).
Explicit confirmation	Confirm the contents of the current slot explicitly.
Confirm all	Confirm the contents of all slots.
Implicit confirmation	Confirm the contents of the current slot implicitly while querying for information on the next slot.
Accept	Accept information in the current slot without confirmation at present. Terminate if a complete transaction has been specified.

Table 2: Actions defined for the application

Variable	Possible values
CurrentFocus	Type, Day, Film, Cinema
Status	Empty, Filled
#Empty	0, 1, 2, 3
#Unconfirmed	0, 1, 2, 3
InfoSource	Default,Negated,Elicited,Unelicited
Confidence	Default, 0.2, 0.3, ..., 1.0
ConfLevel	Default, Low, High

Table 3: Variables used in the different state space representations

state-action values are updated based on the reward at the end of the episode. Q-learning has the advantage of allowing the update for each state to be performed immediately, rather than having to wait until the end of the episode. However, because of its dependence on the next state, it may be more vulnerable to violations of the Markov property.

We used Watkins' $Q(\lambda)$ algorithm with replacing eligibility traces [12]. The algorithm is based on estimating the optimal action value function $Q^*(s,a)$, which describes the expected future reward generated by selecting an action a while in state s and following the optimal policy thereafter. Once this function is known, an optimal policy can be followed by simply selecting the action with the largest Q value in each state.

In order to estimate $Q^*(s,a)$, a function $Q(s,a)$ is initialised arbitrarily and the resulting policy interfaced with the simulation system to generate learning dialogues. After each system action, Q(s,a) is updated using the update equation

$$Q_{t+1}(s,a) = Q_t(s,a) + \alpha\delta_t e_t(s,a), \qquad (2)$$

where α is a variable step size parameter, $e_t(s,a)$ is the *eligibility* of the state-action pair (s,a) to be updated, and δ_t is an error term:

$$\delta_t = r_t + \max_a Q_t(s_{t+1},a) - Q_t(s_t,a_t), \qquad (3)$$

with r_t being the observed reward and s_{t+1} the successor state after action a_t was taken in state s_t at time t.

The eligibility changes to reflect the strength of the causal link between the current state and a particular state-action pair (s,a) from earlier in the episode. It decays exponentially with time, and is set to zero whenever an exploratory action is taken:

$$e_t(s,a) = \begin{cases} 1 & \text{if } s = s_t \text{ and } a = a_t \\ 0 & \text{if } s = s_t \text{ and } a \neq a_t \\ \lambda e_{t-1}(s,a) & \text{if } s \neq s_t. \end{cases} \qquad (4)$$

Here λ is the eligibility trace decay parameter, which determines the nature of the algorithm. For $\lambda = 0$ it reduces to Q-learning, with action values being updated based only on the immediate successor state. For $\lambda = 1$ the algorithm is a version of Monte Carlo learning, which performs updates based on the eventual accumulated reward. Intermediate values of λ produce algorithms that combine the properties these two approaches.

2.5.2 Choice of parameters

The step size was set as $\alpha_k = 1/(p^k)$, where k is the number of times a particular parameter has been updated, and p is a constant between 0.5 and 1.0 (good convergence was obtained with $p = 0.8$). Exploration was done using an epsilon-greedy strategy, with epsilon starting at 1 (random exploration) and decreasing exponentially to a minimum of 0.1 (exploration occurs 10% of the time). These settings satisfy the theoretical requirements to ensure convergence to the optimal policy.

Figure 1 shows how the Q value of the initial dialogue state progresses in a typical training run. After 10^6 episodes the fluctuations are in the order of 0.01, which is sufficient for the purpose of these experiments. The training runs for results presented in the remainder of this paper were performed for a length of 10^6 episodes. To verify the accuracy of these experiments, a number of training runs were also performed for periods of up to 10^7 episodes, with no noticeable change in results.

Policies trained using various values of the eligibility trace decay parameter λ are compared in Figure 2. This illustrates the effect of changing the learning algorithm from Q-learning ($\lambda = 0$) to Monte Carlo learning ($\lambda = 1$) via a set of intermediate algorithms. The graph shows

Name	State variables	Size
Small	Focus, Status, #Empty, #Unconfirmed	209
Information Source	Focus, Status, #Empty, #Unconfirmed, InfoSource	480
Large Confidence	Focus, Status, #Empty, #Unconfirmed, Confidence	1298
Small Confidence	Focus, Status, #Empty, #Unconfirmed, ConfLevel	330
SmallConf + InfoSource	Focus, Status, #Empty, #Unconfirmed, ConfLevel, InfoSource	778

Table 4: State space representations

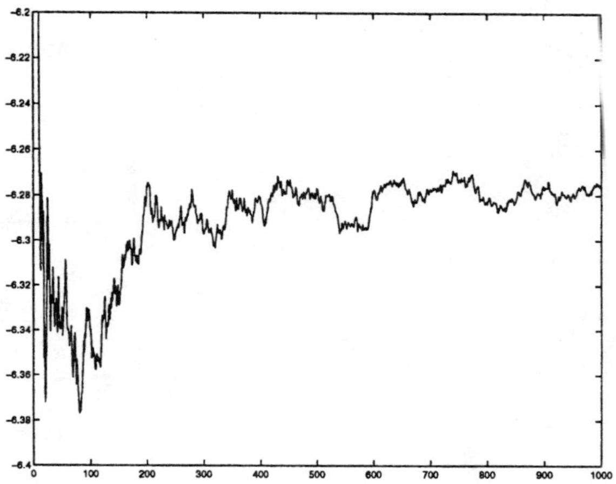

Figure 1: Q value of the initial dialogue state as training progresses

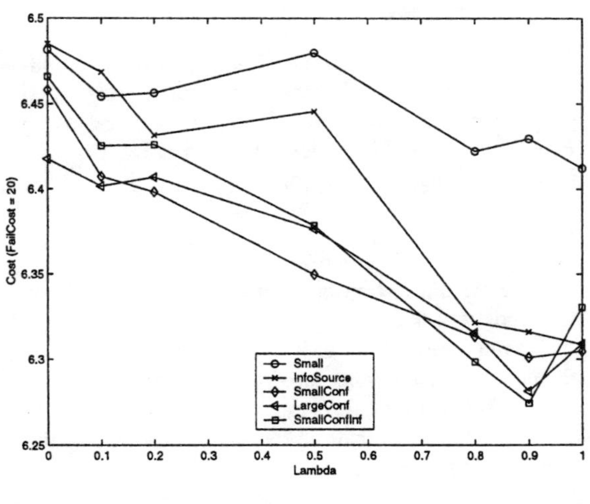

Figure 2: Comparison of policies trained using different eligibility trace decay rates

the performance of policies using each of the state space representations, for the case of $FailCost = 20$. Other cost functions gave similar results.

We observe that different values of λ work well for different state space representations, but overall the best results are obtained for algorithms close to Monte Carlo learning rather than Q-learning, with $\lambda \approx 0.9$. This supports the observation reported in [5] that a value of $\lambda = 0.9$ worked well over a range of problems where memoryless policies were obtained for partially observable MDPs. (Note, however, that the difference in performance for values close to 1 was small and probably not significant. Thus it is not clear whether the use of eligibility traces gives any real improvement over simple Monte Carlo learning.) The remaining experiments presented here use this value for λ.

2.6 Experiments and results

2.6.1 Baseline system

The main baseline system available is the original hand designed application. This uses a large number of internal system variables and advanced strategies such as variable confidence thresholds that depend on the number of times specific fields have been prompted for, etc. Since, in order to keep the design problem tractable, we have restricted ourselves to simple state spaces, comparing with this full system is not entirely fair on the more limited automatically designed policies. For this reason we also constructed several handcrafted systems that operate in the *Small* state space, using our defined action set. These policies are simple, not taking much dialogue context into account, but of the type that a human would implement. They are summarised in Table 5.

2.6.2 Learning experiments

After training policies for each of the different state space representations and cost functions, the performance of each policy was measured by means of simulations (10^5 episodes per evaluation). The results are shown in Figure 3. Each graph represents the cost, shown on the vertical axis, as measured using a different cost function which is indicated by the label on the left. The horisontal axes represent the policies learned using the different algorithms, which are grouped according to the state space representation used (indicated at the top). The solid lines join policies learned using the same state space representation but different values of *FailCost*.

For each cost function, the policies optimised for that function can be expected to outperform those optimised for a different function. Thus, on the first graph, the policies trained using a *FailCost* of 20 should outperform those using other values. The graph shows that this

Policy	Description
Handcraft 1	Mixed initiative with full confirmation at each step.
Handcraft 2	Mixed initiative with explicit confirmation of each slot but no full confirmation at the end.
Handcraft 3	Mixed initiative with explicit confirmation of each slot and full confirmation at the end.
Handcraft 4	Mixed initiative with confirmation only at the end.
Handcraft 5	System initiative with full confirmation at each step.
Handcraft 6	System initiative with explicit confirmation of each slot but no full confirmation at the end.
Handcraft 7	System initiative with explicit confirmation of each slot and full confirmation at the end.
Handcraft 8	System initiative with confirmation only at the end.

Table 5: Handcrafted policies

is indeed the case, and also that the difference in performance between policies optimised for different cost functions is much greater than those between policies that use different state space representations.

Table 6 compares the results for the optimal policies obtained using the different state space representations, as well as the handcrafted policies in the small state space and the original hand designed system, using a much larger state space. Note that the larger state spaces tend to outperform the smaller ones, but the improvement when extra information is added is small. The automatically designed systems outperform the systems handcrafted on the small state space by large margins. They outperform the original design on some cost functions but are beaten on others, highlighting the inflexibility of the hand design which cannot be optimal for all cost functions.

2.6.3 Comparison of learned policies

The different cost functions represent a range of scenarios where the system is expected to learn dialogue strategies ranging from safe (when the cost of a failure is high, it pays to use confirmation thoroughly) to risky (when failures are less crucial, it is better to streamline the dialogue and use confirmation only when really necessary).

The histogram in Figure 4 shows how the relative frequencies of the different actions in the *Small* state space change as the cost of a transaction failure decreases from 20 to 2. While the exact behaviour of a policy cannot easily be predicted, the large scale trends conform to what one would expect: as the cost of failure decreases, confirmation actions are used less frequently while acceptance actions increase. This illustrates how the learning algorithm adapts to different scenarios in a way that is hard for human designers to emulate.

Figure 5 illustrates how these different policies produce different dialogue costs. The histograms show the cost distributions obtained when the four policies of Figure 4 are evaluated using $FailCost = 5$. The first two policies were optimised for $FailCost = 20$ and $FailCost = 10$ respectively. They have high average dialogue length, which produces a noticeable shift to the right, as well as long tails reflecting the existence of exceptionally long dialogues. These correspond to dialogues with multiple confirmation subdialogues containing recognition errors.

The third policy is the one that has been optimised for this particular cost function. It strikes a balance between minimising the average dialogue length and restricting the transaction failure rate, which is visible as a secondary peak emerging to the right. The fourth policy was optimised for $FailCost = 2$ and shortens dialogue length even more, moving the main peak further to the left. However, this comes at the cost of increasing the failure rate such that the secondary peak causes the overall dialogue cost to rise.

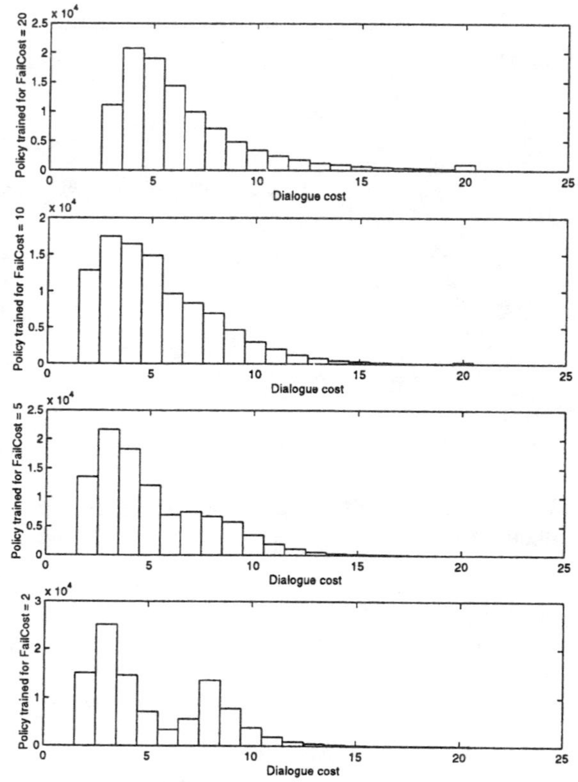

Figure 5: Distribution of dialogue costs for policies optimised for different cost functions: each graph shows a histogram of costs (evaluated using $FailCost = 5$) for policies trained using the cost function indicated on the left

3. CONCLUSIONS

The need for dialogue strategies that are adapted to the specific circumstances of the application, such as the characteristics of the user population and the speech

Policy	Average cost			
	FailCost = 20	FailCost = 10	FailCost = 5	FailCost = 2
Small	6.43	6.12	5.08	4.27
Information Source	6.32	6.08	5.04	4.24
Large Confidence	6.28	5.84	5.00	4.25
Small Confidence	6.30	5.91	4.98	4.25
SmallConf + InfoSource	6.27	5.86	4.99	4.25
Handcraft 1	9.36	8.79	8.50	8.33
Handcraft 2	11.42	9.99	9.27	8.84
Handcraft 3	9.41	8.78	8.47	8.28
Handcraft 4	9.51	8.84	8.50	8.30
Handcraft 5	8.33	7.75	7.46	7.28
Handcraft 6	10.76	9.27	8.52	8.08
Handcraft 7	8.74	8.04	7.67	7.48
Handcraft 8	8.61	7.77	7.34	7.09
Original hand design	6.82	5.52	4.88	4.49

Table 6: Costs obtained for automatically and manually designed systems

recognition performance, is widely recognised. This paper describes how a detailed user and error simulation tool can be used in an MDP reinforcement learning framework to design such strategies. Since the state space representation can be difficult to design, a great advantage of this approach compared to previous work is the ability to explore different state spaces using a single fixed dialogue corpus, transcribed without reference to system state.

We applied the approach to learn dialogue strategies in a real application, automatically selecting among the many possible approaches to confirmation and mixed initiative issues. A number of state space representations were compared, as well as the effect of using different cost functions. The learned policies outperformed handcrafted policies using the same state space, and gave performance similar to that of the original hand design, which used a much richer state space and action set. They also display flexibility, optimising their behaviour according to the cost function being used.

In a real application it will often not be clear what the best choice of cost function is. Ideally, a cost function should be constructed based on user satisfaction studies done in the specific application domain, using methods such as the PARADISE framework [16]. Where such studies have not been done, the designer may have to choose a cost function in an ad hoc way. This is not as disadvantageous as it may seem, since the behaviour of the learned strategy can then be evaluated qualitatively and the cost function adjusted until the learned strategy displays the desired characteristics. Subsequent user trials can then be used to elicit user satisfaction ratings which can be used to refine the cost function further.

Since the automatically learned strategies yield performance similar to the manually designed system, it would be possible to save several design iterations without degrading performance by using only automatic learning. However, even better performance should be obtainable by combining the two approaches: automatic learning is ideal for optimising low level aspects of system behaviour such as determining appropriate confidence levels, confirmation strategy and management of initiative. Optimal treatment of these aspects depend on the user and error parameters encapsulated in the simulation tool and cannot be designed by hand in a principled way.

Methods such as manual design and automated planning, on the other hand, are useful for high level aspects of system design that are not influenced as directly by the simulation parameters. For instance, the order in which the system should request different pieces of information should not be decided by the reinforcement learner, as it is unlikely that the user model will contain information that is particularly relevant to the question. Instead, the issue should be resolved at a higher level without giving the learning algorithm a choice in the matter.

Such integration of automatic learning methods with more traditional approaches can be done by appropriate selection of the state space and action set that is presented to the reinforcement learner: by restricting the options available to the algorithm, it is allowed to focus on the design aspects for which its models contain useful information, without having to try to distinguish between high level strategies for which it is not suited. At the same time, this approach makes the problem more tractable so that a more detailed state space can be used. Closer investigation into the combination of automatic learning with other methods is an important topic for future research.

Another open research question concerns the refinement of the user model, for instance by using separate models for different subsets of the user population, e.g. a naive and an experienced user group. While the idea of basing the system design on an explicit model of user expertise is not new [13], no data-driven versions of such an approach seem to have been investigated yet. Once such models have been constructed, it would be possible to learn strategies that estimate and adapt to user expertise.

The state space of the user model could also be expanded to include more detailed parameters such as the number of times the user has been asked a specific question. Modelling user behaviour this closely is likely to suffer from data sparsity problems, but if accurate models can be constructed it would expand the range of situations to which the learning system is applicable.

We conclude that the automatic learning approach presented here opens a large scope of possibilities for development and optimisation of adaptive dialogue applications.

4. REFERENCES

[1] D. Goddeau and J. Pineau. Fast reinforcement learning of dialog strategies. *Proc. ICASSP*, 2000.

[2] E. Levin and R. Pieraccini. A stochastic model of computer-human interaction for learning dialogue strategies. *Proc. Eurospeech*, pages 1883–1886, 1997.

[3] E. Levin, R. Pieraccini, and W. Eckert. A stochastic model of human-machine interaction for learning dialogue strategies. *IEEE Transactions on Speech and Audio Processing*, 8(1):11–23, 2000.

[4] D. Litman, M. Kearns, S. Singh, and M. Walker. Automatic optimization of dialogue management. *Proc. COLING*, 2000.

[5] J. Loch and S. Singh. Using eligibility traces to find the best memoryless policy in partially observable Markov decision processes. *The 15th International Conference on Machine Learning*, July 1998.

[6] N. Roy, J. Pineau, and S. Thrun. Spoken dialogue management using probabilistic reasoning. *Proc. Association for Computational Linguistics*, 2000.

[7] K. Scheffler. *Automatic design of human-machine dialogue systems*. PhD thesis, Cambridge University, 2002.

[8] K. Scheffler and S. Young. Corpus-based dialogue simulation for automatic strategy learning and evaluation. *Proc. NAACL Workshop on Adaptation in Dialogue*, 2001.

[9] S. Singh, M. Kearns, D. Litman, and M. Walker. Reinforcement learning for spoken dialogue systems. *Proc. NIPS*, 1999.

[10] S. Singh, M. Kearns, D. Litman, and M. Walker. Empirical evaluation of a reinforcement learning spoken dialogue system. *Proc. AAAI*, 2000.

[11] S. Singh, D. Litman, M. Kearns, and M. Walker. Optimizing dialogue management with reinforcement learning: Experiments with the NJFun system. *Journal of Artificial Intelligence Research*, 16, 2002.

[12] R. Sutton and A. Barto. *Reinforcement Learning: An Introduction*. MIT Press, Cambridge, Massachusetts; London, England, 1998.

[13] G. Veldhuizen van Zandten. User modelling in adaptive dialogue management. *Proc. Eurospeech*, 1999.

[14] M. Walker. An application of reinforcement learning to dialogue strategy selection in a spoken dialogue system for email. *Journal of Artificial Intelligence Research*, 12:387–416, 2000.

[15] M. Walker, J. Fromer, and S. Narayanan. Learning optimal dialogue strategies: a case study of a spoken dialogue agent for email. *Proc. Association for Computational Linguistics*, pages 1345–1352, 1998.

[16] M. A. Walker, D. J. Litman, C. A. Kamm, and A. Abella. PARADISE: A general framework for evaluating spoken dialogue agents. *Proc. Conf. of the Association for Computational Linguistics*, pages 271–280, 1997.

[17] S. Young. Probabilistic methods in spoken dialogue systems. *Philosophical Transactions of the Royal Society (Series A)*, 358:1389–1402, 2000.

[18] B. Zhang, Q. Cai, J. Mao, and B. Guo. Planning and acting under uncertainty: A new model for spoken dialogue systems. *Uncertainty in Artificial Intelligence: Proceedings of the 17th Conference*, pages 572–579, 2001.

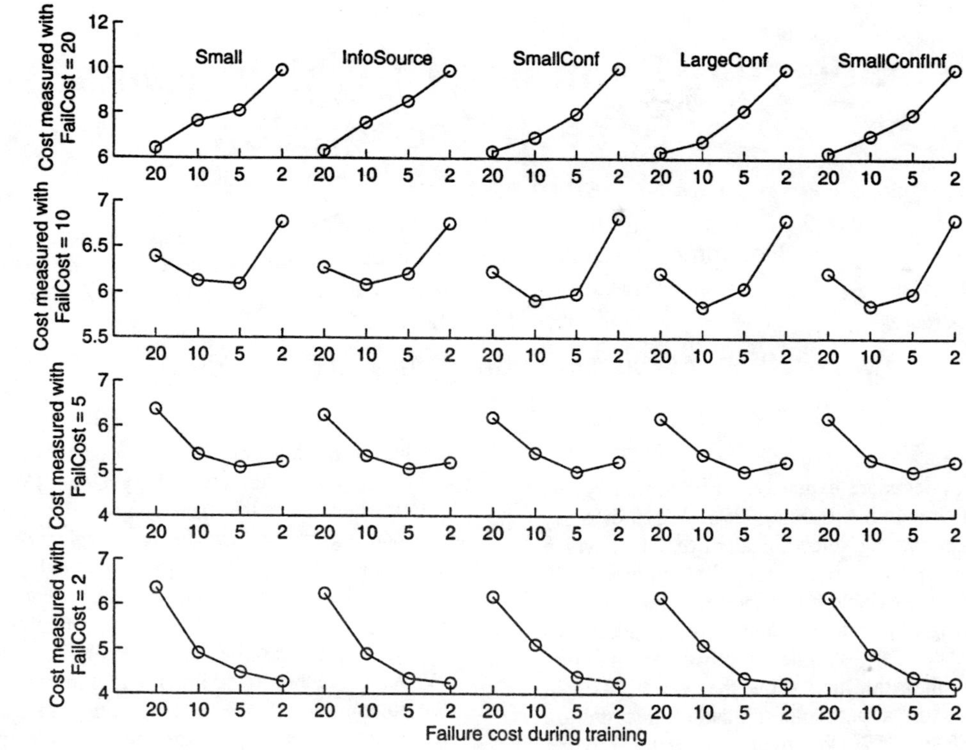

Figure 3: Comparison of policies trained on different cost functions for all state space representations: each graph plots the cost for all the policies, measured using the cost function indicated on the left

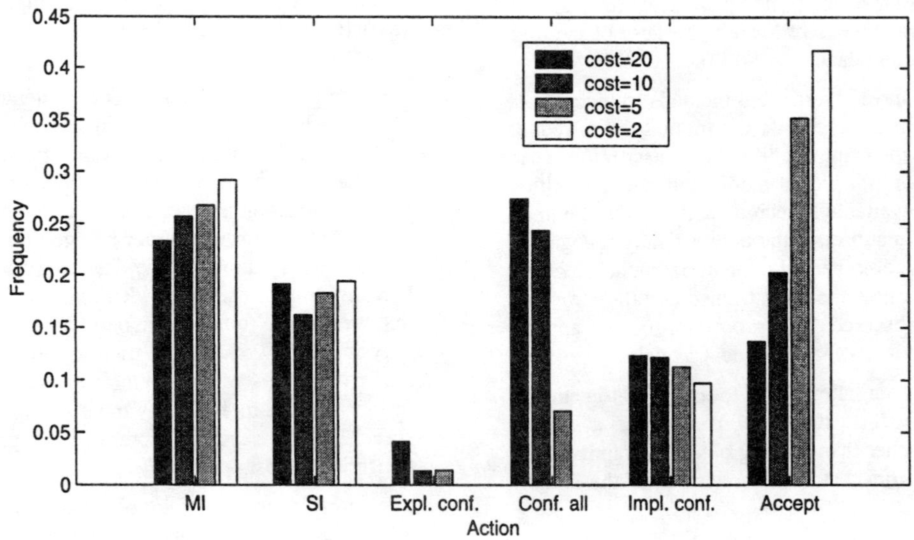

Figure 4: Relative frequencies of actions in policies optimised for different cost functions

Selective Sampling of Training Data for Speech Recognition

Teresa M. Kamm and Gerard G. L. Meyer
Center for Language and Speech Processing
Department of Electrical and Computer Engineering
The Johns Hopkins University
Baltimore, MD 21218, USA

tkamm@clsp.jhu.edu, gglmeyer@jhu.edu

ABSTRACT

Speech recognition systems are expensive to train, mostly due to the high cost of annotating training data. We previously proposed an iterative training selection algorithm [1], which sought to improve speech recognition by automatically selecting a subset of the available humanly transcribed training data, thereby improving error rates without incurring additional transcription cost. We suggest one improvement to that "selective sampling" algorithm and show that we are able to reduce the error rate on a particular alphadigit recognition problem from 10.3% to 9.5%. We then extend the iterative training selection algorithm to work with untranscribed speech, guiding selection of speech that is then transcribed. We show, on a particular alphadigit recognition problem, that it is possible to match the baseline error rate while only incurring 25% of the transcription cost.

1. INTRODUCTION

Conventional wisdom says that incorporating more training data is the surest way to reduce the error rate of a speech recognition system. This, in turn, guarantees that speech recognition systems are expensive to train, because of the high cost of annotating training data.

Several authors [2-4] have investigated methods to incorporate automatically transcribed speech into the training set to reduce error rates without incurring additional transcription cost. These methods start with an initial model and run recognition on a large amount of available speech data. A selection criteria is applied that selects a subset of the automatically recognized material which is then combined with the initial model to create a larger training set. A new model is trained and the error rate of the new model is observed. This procedure may be applied iteratively on unused data to get subsequent models.

In [1], we suggested an alternative to using automatically transcribed data to reduce the cost of training a speech recognition system. Rather than seeking out more training data, we proposed an algorithm that made better use of the already available training data. This approach, which is a "selective sampling" algorithm (coined by Cohn [5]), is to allow the training algorithm to assert control over which examples are used during training and focus the selection on examples that are in the region of uncertainty. In the region of uncertainty, the hypothesis made by the model is very likely to be in error. By identifying the region of uncertainly, training material that lies in that region can be automatically selected, labeled by a human and incorporated into the training set. This approach has the potential to select a set of training data from which to build a model that can outperform a model built on much more, but randomly selected, training data.

In this paper, we review the iterative training selection algorithm proposed in [1], which sought to improve speech recognition by automatically selecting a subset of the available humanly transcribed training data, thereby improving error rates without incurring additional transcription cost. We then propose a secondary selection criterion to remove the inherent randomness in the original algorithm while maintaining the error rate. Using this iterative algorithm, we are able to reduce the error rate on a particular alphadigit recognition problem from 10.3% to 9.5%, and we do this by selecting 35% of the full training set.

We then propose an extension of the iterative training selection algorithm to select untranscribed speech that is then transcribed by humans. We investigate this unsupervised algorithm on the same alphadigit recognition problem. Starting with a seed system trained on a small amount of annotated data, we desire to reduce the error rate of our recognition system by iteratively incorporating automatically selected speech that is then humanly transcribed and added into the training set. We show that we are able to match the baseline error rate of 10.3% while only incurring 25% of the transcription cost, that is, by only transcribing 25% of the available speech. The error rate can be further reduced to 10.0% by transcribing 65% of the available speech. Either scenario represents a significant reduction in transcription cost.

The organization of this paper is as follows. Section 2 introduces the notation used throughout this paper and reviews the automatic training paradigm. Section 3 discusses the corpus and the baseline systems. Section 4 reviews the previously proposed iterative training selection algorithm and presents new results. Section 5 discusses the unsupervised iterative training selection algorithm that does not assume availability of transcribed training data. Finally, a summary and discussion is presented in Section 6.

Proceedings of HLT 2002, Second International Conference on Human Language Technology Research, M. Marcus, ed., Morgan Kaufmann, San Francisco, 2002.

2. AUTOMATIC TRAINING PARADIGM

In order to discuss the Automatic Training Paradigm, which is the core of our iterative algorithm, we first must introduce some notation. Given T, a set of audio speech cuts, or segments, we define:

- |T|: The size of set T.
- H(T): The human transcription of the set T.
- M(H(T)): The model M built using the human transcription of set T. (It is assumed that the transcription is paired with the audio speech cuts and the audio is also used in modeling.)
- A(M,T): Automatic transcription of the set T using the model M.
- S(A(M,T)): The subset of T selected by the selection criterion, based on the automatic transcription of T using model M.
- E(A(M,T)): The error rate of the automatic transcription of set T using model M.

The Automatic Training Paradigm, as described in [1], is comprised of two steps. The first step, Automatic Subset Selection [Figure 1], goes as follows: Given a training set T and a human transcript H(T), train a model M_0=M(H(T)). Given another set of speech U_0 which has human transcription H(U_0), use M_0 to get the automatic transcription A(M_0,U_0). Apply a selection criterion to A(M_0,U_0) to get a subset U_1=S(A(M_0,U_0)) of U_0.

Once the subset is selected the second step, Model Update and Test [Figure 2], goes as follows: Use human transcription H(T) and human transcription H(U_1) to train model M_1=M(H(T) U H(U_1)). Apply the model M_1 to the test set D and observe the error rate E(A(M_1,D)).

3. CORPUS AND BASELINE SYSTEMS

3.1 Data

The speech corpus chosen to perform this study was selected based on four criteria:

1. To focus attention on the acoustic problem.
2. To be a realistic task.
3. To have a standard train/test set defined for comparison with other published results.
4. To be small enough such that experiment turn-around time would be manageable.

The OGI Alphadigit Corpus [6] met these criteria. The corpus is a collection of over 3000 subjects speaking strings of 6 alphadigits over the telephone. The alphadigits are the English letters "A" through "Z" and the digits "0" through "9". The speakers were prompted to speak either 19 or 29 sets of 6 alphadigits. Researchers at ISIP [7] have defined a standard train/test partition of this corpus, and have reported error rates achieved on this corpus [8].

From the ISIP training partition of 51545 sentences, 46730 sentences were selected such that the transcription matches one of the prompts given in the prompt list [6]. This was an inexpensive way to remove possible transcription substitution errors from the training set. In this paper, this training set is denoted as T_{ALL}. From the ISIP evaluation test partition of 3329 sentences, 3112 sentences were selected using the prompt list in the same way. This test set is denoted as D.

3.2 System Description

The training and testing of the systems described in this paper were done using HTK [9]. In general, the procedures used followed the steps given in the HTK documentation.

The systems described in this paper follows [8], with the exception that we choose to build word models rather than syllable models. A word model is created for each alphadigit, plus silence and short pause. The silence/short pause models are built according to the procedure in the HTK documentation [9]. Each word model uses a standard left-right topology including a re-entrant transition, with the number of states based on one-half the mean duration of the word.

The word durations are determined by first training a system with each word model having 10 states. Then a forced alignment of the models to the training data is generated and the word duration statistics are computed from this forced word alignment. All systems discussed in this paper have a total of 825 states.

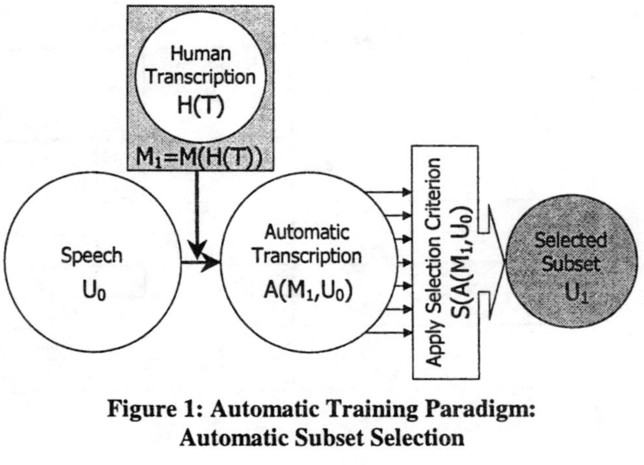

Figure 1: Automatic Training Paradigm: Automatic Subset Selection

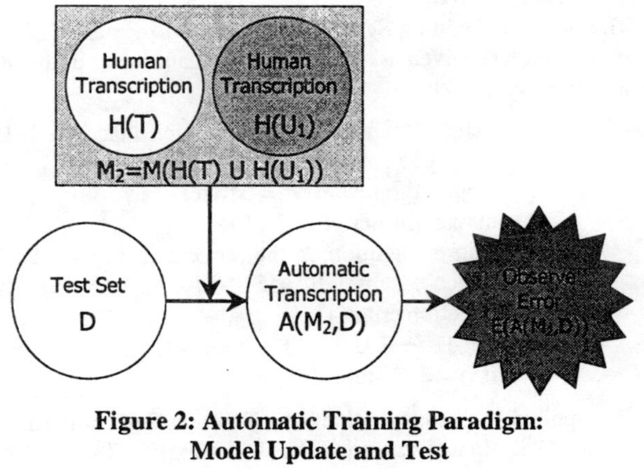

Figure 2: Automatic Training Paradigm: Model Update and Test

The features are 12 mel-frequency cepstral coefficients plus energy, the deltas, and the double deltas to make a feature vector of length 39. In all systems discussed in this paper, 12 gaussians are estimated per feature per state.

An equal probability word network is used to drive recognition. This network is defined as: optional silence, followed by one or more alphadigits, followed by optional silence.

3.3 Baseline Systems

Several systems were built that demonstrate baseline performance for varying amounts of training data. For a balanced (i.e. by sex, type) amount of training data T_b (see [1] for further details), a model $M_b=M(H(T_b))$ was built, comprised of 36 "word" models and 2 silence models, using the human transcription of T_b and standard HTK training procedures [9]. The system error rates $E(A(M_b,D))$ for models M_b based on various balanced training subsets of T_{ALL} are given in Table 1.

Table 1. Relation between Error Rate and Training Size for selected training sizes.

Training Size (% of T_{ALL})	Error Rate (%)
5%	14.3%
10%	11.8%
25%	11.0%
50%	10.4%
100%	10.3%

4. ITERATIVE TRAINING SELECTION ALGORITHM

In [1], we demonstrated that high recognition error is an effective selector of training material that can make a significant improvement in error rate. We then proposed the following iterative training selection algorithm that iteratively selects additional training material that is subsequently incorporated into the recognition model. In Section 4.1, we review the previously proposed iterative training selection algorithm. Then in Section 4.2, we discuss a weakness of that algorithm and propose a secondary selection criterion that addresses the weakness.

4.1 The Iterative Training Selection Algorithm

The Iterative Training Selection Algorithm to generate N models is as follows: Given a set of training data T_0 and the human transcription $H(T_0)$:

1. Select a subset T_1 from T_0 such that it is balanced (i.e. by sex and type) and let i = 1.
2. Obtain the model $M_i = M(H(T_i))$ by using T_i and the human transcription $H(T_i)$.
3. Run recognition on the remaining training T_0-T_i and select a subset $S_i = S(A(M_i,T_0-T_i))$ by applying a selection criteria.
4. Let $T_{i+1} = S_i \cup T_i$ and let i = i + 1.
5. If (i == N) stop, else go to step 2.

We applied the proposed Iterative Training Selection Algorithm to the OGI-alphadigit corpus by 1) letting $T_0=T_{ALL}$, all of the available training data, 2) letting T_1 be the 5% balanced subset selected from T_{ALL}, as described in Section 3 and, 3) replacing the stopping rule in step 5 with a heuristic stopping rule which is: stop if the error is no longer improving on a test set.

We ran the Iterative Training Selection Algorithm using a high error selection criterion where $|S_i| = |T_1|$ for i = 1 to N-1. The sequence of models was judged by applying the model M_i to the test set D and observing the error rate $E_i = E(A(M_i,D))$. The error rate of the sequence of models generated is summarized in column 3 of Table 2.

By iteratively applying the High Error Selection criteria, it is possible to select a subset of the full training from which to build a model that gives better recognition performance (9.4% error) than a model built using the full training set (10.3% error). In fact, it is only necessary to use 35% of the full training to achieve this result.

4.2 Randomness in Selection

When applying the Iterative Training Selection Algorithm to the training of the OGI alphadigits, the high error selection criterion was not sufficient to completely specify the subset to select at each iteration. For example, in the first iteration, the subset consisted of all the sentences that had 8 and 7 recognition errors and a randomly selected portion of the sentences with 6 errors. This random selection can influence the output of the Iterative Training Selection Algorithm, particularly when the selected subset is dominated by random selection. Several runs of the algorithm were made, and the range of minimum error was between 9.4 and 9.5%, at a training size of 35%.

As an alternative to random selection, we propose the use of a confidence measure to guide selection when necessary. In particular, we used the sentence posterior probability as a confidence measure and chose sentences that had a low confidence. This secondary criterion was invoked as necessary, whenever selection of a portion of sentences with the same number of errors was required. The error rates of the sequence of models generated using low confidence and random selection as secondary selection criterion are compared in Table 2.

Table 2: Comparison of Secondary Selection Criteria at each iteration of the Iterative Training Selection Algorithm

Iteration	Training Size (% of T_{ALL})	Error Rate (%)	
		Random Selection	Low Confidence Selection
1	5%	14.3%	14.3%
2	10%	11.8%	11.5%
3	15%	11.1%	10.8%
4	20%	10.4%	10.7%
5	25%	9.9%	10.1%
6	30%	9.5%	9.6%
7	35%	**9.4%**	**9.5%**
8	40%	9.7%	9.8%

The Low Confidence secondary selection criterion removed the inherent randomness of the original Iterative Training Selection Algorithm and an error of 9.5% was achieved using 35% of the training set. This result is comparable to the average result achieved with several runs of original algorithm.

5. UNSUPERVISED ITERATIVE TRAINING SELECTION ALGORITHM

In [1], we suggested that the Iterative Training Selection Algorithm could be extended to enable pragmatic use of future human transcription investment by selecting speech to transcribe which would contribute most to reduce the error rate. By using a low confidence selection criterion rather than a high error selection criterion on a large set of untranscribed speech, a small set of speech could be selected, transcribed by humans and then fed back into training. By observing error on a reasonably large test set, this process could be iterated until no reduction in error rate is observed.

This proposed extension of the Iterative Training Selection Algorithm is more formally stated as follows: Given T_0, a set of untranscribed speech:

1. Select a balanced subset T_1 from T_0 and let i = 1.
2. Transcribe T_i and obtain the model $M_i = M(H(T_i))$ by using T_i and the human transcription $H(T_i)$.
3. Run recognition on the remaining training T_0-T_i and select a subset $S_i = S(A(M_i, T_0-T_i))$ by applying an unsupervised selection criteria.
4. Let $T_{i+1} = S_i \cup T_i$ and let i = i + 1.
5. If (i == N) stop, else go to step 2.

We applied the Unsupervised Iterative Training Selection Algorithm to the OGI-alphadigit corpus by 1) letting T_0=T_{ALL}, all of the available training data, 2) letting T_1 be the 5% balanced subset selected from T_{ALL}, as described in Section 3 and, 3) replacing the stopping rule in step 5 with a heuristic stopping rule which is: stop if the error is no longer improving on a test set. Note that assuming that T_1 is balanced is not always possible without being able to observe the full transcribed training set. In some cases, a balanced set can be obtained by controlling the collected speech. For example, when obtaining speech for the alphadigit problem, a group of speakers with an equal number of males and females could be selected. Then it could be specified which alphadigits each person should say in order to have a balanced set of tokens available for the initial training step.

We ran the Unsupervised Iterative Training Selection Algorithm using a low confidence selection criterion where $|S_i| = |T_1|$ for $i = 1$ to N-1. The sequence of models were judged by applying the model M_i to the test set D and observing the error rate $E_i = E(A(M_i, D))$. The error rates of the sequence of models generated are summarized in Table 3.

From the data in Table 3, we make two observations. First, by selecting, transcribing, and training on only 25% of the speech we can obtain the same error rate we would get if we had transcribed and used the entire training set (10.3% using 100% of the training data). Second, by continuing to select and transcribe additional speech, a minimum error rate of 10.0% is achieved by using 65% of the training data. Either scenario represents a significant reduction in transcription cost with out compromising performance.

By iteratively applying the low confidence selection criteria, it is possible to achieve improved performance and minimize the transcription cost. We demonstrated that we can automatically select (without knowing the transcription) a subset of the full training, which can then be transcribed and used to build a model that gives better recognition performance (10.0% error) than a model built using the full training set (10.3% error). In fact, transcription of only 65% of the full training set is necessary to achieve this result.

Table 3: Comparison of Model Error Rates at each Iteration of the Unsupervised Iterative Training Selection Algorithm

Iteration	Training Size (% of T_{ALL})	Error Rate (%)
1	5%	14.3%
2	10%	11.9%
3	15%	10.9%
4	20%	10.4%
5	25%	**10.2%**
6	30%	10.2%
7	35%	10.2%
8	40%	10.3%
9	45%	10.1%
10	50%	10.1%
11	55%	10.1%
12	60%	10.1%
13	65%	**10.0%**

6. SUMMARY AND DISCUSSION

We have presented an iterative algorithm that automatically selects training material by observing a confidence score, and perhaps the recognition error, and selecting subsequent data that are hard for the current model to recognize. We have successfully demonstrated the algorithm on the OGI-alphadigit corpus in two cases. First, when a large transcribed training set is available, the error rate is reduced from 10.3%, using all of the available training data, to 9.5%, using 35% of the available training data. Second, when a large set of untranscribed speech is available, the baseline error rate of 10.3% can be achieved after selecting, transcribing, and using 25% of the speech, thereby making a significant reduction in transcription cost. Further transcription can reduce the error rate to 10.0%, after selecting, transcribing and using 65% of the speech.

The iterative training selection algorithm described in this paper is an independently derived implementation of the selective sampling theory described in Cohn [5]. In [5], the selective sampling theory is developed in the context of learning a binary concept in the absence of noise, and it is shown how it may be approximately implemented in a neural network. It is also suggested that selective sampling "is well suited to problems such as speech recognition", but gives no indication of how to apply such an approach to the complex problem of speech recognition.

In this paper, we have shown how selective sampling can be applied to a simple speech recognition problem. This is just the first step in attaining the goal of reducing the cost of training a large vocabulary continuous speech recognition (LVCSR) system.

7. REFERENCES

[1] T. M. Kamm and G. G. L. Meyer, "Automatic Selection of Transcribed Training Material," In *Proc. IEEE Workshop Automatic Speech Recognition and Understanding*, 2001

[2] G. Zavaliagkos and T. Colthurst, "Utilizing Untranscribed Training Data to Improve Performance," presented at Broadcast News Transcription and Understanding Workshop, Lansdowne, Virginia, 1998.

[3] L. Lamel, J.-L. Gauvain, and G. Adda, "Lightly Supervised Acoustic Model Training," presented at ISCA ITRW Workshop on Automatic Speech Recognition: Challenges for the New Millennium, Paris, France, 2000.

[4] T. Kemp and A. Waibel, "Unsupervised Training of a Speech Recognizer: Recent Experiments," In *Proc. EUROSPEECH*, 1999, pp. 2725-2728.

[5] D. Cohn, L. Atlas, and R. Ladner, "Improving Generalization with Active Learning," *Machine Learning, 15*(2), pp. 201-221, 1994.

[6] M. Noel, (1997), "Alphadigits," Center for Spoken Lang. Understand., Oregon Graduate Inst. Sci. Technol., Portland, OR, [Online] Available: http://www.cse.ogi.edu/CSLU/corpora/alphadigit

[7] J. Hamaker, A. Ganapathiraju, and J. Picone, (1997), "A proposal for a standard partitioning of the OGI AlphaDigit corpus," Inst. Signal Inform. Process., Mississippi State Univ., [Online] Available: http://www.isip.msstate.edu/projects/speech/software/asr/research/syllable/alphadigits/data/ogi_alphadigits/eval_trans.text

[8] J. Hamaker, et al., "Advances in Alpha Digit Recognition Using Syllables," In *Proc. ICASSP*, 1998, pp. 421-424.

[9] S. Young, et al., *The HTK Book, Version 2.2*: Entropic Ltd., 1999.

DynaSpeak: SRI's Scalable Speech Recognizer for Embedded and Mobile Systems

Horacio Franco, Jing Zheng, John Butzberger, Federico Cesari, Michael Frandsen, Jim Arnold, Venkata Ramana Rao Gadde, Andreas Stolcke, Victor Abrash

SRI International, 333 Ravenswood Ave., Menlo Park, CA 94025, USA

Phone: +1 650 859 3284

Email: hef@speech.sri.com

ABSTRACT

We introduce SRI's new speech recognition engine, DynaSpeak™, which is characterized by its scalability and flexibility, high recognition accuracy, memory and speed efficiency, adaptation capability, efficient grammar optimization, support for natural language parsing functionality, and operation based on integer arithmetic. These features are designed to address the needs of the fast-developing and changing domain of embedded and mobile computing platforms.

Keywords

Speech recognition, scalability, embedded and mobile computing.

1. INTRODUCTION

With the advent of more powerful processors, portable computing devices are gaining widespread use. Some of them, such as the new generation of mobile phones, high-end personal digital assistants (PDAs), and networked systems within automobiles, share the availability of significant computing power as well as information access through wireless networking. Because of the small physical size and the mobile nature of these devices, use of a keyboard may be impractical and sometimes distracting, while speech-driven user interfaces seem the ideal choice. The challenge is to offer a satisfactory user experience, freeing the user from the need to remember predefined commands by allowing the use of naturally constructed sentences, and by providing a robust and accurate recognition capability.

To address this need, we developed a new recognizer, named DynaSpeak™, which would support the use of SRI's state-of-the-art large vocabulary continuous speech recognition (LVCSR) technology on these new platforms with minimal loss of accuracy or robustness. One of our objectives was to have a scalable, flexible recognizer architecture that would not be bounded by any initial design limitations that could make the architecture obsolete when more powerful platforms arrive.

The challenge of supporting our speech technology on the target platforms required tackling several aspects: small memory footprint, addressed in part by a dynamic grammar and dynamic search architecture combined with optimization technology, as well as by the use of compressed acoustic models; integer computation, as most platforms for mobile and embedded systems do not support floating point arithmetic; and low-overhead Gaussian and search pruning, critical for fast decoding in large search spaces. In addition, we implemented full support for our different acoustic and language models (LMs) plus a simple natural language parsing capability. To achieve robustness, we also implemented fast online speaker adaptation and noise compensation capabilities. Finally, a multithread-safe implementation efficiently supports running multiple instances of the recognizer with different grammars and even acoustic models in each instance, a valuable feature for the development of speech-to-speech translation systems. In the following sections we review the most salient characteristics of the DynaSpeak recognizer.

The organization of this paper is as follows: Section 2 describes DynaSpeak's search strategy and grammar representation. Section 3 introduces acoustic and language model support. Section 4 describes an online adaptation algorithm used for speaker and environmental adaptation. Section 5 introduces an efficient algorithm to reduce Gaussian computation and search effort. Section 6 gives a brief description of the grammar optimization algorithm. Section 7 deals with natural language processing support. Section 8 discusses some implementation issues. Section 9 presents a sample mobile application. Section 10 summarizes the paper.

2. DYNAMIC SEARCH AND GRAMMARS

To reduce the amount of memory required for a given recognition task, we use hierarchical data structures that include a top-level word grammar and various related word subgrammars that may be loaded on demand. Each word in turn is described by a probabilistic graph of phones that can also be loaded dynamically. Each phone is represented by a probabilistic graph corresponding to a hidden Markov model (HMM), also loaded dynamically. At all layers of this hierarchy, the graph representation uses the same data structure. Unlike typical speech recognition systems, these grammars and subgrammars are not compiled and expanded into a single large flat network structure before runtime. Instead, during recognition, memory is allocated to a subgrammar when a transition to it is made during the search. The subgrammars may then be expanded and evaluated, and the probability of a match between the speech signal and an element of the subgrammar may be computed. During the search, whenever the maximum probability of all active states of a subgrammar, a word, or a

Proceedings of HLT 2002, Second International Conference on Human Language Technology Research, M. Marcus, ed., Morgan Kaufmann, San Francisco, 2002.

phone falls out of the pruning beam width, the related memory is released to ensure small memory consumption. Because unexpanded grammars and subgrammars take up very little memory, this method enables systems with limited memory to recognize and process a larger vocabulary than would otherwise be possible.

The dynamic search strategy and the hierarchical data structure allow for great flexibility in dealing with dynamic grammars, which means that grammars or subgrammars can be added, deleted, replaced, and selected by the application or the user, while the speech recognition system is operating. This feature enables on-the-fly configuration of a recognition application depending on the current context, which is important for many tasks.

3. ACOUSTIC AND LANGUAGE MODELS

3.1 Acoustic Model

Designed with scalability in mind, the DynaSpeak recognizer supports Gaussian mixture models (GMMs) with generic tying schemes, in particular phonetically tied mixtures (PTM) for small systems, and the more general Genonic models [1] that permit arbitrary tying, with groups of clustered triphone states sharing a common codebook, allowing for robust estimation of the model parameters while maintaining good acoustic resolution. Phone state tied mixtures (PSTMs) are a special case of Genonic model, where triphone state clustering is based on the central phone identity and the HMM state index. When model size must be small because of hardware limitations, PSTM models allow for better acoustic resolution than PTM models with similar-sized Gaussian codebooks. If we choose to use a smaller codebook size for each mixture in a PSTM model, and equate the total number of Gaussians with a PTM model, a PSTM is preferred due to a smaller number of mixture weight parameters, and for being easier to train robustly due to the smaller codebook size. In some of our experiments, with the same training data, PSTM models give equal or better performance than PTM models, with smaller storage requirements.

To satisfy the memory constraints of some applications we have introduced several techniques to make models compact, and yet accurate: First, we developed a decision-tree-based algorithm for mixture weight clustering to reduce the number of distinct probability distributions, thus saving significant storage space. Second, we developed a Gaussian merging algorithm to reduce the number of Gaussian components in different codebooks in an extension of our previous work [2]. The original algorithm was specially designed for PTM models, while the new algorithm allows Gaussian merging in the whole acoustic space, which is more effective in compressing models. Third, we replace mixture weights below a certain threshold with their average value [3], further reducing the number of distinct parameters and enabling compact storage and representation. Finally, we quantize Gaussian and mixture weight parameters to eight bits. This technique must be accompanied by a zero mean/unit variance feature normalization to keep Gaussian parameters within a common range, and with a saturation mechanism in the Gaussian probability computation. Our experiments showed that these model compacting techniques brought very little performance degradation.

Table 1 gives an example of model size compression. The baseline model is a PSTM model trained on 231,000 utterances comprising digit strings, command-and-control words, spellings, and dictations. The acoustic feature vectors are formed by C1-C12 plus normalized C0 mel cepstrum coefficients, with the addition of first- and second-order derivatives, extracted using a 32 ms analysis window and 16 ms frame advance rate on waveforms sampled at 8 kHz. We used a lexicon with 46 phonemes, and three-state left-to-right HMM topology. Thus, the acoustic model has 138 Gaussian codebooks (Genones). We selected a codebook size of 32 Gaussians per Genone. In context-dependent training, 22,194 triphone states were generated, each with 32 mixture weight parameters.

We tested this acoustic model on an unconstrained digit string recognition task with 1000 utterances collected in-house through telephone channels, and obtained a word error rate (WER) of 1.0% and a string error rate (SER) of 7.1%, (second row of Table 1). We then performed the mixture weight clustering and the Gaussian merging procedure, which reduced the parameter size to 10% of the original mixture weights and to 67% of the original Gaussians as shown in the second row. The error rate remained unchanged. A further compression that cut the number of Gaussians by 50% increased the error rate only slightly (last row of Table 1).

Table 1. Effectiveness of acoustic model compression

	# of mixture weights	# of Gaussians	WER in %	SER in %
Baseline	22194x32	4406	1.0	7.1
Compressed 1	2000x32	3000	1.0	7.1
Compressed 2	2000x32	2208	1.1	7.3

3.2 Language Model

Within the DynaSpeak recognizer, grammars are represented as weighted directed graphs, where nodes are associated with words or subgrammars, and arcs with transition probabilities. This representation is general enough for almost all types of grammars used in automatic speech recognition (ASR). As discussed earlier, a hierarchical grammar structure is allowed. At the user interface, DynaSpeak supports two forms of grammar specification: Java™ speech grammar format (JSGF) and DECIPHER™ probabilistic finite state grammar (PFSG) format.

JSGF specifies rule-based grammars, which are typically used for tasks like command-and-control. JSGF uses a textual representation that can be generated by both developers and computer programs. By an extension of the JSGF specification, we also allow pronunciations of new vocabulary items to be loaded dynamically along with the recognition grammars. PFSG is a special form of finite state string-to-weight transducer, in which words are emitted at nodes instead of arcs. This format is used by SRI's research LVCSR system, the DECIPHER recognizer. PFSGs can be conveniently used to represent statistical LMs, such as N-grams. In addition, DynaSpeak's hierarchical grammar structure allows an efficient representation of class-based statistical LMs [4], where word classes can be represented as subgrammars. The advantage of this representation is that word classes can be dynamically updated at runtime, which provides great flexibility for many applications. LM training and PFSG manipulation are supported by the SRI Language Modeling Toolkit [5].

4. ONLINE ADAPTATION

Mismatches between training and working conditions pose challenges to speech recognition technology in real-world applications, especially for embedded and mobile computing. The mismatches could stem from many sources; different speaker characteristics and environmental noise are two major factors. To improve the recognizer's robustness against these mismatches, and therefore promote the usability of speech recognition, acoustic model adaptation techniques have been extensively studied and applied. Based on the operation mode, adaptation approaches can be classified into two categories, online adaptation and offline (batch) adaptation. The former category adjusts model parameters at runtime, incrementally and instantly adapting the acoustic model to match the speaker and the acoustic environment. The latter category modifies the acoustic model based on certain amounts of prerecorded data. Based on the availability of word transcriptions for the speech data, adaptation algorithms can be divided into supervised algorithms, which modify model parameters according to correct word strings, and unsupervised algorithms, which use recognition hypotheses. Clearly, supervised adaptation requires the user's aid and cooperation in the process. In DynaSpeak's application scenarios, the most relevant technique is unsupervised online adaptation, which is also the most difficult; the challenge is to be robust enough to deal with very small amounts of adaptation data and possible recognition errors.

Among the prevailing adaptation techniques, transformation-based approaches have the advantage of needing small amounts of adaptation data and being robust to recognition errors, and are therefore the best candidates for unsupervised online adaptation. As stated in [6], transforms can be applied either to features or to models. We chose to perform feature-based transformation since it does not change the acoustic models, so that we need to save only a single copy of the acoustic models for different adaptation conditions, which is important in keeping a small memory footprint. Although full-matrix or block-diagonal matrix linear transforms proved to be more powerful, we use diagonal transforms because the former require more computation and numerical precision than many current embedded platforms can provide.

We developed an expectation-maximization (EM) algorithm for estimating linear transforms based on the maximum likelihood criterion. This adaptation algorithm was first proposed in [7], where the transforms were applied to the models instead of features. In our implementation, the inverse transform is applied to the acoustic features, which in theory has the same effect. We apply this algorithm in an online unsupervised mode, that is, recognition hypotheses are used to generate the statistics needed by the EM algorithm, and these statistics are accumulated during the use of the system, which produces incrementally refined estimates of the feature transforms. For computational efficiency, Viterbi alignments between HMM states and input speech were used instead of forward-backward alignments, and results proved to be similar. To reduce hardware requirements, we used only integer arithmetic operations in the algorithm implementation. With careful design, this causes little degradation in performance. We also use estimated confidence values to filter out possibly wrong recognition hypotheses, so only the utterances with high confidence values are used to update the transforms. This can improve the robustness of the adaptation algorithm. The transformation-based adaptation brought significant error rate reductions in several tasks.

The following experiment demonstrates the effectiveness of adaptation. We recorded 100 telephone numbers in each of four different conditions using a Compaq iPAQ personal digital assistant: inside a quiet office, off a busy street, at a restaurant, and in a dynamically changing noisy environment. We recognized these 400 utterances using an acoustic model trained as described in Section 3.1 with an unconstrained digit string grammar. Clearly, the training and working conditions are mismatched except for the case of office recordings. Table 2 compares the WER with and without online adaptation.

Table 2. WER comparison with and without online adaptation for different acoustic environments

	Office	Street	Rest.	Noisy	Total
No adapt	0.8%	12.2%	13.5%	20.2%	11.5%
Adapt	0.8%	8.6%	9.2%	13.3%	8.0%

As Table 2 shows, online adaptation brings WER reductions from 30% to 35% in all unmatched conditions.

5. GAUSSIAN AND PHONETIC PRUNING

Aside from memory constraints, limited processing speed also brings challenges to the speech recognition application on current hardware platforms of many embedded and mobile systems. A response time that is too long could affect the usability of an ASR application as seriously as recognition errors. A practical recognition system must strike a compromise between speed and accuracy; the well-known beam pruning technique in the Viterbi search algorithm is one approach to achieve this kind of tradeoff. To achieve better speed and less accuracy loss, we developed other pruning algorithms in addition to beam pruning, in order to reduce Gaussian and search computation. These algorithms are based on Gaussian shortlists and a form of phonetic pruning, both of which use a vector quantization (VQ) of the acoustic space and add little computational overhead.

Through a VQ algorithm, we partition the whole acoustic space into a number of VQ regions. The VQ codebooks are organized as a tree for quickly locating the VQ region in which a given input feature vector falls. For Gaussian shortlist pruning, we associate each VQ region with a list of Gaussians, which is built in a training procedure in which Gaussians having high likelihood scores for training samples falling within that region are put into the list. During recognition, at each frame, a VQ region is first located according to the feature vector of that frame. Then, only the Gaussians in the corresponding list are evaluated, while others are simply ignored. Thus, a significant part of Gaussian computation is avoided. This technique was first proposed in [1] and has been used in SRI's DECIPHER recognizer.

We recently extended the shortlist technique to prune the search space using a phoneme-based method. We compute the average phoneme posterior probabilities for each VQ region according to the training data samples falling into that region, and store the probabilities in a table. With this table, we can estimate phone posterior probabilities at each frame during search. Then, we prune the search hypotheses corresponding to phone posteriors below a chosen threshold. The method of phone-posterior-probability-based pruning was originally proposed in [8], where it was called *phone deactivation pruning*. In that work, a multilayer perceptron (MLP) was used to estimate the desired posterior probabilities. While this method is convenient within the hybrid connectionist/HMM approach, it is harder to apply to the more common GMM/HMM systems, like DynaSpeak. The proposed VQ-based phone posterior probability estimation method has very little computational overhead, and can be used over a window of consecutive frames for improved estimation robustness. Gaussian shortlist pruning and phonetic pruning can be combined, by sharing the same VQ codebook.

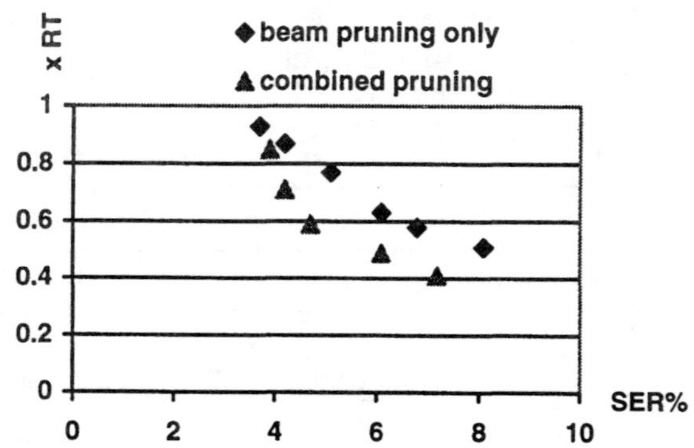

Figure 1: Comparison between two pruning schemes: beam pruning only and the combination of beam pruning, Gaussian shortlist, and phonetic pruning.

The following example shows how Gaussian shortlists and phonetic pruning improve the speed-accuracy tradeoff beyond the standard beam pruning on a task that is constrained by limited processing power. Using the same grammar and acoustic model, we tested two different pruning schemes: standard beam pruning only, and a combination of beam pruning, Gaussian shortlists, and phonetic pruning. Figure 1 shows operating points in terms of SER and real time factor (xRT) obtained with different pruning parameters, using the two pruning schemes. (The recognition experiments were performed on a development platform that is more powerful than the target hardware platform; the target performance therefore lies below 1xRT in this case.) It is clear that the combined pruning scheme is superior since it achieves a smaller error rate with faster recognition speed.

6. GRAMMAR OPTIMIZATION

Although DynaSpeak's hierarchical grammar structure allows for maximum flexibility and minimum static storage space, it causes some computational overhead to the search algorithm because of the frequent grammar expansion operations. More importantly, it impedes effective inter-grammar optimization, which could merge common partial search paths in different grammars to reduce the search effort. For speed-critical tasks where a small memory footprint is not essential, we developed an algorithm to selectively expand subgrammars and reduce the grammar hierarchy. This algorithm is not designed to fully flatten the hierarchical grammar into a word graph, but to remove certain unnecessary hierarchies for achieving better speed-size tradeoff. In fact, DynaSpeak supports some grammars that cannot be flattened, such as grammars with recursion. In some cases complete flattening could result in serious memory inefficiency; for example, a flat word graph is much less efficient in representing class-based trigram LMs with large word classes being referenced multiple times, than using subgrammars to represent word classes. In other cases, users might want to preserve certain subgrammars for special purposes, like online update, while removing other subgrammars for speed. Our algorithm has control parameters that allow the user to select the desired speed-size tradeoff, and to protect critical subgrammars in the expansion procedure. The design of this algorithm again reflects the main features of DynaSpeak, scalability and flexibility.

User-provided grammars, especially manually created ones, could have numerous redundancies, resulting in duplicated partial search paths. Removing these redundancies not only helps to achieve a compact and memory-efficient grammar representation, but also speeds up recognition. The above-mentioned selective grammar expansion procedure will create more room for possible grammar reduction compared to unexpanded hierarchical grammars. A commonly used approach views grammars as weighted finite state acceptors (WFSAs, a form of transducer) and performs the well-known determinization/minimization procedure [9]. We did not choose this approach for the following reasons: First, not all grammars are determinizable, and the determinization procedure has exponential complexity in the worst case. Second, determinization does not necessarily reduce grammar size; instead, it could increase the size exponentially. Third, the speed advantage of deterministic grammars over nondeterministic grammars is not very obvious in the context of speech recognition. Determinism could make pruning more efficient, but grammar size in terms of number of nodes and arcs also plays a big role. Finally, DynaSpeak internally does not represent grammars in WFSAs; bidirectional format conversion is needed in order to apply WFSA algorithms. In DynaSpeak's context, we need an efficient algorithm that can improve grammar compactness and determinism, but not necessarily to the minimal point.

With these considerations in mind, we designed a grammar reduction algorithm based on the following property: In a grammar, we can merge two nodes having identical word or subgrammar labels and the same set of successors or predecessors with the same transition probabilities without changing the grammar's function. This fact was previously used in [10] to reduce word lattices (acyclic directed word graphs); the new algorithm handles general grammars with special treatment for self-transition arcs.

We implemented this algorithm in a very efficient way based on a specially defined lexicographic order in the node space, and a fast sorting algorithm with linear complexity. In addition, we use a *pushing* algorithm [9] to redistribute probabilities across the graph, moving them as close as possible to the beginning of the sentence. This not only improves the pruning efficiency in the search, but also makes the reduction algorithm more effective. To further improve the reduction algorithm, we used a null node removal algorithm before performing grammar reduction, and a null node reintroduction algorithm after that. Here null nodes refer to special nodes without emission, which can be used to save a number of transitions, and thus reduce grammar size. However, they could also cause search overhead. Here, too, we provide control parameters for null node manipulation, and allow users to select the desired tradeoff between speed and size. A detailed description of the grammar optimization algorithm can be found in [11].

This grammar optimization approach has been used in many applications. For instance, in a phrase translation application described below and in [12], containing a grammar of 700 distinct phrases, the grammar optimization algorithms resulted in a speedup of 100%. We also successfully applied this approach to a class-based trigram grammar, and obtained a 140% speedup. In addition, we applied the graph reduction algorithm to generate a compact representation of multiple word pronunciations. The pronunciations of each individual word are organized as a network, with common phonemes shared. This approach achieves both memory and speed efficiency.

7. NATURAL LANGUAGE SUPPORT

In many applications, recognizing word strings from a user's utterance is not the final goal. The application may need to analyze the recognition result, (partly) understand the meaning of the utterance, and take corresponding actions. This capability is referred to as natural language understanding (NLU). A common NLU system parses the input text, generates a parse tree, and interprets the text segment corresponding to each tree node based on rules linked to that node. The parser usually employs its own grammar. In an application that combines ASR and NLU, the input of the NLU module are the recognized words. If the grammar for recognition is the same as the grammar for NLU we can directly use the recognizer as the parser. This, in turn, can save significant overhead and implementation. Although limited, this approach can be useful in many cases, especially for command-and-control and form filling applications.

In DynaSpeak, the support for hierarchical grammar structures allows for a straightforward implementation of this approach, which we call *slot filling*. A slot refers to a subgrammar of semantic interest. The goal of slot filling is to find the portions of the recognition hypothesis that correspond to each of the slots, and then to process them accordingly. In our implementation, we created a special grammar-level backtrace tag identifying grammar names, in addition to the word-level tags needed by the common word recognition. During search, we add grammar-level tags to the backtrace array on entering and exiting each subgrammar. At the end of the search, by retrieving the backtrace array, we can easily determine which segments of the decoded word string correspond to which subgrammars, thus identifying the slot fillers. In the grammar optimization phase, we deliberately preserve the subgrammars corresponding to slots from being expanded, while optimizing other subgrammars for speed. In addition, the DynaSpeak recognizer can output the parse tree along with the recognition hypothesis, to enable more sophisticated NLU postprocessing.

8. IMPLEMENTATION ISSUES

Despite rapid advances, today's hardware platforms for most embedded and mobile computing systems still do not meet the requirements for full-fledged state-of-the-art automatic speech recognition technology, mostly with regard to memory size and processing speed. Also, hardware floating point support is often missing. This gap creates significant engineering challenges to developers, who must carefully consider implementation issues to minimize resource requirements and performance loss. At the same time, the recognizer's architecture should be scalable enough to take advantage of hardware improvements in the future. In DynaSpeak, all aspects of the recognition computation, including front-end processing, observation probability density evaluation, and search are implemented in integer arithmetic. Most model parameters are stored in one-byte-long integers. Runtime estimation of the mean and variance of the acoustic features is used for feature normalization. This allows the model parameters to be kept within a uniform range that is suitable for byte encoding. The implementation is designed to be portable to floating point operation without difficulty when more powerful processors become available.

As the recognizer dynamically scales its use of resources depending on grammar and vocabulary size, we can seamlessly use DynaSpeak in a wide range of tasks, from simple command-and-control applications, to recognition of natural, unconstrained speech using large-vocabulary class-based statistical N-gram LMs. The recognizer has a multithread-safe implementation that allows multiple execution threads to be run efficiently, each with different acoustic models and grammars. The code, written in C++, is modular and portable, allowing rapid migration to new hardware and software platforms. Currently, Unix, Linux, and all versions of Windows are supported on PCs. Windows CE and embedded Linux are supported on Pocket PCs.

9. APPLICATION EXAMPLE

One of the first applications based on DynaSpeak is a phrase translation system, the "Phraselator" [12]. The goal of the system was to provide the capabilities of a voice-activated phrasebook, such that a user would utter a phrase from a set of allowable phrases, the phrase would be recognized among the possible alternatives, and an associated prerecorded translation would be played back. The moderate computational demand and the ubiquitous target environment for such a system make it an ideal application for the current generation of high-end PDAs. The main challenge in developing this system was to achieve real-time speaker-independent recognition for about 700 simultaneously active phrases. We used compressed PSTM acoustic models similar to those described in Section 3.1. These models were trained on 270,000 sentences of general, large-vocabulary English uttered by 7292 speakers.

We explored several recognition strategies to tackle the phrase recognition task: 1. Use a finite state grammar where each sentence is explicitly represented by concatenating the corresponding word models in a unique path; the recognized word sequence immediately corresponds to the recognized phrase. 2. Use a bigram grammar trained on the allowable phrases for recognition of the input utterance; the recognized word string is then matched against the allowable phrase set. The best lexical match is defined as the recognized phrase. 3. Use an approach similar to approach 2, but add a second pass of acoustic rescoring by using a lexical tree HMM formed from the top N candidate sentences obtained from the lexical match following the first recognition pass.

We evaluated the three recognition strategies on a test set of 1000 sentences uttered by 10 speakers. The SER was 6.0%, 11.3%, and

7.1%, respectively. These results favored approach 1, the sentence-based grammar, which was also slightly faster than approach 3. Most of the DynaSpeak features described in earlier sections were critical to the success of this application: grammar optimization, Gaussian and search VQ-based pruning for significant speed gains, speaker and environment adaptation for robustness, and dynamic loading of grammars, to allow on-the-fly change of phrase sets to deal with different translation domains. Given the speaker-independent and phonetic nature of the acoustic models, it is straightforward to create phrase sets for new domains with relatively simple tools. It is also easy to add sentence variations by either defining new sentences associated with the same translation, or by modeling each set of semantically equivalent sentences by a JSGF subgrammar.

10. SUMMARY

We have given a brief description of SRI's new DynaSpeak™ speech recognition engine. Scalability is one of the most important features in DynaSpeak's design and implementation. DynaSpeak supports Gaussian mixture model and hidden Markov model based acoustic models, and has several techniques for building small, yet accurate, models. For language modeling, it supports both rule-based grammars, specified as Java™ speech grammar format (JSGF), and statistical LMs, represented in the DECIPHER™ probabilistic finite state grammar (PFSG) format. DynaSpeak uses a dynamic search strategy based on a hierarchical data structure across grammar, word, phone, and state representations, which generally ensures a small memory footprint. In addition, it provides convenient support for class-based statistical language models. DynaSpeak has an efficient and flexible grammar optimization algorithm that allows the user to improve decoding speed according to the available memory resources. With additional pruning techniques in both Gaussian computation and search, DynaSpeak can achieve real-time recognition on complex tasks. It also provides natural language support, which allows users to develop speech-enabled applications with ease. To provide robustness to environment and speaker variability, DynaSpeak has an online adaptation capability that adjusts the acoustic models to match the input speech during use. DynaSpeak has been designed to run on current mobile computing hardware, without needing floating point support; it also remains highly portable to newly emerging platforms. In sum, the DynaSpeak ASR capabilities provide an effective enabling technology for today's and tomorrow's speech-powered mobile computing applications.

11. REFERENCES

[1] Digalakis, V., Monaco, P., and Murveit, H. Genones: Generalized Mixture Tying in Continuous Hidden Markov Model-Based Speech Recognizers. *IEEE Trans. Speech and Audio Processing* 4(4), 281-289, July 1996.

[2] Sankar, A. Experiments with a Gaussian Merging-Splitting Algorithm for HMM Training for Speech Recognition. In *Proc. DARPA Broadcast News Transcription and Understanding Workshop* (Lansdowne, VA), pp. 99-104, February 1998.

[3] Gupta, S., Soong, F., and Hami-Cohen, R. Quantizing Mixture Weights in a Tied-Mixture HMM, In *Proc. ICSLP* (Phildelphia, PA), pp. 1828-1831, 1996.

[4] Brown, P.F., Pietra, V.J.D., deSouza, P.V., Lai, J. C., and Mercer, R.L. Class-Based n-gram Models of Natural Language. *Computational Linguistics* 18(4), 467-481, December 1992.

[5] Stolcke, A., SRILM -- An Extensible Language Modeling Toolkit. In *Proc. ICSLP* (Denver, CO), vol. 2, pp. 901-904, 2002.

[6] Sankar, A., and Lee, C.-H. Stochastic Matching for Robust Speech Recognition. *IEEE Signal Processing Letters* 1, 124-125, August 1994.

[7] Digalakis, V. V., Rtischev, D., and Neumeyer, L. G. Fast Speaker Adaptation Using Constrained Reestimation of Gaussian Mixtures. 3(5), 357-366, September 1995.

[8] Renals, S. Phone Deactivation Pruning in Large Vocabulary Continuous Speech Recognition. *IEEE Signal Processing Letters* 3, 4-6, 1996.

[9] Mohri, M. Finite-state Transducers in Languages and Speech Processing. *Computational Linguistics* 23(2), 269-312, 1997.

[10] Weng, F., Stolcke, A., and Sankar, A. Efficient Lattice Representation and Generation. In *Proc. of ICSLP* (Sydney, Australia), vol. 6, pp. 2531-2534 November 1998.

[11] Zheng, J., and Franco, H. Fast Hierarchical Grammar Optimization Algorithm Towards Time and Space Efficiency. In *Proc. of ICSLP* (Denver, CO), pp. 393-396, September 2002.

[12] Phraselator. http://www.phraselator.com.

Word and Sub-word Indexing Approaches for Reducing the Effects of OOV Queries on Spoken Audio

Beth Logan, Pedro Moreno and Om Deshmukh*
COMPAQ Cambridge Research Laboratory
One Cambridge Center
Cambridge, Massachusetts, 02142-1612, United States
Beth.Logan@compaq.com, Pedro.Moreno@compaq.com

ABSTRACT

We explore the problem of out of vocabulary (OOV) queries in audio indexing systems by comparing three indexing methods on a broadcast news repository containing 75 hours of audio. Our systems are word-based, phoneme-based and a novel system based on syllable-like units called *particles*. To better examine the performance of these three approaches we use a query set where the percentage of OOVs has been artificially increased to 50%. We additionally investigate whether the combination of the three indexing techniques can yield improvements in retrieval. We explore several simple combination strategies such as weighted combinations. We find that combining word and sub-word based systems results in improved retrieval performance.

Keywords

Speech indexing, sub-word indexing

1. INTRODUCTION

Improvements in speech recognition technology and computing power have enabled the development of usable indexes for vast spoken audio repositories (e.g. [9]). A standard technique is to use speech recognition to transcribe the audio and then to build an index using this transcription. However, this approach suffers from the fact that a speech recognizer has a limited vocabulary so the system cannot retrieve out of vocabulary (OOV) queries.

A popular technique to confront this problem is to use phoneme rather than word recognition. Here, a phoneme recognition system is used to transcribe the spoken audio. Word queries are then converted to phoneme sequences and searched for in the transcriptions.

Since phoneme recognition is less accurate than word recognition, a typical approach consists of generating for each audio segment to be indexed a lattice of phonemes encoding potentially thousands of alternative hypotheses (e.g. [5], [4]). Queries are then matched against the lattice via a scanning procedure. Improved accuracy can be obtained by converting a word recognition lattice to phonemes using a dictionary rather than performing phoneme recognition directly [5]. Additionally, phonetic confusion matrices may be used to expand the query and document representations (e.g. [7], [8]).

While the lattice approach is attractive, searching through many hypotheses and confusions is a double-edged sword. Potentially many false-positives can be generated. This can be quite significant for large repositories. For example, in [4] a false alarm rate of the order of 0.5 per hour of audio indexed is quoted for phoneme queries of length 7-11. For an index of 1,000,000 hours, this would mean that a single query might generate 500,000 or so false alarms. Even for repositories only 10,000 hours long we still would have 5,000 false alarms per query. In addition to these problems lattice based systems suffer from low speeds while searching. Since it is not possible to build a hash table structure for quick access, the cost of search is linear with the size of the audio repository. To alleviate the problem of search speed we can build an index structure of sequences of phonemes or syllables (e.g. [11]). However, the problem of false positives remains as syllable units still occur much more frequently than words.

Ideally we would like to develop systems that have the low OOV rates of lattice based systems while maintaining the good scalability, speed of search, and low false alarm rate properties of word-based of index systems. This paper represents our first attempts in this direction. In the following sections we study three approaches to audio indexing: a word-based system, a novel *particle*-based system and a phoneme-based system. The particle system is syllable-like with particles consisting of automatically determined within-word sequences of phonemes [10]. Our hope is that it can find OOV queries with less false positives than the phoneme system. We also explore some simple schemes that combine the three different indexing approaches.

2. EXPERIMENTAL CONDITIONS

We first describe our experimental setup.

2.1 Audio Databases

We use spoken audio transcribed by the Linguistic Data Consortium (LDC) [1] for our experiments. The transcripts provide us with the ground truth and allow us to estimate precision, recall and false alarm rates. The audio is from broadcast sources and is sampled at 16kHz. For training acoustic models we use 65 transcribed hours of the HUB4_96 training set. Our indexing experiments are performed on about 75 hours of audio composed of the HUB4_96

*Om Deshmukh is a graduate student at the University of Maryland.

Proceedings of HLT 2002, Second International Conference on Human Language Technology Research, M. Marcus, ed., Morgan Kaufmann, San Francisco, 2002.

development and test data and the HUB4_97 training and test data.

2.2 Document and Relevance Definitions

In our system, we index hours-long streams of audio which do not have labeled topic boundaries. Since returning the whole stream is meaningless, we arbitrarily define documents as 10 second segments of audio, similar to the *clips* returned by the *SpeechBot*[1] user interface. If the index returns a clip in which the query word/s were spoken, the query is judged successful.

2.3 Evaluation Metrics

Our primary evaluation metric is 11-pt average precision. This is an estimate of the area under a recall-precision curve. The greater this area, the better the system[2]. It is an overall measure of the quality of a retrieval system, incorporating recall and precision.

Because we are examining sub-word-based systems for which false-positives are a major problem, we also explicitly report the number of false positives even though 11-pt average precision implicitly includes this quantity. The number of false positives for a given query is defined as the number of incorrect hits divided by the total number of hits returned. We average our results over all queries.

For completeness, we also show recall, top 5 precision, and top 10 precision. These measures are also implicitly included in 11-pt average precision since it is an overall figure of merit. For all metrics we average over all queries.

2.4 Query Selection

In [2] it is recommended that at least 25 and preferably 50 queries are used for an evaluation for which average precision is the metric. We therefore use 50 queries. Our aims in query selection are:

- to use proper names for which relevance can be determined automatically;
- to have a high proportion of OOV queries;
- to use 'real-world' queries;
- to have at least 10 hits per query, similar to a Web page of hits.

Comparison of the ground truth to the dictionary used for word recognition yields 23 suitable single word OOV queries (*i.e.* proper names with at least 10 hits). We choose the remaining 27 queries as the most frequent in-vocabulary queries to the *SpeechBot* public site which have at least 10 hits and are proper names. The majority of these queries are single-word queries with only three queries having two words. The *SpeechBot* public site has been in operation for over 18 months and is therefore a reasonable source of real-world queries. Note that our query OOV rate of about 50% is much higher than the 13% rate observed on the *Speechbot* site[6]. The queries and the number of documents in which they appear are listed in Table 4 in Appendix A.

2.5 Indexing Systems

We investigate three systems. The first uses a large vocabulary speech recognizer with a 70,000 word dictionary and a trigram language model, similar to the recognizer used by *SpeechBot* [9]. Its acoustic models are trained on the 65 hour training set. The language model is trained on the transcriptions for this set and additional text sources.

The second system uses our novel particle recognizer [10]. Particles are defined as within-word sequences of characters obtained from orthographic or phonetic transcriptions of words. Our particles are obtained from phonetic transcriptions. They are learned automatically from data. Specifically, they are determined by decomposing words into sub-sequences of phonemes so as to maximize the leaving-one-out likelihood of a particle bigram language model.

The particle dictionary consists of phoneme sequences from single phonemes to full words. Once the dictionary of valid particles is defined the word text corpora is translated into particles. This new particle corpora is used then for training a traditional language model of particles where unigram, bigram and trigram probabilities with back-off weights are learned from data. A similar translation is performed on the transcripts of the acoustic corpora and triphone based large vocabulary acoustic models are then built.

The particles representation is quite flexible. If the dictionary of particles only contains single phoneme particles then the particle recognizer behaves like a phonetic recognizer. If the particles are as long as words then it behaves like a word recognizer. In our implementation we use a dictionary of about 7,000 particles. We have found that this dictionary size with particles of length from one to three phonemes yields optimal results. In effect a particle based recognition system behaves like a syllable based speech recognizer where the basic units are automatically learned from textual data. In our system we use the same audio and text corpora for training as for the word-based recognizer.

Finally, our third system indexes phoneme sequences. We do not run a phoneme recognizer. Instead, we use a dictionary to automatically convert the transcripts from the word recognizer in our first system to phonemes. Preliminary tests indicated that this gives better results than running a phoneme recognizer.

The 75 hours of audio used for testing were transcribed by each system. The time-marked words, particles and phonemes were then fed into three separate indexes. Our index is the same as that used in *SpeechBot* which is a derivative of the AltaVista index [3]. We choose this index, which can quickly handle boolean queries, rather than a standard vector-space index because we are interested in Web-based systems which must scale to millions of queries per day.

3. RESULTS

Figure 1 and the first three lines of Table 1 show the performance of each system averaged over all queries. We see that the word-based system has the best performance overall. However, as Figures 2 and 3 and Tables 2 and 3 demonstrate, the performance of the particle and phoneme systems are worse than the word system for in-vocabulary queries and better for OOV queries. The particle system performs slightly better than the phoneme system on OOV queries.

Since particles are syllable-like, we investigate indexing sequences of phonemes as described in [11]. Specifically, we investigate indexing sequences of from 3-5 phonemes with from 1-4 phonemes overlap. The fourth line of Tables 1, 2 and 3 and Figures 4, 5 and 6 show results for the best of these systems. This indexed phoneme sequences of length 5 with overlap 4. In the figures and tables it is referred to as the 'Phoneme (5/4)' system.

From these results we see that using sequences of phonemes can improve the average precision. The system is at least as good as using particles for OOV words and equivalent to words overall.

However, although both the word index and phoneme sequence index have an average precision of 0.35, they operate at different recall and false positive levels. From Table 1, we see that using phoneme sequences rather than words improves the recall from 0.39 to 0.48. However, this comes at a cost of increasing the number of false positives from 0.08 to 0.57. In some applications this

[1] *http://www.speechbot.com*

[2] An ideal system would have precision 1.0 for all recall values i.e. every document retrieved would be relevant.

increase in false positives could be crippling. In others it might be justified by the increase in recall.

Finally, we consider combining the word-based and best phoneme-based indexes. We consider two simple strategies:

- linearly combining the scores;
- selecting the word index for in-vocabulary queries and the phoneme (5/4) index otherwise.

The last two lines of Table 1, 2 and 3 show the results of these experiments. Both strategies result in improved average precision.

For the linear combination technique, we report results from an exhaustive search of the space of all possible combination coefficients. This result is therefore an upper bound, obtainable only if the coefficients could be optimized on a development query set. The OOV-based combination technique does not rely on the use of a development set and thus could be recommended for all query types. Its performance is equivalent to the best linear combination of systems and is additionally shown in Figure 4.

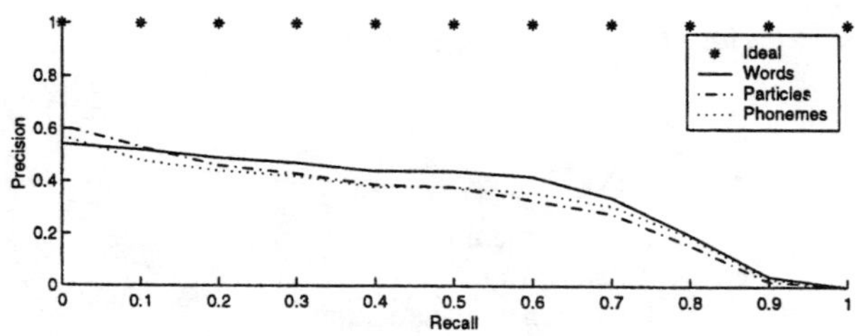

Figure 1: Precision-Recall curves averaged over all queries for the baseline systems and the ideal system.

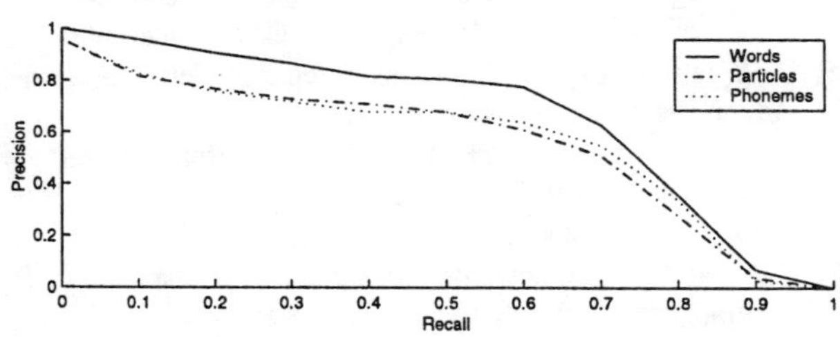

Figure 2: Precision-Recall curves for the in-dictionary queries for the baseline systems.

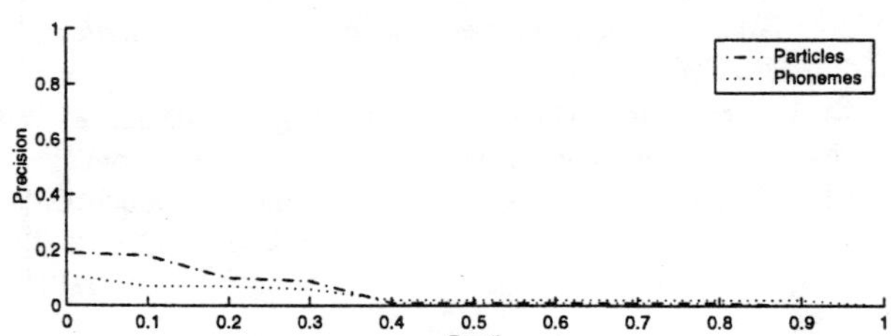

Figure 3: Precision-Recall curves for the OOV queries for the particle and phoneme baseline systems.

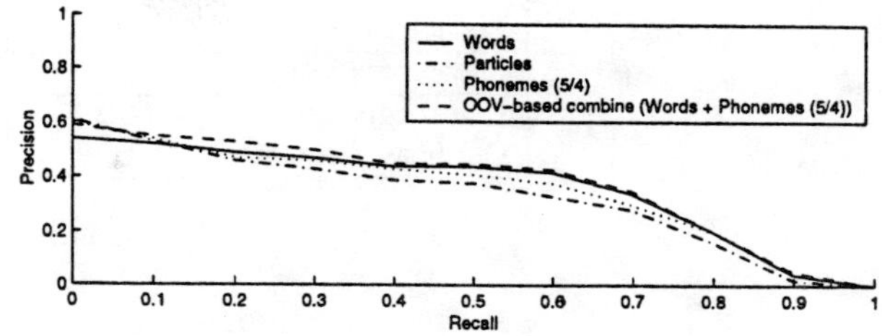

Figure 4: Precision-Recall curves for all queries showing the comparison between the word and particle baseline systems, a system indexing sequences of phonemes and a combination-based system.

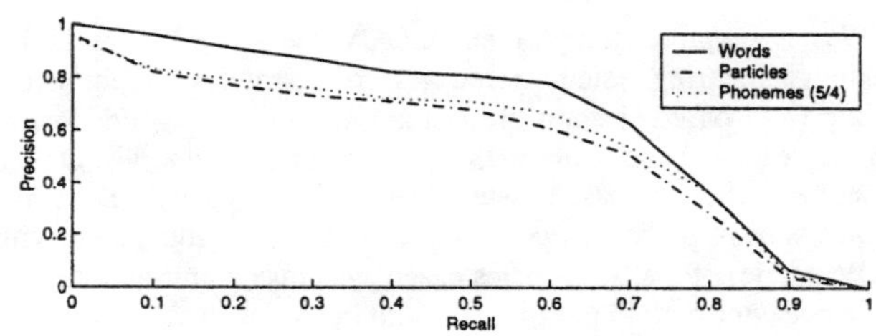

Figure 5: Precision-Recall curves for the in dictionary queries showing the comparison between the word and particle baseline systems and a system indexing sequences of phonemes.

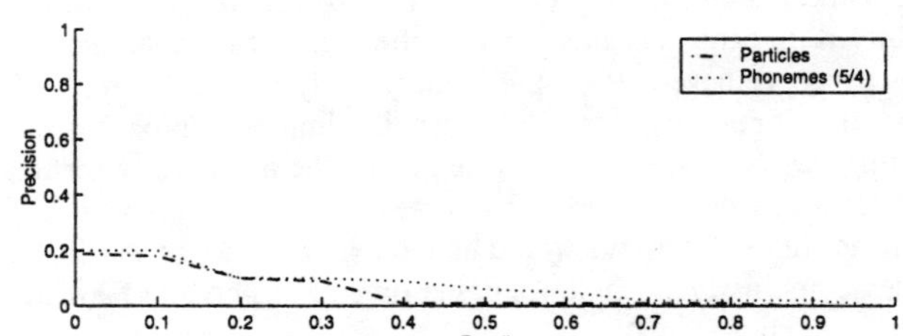

Figure 6: Precision-Recall curves for the OOV queries showing the comparison between the particle baseline system and a system indexing sequences of phonemes.

System	11-pt Avg. Precision	Recall	Top 5 Precision	Top 10 Precision	False Positives
Word	0.35	0.39	0.50	0.48	0.08
Particles	0.33	0.39	0.51	0.47	0.21
Phonemes	0.32	0.42	0.48	0.44	0.27
Phonemes (5/4)	0.35	0.48	0.48	0.45	0.57
Linear combine	0.39	0.48	0.54	0.51	0.57
OOV-based combine	0.39	0.46	0.56	0.53	0.34

Table 1: Results averaged over all queries for various indexing systems.

System	11-pt Avg. Precision	Recall	Top 5 Precision	Top 10 Precision	False Positives
Word	0.66	0.73	0.92	0.89	0.14
Particles	0.55	0.65	0.82	0.79	0.24
Phonemes	0.56	0.71	0.84	0.77	0.29
Phonemes (5/4)	0.58	0.76	0.80	0.76	0.56
Linear combine	0.66	0.76	0.92	0.87	0.14
OOV-based combine	0.66	0.73	0.92	0.89	0.14

Table 2: Results averaged over all in-dictionary queries for various indexing systems.

4. CONCLUSIONS

We have explored the problem of OOV query words in audio indexing, comparing systems based on words, particles and phonemes. While word based systems are fast and have overall good IR performance they cannot work in the presence of OOV queries. On the other hand phonetic based systems offer generally lower IR performance but can partially recover some of the audio documents with OOV queries. Finally, particles based systems exhibit an intermediate behavior both in performance and in complexity.

The IR performance of a phonetic based system can be improved by translating the word queries into a phonetic representation and creating phone sequences 5 phonemes long with a 4 phoneme overlap. However, there is a cost for this improvement. The false alarm rate, a metric often overlooked in IR, is significantly increased. False alarms are implicitly included in traditional IR precision/recall metrics. However, by explicitly measuring it we obtain a more complete view of the performance of these three different systems. In many applications high false alarm rates can render the system unusable or at the very least have a high impact on the perceived usability of the system.

Clearly no approach stands on its own as the correct answer to the audio document IR problem. The combination of word and subword indexing systems perhaps offers us a third approach. In this paper we have made a preliminary study on combining these systems with promising results. Even the simplest approach of detecting the query word as OOV and using the phonetic or particle system for that query works as well as using an optimal weighting scheme. In the future we would like to explore more sophisticated index combination techniques based on data fusion and Bayesian mixing of classifiers.

It is also important to note that the particle based system has not been deeply explored in this paper. We consider our reported results quite preliminary and intend to investigate this approach more in the future. Finally, we have not explored traditional IR techniques such as query expansion and relevance feedback. The role of these approaches in OOV retrieval remains an alternative route for further study.

5. REFERENCES

[1] S. Bird and M. Liberman. Linguistic annotation resources. University of Pennsylvania. See http://www.ldc.upenn.edu/annotation.

[2] C. Buckley and E. Voorhees. Evaluating evaluation measure stability. In *SIGIR2000*, 2000.

[3] M. Burrows. *Method for Indexing Information of a Database*. U.S. Patent 5,745,899, 1998.

[4] M. Clements, P. S. Cardillo, and M. S. Miller. Phonetic searching vs. LVCSR: How to find what you really want in audio archives. In *20th Annual AVOIS Conference*, 2001.

[5] D. A. James. A system for unrestricted topic retrieval from radio news broadcasts. In *Proc. ICASSP*, 1994.

[6] B. Logan, P. Moreno, J. V. Thong, and E. Whittaker. An experimental study of an audio indexing system for the Web. In *Proc. ICSLP*, 2000.

[7] K. Ng and V. Zue. Towards robust methods for spoken document retrieval. In *Proc. ICSLP*, 1998.

[8] S. Srinivasan and D. Petkovic. Phonetic confusion matrix based spoken document retrieval. In *SIGIR2000*, 2000.

[9] J. V. Thong, D. Goddeau, A. Litvinova, B. Logan, P. Moreno, and M. Swain. Speechbot: a speech recognition based audio indexing system for the web. In *Proc. RIAO*, 2000.

[10] E. W. D. Whittaker, J. Van Thong, and P. J. Moreno. Vocabulary independent speech recognition using particles. In *ASRU 2001*, 2001.

[11] M. Witbrock and A. G. Hauptmann. Using words and phonetic strings for efficient information retrieval from imperfectly transcribed spoken documents. In *Second ACM International Conference on Digital Libraries*, 1997.

System	11-pt Avg. Precision	Recall	Top 5 Precision	Top 10 Precision	False Positives
Word	0.00	0.00	0.00	0.00	0.00
Particles	0.06	0.09	0.15	0.10	0.17
Phonemes	0.04	0.08	0.07	0.05	0.24
Phonemes (5/4)	0.08	0.14	0.10	0.09	0.58
Linear combine	0.08	0.14	0.10	0.09	0.58
OOV-based combine	0.08	0.14	0.10	0.09	0.58

Table 3: Results averaged over all OOV queries for various indexing systems.

APPENDIX

A. LIST OF QUERIES

In dictionary	Count	Out of Dictionary	Count
bill clinton	56	cunanan	70
al gore	31	mair	57
clinton	626	fayed	52
microsoft	40	dodi	37
israel	104	tamraz	26
egypt	15	peekskill	23
montreal	23	sankara	18
china	226	plavsic	18
nasdaq	53	reineck	13
paris	101	rutan	16
christmas	97	fenphen	16
jesus	11	lia	13
kennedy	48	mcaleese	14
france	62	bilbao	13
england	86	reesjones	13
germany	37	cortisol	10
switzerland	13	onondaga	10
india	39	hightech	12
nasa	73	zorich	12
australia	25	liderman	12
mexico	121	montserrat	11
cuba	141	boughton	10
florida	198	pazuto	10
canada	106		
iran	66		
texas	151		
stock market	41		

Table 4: Queries to the system

Beyond the Phoneme: A Juncture-Accent Model of Spoken Language

Steven Greenberg, Hannah Carvey, Leah Hitchcock and Shuangyu Chang
International Computer Science Institute
1947 Center Street, Berkeley, CA 94704 USA
{steveng, hmcarvey, leahh, shawnc}@icsi.berkeley.edu

ABSTRACT

Phonemic models of spoken language are incapable of accommodating the patterns of pronunciation variation observed in spontaneous speech (as exemplified by a corpus of American English telephone dialogues, a.k.a. SWITCHBOARD). Variation in pronunciation with respect to segmental identity and duration can be accounted for in terms of a juncture-accent model, in which position of the segment within the syllable (i.e., onset, nucleus, coda), in tandem with knowledge of the associated stress-accent pattern, is used to interpret the inherently ambiguous phonetic information contained in the acoustic signal. Many properties of pronunciation variation can be accounted for in terms of such a model, including: (1) the prevalence of coda deletion, (2) the mutability of vocalic identity and (3) the relative stability of syllable onsets. The melding of phonetic and prosodic features within the syllable provides for efficient and reliable linguistic information coding.

1. INTRODUCTION

In traditional models of spoken language words are represented strictly as phonemic sequences, strung together like "beads on a string" [12], analogous to the orthographic representation in a dictionary, with little (if any) provision made for prosodic and other extra-phonetic features.

Do such linear, phonemic models provide an accurate characterization of spoken language? Probably not – for if they did, current-generation automatic speech recognition (ASR) systems, whose architecture is predicated on such models (at least for English and many other languages) would experience little difficulty decoding the speech signal into its constituent phonemic segments. In fact, most ASR systems rarely recognize more than 75% of the segments correctly, even when the material is carefully enunciated; phonetic classification is even worse when spontaneous speech is involved [9]. For this reason ASR systems generally rely on "language" models to effectively prune lexical alternatives in an effort to achieve reasonable word-recognition performance (for all but limited-vocabulary tasks). However, language models require extensive training material, highly representative of the task domain, in order to be truly effective. Moreover, the collection and annotation of such training material is both time-consuming and expensive to perform, thus limiting the ability to quickly (and inexpensively) develop ASR systems for novel task domains.

Why are phonemic models inadequate for representing words in an utterance? Statistical analysis of five hours of spontaneous dialogue material (the SWITCHBOARD corpus, cf. [3]) suggests that pronunciation variation typical of everyday speech is not readily accommodated within a phonemic-sequence model. Approximately 22% of the canonical phones (i.e., phonemes) in the manually annotated component of SWITCHBOARD are not phonetically realized; there is a decided predisposition for speakers to "delete" segments in the pronunciation of many words, particularly those spoken frequently [6]. Moreover, even in the absence of segmental deletion, phonetic realizations often differ from the canonical (i.e., dictionary) form [6]. In consequence, many words are pronounced in dozens of different ways, depending on such factors as (1) linguistic background of the speaker (i.e., regional dialect or foreign accent), (2) speaking style, (3) rate of speaking, (4) acoustic and/or visual environment, (4) semantic emphasis and (5) idiolect. Keeping track of such variation at the phonetic-segment level is a daunting task, one that is likely to defeat even the most sophisticated pronunciation models currently used in ASR.

If words are inadequately represented in terms of phonemes, how might they be more faithfully characterized? A clue is to be found in the historical development of writing systems. The earliest orthographic systems – from Egypt and Sumer – were based not on phonemes but on supra-phonetic units such as the syllable and the word [16]. Moreover, many contemporary writing systems, such as those employed in China and Japan, are essentially syllabic in nature.

The syllable offers many advantages for characterizing *spoken* language relative to a strictly phonemic representation. It is a remarkably stable unit – only 1% of *canonical* syllables are unrealized (i.e., deleted) in SWITCHBOARD [6]. Moreover, the syllable is eminently compatible with speech production models; speakers articulate in terms of syllables, rather than phonemes [14]. There is also increasing evidence that the syllable is a perceptually important unit for decoding spoken language, perhaps more so than the phone [5].

One of the more interesting properties of the syllable is its capacity for absorbing certain extra-phonetic properties pertinent to the prosody of an utterance. A syllable can be characterized not only as a sequence of phonemes, but also in terms of its "prominence" relative to other syllables. Prominence is a perceptual attribute that largely reflects (for a stress-accent language such as English) a broad constellation of acoustic properties, including amplitude, duration, fundamental frequency and the spectral contour, *relative* to the surrounding syllabic context [1]. The linguistic manifestation of prominence is "accent." Accent is an integral component of a language's prosodic representation and is often relied on for lexical, syntactic and semantic disambiguation [1] [13]. It also provides important information concerning the emotional tone of the speaker.

In English, accent appears to function essentially as a two-level

Proceedings of HLT 2002, Second International Conference on Human Language Technology Research, M. Marcus, ed., Morgan Kaufmann, San Francisco, 2002.

system (i.e., accented vs. unaccented); however, syllables with accent, can assume a graded quantity (such as "heavy" and "light"). For this reason the analyses presented in the current study partition the stress-accent "space" into either two (heavily accented vs. unaccented) or three levels (heavy, light and none), even though the annotation material from which they are derived labeled accent with a finer degree of granularity (cf. Section 2 for a description of the annotation methods).

Traditionally, accent has been thought of as a linguistic parameter largely independent of the phonetic tier, whose realization is functionally orthogonal to the identity of the phonetic constituents through which accent is imparted (e.g., [2]). However, the current study calls this assumption into question; many phonetic properties encapsulated in pronunciation variation observed in spontaneous dialog material can be most readily understood in terms of stress accent and its impact on syllable structure. Many phonetic properties of a segment are governed by its position within the syllable (i.e., whether it is a part of the onset, nucleus or coda) in concert with accent (i.e., accent differentially affects the phonetic realization of syllabic constituents). Together, accent and syllable position, provide the structural framework required to predict (and understand) the pattern of pronunciation variation observed in the SWITCHBOARD corpus. A syllable-based, juncture-accent model of spoken language, incorporating these insights, is described in Section 5.

2. CORPUS MATERIAL AND METHODS

The Switchboard corpus [3] contains many hundreds of brief (5-10 minute) telephone dialogues of a casual nature, spoken by native speakers of American English (from most major dialect regions). A subset of this material (45.43 minutes, consisting of 9,922 words, 13,446 syllables and 33,370 phonetic segments, comprising 674 utterances spoken by 581 different speakers) was hand-labeled (by students in Linguistics from the University of California, Berkeley, using Entropics Software to concurrently display the pressure waveform, spectrogram, word- and syllable-level transcripts) with respect to phonetic-segment identity and level of stress accent (for each vocalic nucleus). The mean duration of each utterance transcribed was 4.76 seconds (the range was 2 to 17 seconds, with ca. 60% of the material between 4 and 8 seconds in length), and the average number of words per utterance was 18.5 (range: 2 to 64 words). The average number of syllables per utterance was 23.25 (range: 5 to 81 syllables). Filled pauses (e.g., "um" and "uh") were excluded from analysis because of the high proportion of non-linguistic attributes associated with such forms.

Three transcribers phonetically labeled and segmented the material. The phonetic inventory used is a variant of Arpabet, originally applied to labeling the TIMIT corpus, but adapted to the exigencies of spontaneous material (cf. [6] for details of the tran-

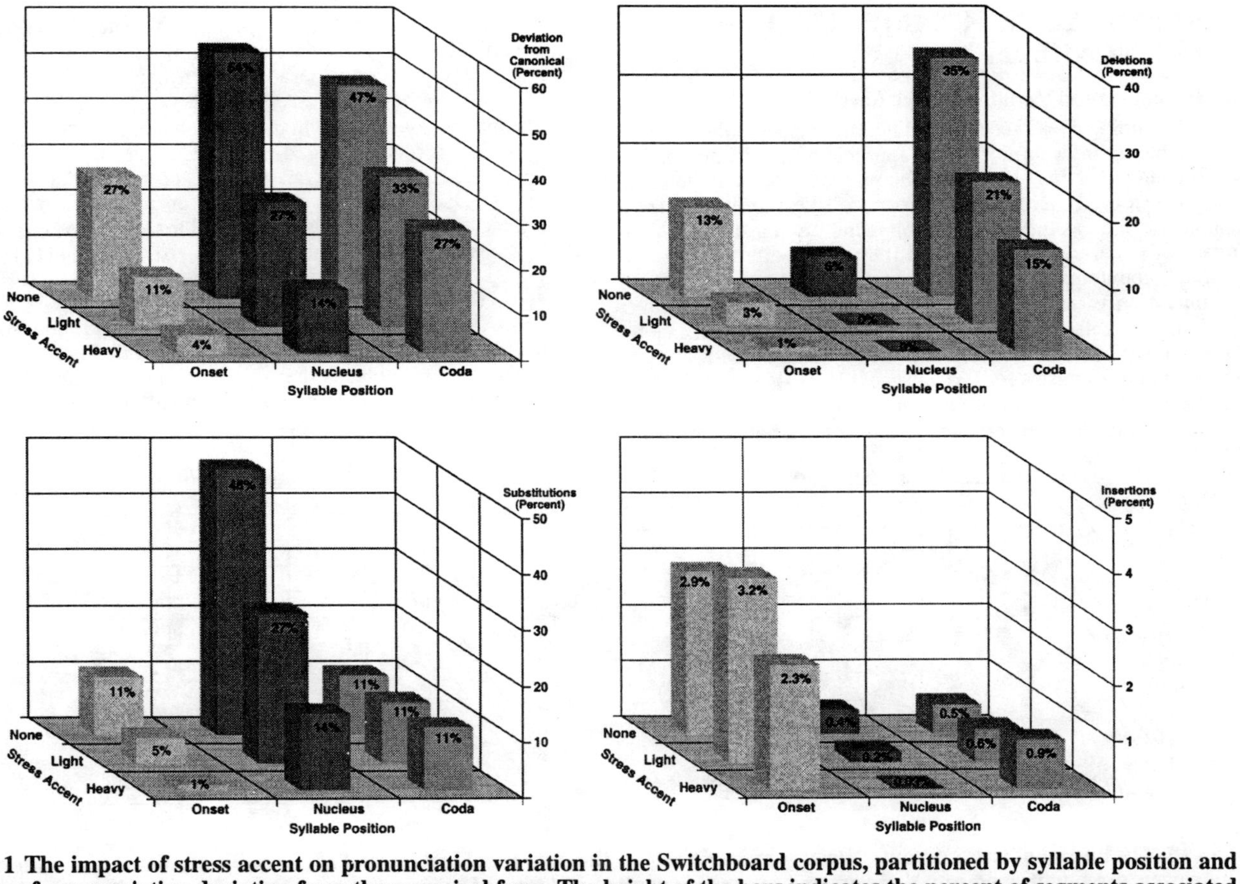

Figure 1 The impact of stress accent on pronunciation variation in the Switchboard corpus, partitioned by syllable position and the type of pronunciation deviation from the canonical form. The height of the bars indicates the percent of segments associated with onset, nucleus and coda components that deviate from the canonical phonetic realization. The magnitude of the deviation is also shown in terms of percentage figures for each bar. Note that the magnitude scale differs for each panel. The sum of the "Deletions," (upper right panel) "Substitutions" (lower left) and "Insertions" (lower right) equals the total "Deviation from Canonical" shown in the upper left panel. Canonical onsets = 10,241, nuclei = 12,185, codas = 7,965. Adapted from [7].

scription orthography). The interlabeler agreement was 74%. An analysis of the pattern of interlabeler disagreement for vocalic segments indicates that, in such instances, labelers typically disagreed only slightly, usually in terms of one level of height or front/back position. Rarely did transcribers disagree about whether a segment is a monophthong or diphthong.

Two individuals (distinct from those involved with the phonetic labeling) marked the same material with respect to stress accent. Three levels of stress were distinguished – (1) fully accented ("heavy"), (2) completely unaccented ("no accent") and (3) an intermediate level of accent ("light"). The transcribers were instructed to label each syllabic nucleus on the basis of its perceptually based accent rather than using knowledge of a word's canonical stress pattern derived from a dictionary. All of the stress-accent material was labeled by both transcribers and the accent labels averaged. In the vast majority of instances the transcribers agreed as to the stress-accent level associated with each nucleus – interlabeler agreement was 85% for unaccented nuclei, 78% for fully accented nuclei (and 95% for any level of accent, where both transcribers ascribed some measure of accent to the nucleus). In those instances where the transcribers were not in complete accord, the difference in their labeling was usually a half- (rather than a whole-) level step of accent. Moreover, disagreement was typically associated with circumstances where there was some genuine ambiguity in accent level (as determined by an independent, third observer).

3. STRESS ACCENT'S IMPACT ON PRONUNCIATION

3.1 Pronunciation Variation at the Level of the Syllable

We first examine stress accent's differential impact at the level of the syllable in order to more fully appreciate (and comprehend) pronunciation patterns observed at the segmental level. In general, heavily accented syllables are far more likely to be realized canonically (i.e., as the primary pronunciation in a standard dictionary of American English) than their unaccented (or lightly accented) counterparts. Figure 1 illustrates the general pattern of pronunciation variation associated with stress accent. Accented *onsets,* in particular, are extremely likely to be pronounced canonically, consistent with models of spoken language that highlight the importance of onsets for lexical access [4][15]. The nuclei and codas are far less likely to be canonically realized, and the likelihood of deviation from the canonical rises dramatically as the magnitude of accent level diminishes.

Further insight is gained when the pronunciation patterns are partitioned according to the *type* of deviation observed – substitutions, deletions and insertions. Most substitution forms of deviations (lower left panel) are to be found in the nucleus and are inherently vocalic in nature (cf. Section 3.2). Substitutions are rarely encountered in either the onset or the coda. Segmental deletion, on the other hand, is rarely observed in either the nucleus or onset, but is quite common in the coda. Insertions occur infrequently and are concentrated in the onset. The absence of stress accent dramatically increases the probability that a nucleus or coda constituent will deviate from the canonical. However, accent's impact is highly selective. Its influence is most apparent for substitutions in the nucleus and deletions in the coda. The probability of insertion, as well as coda substitution, is generally unaffected by accent level (cf. Figure 1).

3.2 Pronunciation Variation in the Vocalic Nucleus

Much of stress accent's impact on phonetic identity is found in the nucleus. Figure 2 illustrates the dramatic changes imposed by accent on the phonetic composition and structure of the vocalic system. In heavily accented syllables there is a relatively even distribution of vocalic segments across the articulatory space, particularly with respect to front vowels. Back vowels are mainly represented in terms of the diphthongs [ow] and [uw]. The articulatory distribution of vowels differs markedly in unaccented syllables. Within this context the overwhelming majority of segments lie in the high-front ([ih], [iy]) and high-central ([ax]) regions of the articulatory space. Moreover, the proportion of low- and mid-height vowels is considerably lower than observed in accented syllables. Among unaccented syllables there is a decided skew in the distribution towards high vowels for both canonical and non-canonical forms (cf. Fig. 4 in [7]). Changes in vowel height are heavily skewed towards raising in unaccented syllables (cf. Fig. 5 in [7]). Overall, there is a tendency for lax, high vowels to occur primarily in unaccented syllables and for low vowels to be present in accented forms, as illustrated in Figure 3 (cf. [7] [11]).

3.3 Pronunciation Variation in the Syllable Onset

As discussed in Section 3.1, onsets are usually pronounced canonically, particularly in accented syllables (cf. Figure 1). Only in unaccented syllables is there a significant tendency for a certain proportion of onsets to be non-canonical pronounced. The overwhelming majority of deviations within this context are in the

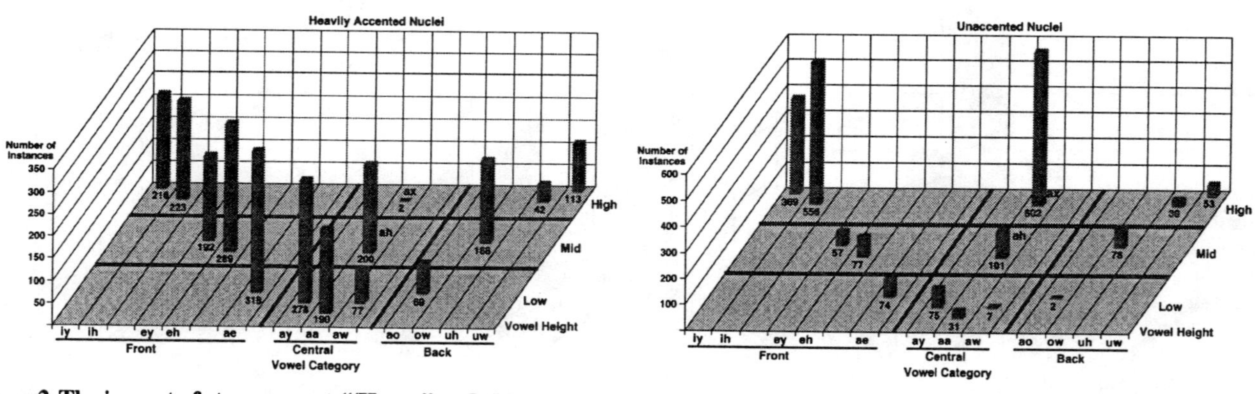

Figure 2 The impact of stress accent ("Heavy" and "None") on the number of instances of each vocalic segment type in the corpus. The vowels are partitioned into their articulatory configuration in terms of horizontal tongue position ("Front," "Central" and "Back") as well as tongue height ("High," "Mid" and "Low"). Note the concentration of vocalic instances among the "Front" and "Central" vowels associated with "Heavy" accent and the association of high-front and high-central vowels with unaccented syllables. The data shown pertain solely to canonical forms realized as such in the corpus. The skew in the distributions would be even greater if non-canonical forms were included. Adapted from [7].

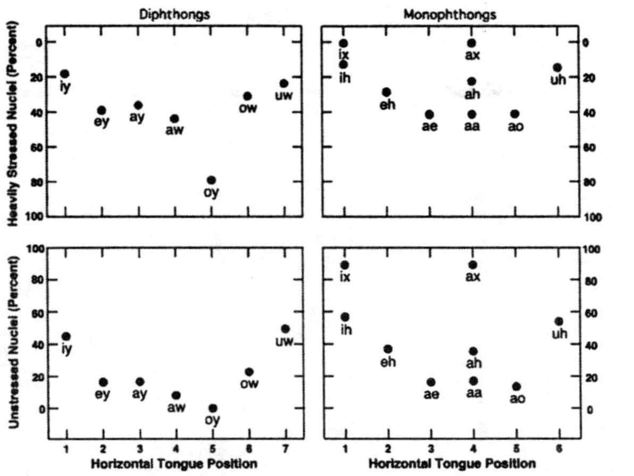

Figure 3 Spatial representation of the mean proportion of nuclei associated with syllables that are heavily stressed or completed unstressed as a function of vocalic identity. Vowels are segregated into diphthongs and monophthongs for illustrative clarity. Note that the polarization of the y-axis scale for the unaccented syllables is the reverse of that associated with the heavily accented syllables (performed in order to highlight the spatial organization of the data). The x-axis refers to the hypothetical position of the tongue in the horizontal place and is intended purely for illustrative purposes. From [11].

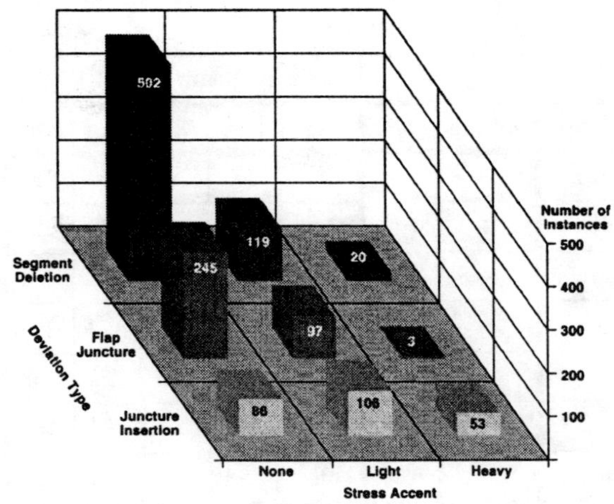

Figure 4 The effect of stress accent on the type of pronunciation deviation from the canonical for syllable onset segments. The three deviation forms shown ("Segment Deletion," "Flap Juncture" and "Juncture Insertion") account for 76% of the non-canonical segments in onset position. Adapted from [7].

form of segmental deletions (cf. Figure 4). Most of these deletions occur in association with common pronominals, such as "them," "they," "him" and "her," the definite article "the," and the demonstratives "these" and "those." The deleted segment is usually either [dh] or [h] (cf. Table 1). Both classes of segment occur in words that occur frequently and are therefore highly predictable from context.

The other common forms of deviation among onsets pertain to either the insertion or substitution of junctures, of which the alveolar ([dx]) and nasal ([nx]) flaps, the glottal stop ([q]) and the glides [w] and [y] are the most common variety. Such junctures are typically associated with a pair of syllables – an unaccented (or lightly accented) one preceded by a more heavily accented precursor. The flaps and glottal stop, in particular, are examples of "pure" junctures in that they serve primarily as syllable separators rather than as phonetic segments *per se* (an issue addressed in more detail in Section 5).

There are two other contexts in which onsets are likely to be non-canonically realized. The centrally articulated segments, [t], [d] and [n], tend to be non-canonically articulated, particularly in unaccented syllables. In many instances such segments are transformed into pure junctures (i.e., the flaps [dx] and [nx]). The other context pertains to the place "chameleons," whose specific articulatory locus depends on the surrounding vocalic context. These liquids, approximants and syllabics have many articulatory and acoustic properties in common with vowels, and under many circumstances behave more like vocalic than consonantal segments. In unaccented syllables many of these segments either become reduced (e.g., reduced liquids) or disappear altogether. Under such circumstances segmental duration may serve as a more sensitive indicator of stress accent's impact on phonetic realization than segmental identity (cf. Section 4 and [8]).

3.4 Pronunciation Variation in the Syllable Coda

The coda is far less likely to be canonically pronounced than the onset (cf. Section 3.1 and Figure 1). Most of the deviations observed are in the form of segmental deletions; their frequency is extremely sensitive to stress accent (cf. Figure 1).

These coda deletions are of a highly selective nature. Virtually none of the anterior or posterior segments are deleted in any great measure. The exceptions are [v], [m] and [ng] in unaccented syllables, all of which behave in a manner similar to flaps (and pure junctures) in this context (the case of [v] is discussed in more detail in Section 5 and Figure 8).

In contrast to the anterior and posterior codas, the centrally articulated segments, particularly [t], [d] and [n], are extremely likely to be non-canonically realized, even in heavily accented syllables (the level of accent exerts a significant impact on the probability of non-canonical pronunciation). In many contexts the default pronunciation of such segments is non-canonical (usually segmental deletion or junctural substitution).

What distinguishes the centrally articulated codas from their more forward (and backward) counterparts (besides place of articulation)? In contrast to the onsets, where in terms of place of articulation there is a relatively even numerical distribution among anterior, central and posterior segments (cf. Table 1), the codas manifest a decided frequency skew towards the central phones. Fully 75% of coda segments are centrally articulated (in canonical form). In other words, the default place of articulation for coda segments is central. Anterior and posterior segments are relatively rare, and in this sense are more "informative" in terms of lexical and syllabic differentiation. It is perhaps not coincidental that the non-central segments most likely to be non-canonically pronounced ([v], [m], [ng]) occur far more frequently than other members of their place-of-articulation class (this relation between coda realization and "information" is discussed further in Section 5).

Place chameleons in the coda behave, in many respects, like vocalic segments, not only in terms of their segmental mutability as a function of accent, but also in terms of duration (cf. Section 4 and [8]). They are likely to either delete or reduce in unaccented

			Stress	Syllable Onset: Heavy		Light		None		Total		Syllable Coda: Heavy		Light		None		Total	
Manner	*Voicing*	*Place*	*Seg*	*Can*	*Tran*	*Can*	*Tran*	*Can*	*Tran*	*Can*	*Tran*	*Can*	*Tran*	*Can*	*Tran*	*Can*	*Tran*	*Can*	*Tran*
Stop	–	ANTERIOR	p	203	205	153	153	94	94	450	452	33	32	39	32	17	13	89	77
Stop	+		b	126	127	227	225	214	190	567	542	9	6	4	4	1	1	14	11
Nasal/J	+		m	137	137	211	211	116	110	464	458	108	96	148	148	**112**	**83**	368	327
Fric	–		f	136	136	104	104	113	103	353	343	37	36	40	40	36	48	113	124
Fric/J	+		v	35	33	58	58	108	93	201	184	63	55	102	87	**172**	**94**	337	236
Fric	–		th	62	61	102	100	28	26	192	187	11	10	24	16	34	20	69	46
Fric/J	+		dh	95	80	311	257	**625**	**451**	1031	788	0	0	0	4	0	5	0	9
Glide	+		y	63	72	135	136	**193**	**145**	391	353	–	–	–	–	–	–	–	–
Stop	–	CENTRAL	t	241	245	276	230	**513**	**276**	1030	751	**322**	**126**	**575**	**191**	**562**	**172**	1459	489
Stop	+		d	141	143	149	134	**173**	**128**	463	405	**200**	**119**	**295**	**127**	**370**	**96**	865	342
Flap/J	+		dx	0	3	**0**	**62**	**0**	**179**	0	244	–	–	–	–	–	–	–	–
Nasal	+		n	133	135	237	196	**194**	**130**	564	461	**311**	**237**	**498**	**381**	**773**	**542**	1582	1160
Flap/J	+		nx	0	2	**0**	**40**	**0**	**73**	0	115	–	–	–	–	–	–	–	–
Fric	–		s	289	290	284	287	187	186	760	763	142	135	202	214	151	155	495	504
Fric	+		z	14	13	16	16	43	45	73	74	179	149	**258**	**208**	**271**	**221**	708	578
Stop	–	POSTERIOR	k	185	186	189	187	170	168	544	541	170	150	196	162	51	39	417	351
Stop	+		g	115	116	138	137	54	51	307	304	10	10	8	10	4	5	22	25
Nasal/J	+		ng	0	0	2	3	1	1	3	4	63	60	139	126	**203**	**129**	405	315
Fric	–		sh	26	26	40	40	73	80	139	146	9	9	2	2	4	6	15	17
Fric	+		zh	0	1	2	9	11	17	13	27	1	0	0	4	0	2	1	6
Affric	–		ch	32	34	19	27	22	23	73	84	26	25	27	25	12	12	65	62
Affric	+		jh	31	30	52	43	58	48	141	121	10	10	11	10	15	12	36	32
Glide	+		w	201	209	310	330	276	287	787	826	0	4	0	2	0	6	0	12
Junct	+		q	**0**	**33**	**0**	**64**	**0**	**38**	0	135	**0**	**42**	**0**	**71**	**0**	**54**	0	167
Liquid	+	CHAMELEON	r	272	269	233	215	**233**	**162**	738	646	205	183	260	216	**181**	**68**	646	467
Liquid	+		l	184	180	226	212	**220**	**162**	630	554	**183**	**90**	**169**	**62**	**120**	**34**	472	186
Aprox	+ (–)		hh	158	156	169	157	**67**	**37**	394	350	–	–	–	–	–	–	–	–
Syllab	+		er	0	0	0	2	0	0	0	2	0	8	0	2	0	1	0	11
Red liq	+		lg	0	2	0	8	**0**	**21**	0	31	**0**	**67**	**0**	**46**	**0**	**10**	0	123
Syllab	+		el	0	1	0	0	0	0	0	1	0	1	0	0	0	1	0	2

Table 1 The impact of stress accent and syllable position (onset vs. coda) on the likelihood of canonical pronunciation as a function of phonetic identity organized by place and manner of articulation, and by voicing. Numbers refer to instances of canonical and transcribed (i.e., actual) instances for each segment. Segments for which there is a significant discrepancy between the number of canonical and transcribed occurrences (indicative of non-canonical pronunciation) are marked in BOLD. Voicing is indicated as either present (+) or absent (–). Abbreviations: Affric – Affricate; Aprox – Approximant; Can – Canonical; Fric – Fricative; Junct – Juncture; J – Juncture; Red liq – Reduced liquid; Syllab – Syllabic; Tran – Transcribed. "/J" – segment can be a pure juncture.

syllables. Such segments behave, in certain respects, like the glide portions of diphthongs. In accented syllables such segments are either substantially reduced in duration (e.g., [lg]) or deleted altogether. In the latter instance, the net result is typically just a slight change in the quality of the preceding vowel. In this sense, deletion of a coda chameleon can often be interpreted as a vocalic transformation (i.e., substitution) rather than as a true segmental deletion.

4. STRESS ACCENT'S IMPACT ON DURATION

Durational variation provides a means separate from segmental identity with which to gauge stress accent's influence on the phonetic properties of the syllable; the patterns observed complement and extend those described in Section 3.

4.1 Durational Variation of the Syllable

The range of durations associated with syllables of variable structure and stress-accent magnitude is shown in Figure 5 (upper left panel). Heavily accented syllables are generally 60-100% longer than their unaccented counterparts. Overall, syllable length is largely dependent on the number of phonetic constituents, but stress accent also plays a decisive role. Syllables of brief duration (< 150 ms) are likely to be unaccented (unless they contain only a single segment), while those longer than 300 ms are likely to be heavily accented. The average duration of a segment (irrespective of its syllabic position) is 60-70 ms in unaccented syllables and 100-150 ms in their heavily accented counterparts. Virtually all syllables shorter than 110 ms are unaccented. The largest disparity between heavily accented and unaccented forms is found in syllables with one or no consonants (i.e., V, CV and VC forms). Such data imply that the vocalic nucleus absorbs much of stress-accent's impact on duration (cf. Figure 5, lower left panel).

4.2 Durational Variation of the Vocalic Nucleus

Vocalic segments associated with heavily accented syllables are, on average, more than twice as long as their unaccented counterparts, irrespective of syllable structure (Figure 5; lower left panel). The average duration of vowels in unaccented syllables is exceedingly short (55-75 ms), particularly for nuclei surrounded by consonantal onsets and codas (i.e., CVC, CVCC and CCVC forms). The duration of vocalic segments in heavily accented syllables is far longer, ranging between 126 and 172 ms (on average). In this sense, the durational properties of vocalic segments depends largely on the stress-accent level of the syllable. However, the detailed relationship between vowel duration and stress accent is more complicated than these data initially imply (cf. Figure 6).

The disparity in duration between vocalic segments in heavily accented and unaccented syllables is illustrated in Figure 6. Diphthongs, as well as low, tense monophthongs exhibit a relatively large disparity between heavily accented and unaccented instances of the same vocalic segment, while there is relatively little difference in duration as a function of stress-accent magnitude for the high and mid lax monophthongs (i.e., [ih], [eh], [ah], [ax], [uh]). These data are interpretable within the framework illustrated in Figure 3, that implies an intimate relationship between stress-accent level and vowel height. The low and mid vowels, be they diphthongs ([ay], [aw], [ey], [oy], [ow]) or monophthongs ([ae], [aa], [ao], [eh], [ah]), are more likely to exhibit full stress accent than their high vocalic counterparts (and conversely, the high vowels are far more likely to lack accent entirely). In a sense, such high, lax monophthongs as [ih], [ix], [ax] and [ux] are inherently unaccented. Therefore, duration, as reflected in stress accent, is unlikely to fully manifest its impact in such segments.

The significance of this relationship between vowel height and stress accent is perhaps most easily understood in light of the cor-

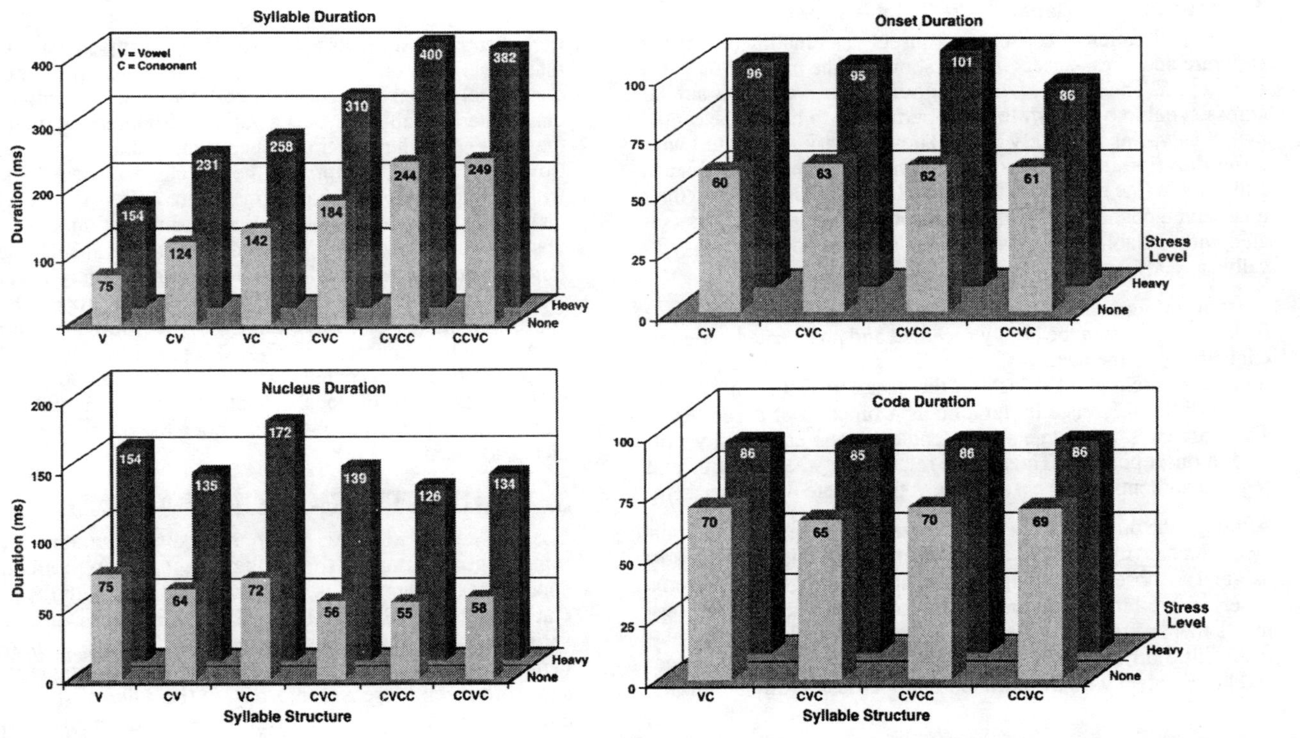

Figure 5 The impact of stress accent on duration of the syllable (upper left panel) and as well as its segmental constituents (onset – upper right panel; nucleus – lower left panel; coda – lower right panel) for a variety of syllable structures. Adapted from [8].

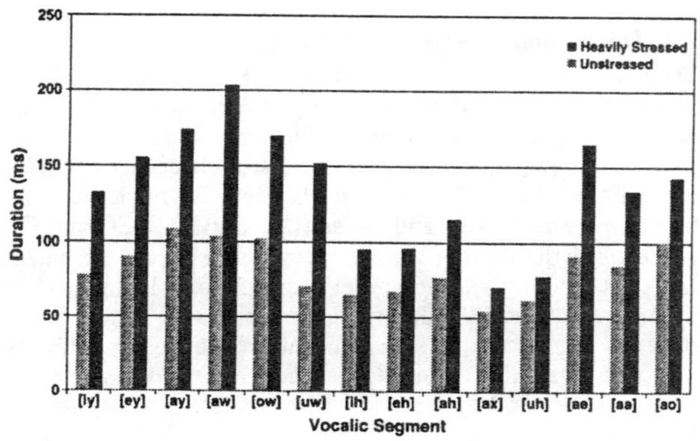

Figure 6 Mean duration of vocalic nuclei in the annotated SWITCHBOARD corpus as a function of stress-accent magnitude. The duration of vowels in heavily stressed syllables is shown in black, while the duration of vowels in unstressed syllables is illustrated in grey. Data shown are associated with canonical realizations of the vowels only. Data associated with the intermediate level of stress accent is omitted for illustrative clarity. From [8].

relation between vowel height and duration (Figure 7). The high vowels, whether they be diphthongs ([iy], [uw]) or monophthongs ([ix], [ih], [ax], [uh]), are considerably shorter in duration than their mid- and low-height counterparts. Moreover, the difference is largely proportional to vowel height – the lower the vocalic segment, the longer it tends to be, all other factors (such as stress-accent level) being equal. The low monophthongs (i.e., [ae], [aa], [ao]) behave more similarly to their low diphthongal counterparts (i.e., [ay], [aw]) than to other monophthongs, suggesting that vowel height is a primary factor underlying vocalic duration (and vice versa).

4.3 Durational Variation of the Syllable Onset

The mean duration of consonantal onsets as a function of syllable structure and stress-accent level is shown in the upper right panel of Figure 5. The average duration of unaccented onsets is similar across syllable types, while those pertaining to heavily accented syllables varies relatively little. The disparity associated with onset duration in heavily accented and unaccented syllables is appreciable (the former are between 41 and 63% longer than their unaccented counterparts), although not quite as large that associated with syllable nuclei (where the durational disparity is typically ca. 100%).

Most onset segments exhibit a modest (but significant) difference in duration between the highly accented and unaccented varieties, comparable to the averages shown in Figure 5. However, certain segments, such as [dh] (as in "the") and [dx] (as in "rider") exhibit little difference in duration as a function of accent level. These are the same segments that tend to be non-canonically realized in onset position. Thus, some relation between duration and segmental identity is likely to exist as they relate to stress accent.

Although the durational disparity between onset segments associated with heavily accented and unaccented syllables is not nearly as great as observed among vocalic nuclei, the general patterns observed are broadly consistent. In both constituent forms, segments that rarely occur in heavily accented syllables exhibit relatively little difference in duration as a function of stress-accent level (consistent with the durational properties of [dh] and [dx]).

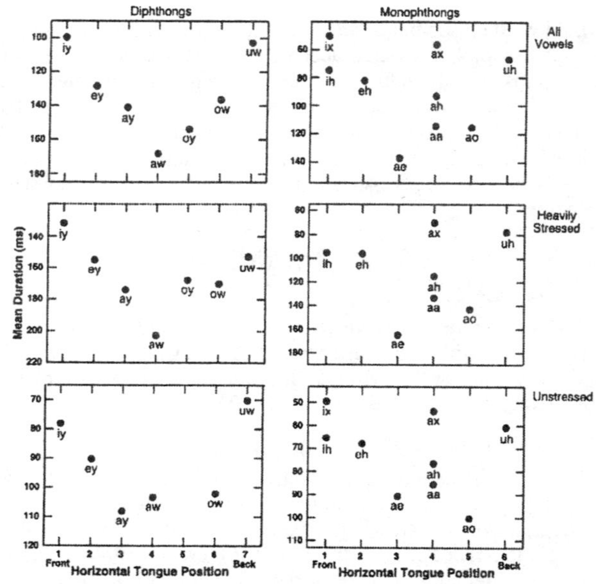

Figure 7 Spatial representation of the mean durational properties of vocalic nuclei organized by stress-accent magnitude and dynamic status of the vowel. The x-axis refers to the hypothetical position of the tongue in the horizontal place and is intended purely for illustrative purposes. Note that the durational scale on the y-axis differs for each of the six plots. From [11].

4.4 Durational Variation of the Syllable Coda

The mean duration of coda segments is shown in the lower right panel of Figure 5 for a variety of syllable structures. The durational patterns observed are rather stable across syllable form. Coda segments in heavily accented syllables are only 23 to 31% longer (on average) than their unaccented counterparts. The duration of coda constituents appears far less sensitive to stress accent than observed in nuclei or onsets. A closer examination of the durational disparities between codas in heavily accented and unaccented syllables reveals a variety of interesting patterns. At the low end of the durational spectrum are the "pure" junctures ([dx], [nx] and [q]) comprising the alveolar and nasal flaps, along with the glottal stop. These segments are uniformly short (40-50 ms) and exhibit virtually no distinction in duration as a function of stress-accent level. As discussed in Section 3.3, such segments function largely as syllable dividers and are largely devoid of a distinctive segmental identity. The durational properties of the approximants ([r] and [l]) exhibit a very different pattern. The duration of both segments is 67-93% longer in accented syllables relative to their unaccented counterparts. This durational disparity is more typical of vocalic nuclei than consonantal codas. A more variable pattern is observed among the remaining coda segments, as discussed in [8].

5. A JUNCTURE-ACCENT MODEL

The data described in this paper are incommensurate with traditional segmental models of spoken language. In particular, the concept of the phoneme is difficult to reconcile with the pronunciation patterns observed in the SWITCHBOARD corpus. The variation observed suggests that the *syllable*, rather than the phoneme is the basic organizational unit of spoken language at the sub-word level. Moreover, prosody, in the guise of stress accent, appears to play a major role with respect to the phonetic specification of pronunciation; accent's influence is differentially distributed across the syllable, both in terms of its magnitude and mode of realization.

A qualitative model, consistent with the pattern of pronunciation variation observed, is illustrated in Figure 8. At the heart of this model is the concept of juncture and accent, which can be likened to a mountain range containing peaks and valleys. A peak's height is associated with the stress-accent level of the syllable. Heavily accented syllables have tall peaks, while unaccented forms are associated with small peaks (as illustrated for the word "seven" in Figure 8). The foothills, ascending to the peak, are associated with the syllable's onset, while the steep crevasse following the peak is linked to the coda. Within this perspective all constituents of the syllable are inextricably linked together. A peak's height affects not only that particular constituent of the topography (i.e., the vocalic nucleus), but also the onset, whose length is directly related to the syllable's magnitude and to a lesser extent the coda. Peaks and valleys are separated by junctures of various types. A "pure" juncture is associated with the [v] in "seven" (Figure 8). Its acoustic signature is a substantial depression of energy across the topography's entire bandwidth, and serves primarily to demarcate one (heavily accented) syllable from another (less accented one). The onsets convey far more lexically distinctive information than the codas by virtue of the distribution of phonetically contrastive features (cf. Sections 3.3 and 3.4). In this sense codas contain relatively little information and are therefore more readily "expendable" than onsets. The nuclei set the "register" for decoding the nuclei and the onsets, providing crucial information for interpreting the acoustic signal associated with the syllable in terms of the *intended* segmental representation; but this interpretative machinery requires an accurate estimate of stress accent to perform at an optimal level.

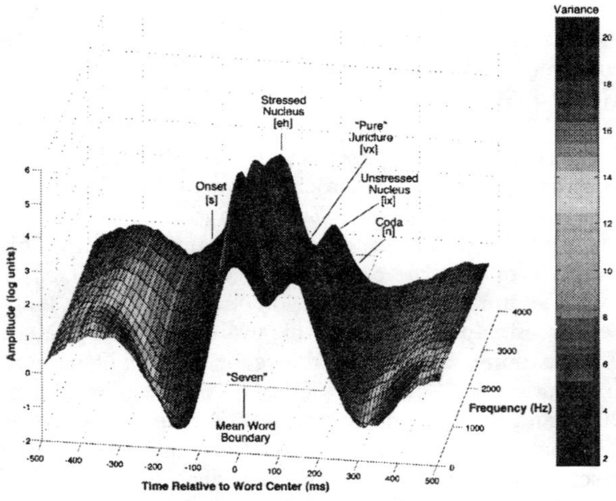

Figure 8 An illustration of a spectro-temporal profile (STeP) for a single, di-syllabic word, "seven" taken from the OGI Numbers95 corpus. The STeP is derived from the energy contour across time and frequency associated with many hundreds of instances of "seven" spoken by many different speakers. Each instance of a word was aligned with the other words at its arithmetic center. The mean duration of all instances of "seven" is shown by the red rectangle. The STeP has been labeled with respect to its segmental and syllabic components in order to indicate the relationship between onset, nucleus, coda and realizations within the syllable and their durational properties. From [8].

6. ACKNOWLEDGEMENTS

This research was supported by the U.S. Department of Defense and the National Science Foundation. We thank Candace Cardinal, Rachel Coulston, Jeff Good and Colleen Richey for transcribing portions of the SWITCHBOARD corpus.

7. REFERENCES

[1] Beckman, M. *Stress and Non-Stress Accent.* Dordrecht: Fortis, 1986.

[2] Clark, J. and Yallup, C. *Introduction to Phonology and Phonetics.* Oxford: Blackwell, 1990.

[3] Godfrey, J.J., Holliman, E.C., and McDaniel, J. SWITCHBOARD: Telephone speech corpus for research and development, *Proc. IEEE Int. Conf. Acoust. Speech Sig. Proc.*, pp. 517-520, 1992.

[4] Gow, D., Melvold, J. and Manual, S. How word onsets drive lexical access and segmentation: Evidence from acoustics, phonology and processing, *Proc. Int. Conf. Spoken Lang. Process. (ICSLP)*, Phila., 1996.

[5] Greenberg, S. Understanding speech understanding – Towards a unified theory of speech perception. *Proc. ESCA Tutorial and Advanced Research Workshop on the Auditory Basis of Speech Perception*, Keele, England, 1996, pp. 1-8.

[6] Greenberg, S. Speaking in shorthand – A syllable-centric perspective for understanding pronunciation variation. *Speech Communication,* 29, 1999, 159-176.

[7] Greenberg, S., Carvey, H.M. and Hitchcock, L. The relation of stress accent to pronunciation variation in spontaneous American English discourse. *Proc. Int. Conf. Speech Prosody*, Aix-en-Provence, 2002.

[8] Greenberg, S., Carvey, H.M., Hitchcock, L. and Chang, S. Temporal properties of spontaneous speech – A syllable-centric perspective, submitted to *Journal of Phonetics*, 2002 (available at: www.icsi.berkeley.edu/~steveng).

[9] Greenberg, S. and Chang, S. Linguistic dissection of switchboard-corpus automatic speech recognition systems, *Proc. ISCA Workshop on Automatic Speech Recognition: Challenges for the New Millennium*, 2000, pp. 195-202.

[10] Greenberg, S., Chang, S. and Hitchcock, L. The relation between stress accent and vocalic identity in spontaneous American English discourse," *Proc. ISCA Workshop on Prosody in Speech Recognition and Understanding,* 2001, pp. 51-56.

[11] Hitchcock, L. and Greenberg, S. Vowel height is intimately associated with stress accent in spontaneous American English discourse," *Proc. 7th Int. Conf. Speech Tech. Comm. (Eurospeech),* 2001, pp. 79-82.

[12] Hockett, C.F. The origin of speech. *Scientific American*, 1960 (Sept.), pp. 88-95.

[13] Lehiste, I. *Suprasegmentals.* Cambridge: MIT Press, 1970.

[14] Levelt, W. *Speaking*. Cambridge: MIT Press, 1989.

[15] Marslen-Wilson, W.D. and Zwitserlood, P. Accessing spoken words: The importance of word onsets. *Journal of Experimental Psychology: Human Perception and Performance*, 15, 1989, 576-585.

[16] Sampson, G. *Writing Systems.* Stanford: Stanford University Press, 1985.

The DUC Summarization Evaluations

Donna Harman, Paul Over
National Institute of Standards and Technology
Gaithersburg, MD 20899

ABSTRACT

There has been a long history of research in text summarization by both the text retrieval and the natural language processing communities, but evaluation of this research has always presented problems. In 2001 NIST launched a new text summarization evaluation effort, guided by a roadmap from the research community and sponsored by the DARPA TIDES project. This paper is a report of the first formal evaluation in a new conference called the Document Understanding Conference (DUC).

1. Introduction

Research in summarization was one of the first efforts to use computers to understand language. Work was done back in the 1950s (see section 1 of [7]) by many groups, including commercial services, to automatically produce abstracts or lists of pertinent keywords for documents. The interest in automatic summarization of text has continued, and currently is enjoying increased emphasis as demonstrated by the numerous summarization workshops held during the last five years.

Along with the research came efforts to evaluate automatic summarization performance. Two major types of evaluation have been used: *intrinsic* evaluation where the emphasis is on measuring the quality of the created summary directly, and *extrinsic* evaluation where the emphasis is on measuring how well the summary performs within a given task.

But evaluation of summarization is extremely difficult to do well. Intrinsic evaluation implies that there is some standard on which to judge summarization quality and usually this standard is operationalized by finding an existing abstract/text data set or by having humans create an "ideal" summary (even though no such ideal exists). The inherent human variability in doing a summarization task requires complex experimental design and analysis to accurately measure differences in machine performance in this task. This problem occurs both for situations using existing abstracts with text [8] and for situations where ideal summaries are created [5].

Extrinsic evaluation requires the selection of a task that could use summarization and then measuring the effect of using automatic summaries instead of the original text. Critical issues here are the task selection and the metrics for measurement. For example the tasks should be time-consuming enough that summaries could be useful, such as deciding whether to read a document based on reading its summary. They also must be sensitive enough to the quality of a summary that differences among a set of well-constructed summaries will show a difference in performance of the task. For examples of extrinsic evaluations, see the TIPSTER SUMMAC evaluation ([3]and [6]) and the Japanese NTCIR evaluation ([4] and [9]).

In 1998 the DARPA TIDES project (Translingual Information Detection, Extraction, and Summarization) specifically called for major advances in summarization technology, both in English and from other languages to English (cross-language summarization). This program offered the opportunity (and requirement) to tackle summarization evaluation once again and a long-term roadmap [1] to guide this evaluation was created. This roadmap provided guidance for the new Document Understanding Conference (DUC), with a pilot run in 2000, and the first major evaluation in the fall of 2001. This paper is a report on the 2001 evaluation, including discussion of what was done, what the outcome was in terms of the evaluation, and what is planned next.

2. Overall Evaluation Design and Data

The roadmap called for evaluation of generic summaries of both single documents and sets of multiple documents, at specified levels of text compression. Summaries can be classified based on characteristics of their input and output. For DUC 2001, fluent, neutral extracts or abstracts were to be produced from largely domain-independent monolingual English newswire and newspaper articles. The summaries were to be generic, i.e., minimally constrained with respect to their pur-

Proceedings of HLT 2002, Second International Conference on Human Language Technology Research, M. Marcus, ed., Morgan Kaufmann, San Francisco, 2002.

pose: situation, audience (educated adult newspaper readers), and use. Whereas this may result in greater variability in human judgments, generic summaries are heavily in use and were felt to be an appropriate first target for evaluation.

The roadmap suggested that the initial evaluation was to be intrinsic, with extrinsic evaluation to be phased in over time, along with requirements of deeper text understanding techniques that can lead to more complicated summaries.

The implementation of this in DUC 2001 was as follows:

1. Sixty sets of approximately 10 documents each were provided as system input for this task. Each document in the set was to be mainly about a single topic and each set of documents was to be centered around a specific event, a set of similar events, a specific subject, a specific person, or a set of opinions about a specific concept. The documents were newspaper or newswire articles from the TREC collection that were at least 10 sentences long.

2. Given such a set of documents, the systems were to automatically create 100-word generic summaries for each document. Additionally they were to create generic summaries of the entire set, one summary at each of four target lengths (approximately 400, 200, 100, and 50 words).

3. The sets of documents were created at NIST by 10 retired information analysts. Each person created six document sets, and then created 100-word manual abstracts for each document, and for the entire document set at the 400, 200, 100 and 50 word lengths.

4. Thirty of the sets (documents and manual abstracts) were distributed as training data on March 1, 2001. The remaining thirty sets of documents (without abstracts) were distributed as test data in mid-June and the system summaries were due two weeks later.

5. NIST then performed manual evaluation of the results (described in next section), returned the results to the participants, and a workshop was held after SIGIR 2001 in mid-September 2001.

3. Evaluation at NIST

The evaluation plan as specified in the roadmap was for NIST to concentrate on manual comparison of the system results with the humanly-constructed abstracts. Manual evaluation was considered critical because there was a general concern that automatic evaluation would not be adequate to deal properly with linguistic devices such as paraphrasing, or with abstracting methods that produce results differing greatly from simple extracts of the initial text. Additionally there was a desire to measure the coherence and organization of generated summaries.

Central to the manual comparison was a new tool developed by Chin-Yew Lin at the Information Sciences Institute, University of Southern California (`http://www.isi.edu/~cyl/SEE/`). This tool allows pairwise comparison of two summaries, and a modified version was used at NIST for the DUC 2001 evaluation. Figure 1 shows one example of this interface. Human evaluation was done at NIST using the same personnel who created the manual abstracts (called model summaries in DUC 2001). These people did pairwise comparisons between their "model" summaries and the "peer" summaries. Peer summaries include system-generated summaries, additional manual abstracts generated by others, and baseline summaries (defined below).

The additional manual abstracts came from two other analysts who were asked to generate "duplicate" manual abstracts. The baseline summaries were defined to be the first 100 words for single documents and the first 50, 100, 200 or 400 words of the most recent document in the document set for the multidocument summaries. An additional baseline of concatentated first, second, etc. sentences from a chronological sequence of documents in the set was also used in the multidocument summaries.

Two specific areas of evaluation were examined using the SEE interface. The first area involved the quality of the summary. Each system-generated summary, baseline summary, and "duplicate" manual summary was judged for grammaticality, cohesion and organization using a five-point scale.

- *Grammaticality*– [All, most, some, hardly any, or none] of the syntactic units (e.g., sentences, clauses, phrases, etc.) follow the rules of English grammatical form (independent of content).
- *Cohesion*– [All, most, some, hardly any, or none] of the sentences fit in as they should with the surrounding sentences.
- *Organization/coherence*– [All, most, some, hardly any, or none] of the summary is well-organized, i.e., the content is expressed and arranged in an effective way.

In the presentation of results the five-point response scale was treated as interval data with equal intervals. Post-evaluation discussions with the evaluators suggest that the intervals near the extremes were in fact felt to be smaller than the others.

The second area of evaluation dealt with coverage, i.e., how well did the peer summaries cover the content of the documents (as expressed by the model summary). The pairwise summary comparison was used in this part of the evaluation and judges were asked to do detailed coverage comparisons. SEE allowed the judges to step through predefined units of the model summary and for each unit of that summary, mark the sentences in the peer summary that expressed [all, most, some, hardly any or none] of the content in the current model summary unit.

The choice of units for the model and peer summaries involved practical as well as theoretical considerations. Researchers wanted units smaller than a

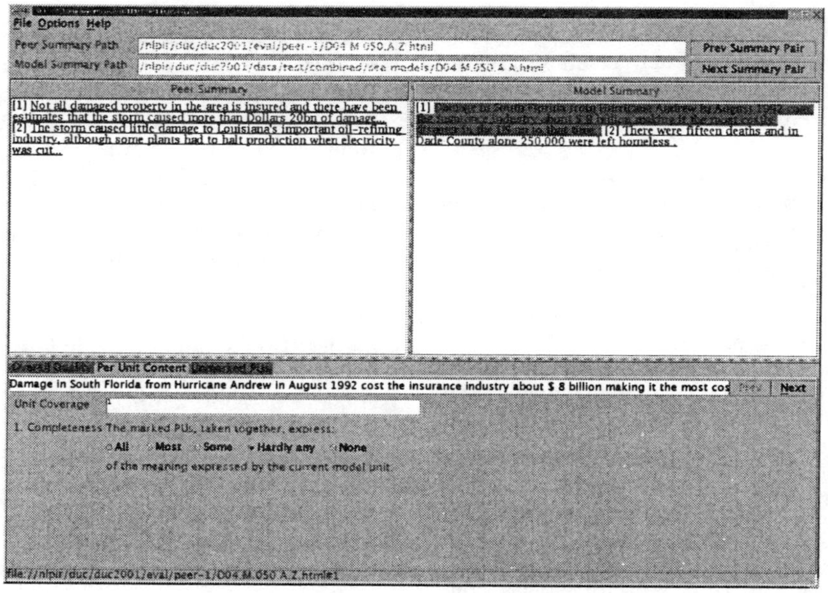

Figure 1: SEE interface for judging per unit coverage

sentence for better diagnostic information. Automatically determined units called elementary discourse units (EDUs) [2] based on rhetorical structure theory were proposed. Because these required some human post-editing, it was only practical to use them for the model summaries, which are many fewer in number than the summaries produced by the research systems. The latter were automatically divided into sentences.

Note that some sentences in the peer summary could be marked as pertinent to multiple units in the model summary, and some sentences in the peer summary might not be marked as being pertinent to any units in the model summary.

This process is much more complex than doing a simple overall comparison, i.e., did the entire summary being judged (the peer summary) express [all, most, some, or hardly any] of the content in model summary. The decision to use this more complicated method sprung from a need for more detail about what parts of automatic summaries matched the model summaries and also because past evaluation experiences indicated that judges had more difficulty making an overall decision than they did making decisions at each unit.

In the final step of the evaluation, the judge reviewed unmarked sentences in the peer summaries and indicated once for the entire peer summary whether [all, most, some, hardly any, or none] of the unmarked peer units really should have been included in the model summary, were related but needn't have been included in the model summary, or are totally unrelated to the model summary.

4. Approaches to Summarization

There were 15 groups that participated in DUC 2001, and an online proceedings (`http://duc.nist.gov`) contains papers from all the groups. The papers are a good sample of the current state-of-the-art in summarization.

Most of the groups produced extracts rather than abstracts. Different techniques were used to select sentences for extraction, such as clustering documents or paragraphs or sentences to locate similarities, or locating important sentences using language modeling. Additionally various non-content features such as document length, sentence position, sentence length, cue word use, and document creation time were used in picking important sentences. Several groups also used these heuristics to improve coherence and organization. There was some effort to remove duplicate information by using the Maximal Marginal Relevance algorithm or by using overlap or similarities to other sentences.

Three groups (Columbia University and two groups at ISI) worked on abstracting as opposed to extracting. It is hoped that more groups will move into abstracting in DUC 2002.

5. Results of the evaluation

One measure of the success of the evaluation is what was individually learned by each group. In terms of the evaluation itself, there are many important questions that need to be examined in this first running of the evaluation. Some are:

1. Were the human summarizers/evaluators able to do the task of writing the abstracts and were they able to use SEE for evaluation?

2. How useful was the information gathered about the quality of the summaries, such as grammaticality, cohesion and organization?

3. How stable were the coverage judgments at a unit

level and would it have been better to work at the whole summary level?

4. Did the coverage part of the evaluation work, i.e., did it provide plausible separation between systems, and between systems and baselines or human-generated abstracts?

5. What effect did the different lengths of summaries (levels of compression) have on the coverage results?

6. What effect did the different types of document sets (single events vs multiple similar events vs biographies, etc) have on the coverage results?

First, the human summarizers/evaluators seemed able to do the summarization task; they understood what was needed and the resulting abstracts are reasonable. They learned to use SEE and in general were able to do the evaluation task. Most of the problems that occurred were due either to the inherent difficulty of the task or to mismatches between the summarization tasks and the specific questions asked in SEE.

Second, the information gathered for quality evaluation was not very useful. The cohesion and organization questions made little sense for very short summaries, and in general judges had difficulty distinguishing between cohesion and organization. Grammaticality was very sensitive to low-level formatting. For example, more than 70% of the baselines were truncated to fit and this resulted in lower grammaticality scores than would have been expected for extraction baselines. In general the scores on the quality metrics were high for grammaticality, which should not have been surprising since most systems used extraction techniques. Similarly cohesion and organization scores for single document summaries were relatively high for all systems, but dropped for multidocument summaries presumably because of the problem of organizing and joining extracts across documents. The cohesion and organization scores reflect the current state-of-the-art for extraction; high for single documents from newspapers and lower for multi-document extracts. The scheme used in DUC 2001 for assessing cohesion and organization, however, did not provide enough detail for success/failure analysis by individual systems.

Third, evaluation of coverage at the per unit level was cognitively difficult. The judges were often in a quandary about how much information to bring to the interpretation of the summaries. Note that the question being asked involves finding a shared meaning between the content in each model summary unit and in the peer summary sentence, and determining how much meaning is shared – a very subjective judgment. The task was also difficult because each model unit was to be treated independently even though each is a part of an interconnected text.

By using multiple judgments of a given peer one can investigate questions like: - how consistent is a judge over time, how much does changing the judge or the model affect the result. There was time for one set of

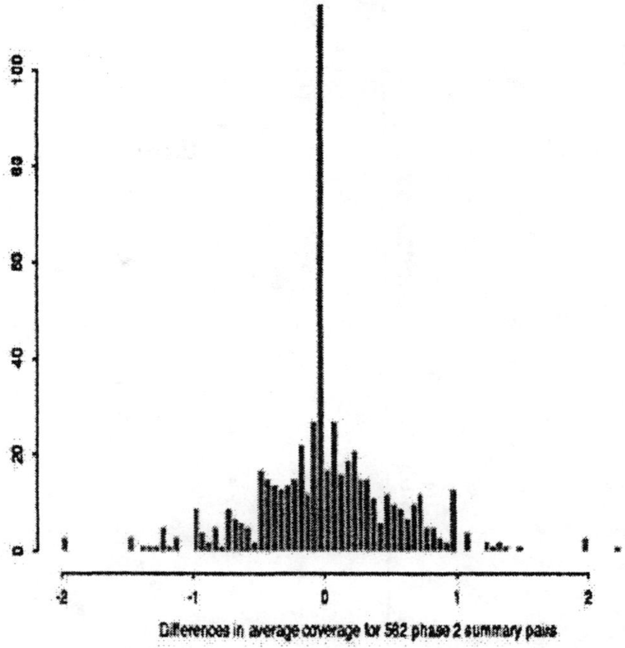

Figure 2: Percentage of average coverage judgments that differed

additional judgments and this was used to examine the effect of the model. When the same judge was asked to repeat the evaluation several days later using a different model (one created by another human), the within-judge differences were small but not zero (see the histogram of these differences in Figure 2).

Would it have been easier to make coverage judgments on the summary as a whole? In discussion with the evaluators afterwards, there was some indication that this would have been much more difficult. Further input from researchers on the usefulness of per unit coverage judgments is needed here to understand the full picture.

Fourth, the coverage differences seen between system-generated summaries, baselines, and human abstracts look plausible. Figure 3 shows the mean average coverage for the thirty test sets both for single document summaries and for multidocument summaries. For single document summaries the system scores are ranged around the baseline score but are lower than the human abstracts. There is an even larger difference between the humans and the systems for the multidocument summaries, with more variation across summaries (both human and automatic). As a final plausibility check, the summaries for the multidocument sets have lower scores than do those for the single documents as would be expected.

As always, it is important to look underneath the averages when measuring and drawing conclusions about system performance. Figure 3 shows that system T has a higher mean average coverage than system S for both single- and multi-document summaries. But as Figure 4 shows, when one looks at the two systems' performance

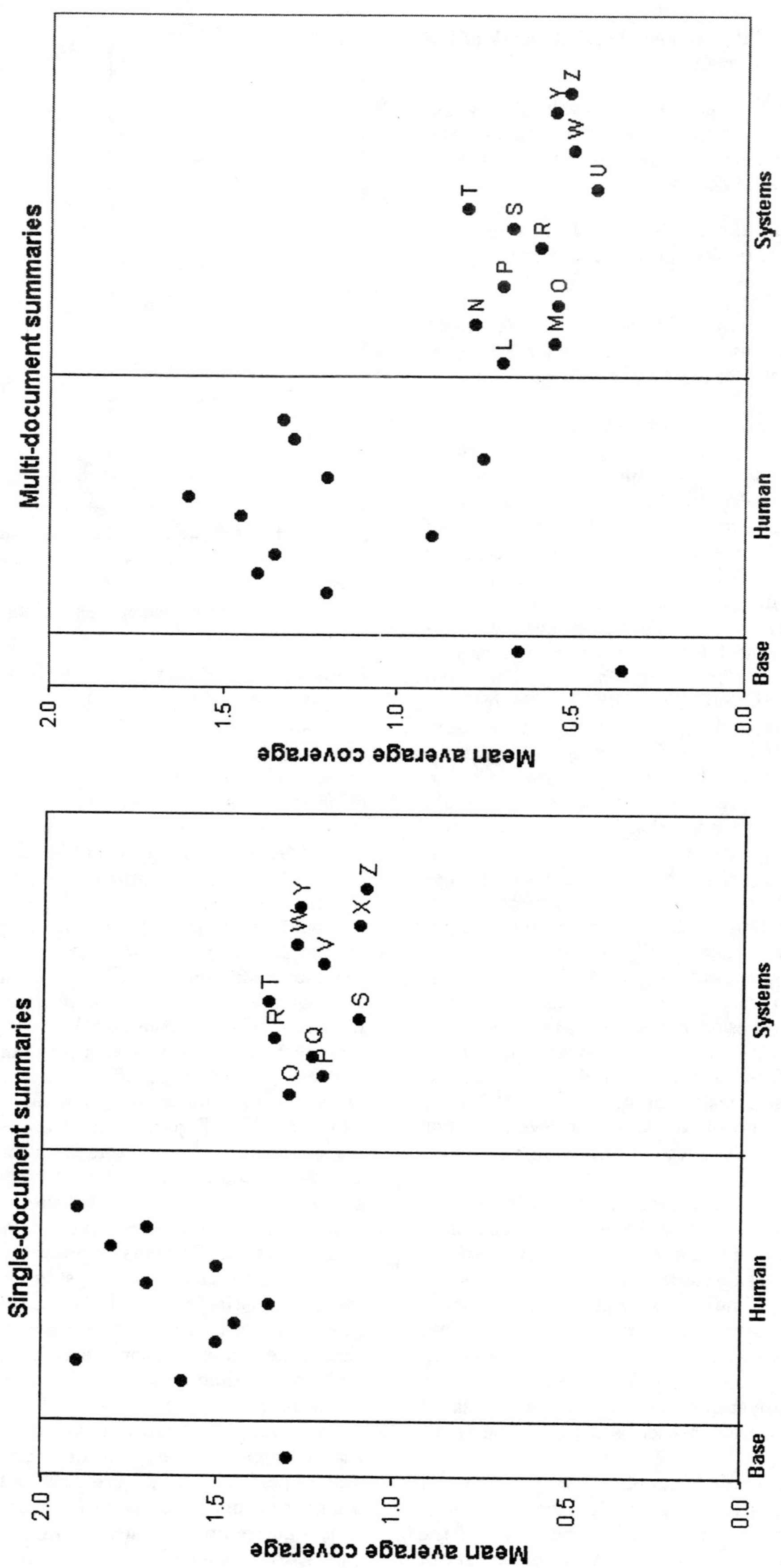

Figure 3: Average coverage for multidocument summaries

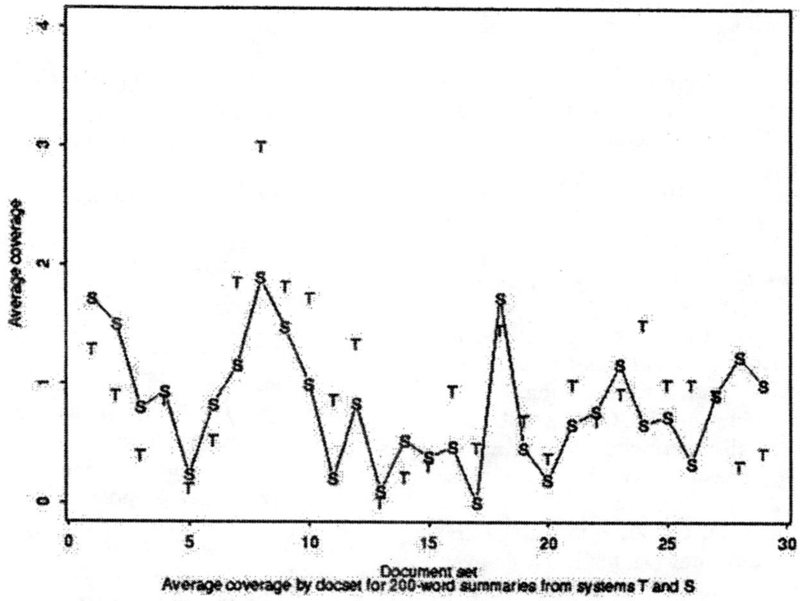

Figure 4: Variation in performance across document sets

Mean Coverage by Length and Summary Type				
	50 words	100 words	200 words	400 words
Baseline 1	0.3655	0.3347	0.3788	0.4059
Baseline 2	0.4632	0.6143	0.6765	0.7707
Systems	0.5008	0.5475	0.6824	0.7738
Humans	1.018	1.175	1.408	1.351

Table 1: Variation of the coverage results across summary lengths.

(in this case just for 200-word multi-document summaries) by document set, S outperforms T in 14 of 29 cases.

Figure 4 also suggests that there is an interaction between system and document set – the effect of the document set depends on which system is chosen. (Note that the model creator, the judge, and the document set are confounded). The presence of such interactions complicates any experimental design and analysis. Large variability due to document set, model, judge, etc., if additive (independent of the levels of other factors), can be addressed by blocking (i.e., within-document set, within-model, etc. comparisons) and analyzed using simple ANOVA models. This is not the case when interactions are present.

Fifth, how did the different target lengths affect the multidocument summarization coverage results? Table 1 shows the average coverage across summary lengths and across source of summaries. The systems perform much worse than the humans and about the same as baseline 2, which is clearly the better baseline for comparison. (Baseline 2 concatenated the first, second, etc. sentences from a chronological sequence of documents in the set.) Human performance, i.e., the agreement between two human summarizers, improves for the longer summaries, as does system performance, but on average never reaches 2 ("some") coverage.

Sixth, in terms of differences across the types of document sets (single events vs multiple similar events vs biographies, etc) there was not enough data to do an analysis: some types of document sets had only three members because of the random way the training and test document sets were split.

What can be learned from DUC 2001 and what is its significance in terms of the overall summarization roadmap? The main significance is that DUC 2001 is the first large-scale intrinsic evaluation of summarization, both for single documents and across multidocument sets. It is large-scale both in the sense of realistic amounts of test data and in the fact that multiple groups participated in the same focused task. The use of human evaluators working with a well-defined mechanism (the SEE interface) to judge the summaries lays the groundwork for a more principled approach to intrinsic evaluation of summaries. And finally DUC 2001 has drawn attention to the multidocument summarization problem, which is important both as a useful application and as a mechanism to allow researchers to more fully address cohesion and organization problems in summarization.

What were the disappointments and weaknesses in DUC 2001? One disappointment was the heavy use of sentence extraction as opposed to the more difficult move to abstracts. Another problem was the poor discrimination of the quality (grammar, cohesion and organization) part of the evaluation. DUC 2002 will hopefully see more attempts at abstracting and will provide a more granular method of measuring the quality of these abstracts.

In terms of the roadmap, DUC 2001 fulfilled the first step: - that of providing a framework for intrinsic evaluation of single and multidocument summaries. The 60 sets of documents and abstracts form an initial data resource; 60 more sets will be added in DUC 2002. The SEE interface has been made publically available as a community platform for human evaluation of summaries and the changes that are being made in SEE for DUC 2002 will strengthen weaknesses in the quality evaluation sections. The issue of human variability in constructing summaries, and therefore the difficulty in evaluation of system-generated summaries, remains a problem for intrinsic summary evaluation.

6. What Next?

There will be a second DUC evaluation effort in 2002 (`http://duc.nist.gov`), with the conference meeting in July following the ACL meeting. The problems found in the DUC 2001 evaluation will be addressed in several different ways.

1. There will be more document sets (60 test sets) as opposed to the 30 sets in DUC 2001. The document sets and manual abstracts will be created in such a way that the 60 sets from DUC 2001 can be used for training. Having more document sets should help in statistical analysis of the results.

2. The target lengths of the summaries have been shortened to eliminate the 400-word summary and to include a headline length summary. It was felt that these were more useful lengths to evaluate; the headline length has many important applications and the 400-word length might be better addressed using extracts.

3. The document sets will be broken into fewer but more tightly specified categories. In particular there will be just four different categories: document sets about a single natural disaster event with all documents created at most in a seven day window, documents about a single event in any domain but with the same time constraint, documents about multiple distinct events of a single type (no time constraint), and documents that present biographical information mainly about a single individual. Having multiple categories will allow groups to specialize their summarization algorithms, but having only four categories will allow more in-depth analysis of the results.

4. SEE will again be used for evaluation, but with major changes in the quality evaluation section to make the results more usable. In particular the grammaticality, coherence and organization items will be evaluated by a series of questions about effective use of pronouns, dangling connectives, subject/verb agreement, etc. These more concrete questions will provide a consistent basis for quality assessment and will allow the participants to more readily pinpoint text generation problems.

5. The five-point intervals [All, most, some, hardly any, or none] will be replaced with percentages [0, 20, 40, 60, 80, 100] to permit better score averaging and more consistent judgment by the evaluators.

6. There will be a new length-adjusted coverage metric for DUC 2002. In addition to measuring how well a peer summary covers the points in the model summary (the coverage metric), brevity will be rewarded.

7. REFERENCES

[1] B. Baldwin, R. Donaway, E. Hovy, E. Liddy, I. Mani, D. Marcu, K. McKeown, V. Mittal, M. Moens, D. Radev, K. Sparck Jones, B. Sundheim, S. Teufel, R. Weischedel, and M. White. An evaluation road map for summarization research. http://duc.nist.gov/roadmapping.html, 2000.

[2] Lynn Carlson, John M. Conroy, Dianne P. O'Leary, Daniel Marcu, Mary Ellen Okurowski, Anthony Taylor, and William Wong. An empirical study of the relation between abstracts, extracts, and the discourse structure of texts. In *Proceedings of the 2001 Document Understanding Conference (DUC2001)*, pages 11–18, 2001.

[3] T. Firmin and M.J. Chrzanowski. An evaluation of automatic text summarization systems. In Mani and Maybury [7], pages 325–340.

[4] Takahiro Fukusima and Manabu Okumura. Text summarization challenge: Text summarization evaluation at ntcir workshop2. In *Proceedings of the Second NTCIR Workshop Meeting on Evaluation of Chinese and Japanese Text Retrieval and Text Summarization*, pages 9–14, 2001.

[5] Hongyan Jing, Regina Barzilay, Kathleen McKeown, and Michael Elhadad. Summarization evaluation methods: Experiments and analysis. In *Intelligent Text Summarization: Papers from the 1998 AAAI Spring Symposium*, pages 51–60, 1998.

[6] I. Mani, T. Firmin, D. House, M.J. Chrzanowski, G. Klein, L. Hirshman, B. Sundheim, and L. Obrst. The tipster text summarization evaluation: Final report. 1999. Morgan Kaufmann Publishing Co. San Mateo, California.

[7] Inderjeet Mani and Mark T. Maybury, editors. *Advances in Automatic Text Summarization.* MIT Press., Cambridge, Massachusetts, 1998.

[8] Daniel Marcu. The automatic construction of large-scale corpora for summarization research. In *Proceedings of the 22th Annual International ACM SIGIR Conference on Research and Development in Information Retrieval*, pages 137–144, 1999.

[9] Yoshio Nakao. How small distinction among summaries can the evaluation method identify. In *Proceedings of the Second NTCIR Workshop Meeting on Evaluation of Chinese and Japanese Text Retrieval and Text Summarization*, pages 235–241, 2001.

Experiments in Multidocument Summarization

Barry Schiffman
Columbia University
New York, NY 10027, U.S.A.
bschiff@cs.columbia.edu

Ani Nenkova
Columbia University
New York, NY 10027, U.S.A.
ani@cs.columbia.edu

Kathleen McKeown
Columbia University
New York, NY 10027
kathy@cs.columbia.edu

ABSTRACT

This paper describes a multidocument summarizer built upon research into the detection of new information. The summarizer uses several new strategies to select interesting and informative sentences, including an innovative measure of importance derived from the analysis of a large corpus. The system also computes concept frequencies rather than word frequencies as an additional measure of importance. It merges these strategies with a number of familiar summarization heuristics to rank sentences. The initial version of the summarizer performed successfully in the evaluation reported at the Document Understanding Conference last year, although the system addressed only the content of the summary and not the presentation. We also discuss here the procedures we are developing to improve the presentation and readability of the summaries.

General Terms

Multidocument summarization

Keywords

Importance metrics, text generation, text analysis

1. INTRODUCTION

The extreme variety in multidocument summarization makes it hard to anticipate all of the demands that would be made on a general purpose summarization system. The input set of articles may be very loosely tied together; for example, it may have the same general topic, such as earthquakes in recent years or third-world debt, or it may be focused on one person or entity but over a long time span. On the other hand, the input set may be narrowly focused on a particular event, such as a mayoral election. The training and test sets for multidocument summarization developed by NIST for the Document Understanding Conference demonstrate the large number of possible variations.

Summarization of document clusters that are tightly focused on a single event is the research focus of Columbia's MultiGen [11], a summarization system that uses information fusion and similarities across input articles. However, since many of the documents in the DUC training corpus in 2001 were only loosely connected, we needed to develop an alternative summarization strategy. Our approach for handling other types of document clusters builds on experiments we were carrying out in detecting new information. One problem for new information detection is that most sentences in one article will be to a great extent different from the sentences in another article [1]. In moving to summarization, we emphasize the problem of determining which of the many different sentences are actually important enough to be included in a general-purpose summary. In turn, our experiments in sentence extraction for summarization will help refine our techniques in new information detection. These experiments were implemented in the DEMS summarizer, the Dissimilarity Engine for Multidocument Summarization.

DEMS produces summaries by extracting the top-ranked sentences until the desired length is met. To do the ranking, DEMS scans all the sentences in the input set of articles and assigns values to features, some of which try to measure the inherent importance and interest of the thought. Some of the features were derived from a large background corpus and will be described in later sections. The combination of innovative features with established techniques, such as increased weight to sentences near the beginning of articles, resulted in a reasonably successful experimental summarizer.

The Columbia Summarizer, used in the DUC evaluation, used different strategies for different types of document clusters. It first examined the document clusters and routed sets to MultiGen if the articles were determined to be on the same event; document clusters on topically related, but different events, were routed to DEMS. In the evaluation in 2001, DEMS was assigned 29 of the 30 sets. In the 2002 evaluation, which is not yet complete, DEMS was assigned 33 of the 59 clusters of articles.

DEMS is now used in tandem with MultiGen in the Newsblaster on-line news browsing system [12]. Document sets with high similarity scores, as measured by the clustering module, are routed to MultiGen, and DEMS gets all others.

In the remainder of this paper, we focus entirely on our work in DEMS, presenting first the overall system and then the evaluation results, both in DUC and in a follow-up evaluation that we carried out of an enhanced DEMS.

2. IMPORTANT AND INTERESTING

Our approach relies on three main techniques to compute significance – identifying importance-signaling words through an analysis of lead sentences in a large corpus of news, identifying high-content verbs through a separate analysis of subject-verb pairs in a

Proceedings of HLT 2002, Second International Conference on Human Language Technology Research, M. Marcus, ed., Morgan Kaufmann, San Francisco, 2002.

Figure 1: **DEMS architecture. The darker boxes represent the system as used at the Document Understanding Conference in 2001. The lighter boxes are the modules added since then.**

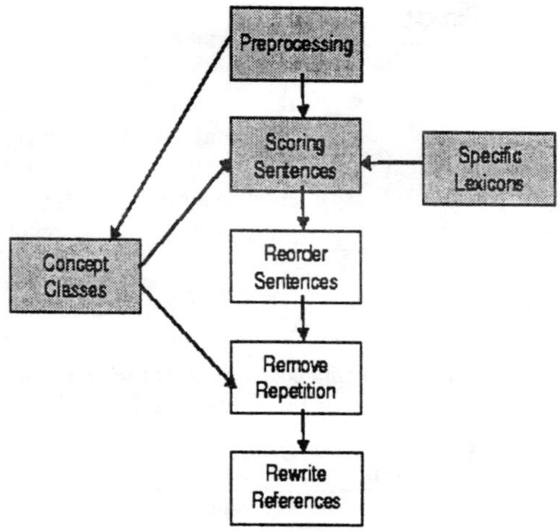

Figure 2: Lead words are those more likely to be found at the beginnings of news articles, and thus are likely to indicate importance in a general or global sense, without reference to the entities and events in a local cluster of articles.

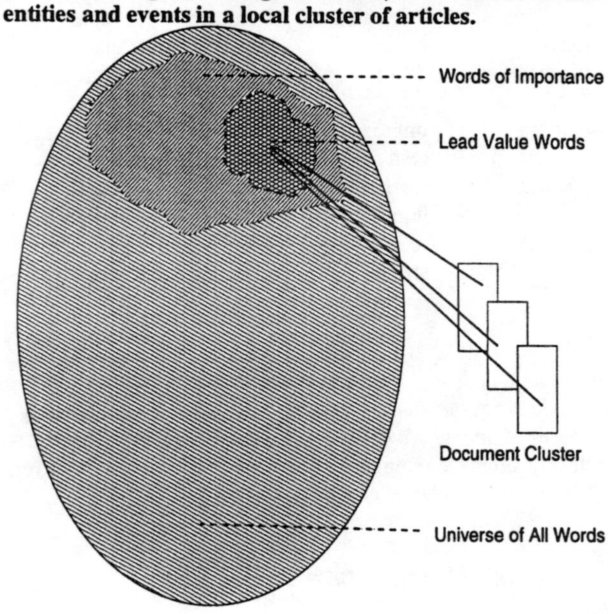

news corpus, and finding the dominant concepts in the input clusters of articles – rather than frequent words. Figure 1 shows how the system is arranged.

2.1 Lead Values

It is well known that the lead sentences of news articles can often make excellent brief summaries [15], but it is difficult to decide which of them to choose in the multidocument setting. Further, the lead sentences do not always indicate the significance of the article. But, if we can identify topics that often appeared in the lead sentences, then by definition these topics should cover important and interesting information. We examined first a large corpus of New York Times articles from 1996, and later a corpus of Reuters articles from the same year to determine what features could distinguish lead sentences from the average sentence [18]. Using just the noninflected forms of the words as the features, we developed lists of 4,600 and 4,900 words from the two corpora that tended, with a reasonable measure of statistical significance, to be in the leads of articles more often than in the full text. We hypothesized that, on average, sentences with more high "lead words" would tend to reflect important events. Table 1 shows a sample of lead words from the Reuters corpus. The criteria for selecting the lead words is:

$$\frac{p(W_{inlead})}{p(W_{anywhere})} > 1$$

The ratios were checked for statistical significance with the binomial test and only those with ratios where $pvalue < 0.05$ were accepted for inclusion in the lexicon.

The lead words are used as binary values, and averaged over the entire article, so that the sentence richest in lead words gets the highest score. By using the lexicon of lead words we are often able to locate secondary topics of interest in the articles, and to make comparisons of importance across documents. Thus, the system goes beyond the simple technique of grabbing the lead sentences – a technique that forms one of the baselines in the DUC evaluation.

We regard the lead words as a beginning of our approach to assess importance in new-information detection, where a statement might have few entities in common with all the material previously seen. We make the distinction between *local importance*, that is importance in the context of the articles we have in a cluster, and *global importance*, or importance is some larger, universal context (Figure 2). The lead-words lexicon is then one way to identify information that is globally important. We are experimenting with others for use in both the summarizer and in new-information detection.

2.2 Verb Specificity

In an effort to put sentences with the maximum amount of content into the summaries, we borrowed an the idea of verb specificity comes earlier work on a a biographical summarizer [19]. In that work, we sought to retrieve from a large corpus a brief description and a short list of interesting events about a person or several people. We first extracted a short description of the person and used the head nouns in that description to select sentences with verbs closely associated with the kind of person the user was interested in, reasoning that these sentences would be more relevant.

In the biography work, we also experimented with the notion of verb specificity. If a verb was closely associated with only a few types of subjects, i.e. one that is highly specific, it would tend to convey information by itself in a sentence, and it would indicate a specific, well-defined event. For example, a verb like "arrest" suggests police activity. But less specific verbs (e.g., "be" or "do") occur with a wide range of subjects and objects.

We found in constructing the biographical summarizer that descriptions could be found with the aid of pattern matching. But representative events important to that person were more difficult to select. In a large corpus, a great number of sentences might mention the particular name the user was interested in, but not all of them were interesting or informative. The system ranked sentences on the basis of how closely tied the verbs were to the terms in the person's description. The association of subject nouns to verbs was computed on the basis of a large corpus study. Mutual information

Table 1: A sampling of the *Lead Value* Lexicon made from the 1996 Reuters news wire. The entries are also used only as binary values.

cynical	coaxing	eerie	renovator	cling	impressionism	cutter	tusker
worn-out	convalescent	vial	unplayable	waterlogged	syphilis	decathalon	dragonfly
gigantic	extricate	unbowed	cherry	waterborne	watershed	phenobarbital	reappearance
rivet	heady	beloved	placid	bloke	caravan	large-scale	windfall
petrol	dame	mend	truffle	chubby	enthral	enunciate	dank
stopgap	freak	pensive	meld	mortuary	well-kept	well-established	one-man
linguist	impresario	ostrich	possess	chump	crestfallen	menu	electronics
nationalize	restive	daub	vile	wizard	finalist	dishevelled	crossroad
autism	workable	reverberate	excitable	trawler	sizeable	insolvent	stewardess
rhyme	fluorescent	sharpen	infighting	setter	electrical	mesa	jeopardize
chunk	rude	rambunctious	polyglot	chivalry	statistical	impressionist	bloodbath
conscription	spectre	crowning	zealotry	intrusion	gutsy	westernmost	showpiece

statistics were collected from a year's worth of newswire.

The data suggested that many verbs were closely tied to a only a few classes of nouns. We derived a "verb specificity" measure that reflects how often the mutual information between a particular verb and one noun or another exceeded a threshold.

$$VerbSpecificity = \frac{Count(V_{mi>T})}{Count(V_{mi>0})}$$

In the DEMS summarizer, the highest verb specificity in a sentence is used as the feature, in order to give increased weight to sentences rich in content. The motivation is to identify sentences that convey a complete thought by themselves, without depending too much on the surrounding context.

2.3 Concepts

A key feature in DEMS was reliance on concepts instead of the individual nouns and verbs. Thus, while we also use two frequency measures, we count the occurrences of concepts rather than words. On a single word basis, many common nouns and verbs will occur only once in a document, but two or more of them might actually be referring to the same idea or entity. Thus, alone, the words might miss the point of the cluster, but when considered as a "Concept Set" would zero in on the main ideas.

To build the Sets, we collect equivalent nouns and verbs into classes of words that conceivably could refer to one another. At present, we use WordNet [13] synonyms, hypernyms and hyponyms, with some simple constraints to decide which words belong together. The constraints are imposed on words that have more than five senses, and therefore large numbers of synonyms – for example "matter" or "issue." The system has no means of disambiguating words and the sets tended to grow unacceptably large. By removing highly polysemous words, manageable sets are obtained. But we noticed that one sense often dominated some words with many senses. At the threshold of 5 senses, we lost words like "father." To restore some of the dropped words, we used the study of subjects and verbs mentioned above to find the words closest in usage to a number of polysemous words, and used that list in place of the WordNet entry.

This strategy, we felt, would provide a truer measure of "aboutness," and would produce higher weights for sentences that talk about the subject of the input set – or at least the topic that ties the articles together . In an ideal world, we would know which words referred to the key entities in the set, but at present we do not have a good way to resolve references either within documents or across documents. We find concept sets an acceptable alternative. Table 2 shows an example of the largest Concept Sets from one article.

Table 2: Sample concepts sets for one article.

war campaign warfare effort cause operation conflict	10
concern carrier worry fear scare	9
home base source support backing	7
arrive reach hand find receive	8
report announce	4
prepare mount launch plunge	4
anger fire fuel dismiss	4

2.4 Other Features

In addition, we used a number of other heuristics, many of which are found in other systems, such as additional value to sentences near the beginnings of articles, or the publication date to make sure the most recent information is included. We diminish the value of sentences that deviate too much from a normal size, which we set at 15 to 30 words, and of sentences with pronouns.

We settled on a set of weights experimentally, although we recognize these may not be ideal. Using machine learning techniques to derive weights or a set of rules for combining the features would incur a tremendous cost of preparing a training corpus.

Here is a list of the additional features:

Location A negative value that penalizes sentences that appear late in the document.

Publication Date Additional value to the most recent documents, on the assumption that users will want the most up-to-date information.

Target Indicates the presence of the central personage in the document cluster, if one exists.

Length A penalty for sentences that are below a minimum (15 words) and above a maximum (30 words). Short sentences are often require some introduction or reference resolution, or else are a kind of interjection. Long sentences can cover multiple thoughts that are often found elsewhere in the document cluster in single sentences.

Others Indicates the presence of any named entity, weighted to the frequency of that entity across all documents.

Pronoun A negative value on sentences that have pronouns in the beginning of the sentence.

Role A positive value in cases where a pronoun follows a named entity.

Lead Value, Set Frequency, Local Frequency and Verb Value are combined with each of the above features in a weighted sum of 11 features in total. The weights are determined experimentally, and have been revised periodically. Different sets of weight form different configurations, with Target and Publication Date emphasized for the biographical sets.

2.5 Ordering

In the initial version of the summarizer used at DUC 2001, we had no time to try to make the output read better or clearer.

Since the conference last year, we implemented a simple ordering scheme to group the sentences from different documents together and then order those from a particular document in order of appearance.

In addition we check for repeated sentences in the output. Repetition was not a serious problem in in the DUC evaluation because the documents were not very similar and the sentences did match across articles. We used only string matching and thus allowed nearly identical sentences in the summary, an occurrence which did happen. In Newsblaster, this repetition is much more of a problem since most of the articles in a cluster are very close matches.

DEMS now uses the Concept Sets instead of individual words to measure the unordered overlap of content words between each new sentence proposed for the summary and all previously selected sentences. By using the Concept Sets, two sentences could be perfectly matched without having any specific words in common. The overlap threshold in DUC 2002 was set at 60%, but it is reduced to 40% in Newsblaster, where the document clusters are usually more cohesive and contain many more passages that have large amounts of overlap.

2.6 Named Entities

References to named entities pose yet another problem to multidocument summarization. Summaries often contain cryptic mentions of people's last names or acronyms and as a result the text becomes unclear. Both intuition and corpus studies (e.g., [14]), suggest that it would be most natural to include people's full name and description at their first mention, and use shorter ways, e.g. last name only, to refer to them at subsequent mentions.

We experimented with an initial algorithm for modification of references to people within the summary. IBM's NOMINATOR system [16] was used to extract named entities from the input cluster.

Titles and premodifier descriptions are also extracted, for example "French President Francois Mitterand", "Actress Elizabeth Taylor", "Los Angeles Police Chief Daryl Gates" (Table 3). In this way, a list of all possible ways to refer to a named entity occurring in the summary is constructed. After ordering the sentences in the summary as described in the previous section, references are substituted so that the longest variant of the name, possibly including a title, appears as first mention and subsequent repeated variants are substituted with the shortest most common name variant.

"Shortest most common" is defined as the shortest way to refer to a person that occurs at least N times in the input documents, and N = number of times the person was referred to by name in the input/number of name variants for that person. This restriction is imposed so that atypical names such as nicknames can be avoided.

Even this simple algorithm seems to improve the clarity and readability of the summary. Immediate future work will focus on coming up with more sophisticated ways of picking variants for subsequent mentions and also ways for identifying and including postmodifying descriptions at first mention.

Table 3: Count of references to the actress Elizabeth Taylor in a cluster in the DUC 2001 test corpus.

Actress Elizabeth Taylor	1
Ms. Taylor	1
Elizabeth	1
Liz Taylor	3
Elizabeth Taylor	8
Liz	11
Taylor	31
Miss Taylor	33

3. RELATED WORK

The closest system in spirit to DEMS is NEATS [7] which used topic signatures. Topic signatures are derived from co-occurence statistics on preselected documents, while DEMS relies on a WordNet-based dictionary. The goal of topic signatures and Concept Sets is similar: to give increased weight to salient statements in the document cluster. Topic signatures focus on associations, like the association between words like restaurant and waiter. Concept Sets focus on equivalent meanings like restaurant and eatery and strives to make finer-grained distinctions. The two systems also use similar ordering schemes. However, NEATS has no equivalent mechanism to the DEMS features that try to assess global importance.

DEMS differs from many summarization systems in that it uses no TF/IDF calculation. Lin and Hovy also found that TF/IDF was less effective than topic signatures in the summarization task [6]. In contrast, many summarization systems do use this measure of importance borrowed from Information Retrieval research, including those developed at the University of Texas [5] and the University of Michigan [3].

A number of systems use similarity to discern importance, but DEMS emphasizes statements that are different, and treats importance as a separate issue, giving no weight to similar passages. Systems that do measure similarity include MultiGen, the University of Texas system [5], focusing on information extraction techniques, and the ISI system [9], which used discourse structure. A group at CMU [4] uses cosine similarity of vectors in the MMR algorithm. A graph representation of several relationships between words is used to find similarities and differences between pairs of articles [8].

The use of the lead-words feature is related to a technique in the machine learning community, in which researchers have used existing corpora that are in some way preselected or partially annotated for one purpose or another. In an information extraction experiment Mark Craven at CMU [2] used what he called "weakly" labeled data to reduce the cost of annotating a training corpus. He was seeking a way to map medical texts into a structured data base. He used a database that contained links to related text articles. Another group working on information extraction at CMU, Seymour and others, sought to build a database of information about computer scientists from "distantly labeled data" composed of the header information on research papers [20]. Ellen Riloff learned textual-syntactic patterns for information extraction by comparing two corpora, a target containing the information she was interested in, and the other a general corpus [17]. The idea is that patterns of specialized words and syntactic structures will show up in greater numbers in the target corpus than in the general corpus.

Table 4: Overall preferences of human judges for reordered and named-entity substitution.

modified	48%
non-modified	13%
no pref	39%

Table 5: Breakdown of judges opinions.

	overall readability	*ordering*	*references*
modified	60%	78%	38%
non-modified	0%	0%	0%
no preference	40%	22%	62%

4. EVALUATION

4.1 At DUC

Our system was evaluated at DUC 2001. Figure 3 and Figure 4 show precision and recall respectively, compared with the averages of all automated systems. The systems were measured against a human-written summary for each cluster. The DEMS system scores are shown in both bar graphs in black and the average of all systems in white. Both charts list the sets in ascending order of the average score to try to reflect a rough scale of difficulty.

In an earlier analysis of the results, we found that either the sets or the human-summaries or the evaluators' judgments varied considerably [10]. In that analysis, the Columbia system was among the four top systems, which all performed in a relatively narrow range. The DUC organizers did not assign any kind of overall score to the participants.

4.2 After DUC

We carried out a post-DUC evaluation to determine whether the changes in presentation that we made to DEMS improved summary quality. The ten top-scoring summaries produced by DEMS for the DUC competition were chosen, the proposed ordering and name substitutions performed and the resulting pairs were given to human judges to assess. Results show that ordering considerably improves the summaries' quality. Named entity substitution also led to improvements, though they made smaller difference.

Three human judges were asked to compare the pairs of modified and non-modified text and to say which one they prefer in terms of 1) overall readability 2) ordering 3) references to people. The judges had the option to either express a preference to a text or state that the two variants are equal. The study was done on 200-word summaries. The overall distribution of preferences is shown in Table 4.

Since we did not define any criteria for good readability, good ordering or appropriate reference sequences, each human used his/her own understanding and the results suggest that those vary substantially– only in 27% of the cases did the opinions of the three judges coincide.

For each question, the majority answer was taken as final; that is, if two humans agreed in a judgment, that was taken as a final judgment for the text. Since there were three choices, the possibility existed that final judgment could not be reached because each human chose a different answer. This happened twice for judgments about references, once for ordering judgments and zero times for overall readability. These facts reveal which assessments are more difficult to make (slight errors in the substitution algorithm can cause disagreement). Table 5 shows the distribution of preferences according to majority opinion.

Even though the experiment was relatively small, it allows us to draw some useful conclusions. First, it shows that even simple methods can improve the quality of the summary and this suggests that it's reasonable to look for ways to assess summaries not only based on content, but also on the basis of readability and naturalness of the text characteristics.

The benefit from name substitution is not immediately evident. There are two major reasons for that – even though the strategy is very sensible in theory, in practice two problems might arise. a) Not all summaries contain (many) names and thus it's not possible to apply substitutions. b) Errors might be introduced in the summary by the substitution algorithms because of occasional errors in the named entity recognition output. In order to get a better sense of the utility of the approach, we applied it on the entire 2001 DUC corpus, both training and testing, totaling 60 sets. Then we manually examined the substitutions suggested by the algorithm for all 60 summaries. We defined the notion of "good substitution" as a substitution of one of the following kinds—1) first mention is a last name, and full name and title are available 2) first mention is a last name and full name is available 3) first mention is an acronym and full name is available 4) full name is used after the first mention and it can be substituted with last name only. Substitutions were possible in 35 of the sixty summaries; a total of 83 good substitutions were suggested, 49 of which involved first mentions and 18 problematic substitutions were proposed.

5. CONCLUSION AND FUTURE WORK

Overall we were pleased with the results, since DEMS was built in about a month. We began work only after reviewing the DUC training sets, when we found that most of the clusters were too diverse for MultiGen, which had been in development for five years.

We are planning improvements along a number of broad areas:

- Categorization of the document clusters. The clusters of articles both in the DUC evaluations and those collected in the Newsblaster system are quite varied, and we need a finer-grained analysis of the relationship between the member articles than we are currently using. The weights for all the features can be easily set automatically once we determine the kind of set we are dealing with. If the set is centered around a person, more weight can be given to sentences which mention that person. If the set is extremely diverse, like a group of articles about different events of the same kind, like volcanoes or political assassinations, more emphasis can be given to global importance while no attention need be paid to publication date.

- Improvement of Concept Sets. We are planning to examine additional ways to refine the data in WordNet and to discover a method for adding new links between less common words. Although we have not conducted an evaluation of the Sets, it is clear that we frequently fail to group words that are in fact linked in the text, and at the same time inappropriate words are added to various sets. Ultimately, the solution would be a comprehensive system to resolve all nominal references in order to get an accurate count of the frequency of a concept in a document. Since we are dealing with sets of documents, the co-reference system would have to be able to operate across the documents.

- We are expanding our rewriting component and will eventually deploy a full-scale text generation capability to the system. The final shaping of the summary is a difficult problem for the kind of diverse document clusters that DEMS

Figure 3: Precision: Dems in the black, compared to average

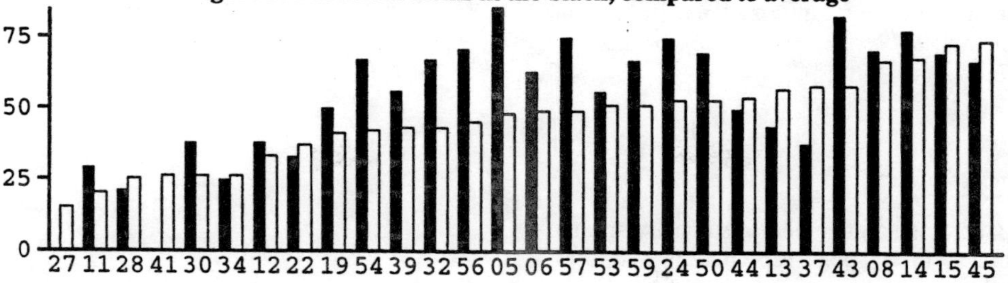

Figure 4: Dems in the black, compared to average.

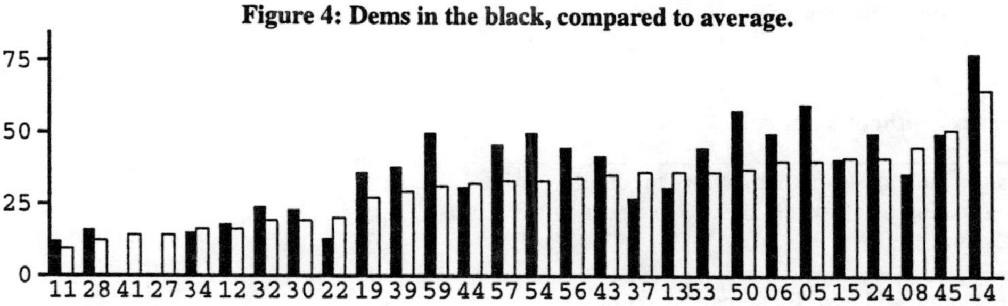

deals with. Since the sentences across documents do not align well, DEMS cannot use an approach like that of MultiGen, which cuts and pastes similar phrases from sentences that cover the same ground. We are exploring alternative approaches to rewriting in this context.

- Ultimately we will add a module to highlight new information, as well as other contrasts, such as different perspectives, between documents.

6. REFERENCES

[1] J. Allan, R. Gupta, and V. Khandelwal. Temporal summaries of news topics. In *Proceedings of the ACM-SIGIR Conference*, 2001.

[2] M. Craven. Learning to extract relations from medline. In *AAAI-99 Workshop on Machine Learning for Information Extraction*, 1999.

[3] H. J. Dragomir R. Radev and M. Budzikowska. Centroid-based summarization of multiple documents: sentence extaction, utility-based evaluation and user studies. In *Proceedings of ANLP/NAACL-2000 Workshop on Automatic Summarization*, 2000.

[4] J. Goldstein, V. Mittal, J. Carbonell, and M. Kantrowitz. Multi-document summarization by sentence extraction. In *Proceedings of ANLP/NAACL-2000 Workshop on Automatic Summarization*, 2000.

[5] S. Harabagiu, D. Moldovan, P. Morarescu, F. Lacatusu, R. Mihalcea, V. Rus, and R. Girju. Gistexter: A system for summarizing text documents. In *Proceedings of the Document Understanding Conference (DUC01)*, 2001.

[6] C.-Y. Lin and E. Hovy. The automated acquisition of topic signatures for text summarization. In *Proceedings of the 18th Annual International Conference on Computational Linguistics*, 2000.

[7] C.-Y. Lin and E. Hovy. Neats: A multidocument summarizer. In *Proceedings of the Document Understanding Conference (DUC01)*, 2001.

[8] I. Mani and E. Bloedorn. Multi-document summarization by graph search and matching. In *Proceedings, American Association for Artificial Intelligence 1997*, 1997.

[9] D. Marcu. Discourse-based summarization in duc-2001. In *Proceedings of the Document Understanding Conference (DUC01)*, 2001.

[10] K. McKeown, R. Barzilay, D. Evans, V. Hatzivassiloglou, B. Schiffman, and S. Teufel. Columbia multi-document summarization: Approach and evaluation. In *Proceedings of the Document Understanding Conference (DUC01)*, 2001.

[11] K. McKeown, J. Klavans, V. Hatzivassiloglou, R. Barzilay, and E. Eskin. Towards multidocument summarization by reformation: Progress and prospects. In *Proceedings of American Association for Artificial Intelligence 1999*, 1999.

[12] K. R. McKeown, R. Barzilay, D. Evans, V. Hatzivassiloglou, J. L. Klavans, C. Sable, B. Schiffman, and S. Sigelman. Tracking and summarizing news on a daily basis with columbia's newsblaster. In *Proceedings of the Human Language Technology Conference*, 2002.

[13] G. A. Miller, R. Beckwith, C. Fellbaum, D. Gross, and K. J. Miller. Introduction to WordNet: An on-line lexical database. *International Journal of Lexicography (special issue)*, 3(4):235–312, 1990.

[14] M. Poesio and R. Vieira. A corpus-based investigation of definite description use. *Computational Linguistics*, 24(2):183–216, 1998.

[15] L. Rau, R. Brandow, and K. Mitze. Domain-independent summarization of news. In *Summarizing Text for Intelligent Communication*, 1994.

[16] Y. Ravin, N. Wacholder, and M. Choi. Disambiguation of proper names in text. In *Proceedings of the 17th Annual ACM-SIGIR Conference*, 1997.

[17] E. Riloff. Automatically generating extraction patterns from untagged text. In *Proceedings of the 13th National Conference on Artificial Intelligence*, 1996.

[18] B. Schiffman. Building a resource for evaluating the importance of sentences. In *Proceedings of the Third Annual Conference on Language Resources and Evaluation*, 2002.

[19] B. Schiffman, I. Mani, and K. J. Concepcion. Producing biographical summaries: Combining linguistic knowledge with corpus statistics. In *Proceedings European Association for Computational Linguistics 2001*, 2001.

[20] K. Seymore, A. McCallum, and R. Rosenfeld. Learning hidden markov model structure for information extraction. In *AAAI-99 Workshop on Machine Learning for Information Extraction*, 1999.

APPENDIX

A. EXAMPLES

Here is an example comparing a nonmodified summary, from a recent Newsblaster summery on weapons inspections in Iraq. Figure A shows an ordered summary for noun-phrase substitution is put in. Figure A shows the result after the references to people are reworked.

Figure 5: Summary without name substitution

Wolfowitz said Iraq is among countries trying to develop weapons of mass destruction that " would make September 11 pale by comparison."

In his State of the Union address, **Bush** named Iraq, Iran and North Korea part of an "axis of evil" bent on developing chemical, nuclear or biological weapons.

Wolfowitz said the **Bush** administration would prefer to find a diplomatic solution to the Iraq issue, but **Hussein** "has shown great resistance to accepting any reasonable outcomes."

Deputy Defense Secretary Paul Wolfowitz told CNN's "Novak, Hunt and Shields" that **President Bush** has not made a decision about military action against Iraq.

Figure 6: Summary with name substitution

Deputy Defense Secretary Paul Wolfowitz said Iraq is among countries trying to develop weapons of mass destruction that "would make September 11 pale by comparison."

In his State of the Union address, **President Bush** named Iraq, Iran and North Korea part of an "axis of evil" bent on developing chemical, nuclear or biological weapons.

Wolfowitz said the **Bush** administration would prefer to find a diplomatic solution to the Iraq issue, but **Iraqi President Saddam Hussein** "has shown great resistance to accepting any reasonable outcomes."

Wolfowitz told CNN's "Novak, Hunt and Shields" that Bush has not made a decision about military action against Iraq.

Automated Multi-document Summarization in NeATS

Chin-Yew Lin and Eduard Hovy
USC Information Sciences Institute
4676 Admiralty Way
Marina del Rey, CA 90292-6695
Tel:+1-310-448-8711/8731
{cyl,hovy}@isi.edu

ABSTRACT

This paper describes the multi-document text summarization system NeATS. Using a simple algorithm, NeATS was among the top two performers of the DUC-01 evaluation.

Keywords

Multi-document text summarization; NeATS

1. OVERVIEW

In this paper we describe work in our NeATS (Next Generation Automated Text Summarization) project on multi-document summarization. To select important content, we used techniques that proved effective in single document summarization such as sentence position [1], term frequency [13], topic signature [11,7], and term clustering. To remove redundancy, we used MMR [3]. To improve cohesion and coherence, we used stigma word filters [4] and time stamps. Although most of the individual techniques are not new, assembling them and applying them to multi-document summarization is new. Also, including lead sentences to ensure coherence is new, and turned out to be important.

For much of the system we re-used modules built in prior work, notable the SUMMARIST single-document summarizer [7] and the Webclopedia question answering system [8,9].

NeATS was evaluated in the Document Understanding Conference DUC-01 [15]. It consistently was among the top performers in the multi-document summarization track. In the aggregating peer-to-peer comparison suggested by [14], NeATS scored first in precision and second in recall among 12 participants. The system also achieved the best F1-measure score across all summary sizes.

2. NeATS

NeATS attempts to extract relevant or interesting portions from a set of documents about some topic and to present them in coherent order. It is tailored to the genre of newspaper news articles, and it works for English, but can be made multilingual without a great deal of effort. At present NeATS produces generic (author's point of view) summaries, but it could be made sensitive to desired focus topics, input by a user.

Proceedings of HLT 2002, Second International Conference on Human Language Technology Research, M. Marcus, ed., Morgan Kaufmann, San Francisco, 2002.

Given an input of a collection of sets of newspaper articles, NeATS applies the following 6 steps.

3. ALGORITHM

3.0 Input

The input is a set of topic groups. Each topic group is a set of approx. 10 newspaper articles selected by the evaluation organizers. A topic group may focus on a single natural disaster (earthquake, hurricane, etc.), a single event (election, car race, etc.), multiple instances of a type of event (many earthquakes, elections, etc.), or a single person (in which case the summary would be a biography).

3.1 Extract and Rank Passages

Given the input documents, form a query, extract sentences, and rank them, using modules of Webclopedia:

1.a identify key words for each topic group: compute unigram, bigram, and trigram topic signatures [11] for each group, using the likelihood ratio λ [2]. A topic signature is a list of words/phrases, each with strengths, that characterizes the group and differentiates it from others [7]

1.b to facilitate fallback (query generalization), remove from the signatures all words or phrases that occur in fewer than half the texts of the topic group

1.c save the signatures in a tree, organized by signature overlap. We use the format of Webclopedia's parser CONTEX [5,6]; see Figure 1.

1.d use Webclopedia's ranking algorithm to rank sentences [8].

3.2 Filter for Content

Given the ranked list of sentences, re-rank or remove those according to the following conditions:

2.a remove all sentences with sentence position > 10. This is a simple version of SUMMARIST's Optimum Position Policy (OPP) [10], which records the relative importance of sentence positions

2.b decrease ranking score of all sentence containing stigma words [4] (day names; time expressions; sentences starting with conjunctions such as "but", "although"; sentences containing quotation marks; sentences containing the verb "say").

3.3 Enforce Cohesion and Coherence

Locate and include a suitable introductory sentence for each remaining sentence:

3.a pair each sentence with the first sentence (lead) of its document; but if the first sentence contains fewer than 5 words, then take the next one. For example (where *x.y* stands for *document number . sentence number*):

`4.3, 6.6, 2.5, 5.2...`

`→ 4.1, 4.3, 6.1, 6.6, 2.1, 2.5, 5.1, 5.2...`

3.4 Filter for Length

Select the required number of sentence pairs using a simplified version of CMU's MMR algorithm [3]:

4.a include first pair

4.b using a simplified version of MMR, find the sentence pair most different from the included ones, and include it too. (In the DUC-2001 implementation, NeATS did not consider the sentence pair, just the sentence. This caused some degradation.)

4.c repeat step 4.b until the summary length criterion is satisfied:

`→ 4.1, 4.3, 2.1, 2.5`

3.5 Ensure Chronological Coherence

Reorder the pairs in publication order, and disambiguate all time words with explicit dates:

5.a reorder pairs in publication order:

`→ 2.1, 2.5, 4.1, 4.5`

5.b for each time word ("today", "Monday", etc.) compute the actual date (from the dateline) and include it in the text in parentheses, in order to signal which day each "today" (etc.) is.

3.6 Format and Print Results

Format and output the final result.

4. DISCUSSION

This simple algorithm gives surprisingly reasonable results. We like the following aspects.

Typical current extractive summarization methods are essentially IR in miniature: from a set of sentences (instead of texts), select and rank the ones most relevant to the query. The major problems are **creating the query** and then **assembling the extracted sentences into a single coherent text** (a step that IR does not have).

For creating the query, we saved a great deal of development time by using existing modules from SUMMARIST [7] and Webclopedia [8,9]. SUMMARIST's topic signature creation techniques [11] allowed us directly to compute a ranked list of words (and bi- and trigrams) most characteristic of each document set. By placing these ngrams (and their sub-ngrams, which form a cluster) into the parse tree format we use for the retrieval stage of Webclopedia (Figure 1), we could directly form increasingly general queries, with which to extract the most relevant sentences from the document set, and rank them.

To assemble the extracted sentences into a single coherent text, we used the fact that a lead sentence, which introduces the article, is a powerful context-setter for each nearby (early) sentence in the article. We therefore paired each extracted sentence with its lead sentence, selected as appropriate.

One further factor interfering with coherence was misleading time words: "today" in articles written on different days means different dates. To disambiguate all time words we therefore computed the actual dates from the articles' datelines and included them after each time word. A typical summary is shown in Figure 2. Note that the sentences span 4 years; without the absolute time references, a very misleading picture of the documents would have been created.

```
( :SURF "WEBCL-SUMMMARIZER-HOSPITAL"
  :CAT S-NP
  :CLASS I-EN-WEBCL-SIGNATURE-HOSPITAL
  :LEX  0.9
  :SUBS  (((HOSPITAL-0)
          (:SURF "Hospital Health Center"
           :CAT S-NP
           :CLASS I-EN-WEBCL-SIGNATURE-HOSPITAL
           :LEX 0.6
           :SUBS  (((HOSPITAL-14)
                    (:SURF "Hospital Health"
                     :CAT S-NP
                     :CLASS I-EN-WEBCL-SIGNATURE-HOSPITAL
                     :LEX 0.6))
                     ((HOSPITAL-24)
                    (:SURF "Health Center"
                     :CAT S-NP
                     :CLASS I-EN-WEBCL-SIGNATURE-HOSPITAL
                     :LEX 0.6))
                   ((HOSPITAL-37)  (:SURF "Hospital" ...))
                   ((HOSPITAL-43)  (:SURF "Center" ...))
                   ((HOSPITAL-44)  (:SURF "Health" ...)))))
        ((HOSPITAL-25)  (:SURF "John Hospital" ...)))
        ((HOSPITAL-42)  (:SURF "doctors"...))
        ((HOSPITAL-47)  (:SURF "April" ...))
        ((HOSPITAL-49)  (:SURF "sinus" ...))))
...
```

"Hospital Health Center" (sub-)ngram cluster

Other (sub-)ngram clusters (compressed)

Figure 1. Portion of topic signature cluster tree for ngrams of "Hospital Health Center".

```
<multi size="100" docset="d45h">
(06/25/90) The republic of Slovenia plans to
  begin work on a constitution that will give
  it full sovereignty within a new Yugoslav
  confederation, the state Tanjug news agency
  reported Monday (06/25/90).
(06/28/91) On Wednesday (06/26/91), the
  Slovene soldiers manning this border post
  raised a new flag to mark Slovenia's
  independence from Yugoslavia.
(06/28/91) Less than two days after Slovenia
  and Croatia, two of Yugoslavia's six
  republics, unilaterally seceded from the
  nation, the federal government in Belgrade
  mobilized troops to regain control.
(02/09/94) In the view of Yugoslav diplomats,
  the normalization of relations between
  Slovenia and the Federal Republic of
  Yugoslavia will certainly be a strenuous and
  long-term project.
</multi>
```

Figure 2. Example 100-word summary (Slovenia's secession from Yugoslavia).

5. RESULTS

We were pleased by the content and readability of the results. Analyzing all systems' results for DUC-2001, we computed Recall, Precision, and F-Measure using the following formulas:

Recall = (# of model units marked with peer units) / (# of model units)

Precision = (# of unique peer units marked with model units) / (# of peer units)

F-Measure = 2*Recall*Precision / (Recall+Precision)

Here 'model unit' denotes an evaluation unit (usually, a sentence) contained in the human-produced model summary and 'peer unit' a unit produced by the system. The DUC organizers used the Summary Evaluation Environment SEE built by one of the authors [12] to rate the relevance of all units in the system summary by comparing them to each model unit.

According to this, NeATS (system N) did not fare badly (though its relative rank may change with different definitions of Recall and Precision). Systems' scores using these formulas are shown in the histogram in Figure 3. Humans did better than any system (both humans over 50%, human X is the average of human 1 and human 2), outscoring the nearest system by about 10%. Only 1 system (NeATS) scored in the mid-40s, with 45%. 5 systems scored between 35% and 41%, and 3 scored between 30% and 35%. Despite the low inter-human agreement (which we take to reflect the undefinedness of the 'generic summary' task), there is obviously still considerable room for systems to improve. We expect that systems that compress their output (unlike NeATS) will thereby gain more space to include additional important material.

NeATS tended to perform best on single-event stories and general topics, across the scale on biographies, and not so well on multi-instance events. A somewhat more targeted strategy is called for in topic groups with internal structure such as the latter two types.

It is interesting to note that systems are separated into two major groups by baseline 2. Baseline 2 forms its summaries by taking the first sentence in the first document, the first sentence in the second document, and so on until the number of sentences in the summary reaches the 50, 100, 200, or 400 word limits. Baseline 1 takes the first 50, 100, 200, 400 words in the last document (by date) of the collection. Almost all systems outperform baseline 1. This result indicates that on average it is necessary to cover most documents in a collection to generate good multi-document summaries.

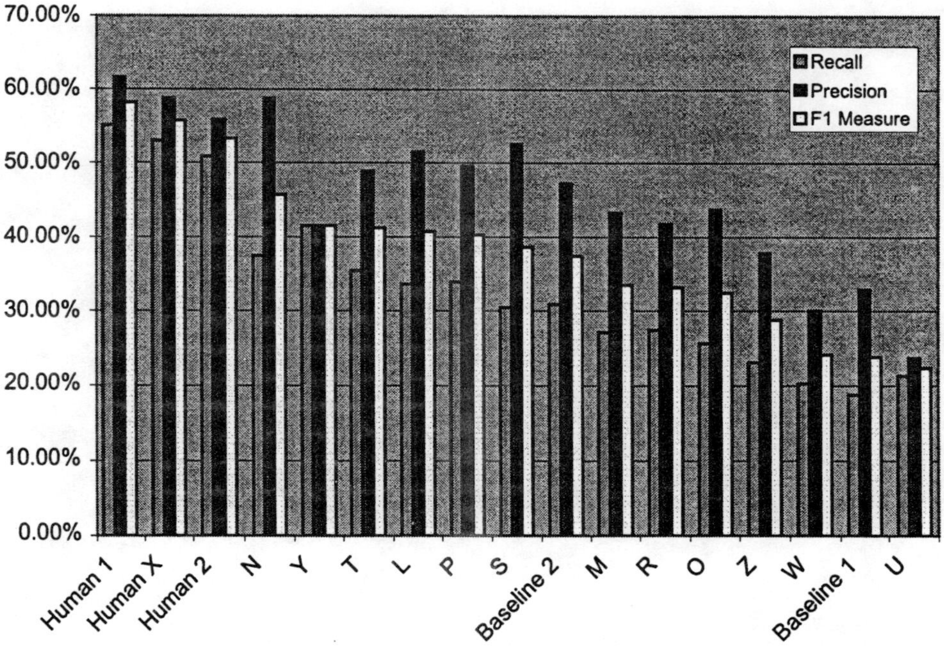

Figure 3. DUC-01 recall, precision, and F1 scores.

6. REFERENCES

[1] Baxendale, P.B. 1958. Machine-Made Index for Technical Literature—An Experiment. *IBM Journal* (October):3, 54–361.

[2] Dunning, T. 1993. Accurate Methods for the Statistics of Surprise and Coincidence. *Computational Linguistics* 19, 61–74.

[3] Goldstein, J., M. Kantrowitz, V. Mittal, and J. Carbonell. 1999. Summarizing Text Documents: Sentence Selection and Evaluation Metrics. *Proceedings of the 22nd International ACM Conference on Research and Development in Information Retrieval (SIGIR-99)*, Berkeley, CA, 121–128.

[4] Edmundson, H.P. 1969. New Methods in Automatic Abstracting. *Journal of the Association for Computing Machinery* 16(2).

[5] Hermjakob, U. 1997. *Learning Parse and Translation Decisions from Examples with Rich Context.* Ph.D. dissertation, University of Texas at Austin. file://ftp.cs.utexas.edu/pub/~mooney/papers/hermjakob-dissertation-97.ps.gz.

[6] Hermjakob, U. 2000. Rapid Parser Development: A Machine Learning Approach for Korean. *Proceedings of the North American chapter of the Association for Computational Linguistics* (NAACL-2000). http://www.isi.edu/~ulf/papers/kor_naacl00.ps.gz.

[7] Hovy, E.H. and C.-Y. Lin. 1999. Automated Text Summarization in SUMMARIST. In M. Maybury and I. Mani (eds), *Advances in Automatic Text Summarization.* Cambridge, MA: MIT Press.

[8] Hovy, E.H., L. Gerber, U. Hermjakob, M. Junk, and C.-Y. Lin. 2000. Question Answering in Webclopedia. *Proceedings of the TREC-9 Conference.* NIST, Gaithersburg, MD. November 2000.

[9] Hovy, E.H., L. Gerber, U. Hermjakob, C.-Y. Lin, and D. Ravichandran. 2001. Toward Semantics-Based Answer Pinpointing. *Proceedings of the DARPA Human Language Technology Conference (HLT).* San Diego, CA. March 2001.

[10] Lin, C.-Y. and E.H. Hovy. 1997. Identifying Topics by Position. *Proceedings of the 5th Conference on Applied Natural Language Processing* (ANLP). Washington, DC.

[11] Lin, C.-Y. and E.H. Hovy. 2000. The Automated Acquisition of Topic Signatures for Text Summarization. *Proceedings of the COLING Conference.* Saarbrücken, Germany. August, 2000.

[12] Lin, C.-Y. 2002. The SEE Summarization Evaluation Environment. In prep.

[13] Luhn, H.P. 1959. The Automatic Creation of Literature Abstracts. *IBM Journal of Research and Development*: 159–165. Also in I. Mani and M. Maybury (eds), *Advances in Automated Text Summarization.* 1999. Cambridge, MA: MIT Press, 15–22.

[14] McKeown, K., R. Barzilay, D. Evans, V. Hatzivassiloglou, M-Y Kan, B, Schiffman, and S. Teufel 2001. Columbia Multi-Document Summarization: Approach and Evaluation. *Workshop on Text Summarization.* New Orleans, LA. September, 2001.

[15] Over, P. 2001. Introduction to DUC-2001: An Intrinsic Evaluation of Generic News Text Summarization Systems. *Workshop on Text Summarization* at the SIGIR Conference. New Orleans, LA. September, 2001.

Formal grammars for estimating partition functions of double-stranded chain molecules

David Chiang
Dept of Computer and Information Science
200 S 33rd St
Philadelphia PA 19104-6389
dchiang@cis.upenn.edu

Aravind K. Joshi
Dept of Computer and Information Science
200 S 33rd St
Philadelphia PA 19104-6389
joshi@cis.upenn.edu

ABSTRACT

This paper looks at an algorithm due to Chen and Dill for estimating the partition functions of a restricted subclass of double-stranded polymers, and shows how it can be translated into a context-free grammar, so that their algorithm reduces to a variant of the CKY parsing algorithm. Our formulation clarifies the structure of Chen and Dill's algorithm, leading to revised complexity analyses and an optimization in one case, and lays a formal foundation for generalizing this method to more complex cases by the use of grammars beyond context-free power such as tree adjoining grammars.

1. INTRODUCTION

An important problem in the statistical mechanics of biomolecules is the computation of the *partition function* of a molecule, which is used to predict various physical properties of the molecule, including its stable conformations and conformational changes. Chen and Dill [1, 2] propose a model for a restricted subclass of molecules which gives an efficient approximate solution to this problem.

The goal of this paper is to show how Chen and Dill's model can be translated into a context-free grammar (CFG), so that their algorithm reduces to a variant of the CKY parsing algorithm [7, 14]. This formulation clarifies the structure of the algorithm, leading to a revised complexity analysis and an optimization in one case, and lays a formal foundation for generalizing this method to more complex cases using, for example, tree adjoining grammars [4, 6].

Molecules like RNAs or proteins are *sequences* of building blocks—nucleotides for RNA or amino acids for proteins—but they do not lie in straight lines in space. Rather, bonds, which we will call *self-contacts*, may form between nonadjacent members of the sequence, folding it into a certain shape in space. A pattern of self-contacts may be represented by a *polymer graph* (see Figure 1) in which straight edges represent the linear structure of the sequence, and curved edges represent the self-contacts. A polymer graph constrains but does not completely determine the shape of a molecule in space. In short, one sequence may correspond to many different polymer graphs, and one polymer graph may correspond to many different shapes or *conformations*.

The partition function of a molecule gives the relative accessibility of the possible conformations of the molecule. It is defined as

$$Q = \sum_j e^{-E_j/kT} \tag{1}$$

where T is the temperature, k is Boltzmann's constant, j ranges over the conformations of the molecule, and E_j is the energy of conformation j. Since all the conformations corresponding to a single polymer graph have the same energy, we may rewrite this as:

$$Q = \sum_j \Omega_j e^{-E_j/kT} \tag{2}$$

where j ranges over polymer graphs, Ω_j is the number of conformations corresponding to polymer graph j, and E_j is the energy of those conformations.

From a computational standpoint, the problem is not simply to find the sum Q, but the contribution of various parts to the sum. For example, if we normalize (1) to sum to 1, the individual terms give us the probabilities of the conformations; likewise, normalizing (2) gives the probabilities of the polymer graphs. Chen and Dill wish to compute the contribution of each energy level to Q, that is, to compute each term of the outer summation in:

$$Q = \sum_E \sum_{\substack{j \\ E_j = E}} \Omega_j e^{-E/kT}. \tag{3}$$

This computation divides into two parts: for each energy level E, we must compute Ω_j, and we must perform the inner summation, which is over all polymer graphs at energy level E.

The key to Chen and Dill's model is that it considers restricted subclasses of polymer graphs. We say that a polymer graph is *nested* if no two curved edges cross each other. For any curved edge e, call the region bounded by e and one or more straight edges the *interior* of e. We say that a nested polymer graph is *linearly nested* if no two curved edges have disjoint interiors. (The polymer graph in Figure 1 is nested, but not linearly nested, because the white regions are disjoint.) RNA secondary structures are conformations of nested poly-

Proceedings of HLT 2002, Second International Conference on Human Language Technology Research, M. Marcus, ed., Morgan Kaufmann, San Francisco, 2002.

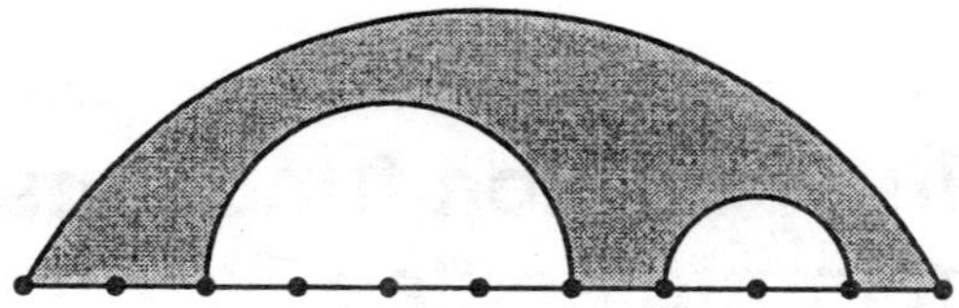

Figure 1: Nested polymer graph, with one face shaded. The straight edges represent covalent bonds, and the curved edges represent self-contacts.

mer graphs; Chen and Dill call the conformations of linearly nested polymer graphs "hairpin conformations."

The restriction to nested polymer graphs allows Chen and Dill's model to decompose a polymer graph into elementary components called *faces* and assume that each folds independently of the others. For nested polymer graphs, a face is the interior of an edge minus the interiors of the edges contained within (e. g., the shaded region in Figure 1).

Then Ω_j, the number of conformations of the polymer graph can be estimated as the product of the number of conformations of each of its faces, and E_j, the energy of the polymer graph, can be estimated as the sum of the energy increments of each of its faces. Moreover, since any restrictions on what types of faces can combine with each other are strictly local, Chen and Dill's algorithm can use dynamic programming to efficiently sum over all possible combinations with a particular energy.

2. DEFINITIONS

This hierarchical decomposition of polymer graphs suggests that nested polymer graphs might be modeled by a CFG (and linearly nested polymer graphs by a linear CFG), following Searls [11]. Under this interpretation, the nonterminal symbols correspond roughly to edges, and the productions correspond roughly to faces.

The computation of Q is accomplished by augmenting each production with a *weight* p, which we write as

$$A \xrightarrow{p} \alpha_1 \cdots \alpha_n$$

where the α_i are either terminals or nonterminals. The weight of a derivation is the product of the weights of the productions used in the derivation, and the weight of a string is the sum of the weights of all possible derivations of the string.

If we assign the weight $\omega e^{-\Delta E/kT}$ to each production of the grammar, where ω is the conformation count of the corresponding face, and ΔE is the energy increment of its outer link, then the weight of the derivation corresponding to polymer graph j will be $\Omega_j e^{-E_j/kT}$, and the weight of the string will be Q.

All this can be computed by a straightforward extension of a standard parsing algorithm like CKY. However, if we want to group polymer graphs according to energy level and compute the contribution to Q from each energy level, we need some more machinery, borrowed from the attribute grammars of Knuth [8].

We attach to each nonterminal symbol a set of *attributes*, and, for each occurrence of a nonterminal A in a derivation, we give each attribute v a value, which we write $v(A)$. These

```
given words w_1, ..., w_n, grammar G
for l = 1 to n do
  for i = 1 to n - l + 1 do
    k = i + l
    for all A -p-> w_i ... w_{k-1} ∈ G do
      c[A, i, k, e(A)] = c[A, i, k, e(A)] + p
    end for
    for all A -p-> w_i ... w_{j1} B w_{j2} ... w_k ∈ G do
      for all E_1 ∈ 𝒱 do
        E = e(A) computed for e(B) = E_1
        c[A, i, k, E] = c[A, i, k, E] + c[B, j_1, j_2, E_1] · p
      end for
    end for
  end for
end for
return {⟨E, c[S, 1, n + 1, E]⟩ | E ∈ 𝒱}
```

Figure 2: Algorithm for linear CFG.

values are defined by *attribute equations* associated with each production $A \rightarrow \alpha_1 \cdots \alpha_n$, which define each attribute of A in terms of the attribute values of the α_i, if any.[1] Define the *v-value* of a derivation rooted by S to be $v(S)$.

Attributes provide a flexible way of computing various functions on derivations, including energies. For example, for every production $A \rightarrow \alpha_1 \cdots \alpha_n$, we can write the attribute equation

$$e(A) = \Delta E + \sum_{\alpha_i \in V} e(\alpha_i)$$

where ΔE is the energy increment due to the outer link of the corresponding face, and V is the set of nonterminals. Then the *e*-value of a derivation will be the total energy of the corresponding polymer graph.

Putting the weights and attributes together, then, we can obtain the terms of the summation (3) simply by computing, for each E, the total weight of those derivations with *e*-value E.

3. ALGORITHMS

To do this, we modify the CKY algorithm to use a separate chart for each energy level, so that it can simultaneously compute $g(E)e^{-E/kT}$ for all values of E. Let $\mathcal{V}$ be the set of possible energy levels of any polymer graph or subgraph, that is, the set of possible *e*-values of any derivation or subderivation. Note that $\mathcal{V}$ must be finite for a given string, or else the algorithm will not terminate. It is sufficient for the grammar to be finitely ambiguous, which is the case for the grammars induced from Chen and Dill's equations (see Appendix A).

The algorithm for linear CFG is shown in Figure 2. Its running time is $O(n^2|G||\mathcal{V}|)$, where n is the length of the input string and $|G|$ is the number of productions in the grammar. The algorithm for a general CFG in Chomsky normal form[2] is shown in Figure 3, whose running time is $O(n^3|G||\mathcal{V}|^2)$. Both of these algorithms are implicit in Chen and Dill's equations,

[1] Knuth calls attributes defined in this way *synthesized attributes*. He also discusses *inherited attributes*, which we do not consider here.

[2] In Chomsky normal form, every production is either of the form $A \rightarrow BC$ or $A \rightarrow a$. Every CFG (which does not generate ϵ) can be converted into this form. Alternatively, we could have started with a more general algorithm instead of CKY.

```
1: given words w_1, ..., w_n, grammar G
2: for l = 1 to n do
3:   for i = 1 to n − l + 1 do
4:     k = i + l
5:     for all A -p-> w_i ··· w_{k−1} ∈ G do
6:       c[A, i, k, ΔE] = c[A, i, k, ΔE] + p
7:     end for
8:     for j = i + 1 to k − 1 do
9:       for all A -p-> BC ∈ G do
10:        for all E_1, E_2 ∈ 𝒱 do
11:          E = e(A) computed for e(B) = E_1, e(C) = E_2
12:          c[A, i, k, E] = c[A, i, k, E]+
                 c[B, i, j, E_1] · c[C, j, k, E_2] · p
13:        end for
14:      end for
15:    end for
16:  end for
17: end for
18: return {⟨E, c[S, 1, n + 1, E]⟩ | E ∈ 𝒱}
```

Figure 3: Algorithm for general CFG in Chomsky normal form (modified CKY).

but here the use of dynamic programming is made explicit.

The grammars, which can be read more or less directly off of Chen and Dill's equations, are shown in Figures 4 and 5 and described in more detail in Appendix A. Our main concern here is in the size of the grammars, since the running time of the algorithms depends on it.

For hairpin conformations, the linear CFG has productions with arbitrarily long right-hand sides. Thus it would seem that the parser (Figure 2) must search through an infinite number of productions in lines 5 and 8. But in fact these productions are instantiations of rule schemata, and if the parser only instantiates each schema as necessary, line 5 only has to consider a bounded number of productions, and line 8 only has to consider $O(n^2)$ productions. This is how Chen and Dill's equations work as well. They analyze this algorithm as running in time $O(n^4)$, but our analysis, which is based on a more precise algorithmic description, gives a running time of $O(n^4|\mathcal{V}|)$.

However, the $O(n^2)$ effective grammar size is due to a single rule schema (for G^*_{Mc}, see Figure 4) which has the form

$$A \xrightarrow{p(l)} a_1 \cdots a_k A' a_{k+1} \cdots a_l.$$

If we replace this schema with the following:

$$A \xrightarrow{p(l)} A^l$$

$$A^i \xrightarrow{1} A^{i-1} a$$

$$A^i \xrightarrow{1} a A^{i-1}$$

$$A^0 \xrightarrow{1} A'$$

the effective $|G|$ becomes $O(n)$ (because the index l ranges from 0 to n). Compacting the grammar in this way improves the running time to $O(n^3|\mathcal{V}|)$.

For RNA secondary structures (general CFG), the grammar size is again $O(n)$, because it contains nonterminals of the form K^l_{tc} (see Figure 5), where l ranges between 2 and n. Chen and Dill analyze this algorithm as running in time $O(n^5|\mathcal{V}|)$, but our analysis gives a running time of $O(n^4|\mathcal{V}|^2)$.

How large is $|\mathcal{V}|$ for a given string? For computing energy levels, $|\mathcal{V}|$ consists of linear combinations (with integer coefficients) of the ΔE's, which are drawn from a fixed, finite set. If there is a number x such that each ΔE can be expressed as an integer multiple of x (e. g., if the ΔE's are all rational), then $|\mathcal{V}|$ will be linear in the number of self-contacts. If the number of self-contacts a single terminal can participate in is bounded (in Chen and Dill's model, it is bounded to two), then $|\mathcal{V}| \in O(n)$, in agreement with Chen and Dill's analysis.

This gives us a running time of $O(n^4)$ for linear CFG (after compacting the grammar) and $O(n^6)$ for general CFG. By coincidence, seemingly, these bounds match Chen and Dill's analysis. However, their analysis underestimates the contribution of $|\mathcal{V}|$ to the overall complexity; moreover, compacting the linear CFG as described above is not merely a difference of analysis, but an optimization of Chen and Dill's original algorithm.

4. EXTENSIONS

4.1 Other groupings

There are other ways to group the terms of the partition function that are of interest, and attribute equations provide enough flexibility to specify a wide variety of such groupings. For example, Chen and Dill elsewhere [3] group conformations according to how many contacts belong to the native structure and how many do not. In this case (assuming as before that the number of self-contacts per terminal is bounded), $|\mathcal{V}| \in O(n^2)$.

4.2 More complex conformations

To generalize to more complicated conformations than RNA secondary structures, like pseudoknots, we must move to more expressive formalisms than CFG, for example, tree adjoining grammar (TAG). The principles set forth here generalize easily to such formalisms. The main challenge lies in identifying the elementary components of these more complicated structures (in other words, what are the "faces" of a non-nested polymer graph?), and finding their energy increments and conformation counts.

Two related approaches may prove useful in this regard. Uemura et al. [12] generate RNA pseudoknots using a tree-adjoining grammar. A standard parsing algorithm for tree adjoining grammars can be modified as we have done for CKY, giving a time complexity of $O(n^6|G|^2|\mathcal{V}|^2)$, where $|G|$ is the number of elementary trees. Rivas and Eddy [10] use a formalism called *crossed-interaction grammar*, which, when formalized, is equivalent to set-local multi-component TAG [13], an extension of TAG. The actual grammar they use for generating RNA pseudoknots is intermediate in formal power between single-component TAG and set-local two-component TAG.[3] Again, their dynamic-programming algorithm [9] can be modified as we have done for CKY, giving the same time

[3]These results are based on some preliminary work of Chiang and Joshi and several discussions at the Workshop on Language Modeling of Biological Data at the University of Pennsylvania in February 2001, and were presented by Joshi in an invited talk at the Pacific Symposium on Biocomputing [5].

complexity as TAG: $O(n^6|G||V|^2)$, where $|G|$ is the number of productions.

Both of these approaches decompose conformations with crossing links into elementary structures and assign energy increments to each structure. However, these energy increments have not all been experimentally determined so far, so that both approaches must make approximations for pseudoknots. It also remains to be seen whether conformation counts can be assigned to such elementary structures that will give good estimates of overall conformation counts.

5. CONCLUSION

In summary, we have given a formally and computationally more precise account of Chen and Dill's method for computing partition functions of double-stranded chain molecules. From a computational standpoint, this account clarifies the structure of the algorithm, leading to a revised complexity analysis and an optimization for the linear case (hairpin conformations). From a formal standpoint, this account separates the principles of the model from the particular restrictions it chooses, laying a foundation for relaxing those restrictions to handle more complex conformations.

6. ACKNOWLEDGEMENTS

This work was partially supported by NSF grant SBR-89-20230. We would like to thank Shi-Jie Chen, Ken Dill, and the two anonymous reviewers, all of whom helped to improve the accuracy and presentation of our paper.

7. REFERENCES

[1] Shi-Jie Chen and Ken A. Dill. Statistical thermodynamics of double-stranded polymer molecules. *J. Chem. Phys.*, 103(13):5802–5813, 1995.

[2] Shi-Jie Chen and Ken A. Dill. Theory for the conformational changes of double-stranded chain molecules. *J. Chem. Phys.*, 109(11):4602–4616, 1998.

[3] Shi-Jie Chen and Ken A. Dill. RNA folding energy landscapes. *Proc. Natl. Acad. Sci.*, 97(2):646–651, 2000.

[4] A. K. Joshi, L.S. Levy, and M. Takahashi. Tree adjunct grammars. *J. Comp. Sys. Sci.*, 10(1):136–163, 1975.

[5] Aravind K. Joshi. Structural descriptions of formal systems and folded structures of biomolecules. In *Pacific Symposium on Bioinformatics*, Kauai, HI, January 2002. Invited talk.

[6] Aravind K. Joshi and Yves Schabes. Tree-adjoining grammars. In Grzegorz Rosenberg and Arto Salomaa, editors, *Handbook of Formal Languages and Automata*, volume 3, pages 69–124. Springer-Verlag, Heidelberg, 1997.

[7] Tadao Kasami. An efficient recognition and syntax algorithm for context-free languages. Technical Report AFCRL-65-758, Air Force Cambridge Research Laboratory, Bedford, MA, 1965.

[8] Donald E. Knuth. Semantics of context-free languages. *Mathematical Systems Theory*, 2(2):127–145, 1968. Corrections published in 5(1):95–96.

[9] Elena Rivas and Sean R. Eddy. A dynamic programming algorithm for RNA structure prediction including pseudoknots. *Journal of Molecular Biology*, 285:2053–2068, 1999.

[10] Elena Rivas and Sean R. Eddy. The language of RNA: a formal grammar that includes pseudoknots. *Bioinformatics*, 16(4):334–340, 2000.

[11] David B. Searls. The linguistics of DNA. *American Scientist*, 80:579–591, 1992.

[12] Yasuo Uemura, Aki Hasegawa, Satoshi Kobayashi, and Takashi Yokomori. Tree adjoining grammars for RNA structure prediction. *Theoretical Computer Science*, 210:277–303, 1999.

[13] David J. Weir. *Characterizing Mildly Context-Sensitive Grammar Formalisms*. PhD thesis, Univ. of Pennsylvania, 1988.

[14] Daniel H. Younger. Recognition and parsing of context-free languages in time n^3. *Information and Control*, 10(2):189–208, 1967.

APPENDIX

A. GRAMMARS

The grammars (that is, rule schemata for the grammars) for hairpin conformations and RNA secondary structures are shown in Figures 4 and 5, respectively. The w_i are terminal symbols, and S is the start symbol. The G_{tc}, G^{*}_{tc}, and K^{l}_{tc} are nonterminals; these symbols and their subscripts are explained by Chen and Dill [2].

The weight of each production is $\omega e^{-\Delta E/kT}$, where ω and ΔE are as listed next to the grammars, and each production $A \rightarrow \alpha_1 \cdots \alpha_n$ has the attribute equations

$$E(A) = \Delta E + \sum_{\alpha_i \in V} E(\alpha_i)$$

$$x = \begin{cases} x(\alpha_1) & \text{if } \alpha_1 \in V \\ \alpha_1 & \text{otherwise} \end{cases}$$

$$y = \begin{cases} y(\alpha_n) & \text{if } \alpha_n \in V \\ \alpha_n & \text{otherwise} \end{cases}$$

where, again, ΔE is as listed next to the grammars. The purpose of the x and y attributes is to keep track of the leftmost and rightmost symbols in the yield of each nonterminal.

In both grammars, $\mathbf{S}_t(l)_{c_1c_2}$, $(\mathbf{Y}_{t_1t_2})_{c_1c_2}$, ω_c, α, and $\Delta E(x, y)$ are parameters which are either experimentally determined or determined by the underlying two-dimensional lattice model for counting conformations, as explained by Chen and Dill [2]. Note that because the weight of a production depends on ΔE, and ΔE depends on the attributes x and y, the weights depend on the attributes, which is not strictly allowed under our definitions. Since x and y are drawn from a finite set, it would be possible to write these attributes into the grammar, but this would complicate the grammar unnecessarily. For the parsing algorithms given here, there is no problem with letting the weights depend on the attributes.

In the second grammar, the productions we have given for $K^{L}_{\mathrm{LR},c}$ when $l > 2$ do not conform exactly to Chen and Dill's equations. Their equations are a simplification from a previous version of their model [1], and the productions we have given here are closer to the older equations. It is possible to reproduce the newer equations exactly, but for us it would be slightly more complicated.

Production	ω	ΔE	
$S \rightarrow G_{tc}$	1	0	
$G_{tc} \rightarrow G^*_{tc}$	ω_c	0	
$G^*_{Lc} \rightarrow G^*_{t'c_2} w_{j'+1} \cdots w_j$	$S_L(j - j' + 2)_{cc_1}$	$\Delta E(x, y)$	$(Y_{Lt'})_{c_1 c_2} = 1$
$G^*_{Mc} \rightarrow w_i \cdots w_{i'-1} G^*_{t'c_2} w_{j'+1} \cdots w_j$	$S_M(j - j' + i' - i + 2)_{cc_1}$	$\Delta E(x, y)$	$(Y_{Mt'})_{c_1 c_2} = 1$
$G^*_{Rc} \rightarrow w_i \cdots w_{i'-1} G^*_{t'c_2}$	$S_R(i' - i + 2)_{cc_1}$	$\Delta E(x, y)$	$Y_{Rt'})_{c_1 c_2} = 1$
$G^*_{Ic} \rightarrow w_i \cdots w_j$	$S_I(j - i + 1)_c$	$\Delta E(x, y)$	

$$t, t' \in \{L, M, R, I\}$$

$$c, c_1, c_2 \in \{1, 2, 3, 4\}$$

Figure 4: Rule schemata for grammar for hairpin conformations.

Production	ω	ΔE	
$S \rightarrow G_{0c} \mid G_{1c} \mid G_{2c}$	1	0	
$G_{0c} \rightarrow G_{0c} w_j \mid G_{1c} w_j$	α	0	
$G_{1c} \rightarrow G^*_{Lc} \mid G^*_{Mc} \mid G_{0c} G^*_{Lc} \mid G_{0c} G^*_{Mc} \mid G_{1c} G^*_{Mc}$	1	0	
$G_{2c} \rightarrow G^*_{Rc} \mid G^*_{LR,c} \mid G_{0c} G^*_{Rc} \mid G_{0c} G^*_{LR,c} \mid G_{1c} G^*_{Rc}$	1	0	
$G^*_{Ic} \rightarrow w_i \cdots w_j$	$S_I(j - i + 1)_c$	$\Delta E(x, y)$	
$G^*_{tc} \rightarrow K^l_{t'c_2}$	$S_t(l)_{cc_1}$	$\Delta E(x, y)$	$l > 2, (Y_{tM})_{c_1 c_2} = 1, t \neq I$
$K^l_{Ic} \rightarrow w_i \cdots w_{i+l-1}$	1	0	
$K^l_{Lc} \rightarrow K^{l-1}_{Lc} w_j \mid K^{l-1}_{LR,c} w_j$	1	0	
$K^l_{Mc} \rightarrow K^{l-1}_{Mc} w_j \mid K^{l-1}_{Rc} w_j$	1	0	
$K^l_{Rc} \rightarrow w_i K^{l-1}_{Rc} \mid w_i K^{l-1}_{LR,c}$	1	0	
$K^l_{LR,c} \rightarrow K^{l-1}_{LR,c_1} G^*_{t'c_2}$	1	0	$l > 2, (Y_{MM})_{cc_2} = 1, t' \notin \{L, LR\}$
$K^l_{LR,c} \rightarrow K^{l-1}_{Lc_1} G^*_{t'c_2}$	1	0	$l > 2, (Y_{MM})_{cc_2} = 1$
$K^2_{LR,c} \rightarrow G^*_{Mc} \mid G^*_{Ic}$	1	0	

$$l > 0$$

$$t, t' \in \{L, M, R, LR, I\}$$

$$c, c_1, c_2 \in \{1, 2, 3, 4\}$$

Figure 5: Rule schemata for grammar for RNA secondary structures.

Massive Bio-Ontology Engineering for NLP

Udo Hahn
Text Knowledge Engineering Lab
Albert-Ludwigs-Universität Freiburg
D-79085 Freiburg, Germany
hahn@coling.uni-freiburg.de

Stefan Schulz
Medical Informatics Department
Universitätsklinikum Freiburg
D-79104 Freiburg, Germany
stschulz@uni-freiburg.de

ABSTRACT

We describe an ontology engineering methodology by which conceptual knowledge is extracted from an informal medical thesaurus (UMLS) and automatically converted into a formally sound description logics system. Our approach consists of four steps: concept definitions are automatically generated from the UMLS source, integrity checking of taxonomic and partonomic hierarchies is performed by the terminological classifier, cycles and inconsistencies are eliminated, and incremental refinement of the evolving knowledge base is performed by a domain expert. We report on knowledge engineering experiments with a terminological knowledge base composed of 164,000 concepts and 76,000 relations.

1. INTRODUCTION

Over several decades, an enormous body of medical knowledge, e.g, disease taxonomies, medical procedures, anatomical terms etc., has been assembled in a wide variety of medical terminologies, thesauri and classification systems. The conceptual structuring of a domain they allow is typically restricted to the provision of broader and narrower terms, related terms or (quasi-)synonymous terms. This is most evident in the UMLS, the *Unified Medical Language System* [14], an umbrella system which covers more than 60 medical thesauri and classifications. Its metathesaurus component contains more than 800,000 concepts which are structured in hierarchies and classified by 134 semantic types (provided by the UMLS *semantic network*). Their semantics is shallow and entirely intuitive, which is due to the fact that their usage was primarily intended for humans as a backbone for various forms of clinical knowledge management, e.g., cross-mapping between different terminologies, medical information retrieval, disease and procedure encoding, etc.

Given the size, the evolutionary diversity and inherent heterogeneity of the UMLS, there is no surprise that the lack of a formal semantic foundation leads to inconsistencies, circular definitions, etc. [2]. This may not cause utterly severe problems when humans are in the loop and its use is limited to disease encoding, accountancy or document retrieval tasks. However, anticipating its use for more knowledge-intensive applications such as natural language understanding of medical narratives [6], medical decision support systems [17], etc., those shortcomings might lead to an impasse.

As a consequence, formal models for dealing with medical knowledge have been proposed, using representation mechanisms based on conceptual graphs, semantic networks or description logics [28, 3, 13, 16]. Not surprisingly, there is a price to be paid for more expressiveness and formal rigor, *viz.* increasing modeling efforts and, hence, increasing maintenance costs. Operational systems making full use of this rigid approach, especially those which employ high-end knowledge representation languages, are usually restricted to rather small subdomains. The most comprehensive of these sources we know of is the GRAIL-encoded GALEN knowledge base which covers up to 9,800 concepts [16]. The limited coverage then hampers their routine usage, an issue which is always highly rewarded in the medical informatics community.

The knowledge bases developed within the framework of the above-mentioned terminological systems have all been designed from scratch – without making systematic use of the large body of knowledge contained in those medical terminologies. An intriguing approach would be to join the massive *coverage* offered by informal medical terminologies with the high level of *expressiveness* supported by formal inferencing systems, as developed in the AI knowledge representation community, in order to develop formally solid medical knowledge bases on a larger scale.

2. PART-WHOLE REASONING

As far as medical knowledge is concerned, two main hierarchy-building relationships can be distinguished, *viz.* is-a (taxonomic) and part-whole (partonomic) relations. Anatomical knowledge, a central portion of medical knowledge, is principally organized along part-whole hierarchies. Hence, any proper medical knowledge representation has to take account of both hierarchy types and the reasoning patterns they imply. [1]

Part-whole knowledge has been an issue within diverse areas ranging from philosophy (mereology), data modeling for database systems and object-oriented programming, to knowledge representation proper in the field of artificial intelligence. Major strands of this work are discussed by Artale et al. [1] under the heading of object-centered representation approaches. This also includes the description logic (DL) paradigm to which we subscribe in our work, too. From our application domain, the need arises to have formally solid inference mechanisms for taxonomic (generalization

[1]In an exploratory quantitative study of the particular text genre we are dealing with, namely medical finding reports, we found [5] that 45% of the (indirect) reference relations between sentences are due to bridging or functional anaphora, which refer heavily to part-whole knowledge. On the other hand, 34% of the (direct) reference relations are due to nominal anaphora, which bring taxonomic knowledge to bear.

Proceedings of HLT 2002, Second International Conference on Human Language Technology Research, M. Marcus, ed., Morgan Kaufmann, San Francisco, 2002.

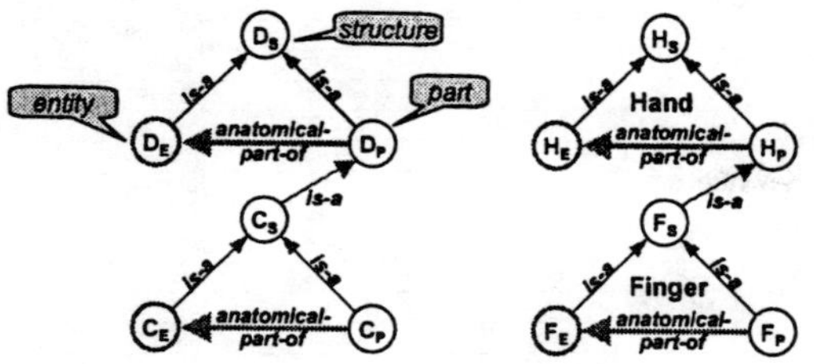

Figure 1: SEP Triplets: Partitive Relations within Taxonomies

hierarchies), as well as partonomic reasoning (part-whole hierarchies) available within a uniform representation model. Second, it is not sufficient for us to have a sound formal platform of knowledge representation, but we also require an inference engine which performs this style of advanced reasoning on large data sets ($\gg$ 10,000 items).[2] Hence, we consider KL-ONE-type descriptions logics [10, 29], at the formal representation level, and LOOM's classification-based inference machine [11, 12], at the system level, the most convenient match of our requirements and the current state of the art.

Unlike generalization-based reasoning in concept taxonomies, no fully conclusive mechanism exists up to now for reasoning along part-whole hierarchies. In the description logics community several language extensions have been proposed which provide special constructors for part-whole reasoning [16, 9]. This seems a reasonable way to proceed, as long as the transitivity property of a relation can be assumed, in general. In the medical [7] as well as commonsense domains [4], however, various exceptions exist such that the transitivity of *part-of* relations cannot be granted, in general. Hence, both the expression of regular transitive use, as well as exception handling for nontransitive *part-of* relations has to be taken into consideration. Motivated by informal approaches sketched by Schmolze & Mark [22] and Schulz *et al.* [24], we formalized a model of part-whole reasoning [7] that incorporates the above requirements and also does not exceed the expressiveness of the well-understood, parsimonious concept language $\mathcal{ALC}$ [21].[3]

Our proposal is centered around a particular data structure, so-called *SEP triplets*, especially designed for part-whole reasoning (cf. Figure 1). They define a characteristic pattern of IS-A hierarchies which support the emulation of inferences typical of transitive PART-OF relations. In this formalism, the relation ANATOMICAL-PART-OF describes the partitive relation between physical parts of an organism.

A triplet consists, first of all, of a composite 'structure' concept, the so-called **S-node** (e.g., HAND-STRUCTURE). Each *structure* concept subsumes both an anatomical *entity* and each of the anatomical *parts* of this entity. Unlike entities and their parts, structures have no physical correlate in the real world — they constitute a representational artifact required for the formal reconstruction of systematic patterns of part-whole reasoning. The two direct subsumees of an S-node are the corresponding **E-node** ('entity') and **P-node** ('part'), e.g., HAND and HAND-PART, respectively. Unlike an **S-node**, these nodes refer to specific ontological objects. The E-node denotes the whole anatomical entity to be modeled, whereas the P-node is the common subsumer of those concepts that have their role ANATOMICAL-PART-OF filled by the corresponding E-node concept, as an existential condition. Hence, for every P-node there exists a corresponding E-node for the role ANATOMICAL-PART-OF. A reconstruction of some basic anatomical relations in terms of SEP triplets is illustrated in Figure 2.

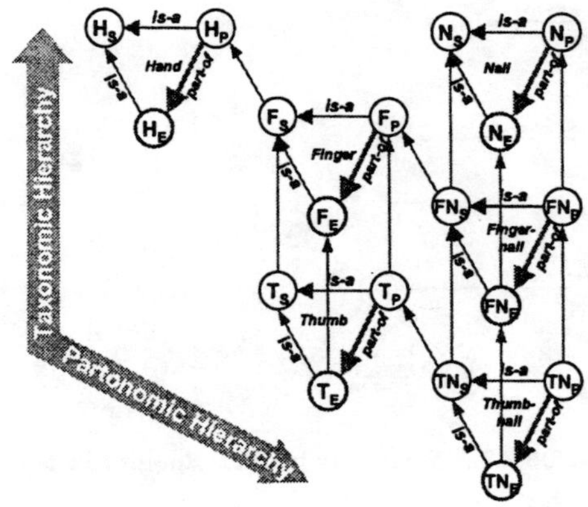

Figure 2: SEP Triplet Model of a Partonomic Hierarchy of the Concept HAND

The reconstruction of the relation ANATOMICAL-PART-OF by taxonomic reasoning proceeds as follows. Let us assume that C_E and D_E denote E-nodes, C_S and D_S denote the S-nodes that subsume C_E and D_E, respectively, and C_P and D_P denote the P-nodes related to C_E and D_E, respectively, via the role ANATOMICAL-PART-OF (cf. Figure 1). These conventions can be captured by the following terminological expressions:

$$C_E \sqsubseteq C_S \sqsubseteq D_P \sqsubseteq D_S \quad (1)$$

$$D_E \sqsubseteq D_S \quad (2)$$

The P-node is defined as follows (note the disjointness between D_E and D_P, i.e., no anatomical concept can be ANATOMICAL-PART-OF itself):

$$D_P \doteq D_S \sqcap \neg D_E \sqcap \exists anatomical\text{-}part\text{-}of.D_E \quad (3)$$

Since C_E is subsumed by D_P (according to (1)), we infer that the relation ANATOMICAL-PART-OF holds between C_E and D_E, too:

$$C_E \sqsubseteq \exists anatomical\text{-}part\text{-}of.D_E \quad (4)$$

This way of modeling allows the knowledge engineer to switch the transitivity property on and off, dependent on whether the E-node or the S-node is addressed as the target concept for a conceptual relation. In the first case, the propagation of roles across part-whole hierarchies is disabled, in the second case it is enabled. As an example (cf. Figure 3), ENTERITIS is defined as HAS-LOCATION INTESTINE. The range of the relation HAS-LOCATION is restricted to the E-node of INTESTINE. This precludes, for instance, the classification of APPENDICITIS as ENTERITIS though the APPENDIX is related to the INTESTINE via an ANATOMICAL-PART-OF relation. GLOMERULONEPHRITIS, however, is classified as NEPHRITIS (HAS-LOCATION KIDNEY), since the GLOMERULUM is an AN-

[2] Our key application deals with knowledge acquisition from medical finding reports [5]. Therefore, a large-coverage ontology and sophisticated reasoning capabilities using such an ontology are indispensable.

[3] $\mathcal{ALC}$ allows for the construction of hierarchies of concepts and relations, where $\sqsubseteq$ denotes subsumption and $\doteq$ definitional equivalence. Existential ($\exists$) and universal ($\forall$) quantification, negation ($\neg$), disjunction ($\sqcap$) and conjunction ($\sqcup$) are supported. Role filler constraints (e.g., typing by C) are linked to the relation name R by a dot, $\exists R.C$.

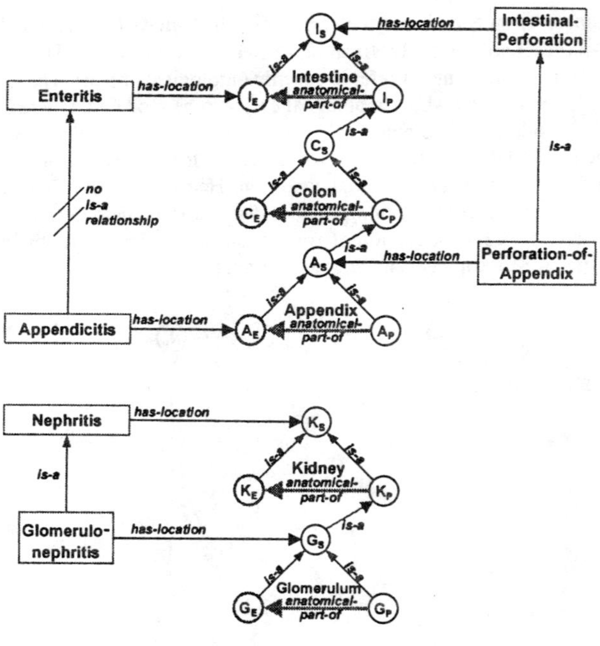

Figure 3: Enabling/Disabling Transitivity in a SEP-Encoded Partonomy

ATOMICAL-PART-OF the KIDNEY. In the same way, PERFORATION-OF-APPENDIX is classified as INTESTINAL-PERFORATION (cf. [7] for a more comprehensive analysis of these phenomena).

3. KNOWLEDGE IMPORT AND REFINEMENT

Our goal is to extract conceptual knowledge from two highly relevant subdomains of the UMLS, *viz.* anatomy and pathology, in order to construct a formally sound knowledge base using a terminological knowledge representation language. This task will be divided into four steps: (1) the automated generation of terminological expressions, (2) their submission to a terminological classifier for consistency checking, (3) the manual restitution of formal consistency in case of inconsistencies, and, finally, (4) the manual rectification and refinement of the formal representation structures. These four steps are illustrated by the workflow diagram depicted in Figure 4.

Step 1: Automated Generation of Terminological Expressions. Sources for concepts and relations are the UMLS semantic network and the *mrrel*, *mrcon* and *mrsty* tables of the 1999 release of the UMLS metathesaurus. The *mrrel* table which contains approximately 7,5 million records (for a fragment, cf. Figure 5) exhibits the semantic links between two UMLS CUIs (concept unique identifier),[4] the *mrcon* table contains the concept names and *mrsty* keeps the semantic type(s) assigned to each CUI. These tables, available as ASCII files, were imported into a Microsoft Access

CUI1	REL	CUI2	RELA	X	Y
C0005847	CHD	C0014261	part_of	MSH99	MSH99
C0005847	CHD	C0014261		CSP98	CSP98
C0005847	CHD	C0025962	isa	MSH99	MSH99
C0005847	CHD	C0026844	part_of	MSH99	MSH99
C0005847	CHD	C0026844		CSP98	CSP98
C0005847	CHD	C0034052		SNMI98	SNMI98
C0005847	CHD	C0035330	isa	MSH99	MSH99
C0005847	CHD	C0042366	part_of	MSH99	MSH99
C0005847	CHD	C0042367	part_of	MSH99	MSH99
C0005847	CHD	C0042367		SNM2	SNM2
C0005847	CHD	C0042449	isa	MSH99	MSH99

Figure 5: Semantic Relations in the UMLS Metathesaurus

relational database and manipulated using SQL embedded in the VBA programming language. For each CUI in the *mrrel* subset its alphanumeric code was substituted by the English preferred term found in *mrcon*.

After a manual remodeling of the 135 top-level concepts and 247 relations of the UMLS semantic network, we extracted, from a total of 85,899 concepts, 38,059 anatomy and 50,087 pathology concepts from the metathesaurus. The criterion for the inclusion into one of these sets is the assignment to predefined semantic types. Also, 2,247 concepts were found to be included in both sets, anatomy and pathology. Since we wanted to keep the two subdomains strictly disjoint, we maintained these 2,247 concepts duplicated, and prefixed all concepts by ANA- or PAT- according to their respective subdomain. This can be justified by the observation that these hybrid concepts exhibit, indeed, multiple meanings. For instance, TUMOR has the meaning of a malignant disease on the one hand, and of an anatomical structure on the other hand. The same applies to congenital and acquired malformations, e.g., *claw foot*, etc.

As target structures for the anatomy domain we chose SEP triplets. These are expressed in the terminological language LOOM which we had previously extended by a special DEFTRIPLET macro (cf. Table 1 for an example). Only UMLS *part-of*, *has-part* and *is-a* relation attributes are considered for the construction of taxonomic and partonomic hierarchies (cf. Figure 4). Hence, for each anatomy concept, one SEP triplet is created. The result is a mixed IS-A and PART-WHOLE hierarchy a straightforward example of which is depicted in Figure 2.

For the pathology domain, we treated *CHD* (child) and *RN* (narrower relation) from the UMLS as indicating taxonomic links. No part-whole relations were considered, since this category does not apply to the pathology domain. Furthermore, for all anatomy concepts contained in the definitional statements of pathology concepts the 'S-node' is the default concept to which they are linked, thus enabling the propagation of roles across the part-whole hierarchy.

```
(deftriplet HEART
   :is-primitive HOLLOW-VISCUS
   :has-part (:p-and
      FIBROUS-SKELETON-OF-HEART
      WALL-OF-HEART
      CAVITY-OF-HEART
      CARDIAC-CHAMBER-NOS
      LEFT-SIDE-OF-HEART
      RIGHT-SIDE-OF-HEART
      AORTIC-VALVE
      PULMONARY-VALVE))
```

Table 1: Generated Triplets in LOOM Format

[4] As a convention in UMLS, any two CUIs must be connected by at least a shallow relation (in Figure 5, CHilD relations in the column REL are assumed between CUIs). Shallow relations may be refined in the column RELA, if a thesaurus is available which contains more specific information. Some CUIs are linked either by *part-of* or *is-a*. In any case, the source thesaurus for the relations and the CUIs involved is specified in the columns X and Y (e.g., MeSH 1999, SNOMED International 1998).

UMLS relation	number of links	Step 1 Automatic generation of Loom definitions, augmented by P-Loom language elements *;;; = comment line*	Step 2 Submission to Loom classifier. Validation for formal consistency by Loom	Step 3 Manual restitution of formal consistency	Step 4 Manual rectification and refinement of the resulting knowledge base
Anatomy Concepts Linked to Anatomy Concepts					
sibling_of	267.218	*;;; SIB*			add negations in order to express taxonomic or partitive disjointness
child_of	59.808	*;;; CHDRN*			include related concepts into :is-primitive or :part-of clause where plausible
narrower_term	24.223	*;;; CHDRN*			
isa	9.755	:is-primitive	check for definitional cycles	remove taxonomic parent concepts	substitute of primitive links by non-primitive ones where possible
location_of	4.803	*;;; LOCATION_OF*			include related concepts into :has-part clause where plausible
has_location	4.803	*;;; HAS_LOCATION*			include related concepts into :part-of clause, where plausible
has_part	4.321	:has-part			check whether this part is mandatory (under "real-anatomy" assumption)
has_conceptual_part	126				
part_of	4.321	:part-of	1. check for partonomic cycles 2. check for disjointness between E and P node	1. remove partonomic or taxonomic parent concepts 2. redefine triplet as single concept	check for plausibility and completeness
conceptual_part_of	126				
parent	59.808	*;;; PARRB*			include related concepts into :has-part clause where plausible
broader_term	24.223	*;;; PARRB*			
inverse_isa	9,755	<do nothing>			
associated_with	14				
mapped_from	2.643				
other_relation	10.908				
qualified_by	1.864				
allowed_ qualifier	1.864				
mapped_to	2643				
<other named relations>	11.886	(:some x)	check for inherited constraints	remove constraints	remove or add constraints
Pathology Concepts Linked to Pathology Concepts					
sibling_of	457.542	;;; SIB			add negations in order to express taxonomic disjointness
child_of	72.426	:is-primitive	check for definitional cycles	remove parent concepts	substitute primitive links by non-primitive ones whenever possible
narrower_term	26.972				
isa	3.635				
inverse_isa	3.635	<do nothing>			
associated_with	13.902				
mapped_to	15.024				
mapped_from	15.024				
part_of	1				
has_part	1				
parent	72.426				
broader_term	28.972				
other_relation	25.796				
qualified_by	6.255				
allowed_qualifier	6.255				
<other named relations>	4.162	(:some x)	check for inherited constraints	remove constraints	remove or add constraints
Pathology Concepts Linked to Anatomy Concepts					
CUIpat = CUIana	2.247	(:some has_enatomic_correlate)			plausibility check of concept "duplication" (assignment to both domains)
<missing>		<do nothing>			add pathology-anatomy links
associated_with	2.314	(:some associated_with <anatomy_concept>_S)		check for consistency	render links complete, link to E-node instead of S-node when role propagation has to be disabled
has_location	9,230	(:some has_location <anatomy_concept>_S)			
<other>		<do nothing>			

Figure 4: Workflow Diagram for the Construction of a LOOM Knowledge Base from the UMLS

As a fundamental semantic assumption all roles generated in this process were considered as existentially quantified. This means that any relation r (PART-OF, HAS-LOCATION,..) which holds between two concepts A and B is mapped to a role $R.B$ which is a necessary condition in the definition of the concept A. All conceptual constraints for a concept definition are mapped to a conjunction of constraints.

In both subdomains, shallow relations, such as the extremely frequent sibling *SIB* relation, were included as comments into the code to give some heuristic guidance for the manual refinement phase.

Step 2: Automatic Consistency Checking by the LOOM Classifier. The import of UMLS anatomy concepts resulted in 38,059 DEFTRIPLET expressions for anatomical concepts and 50,087 DEFCONCEPT expressions for pathological concepts. Each DEFTRIPLET was expanded into three DEFCONCEPT (S-, E-, and P-nodes), and two DEFRELATION (ANATOMICAL-PART-OF-X, INV-ANATOMICAL-PART-OF-X) expressions, summing up to 114,177 concepts. This yielded (together with the concepts from the UMLS semantic network) a total of 240,764 definitory LOOM expressions.

From 38,059 anatomy triplets, 1,219 DEFTRIPLET statements exhibited a :HAS-PART clause followed by a list of a variable number of triplets, containing more than one argument in 823 cases (average cardinality: 3.3). 4,043 DEFTRIPLET statements contained a :PART-OF clause, only in 332 cases followed by more than one argument (average cardinality: 1.1). The resulting knowledge base was then submitted to the terminological classifier and checked for terminological cycles and coherence. In the anatomy subdomain, one terminological cycle and 2,328 incoherent concepts were found, in the pathology subdomain 355 terminological cycles though not a single incoherent concept were determined (cf. Table 2).

	Anatomy	Pathology
Triplets	38,059	—
defconcept statements	114,177	50,087
cycles	1	355
inconsistencies	2,328	0

Table 2: Classification Results for the Concept Import

Step 3: Manual Restitution of Consistency. The inconsistencies in the anatomy part of the knowledge base identified by the classifier could all be traced back to the simultaneous linkage of two triplets by both *is-a* and *part-of* links, an encoding that raises a conflict due to the disjointness required for corresponding P- and E-nodes. In most of these cases the affected parents belonged to a class of concepts that obviously cannot be appropriately modeled as SEP triplets, e.g., SUBDIVISION-OF-ASCENDING-AORTA or ORGAN-PART. The meaning of each of these concepts almost paraphrases that of a P-node, so that in these cases the violation of the SEP-internal disjointness condition could be accounted for by substituting the involved triplets with simple LOOM concepts, by matching them with already existing P-nodes or by disabling IS-A or PART-OF links.

In the pathology part of the knowledge base, we expected a large number of terminological cycles, as a consequence of interpreting the thesaurus-style *narrower term* and *child* relations through taxonomic subsumption (IS-A). Bearing in mind the size of the knowledge base, we consider 355 cycles a tolerable number. Those cycles were primarily due to very similar concepts, e.g., ARTERIOSCLEROSIS *vs.* ATHEROSCLEROSIS, AMAUROSIS *vs.* BLINDNESS, and residual categories ("other", "NOS" = *not otherwise specified*). These were directly inherited from the source terminologies and are notoriously difficult to interpret out of their definitional context, e.g., OTHER-MALIGNANT-NEOPLASM-OF-SKIN *vs.* MALIGNANT-NEOPLASM-OF-SKIN-NOS.

The cycles were analyzed and a negative list which consisted of 630 concept pairs was manually derived. In a subsequent extraction cycle we incorporated this list in the automated construction of the LOOM concept definitions, and given these new constraints, a fully consistent knowledge base was generated.

Step 4: Manual Rectification and Refinement of the Knowledge Base. To set up this high-volume knowledge base including the aforementioned working steps required three months of work for a single person, in total. The fourth step – when performed for the whole knowledge base – is very time-consuming and requires broad and in-depth medical expertise. An analysis of random samples from both subdomains is currently being performed by the second author, a domain expert. The preliminary data we supply refer to the analysis of two random samples of each one-hundred anatomy and one-hundred pathology concepts. This took one person about a single month.

From the experience we gained in the anatomy and pathology subdomains so far, the following workflow can be derived:

- *Checking the correctness of both the taxonomic and partitive hierarchies.* Taxonomic and partitive links are manually added or removed. Primitive subsumption is substituted by non-primitive subsumption whenever possible. This is a crucial point, because the automatically generated hierarchies contain only information about the parent concepts and necessary conditions. As an example, the automatically generated definition of DERMATITIS includes the information that it is an INFLAMMATION, and that the role HAS-LOCATION must be filled by the concept SKIN. An INFLAMMATION that HAS-LOCATION SKIN, however, cannot automatically be classified as DERMATITIS.

  Results: In the *anatomy* sample, only 76 concepts out of 100 could be unequivocally classified as belonging to 'canonical' anatomy. (The remainder, e.g., ANA-PHALANX-OF-SUPERNUMERARY-DIGIT-OF-HAND, referring to pathological anatomy was immediately excluded from analysis.) Besides the assignment to the UMLS semantic types, only 27 (direct) taxonomic links were found. Another 83 UMLS relations (mostly "child" or "narrower" relations) were manually upgraded to taxonomic links. 12 (direct) *part-of* and 19 *has-part* relations were found. Four *part-of* relations and one *has-part* relation had to be removed, since we considered them as implausible. 51 UMLS relations (mostly "child" or "narrower" relations) were manually upgraded to *part-of* relations, and 94 UMLS relations (mostly "parent" or "broader" relations) were upgraded to *has-part* relations. After this workup and upgrade of shallow UMLS relations to semantically more specific relations, the sample was checked for completeness again. As a result, 14 *is-a* and 37 *part-of* relations were still considered missing.

  In the *pathology* sample, the assignment to the pathology subdomain was considered plausible for 99 of 100 concepts. A total of 15 false *is-a* relations was identified in 12 concept definitions. 24 *is-a* relations were found to be missing.

- *Check of the* :has-part *arguments assuming 'real anatomy'.* In the UMLS sources *part-of* and *has-part* relations are considered as symmetric. According to our transformation rules, the attachment of a role HAS-ANATOMICAL-PART to an E-node B_E, with its range restricted to A_E implies the existence of a concept A for the definition of a concept B. On the

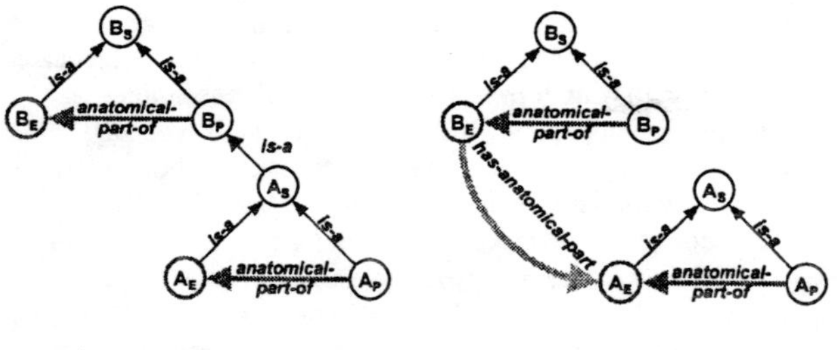

Figure 6: Patterns for Part-whole Reasoning Using SEP triplets

other hand, the classification of A_E as being subsumed by the P-node B_P, the latter being defined via the role ANATOMICAL-PART-OF restricted to B_E, implies the existence of B_E given the existence of A_E. These constraints do not always conform to 'real' anatomy, i.e., anatomical concepts that may exhibit pathological modifications. Figure 6 (left) sketches a concept A that is necessarily ANATOMICAL-PART-OF a concept B, but whose existence is not required for the definition of B. This is typical of the results of surgical interventions, e.g., a large intestine without an appendix, or an oral cavity without teeth, etc.

Results: All 112 *has-part* relations obtained by the automatic import and the manual workup of our sample were checked. The analysis revealed that more than half of them (62) should be eliminated in order not to obviate a coherent classification of pathologically modified anatomical objects.[5] As an example, most instances of ILEUM do not contain a MECKEL'S DIVERTICULUM, whereas all instances of MECKEL'S DIVERTICULUM are necessarily ANATOMICAL-PART-OF ILEUM. Many surgical interventions that remove anatomical structures (appendix, gallbladder, etc.), produce similar patterns. In our formalism, this corresponds to a single taxonomic link between a S-node and a P-node (cf. Figure 6 (left part)). The opposite situation is also possible (cf. Figure 6, right part): the definition of A_E does not imply that the role ANATOMICAL-PART-OF be filled by B_E, but B_E does imply that the inverse role be filled by A_E. As an example, a LYMPH-NODE necessarily contains LYMPH-FOLLICLES, but there exist LYMPH-FOLLICLES that are not part of a LYMPH-NODE. This pattern is typical of the mereological relation between macroscopic (countable) objects, such as organs, and multiple uniform microscopic objects.

- *Analysis of the sibling relations and defining concepts as being disjoint.* In UMLS, *SIB* relates concepts that share the same parent in a taxonomic or partonomic hierarchy. Pairs of sibling concepts may have common descendants or not. If not, they constitute the root of two disjoint subtrees. In a taxonomic hierarchy, this means that one concept implies the negation of the other (e.g., a benignant tumor cannot be a malignant one, *et vice versa*). In a partitive hierarchy, this can be interpreted as *spatial* disjointness, *viz.* one concept does not spatially overlap with another one. As an example, ESOPHAGUS and DUODENUM are spatially disjoint, whereas STOMACH and DUODENUM are not (they share a common transition structure, called PYLORUS), such as all neighbor structures that have a surface or region in common. Spatial disjointness can be modeled so that the definition of the S-node of the concept *A* implies the negation of the S-node of the concept *B* [26].

  Results: We found on the average 6.8 siblings per concept in the anatomy domain, 8.8 in the pathology domain. So far, the analysis of sibling relations has been performed only for the anatomy domain. From a total of 521 sibling relations, 9 were identified as *is-a*, 14 as *part-of*, and 17 as *has-part*, whereas 404 referred to topologically disconnected concepts.

- *Completion and modification of anatomy–pathology relations.* Surprisingly, only very few pathology concepts contained an explicit reference to a corresponding anatomy concept. These relations must, therefore, be added by a domain expert. In each case, the decision must be made whether the E-node or the S-node has to be addressed as the target concept for modification such that the propagation of roles across part-whole hierarchies is disabled or enabled.

  Results: In our random sample we found 522 anatomy-pathology relations, from which 358 (69%!) were judged incorrect by the domain experts. In 36 cases an adequate anatomy-pathology relation was missing. All 164 HAS-LOCATION roles were analyzed as to whether they were to be filled by an S-node or an E-node of an anatomical triplet. In 153 cases, the S-node (which allows propagation across the part-whole hierarchy) was considered to be adequate, in 11 cases the E-node was preferred. The analysis of the random sample of 100 pathology concepts revealed that only 17 were to be linked with an anatomy concept. In 15 cases, the default linkage to the S-node was considered to be correct, in one case the linkage to the E-node was preferred, in another case the linkage was considered to be false.

  The high number of implausible constraints points to the lightweight semantics of HAS-LOCATION links in the UMLS sources. While we interpreted them in terms of a conjunction for the import routine, a disjunctive meaning seems to prevail implicitly in many definitions of top-level concepts such as TUBERCULOSIS. In this example, we find all anatomical concepts that can be affected by this disease linked by HAS-LOCATION. All these constraints (e.g., HAS-LOCATION URINARY-TRACT) are inherited to subconcepts such as TUBERCULOSIS-OF-BRONCHUS. Hence, a thorough analysis of the top-level pathology concepts is necessary, and conjunctions of constraints will have to be substituted by disjunctions where necessary.

4. RELATED WORK

The benefits and problems of importing conceptual knowledge from a semi-formal into a rigorous knowledge representation formalism have been described by Pisanelli *et al.* [15]. They extracted knowledge from the UMLS semantic network, as well as from parts of the metathesaurus and converted it into a description logics system. Spackman *et al.* [27] describe how the SNOMED nomenclature evolves from a multi-axial coding system into a formally founded ontology. Their general goal is to avoid ambiguous or semantically invalid representations of composite concepts. However, both approaches do not provide a special reasoning mechanism for *part-of* relations.

Within the formal framework of GALEN a fragment of the Read Thesaurus was translated into GRAIL, a knowledge representation system also based on description logics [18]. In a cross-validation

[5] In Table 1 the concepts marked by *italics*, *viz.* AORTIC-VALVE and PULMONARY-VALVE should be eliminated from the :HAS-PART list, because they may be missing in certain cases as a result of congenital malformations, inflammatory processes or surgical interventions.

study it was checked, on the one hand, whether the definitions contained in the Read Thesaurus were logically consistent and, on the other hand, whether the GRAIL domain model was rich enough to encode them. Although GRAIL comes with a special-purpose reasoning formalism dedicated to partonomies, the adaptation was limited to simple generic hierarchies as only these structure the Read Thesaurus.

The developers of VOXEL-MAN [23], a multimedia tutoring systems for anatomy, and of the Digital Anatomist (UWDA), an anatomical semantic network [19] have both emphasized partitive hierarchies though at an informal level. Whereas in VOXEL-MAN a fine-grained ontology of *part-of* relations is sketched that accounts for various part-whole relations found in the anatomy domain, the UWDA developers restrict themselves to a small set of relations leading to a precise separation between partitive and generalization hierarchies. They excel with a high granularity of description and a broad coverage.

The approach we introduced here tries to combine the broad coverage and the fine-grained concept descriptions of the UWDA with the formal rigor of description logics. Additionally, we enhance the imported knowledge with part-whole specific reasoning capabilities indispensable within the medical domain, though this has already been described as a hard problem for terminological languages [8].

Several alternatives have been brought forward to solve this problem within the DL framework. The first approach extends a basic language definition (usually, $\mathcal{ALC}$) by generally allowing role hierarchies and transitivity of roles [9] or by supplying dedicated transitive partonomy operators such as for the GRAIL language [16]. This way, the transitivity property is hard-wired to role definitions and assumed to hold, in general. This contradicts empirical data from anatomical ontologies as discussed in [7], which reveal that the same relation may be transitive and nontransitive depending on the anatomical context.

Alternatively, one may want to preserve standard language definitions for reasons of simplicity and parsimony. Accordingly, Schmolze and Mark [22] propose a 'data structure' solution similar to ours using subsumption to obtain inferences resembling those of transitive roles or transitive closure of roles. Artale *et al.* [1] criticize this proposal for the "proliferation of (artificial) concepts" involved. We argue, however, that these additional concepts are necessary from an ontological point of view, as the distinct mechanisms for conditioned specialization modeling reveal (cf. Figure 3).

It remains to be seen, however, whether conservative structural extensions of a stable language platform are able to carry over to the many varieties of partonomic reasoning and different part-whole relations (discussed in a survey by Sattler [20]), or whether newly designed operators or other fundamental language extensions are needed. In the medical domain, at least, where the restriction to one subrelation of PART-OF, viz. ANATOMICAL-PART-OF, is sufficient, a relatively simple "data structure" extension like the SEP triplets yields already adequate results, without the necessity to resort to profound extensions of the terminological language. We have found evidence that the triplet mechanism we here propose can be straightforwardly extended to cover mereotopological and (limited) spatial reasoning, as well [26, 25].

5. CONCLUSIONS

There is a growing demand for high-quality terminology services and their embedding in functionally advanced health information systems. Instead of developing sophisticated medical knowledge bases from scratch, we here propose a 'conservative' approach — reuse existing large-scale resources, but refine the data from these resources so that advanced representational requirements imposed by more expressive knowledge representation languages are met. The resulting knowledge bases can then be used for sophisticated applications requiring formally sound medical reasoning.

The ontology engineering methodology we have proposed in this paper does exactly this. It provides a formally solid description logics framework with a modeling extension by SEP triplets so that both taxonomic and partonomic reasoning are supported equally well. While pure automatic conversion from semi-formal to formal environments causes problems of adequacy of the emerging representation structures, the refinement methodology we propose already inherits its power from the terminological reasoning framework. In our concrete work, we found the implications of using the terminological classifier, the inference engine which computes subsumption relations, of utmost importance and of outstanding heuristic value. Hence, the knowledge refinement cycles are truly semi-automatic, fed by medical expertise on the side of the human knowledge engineer, but also driven by the reasoning system which makes explicit the consequences of (im)proper concept definitions.

We also stipulate that our knowledge engineering methodology is general in the sense that it can be applied to all those domains where, at least, shallow thesauri are available. Our focus on partonomic knowledge and reasoning is, of course, best matched by science and engineering domains (e.g., we might also consider using the INSPEC thesaurus for physics, electronic engineering and computer science).

Acknowledgements. We would like to thank our colleagues in the CLIF group and the Department of Medical Informatics for fruitful discussions. S. Schulz was supported by a grant from DFG (Ha 2097/5-2).

6. REFERENCES

[1] Alessandro Artale, Enrico Franconi, Nicola Guarino, and Luca Pazzi. Part-whole relations in object-centered systems: An overview. *Data & Knowledge Engineering*, 20(3):347–383, 1996.

[2] James J. Cimino. Auditing the Unified Medical Language System with semantic methods. *Journal of the American Medical Informatics Association*, 5(1):41–45, 1998.

[3] James J. Cimino, Paul D. Clayton, George Hripsack, and Stephen B. Johnson. Knowledge-based approaches to the maintenance of a large controlled medical terminology. *Journal of the American Medical Informatics Association*, 1(1):35–50, 1994.

[4] D. Alan Cruse. On the transitivity of the part-whole relation. *Journal of Linguistics*, 15:29–38, 1979.

[5] Udo Hahn, Martin Romacker, and Stefan Schulz. Discourse structures in medical reports – watch out! The generation of referentially coherent and valid text knowledge bases in the MEDSYNDIKATE system. *International Journal of Medical Informatics*, 53(1):1–28, 1999.

[6] Udo Hahn, Martin Romacker, and Stefan Schulz. How knowledge drives understanding: Matching medical ontologies with the needs of medical language processing. *Artificial Intelligence in Medicine*, 15(1):25–51, 1999.

[7] Udo Hahn, Stefan Schulz, and Martin Romacker. Part-whole reasoning: A case study in medical ontology engineering. *IEEE Intelligent Systems & Their Applications*, 14(5):59–67, 1999.

[8] Ira J. Haimowitz, Ramesh S. Patil, and Peter Szolovits. Representing medical knowledge in a terminological language is difficult. In R. A. Greenes, editor, *SCAMC'88* –

Proceedings of the 12th Annual Symposium on Computer Applications in Medical Care, pages 101–105. Washington, D.C.: IEEE Computer Society Press, 1988.

[9] Ian Horrocks and Ulrike Sattler. A description logic with transitive and inverse roles and role hierarchies. *Journal of Logic and Computation*, 9(3):385–410, 1999.

[10] Robert MacGregor. The evolving technology of classification-based knowledge representation systems. In John Sowa, editor, *Principles of Semantic Networks*, pages 385–400. San Mateo, CA: Morgan Kaufmann, 1991.

[11] Robert MacGregor and Raymond Bates. The LOOM knowledge representation language. Technical Report RS-87-188, Information Sciences Institute, University of Southern California, 1987.

[12] Robert M. MacGregor. A description classifier for the predicate calculus. In *AAAI'94 – Proceedings of the 12th National Conference on Artificial Intelligence*, volume 1, pages 213–220. Seattle, WA, USA, July 31 - August 4, 1994. Menlo Park, CA: AAAI Press & MIT Press, 1994.

[13] Eric Mays, Robert Weida, Robert Dionne, Meir Laker, Brian White, Chihong Liang, and Frank J. Oles. Scalable and expressive medical terminologies. In J. J. Cimino, editor, *AMIA'96 – Proceedings of the 1996 AMIA Annual Fall Symposium (formerly SCAMC). Beyond the Superhighway: Exploiting the Internet with Medical Informatics*, pages 259–263. Washington, D.C., October 26-30, 1996. Philadelphia, PA: Hanley & Belfus, 1996.

[14] Alexa T. McCray and S. J. Nelson. The representation of meaning in the UMLS. *Methods of Information in Medicine*, 34(1/2):193–201, 1995.

[15] Domenico M. Pisanelli, Aldo Gangemi, and Geri Steve. An ontological analysis of the UMLS metathesaurus. In C. G. Chute, editor, *AMIA'98 – Proceedings of the 1998 AMIA Annual Fall Symposium. A Paradigm Shift in Health Care Information Systems: Clinical Infrastructures for the 21st Century*, pages 810–814. Orlando, FL, November 7-11, 1998. Philadelphia, PA: Hanley & Belfus, 1998.

[16] Alan L. Rector, Sean Bechhofer, Carole A. Goble, Ian Horrocks, W. Anthony Nowlan, and W. Danny Solomon. The GRAIL concept modelling language for medical terminology. *Artificial Intelligence in Medicine*, 9:139–171, 1997.

[17] James A. Reggia and Stanley Tuhrim, editors. *Computer-Assisted Medical Decision Making*. New York: Springer, 1985.

[18] Jeremy E. Rogers, Colin Price, Alan Rector, W. Daniel Solomon, and Nick Smeijko. Validating clinical terminology structures: Integration and cross-validation of READ THESAURUS and GALEN. In C. G. Chute, editor, *AMIA'98 – Proceedings of the 1998 AMIA Annual Fall Symposium. A Paradigm Shift in Health Care Information Systems: Clinical Infrastructures for the 21st Century*, pages 845–849. Orlando, FL, November 7-11, 1998. Philadelphia, PA: Hanley & Belfus, 1998.

[19] Cornelius Rosse, Linda G. Shapiro, and James F. Brinkley. The Digital Anatomist foundational model: Principles for defining and structuring its concept domain. In C. G. Chute, editor, *AMIA'98 – Proceedings of the 1998 AMIA Annual Fall Symposium. A Paradigm Shift in Health Care Information Systems: Clinical Infrastructures for the 21st Century*, pages 820–824. Orlando, FL, November 7-11, 1998. Philadelphia, PA: Hanley & Belfus, 1998.

[20] Ulrike Sattler. A concept language for an engineering application with part-whole relations. In A. Borgida, M. Lenzerini, D. Nardi, and B. Nebel, editors, *DL'95 – Proceedings of the International Workshop on Description Logics*, pages 119–123, Rome, Italy, 1995, 1995.

[21] Manfred Schmidt-Schauß and Gerd Smolka. Attributive concept descriptions with complements. *Artificial Intelligence*, 48(1):1–26, 1991.

[22] James G. Schmolze and William S. Mark. The NIKL experience. *Computational Intelligence*, 6(1):48–69, 1991.

[23] Rainer Schubert and Karl-Heinz Höhne. Partonomies for interactive explorable 3D-models of anatomy. In C. G. Chute, editor, *AMIA'98 – Proceedings of the 1998 AMIA Annual Fall Symposium. A Paradigm Shift in Health Care Information Systems: Clinical Infrastructures for the 21st Century*, pages 433–437. Orlando, FL, November 7-11, 1998. Philadelphia, PA: Hanley & Belfus, 1998.

[24] Erich B. Schulz, Colin Price, and Philip J. B. Brown. Symbolic anatomic knowledge representation in the Read Codes Version 3: Structure and application. *Journal of the American Medical Informatics Association*, 4(1):38–48, 1997.

[25] Stefan Schulz and Udo Hahn. Mereotopological reasoning about parts and (w)holes in bio-ontologies. In Chris Welty and Barry Smith, editors, *Formal Ontology in Information Systems. Collected Papers from the 2nd International Conference*, pages 210–221. Ogunquit, Maine, USA, October 17-19, 2001. New York, NY: ACM Press, 2001.

[26] Stefan Schulz, Udo Hahn, and Martin Romacker. Modeling anatomical spatial relations with description logics. In J. M. Overhage, editor, *AMIA 2000 – Proceedings of the Annual Symposium of the American Medical Informatics Association. Converging Information, Technology, and Health Care*, pages 779–783. Los Angeles, CA, November 4-8, 2000. Philadelphia, PA: Hanley & Belfus, 2000.

[27] Kent A. Spackman and Keith E. Campbell. Compositional concept representation using SNOMED: Towards further convergence of clinical terminologies. In C. G. Chute, editor, *AMIA'98 – Proceedings of the 1998 AMIA Annual Fall Symposium. A Paradigm Shift in Health Care Information Systems: Clinical Infrastructures for the 21st Century*, pages 740–744. Orlando, FL, November 7-11, 1998. Philadelphia, PA: Hanley & Belfus, 1998.

[28] Françoise Volot, Pierre Zweigenbaum, Bruno Bachimont, Mohamed Ben Said, Jacques Bouaud, Marius Fieschi, and Jean-François Boisvieux. Structuration and acquisition of medical knowledge: Using UMLS in the Conceptual Graph formalism. In C. Safran, editor, *SCAMC'93 – Proceedings of the 17th Annual Symposium on Computer Applications in Medical Care*, pages 710–714. Washington, D.C., October 30 - November 3, 1993. New York: McGraw-Hill, 1994.

[29] William A. Woods and James G. Schmolze. The KL-ONE family. *Computers & Mathematics with Applications*, 23(2/5):133–177, 1992.

Comparative n-gram analysis of whole-genome protein sequences

M. Ganapathiraju, D. Weisser, R. Rosenfeld, J. Carbonell, R. Reddy & J. Klein-Seetharaman
Carnegie Mellon University
Pittsburgh, PA15217
412 383 7325
{madhavi, dweisser, roni, jgc, rr, judithks}@cs.cmu.edu

ABSTRACT

A current barrier for successful rational drug design is the lack of understanding of the structure space provided by the proteins in a cell that is determined by their sequence space. The protein sequences capable of folding to functional three-dimensional shapes of the proteins are clearly different for different organisms, since sequences obtained from human proteins often fail to form correct three-dimensional structures in bacterial organisms. In analogy to the question "What kind of things do people say?" we therefore need to ask the question "What kind of amino acid sequences occur in the proteins of an organism?" An understanding of the sequence space occupied by proteins in different organisms would have important applications for "translation" of proteins from the language of one organism into that of another and design of drugs that target sequences that might be unique or preferred by pathogenic organisms over those in human hosts.

Here we describe the development of a biological language modeling toolkit (BLMT) for genome-wide statistical amino acid n-gram analysis and comparison across organisms (freely accessible at www.cs.cmu.edu/~blmt). Its functions were applied to 44 different bacterial, archaeal and the human genome. Amino acid n-gram distribution was found to be characteristic of organisms, as evidenced by (1) the ability of simple Markovian unigram models to distinguish organisms, (2) the marked variation in n-gram distributions across organisms above random variation, and (3) identification of organism-specific phrases in protein sequences that are greater than an order of magnitude standard deviations away from the mean. These lines of evidence suggest that different organisms utilize different "vocabularies" and "phrases", an observation that may provide novel approaches to drug development by specifically targeting these phrases. The results suggest that further detailed analysis of n-gram statistics of protein sequences from whole genomes will likely – in analogy to word n-gram analysis – result in powerful models for prediction, topic classification and information extraction of biological sequences.

Keywords

Biological language modeling toolkit, genome signatures.

Proceedings of HLT 2002, Second International Conference on Human Language Technology Research, M. Marcus, ed., Morgan Kaufmann, San Francisco, 2002.

1. INTRODUCTION

1.1 Opportunity for human language technologies in biological data analysis

Central to the understanding of complex biological systems are proteins. Their form and function is in principle encoded in characteristic amino acid sequences. The precise relationship between a primary protein sequence, its three-dimensional structure and its function in a complex cellular environment is one of the most fundamental unanswered questions in biology. Large amounts of genomic and protein sequence data for homo sapiens and other organisms have recently become available, together with a growing body of protein structure and function data. The expected exponential increase in the amount of this data in the coming decade creates an opportunity for attacking the sequence-structure-function mapping problem with increasingly sophisticated data-driven methods. Such methods have proven immensely successful in the domain of natural language, and are directly responsible for the success of automatic speech recognition, document classification, information extraction, statistical machine translation and other challenging tasks over the past two decades.

1.2 Introduction: biological language

The mapping of biological sequences to form and function of proteins is conceptually similar to the mapping of words to meaning. This analogy is being studied by a growing body of research ([1] and pointers thereof). Thus, word n-gram analysis has found applications to biological sequences, using various types of "vocabulary", for example the nucleotides or the 61-codon types in the case of DNA (e.g. [2]), and the standard 20 amino acids or reduced 3-letter charge groups of the amino acids in the case of proteins (e.g. [3]). Thus, nearest-neighbor correlation analysis have revealed specific preferences for proximity of certain amino acids in protein sequences [4]. The results from n-gram analysis have been used in some cases to demonstrate that genome or protein sequences follow Zipf law [5-11]. However, since non-deterministic sequences also follow a power law (see e.g. [12]), detection of linguistic features in biological sequence data based on the distribution of n-grams is controversial and the extent to which amino acid sequences can be modeled stochastically is not clear.

The advent of whole-genome sequencing efforts provides a new opportunity to revisit n-gram statistics and Zipf-type analysis in greater detail. In particular, specific questions that can now be addressed are: How characteristic is the amino acid n-gram distribution for specific organisms? Do different organisms tend to use different phrases? Previous determination of global statistics of entire genomes supports that there are genome-specific regularities in n-gram statistics. For example, species-specific regularity in composition ("unigram count") has been identified [13], the typical length of prokaryotic proteins is different from that in eukaryotes [14, 15] and differences in patterns in usage of secondary structure elements [16] by various genomes have been observed. Here we extend global genome sequence analysis to systematically compare n-gram statistics of protein sequences from a larger number of known genomes. The long-term goal is to provide a useful starting point to derive language models with defined vocabulary and phrase preferences and grammatical rules for protein sequences of different organisms.

2. DEVELOPMENT OF A TOOL-KIT FOR BIOLOGICAL LANGUAGE MODELING (BLMT)

Statistical analysis of biological sequence data requires n-gram string matching and string searches. Due to the large size of genomic data, the search for subsequences becomes a computationally challenging problem. Searching for a sub-string from large text data is a well-studied problem in computer science, with applications to diverse areas including data compression, network intrusion detection, information retrieval and word processing [17]. Data structures like suffix trees [18] and suffix arrays [19] have been used as preferred data structures for applications of this kind [19-21] and more recently also for biological data [22]. When suffix arrays are complemented with other data arrays, e.g. the Least Common Prefix (LCP) array [19] and/or Rank arrays [23], they provide additional functionality at reduced computational cost. Thus, it permits search of a sub-string of length P in a string of length N in O(P+log N) time, and requires O(N) space for construction, which is competitive with those of suffix trees [19]. Preprocessed suffix arrays can now be used to efficiently extract global n-gram statistics and compare it amongst various genomes. The method is illustrated in Figure 1 using the organism Aeropyrum pernix as an example (Table 1).

To extract n-gram statistical data from the genome suffices, we have assembled a tool-kit that combines the following functions:
(1) Counting protein number and length
(2) Counting n-grams and most frequent n-grams
(3) Counting n-grams of specified length
(4) Determining relative frequencies of specific n-grams across organisms
(5) Identifying longest repeating sequences
(6) Localization and co-localization of n-grams for grouping proteins
(7) N-gram neighbor (left and right) identification
(8) Distribution of n-gram frequencies in specific protein sequences from global statistics
(9) Preprocessing of sequence data to prepare for analysis in CMU/Cambridge Statistical Language Modeling (SLM) Toolkit [24].

The functions of the toolkit were applied to protein sequences derived from whole-genome sequences of 44 different organisms. Amino acids were treated as words. The numbers of proteins varied from 484 (175,928 amino acids) in Mycoplasma genitalium to 25612 (18,283,879 amino acids) in Homo sapiens.

Table 1. Format of protein sequence input files

>gi|5103389|dbj|BAA78910.1| 241aa long hypothetical protein
MVDILSSLLL
>gi|5103390|dbj|BAA78911.1| 112aa long hypothetical protein
MDPADKLMK
>gi|5103391|dbj|BAA78912.1| 100aa long hypothetical protein
MQA

3. RESULTS: COMPARATIVE GENOME N-GRAM STATISTICS

3.1 Probabilistic models can distinguish organisms

A simple Markovian unigram (context independent amino acid) model from the proteins of Aeropyrum pernix was trained. When training and test set were from the same organism, a perplexity (a variation on cross-entropy) of 16.6 was observed, whereas data from other organisms varied from 16.8 to 21.9. Thus the differences between the 'sub-languages' of the different organisms are automatically detectable with even the simplest language model. This observation is purely based on the large differences in unigram distributions (described in Section 3.2 and Figure 2 below) and is independent of the organism that is used to train the model.

0	1	2	3	4	5	6	7	8	9	10	11	12	13	14	15	16	17	18	19	20	21	22	23	24
M	V	D	I	L	S	S	L	L	L	#	M	D	P	A	D	K	L	M	K	#	M	Q	A	#
19	24	5	8	15	23	22	13	12	11	1	16	7	20	4	6	10	14	17	9	2	18	21	3	0
24	10	20	23	14	2	15	12	3	19	16	9	8	7	17	4	11	18	21	0	13	22	6	5	1
0	1	1	0	1	0	1	1	0	0	1	0	1	1	1	1	0	1	1	1	0	0	0	1	0

Genome String

Suffix (Pos) Array Lexicographical ordering of suffixes: Position 0 is # (24 in original string). Position 1 is #MD... (10 in original string), Position 2 is #MQ... (20 in original string), Position 3 is A# (23 in original string) etc.

Rank Array The suffix A#.... takes position 3 in the suffix array, hence its rank is 3.

LCP Array The number of common leading symbols.

Figure1. Example for genome string organization in suffix arrays: *Aeropyrum pernix*.

3.2 Comparative Zipf-like analysis

We developed a modification of Zipf-like analysis that can reveal differences between word-usage in different organisms. First, the amino acid n-grams of a given length are sorted in descending order by frequency for the organism of choice. An example using the simplest case, n=1, is shown in Figure 2 for two organisms Aeropyrum pernix and Neisseria meningitidis to illustrate the principle. The frequencies of the sorted n-grams are shown in bold red. Thin lines indicate the respective frequencies of n-grams with given rank in Aeropyrum pernix (Figure 2A) or Neisseria meningitides (Figure 2B) in all the other organisms. The same plots for the other 42 organisms studied for n=1 and also for other n (n<5) can be viewed at www.cs.cmu.edu/~blmt. While there is striking variation in rank of certain n-grams in different organisms, the most rare n-grams in one organism are overall rare in all organisms. Specific differences in n-grams other than unigrams are explored in more detail below (Section 3.3).

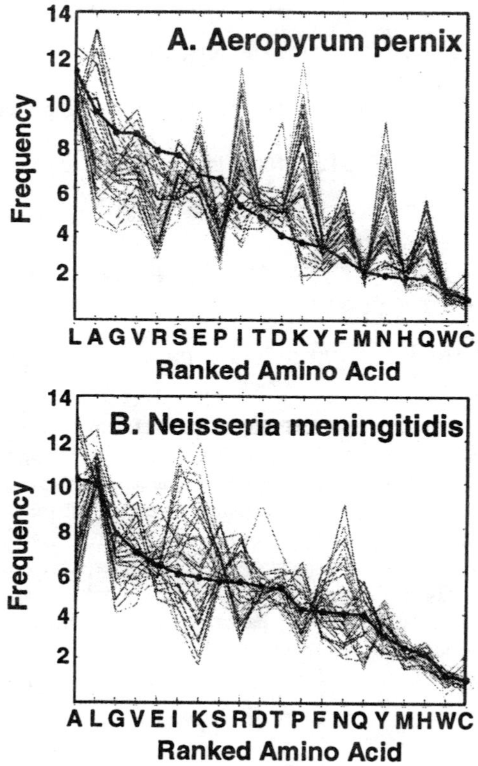

Figure 2. Comparative Zipf analysis: n-grams are ranked according to frequency for one organism (shown as bold, red line). Shown here are two examples for n=1, Aeropyrum pernix (A.) and Neisseria menigitidis (B.). The respective frequencies of n-grams the other 43 organisms studied are drawn as thin lines. The plots for other organisms and other n studied can be viewed at the website www.cs.cmu.edu/~blmt.

3.3 Organism-specific usage of "phrases" in protein sequences

The Zipf-like analysis described above (Section 3.2) allows us to quantify the differences in specific n-gram frequencies across

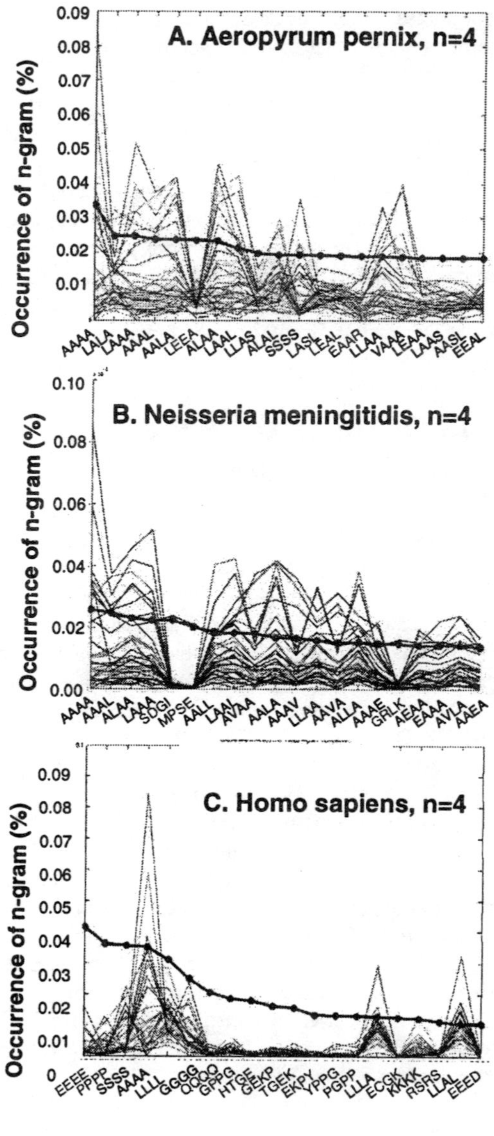

Figure 3. Comparative Zipf analysis: Top 20 most frequently used 4-grams in Aeropyrum pernix (A), Neisseria meningitidis (B) and Homo sapiens (C). Line colors as in Figure 2.

organisms. In particular, as we move to larger contexts, organisms show much more marked differences in the statistics of their n-gram distribution with peculiar outliers. Strikingly, we found n-grams that are very frequent in some organisms yet rare (or completely absent in some cases) in others. Examples are shown in Figure 3 for n=4 in Aeropyrum pernix (Figure 3A), Neisseria meningitidis (Figure 3B) and Homo sapiens (Figure 3C). In A. pernix, the LEEA frequency is strikingly high. In N. meningitidis, MPSE, SDGI and GRLK are amongst the top 20 most frequently used 4-grams, but are used in no other organism with such high frequencies. In human, the differences to the bacterial and archaeal organisms are even more pronounced, presumably due to their evolutionary distance to the unicellular organisms. The investigation of other eukaryotic genomes is underway.

These highly idiosyncratic n-grams suggest "phrases" that are preferably used in the particular organism. The observation of organism-specific phrases is not unique to extremophile or other specialized organisms. Instead, idiosyncratic phrases appear in all the organisms (also see Section 3.4 below), and the results for other organisms (including very common and ubiquitous bacteria such as Escherichi coli) can be viewed at www.cs.cmu.edu/~blmt. Importantly, these phrases can be organism-specific.

3.4 Phrases are not due to random variation

To test if the observation of idiosyncratic n-grams could be explained by chance sampling, we generated two sets of 20 artificial genomes by Monte Carlo simulation using the unigram frequencies of Neisseria meningitidis and Aeropyrum pernix, respectively. Figure 4 shows a Zipf-like comparison as described above for the natural genomes, for Neisseria meningitidis in comparison to the random genomes (A), for Aeropurum pernix in comparison to the random genomes (B) and for one of the random genomes in comparison to the other random genomes and the Neisseria and Aeropyrum genomes (C). As one can see, in both natural genomes the frequencies are well above the baseline variation due to chance sampling.

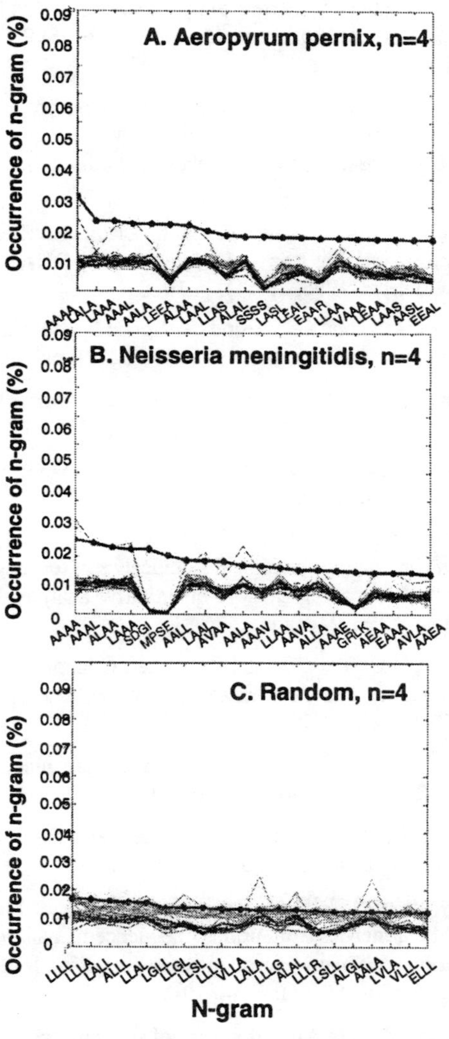

Figure 4. Comparative Zipf analysis of random genomes versus natural genomes: Top 20 most frequently used 4-grams in Aeropyrum pernix (A), Neisseria meningitidis (B) and a random genome (C). Line colors as in Figure 2. Note that both natural genomes strike out, not only the one according to which the n-grams were ranked.

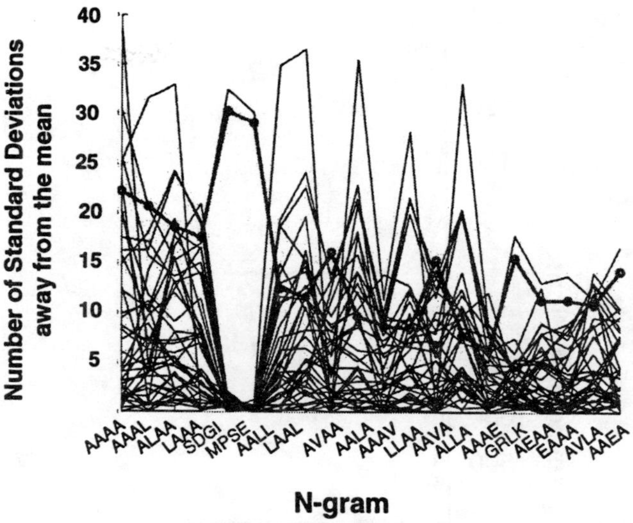

Figure 5. Distance from mean values based on unigram distributions in Neisseria meningitidis. Values are plotted as multiples of standard deviation from mean. The unigram distribution was as in Figure 2A.

3.5 Phrase frequencies can be very distant from mean values

To further strengthen the notion that the phrases are not due to random variation, we calculated the distance of 4-gram frequencies in multiples of standard deviations for the top 20 4-grams in Neisseria meningitidis. The result is shown in Figure 5. The phrases SDGI and MPSE are approximately 30 standard deviations away from the means based on unigram distributions. In contrast, all of the other organism, except for a different strain of Neisseria meningitidis, show only very small standard deviations from mean values based on their own unigram frequencies. GRLK is also more frequent than would be expected based on independent unigram probabilities, although not to the same degree as SDGI and MPSE. The large deviation from mean values clearly shows that phrases are not only organism-specific in absolute terms but are also quantifiably distant from the values predicted by independent unigram frequencies of the same organism.

3.6 How many phrases are there in an organism?

The previous section has shown that there is a correlation between deviation from mean values within the same organism and difference in frequency of certain n-grams in comparison with other organisms. The next step is to identify all the phrases in an organism. Towards this goal, we have quantified the number of n-grams as a function of standard deviation from mean values. The result is shown for one organism (Escherichia coli) in Figure 6, for n=2 (Figure 6A), n=3 (Figure 6B) and n=4 (Figure 6C). Especially 3-gram and 4-gram values are heavily tailed. It is this long tail which gives rise to the large deviations observed in Figure 5.

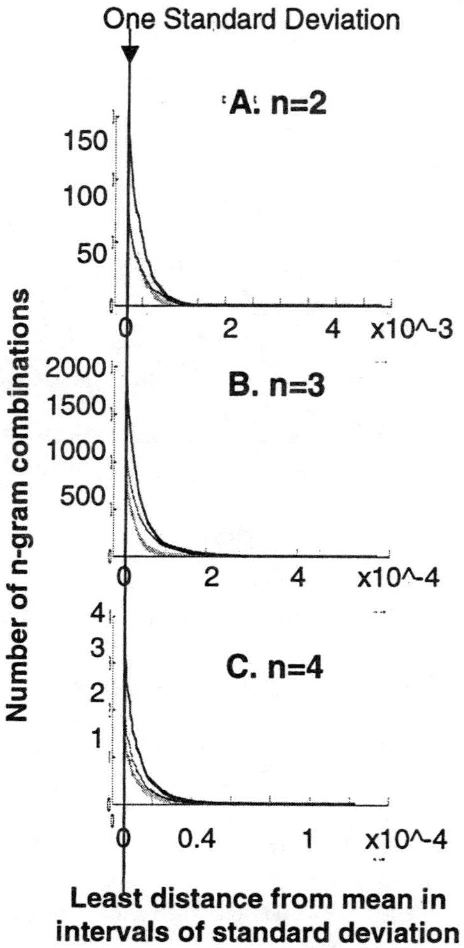

Figure 6. Number of n-grams in dependence of distance from mean value for Escherichia coli. Solid lines, absolute values; dotted lines, negative values (underrepresented n-grams); dashed lines, positive values (overrepresented n-grams).

4. CONCLUSIONS AND FUTURE WORK

Using n-gram statistical analysis of whole-genome protein sequences we have shown that there are organism-specific phrases in direct analogy to human languages. Future work will aim at detailed identification of these phrases to map out the sequence space occupied by proteins in different genomes. We will test experimentally what is the structure space occupied by these sequences to map their biological significance.

5. ACKNOWLEDGMENTS

This work was supported by Information Technology Research Grant 0204078 from the National Science Foundation.

6. REFERENCES

[1] Language Modeling of Biological Data Workshop. ed. D. Searles. 2001, University of Pennsylvania. http://www.ircs.upenn.edu/modeling2001/modeling.shtml,

[2] Burge, C., A.M. Campbell, and S. Karlin, Over- and under-representation of short oligonucleotides in DNA sequences. Proc Natl Acad Sci U S A, 1992. 89(4): p. 1358-62.

[3] Erhan, S., T. Marzolf, and L. Cohen, Amino-acid neighborhood relationships in proteins. Breakdown of amino-acid sequences into overlapping doublets, triplets and quadruplets. Int J Biomed Comput, 1980. 11(1): p. 67-75.

[4] Karlin, S., et al., Statistical methods and insights for protein and DNA sequences. Annu Rev Biophys Biophys Chem, 1991. 20: p. 175-203.

[5] Weiss, O., M.A. Jimenez-Montano, and H. Herzel, Information content of protein sequences. J Theor Biol, 2000. 206(3): p. 379-86.

[6] Li, W., Statistical properties of open reading frames in complete genome sequences. Comput Chem, 1999. 23(3-4): p. 283-301.

[7] Czirok, A., et al., Correlations in binary sequences and a generalized Zipf analysis. Physical Review. E. Statistical Physics, Plasmas, Fluids, and Related Interdisciplinary Topics, 1995. 52(1): p. 446-452.

[8] Israeloff, N.E., M. Kagalenko, and K. Chan, Can Zipf distinguish language from noise in noncoding DNA? Physical Review Letters, 1996. 76(11): p. 1976.

[9] Konopka, A.K. and C. Martindale, Noncoding DNA, Zipf's law, and language. Science, 1995. 268(5212): p. 789.

[10] Mantegna, R.N., et al., Linguistic features of noncoding DNA sequences. Phys Rev Lett, 1994. 73(23): p. 3169-72.

[11] Tsonis, A.A., J.B. Elsner, and P.A. Tsonis, Is DNA a language? J Theor Biol, 1997. 184(1): p. 25-9.

[12] Chatzidimitriou-Dreismann, C.A., R.M. Streffer, and D. Larhammar, Lack of biological significance in the 'linguistic features' of noncoding DNA--a quantitative analysis. Nucleic Acids Res, 1996. 24(9): p. 1676-81.

[13] Karlin, S., B.E. Blaisdell, and P. Bucher, Quantile distributions of amino acid usage in protein classes. Protein Eng, 1992. 5(8): p. 729-38.

[14] Venter, J.C., et al., The sequence of the human genome. Science, 2001. 291(5507): p. 1304-51.

[15] Lander, E.S., et al., Initial sequencing and analysis of the human genome. Nature, 2001. 409:860-921.

[16] Bradley, P., et al., BETAWRAP: successful prediction of parallel beta -helices from primary sequence reveals an association with many microbial pathogens. Proc Natl Acad Sci U S A, 2001. 98(26): p. 14819-24.

[17] Apostolico, A., The Myriad virtues of subword trees, Combinatorial Algorithms on Words. NATO ASI series in Computer and System Sciences, 1985. 12: p. 85-96.

[18] Weiner, P. Linear pattern matching algorithms. in 14th Annual Symposium on Switching and Automata Theory. 1973. University of Iowa.

[19] Manber, U. and G. Myers, Suffix arrays: A New Method for On-Line String Searches. SIAM Journal on Computing, 1993. 22(5): p. 935-948.

[20] Grossi, R. and J.S. Vitter. Compressed Suffix Arrays and Suffix Trees, with Applications to Text Indexing and String Matching. in Proceedings of the 32nd Annual ACM Symposium on Theory of Computing (STOC '00). 2000. Portland, OR.

[21] Larsson, N.J. Extended application of suffix trees to data compression. in IEEE Data Compression Conference. 1996.

[22] Burkhardt, S., et al. q-gram Based Database Searching Using a Suffix Array (QUASAR). in Third Annual Intl. Conference on Computational Molecular Biology, RECOMB'99. 1999. Lyon, France.

[23] Kasai, T., et al. Linear-Time Longest-Common-Prefix computation in Suffix Arrays and Its applications. in Annual Symposium on Combinatorial Pattern Matching CPM-2001. 2001. Jerusalem, Israel.

[24] Clarkson, P.R. and R. Rosenfeld, Statistical language modeling using the CMU-Cambridge toolkit. Proceedings ESCA Eurospeech, 1997.

The GENIA Corpus: an Annotated Research Abstract Corpus in Molecular Biology Domain

Tomoko Ohta
University of Tokyo
Hongo 7-3-1, Bunkyo-ku, Tokyo
113-0033, Japan
okap@is.s.u-tokyo.ac.jp

Yuka Tateisi
CREST, JST
Hongo 7-3-1, Bunkyo-ku, Tokyo
113-0033, Japan
yucca@is.s.u-tkyo.ac.jp

Jin-Dong Kim
CREST, JST
Hongo 7-3-1, Bunkyo-ku, Tokyo
113-0033, Japan
jdkim@is.s.u-tokyo.ac.jp

ABSTRACT

With the information overload in genome-related field, there is an increasing need for natural language processing technology to extract information from literature and various attempts of information extraction using NLP has been being made. We are developing the necessary resources including domain ontology and annotated corpus from research abstracts in MEDLINE database (GENIA corpus). We are building the ontology and the corpus simultaneously, using each other. In this paper we report on our new corpus, its ontological basis, annotation scheme, and statistics of annotated objects. We also describe the tools used for corpus annotation and management.

1. INTRODUCTION

Recently, rapid advances in genome-related field have caused a problem of information overload. Although the databases of proteins, genes, etc. have been constructed, the work of updating them with the latest results published in journals is still largely a manual process, and the use of natural language processing technology to help this process is expected and various attempts of information extraction using NLP has been being made.

We are currently working on the task of extracting event information by using general-purpose natural language processing method[2]. At the same time we are developing the necessary resources or knowledge including domain ontology and annotated corpus from research abstracts in MEDLINE database (GENIA corpus) that can be used as a gold standard for evaluation, training data for machine learning programs, and for other various purposes. We are building the ontology and the corpus simultaneously, using each other; we enhance the ontology with the terms in the annotated corpus, and the tags set for annotation with enhanced ontology.

Text corpus annotated with various levels of linguistic information is required as the process of event information extraction requires syntactic, semantic, and other broad range of levels of natural language processing. As the first step of information extraction, we focused on extracting and classifying the "actors" of events, such as substances. The current version of GENIA corpus is aimed for such application, in which we annotated the named entities in the research abstracts taken from MEDLINE database. We first built a conceptual model (ontology) of substances and sources (substance location), and based on that ontology, we have annotated such named entities involved in biological reactions concerning to transcription factors in human blood cells. The preliminary version of the corpus[16] was used as a learning and test set of a system that extracts the names of substances involved in and their sources from MEDLINE abstracts[3]. In this paper we report on the corpus, its ontological basis, annotation scheme, and statistics of annotated objects. We also describe the tools used for corpus annotation and management.

Proceedings of HLT 2002, Second International Conference on Human Language Technology Research, M. Marcus, ed., Morgan Kaufmann, San Francisco, 2002.

2. THE TAG SET AND UNDERLYING ONTOLOGY

Named entity annotation task can be regarded as identifying and classifying the names that appears in the texts according to a predefined classification. For a reliable classification, the classification must be well-defined and easy to understand by the domain experts who annotate the texts. To fulfill this requirement, we create a concrete data model (ontology) of the biological domain on which the tag sets are based.

In defining the ontology, we required that the classification must be mutually exclusive. For example, the substances can be classified by their biological role or by their chemical structure, which are both important. However, in our initial annotation work, we rather concentrated on one criteria because using two might prevent the mutually exclusive classification or require more complicate tag structures and context dependent semantic tags.

Ontologies of biological terminology has been created to provide a model of biological concept that can be used for integrating the heterogeneous information sources such as multiple databases[1, 14, 15], as a controlled vocabulary for annotating database entries[6, 7, 17, 10], or as templates in information extraction task[12]. However, existing ontologies were not suitable for our task. For example, there are classes of "Organic Chemicals [D02]", "Enzymes, Coenzymes, and Enzyme Inhibitors [D08]", and "Amino Acids, Peptides, and Proteins [D12]" at the same level right under the "Chemicals and Drugs [D]" category in the MeSH term hierarchy, a contorolled vocabulary developed at National Library of Medicine for indexing MEDLINE abstracts. Because an enzyme is a protein in chemical structure and a protein is an organic compound, we must allow a multiple tag or a structured tag to annotate the name of an enzyme if we use this level of classification in annotation. Otherwise, there would be an ambiguity as to which tag (class) should be used to annotate the name. Similar problems were found in several other ontologies[1, 14].

On the other hand, the ontologies for annotating entries in biological databases[17, 7, 6] have focused on describing specific class of entities in depth, because they must be as fine-grained as to distinguish between the entities differently categorized in existing databases, but do not have to treat the entities that are not in the databases. Thus, these ontologies are very specific in one area but not enough for other: some information necessary for information extraction task can be completely out of the scope of these ontologies. Thus, for our current annotation purpose, we could not choose an ontology of this type. We need an ontology that covers broader range of concept at shallower (more general and coarse-grained) level than these ontologies. The ontologies developed at Columbia University[12] or Institute of Medical Science in University of Tokyo[15] are more suitable for out task, but they were not widely available at the time when we started the project.

Thus, we first defined the base ontology as a taxonomy shown in Figure 1. The top level of the ontology is divided into *substance* and *source* subhierarchy, and *other* that is not either a substance or a source.

At the outset of our annotation work we chose to simplify the classification of substances by concentrating on the chemical structure. This is because the chemical structure is more independent of the biological context that the substance appears, and is therefore more stably defined. For example, the chemical characteristics of a protein can be easily defined, but its biological role may vary depending on the biological context, e.g., a substance may work as an enzyme for one species but not for others. In our model we do not classify substance as enzymes, transcription factors, genes, etc. but as proteins, DNAs, RNAs, etc. They are further classified into families, complexes, individual molecules, subunits, domains, and regions.

Based on the ontology, names of substances that appear in MEDLINE abstracts are classified into the names of atoms (e.g., *calcium*), inorganic compounds (e.g., *H2O2*), proteins (e.g. *NF-kappa B*), peptides (e.g., *pml/RAR-alpha peptides*), amino acids(e.g., *tyrosine*), DNAs (e.g., *PML gene*), RNAs (e.g., *Egr-1 mRNA*), nucleotide polymers other than DNAs and RNAs (e.g., *CpG dinucleotide*), nucleotide monomers (e.g., *thymidine*), lipids (*lipopolysaccharide*), carbohydrates (*3-O-methyl-D-glucose*), and other organic compounds (*2,3,7,8-tetrachlorodibenzo-p-dioxin*). Similarly, the names of sources are classified into the names of multi-cell organisms, mono-cell organisms other than the virus, virus, body parts, tissues, cell types, cell subcomponents, cell lines, and other artificial sources.

Sources are biological locations where substances are found and their reactions take place. They are also hierarchically sub-classified into organisms (e.g., *human*), body parts (e.g., *head*), tissues (e.g. *brain*), cells or cell types (e.g., *leukocyte*), cell sub-cations (e.g., *me mbrane*), or artificially cultured cell lines (e.g., *HeLa*). Organisms are further classified into multi-cell organisms, mono-cell organisms other than viruses, and viruses. There is obviously relations other than taxonomy between the classes in the source hierarchy. For example, (multi-cell) organisms, tissues, cells, and sublocations are interrelated with *part-of* relation, a cell line is made from a certain cell type, and so on. However, these relationships are not in Figure 1.

We mark up the terms that appear in abstracts and classify them with this classification. Also, we mark up other terms that are not the names of substances or sources, but yet considered important in the task of information extraction. They are used for further enhancing the ontology.

We adopt the DARPA Agent Mark-Up Language (DAML)[4] as the ontology-defining language for GENIA project. The DAML has been designed as an XML-based se mantic language and the latest release of the language (DAML+OIL) provides a rich set of constructs with which to create ontologies and to markup information. Many ontologies have been written or are being written in DAML. We have therefore decided to manage our ontology in DAML so as for us to utilize the existing ontologies in DAML ontology library and for others to access our products easily.

3. GPML

The classification described in previous section is encoded in GENIA Project Markup Language (GPML)[8], a document type definition (DTD) of XML language that consists of definitions of structural elements for defining logical division of documents, linguistic elements for annotating linguistic (both syntactic and semantic) information, and resource elements for defining language resources that are not the document itself such as ontologies or thesauri. These elements provide the way of annotating corpora with linguistic information and document structure information simultaneously. The structure of GPML elements also supports our strategy to build language resources simultaneously by providing a mecha nism of extending existing ontology and lexicon while annotating corpora. The extended parts of ontology can be defined using the resource elements while annotating the corpus, and will be collected later for complementing the main ontology. In designing GPML, simplicity and extensibility were regarded highly. For the simplicity, we didn't define such entities that are just useful for potential extension but not used for the current GENIA resources. For example, we didn't define structural entities for chapters or sections because the current GENIA corpus consists of MEDLINE abstracts and there are no such structures. For the extensibility, we tried to secure reliable guidelines instead of relying on imperfect predictions about potential extensions. For example, we decided to maintain the structural part of GPML as compatible as possible with DocBook[5], a markup language for technical documentation maintained by OASIS. It is one of th e most popular XML applications supported by a large base of users and developers.

Each abstract (article element) in GENIA corpus comprises four elements: *title*, *articleinfo*, *abstract* and *localresource* (See Figure 2) for an example). A *title* element contains the title of the abstract and an *abstract* element contains the main body of the abstract. An *articleinfo* element contains bibliographic information about the article; currently we use only the *bibliomisc* element (as defined in DocBook) in it, which contains the unique identifier of the abstract in MEDLINE assigned by the National Library of Medicine. A *localresource* element contains ontologic and lexical information for the article.

An abstract element comprises one or more *sentence* elements. A *sentence* element contains a sentence in the abstract, and contain *term* elements and *cons* elements. T he *term* elements are semantically atomic terms which are basic units of linguistic analysis. The *cons* elements are phrases which consist of other *term* or *cons* elements. The *term* and *cons* elements can have their syntactic and semantic information as their attributes.

In the current GENIA corpus, technical terms in the title and the body of the abstracts are tagged as *term* or *cons* elements with conceptual information from the ontology encoded in the *sem* attribute, which is a pointer to an element within the *localresouce* elements as described later. A technical term is considered to be a semantic unit, so that they can be naturally regarded as a *term* element. However, in coordinating clauses, a term is often separated into two or more parts. In such case, we just isolate each part as it is and label

```
+------+-source-+-natural-+-organism-+-multi-cell organism
       |        |         |          +-mono-cell organism
       |        |         |          +-virus
       |        |         |
       |        |         +-body part
       |        |         +-tissue
       |        |         +-cell type
       |        |         +-cell component
       |        |         +-other (natural source)
       |        +-artificial-+-cell line
       |                     +-other (artificial source)
       +-substance-+-compound-+-organic-+-amino acid-+-protein-+-protein family or group
       |           |          |         |            |         +-protein complex
       |           |          |         |            |         +-individual protein molecule
       |           |          |         |            |         +-subunit of protein complex
       |           |          |         |            |         +-substructure of protein
       |           |          |         |            |         +-domain or region of protein
       |           |          |         |            +-peptide
       |           |          |         |            +-amino acid monomer
       |           |          |         +-nucleic acid-+-DNA-+-DNA family or group
       |           |          |         |              |     +-individual DNA molecule
       |           |          |         |              |     +-domain or region of DNA
       |           |          |         |              +-RNA-+-RNA family or group
       |           |          |         |              |     +-individual RNA molecule
       |           |          |         |              |     +-domain or region of RNA
       |           |          |         |              +-polynucleotide
       |           |          |         |              +-nucleotide
       |           |          |         +-lipid-+-steroid
       |           |          |         +-carbohydrate
       |           |          |         +-other (organic compounds)
       |           |          +-inorganic compounds
       |           +-atom
       +-other
```

Figure 1: The underlying ontology

each of them as indicating they are parts of certain terms. After doing so, we assemble or iginal terms with their parts. When we annotate assembled terms, we use *cons* elements instead of *term* elements.

For example, in Figure 2, the term *mitogen- and stress-activated protein kinases* in the title actually means *mitogen-activated protein kinases and stress-activated protein kinases.* In the title, the term *mitogen- and stress-activated protein kinases* is annotated as a *cons* element that is an *and*-coordination of two terms (denoted with pointers #3 and #4 in the *sem* attribute). The actual entities are declared in the *localresource* element (the *class* elements with id=3 and id=4).

The *localresource* element is for createing new concepts reqquired but are not in the base ontology, which is the case of almost every time in current version of the corpus. Lexical variation information has been also stored up in the localresource elements. A newly created subclass or an instance of a class in the base ontology is declared in *class* elements which has a *label* element, the name of the newly created entity (class or instance), and *SubClassOf* element, the superclass of the entity. For example, in the case of the coordinated terms mentioned above, we need to create the concepts of *mitogen-activated protein kinase* and *stress-activated protein kinase*. The full forms of the terms are used a s the label, and in the *SubClassOf* element they are declared as instances of the *protein* class of the GENIA ontology. The base ontology to be used is declared at the top of the *localresource* element as an *imports* element.

Using the *localresource* element, we can add the concepts to the base ontology while annotating the instances which appear in the real-world texts. Later, the information in the *localresource* elements can be gathered to enhance the base ontology itself. In this way, we can create the corpus and the ontology simultaneously.

4. THE CURRENT STATUS OF THE GENIA CORPUS

So far, we have annotated 2,500 abstracts related to the transcription factors in human blood cells. We have marked up 146,505 names with 31 different semantic classes. 77,480 proteins, 23,628 DNAs, 2,432 RNAs, 27,542 sources, 36,683 others are marked up. We have made 670 abstracts out of 2,500 (GENIA Corpus ver. 1.1) available to public[18].

We are currently trying to enhance the corpus in both quantity and quality. As well as increasing the number of abstracts, we have started to annotate syntactic and co-reference structures to the same set of abstracts that the terms were annotated. Then, the corpus can be further annotated with event structures.

Part-of-speach annotation to the same set of abstracts annotated for named entities is under way using Penn Treebank set[13]. The preliminary version of annotation to the base text of GENIA Corpus ver 1.1 was done and the annotated texts are used internally for the experiment of named entity extraction. We just started to define the scheme for annotating the deeper level of syntactic feature and co-reference structures.

The underlying ontology is also under enhancement. We have collected the terms in *other* class in the current corpus and have been re-classifying the terms to broden the coverage of the ontology. Deailed quantitive analysis is yet to be done, but we have found certain classes, like diseases, interaction of substances and cells, and experimental methods, should be added to the base ontology.

```
<article>
<title>
Effects of <term sem="#000">Ara-C</term> on <term sem="#002">neutral sphingomyelinase</term>
and <cons sem="(AND #3 #4)"><term sem="#005">mitogen-</term> and <term sem="#006">stress-</term>
term sem="#007">activated protein kinases</term></cons> in <term sem="#008">T-lymphocyte cell lines</term>.

</title>
<articleinfo>
<bibliomisc>MEDLIN:97107281</bibliomisc>
</articleinfo>
<abstract>
<sentence>
<term sem="#002">Neutral sphingomyelinase</term> (<term sem="#009">SMase</term>) can be
activated by <term sem="#010">extracellular signals</term> to produce <term sem="#011">ceramide</term>,
which may affect <term sem="#012">mitogen-activated protein kinase (MAPK) activities</term>.
</sentence>
        :
</abstract>
<localresource>
<imports resource="http://www-tsujii.is.s.u-tokyo.ac.jp/GENIA/GENIA.daml" prefix="GENIA"/>
<class id="000"><label>Ara-C</label><subClassOf resource="GENIA#other_organic_compounds"/></class>
<class id="001"><label>molecule</label><subClassOf resource="GENIA#protein"/></class>
<class id="002"><label>neutral_sphingomyelinase</label><subClassOf resource="#001"/></class>
<class id="003"><label>mitogen-_activated_protein_kinase</label>
    <subClassOf resource="GENIA#protein"/></class>
<class id="004"><label>stress-_activated
_protein_kinase</label>
    <subClassOf resource="GENIA#protein"/></class>
:
</localresource>
</article>
</set>
```

Figure 2: An annotated abstract in GPML format

5. TOOLS FOR CORPUS ANNOTATION

Although a XML-tagged text can be created by using text editors, semantically annotated corpora must be created by domain experts who are not always familiar with XML tag scheme. A tool for management of the tagged texts is also indispensable for controlling the quality of the corpus and taking the statistics of tag data.

To help annotators, we use a GUI-based tag definition tool TagEdit (Figure 3) and tagging tool JTag (Figure 4)[11].

In the tag definition tool TagEdit, definition of new tag-set, refinement of definition, enhancement of the tag-set by adding or removing tags, and enrichment of tags by adding or removing attributes are available. In TagEdit, a tag set is assumed have hierarchical structure. That is, a tag is defined as a "child tag" of another. The defined tag set is directly corresponding to a taxonomy in an ontology, and this feature is suitable for semantic annotation of named entities.

The tagging tool JTag allows the annotators to choose tags from a tagset defined with TagEdit and annotate texts with them. JTag supports the exporting the annotated data in two forms: An annotated text can be saved as tag-embedded XML document, or the data including the class of tag, the position of tag in the text, and values of attributes can be saved separately from the text to be stored in external database.

The separation of tag information from the text itself allows users to perform various operations on tags, e.g. to compare the annotation by different annotators and to take statistics. For this kind of operations, we developed Tag Information Management System (TIMS) Workbench[9] to perform/view tagging on a particular document. Since tag informations stored separately from original documents and managed using an external database software, various

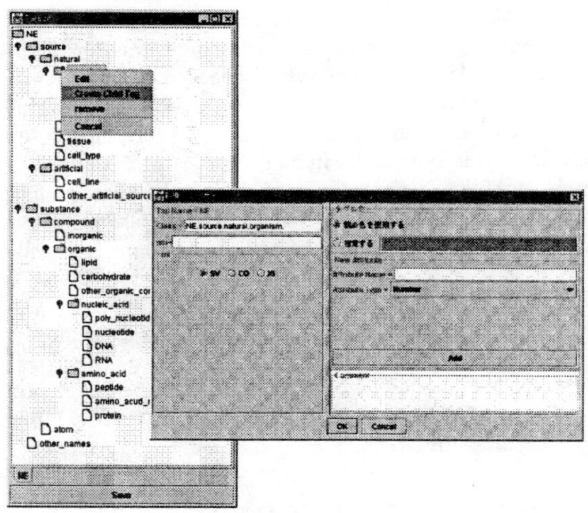

Figure 3: Definition of Tags with TagEdit: select a tag in hierarchy and "create child tag" to add a tag for its child.

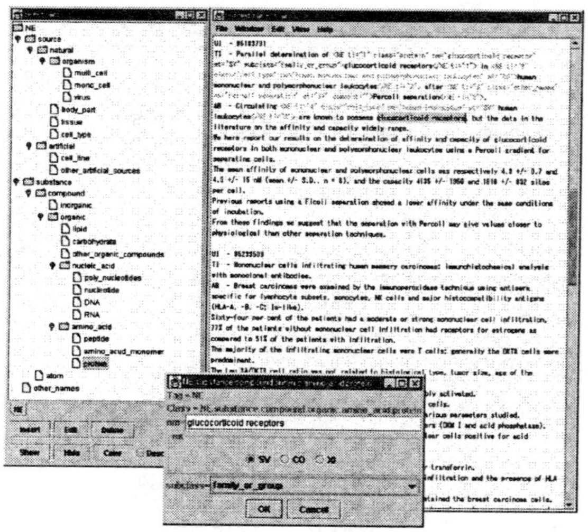

Figure 4: Annotation with JTag: select a range of text in right window and insert one of the tags shown in the left window

different types of tags for the same document can be added. The system also keeps track of the Audit Trail or History, i.e., the date and time, the user or system that performed the tagging etc. TIMS also has facility to search logically for tags, which we call Interval Operations. They are XML specific text/data mining operations which can be performed over documents. The operations can be done over open documents or in batch mode, selecting the files from a list. The TIMS workbench is also available to public[18].

6. CONCLUSION AND FUTURE WORK

We have made a corpus from research abstracts in molecular biology domain annotated with named entities classified based on a ontology of substances and sources, and the tools for tag definition, annotation and corpus management. We have annotated 2500 abstracts from MEDLINE database, and made 670 of them available to public. Since its release in July 2001, the corpus was downloaded 67 times, and TIMS workbench was downloaded 42 times[1].

We have started to annotate syntactic and co-reference information to the same set of abstracts. Using GPML DTD, the syntactic and co-reference information will be integrated to the current corpus as an attribute to *term* and *cons* elements. We plan to anntate the corpus with event structures. The future work also include the enhancement of the underlying ontology and enrichment of the tag set.

7. ACKNOWLEDGMENTS

The research is partially supported with Genome Information Science Project (MEXT, Japan) and Information Mobility Project (CREST, JST, Japan).

8. ADDITIONAL AUTHORS

Additional authors: Hideki Mima (CREST, JST, email: mima@is.s.u-tokyo.ac.jp) and Jun-ichi Tsujii (University of Tokyo and CREST, JST, email: tsujii@is.s.u-tokyo.ac.jp).

9. REFERENCES

[1] as of the end of February 2002

[1] P. G. Baker, C. A. Goble, S. Bechhofer, N. W. Paton, R. Stevens, and A. Brass. An ontology for bioinformatics applications. 15:510–520, 1999.

[2] N. Collier, H. Mima, S.-Z. Lee, T. Ohta, Y. Tateisi, A. Yakushiji, and J. ichi Tsujii. The genia project: Knowledge acquisition from biology texts. pages 448–449, 2000.

[3] N. Collier, C. Nobata, and J. Tsujii. Extracting the names of genes and gene products with a hidden markov model. In *Proceedins of COLING '2000*, pages 201–207, 2000.

[4] DARPA. The DARPA agent markup language. http://www.daml.org/.

[5] DocBook Technical Committee. http://www.oasis-open.org/docbook/.

[6] V. Giudicelli and M.-P. Lefranc. Ontology for immunogenetics: the imgt-ontology, bioinformatics. 15(12):1047–1054, 1999. http://imgt.cines.fr.

[7] P. D. Karp. An ontology for biological function based on molecular interactions. 16(3):269–285, 2000. http://www.ai.sri.com/pkarp/interactions.html.

[8] J.-D. Kim, T. Ohta, Y. Tateisi, H. Mima, and J. Tsujii. Xml-based linguistic annotation of corpus. In *Proceedins of the First NLP and XML Workshop*, pages 47–53, 2001.

[9] H. Mima, S. Ananiadou, G. Nenadic, and J. Tsujii. Xml tag information management system: A workbench for ontology-based knowledge acquisition and integration. In *Proceedins of Human Language Technology Conference (HLT 2002)*, 2002.

[10] National Library of Medicine. Medical subject headings. http://www.nlm.nih.gov/mesh/meshhome.html.

[11] Y. Ohta, T. Nishikawa, and S. Ikehara. Production system for mining in large biological dataset. In *Proceedins of 9th Internationational Conference on Intelligent Systems for Molecular Biology (ISMB 2001)*, page 64, 2001.

[12] A. Rzhetsky, T. Koike, S. Kalachikov, S. M. Gomez, M. Krauthammer, S. H. Kaplan, P. Kra, J. J. Russo, and C. Friedman. A knowledge model for analysis and simulation of regulatory networks. 16(12):1120–1128, 2000. http://genome6.cpmc.columbia.edu/ tkoike/ontology.

[13] B. Santrini. Part-of-speech tagging guidelines for the Penn Treebank project, 1991. included in Penn Treebank II CD-ROM.

[14] S. Schulze-Kremer. Ontologies for molecular biology. In *Proceedins of 3rd Pacific Symposium on Biocomputing*, pages 695–706, 1998.

[15] T. Takai-Igarashi and T. Takagi. Signal-ontology: Ontology for cell signalling. 11:440–441.

[16] Y. Tateisi, T. Ohta, N. Collier, C. Nobata, and J. ichi Tsujii. Building an annotated corpus from biology research papers. In *Proceedins of Workshop on Semantic Annotation and Intelligent Content*, pages 28–34, 2000.

[17] The Gene Ontology Consortium. Gene ontology: tool for the unification of biology. 25:25–29, 2000. http://www.geneontology.org/.

[18] The GENIA project. http://www-tsujii.is.s.u-tokyo.ac.jp/genia/.

A Knowledge-Rich Approach to Understanding Text about Aircraft Systems

Peter Clark, Lisbeth Duncan, Heather Holmback, Tom Jenkins, John Thompson
Boeing Engineering and Information Technology
Boeing, Seattle, WA 98124
{peter.e.clark,lisbeth.e.duncan,heather.holmback,thomas.l.jenkins2,john.a.thompson}@boeing.com

ABSTRACT

As part of a longer-term goal to construct an aerospace knowledge-base (KB), we are developing techniques for interpreting text about aircraft systems and then adding those interpretations to the KB. A major challenge in this task is that much of what is written builds on unstated, shared, general knowledge about aircraft, and such prior knowledge is needed to fully understand the text. To address this challenge, we are using a more general KB about aircraft to create strong, prior expectations about what might be stated in that text, then treating the language understanding task as one of incrementally extending and refining that prior knowledge. The KB constrains the possible interpretations of the text, allowing it to be placed in the appropriate context and helping identify when statements can be taken literally or need to be coerced or modified to be understood correctly. In this paper we present this approach and discuss its underlying assumptions and range of applicability. The significance of this work is twofold: It illustrates the critical role background knowledge plays in fully understanding language, and it provides a simple model for how that understanding can take place, based on the iterative refinement of a representation using information extracted from text.

1. OVERVIEW

Our long-term goal is the construction of a large-scale aerospace knowledge-base (KB), for use in tasks such as concept-based information retrieval (described in [6]) and automated question-answering about aircraft. To help construct this KB, we are developing language processing techniques to interpret text about aircraft [14, 12, 5], e.g., from existing training manuals authored in a restricted version of English or directly from an aerospace engineer. The resulting interpretation is then added to the KB.

A major challenge in this task is that much of what is written builds on unstated, shared, general knowledge about aircraft, and such prior knowledge is needed to fully understand the text. In particular, a literal translation of the text is often either highly incomplete, or worse incorrect, if no further processing is done. For example, consider:

(1) The hydraulic system supplies power to the rudder.

Proceedings of HLT 2002, Second International Conference on Human Language Technology Research, M. Marcus, ed., Morgan Kaufmann, San Francisco, 2002.

Correctly interpreting this sentence is surprisingly difficult: here the author's intent was not to assert that some supplying event is currently ongoing, but to refer to a *typical behavior* of the hydraulic system in action. Moreover, in writing this sentence, the author is appealing to some unstated, shared, general knowledge: Both the author and intended reader already know that a rudder is a powered device, that a powered system typically consists of a power source and a powered device, that the source transmits power via some conduit, etc. The author intended this sentence to build upon this knowledge, so that the reader realizes that what (1) is really describing is a *powered system* within the aircraft (as opposed to just an isolated supplying event), and hence that the many implications of this realization can be inferred. For automated language processing, this ability to interpret text as specializing, refining, and building upon background knowledge is essential for both acquiring the full meaning of text, and for determining which statements can be taken literally or need to be coerced, modified, or set in context.

To address this challenge, we are constructing and using an extensive, but fairly general, knowledge-base about aircraft, called AeroNet [5], to provide the knowledge and expectations required to properly interpret the text. The KB contains general knowledge about aircraft, but does not contain the many detailed facts about specific airplanes or their internal systems. It is this latter knowledge that we wish the system to acquire from text.

In particular, the knowledge base and its underlying inference engine allow the system to construct and incrementally refine a representation of an aircraft or an aircraft subsystem. For example, a (representation of a) specific airplane having n engines may be refined to one having two engines, to one having two jet engines, to one having two jet engines connected to the wings, etc. The mechanism for doing this is structure unification [4] (similar to order-sorted feature unification [2]), with a corresponding semantics in first-order logic. One can think of an initial, general, representation of an airplane as denoting a space of possible airplanes, and the language processing task is to incrementally refine this representation, by fitting (coercing and unifying) the processed text into that representation.

This use of domain-specific, background knowledge to form strong expectations about what might be said in text has similarities with the use of scripts and templates (e.g., [7, 8]) in language interpretation. In a similar way, scripts encode shared, unstated background knowledge, providing the context in which knowledge from text should be placed, and enabling question-answering to go beyond the facts directly stated. What is new here is the treatment of this process as incremental refinement of a representation, rather than "filling in the blanks." Rather than artificially dividing the world into 'known' and 'unknown' facts (as in a template) and then hunting for the unknown, we instead just have levels of approximation, and any part of the representation can be be refined through a process of logical unification. Similar ideas have been explored in the context of constraint logic programming [1]. This approach can also be seen as a particular implementation of the general "interpretation as abduction" framework [13], in which the abductive inferences are unifications (equality assertions) of background knowledge with knowledge from text.

2. APPROACH

2.1 Scope of the Problem

The scope of the problem we are addressing is constrained in several in important ways. First, we are processing text authored in an informally restricted sublanguage of English, rather than full natural language, mainly consisting of full, declarative sentences and without excessive syntactic complexity (authored in this way to enable ease of understanding, in particular for readers for whom English was not their native language). Second, we are working with a constrained domain (aircraft systems), which significantly reduces the scope of the target vocabulary, problems such as word ambiguity, and the amount of knowledge required up front in the AeroNet KB. Our initial work has been further constrained to the subdomain of airplane hydraulic systems, and as data we have been using text taken from three pages of a hydraulics training manual. Third, the nature of this particular application domain itself simplifies the problem: as it essentially concerns mechanical artifacts, we are primarily dealing with text describing the physical structure and behavior of mechanical artifacts, as opposed to (for example) text describing human affairs, or discussing points of view. As a result, the text we are processing uses a constrained vocabulary and is simple, regular, and (from a literary point of view) "boring" in style, and poses fewer representational challenges than might otherwise be the case. Finally we note that the background AeroNet knowledge base itself was already partially constructed from an earlier project, and is fairly large (500 concepts, 1500 axioms). We have further extended it for this work.

2.2 The Knowledge Base

The background KB, AeroNet, is encoded in the representation language KM, a frame-based representation language similar to KRL [3] and with first-order logic semantics [4]. AeroNet contains an ontology (class hierarchy) of aerospace and more general concepts, and axioms about those concepts. The majority of its axioms represent, at a general level, the possible configurations of physical objects, events, and their relationships for aircraft, aircraft components, and behaviors associated with those components. In terms of logic, they assert, for a given concept, the existence of additional objects and relationships associated with that concept (e.g., for all airplanes there will exist a fuselage which is part of that airplane). These axioms are important because they are the building blocks from which representations of a possible, specific aircraft are constructed, which in turn form the the possible targets for interpreting natural language statements (i.e., a statement is understood by identifying which of these possible aircraft configurations it is referring to).

A critical feature of the KB, for this application, is the way these axioms are physically encoded. As well as supporting normal logic axioms, KM also supports the use of *prototypes* as an alternative syntax for expressing the common "forall...exists..." axiom form. In KM, a prototype is a graph data structure describing an example of a concept, and is formed by Skolemizing the existentially quantified variables in the original axiom (thus reducing it to a set of

KM Axiom (standard form)

```
(every Airplane has
  (parts ((a Fuselage)
          (a Tail with
             (connected-to
                ((the Fuselage parts of Self))))
```

KM Axiom (prototype form)

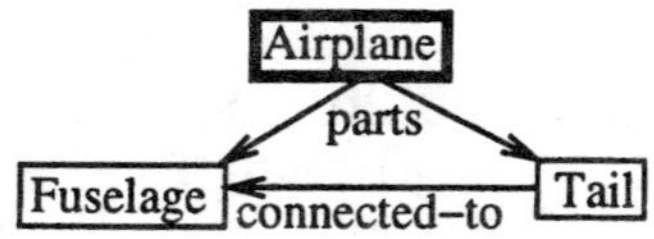

Figure 1: Axioms are converted to a prototype form, encoded using a graph data structure, to enable matching with NLP-generated graph structures. This figure shows the axiom "All airplanes have a fuselage and a tail connected to that fuselage." in both forms.

ground assertions between Skolem constants). KM's inference engine handles prototypes in a special way, by asserting that the those assertions holds for *all* instances of that concept (thus applying the same semantics as the original axiom). An illustration of these encodings is shown in Figure 1. More details are of KM's prototype mechanism are available in [4]. (Prototypes have been used in other AI languages also, e.g., in KRL [3]).

The significance of prototypes is that they form the critical bridge from logical axioms in the KB to the graph-like structures output by our NL processor. By syntactically reformulating sentence-like axioms as prototype graphs, the task of aligning text with axiom-encoded knowledge becomes one of aligning, combining, and reasoning over graphical data structures. Other work in NLP has similarly found that encoding axioms using graphical data structures is helpful for the same reasons, e.g., [16].

2.3 Overview of the Process

Before processing a unit of text, the user first manually specifies the object ("topic") the text describes (either a specific airplane or airplane system). The system then creates an initial, general representation of that airplane/airplane system using the KB (Step 1 of Figure 2).

Processing the text itself then occurs in two stages as follows:

- First, a unit of text is processed to construct an initial, literal, or sometimes underspecified, representation of the text.
- Second, the system searches for a place where this structure can "fit in" with the current representation of the airplane/airplane subsystem, and when one is found, the structure is unified at that point, hence specializing that representation.

This second stage could be described as "model-based interpretation" of text, as it treats language understanding primarily as a process of specializing, instantiating, and combining pre-existing knowledge structures, guided by the content of text. The pre-existing structures provide the reference point for interpreting the input language, allowing determination of what statements can be taken literally, and what statements need to be to be coerced, modified, or set in context.

2.4 Stage 1: Initial Interpretation and Normalization

Consider that the user has stated that the topic is the 777-200 airplane, and entered the aircraft-related sentence discussed earlier:

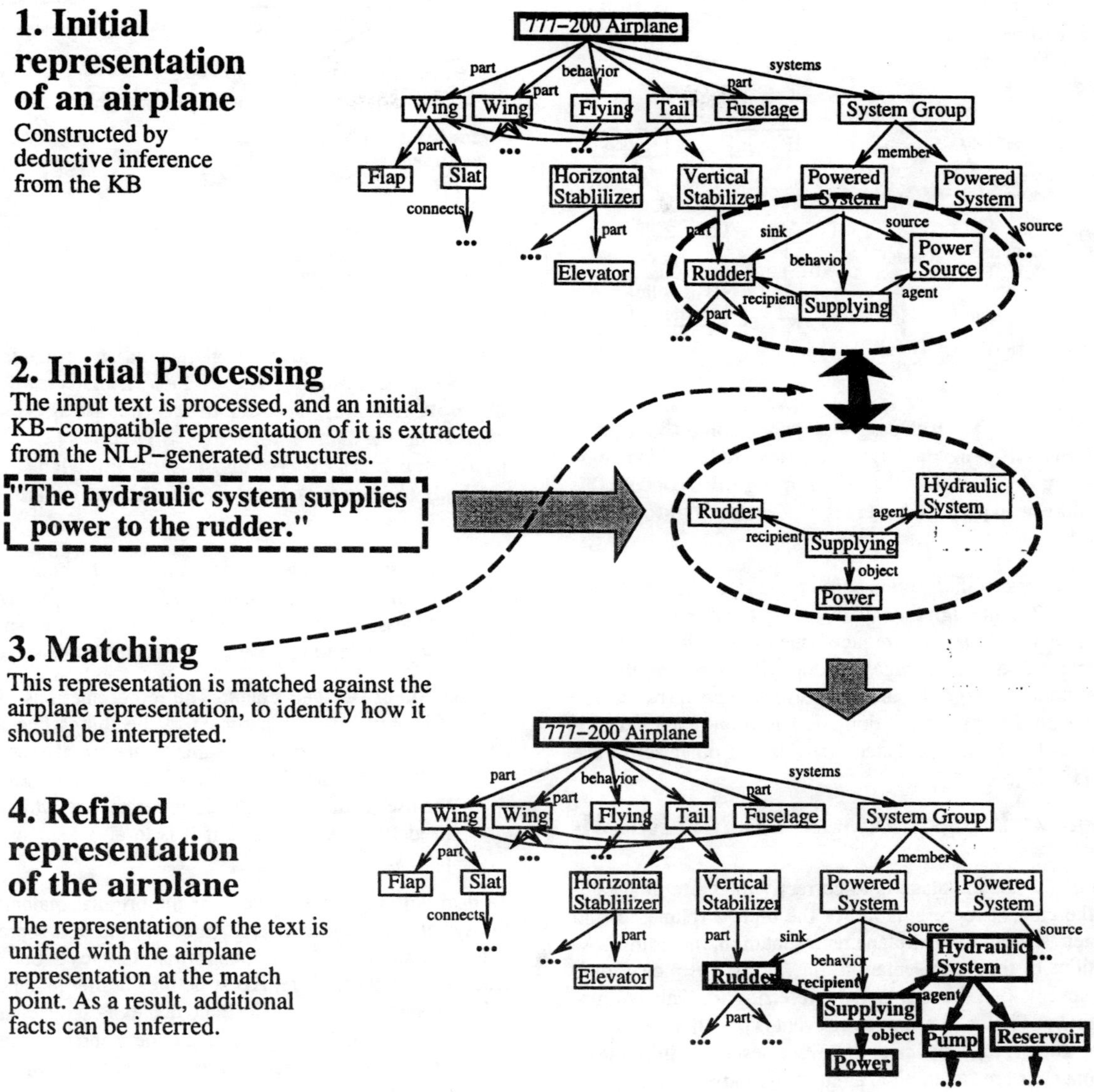

Figure 2: Text is understood by matching a KB-compatible representation of it, extracted from initial language processing, against a representation containing general expectations (derived from background knowledge). As a result, that representation is refined to absorb the new knowledge. (The graphs shown here are much simplified).

(1) The hydraulic system supplies power to the rudder.

(This sentence contains new knowledge as in general rudders can be powered in other ways also, e.g., using mechanical cables, and not all airplanes have hydraulic systems. Although these general possibilities are pre-encoded in the KB, the KB does not know which of these are realized in the 777-200 airplane. It is this knowledge which the sentence conveys and which we wish the system to acquire).

The goal of the first stage in processing is to generate an initial interpretation of this text, expressed in terms of AeroNet's ontology (Figure 3). To do this, the input text is processed using Boeing's natural language understanding system. This system uses a bottom-up chart parser interleaved with semantic interpretation, and produces a full syntactic analysis paired with a semantic analysis showing the relations between the elements of the sentence. Word senses relevant to the domain are also distinguished in this stage [15, 10, 9]. Following this, a set of simple manipulation rules are used to rewrite the relevant information from the resulting structure into a form consistent with AeroNet's pre-built ontology (Step 2 of Figure 2). These rules build a representation of events, entities, locations, properties, etc., in the input, and synthesizes information across the sentences in cases of a multi-sentence unit of text. Contrary to the other applications where we include a large degree of detailed domain inferencing in the sentence-level semantic and discourse-level interpretation phase, in this work the natural language understanding system is designed to produce a more superficial, less specific interpretation of the input text.

One issue with a "pipelined" system like this is how much disambiguation and filling in of information should be done at this stage. In this case, the system attempts to choose an overall parse/syntactic configuration, but may not be able to fill in all the semantic relationships between the constituents. For example, the system will not commit to how elements of a 3-item noun compound are grouped together, or what the semantic relations among the elements are.

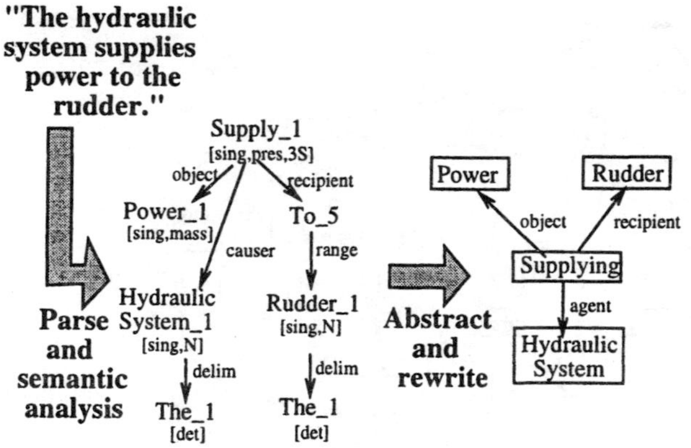

Figure 3: During the first stage of processing, the text is parsed and an NLP-generated structure (logical form) is generated. Following this, simple rewrite/renaming rules convert this structure into one expressed in terms of AeroNet's ontology.

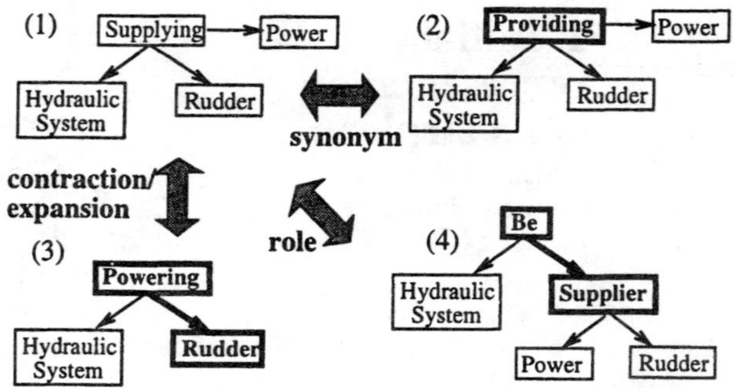

Figure 4: If the initial NLP-generated structure fails to match the KB, the system tries various transformations and reattempts matching, in order to accomodate alternative ways of expressing the same knowledge. Structures (2)-(4) show alternative structures expressing the same knowledge as in (1) (see the body of the paper for their English equivalents).

This remains underspecified at this point, to be resolved later using the KB in stage 2. Although there is of course the risk of mistakes in this stage, the risk is partially reduced due to the constrained application domain and sublanguage targetted. Furthermore, the NL system does include a large amount of information on verbs that are likely to occur in the application domain, based on many years of development to handle maintenance manuals and other aerospace documents [14, 12].

2.5 Stage 2: Integration with Existing Knowledge

The goal of the second stage is to correctly integrate this statement with the current representation of the topic airplane. To do this, the system searches the airplane representation, including possible extensions of that representation, for (in this case) candidate "supplying" events that the user may be referring to. This is illustrated in Step 3 of Figure 2. A matching event is one that is equal or more general than (i.e., subsumes) the event described in the text. If multiple matches are found, then a (currently naive) scoring system determines the best match. In addition, it will also search (and again possibly extend) the airplane representation for the objects playing roles in that event.

If a match is found, then the text representation is unified with the airplane representation at the match point, thus adding details to the airplane representation which were specified in the text. In graphical terms, unification involves maximally merging the two graphs, where two arcs can merge if they denote the same relationship, and two nodes can merge if one subsumes (is more general than) the other. In logical terms, unification involves recursively asserting equality between objects in the text representation and Skolem instances in the current airplane representation, subject to the same constraints. This is illustrated in Step 4 of Figure 2.

For this matching to succeed in this straightforward way, the structure representing the user's statement, produced in stage 1, must correspond exactly with the representational structures used in the KB. However, in practice this condition may not hold for two reasons:

Linguistic Variation: Any piece of knowledge can be expressed in language in a variety of different ways, resulting in a variety of different structures being output by the stage 1 processing, only some of which may neatly correspond to the structures in the KB. Note that although the stage 1 processing removes some of these variations by converting the input text into a more normalized form (e.g., by converting active and passive sentences into the same output structure), it is not possible to remove all variations at this stage.

Expression of Derived Facts: The representations explicit in the KB only describe a subset of the things that a user might state or refine; on top of this, there are also a large number of "derived facts" or "viewpoints" on that knowledge which the user could also potentially refine, and which the matcher needs to have access to if it is to also recognize those user inputs.

To deal with these phenomena, if the original matching fails then the system will try to *coerce* (modify) the text representation to match, by applying simple transformation rules to both the text representation and the target KB structures during matching. This enables the system to also understand text expressing the same knowledge but in alternative ways, and to understand statements concerning the wider body of facts implied by, but not explicitly stated in, the KB structures.

For linguistic variation, the matcher currently tries three types of transformations to modify the text representation, namely the replacement of concepts by near-synonym concepts, expanding verb-object contractions (and vice versa), and removing/adding explicit mention of roles. (There are also other dimensions of linguistic variation which we have not yet accounted for, which we summarize later.). As illustration, these allow the (structures corresponding to) the below sentences to be transformed into each other. In particular, the transformations (1) ↔ (2), (1) ↔ (3), and (1) ↔(4) illustrate the near-synonym, verb-object contractions, and role transformations respectively, illustrated in Figure 4:

(1) The hydraulic system supplies power to the rudder.
(2) The hydraulic system {provides/sends/transmits/gives} power to the rudder.
(3) The hydraulic system powers the rudder.
(4) The hydraulic system is the {supplier/provider} of power for the rudder.

By applying these transformations, alternative structures denoting the user's input are derived and matched with the KB if the original structure fails to match. Note that none of the (structures corresponding to) these sentences is considered to be the "canonical representation" of the input text; rather, the transformations allow these alternative structures to also be tried when searching for a match in the KB. This is important, as the structure of the corresponding knowledge in the KB itself depends on domain-specific design decisions made when building the KB, may vary depending on the particular concepts involved, and may change if the KB itself is later redesigned to change those design decisions. It also allows the stage 1 NLP system to defer application-dependent decisions about (for example) which words are synonyms, and thus remain general-purpose (as opposed to it "hard wiring" those decisions into it, which would make it highly domain-specific).

Concerning derived facts, the matcher needs to account for user statements which may refer to an *implication* of knowledge in the KB, rather than just to knowledge explicitly represented in (i.e., as subgraphs of) the KB prototypes. To do this, it needs to match against an extended version of the KB, extended to contain those implications. This extended KB is not generated in its entirity (it would be impractical to do so); rather it is a "virtual KB" giving the appearance of being there to the matcher, while in practice parts are generated on demand. To generate these extensions, we are currently using just three general rules, although clearly more are needed:

1. "Causal transitivity": If X is the agent in event E, then add a representation of X as the agent in all the causally downstream events of E.
2. "Object as instrument": If X does E to Y, causing Y to do E' to Z, then add a representation of Y as the instrument in X doing E' to Z.
3. "System for system part": If X does E, and X is a part of system Y, then add a representation of Y as doing E.

As a (simplified) example of the first two rules being applied, consider Figure 5. If the KB explicitly contains a representation of the causal chain (for a cable-driven rudder control system's behavior):

(5) The pilot presses a foot pedal.
(6) The foot pedal pulls a cable.
(7) The cable moves the rudder.

Then the virtual KB will also contain representations of:

(8) The pilot moves the rudder using the foot pedal.
(9) The pilot moves the rudder using a cable.
(10)The pilot pulls a cable using the foot pedal.
(11) The foot pedal moves the rudder using a cable.

As a result, the user's statement is matched against all these target structures, thus accommodating statements which refine implicit as well as explicit information in the KB. Some of these derived representations are abstractions of knowledge in the KB, while some are alternative viewpoints on the knowledge in the KB. Also, in a few cases, the derived representation can violate KB constraints, i.e., do not make sense when taken literally (e.g., "The pilot consumes fuel," from "The pilot operates the engines." and "the engines consume fuel."). Rather than discard these, they can be viewed as KB-generated metonymous representations (i.e., where an object stands in place of a closely related object), and used to recognize and correctly interpret similar uses of metonymy in the input text. In this case, the inference rules are playing the role of metonymic transformation rules (similar to those used by Fass [11]).

Returning to the running example (1), as AeroNet already knows that airplanes (in general) contain rudders and some powered system must drive them, the search will find the supplying event that is the behavior of that powered system. As this matches (subsumes) the input text, the text representation is unified with this supplying event, resulting in the rudder's power source being refined to be

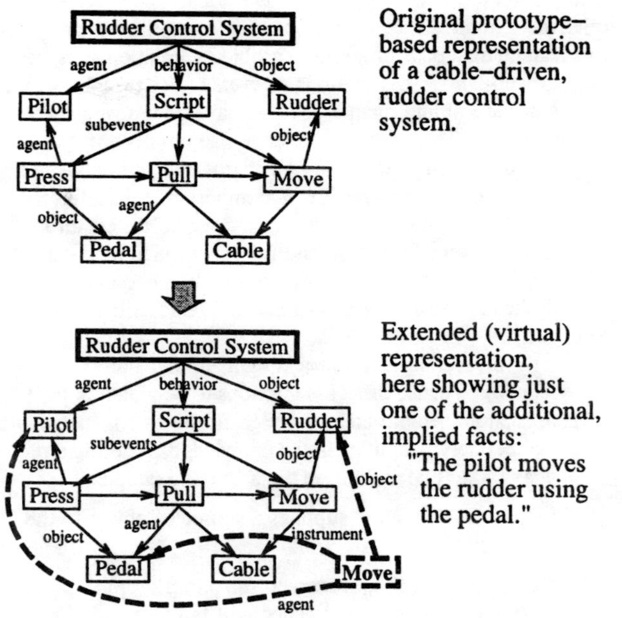

Figure 5: To handle statements referring to facts not explicit in the original representation, the matcher matches against a (virtual) extended version of the representation, extended to also include implied facts.

a hydraulic system. From here, now that the system knows a hydraulic system is in the airplane, additional facts can be inferred (i.e., the graph grown further) using knowledge about hydraulic systems in the KB. This is illustrated in Step 4 of Figure 2.

The significance of this stage 2 processing is that, rather than simply (and erroneously) assert the existence of this supplying event, the system has determined the appropriate context in which that statement belongs, and added it at that point. As a result, a fuller meaning of the text (namely that it is implicitly describing part of the characteristic behavior of rudder's power system) has been acquired by the system, even though that extra information has not been explicitly stated in the text.

3. STATUS AND DISCUSSION

While the stage 1 NL processor is mature and operates on a broad range input language, and the AeroNet KB is also large (500 concepts, 1500 axioms), our work on their integration is still preliminary and we have only achieved full start-to-end throughput on a small number of sentences. Part of the reason for this is simply the implementation not keeping up with the theory, but part of it is due to more fundamental challenges of text understanding which our approach cannot currently handle. In this section, we attempt to distinguish these two aspects by characterizing the scope of the presented approach, and cases where it breaks down.

Our approach relies on several mechanisms and assumptions. First, it relies on the KB creating strong expectations about what knowledge might be expressed, and on the text's author conforming to those expectations. In addition, it relies on the language processing and matching processes to tolerate variations in how that knowledge might be expressed. For the matching process to work, the structure of the processed language (the output of stage 1) must be correct and reasonably close to the structures in the KB, and the sentences need sufficient detail to avoid excessive ambiguity when matching with the KB. To meet these requirements, the input sentences need to be fairly context-independent, accurate, and have a relatively simple structure, for example containing short, declarative statements about properties of objects, relationships between objects, and simple descriptions of events. (The majority of sentences in the training manual text we have been using meet these requirements). The primary challenge has not been in the stage 1 language processing itself, but in bridging the gap between its result and the structures in the KB. An important contribution of this work has been allowing a wider gap to be tolerated through the application of transformation and inference rules in stage 2 (e.g., allowing some types of metonymy to be identified and corrected), but still the gap must not be too great for the described approach to be effective.

There are several phenomena (linguistic and otherwise) which can occur which cause these assumptions to be violated, including:

1. Inaccurate/simplified knowledge. If the user is inaccurate or deliberately simplifies in the knowledge, resulting structures may fail to match those in the KB. For example,

   (12) The pump supplies a source of power to the rudder.

   is, strictly speaking, incorrect (the pump supplies power, not a source of power), and hence will fail to match knowledge in the KB, even using transformations. While here the author may simply have been "sloppy" accidentally, in other cases he/she may deliberately make technically inaccurate statements so as to simplify for pedagogical purposes.
2. Fluctuating ("fuzzy") concept boundaries. Sometimes the precise boundaries of a concept may subtly vary in text. For example, does the "hydraulic system" include its controlled devices (e.g., the rudder) or not? Some text treats the answer as yes, other text as no, in contrast to the KB which has a single, precise answer to this question, and cannot cope if the user deviates from that. Strictly, the user's variations correspond to (subtly) different senses of the phrase "hydraulic system", but it is unrealistic to treat them as a (potentially large) number of different word senses to be disambiguated.
3. Ambiguities which are not locally resolvable. Although the KB significantly restricts ways in which the input text will be understood, there still may be ambiguity (i.e., multiple matches with the KB). For example, in

   (13) The EDP is on the right side of the airplane's engine.

   the reader understands "the airplane's engine" as "the airplane's propulsion engine," although to the matcher it is ambiguous (there are other engines in an airplane besides its propulsion engines). In these cases, the author is additionally relying on context and unstated communication protocol to identify the preferred match, which we have not accounted for.
4. Complex sentence structure. We assume that the organization of constituents of the input sentences will be correctly determined by the stage 1 processing. However this becomes harder to achieve as sentences get longer and more ambiguous. A (rather extreme) example is:

   (14) The RAT blade lock pin behind the turbine locks the turbine blades in a vertical position when the RAT is more than 9 degrees from the extended position.

   As sentences become more complex, it becomes harder for the stage 1 NL system to build a complete semantic representation with all the information packaged so that it can be used easily by the KB.
5. Other linguistic variations. Although the NLP processor will normalize many verb alternations to a common structure, and the transformation rules account for some additional linguistic variations in expressing knowledge, there are still variations which have not been covered, and hence will not be interpreted by the system.

An additional challenge occurs when multiple transformations of the text and KB are required to achieve a match, and this has been the main obstacle to processing multi-sentence input. The challenge here is not so much in generating a single, integrated structure representing the multi-sentence text (which the stage 1 NL processor can do effectively), but in then matching that structure against the KB. While small sentence-based structures can be feasibly transformed to achieve a match, the task becomes highly complex with paragraph-equivalent sized structures. To deal with longer text units, better interleaving of the stage 1 and stage 2 processing is clearly desirable.

4. SUMMARY AND CONCLUSION

We have presented an approach to understanding text about aircraft systems, based on using a KB to create strong, prior expectations about what might be stated in that text, and on treating the language understanding task as one of incrementally refining an airplane representation build using this prior knowledge. The KB constrains the possible interpretations of the text, allowing it to be placed in the appropriate context and helping identify when statements can be taken literally or need to be coerced or modified to be understood correctly. We have also described the assumptions on which this approach is based and which determine its range of applicability.

As a practical means of extending a knowledge-base, it is worth reiterating several factors that simplify the task and make it more feasible: we are working with training manuals, whose language is deliberately simplified (as opposed to technical maintenance manuals, whose language can be more complex); the stage one NLP system has been developed and used to process manuals (for other purposes) for several years; the domain is constrained; and we are not attempting to extract every item of information from the text – rather, the system will simply ignore text that does not match any expectations in the airplane model being constructed, and hence we are not dependent on fully understanding the entire text in order to acquire at least some knowledge using this method (the system will extract what it can, and simply ignore the rest). As an additional benefit, this method opens the possibility of knowledge entry directly from an engineer using a controlled language interface, which we are also exploring, rather than requiring him/her to learn and work with the underlying knowledge representation language.

One of the most difficult challenges has been determining the relationship between the "stage 1" and "stage 2" processing steps, and how much decision-making (e.g., word sense disambiguation, normalization of the logical forms) should be performed during initial, KB-independent text processing (stage 1), and how much with reference to the KB (stage 2). Too much, and the system may make premature and erroneous commitments up front; too little and there may not be enough structure identified for the knowledge-rich processing to operate. In practice, we have deliberately chosen not to exploit the full power of the stage 1 NL processor, instead delaying some decisions (e.g., normalizing the earlier variants (2), (3) and (4)) to the second processing stage, thus avoiding redundantly hard-wiring the required knowledge in the stage 1 lexicon and normalization rules. Similarly, there is clearly scope for the KB to provide additional guidance during the initial processing. These issues are critical for any knowledge-based NLP approach to address.

Although subject to a number of constraints, the approach suggests how a strong interplay between language processing and background knowledge can be achieved. The significance of this work is twofold: it illustrates the critical role background knowledge plays in fully understanding language, and provides a simple model for how that understanding can take place, based on the iterative refinement of a representation using information extracted from text.

4.1 Acknowledgements

Many thanks to Ken Barker and Gary Coen for valuable feedback on earlier versions of this paper.

5. REFERENCES

[1] H. Ait-Kaci and A. Podelski. Towards a meaning of LIFE. *Logic Programming*, 16:195–234, 1993. (also available as http://www.isg.sfu.ca/ftp/pub/hak/prl/PRL-RR-11.ps.Z).

[2] H. Ait-Kaci, A. Podelski, and S. C. Goldstein. Order-sorted feature theory unification. In D. Miller, editor, *Proc. Int. Symp. on Logic Programming*, pages 506–524. MIT, 1993.

[3] D. Bobrow and T. Winograd. An overview of KRL, a knowledge representation language. In R. Brachman and H. Levesque, editors, *Readings in Knowledge Representation*, pages 264–285. Kaufmann, CA, 1985. (originally in Cognitive Science 1 (1), 1977, 3–46).

[4] P. Clark and B. Porter. KM – the knowledge machine: Users manual. Technical report, AI Lab, Univ Texas at Austin, 1999. (http://www.cs.utexas.edu/users/mfkb/km.html).

[5] P. Clark, J. Thompson, H. Holmback, and L. Duncan. AeroNet: Building the aeronet knowledge base. Technical report, Boeing Mathematics and Computing Technology, Seattle, WA, 2000.

[6] P. Clark, J. Thompson, H. Holmback, and L. Duncan. Exploiting a thesaurus-based semantic net for knowledge-based search. In *IAAI-2000*. AAAI Press, 2000. (http://www.rt.cs.boeing.com/~clarkp/papers/iaai00.ps.Z).

[7] R. E. Cullingford. Controlling inference in story understanding. In *IJCAI-77*, page 17, 1977.

[8] G. DeJong. Prediction and substantiation: two processes that comprise understanding. In *IJCAI-79*, pages 217–222, 1979.

[9] L. Duncan, W. Brown, C. Esposito, H. Holmback, and P. Xue. Enhancing virtual maintenance environments with speech understanding. Technical Report TECHNET-9903, Boeing Mathematics and Computing Technology, 1999.

[10] L. Duncan, P. Harrison, H. Holmback, T. Jenkins, A. Kao, S. Miller, S. Poteet, and J. Powell. Message processing and data extraction for the real time information management system (RTIMS) project. Tech Report BCSTECH-94-057, Boeing Computer Services, 1994.

[11] D. Fass. met*: A method for discriminating metonymy and metaphor by computer. *Computational Linguistics*, 1(17):49–90, 1991.

[12] J. Hoard, R. Wojcik, and K. Holzhauser. An automated grammar and style checker for writers of simplified english. In P. Holt and N. Williams, editors, *Computers and Writing: State of the Art*, pages 278–296, Oxford, England, 1992. Intellect.

[13] J. Hobbs, M. Stickel, D. Appelt, and P. Martin. Interpretation as abduction. *Artificial Intelligence*, 63(1–2):69–142, 1993.

[14] H. Holmback, L. Duncan, and P. Harrison. A word sense checking application for simplified english. In *Third International Workshop on Controlled Language Applications*, 2000.

[15] T. A. Nicolino. A natural language processing based situation display. In *Proc. 1994 Symposium on Command and Control Research and Decision Aids*, pages 575–580, Naval Postgraduate School, Monterey, CA, 1994.

[16] J. F. Sowa. *Conceptual structures: Information processing in mind and machine*. Addison Wesley, 1984.

Can We Derive General World Knowledge from Texts?

Lenhart Schubert
University of Rochester
Rochester, NY 14627-0226
schubert@cs.rochester.edu

ABSTRACT

As one attack on the "knowledge acquisition bottleneck", we are attempting to exploit a largely untapped source of general knowledge in texts, lying at a level beneath the explicit assertional content. This knowledge consists of relationships implied to be possible in the world, or, under certain conditions, implied to be normal or commonplace in the world. The goal of the work reported is to derive such general world knowledge (initially, from Penn Treebank corpora) in two stages: first, we derive general "possibilistic" propositions from noun phrases and clauses; then we try to derive stronger generalizations, based on the nature and statistical distribution of the possibilistic claims obtained in the first phase. Here we report preliminary results of the first phase, which indicate the feasibility of our project, and its likely limitations.

1. INTRODUCTION

We think that there is a largely untapped source of general knowledge in texts, lying at a level beneath the explicit assertional content. This knowledge consists of relationships implied to be possible in the world, or, under certain conditions, implied to be normal or commonplace in the world. For instance, the sentence "*He entered the house through its open door*" suggests that it is possible for a person (or at least a male) to enter a house, that houses have doors, that doors can be open, etc. The goal of the present work is to derive such general world knowledge (initially, from Penn Treebank corpora) in two stages: first, we derive general "possibilistic" propositions from noun phrases and clauses; then we try to derive stronger generalizations, based on the nature and statistical distribution of the possibilistic claims obtained in the first phase.

A feature that our initiative shares with standard knowledge extraction work is its scalability and lack of dependence on deep semantic processing. However, it is distinctive in both its aims and its methodology. We are attempting to derive a broad range of general relationships from texts, rather than some predetermined specific kinds of facts; and we are using general phrase structure coupled with compositional interpretive rules to obtain general propositional information, rather than employing specialized extraction patterns targeted at specific relationships (e.g., [1, 2, 3, 6, 8, 14,19]) Our long-range goal is to use the derived knowledge as part of a KB supporting language understanding and commonsense reasoning.

We have reached a stage in our work where we are able to extract large numbers of general propositions from Treebank corpora, and can assess, in a very preliminary and informal way, the prospects for arriving at useful world knowledge by this method, and the limitations of the approach. In the following, we briefly sketch and assess our two-stage technique (with emphasis on the first, implemented stage).

Proceedings of HLT 2002, Second International Conference on Human Language Technology Research, M. Marcus, ed., Morgan Kaufmann, San Francisco, 2002.

2. EXTRACTING GENERAL "POSSIBILISTIC" PROPOSITIONS

The derivation of possibilistic propositions is based on a mechanism very similar to compositional semantic interpretation. The essential difference is that before combining the meanings of the immediate constituents of a phrase, we *abstract* those meanings, i.e., we simplify and generalize them; this involves stripping modifiers and inessential conjuncts, and generalizing individual terms (including named entities) to types. For example (using English glosses of the logical representations), abstraction of "*a long, dark corridor*" would yield "*a corridor*"; "*a small office at the end of a long dark corridor*" would yield "*an office*"; and "*Mrs. MacReady*" would yield "*a woman*". It is this process of abstraction, together with a weakening of the relations involved to a possibilistic form, that often yields general presumptions about the world, underlying the assertions made. At the same time, the fact that modifiers, conjuncts and specific meanings of definite descriptions are allowed to fall by the wayside as the interpretation of a sentence proceeds from lower-level to higher-level constituents greatly simplifies the interpretive process, in comparison with systems that attempt full understanding. Moreover, proposition extraction at lower and higher levels is relatively independent: interpretive failure at a lower level (e.g., for an "inessential" phrase, such as an adverbial) need not prevent proposition extraction from disjoint or higher-level phrases; and conversely, interpretive failure at a higher level leaves intact the propositions extracted from lower levels.

The choice of Treebank corpora as a basis for our initial knowledge extraction work is a natural one, since there exist robust, fairly accurate parsers trained on Treebank corpora (e.g., [7, 10, 9]), and these would eventually allow us to bootstrap our approach to very large unannotated corpora. The major challenge was that of providing reasonably reliable interpretive rules, at least for many of the clausal and other phrasal units that we viewed as potential sources of general possibilistic knowledge. In outline, our current algorithms for processing a bracketed (Treebank) sentence operate as follows:

1. Preprocess the input tree (e.g., mark infinitives, passives, temporal noun phrases and prepositional phrases, categorize prepositional phrases, etc.)
2. Apply a set of ordered patterns to the tree recursively; these amount to phrase structure rules allowing for regular expressions (including negation) on the right-hand side
3. For each successfully matched subtree, abstract the interpretations of the essential constituents, and combine the abstracted interpretations in accord with the semantic rule linked to the pattern that matched the subtree
4. In processing the tree recursively, collect interpretations of phrases expected to provide general "possibilistic" propositions
5. Formulate possibilistic propositions from the collected phrasal interpretations, and output these along with simple English verbalizations.

The following is a simple example of a phrase structure pattern and associated semantic rule that could be used for a verb phrase in step 3:

(VP ((* ADVP (ADV) (PP)) ((V)) (NP) (S-INF) (*)))
(:f 1 (:p 2 3 4))

"Starred" constituents may occur 0 or more times. An example of a phrase from the Brown corpus matched (after preprocessing) by the phrase structure pattern is *"asked Kitti to join him"*. The :f and :p in the semantic rule specify function and predicate application, and the digits are indices for the (abstracted) interpretations of the corresponding pattern constituents. (The possible rightmost, i.e., 5th, constituent or sequence of constituents is ignored by the semantic rule.) The semantic output for the phrase under consideration would be

(:p ASK[V] (:q DET FEMALE-INDIVIDUAL)
(:f KA (:p JOIN[V] (:q DET MALE-INDIVIDUAL)))),

whose gloss is *"ask a female individual to join a male individual"*. (The :q indicates an unscoped quantifier, here the generic DET quantifier.)

An example of a complete and unedited output for a sentence from the Brown corpus is the following:

```
INPUT:

 ((S
   (S
     (NP (NNP Blanche) )
     (VP (VBD knew)
       (SBAR (\-NONE\- \0)
         (S
           (NP (NN something) )
           (AUX (MD must) )
           (VP (VB be)
             (VP (VBG causing)
               (NP
                 (NP (NNP Stanley) )
                 (POS \'s) (JJ new)
                 (\, \,)
                 (JJ strange) (NN behavior) )))))))
   (CC but)
   (S
     (NP (PRP she) )
     (ADVP (RB never) )
     (ADVP (RB once) )
     (VP (VBD connected)
       (NP (PRP it) )
       (PP (IN with)
         (NP (NNP Kitti) (NNP Walker) )))))
 (\. \.) )

OUTPUT:

WORDS OF THE INPUT:

(BLANCHE KNEW 0 SOMETHING MUST BE CAUSING STANLEY 'S NEW ,
 STRANGE BEHAVIOR BUT SHE NEVER ONCE CONNECTED IT WITH
 KITTI WALKER .)

OUTPUT (IN ENGLISH, FOLLOWED BY UNDERLYING LOGICAL FORMS):

 A FEMALE-INDIVIDUAL MAY KNOW A PROPOSITION.
 SOMETHING MAY CAUSE A BEHAVIOR.
 A MALE-INDIVIDUAL MAY HAVE A BEHAVIOR.
 A BEHAVIOR CAN BE NEW.
 A BEHAVIOR CAN BE STRANGE.
 A FEMALE-INDIVIDUAL MAY CONNECT A THING-REFERRED-TO WITH
   A FEMALE-INDIVIDUAL.

((:I (:Q DET FEMALE-INDIVIDUAL) KNOW[V] (:Q DET PROPOS))
 (:I (:F K SOMETHING[N]) CAUSE[V] (:Q THE BEHAVIOR[N]))
 (:I (:Q DET MALE-INDIVIDUAL) HAVE[V] (:Q DET BEHAVIOR[N]))
 (:I (:Q DET BEHAVIOR[N]) NEW[A])
 (:I (:Q DET BEHAVIOR[N]) STRANGE[A])
 (:I (:Q DET FEMALE-INDIVIDUAL) CONNECT[V]
     (:Q DET THING-REFERRED-TO)
     (:P WITH[P] (:Q DET FEMALE-INDIVIDUAL))))
```

In the logical forms, the :I indicates an infix formula, consisting of a subject, predicate, and possible additional arguments. Our logical forms are based on episodic logic [20], a natural logic that facilitates the transduction from language to logic and *vice versa*. As a second example, the following was obtained for a sentence of the Wallstreet Journal Corpus. (The input tree is omitted.)

```
(REP . RONNIE FLIPPO ( D . , ALA . ) , ONE OF THE MEMBERS
 OF THE DELEGATION , SAYS 0 HE WAS PARTICULARLY IMPRESSED
 *-1 BY MR . KRENZ 'S READY ADMISSION THAT EAST GERMANY
 NEEDED *-2 TO CHANGE .)

 AN ELECTED-REPRESENTATIVE MAY SAY A PROPOSITION.
 A DELEGATION MAY HAVE MEMBERS.
 A MALE-INDIVIDUAL MAY BE IMPRESS -ED BY AN ADMISSION.
 AN ADMISSION CAN BE READY.
 A COUNTRY MAY NEED TO CHANGE.

((:I (:Q DET ELECTED-REPRESENTATIVE) SAY[V] (:Q DET PROPOS))
 (:I (:Q DET DELEGATION[N]) HAVE[V]
     (:Q DET (:F PLUR MEMBER[N])))
 (:I (:Q DET MALE-INDIVIDUAL) (:F BE[PASV] IMPRESS[V])
     (:P BY[P] (:Q DET ADMISSION[N])))
 (:I (:Q DET ADMISSION[N]) READY[A])
 (:I (:Q DET COUNTRY) NEED[V] (:F KA CHANGE[V])))
```

These outputs (which are not atypical, quantitatively and qualitatively, for what we obtain for sentences from the Brown corpus or Wall Street Journal corpus) illustrates both the potential of our approach and some of the difficulties still to be overcome. Some of the propositions are arguably general knowledge that any human being is well-aware of, and which could be useful in a general NLU or commonsense reasoning system. For instance, the claims about who may say or know a proposition, about delegations having members, and about being impressed by an admission fall into this category.

On the other hand, a problem with our extracted propositions is that their content is often unclear or ambiguous (as in the case of *"An admission can be ready"*, which intuitively allows for multiple senses of *"admission"* and *"ready"*), or they are true but arbitrary (e.g., the last of the extracted propositions for the Brown sentence certainly seems true enough, but completely arbitrary – not something likely to be useful for language processing or inference). Fortunately, outright falsehoods among the outputs are very rare. We are currently working out a judging scheme that will allow an empirical evaluation of the first-stage output, assessing the coherence, clarity/nonambiguity, nonarbitrariness, and truth of the output propositions, as determined subjectively by human judges (with sufficient consistency across judges). At the same time, we are considering various methods for improving the output, including use of WordNet [11] for type abstraction, better event-noun identification/classification, use of Treebank-3 information on argument roles, and most importantly, use of a coreference module to guess entity types for pronouns. We are also considering methods of filtering out unwanted output, e.g., discarding propositions as arbitrary if they are derived only once from a large corpus, even after certain abstraction operations.

3. THE SECOND STAGE: DERIVING STRONGER PROPOSITIONS

We have formulated several (as yet unimplemented) methods for strengthening some of the extracted propositions based on the types of symbols comprising them and on the occurrence statistics of related propositions. For example, we frequently extract certain simple variants of the first output proposition above, such as "A MALE-INDIVIDUAL MAY KNOW A PROPOSITION". From such sets of variants we expect to be able to infer that (by and large) *only* people or agencies know propositions. Similarly, preliminary examination of the Brown corpus indicates that we should be able to derive such generalities as (for transitive verb "*carry*"): if x carries y, then if y is a gun, then x is probably a person; if y is a bomb, then x is probably an airplane;[1] if y is a group of people, then x is probably a vehicle; etc. This sort of information is closely related to traditional *selectional preferences* (e.g., [5, 13, 16, 17, 21, 22]), but it is explicitly formulated as propositional knowledge by our methods and hence potentially usable not only for linguistic disambiguation but also for inference. Furthermore, extant methods for extracting selectional preferences from texts tend to "lose the connection" between the arguments of 2- or 3-place predicates (if they attempt to correlate multiple arguments at all). This is because of the myriad argument types that can occur (e.g., carriers found in Brown include persons, vehicles, [business] expansion, books, ants, positions, stories, roads, calculations, etc., and objects carried include [body]weight, passports, the economy, disclaimers, titles, responsibilities, traffic, rigging, etc.)

Our other planned methods of deriving stronger propositions depend on details of the propositions obtained in the first stage. For example, certain propositions involving possessive HAVE[V], such as "A FEMALE-INDIVIDUAL MAY HAVE AN ARM", derived from possessive NPs such as "*her arm*" can be directly and fairly safely strengthened to something like "A FEMALE-INDIVIDUAL GENERALLY HAS AN ARM" under certain conditions, for instance when the thing possessed is a part-type, or (less safely) when there is no possible prior coreferent for it.

4. CONCLUDING REMARKS

We have described a new method of obtaining general world knowledge from texts that is aimed at a broader range of facts than methods based on specialized extraction patterns, while still not depending on in-depth NLU.

It is of interest to compare the kinds of information obtainable by our method with the kinds obtained by specialized techniques. In essence, we obtain less specific information, but much more of it. For example, consider Berland and Charniak's techniques for extracting part-whole relations from text corpora [6]. Their extraction patterns relied primarily on genitives (such as "*the school's gymnasium*") and *of*-adjuncts (as in "*the basement of the building*"), and these are precisely the constructs from which we obtain propositions like the one mentioned above, that "*a female individual may have an arm*". However, note that at least in our first-stage processing we do not attempt to particularize HAVE to HAVE-AS-PART. Thus, from the phrase "*her sister*" we would derive the claim that "*a female individual may have a sister*", and as long as we interpret HAVE broadly, this is correct – whereas such an example is problematic if we are interested exclusively in part-whole relations. As indicated above, we intend in the second stage to appeal to occurrence statistics as well as certain kinds of lexical semantic information in deciding whether and how to strengthen first-stage propositions. At that point our output propositions may more nearly match those obtainable by specialized techniques; but to some extent we will continue to trade off specificity for breadth and generality.

Similar comments apply in relation to Girju and Moldovan's very interesting recent work on identifying sentences that express causal relationships [12]. Their targets were primarily sentences of form *NP1 causation-verb NP2*, e.g., "*Earthquakes cause tidal waves*", or "*The assassination led to World War I*" (though they also provide a quite comprehensive discussion of other relevant constructions). Again, our approach would succeed in extracting general propositions from such sentences (assuming we can parse them correctly), but would not, as it stands, explicitly distinguish a causal claims like AN ASSASSINATION MAY LEAD TO WAR from a non-causal one like A TRAIL MAY LEAD TO A LAKE. Girju and Moldovan make use of lexical information, such as that an assassination (unlike a trail) is a human action, to sort out causal from non-causal sentences. This is a prime concern for them, since their motivation for causal sentence identification is to enable text-based question-answering for causal questions such as "*What were the causes of World War I?*". For us, a more immediate concern is the extraction general presumptions, in an explicit logical form, from specific (factual or fictitious) texts, with maximally broad coverage of the relationships encounterd. However, we would expect to use Girju and Moldovan's type of lexical semantic information in deploying our extracted propositions for inference.

One extant system for more general knowledge acquisition from text is MindNet [18]. However, the goal of this system is not the inference of general propositions from specific texts, but rather the direct interpretation of the contents of MRDs such as the *American Heritage Dictionary, 3rd Edition*. As such, it is reported to achieve full coverage, though the available descriptions of its design, capabilities and limitations are somewhat sketchy. In any case, it would certainly be desirable to merge lexicon-derived knowledge with knowledge inferred from texts, since the types of information obtainable by these methods are quite distinct. (A glance at our sample ouput indicates that few of our derived propositions are of the sort found in lexicons.)

As we have indicated, there are some similarities between our derived propositions and the information implicit in selectional preferences. Efforts to extract predicate-argument structure are also related (e.g., Abney's method based on a cascaded finite-state parser [4][2]). However, the attempt to formulate and evaluate the derived information as general propositions about the world is to our knowledge novel.

The quest for general world knowledge also brings to mind CYC [15], but as in the case of MindNet we regard that work as complementary rather than an alternative. Little of the knowledge we are extracting can be found in CYC; and little of the knowledge in CYC is obtainable by our methods. An impediment to merging the two kinds of knowledge, however, is that CYC's invented (and rather heterogeneous) ontology is not easily brought into alignment with linguistically derived knowledge.

[1] For more extensive or recent texts, x may with some likelihood be a person.

[2] Our experimentation on some Brown corpus sentences suggests that this approach yields very sparse information – for many sentences, no more than a subject-verb relation, because of the parser's very conservative phrase attachment policy.

Acknowledgements

This work was supported by the National Science Foundation under grant IIS-0082928, and greatly benefited from discussions with David Ahn, Greg Carlson, Aaron Kaplan, and Henry Kyburg.

5. REFERENCES

[1] *Proc. of the 5th Message Understanding Conference (MUC-5).* Morgan Kaufmann, Los Altos, CA, 1993.

[2] *Proc. of the 6th Message Understanding Conference (MUC-6).* Morgan Kaufmann, Los Altos, CA, 1995.

[3] *Proc. of the 7th Message Understanding Conference (MUC-7).* Morgan Kaufmann, Los Altos, CA, April 29 – May 1, Virginia 1998.

[4] S. Abney. Partial parsing via finite-state cascades. In *Proceedings of the ESSLLI '96 Robust Parsing Workshop.* 1996.

[5] E. Agirre and D. Martinez. Learning class-to-class selectional preferences. In *Proc. of the 5th Workshop on Computational Language Learning (CoNLL-2001),* Toulouse, France, July 6-7, 2001.

[6] M. Berland and E. Charniak. Finding parts in very large corpora. In *Proc. of the 37th Ann. Meet. of the Assoc. for Computational Linguistics (ACL-99),* Univ. of Maryland, June 22 - 27, 1999.

[7] E. Charniak. A maximum-entropy-inspired parser. In *Proc. of the 1st Meet. of the North Am. Chapt. of the Assoc. for Computational Linguistics (NACL-2000),* pages 132–139, Seattle, WA, April 29 - May 4, 2000.

[8] S. Clark and D. Weir. An iterative approach to estimating frequencies over a semantic hierarchy. In *Proc. of the Joint SIGDAT Conference on Empirical Methods in Natural Language Processing and Very Large Corpora,* 1999. Also available at http://www.cogs.susx.ac.uk/users/davidw/research/papers.html.

[9] M. J. Collins. Three generative, lexicalised models for statistical parsing. In *Proc. of the 35th Ann. Meet. of the Assoc. for Computational Linguistics (ACL-97) and 8th Conf. of the Eur. Chapter of the Assoc. for Computational Linguistics (EACL-97),* pages 16–23, 1997.

[10] M. J. Collins. Discriminative reranking for natural language parsing. In *Proc. of the 7th Int. Conf. on Machine Learning (ICML-2000),* 2000.

[11] C. Fellbaum, editor. *WordNet: An Electronic Lexical Database.* MIT Press, 1998.

[12] R. Girju and D. I. Moldovan. Text mining for causal relations. In *FLAIRS 2002,* 2002.

[13] R. Grishman and J. Sterling. Acquisition of selectional patterns. In *Proc. of COLING-92,* pages 658–664, Nantes, France, 1992.

[14] M. A. Hearst. Automated discovery of WordNet relations. In C. Fellbaum, editor, *WordNet: An Electronic Lexical Database,* pages 131–153? MIT Press, 1998.

[15] D. Lenat. CYC: A large-scale investment in knowledge infrastructure. *Comm. of the ACM,* 38(11):33–38, 1995.

[16] P. Resnik. A class-based approach to lexical discovery. In *Proc. of the 30th Ann. Meet. of the Assoc. for Computational Linguistics (ACL-92),* pages 327–329, Newark, DE, 1992.

[17] P. Resnik. Semantic classes and syntactic ambiguity. In *Proc. of ARPA Workshop on Human Language Technology,* Plainsboro, NJ, 1993.

[18] S. D. Richardson, W. B. Dolan, and L. Vanderwende. MindNet: acquiring and structuring semantic information from text. In *Proc. of the 36th Ann. Meet. of the Assoc. for Computational Linguistics and the 17th Int. Conf. on Computational Linguistics (COLING-ACL'98), vol. II,* volume 2, pages 1098–1102, Montreal, Canada, Aug. 10-14, 1998.

[19] E. Riloff and R. Jones. Learning dictionaries for information extraction by multi-level bootstrapping. In *Proc. of the 16th Nat. Conf. on Artificial Intelligence (AAAI-99),* 1999.

[20] L. K. Schubert and C. H. Hwang. Episodic Logic meets Little Red Riding Hood: A comprehensive, natural representation for language understanding. In L. Iwanska and S. Shapiro, editors, *Natural Language Processing and Knowledge Representation: Language for Knowledge and Knowledge for Language,* pages 111–174. MIT/AAAI Press, 2000.

[21] U. Zernik. Closed yesterday and closed minds: Asking the right questions of the corpus to distinguish thematic from sentential relations. In *Proc. of COLING-92,* pages 1304–1311, Nantes, France, Aug. 23-28, 1992.

[22] U. Zernik and P. Jacobs. Tagging for learning: Collecting thematic relations from corpus. In *Proc. of the 13th Int. Conf. on Computational Linguistics (COLING-90),* pages 34–39, Helsinki, 1990.

A Formal Approach to Score Normalization for Meta-search

R. Manmatha and H. Sever
Center for Intelligent Information Retrieval
Computer Science Department
University of Massachusetts
Amherst, MA 01003
[manmatha,sever]@cs.umass.edu

ABSTRACT

Meta-search, or the combination of the outputs of different search engines in response to a query, has been shown to improve performance. Since the scores produced by different search engines are not comparable, researchers have often decomposed the meta-search problem into a score normalization step followed by a combination step. Combination has been studied by many researchers. While appropriate normalization can affect performance, most of the normalization schemes suggested are ad hoc in nature.

In this paper, we propose a formal approach to normalizing scores for meta-search by taking the distributions of the scores into account. Recently, it has been shown that for search engines the score distributions for a given query may be modeled using an exponential distribution for the set of non-relevant documents and a normal distribution for the set of relevant documents. Here, it is shown that by equalizing the distributions of scores of the top non-relevant documents the best meta-search performance reported in the literature is obtained. Since relevance information is not available apriori, we discuss two different ways of obtaining a good approximation to the distribution of scores of non-relevant documents. One is obtained by looking at the distribution of scores of all documents. The second is obtained by fitting a mixture model of an exponential and a Gaussian to the scores of all documents and using the resulting exponential distribution as an estimate of the non-relevant distribution. We show with experiments on TREC-3, TREC-4 and TREC-9 data that the best combination results are obtained by averaging the parameters obtained from these approximations. These techniques work on a variety of different search engines including vector space search engines like SMART and probabilistic search engines like INQUERY.

The problem of normalization is important in many other areas including information filtering, topic detection and tracking, multilingual search and distributed retrieval. Thus, the techniques proposed here are likely to be applicable to many of these tasks.

1. INTRODUCTION

Meta-search, or the combination of the outputs of different search engines to produce a single (combined) ranked list in response to a query, has been shown to improve performance [5, 8, 9, 7, 11, 2]. Many search engines produce scores as a measure of the relevance of the document to a particular query. These scores are then used to generate document rankings. The scores produced by different search engines are usually not comparable since they are often computed using some metric (or non-metric) distance function. Researchers have often decomposed the meta-search problem into a score normalization step followed by a combination step. While the combination step has been studied by a number of researchers [5] there has been little work on the normalization techniques to be used. The normalization step can in fact be more critical for performance in many situations [13]. Existing normalization schemes [8, 9, 13] have been proposed on heuristic grounds and their performance seems to depend somewhat on the dataset used [13]. Thus, the appropriate choice of normalization is not clear.

We propose that the correct way to normalize scores for meta-search is by taking the distributions of the scores into account. Researchers have previously shown that for search engines [11] and for the outputs of filtering systems [1] the score distributions for a given query may be modeled using an exponential distribution for the set of non-relevant documents and a normal distribution for the set of relevant documents. Here, we show that by equalizing the distributions of scores of the top non-relevant documents the best meta-search performance reported in the literature is obtained. The non-relevant distributions can be equalized by mapping the minimum score to zero and equalizing the means of the different exponential distributions. Since relevance information is not available in practice, we show that there are two different ways of obtaining a good approximation to the distribution of scores of non-relevant documents (i.e. of estimating the exponential parameter).

1. The non-relevant distribution may be approximated by fitting an exponential distribution to the scores of *all* documents (rather than fitting only the non-relevant documents). This approximation is usually reasonable because the proportion of relevant documents in search engines is usually small. We show that this approximation is in fact identical with a normalization technique selected by Montague and Aslam [13] on heuristic grounds.

2. An alternative technique for estimating the non-relevant distribution involves fitting a mixture model consisting of an exponential and a Gaussian to the scores of all documents [11] and then using the exponential component as an estimate of the non-relevant distribution. The mixture model is solved using Expectation-Maximization (EM).

The best estimate turns out to be to take an average of those obtained using the above (two) approximations. We show that the combination performance obtained by taking this average is the

In HLT'02. This material is based on work supported in part by the Center for Intelligent Information Retrieval, in part by the National Science Foundation under grant numbers IRI-9619117 and in part by SPAWARSYSCEN-SD grant number N66001-99-1-8912. Any opinions, findings and conclusions or recommendations expressed in this material are the author(s) and do not necessarily reflect those of the sponsor(s).

Proceedings of HLT 2002, Second International Conference on Human Language Technology Research, M. Marcus, ed., Morgan Kaufmann, San Francisco, 2002.

best reported performance for meta-search and is consistently good over all the four (TREC) datasets tested. The techniques used here have been applied to a variety of search engines operating on different principles including vector space engines like SMART and probabilistic search engines like INQUERY.

Surprisingly, the performance of this model is better than one obtained by combining posterior probabilities (computed from the mixture model mentioned above) [11]. Part of the problem stems from errors in estimating the mixture model (consisting of relevant and non-relevant errors).

While our work in this paper focuses on the problem of combining the outputs of different search engines retrieving documents from a common database, score normalization is important in many different contexts. The approach here could be easily extended to the combination of different search engines indexing databases in different languages to produce a multi-lingual search engine or the combination of search engines indexing different databases (distributed retrieval). The score normalization procedure used here may also be useful for the topic detection and tracking task where scores have to be normalized across different topics.

2. PRIOR WORK

We will discuss some of the normalization and combination techniques proposed before describing some score modeling work. A recent and extensive survey of evidence combination in information retrieval is provided by Croft [5].

Fox and Shaw [7] proposed a number of combination techniques including operators like the MIN and the MAX. Other techniques included one that involved setting the score of each document in the combination to the sum of the scores obtained by the individual search engines (CombSum), while in another the score of each document was obtained by multiplying this sum by the number of engines which had non-zero scores (CombMNZ). Note that summing (CombSum) is equivalent to averaging while CombMNZ is equivalent to weighted averaging. Lee [8, 9] studied this further with six different engines. His contribution was to normalize each engine on a per query basis improving results substantially. Lee showed that CombMNZ worked best, followed by CombSum while operators like MIN and MAX were the worst. Lee also observed that the best combinations were obtained when systems retrieved similar sets of relevant documents and dissimilar sets of non-relevant documents. Vogt and Cottrell [14] also verified this observation by looking at pairwise combinations of systems. A probabilistic approach using ranks rather than scores was proposed last year by Aslam and Montague [3, 2]. This involved extensive training across about 25 queries to obtain the probability of a rank given a query. Their results for TREC-3 were close to but slightly worse than Lee's COMBMNZ technique [1]. Aslam and Montague were able to demonstrate that rank information alone can be used to produce good combination results. The main difficulty with this technique seems to be the extensive training required of every engine on a substantial number of queries.

Montague and Aslam [13] proposed three different normalization schemes for meta-search. The methods involved linearly shifting and scaling scores so that the following mappings were achieved:

Name	Method
Standard	Map min to 0 and max to 1.
Sum	Map min to 0 and the sum to 1.
ZMUV	Map mean to 0 and variance to 1.

Table 1: Normalization Methods Suggested by Montague and Aslam

They tested these with some well known combination techniques including CombSum and CombMNZ [7, 8, 9].

Recent (and independent) work by Manmatha et al [11] - for search - and Arampatzis and van Hameren [1] - in the case of filtering - has shown that the scores of non-relevant documents may be approximated by an exponential distribution and the scores of relevant documents by a Gaussian distribution. These experiments (by Manmatha et al [11]) were done by modeling the top 1000 documents for different search engines from the TREC-3 ad hoc track.

These distributions were successfully used for information filtering in [1, 15]. Manmatha et al [11] also showed that the relevant and non-relevant distributions could be recovered by solving a mixture model consisting of an exponential and a Gaussian using Expectation-Maximization (EM). They used mixture model to map scores to probabilities for each engine. The probabilities were averaged for meta-search. The results were as good as the CombMNZ technique with the Standard normalization.

3. EXISTING NORMALIZATION SCHEMES

We first start by looking at Montague and Aslam's normalization schemes. Montague and Aslam [13] reported the results of combining a set of n engines. First, a set of n engines is randomly selected from the set of all available engines and these n engines are then combined. A different set of n engines is then selected and the results combined again. The process is repeated until all possible choices for a given n have been selected. The results for a given n are then averaged and reported. We argue that this is not a useful way of reporting results in meta-search. The average precision for the average combination is often less than the average precision for the best search engine. This happens because many of the sets of n are combinations of search engines with much lower average precision.

In Table 2 we, therefore, compare the performance of the three normalization schemes suggested by Montague and Aslam [13] and two different combination schemes on the top five engines for data from the ad hoc track of TREC-3 data. This track provides scores for the top 1000 documents for all search engines which participated in this track. In the table Sum-CombSum means that the normalization technique used was the 'Sum' technique (see Table 1) and the combination technique was CombSum. The first row gives the average precision for the top engine (in terms of average precision). The second row reports the combination performance in terms of average precision for the top two engines. The third, fourth and fifth rows report the performance for combining the top 3 engines, the top 4 engines and the top 5 engines respectively. The results are also plotted in Figure 1.

From Table 2 it is clear that Sum-CombSum and Sum-CombMNZ perform best (with Sum-CombSum performing slightly better). This is in fact corroborated by experiments on the ad hoc tracks in TREC-4, TREC-5 data and on TREC-9 (web-track) data. From this table, the normalization used appears to be more important than the combination scheme used. That is, the Sum normalization performs best whether CombSum or CombMNZ is selected. [2].

Why should the Sum normalization scheme perform better? The paper by Montague and Aslam [13] does not give any intuition for picking one normalization scheme over another. We argue below that the appropriate normalization involves equalizing the non-

[1]The graph for Lee's technique in [3] is incorrect.

[2]Interestingly, contrary to Lee's claim [9], Standard-CombSum is in fact slightly better than Standard-CombMNZ.

Engines combined	Sum CombSum	ZMUV CombSum	Standard CombSum	Sum CombMNZ	ZMUV CombMNZ	Standard CombMNZ
inq102	0.4226	0.4226	0.4226	0.4226	0.4226	0.4226
inq102, citya1	0.4551	0.4445	0.4495	0.4503	0.4382	0.4464
inq102, citya1, brkly7	0.4807	0.4593	0.4742	0.4742	0.4553	0.4700
inq102, citya1, brkly7, inq101	0.4715	0.4471	0.4683	0.4677	0.4438	0.4648
inq102, citya1, brkly7, inq101, assctv2	0.4773	0.4500	0.4750	0.4713	0.4455	0.4692
average	0.4614	0.4447	0.4579	0.4572	0.4411	0.4546

Table 2: Non-interpolated precision of TREC-3's top 5 engines

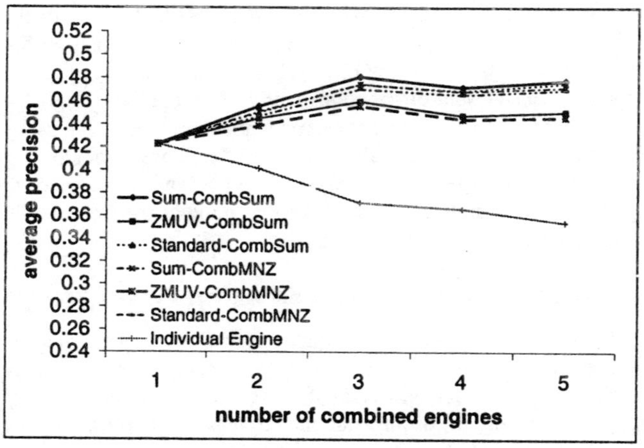

Figure 1: Average precision graphs for the different normalization schemes suggested by Montague and Aslam for combining the best five engines from TREC-3

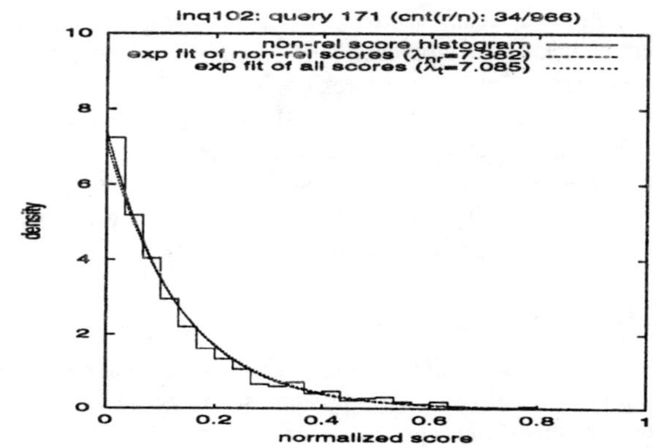

Figure 2: Histogram, exponential fit to non-relevant data and fit for entire data for query 171 INQUERY (inq102)

relevant score distributions of the outputs of different search engines. We show that the 'Sum' normalization is a good way of approximately normalizing the non-relevant score distributions of different search engines. We also show how better approximations may be obtained.

4. FUSION BY EQUALIZING DISTRIBUTIONS

Figure 2 shows a histogram of scores for query 171 for INQUERY from TREC-3. Note that the data are first normalized so that the minimum and maximum score for a query are 0 and 1 respectively. A maximum-likelihood fit of an exponential curve to this data is also shown (see [11] for more details).

The probability density of the exponential distribution is described by the following equation:

$$p(x) = \lambda \exp(-\lambda x) \tag{1}$$

and its mean = $1/\lambda$.

We note that a large variety of search engines based on different principles have non-relevant score distributions described by an exponential (see [11]).

The non-relevant distribution provides information as to how the scores would be distributed even if there are no relevant documents. That is, it provides information as to how a search engine maps a random set of documents to scores for a given query. Relevant documents will tend to get picked more easily if they stand out against this baseline distribution.

Since a good normalization scheme should ensure that random documents are mapped in the same manner, it is appropriate to normalize the random distributions. For a non-relevant distribution which is exponential, this can be done by simply setting the minimum score to 0 and the means of the exponentials to be the same. The retrieved lists from different search engines are now merged based on the normalized scores and CombSum. The results obtained by this technique (top curve labeled EXPML-CombSum) are the best as seen in Figure 3. The figure shows the average precision for the best 5 individual engines from TREC-3 (the individual engine graph). Each combination technique is labeled using the normalization technique followed by the combination technique used. For example, the CombMNZ technique with Standard normalization (Table 1) is referred to as Standard-CombMNZ. This was advocated by Lee [9] as the best fusion technique. EXPML-CombSum provides an improvement of almost 3.5% over Standard-CombMNZ in terms of average precision.

In practice, relevance information is not available. Hence, the non-relevant distribution has to be estimated without relevance information. We discuss three different ways of doing this below.

4.1 Estimate Using Mixture Model Fit

Manmatha et al [11] showed that one could fit a mixture model consisting of an exponential and a Gaussian to the score distributions using Expectation Maximization. This model applies to many different search engines.

The density of a mixture model $p(x)$ can be written in terms of the densities of the individual components $p(x|j)$ as follows: [4, 12]

$$p(x) = \sum_j P(j)p(x|j) \tag{2}$$

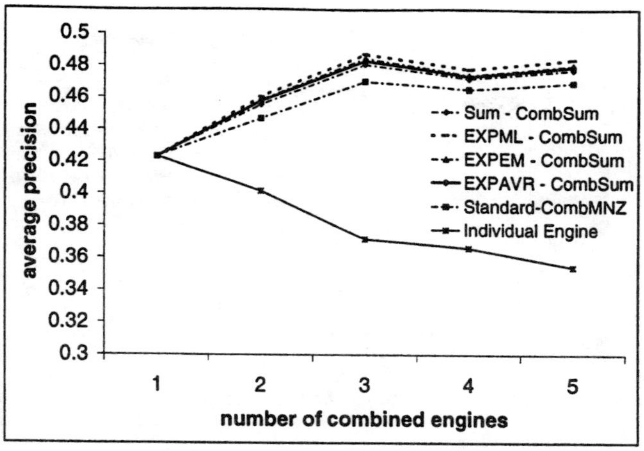

Figure 3: Average precision graphs for combining the best five engines from TREC-3

where j identifies the individual component, the $P(j)$ are known as mixing parameters and satisfy

$$\sum_{j=1}^{2} P(j) = 1, 0 \leq P(j) \leq 1. \tag{3}$$

We will denote densities with a lower case p(x) and probabilities with an uppercase P(x). In the present case, there are two components, an exponential density with mean λ

$$p(x|1) = \lambda \exp(-\lambda x) \tag{4}$$

and a Gaussian density with mean μ and variance σ^2

$$p(x|2) = \frac{1}{\sqrt{2\pi}\sigma} \exp(-\frac{(x-\mu)^2}{2\sigma^2}) \tag{5}$$

The Gaussian part is an estimate of the relevant distribution while the exponential part of the mixture may be used as an estimate of the non-relevant distribution. The mixture model may be solved using Expectation-Maximization which is an iterative procedure to update the parameter values given some initial estimates. The reader is referred to [10] for details on the solution of this mixture model. The parameters of the mixture may be solved using the following update equations:

$$\mu^{new} = \frac{\sum_n P^{old}(2|x^n)x^n}{\sum_n P^{old}(2|x^n)} \tag{6}$$

$$(\sigma^{new})^2 = \frac{\sum_n P^{old}(2|x^n)||x^n - \mu^{new}||^2}{\sum_n P^{old}(2|x^n)} \tag{7}$$

$$\lambda^{new} = \frac{\sum_n P^{old}(1|x^n)}{\sum_n P^{old}(1|x^n)x^n} \tag{8}$$

$$P(1)^{new} = \frac{1}{N}\sum_n P^{old}(1|x) \tag{9}$$

Note that the updated Gaussian parameters are given by μ^{new} and σ^{new} while the updated exponential parameter is given by λ^{new}. $P(1)^{new}$ is the new estimate of the mixing parameter for the exponential ($P(2) = 1 - P(1)$). $P^{old}(j|x^n)j^n$ are estimates of the posterior for component j (j = 1,2) given the current estimates of the parameters.

For our purpose here, we use the exponential part of the mixture as an estimate of the non-relevant distribution. Equalizing the non-relevant distributions of the different search engine outputs is equivalent to equalizing the exponential components of the mixtures describing their outputs. That is, the scores of all documents are rescaled to ensure that the means of the exponential components are the same. In practice, this may be done for a given query on a search engine by by simply dividing the score of every document by the mean of the exponential component. The results obtained using their technique (labeled EXPEM-CombSum) are shown in Figure 3. EXPEM-CombSum is the second curve from the top and the closest in performance to EXPML-CombSum (our theoretical ideal). For various reasons, the exponential distribution obtained using the EM algorithm doesn't converge exactly to the non-relevant distribution.

4.2 Estimate Using Total Distribution

Figure 2 also shows an exponential fit to the scores of *all* documents. This plot is close to the exponential fit to the non-relevant documents. The distribution of all documents is often a good approximation to the distribution of non-relevant documents because the proportion of relevant documents is small in many cases (in this case 34 out of a 1000)

Figure 4 shows a plot of the difference of the means of the two distributions for all 50 queries of INQUERY (depicted as the t - nr curve). This difference is always positive and for many of the queries, but not all, it is small. Figure 4 also shows the difference between means of the exponential model obtained from the mixture model and the one obtained from the non-relevant document scores (labeled as em - nr).

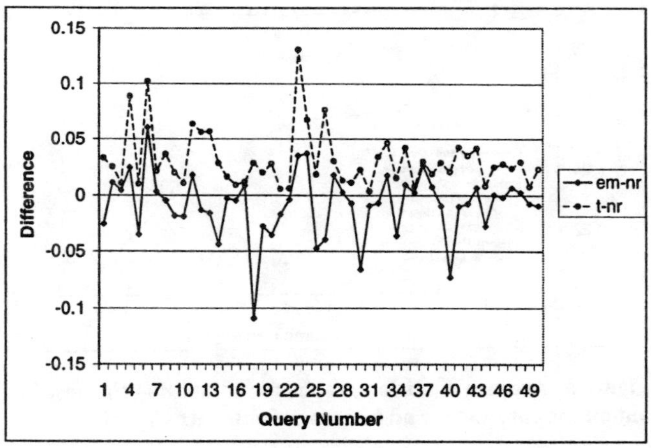

Figure 4: Differences between the means estimated using the two approximation techniques and the mean of the non-relevant distribution for INQUERY (inq102) for TREC-3. em, nr and t refer to the means obtained from the mixture model, non-relevant distribution and the total distribution respectively. Note that the t - nr curve is always positive and that the two differences are un-correlated.

Normalizing using the distribution of all scores is equivalent to setting the minimum to zero and equalizing the mean of all the scores. It is straightforward to show that this is equivalent (in terms of document ranking) to the Sum normalization scheme proposed by Montague and Aslam [13] (see Table 1). The plot labeled as Sum-CombSum in Figure 3 has the fourth best performance (but is really close to the optimal EXPML-CombSum). Our approach here provides the theoretical justification for one of Montague and Aslam's normalization schemes.

Note that for some datasets, Sum-CombSum is better than EXPEM-CombSum as shown in Figure 5 (which shows the average precision graphs for combining the best five automatic runs from the ad hoc track of TREC-4).

The last normalization scheme proposed by Montague and Aslam may be viewed as normalizing the means and variances of two Gaussian distributions. Since we know that the distribution of all scores is definitely not a Gaussian this should not work very well. In fact, the ZMUV-CombMNZ and ZMUV-CombSum are the worst performing combination techniques in Figure 1 and Table 2 and in Figure 5 the performance of ZMUV-CombMNZ actually gets worse as one combines more engines. One could not have predicted this without understanding the nature of the score distributions. We note that in a related area (TDT), this is a common technique for score normalization [6] - and probably a bad choice.

4.3 Estimate by Averaging

Figure 4 shows that the two estimates of the non-relevant distribution often err in different directions. Another estimate can, therefore, be obtained by averaging the two estimates. Normalizing and combining produces the EXPAVG-CombSum plot in Figures 3 and 5. We see that this lies between EXPEM-CombSum and Sum-CombSum. This gives the best consistent performance over all datasets. Note that for Trec-4 we take the top five automatic runs from TREC-4 to show that meta search also works in such cases.

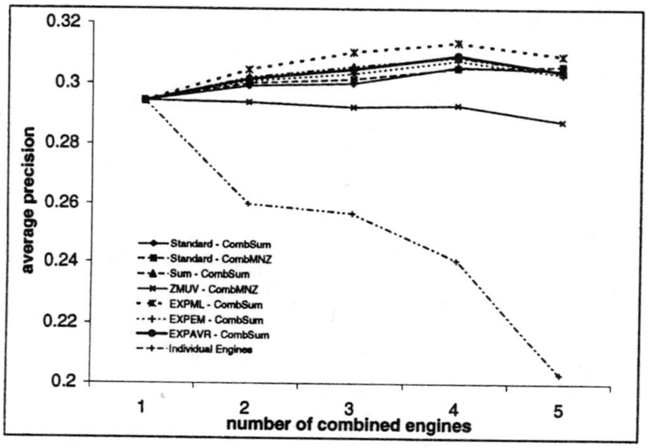

Figure 5: Average precision graphs for combining the best five automatic runs for the ad hoc track from TREC-4

Figure 6 shows the results from the Web Track of TREC-9 and again the best results are obtained by using EXP-ML.

4.4 Discussion of Results

The approach discussed here of equalizing the non-relevant score distributions of different search engines and then averaging the resulting scores clearly produces the best meta search results reported so far. Three different ways of estimating the non-relevant distribution have been discussed above but clearly the easiest technique involves estimating using the total distribution (equivalently, the Sum normalization). We have compared the results with some of the standard ad hoc normalization and combination techniques above. It is interesting to compare the results to a technique based on mapping scores to probabilites and then combining the probabilities as follows.

The mixture model may be used to compute a posterior probability of relevance given the score (see [11]. The different search engines may then be combined by averaging the probabilities. In practice, combination by averaging posterior probabilities does not work as well as the technique proposed here involving equalizing the non-relevant distributions. We believe that the reason for this is the error involved in estimating the mixture model. For estimating the posterior probability both the relevant (Gaussian) and non-relevant (exponential) components of the mixture need to be estimated. As we have seen above, there are errors in estimating the exponential component. There are also errors in estimating the Gaussian component. The Gaussian component is also harder to estimate because the number of relevant documents could be small. Since the posterior probability of relevance given score needs a good estimate of the Gaussian component, there can be errors in it.

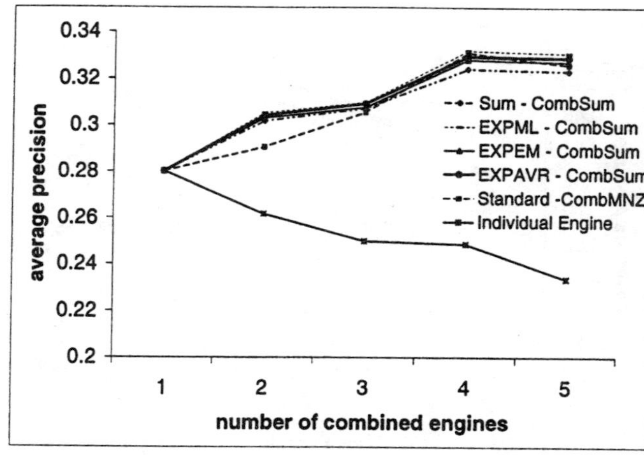

Figure 6: Average precision graphs for combining five runs from the manual interactive track from TREC-9

In the case of multi-lingual retrieval and distributed retrieval, the problem of estimating the Gaussian component for some databases may be really severe. Imagine, for example a French news database, an English news database and an Indonesian news database. In response to a query about the mayor of Nice, the French database may have a number of relevant documents while the Indonesian database may have no relevant documents. In such a situation, the estimates of the posterior probability would be especially poor. However, the techniques described here would still work (the exponential component of the mixture would still be estimated reasonably well).

One could also ask whether equalizing the Gaussian (relevant) distributions works. There does not appear to be any obvious intuitive reason for the relevant distributions to have the same parameters (although they may all belong to the same family of distributions). In practice, this does not work very well as expected.

Combining multiple search engines usually provides substantial improvements over even the best individual search engine. There are exceptions to this rule. For example, when the performance of one search engine is much better than another search engine then combination may not improve performance. Although combining the top few search engines usually improves performance, combining more than about 5 engines does not seem to cause a substantial improvement in performance and may in fact cause degradation. As is clear from the previous figures, as one goes further down the list, the performance of the individual search engines get substantially worse. An interesting question is how many engines should be combined before the performance shows no further improvement.

5. CONCLUSION AND FUTURE WORK

We have described a formal approach to meta search which involves equalizing the distributions of scores of the top non-relevant score distributions of different search engines on a per query basis.' Three different techniques were described for estimating the non-relevant distribution. It was shown that the techniques described here produce the best reported meta search performance in the literature. The approach described here also provides a formal basis for one of the normalization schemes previously described in the literature.

Future work could include the extension of this technique to the combination of results from search engines operating on databases in different databases to produce a multi-lingual search engine and on combining the results from different databases in distributed retrieval.

The problem of score normalization is also important in other information retrieval tasks like topic detection and tracking and the discussion in this paper could provide some insight in such areas.

6. REFERENCES

[1] A. Arampatzis and A. van Hameren. The score-distributional threshold optimization for adaptive binary classification tasks. In *In the Proc. of the 24th ACM SIGIR conf. on Research and Developement in Information Retrieval*, pages 285–293, Sept 2001.

[2] J. Aslam and M. Montague. Models for metasearch. In *In the Proc. of the 24th ACM SIGIR conf. on Research and Developement in Information Retrieval*, pages 276–284, Sept 2001.

[3] J. A. Aslam, , and M. Montague. Bayes optimal metasearch: A probabilistic model for combining the results of multiple retrieval systems. In *the Proc. of the 23rd ACM SIGIR conf. on Research and Developement in Information Retrieval*, pages 379–381, 2000.

[4] C. M. Bishop. *Neural Networks for Pattern Recognition.* Oxford University Press, 1995.

[5] W. B. Croft. Combining approaches to information retrieval. In W. B. Croft, editor, *Advances in Information Retrieval*, pages 1–36. Kluwer Academic Publishers, 2000.

[6] J. Fiscus and G. R. Doddington. Topic detection and tracking evaluation overview. In J. Allan, editor, *Topic Detection and Tracking: Event-based Information Organization*, pages 17–31. Kluwer Academic Publishers, 2002.

[7] E. Fox and J. Shaw. Combination of multiple searches. In *the Proc. of the 2nd Text Retrieval Conference (TREC-2)*, pages 243–252. National Institute of Standards and Technology Special Publications 500-215, 1994.

[8] J. H. Lee. Combining multiple evidence form different properties of weighting schemes. In *the Proc. of the 18th Intl. Conf. on Research and Development in Information Retrieval (SIGIR'95)*, pages 180–188, 1995.

[9] J. H. Lee. Analyses of multiple evidence combination. In *the Proc. of the 20th Intl. Conf. on Research and Development in Information Retrieval (SIGIR'97)*, pages 267–276, 1997.

[10] R. Manmatha, T. Rath, and F. Feng. Modeling score distributions for meta search. *Submitted to ACM TOIS.*

[11] R. Manmatha, T. Rath, and F. Feng. Modeling score distributions for combining the outputs of search engines. In *the Proc. of the 24th ACM SIGIR conf. on Research and Developement in Information Retrieval*, pages 267–275, Sept 2001.

[12] G. McLachlan and D. Peel. *Finite Mixture Models.* John Wiley, 2000.

[13] M. Montague and J. Aslam. Relevance score normalization for metasearch. In *In the Proc. of the ACM Tenth International Conference on Information and Knowledge Management (CIKM)*, pages 427–433, Nov 2001.

[14] C. Vogt and G. Cottrell. Predicting the performance of linearly combined IR systems. In *the Proc. of the 21st ACM SIGIR conf. on Research and Developement in Information Retrieval*, pages 190–196, 1998.

[15] Y. Zhang and J. Callan. Maximum likelihood estimation for filtering thresholds. In *In the Proc. of the 24th ACM SIGIR conf. on Research and Developement in Information Retrieval*, pages 294–302, Sept 2001.

Quantifying Query Ambiguity

Steve Cronen-Townsend and W. Bruce Croft
Center for Intelligent Information Retrieval
Department of Computer Science
University of Massachusetts, Amherst, MA 01003
{crotown, croft}@cs.umass.edu

ABSTRACT

We develop a measure of a query with respect to a collection of documents with the aim of quantifying the query's ambiguity with respect to those documents. This measure, the *clarity score*, is the relative entropy between a query language model and the corresponding collection language model. We substantiate that the clarity score measures the coherence and specificity of the language used in documents likely to satisfy the query. We also argue that it provides a suitable quantification of the (lack of) ambiguity of a query with respect to a collection of documents and has potential applications throughout the field of information retrieval. In particular, the clarity score is shown to correlate positively with average precision in evaluations using TREC test collections. Hence, as one example, the clarity score could serve as a predictor of query performance. Systems would then be able to identify vague information requests and respond differently than they would to clear and specific requests.

1. INTRODUCTION

An important challenge for information retrieval systems is dealing gracefully with ambiguous queries. For example, suppose a user interested in the competitors in the 1988-1989 soccer World Cup gives the query "World Cup" against the AP88 collection of news articles. If those two words are the only evidence the system has about what the user means, it is simply impossible for the system to return the soccer articles consistently higher in the ranked list than the articles about World Cup chess tournaments, that are, in fact, predominant in the chosen collection among the articles that use the query terms frequently. Despite the fact that the user might not have known that there was a World Cup in anything other than the sport of soccer, he or she would, typically, get a ranked list with chess articles predominating near the top and occasional soccer articles farther down the list. Hence, for this collection, the query "World Cup" is significantly more ambiguous (less clear) than than the query "World Cup soccer." However, if there were no articles about World Cup chess tournaments in the collection, the two queries would be similar in ambiguity. Hence ambiguity is a matter of degree, and, furthermore, since the degree of ambiguity depends of the details of the the documents present in the collection all queries are ambiguous to some degree.

Clearly information retrieval systems must act on more user information than just the query words in cases of high query ambiguity. One common approach has been treating all queries the same initially but then refining the document list in response to user feedback on the initial list. We envisage a new approach where vague queries will be handled differently than clear ones from the beginning. In this paper, we address the important first step of automatically identifying queries that are vague with respect to a given collection of documents.

Firstly, we motivate the definition of a clarity score and show how to compute it and give examples and visualizations. Despite the possibility of examining clarity score contributions due to individual terms, we have not developed clarity scores as a term-weighting scheme and show that there is no discernible correlation with a traditional inverse document frequency measure. Then we substantiate that the clarity score measures the coherence and specificity of the language associated with documents likely to satisfy the query and argue that it therefore serves as a suitable quantification of query ambiguity. We then show the positive association between clarity score and performance of a query using test collections, examine related work, and conclude.

2. DEFINING CLARITY SCORES

2.1 Motivation

Starting from a language modeling viewpoint, quantifying the ambiguity of a query rests on the notion of a query language model. By a query language model, we mean a language model representing the collection word usage that is associated with the query. The simplest version of this is a unigram language model, which is an estimated probability distribution for the occurrence of single terms in documents associated with the query.

Counting the number of topics in this language model seems like a sensible quantification of ambiguity, since it captures the idea that a query is ambiguous if it returns documents about many different topics. However, the notion of topic is not mathematically well-defined, since topics are overlapping and depend on a chosen level of topic generality. Some advances have been made in this area by trying

Proceedings of HLT 2002, Second International Conference on Human Language Technology Research, M. Marcus, ed., Morgan Kaufmann, San Francisco, 2002.

to capture latent semantic information[7], but we have not pursued this approach.

Considering the entropy of the query model is a potentially interesting approach, since the entropy of a probability distribution measures directly how much the distribution specifies certain values. So, in this case, the entropy measures how strongly the distribution specifies certain words.

In this approach it is important to remove, as much as possible, the large and fluctuating contributions to the entropy from generic words. This can be done by computing the relative entropy between the query model and the overall collection language model, instead of the entropy of the query language model alone. These considerations lead to a measure where a query whose language model looks like the language model for the whole collection receives a low score, and a query whose language model is very different from the the collection language model receives a high score. Thus we are measuring something like the lack of ambiguity, and we call the measure the *clarity score.*

We believe that a typical way a query language model proves similar to the collection model is that the query selects documents that are about many different topics. The blurring of the individual topic models together creates an overall distribution that is smoother and more similar to the collection language model than the model for a query that selects documents about a single topic. The single-topic model will have large spikes at topic words. Thus, the similarity between the query language model and the collection language model is related to the coherence of the retrieved set, or the degree to which the favored documents are about the same topic.

Query ambiguity, as compared to single word ambiguity, is relatively simple. We believe that it can be fairly well characterized by a single number. Since the notions of clarity and ambiguity are themselves rather vague, we take our measure as the definition of the clarity (lack of ambiguity) of a query with respect to a certain collection of documents. Thus query ambiguity, in our conception, becomes strictly one-dimensional. We now make the definition of clarity scores mathematically precise, leaving the issue of its degree of correspondence to the general connotations of the terms ambiguity and clarity for Section 3.

2.2 Definition

In order to compute a clarity score, one must first create a query language model. We have investigated both of the methods put forward by Lavrenko and Croft[11] for estimating such models[1]. The best all-around way of estimating the query model for the purposes of computing clarity scores is Lavrenko and Croft's *Method 1*[4]. In this approach one, in effect, assumes that the query terms and the words in the documents are sampled identically and independently from the query model unigram distribution.

The query model unigram distribution is estimated by

$$P(w|Q) = \sum_{D \in R} P(w|D)P(D|Q), \qquad (1)$$

where w is any term, D is a document, Q is the query, and R is the set of all documents containing at least one query term. Inside conditional probabilities, D refers to a language model estimated from the corresponding single document.

[1]Lavrenko and Croft refer to these as *relevance models.*

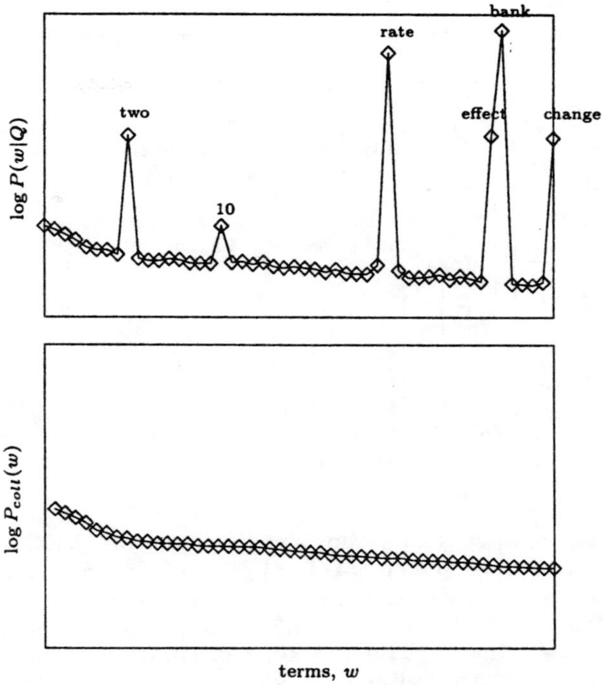

Figure 1: The query language model for query A, "Show me any predictions for changes in the prime lending rate and any changes made in the prime lending rates" in TREC disk 1 and the collection language model for that corpus. The top 50 terms are plotted in order of collection probabilities.

The likelihood of a query given a document is estimated using the language modeling approach of [17] as

$$P(Q|D) = \prod_{q \in Q} P(q|D), \qquad (2)$$

and $P(D|Q)$ is obtained by Bayesian inversion with uniform prior probabilities for documents in R and a zero prior for documents that contain no query terms.

The probabilities $P(w|D)$ and $P(q|D)$ in (1) and (2) are estimated with linear smoothing[12] given by

$$P(w|D) = \lambda P_{ml}(w|D) + (1-\lambda)P_{coll}(w), \qquad (3)$$

where $P_{ml}(w|D)$ is simply the relative frequency of term w in documents D, $P_{coll}(w)$ is the relative frequency of the term in the collection as a whole, and $\lambda = 0.6$ throughout this study. Figure 1 shows a query language model for a clear query and the corresponding collection model.

The clarity score for the query is simply the relative entropy, or Kullback-Leibler divergence[3], between the query language model and the collection language model, given by

$$\text{clarity score} = \sum_{w \in V} P(w|Q) \log_2 \frac{P(w|Q)}{P_{coll}(w)}, \qquad (4)$$

where V is the entire vocabulary of the collection.

In practice the most efficient way to calculate clarity scores is to estimate the query model by sampling documents to produce a query language model using equation (1). Unless otherwise noted, all clarity scores in this paper are calculated by sampling until a limit of 500 unique documents is reached. Alternatively to equation (4), one can compute

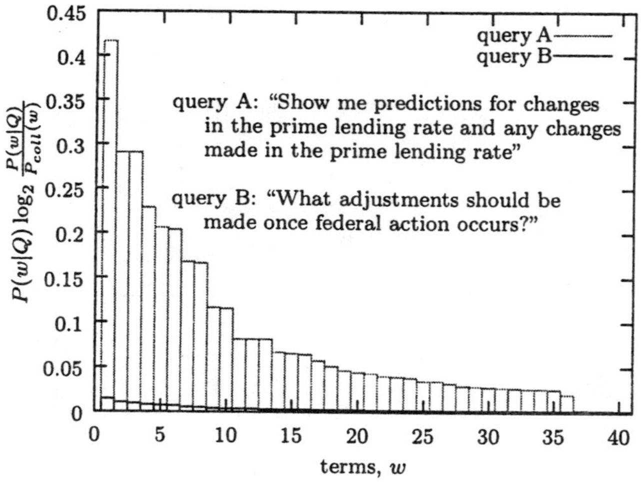

Figure 2: A clear versus a vague query in TREC disk 1 with the top 40 terms in 4) plotted separately. The top six contributions, in order, for query A are for the terms "bank," "hong," "kong," "rate," "lend," and "prime." The top six contributing terms for query B are "adjust," "federal," "action," "land," "occur," and "hyundai."

the divergence with the roles of the query and collection language models reversed. One can also use either the query model of equation (1) or Lavrenko and Croft's *Method 2*-type models. Of the 4 combinations, the definition given above performs slightly better than the others on large collections. See [4] for more details.

2.3 Examples

Consider two queries, A and B against the TREC disk 1 collection of documents. Query A is "Show me any predictions for changes in the prime lending rate and any changes made in the prime lending rates" (see Figure 1 for the query language model). Query B is "What adjustments should be made once federal action occurs?". These queries happen to be two query variants for TREC topic 56 from the query track[2]. Figure 1 shows the language models used in computing the clarity score for query A, which is 2.85 bits. In terms of these figures, the clarity score is the top graph minus the bottom graph, times 2 to the power of the top graph and summed over terms. Just the difference between the two graphs makes a function with spikes at the most topical words and the final step of taking the expectation value of this quantity using the top distribution enhances the peaks further still. This procedure can also be interpreted as computing the number of bits wasted, on average, when one encodes term-occurrence events sampled from the query language model with a code optimally designed for the collection language model.

The best way to visualize the difference between clear and vague queries is to plot the clarity contributions on a term-by-term basis as in Figure 2. Here $P(w|Q) * \log \frac{P(w|Q)}{P_{coll}(w)}$ is plotted for each of the top 40 contributing terms w, sorted in descending order of contribution. In this representation, the clarity score is the total area of the bars leading to a clarity score of 2.85 for query A (grey bars) and 0.37 for query B

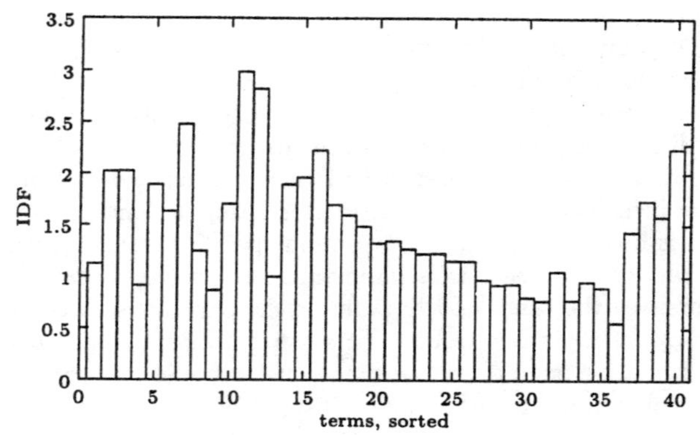

Figure 3: The IDFs of the top 40 contributing terms to the clarity score of query A with the terms plotted in the same order as in Figure 2.

(black bars). The contrast between the high-clarity query A and the low-clarity query B is evident.

It is important to note that we have not developed this method as a weighting scheme for terms. Although the contributions of individual terms to the clarity score of an entire query may be examined (as in Figure 2) these scores do not, for example, correlate with traditional inverse document frequency(IDF) measures. Consider, for example, IDF, defined as

$$IDF(w) = \log_{10} \frac{\text{number of docs}}{\text{number of docs containing } w}. \quad (5)$$

This measure is plotted in Figure 3 for the top 40 clarity score contributing terms for query A. Comparing this graph to the grey bars in Figure 2 shows evidence for only a possible small correlation between IDF and clarity score contributions to this query. Any correlation disappears quickly as one considers more and more terms since the additional terms have uniformily small clarity contributions but often have large IDF values. The leftmost bar, corresponding to "bank", and the fourth bar corresponding to "rate," show relatively modest IDF scores for these two terms, despite their large contributions to the clarity score of query A. A term's clarity score contribution reflects the degree to which that term's probability in the query model rises above its background level. A term's IDF, however, depends on the collection but not on the query under consideration, making it a less specific measure.

Further examples from the TREC-7 ad hoc track are shown in Table 1. The first entry indicates that query that had rank 1 (lowest) score was the title of TREC topic 379, namely "mainstreaming" and it has a clarity score of 0.311. Similarly the last entry indicates that the highest scoring query in the set of 50 queries was "anorexia nervosa bulimia", the title of TREC topic 369, with a score of 2.921.

Some insight into our method can be gained by considering the query at rank 46 "sick building syndrome" where none of the terms individually seem very specific but through documents where they co-occur they generate a fairly spiky language model. On the flip side, the query "drug legalization benefits" scores poorly, at rank 7, even though the terms seem reasonable. In this case, the term "benefit" probably helps the query marginally because it occurs in so many documents and does not probably co-occur extremely strongly with the other two terms. Moreover, the specific meaning of legalization of drugs is lost here by the stemming, which causes "legalization" to match any other words with the stem "legal". This effect might also be exacerbated by a limited number of documents about the legalization of drugs in the collection. Documents that only match one of 'legal" or "drug" or match both but are not about legalization of drugs are about many topics and make a language model similar to the over collection language model, leading to a low clarity score.

rank	topic	query	score
1	379	mainstreaming	0.311
2	354	journalist risks	0.315
3	391	R&D drug prices	0.372
4	359	mutual fund predictors	0.401
5	381	alternative medicine	0.428
6	395	tourism	0.464
7	360	drug legalization benefits	0.481
8	376	World Court	0.490
9	371	health insurance holistic	0.492
10	366	commercial cyanide uses	0.498
41	382	hydrogen fuel automobiles	1.630
42	355	ocean remote sensing	1.700
43	351	Falkland petroleum exploration	1.797
44	353	Antarctica exploration	1.801
45	365	El Nino	1.832
46	396	sick building syndrome	1.882
47	374	Nobel prize winners	1.977
48	368	in vitro fertilization	2.031
49	356	postmenopausal estrogen Britain	2.083
50	369	anorexia nervosa bulimia	2.921

Table 1: The clarity scores of the ten lowest and the ten highest clarity scoring title queries in TREC-7. The query at rank 42 ("ocean remote sensing") made such a peaked P(D|Q) that only 89 unique documents appeared in 250,000 samples and were used to construct the query language model. The query at rank 48 ("in vitro fertilization") was modelled with all the 63 documents that contained either terms matching "vitro" or "fertilize." Similarly, the query at rank 10, "commercial cyanide uses" was modelled with all of the 414 documents that matched the two query terms after the stop word "uses" was removed. All other queries were modelled with the usual 500 documents.

3. QUERY AMBIGUITY AND CLARITY

Figure 4 shows a set of interrelated queries and their clarity scores in the TREC disk 1 collection. Since our system turns turns all text to lower case and morphologically normalizes it[9], the query "jobs" is considered equivalent to "Jobs" and would match documents mentioning the cofounder of Apple Computer or mentioning employment.

The right side from top to bottom shows a typical series of transformations where additional terms are added to reduce the ambiguity of the query. The original query "jobs" would rank highly documents about many topics, whereas "textiles jobs" more narrowly focuses on documents about jobs related to cloth. Finally "denim textiles jobs" narrows down the meaning of the query even further with correspondingly higher clarity scores at each step. The left side of the figure follows a similar progression. The middle query "textiles steve jobs" is an ambiguous combination of the two streams of meaning and its clarity score is lower then either of the two word queries "steve jobs" or "textiles jobs." These examples suggest that the clarity score is related, to some degree, to everyday notions of the ambiguity of a query as a whole, in terms of the number of topics it could be referring to.

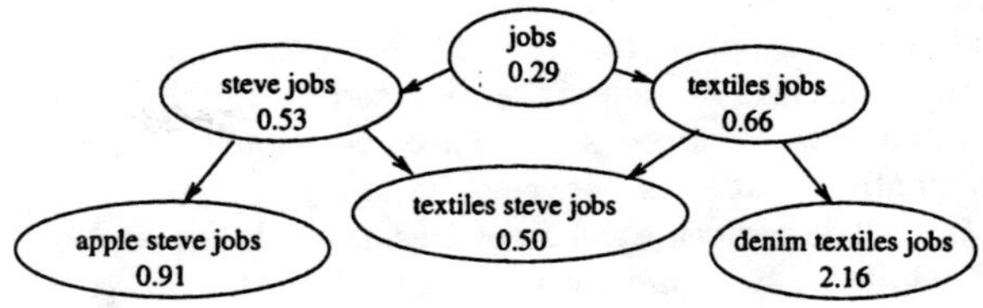

Figure 4: Clarity scores of some queries in the TREC disk 1 collection. Arrows show adding a query term.

Collection	Queries	Number	R	P-value
AP88+89	101 – 200	100	0.368	1.2×10^{-4}
TREC 7	351 – 400	50	0.577	2.7×10^{-5}
TREC 8	401 – 450	50	0.494	2.7×10^{-4}
TREC7+8	351 – 450	100	0.536	4.8×10^{-8}

Table 2: The correlation of clarity scores with average precision in several TREC test collections. The queries are the titles of the TREC topics (usually a few words).

The middle query "textiles steve jobs" offers a way to probe this relationship even further. By hand-labeling the documents and computing the clarity score on the subsets we see some interesting trends. Using just the top 20 documents to estimate the query model, the clarity score of this ambiguous query is 1.39[2]. Using just the top 20 documents mentioning the co-founder of Apple Computer, Steve Jobs, the clarity score is 1.42. Using just the top 20 documents that mention textiles the clarity score is 1.54, while the clarity score using the top 20 mentioning neither is 1.26. In this simple example mixing documents from disparate topics reduces the clarity score, and those documents that are in the miscellaneous category are the lowest scoring subset, presumably since they are a mix of many different subjects. Documents in the miscellaneous category are mainly contain "by Steve Cook" (which increases $P(D|Q)$ since "steve" is a query term) and happen to be about a variety of computer-related topics, or are about employment but do not mention textiles. Experiments like this provide evidence for our assertion that clarity scores provide a suitable quantification of query ambiguity.

4. CLARITY AND RETRIEVAL PRECISION

In order to assess the potential for using clarity scores to predict the performance of a query, we measure the correlation between clarity scores and average precision scores for

[2]This score is higher than that reported in Figure 4 since the artificial certainty created by estimating the query language model with 20 as compared to 500 documents raises the relative entropy.

various TREC test collections. Since the distributions are unknown, an appropriate test is the Spearmann rank correlation test[6]. The scores are replaced by rankings, and one computes what appears to be a correlation coefficient from elementary statistics between the two rankings. A score of 1 indicates perfect agreement in the rankings and a score of −1 indicates opposite rankings. This is a distribution-free statistic whose null distribution (if the two rankings are unassociated) is well-approximated by a normal for sample sizes as large as 50, our smallest sample size, thus it is straightforward to compute the p-values, or probabilities that results as extreme or more extreme occurred by chance. See Table 2 for some results. More details and data may be found in [4].

5. RELATED WORK

Ambiguity has long been of interest in information retrieval[5] and in the larger field of language technologies(see [12]). The information retrieval work focuses on the improvements possible through retrieving documents based on unambiguous word senses(see [10], [15], and [16]). In operation, this approach requires word sense disambiguation, the automatic determination of word senses, when the documents are indexed. The present work is different in that it measures ambiguity without attempting to resolve it, and that it measures the query as a whole.

Another focus of research attention started with the automatic choice of index terms[1] and led to automatic identification of stop words[19] and content-bearing terms[8]. This stream has produced two studies closely related to ours. Pirkola and Jarvelin[13] examine individual term contributions to the retrieval effectiveness of queries and have some success at identifying the most important query term when there is no information as to the actual relevance of the documents to the query. In seeking to classify questions as easy or hard, Sullivan[18] models very long question text directly and compares questions in a sophisticated way to an existing set of questions whose effectiveness at retrieving relevant documents (when viewed as information retrieval-style queries) has been measured.

Additionally, a nearly identical mathematical approach to ours has been used to model selectional preferences in natural language[14].

6. CONCLUSIONS

We have shown that the query clarity score, as defined, corresponds to certain connotations of the lack of ambiguity. The example in Section 3 suggests that queries whose likely documents are a mix of documents from disparate topics receive a lower score than if they resulted in a topically-coherent retrieved set. It has also been shown that the measure correlates strongly and significantly with average precision. Clarity score computation does not refer to the notion of the information need behind the query and may be used to make predictions about the performance of a query in general information retrieval systems, where there is no information as to the actual relevance of documents to certain requests. Based on these initial results, query clarity promises to be a useful tool in many areas of information retrieval and related language technologies.

7. ACKNOWLEDGMENTS

This work was supported in part by the Center for Intelligent Information Retrieval, in part by SPAWARSYSCEN-SD grant number N66001-99-1-8912 and in part by NSF grant #IIS-9907018. Any opinions, findings and conclusions or recommendations expressed in this material are the authors and do not necessarily reflect those of the sponsors.

8. REFERENCES

[1] R. Bookstein and D. R. Swanson. Probabilistic models for automatic indexing. *Journal of the American Society for Information Science*, 25:312–318, 1974.

[2] C. Buckley. The trec-9 query track. In E. Voorhees and D. Harman, editors, *Proceedings of the Ninth Text REtrieval Conference(TREC-9)*, 2000. NIST Special Publication 500-249.

[3] T. M. Cover and J. A. Thomas. *Elements of Information Theory*. Wiley-Interscience, New York, New York, 1991.

[4] S. Cronen-Townsend, Y. Zhou, and W. B. Croft. Predicting query performance. Submitted to SIGIR 2002.

[5] L. Earl. Use of word government in resolving syntactic and semantic ambiguities. *Information Storage and Retrieval*, 9:639–664, 1973.

[6] J. D. Gibbons and S. Chakraborty. *Nonparametric Statistical Inference, 3rd ed.* Marcel Dekker, New York, New York, 1992.

[7] T. Hofmann. Probabilistic latent semantic indexing. In *Proceedings of the 22nd Annual international ACM SIGIR Conference*, pages 50–57, 1999.

[8] W. Kim and W. J. Wilbur. Corpus-based statistical screening for content-bearing terms. *Journal of the American Society for Information Science and Technology*, 52(3):247–259, 2001.

[9] R. Krovetz. Viewing morpholgy as an inference process. In *Proc. of the 16th Annual ACM SIGIR Conference*, pages 191–202, June-July 1993.

[10] R. Krovetz and W. B. Croft. Lexical ambiguity and information retrieval. *ACM Transactions on Information Systems*, 10(2):115–141, 1992.

[11] V. Lavrenko and W. B. Croft. Relevance-based language models. In *Proc. of the 24th Annual ACM SIGIR Conference*, pages 120–127, September 2001.

[12] C. D. Manning and H. Schütze. *Foundations of Statistical Natural Language Processing*. MIT Press, Cambridge, Massachusetts, 1999.

[13] A. Pirkola and K. Jarvelin. Employing the resolution power of search keys. *Journal of the American Society for Information Science and Technology*, 52(7):575–583, 2001.

[14] P. Resnik. Selectional constraints: An information-theoretic model and its computational realization. *Cognition*, 61:127–159, 1996.

[15] M. Sanderson and K. van Rijsbergen. The impact on retrieval effectiveness of skewed frequency distributions. *ACM Transactions on Information Systems*, 17(4):440–465, 1999.

[16] H. Schütze and J. Pederson. Information retrieval based on word senses. In *Proceedings of the 4th Annual Symposium on Document Analysis and*

Information Retrieval, pages 161–175, 1995.

[17] F. Song and W. B. Croft. A general language model for informatioon retrieval. In *Proceedings of the 22nd annual international ACM SIGIR conference*, pages 279–280, 1999.

[18] T. Sullivan. Locating question difficulty through explorations in question space. In *Proceedings of the 1st ACM/IEEE Joint Conference on Digital Libraries*, pages 251–252, 2001.

[19] W. J. Wilbur and K. Sirotkin. The automatic identification of stop words. *Journal of Information Science*, 18(1):45–55, 1992.

An Algorithm for Unsupervised Topic Discovery from Broadcast News Stories

Sreenivasa Sista
Department of Electrical and Computer Engineering,
Northeastern University
Boston, MA
ssista@ece.neu.edu

Richard Schwartz, Timothy R. Leek, and John Makhoul
BBN Technologies,
Cambridge MA
schwartz, tleek, makhoul@bbn.com

ABSTRACT

The cost of annotating a large corpus with thousands of distinct topics is high. In addition, human annotators usually fail to indicate all of the relevant topics for each document. It would be desirable to determine the topics in any new domain or language automatically, given only a large corpus in that domain and language. We present an algorithm called Unsupervised Topic Discovery, which creates topics from a collection of news stories, provides a human understandable topic label and then assigns the topics to the news stories. Finally, we report our results on a collection of broadcast news stories in English and Arabic.

Keywords

Knowledge extraction, topic classification, thematic clustering, text summarization.

1. INTRODUCTION

Topics are subjects or themes that can be used to categorize a document (or a news story). Usually, a news story is about several topics. For example, a news story about the "Oklahoma City Bombing in 1995" can be said to contain topics "Bombings", "Terrorism", "Oklahoma", "Deaths and Injuries". The cost of human annotation of such topics for a large number of documents is very high. In this paper, we present an automatic text categorization method called "Unsupervised Topic Discovery" (UTD) that creates new topic categories.

Extracting themes from text is not a new problem. Word disambiguation was achieved by clustering words (noun and verb pairs) by themes [5][6]. The ITERATE algorithm [7] clusters documents into a hierarchical conceptual cluster tree based on inter-document similarity. Text excerpts from documents that are about a theme were found to be very useful [3] for generating document summaries. All the above approaches extracted thematic information from documents targeted at specific applications e.g., word disambiguation, document categorization and document summarization. In addition, we assert that topics cannot be arranged in a strict tree structure. For example, a group of documents about "illegal steroid usage in Olympics" can be represented in a hierarchical structure in two ways (a) cluster of documents about "drug-abuse", where "drug-abuse" is a sub-category under the category "sports", or (b) a cluster of documents about "sports", where "sports" is a sub-category under the category "drug-abuse".

The proposed method for UTD aims to create a flat list of topics, from a large collection of documents. Each discovered topic is automatically assigned an intelligible topic label and a set of support words, statistically associated with the topic. We employ OnTopic™[1] topic classification system, to generate statistical topic models. The resulting topic models can be used in applications like text categorization [1], document summarization and story segmentation [10].

In section 2, we define the term topic under the UTD framework. Section 3 describes the OnTopic topic classification model used for creating the topic support words. In Section 4, we describe the UTD system. Section 5 describes the evaluation methodology. Section 6 describes UTD experiments for broadcast news stories in English and Arabic.

2. TOPICS

There are many definitions for topics, so it's worth defining what we mean. By "topics", we mean subjects that can be used to categorize a document, much as used by Primary Source Media or by Reuters. Human annotators represent a topic by a single term (a phrase or a word) like "Inhalation Anthrax". Often, the topic label (e.g., Inhalation Anthrax) does not appear, in its exact form, inside a document. The presence of the topic inside a document is judged by several words that are related to the main topic.

Thus, our definition of a topic has the following components:

1. A descriptive and human comprehensible label. 'Birds,' 'aircraft accidents,' 'President Clinton,' 'White House,' 'dinosaurs,' and 'insurance industry' are some topic labels.
2. A set of terms, known as support words, that supports the existence of the topic in a document or text. For example, terms "anthrax," "anthrax spores," "bacteria," and "germ warfare agent" are some of the support terms for the topic "Inhalation Anthrax".

Proceedings of HLT 2002, Second International Conference on Human Language Technology Research, M. Marcus, ed., Morgan Kaufmann, San Francisco, 2002.

3. A statistical measure of significance of the support term for a topic. Some support words carry more information about a topic than others. For example, the term "anthrax" gives a better indication of the presence of the topic "inhalation anthrax" than the term "bacteria". Significance of a support word for a topic is represented by a statistical probability, P(support term | Topic).

3. TOPIC MODEL

There are many methods for determining the topics in a document. The OnTopic™ system at BBN uses a Hidden Markov Model (HMM) to model multiple topics in documents explicitly [1]. The model is pictured in Figure 1. We assume (make believe) that the story is generated by this model. According to this model, when an author decides to write a story, the first thing he does is to pick a set of topics. The topics are chosen according to the prior distribution for topics. There is a HMM with one state for each of the chosen topics, plus an additional state for the General Language topic. Each of the states has a distribution for the language about that topic. In the simplest case, this language model is a unigram distribution on words. However, the state could also contain a higher order n-gram language model for word sequences for that topic. According to the model, the author writes the story one word at a time. Before choosing each word, he first chooses which of the topics that word will be about. This is chosen according to the probability of each topic, given the set of topics in the story. Once the topic is chosen, the author chooses a word from the corresponding topic state according to the distribution of words for the topic. Then the author must choose the topic for the next word, and so on until the story is finished. (If an n-gram model is used, the process is slightly more complicated, but the same principle can be used.)

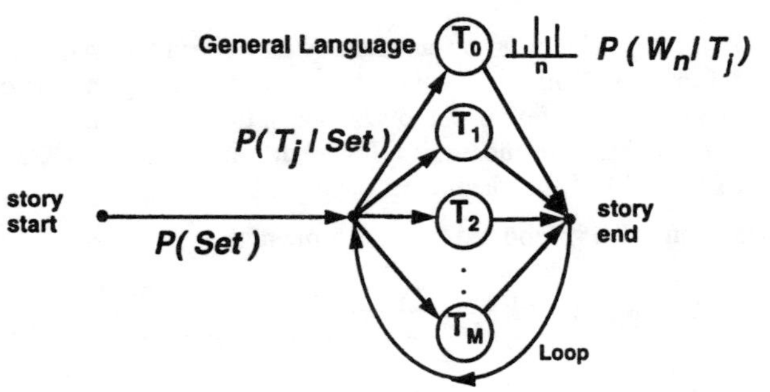

Figure 1: OnTopic topic classification model - HMM for how a story is generated from its topics.

Typically, we are not given the word distributions for the topics. We must determine them from a corpus of stories annotated with topics. We use a modified version of the EM method to determine the distributions. Given a new document, we could determine the most likely set of topics by considering all possible sets of topics exhaustively. Of course, this is too expensive. Instead, we first determine which individual topics are likely enough and then we consider all combinations of those few topics.

These topic models can be used to provide a very concise summary of a story, or as a common set of key terms to be used in searching for documents about a desired combination of subjects (without having to know what words are actually in the document).

4. SYSTEM DESIGN

In this section, we describe the process of Unsupervised Topic Discovery (UTD). UTD is a process by which a system or a machine gains knowledge of or ascertains the existence of previously unknown topics in a collection of documents. The input to the UTD system, typically, is a collection of documents and the output, are topics. The algorithm for finding the themes or topics in the corpus has two high-level steps. First (in section 4.1), we find descriptive phrases (using the MDL criterion) in the corpus. Then, we augment each document with the phrases they contain and identify names of people, places, and organizations. Next, in section 4.2, we determine an initial set of topics, based on the key-phrases that occur in each document. These key-phrases are assigned as the initial topics for each document. We then use the Estimate-Maximize algorithm to determine the full set of words and phrases that are statistically associated with each of the topics.

4.1 Feature Selection

One of the goals of the topic discovery process is to create meaningful topic labels. We choose topic labels from the features of a document. In order to create intelligible topic labels, we first augment a document with names and phrases. Then, we choose words, names and phrases as potential names.

4.1.1 Proper Names

Proper nouns are usually key terms for any document or news story e.g., Bill Clinton. We use IdentiFinder [2], a name extraction system to locate names of persons, places, and organizations. We enhance the person name feature by replacing a partial name of a person with the most recent full name inside the same document. For example, we replace all the later occurrences of the name "Clinton" with the most recent occurrence of the full name "Bill Clinton". We reason that the full name of a person is most often mentioned at the beginning of the document and the later references are only partial references.

4.1.2 MDL Phrases

A Phrase is often more descriptive than a single word. For example, the phrase "aircraft accidents" is more descriptive than the word "accidents". We find those word sequences that have high mutual information, such that they decrease the description length (DL, the number of bits needed to code the corpus) for the corpus [4].

The description length (DL) of a corpus is defined by [11] a sum of the number of bits necessary to represent the coded terms in the corpus plus the number of bits required to represent the mapping between the original and the term for the code. In the UTD system, we represent each term by a 32-bit integer. We join two consecutive terms into a phrase (bigram) if the DL of the system decreases by more than some number of bits. The phrase creation process is iterative. First, we find pairs of words and create a new corpus replacing the individual words with newly created phrases. The process of searching for bigrams in the new corpus and creation of another version of corpus with new bigrams is repeated until the search for bigrams results in a null set. For example, in the first iteration, we create a bigram "RODHAM CLINTON", then, in the next iteration, we create "HILLARY [RODHAM CLINTON]".

4.2 Topic Discovery

Topics are themes that are discussed extensively within a document and that are shared among several documents. The TFIDF measure, used in the information retrieval field, coarsely reflects the characteristics of a topic term. Our algorithm for topic discovery employs the TFIDF measure [12] for selecting the topic labels and the OnTopic training procedure for creating topic support words. The algorithm is shown below:

1. Find the K(=5) key terms for each document. The key terms are the top K terms ranked by their TFIDF score, $TFIDF(w,D) = n(w,D)\log\left(\frac{P}{df(w)}\right)$
   where *n(w,D)* is the frequency of the term (word or phrase) *w* in document *D*, *P* is number of documents in the corpus, *df(w)* is the number of documents that have the term *w*.
2. Prune the key term *w* if it is not a key term for more than Q (=4) documents. The surviving key terms over all the document collection are the topic categories for the document collection. Pruning of key-terms prevents creation of topics from terms that are extremely rare. In addition, pruning also eliminates errors in text due to transcription and errors in feature selection by subsystems like IdentiFinder and MDL phrase finder.
3. Using the OnTopic training procedure [1], create a topic model. The input to the trainer is the list of documents and the initial topic categories (surviving key terms) for each document. The OnTopic trainer employs the Estimate-Maximize procedure to obtain topic distributions for each topic category by maximizing the posterior probability, *P(Set of topics given a Document)*. The training results in 100 support words on an average for each topic.

Table 1: Support words and Likelihood scores for the UTD topic "inhalation_anthrax"

Support Words	P (Term I Topic)
anthrax	0.2671
inhalation_anthrax	0.1346
Lundgren	0.0525
anthrax_spores	0.0228
John_Rowland	0.0215
postal_workers	0.0184
mailroom	0.0175
germ_warfare_agent	0.0168
Kathy_Nguyen	0.0155
Miesel	0.0101
anthrax_attacks	0.0101

The support words along with the topic label completely define a topic. Some of the support words for the topic "inhalation anthrax", created by the UTD system, on a collection of news stories (in English), are shown in Table 1.

5. TOPIC EVALUATION

To evaluate the topics, we assign the topics to the documents by using the OnTopic topic classification system [1]. The topic classification system assigns an expanded set of topics for each document. The expanded set includes the topics we failed to identify at the beginning and topics that are related to the document but the label did not appear in the document. For each document, the topic classification system provides a list of topics ranked by the log-posterior probability, P(topic I document). We choose a set of five topics at the top-rank for each document. For each document, to eliminate duplicate topic sets and improve visual quality of the topics, a sub-string search for duplicate topics is done within the assigned set.

A subjective evaluation of a small sample (=100) of documents, randomly chosen from each test document collection was done. During the evaluation, the evaluators mark the topics as "correct" or "wrong". To determine the quality of topics, the following questions were asked:

- Does the topic label relate to the document? Reject if the label is not related to the document.
- What is the quality of the topic label? We reject topic labels like "British Prime" (if they are created as topic labels).
- We also reject the topic labels if they are too generic e.g., "people".
- Is the topic label similar to another topic label for the same document? We reject one of the "President Clinton" and "Bill Clinton" if they are assigned to the same document.
- If the topic label is too ambiguous and doesn't convey the information from the document, even after placing the topic label in the context of the other labels, then reject the topic. For example, if the topics for a document are STOCK, ZERO, MARKET, then reject the topic ZERO.

A precision value is reported for each topic rank,

$$\Pr ecision(rank\, n) = \frac{\#\, correct\, topics\, at\, rank\, n}{\#\, evaluated\, documents}$$

Another measure of performance that is used in conjunction with precision is the recall measure. Recall is the percentage of topics inside a document that have been hypothesized by a system. To measure recall, human annotation of topics for a document is necessary and the annotated topics should have various levels of granularity. Thus, we refrained from including the recall measure in the UTD system evaluation.

We believe that evaluating randomly sampled 100 documents provides a reasonable understanding of the performance of the UTD system. Using the binomial model, the 95% confidence interval is given by

$$c = 1.92 \cdot \sqrt{\frac{p\cdot(1-p)}{n}},$$

Table 3: UTD Topic Precision for English and Arabic Documents

Topic Rank	English documents	Arabic documents
1	96%	88%
2	96%	78%
3	89%	73%
4	82%	83%
5	82%	73%

Table 4: Comparison of UTD system performance with TFIDF key term selection procedures

Topic rank	TFIDF terms[δ] (baseline performance)	UTD topics
1	92%	96%
2	83%	96%
3	87%	89%
4	81%	82%
5	68%	82%

[δ] Topics are top 5 key terms for the document, ranked according to the TFIDF score (defined in step 1 of UTD algorithm described in section 4.2)

Table 5: Average number of topics assigned to each document

System	UTD on English	UTD on Arabic	TFIDF key-terms
Average number of topics per document	4.887	4.321	4.315

where, c is the confidence interval, p is the probability of error, and n is the sample size (=100). Table 2 shows the 95% confidence intervals for various precision values.

Table 2: 95% confidence interval values for a random sample size of 100

Precision	95% confidence interval
95%	4.1%
90%	5.7%
85%	6.8%
80%	7.7%
70%	8.8%

The confidence interval (shown in Table 2) indicates that for several evaluations, each evaluation done on a randomly chosen sample of 100 documents, 95% of the time the variation in the precision is limited by the confidence interval i.e., at 95%±4.1% or 90%±5.7% or 70%±8.8%. In addition, the evaluation sample size has to be quadrupled to reduce the confidence interval by half, which means a very time consuming subjective evaluation.

6. EXPERIMENTAL RESULTS

The UTD system was tested on both English and Arabic documents. For the test-run, 95,530 English documents were chosen from the Primary Source Media (PSM) data for the duration July 1995 through June 1996 and January 1997 through December 1997. We also added 350 documents from Yahoo daily news during the month of November 2001. The Arabic language UTD run was carried out on 37,057 Arabic documents from the Al-Hayat news source for the period January 2001 to November 2001. We ignored the stop words. The remaining words were stemmed to their common roots using the Porter stemming algorithm [8] for English and the Buckwalter stemming algorithm [9] for Arabic.

UTD run on English produced 24124 topics, with an average of 4.887 topics per document. The evaluation was done on a random sample of 100 documents from each of the English and Arabic document collections. From the precision scores are shown in Table 3, it can be seen that the topics discovered by the UTD system are very good.

For the Arabic data, 21737 topics were created with an average of 4.321 topics per document. The lower precision values (as indicated in Table 3) for the Arabic data, when compared to the results for English data, were mainly due to the presence of orthographic variations, errors in stemming due to multiple inflections of the same word, different character usage for similar looking glyphs and an incomplete stop word list.

In order to determine how valuable it was to find proper nouns, we performed an experiment on English data without the IdentiFinder names as features. We found that the degradation in precision value for the topics at rank 1 and 2 was only 2%.

To assess the importance of support words for finding topics, we compared the performance of UTD system against a baseline system. Our baseline system defines topics as the TFIDF key-terms for a document. For each document, five top ranked TFIDF terms are selected as topics. The evaluation results for the baseline system and the UTD system are shown in Table 4. At the top ranked topic, both the baseline system and the UTD method work well, although the UTD method has half the errors. The 95% confidence interval for the top-1 result is 4%. Thus, these results are significant. At the lower ranks, the difference between the methods is larger. We believe this is because the lower topics, which are often more general, are less likely to include the topic name, or need the supporting evidence of the other words. Thus, the UTD method is better able to find them, while the baseline method using TFIDF makes more mistakes.

From the UTD experiments, we also observed that on an average, 30% of the topics assigned to a document (and subjectively judged as correct) are not in the initial topic set used in training. In addition, for 9% of the correct topics (after subjective evaluation) the topic labels are not present the document, but the support words identified the topic. These two results indicate that (a) the UTD process finds good topic terms that would not have been selected by the TFIDF key-term selection procedure, and (b) the UTD process, by using the support words, finds topics for which the topic label is not in the document. These results reinforce our belief that support words are strong indicators of the presence of a topic inside the documents.

7. CONCLUSIONS

We have described a new method for discovering topics from a document collection. The UTD system performed well on English and Arabic corpora. Our approach of using support words as an additional evidence of a topic, resulted in improved performance when compared with a simple key-term selection approach. We were able to identify topics in documents even if the topic name is not in the document at all.

Our results have shown that names as features improve the performance by a small fraction. Thus, the same system can be used on a new language with minimum resources.

8. ACKNOWLEDGEMENTS

We thank Alex Fraser, Jinxi Xu and Mohammed Noamany for helping us with the Arabic pre-processing (stemming and stop word removal). We thank Mohammed Noamany for the great help in subjective evaluation of the Arabic data.

9. REFERENCES

[1] Schwartz, R., Imai, T., Kubala, F., Nguyen, L. and Makhoul, J. A Maximum Likelihood Model for Topic Classification of Broadcast News, *Eurospeech-97*, Greece, 1997.

[2] Kubala, F., Schwartz, R., Stone, R., and Weischedel, R. Named Entity Extraction from Speech, DARPA Broadcast News Transcription and Understanding Workshop, 1998.

[3] Salton, G., and Singhal, A. Automatic Text Theme Generation and the Analysis of Text Structure, Technical Report 94-1438, Dept. of Computer Science, Cornell University, NY, 1994.

[4] Carl de Marcken. The Unsupervised Acquisition of Lexicon from Continuous Speech, MIT Artificial Intelligence Laboratory, A.I. Memo No. 1558, 1995.

[5] Pereira, F., Tishby, N., and Lee, L. Distributional clustering of English words, *Proceedings of ACM*, 183-190, 1993.

[6] Hang Li, and Abe, N. Word clustering and disambiguation based on co-occurrence data, *Proceedings of COLING-ACL'98*, 749-755, 1998.

[7] Biswas, G., Weinberg, J.B., and Fisher, D.H. ITERATE: A Conceptual Clustering Algorithm for Data Mining, *IEEE Transactions on Systems, Man, and Cybernetics – Part C: Applications and Reviews*, Vol. 28, 219-230, 1998.

[8] Porter, M.F. An algorithm for suffix stripping, *Program*, 14(3), 130-137, 1980.

[9] Buckwalter, T. Personal Communications, 2001.

[10] Srivastava, A. Story Segmentation in Audio Indexing, M.S. Thesis, Northeastern University, Boston, 1999.

[11] Leek, T.R. Minimum Description Length (MDL) Phrases. BBN Technologies, Technical Report 010405TRL, 2001.

[12] Salton, G. The SMART retrieval system: Experiments in Automatic Document Processing. Prentice Hall, 1971.

Relevance Models for Topic Detection and Tracking

Victor Lavrenko, James Allan,
Edward DeGuzman, Daniel LaFlamme, Veera Pollard, and Stephen Thomas

Center for Intelligent Information Retrieval
Department of Comupter Science
University of Massachusetts, Amherst, MA 01003

ABSTRACT

We extend relevance modeling to the link detection task of Topic Detection and Tracking (TDT) and show that it substantially improves performance. Relevance modeling, a statistical language modeling technique related to query expansion, is used to enhance the topic model estimate associated with a news story, boosting the probability of words that are associated with the story even when they do not appear in the story. To apply relevance modeling to TDT, it had to be extended to work with stories rather than short queries, and the similarity comparison had to be changed to a modified form of Kullback-Leibler. We demonstrate that relevance models result in very substantial improvements over the language modeling baseline. We also show how the use of relevance modeling makes it possible to choose a single parameter for within- and cross-mode comparisons of stories.

1. INTRODUCTION

Topic Detection and Tracking (TDT) is a research program investigating methods for automatically organizing news stories by the events that they discuss. TDT includes several evaluation tasks, each of which explores one aspect of that organization–i.e., splitting a continuous stream of news into stories that are about a single topic ("segmentation"), gathering stories into groups that each discuss a single topic ("detection"), identifying the onset of a new topic in the news ("first story detection"), and exploiting user feedback to monitor a stream of news for additional stories on a specified topic ("tracking").

Another TDT evaluation task, Link Detection, requires determining whether or not two randomly selected stories discuss the same topic. Unlike the other tasks that have value in and of themselves, Link Detection is a a component technology: it can be used to address each of the other tasks.[1] For example, in order to recognize the start of a new topic, a candidate story might be compared to all prior stories to see whether the topic appeared earlier. Similarly, tracking stories on a specified topic can be done by comparing each arriving story to the user-supplied list of on-topic stories.

The core of most approaches to Link Detection (and therefore to most of the TDT tasks) is comparing word overlap between the two stories: the more words that are in common, the more likely it is that the two stories are on the same topic. This method is the basis of everything from vector space approaches [4, 17] to statistical language model [19, 12] techniques. As in the field of Information Retrieval, much research focuses on techniques for selecting which words to compare, how they should be weighted, and how best to compare the sets of weighted words.

Another research idea that has become common in TDT is expanding the words in a story to include other, strongly related words. The idea is to increase the likelihood that two stories on the same topic will have important overlapping words. Vector space models use query expansion techniques such as Local Context Analysis [18] to expand the list of words [16]. More theoretically grounded approaches such as statistical language modeling implicitly include related words from a background model as part of the smoothing process [19, 12].

In this paper we explore this technique of expanding the set of words associated with a story using "relevance models," a theoretical extension of statistical language modeling that was developed for the task of document retrieval. In the next section we outline the basic ideas of relevance models. In Section 3 we present how relevance models were adapted to the TDT tasks, where stories are compared to each other rather than a query to a document, and where the comparison method is therefore different. Section 4 describes the experiments that were done and shows how relevance models improve effectiveness on the link detection task. In Section 4.5 we briefly explore how this expansion process is quite different depending on whether the stories come from within a single source and modality, or across them. Section 5 draws conclusions and speculates on future work in this area.

2. RELEVANCE MODELS

Lavrenko and Croft [11] define "relevance model" to be a mechanism that determines the probability $P(w|R)$ of observing a word w in a document that is relevant to a query,

[1]In fact, such relationships exist between several of the tasks. The tracking task can be a basis for the other tasks also [3], though unlike link detection, it has clear value on its own.

Proceedings of HLT 2002, Second International Conference on Human Language Technology Research, M. Marcus, ed., Morgan Kaufmann, San Francisco, 2002.

where R represents the class of documents that are relevant to the query. The difficult aspect of relevance models is estimating the model in the absence of significant amounts of data—typically the system has available only the query and a set of documents without relevance judgments.

One way to address that problem is to make the assumption that in the absence of any training data and given a query $Q = q_1q_2 \ldots q_k$, we can approximate $P(w|R)$ by $P(w|q_1q_2 \ldots q_k)$. That is, by the probability of co-occurrence between the query and the word.

To implement the ideas behind relevance models, a system follows the following steps:

- Use the query, Q, to retrieve a set of highly ranked documents, R_Q. This step yields a set of documents that contain most or all of the query words. The documents are, in fact, weighted by the probability that they are relevant to the query—i.e., $P(D|Q), D \in R_Q$.
- For each word in those documents, calculate the probability that the word occurs in that set. That is, calculate $P(w|R_Q)$, a value that is used to approximate $P(w|R)$:

$$P(w|R_Q) = \sum_{D \in R_Q} P(w|D)P(D|Q) \qquad (1)$$

As with most language modeling approaches, $P(w|D)$ is calculated using a maximum likelihood estimate smoothed with the background model:

$$\begin{aligned} P(w|D) &= \lambda P_{ml}(w|D) + (1-\lambda)P_{bg}(w) \\ &= \lambda \frac{\text{tf}_{w,D}}{|D|} + (1-\lambda)\frac{\text{cf}_w}{\text{coll.size}} \end{aligned} \qquad (2)$$

Here, $\text{tf}_{w,D}$ is the number of times the word w occurs in the document D, cf_w is the total number of times w occurs in a large background collection, and coll.size is the total number of words in that background collection. The value of λ as well as the number of documents to include in R_Q are determined empirically from training data. For all experiments reported here, R_Q is 30. Values of λ are reported below.

3. RELEVANCE MODELS IN TDT

The relevance model described above was built from a small query and then used to estimate the probability that documents are relevant to the query. In TDT's link detection task two stories are being compared to decide if they are on the same topic. We will do this by building a relevance model for *each* story, where that model is intended to capture the topic of the stories. Because we are starting from an entire story rather than from a short query, the estimation must be done slightly differently.

Once the two models are created, we decide whether they discuss the same topic by comparing the models directly. We found it helpful to use a modified form of the Kullback-Leiblar divergence

Finally, we needed to explore the impact of different modalities on the comparisons. In most retrieval tasks, the collection being searched contains a mostly homogeneous set of documents. TDT collections, on the other hand, come from newswire text, speech recognition output, closed captioning, machine translation, and combinations of all of those. Comparisons within and across modalities can have significant impact on the results. We discuss below how we addressed that problem.

3.1 Building the topic models

In order to build a topic (relevance) model for a story, we start with the process described above. The story, $S = q_1q_2 \ldots q_k$, is used as a "query" into all training stories in the news. Each training story, D, is therefore ranked by $P(D|S)$ or $P(D|q_1 \ldots q_k)$. Unfortunately, if those probabilities are used directly, they are generally forced to zero because there are so many terms in the story (i.e., k is large). To see why that is the case, consider how we calculate the probability:

$$P(D|q_1 \ldots q_k) = \frac{P(q_1 \ldots q_k|D)P(D)}{P(q_1 \ldots q_k)}$$

The denominator $P(q_1 \ldots q_k)$ is a constant across different documents D, and following [11] we picked a a uniform prior $P(D)$. Therefore only the probability of the query given the document $P(q_1 \ldots q_k|D)$ has an impact on the value of the posterior. We usually assume independence of the query words and calculate:

$$P(D|q_1 \ldots q_k) \sim P(q_1 \ldots q_k|D) = \prod_{i=1}^{k} P(q_i|D)$$

When k is larger than a few terms, the resulting product becomes very small (recall that $P(q_i|D) < 1$). As a result, we often get floating point underflow and—more importantly—the probability only has a reasonable value for the highest-ranked story. That is, $P(D|q_1 \ldots q_k)$ is driven to zero for all but the highest ranked story, which is almost always the original document $S = q_1 \ldots q_k$. If that happens, then the value of relevance modeling disappears: no stories are mixed into the model.

To address this problem, we "flatten" the probability as $P(q_1 \ldots q_k|D)^{\frac{1}{k}}$. Taking the kth root avoids both problems listed above. This is a heuristic adjustment which we hope to circumvent in our future work on relevance-based models.

3.2 Measuring Topic Similarity

Once we have built models for each topic, we need to compare the models to determine the chance that they represent the same topic. Given two stories, S_1 and S_2, assume that their relevance models are M_1 and M_2, respectively. If we were to parallel the information retrieval use of relevance models, we might calculate either $P(S_1|M_2)$ or $P(S_2|M_1)$ or possibly the average of the two.

However, given that we have two models that were estimated from similar amounts of data (S_1 or S_2) we can instead compare the models directly. The Kullback-Leibler divergence is a standard way to compare two probability distributions, defined as:

$$D(M_1||M_2) = \sum_w P(w|M_1) \log \frac{P(w|M_1)}{P(w|M_2)}$$

KL divergence is asymmetric, which is unacceptable as a link detection metric. We compute a symmetric version by summing the divergence in both directions: $D(M_1||M_2) + D(M_2||M_1)$. Since Kullback-Leiblar divergence is a measure of dissimilarity of the two distributions, we use the negation of the above quantity to measure similarity.

This yields a reasonable approach, but has the problem that if the models are very ambiguous—e.g., if relevance modeling failed and created a model that looks too much like general English—their matching has very little significance. That is, if the two models are both of general English, it is not valuable that they are identical since they do not describe a topic. To address this problem, we leverage a notion of query clarity [8], the KL divergence between a distribution and general English. A distribution is clear (or focused) if it is very unlike general English and unclear if it is identical to general English.

The non-symmetric version of our topic similarity measure is therefore: $[-D(M_1||M_2) + \text{Clarity}(M_1)]$ That is, the degree to which M_2 and M_1 are similar, increased to the extent that M_1 is a clear model that differs from general English. After a very simple algebraic manipulation, the similarity measure can be written as:

$$\sum_w P(w|M_1) \log \frac{P(w|M_2)}{P(w|GE)} \qquad (3)$$

In this form it bears strong resemblance to the length-normalized log-likelihood ratio, which has been used by a number of TDT participants [12, 4]. Note that adding clarity has resulted in the denominator that plays a role similar to the role of *idf* in document retrieval. To get the final similarity measure, we calculate the same quantity the other way (swapping M_1 and M_2) and add them together.

4. APPLYING RELEVANCE MODELS

In this section we evaluate performance of relevance models, as described above, on the Link Detection task of TDT. First, we describe the experimental setup and the evaluation methodology. Then we provide empirical support for the choice of parameters in our system. Finally we show that relevance models significantly outperform simple language models, as well as other heuristic techniques.

4.1 Experimental Setup

4.1.1 Dataset

All of the following experiments were performed on a 4-month subset of the TDT2 [7] dataset. The corpus contains 40,000 news stories totaling around 10 million words. The news stories were collected from six different sources: two newswire sources (Associated Press and New York Times), two radio sources (Voice of America and Public Radio International), and two television sources (CNN and ABC). The stories cover January through April of 1998. Radio and television sources were manually transcribed [7] at closed-caption quality. In a pre-processing stage, the stories were stemmed and 400 stop-words from the InQuery [5, 2] stop-list were removed.

4.1.2 Topics

TDT is concerned with detecting and organizing the topics in news stories. Human annotators identified a total of 96 topics in the TDT2 dataset, ranging from 1998 Asian financial crisis, to the Monica Lewinsky scandal, to an execution of Karla Faye Tucker. Each topic is centered around a specific event, which occurs in a specific place and time, with specific people involved. 56 out of these 96 topics are sufficiently represented in the first four months of 1998 and will form the basis for our evaluation.

4.1.3 Evaluation Paradigm

The system is evaluated in terms of its ability to detect the pairs of stories that discuss the same topic. A total of 6363 story pairs were drawn from the dataset (according to the official TDT2 sampling). 1469 of these were manually [7] judged to be on-target (discussing the same topic), and 4894 were judged off-target (discussing different topics). During evaluation the Link Detection System emits a YES or NO decision for each story pair. If our system emits a YES for an off-target pair, we get a False Alarm error; if the system emits a NO for on-target pair, we get a Miss error. Otherwise the system is correct. Link Detection is evaluated in terms of the decision cost [9], which is a weighted sum of probabilities of getting a Miss and False Alarm:

$$Cost = P(Miss)C_{Miss} + P(FA)C_{FA}$$

In current evaluations of Link Detection, C_{Miss} is typically set to 10×0.02, and $C_{FA} = 1 \times 0.98$. Note that by always answering YES a system would have no misses and therefore a cost of 0.2 (similarly, always answering NO guarantees a cost of 0.98). To penalize systems for doing no better than a simple strategy like that, the cost is normalized by dividing by the minimum of those two values (here, 0.2). A normalized cost value near or above 1.0 reflects of a system of marginal value. An operational Link Detection System requires a threshold selection strategy for making YES / NO decisions. However, in a research setting it has been a common practice to ignore on-line threshold selection and perform evaluations at the threshold that gives the best possible cost. All of our experiments report the minimum normalized detection cost: $Cost_{min}$.

4.2 Value of Clarity-adjusted KL

In Section 3 we describe a clarity-adjusted KL divergence, and provide an argument for why we believe this measure may perform better than straight KL divergence. To evaluate the value of clarity adjustment we perform a simple experiment without constructing relevance models. Given a pair of stories A and B we construct maximum likelihood language models of each story, smooth it with the background model, as described in equation (2), and measure divergence. We consider four different divergence measures:

1. simple KL divergence: $KL_1(A, B) = D(A||B)$
2. symmetric version: $KL_2(A, B) = D(A||B) + D(B||A)$
3. clarity-adjusted: $KL_{c,1}(A, B) = D(A||B) - Clarity(A)$
4. symmetric: $KL_{c,2}(A, B) = KL_{c,1}(A, B) + KL_{c,1}(B, A)$

Figure 1 shows the minimum detection cost ($Cost_{min}$) of the four measures as a function of the smoothing parameter λ from equation (2). We observe that clarity-adjusted KL leads to significantly lower errors for all values of λ. Clarity adjustment also leads to smaller dependency on λ, which makes tuning easier. We also note that for both simple and adjusted KL, we get significantly better performance by using symmetric divergence. The best performance $Cost_{min} = 0.1057$ is achieved by using the symmetric version of clarity-adjusted KL when $\lambda = 0.2$. This

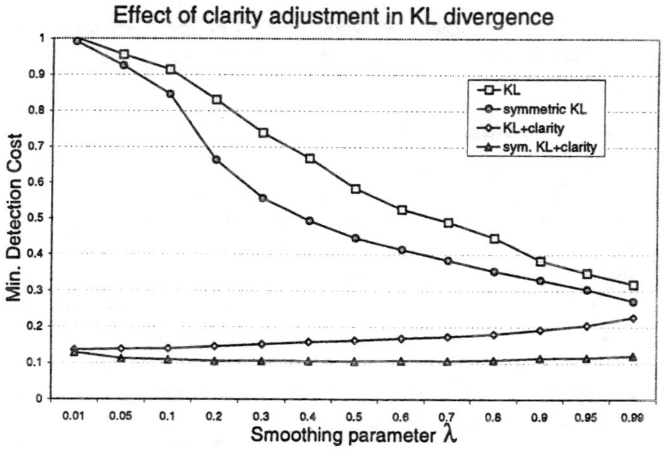

Figure 1: Clarity adjustment leads to significantly lower error rates. Symmetric versions of KL perform better than asymmetric versions. Symmetric KL with clarity is best and most stable with respect to the smoothing parameter λ.

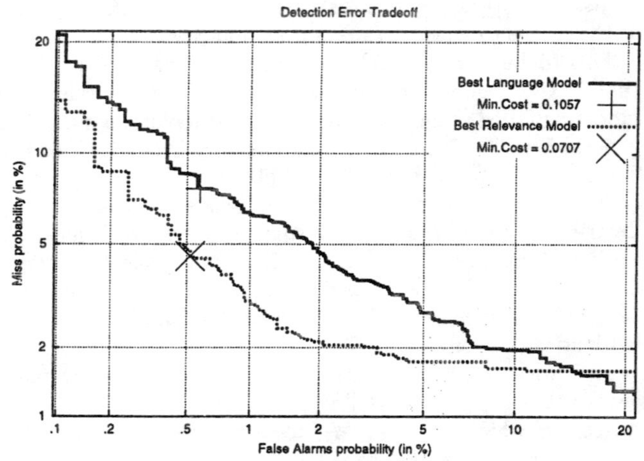

Figure 2: Relevance Models noticeably outperform the baseline for all threshold settings in the region of interest. Minimum Detection Cost is reduced by 33%

performance will be used as a baseline in later comparisons with relevance models. The baseline is competitive with the state-of-the-art results reported in the official TDT evaluations [14].

4.3 Relevance Model Performance

Now we compare our baseline to the performance we can achieve with relevance models. Given a pair of stories A and B, we construct a relevance model from each story as described in Sections 2 and 3. For efficiency purposes, each story was reduced to 30 words with highest frequencies, and these words were used as a query Q to retrieve a set of related stories R_Q. The set R_Q was limited to contain 30 highest-ranked documents. The relevance model was constructed from this set of documents according to equation (1). We use symmetric clarity-adjusted KL as a measure of divergence between the two resulting relevance models. The smoothing parameter λ is set to 0.999. Empirical justifications for these parameter settings are described in section 4.4.

Figure 2 shows the *Detection Error Tradeoff* (DET) [13] curve for the performance of relevance models, compared to the best language modeling baseline. A DET curve is a plot of Miss and False Alarm probabilities as a function of a sliding threshold. The point on each curve marks the optimal threshold, and the corresponding minimum cost $Cost_{min}$. Note that the values are plotted on a Gaussian scale and that the axes only go up to 20% Miss and False Alarm; the full-range DET curves are presented in Figure 6. We observe that a relevance modeling system noticeably outperforms the baseline for almost all threshold settings. The improvements are particularly dramatic around the optimal threshold. The minimum cost is reduced by 33%. Outside of the displayed region, on the high-precision end ($FalseAlarm < 0.01\%$), the relevance modeling system noticeably outperforms the baseline. On the very high-recall end ($Miss < 1.5\%$), the baseline performs somewhat better.

The results in Figure 2 were achieved by careful tuning of parameters on the 4-month subset of the TDT-2 corpus and do not represent a blind evaluation. However, the same parameters were used in the official TDT 2001 blind evaluation on the 3-month TDT-3 corpus. The results in that case were comparable to those described above (see Figure 7 for details). The system based on Relevance Models significantly outperformed a state-of-the-art vector-space system (cosine with Okapi *tf.idf* weighting). The normalized minimum cost was reduced from 0.27 to 0.24. This suggests that our parameter settings generalized reasonably well to the new dataset and the new set of topics.

4.4 Parameter Selection

In this section we provide empirical justification for the values of parameters we used in the estimation of relevance models. We explore three parameters: the number of words we used to represent the document, the size of the retrieved set R_Q, and the smoothing parameter λ.

4.4.1 Query size

Efficiency issues prompted us to represent a document by 30 words with highest frequencies in that document. Ideally, we would like to be able to use all the words in the document, however running the whole document as a query is computationally very expensive, while running a 30-word query is quite feasible. To show that 30 words is a reasonable value, we look at resulting precision in the set R_Q for different sizes of R_Q. Figure 3 shows the precision as a function of the number of words in the query. Precision is the proportion of documents in R_Q that discuss the same topic as the query document. We show precision for the sets R_Q of size 5, 10, 15, 20 and 30. We observe that in all cases precision does not improve significantly if we use more than 30 words. If we use fewer than 30 words, the precision degrades noticeably. In the remaining experiments we use 30-word queries. Note that stopwords have been removed from the documents prior to selecting high-frequency words.

4.4.2 Size of retrieved set

In theory, estimating a relevance model involves computing equation (1) over all the documents D in the dataset, since $P(D|Q)$ is never zero due to the smoothing. In practice this is very expensive and unnecessary. For the vast majority

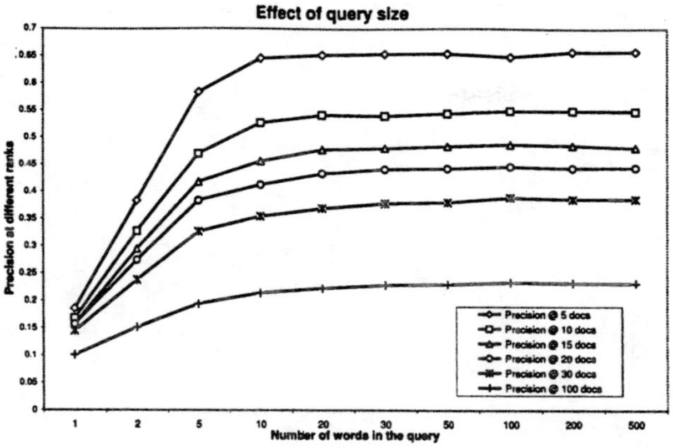

Figure 3: Using more than 30 words to represent the document does not lead to improved precision in the set R_Q. The result is consistent over various sizes of R_Q.

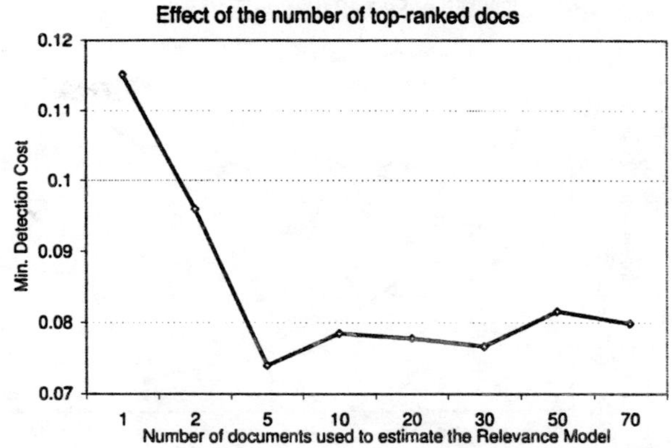

Figure 4: Using anywhere between 5 and 70 top-ranked documents as R_Q results in consistently good performance.

of documents, $P(D|Q)$ is very close to zero, and including it in the summation will have little effect. For this reason we consider limiting R_Q to the n documents with the highest $P(D|Q)$. Figure 4 shows relevance models performance as a function of n (the smoothing parameter λ was fixed at 0.9). We observe that using anywhere between 5 and 70 documents with highest $P(D|Q)$ results in good performance. Using fewer than 5 or more than 100 documents has adverse effects. We settled on using 30 top-ranked documents.

4.4.3 Smoothing

Smoothing is a critical component of any system based on statistical language modeling. Numerous studies [6, 10, 15] have shown that smoothing has a very strong impact on performance of information retrieval systems. In Section 4.2 we observed that the smoothing from equation (2) has a strong effect on performance of maximum likelihood models. Interestingly, smoothing had a very unusual effect with relevance models. We obtained best performance with λ very close to 1, i.e. with almost no smoothing of the document models. This result is somewhat unexpected, and deserves a brief explanation.

According to Zhai and Lafferty [10], smoothing plays a dual role in applications of statistical language models to Information Retrieval. First, smoothing ensures non-zero probabilities for every word under a document model, and acts as a variance-reduction technique. Second, smoothing has an *idf*-like effect on document scoring. Both of these roles are captured by different mechanisms in our model. When we estimate a Relevance Model for some story, we mix together neighboring document models (equation 1). This results in non-zero probabilities for many more words than actually occur in the original story, so there is less value in smoothing to avoid zeros. Also, as mentioned in the end of section 3.2, clarity adjustment on KL divergence has an effect similar to *idf*.

4.5 Cross-modal evaluation

An essential part of TDT is being able to deal with multiple sources of news. The TDT2 corpus that was used in our experiments includes news from six different sources. Two of these (Associated Press and New York Times) are printed sources, the other represent broadcast news, which are transcribed from audio signal. Spoken text has very different properties compared to written sources, and part of the TDT challenge is development of the algorithms that can cope with source-related differences in reporting. To determine how well our algorithms perform on different source conditions, we partitioned the set of 6363 pairs into three subsets:

1. 2417 pairs where both stories come from a broadcast source; this set will be labeled "BN" (broadcast news)
2. 1027 pairs where both stories come from a printed source; this set will be labeled "NW" (newswire)
3. 2919 pairs where one story is from a broadcast source and the other from the printed source; this set will be labeled "NWxBN"

Figure 5 shows performance of the baseline and the relevance modeling systems on the three subsets we described. Performance is shown as a function of the smoothing parameter λ. First we observe that performance varies very significantly from one subset to another. Interestingly, both systems perform best on the "NWxBN" condition, even though it intuitively appears to be more challenging as we are dealing with two different language styles. Another very interesting issue is the value of λ that gives the best performance. Note that for the baseline system the optimal λ value is different for every condition: "BN" is optimized near $\lambda = 0.5$, "NW" - near $\lambda = 0.05$, while "NWxBN" is optimal near $\lambda = 0.7$. This means that for the baseline system we cannot select a single value of λ which will work well for all sources. In contrast to that, for the relevance modeling system all conditions are optimized if we set λ to 0.99, or any value close to 1. This is a very encouraging result, as it shows that relevance models are not very sensitive to source conditions.

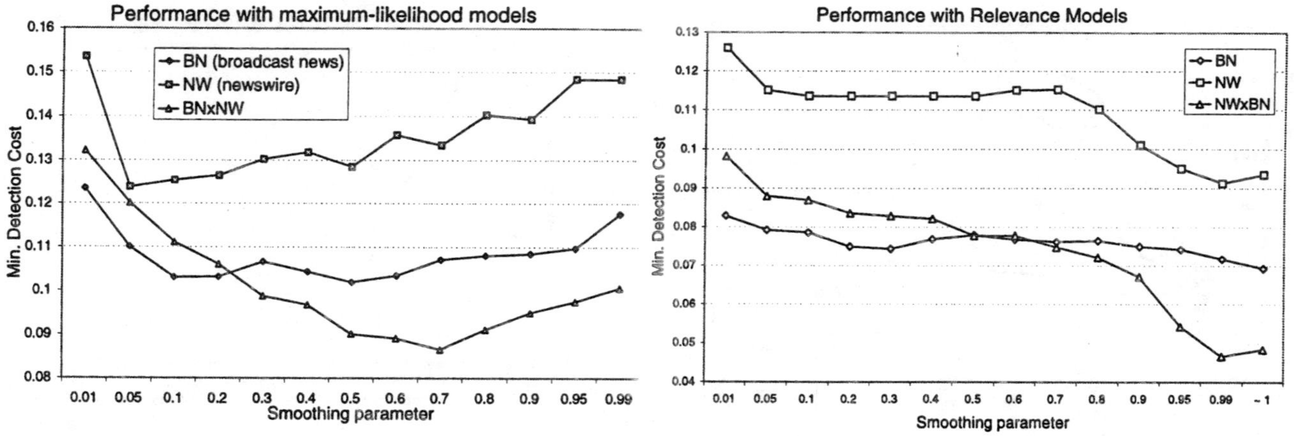

Figure 5: Performance on different source conditions. Left: baseline, optimal smoothing value is different for every condition. Right: Relevance Models, all conditions are optimized as λ approaches 1.

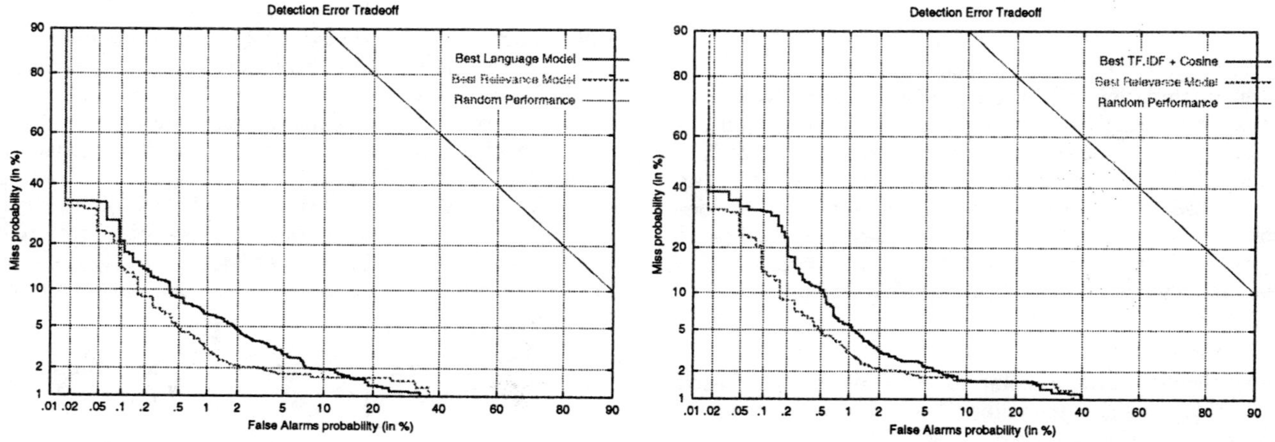

Figure 6: Performance of Relevance Models on the training data. Relevance Models with optimal parameters outperform both the optimal Language Modeling system (left), and the optimal vector-space system using Cosine with Okapi term weighting (right). Minimum Detection Cost was reduced by 33% and 25% respectively (not shown).

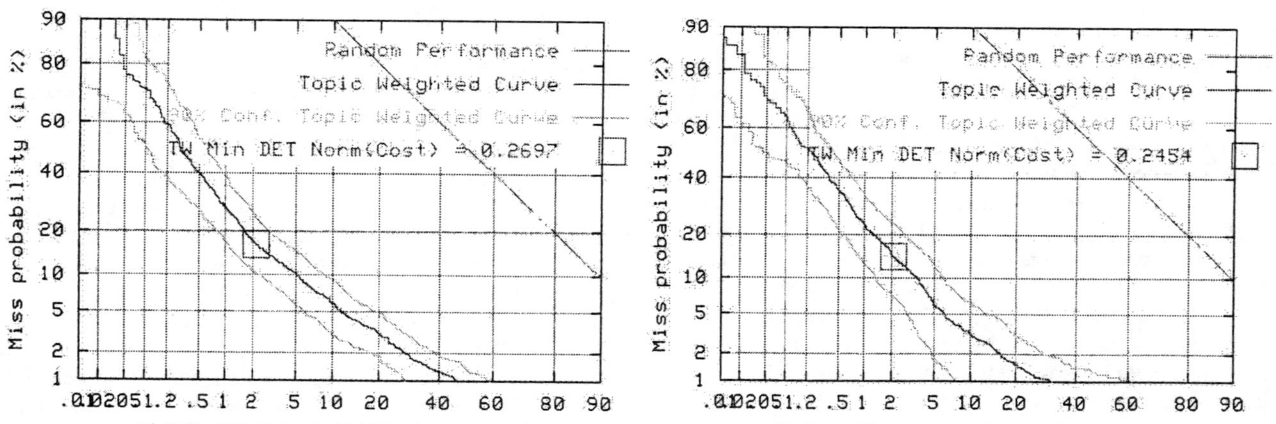

Figure 7: Performance of Relevance Models in the official TDT 2001 evaluation. All the parameters were tuned on the training dataset, and no part of the evaluation dataset was used prior to evaluation. Relevance Models (right) consistently outperform the vector-space model (left). Minimum Detection Cost is reduced by 10%.

5. CONCLUSIONS

In this work we have shown how the relevance model technique can be extended to TDT's link detection task. To do so, the models themselves had to be calculated differently to avoid the problem of very small probabilities due to large "queries". Also, we found it preferable to compare two models directly using a version of KL divergence that incorporates model clarity, or how close the model is to general English.

We demonstrated a substantial performance improvement using relevance models. The parameter selection problem was also shown to be somewhat simpler because the cost values are less sensitive to parameter changes with than without relevance models.

This effect—easier parameter selection—carried over into the problem of within- and cross-mode comparisons of stories. With relevance models, the different choices (both A, both B, or A&B) have much more similar cost values, improving the error tradeoffs.

6. FUTURE WORK

In the course of this work, we encountered a number of interesting questions that we hope to answer in our future research. For one, we were surprised by the gain we achieved by using clarity adjustment over the straight KL divergence, and would like to investigate theoretical implications of its remarkably good performance. Second, we are not satisfied with the heuristic nature of *flattening* of posterior probabilities (section 3.1), and are investigating more formal approaches.

The present work can be extended in a number of important directions. One is dictated by the multi-lingual nature of TDT: a Link Detection system should be capable of dealing with stories in multiple languages. We are actively investigating techniques for estimating multi-lingual relevance models, i.e. language models that contain a mixture of English and non-English words. We are also interested in extending the framework of relevance models to the case where the stories discuss multiple topics. In this case, multiple relevance models would be formed for each story in question.

Acknowledgments

This work was supported in part by the Center for Intelligent Information Retrieval, in part by the National Science Foundation under grant number EIA-9820309, and in part by SPAWARSYSCEN-SD grant number N66001-99-1-8912. Any opinions, findings and conclusions or recommendations expressed in this material are the authors and do not necessarily reflect those of the sponsors.

7. REFERENCES

[1] J. Allan, editor. *Topic Detection and Tracking: Event-based Information Organization.* Kluwer Academic Publishers, Boston, 2002.

[2] J. Allan, M. Connell, W. Croft, F. Feng, D. Fisher, and X. Li. INQUERY and TREC-9. In *Proceedings of the Text Retrieval Conference (TREC-9)*, pages 551–577. NIST, 2001.

[3] J. Allan, V. Lavrenko, and H. Jin. First story detection in TDT is hard. In *Proceedings of the Conference on Information and Knowledge Management (CIKM)*, pages 389–396, 2000.

[4] J. Allan, V. Lavrenko, and R. Swan. Explorations within topic tracking and detection. In Allan [1], pages 197–224.

[5] J. Broglio, J. Callan, and W. B. Croft. INQUERY system overview. In *Proceedings of the Tipster Text Program (Phase I)*, pages 47–67, San Francisco, 1994. Morgan Kaufmann.

[6] S. F. Chen and J. T. Goodman. An empirical study of smoothing techniques for language modeling. In *Proceedings of the 34th Annual Meeting of the ACL*, 1996.

[7] C. Cieri, S. Strassel, D. Graff, N. Martey, K. Rennert, and M. Liberman. Corpora for topic detection and tracking. In Allan [1], pages 33–66.

[8] W. B. Croft, S. Cronen-Townsend, and V. Lavrenko. Relevance feedback and personalization: A language modeling perspective. In *Proceedings of the DELOS-NSF Workshop on Personalization and Recommender Systems in Digital Libraries*, pages 49–54, 2001.

[9] J. G. Fiscus and G. R. Doddington. Topic detection and tracking evaluation overview. In Allan [1], pages 17–31.

[10] J. Lafferty and C. Zhai. A study of smoothing methods for language models applied to ad hoc information retrieval. In *Proceedings on the 24th annual international ACM SIGIR conference*, pages 111–119, 2001.

[11] V. Lavrenko and W. B. Croft. Relevance-based language models. In *Proceedings of ACM SIGIR Conference on Research in Information Retrieval*, pages 267–275, 2001.

[12] T. Leek, R. Schwartz, and S. Sista. Probabilistic approaches to topic detection and tracking. In Allan [1], pages 67–83.

[13] A. Martin, G. Doddington, T. Kamm, and M. Ordowski. The DET curve in assessment of detection task performance. In *EuroSpeech*, pages 1895–1898, 1997.

[14] NIST. Proceedings of the tdt 2001 workshop. Notebook publication for participants only, Nov. 2001.

[15] J. Ponte. Is information retrieval anything more than smoothing? In *Proceedings of the Workshop on Language Modeling and Information Retrieval*, pages 37–41, 2001.

[16] J. Ponte and W. B. Croft. Text segmentation by topic. In *Proceedings of the European Conference on Research and Advanced Technology for Digital Libraries (ECDL)*, pages 113–125, 1997.

[17] J. M. Schultz and M. Y. Liberman. Towards a "universal dictionary" for multi-language IR applications. In Allan [1], pages 225–241.

[18] J. Xu and W. B. Croft. Improving the effectiveness of inforamtion retrieval with local context analysis. *ACM Transactions on Information Systems (TOIS)*, 18(1):79–112, 2000.

[19] J. Yamron, L. Gillick, P. van Mulbregt, and S. Knecht. Statistical models of topical content. In Allan [1], pages 115–134.

Named Entity Translation:

Extended Abstract

Yaser Al-Onaizan Kevin Knight

Information Sciences Institute
University of Southern California
Marina del Rey, CA 90292
{yaser,knight}@isi.edu

Keywords

Named Entity Translation, Named Entities, Machine Transliteration,Machine Translation

1. INTRODUCTION

Named entity phrases are being introduced in news stories on a daily basis in the form of personal names, organizations, locations, temporal phrases, and monetary expressions. While the identification of named entities in text has received significant attention (e.g., [2] and [1]), translation of all named entities has not. This translation problem is especially challenging because new phrases can appear out of nowhere, and because many are domain specific, not to be found in bilingual dictionaries.

In this paper, we describe a system for Arabic-English named entity translation, though the technique is applicable to any language and does not require especially difficult-to-obtain resources.

2. PRODUCING TRANSLATION CANDIDATES

Our translation is carried out by first generating a list of translation candidates, as will be described in this section, then re-scoring them using different monolingual clues (Section 3).

Named entity phrases can be identified fairly accurately. In addition to identifying phrase boundaries, systems also provide the category and sub-category of the phrase (e.g., *Entity Name*, and *Person*). Different types of named entities are translated differently and hence our candidate generator has a specialized module for each type. Numerical and temporal expressions typically use a limited set of vocabulary words (e.g., names of months, days of the week) and can be translated fairly easily using simple translation patterns. Therefore, we will not address them in this paper. Instead we will focus on person names, locations, and organizations. But before we present further details, we will discuss how words can be transliterated (i.e., "sounded-out").

Proceedings of HLT 2002, Second International Conference on Human Language Technology Research, M. Marcus, ed., Morgan Kaufmann, San Francisco, 2002.

2.1 Transliteration

Transliteration is the process of replacing words in the source language with their approximate phonetic or spelling equivalents in the target language. Transliteration between languages that use similar alphabets and sound systems is very simple. However, transliterating names from Arabic into English is a non-trivial task, mainly due to the differences in their sound and writing systems. Short vowels are rarely written in Arabic in newspaper text, which makes pronunciation highly ambiguous. Also, there is no one-to-one correspondence between Arabic sounds and English sounds. For example, English **P** and **B** are both mapped into Arabic "ب"; Arabic "ح" and "ه" into English **H**; and so on.

[3] present an Arabic-to-English back-transliteration system based on the source-channel framework. The transliteration process is based on a generative model of how an English name is transliterated into Arabic. It consists of several steps, each is defined as a probabilistic model represented as a finite state machine. First, an English word is generated according to its unigram probabilities $P(w)$. Then, the English word is pronounced with probability $P(e|w)$, which is collected directly from an English pronunciation dictionary. Finally, the English phoneme sequence is converted into Arabic writing with probability $P(a|e)$.

One serious limitation of this method is that only English words with known pronunciations can be produced. Also, human translators often transliterate words based on how they are spelled in the source language. For example, *Graham* is transliterated into Arabic as "غراهام" and not as "غرام". To address these limitations, we extend this approach by using a new spelling-based model in addition to the phonetic-based model.

The spelling-based model we propose directly maps English letter sequences into Arabic letter sequences $P(a|w)$, which are trained on a small English/Arabic name list without the need for English pronunciations. Since no pronunciations are needed, this list is easily obtainable for many language pairs. We also extend the $P(w)$ to include a letter trigram model in addition to the word unigram model. This makes it possible to generate words that are not already defined in the word unigram model.

2.2 Producing Candidates for Person Names

Person names are almost always transliterated. The translation candidates for typical person names are generated using a transliteration module. For example, the name "بيل كلينتون" is transliterated into: *Bell Clinton*, *Bill Clinton*, *Bill Klington*, etc. Finite-state devices produce lattices containing the candidates, as well as n-best lists.

2.3 Producing Candidates for Location and Organization Names

Words in organization and location names, on the other hand, are either translated or transliterated, and it is not clear when a word must be translated and when it must be transliterated. So to generate translation candidates for a given phrase, words in the phrase are first translated using a bilingual dictionary and they are also transliterated. Our candidate generator combines the dictionary entries and k-best transliterations for each word in the given phrase into a regular expression that accepts all possible permutations of word translation/transliteration combinations. This regular expression is then matched against a large English news corpus. All matches are then scored according to their individual word translation/transliteration scores. The scored matches form the list of translation candidates. For example, the candidate list for "خليج الخنازير" includes *Bay of Pigs* and *Gulf of Pigs*.

3. RE-SCORING CANDIDATES

Once a ranked list of translation candidates is generated for a given phrase, several monolingual English resources are used to help re-rank the list. The first re-scoring factor we use is the normalized straight Web count. For the "بيل كلينتون" example, the top two translation candidates are *Bell Clinton* with transliteration score 1.1×10^{-09} and *Bill Clinton* with score 6.7×10^{-10}. The Web frequency counts of these two names are: 146 and 840,844 respectively. This gives us revised scores of 1.9×10^{-13} and 6.68×10^{-10}, respectively, which leads to the correct translation being ranked highest.

In some cases straight Web counting does not help the re-scoring. For example, the top two translation candidates for "دونالد مارون" are *Donald Martin* and *Donald Marron*. Their straight Web counts are 2992 and 2509, respectively. These counts do not change the candidates list ranking. We next seek a more accurate counting method by counting phrases only if they appear within a certain context. Using search engines, this can be done using the boolean operator **AND**. For the previous example, we use the fact that the person mentioned is the *CEO* of *Paine Webber*. In this case we get the counts 0 and 357 for *Donald Martin* and *Donald Marron*, respectively. This is enough to get the correct translation as the top candidate.

4. EXTENDING THE CANDIDATES LIST

The re-scoring methods described above assume that the correct translation is in the candidates list. When it is not in the list, the re-scoring will fail. To address these situations, we need to be able to extrapolate from the candidate list. We do this by searching for the correct translation rather than generating it. We do that by using sub-phrases from the candidates list or by searching for documents in the target language similar to the one being translated. For example, for a person name, instead of searching for the full name, we search for the first name and the last name separately. Then, we use the IdentiFinder named entity identifier [1] to identify all named entities in the top n retrieved documents for each sub-phrase. All named entities of the type of the named entity in question (e.g., *Person*) found in the retrieved documents and that contain the sub-phrase used in the search are added to the list of translation candidates, and the re-scoring is repeated.

To illustrate this method, consider the name "كوفي عنان." Our translation module proposes: *Coffee Annan*, *Coffee Engen*, *Coffee Anton*, *Coffee Anyone*, and *Covey Annan* but not the correct translation **Kofi Annan**. Using a search engine, we retrieve the top n matching documents for each of the names *Coffee*, *Covey*, *Annan*, *Engen*, *Anton*, and *Anyone*. All person names found in the retrieved documents that contain any of the first or last names we used in the search are added to the list of translation candidates. We hope that the correct translation is among the names found in the retrieved documents. The re-scoring procedure is applied once more on the expanded candidates list. In this example, this leads to the correct translation being ranked as top.

To address cases where neither the correct translation nor any of its sub-phrases can be found in the list of translation candidates, we also perform the above extrapolation procedure using contextual information such as the title of the original document to find similar documents in the target language. This is especially useful when translating named entities in news stories of international importance where the same event will most likely be reported in many languages including the target language.

5. EVALUATION

This section presents our preliminary evaluation results. Our evaluation corpus consists of 21 Arabic newspaper articles with named entity phrases hand-tagged and translated to English. The Arabic phrases are paired with their English translations to create the gold-standard translation. In order to evaluate human performance at this task, we asked a bilingual speaker (a native of Arabic) to translate the Arabic named entity phrases given the text they appear in. The errors made by the original human translator turned out to be numerous, ranging from simple spelling errors (e.g., *Custa Rica* vs. *Costa Rica*) to more serious errors such as transliteration errors (e.g., *John Keele* vs. *Jon Kyl*) and other translation errors (e.g., *Union Reserve Council* vs. *Federal Reserve Board*). The error rates in the human translations were 40%, 13.9%, and 28.3% for person, location, and organization names respectively. The overall error rate was 26.3%.

The translations obtained by our system show promising results. The error rates for the results obtained by the candidate generator were 40%, 45%, and 68.3% for person, location, and organization names respectively. After the re-ranking procedure is applied, the error rates were reduced to 22.8%, 31%, and 56.7% respectively. If we measure how often the correct answer is in the top-20 list of proposed candidates, error rates are 15.2%, 29.5%, and 45%, respectively.

6. REFERENCES

[1] D. M. Bikel, R. Schwartz, and R. M. Weischedel. An algorithm that learns what's in a name. *Machine Learning*, 34(1/3), 1999.

[2] A. Mikheev, M. Moens, and C. Grover. Named Entity Recognition without Gazetteers. In *Proceedings of the EACL*, 1999.

[3] B. G. Stalls and K. Knight. Translating Names and Technical Terms in Arabic Text. In *Proceedings of the COLING/ACL Workshop on Computational Approaches to Semitic Languages*, 1998.

Speaker, Accent, and Language Identification Using Multilingual Phone Strings

Tanja Schultz, Qin Jin, Kornel Laskowski, Alicia Tribble, Alex Waibel
Interactive Systems Laboratories
Carnegie Mellon University
Pittsburgh, PA 15213, USA
{tanja,qjin,kornel,atribble,ahw}@cs.cmu.edu

ABSTRACT

In this paper we investigated the identification of non-verbal cues from spoken speech, namely speaker, accent, and language. For these tasks, a joint framework is developed which uses phone strings, derived from different language phone recognizers, as intermediate features and which performs classification decisions based on their perplexities. Our evaluation on variable distance data proved the robustness of the approach, achieving a 96.7% speaker identification rate. Furthermore, we achieved 93.7% accent discrimination accuracy between native and non-native speakers. For language identification, we obtained 95.5% classification accuracy for utterances 5 seconds in length and up to 99.89% on longer utterances. The experiments were carried out in a language independent nature, on languages not presented to the phone recognizers for training, suggesting that they could be successfully ported to non-verbal cue classification in other languages.

1. INTRODUCTION

The identification of an utterance's non-verbal cues, such as speaker, accent and language, can provide useful information for speech analysis. In this paper we investigate far-field speaker identification, as well as accent and language identification, using multilingual phone strings produced by phone recognizers trained on data from different languages.

Currently, approaches based on Gaussian Mixture Models (GMMs) [4] are the most widely and successfully used methods for speaker identification. Although GMMs have been applied successfully to close-speaking microphone scenarios under matched training and testing conditions, their performance degrades dramatically under mismatched conditions. The term "mismatched condition" describes a situation in which the testing conditions, e.g. microphone distance, are quite different from what had been seen during training. For language and accent identification, phone recognition together with phone N-gram modeling has been the most successful approach in the past [6]. More recently, Kohler introduced an approach for speaker recognition where a phonotactic N-gram model is used.

Proceedings of HLT 2002, Second International Conference on Human Language Technology Research, M. Marcus, ed., Morgan Kaufmann, San Francisco, 2002.

In this paper, we extend this idea to far-field speaker identification, as well as to accent and language identification. We introduce two different methods based on multilingual phone strings to tackle mismatched distance and channel conditions and compare them to the GMM approach.

2. THE MULTILINGUAL PHONE STRING APPROACH

The basic idea of the multilingual phone string approach is to use phone strings produced by different context-independent phone recognizers instead of traditional short-term acoustic vectors [1]. For the classification of an audio segment into one of n classes of a specific non-verbal cue, m such phone recognizers together with $m \times n$ phonotactic N-gram models produce an $m \times n$ matrix of features. A best class estimate is made based solely on this feature matrix. The process relies on the availability of m phone recognizers, and the training of $m \times n$ N-gram models on their output.

By using information derived from phonotactics rather than directly from acoustics, we expect to cover speaker idiosyncrasy and accent-specific pronunciations. Since this information is provided from complementary phone recognizers, we anticipate greater robustness under mismatched conditions. Furthermore, the approach is somewhat language independent since the recognizers are trained on data from different languages.

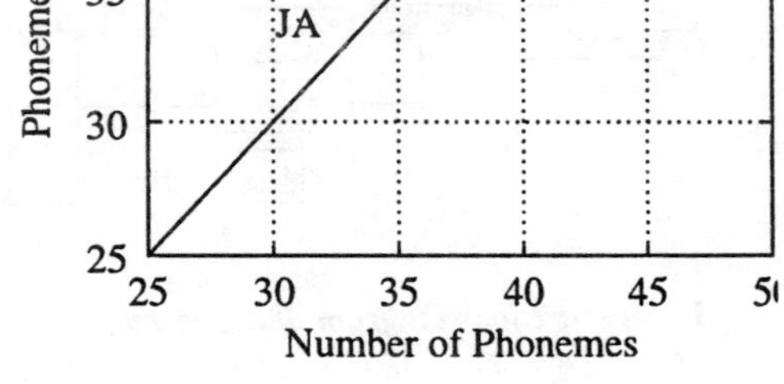

Figure 1: ***Error rate vs number of phones in 10 languages***

2.1 Phone Recognition

For the experiments presented here, the m phone recognizers were borrowed without modification from among the ones available within the GlobalPhone project: Mandarin Chinese (CH), Croatian (CR), French (FR), German (GE), Japanese (JA), Portuguese (PO), Spanish (SP) and Turkish (TU). Figure 1 shows phone error rates per language in relation to the number of modeled phones. See [5] for further details.

2.2 Phonotactic Model Training

In classifying a non-verbal cue C into one of n classes, C_j, our feature extraction scheme requires $m \times n$ distinct phonotactic models $\mathrm{PM}_{i,j}$, $1 \leq i \leq m$ and $1 \leq j \leq n$, one for each combination of phone recognizer PR_i with output class C_j. $\mathrm{PM}_{i,j}$ is trained on phone strings produced by phone recognizer PR_i on C_j training audio as shown in Figure 2. During the decoding of the training set, each PR_i is constrained by an equiprobable phonotactic language model. This procedure does not require transcription at any level.

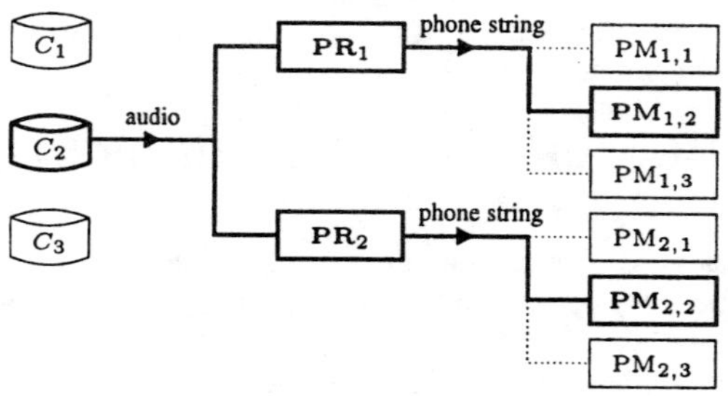

Figure 2: ***Training of feature-specific phonotactic models***

2.3 Classification

We present two multilingual phonotactic model (MPM) approaches to feature extraction, MPM-pp and MPM-dec.

In MPM-pp, each of m phone recognizers $\{\mathrm{PR}_i\}$, as used for phonotactic model training, decodes the test audio segment. Each of the resulting m phone strings is scored against each of n phonotactic models $\{\mathrm{PM}_{i,j}\}$. This results in a perplexity matrix $\mathbf{PP}$, whose $(PP)_{i,j}$ element is the perplexity produced by phonotactic model $\mathrm{PM}_{i,j}$ on the phone string output of phone recognizer PR_i. Although we have explored some alternatives, our generic decision algorithm is to propose a class estimate C_j^* by selecting the lowest $\sum_i (PP)_{i,j}$. Figure 3 depicts the MPM-pp procedure.

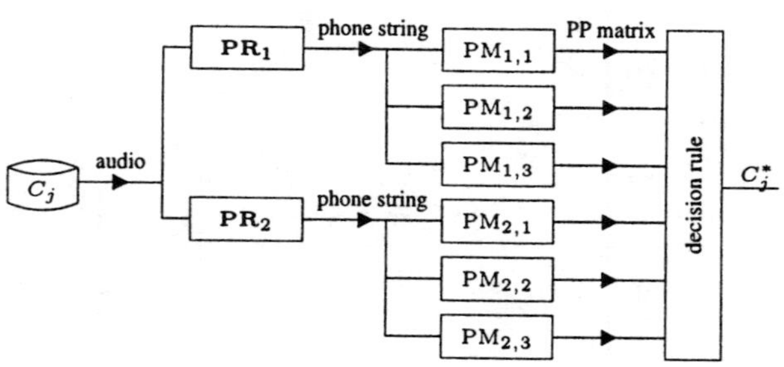

Figure 3: ***Block diagram of MPM-pp***

In MPM-dec, we also use all m phone recognizers $\{\mathrm{PR}_i\}$, but this time when decoding a test utterance we replace the equiprobable phonotactic language model used during phonotactic training with each of the n phonotactic models $\mathrm{PM}_{i,j}$ in turn. The test audio segment is therefore decoded by each of the m phone recognizers n times, resulting in a decoding score matrix $\mathbf{SCORE}$, whose $(SCORE)_{i,j}$ element is the decoding score produced jointly by phone recognizer PR_i and phonotactic model $\mathrm{PM}_{i,j}$ during decoding. As in MPM-pp, the class C_j^* whose $\sum_i (SCORE)_{i,j}$ is lowest is hypothesised. The key behind this method is that a phonotactic model $\mathrm{PM}_{i,j}$ is used directly in the decoding; however, this means that a test utterance must be decoded $m \times n$ times as opposed to only m times for MPM-pp. Furthermore, this procedure relies on the ability to produce reliable phonotactic models $\{\mathrm{PM}_{i,j}\}$ from the training data which are suitable for decoding.

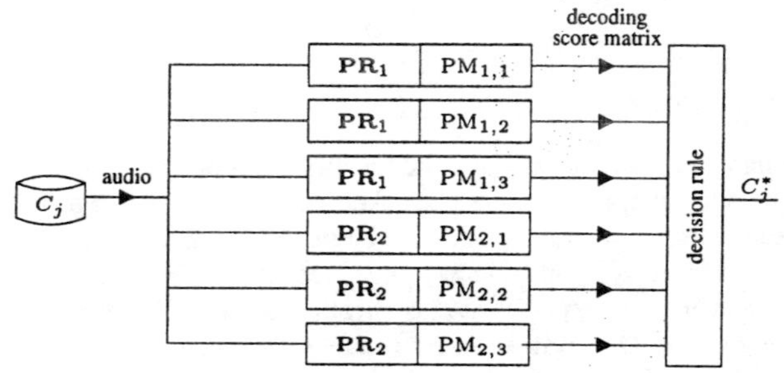

Figure 4: ***Block diagram of MPM-dec***

3. EXPERIMENTS

In this section we apply the described non-verbal cue identification framework to speaker, accent, and language identification.

3.1 Speaker Identification (SID)

Real world speaker identification is expected to work under mismatched conditions, regardless of the microphone distances during training and testing. To investigate robust speaker ID, a database has been collected in our lab containing 30 speakers reading different articles. Each of the five sessions per speaker are recorded using eight microphones in parallel: one close-speaking microphone (Dis 0), one lapel (Dis L) microphone worn by the speaker, and six other lapel microphones at distances of 1, 2, 4, 5, 6, and 8 feet from the speaker. About 7 minutes of spoken speech (approximately 5000 phones) is used for training the PMs, while for training the GMMs one minute was used. The different amount of training data for the two approaches seems to make the comparison quite unfair; however, the training data is used for very different purposes. In the GMM approach, the data is used to train the Gaussian mixtures. In the MPM approach, the data is solely used for creating phonotactic models; no data is used to train the Gaussian mixtures of the phone recognizers.

Testing	Training			
	Dis 0	Dis 1	Dis 2	Dis 6
Dis 0	**100**	43.3	30	26.7
Dis 1	56.7	**90**	76.7	40
Dis 2	56.7	63.3	**93.3**	53.3
Dis 6	40	30	60	**83.3**

Table 1: ***GMM performance under matched and mismatched conditions***

The GMM approach was tested on 10-second chunks, whereas the phone string approach was additionally tested on shorter and longer (up to one minute) chunks. We report results for closed-set text-independent speaker identification. Table 1 shows the GMM results with one minute training data on 10 seconds of test data. It illustrates that the performance under mismatched conditions degrades considerably when compared to performance under matched conditions.

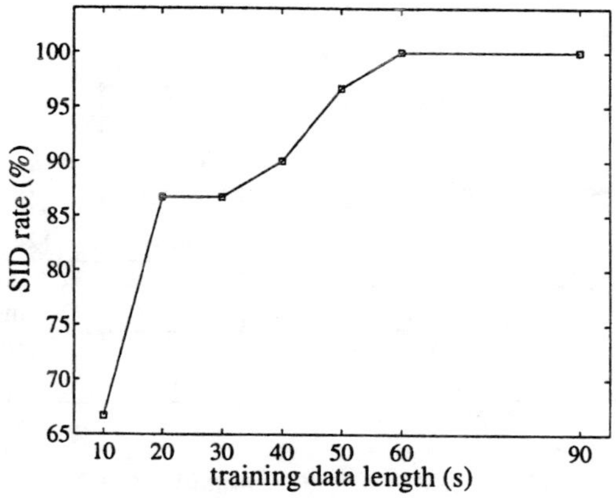

Figure 5: ***GMM performance with increasing training data***

Figure 5 shows the performance of the GMM approach with increasing amounts of training data, from 10 seconds to 90 seconds, on 10 seconds of test data. The graph indicates that for a fixed configuration of GMM structure, adding more training data is not necessary.

Language	60s	40s	10s	5s	3s
CH	100	100	56.7	40.0	26.7
CR	40.0	33.3	30.0	26.7	36.7
FR	70.0	56.7	46.7	16.7	13.3
GE	80.0	76.7	50.0	33.3	26.7
JA	30.0	30.0	36.7	26.7	16.7
PO	76.7	66.7	33.3	20.0	10.0
SP	70.0	56.7	30.0	20.0	16.7
TU	53.3	50.0	30.0	16.7	20.0
Int. of all LM	**96.7**	**96.7**	**96.7**	**93.3**	**80**

Table 2: ***MPM-pp SID rate on varying test lengths at Dis 0***

Table 2 shows the identification results of each phone recognizer and the combination results for eight language phone recognizers for Dis 0 under matched conditions. This shows that multiple languages compensate for poor performance on single engines, an effect which becomes even more important on shorter test utterances.

Table 3 and Table 4 compare the identification results for all distances on different test utterance lengths under matched and mismatched conditions, respectively. Under matched conditions, training and testing data are from the same distance. Under mismatched conditions, we do not know the test segment distance; we make use of all $p = 8$ sets of $\mathrm{PM}_{i,j}$ phonotactic models, where p is the number of distances, and modify our decision rule to estimate $C_j^* = \min_j \left(\min_k \sum_i \mathrm{PM}_{i,j,k}\right)$, where i is the index over phone recognizers, j is the index over speaker phonotactic models, and $1 \leq k \leq p$. These two tables indicate that the performance of

Test Length	60s	40s	10s	5s
Dis 0	96.7	96.7	96.7	93.3
Dis L	96.7	96.7	86.7	70.0
Dis 1	90.0	90.0	76.6	70.0
Dis 2	96.7	96.7	93.3	83.3
Dis 4	96.7	93.3	80.0	76.7
Dis 5	93.3	93.3	90.0	76.7
Dis 6	83.3	86.7	83.3	80.0
Dis 8	93.3	93.3	86.7	66.7

Table 3: ***MPM-pp SID rate on varying test lengths at matched training and testing distances***

Test length	60s	40s	10s	5s
Dis 0	96.7	96.7	96.7	90.0
Dis L	96.7	100	90.0	66.7
Dis 1	93.3	93.3	80.0	70.0
Dis 2	96.7	96.7	86.7	80.0
Dis 4	96.7	96.7	93.3	80.0
Dis 5	93.3	93.3	86.7	70.0
Dis 6	93.3	86.7	83.3	60.0
Dis 8	93.3	93.3	86.7	70.0

Table 4: ***MPM-pp SID rate on varying test lengths at mismatched training and testing distance***

MPM-pp, unlike that of GMM, is comparable for matched and mismatched conditions.

Table 5 compares the performance of MPM-dec at Dis 0 under matched conditions with that of MPM-pp on test utterances of 60 seconds in length. Even though MPM-dec is far more expensive than MPM-pp, its performance is only 60% under matched conditions for close-speaking data while MPM-pp yields 96.7%. The considerably poorer performance of MPM-dec seems to support the assumption made earlier that the phonotactic models we produced, which perform well within the MPM-pp framework, are not sufficiently reliable to be used during decoding as required by MPM-dec. These findings led us to focus on the use of the MPM-pp approach for accent and language identification.

Language	MPM-pp (%)	MPM-dec (%)
CH	100	53.3
CR	40	26.7
FR	70	23.3
GE	80	40.0
JA	30	26.7
PO	76.7	30.0
SP	70	26.7
TU	53.3	26.7
Int. of all PM	**96.7**	**60**

Table 5: ***Comparison of SID rate using MPM-pp and MPM-dec***

3.2 Accent Identification (AID)

In this section we apply our non-verbal cue identification framework to accent identification. In a first experiment, we use the

MPM-pp approach to differentiate between native and non-native speakers of English. Native speakers of Japanese with varying English proficiency levels make up the non-native speaker set [2]. Each speaker was recorded reading several news articles aloud; training and testing sets are disjoint with respect to articles as well as speakers. The data used for this experiment is shown in Table 6.

	use	native	non-native
n_{spk}	training	3	7
	testing	2	5
$\sum n_{utt}$	training	318	680
	testing	93	210
$\sum \tau_{utt}$	training	23.1 min	83.9 min
	testing	7.1 min	33.8 min

Table 6: ***Number of speakers, total number of utterances and total length of audio for native and non-native classes***

We employ six of the GlobalPhone phone recognizers, $PR_i \in \{CR, FR, GE, JA, PO, SP\}$. In training, native utterances are used to produce six phonotactic models $PM_{i,nat}$; the same is done for non-native speech resulting in six $PM_{i,non}$. During classification, the 6×2 phonotactic models produce a perplexity matrix for the test utterance to which we apply our lowest average perplexity decision rule; the class with the lower perplexity is identified as the class of the test utterance.

On our evaluation set of 303 utterances, this system classifies with an accuracy of 93.7%. The separability of the two classes is demonstrated in the average perplexity of each class of phonotactic model over all test utterances. The average perplexity of non-native models on non-native data is lower than the perplexity of native models on that data. Similarly, native models give lower scores to native data than do non-native models. Table 7 shows these averages.

Phonotactic model	Utterance class	
	non-native	native
non-native	29.1	31.7
native	32.5	28.5

Table 7: ***Average phonotactic perplexities for native and non-native classes***

The accented speech experiment is unique among our classification tasks in that it attempts to determine the class of an utterance in a space that varies continuously according to the English proficiency of its speaker. Although classification among native and non-native speakers is discrete, it can be described as identifying speakers who are clustered at the far ends of this proficiency axis. In a second experiment, we attempt to further classify non-native utterances according to proficiency level.

The original non-native data was labelled with the proficiency of each speaker on the basis of a standardized evaluation procedure conducted by trained proficiency raters [2]. All speakers received a floating point grade between 0 and 3, with a grade of 4 reserved for native speakers. The distribution of non-native training speaker proficiencies shows that they fall into roughly three groups and we create three corresponding classes for our new discrimination task. Class 1 represents the lowest proficiency speakers, class 2 contains intermediate speakers, and class 3 contains the high proficiency speakers.

We apply the MPM-pp approach to classify utterances from non-native speakers according to assigned speaker proficiency class. The phonotactic models are trained as before, with models in six languages for each of 3 proficiency classes; our division of data is shown in Table 8.

	use	class 1	class 2	class 3
n_{spk}	training	3	12	4
	testing	1	5	1
$\sum n_{utt}$	training	146	564	373
	testing	78	477	124
$\sum \tau_{utt}$	training	23.9 min	82.5 min	40.4 min
	testing	13.8 min	59.0 min	13.5 min
ave. prof	training	1.33	2.00	2.89
	testing	1.33	2.00	2.89

Table 8: ***Number of speakers, total number of utterances, total length of audio and average speaker proficiency score per proficiency class***

Phonotactic model	Utterance proficiency		
	Class 1	Class 2	Class 3
Class 1	28.35	23.85	25.46
Class 2	23.85	23.86	24.17
Class 3	25.46	23.94	23.91

Table 9: ***Average phonotactic perplexities per proficiency class***

Our results indicate that discriminating among proficiency levels is a more difficult problem than discriminating between native and non-native speakers. Table 9 shows that the class models in this experiment were more confused than the native and non-native models, and classification accuracy suffered as a result. We were able to achieve 84% accuracy in differentiating between class 1 and class 3 utterances, but accuracy on 3-way classification ranged from 34% to 59%.

Overall, the phone string approach worked well for classifying utterances from speaker proficiency classes that were sufficiently separable. Like the other applications of this approach, accent identification requires no hand-transcription and could easily be ported to test languages other than English/Japanese.

3.3 Language Identification (LID)

In this section, we apply the non-verbal cue identification framework to the problem of multiclassification of four languages: Japanese (JA), Russian (RU), Spanish (SP) and Turkish (TU).

We employed a small number of phone recognizers in languages other than the four classification languages in an effort to duplicate the circumstances common to our other non-verbal cue experiments, and to demonstrate a degree of language independence which holds even in the language identification domain.

Phone recognizers in Chinese (CH), French (FR), and German (GE), with phone vocabulary sizes of 145, 47 and 42 respectively, were borrowed from the GlobalPhone project as discussed in [5].

The data for this classification experiment, also borrowed from the GlobalPhone project but not used in training the phone recognizers, was divided up as shown in Table 10. Data set 1 was used for training the phonotactic models, while data set 4 was completely held-out during training and used to evaluate the end-to-end performance of the complete classifier. Data sets 2 and 3 were used as development sets while experimenting with different decision strategies.

	Set	JA	RU	SP	TU
n_{spk}	1	20	20	20	20
	2	5	10	9	10
	3	3	5	5	5
	4	3	5	4	5
$\sum n_{\text{utt}}$	all	2294	4923	2724	2924
$\sum \tau_{\text{utt}}$	all	6 hrs	9 hrs	8 hrs	7 hrs

Table 10: ***Number of speakers per data set, total number of utterances and total length of audio per language***

For phonotactics, utterances from set 1 in each $L_j \in \{\text{JA}, \text{RU}, \text{SP}, \text{TU}\}$ were decoded using each of the three phone recognizers $\text{PR}_i \in \{\text{CH}, \text{FR}, \text{GE}\}$ and 12 separate trigram models were constructed with Kneser/Ney backoff and no explicit cut-off. The training corpora ranged in size from 140K to 250K tokens, and the resulting models were evaluated on corpora constructed from set 2 utterances, of size 27K to 140K tokens. Trigram coverage for all 12 models fell between 73% to 95%, with unigram coverage below 1%.

In order to explore classification in a timeshift-invariant setting, we elected to extract features from segments of audio selected from anywhere in each utterance. For each of $\text{PR}_i \in \{\text{CH}, \text{FR}, \text{GE}\}$, phone strings for all utterances of each speaker in data set 4 were concatenated following decoding. Overlapping windows representing durations of 5, 10, 20 and 30 seconds, offset by 10% of their width, were identified for classification, each leading to a matrix of 3×4 perplexities. Duration was approximated using each speaker's average phone production rate per second for each recognizer PR_i. The number of testing exemplars is depicted per segment length in Table 11.

Set	5 s	10 s	20 s	30 s
4	23541	11689	5765	3789

Table 11: ***Number of test exemplars per segment length***

Classification using lowest average perplexity led to 94.01%, 97.57%, 98.96% and 99.31% accuracy on 5s, 10s, 20s and 30s data respectively, as shown in Figure 6.

For comparison with our lowest average perplexity decision rule, we contructed a separate 4-class multiclassifier, using data set 2, for each of the four durations $\tau_k \in \{5\text{s}, 10\text{s}, 20\text{s}, 30\text{s}\}$; data set 3 was used for cross-validation. With each speaker's utterances concatenated and then windowed as was done for data set 4, this led to audio segments as in Table 12. These were subjected to the same feature extraction as before, yielding a 3×4 perplexity matrix per datum.

Set	5 s	10 s	20 s	30 s
2	48504	24092	11883	7815
3	28180	14003	6917	4556

Table 12: ***Number of ECOC/MLP training and cross-validation exemplars per segment length***

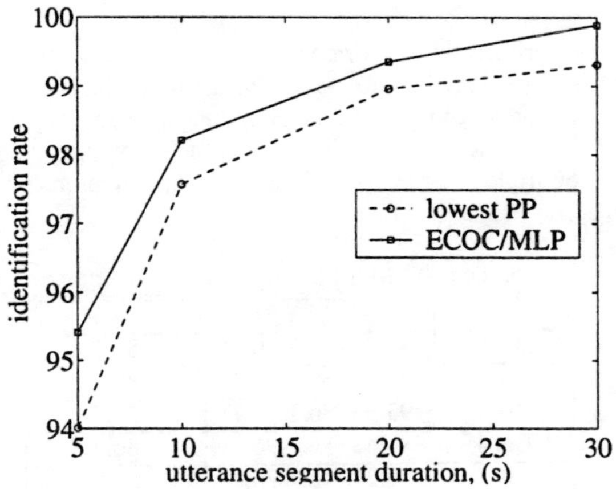

Figure 6: ***Language identification rate vs audio segment duration***

A class space of 4 classes induces 7 unique binary partitions. For each of these, we trained an independent multilayer perceptron (MLP) with 12 input units and 1 output unit using scaled conjugate gradients on data set 2 and early stopping using the cross-validation data set 3. In preliminary tests, we found that 25 hidden units provide adequate performance and generalization when used with early stopping.

The output of all 7 binary classifiers was concatenated together to form a 7-bit code, which in the flavor of error-correcting output coding (ECOC) was compared to our four class codewords to yield a best class estimate. Based on total error using the best training set weights and cross-validation set weights on the cross-validation data, we additionally discarded those binary classifiers which contributed to total error; these classifiers represent difficult partitions of the data. Performance of this ECOC/MLP classification scheme on 5s, 10s, 20s and 30s data from set 4 was 95.41%, 98.33%, 99.36% and 99.89% respectively, shown in Figure 6.

4. LANGUAGE DEPENDENCIES

Implicit in our non-verbal cue classification methodology is the assumption that phone strings originating from phone recognizers trained on different languages yield crucially complementary information. Thus far we have not explored the degree to which the phone recognizers must differ, nor can we state how performance varies with the number of phone recognizers used. In this section we report on two experiments in the speaker identification arena intended to answer these questions.

4.1 Multi-lingual vs Multi-engine

We conducted one set of experiments to investigate whether the reason for the success of the multilingual phone string approach is related to the fact that the different languages contribute useful classification information or that it simply lies in the fact that different recognizers provide complementary information. If the latter were the case, a multi-engine approach in which phone recognizers trained on the same language but on different channel or speaking style conditions might do a comparably good job. To test this hypothesis, we used a multi-engine approach based on three English phone recognizers which were trained on very different conditions, namely: Switchboard (telephone, highly conversational), Broadcast News (various channel conditions and speaking styles), and English Spontaneous Scheduling Task (high quality, spontaneous).

The experiments were carried out on all distances Dis 0 to Dis 8, for the speaker identification task. For a fair comparison between the three English engines and the eight language engines, we generated all possible language triples out of the set of eight languages ($\binom{8}{3} = 56$ triples) and calculated the average, minimum and maximum performance for each.

Approach	Multi-Lingual	Multi-Engine
Dis 0	87.92 (66.7-100)	93.3
Dis L	88.21 (63.3-96.7)	86.7
Dis 1	83.57 (66.7-93.3)	86.7
Dis 2	93.63 (86.7-96.7)	76.7
Dis 4	81.43 (56.7-96.7)	86.7
Dis 5	86.07 (66.7-96.7)	83.3
Dis 6	81.96 (66.7-93.3)	63.3
Dis 8	87.14 (63.3-93.3)	63.3

Table 13: ***Multi-Lingual vs Multi-Engine SID rates***

The results, given in Table 13, show that for all distances the best performance of the multilingual triples always outperforms the performance on the multi-engine triple. Even on average the multilingual approach achieves better identification results than the multi-engine approach for all but three distances (Dis 0, 1,4). For most distances the multi-engine approach lies within the range of the multilingual approach. On Dis 2 and 6, however, the multi-engine approach is outperformed by all $\binom{8}{3}$ language triples. The poor performance of the multi-engine approach on the far distances Dis 6 and Dis 8 is alarming and may indicate some robustness problems.

From these results we draw the conclusion that for our given choice of multiple English engines the multiple language phone recognizers provide more useful information for the classification task than do multi-engine recognizers. However, this results may not hold for other selections of single-language multi-engine recognizers. Further investigations on other engines, as well as on other non-verbal cues, are necessary to fully answer this question.

4.2 Number of involved languages

In a second suite of experiments, we investigated the influence of the number of phone recognizers on speaker identification rate. These experiments were performed on an improved version of our phone recognizers in 12 languages trained on the above described GlobalPhone data.

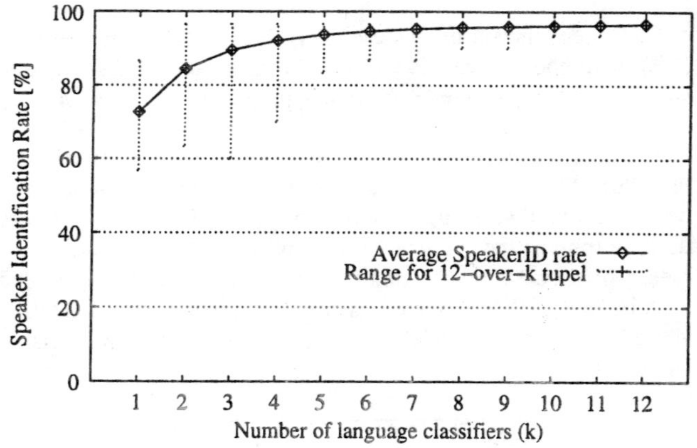

Figure 7: ***SID rate vs number of phone recognizers***

Figure 7 plots the speaker indentification rate over the number m of languages used in the identification process on matched 60 second data at Dis 6. The performance is given in average and range over the $\binom{12}{m}$ language m-tuples. The plot indicates that the average speaker identification rate increases with the number of involved phone recognizers. It also shows that the maximum performance of 96.7% can already be achieved using only two languages; in fact two (out of $\binom{12}{m} = 66$) language pairs gave optimal results: CH-KO, and CH-SP. However, the lack of a strategy for finding the best suitable pair does not make this very helpful. On the other hand, the increasing average indicates that the probability of finding a suitable language-tuple which optimizes performance increases with the number of available languages. While only 4.5% of all 2-tuples achieved best performance, as many as 35% of all 4-tuples, 60% of all 6-tuples, 76% of all 8-tuples and 88% of all 10 tuples were likewise found to perform optimally in this sense.

5. CONCLUSIONS

We have investigated the identification of non-verbal cues from spoken speech, namely speaker, accent, and language. For these tasks, a joint framework is developed which uses phone strings, derived from different language phone recognizers, as intermediate features and which performs classification decisions based on their perplexities.

Our good identification results validate this concept, indicating that multilingual phone strings could be sucessfully applied to the identification of various non-verbal cues, such as speaker, accent and language. Our evaluation on variable distance data proved the robustness of the approach, achieving a 96.7% speaker identification rate on 10s chunks from 30 speakers under mismatched conditions, clearly outperforming GMMs on large distances. Furthermore, we achieved 93.7% accent discrimination accuracy between native and non-native speakers. The speaker and accent identification experiments were carried out on English data, although none of the applied phone recognizers were trained or adapted to English spoken speech.

For language identification, we obtained 95.5% classification accuracy for utterances 5 seconds in length and up to 99.89% on longer utterances, showing additionally that some reduction of error is possible using decision strategies which rely on more than just lowest average perplexity. Additionally, the language identification experiments were run on languages not presented to the phone recognizers for training. The language independent nature of our experiments suggests that they could be successfully ported to non-verbal cue classification in other languages.

6. REFERENCES

[1] Q. Jin, T. Schultz, and A. Waibel, "Speaker Identification using Multilingual Phone Strings", to be presented in: *Proceedings of ICASSP*, Orlando, Florida, May 2002.

[2] M. A. Kohler, W. D. Andrews, J. P. Compbell, and L. Hernander-Cordero, "Phonetic Refraction for Speaker Recognition", *Proceedings of Workshop on Multilingual Speech and Language Processing*, Aalborg, Denmark, September 2001.

[3] L. Mayfield-Tomokyo, "Recognizing Non-Native Speech: Characterizing and Adapting to Non-Native Usage in LVCSR", PhD thesis, CMU-LTI-01-168, Language Technologies Institute, Carnegie-Mellon University, 2001.

[4] D. A. Reynolds and R. C. Rose, "Robust Text-Independent Speaker Identification Using Gaussian Mixture Speaker Models", *IEEE Transactions on Speech and Audio Processing*, Volume 3, No. 1, January 1995.

[5] T. Schultz and A. Waibel, "Language Independent and Language Adaptive Acoustic Modeling for Speech Recognition", *Speech Communication*, Volumne 35, Issue 1-2, pp 31-51, August 2001.

[6] M. A. Zissman, "Language Identification Using Phone Recognition and Phonotactic Language Modeling", *Proceedings of ICASSP*, Volume 5, pp 3503-3506, Detroit MI, May 1995.

Corpus-based Comprehensive and Diagnostic MT Evaluation: Initial Arabic, Chinese, French, and Spanish Results

Kishore Papineni Salim Roukos Todd Ward
IBM T. J. Watson Research Center
{papineni,roukos,toddward}@us.ibm.com

John Henderson Florence Reeder
MITRE
{jhndrsn,freeder}@mitre.org

ABSTRACT

We describe two metrics for automatic evaluation of machine translation quality. These metrics, BLEU and NEE, are compared to human judgment of quality of translation of Arabic, Chinese, French, and Spanish documents into English.

1. INTRODUCTION

Machine Translation (MT) evaluation has long been considered something of a black art. Therefore, MT evaluation (MTE) metrics have been historically conspicuous in their absence. Evaluations have tended to be holistic scoring by committees of raters on the basis of the somewhat vaguely specified parameters of intelligibility and fidelity ([8], [1], [4]). Intelligibility and fidelity have been called fluency and adequacy respectively. While these evaluations represent valid judgments of MT quality, their proper administration and application have been problematic and too expensive to support rapid development paradigms [3]. Furthermore, comparing successive evaluations and evaluations at different sites has often been a fool's errand. Rating committees change, corpora are different, and evaluation criteria are often underspecified and subjective at best. A typical question one encounters during an attempt to compare sets of evaluations could be as simple and as complex as "Does a score of 4 on a 1-5 scale mean the same thing as a 6 on a 1-7 scale?" On the other hand, human judgments are the final indicator of system acceptance and cannot be ignored.

Examination of past MTE strategies and the uses of MT and MTE has yielded some desired characteristics for current MT evaluations: MTE measures should be automated or extremely cheap; they must be replicable; they should correlate well with human judgments of quality; they should be predictive of the possible uses of imperfect MT output; and they should be diagnostic for the improvement of systems. Recently, a number of interesting, useful and rational metrics have appeared. Two of these metrics, BLEU and NEE, meet the desired criteria for MTE. By virtue of the electronic corpora used for their refinement, automation and replicability, we are able to look at both metrics and see what they tell us about different systems and MT. This paper examines these two metrics on four different bilingual corpora.

Proceedings of HLT 2002, Second International Conference on Human Language Technology Research, M. Marcus, ed., Morgan Kaufmann, San Francisco, 2002.

2. BACKGROUND

Before describing the experiments performed, we will describe each of the metrics. First is BLEU[7] and the second is the Named-Entity translation Evaluator, NEE (descended from [5]).

2.1 BLEU

The closer a machine translation is to a professional human translation, the better it is. This is the central idea behind BLEU. To judge the quality of a machine translation, one measures its closeness by a numerical metric to one or more reference human translations. Thus, BLEU requires two ingredients:

1. a numerical "translation closeness" metric
2. a corpus of good quality human reference translations

These reference translations can be reused over and over again and incur only a one-time startup expense. Each evaluation can be accomplished in seconds.

BLEU is fashioned after the highly successful *word error rate* metric used by the speech recognition community, appropriately modified for *multiple* reference translations and allowing for legitimate differences in word choice and word order. The main idea is to use a weighted average of variable length phrase matches against the reference translations. This view gives rise to a family of metrics using various weighting schemes. The baseline BLEU metric uses two key concepts in deciding closeness. The first is a *modified* n-gram precision and the second is a recall on length of the translation. Both are reminiscent of the familiar precision and recall used in information retrieval literature, but have been adapted for *multiple* reference translations.

The intuition behind the recall on length is that a one-word candidate translation is bad if all the reference translations have ten or more words, for example. A good translation roughly matches the reference translations in length. Traditionally, precision has been paired with recall to overcome such length-related problems. However, BLEU considers *multiple* reference translations, each of which may use a different word choice to translate the same source word.

Furthermore, a good candidate translation will only use (recall) one of these possible choices, but not all. Indeed, recalling all choices leads to a bad translation. To account for recall on concepts among multiple reference translations with different word choice and word order, one could align the reference translation for concepts. Such alignment is complicated. Instead, the recall on length couples with the modified n-gram precision to achieve the same effect in a very simple way. The recall on length is implemented as a penalty on the mismatch between the lengths of the candidate translation and the reference translations.

Modified n-gram precision counters against cheating by repeating a phrase in the reference translation to match the expected length of the reference translations. Thus, to score high with BLEU the candidate translation must match a reference translations in length and then in word choice (determined by modified unigram precision) and in word order (determined by higher order modified n-gram precisions). BLEU uses a geometric average of n-gram precisions at various n (1 to 4) multiplied by the length penalty. The details are below.

We first explain the modified unigram precision. To compute modified unigram precision, we first count the maximum number of times a word occurs in any single reference translation. Next, we clip the total count of each candidate word by its maximum reference count:

$$Count_{clip} = min(Count; Max_{Ref}Count).$$

In other words, we truncate each word's count, if necessary, to not exceed the largest count observed in any single reference for that word. We then add these clipped counts up, and divide by the total (unclipped) number of candidate words. This gives us the modified unigram precision. Modified n-gram precision p_n for any n is defined similarly.

When there is only one sentence in the entire test corpus, the above procedure is unambiguous. How do we compute modified n-gram precision on a multi-sentence test set? Although one typically evaluates MT systems on a corpus of entire documents, our basic unit of evaluation is the sentence. A source sentence may translate to many target sentences, in which case we abuse terminology and refer to the corresponding target sentences as a "sentence."

We first compute the n-gram matches sentence by sentence. Next, we add the clipped n-gram counts for all the candidate sentences and divide by the number of candidate n-grams in the test corpus to compute a modified precision score, p_n, for the entire test corpus.

$$p_n = \frac{\sum_{C\in\{Candidates\}} \sum_{n\text{-}gram \in C} Count_{clip}(n\text{-}gram)}{\sum_{C\in\{Candidates\}} \sum_{n\text{-}gram \in C} Count(n\text{-}gram)}.$$

In other words, we use a word-weighted average of the sentence-level modified precisions rather than a sentence-weighted average. As an example, we compute word matches at the sentence level, but the modified unigram precision is the fraction of words matched in the entire test corpus.

Candidate translations longer than their references are already penalized by the modified n-gram precision measure: there is no need to penalize them again. Consequently, we introduce a multiplicative *brevity penalty* factor that only penalizes candidates shorter than their reference translations. With this brevity penalty in place, a high-scoring candidate translation must now match the reference translations in length, in word choice, and in word order. Note that neither this brevity penalty nor the modified n-gram precision length effect directly considers the source length; instead, they consider the range of reference translation lengths in the target language.

The brevity penalty is a multiplicative factor modifying the overall BLEU score. We wish to make the penalty 1 when the candidate's length is the same as any reference translation's length. For example, if there are three references with lengths 12, 15, and 17 words and the candidate translation is a terse 12 words, we want the brevity penalty to be 1. We call the closest reference sentence length the "best match length."

We compute the brevity penalty over the entire corpus to allow some freedom at the sentence level. We first compute the test corpus' effective reference length, r, by summing the best match lengths for each candidate sentence in the corpus. The brevity penalty is a decaying exponential in r/c, where c is the total length of the candidate translation corpus.

We take the geometric mean of the test corpus' modified precision scores and then multiply the result by an exponential brevity penalty factor.

We first compute the geometric average of the modified n-gram precisions, p_n, using n-grams up to length N and positive weights w_n summing to one.

Next, let c be the length of the candidate translation and r be the effective reference corpus length. We compute the brevity penalty BP,

$$\text{BP} = \begin{cases} 1 & \text{if } c > r \\ e^{(1-r/c)} & \text{if } c \leq r \end{cases}.$$

Then,

$$\text{BLEU} = \text{BP} \cdot \exp\left(\sum_{n=1}^{N} w_n \log p_n\right).$$

In the log domain,

$$\log \text{BLEU} = \min(1 - \frac{r}{c}, 0) + \sum_{n=1}^{N} w_n \log p_n.$$

In our baseline, we use $N = 4$ and uniform weights $w_n = 1/N$.

As n increases, BLEU places more emphasis on longer n-grams than unigrams (since n-gramprecision decreases logarithmically).

2.2 NEE

The Named Entity translation Evaluator NEEemerged from testing in named entity translation as an MT metric ([5], [9]). The score reflects the degree to which named entities [6] are translated correctly by a given MT system. The underlying assumptions are that a) named entities are important components in translation quality; b) named entities measurements are indicative of the kinds of downstream tasks for which MT output is suited; c) named entities metrics represent an actionable area for MT improvement . The premise that the NEE metric is a reasonable one for MTE comes from the fact that named entities are relatively objective measures with straightforward definitions and less variation than MT in the whole. Previously, named entities were identified as constrained, yet important nuggets in translation, particularly for TIDES applications [9]. The work presented here takes the prior work to the next level by applying the technique to larger corpora, more diverse language pairs and different levels of granularity.

The process for utilizing this metric is relatively straight-forward: a) identify the named entities within a given corpus; b) pull unique entities from the document[1].; c) find the entities in the system out-

[1] Experiments on French, Spanish showed that a strong correlation between paragraph and document level scores.

put text; and d) compare entities in the output text with those identified in the reference text. Figure 1 shows the flow. Identifying the named entities in the reference translation requires human annotation, and is the only stage of the process to do so. To prepare the corpora for evaluation, two expert annotators used the Alembic Workbench [2] annotation tool to tag occurrences of named entities according to the MUC [6] annotation guidelines. After the named entities are tagged in the reference translation (designated ANNO for our discussions), the metric can be applied.

Figure 1: NEE Flowchart

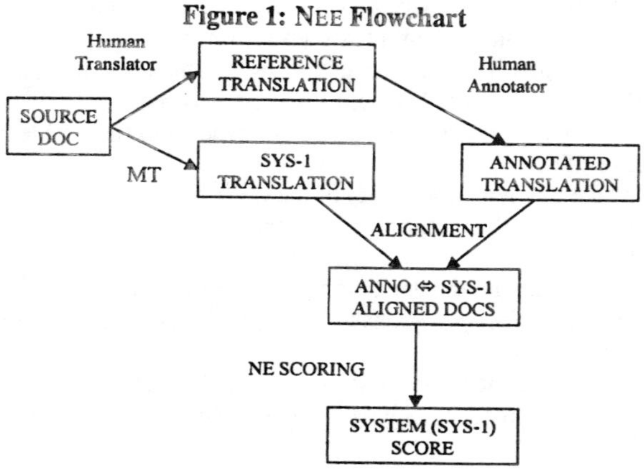

The next stage is to align the ANNO translation text with the evaluation text (SYS-1 for this discussion). This is performed, currently, at either the article (file) level or at the paragraph level within articles. The discussion of the most appropriate granularity follows in the results section. Once the ANNO and SYS-1 have been aligned, the aligned pairs are handed off to the scoring software.

To score the translation, for each article in the aligned pair, the tagged named entities are pulled from the ANNO and a list of unique names for the comparison unit (paragraph or article) is prepared. This is followed by normalization, which becomes more important with increased divergence between language pairs (e.g. [10]). At this time, the normalization steps applied are: a) substitution of non-diacritic marked letters for the equivalent diacritic mark character for Romance languages[2]; b) down-casing[3]; c) the normalization of numeric quantities (particularly for numbers under 100) and d) the removal of possessives. Other normalization steps may be needed, as well as the incorporation of partial match scoring (see [9] for discussion of candidates). Once the named entity list and the SYS-1 tokens have been normalized, the search for named entities in the token lists is straight-forward. Only exact matches given the normalization steps described are considered at this time and all results here reflect this.

3. EXPERIMENTS

Different corpora were used for the development of the two metrics. The corpora were then exchanged for the purpose of running the different evaluators on them. Each corpus will now be described.

The Chinese-English corpus is a collection of documents from various sources including the internet. It consists of 40 documents and 500 sentences, 2 expert human reference translations, 3 system translations, and 2 additional human translations. A subset containing 50 sentences was randomly selected. Translations of these 50 sentence by the 3 systems and 2 humans (250 sentence pairs) were judged by 20 humans on a scale of 1 (very bad) to 5 (very good). Ten of the judges were monolingual native speakers of English and the rest were bilingual native speakers of Chinese. Figure 2 shows the correlation between human judgments and BLEU for this corpus. The correlation coefficient R of BLEU with monolingual human judgment is 0.99 while that with the bilingual judgments is 0.96. It may be noted that there is a high correlation between the monolingual and bilingual judgments. This suggests that we can use monolingual judgments to evaluate the metrics. We also show the *prediction error* ($1 - R^2$) expressed as percent in some of the graphs below.

Figure 2: BLEU vs Bilingual and Monolingual Judgments on Chinese to English

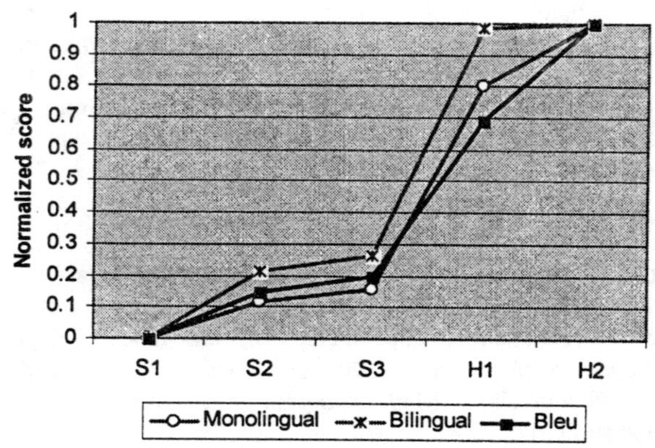

In addition to validating BLEU against human judgments on Chinese-to-English translations, we compared BLEU with human judgments involving two other language pairs. We used the French-English human judgments from the DARPA-94 evaluation for 6 systems and the Spanish-English for 5 systems. BLEU was computed for each system against the one reference provided in the evaluation. One of the systems in each language pair was a human translator labeled "expert".

The French-English and Spanish-English corpora were both from the DARPA-94 evaluation. Each language set consists of 100 documents of newswire text, translated into English by 2 expert translators along with the machine translations from the original evaluation. BLEU was computed for the 100 test documents. Again, BLEU correlates highly with human judgments, particularly for adequacy and fluency. Figures 3 and 4 show the correlation of BLEU with human judgments on the French and Spanish translations respectively.

We summarize the correlation of BLEU with human judgments on DARPA-94 MT evaluation data below. It is remarkable that BLEU and fluency have a correlation of 0.9958 for French-English which we rounded to 1 in Table 1.

Table 1: Correlation of BLEU with Human Judgments of DARPA-94 MT Evaluation

Source	Adequacy	Fluency	Informativeness
French	0.94	1.00	0.86
Spanish	0.98	0.96	0.85

[2]For instance à becomes a.

[3]It has yet to be demonstrated that this is the correct normalization step, although it does increase human-human agreement.

Figure 3: BLEU Prediction Error on Adequacy, Fluency, and Informativeness (F-E)

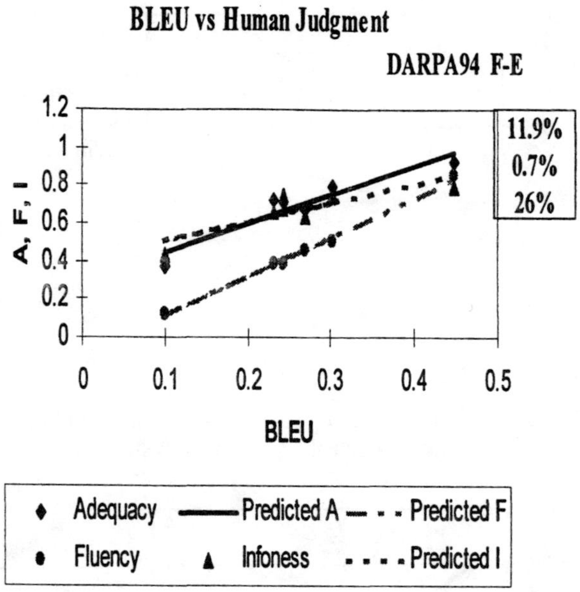

Figure 4: BLEU Prediction Error on A, F, I (S-E)

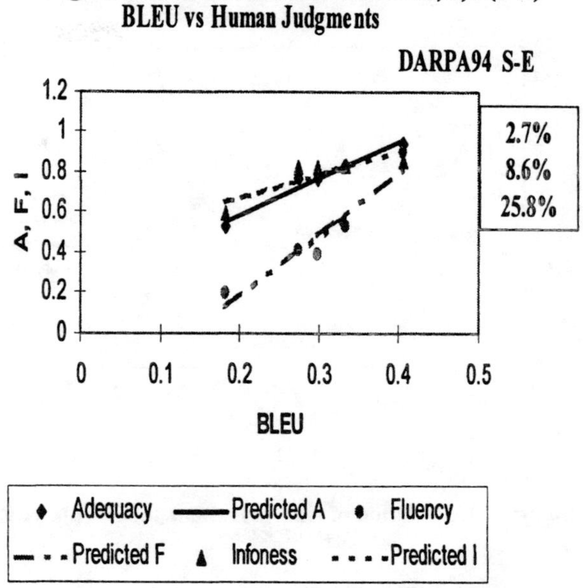

Figure 5: Correlation of NEE vs Human Judgments (C-E)

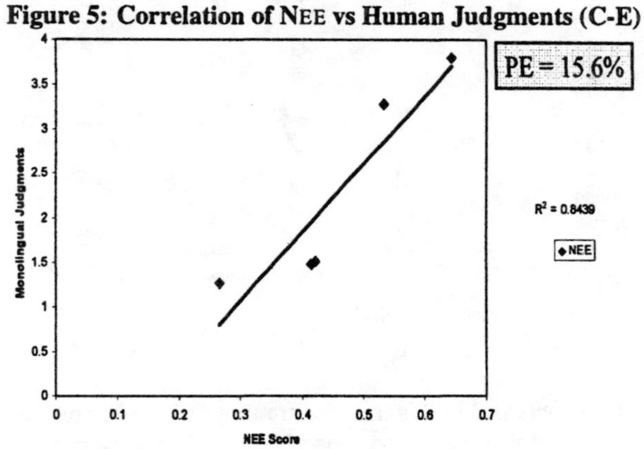

We also computed the correlation of NEE with human judgments of DARPA-94 MT evaluation. For the French-English NEE correlation, we only used 4 systems due to data-formatting issues. Figures 5, 6, 7 show the correlation of BLEU with human judgments on the Chinese, French, and Spanish translations respectively. Table 2 summarizes the results.

Table 2: Correlation of NEE with Human Judgments of DARPA-94 MT Evaluation

Source	Adequacy	Fluency	Informativeness
French	0.86	0.90	0.70
Spanish	0.76	0.93	0.49

Both BLEU and NEE are single number metrics, and cannot be expected to track different quantities such as Adequacy and Fluency (unless the quantities are highly correlated). Since BLEU is parametric in the size of n-grams that are matched, we can look at the effect of the n-gram size (phrase length) on prediction error of BLEU on Adequacy and Fluency. The effect is shown in Figures 8 and 9 for French and Spanish corpora respectively.

BLEU with shorter phrases correlates better with Adequacy whereas with longer phrases it correlates better with Fluency. In fact, $n = 1$ seems the best predictor of Adequacy. This is expected since adequacy is more about getting the words right, and BLEU with unigrams measures just that. This also suggests that as translation quality of the tested systems gets better, we should use BLEU with bigger n for better correlation. Conversely, when testing systems of poor quality, BLEU with smaller n may be better. Interestingly, on the Spanish-English test corpus we could go as far as matching 16-grams. Perhaps Spanish is an easier language to translate into English than French is.

We also tested these metrics on an Arabic-English corpus of 19 documents, containing about 5000 words. We evaluated 5 "systems" out of which two were human translators. We obtained human about 4000 sentence-level judgments from 16 monolingual native speakers of English. Again, we used only one reference translation. Figure 10 shows the correlation of BLEU with human judgments on this corpus.

The correlation coefficient of BLEU with monolingual human judgment is 0.98. This was a surprise to us: BLEU is a simple metric based on counting n-grams and with simple weights for different n-gram precisions. The same BLEU that was developed on the Chinese-English pilot corpus worked well on different test corpora spanning many source languages and systems of varying quality.

Figure 11 shows the correlation of NEE with human judgments on the Arabic-English corpus.

NEE showed for all languages that human translators are completely consistent even in named entity translation only about 80% of the time for Romance languages. For languages such as Arabic and Chinese, the scores drop to around 60% match on human translation agreement. Further study of this and of partial match scoring are indicated.

Acknowledgments This work was partially supported by the Defense Advanced Research Projects Agency and monitored by SPAWAR under contract No. N66001-99-2-8916. The views and

Figure 6: Correlation of NEE vs Human Judgments (F-E)

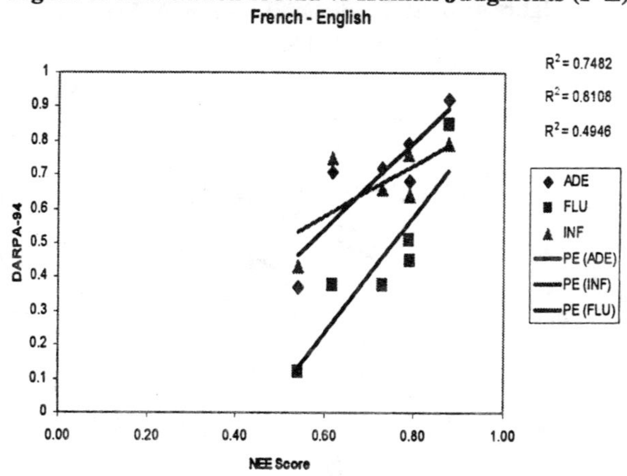

Figure 7: Correlation of NEE vs Human Judgments (S-E)

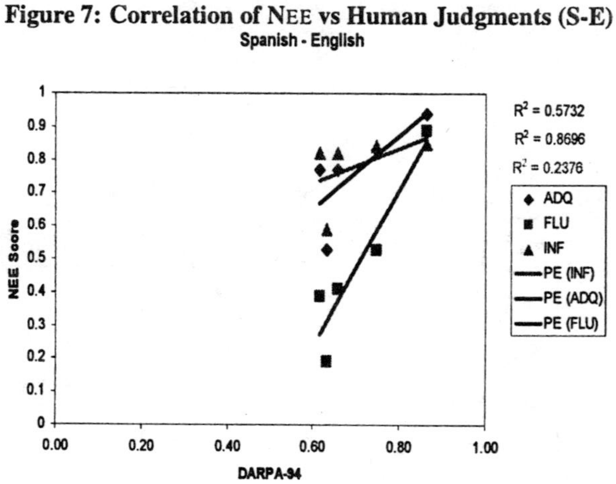

Figure 8: Prediction Error of BLEU vs n-gram length (F-E)

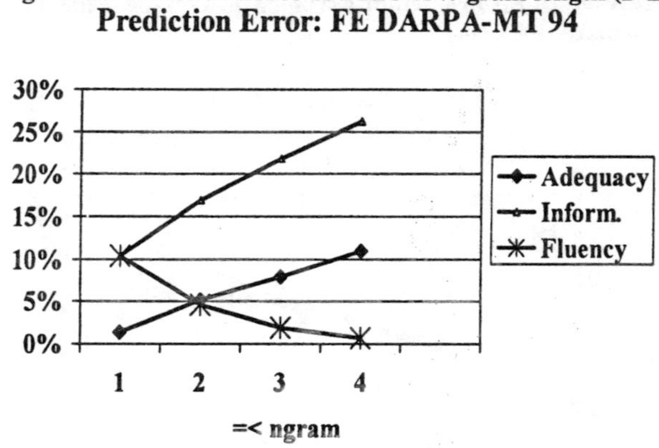

Figure 9: Prediction Error of BLEU vs n-gram length (S-E)

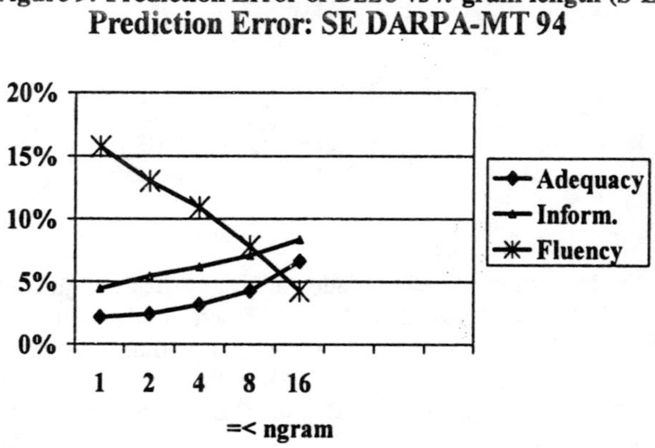

findings contained in this material are those of the authors and do not necessarily reflect the position of policy of the Government and no official endorsement should be inferred.

4. REFERENCES

[1] ALPAC. 1966. Language and machines: Computers in Translation and Linguistics. A Report by the Automatic Language Processing Advisory Committee. Division of Behavioral Sciences, National Academy of Sciences, National Research Council, Washington, D.C.

[2] Day, D., Aberdeen, J., Hirschman, L., Kozierok, R., Robinson, P., & Vilain, M. 1997. Mixed-initiative Development of Language Processing Systems. Proceedings of the Fifth Conference on Applied Natural Language Processing, ANLP.

[3] Doyon, J., Taylor, K., & White, J. 1998. The DARPA Machine Translation Evaluation Methodology: Past and Present. Proceedings of AMTA-98. Philadelphia, PA.

[4] JEIDA, 1989. A Japanese View of Machine Translation in the Light of the Considerations and Recommendations Reported by ALPAC, USA. Japan Electronic Industry Development Association, Tokyo.

[5] Hirschman, L., Reeder, F., Burger, J., & Miller, K. 2000. Name Translation as a Machine Translation Evaluation Task. Proceedings of the Workshop on Machine Translation Evaluation, LREC-2000.

[6] MUC-7. 1998. Proceedings of the Seventh Message Understanding Conference (MUC-7). http://www.muc.saic.com/proceedings/muc_7_toc.html

[7] Papineni, K., Roukos, S., Ward, R. T., Zhu, W.-Z. 2002. BLEU: A Method for Automatic Evaluation of Machine Translation, Proceedings of the 40th Annual Meeting of the ACL, Philadelphia, PA.

[8] White, J. S., T. A. O'Connell, & F. E. O'Mara. 1994. Advanced Research Projects Agency Machine Translation Program: 3Q94. Proceedings of the November 1994 Meeting.

[9] Reeder, F., Miller, K., Doyon, J., White, J. 2001. The Naming of Things and the Confusion of Tongues: An MT Metric. MT-Summit Workshop on MT Evaluation, September.

[10] Knight, K. & J. Graehl. 1998. Machine Transliteration. Computational Linguistics, 24(4), 598-612.

Figure 10: Correlation of BLEU vs Human Judgments (A-E)

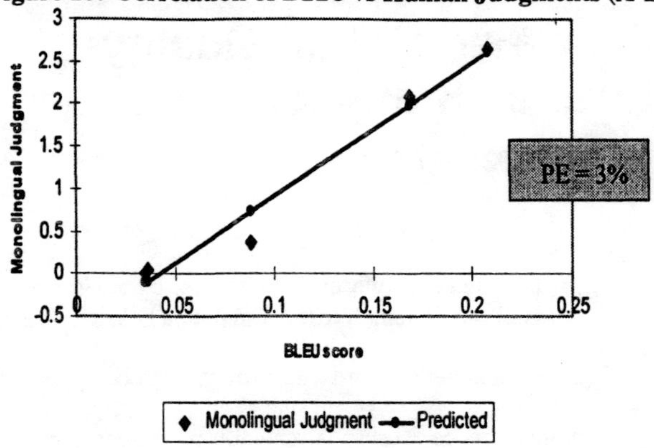

Figure 11: Correlation of NEE vs Human Judgments (A-E)

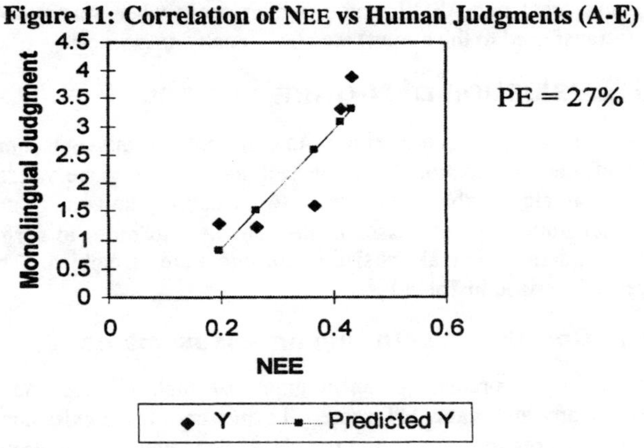

Automatic Evaluation of Machine Translation Quality Using N-gram Co-Occurrence Statistics

George Doddington, doddington@nist.gov, 925/377-5883

1 Introduction

Evaluation is recognized as an extremely helpful forcing function in Human Language Technology R&D. Unfortunately, evaluation has not been a very powerful tool in machine translation (MT) research because it requires human judgments and is thus expensive and time-consuming and not easily factored into the MT research agenda. However, at the July 2001 TIDES PI meeting in Philadelphia, IBM described an automatic MT evaluation technique that can provide immediate feedback and guidance in MT research. Their idea, which they call an "evaluation understudy", compares MT output with expert reference translations in terms of the statistics of short sequences of words (word N-grams). The more of these N-grams that a translation shares with the reference translations, the better the translation is judged to be. The idea is elegant in its simplicity. But far more important, IBM showed a strong correlation between these automatically generated scores and human judgments of translation quality.[1] As a result, DARPA commissioned NIST to develop an MT evaluation facility based on the IBM work. This utility is now available from NIST and serves as the primary evaluation measure for TIDES MT research.[2]

2 N-gram Co-occurrence Scoring

Evaluation using N-gram co-occurrence statistics requires an evaluation corpus of source material along with one (or preferably more) high quality reference translations. Scoring may then be done by tabulating the fraction of N-grams in the test translation that also occur in the reference translations. The IBM algorithm scores MT quality in terms of a weighted sum of the counts of matching N-grams. The IBM algorithm also includes a penalty for translations whose length differs significantly from that of the reference translations. IBM's formula for calculating the score (which IBM has dubbed "BLEU"[1]) is

$$Score = \exp\left\{\sum_{n=1}^{N} w_n \log(p_n) \quad - \quad \max\left(\frac{L^*_{ref}}{L_{sys}} - 1,\ 0\right)\right\} \qquad \text{Eqn 1}$$

where

$$p_n = \frac{\sum_i \left(\begin{array}{l}\text{the number of } n\text{-grams in segment } i,\\ \text{in the translation being evaluated, with}\\ \text{a matching reference cooccurrence in segment } i\end{array}\right)}{\sum_i \left(\begin{array}{l}\text{the number of } n\text{-grams in segment } i,\\ \text{in the translation being evaluated}\end{array}\right)}$$

$$w_n = N^{-1}$$

$$N = 4$$

and

L^*_{ref} = the number of words in the reference translation that is closest in length to the translation being scored

L_{sys} = the number of words in the translation being scored

N-gram co-occurrence scoring is typically performed segment-by-segment, where a segment is the minimum unit of translation coherence, usually one or a few sentences. The N-gram co-occurrence statistics, based on the sets of N-grams for the test and reference segments, are computed for each of these segments and then accumulated over all segments. It is intuitive that the smaller the segment, the better the co-occurrence statistics.

Before scoring, the translated text is conditioned to improve the efficacy of the scoring algorithm. This conditioning is applied both to the translation to be scored and to the reference translations. Here are the conditioning actions that are applied (for English):

- Case information is removed. All text is reduced to lower case.
- Numerical information (in terms of sequences of digits, commas and periods) is kept together as single words.
- Punctuation is tokenized into separate words (except for dashes and apostrophes).
- Adjacent non-ASCII words (which occur when source text is transferred to the output) are concatenated into single words.

3 Evaluation of N-gram Scoring

N-gram co-occurrence scoring is an extremely promising technique for efficient evaluation. But the technique needs to be validated and evaluated further with respect to its stability and its ability to predict human quality assessments reliably. In order to perform this validation, several translation corpora were assembled. These are summarized in Table 1.

3.1 Correlation with Human Assessments

The ability to predict human judgment of quality is the sine qua non of any automatic MT score. To this end, there exist human quality scores for each of the translated documents in the corpora listed in Table 1. These scores may then be averaged across documents to generate system-specific scores that indicate the translation quality of the systems. Human assessors were asked to judge translation quality along several different dimensions. For the 1994 corpora there were three dimensions, namely "Adequacy", "Fluency" and "Informativeness". For the 2001 corpus there were only two dimensions, namely "Adequacy" and "Fluency". Although the procedures used in 2001 differed somewhat from the procedures used in 1994[3], the judgments are basically the same:

[1] Kishore Papineni, Salim Roukos, Todd Ward, Wei-Jing Zhu (2001). "Bleu: a Method for Automatic Evaluation of Machine Translation". This report may be downloaded from URL http://domino.watson.ibm.com/library/CyberDig.nsf/home. (keyword = RC22176)

[2] Visit NIST's MT evaluation web site to download a copy of this utility. The URL is http://www.nist.gov/speech/tests/mt/

[3] The specification used by the LDC for the 2001 human assessment may be accessed from LDC's web site at the URL: www.ldc.upenn.edu/Projects/TIDES/Translation/TranAssessSpec.pdf

- For "Adequacy", the translation being evaluated is compared with a high quality reference translation, segment by segment. Each evaluation segment is scored according to how well (how "adequately") the meaning conveyed by the reference translation is also conveyed by the evaluated segment.
- For "Fluency", the translation being evaluated is judged according to how fluent it is. This is done segment by segment, with no reference to what the translation is supposed to convey.
- For "Informativeness", an assessor is asked to answer a set of questions about the content of each document after reading a translation of it. The Informativeness score is then the fraction of questions that are correctly answered.

Table 1 Primary characteristics of the corpora used to study the performance of N-gram co-occurrence based scoring of translation quality.

Description of Corpus	Source language	# of documents	# of human translations	# of MT systems
The 1994 DARPA corpus used to evaluate French-English MT	French	100	2	5
The 1994 DARPA corpus used to evaluate Japanese-English MT	Japanese	100	2	4
The 1994 DARPA corpus used to evaluate Spanish-English MT	Spanish	100	2	4
The 2001 DARPA corpus used for the Chinese-English dry run	Chinese	80	11	6[4]

The correlation between BLEU scores and human assessments of translation quality for the various systems evaluated in the DARPA 1994 and 2001 evaluations are listed in Table 2. In general, there is very strong correlation between human judgments and BLEU. Note however that the correlation for professional translators is much smaller than for machines. Not that the scores for professional translators aren't distinctly better than for machines. They are, as shown in Figure 1. Rather, the lower correlation means that the N-gram score distinctions between professional translations correlate less well with human judgments than those between different machine translations. A possible explanation for this difference in correlation is that differences between professional translators are far more subtle and thus less well characterized by N-gram statistics.

Other than the low correlation scores for the human translations, the correlations between human judgments and N-gram scores are above 90% for all of the comparisons, with the exception of the fluency score for Japanese. A possible explanation for this low correlation is simply that the Japanese systems seemed to be very similar in quality. Thus the uncorrelated differences account for more of the between-system variance.

[4] These 6 systems are commercial MT systems. There were also 9 research MT systems included in the evaluation. The research systems were not included in the analysis, however, because human assessments were performed only on the output from commercial systems.

Figure 2 shows a scatter-plot of N-gram scores versus human judgments of Adequacy and Fluency for the 6 commercial Chinese-to-English MT systems. Note that, while the correlation is quite high, there are some differences in judgment. Among them is one reversal in ranking with respect to Adequacy, albeit attributable to relatively minor differences in score.

Table 2 Correlation between IBM's BLEU scores and human assessments. The N-gram scores were produced using all (2) of the reference translations for the 1994 corpora MT systems and 8 reference translations for the 2001 Chinese corpus.

The Corpus	The Systems	Adequacy (%)	Fluency (%)	Informativeness (%)
1994 French Corpus	5 MT Systems	95.7	99.7	91.4
1994 Japanese Corpus	4 MT Systems	97.8	85.6	98.3
1994 Spanish Corpus	4 MT Systems	97.5	97.2	94.3
2001 Chinese Corpus	6 Commercial MT Systems	95.2	97.1	-
	7 Professional Translators	70.5	16.6	-

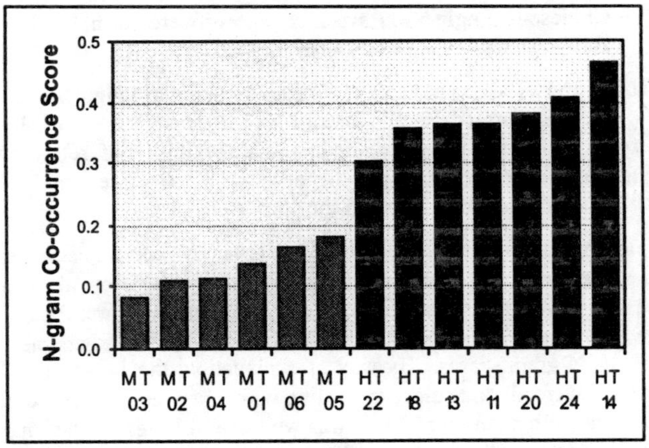

Figure 1 Rank-ordered N-gram co-occurrence scores for the 6 commercial MT systems and 7 professional translators in the 2001 Chinese-English dry run evaluation.

3.2 Sensitivity and Consistency

Ideally, a good score is both sensitive and consistent. That is, a good score will be able to distinguish between systems of similar performance, and this difference will be essentially unaffected by the selection of translations used for reference or documents used for scoring.[5] To measure the sensitivity and consistency of N-gram co-occurrence scoring, we examined the variability of system

[5] For N-gram co-occurrence scoring, such reliable indication of performance can be expected only if the reference translations are all of high quality and the choice of documents is within the same distribution of genre and other relevant parameters.

scores with respect to the choice of documents and the choice of reference translations used to compute the scores. To do this we used the F-ratio measure, namely the between-system score variance divided by within-system score variance. The between-system variance is the variance of average system scores across different systems, and the within-system variance is the variance of document scores for a given system, computed across different documents and different reference translations and then pooled over all systems. Thus the greater the F-ratio, the better the score.

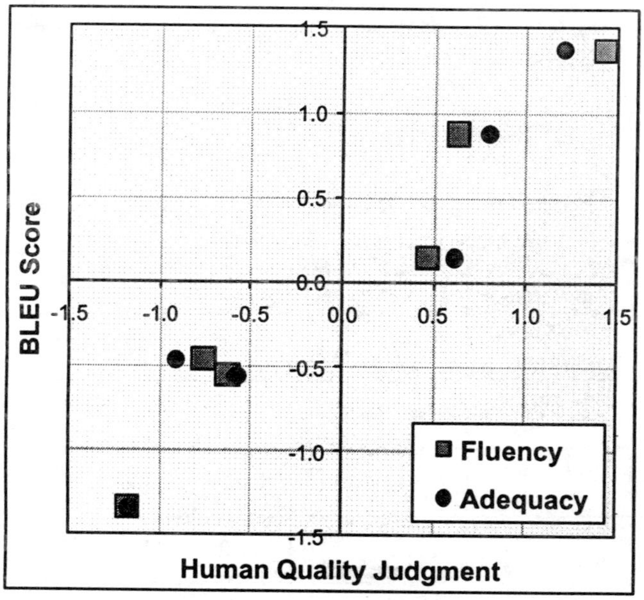

Figure 2 Scatter-plot of IBM's BLEU scores versus human judgments of Adequacy and Fluency for the 6 commercial Chinese-to-English MT systems. Scores were normalized to zero mean and unit variance before plotting.

Table 3 shows a comparison of F-ratios for human judgments and N-gram co-occurrence scores for all four corpora of this study. For purposes of cross-corpus comparison, the number of reference translations used to compute the co-occurrence score was held constant and equal to 2 for all of the corpora.

Note that in general the stability of the co-occurrence scores compares favorably to that of the human judgments. Note also that the F-ratios for the Japanese corpus are significantly poorer than for the French and Spanish 1994 corpora, for both human judgments as well as N-gram scores. By way of explanation, the Japanese MT systems were all quite close in quality, with a between-system score variance (of human scores) that was well over 4 times smaller than either French or Spanish. Also, note the relatively low correlation for Fluency for Japanese in Table 2. Nonetheless, the correlation for Adequacy remained high for Japanese.

On the other hand, note that the correlation between human and N-gram scores was very much smaller for human translations of Chinese than for machine translations. In this case, however, the spread of quality for human translations was comparable to the spread for machines, with between-human score variance (of human scores) being > 50% of N-gram score variance for Adequacy and > 80% of N-gram score variance for Fluency.

There are two sources of variance in N-gram co-occurrence scores shown in Table 3, namely variance due to the use of different sets of documents and variance due to the use of different reference translations. For judging relative translation quality, however, variance from the use of different reference translations may not be so important. This is because the variance due to choice of reference manifests itself primarily as a score offset that affects all systems similarly. Thus the relative ranking of systems remains largely unchanged, as illustrated in Figure 3.

Table 3 Comparison of F-ratios for human judgments versus IBM's BLEU scores.[6] F-ratios for reference variation are available only for the Chinese corpus because this is the only corpus with a number of reference translations that is large enough to support such analysis.

The Corpus	The Systems	F-ratios for Human Judgments			F-ratios for BLEU Scores	
		Adequacy	Fluency	Informativeness	Document variation	Reference variation
'94 French Corpus	All MT Systems	86.7	82.4	36.1	213.4	-
'94 Japanese Corpus	All MT Systems	8.4	14.2	2.8	45.5	-
'94 Spanish Corpus	All MT Systems	62.5	61.5	34.3	226.0	-
2001 Chinese Corpus	Commercial MT Systems	53.7	44.6	-	42.5	45.1
	Professional Translators	19.8	39.5	-	26.5	2.6

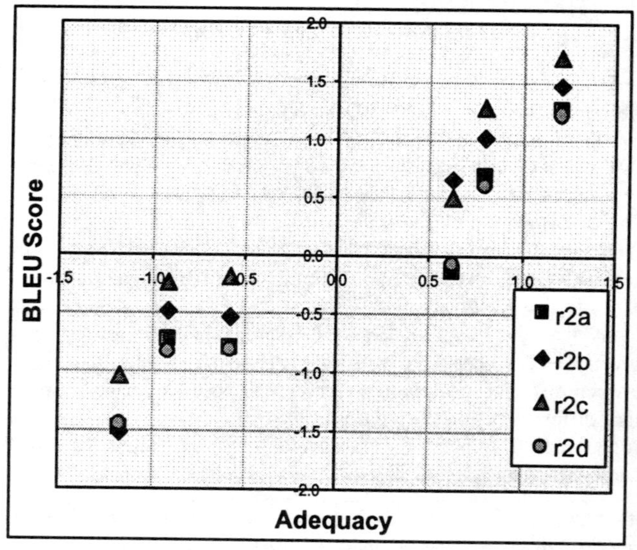

Figure 3 Scatter-plot of IBM's BLEU scores versus human Adequacy judgments for the 6 commercial Chinese-to-English MT systems. Four different sets of BLEU scores are shown, corresponding to the use of four different sets of

[6] There were a total of 11 judges used for the 2001 Chinese corpus. The scores for each of the judges for this corpus were normalized to standard mean and variance individually for each judge. This normalization improved the F-ratios for human judgments by about a factor of 2.

2 reference translations for each of four experiments. Scores were normalized to zero mean and unit variance (over all four experiments) before plotting.

4 The NIST Score Formulation

Several possible variations of N-gram scoring suggest themselves upon reflection on the characteristics of N-gram co-occurrence scores:

- First, note that the IBM BLEU formulation uses a geometric mean of co-occurrences over N. This makes the score equally sensitive to proportional differences in co-occurrence for all N. As a result, there exists the potential of counterproductive variance due to low co-occurrences for the larger values of N. An alternative would be to use an arithmetic average of N-gram counts rather than a geometric average.
- Second, note that it might be better to weight more heavily those N-grams that are more informative – i.e., to weight more heavily those N-grams that occur less frequently, according to their information value. This would, in addition, help to combat possible gaming of the scoring algorithm, since those N-grams that are most likely to (co-)occur would add less to the score than less likely N-grams.

Information weights were computed using N-gram counts over the set of reference translations, according to the following equation:

$$Info(w_1 \ldots w_n) = \log_2\left(\frac{\text{the \# of occurrences of } w_1 \ldots w_{n-1}}{\text{the \# of occurrences of } w_1 \ldots w_n}\right) \quad \text{Eqn 2}$$

Table 4 compares F-ratios and Correlation values for individual N-gram co-occurrence scores for commercial translation systems evaluated on the 2001 Chinese-to-English corpus. Note that the information-weighted N-gram counts provide superior F-ratio and correlation performance for N = 1, about the same performance for N = 2, and poorer performance for N > 2. The poorer performance for the higher values of N may be due to poor estimation of N-gram likelihoods.[7] Note also that the F-ratios for single N-grams, both unweighted and information-weighted, are greater than the F-ratios for IBM's BLEU formulation for N = 1 and 2. Further, the single N-gram correlations also are comparable to the BLEU correlations for N = 1 and 2.

Table 4 F-ratios and Correlation values for individual N-gram co-occurrence scores for commercial translation systems for the 2001 Chinese-to-English corpus. Eight reference translations were used to compute these statistics.

	Unweighted			Information-weighted		
N-gram	F-ratio	Adequacy Correlation (%)	Fluency Correlation (%)	F-ratio	Adequacy Correlation (%)	Fluency Correlation (%)
1	98.6	97.7	97.6	149.2	99.0	97.3
2	94.5	97.1	98.4	97.5	96.1	97.7
3	46.1	94.8	96.3	39.9	84.5	90.4
4	22.4	93.0	95.0	19.5	87.8	92.7
5	9.5	94.7	95.7	5.5	87.6	91.9

Based on the superior F-ratios of information-weighted counts and the comparable correlations, a modification of IBM's formulation of the score was chosen as the evaluation measure that NIST will use to provide automatic evaluation to support MT research. NIST's formula for calculating the score is

$$Score = \sum_{n=1}^{N}\left\{ \sum_{\substack{\text{all } w_1 \ldots w_n \\ \text{that co-occur}}} Info(w_1 \ldots w_n) \Big/ \sum_{\substack{\text{all } w_1 \ldots w_n \\ \text{in sys output}}} (1) \right\} \cdot \exp\left\{\beta \log^2\left[\min\left(\frac{L_{sys}}{\bar{L}_{ref}}, 1\right)\right]\right\} \quad \text{Eqn 3}$$

where

β is chosen to make the brevity penalty factor = 0.5 when the # of words in the system output is 2/3[rds] of the average # of words in the reference translation,

$N = 5$

and

$\bar{L}_{ref}$ = the average number of words in a reference translation, averaged over all reference translations

L_{sys} = the number of words in the translation being scored

Notice that, in addition to the calculation of the co-occurrence score itself, a change was also made to the brevity penalty. This change was made to minimize the impact on the score of small variations in the length of a translation. This preserves the original motivation of including a brevity penalty (which is to help prevent gaming the evaluation measure) while reducing the contributions of length variations to the score for small variations. Figure 4 gives a comparison of the two brevity penalty factors.

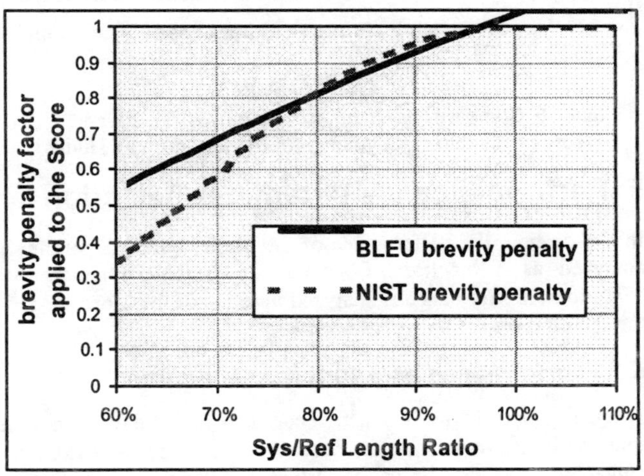

Figure 4 Comparison of the BLEU and NIST brevity penalty factors.

The NIST evaluation score is compared with IBM's original BLEU score in Figure 5 and Figure 6. Figure 5 demonstrates that the NIST score provides significant improvement in score stability and reliability for all four of the corpora studied. Figure 6 demonstrates that, for human judgments of Adequacy, the NIST score correlates better than the BLEU score on all of the corpora. For Fluency judgments, however, the NIST score correlates better than the BLEU score only on the Chinese corpus. This may be a mere

[7] Large amounts of data are required to estimate N-gram statistics for N > 2. In the current implementation, however, the N-gram statistics are computed only from the reference translations for the evaluation corpus.

random statistical difference between corpora. Or alternatively, this may be a consequence of different human judgment criteria or procedures. (The Chinese-to-English translations were judged at LDC using a different procedure than that used by John White at PRC for the 1994 corpora.)

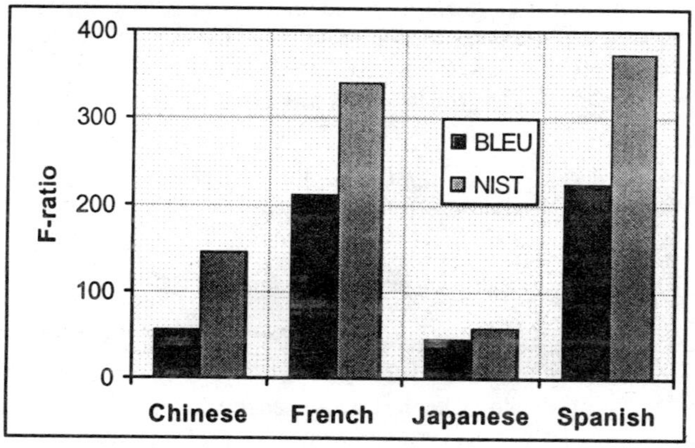

Figure 5 F-ratio comparison of the BLEU and NIST scores for document variance for the four corpora studied.

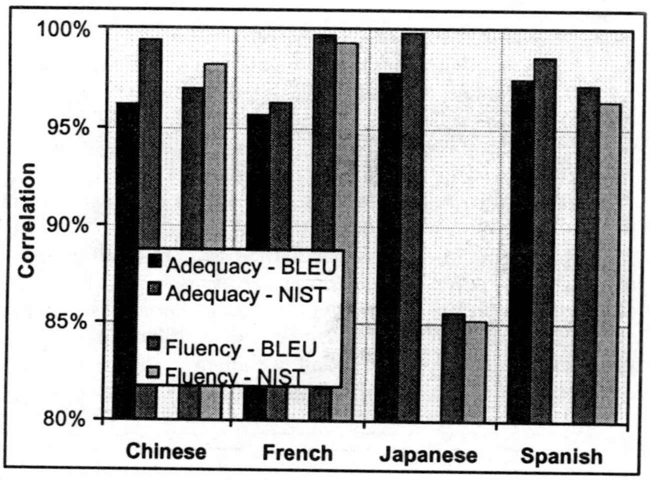

Figure 6 Comparison of the correlation of BLEU and NIST scores with human judgments for the four corpora studied.

5 Performance vs. Parameter Selection

In this section, the performance of the NIST scoring algorithm is analyzed as a function of several important parameters and conditions. Performance is analyzed in terms of the score's F-ratio the score's correlation with human judgment.

5.1 Performance as a function of source

The Chinese-to-English evaluation corpus included data from three sources, as shown in Table 5. Zaobao is a Chinese newswire from Singapore, and the Voice of America data comprises manual transcriptions of broadcasts in Mandarin. Since MT performance is sensitive to genre and style, human assessments of translation quality are broken out according to source and shown in Figure 7 both for professional and machine translations. From this figure it appears that the quality of professional translations of Voice of America transcripts is better than translations of newswire. This might be explained if VOA broadcasts were generally simpler language. The machine translations don't appear to exhibit marked differences between sources, although Fluency assessments of VOA broadcasts are poorer than those of newswire, this despite the better performance on professional translations.

Table 5 The three sources of data for the 2001 DARPA Chinese evaluation corpus.

Source	Number of Documents	Number of Words
Xinhua newswire	27	8411
Zaobao newswire	27	9083
Voice of America transcripts	26	6746

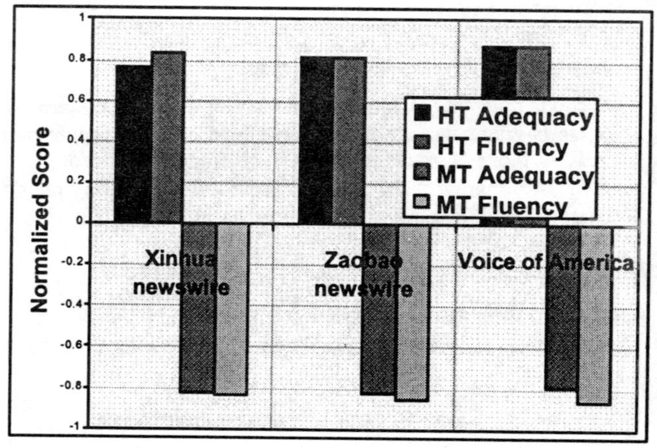

Figure 7 Average human assessment scores for 6 professional translations (denoted "HT") and 6 commercial off-the-shelf MT systems (denoted "MT") for the Chinese corpus, broken out according to source.

More interesting is the relative scoring of different MT systems on the different sources, shown in Figure 8. This figure is a scatter-plot of Adequacy scores for translations of Xinhua newswire and Voice of America transcripts versus Adequacy scores for Zaobao translations. This demonstrates that, while there is a loose agreement in the relative ranking of systems on different sources, the correlation between human assessments on the difference sources is much poorer than the correlation between human assessments and NIST scores, given the source.

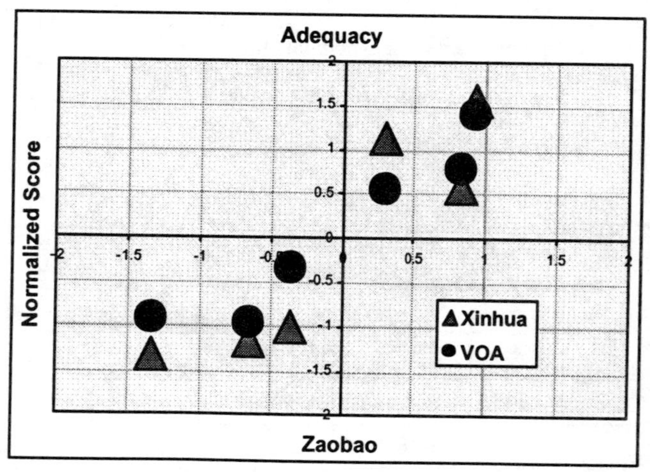

Figure 8 A scatter plot of average human Adequacy scores for 6 MT systems. Average scores for Xinhua and VOA are plotted versus average scores for Zaobao.

A scatter plot of NIST scores for the 6 commercial MT systems versus human Adequacy assessments is shown in Figure 9. Note that the correlation between the NIST score and human Adequacy assessment is much better than the correlation between human Adequacy assessments between difference sources. This contrast is shown quantitatively in Table 6.

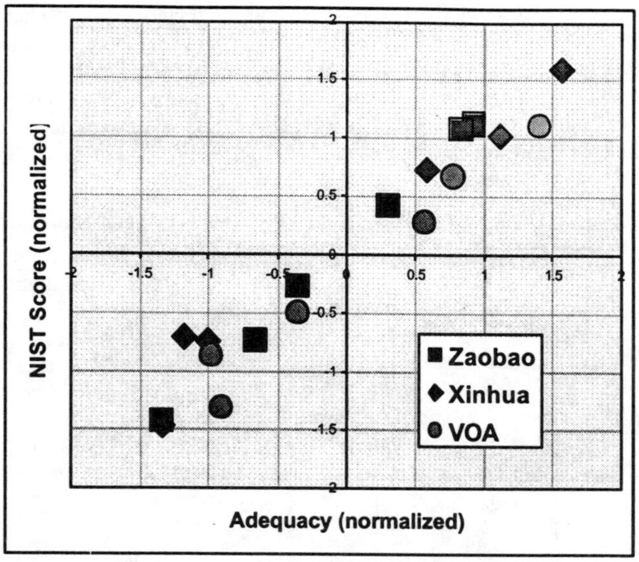

Figure 9 Scatter plot of NIST scores versus human Adequacy scores for the 6 commercial Chinese MT systems, plotted for each of the three different sources of data.

Table 6 Correlations (in percent) of human Adequacy scores for the three sources of data, compared with correlations between human Adequacy scores and NIST scores for each source, for the 6 commercial Chinese MT systems

Source	Xinhua	Zaobao	VOA	NIST score
Xinhua newswire	100.0	86.3	98.3	93.0
Zaobao newswire	-	100.0	91.5	99.8
Voice of America transcripts	-	-	100.0	93.9

5.2 Performance vs. number of references

Because of the wide variety of possible valid translations, the number of reference translations is generally regarded as an important factor in producing valid scores – the more reference translations, the better the performance of the co-occurrence score. However, as shown in Figure 10 and Figure 11, increasing the number of references appears to yield only modest improvements in evaluation performance. Specifically, there appears to be no significant improvement in the correlation with human judgments with the use of more than 1 reference translation. And the increase in F-ratio with increasing numbers of references is modest, at least for document variance. Although there is a great increase in F-ratio for the use of 4 references, this is quite likely an artifact attributable to the small sample of reference sets used in the experiment.[8]

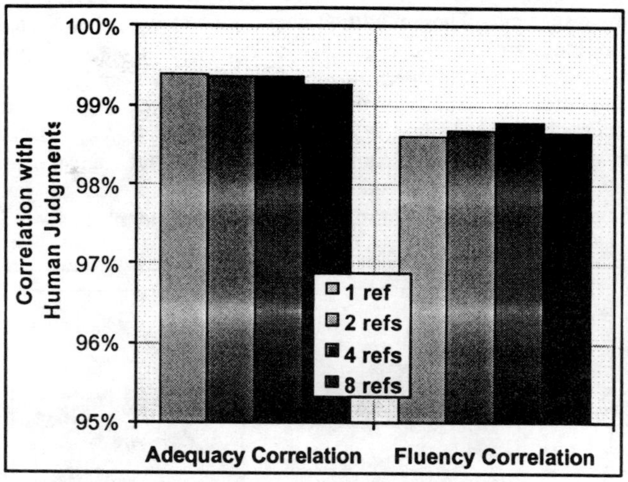

Figure 10 Adequacy and Fluency correlation statistics versus the number of reference translations used for scoring, for NIST scores for the 6 commercial Chinese-to-English MT systems.

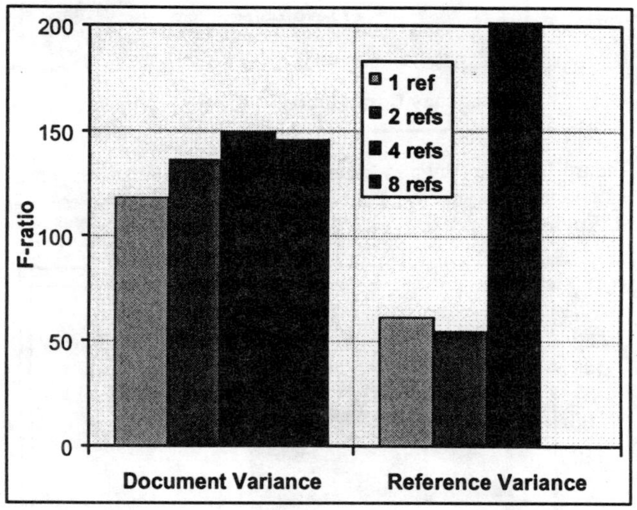

Figure 11 F-ratio statistics versus the number of reference translations used for scoring, for the NIST score on the Chinese-to-English evaluation corpus.

5.3 Performance versus segment size

Segment size is an important consideration. Intuitively, the shorter the segment over which co-occurrence is restricted, the better an N-gram co-occurrence score will perform. But the smaller the segments are made, the more work there is in establishing and maintaining the segments. More importantly, restricting the translation to be synchronous with the segmentation is an unnatural constraint that becomes more onerous as the segments become shorter. Obviously, segments should be no less than one sentence in length. And it would be ideal if the scoring algorithm performed well with no document-internal segmentation at all.

The effect of segmentation was studied by joining each adjacent pair of segments into single segment, thus effectively doubling the size of a segment. (Final odd segments at the end of a document were left as is.) This was done multiple times for the 2001

[8] The experiment in which the number of reference translations was varied was structured as follows: A total of eight reference translations were used. These 8 references were divided into 8 sets of one reference, 4 sets of two references, 2 sets of four references, and 1 set of 8 references. This left only one degree of freedom for computing the variance for 4 references, and none at all for 8 references (which is why there is no bar shown for the 8 reference case).

Chinese-to-English corpus until each document contained only a single segment. These modified document sets were then scored. The results are shown in Figure 12 and Figure 13. It is encouraging to see that correlation performance degrades only slightly, even at 271 words per segment, which corresponds to one segment per document. The decline in F-ratio is more pronounced, but still remains above 100 at 1 segment per document. Of course, using only one segment per document must be expected to yield progressively poorer performance as the average number of words in a document increases.

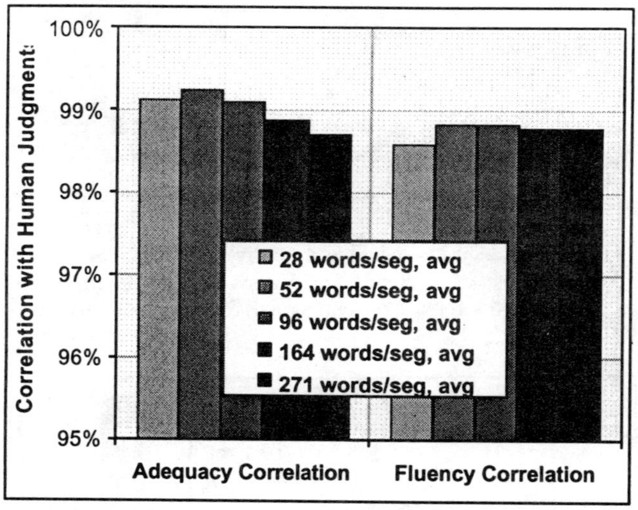

Figure 12 Adequacy and Fluency correlations statistics versus segment size, for NIST scores for 6 commercial Chinese-to-English MT systems.

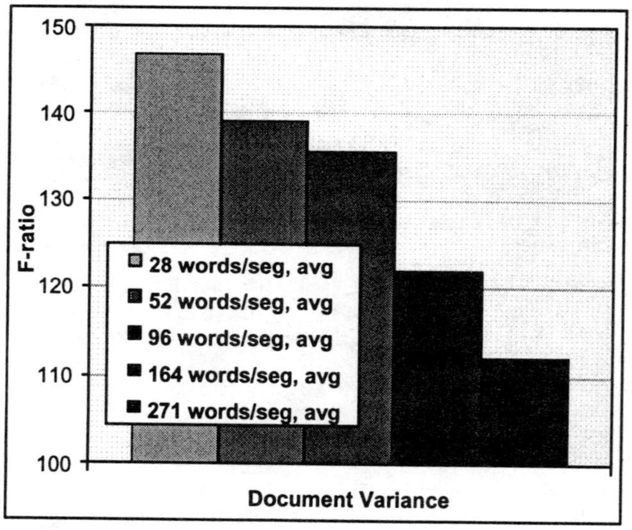

Figure 13 F-ratio versus segment size, for NIST scores for 6 commercial Chinese-to-English MT systems.

5.4 Performance with more language training

Table 4 shows that, while information-weighted N-gram counts are superior to unweighted counts for unigrams, information-weighted counts perform less well for N > 1. This may be attributable to poor information estimates that arise from using only the reference translations as a corpus to estimate N-gram likelihoods. To obtain reasonably accurate estimates, a much larger corpus would be required. To see if more accurate estimates of likelihoods might improve score performance, an auxiliary database comprising the entire English language subset of both the TDT2 and TDT3 corpora[9] was used to estimate N-gram likelihoods. Table 7 show the equivocal results of this experiment. While using the TDT corpus to estimate N-gram likelihoods yields minor (probably insignificant) improvements in the correlation of the NIST score with both Adequacy and Fluency judgments, this is accompanied by a (probably significant) decline in the F-ratio. Regarding individual N-grams, the table shows that there is minor improvement in the F-ratio for all N-grams except for N = 1 where there is a significant reduction in F-ratio. And while the correlation with human judgments is better for N = 2 and 3, it is worse for N = 4 and 5. (Even the TDT corpora may be inadequate to supply meaningful likelihood estimates for N > 3, especially considering the change in topics when switching from the TDT sources to the Chinese MT sources.)

Table 7 F-ratios and Correlation values for individual N-grams and the overall NIST score given different information weighting sources. Values are for commercial translation systems for the 2001 Chinese-to-English corpus. Eight reference translations were used to compute these statistics.

	Information weights computed from the evaluation corpus			Information weights computed from TDT2 and TDT3		
N-gram	F-ratio	Adequacy Correlation (%)	Fluency Correlation (%)	F-ratio	Adequacy Correlation (%)	Fluency Correlation (%)
1	149.2	99.0	97.3	115.4	98.3	96.0
2	97.5	96.1	97.7	105.4	99.2	98.8
3	39.9	84.5	90.4	48.1	92.0	94.9
4	19.5	87.8	92.7	21.2	84.8	89.3
5	5.5	87.6	91.9	5.8	82.2	87.6
NIST	146.8	99.3	98.7	121.5	99.5	98.8

In using the corpus-based likelihoods and resultant information calculations, it often happens that higher order N-grams don't contribute to the score. This occurs whenever the N-1 gram predicts the N-gram without error – i.e., whenever there are the same number of occurrences of both, usually one occurrence. In this case there is no (additional) information conveyed by the Nth word in the N-gram and the information is zero. Since individual N-grams appear to perform better unweighted than weighted, it is possible to force a minimum information contribution for all N-gram tokens by adding a certain minimum number of occurrences to the N-1 gram in Eqn 2. This was attempted for a number of values for the minimum number of occurrences of the N-1 gram. Unfortunately, and rather surprisingly, the performance of the score was virtually unaffected by such changes.

5.5 Performance with preservation of case

The assumption has been that removing case information would provide better N-gram scoring. This is not necessarily true, however. Furthermore, there are languages (other than English) where an argument can be made that case information might be more important than for English. With this in mind, an experiment was conducted to compare scoring performance with and without

[9] http://www.ldc.upenn.edu/Catalog/TDT.html

case information preserved in the translation. The results of this comparison are shown in Table 8. This table shows clearly that there is very little difference in scoring performance, whether case information is preserved or removed.

5.6 Performance with reference normalization

The score variance attributable to choice of reference translations appears to be an offset that applies roughly equally to all systems. Thus it might be the case that this offset might be at least partially mitigated by dividing the system score by the average reference score. However, when this normalization was attempted, the F-ratio remained essentially unchanged. (Correlation of system scores with human assessments is unaffected by this normalization, because the normalization applies to all system scores equally.)

Table 8 A comparison of F-ratio and of Adequacy/Fluency correlations with and with case information, computed for the 6 commercial MT systems on the Chinese corpus using 8 reference translations.

	F-ratio	Adequacy Correlation (%)	Fluency Correlation (%)
Case Info Removed	147	99.3	98.7
Case Info Preserved	148	99.0	98.9

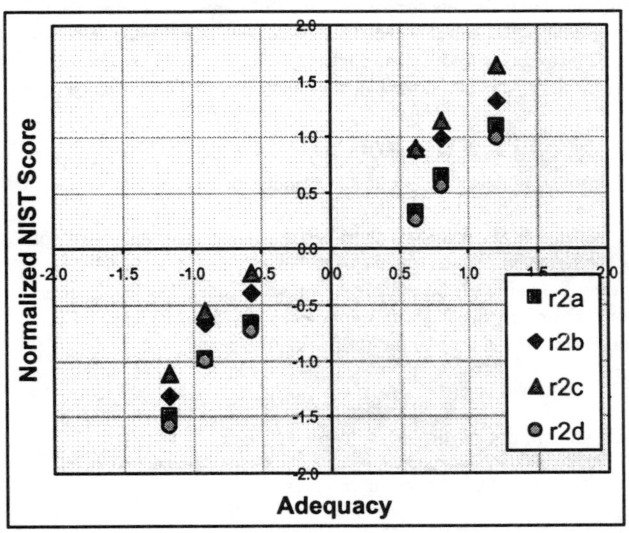

Figure 14 Scatter-plot of NIST scores versus human Adequacy judgments for the 6 commercial Chinese-to-English MT systems. Four different sets of NIST scores are shown, corresponding to the use of four different sets of 2 reference translations for each of four experiments. Scores were normalized to zero mean and unit variance (over all four experiments) before plotting.

6 The NIST MT Evaluation Facility

NIST now provides an evaluation facility that may be used to support MT research for translating various languages into English. This facility includes an N-gram co-occurrence scoring utility, which may be downloaded and used as desired by research sites. This utility requires a corpus of source documents and a corresponding set of one or more reference translations of each source document. The LDC offers corpus support for some source languages, and a research site's own corpora may be used, of course. In addition, formal evaluations of technology are supported with an email-based automatic evaluation utility. In this case, no reference translations are provided. Instead, each participating site receives the source documents, translates the documents, and then sends the translations to be evaluated to NIST via email. NIST then automatically scores the proffered translations and returns the results by email. Details of procedures and data formats are available from the NIST MT web site.[10]

---

[10] http://www.nist.gov/speech/tests/mt

Does Confidence Annotation Meet the Dialog Goal?: A Quantitative Analysis *

Kadri Hacioglu and Wayne Ward
Center for Spoken Language Research
University of Colorado at Boulder
{hacioglu,whw}@cslr.colorado.edu

ABSTRACT

In this paper, we quantify the impact of using confidence annotation on the performance of a dialog system for a given dialog strategy. Although the ultimate goal in a dialog system is to optimize the user satisfaction, it is very difficult to quantify it. Instead, we consider the probability of success and the number of expected turns of a transaction as our dialog performance metrics. In fact, they are fairly strong predictors of user satisfaction. The desired dialog goal in terms of these metrics is mapped onto an operating region on the receiver operating characteristics (ROC) plane of the confidence annotation method. In doing so, one can not only figure out whether the confidence annotation would meet the desired goal at the dialog level but also understand how to tune the system in order to reach that goal. Such an analysis therefore allows the system designer to optimize the use of confidence annotation and tune the system without doing any time consuming online experiments.

1. INTRODUCTION

Confidence annotation, which would be unnecessary if we had perfect speech recognition/understanding performance, has become an important component in spoken dialog systems (SDSs). It allows a SDS to avoid annoying verification turns in cases where the confidence of information items is high. Similarly, it prevents a SDS from acting on an information item with low confidence. Several metrics have been used to assess the performance of confidence annotation. Almost all are related to its correct classification or detection ability. However, its actual impact on the dialog system performance (e.g. user satisfaction, successful completion rate, average number of turns etc.) is not clear without live user experiments. This is a very long process and needs to be repeated if the confidence annotation scheme has changed. So, an analytical analysis that can relate confidence annotation to dialog performance is highly desirable.

This research has been inspired by the work reported in [1]. A finite state model was introduced for information items. Simulation-based statistical analysis was carried out, and speech understanding front-end performance was related to several dialog performance metrics.

In this paper, we extend the work in [1] to a dialog strategy that makes use of confidence annotation. In addition to speech understanding performance metrics, we relate dialog performance metrics to those of confidence annotation. We do not use any simulations to determine the finite state model transition probabilities. Our dialog strategy and assumptions on users' response patterns are simple enough to allow explicit derivation of the transition probabilities in terms of commonly used metrics to assess the speech understanding and confidence annotation components. We finally map a dialog goal, in terms of the probability of success and average number of turns, to a set of operating points on the ROC plane of the confidence annotation scheme, and compare it to the possible operating points of the confidence annotation.

The paper is organized as follows. In section 2, we introduce several finite state models for an information item considering confidence annotation and different user behaviors. A method for statistical analysis is introduced in section 3. Section 4 presents several numerical results, and conclusions are made in the final section.

2. FINITE STATE MODELS

As in [1], we assume a finite state model for an information item. An information item might be known (specified by the user) or unknown to a SDS. A known item can further be classified as "not accepted yet" and "accepted". Another classification is made regarding the value of the information item. The value can either be "correct" or "incorrect". Based on these classifications an information item can be in one of the following five states:

1. unknown; (u,ϕ)
2. known, not confirmed, incorrect; (k,e)
3. known, not confirmed, correct; (k,c)
4. accepted, correct; (a,c)
5. accepted, incorrect; (a,e)

The possible transitions, and their probabilities, among the states are determined by

- user behavior
- speech understanding front-end
- dialog strategy

The simplest dialog strategy, which will serve as the baseline system in this paper, asks for an information item and accepts it

*The work is supported by DARPA through SPAWAR under grant #N66001-00-2-8906.

Proceedings of HLT 2002, Second International Conference on Human Language Technology Research, M. Marcus, ed., Morgan Kaufmann, San Francisco, 2002.

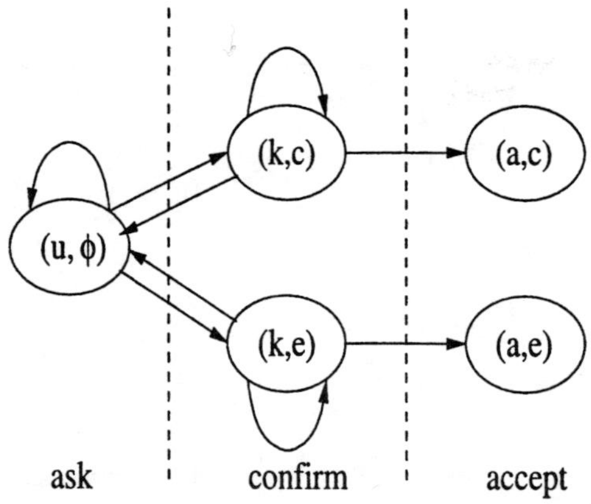

Figure 1: Baseline finite state model (FSM0)

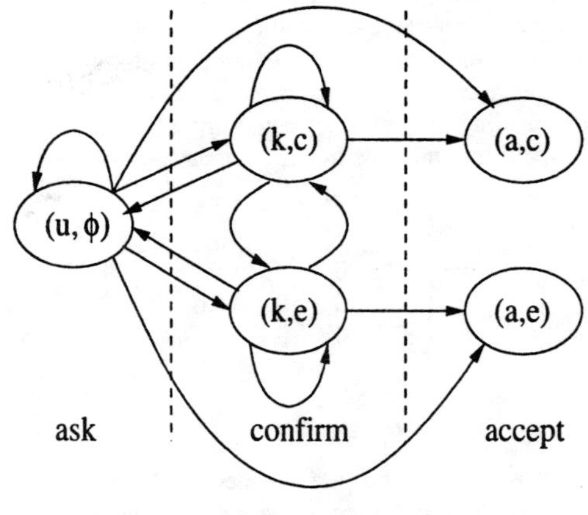

Figure 3: Finite state model considering confidence annotation and different user behavior (FSM2)

after positive verification. Otherwise, the information item is asked again. The user is assumed to be very cooperative and replies "yes" or "no" to any confirmation. The baseline finite state model is shown in Figure 1. Self transitions correspond to "no reply", which is a deletion error at the front-end since the user is assumed to cooperatively reply to any query.

A dialog strategy with confidence annotation may work as follows:

- If $C(I|\text{ask})$ is LOW, confirm I.
- If $C(I|\text{ask})$ is HIGH, accept I.

and

- If $C(I|\text{confirm})$ is LOW, assume "no reply".
- If $C(I|\text{confirm})$ is HIGH, accept I.

where I is the information item and $C(.|.)$ is the confidence score of an information item conditioned on a dialog action. The confidence score is said to be LOW if it is below a certain threshold, say θ_T. Otherwise, it is HIGH. The corresponding finite state model is exhibited in Figure 2.

Another dialog strategy might be the following:

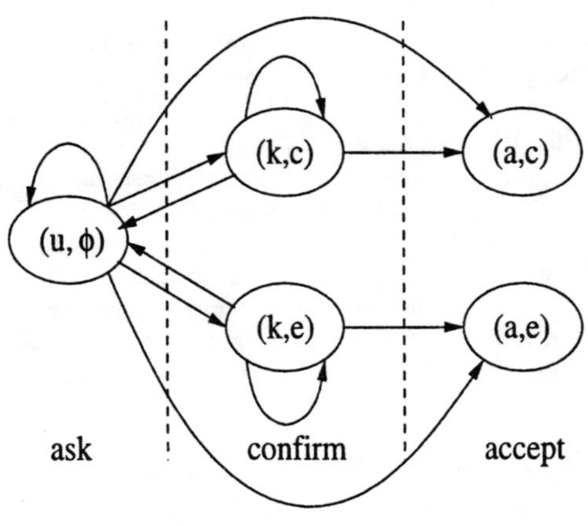

Figure 2: Finite state model considering confidence annotation (FSM1)

- If $C(I|\text{ask})$ is LOW, ask again.
- If $C(I|\text{ask})$ is MEDIUM, confirm I.
- If $C(I|\text{ask})$ is HIGH, accept I.

The confidence score is said to be MEDIUM when

$$\theta_1 < C(I|action) < \theta_2$$

This strategy has the same finite state model as in Figure 2, but the transition probabilities are different.

A simple change in user behavior can result in a different model. For instance, a user might also provide the value of an information in addition to replying "no" to a confirmation. The respective model is depicted in Figure 3. Note the transitions between (k, c) and (k, e).

3. STATISTICAL ANALYSIS METHOD

We base our analysis on the properties of Markov chains [2]. The sequence of states of a transaction can be viewed as a Markov chain. It starts at (u, ϕ) and ends at either (a,c) or (a,e). The former state is called the initial state and the latter states are called absorbtion states. The transaction is considered successful if the sequence ends at (a,c). The transaction is assumed to end when the sequence hits one of the absorbtion states. For the sake of analysis, self loops (not shown) with probability one are assumed for each absorbtion state.

We are interested in the following two metrics:

- $P_s = Pr\{state = (a, c)\}$
- $N_t = \sum_n nPr\{state \in A)\}$

where P_s is the probability of success, N_t is the average number of turns and A is the set of absorbtion states. In order to calculate the required metrics it is sufficent to know the initial probability distribution of the states, π_0, and the transition probability matrix, T.

The probability distrubition of the states at time n is given by

$$\pi_n = \pi_0 T^n \tag{1}$$

Those probabilities at equilibrium satisfy

$$\pi = \pi T \tag{2}$$

The equilibrium probability of (a, c) gives P_s.

In the baseline model, the transition probabilities depend on the performance of the speech understanding front-end. We quantify the performance of the front-end in terms of the probability of correct understanding, P_c, and the probability of deletion, P_d. Given those probabilities, the transition matrix can be written as

$$T = \begin{bmatrix} P_d & P_e & P_c & 0 & 0 \\ P_c & P_d & 0 & 0 & P_e \\ P_e & 0 & P_d & P_c & 0 \\ 0 & 0 & 0 & 1.0 & 0 \\ 0 & 0 & 0 & 0 & 1.0 \end{bmatrix} \quad (3)$$

where

$$P_e = 1 - P_c - P_d \quad (4)$$

We need to quantify the performance of the confidence annotation for the system that uses it. We define P_{CR} and P_{FR} as the correct and false rejection probabilities, respectively. Similarly, one can define $P_{CA} = 1 - P_{FR}$ as the probability of correct acceptance, and $P_{FA} = 1 - P_{CR}$ as the probability of false acceptance. It is not uncommon to report the performance of confidence annotation as the plot of P_{CR} with respect to P_{FR}. This plot is known as the receiver operating characteristics (ROC). Each point on the plot corresponds to a different threshold setting. With confidence annotation as used in the model shown in Figure 2, the transition probability matrix becomes

$$T = \begin{bmatrix} P_d & P_e P_{CR} & P_c & P_c P_{CA} & P_e P_{FA} \\ P_c P_{CA} & P_{d'} & 0 & 0 & P_e P_{FA} \\ P_e P_{FA} & 0 & P_{d'} & P_c P_{CA} & 0 \\ 0 & 0 & 0 & 1.0 & 0 \\ 0 & 0 & 0 & 0 & 1.0 \end{bmatrix} \quad (5)$$

where

$$P_{d'} = P_d + P_e P_{CR} + P_c P_{FR} \quad (6)$$

The initial probability distrubition of the states is obvious; the probability of the initial state is one and probabilities of all other states are zero.

Finally, we define the goal G of a dialog system as follows:

$$G = \{P_s > P_s^*, N_t < N_t^*\} \quad (7)$$

where P_s^* is the minimum and N_t^* is the maximum acceptable values of the respective metrics. We are interested in the region on the plane (P_{CR}, P_{FR}) over which G is satisfied. This region can easily be obtained by numerical evaluation using equations given above.

The models assume a single information item. However, a transaction might need multiple information items. Assuming that

- SDS needs n_i information items to complete a transaction
- Information items are asked one at a time and are independent
- Speech understanding and confidence annotation performances are the same for all pairs of information items and actions

we can easily extend the analysis to multiple information items as

$$\begin{aligned} P_s &= (Pr\{state = (a, c)\})^{n_i} \\ N_t &= n_i \textstyle\sum_n nPr\{state \in A)\} \end{aligned} \quad (8)$$

To be more realistic one can relax the assumptions to obtain a relatively complex FSM. For instance, one can allow the SDS to simultaneously query multiple information items.

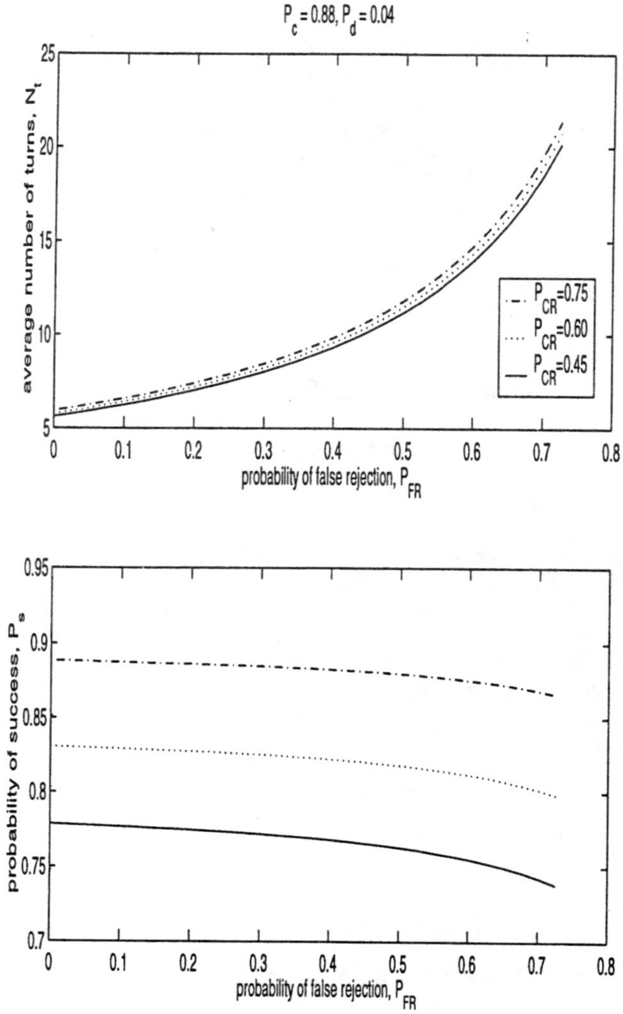

Figure 4: The dependency of dialog metrics to confidence annotation metrics

4. NUMERICAL RESULTS

We first consider the baseline system (FSM0) shown in Figure 1. Assuming typical values of 0.88 and 0.04 for P_c and P_d, respectively, and $n_i = 5$, we numerically evaluate $N_t = 12.3$ and $P_s = 0.96$. We compare this result to the result of FSM1. We consider a typical setting of the confidence threshold that leads to $P_{CR} = 0.63$ at $P_{FR} = 0.05$. The respective results are $N_t = 6.1$ and $P_s = 0.84$. There is a significant drop in the number of average turns at the expense of the probability of success.

Figure 4 shows the dependency of the dialog metrics on P_{FR} for different values of P_{CR}. We conclude that the probability of success is very sensitive to P_{CR}. However, the average number of turns changes very slowly with P_{CR} but increases rapidly with P_{FR}.

As we mentioned earlier it is very common to use a ROC to assess a confidence annotation method. The ROC of the confidence annotation method that we have recently developed [3] within the context of CU Communicator [4] is shown in Figure 5. We wonder how good the annotation scheme is as compared to a given dialog

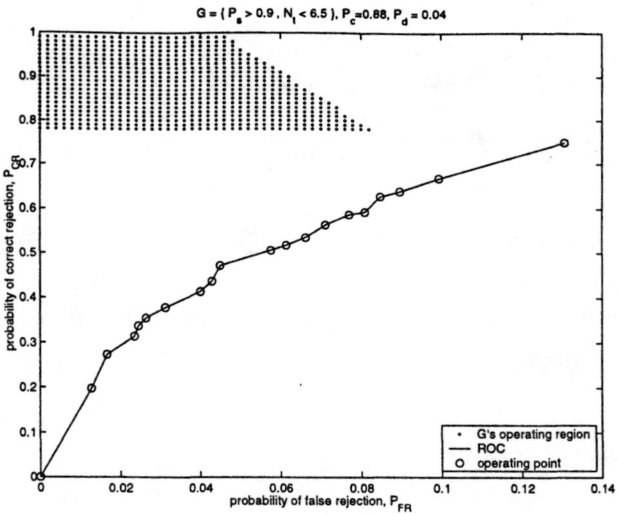

Figure 5: The ROC of the confidence annotation and the operating region of the dialog goal $G = \{P_s > 0.9, N_t < 6.5\}$. The front-end performance is $(P_c = 0.88, P_d = 0.04)$.

goal G. The set of points on (P_{FR}, P_{CR}) plane that satisfy the goal constitutes the so called operating region. We say that the goal is achived if there is at least one operating point of the ROC that falls within that region. The operating region of $G = \{P_s > 0.9, N_t < 6.5\}$ is also shown in Figure 5. It clearly shows that our confidence annotation scheme does not meet the goal and must be improved if we are not willing to lower the goal.

Another possibility is to improve the performance of the speech understanding front-end. The impact of lowering the goal and improving speech understanding are shown in Figure 6 and 7, respectively.

5. CONCLUSIONS

We have presented a quantitative method that can be used to relate confidence annotation metrics to dialog metrics. This method avoids time consuming online experimentation and allows the SDS designer to optimize the use of confidence annotation by either selecting an appropriate dialog strategy or tuning the speech understanding front-end. The framework is so general that it can be extended to account for different user behaviors and more complex dialog strategies. Our research is continuing in those directions.

6. REFERENCES

[1] B. Lin and L. Lee, "Computer-aided analysis and design for spoken dialogue sysyems based on quantitative simulations," *IEEE Transactions on Speech and Audio Processing*, vol. 9, no. 5, pp. 534–548, July 2001.

[2] James R. Norris, *Markov Chains*, Cambridge University Press, 1998.

[3] K. Hacioglu and W. Ward, "A concept graph based confidence measure," to appear in *International Conference on Acoustics, Speech, and Signal Processing*, Orlando, Florida, May 2002.

[4] W. Ward and B. Pellom, "The CU communicator system," in *IEEE Workshop on Automatic Speech Recognition and Understanding*, Keystone, Colorado, 1999.

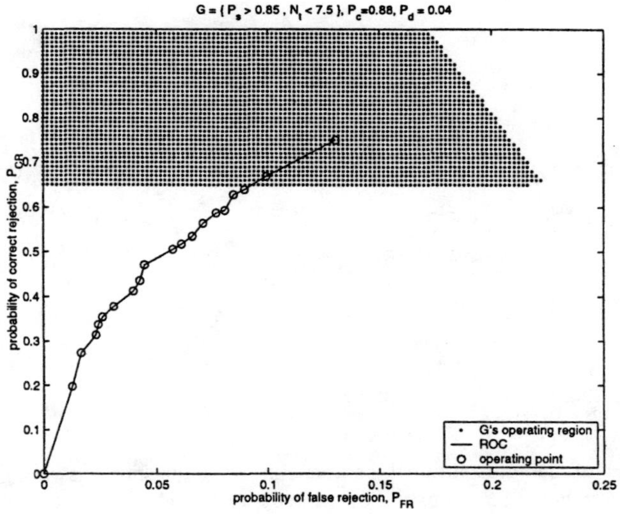

Figure 6: The ROC of the confidence annotation and the operating region of the dialog goal $G = \{P_s > 0.85, N_t < 7.5\}$. The front-end performance is $(P_c = 0.88, P_d = 0.04)$.

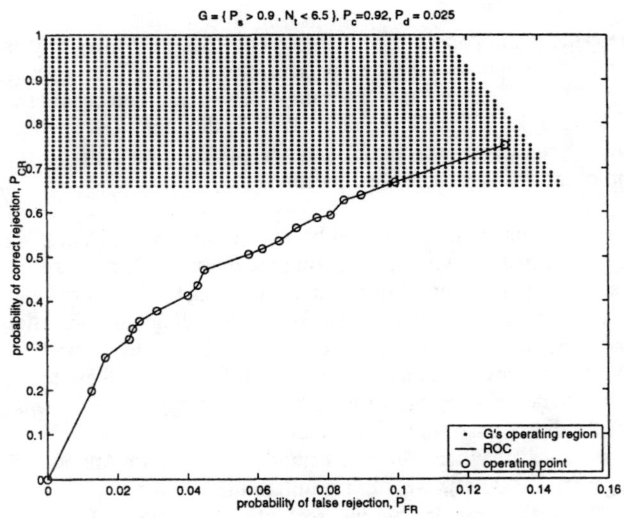

Figure 7: The ROC of the confidence annotation and the operating region of the dialog goal $G = \{P_s > 0.9, N_t < 6.5\}$. The front-end performance is $(P_c = 0.92, P_d = 0.025)$.

Statistical Answer-Type Identification in Open-Domain Question Answering

John Prager
IBM T.J. Watson Research Center
Yorktown Heights, N.Y. 10598
jprager@us.ibm.com

Jennifer Chu-Carroll
IBM T.J. Watson Research Center
Yorktown Heights, N.Y. 10598
jencc@us.ibm.com

Krzysztof Czuba
Carnegie-Mellon University
Pittsburgh, PA 15213
kczuba@cs.cmu.edu

ABSTRACT

One of the most critical components of a question-answering system is the identification of the type, or semantic class, of the answer sought. Systems today use widely-varying numbers of such classes, but all must map the question to one or more classes in their repertoire. In this paper, we present a statistical method of associating question terms with candidate semantic classes that has been shown to achieve a high degree of accuracy and to be applicable to different underlying semantic classifications.

Keywords

Question-Answering, Information Retrieval, Ontologies

1. INTRODUCTION

One critical component of a question-answering (QA) system is the identification of the type, or semantic class, of the answer sought. In all current top-performing QA systems (see e.g [Pasca and Harabagiu, 2001; Clarke et al., 2001]), the identified answer type is used in search and/or answer selection to help select appropriate answers to a given question.

These systems consist essentially of the following stages: 1) identify the answer type by analyzing the question, 2) process the question by elimination of stop-words, including the wh-words that indicate the question type, 3) perform morphological and other expansions on the question, 4) perform a bag-of-words search to return a number of documents or passages, 5) examine these texts for candidate answers of the earlier-identified type, and 6) rank these candidate answers with a metric based on linguistic, logical and statistical features. In our method of Predictive Annotation [Prager et al., 2000], we further utilize the answer type during indexing time by indexing the semantic class labels for each recognized named entity along with the text. During search time, we include in the bag-of-words the desired answer-type, thus guaranteeing that the resulting passages contain at least one candidate answer of the correct semantic class, in the context of the other terms in the question. Regardless of the usage of answer types in the rest of the system, however, answer type identification is integral to the selection of answer candidates in all current prominent question answering systems.

Although the technique of answer type identification is widely employed, there is no generally agreed upon classification used by these systems. The issues influencing the creation of such a set are granularity and coverage. For example, it is clear that for answering "Where" questions, a class of type PLACE is needed. In a context where there are likely to be questions of the kind: "What state ... " and "Name a country that ... ", it seems reasonable that classes STATE and COUNTRY would be useful. However, this argument can be applied to an almost indefinite level of granularity, suggesting classes: CONTINENT, OCEAN, COUNTY, CAPITAL, CITY, TOWN, VILLAGE, ISLAND, PORT, STADIUM, DESERT, MOUNTAIN, RIVER, LAKE, STREET, BUILDING, PLANET and so on, not to mention the different kinds of organization (e.g. FACTORY, MUSEUM, SCHOOL) that can be locations. Furthermore, though no named-entity-based system would get far without the basic notions such as PLACE, PERSON, TIME and NUMBER, with appropriate subclasses, it is not so obvious whether classes such as COLOR, DISEASE and METAL are necessary too.[1]

The number of classes employed by systems participating in the QA track of TRECs 8-10 [Voorhees and Harman, 2000-2] ranged from approximately 10 to 100 (see, e.g. [Ittycheriah et al. 2001] and [Hovy et al. 2001]). However, there is no clear correlation between classes and system performance. We thus conclude that for the foreseeable future, systems will vary in the semantic classes they use, with no guarantee that a close-matching class exists for any given question. This paper addresses the problem of finding the "best" class to match a question's answer type from a system's own inventory of classes. Although in the rest of the paper, the examples draw on the semantic classes used in our system, the algorithm we discuss is independent of this classification and can be easily adopted by other existing systems.

We focus on fact-based questions seeking a named entity whose type is easily (at least to a human) determined from the question, for example, "What is the wingspan of a condor?" and "What metal has the highest melting point?". These questions are by-and-large either asking for the value of a property of an object or to select one item from an enumerable set. "Definitional"

[1] One can transform the coverage problem to a granularity problem by inventing general classes such as PROPERTY and THING.

questions (such as "What is a meerkat?") are not appropriate to this treatment since the question does not indicate the type of the answer being looked for; such questions can be answered by using different approaches, such as Virtual Annotation [Prager et al., 2001].

2. METHODOLOGY

To determine the mapping between an answer type specification in the question (such as **wingspan**) and a semantic class, we had previously employed a WordNet-based manual tagging method. We manually associated with about a hundred mid-level WordNet synsets [Miller, 1995] one or more semantic classes. Given a question term we traversed its hypernym tree until a tagged synset was found, and returned the associated semantic class(es). Thus to answer the TREC8 question "What debts did the Qintex group leave?" we would look up **debts** and find its ancestor **financial condition** which was mapped to our class MONEY.

There were two major problems with this manual tagging method. First, it requires deriving by hand the synset-class mapping, which is a labor-intensive task that resulted in many gaps in coverage (i.e. for some terms, none of its ancestors were associated with any semantic class). This coverage problem can be reduced by applying additional manual effort, but must be revisited whenever semantic classes change. The work must also be replicated if another ontology is used, and may not be feasible if a domain-specific ontology is unavailable. The second problem was that, especially for compound nouns such as **death toll**, not all terms had entries in WordNet. Using just the head noun was not necessarily effective either: the parentage of **toll** consists of the two branches: {**fee, fixed charge, charge, cost, expenditure, financial loss, loss, transferred possession, possession**} and {**value, worth, quality, attribute, abstraction**}. Neither branch is useful in directing a QA system to find numbers of people, or just numbers. Since this approach is neither automatable nor easily extensible, we investigated an alternative statistical approach.

Our new approach follows from the observation that frequently in text, entities are mentioned in conjunction with other entities of the same or similar[2] semantic class. This could be because an entity is contrasted with another entity, is presented in a list with another entity, or shares a relationship with some other entity. For instance, in "What is the wingspan of a condor?", the term **wingspan** occurs frequently with entities labeled LENGTH in the corpus, such as "9-foot". We hypothesize that local co-occurrence counts of the question term T and each semantic class label L_i used by the system will indicate the degree of association between T and L_i, and that those classes highly associated with T would be good candidate classes for T itself.

Our approach specifically targets questions that include a single or multi-word term T that explicitly names the answer type, such as **wingspan.** After extracting T, our goal is to determine, given a system's underlying semantic classification, the most plausible class(es) that represents answers of type T. For example, for "What was the death toll at the eruption of mount Pinatubo?", we extract **death toll** as the term T. Given our semantic classification, the correct classes are either WHOLENO or POPULATION, specifying either a cardinal number or, more specifically, a number recognized as population size.[3]

Our algorithm seeks to determine the semantic class of T based on the co-occurrence counts of T and each semantic class label L_i, relative to total occurrences of L_i in the TREC corpus. First, each class label receives a score based on a scoring function S, which is compared with the expected score for that class. The greater the score for L_i deviates positively from its expected value, the higher the degree of positive association is between T and L_i, and thus the better L_i is as a candidate answer type.

We implemented three variations of the scoring function as follows, where C represents the TREC corpus:

> S1 counts the number of co-occurrences of T with L_i in the same or consecutive lines of each document in C.
>
> S2 counts the number of documents in C where both T and L_i occur in the same sentence.
>
> S3 counts the number of documents in C where both T and L_i occur either adjacent or separated by a single word.

These scoring algorithms differ in two aspects. First, they differ in the window size that defines the context in which we search for co-occurrences. Second, they differ in terms of whether actual co-occurrence counts or the number of documents containing term co-occurrences are used. In S1-S3, all counts are transformed into a deviation from the expected frequency given a uniform distribution of class labels in the corpus. The class labels are then scored and sorted and the top classes may be used as candidate answer types for a QA system. Additionally, we implemented a fourth algorithm, AVERAGE, based on the outcome of the three S_j scoring algorithms.

The specific algorithms used are as follows.

S1 – Occurrences

Using the GREP utility we found all three-line text segments containing T in the middle line, and collected these segments in a file F. We ran our named-entity-recognizing indexer on F to generate an index whose statistics we could query. For each semantic class label L we calculated the ratio

$$R_l = \frac{\text{occs of L in F} / \text{total terms in F}}{\text{occs of L in C} / \text{total terms in C}} \quad \ldots\ldots (1)$$

This ratio represents, for each semantic class L, how its distribution in the text segments in F differs from its distribution in the TREC corpus as a whole. The larger this ratio is, the higher the co-occurrence is between T and L, and therefore the likelier L is as a candidate semantic type for the question term T.

[2] I.e. they may share a hypernym or meronym relationship.

[3] Our named entity recognizer/annotator can (and frequently does) tag text strings with multiple semantic labels.

Table 1 Results for "death toll"

	S1 - Occurrences		S2 - Sentences		S3 - Phrases		AVG - Average	
1	POPULATE	10.55	WHOLENO	3.00	WHOLENO	0.96	WHOLENO	0.22
2	SPEED	6.00	SMALLNO	2.74	SMALLNO	0.92	SMALLNO	0.21
3	SMALLNO	4.87	DISEASE	2.65	DISEASE	0.74	DISEASE	0.14
4	WHOLENO	4.86	THING	2.17	SPEED	0.61	LARGENO	0.14
5	LARGENO	4.82	LARGENO	1.98	LARGENO	0.37	SPEED	0.12

Table 2 Results for "cancer"

	S1 - Occurrences		S2 - Sentences		S3 - Phrases		AVG - Average	
1	DISEASE	83.78	CONSTELL	208.32	MEDICAL	24.91	DISEASE	0.39
2	MEDICAL	20.93	DISEASE	108.92	DISEASE	16.13	MEDICAL	0.26
3	CONSTELL	20.29	MEDICAL	53.03	SYMPTOM	2.66	CONSTELL	0.22
4	STAR	13.00	MEDICINE	19.39	ROLE	2.63	STAR	0.05
5	MEDICINE	12.29	SYMPTOM	14.08	STAR	2.63	MEDICINE	0.04

S2 – Sentences

For S2 and S3 we used a utility *doc_cnt* in our GuruQA search-engine package [Prager et al., 2000]; doc_cnt takes a GuruQA query and returns the number of documents that the query matches exactly. For S2 we used the query

```
@win(1 T L)
```

which finds occurrences of T and L within a window size of 1, i.e., when they co-occur in the same sentence. For each semantic class label L, if doc_cnt used as above returned a count of M documents, we calculated the ratio

$$R_2 = \frac{M/1000}{docs\ containing\ L\ in\ C / total\ docs\ in\ C} \quad \ldots\ \ldots\ (2)$$

S3 – Phrases

For S3 we used the GuruQA query

```
@win(1 @phr(1 T L))
```

which finds occurrences of T and L in the same phrase with at most one intervening term. For each semantic class label L, if doc_cnt as used above returned a count of N documents, we calculated the ratio

$$R_3 = \frac{N/1000}{docs\ containing\ L\ in\ C / total\ docs\ in\ C} \quad \ldots\ \ldots\ \ldots\ (3)$$

Equivalently, equations (2) and (3) are seeking the L which maximizes

$$|T \text{ and } L| / |L| \quad \ldots\ \ldots\ \ldots\ \ldots\ \ldots\ (4)$$

for the respective kind of intersection. The factor (1000/total docs in C) is constant and just serves to scale the numbers.

AVERAGE

We gathered the top 5 semantic categories according to each scoring scheme. We noticed that the best-performing scoring algorithm S_j depended on L_i, but in a non-obvious way, and also that the correct L_i for a given T would often occur in two or three of the top-5 lists, even if never in first place. We therefore decided to compute the average of the S_j. Since the scales of the S_j were not directly compatible, we normalized the S_j scores R_{ji} by dividing each score by the sum of the top 5 placed L_i. The AVG score for a given L_i is the average of its normalized R_{ji} scores. The sum of the top 5 AVG scores equals 1 only if the top 5 L_i entries for each of the S_j contain the same 5 L_i, in some permutation.

Scores for sample question-terms are presented in Table 1 and Table 2. It should be noted that for the S_j scores, the absolute values of the numbers are not as meaningful as their relative values, within a column. Values across columns cannot be compared. The absolute values in the AVG column, on the other hand, can be thought of as rough estimates of confidence.

3. EXAMPLES

As illustration of some of the properties and behaviors of our approach, we present in Table 3 the top-5 results for certain selected question terms. The rows in the table are split into three groups to facilitate discussion. For each question term, we show the top 5 semantic classes returned by the system, along with their respective scores using the AVERAGE scoring algorithm,

Table 3 Top 5 Results for Selected Question Terms

Question Term T	1st		2nd		3rd		4th		5th	
	Class	S	Class	S	Class	S	Class	S	Class	S
Wingspan	*LENGTH*	*0.67*	SPEED	0.12	WEIGHT	0.06	POWER	0.05	VEHICLE	0.05
Cancer	*DISEASE*	*0.39*	*MEDICAL*	*0.26*	CONSTELL	0.22	STAR	0.05	MEDICINE	0.04
Culture	*DURADATE*	*0.19*	*NATIONAL*	*0.16*	THING	0.14	ROLE	0.12	COMPOS	0.07
Season	SPORTSTEAM	0.34	*TIMEOFYEAR*	*0.19*	WEIGHT	0.12	TIME	0.10	SPORT	0.06
Bone	MUSICAL	0.38	DISEASE	0.28	MEDICAL	0.12	*BODYPART*	*0.10*	SYMPTOM	0.05
Plant	POWER	0.52	PROVINCE	0.08	ROLE	0.07	WEIGHT	0.07	AREA	0.06
Continent	*CONTIN*	*0.47*	PLACE	0.11	MOUNTAIN	0.10	REGION	0.09	OCEAN	0.08
Country	REGION	0.22	CONTIN	0.14	PLACE	0.10	ROLE	0.10	THING	0.08
State	NICKNAME	0.19	ROLE	0.14	PLACE	0.11	COUNTRY	0.10	POWER	0.10
Movie	*COMPOS*	*0.45*	THING	0.09	CONSTELL	0.09	PERSON	0.09	DURADATE	0.09
Film	*COMPOS*	*0.29*	PERSON	0.10	CONSTELL	0.10	DURADATE	0.10	THING	0.10
Best-selling book	*COMPOS*	*0.67*	PERSON	0.12	THING	0.16	RELIGION	0.05	YEAR	0.05
Novel	*COMPOS*	*0.28*	DURADATE	0.19	RELIGION	0.17	PHONE	0.15	PERSON	0.09
Sitcom	*COMPOS*	*0.60*	THING	0.09	ROLE	0.07	PERSON	0.06	MOST	0.04
Television show	*COMPOS*	*0.50*	MOON	0.17	THING	0.09	ROLE	0.07	PERSON	0.07
Song	*COMPOS*	*0.34*	STAR	0.26	MUSICAL	0.12	PERSON	0.09	THING	0.05

which indicates relative confidence. The semantic classes in italics are those considered correct for the given question term.

The first group of question terms in Table 3 contains examples that show certain system successes and failures. The clear winner for **wingspan** is LENGTH, as desired. Note that the runner-up candidates all are related in reasonable ways, in particular when the word is used in the context of wingspans of aircrafts. The results for **cancer** ("What is the most common cancer?") returned highly relevant semantic classes that represent diseases and medical conditions in first and second places. Interestingly, the two semantic classes in top 5 positions that are considered irrelevant for this example are STAR and CONSTELL(ATION), which correspond to a different, but also fairly common sense of the word. **Culture** ("What culture developed the idea of potlatch?") did well, in our opinion, with a fuzzy category. Its best candidates, DURADATE[4] and NATIONAL, address the temporal and spatial aspects of the question. For the next two question terms, the correct semantic class is found, but not in the top position. For the question term **season** ("What is the busiest air travel season?"), the system found the correct semantic class TIMEOFYEAR in second position. The first place answer is SPORTSTEAM, at first glance an unlikely candidate. However, we believe this is because journalists often compare sports teams by season, or refer to a team's perfo rmance in the "1995 baseball season". On the other hand, when the four seasons are mentioned in text, the word "season" is so strongly implied by "spring" and "summer" that it is often not explicitly mentioned. The next two examples, **bone** and **plant**, suffer from problems with polysemy, which we elaborate further in Section 5.

The second group of examples contains three question terms, **continent** ("What continent is Bolivia on?"), **country** ("In what country is a stuck-out tongue a friendly greeting?"), and **state** ("What state produces the best lobster to eat?"). Of these three terms, the system found a suitable semantic class only for **continent** (not considering the generic semantic class PLACE). Similar to the **season** example, we presume that this is because we talk about "the African continent" but not the "French country" or the "Massachusetts state", for example [5]. We will discuss this issue of failure due to stylistic factors in Section 5. However, note that the scores for the top candidates in the **country** and **state** examples are relatively low, compared to most other examples for which the top semantic class is correct.

The final group of examples illustrates a wide range of question terms for which our system returns COMPOS, our generic class for titled works (compositions), as the top candidate semantic class. These question terms include **movie, film, best-selling book, novel, sitcom, television show**, and **song**. Note that not only did our system return COMPOS for all these examples, it also did so with high confidence. This set of examples illustrates the powerfulness of our methodology --- though it is possible to manually derive pattern-matching rules to associate question terms with candidate semantic classes, we conjecture that terms such as **sitcom** is unlikely to be in a QA-system's pattern repertoire for all but those with the most complete coverage.

---

[4] DURADATE is the intersection of DURATION and DATE – time references that can be viewed either as points in time or extents, such as "The 12th century" and "The Renaissance".

[5] Although admittedly the expression "state of X" is us ed somewhat, a rough calculation shows it to be used less that 2% of times a state is mentioned.

4. EXPERIMENTAL RESULTS

To evaluate the performance of our algorithm, we chose questions from the TREC9-10 QA tracks[6] that fit our criterion, that a term in the question explicitly states the answer type. These questions fall into two categories: *Set* questions, which seek a member of a set of instances ("What metal has the highest melting point?") and *Property* questions, which seek the value of a property ("What is the wingspan of the condor?").

We applied our algorithm to all qualifying questions using all three scoring functions, plus the average. The algorithm returned the top 5 candidates, and each question received a score equal to the reciprocal rank of the correct answer (or 0 if it failed to show). The scores in the following tables are the mean reciprocal ranks (MRRs) in each test condition. The column labeled N shows the number of questions processed (in Table 5 and Table 7, multiple questions with the same term T are counted only once).

Table 4 MRRs for TREC9 questions, counting instances

	N	S1	S2	S3	AVG
Property	27	.63	.66	.70	.67
Set	106	.42	.55	.62	.60
All	133	.46	.58	.64	.62

Table 5 MRRs for TREC9 questions, counting types

	N	S1	S2	S3	AVG
Property	15	.53	.56	.64	.61
Set	73	.50	.65	.67	.72
All	88	.50	.63	.66	.70

Table 6 MRRs for TREC10 questions, counting instances

	N	S1	S2	S3	AVG
Property	49	.72	.81	.91	.89
Set	103	.33	.42	.48	.46
All	152	.46	.55	.62	.60

Table 7 MRRs for TREC10 questions, counting types

	N	S1	S2	S3	AVG
Property	21	.65	.74	.83	.88
Set	49	.40	.49	.56	.55
All	70	.48	.56	.64	.65

In most cases, *Property* questions fared much better than *Set* questions. Furthermore, S3 universally outperformed S2, which in turn outperformed S1, suggesting that very close proximity is a key feature for success. In about half of the experimental conditions the AVERAGE column performed best. We plan to investigate whether the scoring functions combined with the manual tagging method will lead to further improvement.

[6] These questions are familiar to the community, have answer sets, and are derived (by NIST) from logs of questions from real users.

5. DISCUSSION

The results show that our methodology works very well on the kinds of factual questions in TREC QA - on average, a correct answer type is proposed in first or second place. The errors typically fall into two categories: those resulting from polysemy and those resulting from stylistic or domain-dependent factors. The first category is typified by **plant**, as in "Material called linen is made from what plant?" Our algorithm strongly suggests type POWER, since most mentions of **plant** in the TREC corpus are about power plants and their power output. The second category is typified by **bone**, as in "What is the longest bone in the human body?" Instead of BODYPART, the algorithm suggests MUSICAL (instrument), due to polysemy of words such as "pipe", "horn", "wood", "organ" etc., and DISEASE, since mentions of bone diseases are more common than phrases such as "the ulna bone". Examples such as **season, country,** and **state** discussed earlier in the paper also fall into this category. This contrasts with **metal**, which frequently occurs in sentences such as "Among the precious metals, platinum futures showed ... ". We observe that *Set* questions are much more prone to such problems than *Property* questions.

5.1. Local Context Analysis

It was hypothesized that these problems, particularly those deriving from polysemy, can be ameliorated by using the context of the entire question to disambiguate senses, following the work in Local Context Analysis of Xu and Croft (1996). To test this hypothesis, we used the original questions (from which our focus terms T were derived) to query the corpus and generate document sets. We used hit-lists of size 1000, which resulted in sets of $1000n$ documents, where n was the number of questions focusing on a given query term. We used these document sets as substitutes for the TREC corpus C in equations (1)-(3); we indexed the document sets and applied the four scoring functions described in Section 2. Our results were (by type) almost uniformly worse than using the entire corpus.

The reasons for the deterioration appear to be many, but with two main variations, both concerning the frequency of the question term T. Based on equation (4), in order for the score for the correct semantic class L to improve with the application of local context analysis, either 1) T and L must co-occur more frequently in the sub-corpus than in the entire TREC corpus, or 2) L itself must occur less frequently in the sub-corpus than in the whole corpus. When the question term T is frequent, we observe that the number of co-occurrences of T and each semantic class tend to remain fairly constant between the sub-corpus and the main corpus. On the other hand, when T is very infrequent, its co-occurrence with each semantic class is constant – all of its instances occur in the filtered corpus. In either case, the numerator of (4) will be constant (modulo scaling). However, since the filtered corpus is biased toward the subject-matter of the question term, the denominator of (4) will tend to be the maximum possible for highly correlated classes, i.e., $|L|$ will become greater for more relevant semantic classes, resulting in lower scores for the very semantic classes whose scores we are seeking to improve!

5.2. Frequency Correlation

We hypothesize that explicit mention of the semantic class with a term may be correlated with the frequency of that term. Noticeably, the two most frequently occurring terms (**year** and **state**) each got a score of 0, since it usually goes without saying that, for example, 1960 is a year and that California is a state. To validate our hypothesis, we plotted the score for a question term against the document frequency (DF) of the term, with appropriate smoothing. Figure 1 shows the MRR of a moving window of 30 terms against log of DF. Figure 2 shows a "cumulating" MRR for all question terms of equal or lesser DF. This allows one to see what the effective accuracy of the system is if applied to all question terms with a DF below a given threshold.

Despite the obvious kinks in the curves, there is a clear downward trend of MRR with DF, although it appears that two or more competing forces are at play. The steep rise in both figures at log DF of around -5 is an artifact of the smoothing. In fact there is a jump from average performance of about .7 to near-perfect performance for all terms with log DF -5.0 to -3.5. This is illustrated in Figure 3, which is like Figure 2 but only applied to terms with log DF greater than -5 (i.e. occurring in more than 1 in every 150 documents). The cumulating MRR for terms in this range is clearly monotonic.

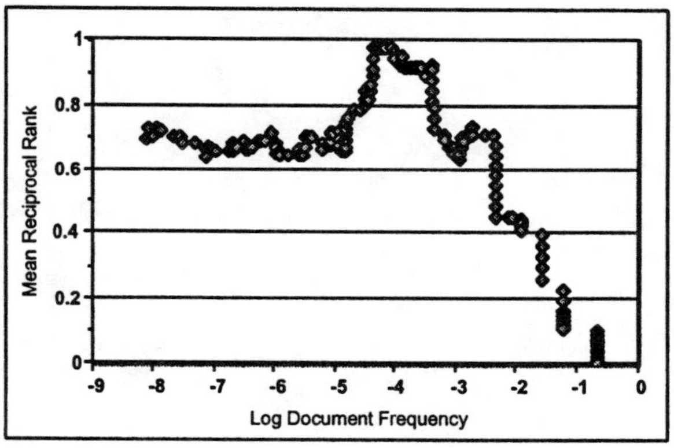

Figure 1. Question terms arranged in increasing order of their DF. Graph shows the MRR of a sliding window of 30 terms against the log DF of the right-most term in the window.

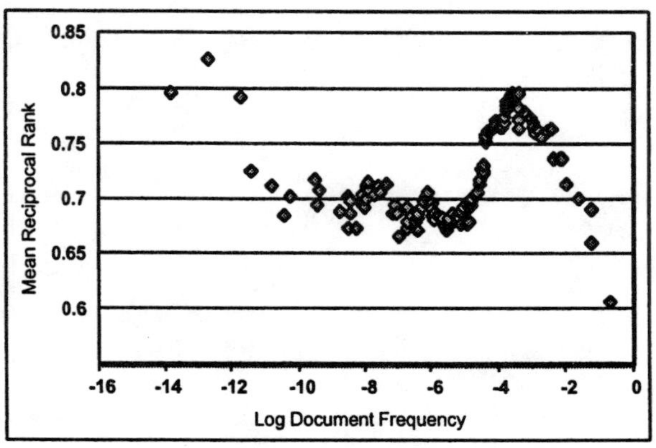

Figure 2. With the same ordering as in Figure 1, the MRR of all of the terms to the left of a given term is plotted.

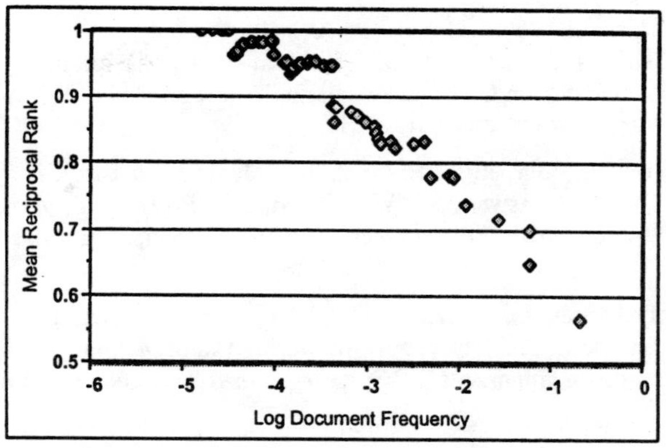

Figure 3. As Figure 2, but only for the most frequent terms.

It seems quite likely from these figures that there are at least two different phenomena, or possibly a single phenomenon with different controlling parameters in different frequency ranges. It is possible there is some relation with Rosch et al.'s [1976] Basic Categories, which is to say that the most natural level of description of an object is both used most frequently and is least in need of a semantic description. A full investigation of these phenomena is beyond the scope of this paper.

We can use the results presented in these figures to choose a performance threshold for deciding when to apply our algorithm, based on how frequently the question term occurs in text.. For example, if we choose a threshold of log DF = -2.5, corresponding to a frequency of less than 1 document in 12, we can predict an MRR of greater than .6 for any such question term, or an average MRR of about.75 across all such terms.

6. SUMMARY

We presented a statistical method of determining the appropriate semantic types corresponding to a term given any underlying semantic classification. When utilized by a QA system, our algorithm establishes the identity of a candidate answer type sought by a natural language question. We have shown that our algorithm, on average, proposes a correct answer type in either first or second place on a subset of the TREC9-10 questions. Furthermore, for especially the more frequent terms, the rarer the term, the better the algorithm performance. These figures provide a thresholding mechanism for a given desired success rate, based on the corpus document frequency of the term.

7. ACKNOWLEDGMENTS

We would like to thank Dave Ferrucci and the anonymous reviewers for their very helpful comments and suggestions. This work was supported in part by the Advanced Research and Development Activity (ARDA)'s Advanced Question Answering for Intelligence (AQUAINT) Program under contract number MDA904-01-C-0988.

8. REFERENCES

[1] Clarke, L.A., Cormack, G.V. and Lynam, T.R. "Exploiting Redundancy in Question Answering", *Proceedings of SIGIR 2001*, New Orleans, LA, 2001.

[2] Hovy, H., Gerber, L., Hermjakob, U. Junk, M. & Lin, C-Y. "Question Answering in Webclopedia. In *Proceedings of the 9th Text Retrieval Conference (TREC9)*, Gaithersburg, MD, 2001.

[3] Ittycheriah, A., Franz, M., Zhu, W-J., Ratnaparkui, A. and Mammone, R.J. "Question Answering Using Maximum Entropy Components", *Proceedings NAACL*, Pittsburgh, PA, 2001.

[4] Mihalcea, R. and Moldovan, D. "A Method for Word Sense Disambiguation of Unrestricted Text", *Proceedings of the 37th Annual Meeting of the Association for Computational Linguistics (ACL-99)*, pp. 152-158, College Park, MD, 1999.

[5] Miller, G. "WordNet: A Lexical Database for English", *Communications of the ACM* 38(11) pp. 39-41, 1995.

[6] Pasca, M.A. and Harabagiu, S.M. "High Performance Question/Answering", *Proceedings of SIGIR 2001*, New Orleans, LA, 2001.

[7] Prager, J.M., Brown, E.W., Coden, A.R., and Radev, D.R. "Question-Answering by Predictive Annotation", *Proceedings of SIGIR 2000*, pp. 184-191, Athens, Greece, 2000.

[8] Prager, J.M., Radev, D.R. and Czuba, K. "Answering What-Is Questions by Virtual Annotation", *Proceedings of HLT 2001*, pp. 26-30, San Diego, CA 2001.

[9] Radev, D.R., Prager, J.M. and Samn, V. "Ranking Suspected Answers to Natural Language Questions using Predictive Annotation", *Proceedings of ANLP00*, Seattle, WA, 2000.

[10] Rosch, E. et al. "Basic Objects in Natural Categ ories", *Cognitive Psychology* 8, pp. 382-439, 1976.

[11] TREC8 - "The Eighth Text Retrieval Conference", E.M. Voorhees and D.K. Harman Eds., NIST, Gaithersburg, MD, 2000.

[12] TREC9 - "The Ninth Text Retrieval Conference", E.M. Voorhees and D.K. Harman Eds., NIST, Gaithersburg, MD, 2001.

[13] TREC2001 - "The Tenth Text Retrieval Conference", E.M. Voorhees and D.K. Harman Eds., NIST, Gaithersburg, MD, to appear in 2002.

[14] Xu, J. & Croft, W.B. "Query expansion using local and global document analysis", *Proceedings of SIGIR 96*., pp 4-11, 1996.

Japanese Spoken Document Retrieval Considering OOV Keywords Using LVCSR System with OOV Detection Processing

Hiromitsu NISHIZAKI and Seiichi NAKAGAWA
Department of Information and Computer Sciences
Toyohashi University of Technology
1-1 Hibarigaoka, Tempaku-cho, Toyohashi-shi, Aichi, JAPAN 441-8580
{nisizaki,nakagawa}@slp.ics.tut.ac.jp

ABSTRACT

This paper describes a Japanese spoken document retrieval system that is robust for Out-of-Vocabulary (OOV) words. A standard approach to spoken document retrieval is to automatically transcribe spoken documents into word sequences, which can be directly matched against queries. In this approach, the documents including OOV words and words mis-recognized as other words can not be retrieved. To avoid this problem, we propose a novel method of spoken document retrieval considering OOV keywords. One of our approach is to create a index from multiple recognizers' outputs to deal with transcribed documents including mis-recognized words. The index becomes better to use multiple recognizers which have different characteristics to one another. The other is to use both word based indexing for in-vocabulary keywords and syllable based indexing for OOV keywords, and to switch them according to in-vocabulary/OOV keywords in the query. Evaluation results clearly show that this approach benefits from advantages of both indexing methods and that the proposed technique is quite effective in robustly retrieving spoken documents.

Keywords

Spoken Document Retrieval, OOV Detection, Multiple Recognizers, DTW matching, HMM based word spotting

1. INTRODUCTION

Recently, environments in which a large number of audio and multimedia archives such as video tapes, digital libraries and so on can be easily used have been prepared. Especially, a rapidly increasing number of spoken documents, such as broadcast radio and television programs, are archived, and many of them can be accessed through the Internet. The needs for retrieving such speech information have been more and more growing, while it is definitely true that the effective retrieval technique is lacking at present, and the development of technology for retrieving such speech information is becoming more and more important.

In the TREC Spoken Document Retrieval track[1], a number of studies were presented on the subject of English and Mandarin broadcast news documents. A standard approach to spoken document retrieval (SDR) is to automatically transcribe spoken documents into word sequences, which can be directly matched against queries. In this approach, however, a serious problem arises when both the queries and the documents include out-of-vocabulary (OOV) keywords[1], where matching against OOV keywords always fails, because the OOV keyword can not be transcribed as a word. Many previous studies handled an OOV problem in spoken document retrieval. In most of them, spoken documents were not transcribed into word sequences, but into phoneme / syllable sequences using phoneme / syllable recognizers[11, 9, 6, 8]. Wechsler et al.[11] used a phoneme recognizer to transcribe spoken documents. K. Ng et al.[9] worked on the use of sub-word unit representation based on phonemes in spoken document retrieval. H. M. Wang[6] also investigated syllable-based indexing for retrieval of spoken documents in Mandarin Chinese using a syllable lattice. C. Ng et al.[8] reported, however, that better retrieval performance in terms of average precision was obtained using word-based indexing rather than using phoneme/syllable based indexing. Furthermore, word based retrieval must be faster than that based on phoneme/syllable.

This paper describes a Japanese spoken document retrieval system for broadcast news articles that uses both word based indexing for in-vocabulary keywords and syllable based indexing for OOV keywords. Our approach of combining word based and syllable based indexing has advantages of both indexing. The syllable index is created by recognizing spoken documents using a speech recognizer with OOV detecting process, i.e., detected OOV words are indexed as a syllable sequence. We suppose that a recognizer's lexicon is equivalent to a lexicon which is used to identify whether an input keyword is OOV or not in retrieving process. When a keyword included in a query does not belong to OOV, it is matched directly against word index, where neither retrieval speed nor accuracy is harmed. When a keyword belongs to OOV, spoken documents including OOV words can be robustly retrieved to use a DTW (Dynamic Time Warping) matching technique by which the keyword is matched against

[1] In this paper, we define a set of words input to a retrieval system as "a query" and a constituent word of a query as "a keyword".

syllable index, or an HMM-based word spotting technique is also applied. In the latter case, this technique is applied for the speech segments detected as OOV only.

For spoken document retrieval, a mis-recognition problem is also fatal as far as word based indexing is used. We propose to utilize multiple recognizers' outputs in SDR, and investigate whether or not combining two recognizers that are different in their natures can help improve the performance of SDR. It is well known that a voting scheme such as ROVER (Recognizer Output Voting Error Reduction) for combining multiple speech recognizers' outputs can achieve word error reduction[2]. A method which attaches a confidence measure to each hypothesized word from a recognizer's output by utilizing multiple recognizers' outputs is also proposed[5]. In the proposed method in this paper, indexes are created by taking the union as well as the intersection of two different recognizers' outputs. By taking the union of the transcripts, word correct rate improves, while insertion errors increase. By taking the intersection of the transcripts, on the other hand, both word correct rate and insertion errors decrease. We evaluate both the union index and the intersection index, and show that it is effective to utilize multiple recognizers' outputs in SDR. In the evaluation result, the retrieval performance of the union index, which is improved in terms of correct and deletion rates, outperforms that of the intersection index with fewer insertion errors. This result claims that, in SDR, it is the most important to achieve the word correct rate as high as possible, even if insertion errors increase.

2. JAPANESE SPOKEN DOCUMENT RETRIEVAL SYSTEM

2.1 System Overview

Figure 1 shows the system overview. First, two types of databases are prepared by two types of recognizers as shown in Figure 1, where one consists only of word sequences (Database1), and of the mixture of word and syllable sequences (Database2). One database is transcribed by a recognizer without OOV detection processing, while the other is transcribed by a recognizer with OOV detection processing, by which the portion of OOV in spoken documents is represented as a suitable syllable sequence. If a keyword included in a query is in-vocabulary, it is matched directly against word index in the Database1 transcribed only in word. If a keyword belongs to OOV, on the other hand, its syllable form is matched against syllable index by DTW matching in the Database2 transcribed in the mixture of words and syllables, or concatenated HMMs which correspond to a syllable form of the keyword are directly matched against parts of spoken documents detected as OOV using an HMM-based word spotting technique. By combining word based index with syllable based index, spoken documents including OOV keywords may be retrieved robustly.

2.2 LVCSR systems

As the Japanese LVCSR systems, we use the one named Julius, which is provided by IPA Japanese dictation free software project[4], as well as the one named SPOJUS[3], which has been developed in our laboratory. As the acoustic models of those two recognizers, we use the phoneme-unit based HMMs for Julius and the syllable-unit based HMMs for SPOJUS, respectively. The phoneme (tri-phone-based) HMMs (43 Japanese phonemes) are provided by IPA Japanese dictation free software project, where their acoustic feature vectors consist of 25 dimensions: 12 dimensional Mel-frequency cepstrum coefficients (MFCCs) , the cepstrum difference coefficients (delta MFCCs), and delta power, and they are calculated every 10 msec. The speech data used for training phoneme HMMs are sampled at 16kHz and 16bits. On the other hand, the syllable HMMs (116 Japanese syllables) have been developed in our laboratory[7] using 16kHz sampled speech, where their feature vectors consist of 50 dimensions: 24 dimensional Mel-frequency cepstrum coefficients (MFCC) segmented from 4 successive frames, delta 12 dimensions calculated over 9 successive frames, delta delta 12 dimensions and delta, delta delta powers, and they are calculated every 10msec (this model is called 'MFCC-segment model'). The distribution of the acoustic features are modeled using mixtures of diagonal covariance Gussians for the phoneme HMMs, and full covariance Gussians for the syllable HMMs, respectively. As the language models for both recognizers, the word bigram and trigram language models for 20k vocabulary size (coverage of 96.7%) are trained using 5 years Japanese NHK broadcast news scripts (approximately 120,000 sentences). Those recognizers run in two decoding passes, where the first pass uses the word bigram, and the second pass uses the word trigram.

The SPOJUS has the function of OOV word detection, which is called as "OOV detection processing". In the SPOJUS with OOV detection processing, if the transition probability from preceding word to the current processing word is low in the bigram language model and the acoustic likelihood is also low, this portion is not transcribed in a word sequence but in a syllable sequence, that is, OOV.

2.3 Speech Data Corpus

The speech data used in this work is Japanese NHK (Japan Broadcasting Corp.) broadcast TV news from June 1 to July 14, 1996. The data is partitioned into separate news stories, and includes 976 stories (7,099 sentences, approximate 18 hours) in total, half of which are utterances with noise such as background music. It is very difficult to transcribe certain portions of those spoken documents, because utterances with dialogue speech and field reports are also included in this data.

2.4 Retrieval without OOV Keywords

In the retrieval engine, a keyword in a query is matched against an index word made of transcripts from recognizers' outputs. This is a very simple engine to retrieve target spoken documents which include the input keyword, where any kinds of similarities between query and documents are not calculated at all[10]. This is simply because our primary goal is to evaluate effects of various speech processing techniques upon spoken document retrieval performance. Improving the absolute performance of spoken document retrieval is not very important in this study.

A system architecture as shown in Figure 2 is used in a retrieval experiment, where OOV keywords are not treated to examine that some recognition errors in transcriptions of spoken documents affect a retrieval performance. The OOV keywords described in this paper are defined as keywords which are not listed in the recognizer's lexicon.

The *combination module* generates an index which is used in the retrieval engine by taking either union (**OR**) or insertion (**AND**) among the two recognizers' outputs, or by selecting (**SELECT**) the one from the two outputs.

The set of documents transcribed only in words is denoted as *DW*, where the DW transcribed by the SPOJUS is represented

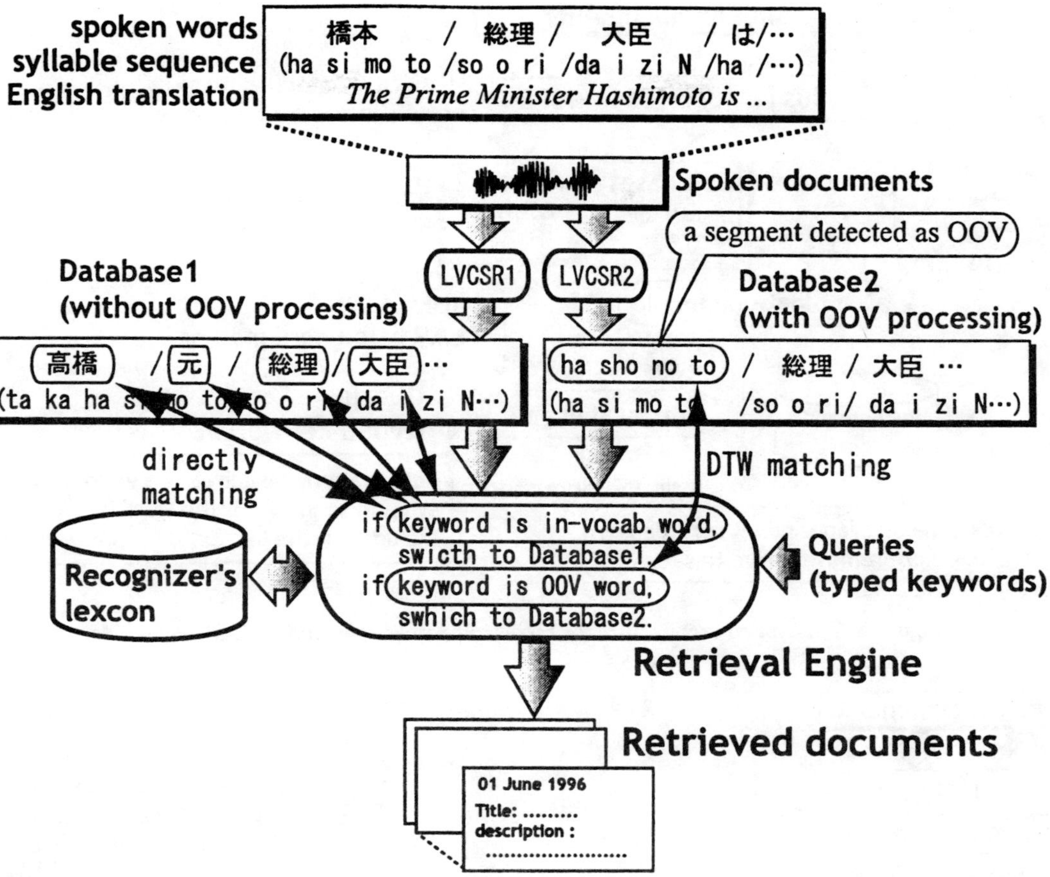

Figure 1: The system overview.

as "DW_{spo}", and the DW transcribed by the Julius is represented as "DW_{jul}". and that transcribed in the mixture words and syllables as DWS (the DWS transcribed by two recognizers are denoted as "DWS_{spo}" and "DWS_{jul}" respectively). If a keyword included in a query is in-vocabulary, it is matched directly against indexes in DW. In this study, we evaluate the following four types of indexes as DW.

$$DW \in \{DW_{jul}, DW_{spo}, DW_{jul} \vee DW_{spo}, DW_{jul} \wedge DW_{spo}\}.$$

These four indexes are evaluated in terms of the performance of SDR.

2.5 Retrieval by Queries Including OOV Keywords

A system architecture as shown in Figure 3 is used in a retrieval experiments by queries including OOV keywords. In addition to the system shown in Figure 2, the SPOJUS with OOV detection processing function creates the *Database2* (denoted as DWS_{spo}). The Database2 is composed of words and syllable sequences, however, syllable sequences are only used in the matching process for an OOV keyword. We also prepare the Database2 composed of only syllables using the syllable recognizer (the one of functions of the SPOJUS) which generates syllable sequence only, denoted as DS_{spo}. The Database2 is represented as "$DWS \in \{DWS_{spo}, DS_{spo}\}$".

When a keyword belongs to OOV, i.e., the keyword is not included in recognizer's lexicon, spoken documents including OOV words can be robustly retrieved to use a DTW matching technique considering syllable confusions by which the keyword is matched against syllable index, or to apply an HMM based word spotting technique for the speech segments detected as OOV corresponding to the syllable index in the Database2. When a keyword included in a query does not belong to OOV, i.e., the keyword is included in the lexicon, on the other hand, it is matched directly against word index generated from the combination module.

Let us denote a query as q, and a keyword included in a query as w ($w \in q$). Also, a document transcribed only in word is denoted as dw' (i.e., $dw' \in DW'$), and that transcribed in the mixture of words and syllables as dws (i.e., $dws \in DWS$). In the proposed method, according to whether a keyword in a query is in-vocabulary/OOV, the document index to be matched against the keyword is switched between dw' and dws. So, let us introduce a notation for switching between dw' and dws and denote it as dw'/dws.

$$dw'/dws = \begin{cases} dw' & \text{(if } w \text{ is an in-vocabulary keyword)} \\ dws & \text{(if } w \text{ is an OOV keyword)} \end{cases}$$

Let us also introduce a notation for switching between the set DW' of documents transcribed only in words, and the set DWS of those transcribed in the mixture of words and syllables, and

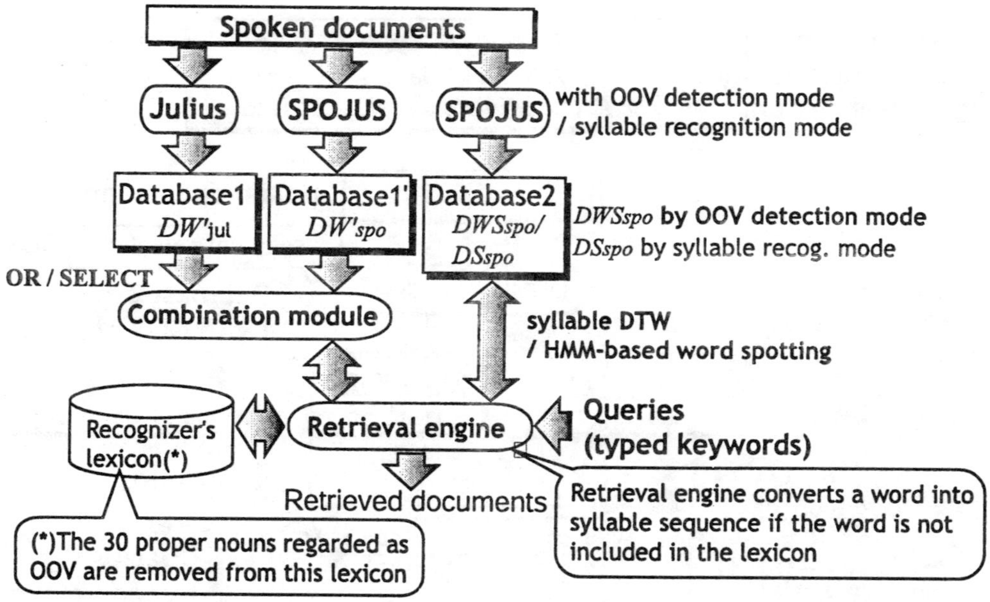

Figure 3: The system architecture for retrieval by queries including OOV keywords.

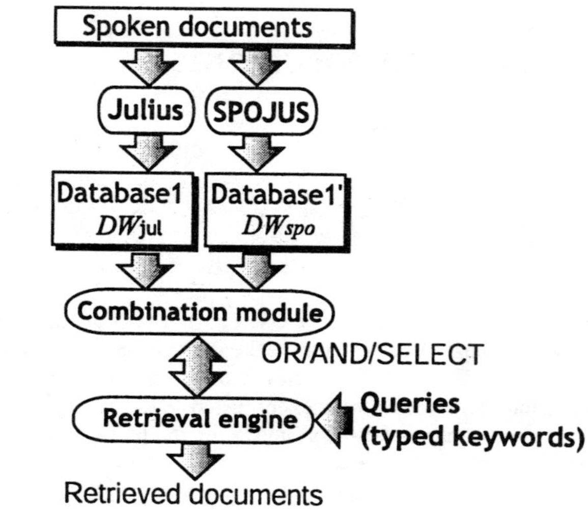

Figure 2: The system architecture for retrieving without OOV keywords.

denote it as DW'/DWS.

$$DW'/DWS = \{dw'/dws | dw' \in DW', dws \in DWS\}$$

In this study, we evaluate the "DW'_{spo}/DWS_{spo}" and "$\{DW'_{jul} \vee DW'_{spo}\}/DWS_{spo}$".

Table 1 shows notations described above which represent transcript types of spoken documents. In the retrieval experiment without OOV keywords described in Section 2.4 and Section 3.3, we use only the DW which is recognized by both the SPOJUS and Julius with a lexicon in which words handled as OOV words (30 proper nouns) in Section 3.4 are included. By contrast with DW, DW', DS and DWS are used in the retrieval experiments with OOV keywords described in Section 2.5 and Section 3.4. The DW' is recognized by both the recognizers with a lexicon which differs from the lexicon for the transcription of DW.

Table 1: Notations of various transcripts

transcript's unit	OOV keyword	
	not included	included
word	DW	DW'
syllable	—	DS
word&syllable	—	DWS

2.5.1 *DTW matching considering syllable confusions*

Figure 4 shows an overview of the syllable based DTW matching. Let us denote a syllable sequence, which is detected as an OOV word using the OOV detection, as $X = \{x_1, x_2, \cdots, x_I\}$ (I is the number of syllable in X, $x_i \in X$) and syllable sequence of the OOV keyword as $Y = \{y_1, y_2, \cdots, y_J\}$ (J is the number of syllable in Y, $y_j \in Y$). As shown in Figure 4, we apply the syllable based DTW matching on the syllable sequence X against the syllable sequence Y. In this DTW matching, the likelihood $G(i, j)$ of arriving at the point (i, j) in a DTW lattice matrix is maximized:

$$G(i,j) = \begin{cases} 1.0 \quad i \geq 0, j = 0 \\ G(0, j-1) \cdot P(y_j, \phi) \quad i = 0, i > 0 \\ \max \begin{cases} G(i-1, j) \cdot P(\phi, x_i) \\ G(i-1, j-1) \cdot P(y_j, x_i) \quad i > 0, j > 0 \\ G(i, j-1) \cdot P(y_j, \phi) \end{cases} \end{cases}$$

where $P(r, h)$ is the probability of mis-recognizing syllable r as h. Syllable sequences are obtained using a syllable recognizer for a held-out data whose size is similar to the evaluation set. By comparing those sequences with the references, the syllable recognition error confusion matrix is calculated as bellow:

$$P(r,h) = \frac{C(r,h)}{\sum_{k \in h} C(r,k)}.$$

,where $C(r,h)$ is the number to misrecognize syllable r as h. When the DTW score $G(i,J)$ is larger than a given threshold, the OOV keyword is judged to be in the spoken document.

2.5.2 HMM-based word spotting

In the HMM-based word spotting, on the other hand, we apply the word spotting technique to the segment of speech corresponding to the syllable sequence detected as an OOV word. The concatenated HMMs generated from the syllable sequence of the OOV keywords are matched against the speech segment. Figure 5 shows an overview of the HMM based word spotting. The score S_{oov} is a likelihood of concatenated HMMs represented as the OOV keywords for the speech segment detected as OOV. On the other hand, the score S_w is the best likelihood out of concatenated HMMs represented as arbitrary syllable sequences. The difference between S_{oov} and S_w corresponds to the likelihood of the *posteriori* probability for the OOV keywords. The smaller the difference of S_{oov} and S_w becomes, the higher the possibility of including the OOV keyword in the speech segment becomes. When the difference of the scores is smaller than a given threshold, the OOV keyword is judged to be in the spoken document.

3. RETRIEVAL EVALUATION

3.1 Experimental Setup

A set of 50 queries (each of which consists of three to five keywords, and 175 distinct keywords in total) is created. The queries were created by a few subjects who chose words from the titles of randomly selected 50 news documents out of the whole 976 stories. We prepared the correct documents for a query as *references*, where all keywords in the query were included. The retrieval performance is evaluated by recall-precision curve (ROC curve).

Whether or not a keyword w ($w \in q_i, q_i \in Q, Q = \{q_i, \cdots, q_{50}\}$,) is included in a document d is denoted as follows:

$$hit(d,w) = \begin{cases} 0 & (\text{if } w \text{ is not in } d) \\ 1 & (\text{if } w \text{ is in } d) \end{cases}$$

,then the total number of words included in d is calculated as bellow:

$$hit(d,q_i) = \sum_{w \in q_i} hit(d,w)$$

In this evaluation, it is required that documents to be retrieved satisfy the condition $hit(d,q_i) \geq n$, and the set of retrieved documents is represented as follows:

$$output(q_i,n) = \{d | hit(d,q_i) \geq n\}.$$

Recall and precision rates for the retrieved documents set $output(q_i,n)$ are calculated as follows:

$$Recall_{q_i,n} = \frac{|\text{references for } q_i \wedge output(q_i,n)|}{|\text{references for } q_i|}$$

$$Precision_{q_i,n} = \frac{|\text{references for } q_i \wedge output(q_i,n)|}{|output(q_i,n)|}$$

,where references for $q_i \wedge output(q_i,n)$ denotes is the intersection of the set of the references and $output(q_i,n)$. $Recall_n$ and $Precision_n$ for all the queries are calculated by averaging $Recall_{q_i,n}$ and $Precision_{q_i,n}$ respectively.

$$Recall_n = \frac{1}{N}\sum_{i=1}^{N} Recall_{q_i,n}$$

$$Precision_n = \frac{1}{N}\sum_{i=1}^{N} Precision_{q_i,n}$$

Using various values of n, recall-precision curves are plotted.

3.2 Speech Recognition Rates

We evaluate the two recognizers' performance for the corpus described in Section 2.3 by comparing the their outputs with the manual transcriptions. Word recognition rates of individual recognizers without OOV detection processing as well as those of the union /intersection (to be described in the next section) of their outputs are shown in Table 2. In the table, transcribed databases are denoted as DW_{jul} (transcribed by Julius), DW_{spo} (transcribed by SPOJUS), $DW_{jul} \vee DW_{spo}$ (union of DW_{jul} and DW_{spo}) and $DW_{jul} \wedge DW_{spo}$ (intersection of DW_{jul} and DW_{spo}). Note that the $DW_{jul} \vee DW_{spo}$ and $DW_{jul} \wedge DW_{spo}$ are calculated for the word sequences which are generated by making an alignment of the two recognizers' outputs using DTW matching. By taking the union of the transcripts from the two recognizers, the word correct rate improves while insertion errors increase. On the other hand, by taking the intersection of those two transcripts, word correct rate decreases, while insertion errors decrease.

Table 2: Word recognition rates[%]

decoder	Acc.	Cor.	Sub.	Ins.	Del.
DW_{Jul}	56.3	66.1	27.1	9.8	6.8
DW_{SPO}	63.3	72.1	23.3	8.8	4.6
$DW_{Jul} \vee DW_{SPO}$	36.4	78.1	19.7	41.6	2.3
$DW_{Jul} \wedge DW_{SPO}$	57.7	58.8	7.7	1.1	33.6

Acc. = 100 - Sub. - Ins. - Del.
Cor. = 100 - Sub. - Del.

3.3 Retrieval without OOV Keywords

The performance in terms of recall and precision is shown in Figure 6. Comparing the retrieval performance of Figure 6 with the word recognition rates listed in Table 2, it is interested that the retrieval performance becomes better according to the increase of the word correct rates. In total, the best curve is $DW_{Jul} \vee DW_{SPO}$ which coincides with the fact that $DW_{Jul} \vee DW_{SPO}$ is the one with the greatest correct rate and the least deletion rate in Table 2. It can be also seen from the Figure 6 that $DW_{Jul} \vee DW_{SPO}$ outperforms $DW_{Jul} \wedge DW_{SPO}$ quite well, where $DW_{Jul} \vee DW_{SPO}$ contains much more insertion errors than $DW_{Jul} \wedge DW_{SPO}$. This result shows that insertion errors cause little damage to the retrieval performance. These evaluation results clearly claim that, in SDR, it is the most important to achieve the word correct rate as high as possible, even if insertion errors increase.

3.4 Retrieval by Queries Including OOV Keywords

We describe the results of evaluation of SDR when an OOV keyword is included in the query sets. To compare with the results of evaluating SDR without OOV keywords described in Section 3.3, 30 proper nouns in the query set were removed

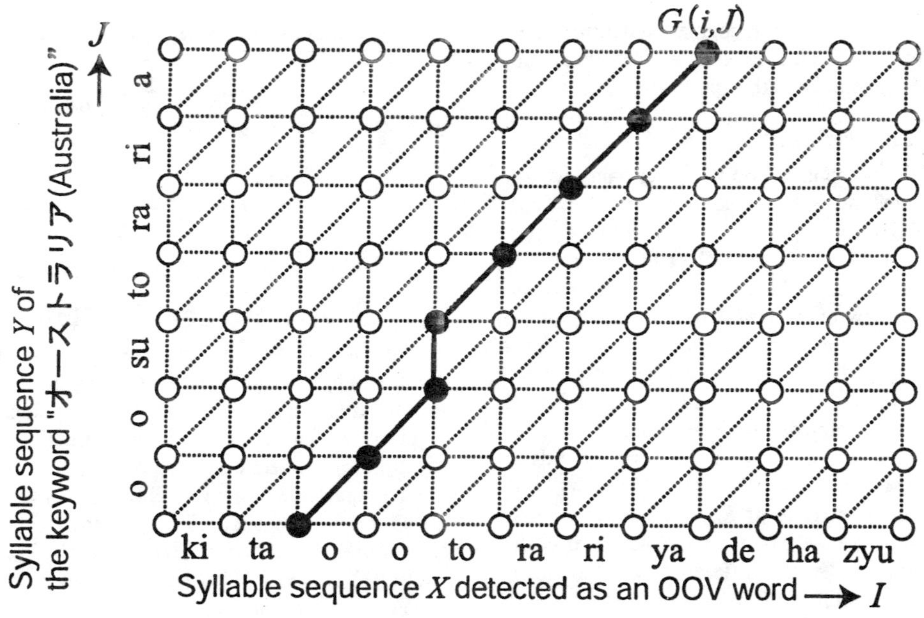

Figure 4: Syllable based DTW matching

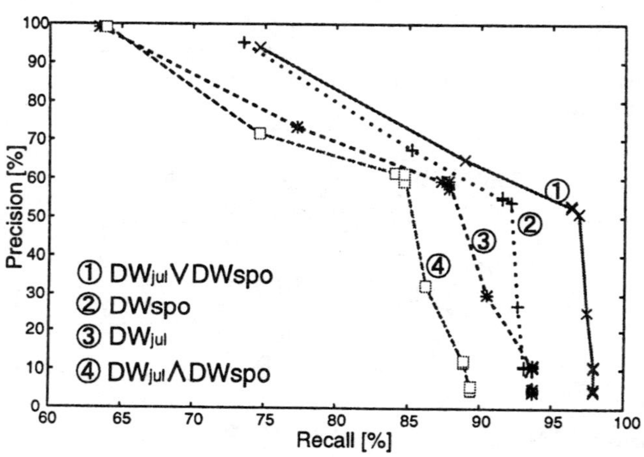

Figure 6: Recall-precision curve for the retrieval without OOV keywords

from the recognizer's lexicon. Transcribed databases consisting of the mixture of words and syllables were prepared by the SPOJUS with OOV detection processing. Those removed 30 proper nouns were observed 1019 times in the whole spoken documents. Out of those 1019 occurrences, 495 (about 48.6%) were detected as OOV words (syllable sequences) correctly, and 18575 syllable sequences (about 4.5 hours) were detected falsely. In other words, the recall/precision rates of OOV detection were 48.6%, 2.6%($= 495/(18575 + 495)$) respectively.

3.4.1 DTW matching considering syllable confusions

Figure 7 shows the recall-precision curves of SDR by queries including OOV keywords using syllable DTW matching. The "*baseline*" curves indicate that OOV keywords (the 30 proper nouns) are included in queries and documents and are not processed at all. The "*ideal*" curves show that OOV keywords are not included in queries and documents, in other words, that these OOV keywords are registered in the lexicon, similar to the curves shown in Figure 6. From the comparison of the pair of DW_{spo} and DW_{spo}/DWS_{spo}, or the pair of $DW_{spo} \vee DW_{jul}$ and $\{DW_{jul} \vee DW_{spo}\}/DWS_{spo}$, switching between DW and DWS_{spo} according to the types of keywords (OOV keywords or in-vocabulary keywords) contributes to improving the recall-precision curve without OOV detection processing. From the comparison of $\{DW_{jul} \vee DW_{spo}\}\ /DWS_{spo}$ and DW_{spo}/DWS_{spo}, furthermore, it can be seen that taking the union of the two transcripts of word index forms contribute to improving the total performance of $\{DW_{jul} \vee DW_{spo}\}/DWS_{spo}$. These results clearly claim that the proposed techniques are quite effective in robustly retrieving spoken documents by queries including OOV keywords. It is also expected that the retrieval performance can be further improved by increasing the precision of OOV detection, because the current precision rate of OOV detection is quite low and the insertion errors cause many false matches.

We can compare the ROC curves by DWS_{spo} with DS_{spo} in Figure 8. In spite of quite low detection rate of OOV, using the index (DWS_{spo}) by detecting OOV segments from spoken documents improve the retrieval performance rather than using the index (DS_{spo}) which consists of only syllable sequences by the syllable recognizer. To compare related works with the proposed method in this paper, furthermore, we drew the ROC using the specific queries consisting of the 175 syllable formed keywords (represented as "DS_{spo}"(the lowest performance) in Figure 8). This result claims that using both the word index and the syllable index is quite effective to improve retrieval performance.

3.4.2 HMM-based word spotting

Figure 9 shows the ROC curves of SDR by queries including OOV keywords using the HMM-based word spotting technique we proposed here. In the same cases as the result shown in Figure 9, these results by the proposed technique contribute

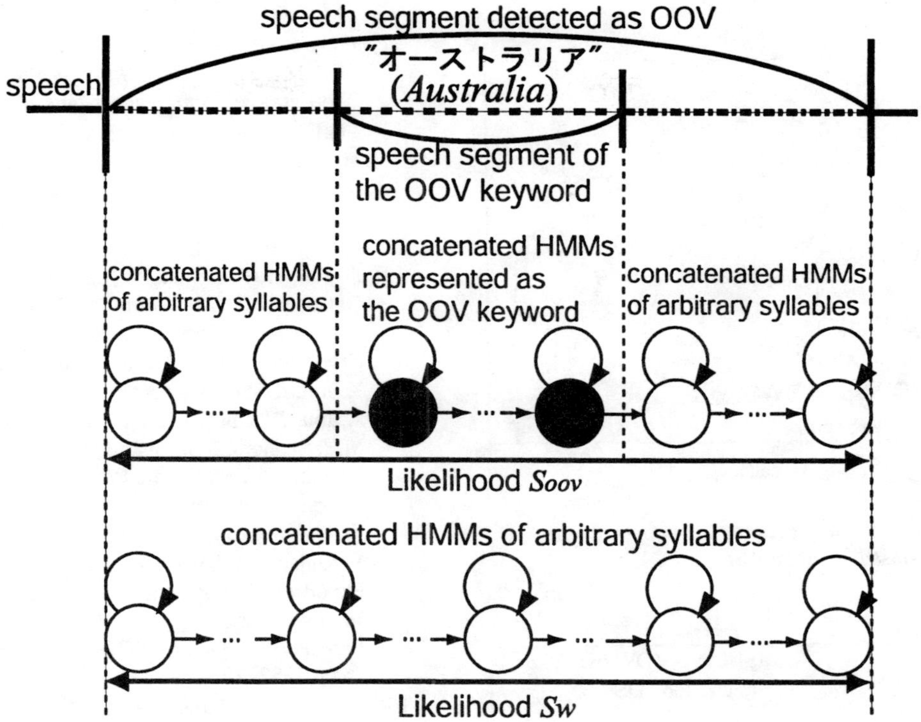

Figure 5: HMM-based word spotting

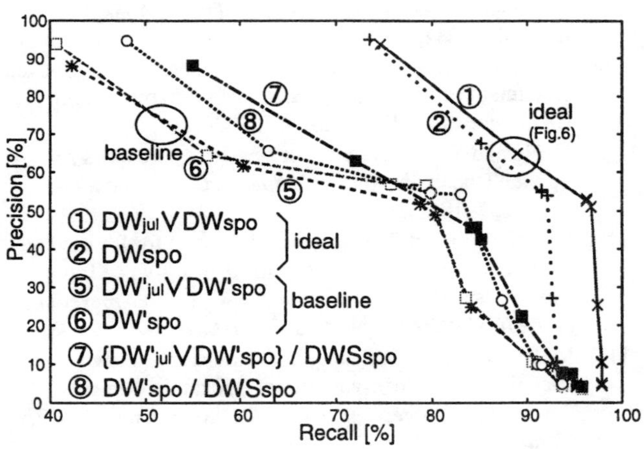

Figure 7: Recall-precision curves for the retrieval with OOV keywords (syllable-based DTW matching)

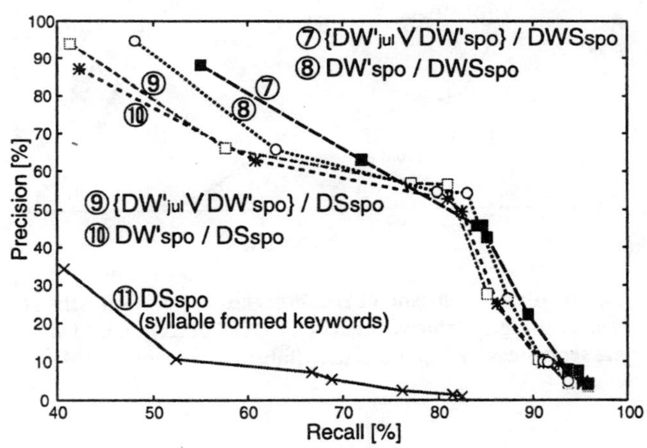

Figure 8: Comparison of recall-precision curves for the retrieval using syllable sequences by OOV detection and syllable sequences by a connected syllable recognizer (DTW matching)

to improving the recall-precision curves without OOV detection processing.

If the type of input keyword is OOV, the concatenated HMMs generated from the syllable sequence of the OOV keyword are matched against either DWS_{spo} (the speech segments detected as OOV) or DS_{spo} (overall speech documents [2]). In Figure 10, the ROC curve is improved using DS_{spo} rather than using DWS_{spo} because HMM-based word spotting is superior to DTW-based spotting. However, to make a matching the whole speech documents (approximate 18 hours) against a keyword by the word spotting consumes a lot of hours. As the number of spoken documents increase, impractical time will be spent for retrieving documents. From a practical point of view, therefore, we need to limit the number of candidates, which are detected by the HMM-based word spotting, using the DTW matching of between syllable formed keywords and syllable sequences detected as OOV, where faster matching is available. To perform the HMM-based word spotting for the candidates which have high likelihood of the DTW matching will reduce the time con-

[2]The HMM-based word spotting technique was applied to the overall speech documents (as well as denoted as "DS_{spo}") for the concatenated HMMs of the keyword.

cerning the retrieval.

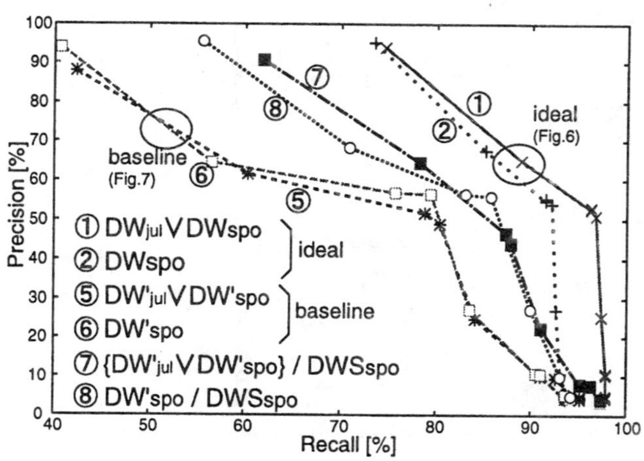

Figure 9: Recall-precision curves for the retrieval with OOV keywords(HMM-based word spotting)

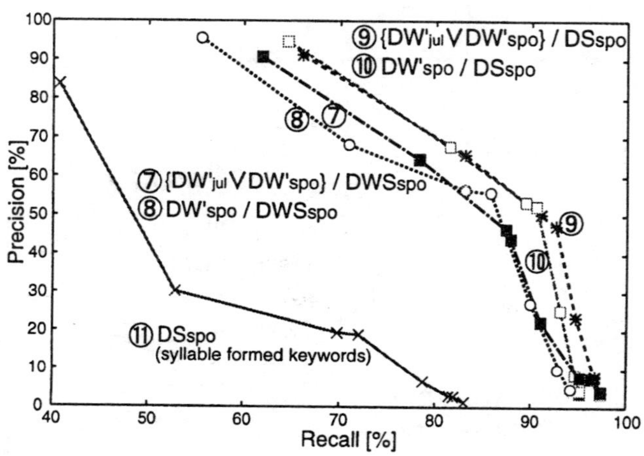

Figure 10: Comparison of recall-precision curves for the retrieval using syllable sequences by OOV detection and syllable sequences by a connected syllable recognizer(HMM)

4. CONCLUSIONS

In this paper, we investigated robust methods to improve Japanese spoken document retrieval performance when speech recognition errors and OOV words are contained in spoken documents. The results of experimental evaluation showed that the index created by taking the union of the two recognizers' outputs improved the retrieval performance. From these results we conclude that it is the most important to achieve the word correct rate as high as possible, even if insertion errors increase.

To resolve the OOV problem in SDR, we created the syllable index by recognizing spoken documents using a speech recognizer with OOV detecting processing. By switching the word index and the syllable index according to the types of keywords (OOV / in-vocabulary words) in a query, furthermore, the performance of retrieving documents including OOV keywords improved using both DTW matching and HMM-based word spotting techniques.

5. REFERENCES

[1] J. Garofolo, C.G.P.Auzanne, and E. Voorhees. The TREC SDR Track: A Success Story. *In Proceedings of the 8th Text Retrieval Conference*, pages 107–129, 2000.

[2] J.G.Fiscus. A Post-processing System to Yield Reduced Word Error Rates: Recognizer Output Voting Error Reduction (ROVER). *In Proceedings of the IEEE Workshop on Automatic Speech Recognition and Understanding*, pages 347–354, 1997.

[3] A. Kai, Y. Hirose, and S. Nakagawa. Dealing with Out-of-vocabulary Words and Speech Disfluencies in an N-gram based Speech Understanding System. *In Proceedings of the ICSLP'98*, pages 2427–2430, 1998.

[4] K.Itoh, K.Shikano, T.Kawahara, K.Takeda, A.Yamada, A.Itou, T.Utsuro, T.Kobayashi, N.Minematsu, M.Yamamoto, S.Sagayama, and A.Lee. IPA Japanese Dictation Free Software Project. *Proc. of the 2nd International Conference on Language Resourses and Evaluation*, pages 1343–1350, 2000.

[5] Y. Kodama, T. Utsuro, H. Nishizaki, and S. Nakagawa. Experimental Evaluation on Confidence of Agreement among Multiple Japanaese LVCSR Models. *In Proceedings of the EUROSPEECH 2001*, pages 2549–2552, 2001.

[6] H. min Wang. Experiments in Syllable-based Retrieval of Broadcast News Speech in Mandarin Chinese. *Speech Communication*, 32(1-2):49–60, 2000.

[7] S. Nakagawa and K. Yamamoto. Evaluation of Segmental Unit Input HMM. *In Proceedings of the ICASSP'96*, pages 439–442, 1996.

[8] C. Ng, R. Wilkinson, and J. Zobel. Experiments in Spoken Document Retrieval using Phoneme N-grams. *Speech Communication*, 32(1-2):61–77, 2000.

[9] K. Ng and V. W. Zue. Subword-based Approaches for Spoken Document Retrieval. *Speech Communication*, 32(3):157–186, 2000.

[10] H. Nishizaki and S. Nakagawa. A System for Retrieving Broadcast News Speech Documents using Voice Input Keywords and Similarity between Words. *In Proceedings of the ICSLP'2000*, pages 1073–1076, 2000.

[11] M. Wechsler, E. Munteanu, and P. Schauble. New Techniques for Open-vocabulary Spoken Document Retrieval. *In Proceedings of the SIGIR'98*, pages 20–27, 1998.

An Adaptive Approach to Named Entity Extraction for Meeting Applications

Fei Huang, Alex Waibel
Language Technologies Institute
Carnegie Mellon University
5000 Forbes Ave. Pittsburgh,PA 15213
fhuang@cs.cmu.edu, ahw@cs.cmu.edu

ABSTRACT

Named entity extraction has been intensively investigated in the past several years. Both statistical approaches and rule-based approaches have achieved satisfactory performance for regular written/spoken language. However when applied to highly informal or ungrammatical languages, e.g., meeting languages, because of the many mismatches in language genre, the performance of existing methods decreases significantly.

In this paper we propose an adaptive method of named entity extraction for meeting understanding. This method combines a statistical model trained from broadcast news data with a cache model built online for ambiguous words, computes their *global context* name class probability from *local context* name class probabilities, and integrates name lists information from meeting profiles. Such a fusion of supervised and unsupervised learning has shown improved performance of named entity extraction for meeting applications. When evaluated using manual meeting transcripts, the proposed method demonstrates a 26.07% improvement over the baseline model. Its performance is also comparable to that of the statistical model trained from a small annotated meeting corpus. We are currently applying the proposed method to automatic meeting transcripts.

Keywords

named entity extraction, meeting application, cache model

1. INTRODUCTION

Named entity extraction, i.e., extracting specific information structures, such as proper names, time and numerical expressions, from written or spoken languages, has been intensively investigated in the past several years [8, 6]. Much of the previous work on name finding is based on one of the following approaches: (1) hand-crafted or automatically acquired rules or finite state transducers([1, 2]); (2) lookup from large name lists or other specialized resources [11]; (3) statistical models[3, 5]. Both statistical approaches and rule-based approaches have achieved very good performance, with 93 F-score on written English newswire articles compared with the 97 F-score achieved by humans[4], where F-score is a combined measure of precision and recall. When applied to manual broadcast news (**BN**) transcripts (0% WER), the F-score is only slightly lower, at 91[10]. However when applied to languages that are highly informal and contain strong spoken language characteristics, the performance of existing methods degrades significantly.

Meeting understanding is one application with these language characteristics. Unlike written newswire articles, meeting transcripts/hypotheses have no case and punctuation information available to facilitate named entity extraction. Even compared with broadcast news (**BN**), the language used in meetings(**MT**) is more informal[13]. Generally speaking, meeting language is characterized by:

- Shorter sentences,
  (7.7 words per sentence in MT vs. 12.1 in BN);
- Fewer sentences per turn,
  (2.2 in MT vs. 4.1 in BN);
- More disflunecies,
  (0.87 per sentence in MT vs. 0.48 in BN);
- More repairs,
  (29.0% in MT vs. 13.8% in BN);
- More non-lexicalized filled pauses, e.g., "uh,um",
  (29.5% in MT vs.0.7% in BN).

Considering the many mismatches in language genre, the rules and statistical models acquired from formal written or spoken languages can not be directly used for meeting applications. Unfortunately it would be very expensive to record lots of meetings, transcribe them and build a corpus for training. Therefore we propose an adaptive method for named entity extraction for meeting understanding. This method is based on a statistical model trained from broadcast news data, but additionally makes use of meeting level global context information and name lists information in meeting

Proceedings of HLT 2002, Second International Conference on Human Language Technology Research, M. Marcus, ed., Morgan Kaufmann, San Francisco, 2002.

profiles to improve performance. This combination of supervised and unsupervised learning proved to be very effective. The experimental result on manual meeting transcripts is significantly better than the baseline model, which is trained from a large annotated broadcast news corpus. Its performance is also comparable to that of a statistical model trained from a small annotated meeting corpus.

In the following sections, we will introduce the baseline statistical model (Section 2), describe the proposed method (Section 3), present the experimental results and analysis (Section 4), and finally draw some conclusions (Section 5).

2. BASELINE MODEL

The baseline model adopts the Hidden Markov Model framework described in [3]. Eight internal states represent 7 classes of named entities (*PERSON,LOCATION, ORGANIZATION, TIME, DATE, MONEY* and *PERCENT*) as well as one remaining class (*NOT_A_NAME*). This generative model assumes the following generation process of a given sentence:

- current name class NC is selected according to the previous word and its name class,
- the first word in a name class is generated according to the current and previous name classes,
- each subsequent word in this name class is generated from a class-dependent bigram model.

Thus the task in the training procedure is to estimate 3 probabilities:

1. $P_c(NC|w_{-1}, NC_{-1})$, class transition probability,
2. $P_f(w_1|NC, NC_{-1})$, first word generation probability,
3. $P_b(w|w_{-1}, NC)$, class-dependent bigram probabilities.

In the above notations, NC and NC_{-1} represent the current and previous name classes respectively, w_1 represents the first word in the current name class, w represents the current word, and w_{-1} represents the previous word. To deal with data sparseness, different smoothing techniques, such as back-off and interpolation strategies, are used in the baseline model.

In the decoding process, the Viterbi decoding algorithm [12] is applied to find the name class sequence which maximizes the probability of generating the whole sentence with L words,

$$\begin{aligned} \text{NC} &= argmax_{\vec{NC}}\ P(\vec{W}, \vec{NC}) & (1)\\ &= argmax_{\vec{NC}}\ p(NC_1) \times p(w_1|NC_1) \times \\ & \prod_{i=2}^{L} \tilde{p}(w_i, NC_i|w_{i-1}, NC_{i-1}), & (2) \end{aligned}$$

where $\vec{W}$ stands for word sequence $(w_1, w_2, \ldots, w_L)$, $\vec{N}$ denotes name class sequence $(NC_1, NC_2, \ldots, NC_L)$, and $\tilde{p}(w_i, NC_i| w_{i-1}, NC_{i-1})$ represents the transition probability from w_{i-1} to w_i, assuming class transition from NC_{i-1} to NC_i.

When the transition is between different classes,

$$\begin{aligned} \tilde{p}(w_i, NC_i|w_{i-1}, NC_{i-1}) &= P(end|w_{i-1}, NC_{i-1}) \times \\ P_c(NC_i|w_{i-1}, NC_{i-1}) &\times P_f(w_i|NC_i, NC_{i-1}). \quad (3) \end{aligned}$$

When the transition is within the same class, i.e., $NC_i = NC_{i-1}$,

$$\begin{aligned} \tilde{p}(w_i, NC_i|w_{i-1}, NC_{i-1}) &= \\ P(no\_end|w_{i-1}, NC_{i-1}) &\times P_b(w_i|w_{i-1}, NC_i). \quad (4) \end{aligned}$$

The $P(end|w_{i-1}, NC_{i-1})$ and $P(no\_end|w_{i-1}, NC_{i-1})$ denote the probability of exiting or remaining in the previous name class given the previous word.

Working with *spoken* language, a lot of informative format information, like punctuation, case information and Arabic numerical expression (e.g.,10/23/1997), is no longer available. Therefore, our model only considers words as the basic modeling unit, and disregards format feature representations. This is different from BBN's IdentiFinder system[3].

As in most statistical NLP work, data sparseness is also a serious problem. We adopt both interpolation strategies (interpolate the best-fit model with the more general model to reduce over-fitting), and back-off strategies for smoothing. Back-off paths for each of the three probabilities are:

- $P_c(NC|w_{-1}, NC_{-1}) \rightarrow P_c(NC|NC_{-1}) \rightarrow P_c(NC) \rightarrow \frac{1}{number\_of\_name\_classes}$
- $P_f(w_1|NC, NC_{-1}) \rightarrow P_f(w_1|NC) \rightarrow P_f(w_1) \rightarrow \frac{P(NC)}{Vocabulary\_size}$
- $P_b(w|w_{-1}, NC) \rightarrow P_b(w|NC) \rightarrow \frac{P(NC)}{Vocabulary\_size}$

When tested on broadcast news data, the performance of the baseline model is comparable to the IdentiFinder. Detailed results are presented in Section 4.

3. ADAPTATION MODEL

To deal with the mismatch between formal and informal language, the proposed adaptation model uses the meeting level global context information as well as meeting profile information to improve the performance of named entity extraction.

3.1 Unsupervised Adaptation: Cache model

Cache models were first proposed for dynamic language modeling for speech recognition in [7], where the pre-computed general trigram model is interpolated with the local trigram model. The so-called *cache model* is trained from on-line generated word hypothesis, to "capture the short-term fluctuation in word frequency"[7]. Our cache model adaptation procedure also makes use of global context information from whole meeting transcripts, e.g., topical information, consistency of name class for a given word, to improve name class annotation in local contexts, but with different theory and model implementations.

The basic assumption of the proposed model is that each meeting will have some coherent topics, and even if a word or word sequence could have more than one name class in general, the name class of its every instance in a specific context (e.g. throughout a meeting) will tend to be consistent. This class will be in line with the topic of the scenario. Although the topic mismatches and the disfluency of spoken language in meetings will reduce the accuracy of the probability estimation, the average probabilities over the whole meeting, which is supposed to be internally coherent, may help give a reliable estimation, and possibly correct some errors in annotation. Therefore, the adaptation model will identify ambiguous words from first-pass annotation, build a cache to store their probability of belonging to each name class in each instance, estimate their global name class probability, and then relabel their name classes accordingly.

Formally, for a given word w, the best name class estimation in terms of the whole meeting context should satisfy

$$\begin{aligned} \hat{NC}(w) &= argmax_{NC}\ P(NC|w) \\ &= argmax_{NC} \prod_i P(NC_i = NC|w_i = w). \quad (5) \end{aligned}$$

$P(NC|w)$, the *global name class probability* for word w, is computed from the product of its *local name class probability* at position i, $P(NC_i = NC|w_i = w)$, under the independent assumption. The latter could be represented as the composition of 2 probabilities: *forward* NC probability $P(NC_i|w_i, w_{i-1})$ and *backward* NC probability
$P(NC_i|w_i, w_{i+1})$. This model tries to estimate the current class probability from its past and future context.

For forward probability,

$$P(NC_i|w_i, w_{i-1}) = \frac{P(w_i, NC_i|w_{i-1})}{P(w_i|w_{i-1})}, \quad (6)$$

where

$$\begin{aligned} P(w_i, NC_i|w_{i-1}) &= \frac{P(w_i, NC_i, w_{i-1})}{P(w_{i-1})} \\ &= \frac{\sum_{NC'_{i-1}} P(w_i, NC_i, w_{i-1}, NC'_{i-1})}{P(w_{i-1})} \\ &= \frac{\sum_{NC'_{i-1}} P(w_i, NC_i|w_{i-1}, NC'_{i-1})P(w_{i-1}, NC'_{i-1})}{P(w_{i-1})} \\ &= \sum_{NC'_{i-1}} \tilde{p}(w_i, NC_i|w_{i-1}, NC'_{i-1})p'(NC'_{i-1}|w_{i-1}) \quad (7) \end{aligned}$$

and

$$P(w_i|w_{i-1}) = \sum_{NC'_i} P(w_i, NC'_i|w_{i-1}). \quad (8)$$

For backward probability,

$$\begin{aligned} P(NC_i|w_i, w_{i+1}) &= \frac{P(w_{i+1}, w_i, NC_i)}{P(w_{i+1}, w_i)} \\ &= \frac{P(w_{i+1}|w_i, NC_i)P(w_i, NC_i)}{P(w_{i+1}, w_i)} \\ &= \frac{[\sum_{NC'_{i+1}} \tilde{p}(w_{i+1}, NC'_{i+1}|w_i, NC_i)]p'(NC_i|w_i)}{P(w_{i+1}|w_i)} \quad (9) \end{aligned}$$

In the above functions, $\tilde{p}$ is the transition probability, and $p'(NC|w)$ is a context-independent *prior* name class probability for word w, which is computed from the general domain broadcast news training data.

Thus, the local name class probability for word w at position i is the interpolation between the forward and backward probabilities, and w's name class probability over the whole meeting is the average probability over all the occurrences of word w. Such a global probability will be utilized for the re-estimation of w's name classes.

In summary, the whole name class annotation proceeds in the following way:

- Apply the baseline model on the test data;
- Identify ambiguous words, which have both:
  - different class labels over the whole meeting according to the first-pass decoding;
  - low class assignment confidence, which is defined in terms of the ratio between top 2 class-dependent word generation probabilities;
- Apply cache model re-estimation on those ambiguous words to compute their global name class probability;
- Select the winning class, which has the highest global name class probability, weighted by the frequency of that class label in the first-pass decoding;
- Relabel the ambiguous words with the winning class label.

3.2 Supervised Adaptation: Learning from Meeting Profile

Cache model adaptation works well when the true name class has the highest average probability among all labeled name classes after the first-pass decoding. However, when indicative information is not available (particularly for some OOV words), and thus first-pass labels are mostly incorrect, the model becomes less effective. However, some indicative information could be extracted from meeting profiles, which usually contain the attendants' names, the topics to be discussed, or even a concise summary of the meeting. When such information is taken into the model in the form of probabilistic name lists (e.g., person/location/organization name lists), in which each word is associated with the *prior* probability of belonging to this name class, more certainty about class annotation is obtained and therefore the named entity extraction performance

Table 1: Baseline model on BN and MT data

	BN	MT1	MT2
IdF	87.91	27.14	47.03
Baseline	88.35	37.93	60.37

Table 2: Adaptation on baseline model for MT data I

	MT1	MT2
BL	37.93	60.37
BL+MP	50.07	65.65
BL+MP+CM	66.67	68.33

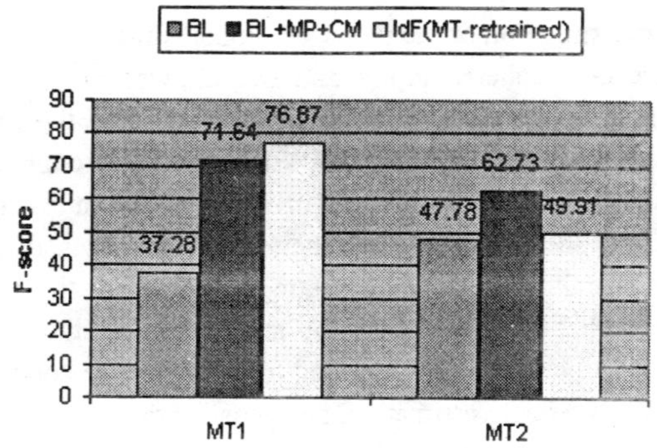

Figure 1: F-score comparison on ENAMEX class.

will accordingly be improved.

In our current implementation, only attendees' name information is added to the meeting profile, and assigned to the *PERSON* name class with probability 0.9. The remaining probability mass, 0.1, is equally distributed among the rest name classes. These class-dependent unigram probabilities, $P(w|NC)$, are used in the computation of word generation probabilities.

4. EXPERIMENTAL RESULT

To evaluate the performance of the baseline model and the adaptation approach, we performed several experiments. We trained our baseline model using Hub4 NE-IE training data (52 broadcast news transcripts, about 260K words), and tested it on one manual broadcast news transcripts (2318 words, 106 named entities), obtained the **Baseline** result. We also ran the IdentiFinder (re-trained with the same broadcast news training data)on the same test data, obtained **IdF** result. Then, we ran the same experiment on two manual meeting transcripts, **MT1** (10554 words,137 named entities) and **MT2** (11146 words, 240 named entities). Table 1 summarizes the F-scores of these experiments.

As shown in Table 1, both IdentiFinder and the baseline model work reasonably well on broadcast news data, but their performances drop considerably when tested on the meeting data. Furthermore, their performances vary from meeting to meeting. This is understandable due to the various mismatches in language characteristics and the nature of different meetings.

Table 3: Adaptation on baseline model for MT data II

	BL	BL+MP+CM	Improvement	IdF(retrained)
MT1	37.93	66.67	75.77%	67.90
MT2	60.37	68.33	13.18%	61.11
MT3	47.76	54.99	15.13%	56.99
MT4	53.61	59.49	10.96%	63.87
MT5	53.87	58.23	8.09%	69.69
MT6	38.98	52.18	33.86%	66.10
MT7	60.33	61.13	1.32%	58.27
MT8	27.57	58.60	112.55%	68.32
Avg.	**47.55**	**59.95**	**26.07%**	**64.03**

Table 2 demonstrates the experimental result when different adaptation strategies are applied. **BL**, **MP** and **CM** represent the baseline model, the meeting profile model and the cache model respectively. When the meeting profile information-in this case, the participant name lists-is integrated into the baseline model, the performance is improved, especially for person names. Specifically, in **MT1** the name list contains 45 instances of the 137 named entity instances, improving F-score by 32%, while in **MT2**, the name list contains 24 of the 240 named entity instances, improving F-score by 8.7%, respectively. Such difference in name list coverage also explains why name lists lead to more significant improvement in **MT1** than in **MT2**. When cache model adaptation is additionally applied on **BL+MP**, most of the local annotation errors are corrected as long as the true name classes are assigned higher probabilities on average during their baseline annotations. Thus performance is further improved. Figure 1 illustrates the F-scores of different systems on *ENAMEX*, which contains three name classes: *LOCATION*, *ORGANIZATION* and *PERSON*.

More experimental results are presented in Table 3, which shows that the cache model plus meeting profile information is very effective in **MT1**, **MT6** and **MT8**, and less effective in **MT7**. But in general, empirical experiments indicate that the proposed adaptive approach increases the named entity extraction accuracy by an average of 26.07% over the baseline system.

In Table 3, the performance of the proposed model is also compared with the IdentiFinder system (denoted as **IdF(retrained)**) retrained using a small number of manual meeting transcripts. Among all 8 meeting transcripts, which share similar topics and genres, 6 are left as training data, and the rest 2 are evaluated as test data. In each "fold" of such 4-fold cross validation experiments, the training set contains roughly same number (about 90K) of words, and includes most of the attendees' names in the test meetings, ranging from 58% to 100% instance coverage. Trained with such adaptation data, the **IdF** model demonstrates much better accuracy than the baseline system. Experimental result also shows that, although in general the performance of the proposed method, without using any adaptation data, is not as good as that of the IdF system trained with adaptation corpus, in some applications it is possible that the former is comparable(as in **MT1**, **MT3**, **MT4**), even outperforms

Example 1

BL: uh <b_enamex TYPE="PERSON">john <e_enamex> is on <b_enamex TYPE= "ORGANIZATION"> **channel one** <e_enamex> uh ***ty*** number two ***susi*** three ***nils*** four and myself five

BL+MP: uh <b_enamex TYPE="PERSON"> john <e_enamex> is on <b_enamex TYPE= "ORGANIZATION"> **channel one** <e_enamex> uh <b_enamex TYPE="PERSON"> ***ty*** <e_enamex> number two ***susi*** three ***nils*** four and myself five

BL+MP+CM: uh <b_enamex TYPE="PERSON"> john <e_enamex> is on **CHANNEL ONE** uh <b_enamex TYPE="PERSON"> ***TY*** <e_enamex> number two <b_enamex TYPE="PERSON"> ***SUSI*** <e_enamex> three <b_enamex TYPE="PERSON"> ***NILS*** <e_enamex> four and myself five

Reference: uh <b_enamex TYPE="PERSON"> john <e_enamex> is on channel one uh <b_enamex TYPE="PERSON"> ty <e_enamex> number two <b_enamex TYPE="PERSON"> susi <e_enamex> three <b_enamex TYPE="PERSON"> nils <e_enamex> four and myself five

Example 2

BL/BL+MP: is ***bbn*** a name
<b_enamex TYPE="PERSON"> ***bbn*** <e_enamex> 'S the name of a company
yeah then it 'S just ***bbn*** without spaces

BL+MP+CM: is ***bbn*** a name
BBN 'S the name of a company
yeah then it 'S just ***bbn*** without spaces

Reference: is <b_enamex TYPE="ORGANIZATION"> bbn <e_namex> a name
<b_enamex TYPE="ORGANIZATION ">bbn <e_enamex> 'S the name of a company
yeah then it 'S just <b_enamex TYPE="ORGANIZATION "> bbn <e_enamex> without spaces

Figure 2: Some examples excerpted from test data .

the latter(as in **MT2, MT7**).

Some segments excerpted from the test data are presented in Figure 2, where we can find that

- It is possible for the baseline model to detect common named entities, like "*john*", from informal/ungrammatical context, but the result resembles some named entity patterns from broadcast news, e.g., "*channel one*";
- Additional information from meeting profiles, although quite limited in amount, can be very helpful because of its high relevance to the meeting;
- Within the probabilistic model, name lists alone can not guarantee that every instance of their entries is correctly labeled, especially in the context with strong spoken language features, e.g."*...susi three nils four...*". But cache models can recover from such local annotation errors.
- The cache model adaptation works best when correct name classes are assigned higher probabilities on average. Otherwise — especially for the OOV words— it isn't helpful, even detrimental to the annotation, as in the case of "*bbn*".

5. DISCUSSION

5.1 Analogy to the forward/backward variables

The reader may have noticed the analogy between forward/backward probabilities and the $\alpha_t(i)/\beta_t(i)$ in forward-backward algorithm[9]. The forward variable$\alpha_t(i)$, the probability of generating the partial observation sequence $o_1, o_2, \ldots, o_t$ assuming the underlying state is i at time t, given the model λ, is defined as:

$$\alpha_t(i) = P(o_1, o_2, \ldots, o_t, q_t = i|\lambda). \tag{10}$$

The inductive computation for $\alpha_t(i)$ is

$$\alpha_t(j) = [\sum_{i=1}^{N} \alpha_{t-1}(i) a_{ij} b_j(o_t)], \tag{11}$$

where N is the number of states, a_{ij} is the transition probability from state i to state j, and $b_j(o_t)$ is the probability of generating output o_t at state j.

Similarly, the backward variable$\beta_t(i)$, the probability of generating the partial observation sequence $o_{t+1}, o_{t+2}, \ldots, o_T$, given the underlying state is i at time t,and the model λ. is defined as :

$$\beta_t(i) = P(o_{t+1}, o_{t+2}, \ldots, o_T|q_t = i.\lambda), \tag{12}$$

The inductive computation for $\beta_t(i)$ is

$$\beta_t(i) = [\sum_{j=1}^{N} a_{ij} b_j(o_{t+1}) \beta_{t+1}(j)]. \tag{13}$$

Compared with formula (7), $\tilde{p}(w_i, NC_i|w_{i-1}, NC'_{i-1})$ and $a_{ij}b_j(o_t)$ both represent the probability of transiting between 2 states and generating new output in the new state, while $\alpha_{t-1}(i)$ and $p'(NC'_{i-1}|w_{i-1})$ denote the recursive probability corresponding to the previous state. Similarly, the analogy between backward probability and $\beta_t(i)$ also exists, but $\beta_{t+1}(j)$ is replaced by the constant prior probability $p'(NC|w)$.

5.2 Information retrieval based on meeting profiles

Meeting profiles usually contain limited information, and thus offer limited direct benefits. Nevertheless, some topic-related information in meeting profiles, e.g., scheduled topics, meeting summary, could be used as queries to retrieve relevant documents, on which the baseline model could be applied to extract topic-related named entities. Since most of the retrieved documents are written text, we would expect the baseline model attain more accurate annotations on them. Such additionally extracted named entities, together with their annotation confidence, could be integrated into the probabilistic name lists. This experiment will be carried out in the future.

5.3 Advantages and disadvantages

While the IdentiFinder system achieves good performance for general domain applications when enough training data is available, the proposed adaptive strategy works well with domain-dependent applications when no training data is available. This is achieved by the following:

- build a domain-independent model with general domain text;
- develop an adaptation model by "training on the fly", i.e., conducting supervised and unsupervised learning from test data;
- integrate the domain-independent model and the adaptation model for better named entity annotations.

However, utilizing this model prerequisites higher average probabilities for correct name classes, and assumes each word has one name class throughout the meeting, which may not be the case in some situation.

6. CONCLUSIONS

In this paper, we proposed an adaptive method of named entity extraction. This method combines a statistical domain-independent model with an adaptation model trained on the fly. For the latter, we build a cache model for ambiguous words, re-estimate their global context name class probability from local context name class probabilities, and integrate additional information from meeting profiles. We have demonstrated that such a combination of supervised and unsupervised learning greatly increases the performance of named entity extraction for manual meeting transcripts.

7. ACKNOWLEDGMENTS

The authors would like to thank the anonymous reviewers for their valuable comments and suggestions, thank Jie Yang and other members in Interactive System Labs for their inspiring discussions and support, especially thank the data collection group for collecting, transcribing and annotating the meeting data. This research is supported by the DARPA TIDES project.

8. REFERENCES

[1] D. Appelt, J. Hobbs, D. Israel, and M. Tyson. Fastus: A finite-state processor for information extraction from real world texts. In *Proceeding of IJCAI-93*, 1993.

[2] S. Baluja, V. O. Mittal, and R. Sukthankar. Applying machine learning for high performance named-entity extraction. In *Pacific Association for Computational Linguistics*, 1999.

[3] D. Bikel, S. Miller, R. Schwarz, and R. Weischedel. Nymble: A high-performance learning name-finder. In *Proceedings of Applied Natural Language Processing*, pages 194–201, 1997.

[4] N. Chinchor. Overview of muc-7/met-2. In *Proceedings of the Seventh Message Understanding Conference(MUC7), http://www.itl.nist.gov/iaui/894.02/related_projects/muc/ proceedings/muc_7_proceedings/overview.html*, 1998.

[5] Y. Gotoh and S. Renals. Information extraction from broadcast news. In *Philosophical Transactions of the Royal Society of London*, A 358, pages 1295–1310, 2000.

[6] R. Grishman and B. Sundheim. Design of the muc-6 evaluation. In *Proceedings of MUC-6*, 1995.

[7] R. Kuhn and R. D. Mori. A cache-based natural language model for speech recognition. *IEEE Transactions on Pattern Analysis and Machine Intelligence*, PAMI-12(6):570–583, 1990.

[8] N.Chinchor, P. Robinson, and E. Brown. The hub-4 named entity task definition, version 4.8. In *Proceedings of DARPA Broadcast News Workshop http://www.nist.gov/speech/ hub4_98*, 1999.

[9] L. Rabiner. A tutorial on hidden markov models and selected applications in speech recognition. *Proceedings of the IEEE*, 77(2):257–285, Feburary,1989.

[10] P. Robinson, E. Brown, J. Burger, N. Chinchor, A. Douthat, L. Ferro, and L. Hirschman. Overview: Information extraction from broadcast news. In *Proceedings of DARPA Broadcast News Workshop*, pages 27–30, 1999.

[11] M. Stevenson and R. Gaizauskas. Using corpus-driven name lists for name entity recognition. In *Proceedings of 6th Applied Natural Language Processing and 1st North American Chapter of the Association for Computational Linguistics*, 2000.

[12] A. Viterbi. Error bound for convolutional codes and asymptotically optimum decoding algorithm. *IEEE Transaction on Information Theory*, 13:260–269, 1967.

[13] K. Zechner. Automatic summarization of spoken dialogs in unrestricted domains. In *Ph.D Thesis, Language Technology Institute, Carnegie Mellon University*, 2001.

POSTERS
(in alphabetical order)

Natural Language Interaction in Goal–Directed C&C: A Comparative Analysis of Semantic Inference

Jerome R. Bellegarda

Spoken Language Group
Apple Computer, Inc.
Cupertino, California 95014

jerome@apple.com

ABSTRACT

In sufficiently limited domains, natural language interaction is possible even in the absence of actual natural language understanding. This is particularly true for goal-directed command and control, where the understanding task can essentially be cast as an N-way classification problem. The notion of *data-driven semantic inference* was recently introduced as an approach to such tasks which in principle allows for unrestricted command/query formulation. This approach relies on a latent semantic analysis framework, whereby each unconstrained word string is automatically mapped onto the intended action through a semantic classification against the set of supported concepts. The objective of this paper is to compare semantic inference with other like-minded N-way classification methods, such as those based on finite-state grammars or nearest neighbor techniques. All experiments are conducted in the context of a desktop user interface control task involving 113 different actions. Results illustrate some of the benefits of semantic inference, specifically in terms of performance and robustness.

Keywords

Data-driven classification, latent semantic analysis, language understanding methods, command and control speech recognition

1. INTRODUCTION

Command and control (C&C) tasks can be broadly grouped into two categories, according to the mode of interaction they entail. In "process-directed" mode, the user's ultimate goal is not necessarily well-formulated at the outset of the interaction; it tends to be an emergent property of the ensuing dialog between user and machine. In contrast, in "goal-directed" mode, the user typically knows what is to be accomplished and formulates it precisely in a single command or query; there is no provision for dialog, and therefore no opportunity for correction or refinement.

The process-directed mode is exemplified in such conversational systems as *RailTel* (for rail travel information [1]), *How May I Help You?* (for call routing [2]), *AutoTutor* (for introductory computer literacy tutoring [3]), and *Jupiter* (for weather information [4]). In these applications, tracking the underlying dialog state is of utmost importance, because it is instrumental in resolving pronouns and detecting topic switches [2]. The goal-directed mode is more prevalent in systems involving critical-response decision-making (as in, e.g., many military applications) or direct manipulation (cf. the spoken control of desktop user interface elements [5]). Such tasks inherently call for a finer level of command granularity and more stringent rejection capabilities.

Since goal-directed C&C precludes the possibility of clarification (much less error recovery!), it is presently unable to support natural language interaction; instead, typical applications focus on ensuring good recognition performance. This is commonly achieved by relying on a (finite-state) grammar for the underlying language model, which effectively constrains what can be said to a limited number of pre-defined patterns. Unfortunately, most users are not naturally inclined to remember the exact syntax of every command. This can lead to many utterances that are syntactically out-of-grammar, and therefore get either rejected or misrecognized, despite being semantically adequate for the intended action.

To address this issue, we have recently introduced the concept of *data-driven semantic inference*, an approach to C&C which allows, in principle, for any word constructs in command/query formulation [5], [6]. In contrast with usual inference engines (cf. [7]), semantic inference does not rely on formal behavioral principles extracted from a knowledge base. Instead, the domain knowledge is automatically encapsulated in a data-driven fashion within a low-dimensional vector space. Thus, "classical" natural language understanding is forgone in favor of a "simpler" N-way classification problem based on the representation of the input in this vector space. Semantic inference was successfully applied to a desktop user interface control task involving 113 different actions [6].

The main objective of this paper is to compare this approach with other like-minded N-way classification methods. The next section reviews the salient characteristics of semantic inference against conventional C&C. In section 3, we describe in more details the underlying framework and the mechanics of classification. Section 4 gives an analysis of the data used in the experiments. Finally, in Section 5 we compare the performance of semantic inference with that of (i) traditional grammar-based C&C, and (ii) less sophisticated nearest neighbor classification.

2. OVERVIEW

Conventional C&C is illustrated in Fig. 1. The typical system comprises a (grammar-based) speech recognition engine, a map-

Proceedings of HLT 2002, Second International Conference on Human Language Technology Research, M. Marcus, ed., Morgan Kaufmann, San Francisco, 2002.

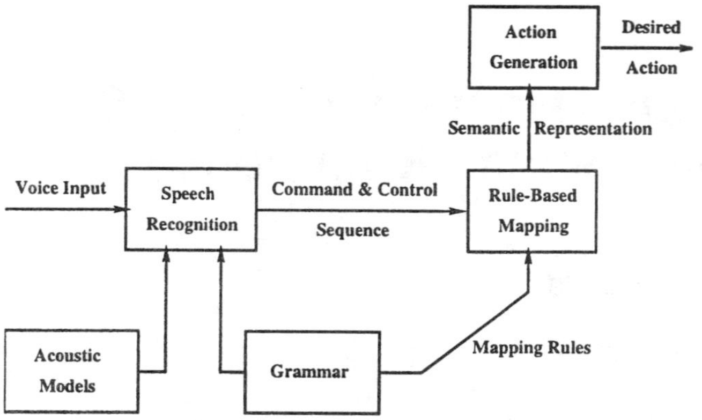

Figure 1: *Conventional Command and Control.*

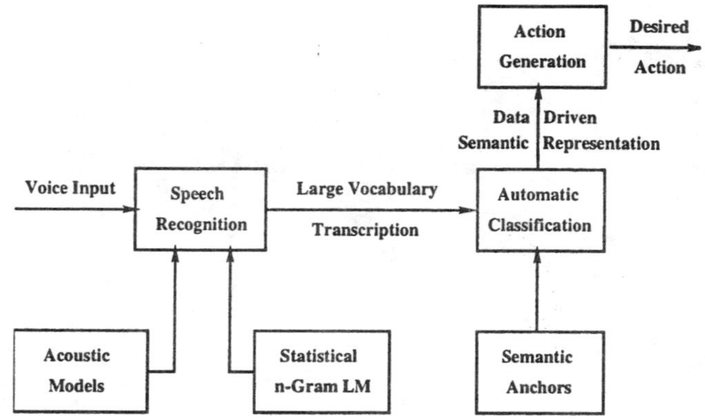

Figure 2: *Semantic Inference Framework.*

ping module, and an action generation engine. The role of speech recognition is to determine which command/query sequence (among those supported by the grammar) the user's voice input corresponds to. For example, "*what's the time?*" might be recognized as "*what is the time?*". This (supported) sequence is then transformed into a semantic representation through some task-specific mapping rules. Obviously, these rules are closely tied to what can be parsed by the grammar. Finally, the action generation engine converts the semantic representation into the desired action, e.g., the appropriate operating system call to query the time.

In contrast, in semantic inference, the recognition of what is said is decoupled from the semantic interpretation of what is to be accomplished. The resulting framework, illustrated in Fig. 2, articulates around two independent components: a recognition component, to perform large vocabulary transcription, and an inference component, to classify the resulting word string. While the (looser) statistical n-gram language model typically entails more errors than a conventional grammar, the word error rate is still reasonably low due to the limited domain of discourse. Furthermore, most of the errors do not seem to materially affect the basic meaning of the utterance. Continuing with the previous example, an unexpected (i.e., out-of-grammar) input such as, for instance: "*how late is it?*" might be transcribed as "*how late is this?*". The major difficulty now is to recognize the action intended to be taken. This is done through semantic classification, whose role is to extract the data-driven semantic representation closest in meaning to the user's utterance. The intended action is then generated as previously.

Semantic classification relies on evidence extracted from some training text by latent semantic analysis (LSA) [8]. Each supported action gives rise to a different vector (*semantic anchor*) in a suitable vector space. Thus, mapping (the transcription of) a command/query onto an action amounts to comparing the corresponding (command) vector with each semantic anchor. This makes the procedure entirely data-driven.

3. SEMANTIC INFERENCE

Let $\mathcal{V}$ be a vocabulary of size M, and $\mathcal{T}$ a collection of utterances used to invoke N actions in some domain of interest. Each of these actions is uniquely associated with a *command*, which may comprise several alternative wordings, or *variants*, each in turn comprising multiple utterances, or *instances*, of that command. (For example, a time query may be associated with a set of variants like "*what's the time?*" and "*how late is it?*" that all convey the proper meaning, each multiply represented in the collection $\mathcal{T}$.) Typically, M and N are on the order of a few hundreds to a few thousands, with scores of different variants for each command.

The LSA formalism defines a mapping between the (discrete) sets $\mathcal{V}$, $\mathcal{T}$ and a (continuous) vector space $\mathcal{S}$, whereby each word $w_i \in \mathcal{V}$ and each command $d_j \in \mathcal{T}$ is represented by a vector in $\mathcal{S}$. This is done by constructing a $(M \times N)$ word-command matrix W, whose entries w_{ij} suitably reflect the extent to which word w_i appeared in command d_j, and performing the SVD of W as [8]:

$$W \approx \hat{W} = U\,S\,V^T\,, \tag{1}$$

where U is the $(M \times R)$ left singular matrix with row vectors u_i $(1 \leq i \leq M)$, S is the $(R \times R)$ diagonal matrix of singular values $s_1 \geq s_2 \geq \cdots \geq s_R > 0$, V is the $(N \times R)$ right singular matrix with row vectors v_j $(1 \leq j \leq N)$, $R \leq \min(M, N)$ is the order of the decomposition, and ^{T} denotes matrix transposition. As is well known, the column vectors of U and V each define an orthornormal basis for the space of dimension R spanned by the u_i's and v_j's. This is the LSA space $\mathcal{S}$, in which the scaled row vectors $\bar{u}_i = u_i S$ and $\bar{v}_j = v_j S$ characterize the position of word w_i and command d_j. We refer to $\bar{u}_i$ and $\bar{v}_j$ as a *word vector* and *command vector*, respectively. Thus, each command vector $\bar{v}_j$ is the *semantic anchor* of the action uniquely associated with the command $d_j \in \mathcal{T}$.

Since $\hat{W}$ captures the major associational structure in W, the "closeness" of vectors in $\mathcal{S}$ is determined by the overall pattern of the language used in $\mathcal{T}$, as opposed to specific constructs. This tends to reveal meaningful associations (not just particular co-occurrences) between words and commands. In particular, a variant is "close" to a semantic anchor if that is otherwise consistent with the expected language structure (e.g., if the variant, despite using a different wording, would tend to invoke the same action).

To illustrate, consider an application with $N = 4$ actions (commands), each associated with a unique command variant: (i) "*what is the time,*" (ii) "*what is the day,*" (iii) "*what time is the meeting,*" and (iv) "*cancel the meeting.*" In this simple example, there are only $M = 7$ words in the vocabulary, with some interesting patterns: "*what*" and "*is*" always co-occur, "*the*" appears in all four commands, only (ii) and (iv) contain a unique word, and (i) is a proper subset of (iii). Constructing the (7×4) word-command matrix as described in [8], and performing the SVD, we obtain the 2-dimensional space shown in Fig. 3.

This figure shows how each word and each command is represented in the space $\mathcal{S}$. Note that the two words which each uniquely

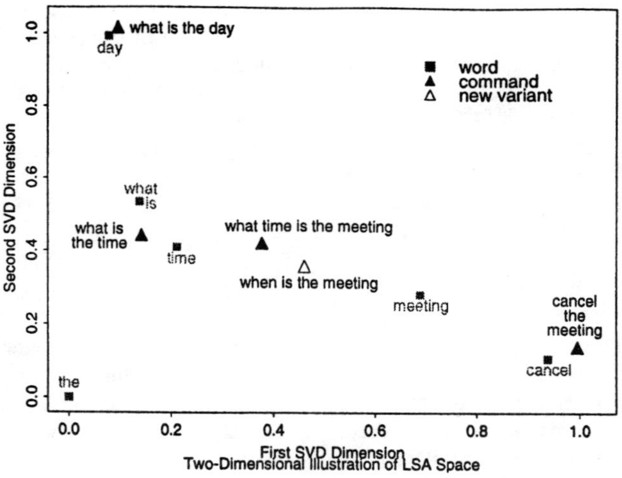

Figure 3: *Typical Behavior in Space S ($R = 2$)..*

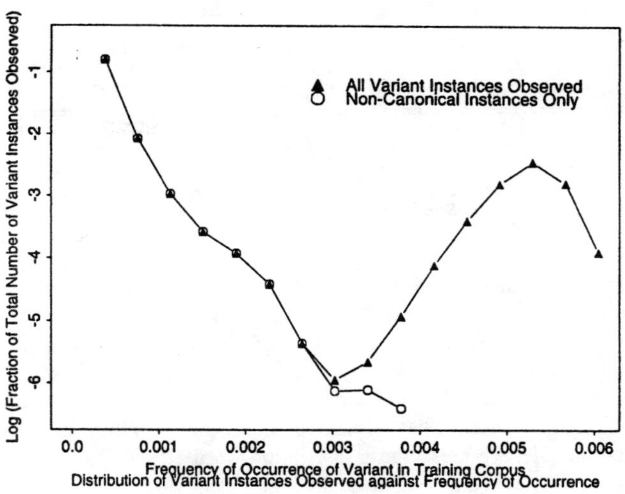

Figure 4: *Bi-Modal Usage Pattern.*

identify a command—"*day*" for (ii) and "*cancel*" for (iv)—each have a high coordinate on a different axis. Conversely, the word "*the*," which conveys no information about the identity of a command, is located at the origin. On the other hand, the semantic anchors for (ii) and (iv) fall "close" to the words which predict them best—"*day*" and "*cancel*", respectively. Similarly, the semantic anchors for (i) and (iii) fall in the vicinity of their meaningful components—"*what–is*" and "*time*" for (i) and "*time*" and "*meeting*" for (iii)—with the word "*time*," which occurs in both, indeed appearing "close" to both.

Now suppose that a user says something outside of the variants observed during training, such as "*when is the meeting*" rather than "*what time is the meeting*." This new word string turns out to have a representation in the space S indicated by the hollow triangle in Fig. 3. Note that this point is closest (in a variety of metrics) to the representation of command (iii). Thus, the new variant can be considered semantically most related to (iii), and the correct action can be automatically inferred.

To perform semantic classification, it is thus sufficient to determine, for a given variant $\tilde{d}_p$, which semantic anchor $\bar{v}_j$ the variant is most closely aligned with. (In this notation, the tilde symbol reflects the fact that the new variant was not, ordinarily, part of the training data.) By construction, the feature vector $\tilde{d}_p$ is a column vector of dimension M, which can be treated as if it were an additional column of W. Provided the matrices U and S do not change,[1] the SVD expansion (1) then implies: $\tilde{d}_p = US\tilde{v}_p^T$, where the R-dimensional vector $\tilde{v}_p^T$ acts as an additional column of the matrix V^T. Hence the *variant vector*:

$$\bar{\tilde{v}}_p = \tilde{v}_p \, S = \tilde{d}_p^T \, U \,, \tag{2}$$

corresponds to the representation of the variant $\tilde{d}_p$ in S. This is consistent with training: if an action is invoked with only one variant, the resulting vector reduces to the semantic anchor for that action.

Once (2) is obtained, classification occurs by assigning the variant vector $\bar{\tilde{v}}_p$ to the semantic anchor $\bar{v}_j$ which maximizes, over $1 \leq j \leq N$, the closeness measure [8]:

$$K(\bar{\tilde{v}}_p, \bar{v}_j) = \cos(\tilde{v}_p S, v_j S) = \frac{\tilde{v}_p \, S^2 \, v_j^T}{\|\tilde{v}_p S\| \, \|v_j S\|} \,. \tag{3}$$

[1]The reader is referred to [6], [8] for a discussion of this relatively mild assumption.

This closeness measure corresponds to the cosine of the angle between the two vectors $\bar{\tilde{v}}_p$ and $\bar{v}_j$.

Semantic inference has a number of useful properties. Not only is there no *a priori* constraint on what the user can say, but it can generalize well from a tractably small amount of training data. For example, it can learn synonyms and apply them in new contexts. Suppose for instance that the training data contained "*cancel the meeting*" and "*undo the meeting*" as variants of one command, but only "*cancel the last command*" as a variant of another command. Because the variants for the former command indicate that "*cancel*" and "*undo*" are synonyms, the new variant "*undo the last command*" would still be correctly mapped.

4. EXPERIMENTAL CONDITIONS

All experiments discussed below were conducted using 113 actions from the "Speakable Items" desktop user interface control task defined on the MacOS operating system. For each action, we collected about 5 variants of the associated canonical command, from 10 different speakers. This produced a total of 4,755 instances, comprising 2,676 distinct variants and 2,079 instances arising from the repetition of (some of) these variants. This formed the training data used for deriving the underlying LSA space.

Fig. 4 shows a histogram of all resulting variant instances (black triangles), as well as non-canonical instances only (hollow circles). The black triangles follow a bi-modal distribution, skewed in favor of low frequency occurrences. The second mode (right-hand side of Fig. 4) arises because some variants are universally accepted across the 10 speakers, and thus tend to be used repeatedly. This is primarily the case for the original 113 canonical commands, which were known to all speakers and whose constituent words largely appeared in all the prompts for variants. (In fact, users resorted to them as natural default choice when they could not think of enough variations.) On the other hand, the vast majority of the 2563 remaining distinct variants (hollow circles in Fig. 4) are highly idiosyncratic, and appear very infrequently in the training corpus. This underscores a surprisingly small degree of overlap between speakers in the way they choose to express the various commands.

For each action, we also collected 4 command instances from 2 additional speakers, comprising both the associated canonical command and 3 variants of the speakers' choosing. This formed eight test sets of 113 utterances each, comprising variants generally sim-

Table I. Average Classification Error Rates.

Underlying Framework	Test Set $\mathcal{T}_0$	Test Set $\mathcal{T}_1$
Semantic Inference	4.0 %	4.7 %
Conventional Grammar	1.8 %	77.4 %
Nearest Neighbor	3.1 %	31.9 %

ilar, but for the most part not exactly identical, to those observed during training. This test suite was labelled as $\mathcal{T}_1$. We also defined the control test suite $\mathcal{T}_0$, comprising the two test sets formed with canonical commands only. In both cases, the objective was to classify each test command variant against the appropriate action.

Since this classification depends on the accuracy of the transcription module, we measured transcription word error rates on both test sets. They were found to be 6.8% on $\mathcal{T}_0$ and 6.7% on $\mathcal{T}_1$. Given the small underlying vocabulary, this is a relatively high error rate. It appears to be due primarily to: (i) the variable fidelity of the low-cost (external or built-in) PlainTalk far-field microphone used for data collection, (ii) the generally poor quality of the acoustic environment (comprising computer fan noise, room reverberation, etc.), and (iii) the semi-spontaneous nature of command elicitation. Function words, in particular, tended to be heavily co-articulated, and therefore prone to errors. As they represented close to 50% of all words spoken in this task, this had a deleterious effect on the overall word error rate. Fortunately, such errors have little impact on semantic inference results, as further discussed below.

5. EXPERIMENTAL RESULTS

Following the implementation described in Section 3,[2] semantic inference led to a word-command matrix W of size (545×113). For consistency with earlier experiments (cf. [5]), the dimension of the LSA space was chosen to be $R = 62$. Classification was then performed using the standard semantic similarity measure (3). The first row of Table I summarizes the average classification error rates (CER) obtained, both on $\mathcal{T}_0$ and on $\mathcal{T}_1$.

To put these results in perspective, we conducted two additional series of experiments. The first one evaluated whether the basic concept advocated in this paper, i.e., decoupling utterance recognition from action inference, indeed translated into better performance. For this, a reasonable baseline is the conventional C&C paradigm operating with a (finite-state) grammar defined on canonical commands only. This is particularly useful to determine: (i) how much semantic variation can be captured through semantic inference, and (ii) how much transcription word error rate affects performance. The resulting performance is reported in the second row of Table I, again in terms of average CER on $\mathcal{T}_0$ and $\mathcal{T}_1$.

While the grammar-based system performs well on in-grammar items ($\mathcal{T}_0$), it—unsurprisingly—fails on the task comprising a majority of out-of-grammar variants ($\mathcal{T}_1$). In contrast, semantic inference performs only slightly worse on $\mathcal{T}_1$ than $\mathcal{T}_0$. We conclude that semantic inference does indeed satisfactorily handle much of the semantic variation present in the variants. In addition, transcription error rate does not seem to appreciably affect performance. This is likely due to the fact that a majority of errors involved function word substitutions like "this/it," "what's/what," "by/my," etc. Because such substitutions do not affect the basic meaning of the commands, they prove relatively harmless from the point of view of semantic classification.

[2]For simplicity, and without loss of generality, word agglomeration (cf. [6]) was not performed.

The above comparison therefore validates the decoupled recognition/inference framework underlying semantic inference. As a next step, the second series of experiments more specifically assessed the effectiveness of the classification paradigm based on (3) in LSA space. For this, a reasonable baseline is a simple nearest neighbor classification using the edit distance measure.[3] This is particularly useful to test the generalization properties of semantic inference. The last row of Table I summarizes the results obtained, again in terms of average CER on $\mathcal{T}_0$ and $\mathcal{T}_1$.

Comparison with the first row of Table I shows that semantic inference indeed proves much better than nearest neighbor at generalizing from the seen (as represented by $\mathcal{T}_0$) to the unseen (as exemplified by $\mathcal{T}_1$). It is interesting to note, however, that the latter slightly outperforms the former in the case of $\mathcal{T}_0$. This can likely be traced to the more central role that canonical commands play in the nearest neighbor approach. In contrast, in semantic inference they are treated just like any other variants.

6. CONCLUSION

In C&C applications which can be characterized as N-way classification problems, semantic inference provides a way to make natural language interaction possible. It works by decoupling the two traditionally tied processes of utterance recognition and action mapping. This is achieved by replacing the usual grammar-driven recognition by a large vocabulary transcription followed by a semantic classification. The latter is implemented within the LSA paradigm. During training, one semantic anchor per supported action is computed in an appropriate LSA space of relatively low dimension. Then, each input utterance is mapped onto an action by comparing the corresponding (command) vector with each semantic anchor, using the closeness measure (3).

This approach has been evaluated in the context of a desktop user interface task involving 113 different actions. Classification results illustrate the robust performance of semantic inference, as compared to both grammar-based processing and nearest neighbor classification. This is largely due to the parsimonious nature of the approach: by leveraging the semantic knowledge of the domain, as encapsulated in the LSA space, it can generalize well from the seen to the unseen. By the same token, however, it is inherently unable to recover deep logical and predicate-argument structure. Future efforts will concentrate on possible extensions to address this important limitation.

7. REFERENCES

[1] L. Lamel *et al.*, "The LIMSI RailTel System: Field Trial of a Telephone Service for Rail Travel Information," *Speech Communication*, Vol. 23, pp. 67–82, 1997.

[2] G. Riccardi and A.L. Gorin, "Stochastic Language Adaptation over Time and State in Natural Spoken Dialog Systems," *IEEE Trans. Speech Audio Proc.*, Vol. 8, No. 1, pp. 3–10, January 2000.

[3] A.C. Graesser *et al.*, "AutoTutor: A Simulation of A Human Tutor," in *J. Cognit. Syst. Research*, Vol. 1, pp. 35–51, 1999.

[4] V. Zue *et al.*, "JUPITER: A Telephone–Based Conversational Interface for Weather Information," *IEEE Trans. Speech Audio Proc.*, Vol. 8, No. 1, pp. 85–96, January 2000.

[5] J.R. Bellegarda and K.E.A. Silverman, "Toward Unconstrained Command and Control: Data–Driven

[3]Of course, other metrics could also be considered, such as the Kullback–Leibler divergence as proposed in [9].

Semantic Inference," in *Proc. ICSLP*, Beijing, China, pp. I258–I261, October 2000.

[6] J.R. Bellegarda and K.E.A. Silverman, "Data–Driven Semantic Inference for Unconstrained Desktop Command and Control," in *Proc. Eurospeech*, Aalborg, Denmark, pp. 455–458, September 2001.

[7] R. De Mori, "Recognizing and Using Knowledge Structures in Dialog Systems," in *Proc. ASRU Workshop*, Keystone, CO, pp. 297–306, December 1999.

[8] J.R. Bellegarda, "Exploiting Latent Semantic Information in Statistical Language Modeling," *Proc. IEEE*, Vol. 88, No. 8, pp. 1279–1296, August 2000.

[9] A. Pargellis *et al.*, "Metrics for Measuring Domain Independence of Semantic Classes,"in *Proc. Eurospeech*, Aalborg, Denmark, pp. 447–450, September 2001.

Design of a Multi-lingual, Parallel-processing Statistical Parsing Engine

Daniel M. Bikel
Department of Computer and Information Science
University of Pennsylvania
200 South 33rd Street, Philadelphia, PA 19104-6389
dbikel@cis.upenn.edu

1. INTRODUCTION

Ever since the widespread availability of the Penn Treebank [9], there have been numerous, statistical parsers developed for English, *e.g.* [8, 5, 3]. To varying degrees, these parsers and others—while very successful at the tasks for which they were designed—had the following limitations:

- they had a fairly fixed probabilistic structure, which could only be changed by re-coding some significant portion of the program[1]
- they had hard-coded features specific to English
- they had hard-coded features specific to the Penn Treebank
- they were designed only for a uniprocessor environment

Building on our work in [1] and [2], we have developed a design for a head-driven, chart parsing engine that addresses all of the above limitations, and we present this design here. In particular, our design provides

- appropriate layers of abstraction and encapsulation for quickly porting to different languages and/or Treebank annotation styles,
- has "plug-'n'-play" probability structures and
- is multi-threaded for use in a multiprocessor and/or multi-host environment for throughput far superior to traditional uniprocessing parsers.

2. BACKGROUND

[1]Based on remarks by Charniak at the NAACL 2000 conference, the parser of [3] does not appear to have this limitation, possessing some flexible mechanism to specify different probability structures.

Proceedings of HLT 2002, Second International Conference on Human Language Technology Research, M. Marcus, ed., Morgan Kaufmann, San Francisco, 2002.

2.1 Probability structures and sentence-level parallelism

In preparation for the work presented in [1], we explored a variety of lexical probability structures involving WordNet synsets. To facilitate this experimentation, we developed a "plug-'n'-play" lexical probability structure architecture. The model we were extending was extracted from BBN's SIFT system [10], which is a history-based model that is derived in large part from Model 2 of [5].

For the computation of probability estimates, the BBN parser had hard-coded construction of data objects to represent the future and history events, computing a maximum-likelihood estimate of $P(X|Y)$ by $\frac{c(X,Y)}{c(Y)}$, where $c(\cdot)$ delivers the count of its argument in the training data. The architecture of [1] placed a layer of abstraction at the computation of the histories for the various back-off levels of the parser: in pseudocode, the construction of a history object for a particular back-off level became simply

```
history =
  probabilityStructure.get(backOffLevel,
                           fullContext);
```

We also made an initial foray into parallel-processing by developing a multi-threaded *sentence server*, to provide parallelism at the sentence level in a cluster computing environment. This work paved the way for the significantly greater degree of parallelism in the architecture of our current parsing engine.

2.2 Language independence

For [2], we took two parsing models, BBN's SIFT-derived parser and David Chiang's stochastic TAG parser [4] and adapted them to parse Chinese. The results were that the Chinese-adapted models performed with accuracy close to their English counterparts when trained on comparably-sized corpora and tested on their respective domains.[2] The main difficulty of the project was ferreting out and replacing all traces of English-specific or Treebank-specific code in the parsers, such as replacing code dependent on the default character encoding and finding and abstracting away from language-specific word features and parts of speech. This project greatly influenced the language-independent design of our current architecture, which allows for a "language package" that contains all data and methods specific to a particular language and/or Treebank annotation style.

[2]Our two comparably-sized corpora were: ~100k words of WSJ text from the (English) Penn Treebank and ~100k words of Xinhua newswire text from the Chinese Treebank. The stochastic TAG model performed at 77%/78% labeled precision/recall on the Xinhua test set, compared to 79%/80% on the English test set. See [2] for more details.

3. DESIGN OVERVIEW

The parsing engine we have developed supports a wide range of head-driven parsing models, including that of BBN's SIFT system, as well as both Models 2 and 3 of [7]. Figure 1 gives a pictorial overview of the design.

3.1 Language package

The most significant data encapsulation of the design is that of the language package. The language package, which will typically be an actual Java package,[3] is a collection of Java classes that are extensions of several abstract classes which provide the specification of data and methods specific to a particular language and Treebank annotation style. There are four such required classes: `Treebank`, `Training`, `HeadFinder` and `WordFeatures`. The `Treebank` class provides all data and methods specific to a particular Treebank, such as predicates for preterminals and complex nonterminal labels. The `Training` class provides methods and data specific to preprocessing training trees. The primary function of the `HeadFinder` class is to read a data (text) file specifying head rules specific to a particular language's Treebank and provide a head-finding method. Finally, the `WordFeatures` class provides a mapping of lexical items of a particular language to orthographic/morphological word-feature–vectors, to aid part-of-speech tagging.[4] As an additional language-independent design criterion, all relevant input and output files are written to and read from with a user-settable character encoding.[5] Our goal is, for treebanks that are not too radically different from the Penn Treebank (the Chinese Treebank [13] and possibly the Korean Treebank have this property, *e.g.* [12]), to be able to create a new language package in about 1–2 weeks. The one language-dependent module that currently does not sit inside the language package is WordNet; this is simply due to the fact that we have yet to implement our WordNet-extended model. Now that the initial implementation is complete, we will make language-specific lexical resources part of the language package framework.

3.2 Probability structure objects

Every type of output element of the models supported by our engine—including nonteminals, preterminals (parts of speech), words, word-features, gaps and subcat frames—has an associated `ProbabilityStructure` object, that specifies how to form the data objects representing the future and history at all possible back-off levels for that output element. Objects containing maximal context—called `TrainerEvent` objects—are passed in to a single method which then delivers the appropriate history or future for a specified back-off level, as per the pseudocode example above in Section 2.1. A layer of abstraction also exists for these probabilistic events: objects that represent events must conform to an `Event` interface.[6] This abstraction allows for maximum flexibility in the underlying types and representation of event elements, which are typically the output elements of the parser, but can also include other features derived from those output elements. In this way, the user can not only easily test new probability structures in our architecture, but also new events with new *types* of event elements.

3.3 Probability-level parallelism

The simplest form of parallelization is to increase a parser's throughput by splitting up a test file into multiple segments and have multiple executables run on these segments, each on a separate host. Our sentence server provided a finer granularity of parallelism, but still required a separate parser on each host. Schemes such as these are a monumental waste of memory resources: each parser contains the same massive tables containing counts of events observed in the training data. Our current design exhibits a much finer degree of parallelism by introducing a *probability server*. The idea is that a `DecoderServer` object can sit on a multiprocessor with a large amount of RAM, providing smoothed top-level probability estimates to mutliple, small chart parsing clients. The architecture also supports load-balancing if multiple, large multiprocessing hosts are available. Java provides an elegant solution to such distributed computing via a built-in technology called *remote method invocation*, or RMI.

An additional feature of our distributed-computing parsing engine is that it is fully *fault-tolerant*: any of the `DecoderServer` objects or parsing clients can fail and the system will keep on operating. Even the `Switchboard` itself can fail (see Figure 1), since the servers and clients will patiently wait to reconnect to a switchboard and to each other, and a new switchboard, when it is brought up, will recover the same state of the old switchboard at the time of its failure.

Finally, the distributed system need not be a collection of closely-knit, identical hosts. Given that the Java runtime environment is available for virtually any operating system and architecture, the parsing engine can and has been run on a disparate set of hosts, running, for example, Solaris, Linux, Windows and MacOS X, where the only requirement is internet connectivity.

4. BUILT FOR SPEED

We did not want all the flexibility above to compromise the efficiency of our system; thus, we spent significant effort at optimizing the decoder.[7] We employed the following categories of optimizations:

1. precomputation of all log-probability estimates and log-lambdas, necessitating only floating-point add operations for computing probability estimates during decoding

2. creation and use of hash maps optimized for mapping arbitrary Java objects to primitive types, achieving spatial locality in probability lookups and eliminating the need for primitive wrapper objects

3. short-circuiting all decoding operations when it is evident that the resulting new chart item will have a zero probability

4. elimination of almost all new-object creation during decoding, including the use of an object pool for efficient recycling of chart item objects

5. smaller optimizations based on profiling

[3] A Java *package*, much like its Lisp progenitor, provides a separate name space for a collection of classes and their data members, as well as providing yet another level of access control for data and methods (i.e., data and methods can be made accessible only within their enclosing package).

[4] Unlike [5, 6], part-of-speech tagging can be fully integrated into the models supported by our architecture. Along these lines, word features have been shown to reduce part of speech ambiguity for unknown words [11] and may be employed by models in our architecture.

[5] Java stores all characters internally as unicode characters, and most runtime environments support a very wide variety of character encodings, supporting an even wider variety of the world's languages, making Java an ideal language with which to implement internationalizable software.

[6] An *interface* is a Java construct (borrowed from the Smalltalk programming language) that specifies a contract for implementations to follow, in the form of a set of method (function) signatures, augmented as needed by API documentation.

[7] Our thanks to Scott Miller of BBN for his invaluable advice for parser optimization.

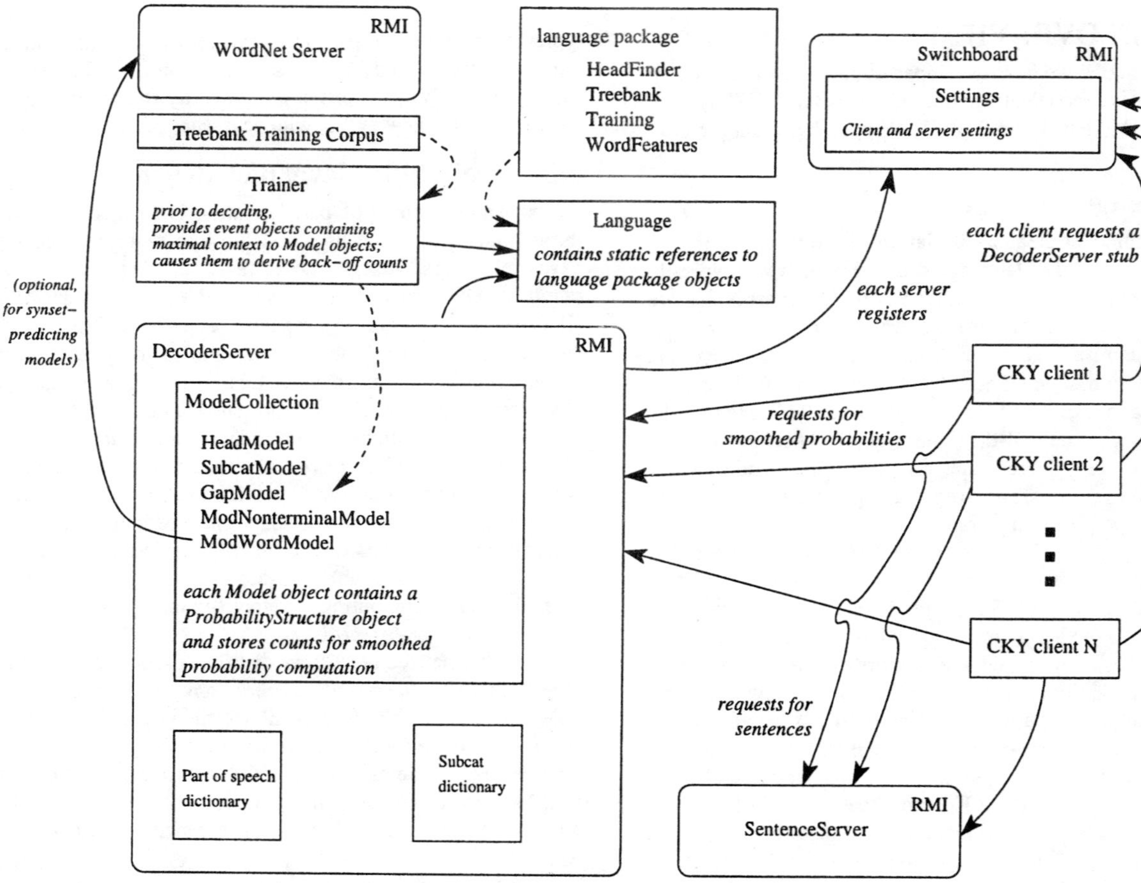

Figure 1: Pictorial design overview. Arrows indicate functional relationships. While there is necessarily always a bi-directional flow of information, the solid arrows indicate the direction of requests from a client to a server (or from a consumer to a producer). Dashed arrows explicitly indicate the flow of information or objects.

Parser	≤ 40 words		≤ 100 words	
	LR	LP	LR	LP
Collins	89.75	90.19	88.47	89.30
Bikel	89.89	90.14	88.72	89.03

Figure 2: Results of Collins' thesis Model 2 and our replication of this model on Section 00 of the Penn Treebank. LR = labeled recall. LP = labeled precision.

Optimization technique 3 was of crucial importance, achieving the single greatest speed improvement of them all. In particular, before the computation of the modifier-generation probability, the decoder first checks to see if the last level of back-off for the modifier-generation model (the history) ever occurred with the particular modifier being generated (the future) in training. If not, then it will be impossible for the model to deliver anything but a zero probability. Put another way, if the coarsest context never occurred with the future being generated, then certainly more specific contexts could never have occurred, and thus the model would delive a zero probability for the entire smoothed estimate. This optimization alone resulted in a five-fold speedup, and so it was also implemented for the subcat-generation model, resulting in an even greater speedup.

5. FLEXIBILITY PUT TO THE TEST

5.1 Replicating Collins' thesis model

The models described in [7] have been used for many tasks and are thus of great importance in the field. As a baseline for our own research, we attempted to replicate Model 2 from Collins' thesis using our new engine. Although this replication turned out to be more difficult than anticipated, happily, we have now achieved results on the development test set that are nearly identical to those reported in Collins' thesis (see Figure 2). [8]

We have documented all our implementation efforts with extreme thoroughness using `javadoc`, a documentation tool that is integrated with the standard Java software development kit. So that Collins' important model will be fully described in the public domain, we aim to release our system to the public for research purposes next year, both as a means to provide a fully documented version of Model 2 from Collins' thesis, and also as a resource for other researchers interested in statistical parsing or language processing in general. We hope that, given its flexibility, our engine will be a useful research testbed for others.

5.2 Developing a language package for Chinese

As mentioned in Section 3.1, a desideratum of our engine was to be able to implement a new language package in 1–2 weeks. We recently implemented a language package for Chinese for use with the Chinese Treebank in only *one and a half days*. Not only was this significantly shorter than our expected implementation time, but we also achieved state-of-the-art results. Using the division of data into training and test sets set up in our previous work [2], on the sentences of length ≤ 40, our engine achieved a labeled recall of 77.0% and a labeled precision of 81.6%. In comparison to the other parsers of which we are aware that have trained and tested on these same data, our parser's recall is equivalent and the precision is significantly higher. With these encouraging results, we hope to improve Chinese parsing performance even further, and also to implement several more language packages for the rapidly-expanding set of treebanks in other languages.

[8] After reading [7] thoroughly—it is a very detailed and well-written document—and then implementing its Model 2, there was a puzzling gap between the performance of our parser and the model's documented performance. As it happened, the replication of Model 2 required a painstaking analysis of the data files output by Collins' trainer in order to reconstruct what the trainer was doing, as well as a detailed analysis of the parser code. These analyses revealed, among other things, discrepancies between details described in [7] and their actual implementation. Additionally, the replication required several e-mail exchanges with Collins himself to clear up ambiguities in both his thesis and the parser code. Many thanks to Mike Collins for his invaluable advice during our efforts to replicate his model.

6. CONCLUSION

In the design presented here, we have shown how using various engineering practices and technologies of modern computer science, we can address several limitations of current statistical parsers. Indeed, almost all of the techniques and technologies we used here can be applied to NLP software in general, particularly in light of the growing need to develop efficient, internationalizable software. By abstracting away from the idiosyncrasies of training data and from a particular probability structure for parser output elements, we provide parser developers a means to test various probability structures, using features and back-off schemes that are the result either of pure theorizing or empirical study or (presumably) both, and we allow this experimentation while maintaining a high degree of computational efficiency. As has been shown in [6], choosing linguistically-motivated features and independence assumptions can often result in a well-estimated, high-performance model. It is thus our hope that continued application of sound engineering practices will not only lead to more efficient, scalable and portable NLP software, but will also benefit the exploration and testing of linguistic theories.

7. REFERENCES

[1] Daniel M. Bikel. A statistical model for parsing and word-sense disambiguation. In *Joint SIGDAT Conference on Empirical Methods in Natural Language Processing and Very Large Corpora*, Hong Kong, October 2000.

[2] Daniel M. Bikel and David Chiang. Two statistical parsing models applied to the Chinese Treebank. In Martha Palmer, Mitch Marcus, Aravind Joshi, and Fei Xia, editors, *Proceedings of the Second Chinese Language Processing Workshop*, pages 1–6, Hong Kong, 2000.

[3] Eugene Charniak. A maximum entropy–inspired parser. In *Proceedings of the 1st Meeting of the North American Chapter of the Association for Computational Linguistics*, pages 132–139, Seattle, Washington, April 29 to May 4 2000.

[4] David Chiang. Statistical parsing with an automatically-extracted tree adjoining grammar. In *Proceedings of the 38th Annual Meeting of the Association for Computational Linguistics*, 2000.

[5] Michael Collins. Three generative, lexicalised models for statistical parsing. In *Proceedings of ACL-EACL '97*, pages 16–23, 1997.

[6] Michael Collins. Discriminative reranking for natural language parsing. In *International Conference on Machine Learning*, 2000. (to appear).

[7] Michael John Collins. *Head-Driven Statistical Models for Natural Language Parsing*. PhD thesis, University of Pennsylvania, 1999.

[8] D. Magerman. Statistical decision tree models for parsing. In *33rd Annual Meeting of the Association for Computational*

Linguistics, pages 276–283, Cambridge, Massachusetts, 1995. Morgan Kaufmann Publishers.

[9] Mitchell P. Marcus, Beatrice Santorini, and Mary Ann Marcinkiewicz. Building a large annotated corpus of English: The Penn Treebank. *Computational Linguistics*, 19:313–330, 1993.

[10] Scott Miller, Heidi Fox, Lance Ramshaw, and Ralph Weischedel. SIFT – Statistically-derived Information From Text. In *Seventh Message Understanding Conference (MUC-7)*, Washington, D.C., 1998.

[11] R. Weischedel, M. Meteer, R. Schwartz, L. Ramshaw, and J. Palmucci. Coping with ambiguity and unknown words through probabilistic methods. *Computational Linguistics*, 19(2):359–382, 1993.

[12] Fei Xia, Chung-hye Han, Martha Palmer, and Aravind Joshi. Comparing lexicalized treebank grammars extracted from Chinese, Korean, and English corpora. In Martha Palmer, Mitch Marcus, Aravind Joshi, and Fei Xia, editors, *Proceedings of the Second Chinese Language Processing Workshop*, pages 52–59, Hong Kong, 2000.

[13] Fei Xia, Martha Palmer, Nianwen Xue, Mary Ellen Okurowski, John Kovarik, Shizhe Huang, Tony Kroch, and Mitch Marcus. Developing Guidelines and Ensuring Consistency for Chinese Text Annotation. In *Proceedings of the 2nd International Conference on Language Resources and Evaluation (LREC-2000)*, Athens, Greece, 2000.

TONGUES: Rapid Development of a Speech-to-Speech Translation System

Alan W Black,
Ralf Brown,
Robert Frederking,
Language Technologies Institute
Carnegie Mellon Univertsity

Rita Singh,
School of Computer Science
Carnegie Mellon Univertsity

John Moody,
Eric Steinbrecher,
Lockheed Martin Systems Integration
Owego, NY

ABSTRACT

We carried out a one-year project to build a portable speech-to-speech translation system in a new language that could run on a small portable computer. Croatian was chosen as the target language. The resulting system was tested with real users on a trip to Croatia in the spring of 2001. We describe its basic components, the methods we used to build them, initial evaluation results, and related significant observations. This work was done in conjunction with the US Army Chaplain School; chaplains are often the only personnel in a position to communicate with local people over non-military issues such as medical supplies, refugees, etc. This paper thus reports on a realistic instance of rapidly deploying and field-testing a speech-to-speech translator using current technology.

1. INTRODUCTION

With speech recognition, synthesis and translation beginning to work well enough for small tasks, this paper describes a short project to build a portable speech-to-speech translation system in a new language. We describe its basic components, the methods we used to build them and related significant observations. The end system was tested with real users on a trip to Croatia in the spring of 2001.

This work was done in conjunction with the US Army Chaplain School. Army chaplains are often among the advance party of troop deployment. In many cases, the chaplains are the only personnel in a position to communicate with local people over non-military issues such as medical supplies, refugees, etc. Often the chaplain has no knowledge of the local language, and due to immediacy requirements, no human translator is available. Thus the chaplain must communicate as best possible, perhaps without even a bilingual dictionary.

Given this domain, our task was to build a speech-to-speech translation system that could run on a small portable computer that will aid conversations between a chaplain and a native. Such a task requires

- speech recognition systems for English and the target language
- speech synthesizer for English and the target language
- a translation system from English to the target language, and the reverse translation system
- an interface that allows these components to be used effectively in communication

The entire project, from start to finish, was allowed to take only one calendar year, including initial contractual arrangements, hiring language experts, etc. All of these systems had to run on a single small sub-notebook computer, in a reasonable time; this added further interesting constraints on the project.

For topical reasons, Croatian was chosen as the target language. Although spoken by around 5 million people, it does not command enough economic weight that the commercial speech and language community has produced recognizers, synthesizers and translation engines for it. Thus it is a realistic language type to use as an example. From a testing standpoint, although Croatia is still of interest to the US military, there are no current hostilities there, thus enabling a realistic field-test under safe conditions.

2. PREPARATION

As we were to build these system in a short period and on a small budget, data driven approaches were the only reasonable method. Such techniques must be used for each of the three core components: machine translation, speech recognition engines, and speech synthesis engines.

Thus at the very start we arranged to record a number of chaplains in role-playing conversations of the type we expected the device to encounter. Fortunately, the chaplains were familiar with role-playing exercises, and all had relevant field experiences to re-enact. Both sides of the conversations were in English. These were digitally recorded with head mounted microphones at 16KHz in stereo (one speaker on each channel), as this was closest to the intended audio channel characteristics of the eventual system. In all, we recorded 46 conversations, ranging from a few minutes to 20 minutes length. In total there was 4.25 hours of actual speech.

These conversations were then hand-transcribed at the word level, identifying false starts, filled pauses and the complete words.

Next the transcriptions of these English-English conversations were translated into Croatian by native Croatian speakers by hand.

This data provided the basic information from which we could boot strap the rest of the speech-to-speech translation system.

Proceedings of HLT 2002, Second International Conference on Human Language Technology Research, M. Marcus, ed., Morgan Kaufmann, San Francisco, 2002.

3. COMPONENTS

3.1 Recognition

For speech recognition, we used the CMU Sphinx II system [8], a relatively light-weight recognizer that works in real time even on machines with relatively small memory and modest-speed processors. For Automatic Speech Recognition (ASR) to work we need to build two basic types of models. **Acoustic Models** which model the acoustic phonetic space for the given language and **Language Models** which model the probability of word sequences. In addition to these models we also need two lexicons one for English and one for Croatian that map words to their pronunciations.

For the English acoustic models, we could have used existing acoustic models trained from similar wide-band speech, but as there were not any readily available conversational wide-band speech databases in the intended domain, it was felt better to train on the chaplain dialogs directly rather than use existing models and some form of adaptation. Although such adaptation techniques may have been beneficial and feasible for English, we knew that for the Croatian no such data was available, and part of this exercise was to develop speech-to-speech translation systems for languages that did not already have speech resources constructed for them. Thus for English we took **only** the 4.25 hours of chaplain speech and directly trained semi-continous HMM models for Sphinx2.

For the English language model we required a larger collection of in-domain text. We used the dialog transcriptions themselves but also augmented that with text from chaplain handbooks that were made available to us. Although we knew we could provide better recognition accuracy by using more resources, we were interested in limiting what resources were necessary for this work, and also (see below) we found the trained models from this data adequate for the task.

Building Croatian models was harder. As we were aware that our resource of Croatian speakers was limited, and they had less skill in carrying out full word transcription of conversational speech, we wished to find a simpler, less resource-intensive method to build Croatian acoustic models. From the the translated chaplain transcripts, we wished to select example utterances that when recorded would give sufficient acoustic coverage to allow reasonable acoustic models to be trained. To do this, we used a technique originally developed for selecting text to record for speech synthesis [2]. By using the initially developed Croatian speech synthesizer, we could find the phonemes that would be used to say each utterance. We then ran a greedy selection algorithm that selects utterances that would best cover the acoustic space [2]. From a list of several thousand utterances, we selected groups of 250 utterances that were phonetically rich. These sets were then read by a number of Croatian speakers. Using read speech avoided the process of hand-transcription of the speech, though it does make it less like the intended conversational speech. Due to the relative scarcity of native Croatian speakers, we recorded only 15 different speakers, of which 13 were female and 2 were male. This resulted in a gender imbalance, which was not however observed to affect the system's performance greatly. In all, a total of 4.0 hours of Croatian speech was collected. This data **alone** was then used to train new acoustic models for Croatian.

For both English and Croatian recognition systems, semi-continuous 5-state triphone HMMs were trained. The number of tied states used in each case was commensurate with the amount of training data available. Although the English models did have explicit modeling of filled pauses (non-linguistic verbalized sounds such as "um", "uh" etc.), none were trained for Croatian. This was partially because the recorded speech was read, and had minimal spontaneous speech phenomena such as filled pauses.

Language models in both cases were word-trigrams built with absolute discounting. The language-model vocabularies consisted of 2900 words for English and 3900 words for Croatian. In pilot experiments with heldout test sets, the word error rates were found to be below 15% for English and below 20% for Croatian.

We note that as the utterances used in the training were not spontaneous, the system was more easily confused by hesitations and filled pauses. However in the actual user tests of the system this proved to be less of a problem than we expected. As turns in a conversation through a speech-to-speech translation system are slower and less spontaneous compared to single language conversations, speakers were more careful in their delivery than they might be in full conversations.

3.2 Synthesis

For English synthesis, we used an existing English voice in the Festival Speech Synthesis System [3]. Although there may have been a slight advantage in building a targeted synthesizer for conversations, it would not have been significantly different in quality. A few lexicon additions were made for the particular domain, but the existing English voice was essentially used unchanged.

For Croatian, it was necessary to build a complete new speech synthesis voice. To do this, we used the tools available in the CMU FestVox project [1], which is designed to provide the necessary support for building new synthetic voices in new languages. Synthetic voices require: text processing, lexicons, a method for waveform synthesis, and prosodic models.

In this case, the text processing was minimal, as the type of language being given to the synthesizer was fairly regular, since it would be generated by the translation system (or the Croatian recognizer).

Luckily, orthographic-to-phoneme rules for Croatian are relatively easy and could be written by hand, so building a lexicon was much easier than it might be for some other languages. (The same lexicon and letter-to-sound rules were used by the recognition engine).

The waveform synthesis was done using a constrained version of general unit selection techniques. From the translated utterances from chaplain dialogs and other Croatian text, we selected 1000 utterances that best covered the phonetic space (using the technique more fully described in [2]). These were spoken by a native male Croatian and automatically labelled by a simple dynamic time warp technique using cross-linguistic prompts (as decribed in [1]). These were then hand corrected.

The final required piece was a set of prosodic models for Croatian; we found a very simple rule-based method of phrasing adequate for this domain (mostly shorter sentences). We trained duration models from the recorded Croatian speech, which worked well. However, the intonation model was harder. We found that a model trained from the relatively small amount of speech in the Croatian database did not produce a good intonation model. Thus we fell back on a different technique: we simply used our English intonation model modified to the range of our Croatian speaker. On listening tests, native Croatians preferred this over the natively-trained model. For other languages such short cuts may not be so acceptable.

The resulting quality–although not always fluent–was understandable almost all the time, and much better than a standard diphone synthesizer. It also readily captured the voice quality of the original Croatian speaker.

3.3 Machine Translation

Again due to the requirement of rapid development, data-driven approaches were preferred. Thus we used a Multi-Engine MT (MEMT) system [7], whose primary engines were an Example-Based MT (EBMT) engine [4] and a bilingual dictionary/glossary. Carnegie

Mellon's EBMT system uses a "shallower" approach than many other EBMT systems; examples to be used are selected based on string matching and inflectional and other heuristics, with no deep structural analysis. The MEMT architecture uses a trigram language model of the output language to select among competing partial translations produced by several engines. It is used in this system primarily to select among competing (and possibly overlapping) EBMT translation hypotheses.

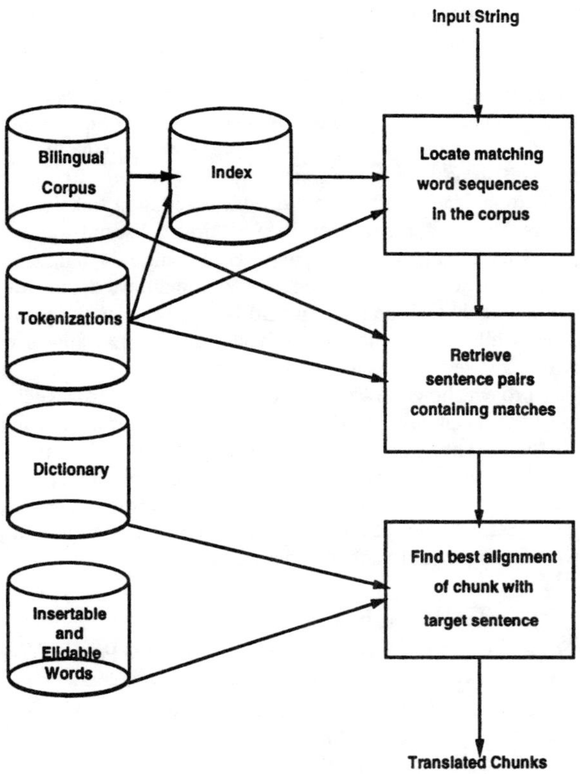

EBMT Architecture

For translation into Croatian, we incorporated a finite-state word reordering mechanism, applied during the language model-driven selection of partial translations, to place clitics in a cluster in the appropriate location. (Croatian syntax requires a very specific ordering of clitics in a cluster in a specific position in the sentence.)

The training corpus for the EBMT engine consisted of the translated chaplain dialogs plus pre-existing parallel text from the DIPLOMAT project [6] and newly-acquired parallel text from the web. The dictionary/glossary engine used both statistically-extracted translations and manually-created entries. The English trigram model already existed, and had been generated from newswire and broadcast news transcripts. Finally, the Croatian trigram model was built from the Croatian half of the EBMT corpus, some Croatian text found on the web, and the full text of some sixty novels and other Croatian literary works (in total, approximately six million words).

3.4 Integration and Interface

Simply stringing together a recognizer, translator, and synthesizer does not make a very useful speech-to-speech translation system. A good interface is necessary to make the parts work together in such a way that a user can actually derive benefit from it. Using our experience from the earlier DIPLOMAT system, we designed the interface to be asymmetric, with the Croatian side being as simple as possible, and any necessary complexity handled on the English side, since the chaplain would be trained and practiced in using the system.

We included back-translation, to allow a user with no knowledge of the target language to better assess the quality of the translation. We also included several user-requested features, such as built-in pre-recorded instructions and explanations for the Croatian (since the Croatian speaker is completely naive regarding the device and the chaplain's intentions), emergency key phrases (such as "Don't move!"), and enhancements such as being able to modify the translation lexicon, so that the system could be tuned to more specific tasks.

The final system ran on a Windows-based Toshiba Libretto, running at 200MHz with 192MB of memory. At the time of the project (2000) this was the best combination of speed and size that was readily available. The system was equipped with a custom touch-screen, so that the Croatian-speaker would not need to type or use a mouse at all. Aware that the system may be used in situations where the non-English participant may be unfamiliar with the technology, we include a microphone/speaker handset that looks like a conventional telephone handset. This has the advantage of provided a close-talking microphone, thus making speech recognition easier, and coming in a format that will be familiar to most people.

4. EVALUATION

In April 2001, a group organized by the US Army Chaplain school took two versions of the device to Zagreb, where it was tested with non-English-speaking Croatians. A number of scenarios were prepared in English and Croatian, and were given to each participant to act out using the translation device. The scenarios were in the intended domain, involving refugees, medical supplies and getting general directions.

In all, 21 dialogs took place, between different Croatian speakers and one of 5 chaplains. After the test, the Croatian participants were given a questionnaire to fill out. Their overall impression was as follows:

Overall	
Good	5
OK	11
Bad	3

Our own observations of the basic system were that it did actually work to a level that was useful about one half of the time (it was not clear in advance that this necessarily would be the case). The participants were capable of communicating through the system and real information was transferred.

However, as expected, there were a number of specific problems. One that we noted immediately was a frustrating slowness of communication, due to required user clarifications, though it was much faster than if a bi-lingual dictionary were the only translation device available.

On asking the participants to identify the most difficult problems, they replied as follows:

User difficulties	
grammar/case	5
loudspeakers	4
translation	3
recognition	2
synthesis	2
speed	1

Hardware issues with the volume of the built-in speakers were a clear (and easily solvable) problem. But other aspects of the core technology were both harder to identify and harder to fix. The system includes a facility to allow the user (typically the chaplain) to explicitly add new words and phrases to the system so that common errors can be minimized over time. Although this facility was not used often, it is clear that supporting a greater level of adaptation would allow the device to become more useful over time.

Unlike the English recognizer, the Croatian recognizer did not support filled pauses and hesitations. The effect was that extra short words (typically function words) were often erroneously hypothesized by the system. As the system displayed what was being recognized, it was easy for the speaker to delete those extra words by hand, which they often did. However the speakers also learned to speak more fluently and less conversationally as they used the system, improving recognition accuracy.

Similarly, we asked what they found easy:

What works?	
short sentences	10
nothing	4

It was quickly discovered by most participants that the system did not translate long, rambling sentences well. Short, direct sentences were much more likely to produce good translations. This was not surprising, given the limitations of the platform and the deliberate limiting of development time to see if such limitations still allowed a useful translation device. We were actually pleased to see that the system provided adequate coverage for successful translation of unrehearsed, naive dialogues.

Other specific observations we noted were that the users could not easily identify where the problems lay with the system. (For example, if speech recognition produced and displayed a correct transcript, and then translation produced an unacceptable result, they would usually *respeak* the same utterance using the same words.) Thus even if we provided separate user methods to add words to the recognizer, language model and translation engine, it is clear that the user would not be able to identify which part (or parts) need to be updated. As we feel that such systems need to provide methods of adaptation in the field, it is clear that the interface presented to the user to offer that adaptation needs more work.

Although there were problems with the volume of the output through the small built-in speakers on the device, which many users commented on, mistakes in the synthesizer were often erroneously attributed to the translator (and vice versa).

A second observation was that the participants continued to use speech and did not resort to the alternative typing interface (although they were clearly aware of it), and only resorted to typing as a last resort. This may have been due to the fact the participants were told to use the speech-to-speech translation device rather than have the more abstract goal of successful communication by the best means. The very small keyboard on the (required) small device may also have been a factor.

Use of system in Croatia

Further details of the evaluation are described in [5].

5. CONCLUSION

As one of the goals of this work was to rapidly develop a speech-to-speech translation system we also wished to account for the effort spent in building this system. Although the work took part over one calendar year, not everyone was working full time on the system during that period. In total there were 6 technical staff involved (the authors of this paper), each bringing their particular expertise. We estimate that in total there was about 2 person-years total effort from the senior staff. In addition to this there was also part-timer Croatian informants, chaplains and some student helpers. We also should note that some of the translation datra used to train the system was collect for a previous project.

Most of the basic systems that were used in development of this system already existed and this was basically a test of how well they perform on new data. However some problems with the tools were found and some new development was carried out. Interestingly it is the organization of data collection, scheduling translators and labellers that is actually one of the most time consuming parts.

If this technique were to be applied to some new language we believe less resources would be required, though we do not want to claim that each new language would be the same as the previous, and hence different possibly non-trivial problems may appear when moving these techniques to new languages.

This project shows how a relatively simple speech-to-speech translation system can be rapidly and successfully constructed using today's tools. The system was indeed constructed in less than one year. The results of the 2001 evaluation in Croatia indicated that, while the system was not ready for actual field use, it was actually impressively close to that level of performance, and worthy of further development to achieve that capability.

6. REFERENCES

[1] A. Black and K. Lenzo. Building voices in the Festival speech synthesis system. http://festvox.org/festvox/, 2000.

[2] A. Black and K. Lenzo. Optimal data selection for unit selection synthesis. In *4rd ESCA Workshop on Speech Synthesis*, Scotland., 2001.

[3] A. Black, P. Taylor, and R. Caley. The Festival speech synthesis system. http://festvox.org/festival, 1998.

[4] R. Brown. Example-based machine translation in the Pangloss system. In *Proceedings of COLING-96*, pages 169–174, Copenhagen, Denmark, 1996.

[5] R. Frederking, A. Black, R. Brown, J. Moody, and E. Steinbrecher. Field testing the tongues speech-to-speech machine translation system. In *LREC 2002*, 2002.

[6] R. Frederking, A. Rudnicky, C. Hogan, and K. Lenzo. Interactive speech translation in the diplomat project. *Machine Translation Journal*, special issue on spoken language translation, 2000.

[7] R. E. Frederking and R. D. Brown. The Pangloss-Lite Machine Translation System. In *Proceedings of the Second Conference of the Association for Machine Translation in the Americas (AMTA)*, pages 268–272, Montreal, Quebec, Canada, October 1996.

[8] X. Huang, F. Alleva, H.-W. Hon, K.-F. Hwang, M.-Y. Lee, and R. Rosenfeld. The SPHINX-II speech recognition system: an overview. *Computer Speech and Language*, 7(2):137–148, 1992.

Rapid Annotation through Human-Machine Collaboration

Elizabeth Boschee, Scott Miller, Lance Ramshaw, Ralph Weischedel

BBN Technologies
10 Moulton Street
Cambridge, MA 02138
617-873-5513

eboschee, szmiller, lramshaw, weischedel@bbn.com

ABSTRACT

This paper addresses the problem of efficiently obtaining training data for a new entity type or relation. We describe a methodology for rapidly obtaining annotation by using seed examples and human feedback, and we show that this method allows annotation to be performed approximately 20 times faster than manual annotation alone, with small degradation in annotation accuracy.

1. INTRODUCTION

The successful application of trainable language processing algorithms (e.g. algorithms for named entity recognition, part-of-speech tagging, parsing, and anaphor resolution) depends crucially on the availability of large annotated corpora. Developments in machine learning such as co-training [1] and active learning [2] hold the promise of far more efficient linguistic annotation than current methods that rely predominantly on human effort. Previous work [3] successfully demonstrated a co-training algorithm for learning a named entity recognition task from unlabeled data with no human intervention. However, the set of contexts in which the algorithm was applied was limited to two specific syntactic constructions. In this paper, we report on a technique in which a human annotator works cooperatively with a machine-learning algorithm to annotate data far more rapidly than a human alone, while more completely and accurately than an unsupervised algorithm alone.

2. APPROACH

The rapid annotation procedure begins with a small set of instances in which we are highly confident. The goal is to iteratively expand the set, adding high precision new instances at each stage. At each stage, the machine generalizes from the current set of instances to conjecture patterns for new instances. Examples covered by these potential patterns are presented for human verification. The results of the human review are used to identify new high reliability patterns, which are then used to add new instances to the set.

3. TEST PROBLEM

To evaluate our system, we worked with 500,000 words of the TDT II corpus. This corpus had been previously annotated with names and descriptions of people, organizations, locations, and geo-political entities such as countries. To simulate the problem of adding of a new entity class to a previously annotated corpus, we removed the person descriptions from the corpus and then attempted to tag them with our system. Since the correct annotation was available, the performance of the system was easily evaluated.

Proceedings of HLT 2002, Second International Conference on Human Language Technology Research, M. Marcus, ed., Morgan Kaufmann, San Francisco, 2002.

4. PATTERN REPRESENTATION

Candidate instances to be tagged include all the noun phrases in the corpus. Each NP is represented as a vector of features, including:

- Parent category and parent headword
- The NP's headword and its tag
- Premodifiers of the core NP
- The word that follows the core NP within the full NP
    - when the word is a preposition, we append to it the category of its object (e.g. *among.NP* or *of.ORG*).

For example, in the sentence "Some analysts expressed caution", the noun phrase "Some analysts" would be represented as the following feature vector:

Parent-category = S
Parent-headword = expressed
Headtag = NNS
Headword = analysts
Premodifiers = Some
Following-word = NULL

or just `(S expressed NNS analysts Some NULL)`.

In general, a pattern has the same format as a feature vector. Pattern feature values can either be specified or wild-card. For example, the pattern

```
(* expressed * * * *)
```

would cover all noun phrases whose parent headword is "expressed".

The SIFT parser [4] was used to determine the syntactic structure used for the context vectors.

5. ALGORITHM

5.1 Pattern Generation

At each stage, the machine tags a set of elements in the corpus that are likely to be correct. For the first iteration, we begin with a set of seed patterns that are generated manually. In the case of our test problem, the seed patterns each specified just a single headword. Four common headwords of person descriptions were used: *president, officials, person, and people.* Fully written out, the seed patterns looked like:

```
(* * * president * *)
(* * * officials * *)
(* * * person * *)
(* * * people * *)
```

On the first iteration, the seed patterns are applied to the entire corpus to yield the set of tagged elements. For other iterations, the set of tagged elements is generated both by a set of patterns currently trusted by the machine, along with any truth values previously manually assigned to specific instances during human review.

The context vectors of these tagged elements are then combined to generate new possible patterns. Combinations are simple—if feature values match, keep that feature value in the combined pattern; if feature values do not match, the combined pattern has a wildcard for that feature.

5.2 Selecting Patterns for Human Review

We wish to present and test patterns where the probability of the class, P(class | pattern), is high. By Bayes rule,

$$P(\text{class} \mid \text{pattern}) = P(\text{class})\, P(\text{pattern} \mid \text{class}) / P(\text{pattern})$$

Since the prior probability of the class is constant, we seek patterns with high values for:

$$P(\text{pattern} \mid \text{class}) / P(\text{pattern})$$

In other words, we seek patterns that cover a disproportionately high number of the previously tagged examples, compared with the pattern's occurrence in general.

We sort patterns by this metric, excluding those for which a certain percentage of previously hand-reviewed examples (if any) have already been judged to be wrong. To maximize the efficiency of human review, we also exclude patterns that cover less than a certain minimum number of examples. We also eliminate patterns that are subsumed by patterns we have already judged to have extremely high precision (they gain us nothing) and patterns that are subsumed by patterns that we have already selected for this iteration. We also obviously eliminate patterns that have been previously evaluated. From the remaining patterns, we then select the top N.

5.3 Human Review

We present 5 random instances of each selected pattern for human review. These examples are shown in sentence context to the user, who makes a binary correct/incorrect decision for each NP displayed.

Only one example of any particular context feature vector is ever displayed to the user. Contexts that are already covered by rules judged to have extremely high precision are not displayed as examples for other rules. These guidelines minimize the number of examples seen by the user that do not generate any new information.

5.4 Pattern Evaluation

Based on human correctness judgments from this iteration and all previous iterations, we then classify the selected patterns into four categories:

1) Very good: at least 95% correct and ≥ 20 instances marked as correct by user

   Trust the pattern absolutely. Never show another example covered by this pattern and never test a pattern subsumed by this pattern.

   Example: `(* * * * * who)`
   - "an executive who disagrees"
   - "the fans who rioted"

2) Provisionally good: at least 85% correct

   Trust the pattern for now, but reevaluate if other overlapping patterns provide more information.

   Example: `(S said * * * *)`
   - "reporters said…"
   - "Italian officials said…"
   - "the news agency said…" (incorrect)

   After gathering further information, we might reevaluate this pattern and determine that it covers too many incorrect examples to be reliable. Meanwhile, however, temporarily trusting the pattern (and thus temporarily tagging all noun phrases whose parent headword is "said") allows us to generate and test the rules:

   `(S said NNS * * *)` – "analysts said"
   `(S said NN * * a)` – "a spokeswoman said"
   `(S said NN * * an)` – "an executive said"

   These refinements of the first rule are more reliable than the first, and, in fact, between them cover the majority of the correct instances covered by the original rule. Thus, when the first rule is discarded, we lose only those instances not covered by these new rules, many of which were indeed incorrect.

3) Marginal: between 50% to 85% correct

   Optionally allow user to hand-mark all examples covered by the pattern. This is only performed late in the process (see below).

4) Bad: less than 50% correct

   These patterns are never considered again.

Very good patterns and provisionally good patterns thus make up the set of patterns used to tag the corpus in the next iteration. This entire process of rule generation, pattern selection, human review, and pattern evaluation is repeated either until manually stopped or until no useful patterns can be generalized from the current information.

6. MARGINAL PATTERN EVALUATION

While not good enough to be trusted, marginal patterns still contain useful information. For example, the pattern

```
(* * * * former *)
```

covers such examples as:

- "the former attorney"
- "a former defense correspondent"
- "the former Soviet republic"
- "his former village"

Although marginal patterns cover too many incorrect instances to allow them to be trusted, they still cover a much higher percentage of correct instances than a random pattern would, and thus we can still gain on manual annotation by hand-marking all examples covered by such patterns.

To determine which such marginal patterns should be hand-marked, we do *not* use information previously gathered about examples covered by the pattern, because it is almost definitely skewed (if the program is working correctly, we will have shown the user more correct examples than incorrect). We instead attempt to roughly determine the percentage of currently unknown contexts that would be correctly covered by this pattern. We do this by showing the user a small number of examples covered by a marginal pattern. Based on the number of such examples which are marked correct by the user, we decide whether to show all contexts covered by this pattern.

7. RESULTS

We evaluated the system's performance on a random subset of the data. The test run of this program found 90.3% of the actual person descriptions. Of these, 82% were exactly correct, while 8.3% were found with incorrect boundaries, usually as a result of a bad parse or because of confusion over lists and conjunctions. Precision was 95%.

Table 1 summarizes progress at various stages of the experiment. The four seed patterns provided 1658 initial instances of person descriptions—all noun phrases headed by *president*, *officials*, *person*, or *people*. In total, 6110 examples were hand-corrected in order to generate 11579 person descriptions. Of these 11579 instances, 7914 were tagged automatically without being seen by the user.

Using an annotation tool designed to facilitate the rapid acceptance or rejection of instances, a human annotator required less than 200 minutes to correct the 6110 examples presented by the system. Even with the overhead of computational delays between iterations, the entire corpus was annotated in about a day. This rate is about 20 times faster than we have previously experienced using strictly manual annotation.

8. CONCLUSIONS

We have described a collaborative human-machine procedure for rapidly annotating references to entities in a large corpus. Experimental results were presented for annotating person descriptions in a 500,000-word corpus. Recall of the procedure was approximately 90%; precision was 95%. The collaborative procedure permitted the annotation to be performed approximately 20 times faster than manual annotation alone.

9. REFERENCES

[1] A. Blum and T. Mitchell. 1998. Combining Labeled and Unlabeled Data with Co-Training. In *Proceedings of the 11th Annual Conference on Computational Learning Theory.*

[2] D. Cohn, L. Atlas, and R. Ladner. 1994. Improving Generalization with Active Learning. In *Machine Learning*, 15(2):201-221.

[3] M. Collins and Y. Singer. 1999. Unsupervised Models for Named Entity Classification. In *Proceedings of the Joint SIGDAT Conference on Empirical Methods in Natural Language Processing and Very Large Corpora.*

[4] S. Miller, H. Fox, L. Ramshaw, and R. Weischedel. 2000. A Novel Use of Statistical Parsing to Extract Information from Text. In *Proceedings of the North American Association for Computational Linguistics.*

Table 1. Progress of the algorithm over 91 iterations

Number of iterations	0	10	30	50	70	91
Marked right by human (cumulative)	0	57	1483	2385	3315	3665
Marked wrong by human (cumulative)	0	7	512	987	1594	2445
Total marked by human (cumulative)	0	64	1995	3372	4909	6110
Number of descriptions found (cumulative)	1658	1988	6699	9196	11184	11579
Marked right by human (Δ)	0	57	1426	902	930	350
Marked wrong by human (Δ)	0	7	505	475	607	851
Total marked by human (Δ)	0	64	1931	1377	1537	1201
Number of descriptions found (Δ)	1658	330	4711	2497	1988	395

Dynamic Stopwording for Story Link Detection

Ralf D. Brown
Language Technologies Institute
Carnegie Mellon University
5000 Forbes Avenue
Pittsburgh, PA 15213-3890 USA
ralf@cs.cmu.edu

ABSTRACT

Carnegie Mellon University entered two systems in the Story Link Detection track of the 2001 Topic Detection and Tracking (TDT) evaluation. These systems were one of our systems from the 1999 TDT evaluation [1], retuned for the new corpus, which had the third-best cost measure; and a new system that adds clustering and dynamically-generated stopwording, which had the best cost measure among all submissions for the default evaluation condition. This paper describes the enhancements which were made and some which were attempted but not used in the evaluation.

1. INTRODUCTION

With the ever-growing flood of information competing for a fixed amount of human attention, there is great interest in developing systems which can provide just the information a user is interested in from a real-time stream of data. The Topic Detection and Tracking project has been investigating various approaches to finding news stories which report on breaking events (topic detection, first-story detection) and those with continued coverage of events which the user has indicated are of interest (topic tracking). In 1999, an additional task was added to focus attention on the underlying primitive operation in all of the above – determining whether two news stories discuss the same thing (story link detection). Link detection is considered to be a primitive operation because if one can reliably determine linkages among stories, one can generate detection and tracking systems by checking whether incoming stories are linked to any previous stories. A story which has no links with any previous stories must be the first story about a new event, while a story which is linked to any of the stories which have already been tracked for an event should be tracked as well.

For the 2001 TDT evaluation, Carnegie Mellon University (CMU) entered two link-detection systems. One was a system from the 1999 TDT evaluation [1], retuned for the new corpus, and a new system that adds clustering and dynamically-generated per-cluster stopwording to the 1999 system. The motivation for the additions is that different events within a single class (such as different bombings or different airplane crashes) will use many of the same terms ("explosion", "crash"). If we can first determine a broad type of event for each story and then ignore the terms which stories in that class have in common, we should be better able to discriminate among similar events.

Proceedings of HLT 2002, Second International Conference on Human Language Technology Research, M. Marcus, ed., Morgan Kaufmann, San Francisco, 2002.

2. SYSTEM DESCRIPTION

The older system uses cosine similarity (after stopword removal) between TF*IDF-weighted term vectors to decide whether two news stories discuss the same subject. In addition to the actual words occurring in the story, terms are added to the vectors for words appearing within the first N words of each story to provide additional weight to the beginning of the story. The TF*IDF weights are updated each time a new source file (containing all stories from a news broadcast or half-hour sample of newswire) is added to the portion of the corpus which the link detector is permitted to examine. A dual threshold is used to determine whether the computed cosine similarity indicates a linkage between the two stories; one threshold is used when the two documents originate from the same type of source, and the other (typically lower) threshold is used for documents from different sources. For the 2001 evaluation, all Mandarin-language sources were grouped together, as were all English-language sources (i.e. a news story from Mandarin-language Voice of America would be treated as coming from the same source as a news story from Xinhua newswire).

The new system also uses cosine similarity, incrementally-updated TF*IDF weights, a global stopword list, and a dual threshold, but additionally performs clustering and cluster-specific stopwording. A single-pass incremental clustering method with configurable cluster-similarity metrics is used; for the TDT evaluation, the similarity metric selected was the root-mean-square of the cosine similarities between the new document and the members of each existing cluster. The resultant clusters have two uses in the link-detection system: selecting stopwords and applying a penalty when the two documents under test are in different clusters.

To select dynamic stopwords, the term frequencies for each individual cluster are computed. The N highest-frequency terms for each cluster which appear in no other cluster are made stopwords for that cluster. Since these terms appear only in the one cluster, they may actively harm recognition of a link to stories about the same event which happen to fall into a different cluster. And because they are common within the cluster, they reduce the differences between sto-

System YES/NO decisions

System	Miss	F.Alarm	Norm.Cost
1999	0.2381	0.0106	0.2899
2001	0.1778	0.0131	0.2421
change	-25.3%	+23.6%	-16.5%

Optimum According to DET Graph

System	Miss	F.Alarm	Norm.Cost
1999	0.1793	0.0175	0.2653
2001	0.1586	0.0159	0.2368
change	-11.5%	-9.1%	-10.7%

Table 1: System Performance Metrics

ries which are *not* linked.

Each test document then has the weights of the stopwords for the cluster containing it set to zero in its term vector prior to computing the cosine similarity, effectively removing the stopwords without actually altering the document stored in memory. After computing the similarity measure, a penalty is applied if the two test documents belong to different clusters.

Before using the highest-frequency cluster-unique terms, we implemented stopword selection by selecting for each cluster the terms with the highest information gain relative to that cluster. Unfortunately, this proved to be computationally intractable – even after several optimizations, a complete run would have taken an estimated 600 hours of CPU time, or very nearly the entire evaluation period.

A further enhancement which was disabled for the evaluation was a finite-state document rewriting engine for normalizing relative time expressions ("yesterday", "Tuesday", "last week", etc.). The normalization was expected to allow the system to better distinguish between different events using similar vocabulary, but proved to slightly worsen performance as measured by the TDT cost metric. There may simply not have been enough rewriting rules, as the existing rules are known not to handle all relative time expressions.

Based on experimental tuning, the parameters used for the evaluation were:

- prefer the first 100 words of the story
- 80 clusters
- 40 stopwords per cluster
- different-cluster penalty of 0.062

3. PERFORMANCE

The performance of the two systems in terms of missed links, false alarms, and the TDT cost metric is summarized in Table 1. This table shows both the cost computed from the systems actual YES/NO decisions and the cost computed using the threshold that minimized the cost while generating the DET curve.

Figure 1 shows the Decision-Error Tradeoff (DET) curve for the system with dynamic stopwording, while Figure 2 shows the performance without. Figure 3 compares the performances of all submitted systems for the default evaluation condition[1]. A DET curve is generated by applying a continuously-variable threshold to the scores output by the system, arbitrarily setting the decision to YES for all scores above the threshold and to NO for scores below the threshold, and computing miss and false alarm rates for each value of the threshold. The minimum TDT cost metric over all thresholds is also computed, and is displayed in the figures as the minimum DET cost (*Min DET* or *MDC*). This minimum cost is usually lower than the cost metric for the system's actual decisions and represents the best the system could perform under the assumption that its hard YES/NO decisions are made by thresholding on the reported score for the story pair. (If the system makes its YES/NO decisions from information other than the confidence score, the point representing the system's actual miss/false-alarm performance will lie off the DET curve.)

The discontinuity or "knee" in Figure 1 is the result of the binary nature of the different-cluster penalty. Since some linked stories end up in different clusters, the penalty is applied to these cases and thus the sliding threshold used to generate a DET curve does not reach those pairs until after a large number of non-linked stories have scores above the threshold. This raises a portion of the DET curve. It is clear that the penalty used in the evaluation was too large; brief experiments performed since the evaluation indicate that reducing the penalty from 0.062 to 0.03 will slightly lower the overall cost metric.

Although the dynamic stopwording improved the TDT cost metric from 0.2899 to 0.2421 (a 16.5% reduction), that improvement came at a huge cost in runtime – the time to process the evaluation test set increased from 36 minutes to 23 hours, a factor of 40. On the other hand, the more sophisticated system also may have more stable performance with varying data, as the minimum cost found by varying the threshold to generate the DET curve was 0.2368 (-2.2% compared to the system's hard YES/NO decisions) with dynamic stopwords and 0.2653 (-8.5%) without. Thus, if one could tune on the evaluation data to use the optimum parameters for the test data rather than the optimum parameters for the training data, the gap between the two systems would be smaller (only a 10.7% reduction).

4. FUTURE WORK

As of this writing, we are in the process of tuning a new system which uses cluster-specific term weighting rather than cluster-specific stop words. The idea is to adjust the impact of all terms rather than just zeroing out a limited number of terms. As yet, per-cluster TF*IDF weighting has not yet been able to match the performance achieved by the submitted system.

Because a section of the DET curve for simple cosine similarity without dynamic stopwords lies well below the curve for dynamic stopwording, it should be possible to combine the two systems, selecting the decision from one or the other depending on the range of scores. Previous work in combining multiple engines [2] has shown that such a combination yields a system with more stable performance on varying test data and sometimes even improves overall performance on the development data.

[1]All figures and performance measures are available at `ftp://jaguar.ncsl.nist.gov/tdt/tdt2001/eval/tdt2001_official_results_20011029/index.htm`

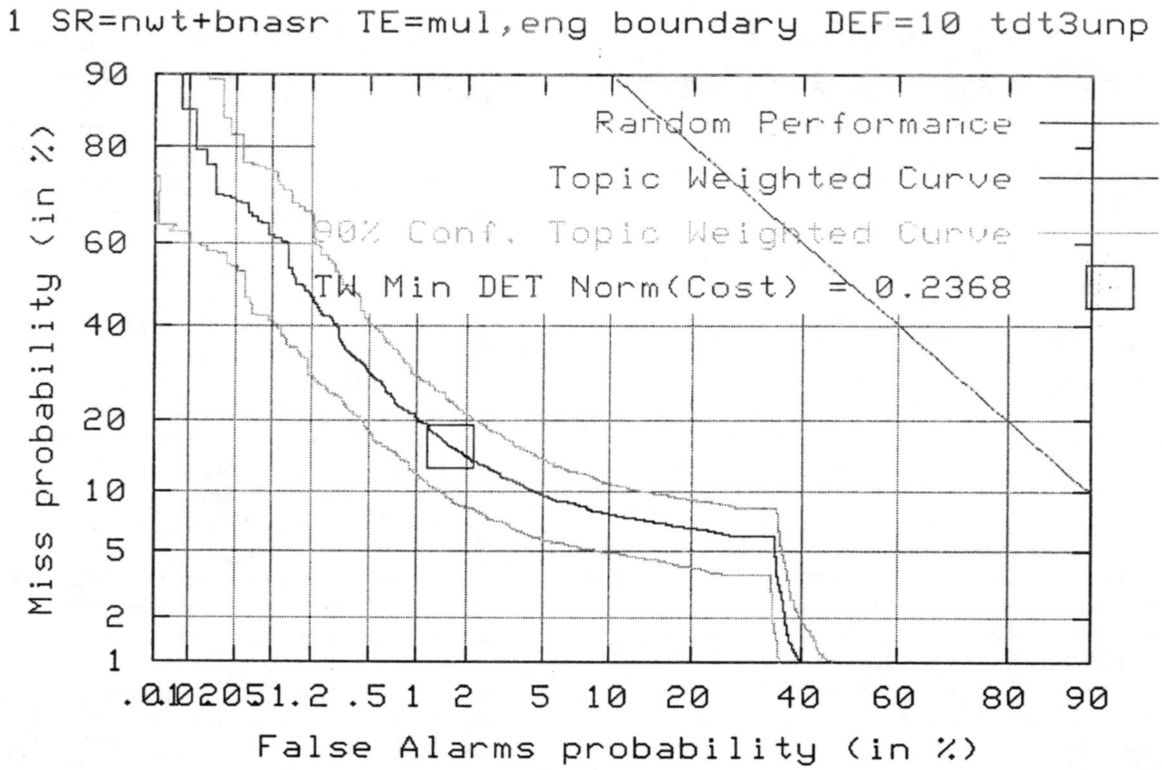

Figure 1: Performance with Dynamic Stopwording

5. REFERENCES

[1] R. D. Brown, T. Pierce, Y. Yang, and J. G. Carbonell. Link Detection – Results and Analysis, 2000. `http://www.nist.gov/speech/tests/tdt/tdt99/-papers/cmu_sld/`.

[2] Y. Yang, T. Ault, T. Pierce, and C. W. Lattimer. Improving Text Categorization Methods for Event Tracking. In *Proceedings of ACM SIGIR Conference on Research and Development in Information Retrieval*, 2000.

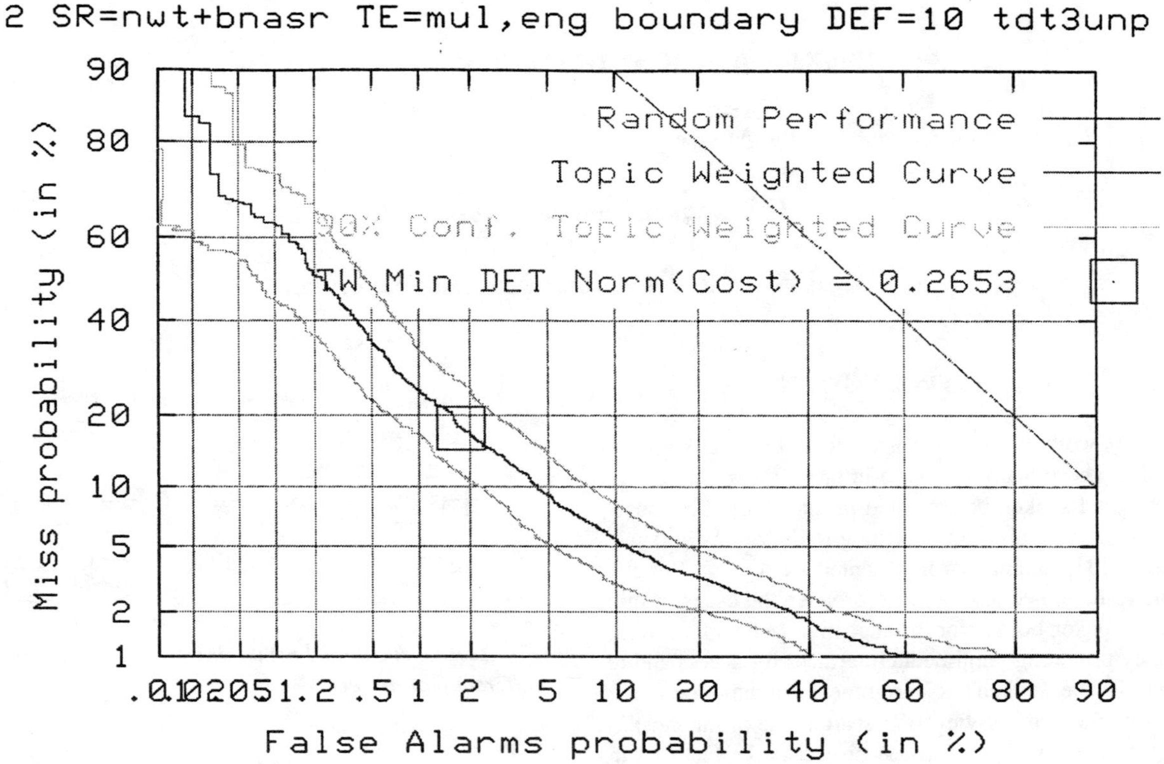

Figure 2: Performance without Dynamic Stopwording

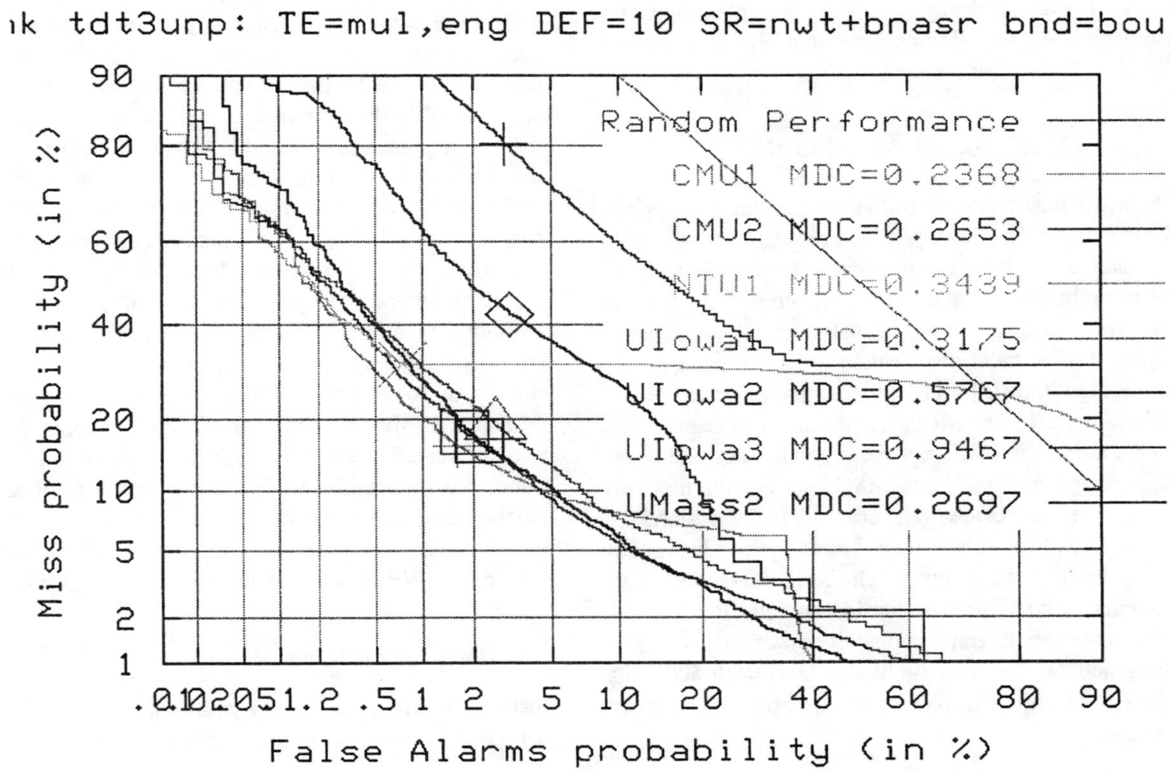

Figure 3: Cross-System Performance Comparison

SPOKEN BOOK ALIGNMENT USING WFSTS

Diamantino Caseiro, Hugo Meinedo, António Serralheiro, Isabel Trancoso, João Neto

L^2F Spoken Language Systems Lab.
INESC-ID/IST
Rua Alves Redol 9, 1000-029 Lisbon, Portugal

1. INTRODUCTION

The framework of this paper is a national project known as IPSOM, whose main goal is to improve the access to digitally stored spoken books, used primarily by the visually impaired community, by providing tools for easily detecting and indexing units (words, sentences, topics). Simultaneously, the project also aims to broaden the usage of multimedia spoken books (for instance in didactic applications, etc.), by providing multimedia interfaces for access and retrieval. Hence, spoken book alignment is a major task.

From the point of view of research, one of the most interesting aspects of the IPSOM project is the fact that indexed spoken books provide an invaluable resource for data-driven prosodic modelling and unit selection in the context of text-to-speech synthesis. This motivated doing the alignment not only on the basis of words, but rather sub-word units and also automatically generating multiple pronunciations by applying phonological rules in a WFST (Weighted Finite State Transducer) framework.

2. ACOUSTIC MODELLING

The hybrid acoustic model used in the alignment of spoken books was originally developed for a dictation task [1]. The model uses a topology where context-independent phone posterior probabilities are estimated by three MLPs (Multi-Layer Perceptrons) given the acoustic data at each frame. The streams of probabilities are then combined using an appropriate algorithm [2]. The processing stages are represented in Figure 1. The MLPs use the same basic structure and are trained with different feature extraction methods: PLP [3], Log-RASTA [3] and MSG [4]. For the first two processes, the features are log-energy and PLP/Log-RASTA 12th order coefficients and their first temporal derivatives summing up to 26 parameters. The MSG method uses 28 coefficients. Each MLP classifier incorporates local acoustic context via a multi-frame input window of 7 frames. The resulting network has a single hidden layer with 500 units and 39 output units (38 phones for European Portuguese plus silence).

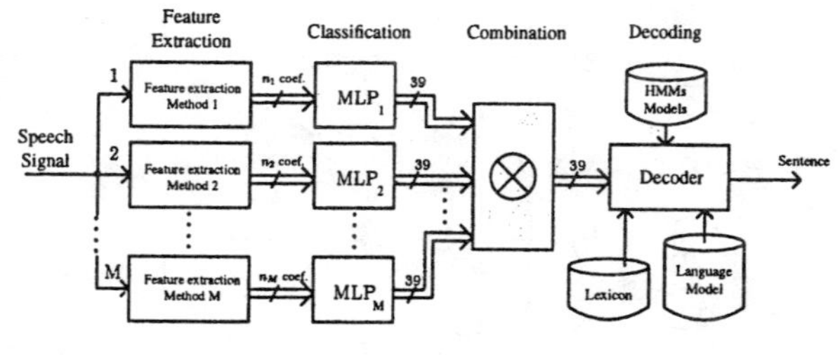

Fig. 1. *Acoustic model combining several MLPs trained on different feature sets.*

3. ALIGNMENT

An aligner is just a decoder, that keeps track of the time boundaries between words or phones. Our decoder is based on WFSTs [5] in the sense that its search space is defined by a distribution-to-word transducer that is built outside the decoder. That search space is usually constructed as $H \circ L \circ G$, where H is the HMM or phone topology, L is the lexicon and G is the language model. For alignment, G is just the sequence of words that constitute the orthographic transcription of the utterance. The main advantage is that no restrictions are placed on the construction of the search space, which means that it can easily integrate other sources of knowledge, and the network can be optimised and replaced by an optimal equivalent one. This last advantage is a disadvantage from the perspective of alignment, as there are no warranties that the output and input labels are synchronised. To solve this problem, the decoder was extended to deal with special labels, on the input side, that are internally treated as epsilon labels, but are used to mark time transitions or boundaries. Whenever such end-of-segment labels are crossed, the time is stored in the current hypothesis. The user may choose to place those labels at the end of each phone WFST or at the end of each word WFST.

3.1. Phonological Rules

Instead of building a lexicon with multiple pronunciations per word, our goal is to develop phonological rules that can

```
$Vocalic = $Vowel | $NasalVowel | $Glide | $NasalGlide;
DEF_RULE SANDHI_ch_z, ( $Vocalic (ch -> z) WORD_BREAK  $Vocalic)
```

Fig. 2. Example of a rule specified using the *rule specification language*.

be used with a lexicon of canonical forms, in order to account for alternative pronunciations. These rules are specified using a finite-state grammar whose syntax is similar to the Backus-Naur-form augmented with regular expressions. Each rule is represented by a regular expression, and to the usual set of operators we added the operator $\rightarrow$, simple transduction, such that $(a \rightarrow b)$ means that the terminal symbol a is transformed into the terminal symbol b. The language allows the definition of non-terminal symbols (e.g. *$vowel*). All rules are optional, and are compiled into WFSTs.

Figure 2 presents an example of the specification of a rule; that specification is first transformed into a transducer T, and then compiled into $R_T = \Sigma^*(T\Sigma^*)^{*1}$. That transducer, when composed with the canonical phone transducer S will produce $S_T = \pi_2(S \circ R_T)$ that allows new pronunciation alternatives.

We do not apply the rules one by one on a cascade of compositions, but rather build their union $R = R_{T_1} \cup R_{T_2} \cup \cdots \cup R_{T_n}$. R is applied 3 times ($S_R = \pi_2(R \circ (R \circ (R \circ S)))$), to allow the application of one rule to the results of another. By performing the union of the rules we avoid the exaggerated growth of the resulting transducer, which can be exponential with the length of the composition cascade.

The main phonological aspects that the rules are intended to cover are vowel reduction and word coarticulation phenomena. Vowel reduction is specially important for European Portuguese, being one of the features that distinguishes it from Brazilian Portuguese and that makes it more difficult to learn for a foreign speaker. In our experiments, we used 37 such rules.

4. EXPERIMENTAL RESULTS

A small pilot corpus (*O Senhor Ventura*, by Miguel Torga) was chosen as a test bed for spoken book alignment. The high-quality DAT recordings were manually edited to remove reading errors and extraneous noises, amounting to a total of 2h15m (around 138k words, corresponding to 5k different forms). Although very intelligible, as expected from a professional speaker, the speaking rate was relatively high - 174 words per minute.

This spoken book allows us to do alignment tests at a word level, but not at a phone level, as required for TTS research. In order to evaluate the quality of the phone level transcriptions obtained using the pronunciation rules, we used a fragment of the EUROM.1 corpus [6], for which we have manual alignment.

[1] Σ is the identity transducer, that converts each input symbol into itself.

4.1. Alignment experiments with spoken books

A major advantage of our approach is that it allowed us to align the full audio version of the book in a single step. This is specially important if we take into account that the memory limitations of our previous alignment tool imposed a maximum of 3-minute audio segments. We thus avoid the tedious task of manually breaking-up the audio into smaller segments with their associated text.

The word segmentation of the book took 197.5 seconds in a 600MHz Pentium III computer (0.024 xRT), and required 200MB of RAM. The phone level alignment of the book ran at 0.027 xRT when using the canonical pronunciations of the lexicon, and 0.03 xRT when using also the pronunciation rules.

4.2. Recognition experiments with spoken books

The edition of recordings to remove reading errors and extraneous noises produced by the speaker is a very labour intensive task. As a first step to automate this procedure, we tried to match text recognized using a dedicated recogniser with the original text in order to detect incorrect audio portions. The dedicated recogniser uses a lexicon and an n-gram language model estimated from all the book's text and achieved a word error rate (WER) of 17.2%.

Significant improvements were obtained by using the automatic alignment labels for speaker adaptation of the acoustic model, using only 80% of the available audio. The adapted model created using the alignment made with the canonical pronunciation lexicon achieved 7.8%, and the one using the phonological rules obtained 7.1%.

4.3. Phone-level alignment evaluation

Our experiments with the EUROM.1 corpus showed us that the phone-level alignment using the phonological rules is closer to the manual transcriptions than the canonical one (95.62% vs. 93.65% phone correction, respectively). The same conclusion was drawn when we analysed the time deviation of the alignments: 38.6% (vs. 37.4%) of the deviations are less than 10ms and the maximum deviation obtained for 90% of the segments was 44ms (vs. 52ms).

We also compared the WFSTs generated by the rules with the manual transcriptions, in order to obtain the oracle performance of the rules (i.e. the performance of a perfect decoder, using all the possible paths in the phone lattices allowed by the rules): 97.73% correctness and 82.11% accuracy. Most of the errors are due to deletions observed in what the speakers said, that are neither allowed by the canonical lexicon nor by the rules.

5. CONCLUSIONS

The paper described our efforts towards aligning spoken books. We verified that the alignment task can be fully automated in a very fast single-step procedure, even for a 2-hour long recording. The use of phonological rules seems to provide reasonably good alternative pronunciations. However, a more exhaustive comparison with manual labelling still needs to be conducted in order to improve these rules.

6. REFERENCES

[1] Neto, J., Martins, C. and Almeida, L., *A Large Vocabulary Continuous Speech Recognition Hybrid System for the Portuguese Language*, in Proc. ICSLP 98, Sydney, Australia, 1998.

[2] H. Meinedo and J. Neto, "Combination of acoustic models in continuous speech recognition hybrid systems", In Proc. ICSLP 2000, Beijing, China, 2000.

[3] H. Hermansky, N. Morgan, A. Baya and P. Kohn, "RASTA-PLP Speech Analysis Technique", In Proc. ICASSP 92, San Francisco, USA, 1992.

[4] B. E. Kingsbury, N. Morgan, and S. Greenberg, "Robust speech recognition using the modulation spectrogram", Speech Communication, 25:117–132, 1998.

[5] M. Mohri, M. Riley, D. Hindle, A. Ljolje, F. Pereira, "Full Expansion of Context-Dependent Networks in Large Vocabulary Speech Recognition", In Proc. ICASSP 98, Seattle, Washington, 1998.

[6] C. Ribeiro, I. Trancoso and M. Viana, *EUROM.1 Portuguese Database*, Report of ESPRIT Project 6819 SAM-A, 1993.

Interdependencies among Dialog Acts, Task Goals and Discourse Inheritance in Mixed-Initiative Dialogs

Shuk Fong Chan
Human-Computer Communications Laboratory
The Chinese University of Hong Kong
chansf@se.cuhk.edu.hk

Helen M. Meng
Human-Computer Communications Laboratory
The Chinese University of Hong Kong
hmmeng@se.cuhk.edu.hk

ABSTRACT

This paper describes a study of the interdependencies among dialog acts, task goals and discourse inheritance in mixed-initiative dialogs in the restaurants domain. Our study is based on 199 dialogs, with disjoint training (169 dialogs) and test sets (30 dialogs). The training set is annotated manually in terms of task goals and dialog acts and tagged automatically in terms of semantic and syntactic categories for each request (from the customer) and response (from the waiter). Based on observations from the process of annotation, we have written a set of category inheritance and refresh rules, which constitute our *selective* inheritance strategy. We compared the selective strategy with two control strategies – (i) no categories are inherited; and (ii) all categories are inherited throughout the dialog session. Comparison is based on the automatic identification of task goals and dialog acts. The selective inheritance strategy outperformed the two control strategies and identified the correct task goals for 92.6% of the dialog turns and the correct dialog acts for 97.8% of the utterances in the test set. We have also developed a discourse inheritance procedure which correctly handled 95.9% of the dialog turns in the test set.

1. INTRODUCTION

Continual advancements in multilingual speech and language technologies have brought the emergence of a diversity of spoken dialog systems (SDS). These systems typically support goal-oriented human-computer conversations regarding restricted application domains, e.g. real-time stock quotations, travel planning, etc. The *dialog model* in a SDS is the most critical component for the system's usability. It determines what the user is able to request from the system, in which way and at what time during the dialog session. The *mixed-initiative* dialog model allows the dialog's initiative to shift strategically in between system and user with the aim to converge on a solution for the task at hand. Hence the mixed-initiative model has good potential in achieving high task completion rates as well as user satisfaction. While it is possible to *handcraft* a sophisticated mixed-initiative dialog flow, the task is expensive, and may become intractable for complex application domains. Consequently, significant efforts have recently been devoted towards understanding mixed-initiative structures in human-human dialogs and human-computer dialogs [1-3]. Such knowledge may be incorporated in the design of mixed-initiative dialog strategies, and to help reduce handcrafting in spoken dialog systems development [4].

Proceedings of HLT 2002, Second International Conference on Human Language Technology Research, M. Marcus, ed., Morgan Kaufmann, San Francisco, 2002.

In this work, we study the interdependencies among dialog acts, task goals and discourse inheritance for mixed-initiative dialogs in the restaurants domain. Typically, the user presents various requests to the system that tries to fulfill them. The interaction shares many commonalities with human-human mixed-initiative dialogs involving requests from the customer and responses from the service provider / agent. In the framework of our study, communication for every request or response is characterized by its categories, dialog act(s) and task goal(s). As the dialog progresses from one turn to the next, selected categories need to be inherited in the discourse and inheritance may be dependent on the task goal or dialog act. The inherited categories augment those in the current (context-dependent) request to help determine its task goal and dialog act. The categories, task goal(s) and dialog act(s) from the request should be useful for the automatic generation of a coherent response. Understanding the interdependencies among dialog acts, task goals and discourse inheritance should enable us to design a mixed-initiative dialog model in a more principled way. Furthermore, orthogonal considerations in our framework for the *domain-dependent* task goals and *domain-independent* dialog acts facilitate separation between the *generic* and *task-specific* components in the dialog model.

2. THE CU RESTAURANTS DOMAIN

Our study is based on 199 dialogs in the restaurants domain (CU Restaurants), collected from websites and books for English learning [5-8]. The dialogs capture interactions between the customer and waiter in a restaurant, and consist of 1109 customer requests and 1320 waiter responses in total.

Table 1. An example dialog in the restaurants domain.

$Customer_1$	Can I have the menu, please?
$Waiter_1$	Yes, sir. Here. Have you decided on something, sir?
$Customer_2$	What is today's special?
$Waiter_2$	Abalone soup and stuffed tofu with rice.
$Customer_3$	I think it would be better to have seafood for a change. I'd like an abalone soup and a grilled fish.
$Waiter_3$	Anything else, sir?
$Customer_4$	No, thanks.
$Waiter_4$	You're welcome.

We divide the corpus into disjoint training (169 dialogs, with 893 customer requests and 1054 waiter responses) and test (30 dialogs, with 216 customer request and 266 waiter responses) sets. The average number of waiter and customer dialog turn pair is 5. Table 1 shows an example dialog from the corpus. The subscripts denote the counter for the dialog turns.

3. TASK GOALS, DIALOG ACTS, CATEGORIES AND ANNOTATION

3.1. Task Goals and Dialog Acts

The task goal (TG) shows the domain specific goal of the user's request. There are 6 task goals in the CU Restaurants domain – ASK_INFO, BILL, COMPLAINT, ORDER, RESERVATION and SERVING.

The dialog act (DA) expresses the primary communicative intention of the customer's request. We have studied a number of annotation schemes proposed for tagging dialog acts, including VERBMOBIL [11,12], VERBMOBIL-2 [9], the summer Johns Hopkins LVSCR Workshop-97 summer project (WS97 project) [12-15], DATE [2-3,16], and MITRE [1,17]. We decided to reference the VERBMOBIL-2 scheme due to the availability of detailed guidelines for tagging and their applicability to our domain. We have adopted 14 dialog acts from VERBMOBIL-2, including BACKCHANNEL, BYE, DEFER, NEGATIVE_FEEDBACK, POSITIVE_FEEDBACK, GREET, INFORM, PREFER, REQUEST_ACTION, REQUEST_INFO, REQUEST_COMMENT, REQUEST_SUGGEST, SUGGEST and THANK.

3.2. Semantic and Syntactic Categories

We have hand-defined 118 semantic and 3 syntactic categories for punctuations,[1] to be extracted from the input customer requests. Examples are shown in Table 2. Within this set of categories, 88 are used for inferring the task goal of the customer's request, and 33 are used for inferring the dialog act.

Table 2. Examples of Semantic and Syntactic Categories.

	Category		Terminals
Semantic	COOKING_STYLE	→	stir fried | marinated | steamed | baked | ...
Semantic	COMPLAIN	→	complain | complained | complaint|
Semantic	THANK	→	thanks | thank you | thank you very much | ...
Syntactic	QUEST_MARK	→	?
Syntactic	EXCLAM_MARK	→	!
Syntactic	PERIOD	→	.

As mentioned earlier, each customer request in our training set is annotated with task goals and dialog acts. We also extracted semantic / syntactic categories from the training query automatically according to rules such as those shown in Table 2.

[1] One may not be able to use punctuations directly if the input request is spoken, but it may be possible to detect similar information from the prosody of the utterance.

The training queries are used to train Belief Networks for automatic identification of the task goals or dialog acts based on the input semantic and syntactic categories.

3.3. Annotating the Training Sentences

Based on the definition in VERBMOBIL-2 [9], an *utterance* is an individual unit that corresponds to a dialog act and a task goal. We segmented the dialog example from Table 1 into utterances, as shown in Table 3.

Table 3. The same example dialog shown in Table 1 after utterance segmentation.

Customer$_1$	Can I have the menu, please?
Waiter$_1$	Yes, sir.
Waiter$_1$	Here.
Waiter$_1$	Have you decided on something, sir?
Customer$_2$	What is today's special?
Waiter$_2$	Abalone soup and stuffed tofu with rice.
Customer$_3$	I think it would be better to have seafood for a change.
Customer$_3$	I'd like an abalone soup and a grilled fish.
Waiter$_3$	Anything else, sir?
Customer$_4$	No,
Customer$_4$	Thanks.
Waiter$_4$	You're welcome.

Table 4. An example dialog segment from Table 1 and its task goals, dialog acts and category annotations.

Customer$_1$	What is today's special? **Categories:** {<WHAT = "what"> <TODAYSPECIAL = "today's special"> <QUEST_MARK = "?">} **Annotated Task Goal:** ORDER **Annotated Dialog Act:** REQUEST_INFO
Waiter$_1$	Abalone soup and stuffed tofu with rice. **Categories:** {<FOOD_DRINK = "abalone soup"> <FOOD_DRINK = "stuffed tofu with rice"> <PERIOD = ".">} **Annotated Task Goal:** ORDER **Annotated Dialog Act:** INFORM
Customer$_2$	I think it would be better to have seafood for a change. **Categories:** {<PREFERENCE_PHRASE = "I think"> <FOOD_DRINK = "seafood"> <CHANGE = "change"> <PERIOD = ".">} **Annotated Task Goal:** ORDER **Annotated Dialog Act:** NEGATIVE_FEEDBACK
Customer$_2$	I'd like an abalone soup and a grilled fish. **Categories:** {<PREFERNCE_PHRASE = "I'd like"> <FOOD_DRINK = "abalone soup"> <FOOD_DRINK = "grilled fish"> <PERIOD = ".">} **Annotated Task Goal:** ORDER **Annotated Dialog Act:** PREFER

For example, the waiter response *Waiter₁* {"Yes, sir. Here. Have you decided on something, sir?"} in Table 1 can be divided into three utterances in Table 3, including {"Yes, sir."}, {"Here."} and {"Have you decide on something, sir?"}.

In our annotation process, we labeled each utterance with a dialog act and a task goal respectively. In our training corpus, we found cases where a single dialog turn contains multiple utterances. While the task goals of the multiple utterances are always consistent, the dialog acts are not. Hence, each dialog turn is associated with a single task goal, but possibly multiple dialog acts to reflect the user's intention. Additionally, since the waiter always tries to serve the customer in a restaurant, we further assume that in a given dialog turn *t*, the task goal of the waiter's response is always identical to that of the customer request, i.e. $TG_{Waiter,\ t} = TG_{Customer,\ t}$. An example of an annotated customer-waiter interaction from our training set is shown in Table 4.

4. SELECTIVE INHERITANCE STRATEGY

While annotating our training set, we observed that:

(i) Given a *context-independent* (self-contained) customer request, the *task goal* can be identified from its semantic and syntactic categories. A *context-dependent* request does not have its full set of categories for determining the task goal. We observed that the task goal of the context-dependent query in our training set is always identical to that in the previous dialog turn.

(ii) The *dialog act* of a customer request can always be identified straight from its categories. We have not seen any context-dependent requests in terms of dialog acts. See Table 5 for an illustration.

(iii) Discourse inheritance in the CU Restaurants corpus involves inheriting appropriate categories from the previous dialog turn(s) to the current dialog turn. In particular, the dialogs in our corpus seem to indicate that it is sufficient to consider only the *previous* dialog turn and its inherited discourse. Furthermore, categories that need to be inherited largely dependent on the task goal. By considering the task goal of the current customer request, we can determine the appropriate categories to inherit.

Table 5. An example dialog showing that category inheritance is not required for dialog act identification.

Customer₁:	*"I'd like a seafood platter, please."* **Categories:** {<PREFERENCE_PHRASE = "I'd like">, <PLEASE = "please">, <PERIOD = ".">} **Dialog Act (DA):** INFORM (This query is self-contained and states the user's preference.)
Waiter₁:	*"Anything else, sir?"* **Categories:** {<QUEST_MARK = "?">} **DA:** REQUEST_INFO
Customer₂:	*"What would you recommend?"* **Categories:** {<WH_WORD = "What">, <SUGGEST = "recommend">, <QUEST_MARK = "?">} **DA:** REQUEST_SUGGEST (This query is self-contained and asks for suggestions.)

Based on these observations, we wrote five *selective* inheritance rules. Each rule corresponds to one of the task goals in the CU Restaurants domain, except for the goal of ASK_INFO, which requires no inheritance (see Table 6 for an example).

Table 6. An example dialog showing the queries with task goal ASK_INFO requires no category inheritance.

Customer₁:	*"What kind of food do you serve?"* **Categories:** {<WHAT = "what">, <FOOD = "food">, <SERVE = "serve">} **Task Goal (TG):** ASK_INFO
Waiter₁:	*"We serve a great variety of popular Japanese dishes in set courses and a la carte."* **Categories:** {<SERVE = "serve"> <RELATIVEAMOUNT = "variety">, <COUNTRY = "Japanese">, <DISH = "dishes">, <SETCOURSE = "set courses">, <FOODSTYLE = "a la carte">} **TG:** ASK_INFO
Customer₂:	*"When is the restaurant open for breakfast?"* **Categories:** {<WHEN = "when">, <RESTAURANT = "restaurant">, <OPEN = "open">, <MEALDESCRIPTION = "breakfast">} **TG:** ASK_INFO

The categories to be inherited selectively for each task goal are shown in Table 7. As an example, if the task goal of the customer request is BILL (i.e., an inquiry about billing), the categories <BILL>, <HOWMUCH> and <PRICEVALUE> should be inherited. This is illustrated in Table 8 with a dialog example, where categories takes on values from the latest dialog turn.

Table 7. Selective inheritance categories for each task goal.

Task Goal	Categories selected for inheritance
BILL	<BILL>, <HOWMUCH>,and <PRICEVALUE>
COMPLAINT	<COMPLAIN>, <COURSE>, <CRITICISM> and <MEALDESCRIPTION>
ORDER	<COURSE>, <MEALDESCRIPTION> and <FOOD_DRINK>
RESERVATION	<ARRANGE>, <LOCATION>, <MEALDESCRIPTION>, <NAME>, <NUMBER>, <NUMBERVALUE>, <PERSON>, <RELATIVEDATE>, <RELATIVETIME>, <RESERVE>, <SIZE>, <SMOKEOPTION>, <TABLE> and <TIME>
SERVING	<UTENSILS> and <FOOD_DRINK>

However, *over-inheritance* is found in some training dialog turns even when selective inheritance rules are applied. Over-inheritance occurs in the dialogs with confirmation (POSITIVE_FEEDBACK) or rejection (NEGATIVE_FEEDBACK). These occurrences show that although category inheritance is largely dependent on the task goal of the customer query, inheritance may also be influenced by the dialog act, i.e. both the task goal and dialog act together influence category inheritance. Table 9 shows an example dialog where over-inheritance of the category <FOOD_DRINK> occurred after the customer rejected (NEGATIVE_FEEDBACK) the waiter's suggestion.

Table 8. Categories <BILL>, <HOWMUCH> and <PRICEVALUE> are selectively inherited for queries with task goal BILL.

Customer_1:	*"Let me have the bill, please. How much is it?"* **Categories:** {<BILL = "bill">, <HOWMUCH = "how much">} **Task Goal:** BILL
Waiter_1:	*"Thank you, sir. One hundred fifty dollars, please."* **Categories:** {<PRICEVALUE = "one hundred fifty dollars">} **Task Goal:** BILL
Customer_2:	*"Here it is."* **Categories:** {<HERE = "here">, *<BILL = "bill">,* *<HOWMUCH = "how much">,* *<PRICEVALUE = "one hundred fifty dollars">*} **Task Goal:** BILL

Table 9. An example dialog showing over-inheritance.

Waiter_1:	*"Today we have fresh mushrooms too."* **Categories:** {<RELATIVEDATE = "today"> <FOOD_DRINK = "mushrooms>"} **Task Goal:** ORDER (from annotation) **Dialog Act:** SUGGEST (from annotation)
Customer_2:	*"I prefer something else."* **Categories:** {<PREFERENCE = "prefer">, <ELSE = "something else">, *<FOOD_DRINK = "mushrooms">* ***(Over-inheritance)***} **Task Goal Inferred:** ORDER **Dialog Act Inferred:** NEGATIVE_FEEDBACK

We have developed four refresh rules to undo over-inheritance. These rules incorporate the independencies among task goals, dialog acts, semantic and syntactic categories. Table 10 summarizes the four refresh rules. For example, the refresh rule of the task goal ORDER specifies that if the customer rejects the suggestion from the waiter, the category <FOOD_DRINK> should be disinherited, like the example dialog shown in Table 9.

Table 10. Four refresh rules that specify categories to disinherit given the task goals and dialog acts. (NEG_FEEDBACK abbreviates negative feedback).

$TG_{Customer,t}$	$DA_{Customer,t}$	$DA_{Waiter,t-1}$	Disinherited Categories
ORDER	NEG_FEEDBACK	SUGGEST	<FOOD_DRINK>
RESERVATION	NEG_FEEDBACK	SUGGEST	<LOCATION>
RESERVATION	NEG_FEEDBACK	SUGGEST	<SMOKEOPTION>
$TG_{Customer,t}$	$DA_{Customer,t-1}$	$DA_{Waiter,t}$	Disinherited Categories
BILL	REQUEST_INFO	NEG_FEEDBACK	<PRICE_VALUE>

5. TASK GOAL AND DIALOG ACT IDENTIFICATION

We used Belief Networks (BNs) to infer the task goal and dialog act(s) for a customer request based on its inherent and inherited categories. The detailed experimental setup is adapted from that used in our previous work for the ATIS domain [17]. We have trained six BNs for each task goal. Each BN is used to infer the presence / absence of its corresponding task goal, based on the input categories. The binary decisions across all BNs are combined to identify the task goal of the customer request. If all BNs vote negative for their respective goals, the request may be context-dependent or out-of-domain (OOD). Similarly, we have trained thirteen BNs to identify the dialog act for each customer request except for INFORM. If all thirteen BNs vote negative, the dialog act is set to INFORM – a catch-all category as used in VERBMOBIL-2. We have used the simplified topology of BNs which is identical to a naïve Bayes setup. Figure 1 illustrated a simplified BN for the task goal ORDER.

Figure 1. A simplified BN for the task goal ORDER.

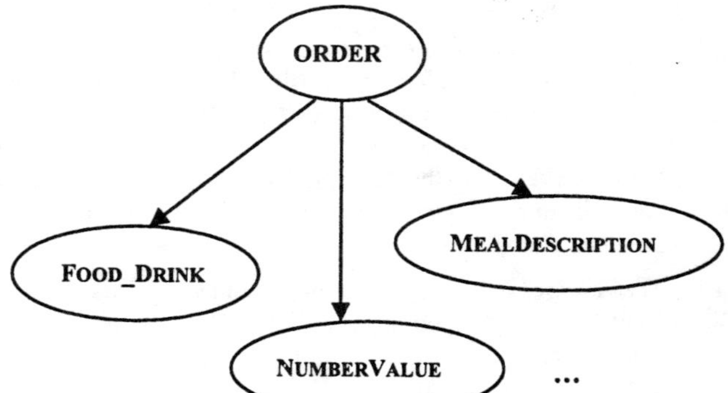

Evaluation indicates 97.8% of the test set *utterances* have correctly identified dialog acts. Since task goal identification can be affected by category inheritance, we experimented with three inheritance strategies. We trained a set of BNs for each inheritance strategy. We also applied the corresponding inheritance strategy to the test set. Figure 2 shows the average task goal identification performance for the three inheritance strategies based on the test set. Selective inheritance gave the best performance.

Figure 2. Test set accuracies for task goal identification based on different category inheritance strategies. Performance in task goal identification is measured in terms of the *dialog turns*, because each turn has a single task goal only.

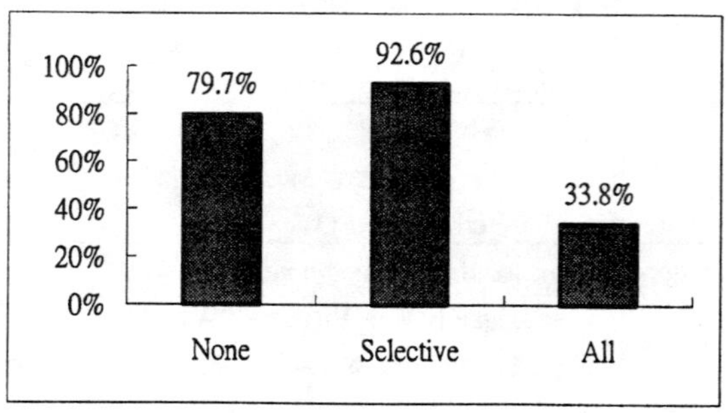

Table 11 provides an example of how the selective inheritance strategy gave rise to the correct task goal, but other strategies identified an incorrect task goal. The categories in italics are inherited from discourse.

Table 11. The use of different inheritance strategies for task goal identification.

$Waiter_1$:	*"Your seafood platter costs one hundred dollars. I'm afraid this voucher cannot cover the cost of your meal. Would you mind paying the extra in cash?"*
	Categories: {<FOOD_DRINK = "seafood platter> <COST = "costs"> <PRICEVALUE = "one hundred dollars"> <PAYMETHOD ="voucher"> <COST = "cost"> <MEALDESCRIPTION = "meal"> <PAY ="paying"> <EXTRA = "extra"> <PAYMETHOD = "cash"> "} **Task Goal:** BILL
$Customer_2$:	*"OK. But how much is the voucher worth?"*
	No inheritance **Categories:** {<HOWMUCH = "how much">, <PAYMETHOD = "voucher">} **Task Goal inferred:** OOD (out-of-domain)
	Selective inheritance **Categories:** {<HOWMUCH = "how much"> <PAYMETHOD = "voucher"> *<PRICEVALUE = "one hundred dollars">*} **Task Goal inferred: BILL**
	All inheritance **Categories:** {<HOWMUCH = "how much"> <PAYMETHOD = "voucher"> *<FOOD_DRINK = "seafood platter> <COST = "costs"> <PRICEVALUE = "one hundred dollars"> <PAYMETHOD="voucher"> <COST = "cost"> <MEALDESCRIPTION= "meal"> <PAY="paying"> <EXTRA = "extra"> <PAYMETHOD = "cash">*} **Task Goal inferred:** OOD

6. PROCEDURE FOR DISCOURSE INHERITANCE

We have developed the following discourse inheritance procedure for handling customer requests in our mixed-initiative dialog corpus. Discourse inheritance includes both category inheritance and task goal inheritance. Table 12 describes the discourse inheritance procedure.

Step 2 specifies *task goal inheritance*, which we found to be necessary for context-dependent customer requests. The BNs often label these requests as OOD, i.e. all BNs vote negative for their corresponding task goals. Under such circumstances, we inherit the task goal of the previous dialog turn, i.e. $TG_{Customer,t}=TG_{Waiter,t-1}$. With task goal inheritance, we improved task goal identification of the test set from 92.6% (see Section 5) to 93.2%.

The discourse inheritance procedure incorporates our findings in the interdependencies among task goals, dialog acts and category inheritance. Evaluation shows that this procedure correctly handled 95.9% of dialog turns in our test set.

Table 12. Discourse inheritance procedure determined based on the CU Restaurants Corpus.

Step 1	Parse for **categories** in the incoming customer request ($C_{Customer, t}$)
Step 2	Infer the **task goal** ($TG_{Customer, t}$) of the request using the trained BNs and $C_{Customer, t}$ If $TG_{Customer, t}$ = nil (all BNs vote negative), then $TG_{Customer, t} = TG_{Waiter, t-1}$ (treat request as context-dependent, perform **task goal inheritance** based on previous dialog turn.)
Step 3	Infer the **dialog act** ($DA_{Customer, t}$) of the request using the trained BNs and $C_{Customer, t}$ If $DA_{Customer, t}$ = nil (all BNs vote negative), $DA_{Customer, t}$ = INFORM
Step 4	Apply selective **category inheritance rules** based on $TG_{Customer, t}$ and $DA_{Customer, t}$. and **category refresh rules** based on $TG_{Customer, t}$, $DA_{Customer, t}$, $DA_{Customer, t-1}$, $DA_{Waiter, t}$ or $DA_{Waiter, t-1}$

7. CONCLUSIONS AND FUTURE WORK

This paper describes a study of the interdependencies among dialog acts, task goals and discourse inheritance in mixed-initiative dialogs in the CU Restaurants domain. Our study is based on 199 dialogs in the restaurants domain, with disjoint training (169 dialogs) and test sets (30 dialogs). Our training set is first annotated manually in terms of task goals and dialog acts and tagged automatically in terms of semantic and syntactic categories for each customer request and waiter response. Based on the annotation process, we observed the following:

1. The task goal of a context-independent customer request can be identified from its categories, while the task goal of a context-dependent request can be inherited from the previous dialog turn.
2. Dialog act identification does not require category inheritance, while task goal identification does.
3. Category inheritance is largely dependent on the task goals of the current query. However in some cases it is also influenced by the dialog act in the cases of confirmation or rejection.

We have written a set of category inheritance and refresh rules, which constitute our *selective inheritance strategy*. We used Belief Networks (BNs) to automate identification of task goals and dialog acts based on input categories. Selective category inheritance outperformed two alternate control strategies where none or all of the categoreis are inherited. The selective strategy achieved correct task goal identification for 92.6% of the dialog turns and correct dialog act identification for 97.8% of the utterances in the test set. We have also developed a *discourse inheritance procedure*, which can correctly handle 95.9% of the dialog turns in the test set. In the near future, we will work on cooperative response generation in the CU Restaurants domain.

ACKNOWLEDGMENTS

This project is supported by the Hong Kong SAR Government Research Grants Council Earmarked Grant CUHK4177/00E and a Direct Grant from The Chinese University of Hong Kong.

REFERENCES

1. Doran, C., J. Aberdeen, L. Damianos and L. Hirschman, "Comparing Several Aspects of Human-Computer and Human-Human Dialogs," Proceedings of the 2nd Sigdial Workshop on Discourse and Dialog, Aalborg, 2001.
2. Walker, M. et al., "DARPA Communicator Dialog Travel Planning Systems: The June 2000 Data Collection," Proceedings of Eurospeech, Aalborg, 2001.
3. Walker, M. and R. Passonneau, "DATE: A Dialog Act Tagging Scheme for Evaluation of Spoken Dialog Systems," Proceedings of the 2nd Sigdial Workshop on Discourse and Dialog, Aalborg, 2001.
4. Pieraccini, R., S. Caskey, K. Dayanidhi, B. Carpenter and M. Phillips, "Etude, A Recursive Dialog Manager with Embedded User Interface Patterns," Proceedings of the Automatic Speech Recognition and Understanding Workshop, Trento, 2001.
5. 史濟蘭, "英語會話入門," 學習出版社有限公司, March 1996.
6. 林志輝, "酒樓餐廳英語," 星輝圖書有限公司, January 1996.
7. 商務編輯部, "速成英語會話," 精英, September 2001.
8. 鄭慧思, "各行各業售貨員英語手冊," 通用語言唱片公司, December 2001.
9. Alexandersson, J. et al, "Dialog Acts in VERBMOBIL-2 Second Edition," Verbmobil Report 226, Universitat Hamburg, DFKI Saarbrucken, Universitat Erlangen, TU Berlin, July 1998.
10. Core, M. G. and J. F. Allen, "Coding Dialogs with the DAMSL Annotation Scheme," Proceedings of the American Association for Artificial Intelligence Conference, 1997.
11. Jekat, S. et al., "Dialog Acts in VERBMOBIL," Verbmobil Report 65, Universitat Hamburg, DFKI Saarbrucken, Universitat Erlangen, TU Berlin, April 1995.
12. Schmitz, B. and J. J. Quantz., "Dialog Acts in Automatic Dialog Interpreting," Verbmobil Report 173, Universitat Hamburg, DFKI Saarbrucken, Universitat Erlangen, TU Berlin, September 1996.
13. Jurafsky, D. et al, "Automatic Detection of Discourse Structure for Speech Recognition and Understanding," Proceedings of the Automatic Speech Recognition and Understanding Workshop, 1997.
14. Jurafsky, D., E. Shriberg and D. Biasca, "Switchboard SWBD-DAMSL Shallow-Discourse-Function Annotation Coders Manual, Draft 13," University of Colorado, Boulder, Institute of Cognitive Science Technical Report, August, 1997.
15. Stolcke, A. et al., "Dialog Act Modelling for Automatic Tagging and Recognition of Conversational Speech," Computational Linguistics, 26:3, 339-371, 2000.
16. Walker, M., R. Passonneau and J. Boland, "Quantitative and Qualitative Evaluation of DARPA Communicator Spoken Dialog Systems," Proceedings of the Human Language Technology Conference, 2001.
17. Doran, C. et al, "Guidelines for Tagging Dialog Acts in Human-Human and Human-Computer Travel Dialogs", Feb 7, 2001.
18. Meng, H., W. Lam and C. Wai, "To Believe is to Understand," Proceedings of the 6th European Conference on Speech Communication & Technology, 1999.

Drug Discovery through Information Extraction Technology

Lois C. Childs, Carl E. Weir
Lockheed Martin Management and Data Systems
lois.childs@lmco.com /
carl.e.weir@lmco.com

Robin McEntire, Paula Matuszek, James Butler, Richard Moore
GlaxoSmithKline
Robin_A_McEntire@gsk.com /
Paula_A_Matuszek@gsk.com /
James_Butler@gsk.com /
Richard_Moore@gsk.com

ABSTRACT

Increasingly, the pharmaceutical industry is a knowledge-based discipline. Knowledge, and information, is kept in both structured and unstructured form. For example, the results of experiments and clinical studies, are most often stored in structured database management systems or spreadsheets. In addition, more scientific information, such as chemical structures and properties are kept in structured form and are accessible through query languages such as SQL. However, a great deal of the most current, and most valuable, information resides not in a structured data source, but only in unstructured text, typically in the scientific literature. The ability to automatically and accurately extract information from unstructured text is of great value at every point in the drug discovery and development process.

1. INTRODUCTION

A major focus of the early drug discovery process is the identification and prioritization of appropriate molecular targets for eventual development into drugs. In antibiotic development, for instance, it is highly desirable both to identify good potential targets and eliminate those compounds that do not have the potential to produce good drugs, since they have the potential to draw on significant resources without producing valuable results. Key information about potential targets, such as essentiality, inhibition relationships, toxicity, observed links between genes or enzymes and disease, protein/protein interactions are all found in the literature, but currently there is a tremendous expenditure of resources and time to extract that information.

Information extraction can also have great benefit to other areas of the pharmaceutical industry. For instance, the pharmacokinetic properties of an inhibitor may determine whether an appropriate dose can be established which will be effective without causing unacceptable side effects. Also, knowledge of the current status of patents for a compound will have a major impact on decisions about which compounds should be moved forward through the drug development process.

Proceedings of HLT 2002, Second International Conference on Human Language Technology Research, M. Marcus, ed., Morgan Kaufmann, San Francisco, 2002.

Information extraction and text mining can also be of great benefit in other areas of the biotech industry such as tracking reports of adverse events, providing notification of the competitive situation in the marketplace, identifying key opinion leaders, finding relevant information on intellectual property issues and providing information on potential collaborators and in-licensing opportunities.

This is a large problem set in which information extraction and text mining can provide significant advantage to organizations within the highly competitive pharmaceutical/biotech industry.

2. Pilot Study

A pilot research and development project was conducted that applied information extraction technology to the MEDLINE abstract repository. Our goal was to automatically create a database of protein inhibitor information. Many medicines are based on their ability to inhibit proteins, because proteins are often catalysts of disease-causing chemical reactions. Prior to this project, there was not a complete database of information pertaining to protein inhibitors available to researchers.

An initial query of MEDLINE for terms such as "enzyme inhibitor" and "Ki" retrieved over 40,000 abstracts. In a demonstration system, 22,000 of these abstracts were processed and stored within a database within ninety minutes. This resulted in a database of approximately 42,000 inhibition relations. Based on a controlled test set, we have estimated that over 90% of these are valid relations.

MEDLINE is the National Library of Medicine's bibliographic database covering the fields of medicine, nursing, dentistry, veterinary medicine, the health care system, and the pre-clinical sciences. It was developed as a search tool for accessing literature citations and linking to full-text journal articles at web sites of participating publishers. MEDLINE contains bibliographic citations and author abstracts from more than 4,300 biomedical journals published in the United States and 70 other countries. It contains over 11 million citations dating back to the mid-1960's. Coverage is worldwide, but most records are from English-language sources or have English abstracts.

3. Information Extraction

In order to create a domain corpus, a query was developed to retrieve all abstracts describing research on protein inhibition. This query retrieved over 40,000 abstracts. From this corpus, 200 abstracts were randomly selected as answer key documents: 100 for training and 100 for testing. 400 answer keys were then generated with the help of the domain expert, i.e., a training and testing set for each type of extraction: entity (proteins, chemical compounds, compound classes etc.) and relationship (inhibition). A knowledge base was developed using the training set and then blind-tested against the testing set. At the end of the pilot, the following scores for the knowledge base were reported, based on the 200 randomly selected abstracts.

Extracted Item	Test Set		Training Set	
	Recall	Precision	Recall	Precision
Proteins	65.83	63.5	80.78	82.99
Compounds	74.88	63.65	89.43	90.03
Inhibitions	60.21	100	86.69	92

Recall is the metric that represents the percentage of all of the possible items that were correctly extracted. Precision is the metric that represents the percentage of all of the extracted items that were correct.

The information extraction system used was Lockheed Martin's AeroText^{TM} text-mining product. This product is a flexible tool that enables knowledge engineers to build an example-based knowledge base using a wizard-like interface. The knowledge base is then compiled and applied by the AeroText engine to provide a fast extraction capability. The engine can perform character-based analysis to identify the lexical tokens of a document, as well as perform single and multi-term look-up of dictionary information. The engine employs a single pattern matching mechanism that can accommodate any kind of linguistic analysis.

The AeroText text-mining tool's design is data-independent, which means it does not rely on or have a bias towards a particular domain, document type, document source, or natural language. The AeroText architecture maintains a strict separation between its text processing software and the linguistic information required for a text-processing task. The software is data-independent and requires a knowledge base to define and control its text-processing operation. The knowledge base contains all of the linguistic information needed for the text-processing task. The content of the knowledge is user-defined and depends greatly on the type of text-processing task, as well as the type of documents that are processed.

AeroText provides an integrated environment with all the necessary components for the knowledge base development cycle rather than a mixture of tools, editors, scripts, and demos. The Integrated Development Environment (IDE) is a graphical user interface that offers object-oriented editors, visual displays of extracted data, visual tools for debugging linguistic data, and various other displays to support analysis of knowledge base performance. Within one environment, developers create linguistic data using editors, build knowledge bases with the compiler, review and debug knowledge bases with single documents, and review performance across multiple documents.

Knowledge acquisition is the process of encoding the linguistic data that the AeroText System needs for analyzing text. The knowledge must be *acquired* from examples of the analysis problem since it is not provided explicitly in the text or other data sources. As more examples are reviewed, the knowledge either generalizes further or splits into separate classes. If counter-examples occur, the knowledge must either restrict in order to eliminate the example or expand to include "negative" rules. This process is time-consuming and often leads to problems caused by poorly encoded knowledge. The AeroText product suite supports this process in several fundamental ways. It represents linguistic patterns as an example string with annotations of additional knowledge and it provides acquisition tools that are invoked from example text. It provides analysis tools that display examples and counter-examples of each pattern. It also offers mechanisms to automate the acquisition of knowledge to reduce the development time and increase its quality. Fully automatic mechanisms often lead to other problems, so a user-in-the-loop model was chosen to allow developers to review, modify, reject or accept the automatically generated knowledge.

The Integrated Development Environment offers wizards to guide the developer through common knowledge base development tasks. The IDE includes wizards for adding terms to the lexicon, adding new rule bases, and setting up batch processing runs. The most important wizard guides the developer through the process of adding a new pattern to a rule base. In addition to step-by-step instructions, this wizard invokes the automated knowledge acquisition mechanism to automate the construction of the pattern.

The AeroText IDE is designed for maximum flexibility and allows the developer to construct a complete knowledge base from start to finish. However, it may be more effective to build the knowledge base upon a common collection of linguistic data so that each developer is not re-encoding the same knowledge. In this way, the knowledge base is constructed by bootstrapping from existing linguistic data. It supports this process by enabling developers to separate linguistic files into data sets that can be selectively imported into knowledge base projects. For example, a developer could import a data set representing general-purpose grammatical knowledge, such as common parts of speech. This process was especially effective for the protein inhibition knowledge base.

4. Domain-Specific Implementation

The life science domain has presented a number of challenges to the knowledge engineers. The language used in medical research literature is like an obscure dialect of English, not easily discernible by non-biochemists. Knowledge engineers and domain experts collaborated to produce a protein inhibition knowledge base. The domain experts provided answer keys and term lists, as well as background information and consultation while the knowledge engineers constructed the knowledge base. In a parallel effort, the domain experts also constructed their own proprietary knowledge base using AeroText.

In the following example, while the rules of English syntax are being followed, the vocabulary is so unfamiliar that casual reading is difficult.

To examine the role of platelet-derived growth factor (PDGF) and the polyol pathway in the growth activity of smooth muscle cells (SMCs), [(3)H]-thymidine incorporation, [(125)I]-PDGF-BB binding and expression of PDGF-beta receptor protein were measured in rat aortic SMCs cultured with 5.5 or 20 mM glucose with or without anti-PDGF antibody or an aldose reductase inhibitor, epalrestat.

For the purposes of the pilot, the information to be extracted from this example is that *epalrestat* is an inhibitor of *aldose reductase*. In order to do this, we must first recognize that *aldose reductase* is a protein and *epalrestat* is a chemical compound. The extraction of the inhibition relationship is then relatively simple. The relationship resides within the pattern: <PROTEIN> inhibitor, <CHEMCOMPOUND>.

The protein inhibition knowledge base uses a combination of term look-up, bottom-up analysis and regular expression operations using known terms, as well as context. Useful stored terms are protein and compound endings, solo proteins and compounds, as well as terms that can appear within a chemical compound name. The latter term list, called "chemterm," comprises approximately 90,000 terms. Features are lists of items whose categories are frequently found in extraction patterns. In the compound name, *"2,4-dioxo-5-acetamido-6-phenylhexanoic acid"*, the terms *dioxo*, *acetamido*, and *phenylhexanoic* are found in the chemterm list. The feature "Chemterm" is then used as a constituent of a pattern to recognize this particular compound.

The knowledge base can also generate its own patterns for novel terms, such as those frequently found in *ad-hoc* acronyms. An example of this is *PKC* when it appears in the following phrase: *protein kinase C (PKC)*. The knowledge base sets up a co-reference relationship between the full term and its references throughout the text. This allows it to extract *Ro31-8220* as an inhibitor of *protein kinase C* from the statement: *Ro31-8220, a specific inhibitor of PKC.*

5. Information Extraction Lessons Learned

The greatest challenge in the protein inhibitor domain is the extraction of long chemical compound formulae. The length of the formulae, plus the use of unusual punctuation, make these very difficult. Additionally, the use of an acronym for the entire expression, placed either before or after the full expression, introduces much ambiguity. The following are examples.

- ethyl-eneglycol-bis(beta-aminoethyl ether)-N,N,N',N'-tetraacetic acid (EGTA)
- R94138 ?N-methyl-(3S)-2-[(2R)-2-hydroxycarbamoylmethylundecanoyl] hexahydropyridazine-3-carboxamide?

A bottom-up approach has been developed that recognizes possible components of a formula and strives to assemble them into a complete expression. This approach often breaks down, however, due to multiple nesting. An extension of this approach is under consideration. Since the current approach is usually successful in recognizing pieces of the formula, another level of processing could be introduced that uses these pieces as pattern components. This would simplify recognition of the entire expression.

6. Database Generation

Via AeroText's published APIs, the extracted information was stored within an Oracle database which can be accessed via a web-like user interface, illustrated in Figure 1.0. This interface provides tools for querying the database and analyzing query results. The pilot study resulted in the extraction of 32K distinct proteins, 22K inhibition relations, and 12K distinct relations. The system processed 400MB of text per hour.

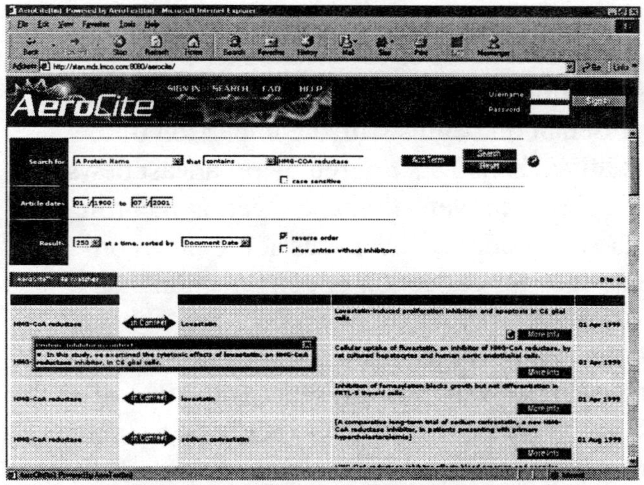

Figure 1. Interface to Protein Inhibitor Database

7. Future Work

In the short term, GlaxoSmithKline (GSK) will roll out the database created by the pilot to scientists within its organization for use in daily work. This roll-out will occur after verification and cleaning of the initial database and KB used to create it. In addition, the roll-out will include more MEDLINE abstracts to provide greater coverage. The areas in which we will concentrate our efforts for future research are:

- Improve compound recognition;
- Improve searching by enzyme class and through elimination of duplicate entries;
- Move on to a more difficult extraction problem such as:
- Relating genes to disease families
- Adverse event reports
- Web site monitoring for competitive intelligence alerting.

Research Methodologies, Observations and Outcomes in (Conversational) Speech Data Collection

Christopher Cieri
University of Pennsylvania
Linguistic Data Consortium
3615 Market Street
Philadelphia, PA 19026
+1 215-573-5489
ccieri@ldc.upenn.edu

David Miller
University of Pennsylvania
Linguistic Data Consortium
3615 Market Street
Philadelphia, PA 19026
+1 215-573-9182
damiller@ldc.upenn.edu

Kevin Walker
University of Pennsylvania
Linguistic Data Consortium
3615 Market Street
Philadelphia, PA 19026
+1 215-573-4172
walkerk@ldc.upenn.edu

ABSTRACT

This paper presents research methodologies for collecting speech data and gives observations from a recent set of conversational speech collections before describing their outcomes. The presentation begins with a comparison of the relative challenges offered by broadcast news, telephone conversation and meeting recordings. The remainder of the discussion focuses on methods for collection of conversational data with special focus on two recent Switchboard collections. We identify method that have allowed for very cost-efficient collection of Switchboard data. We conclude with a summary of generally available resources that result from the efforts described herein.

Keywords

Speech data, audio, telephone collection, meeting data, human subjects, ASR, collection methodology, speaker identification, speech recognition

1. Introduction

Large volumes of speech data are crucial to progress in speech technologies such as speech recognition and speaker identification, to research programs that rely on speech recognition output such as: Topic Detection and Tracking (Wayne 1998, 2000), Automatic Content Extraction (NIST 2000) and to applications such as speech-to-speech translation. This paper discusses methodologies for collecting speech data that have evolved over dozens of collection projects involving thousands of speakers. It begins by identifying challenges present in collecting digital audio from both broadcast news and conversational speech. The discussion focuses primarily on techniques for collecting conversational speech. Observations of human subjects' responses to collection procedures identify methods that yield more natural data while reducing cost. All of the data sets described herein are or will be available for use in linguistic education, research and technology development.

2. Communicative Interactions in Data Supporting Speech Technology Development

Recordings of human communicative interactions used in speech research vary along a number of dimensions. The acoustic properties of a speech signal vary with the channels through which the speech passes on the way from speaker to hearer. Each human language presents its own set of problem including new phoneme inventories and word formation rules and co-occurrence patterns to be modeled. Differences in communicative situation are reflected in vocabulary, speech rate and voice quality. Demographic factors such as age, sex and region of origin affect phonology, lexical choice and sentence formation. Finally the application in which the recognition technology will be used affects vocabulary size and the requirements for the system's speech, accuracy and output format. These concerns are equally present for recognition of broadcast news, telephone conversations and multi-party meetings.

There are other dimensions along which broadcast news, telephone conversations and multi-party meetings vary, rendering each either more or less challenging to speech researchers. Figure 1 lists several of the dimensions and indicates how they affect the degree of challenge each type presents to human annotators and ASR systems alike. Here we will describe just a subset. Rows one and two refer to the degree of variability present in the physical environment and in the audio capture equipment used. In broadcast news, most speech takes place in the studio environment where high quality equipment and quiet prevail. In contrast, recognition of telephone speech suffers from the greater variability present in the physical environment in which the speakers find themselves. Rows three and four point to both movement in place and change of location as factors affecting the difficulty of speech data. Broadcast news personalities tend to sit in a single place and minimize movements that would create noise. Conversational speech lacks this level of discipline. Not only may participants generate additional noise through movements but they may also change their location relative to the data capture devices by moving a phone away from their mouths, by walking out of the range of a wireless phone base or, in the meeting environment, by walking alternately toward and away from room microphones. Broadcast news does present a greater challenge than telephone conversation in its multi-modal signal. The modern television broadcast may contain not only the video of the on-air personality but also background images, closed captioning, sidebar text and the horizontally scrolling text, or "crawl", that CNN has conspicuously employed recently. Integrating these sources of information is an open research problem for information management technologies. Broadcast news speech, relatively formal and well-rehearsed, contains a narrower variety of linguistic styles and fewer disfluencies and rapid speech phenomena than conversational speech. In telephone conversations the number of speakers is usually small and fixed while in broadcast news there may be studio-guests, call-ins and man-on the-street interviews. The *information handicap* in Figure 1 refers to the paucity of information the annotator or recognition system has relative to the participant in a communicative interaction. For telephone conversations, a recognition system has as much signal data as the interlocutors. However in meetings and broadcast television, the facial expressions, maps, etc. that help to disambiguate the audio for participants are lacking in the audio signal. The *Observer's Paradox* states that in order to understand human communication one must study it but the very act of observation affects the phenomenon under study. One assumes that in broadcast news the effect of observation is essentially zero. In LDC telephone collections, there is both evidence that participants believe they should monitor their speech and evidence that they sometime forget to do so. The effect of observation has the potential to be the most profound in meetings where special rooms may be required and where microphones may be in plain site.

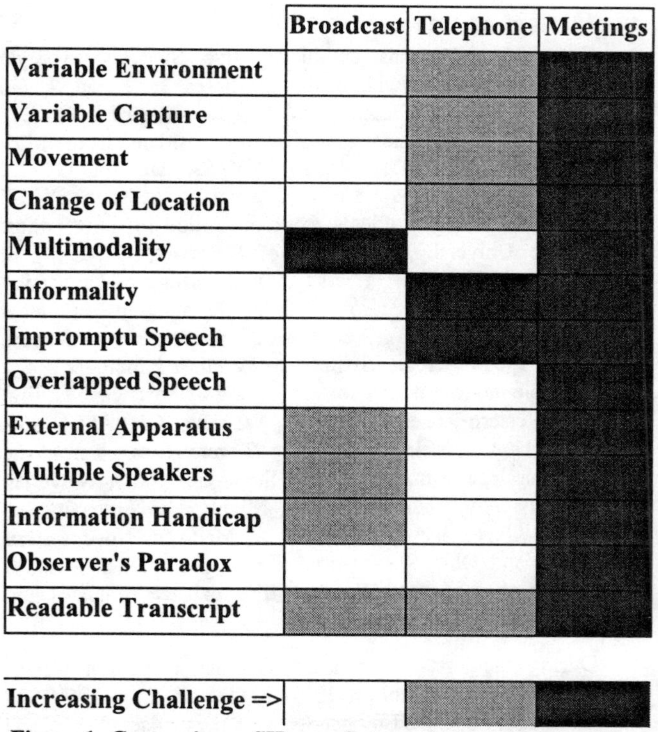

Figure 1: Comparison of Human Interactions underlying three speech data types.

3. Collection Types

In the sections that follow, due to time and space limitations, we will focus our attention on collections of conversational speech, specifically on Switchboard style telephone collections and GroupTalk and GroupMeet style collections of meetings.

The Switchboard call collection protocol is optimal for speaker identification research although researchers in speech recognition, discourse analysis and sociolinguistics, among others, have used Switchboard data. Switchboard targets from 200 to 700 speakers each participating in 10 telephone calls with other participants whom they, typically, do not know. Calls last 5-6 minutes and interlocutors discuss assigned topics. These features distinguish Switchboard from the CallHome and CallFriend protocols that are optimized for large vocabulary speech recognition. CallHome and Call Friend target 100 to 200 participants each of whom makes a single 20-30 minute call to a close friend or family member. Participants are native speakers of the target language of the study; topics are not constrained.

GroupTalk and GroupMeet are protocols for collecting conversational speech during face-to-face meetings. GroupTalk collects facilitated discussions. Under the GroupTalk protocol, an interviewer joins a group of 2 to 4 friends or family members introducing a variety of topics with the goal of identifying a few that truly interest the group and engage them in extended discussions. During GroupTalk sessions we tend to use less obtrusive microphones. Successful GroupTalk sessions will contain relaxed and informal speech. GroupMeet targets planning meetings. The goal of GroupMeet is to identify groups that meet regularly or were planning to hold a specific meeting and gain their permission to record that meeting for research purposes. During GroupMeet sessions, we deploy a variety of microphones. Speech tends to be more formal than in Group Talk.

4. Collection Procedures

A conversational data collection can be divided into two obvious phases, recruitment and collection. Participant recruitment is a crucial and sometimes overlooked aspect in this process for, without participants, there are no data. Our experience over multiple Switchboard collections has shown that several factors in the recruitment process can have profound effects on the collection's outcome. These include 1) determining the best time of year to undertake a collection 2) determining the hours of the day when collection is possible 3) the number of recruits necessary 4) setting the compensation to encourage participants to complete the terms of the study. During the first Switchboard Cellular (1999-2000), our requirement that participants make a certain number of phone calls while outdoors lead us to begin this study three months earlier than we had hoped simply to avoid beginning the study during the coldest months of winter. Under the Switchboard model, we also observed that restricting the hours during which participants can make calls raised the probability that they would actually reach another available participant.

Ideally, participant recruitment occurs a few weeks prior to a collection's commencement. If recruitment occurs too far in advance of a collection's commencement, participant interest is likely to wane. If a telephone collection begin too soon after recruitment begins, the lack of a critical mass of available participants may frustrate callers. The best recruitment efforts, however, are only as good as the technology that supports them. Before recruitment begins, it is imperative to have a reliable subject database and a user-friendly interface to support the recruitment team. Subject data includes: name, gender, age, education, country born/raised in. For purpose of payment and participant care, social security number and contact information are also crucial. Generally speaking, this data is collected during the initial discussion between the participant and the recruitment staff. Indeed, for a telephone collection, that may also be the only time the recruiters speak directly with a participant.

LDC generally advertises via print media and electronic announcements. Potential participants then contact the LDC via phone or e-mail whence they learn: 1) that speech will be recorded for research and educational purposes, 2) that personal information will be kept confidential, not be released with the data, 3) when the study begins and ends and how to participate, 4) how, how much and when they will be compensated.

After initial contact with the recruitment staff, each potential participant receives a set of written detailed instructions that reiterate everything above. In telephone studies, the instructions include the participant's unique number (PIN) and the series of prompts that will be heard. Certain conversational studies (Switchboard) require a critical mass of recruits before they can begin. In other studies, such as CallHome and CallFriend, a participant can begin immediately after registering. For GroupTalk and GroupMeet studies, where either subjects come to LDC or LDC staff go to the subjects' meeting room, the subjects sign an informed consent form. In telephone collections, participants indicate their consent to have their voices recorded multiple times. After receiving their written instructions, subjects must call the robot operator to indicate their consent and activate their PINs. When making or receiving a call subject must again indicate their consent to be recorded. In each type of study, participant compliance is closely monitored to ensure a successful study. If a study does not proceed according to plan, adjusting study parameters including the number of recruits, their demographics and their compensation may be helpful

5. Collection Technology

Conversational speech collection systems must be accurate, reliable, economical, and capable of delivering real world data. For both telephone speech and meeting collection, LDC has developed a robust system that leverages off-the-shelf hardware. The system consists of customized software, telephony hardware, and a project database and can record multiple simultaneous conversations with no need for operator intervention. The project database containing demographic information and call activity statistics for each participant, supports all recruitment, collection and reporting software. The demographic information is entered during recruitment. The call activity statistics are updated each time a participant tries to make a call, or receives one; the call logic software requires accurate, timely information.

The current collection platform is a Windows NT server with a high capacity RAID, Dialogic telephony hardware, and telephony libraries/API. Calls arrive via leased T-1 line. The platform can record up to 12 simultaneous conversations. Processes such as participant validation, T-1 signaling, initiation and termination of recording, and error handling are processed by call logic software developed at LDC. The telephony software is written in VOS, a programming language developed by Parity Software (this has since been purchased by Dialogic and re-branded as CT-ADE). VOS is easy to use, but provides the flexibility to develop complex and robust applications. Based on our experience so far, VOS is quite reliable.

In an effort to accommodate data collection informants, several improvements have been made to the LDC's telephony applications. In the case of the Switchboard application, we have tried to make the participation process less onerous by improving database performance, adding music on hold, and allowing participants to check their participation statistics when they call into the platform. We have also redesigned the callee selection routine. A caller on hold is notified as each potential callee is polled. After a certain number of callees have been tried, the caller is given an opportunity to quit and try their call at a later time, or continue waiting. Adopting a customer-service approach to participants encourages them to complete their role in the study.

The LDC's meeting recording system can record 16 tracks of digital audio. The system features a mixture of wireless and far-field wired microphones. Depending upon the session, either lavalier or head-mounted microphones are used for close-micing of each participant. Room microphones, including a microphone array, PZM, omni-directional and directional microphones are also used. The meeting recording system consists of a digital mixer, a multi-track digital tape recording deck, wireless microphone receivers, a microphone preamplifier, and a multi-channel digital audio computer interface. Meeting sessions are recorded as 16bit/44kHz PCM audio.

6. Observations

To date, LDC has conducted five Switchboard style collections in-house: Switchboard 2 Phases 1, 2 and 3 and Switchboard Cellular Phases 1 and 2. Switchboard 2 Phase 1 included 657 speakers most of whom were residents in the Mid-Atlantic area: (PA=303, NJ=116, NY=53, DE=13, CT=12, MD=14, OH=13, MA=8). Many of the participants in SWB-2 Phase I were college students from the following universities: Penn State University, University of Delaware, University of Pennsylvania, Drexel University, and Rutgers University. However, there was also a large contingent of local Philadelphians in Phase 1. Of the 657 participants, 358 were female and 299 were male. Switchboard 2 Phase 2 included 4,472 5-minute telephone conversations involving 679 participants from the Mid-Western states (MN=156, WI=105, OH=70, IA=64, MI=41, IL=37). Participants in Phase II were recruited from the following college campuses: Iowa State University, Michigan State, University, University of Michigan, University of Minnesota, University of Wisconsin at Madison, Northwestern University, and Ohio State University. Switchboard 2 Phase 3 recruited in the American South with a balance of males and females.

During the first Switchboard Cellular collection (1999-2000), our goal was to collect 10 6-minute calls from 190 GSM cell-phone users balanced by gender. Our most successful means of recruitment was among the employees of a local GSM provider. However, we were still only able to recruit 293 participants, not enough to compensate for participant non-compliance. In a Switchboard study, participant non-compliance generally means that participants either do not make calls or do not receive calls. In the case of Switchboard Cellular, we found that the phones of many of many participants were unavailable during those times the participants themselves had agreed to receive calls. We discovered that this was a result of participants' habit of turning off their cell phones when not using them. To counter this problem and to reduce the frustration of those who subject who were initiating call, LDC recruiters contacted participants on multiple occasions via phone and mailings to remind participants to: 1) change their availability schedule to better reflect those times when they really could receive calls, 2) leave their phones on during the their "available" times, 3) be sure to initiate calls. In a further effort to encourage participation, we instituted a participant lottery for those who completed the study (10 calls). While this study proved to be one of our most efficient in terms of the number of subjects who finished the study, it was also our most labor-intensive study. To counter this participant non-compliance, we decided to over-recruit for the next phase of Switchboard Cellular conducted in the Fall 2000.

The goal in Switchboard Cellular 2 was to collect 10 calls each from 210 participants balanced by gender but with no restriction on cellular networks represented. We recruited a total of 591 participants and instituted a sliding pay scale that 1) covered subject costs for each call 2) offered a large bonus for completing the study (the 10th call) and 3) offered smaller bonuses for participation after the subject had completed the required number of calls. These measures provided strong motivation to the subjects and minimized the LDC's investment in under-performers. As a result, we were able to complete Switchboard Cellular Phase 2 in about one month.

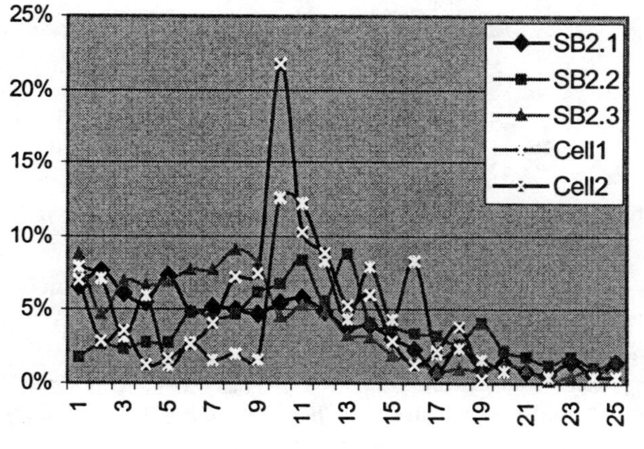

Figure 2 shows participant behavior in each of the Switchboard collections. Switchboard Cellular 2 has the tightest distribution of subjects around the goal of 10 calls. For Switchboard 2.1 through 2.3, the goal was to collect an average of ten calls per participant. Although these studies eventually met their goals, Figure 2 reveals a very diffuse distribution of participant performance. In the Cellular studies, the goal became having a minimum number of subjects who participated in at least 10 calls. The labor intensive approach adopted in Switchboard Cellular 1 produced a funny distribution of subject performance and was costly in terms of recruiter effort. The approach used in Switchboard Cellular 2 produced a distribution that is very tightly centered around a mode at ten calls and was in every other way, more efficient. Figure 2: Switchboard call summary. The vertical axis shows the number of participants who made the number of calls on the horizontal axis.

Figure 3 compares five Switchboard studies showing the ratio of completed subjects to total subjects and the normalized costs overall, per call and per subject who completed the study. The columns in Figure 3 refer to five Switchboard phases. "C1" and "C2" mean Switchboard Cellular Phase 1 and 2 respectively. The rows show the number of subjects, the subset of those who completed 10 calls, the ratio of those two numbers and the total number of calls collected. The second set of rows gives costs associated with participant fees for each of these studies. These costs are normalized for inflationary increases in the base compensation rate. The overall costs were first normalized for inflation and then scaled with respect to Switchboard 2 Phase 2, the largest and therefore most expensive collection. Cost per call was calculated by taking overall costs due to participant fees, normalizing them for inflation and then dividing by the number of successful calls. The cost per completed subject is the inflation-normalized sum of costs due to participant fees divided by the number of subject who completed 10 calls. These last two rows show that problems in the Switchboard Cellular Phase 1 collection caused an 8% increase in the cost per call relative to previous studies. However Cellular Phase 1 was relatively efficient with respect to completed subjects. Switchboard Cellular Phase 2 is the most cost-efficient study by both measures. The sliding scale compensation does seem to have had the effect of encouraging subject in Switchboard Cellular Phase 2 to make all of their 10 calls.

	2.1	2.2	2.3	C1	C2
Subjects	661	684	640	254	418
Completed Subjects	314	463	216	170	261
Ratio Subjects/Completed	0.48	0.68	0.34	0.67	0.62
Calls	1189	1322	1150	462	780
Normalized Participants Costs					
Overall	0.81	1.00	0.60	0.31	0.43
Cost/Call	1.00	1.00	1.00	1.08	0.97
Cost/Completed Subject	0.93	0.78	1.00	0.66	0.59

Figure 3: Summary of five Switchboard collections and their normalized costs.

The five Switchboard studies reported here all differ with respect to the hours of the day during which calls were completed. The policy established for Switchboard 2 Phase 1 and retained in Phase 2 allowed calls between the hours of 12:00 noon and 2:00AM. In Phase 3, the schedule was abbreviation to noon to midnight. In each of these studies, however, this was merely a policy statement, the robot operator was available around the clock and subject could give hours of availability outside the suggested times. In the Cellular phases, we converted our recommendation into a hard limit. Generally, the robot operator would not accept calls and recruiters would not enter availability times after midnight and before noon. We believed these time restrictions were necessary in the smaller Cellular studies to ensure that there was a critical mass of participants making and receiving calls during a smaller block of time. Figures 4 through 8 show call activity as a function of hour of the day in each of five Switchboard studies. The 24 hours of the day run clockwise around the circumference of the graph. For each hour of the day, the percentage of successful calls made during that hour is plotted as distance from the center of the circle. The points are then connected to form an area graph. These graphs are described below.

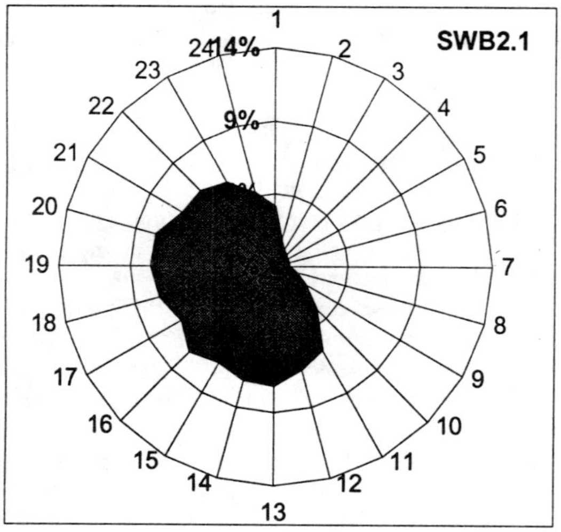

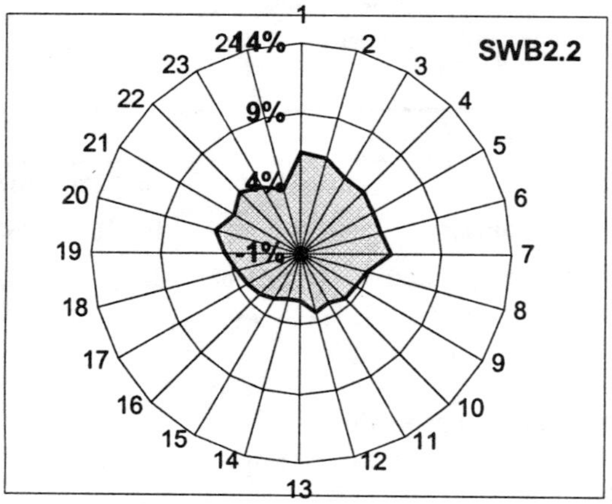

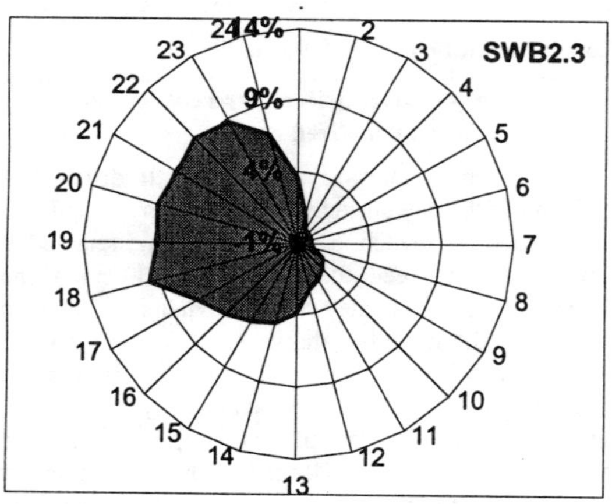

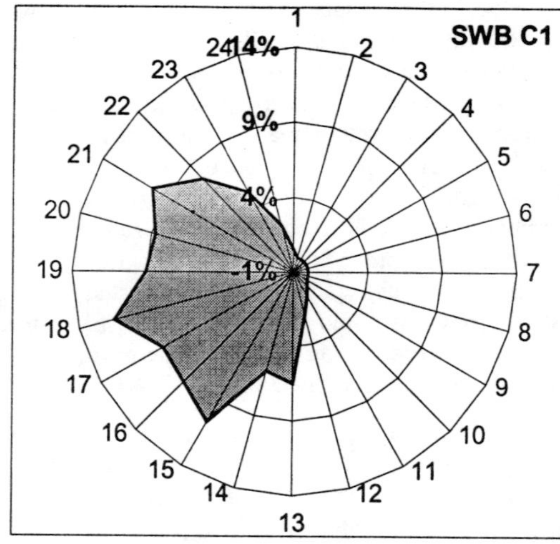

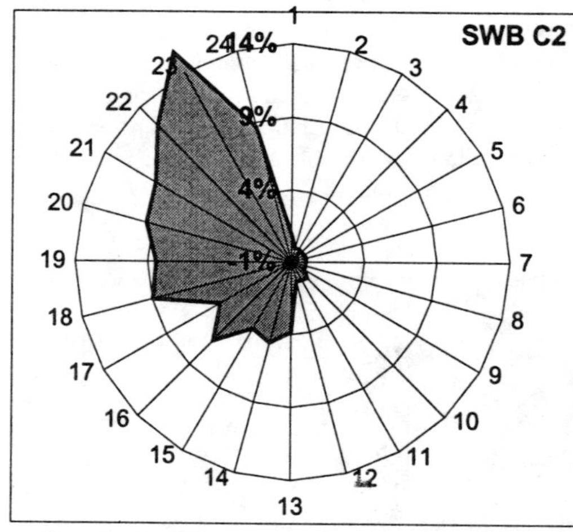

Figure 4-8: Call activity as a function of hour of day in five Switchboard collections

In Switchboard 2 Phase 1 call activity is concentrated in the time between 11:00AM and 1:00AM. In Phase 2, there is more call activity outside the suggested hours than there is within. It is important to note here that we are reporting local time, that is Eastern Standard Time. Many participants in Phase 2 were calling from and to areas that were one or two time zones west of the robot operator. Even so, Phase 2 stands out for the number of late night activity. Phase 3, focussed on the American South does return to the calling pattern of Phase 1. Indeed calls are more tightly clustered in the hours between 2:00PM and 11:00PM. In the Cellular phases, there is essentially no activity between midnight and noon. Note however, that the distribution of calls by hour of the day is different in the two studies. Many of the participants in Cellular Phase 1 were employee of a local call center for a cellular phone service provider. One can observe peaks of activity at 1:00PM, 3:00PM and 6:00PM and 9:00PM that presumably correspond to lunch, break-time, end-of-day and the hour after dinner. In Cellular Phase 2 we see similar peaks and one additional peak at 11:00 PM just before the robot operator shut down for the day.

By analyzing call activity in the previous studies, we were able to adjust the rules of Cellular Phase 2 participation to increase the chance that a caller would quickly connect with a callee.

Comments from subjects collected after the studies ended, reflect the difference between Cellular Phases 1 and 2. In the former, many subjects commented that it was difficult to find someone to talk to. Such problems all but disappeared in Cellular Phase 2.

7. Outcomes

Speech data is crucial to speech technology. This paper compared methodologies for collecting speech data across more than two-dozen studies showing LDC procedures for several collection types and the relative efficiency of various approaches. This section will enumerate some of the resources that these efforts have produced including those that are generally available and those that will be. All for the data described herein is or will shortly be available for research and technology development. The parenthetical notes after each corpus name are the LDC Catalog number and the ISBN number

The CallFriend corpora created for language identification are available in American English-Non-Southern Dialect (LDC96S46 isbn:1-58563-061-6), American English-Southern Dialect (LDC96S47 isbn:1-58563-062-4), Canadian French (LDC96S48 isbn:1-58563-063-2), Egyptian Arabic (LDC96S49 isbn:1-58563-064-0), Farsi (LDC96S50 isbn:1-58563-065-9), German (LDC96S51 isbn:1-58563-066-7), Hindi (LDC96S52 isbn:1-58563-067-5), Japanese (LDC96S53 isbn:1-58563-068-3), Korean (LDC96S54 isbn:1-58563-069-1), Mandarin Chinese-Mainland Dialect (LDC96S55 isbn:1-58563-070-5), Mandarin Chinese-Taiwan Dialect (LDC96S56 isbn:1-58563-071-3), Spanish-Caribbean Dialect (LDC96S57 isbn:1-58563-072-1), Spanish-Non-Caribbean Dialect (LDC96S58 isbn:1-58563-073-X), Tamil (LDC96S59 isbn:1-58563-074-8), Vietnamese (LDC96S60 isbn:1-58563-075-6)

The CallHome corpora were created for large vocabulary continuous speech recognition. For each CallHome language, LDC has released audio, transcripts and a lexicon. Due to space constraints, the identifying information for only the audio follows. The LDC Catalog (www.ldc.upenn.edu/Catalog) gives links from the audio to the transcripts and lexicons. CallHome corpora are available in the following: American English (LDC97S42 isbn:1-58563-111-6), Egyptian Arabic (LDC97S45 isbn:1-58563-114-0), German (LDC97S43 isbn:1-58563-117-5), Japanese (LDC96S37 isbn:1-58563-077-2), Mandarin Chinese (LDC96S34 isbn:1-58563-080-2) and Spanish (LDC96S35 isbn:1-58563-083-7).

The Hub-5 training and evaluation corpora for large vocabulary continuous speech recognition are available in: Mandarin (LDC98S69 isbn:1-58563-131-0) and Spanish (LDC98S70 isbn:1-58563-133-7)

Switchboard 1 (LDC97S62 isbn:1-58563-121-3), three phases of Switchboard-2 Phase 1 (LDC98S75 isbn:1-58563-138-8), Phase II (LDC99S79 isbn:1-58563-144-2), Phase III (LDC2002S06 isbn:1-58563-222-8) and one Switchboard Cellular Phase 1 (LDC2001S13 isbn:1-58563-213-9) have been published. LDC has also released a subset of transcribed Switchboard Cellular calls both audio (LDC2001S15 isbn:1-58563-215-5) and transcripts (LDC2001T14 isbn:1-58563-214-7).

NIST's Speaker Recognition Benchmarks for 1996 (LDC96S61 isbn:1-58563-059-4), 1997 (LDC99S80 isbn:1-58563-142-6), 1998 (LDC98S76 isbn:1-58563-129-9), 1999 (LDC99S81 isbn:1-58563-152-3) and 2000 (LDC2001S97 isbn:1-58563-192-2) have all been released.

To date about 30 hours of meetings involving more than 90 unique speakers have been collected under the GroupTalk and GroupMeet protocols. Some of this material will be included in NIST's Rich Text 2002 Metadata Annotation Experiment.

8. References

[1] Doddington, George, 1998, The Topic Detection and Tracking Phase 2 (TDT-2) Evaluation Plan: Overview & Perspective, Proceedings of the Broadcast News Transcription and Understanding Workshop, Lansdowne, Virginia, February 1998.

[2] Garofalo, et. Al., 2000, The TREC Spoken Document Retrieval Track : A Success Story, April 2000.

[3] NIST - National Institute for Standards and Technology, 2002, Rich Text 2002 Metadata Annotation Experiment http://www.nist.gov/speech/tests/rt/rt2002/experiment.htm

[4] NIST - National Institute for Standards and Technology, 1999, 1999 NIST Broadcast News Evaluation, http://www.nist.gov/speech/tests/bnr/bnews_99/bnews_99.htm

[5] NIST - National Institute for Standards and Technology, 2000, ACE - Automatic Content Extraction, http://www.nist.gov/speech/tests/ace/

[6] NIST - National Institute for Standards and Technology, 2000, The 2000 NIST Hub-5 Evaluation, http://www.nist.gov/speech/tests/ctr/h5_2000/index.htm

[7] Wayne, Charles, 1998, Topic Detection & Tracking: A Case Study in Corpus Creation and Evaluation Methodologies, Proceedings of LREC 1998: The First International Conference on Language Resources and Evaluation, Granada, Granada, Spain, May 1998.

[8] Wayne, Charles, 2000, Multilingual Topic Detection and Tracking: Successful Research Enabled by Corpora and Evaluation, Proceedings of LREC 2000: The Second International Conference on Language Resources and Evaluation, Athens, Greece, May 2000.

Speech in Noisy Environments (SPINE) Adds New Dimension to Speech Recognition R&D

Thomas H. Crystal
Consultant
Arlington, VA 22202-2103
thcrystal@ieee.org

Astrid Schmidt-Nielsen
Naval Research Laboratory
Washington, DC
20375-5337
schmidtn@itd.nrl.navy.mil

Elaine Marsh
Naval Research Laboratory
Washington, DC
20375-5337
marsh@aic.nrl.navy.mil

ABSTRACT

The Naval Research Laboratory, with DARPA sponsorship, conducted the SPINE-1 and SPINE-2 evaluations to measure the performance of automatic speech recognizers to process military-style speech in simulated military environments. Nine different organizations ran a total of 27 systems on the test material. The overall WER for the primary system from each site was 39.6%. The best performing system's WER was 27.5%. The environments included both background noise and voice coders. The more difficult coder-noise combinations generally had fewer speech turns and fewer words/ s than the easier ones. The easier environments appeared to have more chit-chat than the more difficult ones, but because of other compensations, type counts were similar for easy and difficult environments. The changes in talker behavior influenced the accuracy of speech recognizers.

Keywords
Speech recognition, background noise, voice coders.

1. INTRODUCTION

For speech recognition to be useful for communications monitoring or as a training aid for military operations, it must accommodate: (1) the patterns of military speech, (2) degradation of the signal by digital voice coders and by military microphones, including noise-canceling ones, (3) acoustic noise introduced into the signal from the tactical environment (helicopters, tanks, etc.), and (4) changes talkers make to their speech (acoustic patterns, word selection, pronunciation, etc.) to compensate for the distortions, high-noise environments and loss of intelligibility. The Naval Research Laboratory, with DARPA sponsorship, conducted the SPINE-1 (summer of 2000) and SPINE-2 (summer of 2001) evaluations to measure the performance of automatic speech recognizers to process military-style speech in simulated military environments [4].

Proceedings of HLT 2002, Second International Conference on Human Language Technology Research, M. Marcus, ed., Morgan Kaufmann, San Francisco, 2002.

2. DATA COLLECTION FOR SPINE-2

The SPINE data collection used the ARCON Communicability Exercise (ACE), originally developed for testing digital communications systems [1, 2]. Speech was collected from pairs of talkers doing a collaborative task -- a cooperative version of the game Battleship -- while seated in separate sound booths and communicating over low-bit-rate digital coders. Noise from military environments was accurately reproduced over loudspeakers in each booth, and the participants used military headsets or handsets and hearing protectors appropriate for the environment. The talker on one side had the role of Fire Officer (FO): operator of the mine and laser-gun; on the other side was the Search Officer (SO), the radar and sonar operator. Characteristics of SPINE-1 and SPINE-2 are given in Table 1.

Table 1. SPINE Data Statistics

	Talk-ers	Conver-sations (sides)	Conv. Time	Speech Time	Elapsed Time
SPINE1	40	120 (240)	5 min.	21,353 s	32,862 s
SPINE2	32	64 (128)	3 min.	10,101 s	12,646 s

A crucial part of the game was declaring and confirming grid coordinates. SPINE-1 used existing ACE data, for which highly confusable Diagnostic Rhyme Test (DRT) words were used as the grid labels. SPINE-2 differed from SPINE-1 by (1) using less confusable military words for the grid labels, (2) using more severe tactical noise environments, and (3) in some test administration details.

Recognizer evaluation was done using a subset of the full data set for SPINE-2, which consisted of 16 x 4 x 4 x 2 = 512 conversations, 1024 conversation sides -- 16 noise-pair coder combinations and four groups of four talker pairs with each talker being both FO and SO. In this evaluation, only one group of talkers was used in each condition and only one side for each talker. Thus, there were 16 x 4 x 1 x 1 = 64 conversations, 128 sides. Each talker group used each coder once and each noise-pair once, but not all combinations, as shown in Table 2.

Table 2. Speaker Group for each Combination of Coder and Noise Pair in SPINE-2. FO and SO are the roles. A group has four talker pairs one of each is always FO, the other always SO.

	CVSD	CELP	MEL P	LPC
FO: Quiet *SO*: Office	B	A	D	C
FO: Car *SO*: Street	A	D	C	B
FO: Carrier *SO*: F-16	D	C	B	A
FO: Bradley *SO*: Helicopter	C	B	A	D

This means that an analysis of overall noise effects or overall coder effects includes all 16 talker pairs (32 talkers). However, analysis of coder/noise-pair interactions is confounded with talker effects, and there were significant differences among talkers. The talker differences were highly correlated across sites, with the same talkers being consistently recognized well or poorly.

3. SYSTEM EVALUATION

3.1 Primary systems

Even though the talkers always heard one another's voices as transmitted by one of the coders, both uncoded and coded speech was used in the SPINE-2 evaluation. The primary evaluation was done using uncoded speech, and recognizing the coded speech was an option. Nine organizations submitted a total of 27 systems for SPINE-2 evaluation [4]. Of these, nine primary systems recognizing uncoded speech were selected for analysis here. Summing the error counts for these 9 sites over 128 conversation sides and dividing by the total reference words gives an overall WER of 39.6. The nine system's WER's and rates of the various types of errors are shown in Figure 1. The systems group into four clusters. The best site (27.5% WER), 2nd best (30.1%), 6 typical sites (37.5-44.0%) and a final site (56.9%).

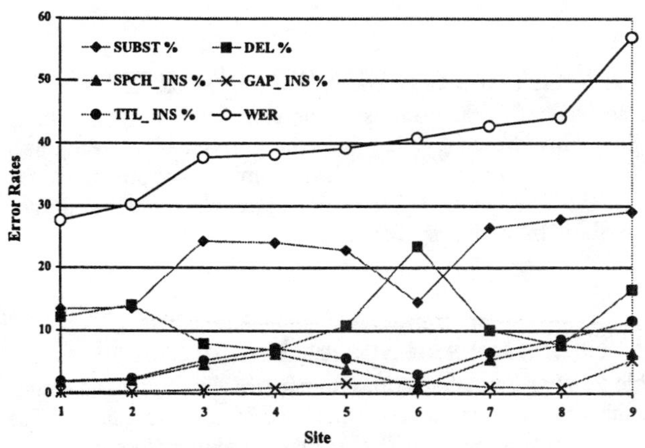

Figure 1. Error Rates of Primary Systems from Different Sites.

The two best sites balance substitutions and deletions and to minimize insertions, particularly gap insertions -- insertions during periods of background noise, which may include background speech. Site 6 has similarly low substitutions and insertions, but at the expense of a high deletion rate, being the only system where deletions significantly exceed substitutions.

3.2 Systems vs. Conversation Sides

Each of the 128 conversation sides affects the individual systems in different ways. This can be seen in Figure 2, which is a scatter plot of the WER's for each of the 1152 combinations of systems (N=9) and conversation sides (N = 128) plotted as a function of the average over systems of the WER for a side. The WER's range from a minimum of 18.3% to a maximum of 90.9%, with the 25th percentile, 31.4%; median, 38.3%; 75th percentile,44.7%.

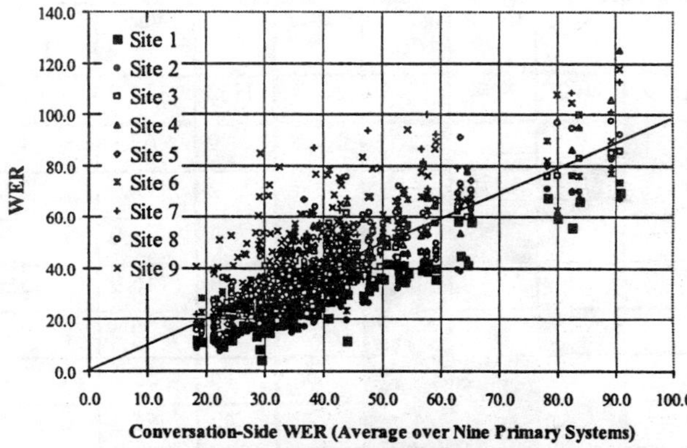

Figure 2. Error Rates of Nine Primary Systems by Converstaion Side

The preponderance of WER's is in the range 26-46%. Within this range, individual systems' error rates for a conversation side cluster within a 25%-wide band around the average for that conversation side. Outliers extend from about 25% below to about 45% above the average.

Systems seem to be differentiated by their outliers. The system with the lowest overall error rate (solid rectangles on the graphs) has a number of conversation sides with WER's significantly below the average. Sites 7 and 9, but not 8, have sides with WER's noticeably above the average. Sites 1 and 2 have the lowest and Site 4 the highest WER's for the side with the highest average WER. The WER's for Sites 3and 6 are quite close to the average, with no high outliers and similar low outliers to the best two sites. Site 6 was noted above to have a similar substitution rate to the best two sites, at the expense of a higher deletion rate.

4. EFFECTS of TEST CONDITIONS

Table 3 shows means for the different roles, coders and noise pairs.

Table 3. Mean WER's for Test Parameters and All Sides.

Role	WER	Coder	WER	Noise_Pair	WER
FO	38.1	lpc	39.5	car<>street	36.3
SO	43.4	cvsd	39.9	office<>quiet	38.9
		celp	41.4	carrier<>f16	40.2
		melp	42.0	bradley<>helo	47.4

The 128 conversation sides are themselves the product of 32 conditions (2 roles (sides) x 4 coders x 4 noise pairs) by 4 sets of talker pairs drawn from a pool of 16 talker pairs. The mean, variance and standard deviation of the 1152 individual WER's are 40.7, 319.7 and 17.9, respectively.

Table 4 shows the contributions to the total variance for various combinations of parameters. The sum of the first four entries in the last column shows that first order means from the sites and the test conditions accounts for only 29.5% of the variance, the remaining 70.5% arising from talker differences and interaction among the factors and sites.

Table 4. Contributions of Parameter Combinations to the Overall Variances.

Sites	Side	Coder	Noise Pair	Talker	N	Var.	Per Cent of Total
N=9	N=2	N=4	N=4	N=4	1152	319.7	100.0%
■					9	67.6	21.1%
	■				2	8.9	2.8%
		■			4	1.0	0.3%
			■		4	16.9	5.3%
	■		■		8	29.3	9.2%
		■	■		16	35.1	11.0%
	■	■	■		32	55.2	17.3%
	■	■	■	■	128	195.3	61.1%

4.1 Coded Speech

In addition to recognizing the uncoded speech, a few sites elected to recognize the output of the voice coders as well. The results for two sites are shown in Figure 3. WER's were greater for coded than for uncoded speech, but differences among coders were small, both for coded and for uncoded speech.

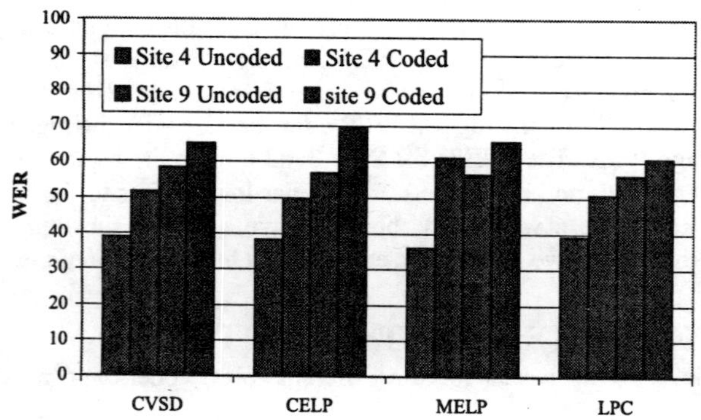

Figure 3. Coder Effects, Coded vs. Uncoded Speech for Two Sites.

4.2 Noise Effects

Figure 4 shows the effect of background noises on recognizer performance for each of the four noise pairs, and Figure 5 shows the effect for the eight different noises.

For each noise pair, one noise was always used as side a and the other as side b. Therefore, within a given noise pair, noise effects

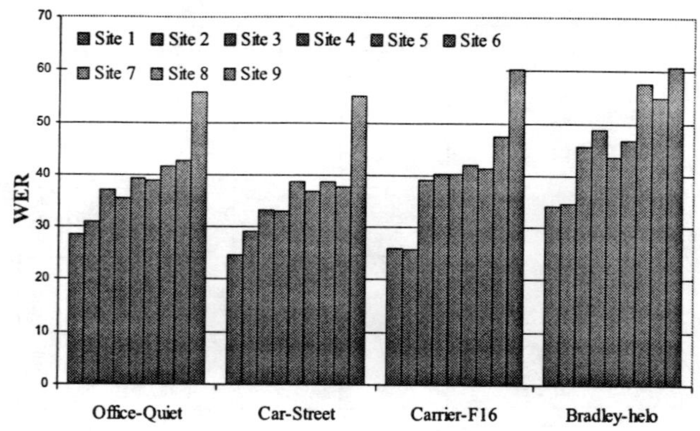

Figure 4. Effect of Noise Pair for Nine Primary Sites.

are confounded with talker differences and possible vocabulary differences for the different game roles. That is, differences between noises within a noise pair reflect talker and role differences as well as the effect of the background noise.

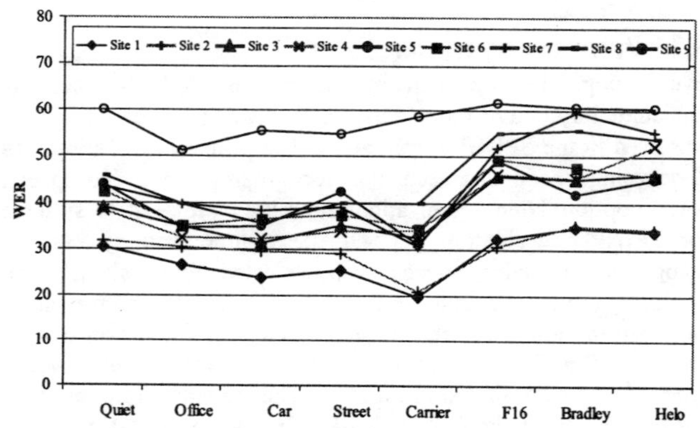

Figure 5. Effect of Different Noise Environments.

5. ANALYSIS OF THE TRANSCRIPTS

An analysis of the transcripts of the conversations was made to explore how different talker behaviors might affect recognizer performance. As is the case with most military applications, the talkers' task is quite constrained and requires only a limited vocabulary. Individual speech turns are quite short.

5.1 Language and Speech Production

Table 5 shows gives the various timing measures and token counts for the conversations and for the individual roles (sides). The average turn was less than 2 s. and the vocabulary less than 1100 words (types). The FO had more to say than the SO and each had a vocabulary of about 800 words. Game words are 118 types considered important for playing the game, e.g., ammo, arm, heading, radar.

Table 5. Language and Speech Production Measurements from Transcripts. Analysis of 64 conversations (128 conversation sides). Elapsed time: 12,646.17 s. (3:30:46.17)

	Both Sides	FO	SO
Speech Time	10,100.56	5,694.23	4,406.33
Speech/Elapsed Time	0.799	0.450	0.348
Turns	5,748	3,098	2,650
Seconds/Turn	1.757	1.838	1.663
Types Total	1,089	812	802
Grid Tokens	3,465	2,043	1,422
Game Tokens	4,119	2,330	1,789
Regular Tokens	16,171	9,208	6,963
Grid Words Spelled	4	4	0
Other Words Spelled	13	5	8
Letters in spelled words	49	36	13
Tokens Total (Each spelled word is 1)	23,772	13,590	10,182
Tokens Total (Each spelled letter is 1)	23,808	13,621	10,187
Tokens/Second of Speech	2.356	2.39	2.31
Tokens/Turn	4.14	4.39	3.84
Spelled/All Grids	0.001	0.002	0
Game+Grid /All Tokens	0.319	0.322	0.315

Table 6 shows ranked word usage. The top ten word types account for 24% of the total tokens; the top 500, over 96%.

Table 6. Word Types Ranked by Frequency of Use

Rank of Type	Cumulative % of Total Types	Number of Tokens	Frequency of Tokens	Cumulative % of Total Tokens
1	0.1%	1086	0.04568	4.6%
10	0.9%	413	0.01737	24.3%
30	2.8%	162	0.00681	45.4%
100	9.2%	51	0.00215	70.7%
250	23.0%	15	0.00063	88.5%
500	45.9%	3	0.00013	96.3%
575	52.8%	2	0.00008	97.2%
722	66.3%	1	0.00004	98.5%
1089	100.%	1	0.00004	100.0%

5.2 Talker behaviors

In the more severe environments, talkers adapted their speech patterns. A major difference between SPINE-1 and SPINE-2 was that SPINE-1 used confusable, rhyming words for the grid labels, whereas SPINE-2 used distinctive military vocabulary for the grid labels. This led to very different compensations by the talkers. In SPINE-1, talkers had to alter their vocabulary to convey the confusable grid labels. The example below illustrates the inventive talk-arounds that were used to convey the highly confusable grid labels in SPINE-1.

SO: Rue veal.

FO: Wow, I can't understand you at all.

....

SO: R as in Robert, U as in underwear, E as in egg. All right and veal as in ah dead baby cow.

In both SPINEs, there tended to be more chit-chat in the less severe environments, and consequently, for SPINE-2, severe environments led to a less varied, rather than a more varied, vocabulary. Figure 6 shows how talker behavior in SPINE-2 changed with increasingly severe noise environments.

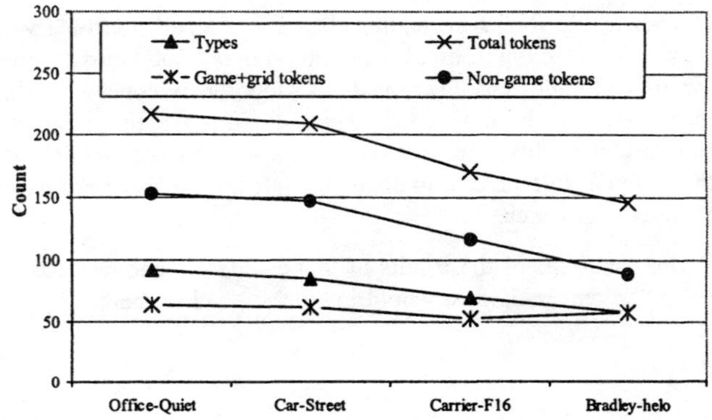

Figure 6. Talker Behaviors by Noise Environment.

In increasingly severe noise environments, the talkers said less, and the conversations were more limited to task-related activities. This was reflected in the use of significantly fewer sentences and turns, fewer total tokens, fewer types, and fewer non-game-related tokens. Speaking rate (words/ s) also decreased. Game-related tokens, including grid labels did not decrease significantly with more severe noise environments. Correlations (by conversation side) between talker behaviors and WER for the different sites were generally small. There were, however, significant correlations with WER for number of game tokens, total tokens, number of turns, and speaking rate for several of the sites.

6. CONCLUSIONS

The SPINE data and evaluation has provided the challenge to developers of automatic speech recognizers to process military-style dialogue when the talkers' speech production and the speech signals are affected by noisy environments and the use of military communication equipment. The lowest WER of 27.5% is 3.0% to 7.7% (absolute) worse than was reported in May 2001, for two different corpora of regular phone conversations. SPINE, with its controlled dimensions – talker roles, environmental noise, and communication channel – provides a wealth of data for investigating relationships among test conditions, talker behavior and recognizer performance. This paper has presented a start at mining this data, primarily with regard to reconizing uncoded speech.

Talker behavior is affected by the role played by the talker, all parts of the equipment (microphone, earphone and coder), and the noise. WER is affected by talker behavior, the microphone, and any noise entering the microphone. Unlike the results reported earlier for SPINE-1 [4], the span of WER's for the coders (uncoded speech) in SPINE-2 was only 2.1%, leading to the conclusion that ways in which the talkers adapted their speech to compensate for coder distortion did not significantly affect recognizer performance. SPINE-2 included more severe noise combinations than SINE-1, and adaptation was shown for noise, where a 40% reduction in word types and a 30% reduction in total tokens were found in the higher noise conditions. Despite this compensation, the span of WER's across noise conditions was 8.5%, undoubtedly also influenced by noise picked up by the microphone. The SO role had a 5.3% higher WER than the FO role but approximately 30% less spoken tokens and speech time.

Overall the SPINE-2 evaluation data has a small vocabulary of only 1089 word types, of which the top-ranked 500 types account for 96% of the tokens. This analysis supports the conclusion that techniques can be developed to greatly improve the automatic recognition of this type of speech. Separate language models for the different roles and/or dialogue models appear to be profitable avenues of research.

Further analyses of the results of this evaluation and evaluations using the remaining data would invariably lead to more ideas for improvement, as well as improvement in recognition performance. Military applications include the monitoring and evaluation of training exercises and actual operations and man-machine interfaces for severe environments. It is also useful for non-military applications of speech technology in environments that use a specialized limited vocabulary in high background noise.

7. ACKNOWLEDGMENTS

NRL's participation in this research and the data acquisition and preparation was funded by DARPA. The authors thank ARCON Corp. for the data collection, the Linguistic Data consortium for doing the transcriptions and distributing the data to the participants and all of the sites that participated in the evaluation.

8. REFERENCES

[1] DoD Digital Voice Processor Consortium. http://www.arcon.com/ddvpc.

[2] Kreamer, E. W., Tardelli, J. D., and Gatewood, P. D. Communicability Testing Using the ARCON Communicability Exercise (ACE) - 95. Tech. Rpt. ARCON Corp., 260 Bear Hill Road, Waltham, MA 02451.

[3] LDC Catalog, Linguistic Data Consortium. http://www.ldc.upenn.edu/Catalog.

[4] Speech in Noisy Environments (SPINE). http://elezar.itd.navy.mil/spine/index.html.

Using Heuristics, Syntax and a Local Dynamic Dictionary for Protein Name Tagging

Gunnar Eriksson
guer@sics.se

Kristofer Franzén
franzen@sics.se

Fredrik Olsson
fredriko@sics.se

Swedish Institute of Computer Science
Box 1263
SE-164 29 Kista, Sweden

ABSTRACT

A prerequisite for all higher level information extraction tasks is the identification of unknown names in text. This paper presents a method for extracting protein names from abstracts of articles in the biomedical domain. These names present several interesting difficulties because of their variant structural characteristics and the lack of common naming standards and fixed nomenclatures in the domain.

The method presented is based on three main components: The use of heuristic rules and knowledge bases, the use of syntactic analysis, and the use of a document-local dynamic dictionary.

The implementation of the method, the protein name tagger Yapex, is evaluated on a set of MEDLINE abstracts, using KeX, a freely available protein name tagger, as a reference system.

The systems are evaluated under two different notions of correctness, and are shown to perform equally well under the more liberal notion, while the Yapex system performs significantly better under the stricter notion of correctness.

Keywords

Named Entity Recognition, Information Extraction, Protein names, Bioinformatics

1. BACKGROUND

The detection and categorization of named entities, such as names of people, organisations and places, in classical MUC-style information extraction tasks [3] might be regarded a solved problem. But names of proteins present a slightly different challenge because of their variant structural characteristics and the specifics of the text domains in which they appear. This certainly holds true for other biological substances, and probably for many other kinds of terminology as well. For a extended discussion on this subject, cf., [6].

The roles and functions of proteins are important study objects in many areas of the life sciences, as well as for the pharmaceutical industry. In view of the vast amount of scientific text produced in these areas, it is essential to find methods for automatic structuring and extraction of information found therein.

One common reason for developing methods for automatic detection of protein names in text, has been the desire to build systems for automatic extraction of interactions between proteins [2, 11]. However, the detection of protein names is in itself useful in, e.g., applications to support browsing, searching and linking in abstracts from the National Library of Medicine's MEDLINE database[1].

Proceedings of HLT 2002, Second International Conference on Human Language Technology Research, M. Marcus, ed., Morgan Kaufmann, San Francisco, 2002.

2. PROTEIN NAMES

Despite the lack of common standards and fixed nomenclatures, protein names exhibit several regularities that can be exploited in order to identify previously unseen instances. Most importantly, protein names are almost always descriptive in some way. Characteristics such as function (e.g., *growth hormone*), localization or cellular origin (such as *HIV-1 envelope glycoprotein gp120*), physical properties (*salivary acidic protein-1*), or similarities to other proteins (*Rho-like protein*) are commonly reflected in the name. Names are also constructed using combination and/or abbreviations of the above. As the examples show, protein names often consist of multiple words.

There is no obvious definition of what is to be treated as a protein name, and for the purpose of this study we use a combination of criteria. A protein name is defined semantically as something that denotes a single biological entity composed of one or more amino acid chains. Protein fragments or protein families are not included in this definition. Furthermore, since names of genes and the names of their protein products are used equivocally we make no attempt to distinguish between them.

In addition to the semantic definition above, from a text structural point of view, we define a protein name as a sequence of words denoting a specific, individual protein entity. We also include some less direct references to individual protein entities in the protein name definition, (e.g., `<prot>`*importin beta1*`</prot>` *derivatives*). The definition excludes non-specific reference to individuals (*transcription factor, a 89 kD protein*). It also excludes most references to groups or classes of proteins (*protein kinases, globulins*), although phrases denoting small groups of nearly identical proteins are included (*eukaryotic RhoA-binding kinases*).

[1]MEDLINE is a bibliographic database owned by the U.S. National Library of Medicine. MEDLINE can be searched via PubMed:
`http://www.ncbi.nlm.nih.gov/entrez/query.fcgi`

Finally, our definition of a protein name excludes anaphoric reference to proteins (*this protein*).

3. METHOD

Arguably, information extraction tasks are always a trade-off between recall and precision, and depending on the application, one may want to focus on one or the other. When trying to extract protein interactions from MEDLINE abstracts, Thomas *et al.* [11] claim that precision is more important, since the amount of text (11 million abstracts) makes it likely that if an interaction is not correctly detected in one abstract it can be found in another. de Bruijn and Martin [5], on the other hand, aim at high recall and a fair precision, arguing that filtering techniques can be used to separate plausible hits from dubious ones at a later stage.

In our case, the first application at hand was a browsing support system, to link protein names in MEDLINE abstracts to entries in SWISS-PROT [1]. Since the intended user is likely to be a domain expert able to judge if a hyperlink actually refers to a protein, we could accept some false links. On the other hand, too many words erroneously marked as proteins would give the user sore eyes and little confidence in the system. The current algorithm initially strives for high recall with the consequence of poor precision. Later modules in the pipelined system use filtering techniques to boost precision, and a local dictionary is eventually applied to increase recall. The algorithm can be described as consisting of the following seven steps: the first four steps are concerned with the lexical analysis of single word tokens, and the first two of these are implementations of some of the heuristic steps in the algorithm described by Fukuda *et al.* [7], from which the terminology of these steps is borrowed. Steps five and six are concerned with the syntactic analysis of noun phrases and of the lexical categories derived in the previous steps, and the final step utilizes the syntactic information to build patterns that identify new single- and multi-word protein names. Each step will be described in the following subsections.

3.1 Lexical analysis of feature terms

Feature terms are words such as *receptor* and *enzyme*, which describe the function or characteristics of a protein. These words often occur in or near a protein name and can be used as indicators of the presence of such a name. Two types of feature terms are distinguished: internal and external, internal terms being words that belong to the name, like *protein, particle* and *receptor*. External feature terms are words — e.g., *peptide, domain* and *terminal* — that act as indicators of a protein name but, most often, do not constitute a part of the name itself, according to our protein name definition. A subset of the internal feature terms (*factor, receptor* and *enzyme*) are considered strong feature terms, being particularly strong indicators of protein names.

3.2 Lexical analysis of core terms

A core term constitutes the nucleus of a protein name. These terms are the parts of a protein name that show the closest resemblance to regular proper names. As candidates for these terms we pick words ending in *-ase* and *-in*, or strings with characteristics typical of protein names, i.e., strings containing instances of upper case letters or numbers, found in names of proteins like *HsMad2* and *U3-55k*. Protein names which do not conform to these patterns are identified by means of a list of established protein names (e.g., *interferon*).

Two general filters are applied to these core term candidates to avoid over-generation: words consisting of $\geq 50\%$ non-word characters, and measuring units are discarded as core terms.

3.3 Lexical analysis of specifiers

We also recognizes a third lexical category, the specifier. Specifiers are terms that often occur at the beginning or end of a protein name, for instance to specify an individual protein. We treat Arabic and Roman numerals, single letters, Greek letter names, and combinations of these as specifiers.

3.4 Applying filters and knowledge bases

As will be seen in the evaluation (Section 5.3, Figure 2), applying the lexical analysis of the previous steps results in a large number of false hits. To remedy this low precision, a set of some 30 lexical analysis filters is applied. Some filters use regular expression patterns of word suffixes to rule out things like names of chemical substances. Other filters match whole words or expressions to filter out bibliographical references, chemical formulas, arithmetic expressions, and amino acid sequences. A third group of pattern-matching filters remove the core-term annotation on words unlikely to function as core terms: words ≥ 6 characters long consisting solely of upper-case letters, or consisting of upper-case letters and more than one hyphen are discarded.

Short core terms (≤ 3 characters) get special treatment. Only those found in our short-protein-name knowledge base drawn from SWISS-PROT [1] are considered core terms. All the others are tagged as potential core terms to be used later in the protein name identification process. Core terms resembling regular proper names are treated in the same way.

3.5 Finding protein name sites

To find all possible locations of protein names in a text, this step takes advantage of the English Functional Dependency Grammar parser (ENFDG version 3.6) from Conexor Oy [9] to locate all noun phrases in the text. For every noun phrase, the procedure identifies the phrase head and its preceding lexical modifiers. This constitutes the minimal noun phrase — the noun phrase without any subordinate noun phrases — and is considered a potential protein name location.

3.6 Identifying protein names

To identify the protein name, the procedure starts off by adjoining all specifiers to their preceding core, potential core, or feature term. Then all external or plural feature terms, their adjoined specifiers, and words without an analysis from the previous steps are stripped off from the right edge of the minimal noun phrase. From the left edge, lexical modifiers earlier identified as numerals together with measuring units are stripped off. The remaining part of the minimal noun phrase is considered a potential protein name. It is selected as such if it contains a core term, a strong feature term together with at least one other word token, a feature term with an adjoined specifier, or a potential core term together with a feature term somewhere in the full, unstripped noun phrase.

3.7 Applying a local dynamic dictionary

The relevant terms in the protein names identified in the previous step are stored in a local dictionary as regular expressions. For every document, the dictionary is used in an additional tagging pass over the text to make possible flexible matching of protein names in noun phrases undetected or misinterpreted by the ENFDG parser.

4. YAPEX

The method described in the previous section is implemented as the protein name tagger Yapex. Awaiting an open source release,

the Yapex system is available for testing at:
`http://www.sics.se/humle/projects/prothalt/`.

The data sets that where used during development and evaluation are published on the same URL.

5. EVALUATION

5.1 Reference and test corpora

Tagging of protein names in running text is cumbersome even for human domain experts, and evaluation of a protein tagger requires a tagged corpus. For an exhaustive discussion on the problems of building annotated corpora for the molecular-biology domain, and results on inter-annotator agreement, cf., Tateisi *et al.* [10].

From the set of answers obtained by posing the following query to MEDLINE, 99 abstracts were drawn randomly to form a reference (training) corpus used during development of Yapex:

```
protein binding [Mesh term] AND interaction
AND molecular
```

with the parameters *abstract, english, human, publication date 1996-2001.* The reference corpus, as well as the test corpus (described below), were annotated by domain experts connected to the Yapex project.

The test corpus consists of 101 MEDLINE abstracts and it is divided into two distinct parts, the first of which contains 48 abstracts obtained as part of the result when posing the above query to MEDLINE. This part contains a total of 1213 annotated protein names. The remaining 53 abstracts of the 101 in the test corpus correspond to a randomly chosen, re-tagged sub-set of the GENIA corpus [4] containing 723 annotated protein names. The reference and test corpora are mutually exclusive.

5.2 Notions of correctness

This evaluation presents performance figures for Yapex and KeX[2] on the test corpus using two different notions of correctness, that is, two ways of talking about the result in terms of what is actually tagged by the tagger and what should have been tagged according to the answer key.

SLOPPY: If any token of the proposed hit, as suggested by the tagger, matches some token of the answer key, constructed by domain experts, the hit is counted as a match.

STRICT: If a proposed hit matches one answer key exactly, the hit is counted as a match.

For an extended discussion on different notions of correctness when evaluating protein name taggers, cf., [8].

5.3 Results

In Figure 1, Yapex and KeX are compared in terms of F-score[3]. Looking at the SLOPPY bars in the chart, we can see that this is

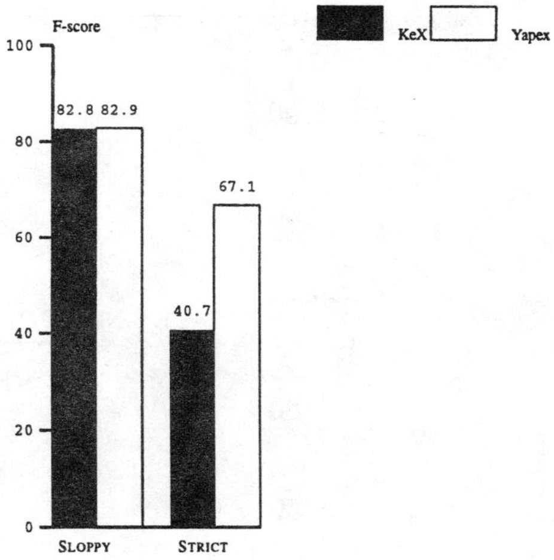

Figure 1: F-score for Yapex and KeX when evaluated along the SLOPPY and STRICT notions.

	YAPEX	KEX
SLOPPY	$R = 82.1\%$	$R = 83.5\%$
	$P = 83.8\%$	$P = 82.1\%$
	$F = 82.9\%$	$F = 82.8\%$
STRICT	$R = 66.4\%$	$R = 41.1\%$
	$P = 67.8\%$	$P = 40.4\%$
	$F = 67.1\%$	$F = 40.7\%$

Table 1: Results for Yapex and KeX given in recall (R), precision (P), and F-score (F).

the only notion under which Yapex and KeX yield similar results. The difference between the systems is more obvious, in favour of Yapex, when the other notion of correctness is reviewed — the figure for Yapex is substantially better when measuring the taggers' performance in terms of the STRICT notion. We notice also that it is only under the SLOPPY condition that KeX performs close to the results reported in [5], but not at all close to what its authors reported in [7].

The result under the STRICT condition, suggests that Yapex is much better at finding the exact edges of the protein names.

Table 1 shows that both systems promote precision and recall equally.

In Figure 2, there are two quadrangles illustrating the possible combinations of using filters and knowledge bases (FKB, cf., Section 3.4) and a Local Dynamic Dictionary (LDD, cf., Section 3.7) for the STRICT and SLOPPY notions.

The way to understand a quadrangle is this: for any of the two notions in the figure, the lower left corner describes the performance of Yapex when neither filters and knowledge bases, nor the Local Dynamic Dictionary are used. The case of using Yapex with FKB, but without the LDD is represented by the upper left corner of the quadrangle. Analogously, the lower right corner denotes the use of Yapex with the LDD, but without FKB. Finally, the upper right corner represents the use of Yapex employing both FKB and LDD.

In Figure 2, we can see that the use of filters and knowledge bases promote a gain in precision, but that they at the same time contribute to lower recall. Even more interesting than the use of FKB, is the use of the Local Dynamic Dictionary. The motivation

[2]KeX is a freely available protein name tagger based on the algorithms presented by Fukuda *et al.* [7]. KeX can be downloaded from:
http://www.hgc.ims.u-tokyo.ac.jp/service/tooldoc/KeX/intro.html.

[3]F-score is a measure combining precision and recall:

$$F = \frac{(\beta^2 + 1)PR}{(\beta^2 P + R)}$$

where β is a parameter that represents the relative importance of Precision (P) and Recall (R), in our case equally important.

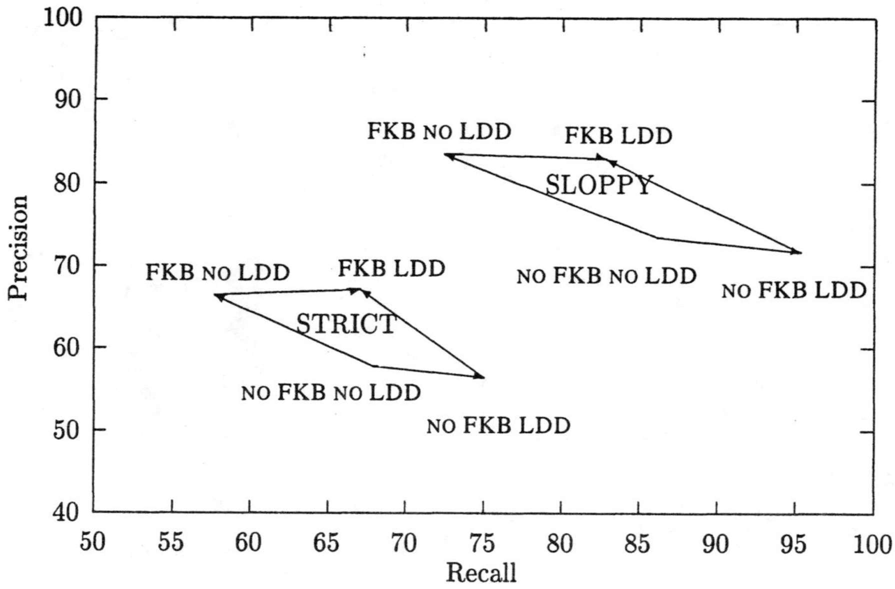

Figure 2: How the Filters and Knowledge Bases (FKB) and the Local Dynamic Dictionary (LDD) influence Recall and Precision.

for using an LDD is to increase recall, and contrary to our intuition, precision did not drop severely even though recall increased substantially when using Yapex with an LDD.

6. DISCUSSION

In this paper we have described a technique for identifying protein names in running text. The good results from the evaluation described above, may be attributed to the three main components of the system: The use of heuristic rules and knowledge bases, the use of syntactic analysis, and the use of a document-local dynamic dictionary.

The evaluation results suggest that it is possible to get quite a good identification rate with a system based on a modest number of heuristic and knowledge-based rules. Such a system may be fine-tuned for either high recall or high precision by the number and nature of the filtering rules.

Due to the nature of such textual entities as name of proteins, there is also an independent need for this kind of heuristics component; a system that relies on knowledge of the syntactic structure of texts has to have some kind of knowledge of prototypical traits of protein names — at least as a fall-back way of identifying unknown or newly coined names.

A system based solely on heuristics of this kind is useful for named entity extraction as long as the aim is to decide whether a given sequence of words contains the name of an entity or not. In settings where the identification of the exact start- and end-points of a name is essential, the usefulness no longer holds. The results from the comparison with the KeX tagger suggest that adding the powers of a full syntactic analysis is a way of improving the detection of name edges. There is nothing surprising about a syntactic parser being able to aid in the detection of protein names: names are only ever found in noun phrases. If we had a perfect parser that identified all minimal noun phrases, the problem would be reduced to deciding if the noun phrase is a protein name or not.

The use of the ENFDG parser is a way of reducing the burden on the heuristic component. By delimiting the search for characteristic parts of protein names to noun phrases, it is possible to limit the heuristic component to the identification of characteristic endings, words, and phrases within a potential name. This enables a simpler rule set with a higher degree of generality.

Another encouraging result is the fact that a general purpose syntactic analysis tool can be used without modifications to good effect in this highly specialized task of analyzing abstracts in the biomedical domain.

That the parsing of these texts is far from perfect, however, is shown in Figure 2 by the performance achieved by the document-local dynamic dictionary. If the texts had been parsed perfectly, there would be no performance gain when adding the LDD component.

Still, the performance of the syntactic parser in the identification of name edges is quite sufficient for building the specific patterns which the LDD uses to find yet other instances of proteins already mentioned in the text. This is a important reason to the large contribution to the performance by the LDD component.

Another reason for the success of the LDD may be its restriction to a single document. We assume that the homonymy rate in a given document is rather low, i.e., a sequence of word tokens already analyzed as a protein name is not likely to have any other function when reoccurring in the same document.

7. ACKNOWLEDGMENTS

Partial funding for this project has been provided by VINNOVA, the Swedish Agency for Innovation Systems.

8. ADDITIONAL AUTHORS

Additional authors: Per Lidén (Virtual Genetics Laboratory AB, email: `per.liden@compumine.com`) and Lars Asker (Virtual Genetics AB, email: `lars.asker@compumine.com`).

9. REFERENCES

[1] A. Bairoch and R. Apweiler. The SWISS-PROT protein sequence database and its supplement TrEMBL in 2000. *Nucl. Acids. Res.*, 28:45–48, 2000.

[2] C. Blaschke, M. A. Andrade, C. Ouzounis, and A. Valencia. Automatic extraction of biological information from

scientific text: protein—protein interactions. In *Proceedings of the Seventh International Conference on Intelligent Systems for Molecular Biology (ISMB'99)*, pages 60–67, Heidelberg, Germany, August 6-10 1999.

[3] A. Borthwick, J. Sterling, E. Agichtein, and R. Grishman. NYU: Description of the MENE named entity system as used in MUC-7. In *Proceedings of the Seventh Message Understanding Conference (MUC-7)*, Fairfax, VA, USA, April 29 - May 1 1998.

[4] N. Collier, H. S. Park, N. Ogata, Y. Tateishi, C. Nobata, T. Ohta, T. Sekimizu, H. Imai, K. Ibushi, and J. Tsujii. The genia project: corpus-based knowledge acquisition and information extraction from genome research papers. In *Proceedings of the European Association for Computational Linguistics (EACL) conference*, 1999.

[5] B. de Bruijn and J. Martin. Protein name tagging. Presented as a poster at the Eighth International Conference on Intelligent Systems for Molecular Biology (ISMB'00), 2000.

[6] K. Franzén, G. Eriksson, F. Olsson, L. Asker, P. Lidén, and J. Cöster. Protein names and how to find them. *International Journal of Medical Informatics*, 67(1-3):49–62, December 2002.

[7] K. Fukuda, T. Tsunoda, A. Tamura, and T. Takagi. Toward information extraction: Identifying protein names from biological papers. In *Proceedings of the Pacific Symposium on Biocomputing (PSB'98)*, pages 705–716, Maui, Hawaii, January 4-9 1998.

[8] F. Olsson, G. Eriksson, K. Franzén, L. Asker, and P. Lidén. Notions of correctness when evaluating protein name taggers. In *Proceedings of the 19th International Conference on Computational Linguistics (COLING 2002)*, Taipei, Taiwan, August 24 - September 1 2002.

[9] P. Tapanainen and T. Järvinen. A non-projective dependency parser. In *Proceedings of the 5th Conference on Applied Natural Language Processing*, pages 64–71, Washington D.C., April 1997. Association for Computational Linguistics.

[10] Y. Tateisi, T. Ohta, N. Collier, C. Nobata, and J. Tsujii. Building an annotated corpus in the molecular-biology domain. In *Proceedings of Workshop on Semantic Annotation and Intelligent Content*, Centre Universitaire, Luxembourg, August 2000. ACL. The workshop was held in conjuntion with the 18th International Conference on Computational Linguistics (COLING-2000).

[11] J. Thomas, D. Milward, C. Ouzounis, S. Pulman, and M. Carroll. Automatic extraction of protein interactions from scientific abstracts. In *Proceedings of the Pacific Symposium on Biocomputing (PSB 2000)*, pages 538–549, Oahu, Hawaii, January 4-9 2000.

The Arizona Virtual Patient: Using Question-Answering Technology to Enhance Dialogue Processing

Scott Farrar
University of Arizona
1049 N. Jacobus Ave
Tucson, AZ 85705
(520) 903-2925
farrar@u.arizona.edu

ABSTRACT

The Arizona Virtual Patient (AVP) is a dialogue-based patient simulator for training pharmacy students. The AVP uses state-of-the-art question-answering techniques, including a taxonomy of expected answer types. After the user enters a question, a database of patient profiles is queried and an appropriate answer in the form of a video is displayed. The patient database can be augmented by non-programmers. It is argued that the AVP is an effective tool for instructing pharmacy students in pharmacist-patient interaction.

Keywords

Dialogue processing, intelligent tutor, question-answering, pharmacy.

1. INTRODUCTION

The Arizona Virtual Patient (AVP) is a dialogue-based patient simulator for the pharmacy domain. It was developed in conjunction with pharmacy educators as a tool for instructing students of pharmacy in the basics of patient counseling. Student input is via the keyboard, but the patient's responses are displayed as short video clips that show non-verbal information particular to the pharmacy domain. The design of the language component draws on technology from question-answering (Q-A) systems. Since the AVP's primary task is to retrieve answers from a patient response database, it is well-suited for Q-A approaches. The most important, based on [5], is the mapping of question types (input) to expected answer types (output).

2. THE PHARMACY DOMAIN

In an early study, [3] show patient simulators to be an effective tool for training pharmacy students in the pharmacist-patient interaction process. Traditional methodology requires either the use of expert human simulators (usually a pharmacy faculty) or access to real patients. Only the former is extensively used in pharmacy programs. Due to time constraints, pharmacy instructors usually require students to practice among themselves in preparation for more focused training with faculty. Other patient simulators are available to pharmacy students but are in the form of interactive multi-media programs [1], [6]. The major shortcoming of these systems is that they have no interactive dialogue capability.

Proceedings of HLT 2002, Second International Conference on Human Language Technology Research, M. Marcus, ed., Morgan Kaufmann, San Francisco, 2002.

2.1 Verbal Techniques for Interaction

Pharmacists interact with patients on a variety of levels: (1) pharmacists are primary care-givers to patients who come to the pharmacy with an acute complaint; (2) pharmacists take medical histories to ensure that there will be no side-effects with existing conditions or interactions with other prescribed medications; and (3) pharmacists counsel patients with chronic conditions on how to manage their disease(s). The AVP can simulate each of the above cases and act as a metric to measure student progress. Based on guidelines developed by [2], optimal pharmacist-patient interaction can be achieved when pharmacists adhere to proven communicative techniques.

The following outlines the desired sequencing of conversation during a typical consultation visit, or when a patient comes to the pharmacist for the first time with an acute complaint. The optimal sequence consists of an **introduction**, the posing of **prime questions**, followed by asking for **final verification**, then finally a **show and tell** session to demonstrate proper use of the medication. The introduction sets the stage for the consultation and requires the pharmacist to introduce him/herself and to verify basic patient information such as name and purpose of the visit. The introduction is followed by the prime questions which must include the following:

> "What did your doctor tell you the medication is for?"
> "How did your doctor tell you to take the medication?"
> "What did your doctor tell you to expect?"

Asking for final verification is the most important step in the consultation. The pharmacist asks the patient to "play back" everything that he or she has learned in order to check for accuracy.

> "Just to make sure that I did not forget to tell you anything important, will you go over how you are going to use the medication?"

Finally in the show and tell step, the pharmacist demonstrates proper use of the medication. This step obviously is not fully carried out, but the pharmacist directs the dialogue by modifying the three prime questions. Besides the proper sequencing of consultation dialogue, the pharmacist can use certain discourse techniques to enhance the interaction. For example, pharmacists are instructed to praise the patient for what he or she knows.

> "Taking it three times a day is correct, but it's best to take it evenly spaced, every 8 hours."

Furthermore, it is the pharmacist's task to draw as much information from the patient as possible. This can be achieved by avoiding **open-ended** questions and opting instead for **closed-ended** ones. Open-ended questions are usually *wh*-questions and demand more than a simple answer, while closed-ended questions prompt for short, yes/no answers. Compare the following:

> *Open-ended:*
>
> "What did the doctor tell you the medication is for?"
>
> "He said it was for my chest pain."
>
> ***Closed-ended***
>
> "Did the doctor tell you what the medication is for?"
>
> "Yes."

Like closed-ended questions, leading or restrictive questions narrow the response options of the patient. These are often in the form of a tag questions.

> ***Leading/restrictive questions:***
>
> "You're taking two of these day, right?"
>
> "I'll bet you're feeling much better, aren't you?"
>
> ***Open-ended questions:***
>
> "How many do you take?"
>
> "How have you been feeling?"

Other good communicative techniques include the use of paraphrasing, a form of active listening. Here are some examples:

> ***Patient's statements:***
>
> "I just wish Dr. Nelson would put me back on aspirin. These fancy new drugs aren't working anyway."
>
> ***Pharmacist's paraphrase:***
>
> "You would rather take aspirin than what you're taking now."

Finally the use of summarization is effective to correct any mistakes and prompts the patient for additional information.

> "From what you've told me, Mrs. Smith, this new medication has upset your stomach and made you feel light-headed, ..."

2.2 Assessing Verbal Skills

In order to use the Arizona Virtual Patient as a measure of the student's performance, it is necessary to attach a quantitative value to the language employed during the consultation. Students can earn up to 100 points per interaction. Points are assigned, for example, when students correctly sequence the dialogue (crucial when performing an on-the-spot diagnosis), employ open-ended questions, and use paraphrasing. Students lose points when they do not adhere to the above guidelines. The quantitative evaluation is one way to provide feedback to the pharmacy student. Another way is by giving the student examples of best-practice dialogue when they run into problems.

3. THE DIALOGUE SYSTEM

Within the pharmacy domain, I designed a patient simulator that can take part in interactive dialogue with the pharmacy student. The following section gives an overview of the system and presents the computational techniques employed.

3.1 System Architecture

The Arizona Virtual Patient is an application designed with the Java™ 2 Standard Development Kit[1] and Quicktime™ for Java[2]. The major components of the AVP are the graphical user interface (GUI), the language processing module, the video database, the knowledge base of patient profiles, the query engine (see Figure 1).

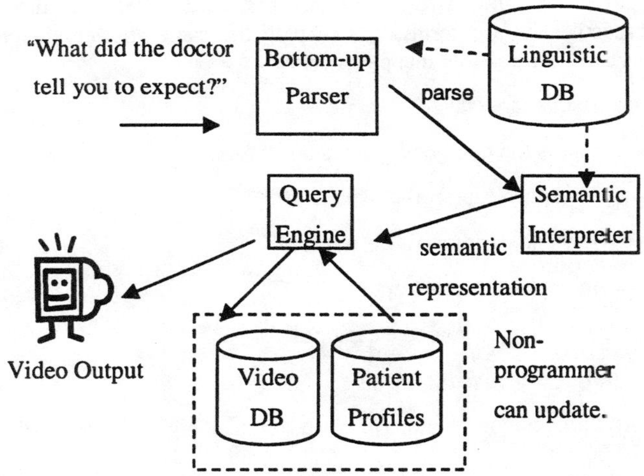

Figure 1: Process Model for the Virtual Patient

The GUI includes a text field for user input, a large window for displaying patient response videos, and a window for on-the-spot tutoring (see Section 3.2 for a discussion of NLP).

3.2 Video Versus Language Generation

I chose to use pre-recorded videos as responses for two reasons. First, the testing of a text-only prototype system against a mixed, text/video prototype revealed that text responses were not an

---

[1] The SDK is available for download at http://java.sun.com/j2se/.

[2]Quicktime for Java is available for free at http://developer.apple.com/sdk/index.html#QTJava.

effective means for involving the student in the dialogue. Students evaluated video interaction as more realistic than text despite the shortcomings of video—the most serious of which was the "canned" nature of the video response. Second, in order to simulate the patient's physical condition and affect (posture, attitude, personality), video is crucial. Quicktime™ for Java allows for a seamless inclusion of video players in a Java application. A typical session requires the recording of approximately 50 videos that are on average 8 seconds long.

3.2 The Language Processing Component

For the initial language processing, I employed a lexicalized, bottom-up parser. The lack of multiple word senses allows for relatively uncomplicated lexicalized parsing. That is, there are relatively few argument-bearing lexical items that are ambiguous. An exception to this is the verb *take,* which is used in two ways in the AVP: "Take this medication and show it to your doctor" and "You need to take this medication daily." Local context, as in the presence of the *to*-phrase, is used to disambiguate such cases. Furthermore, the bottom-up approach works well in the limited domain because the system does not need to deal with structural ambiguities. I handcrafted the grammar based on student interaction with the text-based prototype.

The difficulty with a patient simulator is the need for processing a wide variety of input utterances. Questions can be phrased in many ways. Thus, two input utterances, quite different in their respective surface forms, can map to the same answer video. Consider the possible mappings below:

> *Possible inputs:*
>
> "What's the dosage of the captopril?"
>
> "How much captopril do you take?"
>
> "How many captoprils do you take?"
>
> "How strong is your captopril?"
>
> "How often do you take captopril?"
>
> *Output (video transcripts):*
>
> "Well, one in the morning and one at night—I think it's 50mg."
>
> "I take 50mg. of captopril everyday."

The mapping task is quite similar to what is required in an open-domain question-answering (Q-A) system, in which the user queries large collections of data for factual knowledge. Q-A systems have been quite successful in open-domain tasks as illustrated by the Message Understanding Conference (MUC) [7]. Since over 90% of the input utterances in a pharmacist-patient interview are questions, Q-A strategies were easily adapted to fit the needs of a patient simulator. The primary strategy from the Q-A domain is the use of a taxonomy of **expected answer types** [5] (see Figure 2).

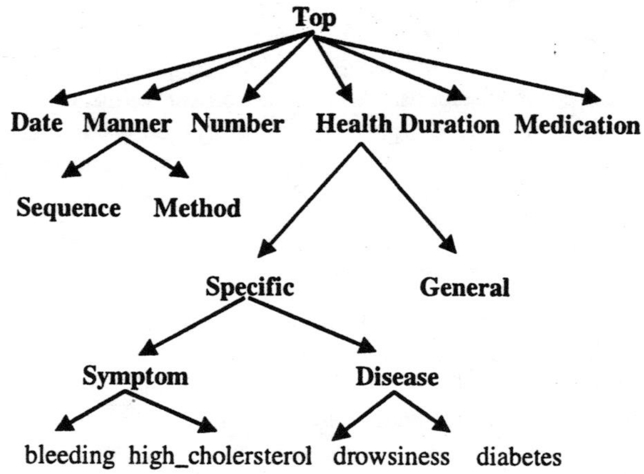

Figure 2: Hierarchy of Expected Answer Types

The advantage of using the taxonomy is that the many-to-few mapping between questions and answers is facilitated. After the input is parsed, a semantic representation (e.g., AMOUNT-captopril- take) is generated based on the taxonomy of answer types. Next, a preprocessed answer database is queried for an appropriate video. The answer database consists of the transcriptions of the videos. Difficulties arise due to two factors. The first is the use of non-canonical question types, such as:

> "And the dosage of your captopril?"
>
> "What about the captopril?"

Based on insights from [4], these questions are mapped onto a hierarchy of question types based on form (cf. the taxonomy of answer types based on semantic content). The observation is that noun phrases, possibly combined with *Wh*-words and/or prepositions, are just as likely to be questions as well-formed interrogatives are, especially in conversation.

3.3 Knowledge Base of Patient Profiles

An important requirement for educational software such as the Arizona Virtual Patient is to allow for development by non-programmers. The design of the AVP allows for such development by including an augmentable knowledge base of patient profiles. A patient profile is a schema that contains information on a particular patient's medical condition, drug history, and general information relevant to a pharmacist-patient interview, such as the patient's name or physician's name. The profile provides the basis for choosing the correct response video. The rationale is that new lexical items (mostly new nouns) will accompany a new patient, such as drug names or names of diseases, but the basic language for interacting with the patient will remain relatively constant. Accompanying the patient profile is the collection of videos that makes up the patient's responses. When a new patient is constructed, the video transcripts are preprocessed only once. An important requirement for educational software is to allow for development by non-programmers. The AVP allows for such development by including an augmentable database of **patient profiles**. A patient profile is a schema that contains information on a particular patient's medical condition, drug history, and general information relevant to a pharmacist-patient counseling session, such as the physician's name or patient's age. The profile provides the basis for choosing the correct response video. The rationale is that new lexical items (drug names or names of diseases) will accompany a new patient, but the basic language for interacting with the patient will remain relatively constant.

4. EVALUATION OF THE SYSTEM

The Virtual Patient was developed by capturing hundreds of interactions of pharmacy students with an early prototype. Effectiveness of the system can be measured in IR terms. One group of students was asked to choose response videos manually from a list of possible questions. This was compared against another group's interaction with the program. **Precision** was initially 93% for the test group (but increased for each students as they used the tool), while **recall** was 89%. Precision is the number of correct answers divided by the total number of possible answers. Recall is the number of correct response videos retrieved divided by the total number of possible correct videos.

5. FURTHER DEVELOPMENT

The Arizona Virtual Patient is an interactive patient simulator that offers a number of advantages over traditional intelligent tutors in the pharmacy domain. Namely, the AVP allows pharmacy students to practice their verbal interaction skills. The AVP goes beyond purely text-based simulators by employing video responses. The result is a more realistic, interactive experience. Another major strength of the AVP is that it can be augmented by non-programmers, viz. pharmacy faculty.

During the next phase of development, I will add automatic speech recognition so students can interact more naturally with the AVP. Another possible direction is to use natural language generation in conjunction with real-time **video animation**. Video animation gives the illusion that the person in the video is actually speaking. Merging these two features will greatly increase the virtual reality of the system and hopefully make the tool more appealing to students.

6. ACKNOWLEDGMENTS

Special thanks to Dr. Richard Herrier who conceived the project and to Dr. John Gilkey who gave special assistance especially with video editing.

7. REFERENCES

[1] Fuhrman, L.C., Eaddy, M., and Dollar, M. Interactive virtual patient database in a Web based environment to teach pharmaceutical care. American Association of Colleges of Pharmacy Annual Meeting, 101 (July 2000), 216.

[2] Gardner, B. and Herrier, R. Pharmacist-Patient Consultation Program PPCP—Unit I: An Interactive Approach to Verifying Patient Understanding. Pfizer Educational Services, 1997.

[3] Gardner, M.E. and Burpeau-Di-Gregorio, M.Y. Objective assessment of pharmacy students' interviewing skills. American Journal of Pharmaceutical Education, 49 (Spring 1985), 137-144.

[4] Ginzburg, J. and Sag, I.A. Interrogative Investigations: The Form, Meaning, and Use of English Interrogatives. Stanford: CSLI, 2000.

[5] Harabagiu, S., Moldovan, D., Pasca, M., Mihalcea, R., Surdeanu, M., Bunescu, R., Girju, R., Rus, V., and Morarescu, P. The role of lexico-semantic feedback in open-domain textual question-answering in Proceedings of the 39th Annual Meeting of the Association for Computational Linguistics (2001), 274-281.

[6] Kolesar, J.M. and Pitterle, M.E. Development and evaluation of a virtual oncology patient. American Association of Colleges of Pharmacy Annual Meeting, 101 (July 2000), 212.

[7] Pasca, M. and Harabagiu, S. High performance question/answering in Proceedings of the 24th Annual International ACL SIGIR Conference on Research and Development in Information Retrieval (SIGIR-2001), 366-374.

Annotating Temporal Information – From Theory to Practice

Lisa Ferro, Robyn Kozierok
The MITRE Corporation, K329
202 Burlington Road, Rte. 62
Bedford, MA 01730-1420, USA
+1-781-271-5875
lferro, robyn@mitre.org

Laurie Gerber
Northrop Grumman
4065 Hancock Street
San Diego, California 92110, USA
+1-619-200-8344
lgerber@gerbersite.com

Beth Sundheim
SPAWAR Systems Center, 244207
53560 Hull Street
San Diego, CA 92152-5001, USA
+1-619-553-4145
sundheim@spawar.navy.mil

Inderjeet Mani, George Wilson
The MITRE Corporation, W640
11493 Sunset Hills Road
Reston, Virginia 20190-5214, USA
+1-703-883-6149
imani, gwilson@mitre.org

ABSTRACT
This paper expands on and updates a report on a set of guidelines for annotating time expressions [3]. Recent developments in the annotation guidelines, development of corpora, and annotation software are described, along with results on inter-annotator agreement in applying the tagging scheme.

Keywords
Annotation, annotation tools, temporal information, ISO-8601

1. INTRODUCTION
In [3][4][5], the authors outlined a set of annotation guidelines for creating normalized representations of temporal expressions in free text. This scheme, called TIMEX2, was originally developed under the DARPA TIDES Program. This paper reports on progress over the past year in three areas: guidelines, corpora, and annotation software. The developments reported here occurred both in preparation for a new tagging effort, and through the initial stages of applying the guidelines to two different genres of text.

2. BACKGROUND
In addition to the goal of marking the textual extent of a temporal expression, the TIMEX2 scheme has the goal of normalizing the VALUE of the expressions for use in applications such as question-answering, machine translation and summarization. The scheme also includes representations for sets of times and various kinds of vague temporal expressions. Where possible, the information recorded in the tags adheres to *ISO 8601: Information Interchange – Representation of Dates and Times* (1997) [6].

Proceedings of HLT 2002, Second International Conference on Human Language Technology Research, M. Marcus, ed., Morgan Kaufmann, San Francisco, 2002.

3. RECENT DEVELOPMENTS
Extended guidelines. The annotation scheme laid out in [5] has been extended to provide greater specificity in characterizing when events and relations hold true. The tagging conventions now allow certain expressions to be more precisely anchored on a timeline by normalizing them in relation to the narrative time or the timestamp of the document. One advantage of this extension is that the representation can now anchor a duration on a timeline. For example, the expression "the past three weeks" formerly had a normalized value of "P3W" (meaning "a period of 3 weeks"). It will now also contain the anchor time, ANCHOR_VAL="2002-W02" (if the phrase were uttered during the second week of January 2002), as well as the relative direction of the period with the respect to the anchor, namely ANCHOR_DIR="BEFORE".

Fuzzy expressions like "past," "present," and "future" are similarly pinned down. For example, <TIMEX2 VAL="PAST_REF" ANCHOR_VAL="2002-01-07" ANCHOR_DIR="BEFORE">the past</TIMEX2> Formerly, this expression would only have VAL="PAST_REF".

The complete set of tag attributes is shown in Table 1.

New corpora. Two new annotated corpora have been prepared and a third is in preparation. The TIDES Temporal Corpora include the following:

(1) a parallel corpus of 95 Spanish dialogs, their English translations, and temporal annotations of all the dialogs and their translations (44,081 words of raw text in all). This corpus is freely available at [9]. The raw Spanish dialogs are part of the Enthusiast corpus collected earlier at Carnegie-Mellon University under U.S. government funding.

(2) 193 documents of the English TDT-2 corpus [8] with temporal annotations (171,535 words of raw text). This

corpus will be released in cooperation with the Linguistic Data Consortium.

There are 8243 TIMEX2 tags in these corpora.

An additional corpus is being annotated with TIMEX2 tags under the auspices of the Automatic Content Extraction (ACE) program's Relation Detection and Characterization (RDC) task. The corpus consists of 180,000 words of newswire, newspaper, and transcribed broadcast news texts. Information on that corpus is available at [1].

Table 1: Tag Attributes

Attribute	Function	Example
VAL	Contains a normalized form of the date/time.	VAL= "1964-10-16"
MOD	Captures temporal modifiers.	MOD= "APPROX"
SET	Identifies expressions denoting sets of times.	SET= "YES"
PERIODICITY	Captures the period between regularly recurring times.	PERIODICITY = "P1M"
GRANULARITY	Captures the unit of time denoted by each set member in a set of times.	GRANULARITY = "G3D"
ANCHOR_VAL	Contains a normalized form of an anchoring date/time.	ANCHOR_VAL= "1964-10-16"
ANCHOR_DIR	Captures the direction of offset from ANCHOR_VAL.	ANCHOR_DIR= "BEFORE"
NON_SPECIFIC	Identifies non-specific expressions.	NON_SPECIFIC= "YES"
COMMENT	Contains any comments the annotator wants to add.	COMMENT= "context garbled"

Temporal annotation software. A Temporal Attributes Entry window has been added to the Alembic Workbench text annotation tool, an open source product built and made available by The MITRE Corporation [2]. The special window, shown in Figure 1, is designed to increase annotator accuracy, consistency, and productivity over manual annotation. The window is currently being used in the preparation of the ACE RDC corpus mentioned above. The data entry window is fully compliant with [5] but also flexible enough for any scheme that uses the ISO-8601 format.

As an example of its versatility, the data entry window is currently being used for two types of temporal tagging. The first marks explicit temporal entities referred to as "TIMEX2 markable." These include specific or fuzzy calendar and clock time references, as well as durations and sets.

The second use is in annotating the time attributes of relations. A relation here means a certain type of association between a pair of entities, such as PERSON AT LOCATION. The time attributes encode when a relation occurred or was true, based on temporal evidence in the text. For this second purpose, evidence may appear in the form of TIMEX2 markable expressions, expressions that contain TIMEX2 markable expressions (leading prepositions such as "*in* 2002" are not part of TIMEX2 markable expressions), and finite verb forms. The time attributes assigned to relations are in some cases simpler than the full TIMEX2 annotation; for example, relations are not tagged with the SET attribute. Data annotated with both TIMEX2 tags and time attributes on relations are being developed in support of the ACE program's RDC task.

The window's structured input fields and drop-down menus allow for rapid and accurate entry of tag attributes. The "Copy VAL" and "Save This Timestamp" buttons allow the annotator to reuse previously entered values. There is a calendar widget [10], shown in Figure 2, that allows the user to click directly on a day and have its value automatically converted to ISO format.

Figure 2: Temporal attributes calendar

A built-in error checking procedure also helps improve compliance with the annotation standard. The Alembic Workbench software is available for Windows (DOS), Unix, and Linux.

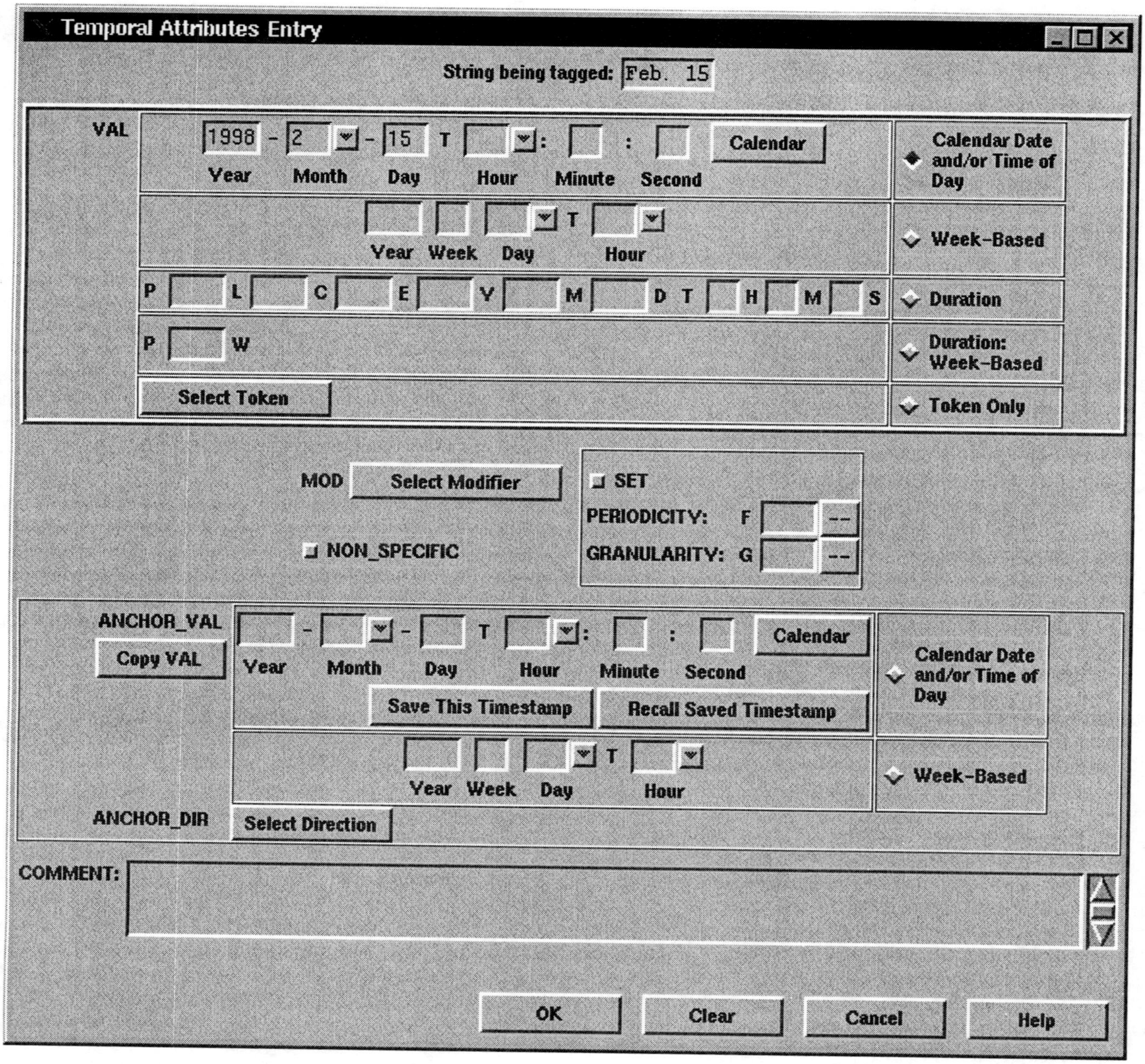

Figure 1: Alembic Workbench Temporal Attributes Entry interface

4. ROBUSTNESS

One of the stated goals for the system introduced in [3] was "reproducibility": the system itself should promote consistency among annotators. To that end, a preliminary assessment was conducted on the TIDES Temporal Corpora mentioned earlier. The documents were annotated by six human annotators, using guidelines and instructions developed under the TIDES program [4][5]. The F-measures, showing the average inter-annotator agreement across five annotators (covering 182 TDT2 documents in all), are shown in Table 2.

Table 2: F-measures for inter-annotator accuracy for human annotators (TDT2)

	Human
TIMEX2	0.73 (17,604)
TIMEX2:GRANULARITY	0.35 (286)
TIMEX2:MOD	0.65 (393)
TIMEX2:NON_SPECIFIC	0.26 (160)
TIMEX2:PERIODICITY	0.90 (346)
TIMEX2:SET	0.67 (326)
TIMEX2:VAL	0.83 (13,037)

The two most important results are shown in the first and the last rows. The row labeled TIMEX2 represents performance on simply marking the expressions as time expressions. The scoring is strict; if the two annotators under comparison have not assigned identical extents to the expression, the scorer will generate at least one (and frequently two) errors. The average F-measure across all pairings of human annotators is 0.73. The last row, TIMEX2:VAL, represents performance on assigning normalized values to those expressions on whose extent the two humans under comparison had agreed. The average agreement across all scoring runs was 0.83. In each row, the number of instances which were compared are shown in parentheses.

The other rows show the results for secondary attributes of TIMEX2 tags. On the whole, we expected there to be less agreement on these attributes than on VAL and on TIMEX2 extent identification. However, it is worth noting that the number of instances of these other attributes is much fewer compared to VAL and TIMEX2 extent.

While the 95 annotated dialog documents all had multiple human annotations, only 51 of the multiple-annotated ones have been converted so far from Word (the Alembic Workbench Temporal Attributes Entry was not yet available for the above annotation effort). While the agreement on dialog TIMEX2 extents is high (F-measure .84), the agreement on dialog VALs is much lower (F-measure of .51) than on TDT2 VALs. The reasons for this will be investigated, but we suspect they may include the relatively smaller number of dialog examples, as well as different assumptions about the dialog reference date.

It is expected that the Alembic Workbench Temporal Attributes Entry window will improve robustness. The window relieves the annotator of much of the mental burden required to adhere to the tag format. It also eliminates typographical errors.

5. FUTURE WORK

As the guidelines are refined through work on the ACE corpus, it will be important to address specific difficulties that humans could experience in applying the guidelines. A recent study on temporal annotation [7] notes that 30-40% of annotator errors may be attributed to ambiguity of the particular guidelines used or to mistakes in applying them. The issues that need to be resolved in our guidelines include:

1. *More consistent criteria for distinguishing markables from non-markables*: currently, modifiers like "former" are markable, while "previous" is not markable; expressions in idioms like "a man ahead of his time" are markable, while "in time" and "good evening" aren't. Expressions headed by category words ("time", "period", etc.) are often vague or idiomatic and hard to normalize. They are currently markable depending on context.
2. *Improved representation for sets*: currently, sets of times can be represented as periods when they are without gaps (e.g., "the last 3 weeks" but not "the last 3 summers"), or as sets of regularly or irregularly occurring points (e.g., "every Thursday" or "Thursdays when the weather is good"), but sets that are bounded or quantified (e.g., "three summers in the 1990's") aren't adequately represented.
3. *Coreference and Granularity*: the guidelines do not address the question of whether times expressed at different granularities should be considered strictly coreferential. Consider, as an example, "kidnapped almost two years ago…abducted in March 1996…captured on March 26, 1996". It is unclear which, if any, of those expressions should be used to provide a value for a subsequent anaphor such as "then" ("Pol Pot, then the guerrila group's leader").
4. *More explicitness about fuzziness*: Fuzzy expressions like "six weeks ago" are normalized by counting back to six weeks prior to the current ISO week (likewise, "last night" is given the day of "yesterday"). A tag VAL like "2002-02" may arise from a precise date expression like "January 2002" or a fuzzy expression like "two months ago". In the fuzzy cases, it would be useful to record the fact of the fuzziness somewhere in the tag.
5. *ISO-related limitations*: the representation doesn't accommodate dates prior to the first century A.D., and fails to normalize expressions based on alternative calendar systems.

Recently, the Advanced Research and Development Activity (ARDA) of the U.S. government, as part of the AQUAINT (Advanced Question and Answering for Intelligence) program, has launched a six-month research project called TERQAS (Time and Event Recognition for Question Answering Systems). The goal of this project is to outline a temporal annotation language called TenseML (for "Tense Markup Language"). The TIMEX2 annotation scheme is being leveraged as a starting point for that effort.

6. REFERENCES

[1] Automatic Content Extraction (ACE) program URL: http://www.nist.gov/speech/tests/ace/index.htm

[2] Alembic Workbench, available for download at http://www.mitre.org/technology/ alembic-workbench/

[3] Mani, I., Wilson, G., Sundheim, B., and Ferro, L. (2001). "Guidelines for Annotating Temporal Information ". In *Proceedings of HLT 2001, First International Conference on Human Language Technology Research*, J. Allan, ed., Morgan Kaufmann, San Francisco, 2001.

[4] Ferro, L. (2001). "Instruction Manual for the Annotation of Temporal Expressions." MITRE Technical Report MTR 01W0000046. McLean, Virginia: The MITRE Corporation.

[5] Ferro, L., Mani, I., Sundheim, B. and Wilson G. (2001). "TIDES Temporal Annotation Guidelines - Version 1.0.2". MITRE Technical Report MTR 01W0000041. McLean, Virginia: The MITRE Corporation.

[6] ISO-8601 ftp://ftp.qsl.net/pub/g1smd/8601v03.pdf 1997.

[7] Setzer, A. and Gaizauskas, R (2001). "A Pilot Study on Annotating Temporal Relations in Text." In *Proceedings of ACL Workshop on Temporal and Spatial Information Processing.* Toulouse, France. July 7, 2001.

[8] TDT-2. Topic Detection and Tracking Program http://morph.ldc.upenn.edu/Catalog/LDC99T37.html 1999.

[9] Tides Temporal Corpus, Spanish and English dialogs. http://www.nist.gov/speech/tests/ace/phase2/resource/index.htm. See *tides-temporal-corpus.tar.*

[10] The calendar widget illustrated in Figure 2 was written by Richard Suchenwirth and made available at http://mini.net/tcl/1816.html.

A Trainable Approach for Multi-Lingual Speech-To-Speech Translation System

Y. Gao, J. Sorensen, H. Erdogan, R. Sarikaya, F. Liu, M. Picheny
IBM T. J. Watson Research Center
yuqing@us.ibm.com

B. Zhou
Center for Spoken Language Research
Univ. of Colorado at Boulder
zhoub@cslr.colorado.edu

Z. Diao
Department of Mathematics
Texas A&M University

ABSTRACT

This paper presents a statistical speech-to-speech machine translation (MT) system for limited domain applications using a cascaded approach. This architecture allows for the creation of multilingual applications. In this paper, the system architecture and its components, including the speech recognition, parsing, information extraction, translation, natural language generation (NLG) and text-to-speech (TTS) components are described. We have implemented the described system for translating speech between Mandarin and English language pair in an air travel application domain. We are current porting the system to the military domain. Encouraging experimental results have been observed and are presented.

Keywords

speech-to-speech translation, statistical natural language understanding based translation, statistical natural language generation

1. INTRODUCTION

Commerce and travel have created an ever increasing need for translation between languages. Recently, progress in the fields of speech and language processing have begun to allow the creation of automated systems to accomplish this task. However, the technical challenges of creating a useful speech-to-speech translation device pushes against the limitations of current technologies such as speech recognition, natural language understanding, machine translation, natural language generation, and text-to-speech synthesis. In this paper, we present a speech translation system employing a statistical framework appropriate for use in language restricted domains. In our cascaded approach, the recognition results obtained in the speaker's language are analyzed and then, through a series of distinct abstract representations, corresponding sentences are generated in the language of the listener.

Compared to other speech translation systems [1], [2], [3], [4] developed by other researchers, our system has several distinguished features. First, all the components in our system, including parser and language generation, are statistics based, and therefore are trainable from speech or text corpus. No handcrafted rules, grammars, or templates are needed. This makes our system flexible, scalable, and robust as the application domain changes. We have built the system for the air travel domain and are currently porting it to the military domain to verify the robustness. Another feature is that our translation is based on the understanding of the meaning of the sentence. It avoids the literal translation and the correct grammar assumption of the transcribed text from the input speech, as it most likely includes recognition errors, and emphasizes meaning preservation. When the automatic transcribed speech script is parsed, the statistical parser focuses on the meaningful phrases and automatically ignores irrelevant portions or out-of-domain concepts in the script. Another innovative characteristic of our system is that we are trying to use the natural language understanding component to help the speech recognizer, as we believe the language structure and conversation structure can be utilized to improve speech recognition performance.

This paper is organized as follows: In Sec. 2, we describe the system architecture and its components, including the speech recognition, parsing, information extraction, translation, natural language generation (NLG) and text-to-speech (TTS) components. Sec. 3 presents the evaluation results and discussions and Sec. 4 contains concluding remarks.

2. SYSTEM OVERVIEW

Figure 1 shows the architecture of our speech translation system. The input speech is recognized through an automatic speech recognizer and parsed by a statistical natural language understanding (NLU) model. An information extraction component is responsible for analyzing the semantic tree that was obtained from the NLU, and extracting two kinds of information from the tree. The first kind of information is a language independent "interlingua" representation. This, combined with a canonical representation of the language dependent attributes instantiated within the semantic model, is sent to a natural language generation (NLG) engine to render in the target language. Both types of information are translated using distinct models, with the specific attributes of items, such as times and dates, using conventional techniques familiar to the machine translation community. The interlingua translation, however, takes place at a semantic level and can result in considerable surface changes in the final result. Finally, when a text representation of the utterance in the target language is completed, a text-to-speech synthesizer is used to produce spoken output.

For a cascaded approach to machine translation to work, the hierarchical information represented in the semantic tree for a sentence

Proceedings of HLT 2002, Second International Conference on Human Language Technology Research, M. Marcus, ed., Morgan Kaufmann, San Francisco, 2002.

must be invariant across translations, at least in the application domain of interest. This invariance has been validated, in part, by work involving translation between English and certain European languages [4]. A more complete test of this assumption would require dissimilar languages that have quite different phrase order conventions, such as Chinese and English, as in the work presented here. Part of the design of our system is reflected in the annotation of the training corpus, which forms the embodiment of a particular interlingua style.

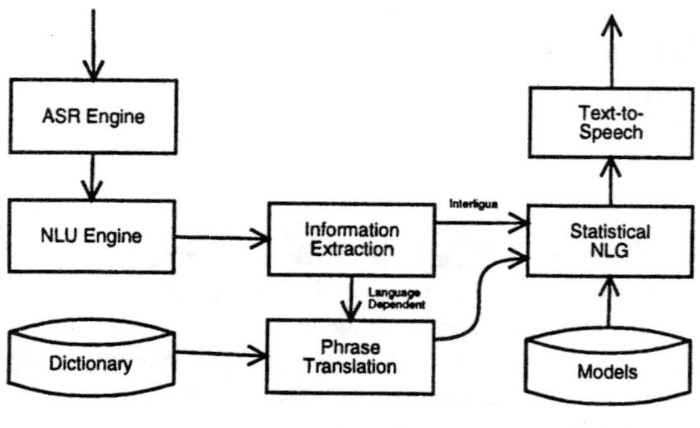

Figure 1: Statistical Speech-to-Speech Translation System Architecture

2.1 Statistical NLU Classer and Parser

The natural language understanding component is one of the most important parts of a machine translation system. The NLU component includes a statistical classer as well as a semantic parser [5], [6], both are decision-tree based. The "classer" is used to replace specific categories of phrases in a sentence that have high word variability with a single token identifying the phrase class. Typical classes in the air travel domain include locations, dates, and times. Following classing, the separate "parser" is used to determine the meaning and structure of the classed sentence by assigning a specific hierarchical tree structure to the sentence as predicted by a statistical model. The classer and parser are trained from hand-annotated sentences from the source language.

For the translation from English to Mandarin, a classer and a parser for English are trained using over 100,000 well-annotated sentences in the air travel domain. This allows our system to train a high accuracy classer that achieves a 96% recall and 95% precision, and an accurate parser that achieves a 87% recall and 88% precision. However, for the translation from Mandarin to English, only 2000 Chinese sentences have been collected and manually annotated for the training of both classer and parser. 1800 sentences were used for training the statistical models and another 200 sentences were used for smoothing the resulting decision tree models. The parser and classer performances are yet to be improved. Figure 2 shows a typical parsing example for a Chinese sentence, where the words "QUERY" or "SEGMENT" denote sentence or phrase type, and words that start with "%" such as "%loc-fr" or "%loc-to" represent specific annotation attributes.

2.2 Information Extraction

Information extraction is the task of analyzing the classer and parser outputs to extract appropriate information required in subsequent processing. Two associative arrays are used to store both the classer and parser results. The first array maps the class tags to the phrases in the original sentence for which they were substituted, such as locations and times. The second array maps the concepts contained in the semantic tree to the specific values that appeared in

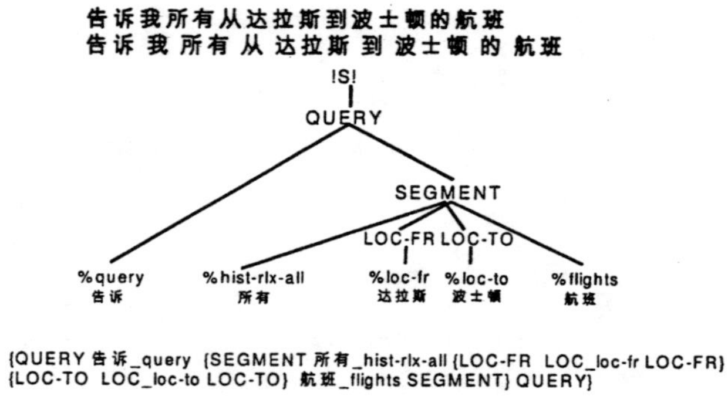

Figure 2: Example for Chinese sentence - The Semantic Tree Representation

the sentence, including speech actions, for example. The semantic concept representation, along with the class constituents, captures the information contained in the parsed sentence. This representation allows direct phrase translation to be applied to the class constituents, but a more general conceptual translation should occur at the second level. Thus this design should allow for the rearrangements that occur when concepts are presented in different order in different languages.

2.3 Attribute Translation

Only the named attributes at the leaf nodes in the semantic tree need to be translated in the traditional sense of word-for-word translation. This is currently performed using language to language dictionaries. In cases where phrases or words may be ambiguous, a semantic tag specific phrase translation dictionary is created. That is, a phrase or word may have different translations when considered generally, but usually not within a specific semantic context. Our sets of Chinese-to-English and English-to-Chinese tag-dependent dictionaries were created semi-automatically from general Chinese-to-English and Chinese-to-English dictionaries which were subsequently audited to remove erroneous translations.

2.4 Automatic Speech Recognition and Synthesis

The English and Mandarin speech recognizers were developed for large vocabulary (over 64K words) continuous dictation speech. The baseline speaker-independent systems are trained on over 200 hours of speech collected from over 2000 speakers for each language [7]. The English recognizer uses an alphabet of 52 phones, while the Mandarin system uses 162 phones, including some tone-dependent phones [8]. Each phone is modeled with a 3-state left-to-right HMM. Both systems have approximately 3000 context-dependent states modeled using 40K Gaussian distributions. The acoustic front-end uses a 24-dimension cepstral feature vector and transformed using LDA.

To improve the recognition accuracy, a LM trained for the DARPA Communicator [9] air travel task was substituted for the general English LM. Unfortunately, for Mandarin system, we do not have a similar domain specific LM; therefore the general dictation Chinese LM is used.

One distinguished feature our system has is that our speech recognizer is coupled with the NLU analyzer, rather than separated as in other systems [2, 10, 1]. The NLU classer and parser results are sent back to the recognizer in order to activate a dialog-state-dependent LM [9], or a turn-based LM [11], to futher improve the recognition accuracy. This is motivated by the fact that task oriented conversations often have clear conversation structures which can help to limit the search space for speech recognition. We are also exploring the use of semantic classer and parser information for a better LM that utilizes the language structure.

For speech synthesis, a trainable, phrase-splicing nad variable substitution system [12] is used to synthssize Mandarin or English speech from the translated Chinese or English sentence. Because of the fact that sometimes the translation output is in the form of mixed input and output languages, for example, when there are untranslatable names of locations, our text-to-speech system has the unusual ability to generate speech across language boundaries seamlessly.

2.5 Statistical Natural Language Generation

The high level semantic translation is accomplished by natural language generation of the semantic representation in the target language. More specifically, statistical NLG is used to discover the preferred concept ordering and to assign the lexical form of a grammatical sentence in the target language. Our statistical NLG models [13] are directly learned from a training corpus, using no manually designed grammars or knowledge base.

This work uses a maximum entropy [14] probability model extended from the "NLG2" model described in [13], [15]. It uses a conditional distribution over $V \cup$ *STOP* for the current symbol to be generated, where V is the vocabulary of all possible symbols and *STOP* is an artificial symbol to mark the end of an independent generation. In this context, *symbols* refer to the introduction of semantic concepts or individual target words into the output word sequence. Output begins with a particular sentence type, as identified in the parsed input. Examples of the sentence type in the air travel domain include *Query*, *Action*, *Book* and *Define*. By including the sentence or phrase type in our generation scheme, we can narrow the probability space. The details of the NLG model training and search are in [15].

3. EVALUATION

Defining a useful performance metric for a language to language translation system is a challenging problem in itself. One such metric, *Bleu* [16], recently proposed by our colleagues for use in text-to-text machine translation was used for evaluation. The *Bleu* metric requires human translated scripts as reference, and for our tests, the modified unigram precision (MUP) measure was used. However, the domain specific translation task with spoken word input has many characteristics that present particular challenges. One issue relates to the problem of spontaneous speech recognition, errors due to disfluencies are considered beyond the scope of this paper.

Because the algorithm presented here is trained on a domain specific corpus, the system is more likely to insert domain-specific words such as words pertaining to flights and booking (in our example) even in the case where these words were not spoken explicitly. For this reason, we have also compared the performance against the online *Babel Fish* system [17]. More complete evaluation requires human judges and, for illustration, we include two examples of translations in Fig 3.

Source	Text	MUP
Chinese	星期六从波士顿飞往匹兹堡的航班都有哪些	
Human 1	Which flights are available from Boston to Pittsburgh on Saturday?	
Human 2	What are the flights from Boston to Pittsburgh this Saturday?	
Babel Fish	Which Saturday flies to Pittsburgh from Boston the scheduled flight all has?	58%
New System	Which ones flight from Boston to Pittsburgh on Saturday?	83%
Chinese	我想了解星期五从费城去加州奥克兰的航班信息	
Human 1	Show me all the flights from Philadelphia to Oakland, California on Friday.	
Human 2	Give me a list of flights from Philadelphia to Oakland, California on this Friday.	
Babel Fish	I want to understand Friday goes to the the California Oakland from the Philadelphia the scheduled flight information.	47%
New System	I want to know flights from Philadelphia to Oakland California on Friday.	67%

Figure 3: Example Translations

4. CONCLUSIONS

The new statistical translation model presented in this paper shows great promise due to its ability to build semantic representations of spoken phrases and to allow general transformations on these representations when creating statements in the target language. This ability has been demonstrated by choosing the highly dissimilar language pair, English and Chinese. In addition, because the presented translation system is based on statistical models trained using corpora, developing translations systems for new languages should require only a fraction of the effort normally invested in building language to language translation systems.

5. ACKNOWLEDGEMENT

Thanks to Drs J. Hansen and W. Ward at CSLR, Univ. of Colorado for their valuable comments and discussions. Thanks to Drs. A. Ratnaparkhi, W. Zhu and X. Luo from IBM Research for their help with this work.

6. REFERENCES

[1] Federal Ministry of Education, Science, and Technology, "http://verbmobil.dfki.de," website.

[2] Carnegie Mellon University, "http://www.is.cs.cmu.edu/js/janus.html," website.

[3] F. Casscuberta et al, "Speech-to-speech translation based on finite-state transducers," in *ICASSP2001*, Salt Lake City, Utah, May 2001.

[4] L.M. Tomokiyo, M. Gavaldà, W. Ward, and A. Waibel, "Concept based speech translation," in *ICASSP*, May 1995.

[5] D. Magerman, *Natural language parsing as statistical pattern recognition*, Ph d desertation, Stanford University, 1994.

[6] K. Davies et al, "The ibm conversational telephony system for financial applications," in *Eurospeech1999*, Budapest, Hangary, Sept 1999, vol. 1, pp. 275–278.

[7] Y. Gao et al, "New adaptation techniques for large vocabulary continuos speech recognition," in *ASR workshop 2000*, Paris, France, September 2000, pp. 107–111.

[8] J. Chen et al, "New methods in continuous mandarin speech recognition," in *EuroSpeech1997*, Rhodes, Greece, September 1997, pp. 1543–1546.

[9] Y. Gao et al, "Recent advances in speech system for ibm darpa communicator," in *EuroSpeech2001*, Aalborg, Denmark, September 2001, pp. 503–506.

[10] Carnegie Mellon University, "http://www.c-star.org," website.

[11] R. Sarikaya et al, "Turn-based language modeling for spoken dialog systems," in *submitted to ICASSP2002*.

[12] R. Donovan et al, "Phrase splicing and variable substitution using the ibm trainable speech synthesis system," in *ICASSP1999*, Phoenix, Arizona, March 1999, pp. 373–376.

[13] A. Ratnaparkhi, "Trainable methods for surface natural language generation," in *Proc. of the 1st Meeting of the North American Chapter of the Association of Computational Liguistics*, Seattle, WA, 2000, pp. 194–201.

[14] A. Berger, S. A. Della Pietra, and V. J. Della Pietra, "A maximum entropy approach to natural language processing," *Computational Linguistics*, vol. 22, no. 1, pp. 39–71, 1996.

[15] B. Zhou et al, "Statistical natural language generation for speech-to-speech machine translation," in *ICSLP2002*, Denver, Colorado, Sept. 2002, pp. 1897–1900.

[16] K. Papineni, "Blue: A method for automatic evaluation of machine translation," Research Report RC22176, IBM, Sept 2001.

[17] Systran Technologies, "http://world.altavista.com," website.

Summarizing Large Document Sets Using Concept-Based Clustering

Hilda Hardy†, Nobuyuki Shimizu†, Tomek Strzalkowski†, Liu Ting†, G. Bowden Wise‡, and Xinyang Zhang†

†NLIP Laboratory, University at Albany, SUNY
1400 Washington Avenue
Albany, NY 12222

‡GE Global Research Center
1 Research Circle
Niskayuna, NY 12309

hardyh@cs.albany.edu

ABSTRACT

This paper describes our multi-document summarizer XDoX designed to summarize large sets of documents (50-500). These documents are typically obtained from routing or filtering systems run against a continuous stream of data, such as a newswire. XDoX identifies the most salient or often-repeated themes within the set and composes an extraction summary reflecting these main themes. The summarizer uses a unique *n*-gram scoring method to give greater importance to clusters of passages that have significant common phrases. Our methods are robust, topic-independent, and easily extensible to multilingual applications. We show examples of summaries obtained in our tests as well as from our participation in the first Document Understanding Conference (DUC).

1. RELATED WORK

An automated multi-document summarization system requires techniques different from those necessary to summarize a single document. Many newswire articles on the same topic, for example, are likely to contain redundant material. Articles may reveal new developments of events over time, or they may include various information and opinions on an issue or a person. Most current automated systems work by identifying the most important sentences or paragraphs in the set of documents and building a summary with these passages. Several systems use Carbonell and Goldstein's Maximal Marginal Relevance measure [1], which selects passages based on a combination of relevance and anti-redundancy. Columbia's SIMFINDER [4] uses several varieties of word overlap in addition to other features to determine similarity values between passages in order to form clusters, followed by sentence extraction (CENTRIFUSER) or reformulation (MULTIGEN, FUF/SURGE). Radev et al's WebInEssence [12] clusters documents according to keyword overlap and performs centroid-based sentence extraction. Marcu [8] selects important sentences based on the discourse structure of the text. Lin and Hovy's NEATS system [7] creates a query based on single terms, bigrams and trigrams most characteristic of each document set, finally producing a ranked list of sentences. TNO's system [6] scores sentences by combining a unigram language model approach with a Bayesian classifier based on surface features. Our XDoX system clusters passages based on our unique *n*-gram scoring methods, and forms an extraction summary based on a representative passage from each cluster.

Proceedings of HLT 2002, Second International Conference on Human Language Technology Research, M. Marcus, ed., Morgan Kaufmann, San Francisco, 2002.

2. XDOX OVERVIEW

The XDoX system (Cross Document Summarizer) was built for information analysts and designed to summarize sets of 50-500 documents that have been retrieved or routed from a text database, the Internet, or a news source, according to a query or a user-defined profile. The system uses clustering techniques to subdivide the documents into groups of passages representing meaningful topics and themes, and to separate unrelated material. XDoX presents the user with two kinds of overall summary, one with more detail related to the complexity of the document set, and one with fewer details and limited length. In addition, a Graphical User Interface allows the user to view individual passages, full documents, and a summary of each topical cluster. Thus the system answers both the indicative and the exploratory needs of our customers.

XDoX has been developed over the last two years with several intermediate designs considered. An early version of the system [15] produced clusters of documents according to their mutual similarity, which was based primarily on straightforward term overlap between documents. In addition, WordNet lexical database [2] [10] was used to facilitate the matching of synonyms and other related terms. This early work focused on evaluating various document clustering techniques, but we found that most known clustering methods could not alone support an effective summarizer. Whether or not WordNet is used, the resulting clusters were often of poor quality, formed around common but semantically unimportant terms.

Our new approach improves the quality of the clusters and the summaries by implementing concept-based clustering and summarization. Instead of clustering entire documents or summaries of documents, we cluster passages [11], or sequences of text, which usually correspond to the natural paragraphs designed by the author or editor, or that may be obtained automatically [5]. Our similarity metric is based on *n*-gram matching rather than just single-term overlap. For example, a word in a sequence of six words receives proportionately more weight than the same word occurring in two distinct three-word sequences, which in turn is weighted more heavily than if it were found in three bi-grams, and so on. Individual term weights are computed at the document level using a variant of pivoted document length normalization metric [14] and added to n-gram weights.

We have found that our new approach produces excellent summaries in most cases. The summaries are based on high-quality clusters that form around significant common concepts or themes that occur repeatedly across the set of documents. The paragraph is a useful semantic unit for conceptual clustering, because most writers view a paragraph as a topical unit, and organize their thoughts accordingly. A few examples of themes detected in large document sets are: "lie detector test", "South Georgia and South Sandwich Islands", and "blood alcohol levels".

3. XDOX SYSTEM ARCHITECTURE

The XDoX system is written in Java, except for our single document summarizer, which is written in C++. The system has several distinct modules. Their basic tasks, inputs and outputs are shown in Figure 1.

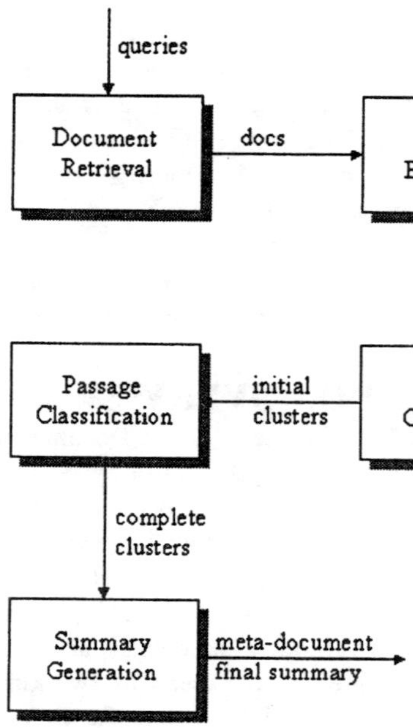

Figure 1. XDoX System Architecture

4. PASSAGE EXTRACTION, TEXT PROCESSING

Documents are first chunked into passages, according to existing paragraph boundaries. Passages are normalized by removing SGML tags, lists of keywords, author by-lines, news sources, locations, etc. Subtitles and one-line paragraphs are merged with the following text.

In preparation for comparing n-grams in passages, the Text Processing module removes stopwords and stems the remaining words, using the Porter algorithm. Each stem is mapped to a unique integer code. The stemmed words are represented as nodes in a simple binary `Word Tree` structure, using Java's red-black `TreeMap` class. The value for each node is an ordered list of occurrences of the stem, including positional information and term weights.

We chose a term weighting scheme that uses average term frequency in a document as the normalization factor. In the function

$$\frac{1+\log(tf)}{1+\log(average(tf))},$$

$tf(t)$ is the actual frequency of term t in document D. This normalization method has been shown to perform 5.7% better than maximum term frequency based normalization for 200 TREC queries on the entire TREC collection [14]. Combining this tf factor with the pivoted normalization used in the SMART system, we arrive at the weighting strategy:

$$\frac{\dfrac{1+\log(tf)}{1+\log(average(tf))}}{(1-c)average(L)+c\times L},$$

where L is the number of unique terms in document D and c is a constant between 0 and 1. This weighting scheme is related to BM25 used in the Okapi system [13], which has been reported to perform consistently better than standard cosine normalization in document retrieval applications.

5. PASSAGE MATCHING

The Passage Matching module compares passages and assigns similarity scores to every pair of passages in the document set (not including pairs from the same document). The output is a table of paragraph pairs and their similarity values, represented as a matrix.

In order to compare large numbers of documents efficiently using *n*-gram matching, we chose to work with a very small subset of all possible substrings in the documents: we look only at *n*-grams, where *n* is 1 to 6, that are actually matched somewhere among the passages in the document set. We construct *n*-grams on the fly, in a bottom-up manner, from the `Word Tree` data structure. The algorithm is as follows:

For each document D_i (D_1 to D_{n-1}):

a. Get the first word w in the first paragraph.
b. From the Word Tree, get a list a of all instances of w occurring in documents D_{i+1} to D_n. These are 1-grams.
c. For each word v which follows w in D_i:
    1) From the Word Tree, get a list b of all instances of v in documents D_{i+1} to D_n. Each v either continues an *n*-gram, wv, or begins a new 1-gram.
    2) Add or insert each v from list b in the proper place in list a. If an *n*-gram in list a cannot be extended by an occurrence in list b, or if it would create a sequence longer than *n*, then the *n*-gram is removed and stored in a matrix structure.

The goal is to find the best matches between any two paragraphs, where "best" is defined as maximum length. For example, the phrase *Federal Reserve Board Chairman Alan Greenspan*, when found in two passages, is counted as a 6-gram and not six 1-grams, or three bi-grams, or any other combination.

For computing the similarity between any two passages, we use a cosine coefficient function, modified according to *n*-gram weights. The *n*-gram weight is given as $(n_i)/n^2$, where n_i is the length of the *n*-gram of which term T_i is an element, and *n* is the length of the maximum *n*-gram. The weight of term T_i in passage X_i is the weight of T_i in document *X* plus the *n*-gram weight. The final passage similarity function is as follows:

$$sim(X_i, Y_i) = \frac{\sum_{j=1}^{t} x_{ij} \times y_{ij}}{\sqrt{\sum_{j=1}^{t} (x_{ij})^2 \times \sum_{j=1}^{t} (y_{ij})^2}},$$

where x_{ij} is the weight of term T_j in paragraph X_i and y_{ij} is the weight of term T_j in paragraph Y_i.

6. SEED-CLUSTERING

In order to form small, initial seed clusters we apply the well-known complete-link algorithm to our similarity matrix [17]. This algorithm becomes computationally expensive when used over large numbers of multi-paragraph documents. We have found it both practical and effective to run the complete-link only to the point at which we reach a target number of candidate seed clusters. We want a target that avoids over-generalization on the one hand and too much detail on the other. For most sets of documents, a good target is $\log_2 N$, where *N* is the number of documents. Initially, each passage is a cluster. We run the algorithm as follows:

1. Merge the most similar two clusters (clusters i and j).
2. Update the similarity matrix to reflect the pairwise similarity between the new cluster (ij) and the original clusters. We remove all the entries for i and j and replace them with new ij entries.
3. Repeat steps 1 and 2 until the target number of seed clusters is reached.

We add the restrictions that a seed cluster must contain three or more passages, and that there must be at least two common terms among the first three passages in the cluster. Clusters with larger common stem sets are preferred, as well as clusters whose common stem sets do not overlap much with another cluster.

7. PASSAGE CLASSIFICATION

In order to complete the clusters, all remaining passages are classified as satellites around the seed clusters. For this stage we perform M-bin classification, where M is the number of seeds. If a passage has no similarity to any of the seeds, it is placed into a miscellaneous 'trash cluster". Passages in a cluster are presented in descending order: seed passages come first, in the order in which they were added to the cluster, so that those with the tightest similarity to one another are shown first. Next come the satellite passages, ordered according to their degree of similarity with the seed cluster.

8. GENERATING 2 KINDS OF SUMMARY

After the clusters are formed, we create a 'meta-document", selecting one of the highest-scoring, or most characteristic, passages from each cluster, and concatenating them together. Next, our single-document summarizer creates a summary of this meta-document, using the query terms, if any, as the 'title". The user, then, has two types of summary to view. The meta-document is more suitable for groups of documents that describe similar but isolated events, such as alcohol-related traffic accidents, or different people who have something in common, such as winners of the Nobel Peace Prize. The summary of the meta-document is more appropriate for groups of documents which are all related to the same topic or event, such as oil exploration in the Falkland Islands, or the U.S. Presidential election in the year 2000.

9. DUC PARTICIPATION, EVALUATION

In August 2001 NIST completed the evaluation of single- and multiple-document summaries submitted by DUC participants. For the multiple-document summarization track, participants were required to submit fixed-length summaries of 50, 100, 200, and 400 words. Of the 25 groups who signed up, 12 submitted multi-document summaries, and 11 submitted single-document summaries. Ten information analysts from NIST compared human-written model summaries with peer summaries (system-created, baseline, or human). The analysts formed intrinsic judgments based on peer grammaticality, cohesion, and organization; coverage of each model unit by the peer (recall);

and other characteristics of peer material. In Figures 2 and 3, R represents the Albany/GE summarizers.

On grammaticality, our XDoX system ranked 6th of 12. Because we used only text extraction, no language generation, any grammatical errors must have come from the documents themselves. We chose to group subtitles and one-line text units, such as dates standing alone, with the following text, so these may have been interpreted as sentence fragments. On cohesion and organization our system ranked 3rd and 2nd. We attribute these high numbers to our method of extracting paragraphs as a whole, rather than individual sentences.

On per-unit content, assessors marked peer units—simple, automatically determined sentences—which expressed at least some of the same facts as the current model unit, or elementary discourse unit. When recall is defined as dividing the number of model units matched with peer units by the total number of units in the model summary, our single-document summarizer ranked 2nd of the 11 participants. Like our multi-document summarizer, the single-document system segments text into passages or equal-sized chunks. Adjacent passages that are strongly linked to one another are reconnected. All passages are scored with respect to a query derived from the title, topic description, and terms occurring frequently in the text. Scores are then normalized by the length of the passage. Passages are combined into groups of two or more and re-scored, until a clear winning passage or passage group emerges to form the summary. Our techniques have been shown to achieve an excellent balance between text compression and content preservation [16]. The DUC evaluation confirms this assessment.

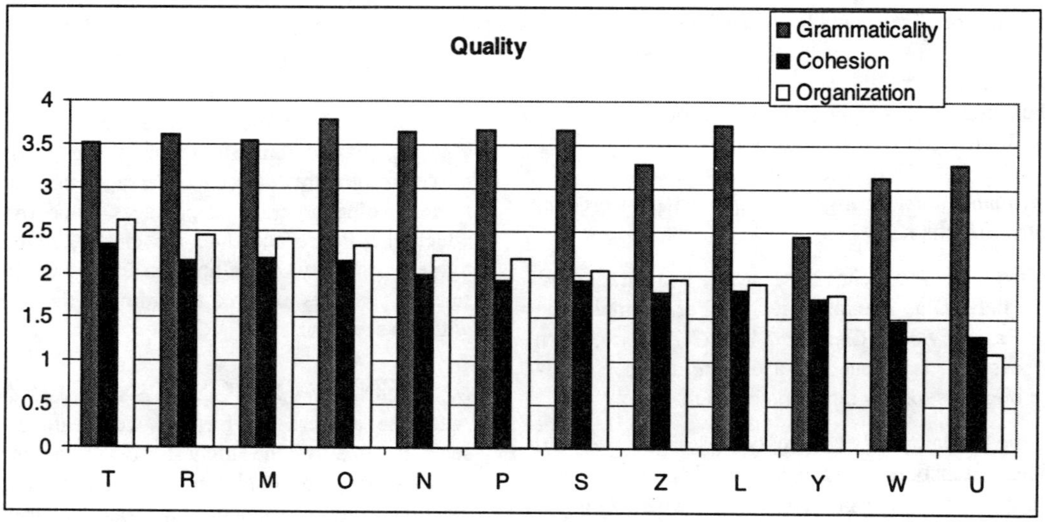

Figure 2. NIST intrinsic quality assessments for multi-document summarization systems.

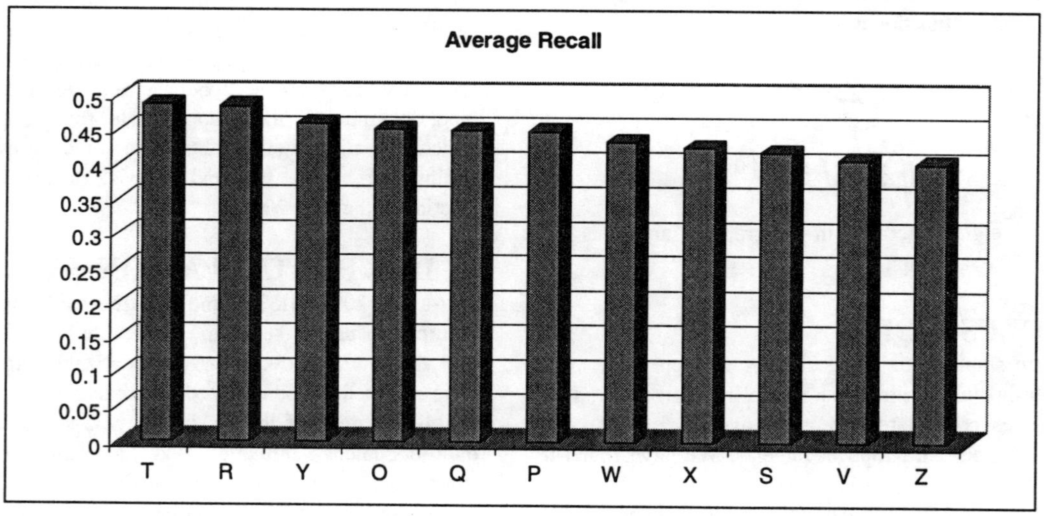

Figure 3. Average recall for single-document summarization systems.

On the whole, we are pleased with our performance in the 2001 Document Understanding Conference. We consider our summaries readable, coherent, and excellent at capturing the main points of the document sets. We think the DUC assessors did well given the program guidelines and the difficulties inherent in judging summaries. We look forward to extrinsic methods of evaluation being incorporated into future DUC conferences.

10. EXAMPLES

The following examples were generated by the XDoX system from the DUC 2001 data.

`docset="d13c"`

President Bush on Monday nominated Clarence Thomas, a conservative Republican with a controversial record on civil rights, to replace retiring Justice Thurgood Marshall on the Supreme Court.

CLARENCE THOMAS; Born: June 23, 1948, in Pinpoint, Ga. Education: B.A. from Holy Cross College, 1971; J.D. from Yale Law School, 1974.

`docset="d39g"`

Officials estimate the tunnel trains may carry 28 million passengers in the first year of operation. Eurotunnel doesn't expect a profit until the end of the century.

In London, the conservative Daily Express newspaper noted today that Britons will be able to walk to France for the first time since the Ice Age.

The tunnel's cost has soared from an initial estimate of $9.4 billion to $16.7 billion, including an extra $1.97 billion in case of unforeseen cost overruns.

Eurotunnel PLC announced Oct. 8 that it had reached an agreement with its banks on $3.5 billion in new credit. More than 200 banks are involved in financing the world's costliest tunnel.

The following summary was obtained from the set of top 100 documents retrieved from the TREC data collection with Topic 358 on the subject of alcohol related driving fatalities.

`docset="TRECtopic358"`

Drinkers beware. When the New Year begins at midnight, a tough new law will take effect making it all the more risky to drink and drive.

Under the new law that takes effect Jan 1, a driver with 0.08% or higher is presumed to be drunk; however, those with lower levels could also be cited for drunk driving.

According to court records, Giunta's blood-alcohol content was 0.29%, more than three times the level at which a motorist is considered legally drunk.

The Department clearly and specifically limited the NPRM to consideration of whether blood testing should be used for situations in which breath testing was not readily available for reasonable suspicion and post-accident tests, or in shy lung situations. For this reason, the issue raised by some commenters of whether employers should have the flexibility or discretion to use blood testing as an alternative to breath testing, even when breath testing is readily available in reasonable suspicion and post-accident testing or even in random or pre-employment testing, is outside the scope of the rulemaking.

The author, Sen. Bill Leonard (R-Big Bear), predicted that the measure will win legislative approval and be sent to Gov. George Deukmejian, whose Administration supports it.

11. CONCLUSION

Our latest version of the XDoX system, using our new passage-clustering techniques, implements a reasonable approximation of conceptual clustering. The overall quality is significantly better than that of our previous version, and compares favorably with the other DUC participants. The summaries are more readable and coherent. In most cases the system successfully presents main points, skips over minor details, and avoids redundancy. XDoX works best on large document sets that have multiple themes. For sets that have fewer than 20 documents, as in the DUC data, our system works well with some parameter adjustments, as long as the documents contain sufficient common concepts around which to form clusters. We have seen excellent results from document sets pertaining to a single event, topic, or person, such as gun control, the eruption of Mt. Pinatubo, the Charles Keating scandal, or the Rodney King beating. XDoX has difficulty generating a longer, more detailed summary when there are 10 or fewer documents concerning isolated incidents, such as gas explosions or earthquakes, or when there is little repetition. We are considering augmenting the system with selective use of our single-document summarizer [16].

12. ACKNOWLEDGMENTS

This paper is based on work supported in part by the Defense Advanced Research Projects Agency (DARPA) and by the Advanced Research and Development Activity (ARDA). Any opinions, findings, and conclusions or recommendations expressed in this material are those of the authors and do not necessarily reflect the views of the U.S. Government.

13. REFERENCES

[1] Carbonell, J., and Goldstein, J. The use of MMR, diversity-based reranking for reordering documents and producing summaries. In Proceedings of SIGIR (1998), 335-336.

[2] Fellbaum, C. (ed.). WordNet – An Electronic Lexical Database. MIT Press, 1998.

[3] Firmin, T., and Chrzanowski, M. J. An Evaluation of Automatic Text Summarization Systems. In I. Mani and M. Maybury (eds.), Advances in Automatic Text Summarization. MIT Press, 1999.

[4] Hatzivassiloglou, V., Klavans, J. L., Holcombe, M. L., Barzilay, R., Kan, M., and McKeown, K. R. SIMFINDER: A Flexible Clustering Tool for Summarization. In NAACL 2001 Workshop on Automatic Summarization (Pittsburgh, PA), 41-49.

[5] Hearst, M. Multi-paragraph segmentation of expository text. In Proceedings of the 32nd Annual Meeting of the Association for Computational Linguistics (Las Cruces,

NM, 1994), Association for Computational Linguistics, 9-16.

[6] Kraaij, W., Spitters, M., and van der Heijden, M. Combining a mixture language model and Naïve Bayes for multi-document summarization. In SIGIR 2001 Workshop on Text Summarization (New Orleans, LA), 95-103.

[7] Lin, C. and Hovy, E. NEATS: A Multidocument Summarizer. In SIGIR 2001 Workshop on Text Summarization (New Orleans, LA), 131-134.

[8] Marcu, D. Discourse-Based Summarization in DUC–2001. In SIGIR 2001 Workshop on Text Summarization (New Orleans, LA), 109-116.

[9] McKeown, K. and Radev, D. Generating summaries of multiple news articles. In Proceedings, 18th Annual International ACM SIGIR Conference on Research and Development in Information Retrieval (Seattle, WA, 1995), 74-82.

[10] Miller, G.A. WordNet: A Lexical Database. Communication of the ACM 38, 11(1995), 39-41.

[11] Mitra, M., Singhal, A., and Buckley, C. Automatic text summarization by paragraph extraction. In Proceedings of the ACL' 97/EACL' 97 Workshop on Intelligent Scalable Text Summarization (Madrid, Spain, 1997).

[12] Radev, D. R., Fan, W., and Zhang, Z. WebInEssence: A Personalized Web-Based Multi-Document Summarization and Recommendation System. In NAACL 2001 Workshop on Automatic Summarization (Pittsburgh, PA), 79-88.

[13] Robertson, S. E., Walker, S., Jones, S., Hancock-Beaulieu, M. M., and Gatford, M. Okapi at TREC-3. In Harman, D. (ed.), The Third Text Retrieval Conference (TREC-3). National Institute of Standards and Technology Special Publication 500-225, 1995, 219-230.

[14] Singhal, A., Buckley, C., and Mitra, M. Pivoted Document Length Normalization. SIGIR 1996, 21-29.

[15] Stein, G., Strzalkowski, T., and Wise, B. Interactive, Text-Based Summarization of Multiple Documents. Computational Intelligence 16, 4 (2000), 606-613.

[16] Strzalkowski, T., Stein, G., Wang, J., and Wise, B. A Robust, Practical Text Summarizer. In I. Mani and M. Maybury (eds.), Advances in Automatic Text Summarization. MIT Press, 1999, 137-154.

[17] Willett, P. Recent trends in hierarchical document clustering: A critical review. Information Processing and Management, 24, 5 (1988).

Automatic Summarization of English Broadcast News Speech

Chiori Hori†, Sadaoki Furui†, Rob Malkin‡, Hua Yu‡ and Alex Waibel‡

†Department of Computer Science, Tokyo Institute of Technology,
2-12-1, O-okayama, Meguro-ku, Tokyo, 152-8552 Japan
{chiori,furui}@furui.cs.titech.ac.jp
‡Interactive Systems Labs, Carnegie Mellon University, Pittsburgh, PA 15213, USA
{malkin,hua,ahw}@cs.cmu.edu

ABSTRACT

This paper proposes an automatic speech summarization technique for English. In our proposed method, a set of words maximizing a summarization score indicating appropriateness of summarization is extracted from automatically transcribed speech and concatenated to create a summary. The extraction process is performed using a Dynamic Programming (DP) technique according to a target compression ratio. In this paper, English broadcast news speech transcribed using a speech recognizer is automatically summarized. In order to apply our method, originally proposed for Japanese, to English, the model of estimating word concatenation probabilities based on a dependency structure in the original speech given by a Stochastic Dependency Context Free Grammar (SDCFG) is modified. A summarization method for multiple utterances using two-level DP technique is also proposed. The automatically summarized sentences are evaluated by a summarization accuracy based on the comparison with the manual summarization of correctly transcribed speech by human subjects. Experimental results show that our proposed method effectively extracts relatively important information and remove redundant and irrelevant information from English news speech.

Keywords

Speech summarization, Summarization scores, Two-level Dynamic Programming, Stochastic Dependency Context Free Grammar, Summarization accuracy

1. INTRODUCTION

Recently, large-vocabulary continuous-speech recognition (LVCSR) technology has made significant advancement. Real time systems can now achieve word accuracy of 90 % and above for speech dictated from newspapers. Currently various applications of LVCSR systems, such as automatic closed captioning [1], meeting/conference summarization [2][3] and indexing for information retrieval [4], are actively investigated. Transcribed speech usually includes not only redundant information such as disfluencies, filled pauses, repetitions, repairs, and word fragments, but also irrelevant information caused by recognition errors. Therefore, practical applications using LVCSR systems require a process of speech summarization which removes redundant and irrelevant information and extracts relatively important information depending on users' requirements, especially for spontaneous speech.

Proceedings of HLT 2002, Second International Conference on Human Language Technology Research, M. Marcus, ed., Morgan Kaufmann, San Francisco, 2002.

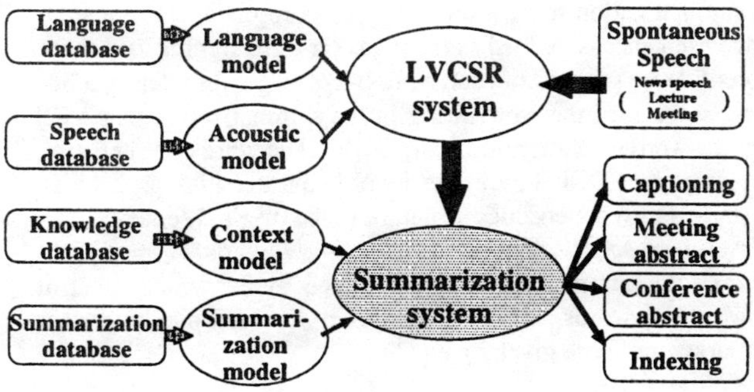

Figure 1: *Automatic speech summarization system.*

Our goal is to build a system that extracts and presents information from spoken utterances according to users' desired amount of information. Figure 1 shows our proposed system. The output of the system can be a summarized sentence for each utterance or summarization of an article consisting of multiple utterances. These outputs can be used for indexing, making closed captions and abstracts, etc. In the closed captioning of broadcast news, the number of words spoken by professional announcers sometimes exceeds the number of words that people can read and understand if all of them are presented on the TV screen. Therefore, reduction of the number of words in speech is indispensable. Meeting/conference summarization should be useful if it can extract relatively important information scattering about in the original speech.

Techniques of automatically summarizing written text have been actively investigated in the field of natural language processing [5]. One of the major techniques for summarizing written text is the process of extracting important sentences. Recently a sentence compression technique using a pair of text and abstract has been proposed [6]. A major difference between text summarization and speech summarization exists in the fact that transcribed speech is sometimes linguistically incorrect due to the spontaneity of speech and recognition errors. A new approach to automatically summarizing speech is needed to cope with such problems.

We have already proposed an automatic speech summarization technique for Japanese speech [7] [8] [9]. Japanese broadcast news speech and lecture speech can be summarized effectively by our proposed method. Since our method is based on a statistical approach, it can be also applied to other languages. In this paper, English broadcast news speech transcribed using a speech recognizer [10] is automatically summarized and its performance is evaluated.

2. SUMMARIZATION OF EACH SENTENCE UTTERANCE

Our method to summarize speech, sentence by sentence, extracts a set of words maximizing a summarization score from an automatically transcribed sentence according to a summarization ratio and concatenates them to build a summary. The summarization ratio is the number of characters/words in the summarized sentence divided by the number of characters/words in the original sentence. The summarization score indicating the appropriateness of a summarized sentence is defined as the sum of a word significance score I, a confidence score C of each word in the original sentence, a linguistic score L of the word string in the summarized sentence [7] [8] and a word concatenation score T [9]. The word concatenation score given by SDCFG indicates a word concatenation probability determined by a dependency structure in the original sentence.

Given a transcription result consisting of N words, $W = w_1, w_2, \ldots, w_N$, the summarization is performed by extracting a set of $M(M < N)$ words, $V = v_1, v_2, \ldots, v_M$, which maximizes the summarization score given by eq.(1).

$$S(V) = \sum_{m=1}^{M} \{L(v_m|\ldots v_{m-1}) + \lambda_I I(v_m) + \lambda_C C(v_m) + \lambda_T T(v_{m-1}, v_m)\} \quad (1)$$

where λ_I, λ_C and λ_T are weighting factors for balancing among L, I, C and T.

This method is effective in reducing the number of words by removing redundant and irrelevant information without losing relatively important information. A set of words maximizing the total score is extracted using a DP technique [7].

2.1 Word significance score

The word significance score I indicates relative significance of each word in a original sentence [7]. The amount of information based on the frequency of each word given by eq. (2) is used as the word significance score for topic words.

$$I(w_i) = f_i \log \frac{F_A}{F_i} \quad (2)$$

where,

w_i : a topic word in the transcribed speech
f_i : number of occurrences of w_i in the transcription
F_i : number of occurrences of w_i in all the training documents
F_A : summation of all F_i in all the training documents ($= \sum_i F_i$)

w_i which occurs frequently over all documents is deweighted by our measure given by eq. (2). Our preliminary experiment showed that this measure is more effective than the tf-idf measure in which w_i homogeneously occurring among documents in the collection data is deweighted.

In this study we choose nouns and verbs as topic words for English. A flat score is given to words other than topic words. To reduce the repetition of words in the summarized sentence, a flat score is also given to each reappearing noun and verb.

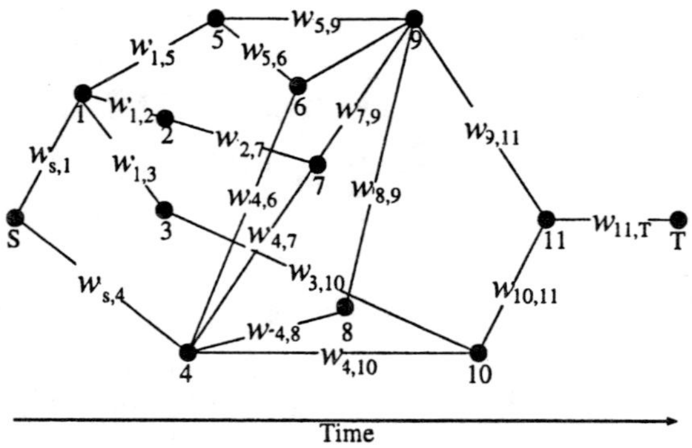

Figure 2: *An example of word graph.*

2.2 Linguistic score

The linguistic score $L(v_m|\ldots v_{m-1})$ indicates the appropriateness of the word strings in a summarized sentence and is measured by n-gram probability $P(v_m|\ldots v_{m-1})$ [7]. In contrast with the word significance score which focuses on topic words, the linguistic score is helpful to extract other words necessary to construct a readable sentence.

2.3 Confidence score

The confidence score $C(v_m)$ is incorporated to weight acoustically as well as linguistically reliable hypotheses [8]. Specifically, a posterior probability of each transcribed word, that is the ratio of a word hypothesis probability to that of all other hypotheses, is calculated using a word graph obtained by a decoder and used as a confidence measure [11]. A word graph consisting of nodes and links from a beginning node S to an end node T is shown in Figure 2.

Nodes represent time boundaries between possible word hypotheses and links connecting these nodes represent word hypotheses. Each link is given acoustic log likelihood and linguistic log likelihood of a word hypothesis.

The posterior probability of a word hypothesis $w_{k,l}$ is given by:

$$C(w_{k,l}) = \log \frac{\alpha_k P_{ac}(w_{k,l}) P_{lg}(w_{k,l}) \beta_l}{\mathcal{G}} , \quad (3)$$

where,

k, l : node number in a word graph ($k < l$)
$w_{k,l}$: word hypothesis occurred between node k and node l
$C(w_{k,l})$: log of the posterior probability of $w_{k,l}$
α_k : forward probability from the beginning node S to node k
β_l : backward probability from node l to the end node T
$P_{ac}(w_{k,l})$: acoustic likelihood of $w_{k,l}$
$P_{lg}(w_{k,l})$: linguistic likelihood of $w_{k,l}$
$\mathcal{G}$: forward probability from the beginning node S to the end node $T(= \alpha_T)$

2.4 Word concatenation score

Suppose "the beautiful cherry blossoms in Japan" is summarized as "the beautiful Japan". The latter phrase is grammatically correct but a semantically incorrect summarization. Since the above linguistic score is not powerful enough to alleviate such a problem, a word concatenation score $T(v_{m-1}, v_m)$ is incorporated to give a penalty for a concatenation between words with no dependency in the original sentence. Since every language has its own dependency structure, a basic computation of the word concatenation score independent of the type of language is described below.

Figure 3: *An example of dependency structure.*

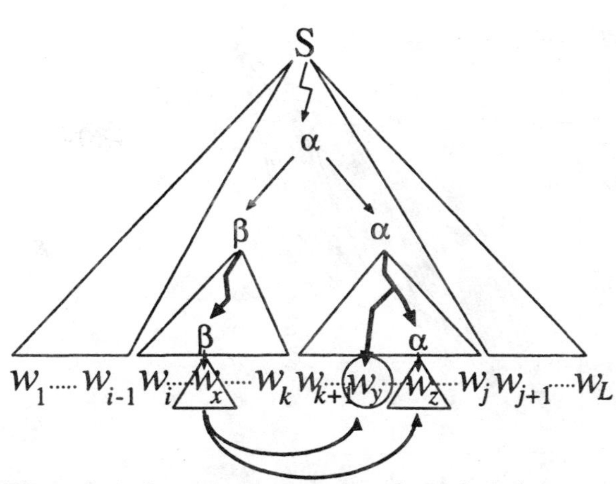

Figure 4: *A phrase structure tree based on a dependency structure.*

Dependency structure

An example of the dependency structure represented by a dependency grammar is shown as the curved arrows in Figure 3. In a dependency grammar, one word is designated as the head of a sentence, and all other words are either a dependent of that word, or dependent on some other word which connects to the head word through a sequence of dependencies [12]. The word at the beginning of an arrow is named the "modifier" and the word at the end of the arrow is named the "head" respectively. For instance, the dependency grammar of English consists of both "right-headed" dependency indicated by right arrows and "left-headed" dependency indicated by left arrows as shown in Figure 3. These dependencies can be represented by a phrase structure grammar, DCFG (Dependency Context Free Grammar), using the following rewrite rules based on Chomsky normal form.

$$\alpha \rightarrow \beta\alpha \quad \texttt{(right-headed)}$$
$$\alpha \rightarrow \alpha\beta \quad \texttt{(left-headed)}$$
$$\alpha \rightarrow w$$

where α and β are nonterminal symbols and w is a terminal symbol (word). Figure 4 illustrates an example of a phrase structure tree based on a word-based dependency structure for a sentence which consists of L words, $w_1, \ldots, w_L$. The w_x modifies w_z, when the sentence is derived from the initial symbol S and the following requirements are fulfilled: 1) the rule of $\alpha \rightarrow \beta\alpha$ is applied; 2) $w_i \ldots w_k$ is derived from β; 3) w_x is derived from β; 4) $w_{k+1} \ldots w_j$ is derived from α and 5) w_z is derived from α.

Dependency probability

Since dependencies between words are usually ambiguous, whether dependencies exist or not between words must be estimated by a dependency probability that one word is modified by others. In this study, the dependency probability is calculated as a posterior probability estimated by the Inside-Outside probabilities [13] based on SDCFG. The probability that the w_x and w_z relationship has a "right-headed" dependency structure is calculated as a product of the probabilities of the above-mentioned steps from 1) to 5). On the other hand, the "left-headed" dependency probability is calculated as the product of the probabilities when the rule of $\alpha \rightarrow \alpha\beta$ is applied. Since English has both right and left dependencies, the dependency probability is defined as the sum of the "right-headed" and "left-headed" dependency probabilities. If a language has only "right-headed" dependency, the "right-headed" dependency probability is used for the dependency probability. For simplicity, the dependency probabilities between w_x and w_z is denoted by $d(w_x, w_z, i, k, j)$, where i, k are the indices of the initial and final words derived from β, and j is the index of the final word derived from α. The dependency probability is calculated as follows:

$$d(w_m, w_l, i, k, j) = \left\{ \sum_{\alpha\beta} f(i,j|\alpha)P(\alpha \rightarrow \beta\alpha)h_m(i,k|\beta)h_l(k+1,j|\alpha) + \sum_{\alpha\beta:\alpha\neq\beta} f(i,j|\alpha)P(\alpha \rightarrow \alpha\beta)h_m(i,k|\alpha)h_l(k+1,j|\beta) \right\} \quad (4)$$

where P is a rewrite probability and f is outside probabilities given by eq. (A-2) in the Appendix. h is a head-dependent inside probability that w_n is a head of a word string derived from α is defined as follows:

$$h_n(i,j|\alpha) = \begin{cases} \sum_{\beta} \left\{ \sum_{k=i}^{n-1} P(\alpha \rightarrow \beta\alpha)e(i,k|\beta)h_n(k+1,j|\alpha) + \sum_{k=n}^{j-1} P(\alpha \rightarrow \alpha\beta)h_n(i,k|\alpha)e(k+1,j|\beta) \right\} & \text{if } i < j \\ b(\alpha \rightarrow w_n) & \text{if } i = j = n \\ 0 & \text{otherwise} \end{cases} \quad (5)$$

where e is the inside probability given by eq. (A-1) in the Appendix.

Word concatenation probability

In general, as shown in Figure 4, a modifier derived from β can be directly connected with a head derived from α in a summarized sentence. In addition, the modifier can be also connected with each word which modifies the head. The word concatenation probability between w_x and w_y is defined as a sum of the dependency probabilities between w_x and w_y, and between w_x and each of the $w_{y+1} \ldots w_z$. Using the dependency probabilities $d(w_x, w_y, i, k, j)$, the word concatenation score is calculated as a logarithmic value of the word concatenation probability given by:

$$T(w_x, w_y) = \log \sum_{i=1}^{x} \sum_{k=x}^{y-1} \sum_{j=y}^{L} \sum_{z=y}^{j} d(w_x, w_z, i, k, j). \quad (6)$$

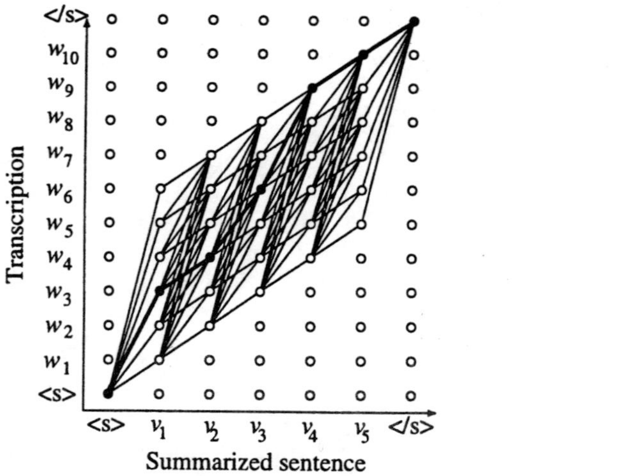

Figure 5: *An example of DP process for speech summarization.*

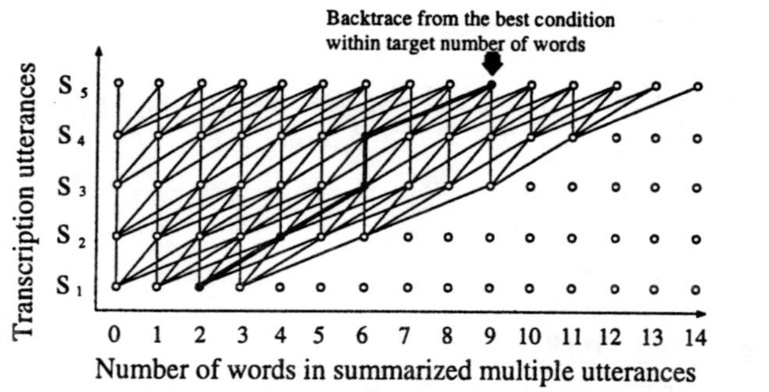

Figure 6: *An example of DP process for summarization of multiple utterances.*

SDCFG

SDCFG is constructed using a manually parsed corpus. Parameters of SDCFG are estimated using the Inside-Outside algorithm. In our SDCFG [14], only the number of non-terminal symbols is determined and all possible phrase trees are considered. The rules consisting of all combinations of non-terminal symbols are applied to each rewriting symbol in a phrase tree. In this method, the non-terminal symbol is not explicitly given a specific function such as a noun phrase function, and the function of non-terminal symbols are automatically learned from data. Probabilities for frequently used rules become bigger, and those for rarely used rules become smaller. Since words in the learning data for SDCFG are tagged with POS (part-of-speech), the dependency probability of words excluded in the learning data can be calculated based on their POS. Even if the transcription results obtained by a speech recognizer are ill-formed, the dependency structure can be robustly estimated by the SDCFG.

2.5 Dynamic programming for automatic summarization

Given a transcription result consisting of N words, $W = w_1, w_2, \ldots, w_N$, the summarization is performed by extracting a set of $M(M < N)$ words, $V = v_1, v_2, \ldots, v_M$, which maximizes the summarization score given by eq. (1). The two-dimensional space for performing the dynamic programming process is shown in Figure 5. The vertical axis indicates the transcription result consisting of 10 words ($N = 10$), and the horizontal axis indicates the summarized sentence having 5 words ($M = 5$). All possible sets of 5 words extracted from the 10 words are indicated by the paths from the bottom-left corner to the top-right corner. One of the paths which maximizes the summarization score is selected.

3. SUMMARIZATION OF MULTIPLE UTTERANCES

Our proposed automatic speech summarization technique for each sentence has recently been extended to summarize a set of multiple utterances (sentences) [9]. A set of words maximizing the summarization score is extracted from multiple utterances under some restrictions applied at the sentence boundaries. These restrictions realizes the summarization of multiple utterances by handling them as a single long utterance. This results in preserving more words inside information rich utterances and shortening or even completely deleting less informative ones. This summarization technique can be considered as a combination of the summarization method extracting important sentences investigated in the field of natural language processing and the sentence-by-sentence summarization method. The multiple utterance summarization method should be especially useful for making lecture abstracts, meeting minutes, etc.

However, the amount of calculation for selecting the best combination among all possible combinations of words in the multiple utterances increases as the number of words in the original utterances increases. In order to reduce the amount of calculation, we proposes a new method in which each utterance is summarized according to all possible summarization ratio and then the best combination of summarized sentences is determined according to a target compression ratio using a two-level DP technique. Figure 6 illustrates the two-level DP technique for summarizing multiple utterances.

4. EVALUATION

4.1 Word network of manual summarization results for evaluation

In order to automatically evaluate summarized sentences, correctly transcribed speech are manually summarized by human subjects and used as correct targets. The manual summarization results are merged into a word network which approximately expresses all possible correct summarization including subjective variations. A "summarization accuracy" of automatic summarization is calculated using the word network [9]. A word string that is the most similar to the automatic summarization result extracted from the word network is considered as a correct target for the automatic summarization. The accuracy, comparing the summarized sentence with the target word string, is used as a measure of linguistic correctness and maintenance of original meanings of the utterance.

4.2 Evaluation data

English TV broadcast news utterances (CNN news) recorded in 1996 given by NIST as a test set of Topic Detection and Tracking (TDT) were tagged by Brilltagger [16] and used to evaluate our proposed method. Five news articles consisting of 25 utterances in average were transcribed by the JANUS [10] speech recognition system. The multiple utterance summarization was performed for each of the five news articles at 40% and 70% summarization ratio. 50 utterances arbitrarily chosen from the five news articles were used for the sentence by sentence summarization with the summarization ratios of 40% and 70%. Mean word recognition accuracies of the utterances used for the multiple utterance summarization and those for sentence by sentence summarization were 78.4%

Table 1: *Examples of automatic summarization and the corresponding target extracted from a manual summarization word network.* upper: a set of words extracted from the correct summarization network which is the most similar to the automatic summarization, lower: automatic summarization of recognition result.

Recognition result	VICE PRESIDENT AL GORE SAYS THE GOVERNMENT HAS A PLAN TO AVOID THE INEVITABLE PROSPECT OF INCREASED AIRPLANE CRASHES AND FATALITY IS
70% summarization	VICE PRESIDENT AL GORE SAYS THE GOVERNMENT HAS A PLAN TO AVOID THE INCREASED AIRPLANE CRASHES
	VICE PRESIDENT AL GORE SAYS THE GOVERNMENT HAS A PLAN TO AVOID <DEL> INCREASED AIRPLANE CRASHES
40% summarization	<INS> THE GOVERNMENT HAS A PLAN TO AVOID THE INCREASED AIRPLANE CRASHES
	GORE THE GOVERNMENT HAS A PLAN TO AVOID THE INCREASED AIRPLANE CRASHES

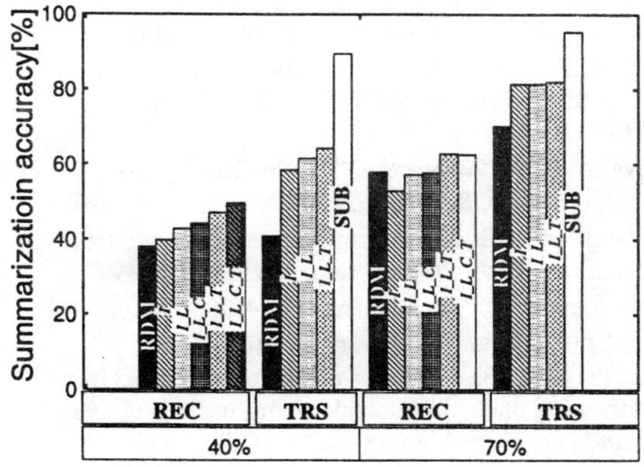

Figure 7: *Each utterance summarization at 40% and 70% summarization ratio.*

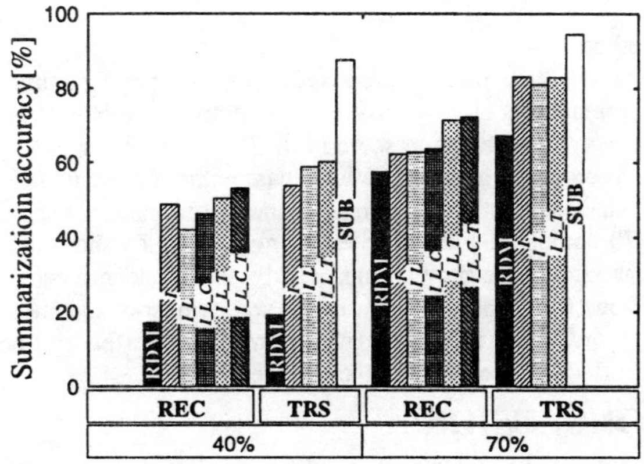

Figure 8: *Article summarization at 40% and 70% summarization ratio.*

and 81.4%, respectively. In order to build word networks of manual summarization results, 17 native English speakers generated manual summarization by removing or extracting words.

4.3 Structure of transcription system

English broadcast news speech was transcribed by the JRTk (Janus Speech Recognition Toolkit) [10] with the following conditions.

Feature extraction

Sounds were digitized with 16kHz sampling and 16bit quantization. Feature vectors had 13 elements consisting of MFCC. Vocal Tract Length Normalization (VTLN) and cluster-based cepstral mean normalization were used to compensate for speaker and channel. Linear Discriminant Analysis (LDA) was applied to reduce feature dimensions in each segment consisting of 7 frames to 42.

Acoustic model

A pentphone model with 6000 distributions sharing 2000 codebooks were used. There were about 105k Gaussians in the system. The training data was comprised of 66 hours of Broadcast News(BN).

Language model

Bigram and trigram were built using BN corpus. Its vocabulary size was 40k.

Decoder

A word-graph-based 3-pass decoder which was composed with JRTk was used for transcription. In the first pass, frame-synchronous beam search was performed using a tree-based lexicon, the above-mentioned HMMs and a bigram model to generate a word graph. In the second pass, frame-synchronous beam search was performed again using a flat lexicon hypothesized in the word graph by the first pass and a trigram model. In the third pass, the word graph was minimized and rescored using the trigram language model.

4.4 Training data for summarization models

A word significance model, a bigram language model and SDCFG were constructed using roughly 35M words (10681 sentences) of the Wall Street Journal corpus and the Brown corpus in Penn Treebank[15].

4.5 Evaluation results

Manual transcription (TRS) and automatic transcription (REC) were both summarized. Table 1 shows examples of automatic summarization and the corresponding target extracted from a manual summarization word network. Figure 7 shows summarization accuracies of utterance summarization at 40% and 70% summarization ratio and Figure 8 shows those of summarizing articles having multiple utterances at 40% and 70% summarization ratio. In these figures, I, L, C and T indicate that the word significance score, the linguistic score, the confidence score and the word concatenation score are used, respectively. In the summarization of REC, conditions with and without the word confidence score, (*I_L_C_T*) and (*I_L_T*), were compared. In summarization for both TRS and REC, conditions with and without the word concatenation score, (*I_L_T*, *I_L_C_T*) and (*I_L*, *I_L_C*), were compared.

The summarization accuracies for manual summarization (SUB) is considered to be the upper limit of the automatic summarization accuracy. To ensure that our method is sound, we made randomly generated summarized sentences (RDM) according to the summarization ratio and compared them with those obtained by our pro-

Table 2: *Number of recognition errors in summarized sentences (): number of sentences including recognition errors)*

REC	Each utterance 180(45)		Multiple utterances 326(94)	
Summarization ratio	40%	70%	40%	70%
I	42 (27)	111 (40)	99 (56)	199 (71)
I_L	44 (28)	87 (37)	86 (53)	166 (69)
I_L_C	23 (15)	49 (22)	34 (28)	82 (47)
I_L_T	46 (27)	84 (37)	90 (56)	173 (69)
I_L_C_T	22 (13)	51 (24)	25 (17)	80 (47)
RDM	82 (30)	87 (21)	89 (45)	169 (65)

posed method.

These results show that our proposed automatic speech summarization technique is significantly more effective than RDM. By using the word concatenation score (*I_L_T*, *I_L_C_T*), meaning alteration is reduced compared with the case without using it (*I_L*, *I_L_C*). The result obtained when using the word confidence score (*I_L_C_T*) compared with those not using it (*I_L_T*) shows that the summarization accuracy is improved by the confidence score. Table 2 shows the number of word errors and number of sentences including word errors in the automatic summarization. Recognition errors are effectively reduced by the confidence score.

5. CONCLUSIONS

Each utterance and a whole news article consisting of multiple utterances of English broadcast news speech were summarized by our automatic speech summarization method based on the following scores: word significance score, linguistic likelihood, word confidence measure and word concatenation probability. Experimental results show that our proposed method can effectively extract relatively important information and remove redundant and irrelevant information from English news speech in the same way as for Japanese new speech.

In contrast with the confidence score which has been incorporated into the summarization score to exclude word errors by a recognizer, the linguistic score is effective to reduce out-of-context word extraction both from recognition errors and human disfluencies. In summarizing Japanese news speech, the confidence measure could improve the summarizing performance by excluding in-context word errors. In the English case, the confidence measure can not only exclude word errors but also help extracting clearly pronounced important words. Consequently the use of the confidence measure yields a larger increase in the summarization accuracy for English than Japanese.

6. ACKNOWLEDGMENT

The authors would like to thank Dr. Yoshi Gotoh (Sheffield University) for an arrangement of generating the correct answers for automatic summarization.

7. REFERENCES

[1] T. Imai et al., "Progressive 2-pass Decoder for Real-Time Broadcast News Captioning," *Proc. ICSLP2000*, vol.I, pp.246–249, Beijing, 2000.

[2] Z. Klaus, "Automatic Generation of Concise Summaries of Spoken Dialogues in Unrestricted Domains," *Proc. SIGIR2001*, New Orleans, 2001.

[3] S. Furui et al., "Toward the Realization of Spontaneous Speech Recognition -Introduction of a Japanese Priority Program and Preliminary Results-," *Proc. ICSLP2000*, vol.III, pp.518–521, Beijing, 2000.

[4] R. Valenza et al., "Summarization of Spoken Audio through Information Extraction," *Proc. ESCA Workshop on Accessing Information in Spoken Audio*, pp.111–116, Cambridge, 1999.

[5] I. Mani et al., "Advances in Automatic Text Summarization," *The MIT Press*, 1999.

[6] K. Knight et al., "Statistics-Based Summarization — Step One: Sentence Compression," *Proc. National Conference on Artificial Intelligence* (AAAI), 2000.

[7] C. Hori et al., "Automatic Speech Summarization Based on Word Significance and Linguistic Likelihood," *Proc. ICASSP2000*, vol.III, pp.1579–1582, Istanbul, 2000.

[8] C. Hori et al., "Improvements in Automatic Speech Summarization and Evaluation Methods," *Proc. ICSLP2000*, vol.IV, pp.326–329, Beijing, 2000.

[9] C. Hori et al., "Advances in Automatic Speech Summarization," *Proc. EUROSPEECH2001*, vol.III, pp.1771–1774, Aalborg, 2001.

[10] A. Waibel et al., "Advances in Meeting Recognition," *Proc. HLT2001*, pp.11–13, San Diego, 2001.

[11] T. Kemp et al., "Estimating confidence using word lattices," *Proc. 5th Eurospeech*, Rhodes, Vol.II, pp.827–830, 1997.

[12] C. Manning et al., "Foundations of Statistical Natural Language Processing," *The MIT Press*, 2000.

[13] K. Lari et al., "The estimation of stochastic context free grammars using the Inside-Outside algorithm," *Computer Speech and Language*, 4, pp.35–56, 1990.

[14] A. Ito et al., "Language Modeling by Stochastic Dependency Grammar for Japanese Speech Recognition," *Proc. ICSLP2000*, Beijing, Vol.I, pp.246–249, 2000.

[15] http://www.cis.upenn.edu/~treebank/

[16] http://www.cs.jhu.edu/~brill/

APPENDIX

Inside probability e and outside probablitie f are given by eqs. (A-1) and (A-2), respectively.

Inside Probabilities

$$e(i,j|\alpha) = \begin{cases} \sum_{k=i}^{j-1} \left\{ \sum_{\beta} P(\alpha \to \beta\alpha) e(i,k|\beta) e(k+1,j|\alpha) \right. \\ \quad \left. + \sum_{\beta:\alpha\neq\beta} P(\alpha \to \alpha\beta) e(i,k|\alpha) e(k+1,j|\beta) \right\} & if\ i<j \\ b(\alpha \to w_i) & if\ i=j \end{cases} \quad \text{(A-1)}$$

Outside Probabilities

$$\begin{aligned} f(i,j|\alpha) &= \sum_{k=1}^{i-1} \left\{ \sum_{\beta} P(\alpha \to \beta\alpha) e(k,i-1|\beta) f(k,j|\alpha) \right. \\ &\quad \left. + \sum_{\beta:\alpha\neq\beta} P(\beta \to \beta\alpha) e(k,i-1|\beta) f(k,j|\alpha) \right\} \\ &+ \sum_{k=j+1}^{L} \left\{ \sum_{\beta} P(\beta \to \alpha\beta) e(j+1,k|\beta) f(i,k|\alpha) \right. \\ &\quad \left. + \sum_{\beta:\alpha\neq\beta} P(\alpha \to \alpha\beta) e(j+1,k|\beta) f(i,k|\alpha) \right\} \end{aligned} \quad \text{(A-2)}$$

A Question/Answer Typology with Surface Text Patterns

Eduard Hovy, Ulf Hermjakob, and Deepak Ravichandran

USC Information Sciences Institute
4676 Admiralty Way
Marina del Rey, CA 90292-6695
Tel: +1-310-448-8711/8731
{hovy,ulf,ravichan}@isi.edu

ABSTRACT

In this paper we announce the release of ISI's QA Typology, which is being made available on the web to support the rapid construction of new QA systems. The Typology has been augmented with surface-level patterns associated with answer types, allowing systems to locate answers of the desired type in text by simple string matching. These patterns are extracted from the web automatically. We describe the process of their extraction, compression, and accuracy determination.

Keywords

Question answering; QA typology; answer patterns

1. QA TYPES AND TYPOLOGIES

The recent TREC-10 Question Answering competition included over 65 participating systems. The vast majority (if not all) performed some variant of answer typing, in which a process analyzes the input question to determine the desired type of the answer. Answer types are used by systems as a matching criterion to filter out candidate answers that look likely. For example, "Who is the richest person in the world?", "Where is Cambodia?", and "When did Marilyn Monroe marry Arthur Miller?" may have answer types *ProperPerson*, *Location*, and *Date* respectively.

The same answer type can be intended by various forms of question, as in "What is the name of the person who invented xeroxing?", "Who invented xeroxing?", and "Who was the inventor of xeroxing?". Similarly, the answer can occur in different forms, such as "Chester F. Carlson invented xeroxing", "the man who invented photocopying was Chester Carlson", and "Inventing the xeroxing process was a high point of Chester F. Carlson's life". What we called an answer type is thus a kind of equivalence class of all these phrasings, or a relation that links all the question forms to all their answer forms. We call this equivalence class a *Qtarget*; for this example it might be *Person*. Most QA systems include a list of such Qtargets, typically ranging in number from around 10 to around 50, and starting with *Who, When, Where,* and *What*.

Since many QA systems associate specific matching information (indicative words, surface word patterns, etc.) with their Qtargets, it is useful to create more specific alternatives that narrow the equivalent sets. Thus *Person* might be specialized to *Inventor*, and be associated with words such as "invent", "invention", "discover", "discovery", and "create". Other specializations of *Person* might be *Artist* (with "perform", "sing") and *Author* ("write", "book", "publish"). In addition, questions often explicitly require more or less specific answers ("Where is Vesuvius?" vs. "In which country is Vesuvius?")

The hierarchicalized Qtargets form a typology that defines the types of questions the system can handle. The hierarchicalization can be exploited for backoff matches, to allow more general Qtargets to apply in cases where specific ones fail. QA lists or typologies are reported in almost all QA system papers; see for example [4,1].

Proceedings of HLT 2002, Second International Conference on Human Language Technology Research, M. Marcus, ed., Morgan Kaufmann, San Francisco, 2002.

2. ISI'S QA TYPOLOGY

Over the past two years, we have created at ISI a QA Typology that currently contains 180 Qtargets. Our initial Typology of about 75 nodes was derived from an analysis by one of our students of over 17,000 questions, downloaded from answers.com [7,8]; see http://www.isi.edu/natural-language/projects/webclopedia/Taxonomy/taxonomy_toplevel.html.

Subsequently, we have been restructuring and extending the Typology to its current form.

Qtargets are of five types.

Abstract Qtargets. Some qtargets are not typical semantic types but are specific to QA. For example, the usual reading of "who was Mother Theresa?" is "why is the individual known as Mother Theresa famous?". The Qtarget *WhyFamous* is not a semantic class. These Qtargets are shown in Figure 1.

Semantic Qtargets. These Qtargets, the largest class, limit the search space to sentence constituents that satisfy a particular semantic class with respect to the Webclopdia ontology, which currently contains about 10,000 items, mostly extracted from WordNet. Some semantic Qtargets are shown in Figure 2.

Syntactic Qtargets. Other Qtargets apply when the system cannot determine a specific semantic type for the answer, but can specify the desired syntactic type. Syntactic qtargets are

```
Abstract qtargets
        WHY-FAMOUS
            WHY-FAMOUS-PERSON
            - Who was Jane Goodall?
            - What is Jane Goodall famous for?
        DEFINITION - What is platinum?
        ABBREVIATION-EXPANSION - What does NAFTA stand for?
        ABBREVIATION - What's the abbreviation for limited partnership?
        SYNONYM - Aspartame is also known as what?
        CONTRAST - What's the difference between DARPA and NSF?
        POPULATION - How many people live in Greater Tokyo?
        VERACITY
            YES-NO-QUESTION - Does light have weight?
            TRUE-FALSE-QUESTION - Chaucer was an actual person. True or false?
        PHILOSOPHICAL-QUESTION - What is the meaning of life?
```

Figure 1. QA typology: Abstract Qtargets.

```
Semantic qtargets
   TEMP-LOC - before the conference
        DATE - July 4
             DATE-WITH-YEAR - July 4, 1776
             ...
        YEAR-RANGE
             DECADE - in the 1980s
             ...
        TEMP-LOWITH-YEAR - July 1776
             DATE-WITH-YEAR
        DATE-RANGE - July 12-14
        TIME - at 2:15pm EST
   AT-LOCATION - under the bed
   PROPER-NAMED-ENTITY
        PROPER-PERSON - John F. Kennedy
        PROPER-LANGUAGE - Afrikaans
        PROPER-ANIMAL - Lassie
        PROPER-PLACE
             CONTINENT - Africa
             WORLD-REGION - Middle East
             ...
             PROPER-COUNTY - Orange County
             PROPER-CITY - Chicago
             PROPER-BODY-OF-WATER
                  PROPER-OCEAN
                  ...
             PROPER-ISLAND
             PROPER-MOUNTAIN
        ...
             PROPER-STAR-CONSTELLATION - Orion
             ...
             PROPER-AMUSEMENT-PARK - Disneyland
             PROPER-HOTEL - Holiday Inn
             PROPER-UNIVERSITY - Harvard
             ...
             PROPER-AIRPORT - LAX
        PROPER-ORGANIZATION
             PROPER-SPORTS-TEAM
                  ...
             PROPER-POLITICAL-PARTY
          PROPER-COMPANY
               PROPER-BROADCASTING-COMPANY
               ...
          GOVERNMENT-AGENCY - House of Representatives, OSHA
  PLANT-FLORA
      FLOWER
      TREE
  SUBSTANCE
      SOLID-SUBSTANCE
          METAL
      LIQUID
          BEVERAGE
```

```
QUANTITY
    MONETARY-QUANTITY - How much does one ton of cement cost?
    SPATIAL-QUANTITY
        DISTANCE-QUANTITY
          - How far is it from Denver to Aspen?
          - How tall is the Sears Building?
        AREA-QUANTITY - How big is Australia?
        VOLUME-QUANTITY - How much milk did you buy?
    TEMPORAL-QUANTITY
    - How long did Desert Storm last?
    - What is the life expectancy for crickets?
    SPEED-QUANTITY - How fast is sound?
    ACCELERATION-QUANTITY - What's the gravity on the moon?
    NUMERICAL-QUANTITY/I-ENUM-CARDINAL
        - How many moons does Jupiter have?
    FREQUENCY-QUANTITY
    - How often does Old Faithful erupt at Yellowstone National Park?
    SCORE-QUANTITY
    - What was the score of the World Cup final Germany vs. Netherlands?
    PERCENTAGE - What is the sales tax rate in New York?
    TEMPERATURE-QUANTITY - How hot is the core of the earth?
    MASS-QUANTITY - What is the average weight of a Yellow Labrador?
    POWER-QUANTITY
    - How many megawatts will the new power plant in Indonesia produce?
    ...
C-LOCATOR
    C-PHONE-NUMBER, C-ADDRESS, C-ZIP-CODE, C-EMAIL-ADDRESS, C-URL
UNIVERSITY-AGENCY - biology department
SPIRITUAL-BEING
OCCUPATION-PERSON - computer scientist
ANIMAL
HUMAN-FOOD
BODY-PART
TEMPORAL-INTERVAL
    DAY-OF-THE-WEEK, MONTH-OF-THE-YEAR, SEASON ...
DISEASE - arthritis
INSTRUMENT - hammer
MUSICAL-INSTRUMENT -trumpet
SPORT - football
LEFT-OR-RIGHT - left, right
I-EADJ-COLOR - blue
I-EADJ-NATIONALITY - German
```

Figure 2. QA Typology: Some Semantic Qtargets.

fairly weak, in that they generally don't restrict the search space much. Webclopedia uses *S-NP* as the default Qtarget. The four syntactic Qtargets are:

```
S-NP, S-NOUN
  What does Peugeot manufacture?
S-VP
  What did John Hinckley do to impress
  Jodie Foster?
S-PROPER-NAME
```

Role Qtargets. These Qtargets specify constituents of the parse tree of the question and candidate answer:

```
ROLE REASON
  Why did David Koresh ask the FBI for a
  word processor?
ROLE MANNER
  What's the easiest way to remove
  wallpaper?
```

For example, in the (simplified) parse tree

```
The tournament was cancelled due to bad
   weather.
 ((SUBJ LOG-OBJ) [2] The tournament
  (PRED) [5] was cancelled
  (REASON) [6] due to bad weather
  (DUMMY) [14] .
 )
```

the phrase "due to the bad weather" satisfies the Qtarget *Role Reason*. This constraint is independent of the syntactic category, which also could have been a subordinate clause ("because the weather was so bad") or a verb phrase ("to avoid injuries").

Slot Qtargets. Slot Qtargets refer to non-syntactic information associated with sentence constituents. Slots may be filled during parsing or later. Some examples are:

```
SLOT TITLE-P TRUE
   Name a novel written by Proust.
SLOT QUOTE-P TRUE
   What did Richard Feynman say upon
   hearing he would receive the Nobel Prize
```

```
   in Physics?
 SLOT POSSIBLE-REASON-P TRUE
```

ISI's QA systems Webclopedia [8] and TextMap [9] both employ the Typology. Both systems can combine Qtargets, using variable strengths:

Question: Where is the Getty Museum?

Qtarget: ((*Proper-city* 1.0) (*At-location* 0.7)
(*Proper-place* 0.7) …)

indicating that the system would prefer a proper city, but could accept something tagged by the named entity tagger just as a general location, or as a place with a name [5].

3. ANSWER PATTERNS

At the recent TREC conference, several systems emphasized the value of a surface-oriented pattern matching approach to QA. The Insight system from Moscow [11] used some hundreds of surface-level patterns to identify answer strings without (apparently) applying Qtargets or similar reasoning. For example, for *BirthYear* questions such as "which year was Mozart born?" the phrase "Mozart (1756 – 1791)…" provides the answer using the general template

NAME_OF_PERSON (BIRTHYEAR – DEATHYEAR)

Several other systems also defined word-level patterns indicating specific Qtargets; e.g., [10]. The Microsoft system [3] extended the idea of a pattern to its limit, by reformulating the input question as a declarative sentence and then retrieving the sentence verbatim, with its answer as a completion, from the web using the normal search engines. For example, "who was Chester F. Carlson?" would be transformed to "Chester F. Carlson was" and submitted. Although this approach might yield many wrong answers (including "Chester F. Carlson was born February 8, 1906, in Seattle"), the sheer number of correct answers often wins the day.

We estimate that word-level patterns can provide at least 25% of the MRR score defined for TREC (although some systems claimed considerably higher results; see [11] and discussion in [6]). In order to determine their power and reap their benefits, we collected all the patterns associated with as many Qtargets as made sense (some Qtargets, such as *Planets* and *Oceans*, are known closed sets that require no patterns).

We developed an automated procedure to learn such patterns from the web, using Altavista (because it returns 1000 documents per query), and to measure their Precision. More formally this experiment can be phrased as "Given a QA pair such as (NAME_OF_PERSON BIRTHYEAR), extract from the web all the different patterns (TEMPLATEs) that contain this QA pair along with the precision of each pattern". We have inserted into the Typology the patterns for approx. 20 Qtargets, recording their Precision scores and relative frequencies of appearance.

The procedure contains two parts:

1. Extracting the patterns
2. Calculating the precision of each pattern

Algorithm 1: Extracting patterns

1. An example of the question-answer pair for which the pattern is to be extracted is passed to a search engine. To learn the pattern for the pair (NAME_OF_PERSON BIRTHYEAR) we submit the query "Gandhi 1869" to Altavista.

2. The top 1000 documents returned by the search engine are retrieved.

3. These documents are broken into sentences by a simple sentence breaker. Only sentences that contain both the Question and the Answer term are retained. BBN's IdentiFinder named entity tagger [2] is used to remove the variations caused by writing a name or a date in different forms.

5. Each of these sentences is converted into a Suffix tree, to collect counts on all phrases and subphrases present in the document.

6. The phrases obtained from the Suffix tree process are filtered so that only those containing both the Question and the Answer terms are retained. This yields the set of patterns for the given QA pair.

Algorithm 2: Calculating the precision of each pattern

1. The Question term alone (without the Answer term) is given as query to Altavista.

2. As before, the top 1000 documents returned by the search engine for this query are retrieved.

3. Again, the documents are broken into sentences.

4. Only those sentences with the Question term are saved.

5. For each pattern obtained in step 6 of Algorithm 1, a pattern-matching check is done against each sentence obtained from step 4 here, and only the sentences containing the Answer are retained. This is used to calculate the precision of each pattern according to the formula

Precision = # patterns matching the Answer
/ total # matches for every pattern

6. Only those patterns are retained for which sufficient examples are obtained in step 5.

To increase the size of the data, we apply the algorithms with several different examples of the same Qtarget. Thus in Algorithm 1 for *BirthYear* we used Mozart, Gauss, Gandhi, Nelson Mandela, Michelangelo, Christopher Columbus, and Sean Connery, each with its birth year. We then applied Algorithm 2 with just these names, counting the yields of the patterns on the exact birth years (no additional words or reformulations, which would increase the yield score).

The results were quite good in some cases. For the rather straightforward *BirthYear* patterns are:

Precision	#Correct	# Found	Pattern
1.0	122	122	<NAME> (<BD> - <DD>
1.0	15	15	<NAME> (<BD> - <DD>),
1.0	13	13	, <NAME> (<BD> - <DD>)
0.9166	11	12	<NAME> was born on <BD> in
0.9090	10	11	<NAME> : <BD> - <TIME>
0.6944	25	36	<NAME> was born on <BD>

Note the overlaps among patterns. By not compressing them further we can record different precision levels.

The *Definition* Qtarget posed greater problems. E.g., disease (the names *jaundice, measles, malaria, and tuberculosis* were paired with the term *disease*, but not also with *illness, ailment,* etc., although this would have increased the yield):

1.0	46	46	heart <TERM> , <NAME>
1.0	35	35	<NAME> & tropical <TERM> weekly
1.0	30	30	venereal <TERM> , <NAME>
1.0	24	24	lyme <TERM> , <NAME>
1.0	22	22	, heart <TERM> , <NAME>
1.0	21	21	' s <TERM> , <NAME>
0.9565	22	23	lyme <TERM> <NAME>
0.9	9	10	s <TERM> , <NAME> and
0.8815	67	76	<NAME> , a <TERM>
0.8666	13	15	<TERM> , especially <NAME>

4. EXTENDING THE TYPES OF TYPES

This work has necessitated extensions to the original Typology. Because the Typology initially focused on matching of answers, most Qtargets express requirements on a single entity: the answer. In this regard the Typology resembles the typical question type hierarchies of QA systems.

The patterns, however, represent relationships between the two anchor points of each pattern. As a result, patterns pick out subsets of Qtargets and cannot easily be incorporated into the Typology. For example, the general Qtarget *Date* has to be split up into *BirthDate, DeathDate, WeddingDate, Discover-Date, GraduationDate, ConstructionDate*, and so on. All the generalizations captured in the Typology under *Date* about the different forms in which dates can be expressed (day+month+year, month+year, year, etc.) have to be repeated for each pattern Qtarget. Naturally, this forces the patterns to contain not only surface forms (words and punctuation, but also type markers (*Date, NumericalAmount, MoneyAmount...*). Work is underway to automatically recognize occurrences of such expressions and replace them with type markers.

5. CONCLUSIONS

Overall, we are satisfied with the coverage of the Typology, and with its utility in Webclopedia's QA processing. A survey of the papers in the TREC 9 and 10 proceedings shows that most systems tend to use more than a dozen Qtargets, while only one system [4] uses in the order of 1000 (in essentially a semantic answer type ontology).

By making public the QA Typology and its patterns we hope to enable a wider range of people to build basic QA systems quickly, and then to help investigate the question of QA.

6. REFERENCES

[1] Abney, S., M. Collins, and A. Singhal. 2000. Answer Extraction. *Proceedings of the Applied Natural Language Processing Conference (ANLP)*. Seattle, WA (296–301).

[2] Bikel, D., R. Schwartz, and R. Weischedel. 1999. An Algorithm that Learns What's in a Name. *Machine Learning—Special Issue on NL Learning*, 34, 1–3.

[3] Brill, E., J. Lin, M. Banko, S. Dumais, and A. Ng. 2001. Data-Intensive Question Answering. *Proceedings of the TREC-10 Conference.* NIST, Gaithersburg, MD (183–189).

[4] Harabagiu, S., M. Pasca, and S. Maiorano. 2000. Experiments with Open Domain Textual Question Answering. *Proceedings of the 18th COLING Conference.* Saarbrücken, Germany (292–298).

[5] Hermjakob, U. 2001. Parsing and Question Classification for Question Answering. In *Proceedings of the Workshop on Question Answering at the Conference ACL-2001.* Toulouse, France.

[6] Hermjakob, U. 2002. Open Questions Regarding Precision of the Insight Q&A System http://www.isi.edu/natural-language /projects/webclopedia/pubs/01insight-reimpl.pdf *or* .ps

[7] Hovy, E.H., L. Gerber, U. Hermjakob, M. Junk, and C.-Y. Lin. 2000. Question Answering in Webclopedia. *Proceedings of the TREC-9 Conference.* NIST. Gaithersburg, MD.

[8] Hovy, E.H., U. Hermjakob, and C.-Y. Lin. 2001. The Use of External Knowledge in Factoid QA. *Proceedings of the TREC-10 Conference.* NIST, Gaithersburg, MD (166–174).

[10] Oh, JH., KS. Lee, DS. Chang, CW. Seo, and KS. Choi. 2001. TREC-10 Experiments at KAIST: Batch Filtering and Question Answering. *Proceedings of the TREC-10 Conference.* NIST, Gaithersburg, MD (354–361).

[11] Soubbotin, M.M. and S.M. Soubbotin. 2001. Patterns of Potential Answer Expressions as Clues to the Right Answer. *Proceedings of the TREC-10 Conference.* NIST, Gaithersburg, MD. (175–182)

Adding Predicate Argument Structure to the Penn TreeBank

Paul Kingsbury
University of Pennsylvania
Department of Linguistics
619 Williams Hall
Philadelphia PA 19104
1–267–738–8262
kingsbur@unagi.cis.upenn.edu

Martha Palmer
University of Pennsylvania
Department of Computer Science
256 GRW
Philadelphia PA 19104
1–215–898–9513
mpalmer@linc.cis.upenn.edu

Mitch Marcus
University of Pennsylvania
Department of Computer Science
461A GRW
Philadelphia PA 19104
1–215–898–2538
mitch@linc.cis.upenn.edu

ABSTRACT

This paper presents our basic approach to creating Proposition Bank, which involves adding a layer of semantic annotation to the Penn English TreeBank. Without attempting to confirm or disconfirm any particular semantic theory, our goal is to provide consistent argument labeling that will facilitate the automatic extraction of relational data. An argument such as *the window* in *John broke the window* and in *The window broke* would receive the same label in both sentences. In order to ensure reliable human annotation, we provide our annotators with explicit guidelines for labeling all of the syntactic and semantic frames of each particular verb. We give several examples of these guidelines and discuss the inter–annotator agreement figures. We also discuss our current experiments on the automatic expansion of our verb guidelines based on verb class membership. Our current rate of progress and our consistency of annotation demonstrate the feasibility of the task.

Keywords

Predicate argument structure, semantic annotation, verb classes.

1.INTRODUCTION

Recent years have seen major breakthroughs in natural language processing technology based on the development of powerful new techniques that combine statistical methods and linguistic representations [1,2,3,11]. A critical element that is still lacking, however, is detailed predicate–argument structure. In the same way that the existence of the Penn TreeBank [8,9] enabled the development of extremely powerful new syntactic analyzers, moving to the stage of accurate predicate argument analysis will require a body of publicly available training data that explicitly annotates predicate argument positions with labels. A consensus on a task–oriented level of semantic representation has been achieved with respect to English, under the auspices of the ACE program (involving research groups at BBN, MITRE, New York University, and Penn). It was agreed that the highest priority, and the most feasible type of semantic annotation, is co–reference and predicate argument structure for verbs, participial modifiers and nominalizations, to be known as Proposition Bank, or PropBank. This paper describes the PropBank verb predicate argument structure annotation being done at Penn. Similar projects include Framenet [7] and Prague Tectogrammatics [4].

Proceedings of HLT 2002, Second International Conference on Human Language Technology Research, M. Marcus, ed., Morgan Kaufmann, San Francisco, 2002.

2.PREDICATE ARGUMENT STRUCTURE

The verb of the sentence typically indicates a particular event and the verb's syntactic arguments are associated with the event participants. In the sentence *John broke the window*, the event is a breaking event, with *John* as the instigator and a *broken window* as the result. The associated predicate argument structure would be **break(John, window)**. Recognition of predicate argument structures is not straightforward since a natural language will have both several different lexical items that can be used to refer to the same type of event as well as several different syntactic realizations of the same predicate argument relations. For example, a meeting between two dignitaries can be described using the verbs *meet, visit, debate, consult*, etc.[1], each of which are syntactically interchangeable while lending their own individual semantic nuances. Thus, variations such as the following are seen:

John *will [meet/visit/debate/consult] (with)* Mary.
John *and* Mary *[met/visited/debated/consulted]*
There was a [meeting/visit/debate/consultation] between John *and* Mary.
John *had a [meeting/visit/debate/consultation] with* Mary.

At the same time, not all syntactic frames of a given verb are interchangeable with those of related verbs:

Blair *[met/consulted/visited] with* Bush.
The proposal *[met/*consulted/*visited] with* skepticism.

In determining consistent annotations for argument labels of several different syntactic expressions of the same verb, we are relying heavily on recent work in linguistics on word classifications that have a more semantic orientation, such as Levin's verb classes [6], and WordNet [10]. The verb classes are based on the ability of the verb to occur or not occur in pairs of syntactic frames that are in some sense meaning–preserving (diathesis alternations) [6]. The distribution of syntactic frames in which a verb can appear determines its class membership, to a finer degree than mere semantic similarity can provide. The fundamental assumption is that the syntactic frames are a direct reflection of the underlying semantics; the sets of syntactic frames associated with a particular verb of a particular Levin class reflect underlying semantic components that constrain allowable arguments. These classes, and our refinements on

[1] These are representative of the *meet* class (36) of [6].

them as captured in VerbNet, [5], provide the key to recognizing the common basis for the myriad ways in which a concept can be expressed syntactically.

3.PROPOSITION BANK

We are annotating predicate argument structure for the Penn TreeBank II Wall Street Journal Corpus of a million words, [8,9]. For the sake of ramping up production, training annotators and working out necessary guidelines and procedures while still producing a coherent product, we have extracted a 300k–word subcorpus, comprising mostly financial reporting, which will be completed and delivered first. This financial subcorpus had an alpha release in December of 2001 and will have a final release in June of 2002. The remainder of the re-annotated TreeBank will be released by June of 2003. PropBank currently annotates all sentential verbs, leaving adjectives and nominalizations for a later stage.

The annotation scheme requires first that verbs be coarsely disambiguated. This disambiguation is done largely on the basis of differing argument structures and as such avoids the subjectivity of other word–sense distinctions such as those found in WordNet. For example, while the verb **leave** has two major senses (DEPART and GIVE), in the following sentence only one is possible: *Vandenberg and Rayburn were wise enough *TRACE* to leave specific operations to presidents.* This is easily determined by the fact that there are three arguments, labeled atheoretically as Arg0, Arg1, and Arg2.

The predicate argument annotation of the embedded clause is, roughly,

base=leave2; tense=infinitival;
arg2=presidents;
arg1=specific operations;
arg0=*TRACE* –> Vandenberg and Rayburn;

(Notice also that the annotation makes explicit the referent of the **TRACE** which instantiates the *Arg0* of *leave.*) These labels allow us to capture the similarity between transitivity alternations as in, for example, *John (Arg0) broke the window (Arg1)* and *The window (Arg1) broke*, [6]. Whenever possible, when transitivity alternations do not occur, we use the same predicate argument structure for all instances of a verb. With *carry*, there are two arguments, *Arg0, Arg1* whether *a mother is carrying a baby, a bond is carrying a yield, crystals are carrying currents*, or *viruses are carrying genes.*

4.DATA

The end product of the project is twofold, containing both the annotated text itself and a linked lexical resource called Frames Files.

4.1Annotation

All annotations are given in the form of a standoff notation referring to the syntactic terminals within the original TreeBank files:

wsj/08/wsj_0810.mrg 16 16 denationalize ----- 16:0–rel
14:1*17:0–ARG1 18:1–ARGM–TMP

This corresponds to the following more human–readable form:

Mr. Fournier also noted that Navigation Mixte joined Paribas's core of shareholders when Paribas was denationalized in 1987, and said it now holds just under 5% of Paribas's shares.[2]

rel: denationalized
ARG1: *trace* –> Paribas
ARGM–TMP: in 1987

4.2Frames Files

4.2.1 Labels

In order to ensure consistent annotation, we provide our annotators with detailed and comprehensive examples of all of a verb's syntactic realizations and the corresponding argument labels. Starting with the most frequent verbs, a series of frames are drawn up to describe the expected arguments, or roles. The general procedure is to examine a number of sentences from the corpus and then select the roles which seem to occur most frequently and/or are semantically necessary. These roles are then numbered sequentially from Arg0 up to (potentially) Arg5, and each role is given a mnemonic label. These labels tend to be verb–specific, although, following the lead of Framenet, some labels tend to be general to verb classes, while other labels follow the naming conventions of, e.g., theta–role theory. The number of roles varies by verb, from a minimum of zero to a maximum of six. Most typically, verbs take two or three roles, such as *hit*:

HIT (sense: strike)
Arg0: hitter
Arg1: thing hit
Arg2: instrument, hit with

It might seem odd for a verb to take no arguments, but that is the normal state of affairs for, eg, weather verbs:

HAIL (sense: pellets of ice from the sky)

(eg, It is hailing outside.)

Maximally, some verbs of "quantifiable motion" can take up to six arguments:

EDGE (sense: move slightly)
Arg0: causer of motion[3]
Arg1: thing in motion
Arg2: distance moved
Arg3: start point
Arg4: end point
Arg5: direction

The publishing unit reported revenue edged up 2.6% to $263.2 million from $256.6 million.

The verb *buy* is expected to have up to five roles:

BUY
Arg0: buyer
Arg1: thing bought
Arg2: seller, bought–from
Arg3: price paid
Arg4: benefactive, bought–for

[2] This and all subsequent examples are taken from the TreeBank.

[3] The agentive argument does not often occur with such verbs of quantifiable motion, but it certainly possible: *John edged the car 3 feet forward from in front of the fire hydrant to behind the UPS truck.*

PURCHASE	BUY	SELL
Arg0: buyer	Arg0: buyer	Arg0: seller
Arg1: thing bought	Arg1: thing bought	Arg1: thing sold
Arg2: seller	Arg2: seller	Arg2: buyer
Arg3: price paid	Arg3: price paid	Arg3: price paid
Arg4: benefactive	Arg4: benefactive	Arg4: benefactive

Table 1: comparison of arguments of semantically related verbs

Rarely, however, will all of these roles occur in a single sentence. For example:

The company bought a wheel–loader from Dresser.

Arg0:	The company
rel:	bought
Arg1:	a wheel–loader
Arg2–from:	Dresser

TV stations bought "Cosby" reruns for record prices.

Arg0:	TV stations
rel:	bought
Arg1:	"Cosby" reruns
Arg3–for:	record prices.

As much as possible, rolesets are consistent across semantically related verbs. Thus, the *buy* roleset is the same as the *purchase* roleset, and both are similar to the *sell* roleset, as seen in Table 1 above.

One detail of note is that, in any transaction, the Arg2 "seller" role of *buy* is equivalent to the Arg0 "seller" role of *sell*, and vice–versa. An Information Extraction application could use a specific rule showing the mapping between these arguments and their relationship to a "commodity transaction" template. For both Machine Translation and Information Extraction, the buyer and seller need to remain distinct, but for other applications, such as Information Retrieval, they can be merged into a superset or Metaframe as given below, which could easily be regarded as equivalent to the verb roles in the Commerce frame in Framenet:

PropBank: EXCHANGE OF COMMODITIES FOR CASH[4]	**FrameNet**: COMMERCE
Arg0: one exchanger	Buyer
Arg1: commodity	Seller
Arg2: other exchanger	Payment
Arg3: cash, price	Goods
Arg4: benefactive	Rate/Unit

Table 2: comparison on PropBank and Framenet

The many–to–many correspondence between the Framenet and PropBank roles is not insignificant. Because the PropBank Metaframe is derived from many verb–specific frames, it is relatively easy to reconstruct what the subject (agent) role should be for any of those specific verbs. That is, each of buy, sell, purchase, etc., indicate whether it is the buyer or the seller which appears in the subject position. This information is not as easily obtained from the Framenet role descriptions, because their labels are defined at the superset level. On the other hand, because of the specificity of PropBank frames it can be difficult to determine larger classes of verbs.

A variety of additional roles are assumed to apply across all verbs and are given the label ArgM with a variety of secondary tags. These tags augment the function tags of the TreeBank and can be considered either as fundamentally different from the numbered arguments (a more theoretical argument/adjunct distinction) or as merely arguments which are always numbered higher than 5. They include:

LOC:	location	NEG:	negation marker
TMP:	time	MOD:	modal verb
MNR:	manner	EXT:	extent, numerical role
DIR:	direction	PRP:	purpose
CAU:	cause	ADV:	general–purpose modifier

Table 3: secondary tags

In addition, we use a tag PRD marking "secondary predication," for those cases where one argument of a verb is a predicate upon another argument of the same verb. This helps underline the important distinction between the following:

Mary called John an idiot. (LABEL)	*Mary called John a cab.* (SUMMON)[5]
Arg0: Mary	Arg0: Mary
Rel: called	Rel: called
Arg1: John (item being labeled)	Arg2: John (benefactive)
Arg3–PRD: an idiot (attribute)	Arg1: a cab (thing summoned)

Table 4: use of PRD tag

4.2.2 *Comparison with other resources*

Use of a large corpus of actual usage enables the discovery of senses not previously predicted by other resources. For example, while both VerbNet and FrameNet have equivalents to PropBank's "Quantifiable Motion" frame, including such verbs as *rise*, *fall*, *increase*, *decrease*, and so forth, neither resource predicted the existence of *add* in the following sentence:

The Nasdaq composite added 1.01 to 456.6 in heavy volume.

Context made it clear that 456.6 was the end point, not the second operand of a mathematical function.

[4] This superset is almost identical to the roleset for "trade."

[5] This sense is absent from Framenet.

Framenet, in contrast, is based on a small subset of sentences, usually picked to best illustrate the roles of the verb in question. While this approach does make the examples clearer and more informative, it does frequently miss interesting or important senses. The different corpora used by FrameNet and PropBank also make it difficult to compare the results of the two projects, since FrameNet's corpus is chosen to avoid ambiguous and complex sentences.

Another benefit of basing semantic classes on real data is avoiding spurious membership. VerbNet, by following [6] quite closely, has propagated some of the errors made by that work. Levin tends to include every conceivable verb within some classes, while neglecting them from others, ending up with oddities such as *stalk* being included not in the same class as *follow* but in the same class as *pit* and *peel*.

PropBank's practice of framing the verbs based on frequency in the corpus, rather than membership in some semantic class, has also served to quickly cover most of the semantic classes of English, a statement which is not true for FrameNet or VerbNet. Over a quarter of the verbs which have been framed by PropBank have no corresponding entry in VerbNet, and FrameNet's coverage is even smaller than VerbNet's. This coverage does come at a price, in that each of the classes has only incomplete membership. Thus, while VerbNet may have X number of verbs in a given class, PropBank will usually have only a small fraction of X. This shortcoming can be solved by using VerbNet's class information to generate frames files automatically, as discussed below.

Finally, PropBank includes a large number of phrasal verbs, such as *go off*, *blow up*, and *pass out*, currently numbering over 200. These phrasal verbs usually have syntax and semantics quite distinct from the non–phrasal bases. Most other resources neglect these altogether.

4.2.3 *Automatic expansion of Frames*

Frames are currently in place for nearly 1000 verbs, with an average of 30–50 added each week. A combination of the existing frames and other resources such as VerbNet [5], allows these frames to be quickly extended to cover over 1200 verbs. For example, the verb *destroy* shares a class with 13 other verbs, of which 9 occur in the TreeBank: *decimate, demolish, devastate, obliterate, ravage, raze, ruin, waste,* and *wreck.* Frames for these latter verbs were created as exact copies of the DESTROY frame with no loss of accuracy except in the case of *waste,* which required a second sense to handle examples such as "waste away". Similarly, a great number of repeated or negated actions (*state/restate, load/unload*) can be generated automatically.

This approach has also highlighted some of the mistaken assumptions inherent in previous efforts at verb classification. Verbs are often grouped on the basis of semantic or syntactic similarity, neglecting the intersection of the two considerations. For example, the "quantifiable motion" verbs obviously include verbs such as *rise* and *fall,* each of which takes four arguments (object in motion, distance, start and endpoints). A separate class holds verbs such as *drop,* taking just two arguments (agent and thing dropped, possibly with adjuncts describing direction, goal, or source). While this is the most common usage, it is equally true that *drop* is synonymous with fall, as in sentences such as *The governments' borrowing authority dropped to $2.8 billion from $2.87 billion.* However, *drop* can be regarded as nothing more than *cause to fall,* thus allowing the two syntaxes to be merged into a single five–argument verb. Under this analysis, the elements that were previously regarded as adjuncts of direction, source, and so forth, are now treated as arguments. Similarly, verbs such as *edge* and *inch* are quantifiable motion verbs, bearing the inherent meaning that the motion be fairly minimal. Unlike *rise* and *fall,* however, which inherently carry the direction of motion, *inch* and *edge* can describe motion in almost any direction—-it is just as possible to *edge forward* as to *inch downward* and so forth. These verbs should then follow the same framing conventions as *rise* and *fall,* with the necessary addition of another argument describing the direction. The resulting class of quantifiable motion verbs is therefore only partially syntactically consistent, but the combination of semantics and syntax is consistent across all the member verbs.

5.PROCEDURE AND ACCURACY

A number of annotators, mostly undergraduate linguistics majors, extend the templates in the frames to the remainder of the examples from the corpus. The rate of annotation is reasonable and rising, with about 50 predicates per person/hour currently being tagged. The learning curve is steep, with most annotators requiring about three days to master most aspects of the task, although of course the occasional bizarre syntax can still confuse even the most experienced annotators. Interannotator agreement varies widely but is generally high, ranging from a low of 60% to a high of 100%, measured by the number of constituents with the agreeing/disagreeing tags per verb lemma.[6] The agreement rate is generally rising, although a high rate of annotator turnover can obscure that fact, and the average runs slightly above 80%. This places predicate–argument tagging accuracy below the accuracy of part–of–speech tagging but well above that of word sense tagging.

Discrepancies tend to arise from misunderstandings on the part of the annotators as to the proper annotation style rather than actual disagreements on what the proper tagging is. As such, these errors are easily caught and corrected. For example, one annotator consistently and incorrectly included complementizers in verbs of saying:

Source sentence: *Intel told analysts that the company will resume shipments of the chips within two to three weeks .*

*** Kate said:
arg0 : Intel
arg1 : the company will resume shipments of the chips within two to three weeks
arg2 : analysts
*** Erwin said:
arg0 : Intel
arg1 : **that** the company will resume shipments of the chips within two to three weeks
arg2 : analysts

Annotation uses a double–blind procedure followed by adjudication to catch and correct discrepancies. This last step takes less than one hour per verb, almost regardless of the number of sentences for that verb. It is found that usually one annotator's output is very close to the adjudication Gold Standard, although the identity of that annotator varies from

[6] A sentence such as John gave Mary the flowers would therefore count as four possible disagreement points, one for each of the arguments and one for the verb itself. Inclusion of the verb in the scoring metric is necessary for catching correct use of phrasal variants.

verb to verb. Agreement rates between annotators and the Gold Standard varies from a low of 45% to a high of 100%. There does not seem to be any correlation between the number of sentences tagged and the rate of agreement, although there is unsurprisingly a degradation in agreement as the number of arguments in a verb's frames increases. Thus, a verb with five expected arguments naturally shows higher disagreement rates than a verb with only one or two, reflecting the complexity of the task.

6.SUMMARY

We have described our approach to the development of a Proposition Bank, which involves the addition of semantic information to the Penn English TreeBank. In order to achieve consistent annotation we rely on explicit Frames Files for each verb which provide the annotators with labeled examples for all of the syntactic and semantic variations of that verb. We presented a detailed comparison of our Frames Files to Framenet Frames and discussed our attempts to use verb classes to automatically extend the Frames Files. We concluded with a summary of the current status of the annotation process. The rate of progress achieved and the inter-annotator agreement figures provide reassuring evidence of the task feasibility.

7.ACKNOWLEDGEMENTS

We gratefully acknowledge guidance from Christiane Fellbaum, programming support from Scott Cotton, and tireless labor from our many annotators, especially Betsy Klipple, Olga Babko-Malayo, and Kate Forbes. This work has been funded by NSF Grant IIS-9800658, VerbNet, and a Department of Defense Grant, MDA904-00C-2136.

8.REFERENCES

[1] Eugene Charniak. Parsing with Context-Free Grammars and Word Statistics. In Technical Report: CS-95-28, Brown University, 1995.

[2] M. Collins. Three generative, lexicalised models for statistical parsing. In Proceedings of the 35th Annual Meeting of the Association for Computational Linguistics, Madrid, Spain, July 1997.

[3] Michael Collins. Discriminative reranking for natural language parsing. In International Conference on Machine Learning, 2000.

[4] Eva Hajicova, Jarmila Panevova, Petr Sgall. Tectogrammatics in Corpus Tagging. In Perspectives on Semantics, Pragmatics, and Discourse: A Festschrift for Ferenc Keifer, I. Kenesei and R.M. Harnish eds.

[5] Karin Kipper, Hoa Trang Dang, Martha Palmer. Class-Based Construction of a Verb Lexicon. AAAI-2000, Seventeenth National Conference on Artificial Intelligence, Austin TX, July 30 – August 3, 2000.

[6] Beth Levin. English Verb Classes and Alternations A Preliminary Investigation. 1993.

[7] J.B. Lowe, C.F. Baker, and C.J. Fillmore. A frame-semantic approach to semantic annotation. In Proceedings 1997 Siglex Workshop/ANLP97, Washington, D.C., 1997.

[8] Mitch Marcus. The Penn TreeBank: A revised corpus design for extracting predicate-argument structure. In Proceedings of the ARPA Human Language Technology Workshop, Princeton, NJ, March 1994.

[9] M. Marcus, B. Santorini, M.A. Marcinkiewicz. Building a large annotated corpus of English: the Penn TreeBank. Computational linguistics. Vol 19, 1993.

[10] G. Miller, R. Beckwith, C. Fellbaum, D. Gross, and K. Miller. Five papers on wordnet. Technical Report 43, Cognitive Science Laboratory, Princeton University, July 1990.

[11] Scott Miller, Heidi Fox, Lance Ramshaw, and Ralph Weischedel. Sift — statistically-derived information from text. In Seventh Message Understanding Conference (MUC-7), Washington, D.C., 1998.

OCR Error Correction Using a Noisy Channel Model

Okan Kolak
Computer Science and UMIACS
University of Maryland
College Park, MD 20742, USA
okan@umiacs.umd.edu

Philip Resnik
Linguistics and UMIACS
University of Maryland
College Park, MD 20742, USA
resnik@umiacs.umd.edu

ABSTRACT

In this paper, we take a pattern recognition approach to correcting errors in text generated from printed documents using optical character recognition (OCR). We apply a very general, theoretically optimal model to the problem of OCR word correction, introduce practical methods for parameter estimation, and evaluate performance on real data.

General Terms

OCR error modeling and correction

Keywords

OCR, noisy channel, parameter estimation, pattern recognition

1. INTRODUCTION

Optical character recognition (OCR) provides the means to make printed material available for on-line retrieval [16] and to extract valuable language data from hardcopy sources such as printed dictionaries [7]. Unfortunately, despite the claims of commercial vendors, OCR error rates are far from perfect, particularly as we move to more challenging languages such as Chinese and Arabic [8]. Moreover, almost all available systems are black boxes, and may not even permit customer-specific retraining. These constraints suggest an approach to OCR performance improvement based on post-processing of system output.

In this paper, we take a pattern recognition approach to correcting errors in OCR-generated text. We apply a very general, theoretically optimal model [14] to the problem of OCR string correction, provide practical methods for parameter estimation, and evaluate performance on real data.

2. OCR ERROR CORRECTION

Our pattern-recognition approach treats OCR as within the framework of the noisy channel model. Noisy channel approaches view a recognition problem generatively: the first step is to model the process by which an observed sequence of symbols $\mathcal{O}$ is generated from a true underlying sequence of symbols $\mathcal{T}$, and the second, at run time, is to identify the true sequence that is most likely given a particular observed sequence. More formally, given observed $\mathcal{O}$, one seeks to find the $\mathcal{T}$ that optimizes

$$\Pr(\mathcal{T}|\mathcal{O}) = \frac{\Pr(\mathcal{O}|\mathcal{T})\Pr(\mathcal{T})}{\Pr\mathcal{O}}$$

Since $\Pr(\mathcal{O})$ is constant across all possible $\mathcal{T}$, we can ignore it.

We focus on error correction at the word level: the problem is to identify the true word T given an observed word O in the output of an OCR system. In the approach presented here, we actually optimize $\Pr(O|T)$, which reflects two assumptions. First, we are assuming that there are no word-level merge or split errors (e.g. misrecognizing `forgive` as `for give`) — in the Appendix we give an algorithm for linking tokens in ground truth data with tokens in OCR output in the presence of missing/extra tokens.[1] Second, optimizing $\Pr(O|T)$ to find the best $\Pr(T|O)$ is justified by assuming that $Pr(T)$ is uniform; we will take up better prior estimates for $\Pr(T)$ in future work.

Words O and T are presumed to be strings over a given alphabet of characters. Character-level splits and merges (e.g. recognizing `m` as `in` or `cl` as `d`) are approximated as combinations of insertion, deletion, and substitution errors.

2.1 OCR Error Correction as Syntactic Pattern Recognition

Oommen and Kashyap [14] introduce a general framework for syntactic pattern recognition that is well suited to the problem of OCR error correction. They provide a probabilistic generative model, M^*, that characterizes $P(O|T)$ for input and output strings T and O over a finite alphabet A. They also give an efficient dynamic programming algorithm for calculating this probability of transforming one string to another.[2]

M^* is defined in terms of three probability distributions. The *quantified insertion distribution*, G, controls insertions during the transformation process; in the most general case, it can be conditioned on the input string. The *qualified insertion distribution* defines the probability $Q(a)$, $a \in A$, that symbol a will be inserted, given that an insertion will be performed. The *substitution and deletion distribution* $S(b|a)$ governs the probability that symbol a in the input string will be transformed into symbol b in the output string; deletion is represented as a transformation into a special null symbol, λ. Let us define and illustrate the generative process step by step, supposing the input string T is abc.

1. Randomly determine z, the number of insertions, using G.

[1]Doermann et al. [7] discuss learning-based approaches to zoning and segmentation.

[2]We have modified their notation slightly for consistency with ours.

Proceedings of HLT 2002, Second International Conference on Human Language Technology Research, M. Marcus, ed., Morgan Kaufmann, San Francisco, 2002.

Let us say z is 2 in this case.

2. Insert z instances of the special insertion symbol ξ into randomly selected positions in T, giving T'.

   Let us say we randomly selected positions 0 and 2, giving us ξabξc.

3. Randomly and independently substitute non-ξ symbols in T' using S to get T''.

   Suppose that a is substituted for a, λ substituted for b, and d is substituted for c. This gives us ξa$\lambda\xi$d. Recall that λ is the special null symbol that is used to represent deletion.

4. Randomly and independently transform all occurrences of ξ in T'' to symbols in A using Q, giving O'.

   Assume the first ξ is transformed into e, and the second one is transformed into f, giving eaλfd as O'.

5. Remove all occurrences of λ from O', giving O.

   We finally get eafd, which is the output string O.

Oommen and Kashyap [14] prove M^* is stochastically consistent, optimal, and that it attains the information theoretic upper bound, and they do a simple study in the domain of correcting typographical errors using a simple uniform distribution for insertion and a confusion matrix for substitution. To our knowledge the work we are presenting here is the first published attempt at obtaining empirical parameter estimates for their model.

3. PARAMETER ESTIMATION

We assume that parameters of M^* are to be estimated from pairs $\langle t, o \rangle$, representing noisy channel input and output. In our setting t is the true word and o is the token recognized by the OCR algorithm, and maximum likelihood parameter estimation requires estimating event frequencies based on the word pairs. Since there are many ways of transforming t into o, it is necessary to distribute credit among all the possible sequences of events for the pair.

We investigated two methods for doing so. A simple first approach is to compute the lowest cost edit sequence based on edit distance, and assign all the weight to the events in that sequence. A second approach is to do iterative estimation over all sequences via an expectation-maximization (EM) approach [6].

3.1 Estimation Based on Levenshtein Distance

We base *edit distance estimation* (EDE) on picking the edit sequence for each $\langle t, o \rangle$ with the lowest Levenshtein edit distance [10]; this may not be optimal, but it is a likely sequence and efficient to compute. In our experiments, we assigned 0 cost to copy, and unit cost to insertion, deletion, and substitution events. Once the edit sequences are computed, calculating the event counts from edit sequences is quite simple. We smooth parameter estimations using Witten-Bell discounting [17].

3.2 Estimation based on Translation Models

It is interesting to note that our parameter estimation problem shares a great deal with the estimation problem for the IBM statistical machine translation models [2, 3]. For example, Figure 1 shows a word-level alignment representative of the IBM models and a character-level alignment consistent with M^*. Moreover, efficient parameter estimation algorithms for the IBM models have already been implemented in the GIZA++ software package [13].[3]

[3]For an introduction to the IBM translation models, see [9]

This suggests the possibility of using translation models as the basis for parameter estimation in the new setting of OCR error correction.

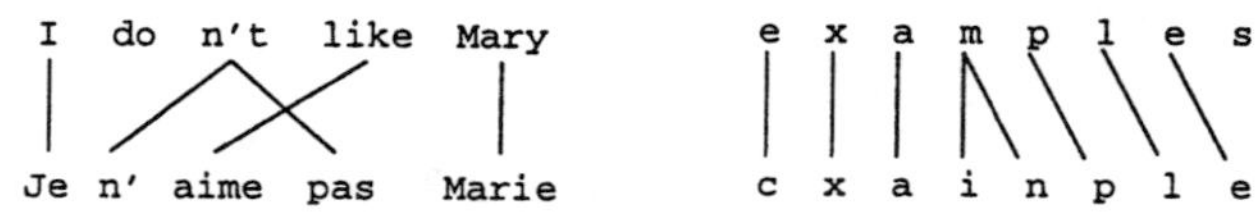

Figure 1: Examples of Alignment in Translation and OCR

The match between models is not perfect; for example, symbol re-ordering is crucial in translation but not OCR, and the IBM fertility model allows one-to-many symbol alignments (splits) but not many-to-one (merges). However, by treating characters as "words" in the translation model's vocabulary, it is possible to use unmodified IBM-style model training on a parallel corpus of "sentence" pairs $\langle t, o \rangle$. The trained IBM model parameters can then be used to estimate the event counts to be used in maximum likelihood parameter estimation for G, Q, and S. We call this strategy *translation model estimation* (TME). EDE and TME are different in the way they estimate the event counts, but the rest of the computation is the same.

Estimation of the frequency of insertion counts is done using the Viterbi alignment between OCR and ground truth characters. All the OCR characters that are mapped from NULL, and all but one of multiple characters that are mapped from a single ground truth character are counted as insertions. For instance, if ground truth symbol a is mapped to symbols p and q, we can assume there is one insertion; however, we cannot tell which OCR symbol is the inserted one.[4] Therefore, we use the translation probability of NULL to a particular symbol as an approximation to that symbol's insertion probability. It is only an approximation, since it ignores the insertion cases that do not involve NULL. Specifically, we estimate the insertion count of a symbol s as

$$\begin{aligned} insertionCount(s) &= round(translationProb(NULL, s) \\ &\quad \times TotalInsertionCount) \end{aligned}$$

Note that we have three sets of insertion counts:

1. Total insertion count
2. Insertion count for each character
3. Insertion count frequencies

and they need to be consistent with each other. Informally, the total number of insertions implied by both insertion counts of symbols and frequencies of insertion counts should be consistent with the total insertion count. More formally:

$$\begin{aligned} TotalInsertionCount &= \sum_{i>0} insertionCountFreq(i) \times i \\ &= \sum_{s \in \{symbols\}} insertionCount(s) \end{aligned}$$

where $insertionCountFreq(i)$ is the number of edit sequences with i insertions.

We estimate the total number of insertions and insertion count frequencies together, so that they are consistent. We then round insertion counts for some symbols up or down to make their sum consistent with the total insertion count.

[4]We are ignoring less likely cases such as one deletion with two insertions.

For substitution counts, we will use the translation probabilities. However, deletion is considered a special case of substitution, and there is no symbol-to-NULL translation probability; therefore, we use the 0-fertility probability of a symbol to estimate its deletion count. If a symbol s appears n times in the corpus, then its deletion count is estimated as

$$deletionCount(s) = round(symbolCount(s) \times fertilityProb(s, 0))$$

Once having accounted for deleted symbols, we can distribute the remaining counts to substitutions. This means that substitution count of a symbols s with a symbol t is estimated as

$$substitutionCount(s,t) = round((symbolCount(s) - deletionCount(s)) \times translationProb(s,t))$$

Note that for any symbol, the sum of deletion and substitution counts should be equal to the symbol count for that symbol.

$$symbolCount(s) = deletionCount(s) + \sum_{t \in \{symbols\}} substitutionCount(s,t)$$

This consistency is trivially achieved by setting the symbol count to the number imposed by deletion and substitution counts. Also note that we ignore the consistency of our estimated counts and actual counts in the data for simplicity, since it is not crucial for validity of our estimates.

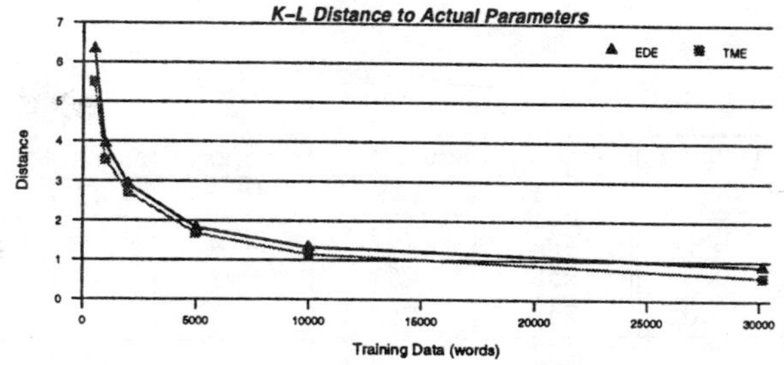

Figure 2: K-L Distance between Original and Learned Parameters

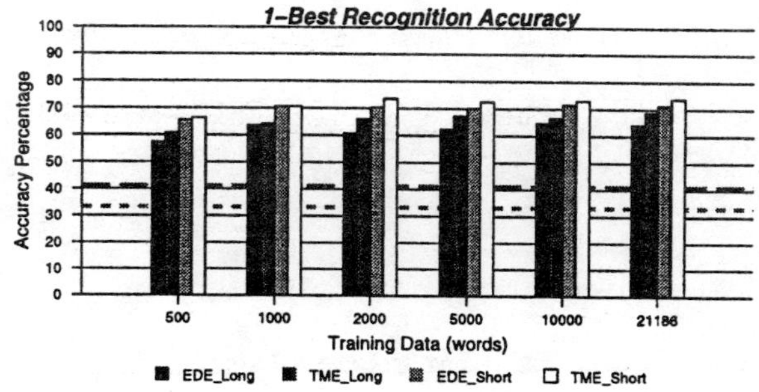

Figure 3: Accuracy of 1-Best Recognition for OCR Data

4. EVALUATION

We performed several sorts of evaluations of our approach. First, as a preliminary evaluation on artificial data, we performed a "reality check" experiment very similar to Oommen and Kashyap's [14] study. The goal here was to see how well the parameter estimation techniques could recover a set of known parameters by training on a data set generated artificially using those parameters. Our results were very similar to Oommen and Kashyap's. We created our training data set by using M^* with a fixed set of parameters similar to theirs to generate a noisy version of 30158 common English words with lengths between 7 and 14 characters. We then estimated the values of the parameters using our two training methods, varying the quantity of training data. The Kullback-Leibler (K-L) distance between the parameter estimates and the true parameters that generated the data are given in Figure 2 as a function of the quantity of training data. There was no significant difference between EDE and TME training methods; both methods perform quite well when the M^* model is known to be a good characterization of the data.

In our second evaluation scenario, largely because the IBM translation modeling framework made it an easy experiment to perform, we looked at whether or not a straightforward statistical MT decoding approach would succeed in recovering an original ground truth string from its OCRed counterpart. Treating characters as "words" in the vocabulary, we used the CMU-Cambridge Toolkit [5] for language modeling, GIZA++ for translation modeling, and the ISI ReWrite Decoder [12] for decoding. This approach performed very poorly, with decoder output on a test set rarely producing the ground truth word, possibly because it does not require that the decoded sequence of characters actually form a word. Modifying the language model component could solve the problem, but for the time being we are not pursuing this route.

Instead, our third evaluation scenario was to take an incorrectly recognized word w and to select the correct word d from a dictionary D by ranking the choices according to $\Pr_{M^*}(w|d)$.[5] We present accuracy figures for selecting the correct d as the top choice (1-best), and as one of the top 3 choices (3-best).

For artificial training and test data, where noisy English strings are generated from ground truth English words as described in the first evaluation, above, the 1-best recognition accuracy was around 96%. This confirms that both training methods perform quite well in an artificial scenario where the generative process is known to be an instance of the M^* model.

More realistically, we also experimented on actual OCR data generated by scanning a hardcopy of the book of Genesis in French using a commercial OCR package, OmniPage 8.0 (which supports French). Measuring against ground truth, the word error rate on these data is approximately 20%. We used disjoint training and test sets, varying the size of the training data to explore sensitivity to training set size; the test set included 423 misrecognized words. We experimented with a short dictionary (1005 words) and a long dictionary (4300 words) in order to explore sensitivity to the number of alternatives for d. The number of valid-word errors was 8 for the short dictionary and 17 for the long dictionary, and these are not included in accuracy computations. The results in Figure 3 and Figure 4 respectively show the percentage of the time that the correct word d is the first choice, and the percentage of the time that it occurs among the top 3 choices. Actual word counts are given in Table 1 and Table 2.

Dashed horizontal lines in the figures are baseline performance of picking d as the word with the lowest Levenshtein edit distance. Baseline 1-best recognition accuracy is 41.20% for the long dictionary and 33.25% for the long one; for the 3-best case, the numbers

[5]Incorrect tokens are identified because they are not in the dictionary. As in many approaches to spelling correction, we are not considering valid-word errors here; see Section 5.

Training Size	Long Dictionary		Short Dictionary	
	EDE	TME	EDE	TME
500	233	247	272	275
1000	258	261	293	293
2000	247	268	292	305
5000	253	273	291	301
10000	263	270	297	303
21186	261	279	296	306

Table 1: 1-Best Recognition Count for OCR Data

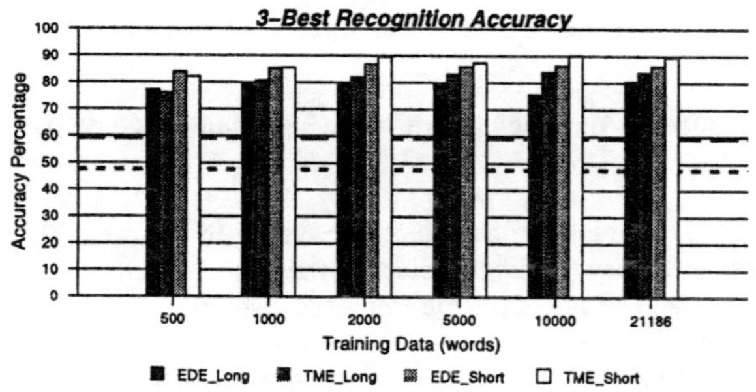

Figure 4: Accuracy of 3-Best Recognition for OCR Data

Training Size	Long Dictionary		Short Dictionary	
	EDE	TME	EDE	TME
500	313	309	348	341
1000	322	328	354	355
2000	324	333	361	372
5000	323	338	357	363
10000	307	341	359	374
21186	327	340	358	372

Table 2: 3-Best Recognition Count for OCR Data

are 59.27% and 47.53%, respectively. The difference between our methods and the baseline is clear: we nearly double the baseline performance one would obtain in correcting OCR word errors by picking the word in the dictionary with the lowest Levenshtein edit distance. In addition, TME training consistently performs a bit better than edit distance training (The difference is statistically significant when aggregated across all experimental conditions, but not condition-by-condition). This is most likely because EDE ignores all but one of the possible edit sequences that could transform an original word to the noisy one, and it may also reflect the fact that the IBM translation models are able to capture the split errors in OCR.

The figures suggest that the size of the candidate dictionary has a significant effect on accuracy, hence one can expect to improve accuracy by using a clever candidate selection mechanism or incorporating evidence from a language model. We were interested to observe that the results do not improve much with the size of the training data amount: training with 2000 words produces reasonable results, which makes practical the creation of manually generated ground truth for training.

5. RELATED WORK

We are unaware of published work on post-recognition error correction for OCR generated text, nor of other work that combines the theoretical guarantees of M^* with the practical aspects of our estimation methods. The spelling correction literature provides methods which could be applied to the OCR correction problem, however, so we briefly compare our method with some spelling correction methods.

Church and Gale [4] used probability scores for spelling correction for the first time. However, their work is limited to the correction of words with a single spelling error and cannot be used to correct OCR text that may contain multiple errors per word.

Mangu and Brill [11] proposed a rule-based approach for spelling correction. Unlike models based on character edit operations, their method is capable of correcting valid-word errors. Moreover, the output of the model is understandable by humans. However, it is based on word usage errors and requires pre-specified confusion sets, which severely limits its utility for OCR correction.

Ristad and Yianilos [15] proposed a stochastic edit distance model and methods to learn model parameters from a training corpus. They achieved a much lower error rate for a word pronunciation problem compared to non-probabilistic edit distance. Our method is very similar; however, their model restricts the possible probability distributions, whereas the model we use permits arbitrarily distributed syntactic errors.

Brill and Moore (B&M) [1] introduced an improved noisy channel model for spelling correction that allows arbitrary string-to-string edit operations. They get better error correction results compared to methods that use only character edits. The authors kindly trained their system on two of our training corpora (with 2000 and 21186 words) and tested on our test data.[6] Their method, unlike ours, only trains on pairs containing recognition errors; there were 371 such pairs in the small (2000-pair) set and 3826 in the large (21186-pair) set. The comparison between TME and their method is given in Table 3. B&M performs significantly better for the larger training set, though the difference in performance for the smaller training set is not statistically significant.

We performed a more detailed analysis on the performance of

[6]Their spell checker had only been developed for and debugged/tested on English, and was used on our French data without modification.

Training Set Size	1-Best		3-Best	
	B&M	TME	B&M	TME
371/2000	281	268	333	333
3826/21186	327	279	365	340

Table 3: Recognition Counts for Brill & Moore vs. TME

EDE, TME, and B&M, for the large training set and 3-Best recognition. We found that 26 of the test words could not be recognized by any of the methods, 310 were recognized by all, and 25 were recognized by two of the three. Each cell in Table 4 shows how many words recognized by one method (rows) were not recognized by the other methods (columns); for example, TME was correct on 12 words that B&M missed. The fact that all three methods are recognizing some words not recognized by other methods means a combination of the three might perform better. Although a straightforward voting scheme is not enough (only 325 words get a majority vote, lower than individual scores), some other combination method may prove useful.

	EDE	TME	B&M
EDE	0	6	10
TME	20	0	12
B&M	52	40	0

Table 4: Pairwise Exclusive Word Recognition Comparison

6. FUTURE WORK

We currently use uniform prior probabilities for the correction candidates. Using a scoring and/or elimination method for candidates, e.g., based on an n-gram language model for words, would almost certainly improve performance. Such potential scoring methods and their effect on correction performance requires further work.

For some languages, necessary resources, including an appropriate online dictionary, may not be available. Creating correction candidates with limited resources, possibly using the OCR documents being corrected, is very appealing and deserves further investigation.

7. CONCLUSIONS

We have presented an approach to string error correction that is based on a model with attractive theoretical properties, contributing new techniques for empirical parameter estimation and investigating application to OCR errors. The approach requires a practical quantity of manually generated training data, is efficiently computed, and works significantly better than the naïve approach of correcting errors by finding the most similar dictionary entry according to simple edit distance. We observed that the size of the candidate dictionary significantly affects correction accuracy, and, since the model provides well defined probabilities, the door is open to integration with language model predictions or other stochastic criteria for ranking likely correction candidates.

Acknowledgments

This research was supported in part by DARPA/ITO Cooperative Agreement N660010028910 and Department of Defense contract MDA90496C1250.

We are grateful to F. Och and H. Ney for GIZA++, D. Marcu for the ISI decoder, P. Clarkson and R. Rosenfeld for the CMU-Cambridge toolkit, E. Brill for his kind assistance in comparative evaluation, and B. Byrne and B. Oommen for useful discussion.

8. REFERENCES

[1] E. Brill and R. C. Moore. An improved model for noisy channel spelling correction. In *38th Annual Meeting of the Association for Computational Linguistics*, pages 286–293, Hong Kong, China, October 2000.

[2] P. F. Brown, J. Cocke, S. A. D. Pietra, V. J. D. Pietra, F. Jelinek, J. D. Lafferty, R. L. Mercer, and P. S. Roossin. A statistical approach to machine translation. *Computational Linguistics*, 16(2):79–85, 1990.

[3] P. F. Brown, S. A. D. Pietra, V. J. D. Pietra, and R. L. Mercer. The mathematics of machine translation: Parameter estimation. *Computational Linguistics*, 19(2), 1993.

[4] K. Church and W. Gale. Probability scoring for spelling correction. *Statistics and Computing*, (1):93–103, 1991.

[5] P. Clarkson and R. Rosenfeld. Statistical language modeling using the CMU-Cambridge Toolkit. In *ESCA Eurospeech*, 1997.

[6] A. P. Dempster, N. M. Laird, and D. B. Rubin. Maximum likelihood from incomplete data via the EM algorithm. *Journal of the Royal Statistical Society, Series B*, 39(1):1–38, 1977.

[7] D. Doermann, H. Ma, B. Karagöl-Ayan, and D. W.Oard. Translation lexicon acquisition from bilingual dictionaries. In *Ninth SPIE Symposium on Document Recognition and Retrieval*, San Jose, CA, 2002. to appear.

[8] T. Kanungo, P. Resnik, S. Mao, D. wan Kim, and Q. Zheng. The Bible, truth, and multilingual optical character recognition. submitted for publication.

[9] K. Knight. A statistical MT tutorial workbook, April 1993. http://www.isi.edu/natural-language/mt/wkbk.rtf.

[10] V. I. Levenshtein. Binary codes capable of correcting deletions, insertions and reversals. *Soviet Physics Doklady.*, 10(8):707–710, 1966.

[11] L. Mangu and E. Brill. Automatic rule acquisition for spelling correction. In *14th International Conference on Machine Learning*, pages 187–194. Morgan Kaufmann, 1997.

[12] D. Marcu and U. Germann. The ISI ReWrite Decoderrelease 0.7.0b. http://www.isi.edu/~germann/software/ReWrite-Decoder/.

[13] F. J. Och and H. Ney. Improved statistical alignment models. In *ACL00*, pages 440–447, Hong Kong, China, October 2000.

[14] B. Oommen and R. Kashyap. A formal theory for optimal and information theoretic syntactic pattern recognition. *Pattern Recognition*, 31:1159–1177, 1998.

[15] E. S. Ristad and P. N. Yianilos. Learning string edit distance. *IEEE Transactions on Pattern Recognition and Machine Intelligence*, May 1998.

[16] Y.-H. Tseng and D. W. Oard. Document image retrieval techniques for chinese. In *Fourth Symposium on Document Image Understanding Technology*, pages 151–158, Columbia, MD, April 2001.

[17] I. H. Witten and T. C. Bell. The zero-frequency problem: Estimating the probabilities of novel events in adaptive text compression. *IEEE Transactions on Information Theory*, 37(4):1085–1093, July 1991.

APPENDIX

Word Pairing with Missing Word and Extra Word Errors

The parameter estimation methods we propose require word pairs $\langle t, o \rangle$ for training. Automatically extracting these word pairs from OCR/ground-truth document pairs is not a trivial task owing to missing and extra word errors. These errors can be caused by merging or splitting words as a result of whitespace recognition errors, missing words, and misrecognizing stains and marks as words. The possibility of having missing or extra words renders useless any simple position-based pairing between OCR tokens and ground truth tokens. Therefore, we designed a simple algorithm to compute a likely pairing. The algorithm assumes that many words are recognized correctly for each line in the OCRed document, and uses these words as anchor points for pairing.

Correctly recognized words are identified by finding a sequence of word copy, insertion, deletion, and substitutions operations that converts ground truth into OCR version with the minimum cost. Copied words in this edit sequence are assumed to be correctly recognized (and momentarily we will generalize this to non-identical but similar words). Owing to the space requirements of the edit distance algorithm, we assume OCR and ground truth files are aligned at the line level, and work on one line pair at a time.

Let us present the algorithm using a sample execution where the original (ground truth) line is `a b c d e` and the OCRed line is `p b q e r`.

- Find an edit sequence that has the minimum cost. In case of equality, the sequence with more copy operations is favored.

```
Substitution : a --> p
Copy         : b --> b
Deletion     : c -->
Substitution : d --> q
Copy         : e --> e
Insertion    :   --> r
```

- For each copy operation, create a bracketed component on both sides that contains only the copied word.

```
a [b] c d [e]
p [b] q [e] r
```

- Do the following for both the original and noisy lines:
  - For each existing bracketed component, create a new bracketed component that contains everything to its right up to the next bracket, or up to the end of the line if there is no next bracket.

```
a [b] [c d] [e] []
p [b] [q] [e] [r]
```

  - Create a bracketed component that contains everything from the beginning of the line to the first existing bracket, or to the end of the line if there is none.

```
[a] [b] [c d] [e] []
[p] [b] [q] [e] [r]
```

- For each bracketed component in the original line, pair its contents with the corresponding (left-to-right) component in the noisy line, ignoring empty bracket pairs.

```
'a'      -->    'p'
'b'      -->    'b'
'c d'    -->    'q'
'e'      -->    'e'
NULL     -->    'r'
```

Since pairing is based on the edit sequence generated by the edit distance algorithm, one can tweak it by modifying the edit distance algorithm or its parameters.

One such useful modification is to use a similarity threshold instead of exact match to decide if two words match. To give an example, let `to illustrate this` be the original line and `lo ilustrate ths` be the OCR line. With exact matching, we would get the following edit sequence

```
Substitution : to         --> lo
Substitution : illustrate --> ilustrate
Substitution : this       --> ths
```

and the pairing `to illustrate this` → `lo ilustrate ths`, where the whole string is mapped over as a single chunk. However, if we assume that two words match if their edit distance is less than 20% of the length of the longer one, the edit sequence would become

```
Substitution : to         --> lo
Copy         : illustrate --> ilustrate
Substitution : this       --> ths
```

giving the more desirable pairing `to` → `lo`, `illustrate` → `ilustrate`, and `this` → `ths`.

Another useful modification is to change the cost of the copy operation. Assume the original line is `a b c d e` and the OCR line is `e p q r s`. With 0 copy cost, we would get the following edit sequence:

```
Substitution : a --> e
Substitution : b --> p
Substitution : c --> q
Substitution : d --> r
Substitution : e --> s
```

and the corresponding pairing would be `a b c d e` → `e p q r s`. If we use -4 as the copy cost, the edit sequence would become

```
Deletion     : a -->
Deletion     : b -->
Deletion     : c -->
Deletion     : d -->
Copy         : e --> e
Insertion    :   --> p
Insertion    :   --> q
Insertion    :   --> r
Insertion    :   --> s
```

and the pairing would be `a b c d` → NULL, `e` → `e`, and NULL → `p q r s`. By changing the cost of the operations, one can tune how far an original word and its correctly recognized version on the noisy side can be.

Recent Improvements to the ATLAS Architecture

Christophe Laprun, Jonathan Fiscus,
John Garofolo, Sylvain Pajot
National Institute of Standards and Technology
100 Bureau Drive Mail Stop 8940
Gaithersburg, MD 20899-8940
(+1) 301 975 3191

{claprun, jfiscus, jgarofolo, pajot}@nist.gov

ABSTRACT

We examine the recent improvements that were made to the ATLAS (Architecture and Tools for Linguistic Analysis Systems) architecture. We first introduce the architecture and the historical context for this work. Next, we describe NIST's initial implementation of the framework before analyzing it. We then focus on three important improvements (relating to multi-dimensional signals, hierarchical structures and validation) we have made to the architecture to make it more usable. We conclude by summarizing the major points covered and discuss plans for future work.

Keywords

ATLAS, MAIA, Linguistic infrastructure

1. INTRODUCTION

Annotated corpora are a central component of research in human language technology. As corpora have proliferated across languages, disciplines, and technologies, the lack of common exchange and storage formats has become a critical problem. This profusion of formats has made reusing annotated data or adapting existing tools for new annotation tasks significantly more difficult.

The standardization of tag sets (an approach we tried with our Universal Transcription Format [5]) is of moderate usefulness since language research is by necessity an open-ended task, subject to constant revision as the research domains change and the theories evolve.

Proceedings of HLT 2002, Second International Conference on Human Language Technology Research, M. Marcus, ed., Morgan Kaufmann, San Francisco, 2002.

A solution to this "bazaar of tools and formats" [2] is to interpose a generic annotation model via which annotation data is manipulated. ATLAS (Architecture and Tools for Linguistic Analysis Systems) makes use of such a generic data model. We first examine the historical context that led to the creation of the project. We then briefly describe the first implementation of the architecture, singling out three aspects of the architecture that needed to be improved: handling of complex signals and hierarchical structures and validation. Each of these aspects is then discussed in detail in subsequent sections. We conclude by summing up the major points we covered and suggest future work.

2. HISTORICAL CONTEXT

The ATLAS project started as a collaboration between the LDC, MITRE and NIST in 1999 following Bird and Liberman' s seminal work on Annotation Graphs (AGs)[1] that demonstrated commonality across a diverse range of annotation practices and defined a formalism based on labeled, directed acyclic graphs.

The three parties recognized the urgent need for a consistent way to represent and process annotation data. NIST needed such a framework to accommodate constantly evolving needs in linguistic evaluation. The LDC was developing the AG formalism in order to develop an infrastructure that would help reduce the cost of linguistic annotation while MITRE was interested in extending their Alembic Workbench annotation tool to support new domains.

NIST recognized the importance of the LDC's work on AGs and decided to form a working group to explore the creation of a generic annotation framework and toolset that would address three important issues for the linguistic research community. First, ATLAS would promote language corpora reuse and exchange. By providing a generic annotation framework, ATLAS would make it easier to share data since data annotated with a generic representation could be reused in new contexts. Second, reusable tools could be written in terms of the generic data model thus easing tool development. Finally, given its genericity, ATLAS would be able to gracefully accommodate changing domains and annotation schemes.

As the result of this collaboration, ATLAS Level 0 (based on AGs) and the basis for a generalized version (ATLAS Level 1) were formally introduced at the second international conference on Language Resources and Evaluation (LREC 2000) in Athens, Greece and were the subject of [2].

After LREC, the LDC moved on to implement an architecture based on Annotation Graphs (also called *AGs* or *ATLAS level 0*, [4]). NIST decided to pursue the development of the generalized version of ATLAS encompassing signals of arbitrary dimensions. A first implementation of the generalized framework (subsequently referred to as 'ATLAS') was made available in April 2001. Based on feedback gathered on this first implementation, a redesigned implementation was released, in Beta form, at the end of January 2002 followed by regular updates in the following months.

3. BASIC CONCEPTS

At the time of its introduction, only the premises for the generic framework were defined. The LDC had developed a prototype C++ implementation for ATLAS level 0. But, the implementation of the generic model had just begun. The remainder of this paper will address only NIST's implementation of the generalized version of ATLAS. We will discuss later how some of these components have evolved.

ATLAS provides an architecture targeted at facilitating the development of linguistic annotation applications[1]. When it was first introduced, the architecture was comprised of three main components that are still present in the newer implementation:

1. a generic linguistic annotation ontology,
2. an Application Programming Interface (API),
3. the ATLAS Interchange Format (AIF, [7]).

The ontology at its core provides the constructs on which the rest of the framework is built. The paradigm is simple but is surprisingly powerful when it comes to expressing complex annotation schemes. This provides a level of indirection separating physical storage and application logic that did not exist when most tools were written to directly read and write data using a specific format. Tools developed in terms of the ATLAS ontology can therefore work with any data conforming to ATLAS' paradigm, which is summarized as follows:

> An annotation is the fundamental act of associating some content to a region in a signal.

Paralleling this ontology, an ATLAS ***Annotation*** references a ***Region*** in a ***Signal*** and associates it with a *Content* element. The preceding notation defines a convention that we follow in this paper: ATLAS concepts are formatted using ***this font and style***. ***Annotation***s are organized in ***Analysis*** elements, which are themselves contained in ***Corpus*** elements. ***Corpus*** also manages ***Region***s and ***Anchor***s. ***Children*** elements will be discussed later. Figure 1, below, presents a pictorial view of the conceptual model.

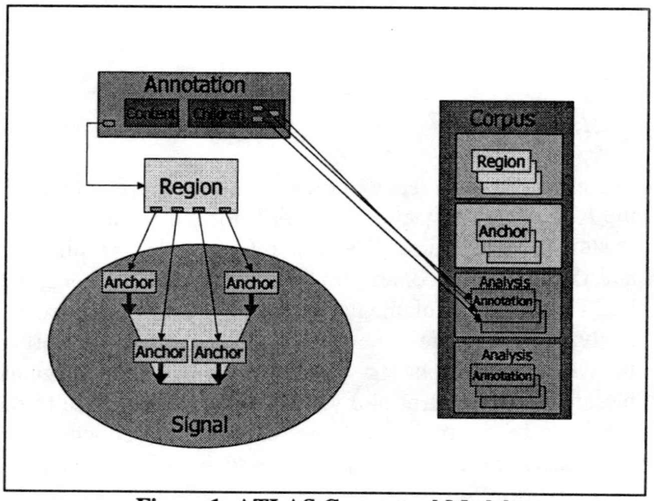

Figure 1: ATLAS Conceptual Model

These constructs can be implemented using a variety of programming languages. The ATLAS API defines ways to manipulate these constructs while the ATLAS Interchange Format provides a way to serialize ATLAS structures so that they can be reused and exchanged.

4. INITIAL IMPLEMENTATION

NIST's first implementation of the ATLAS architecture was made available in April 2001. This first implementation provided us with a starting point allowing us to gather feedback and from which we could mature the framework.

NIST's implementation (called jATLAS) provides a Java instantiation of these constructs in the form of objects that can be used to quickly develop linguistic applications.

Each of these objects publishes operations via which its data can be manipulated and behavior controlled. The ensemble of these operations defines the ATLAS API. Developers can thus access the components of the framework via a well-established interface, permitting alternate implementations to be developed without impacting client applications.

[1] Atlas was (in the Greek mythology) the Titan condemned to bear heavens upon his shoulders. ATLAS is supposed to bear the complexity of annotation management for the benefit of linguistic applications!

jATLAS can serialize the object structures it manipulates so that these structures can be easily shared and reused. The first implementation provided a single modality for serialization: the ATLAS Interchange Format. AIF is an XML-based file format optimized for the serialization of ATLAS structures. XML was chosen as the (then emergent but now well established) standard data interchange format.

jATLAS' first implementation provided NIST with a proof of concept as well as a full-scale model for experimentation. This implementation permitted us to create some initial tools that gave us a deeper understanding of the issues involved in the creation of a generic annotation infrastructure. The development of the framework was not, by its very nature, driven by a particular application, making it rather complex to make the right design choices and understanding their consequences before actually putting the architecture to use.

Both implementation and usage made us realize that the framework exhibited limitations of two kinds: *extrinsic* and *intrinsic*. *Extrinsic* limitations are problems that appear as part of the development process. *Intrinsic* limitations are problems that derive from the data model itself.

4.1 Extrinsic limitations

Extrinsic limitations revealed themselves as our development work progressed. Even though we realized at the time that some problems existed, we wanted to push ahead to explore the issues more deeply and create an architecture with which we could experiment.

The first limitation that we identified was related to compatibility with Annotation Graphs. ATLAS started as a conceptual framework based on the Annotation Graph formalism. Consequently, ATLAS' first instantiation was still very much influenced by the Annotation Graph formalism. Lots of effort had been made, during our collaboration with the LDC and MITRE, to ensure that the data model would be as isomorphic to AGs as possible. In particular, the expressiveness of the data model was restricted in order to respect the constraints imposed by the AG formalism. But, over time, it became clear to NIST that in order to fully generalize the data model, some of these constraints needed to be relaxed. In particular, we decided that strict conformance to the AG model was not required provided that ATLAS could express everything that could be expressed with AGs without loss of information.

The second extrinsic limit that we identified was that the data model was too strongly tied to the serialization format. The reason for this was that our early design work focused on the exchange format rather than the data model. The work on AIF was, in effect, driving the development of the data model, because, even though this was not a conscious effort, the AIF DTD was more or less used as the ATLAS data model. This restricted the expressive power of the framework to XML's.

These issues led us to re-examine the data model from a fresh perspective. We re-designed it starting with the core ontology and only adding new constructs as deemed necessary. The serialization format became then an outgrowth of the stabilized data model.

4.2 Intrinsic limitations

Extrinsic limitations aside, several limitations also existed with the data model itself. These were, however, more difficult to identify and appeared only after we put the architecture to work in building applications.

The first limitation that we will examine was the need to develop the support of complex signal types.

The next limitation, we will then turn our attention to, was the creation of hierarchical annotation structures. Although ATLAS' first data model allowed the creation of hierarchical annotations, it was not as intuitive as it could have been.

The last limitation was the management of semantic information. We initially considered deferring semantic validation to the XML layer. However, this proved to be insufficient and we decided to introduce a meta-annotation concept, implemented in ATLAS by the Meta-Annotation Infrastructure for ATLAS (MAIA), to efficiently address semantic issues.

We discuss each of these points in turn in the next sections and present the solutions that were implemented in the redesign version of ATLAS.

5. MULTI-DIMENSIONAL SIGNALS

Traditionally, linguistic resources have focused on a linear class of signals (e.g., text or audio) that can be indexed via a simple offset into a file. However, as technical capabilities and processing power have increased, so has interest in multi-modality and signals that cannot be reduced to a single dimension.

From the beginning, NIST and the ATLAS Working Group recognized the need for a framework that would be able to evolve gracefully as research interests moved toward more complex, multi-modal signal types. Initially, we believed that the AG formalism could be employed for all signal types. However, as we began working with AGs, it became apparent that although they were well-suited to linear signals, they did not scale well for more complex signal types. The basic premise of multi-dimensional signal handling was included in the first ATLAS implementation. However, many details were yet to be worked out

5.1 Signals and SignalGroups

Annotation sources are represented in ATLAS by the *Signal* construct. An ATLAS *Signal* is an immutable, N-dimensional space containing phenomena that are the target of *Annotations*. Even though typical *Signals* can be equated to physical signal files (speech waveforms, newswire text, video or other more complex data with higher dimensionality), it is not a necessity. In ATLAS, a *Signal* is an entity that identifies a logical (as opposed to a physical file) target for *Annotations* and can thus refer, for example, only to the left track of a stereo recording. ATLAS also does not prescribe to any single format or dimensionality for physical signals, but there must be a way to define an unambiguous coordinate system for the *Signal*.

Furthermore, groups of related *Signals* can be formed to create targets for *Annotations* spanning several logical signals. The *SignalGroup* construct is used to model this grouping. *SignalGroups* constitute new logical signals themselves and are treated as such by the framework. However, some constraints need to be imposed to make them manageable. In particular, since ATLAS *Signals* need to be immutable, once a *SignalGroup* is created and referenced, it cannot be changed. Moreover, in order to ensure consistency, only *Signals* that share common dimensions can be grouped together. An obvious use of *SignalGroup* is the alignment of different signals along a given time line. An example of an index into a stereo audio signal is a simple example.

5.2 Regions and Anchors

Once *Signals* have been identified, linguistic phenomena of interest are identified via *Region* constructs. A *Region* is an abstraction for identifying an area of the *Signal* space. *Regions* are delimited by a set of coordinates that mark specific areas of interest. These markers are modeled by the *Anchor* construct, thus named because they are used to "anchor" annotations to *Signals*.

Anchors are the only ties that annotations have to the physical structure of the signal and the only ATLAS concept that is signal-specific. *Regions* use as many *Anchors* as needed to index into *Signals*. Thus, the *Region* construct encapsulates the specificity of the underlying signal. This is a particularly important aspect of ATLAS since it allows the framework to evolve and scale gracefully, when confronted with new classes of signals, without requiring change to the basic ontology. It is also worth noting that *Regions* can reference other *Regions* as well.

Suppose, for example, that a given television signal has been modeled in ATLAS using three *Signals*: one for each of the two audio tracks and one for the video signal. One might want to annotate a phenomenon occurring only on the audio part of the television signal. If the phenomenon of interest spans both audio channels, one could create a *SignalGroup* grouping them together. Since the video frames can be projected along the time dimension, a grouping of the three *Signals* can be made to annotate time-based phenomena for the entire television signal. However, if the annotation task is to track hand movements, the *Regions* of interest could be defined using both a temporal *Anchor* to mark the frames of interest and another *Region* to define the area of interest within each video frame. The complete *Region* of interest would then be the composition of the temporal *Anchors* and 2D *Regions*. Figure 2, below, presents a graphical view of this example.

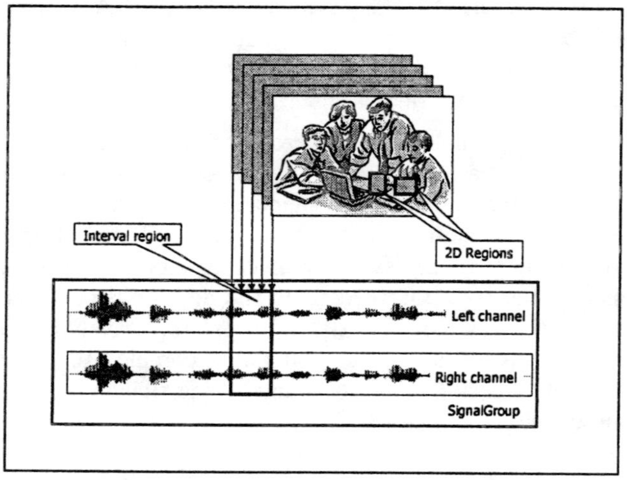

Figure 2: Video Annotation Example

6. HIERARCHICAL STRUCTURES

Support for the representation of inter-annotation relations (in particular, annotation hierarchies) was somewhat limited in the first jATLAS' implementation that constrained such relationships to be represented as part of an *Annotation's Content* in a way that was neither intuitive nor explicit.

As a result of the experience we gained with this implementation, we introduced the *Children* construct to model relations between *Annotations*. *Children* constructs maintain a list of references to *Annotations* that are descendants of a parent *Annotation*. Since references (rather than actual annotations) are used, it is possible to build overlapping hierarchies. Reuse is therefore improved since already created *Annotations* can be reused in new contexts.

Parent *Annotations* can also use their *Children* elements to derive their *Content* and/or *Region*. It is therefore possible to dynamically update *Content* and/or *Region* information of a parent based on changes to its set of *Children*, thus avoiding redundancy and simplifying annotation management.

The TIMIT Acoustic Phonetic Corpus ([3]) provides a simple example of parent/child annotation relationships. In TIMIT, words are composed of a set of phones. This relationship is modeled quite simply in ATLAS by creating a *Children* element of a word *Annotation* that contains a list of references to the phone *Annotations* for that word. Further, this makes it possible for TIMIT word *Annotations* to be reused in the context of morphological analysis – thus creating overlapping yet separate hierarchies. Moreover, since a sentence in TIMIT could be defined as the set of its subordinate words, a sentence *Annotation* could be created by deriving its *Region* (and

Content) from the union of the *Regions* referenced by its subordinate word *Annotations*.

7. META-ANNOTATION INFRASTRUCTURE FOR ATLAS

7.1 Motivation

ATLAS defines a very generic data model that is designed to be able to model a wide range of annotation tasks. Because of this genericity, ATLAS' constructs are minimally constrained. ATLAS provides enough expressive power to represent extremely complex annotations. However, this capability did not come, in the first implementation, without a significant development cost since the responsibility for such issues as structural integrity and consistency checking were pushed up to the application level. To unburden application developers, a means of constraining ATLAS constructs was therefore needed so that ATLAS applications could interpret a particular *Annotation* as a word, for example. The Meta-Annotation concept was introduced to address these needs.

A Meta-Annotation is a piece of meta-information about a kind of linguistic annotation. In the context of ATLAS, meta-annotations are concretized in the form of the *ATLASType* construct. The Meta-Annotation Infrastructure for ATLAS (MAIA[2], [9]) implements the Meta-Annotation concept for ATLAS. It provides a scheme language that allows type definitions to be declared using a simple, XML-based syntax. The ATLAS framework can then dynamically interpret these type definitions. MAIA also provides services (such as the loading and saving of types) that can be utilized by ATLAS implementations.

7.2 ATLASTypes

A rudimentary placeholder existed in the first jATLAS implementation for types. However, the implementation of types and type-checking was left completely up to application developers. We realized, however, when we started working with the framework that this required a considerable amount of work and resulted in a lot of code duplication.

We also explored the idea of deferring semantic validation to the XML layer. However, this provided only limited validation. Worse, it necessitated that validation could only occur on XML file read/writes and could not be used for internal operations.

We realized that to be maximally useful, ATLAS applications need to be able to automatically interpret type information without requiring user intervention or developer effort. Further, we realized that such information more properly belonged at the corpus definition layer than in the application layer. We decided, therefore, to re-design the framework to incorporate support for data typing. This was accomplished via the addition of MAIA and *ATLASTypes* to ATLAS.

An *ATLASType* is a piece of metadata associated with an ATLAS construct to describe attributes of, and permitted operations for a specific annotation element. This provides the kind of data typing supported in most object-oriented languages. *ATLASTypes* are thus very similar to classes in object-oriented parlance.

By definition, elements with the same *ATLASType* share the same structure. *ATLASTypes* also enforce constraints on relationships between ATLAS constructs. For example, from our TIMIT example above, we want to require that sentence annotations can contain only word annotations and, word annotations, in turn, can contain only phone annotations.

7.3 MAIA

MAIA provides a mechanism for the creation and management of *ATLASTypes*. Its type definition language provides a formalism for the specification of an annotation corpus which can be used to validate operations during the creation and modification of the corpus. It permits the ATLAS framework (and ATLAS-based applications) to perform validation to ensure that elements that are supposed to be of a given type have the correct structure and behave as expected. The MAIA type definition language provides a mechanism to create a self-documenting, concise definition of a corpus usable by both human designers/users and ATLAS-based tools.

Essentially, MAIA adds a semantic layer on top of ATLAS' generic structures. This enables developers to focus on higher-level issues, such as user-interaction, without the burden of having to attend to low-level data management.

We see MAIA as a major step towards the development of more generic tools that can be tailored to specific needs at the data level, rather than at the application level. For example, a generic annotation editor could be created which dynamically builds specific interfaces based on the MAIA definition of the data it is to work with.

MAIA is clearly a work in progress and we already have several ideas about how it can be made more powerful and expressive. Currently, it supports only basic data type and position constraints. However, it would be more useful if it supported relationship- and content-dependent constraints. For example, in TIMIT, the time for the first word of a sentence should align with the sentence boundary and we should be able to define what constitutes a legal word. In particular, MAIA will eventually support more elaborate typing for value and range constraints and more accurate description of inter-annotation dependencies. Our ultimate goal is to make MAIA so comprehensive that application developers will have to write no corpus-specific code. MAIA will be detailed in a forthcoming paper.

---

[2] Maia was one of Atlas' daughter in the Greek mythology.

8. CONCLUSION

Since it was first introduced at LREC 2000, the ATLAS framework has evolved to incorporate numerous enhancements including support for hierarchical relationships, multi-dimensional signal types, and data typing via MAIA.

The Java instantiation of ATLAS (jATLAS [8]) has been updated with these enhancements and is now currently in Beta version, available for download, along with more information on the architecture, on the ATLAS web site [6].

Although, ATLAS has matured into a powerful and very usable annotation framework, we are still working to improve it. In particular, we are investigating extending the current framework into a full-fledged annotation server that would allow multiple users to concurrently work on the same annotations in a fully distributed annotation environment. We are also working to make MAIA more expressive by tying it to a query language we intend to develop for ATLAS – thus providing a complete annotation data development/research environment. Work is also in progress on defining a widget library for visualization and editing of ATLAS elements to further improve the ease of application development.

At this time, we would like to invite people interested in using ATLAS to send us descriptions of their annotation corpora. We will work with them to develop MAIA definitions for their data and build a sample ATLAS version of their corpus. This will also provide us with a diversity of data so that we can further improve the framework.

9. REFERENCES

[1] Bird, S. and Liberman, M., 1999. A formal framework for linguistic annotation. Technical report MS-CIS-99-01, Department of Computer and Information Science, University of Pennsylvania. Revised version appeared in Speech Communications 33 (1,2), pp 23-60.

[2] Bird, S., Day, D., Garofolo, J., Henderson, J., Laprun C. and Liberman, M., 2000. ATLAS: A flexible and extensible architecture for linguistic annotation in Proceedings of LREC 2000 (Athens, Greece, May 2000), pp 1699-1706.

[3] Garofolo, J., Lamel, L., Fisher, W., Fiscus, J., Pallett, D., Dahlgren, N., NIST, 1986. The DARPA TIMIT acoustic-phonetic continuous speech corpus CDROM. [http://www.ldc.upenn.edu/lol/docs/TIMIT.html]

[4] LDC, 1999. Annotation Graphs. [http://www.ldc.upenn.edu/AG/]

[5] NIST, 1998. A Universal Transcription Format (UTF) annotation specification for evaluation of spoken language technology corpora. [http://www.nist.gov/speech/tests/bnr/hub4_98/utf-1.0-v2.ps]

[6] NIST, 1999. Architecture and Tools for Linguistic Analysis Systems. [http://www.nist.gov/speech/atlas/]

[7] NIST, 1999. ATLAS Interchange Format. [http://www.nist.gov/speech/atlas/develop/aif.html]

[8] NIST, 2000. jATLAS, a Java implementation of the ATLAS framework. [http://www.nist.gov/speech/atlas/jatlas/]

[9] NIST, 2002. Meta-Annotation Infrastructure for ATLAS. [http://www.nist.gov/speech/atlas/develop/maia.html]

Enhancing the Usability and Performance of NESPOLE! — a Real-World Speech-to-Speech Translation System

Alon Lavie
Language Technologies Institute
Carnegie Mellon University
Pittsburgh, PA, USA
alavie@cs.cmu.edu

Florian Metze
Interactive Systems Laboratories
Universität Karlsruhe (TH)
Karlsruhe, Germany
metze@ira.uka.de

Fabio Pianesi
ITC-irst
Trento, Italy
pianesi@itc.it

1. INTRODUCTION

NESPOLE! [1] is a speech-to-speech machine translation project designed to provide fully functional speech-to-speech capabilities within real-world settings of common users involved in e-commerce applications. The project is a collaboration between three European research groups (IRST in Trento, Italy; ISL at Universität Karlsruhe (TH); and CLIPS at Université Joseph Fourier in Grenoble, France), one US research group (ISL at Carnegie Mellon University in Pittsburgh, PA) and two industrial partners (APT; Trento, Italy – the Trentino provincial tourism board, and AETHRA; Ancona, Italy – a tele-communications company). The project is funded jointly by the European Commission and the US NSF. Over the past year, we have developed a fully functional showcase of the NESPOLE! system within the domain of travel and tourism[2], and have significantly improved system performance and usability based on a series of studies and evaluations with real users. Our experience has shown that improving translation quality is only one of several important issues that must be addressed in achieving a practical real-world speech-to-speech translation system. This paper describes how we tackled these issues and evaluates their effect on system performance and usability. We focus on three main issues: (1) a study on the usage and utility of multi-modality in the context of multi-lingual communication; (2) assessing system performance under various network traffic conditions and architectural configurations; and (3) an end-to-end evaluation of the demonstration system.

2. THE NESPOLE! SYSTEM

The design principles of the NESPOLE! [4] system were already described in [3]. The system uses a client-server architecture to allow a common user, who is initially browsing through the web pages of a service provider on the Internet, to connect seamlessly to a human agent of the service provider who speaks another language, and provides speech-to-speech translation service between the two parties. Standard commercially available PC video-conferencing technology such as Microsoft's NetMeeting® is used to connect between the two parties in real-time.

In the first showcase which we describe in this paper, the scenario is the following: a client user is browsing through the web-pages of APT – the tourism bureau of the province of Trentino in Italy – in search of winter-sport tour-packages in the Trentino region. If more detailed information is desired, the client can click on a dedicated "button" within the web-page in order to establish a video-conferencing connection to a human agent located at APT. The client is then presented with an interface consisting primarily of a standard video-conferencing application window and a shared whiteboard application. Using this interface, the client can carry on a conversation with the agent, where the NESPOLE! server provides two-way speech-to-speech translation between the parties. In the current setup, the agent speaks Italian, while the client can speak English, French or German.

A key component in the NESPOLE! system is the "Mediator" module, which is responsible for mediating the communication channel between the two parties as well as interfacing with the appropriate Human Language Technology (HLT) speech-translation servers. The HLT servers provide the actual speech recognition and translation capabilities. This system design allows for a very flexible and distributed architecture: Mediators and HLT-servers can be run in various physical locations, so that the optimal configuration, given the locations of the client and the agent and anticipated network traffic, can be taken into account at any time. A well-defined API allows the HLT servers to communicate with each other and with the Mediator, while the HLT modules within the servers for the different languages are implemented using very different software packages.

For example, let us suppose an English-speaking client in the US is connecting to an APT agent in Italy. A connection request from the client's PC (in the US) would be

[1]NESPOLE! – NEgotiation through SPOken Language in E-commerce. See the project web-site at http://nespole.itc.it for further details.

[2]A demonstration of this showcase system will be shown at the HLT-2002 conference

Proceedings of HLT 2002, Second International Conference on Human Language Technology Research, M. Marcus, ed., Morgan Kaufmann, San Francisco, 2002.

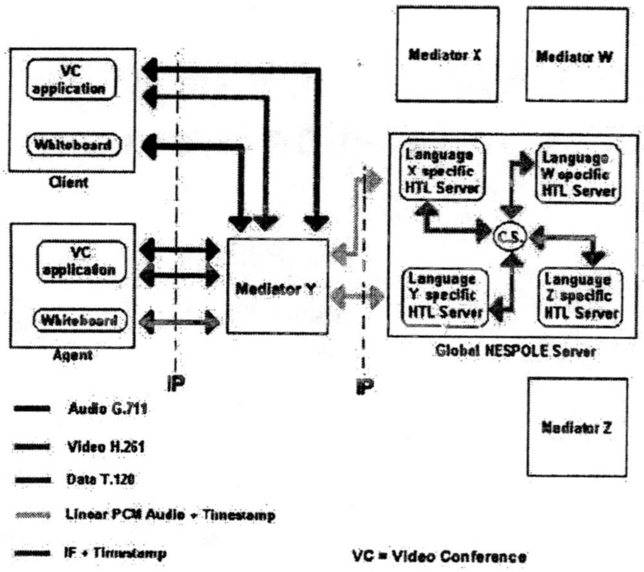

Figure 1: The Nespole! System Architecture

made to the Mediator, which can be physically located anywhere on the net (but practically most likely located either in the US or in Italy). The Mediator establishes a connection over the internet with both an English HLT server and the Italian HLT server (which can again be physically located anywhere on the internet), before calling the agent in Trento. The English HLT server provides English speech recognition, translation from English text into our Interlingua "IF" (Interchange Format) as well as English generation and speech synthesis from IF. The Italian HLT server provides similar functionalities to and from Italian. This basic system design is shown in Figure 1.

The computationally intensive part of speech recognition and translation is done on dedicated server machines, whose nature and location is of no concern to the user. A wide range of client-machines, even portable devices or public information kiosks, are therefore able to run the client software, so that the service can be made available nearly everywhere. The main technical difficulty for VoIP ("Voice over Internet Protocol") applications is coping with adverse internet bandwidth conditions. In order to guarantee real-time communication under insufficient bandwidth conditions, videoconferencing software often drops short segments of speech that were delayed in transport. This, however, can be very detrimental to the performances of speech recognizers [7]. Later in this paper, we present performance statistics, collected with the actual system, that investigate the performance effects of this problem within our system . In order to reduce bandwidth requirements, it is possible to use the NESPOLE! system without video transmission, as we currently do not transmit critical information over this channel.

3. ENHANCING PERFORMANCE AND USABILITY OF THE NESPOLE! SYSTEM

During a preliminary user study conducted in Summer-2001 to evaluate the initial version of our system, several key points emerged that allowed us to improve the system to its current configuration. The resulting "First Showcase" of our system has been demonstrated at several events (e.g. the IST conference in Düsseldorf, Germany, in December 2001) and is also presented at the HLT-2002 demonstration session [6]). The recent improvements allow the users to retain control of the interaction in all situations, and permit a smooth integration of multi-modal and multi-lingual communication. In the following subsections, we describe the main issues we have addressed in the course of developing the current showcase system.

3.1 System Response Time

The standard Video-conferencing setup which we use in the NESPOLE! system allows transmission of both audio and video streams between the participants. In order to limit bandwidth requirements, we currently do not use the video channel and transmit only audio. The system architecture shown in figure 1 contains two different types of Internet connections with different characteristics:

- The "left" IP connection between Client/Agent PCs and the Mediator is a standard video-conferencing connection that uses H323 and UDP protocols. In cases of insufficient network bandwidth, these protocols compromise performance by allowing delayed or lost packets of data to be "dropped" on the receiving side, in order to minimize delays and ensure close to real-time performance.
- The "right" IP connection between the Mediator and the HLT servers uses TCP over IP in order to achieve lossless communication between the Mediator, which interfaces with the UDP channels, and the translation components. For practical reasons, Mediator and HLT servers in our current system usually run in separate and distant locations, which can introduce some time delays, in addition to the time needed for actual data processing by the HLT components.

Speech-packets transmitted over the H323 protocol can be processed as soon as they arrive without waiting for subsequent packets that contain the remaining speech. The inclusion of "Run-On" processing in the speech recognizers and the optimization of inter-process communication within the HLT servers reduced the answering times of the overall system to approximately three times real-time in recent demonstrations.[3] Our experience indicates that users appreciate the fact that the system provides some feedback on its progress in the form of text messages (i.e. recognition results), even before paraphrasing and translation are complete.

3.2 Adaptation of Automatic Speech Recognition Engines

The Speech Recognition modules of the Nespole! system were developed separately at the different participating sites, using different toolkits, but communicate with the Mediator using a standardized interface. The French and German

[3]For comparison, German Speech recognition runs in about real-time on a standard 1GHz Pentium-III machine using a 12k vocabulary.

	English	French	German	Italian
Vocabulary size	8,000	20,000	12,000	4,000
OOV rate	0.3%		<1%	3.0%
LM training Data	Verbmobil (E), C-Star 550k words	Internet 1,500M words	Verbmobil (D) 500k words	Nespole 1500 sentences
+ adaptation	Nespole	Nespole	Nespole	
Perplexity	33		98	150
Microphone type	head-set	head-set	table-top	head-set
Speaking style	spontaneous	read	spontaneous	read
Ac. training Data	16kHz 90h	G711 recoded 12h	16kHz 65h Verbmobil-II	G711 recoded 11h C-Star
+ adaptation	Upsampling of G711		MLLR 80min. + FSA	
Real-time factor	2.5, 1GHz P-III		1.1, 1GHz P-III	1.8, 650Mhz P-III
Memory consumption	280Mb	200Mb	100Mb	
WER on clean data	19.9%	18% (read speech)	29.8%	31.5%

Table 1: Speech Recognizers Used in the NESPOLE! System

ASR modules are described in more detail in [9, 7]. The German engine was derived from the UKA recognizer developed for the German Verbmobil Task [10].

All systems were derived from existing LVCSR recognizers and adapted to the Nespole! task using less than 2 hours of adaptation data. This data was collected during an initial user-study, in which clients from all countries communicated with an APT agent fluent in their mother tongue through the Nespole! system, but without recognition and translation components in place. Segmentation of input speech is done based on automatic silence detection performed by NetMeeting at the site of the originating audio. The audio is encoded according to the G.711 standard at a sampling frequency of 8kHz. The characteristics of the different recognizers are summarized in Table 1.

The word accuracy rates obtained by the recognition engines for the various languages are presented together with the results of the end-to-end evaluation in Section 4.3.

3.3 Improved Analysis Accuracy

The analysis engines for the various languages handled by our system are developed independently by our research groups and follow different approaches. We describe here some recent novel common aspects of the analysis modules developed for English, German and Italian[4]. The analysis process in our system involves mapping input utterances into an interlingua representation ("IF"), which consists of two main pieces of information: (1) the Domain Action (a speech act and a sequence of concepts); and (2) arguments, consisting of feature-value information. Our analyzers apply two separate stages to extracting these two types of information from an input utterance. Statistical models and classifiers are used for the former, while a knowledge-based approach is employed for the latter. Decomposing the problem of IF construction into two separate and independent sub-tasks has the advantage of allowing specialized techniques to be applied to each sub-task, while reducing the amount of needed human grammar development. The main drawback, however, is that the information extracted by the two separate sub-tasks may be inconsistent when combined together, resulting in illegal IFs. Particular attention has thus been given to the problem of the production of legal IFs, since it has a crucial impact on the practical use of the system. The analyzers for English, German and Italian employ procedures for using the well-formedness constraints defined by the Interlingua formalism in order to select the best scoring Domain Action that is most compatible with the extracted arguments [2].

[4]The French analyzer uses a significantly different approach than the one described here.

3.4 Multi-Modality

The nature of the e-commerce scenario and application in which our system is situated requires that speech-translation be well-integrated with additional modalities of communication and information exchange between the agent and client. Significant effort has been devoted to this issue within the project. The main multi-modal component in the current version of our system is the AeWhiteboard – a special whiteboard, which allows users to share maps and web-pages. The functionalities provided by the AeWhiteboard include: image loading, free-hand drawing, area selecting, color choosing, scrolling the image loaded, zooming the image loaded, URL opening, and Nespole! Monitor activation. The most important feature is that each operation the user does is shared with his remote interlocutor, so they can communicate while viewing the same images and drawing on identical-image whiteboards.

Typically, the client asks for information regarding locations, distances between locations, and navigation directions, e.g., how to get from a proposed hotel to the ski slopes. By using the whiteboard, the agent can indicate the locations and draw routes on the map, point at areas, select items, draw connections between different locations using a mouse or an optical pen, and accompany his/her gestures with verbal explanations. Supporting such combined verbal and gesture interactions has required modifications and extensions of both HLT modules and the IF. In summer 2001, we conducted a detailed study to evaluate the effects of multi-modality on the communication effectiveness and usability of our system. The main results of this study are presented in the evaluation section of this paper.

3.5 User interface

Significant attention was also devoted to designing an appropriate front-end user interface for the system, that allows both clients and agents an intuitive and relatively simple control over their communication process.

The user interface display is designed for Windows®and consists of four windows: (1) a Microsoft®Internet Explorer web browser; (2) a Microsoft®Windows NetMeeting videoconferencing application; (3) the AeWhiteboard; and (4) the Nespole Monitor. Using Internet Explorer, the client initiates the audio and video call with an agent of the service provider, by a simple click of a button on the browser page. Microsoft Windows Netmeeting is automatically opened and the audio and video connection is established. The two additional displays – the AeWhiteboard and the Nespole Monitor are also launched at the same time. Client and agent can then proceed in carrying out a dialogue with the help of the speech translation system. For a screen snapshot of these four displays, see [6].

We found it important to visually present aspects of the speech-translation process to the end users. This is accomplished via the Nespole Monitor display. Three textual representations are displayed in clearly identified fields: (1) a transcript of their spoken input (the output from the speech recognizer); (2) a paraphrase of their input – the result of translating the recognized input back into their own language; and (3) the translated textual output of the utterance spoken by the other party. These textual representations provide the users with the capability to identify mistranslations and indicate errors to the other party. A bad paraphrase is often a good indicator of a significant error in the translation process. When a mis-translation is detected, the user can press a dedicated button that informs the other party to ignore the translation being displayed, by highlighting the textual translation in red on the monitor display of the other party. The user can then repeat the turn. The current system also allows the participants to correct speech recognition and translation errors via keyboard input, a feature which is very effective when bandwidth limitations degrade the system performance.

4. EVALUATION

Several different evaluation experiments have been conducted, targeting different aspects of our system: (1) the impact and usability of multi-modality; (2) experiments for assessing the impact of network traffic and the consequences of real packet-loss on system performance; and (3) end-to-end performance evaluations. The database collected during the project and which is being used in the various evaluations is described in [1].

4.1 Experiments on Multi-Modality

During July 2001, we conducted a detailed study to evaluate the effect of multi-modality on the communication effectiveness and usability of our system. The goals of the experiment were to test: (1) whether multi-modality increases the probability of successful interaction, especially when spatial information is the focus of the communicative exchange; (2) whether multi-modality helps reduce ambiguities and disfluencies; and (3) whether multi-modality supports a faster recovery from recognition and translation errors. For these purposes, two experimental conditions were devised: a speech-only condition (SO), involving multilingual communication and the possibility for users to share images; and a multi-modal condition (MM), where users could additionally perform pen-based gestures on shared maps to convey spatial information.

The setting for the experiment was the NESPOLE! scenario described earlier, involving clients searching for winter tour-package information in the Trentino province. The client's task was to select an appropriate resort location and hotel within the constraints specified a priori concerning the relevant geographical area, the available budget, etc. The agent's task was to provide the necessary information. Novice subjects, previously unfamiliar with the system and task were recruited to play the role of the clients. Subjects wore a head-mounted microphone, using it in a push-to-talk mode, and drew gestures on maps by means of a table-pen device or a mouse. Each subject could only hear the translated speech of the other party (original audio was disabled in this experiment). The experiment was conducted on a total of 28 recorded dialogues, with 14 dialogues each for English and for German clients, and Italian agents in all cases. Each group contained seven SO and seven MM dialogues. The dialogue corpus consisted of 16.5 hours of dialogue length: 8.5 hours of English-Italian, 8 hours of German-Italian. The average duration of dialogues was 35 minutes. On average, a dialogue contained 35 turns, 247 tokens and 97 token types per speaker. The dialogue transcriptions include: orthographical transcription, annotations for spontaneous phenomena and disfluencies, turn information and annotations for gestures. Translated turns were classified into successful, partially successful and non-successful, by comparing the translated turns with the responses they generated. Repeated turns were counted as well.

The analysis of the results indicated that both the SO and MM versions of the system were effective for goal completion: 86% of the users were able to complete the task's goal by choosing a hotel meeting the pre-specified budget and location constraints. This demonstrates that the system is sufficiently adequate for novice users to accomplish the given task with minimal written instructions, a very short initial training on using the whiteboard, and no further assistance during the interaction. The average number of gestures per dialogue was 7.6. Gestures were performed only when spatial information was involved, and this ocurred in only a few of the dialogue segments. The agents performed almost all drawing, with a clear preference for area selections. Almost every gesture followed a dialogue contribution. Overall, few or no deictics were used. We believe that these findings are related to the push-to-talk procedure and to the time needed to transfer gestures across the network. Gestures were always preceded by appropriate verbal cues—e.g., "I'll show you the ice skating rink on the map". This shows that gestures were well integrated in the communication.

Data analysis also indicated that the number of turns, the number of words and the dialogue length were similar across conditions and languages. An analysis of the impact of MM on the language used revealed that there were fewer repeated turns (indicating a better reciprocal understanding of the two parties) and smoother dialogues (with fewer returns to already discussed topics) under the MM condition. MM also exhibited fewer ambiguous utterances. Furthermore, the ambiguities in MM conditions were often immediately solved by resorting to MM resources. This was not the case in SO, where ambiguous or mis-understood utterances often remained unresolved. The experiment subjects, given the choice between the MM and the SO system, expressed a clear preference for the former. In summary, the results clearly indicate that multi-modal and multi-lingual features were smoothly integrated. Furthermore, MM had a positive effect on the quality of interaction by reducing ambiguity, making it easier to resolve ambiguous utterances, improving the flow of the dialogue, and enhancing the mutual comprehension between the parties.

4.2 Network Traffic Impact

In our various user studies and demonstrations, we have been forced to deal with the detrimental effects of network congestion on the transmission of Voice-over-IP in our system. The critical network paths are the H323 connections between the Mediator and the client and agent, which rely on the UDP protocol, in order to guarantee real-time human-to-human communication. The communication between the Mediator and HLT servers can, in principle, be within a local network, although we currently run the HLT servers at the sites of the developing partners. This introduces time delays, but no packet loss, due to the use of TCP, in contrast with the UDP used for the H323 connections.

To quantify the influence of UDP packet-loss on system performance, we ran a number of tests between German client installations in the USA (CMU at Pittsburgh) and Germany (UKA at Karslruhe) calling a Mediator in Italy (IRST), which in turns contacted the German HLT server located in Karlsruhe, Germany. The tests were conducted by feeding a high-quality recording of the German development-test set collected at the beginning of the project into a computer set-up for a video-conference, i.e. we replaced the microphone by a DAT recorder (or a computer) playing a tape, while leaving everything else as it would be for sessions with real subjects. In particular, segmentation was based on silence detection performed automatically by NetMeeting. The resulting segments were recognized separately by the HLT servers and the hypotheses concatenated to calculate the WER over the whole dialogue. These tests (a total of more than 16 hours) were conducted at different times of the day on different days of the week, in an attempt to investigate a wide as possible variety of real-life network conditions.

All in all, we were able to run 16 complete tests, resulting in an average word accuracy of 60.4%,[5] with single values in the 63% to 59% range for packet-loss conditions between 0.1% and 5.2%. Higher packet-loss ratios, resulting from generally bad network conditions, usually led to a breakdown of the Client-Mediator or Mediator-HLT server link due to time-out conditions being reached, or the inability to establish a connection at all. We were able, however, to record one dialogue with 21.0% packet loss, which resulted in a word accuracy of 50.3%. This dialogue is very difficult to understand even for humans. From the recorded statistics we conclude that at least for packet-loss ratios below

[5]The word accuracy on the clean 16kHz recording is 71.2%.

Language	WARs	SR Graded (% Acc)
English	61.9%	66.0%
German	63.5%	68.0%
French	71.2%	65.0%
Italian	76.5%	N/A

Table 2: Speech Recognition Word Accuracy Rates and Results of Human Grading (Percent Acceptable) of Recognition Output as a Paraphrase

Language	Transcribed	Speech Rec.
English-to-English	58%	45%
German-to-German	46%	40%
French-to-French	54%	41%
Italian-to-Italian	61%	48%

Table 3: Monolingual End-to-End Translation Results (Percent Acceptable) on Transcribed and Speech Recognized Input

5%, this number alone is not sufficient to predict word-error rate. For 20% packet-loss, the loss in WER is significant, but we still observe less degradation than reported in [8] on synthetic data. In most cases, our experience indicates that we are likely to face packet-loss ratios below 5%, where there is no clear correlation between packet-loss and word-error rate (WER), and WERs remain at levels close to those experienced under optimal bandwidth conditions.

4.3 End-to-End System Evaluation

In December 2001, we conducted a large scale multi-lingual end-to-end translation evaluation of the Nespole first-showcase system. For each of the three language pairs (English-Italian, German-Italian and French-Italian), four test dialogues that were not previously seen by the system developers were used to evaluate the performance of the translation system. The dialogues included two scenarios: one covering winter ski vacations, the other about summer resorts. One or two of the dialogues for each language contained multi-modal expressions. The test data included a mixture of dialogues that were collected mono-lingually prior to system development (both client and agent spoke the same language), and data collected bilingually (during the July 2001 MM experiment), using the actual translation system. This mixture of data conditions was intended primarily for comprehensiveness and not for comparison of the different conditions.

We performed an extensive suite of evaluations on the above data. The evaluations were all end-to-end, from input to output, not intended to assess individual modules or components. We performed both mono-lingual evaluation (where the generated output language was the same as the input language), as well as cross-lingual evaluation. For cross-lingual evaluations, client utterances were evaluated on translation from English German and French to Italian, and agent utterances were evaluated from Italian to each of the three languages. We evaluated on both textual manually transcribed input as well as on input from actual speech-recognition of the original audio. We also graded the speech recognized output as a "paraphrase" of the transcriptions, to measure

Language	Transcribed	Speech Rec.
English-to-Italian	55%	43%
German-to-Italian	32%	27%
French-to-Italian	44%	34%
Italian-to-English	47%	37%
Italian-to-German	47%	31%
Italian-to-French	40%	27%

Table 4: Cross-lingual End-to-End Translation Results (Percent Acceptable) on Transcribed and Speech Recognized Input

the levels of semantic loss of information due to recognition errors. Speech recognition word accuracies and the results of speech graded as a paraphrase appear in Table 2. Translations were graded by multiple human graders at the level of Semantic Dialogue Units (SDUs). For each data set, one grader first manually segmented each utterance into SDUs. All graders then used this segmentation in order to assign scores for each SDU present in the utterance. We followed the three-point grading scheme previously developed for the C-STAR consortium, as described in [5]. Each SDU is graded as either "Perfect" (meaning translated correctly and output is fluent), "OK" (meaning is translated reasonably correct but output may be disfluent), or "Bad" (meaning not properly translated). We calculate the percent of SDUs that are graded with each of the above categories. "Perfect" and "OK" percentages are also summed together into a category of "Acceptable" translations. Average percentages are calculated for each dialogue, each grader, and separately for client and agent utterances. We then calculated combined averages for all graders and for all dialogues for each language pair.

Table 3 shows the results of the monolingual end-to-end translation for the four languages, and Table 4 shows the results of the cross-lingual evaluations. The results indicate acceptable translations in the range of 27–43% of SDUs (interlingua units) with speech recognized inputs. While this level of translation accuracy cannot be considered impressive, our user studies and system demonstrations indicate that it is already sufficient for achieving effective communication with real users. We expect performance levels to reach a range of 60–70% within the next year of the project.

5. ACKNOWLEDGMENTS

The research work reported here was supported by the National Science Foundation under Grant number 9982227 and the European Union under Grant number IST 1999-11562 as part of the joint EU/NSF MLIAM research initiative. Any opinions, findings and conclusions or recommendations expressed in this material are those of the author(s) and do not necessarily reflect the views of the EU or the NSF.

6. ADDITIONAL AUTHORS

S. Burger, D. Gates, L. Levin, C. Langley, K. Peterson, T. Schultz, A. Waibel and D. Wallace (Carnegie Mellon; Pittsburgh, PA, USA; email: {sburger|dmg|lsl|clangley|kay+|tanja+|ahw|dorcas}@cs.cmu.edu), and J. McDonough, and H. Soltau (UKA, Karlsruhe, Germany; email: {jmcd|soltau}@ira.uka.de), and R. Cattoni, G. Lazzari, N. Mana, and E. Pianta (ITC-irst, Trento, Italy; email: {cattoni|lazzari|mana|pianta}@itc.it), and E. Costantini (University of Trieste, Italy; email: costanti@psico.univ.trieste.it), and L. Besacier, H. Blanchon, and D. Vaufreydaz (CLIPS; Grenoble, France; e-mail: {Laurent.Besacier|Herve.Blanchon|Dominique.Vaufreydaz} @imag.fr), and L. Taddei (AETHRA; Ancona, Italy; e-mail: l.taddei@aethra.it).

7. REFERENCES

[1] S. Burger, L. Besacier, P. Coletti, F. Metze, and C. Morel. The NESPOLE! VoIP Dialogue Database. In *Proc. EuroSpeech 2001*, Aalborg, Denmark, 2001. ISCA.

[2] R. Cattoni, M. Federico, and A. Lavie. Robust Analysis of Spoken Input combining Statistical and Knowledge-based Information Sources. In *Proceedings of the 2001 IEEE Workshop on Automatic Speech Recognition and Understanding (ASRU 2001)*, Madonna di Campiglio, Italy, December 2001.

[3] A. Lavie, F. Pianesi, and al. Architecture and Design Considerations in NESPOLE!: a Speech Translation System for E-Commerce Applications. In *Proc. of the HLT2001*, San Diego, CA, 2001. ACM.

[4] G. Lazzari. Spoken translation: challenges and opportunities. In *Proc. ICSLP 2001*, Beijing, China, October 2001.

[5] L. Levin, D. Gates, A. Lavie, F. Pianesi, D. Wallace, T. Watanabe, and M. Woszczyna. Evaluation of a Practical Interlingua for Task-Oriented Dialogues. In *Proceedings of NAACL-2000 Workshop On Interlinguas and Interlingual Approaches*, Seattle, WA, 2000. ACL.

[6] F. Metze, C. Langley, A. Lavie, J. McDonough, H. Soltau, L. Levin, T. Schultz, A. Waibel, R. Cattoni, G. Lazzari, N. Mana, F. Pianesi, E. Pianta, L. Besacier, H. Blanchon, D. Vaufreydaz, and L. Taddei. The NESPOLE! Speech-to-Speech Translation System. In *Proceedings of Human Language Technology Conference (HLT-2002)*, March 2002.

[7] F. Metze, J. McDonough, and H. Soltau. Speech Recognition over NetMeeting Connections. In *Proc. EuroSpeech 2001*, Aalborg, Denmark, 2001. ISCA.

[8] B. Milner and S. Semnani. Robust Speech Recognition over IP Networks. In *Proc. ICASSP 2001*, Salt Lake City, USA, May 2001.

[9] S. Rossato, H. Blanchon, and L. Besacier. Evaluation of a Speech to Speech Translation System: French Experience in the NESPOLE! Project. In *Submitted to Proc. 19th International Conference on Computational Linguistics (COLING 2002)*, Taipei, Taiwan, August 2002.

[10] H. Soltau, T. Schaaf, F. Metze, and A. Waibel. The ISL Evaluation System for Verbmobil - II. In *Proc. ICASSP 2001*, Salt Lake City, USA, May 2001.

Spoken Dialogue Evaluation for the Bell Labs Communicator System

Sungbok Lee, Egbert Ammicht, Eric Fosler-Lussier, Hong-Kwang Kuo, Alexandros Potamianos
Bell Labs, Lucent Technologies, NJ 07974, USA
sungbok, egbert, fosler, kuo, potam@research.bell-labs.com

ABSTRACT

Task-oriented dialogues collected by the Bell Labs Communicator system are analyzed based on objective dialogue metrics and user survey data on system usability. Analyses are presented that confirm and extend some of the previous results shown for other systems. An "error correction metric" is also introduced, and its effectiveness as an objective metric for system performance evaluation is investigated. Results indicate that both user satisfaction and task completion are better correlated with the error correction metric than with the recognition accuracy at the word or sentence level. Multiple regression analysis reveals that the most effective predictors of user satisfaction (among objective dialogue metrics tested in the study) are the number of user words in dialogue and the recognition accuracy at the "concept" level. These two metrics explain 27.2% of variation in user satisfaction. When perceived task completion judgment (a subjective measure that is the single best predictor of user satisfaction) is included in the regression, 45.6% of variation is explained. Adding more variables, such as dialogue duration, is found to have marginal or negative effects. Overall, recognition accuracy at the concept level (as opposed to plain word or sentence accuracy) is shown to be an important metric for dialogue evaluation. In this study, the dialogue system is also evaluated using subjective metrics at each dialogue turn to identify "hot-spots" in the dialogue. We also measure inter-labeler agreement with Communicator callers. Results indicate that it is difficult for independent human raters to reproduce the Likert ratings given initially by the Communicator callers. Thus, given the noisy nature of subjective metrics, an open question is how well objective metrics will ultimately be able to explain the individual variation in subjective evaluation.

General Terms

Dialogue evaluation, Communicator

Keywords

Dialogue metrics, error correction metric, system usability

Proceedings of HLT 2002, Second International Conference on Human Language Technology Research, M. Marcus, ed., Morgan Kaufmann, San Francisco, 2002.

1. INTRODUCTION

Evaluation of the quality of spoken dialogue systems continues to be a difficult task because of several factors: it is difficult to sum up the results of a human-conversation into one number expressing the quality of interaction. It is also hard to assign credit or blame to sub-parts of the system due to the complexity of inter-operating subparts of the system (e.g., the ASR engine, understanding module, spoken language generation, and world knowledge representation), particularly when only summary statistics are available for a particular conversation.

In the DARPA Communicator project, multiple sites have developed spoken dialogue systems that give information about travel reservations.[1] For each system, both objective and subjective metrics were collected for each dialogue; the objective measures were derived from system statistics such as duration of dialogue, number of user words, and recognition error, while the subjective measures were derived from user satisfaction surveys. While these two classes of variables are related, a linear regression framework [11] was only able to explain 38% of the variance in user satisfaction using the objective measures [9].

In the first part of this paper, we introduce an objective dialogue metric and expand on some of the analyses in [9], using the dialogues collected by the Bell Labs Communicator system [1, 6] during the DARPA 2001 Communicator Evaluation period. Since task completion, in addition to user satisfaction, is generally considered to be one of the most important factors in deploying a dialogue system, [2] we decided to investigate the effects of task completion on objective and subjective measures.

Dialogue-level metrics, however, do not really help system designers pinpoint "hot spots" in the dialogue where the system needs improvement. Thus, we initiated a second study where three naive subjects and three expert subjects evaluated the system responses in a given dialogue on a turn-by-turn basis. The findings presented in the second part of the paper suggest that although the averaged score of the turn-by-turn rating of each system response and the overall system usability rating at the end of a given dialogue are consistent for individuals, the inter-subject variation is large. Therefore, subjective judgments of dialogue quality may be difficult to reproduce due to the inter-subject variability.

2. BELL LABS COMMUNICATOR SYSTEM AND DIALOGUE COLLECTION

[1] See the Web pages: http://www.darpa.mil/ito/research/com/index.html, http://fofoca.mitre.org for detailed information about the DARPA Communicator project.

[2] Task completion was also found to be one of the significant factors in the multiple linear regression analysis of user satisfaction [9].

2.1 System Description

The Lucent Bell Labs Communicator system is a mixed-initiative spoken dialogue system applied to a travel reservation domain. The main components of the system are a semantic parser/interpreter, the context tracking/pragmatic analysis module, the dialogue manager, and the system response generation module, in addition to the ASR and TTS engines. Novel features of the system include a domain-independent understanding module with ambiguity resolution and pragmatic analysis that allows the user to provide values for specific attributes, and to directly or indirectly refer to attributes and/or values [1]. These features allow the user to change the system focus and to ask for information about existing attributes and values. It further provides a powerful error correction capability that can handle system errors without explicit confirmation, thus minimizing unnecessary interactions with user.

The system takes in spoken or typed natural language text, and derives candidate attribute-value (AV) pairs (e.g., "Fly to Atlanta in the morning" produces <TOCITY>=Atlanta and <TIME>=morning). We model two types of ambiguities in the system: *value ambiguities*, where the system is unsure of the value for a particular attribute, and *position ambiguities*, where the attribute corresponding to a particular value is ambiguous. We score candidate values based on supporting evidence for or against the candidate. Raw AV pairs may have any number of scores attached (e.g., acoustic confidences and distribution frequencies). The raw AV data are used as evidence; the scores (possibly from multiple dialogue turns) are combined to derive a single individual score p with range [0, 1] for each AV candidate. Additional evidence is provided by pragmatic analysis and by matching a hypothesis to the current context.

The system carries out a pragmatic analysis of the user response to a particular system prompt. Individual candidates that may be in error are identified, and candidate scores are modified based on the derived evidence. For example, a "no" response to an explicit value ambiguity disambiguation question, (e.g., "Are you leaving from Atlanta or from New York?") is taken as strong evidence against both values and the pragmatic confidence for both ('departure.city','Atlanta') and ('departure.city','New York') is reduced.

The user can also talk about attributes directly, and request specific actions from the system. In particular, we allow *information requests*, e.g., "what is the departure city?" to ascertain the value for a specific attribute; *clear requests*, e.g., "clear the departure city," to force the removal of all candidate values for a given attribute; *freeze requests*, e.g., "freeze the departure city," to inhibit the system from further changing the value of a particular attribute; *change requests*, e.g., "change Atlanta to New York," "change the departure city to New York," or even "not Atlanta, New York!"

Other features of the system not discussed here are an agenda-driven dialogue manager, dynamic and adaptive electronic forms, and an adaptive initiative module [2]. The system uses the Galaxy-II hub architecture as outlined in [8]. The system is highly modular; most modules are domain-independent. Some of the design principles used in the Bell Labs Communicator system design are outlined in [5]. For more information on the Bell Labs and other Communicator systems see [1, 6, 9, 7, 12].

2.2 Dialogue Collection

During the DARPA Communicator 2001 evaluation period of about six months, 215 calls were made by 28 paid subjects. For each call the recognized user utterances and corresponding system responses were logged with associated dialogue events (such as the start and end time of user turns) so that objective dialogue metrics can be measured from the log files [10]. After the completion of each call, callers also judged whether the travel task was completed or not and answered a set of five user satisfaction survey questions on the system usability based on the NIST-derived Likert paradigm [3, 10].

TABLE I: MEAN AND STANDARD DEVIATION OF OBJECTIVE DIALOGUE METRICS

	Task Comp.		No Comp.	
Metric	mean	std	mean	std
Dialogue Duration (secs)	547	428	429	423
# of User Turns	33.6	25.8	31.2	24.8
# of User Words	85.6	79.4	94.3	99.7
# of User Words per Turn	2.61	1.36	3.33	1.42
# of Concepts	35.2	27.9	28.7	20.2
# of Concepts per Turn	1.13	0.23	1.18	0.31
Word Error Rate	23.5	12.9	24.9	12.7
Sentence Error Rate	28.8	15.6	34.3	15.9
Concept Err. Rate (CER)	16.5	11.9	20.9	15.9
Sentence CER	15.5	11.2	18.9	15.9
Error Correction Metric	4.7	5.9	8.0	9.9

Among the 215 dialogues, 139 dialogues for which the user survey data on system usability exist are analyzed in this study. Of 139 dialogues, in 115 the assigned task of finding a suitable travel itinerary was completed, while in 24 dialogues the task was not completed.

3. DIALOGUE EVALUATION

3.1 Measurement of Objective Dialogue Metrics

Objective dialogue metrics computed for each dialogue included dialogue duration, the number of user turns, the number of user words, the number of user words per turn, the number of user concepts, and the number of user concept per turn. Additionally, accuracy metrics, such as word and concept error rates, were considered at both the word and sentence level. Except for concept accuracy, each metric can be computed directly from corresponding log files. The concept accuracy error rates are computed based on the outputs of the semantic parser of recognized and transcribed user utterances.

An additional objective metric introduced in this study is the number of redundant occurrences of a given concept such as "cityname" or "date" in user utterances in a dialogue. The so-called "error correction metric" is computed by subtracting the default number of a concept required to complete the travel task from the total number of the occurrences of the concept. For example, two occurrences of two different city names are enough for a round trip. More than two occurrences of the "city" concept indicate that a user tried to correct system errors (e.g., "not Boston, Austin") or that the user abandoned the current dialogue and began a new dialogue by saying "start over". The metric can be computed using the outputs of the semantic parser of either transcribed user utterances or recognized utterances in a dialogue. The error-correction metric is computed in this study only for the two concepts, "city" and "date"[3], using human-transcribed user utterances.

Mean value and standard deviation of each objective dialogue metric are shown in Table I.

It is observed that task-completed dialogues have a longer dialogue duration and a larger number of user turns, although ANOVA

[3]The two concepts account for 61% of the total number of concepts in this set of dialogues.

analysis indicates that the differences are not significant. However, the number of user words is larger for task-incomplete dialogues. Moreover, the number of user words per turn, which is independent of dialogue duration or the number of user turns, is found to be significantly greater for the incomplete dialogues (F=5.94, p=0.01). The number of concepts per turn also shows the same tendency. These observations indicate that a user is more verbose when the system is in trouble (or that verbosity gets the user into more trouble!).

In [9], sentence accuracy was found along with task completion to be a significant predictor of user satisfaction. Here, we see that word error rates for task completion and non-completion do not differ significantly, but the concept error rate increases greatly for non-completion; this rise correlates with sentence accuracy (r=0.759, p=0.01), suggesting that in [9], sentence accuracy was substituting for concept accuracy. In fact, it can be shown that accuracy in concept level is more strongly correlated with user satisfaction than the plain word level or sentence level. This will be discussed in more detail later.

The error correction metric is found to be significantly less for task-completed dialogues (F=5.25, $p < 0.05$). Its correlation to user satisfaction is stronger (r=-0.403, p=0.01) when compared to that of sentence error rate (r=-0.336) or word error rate (r=-0.278). Its correlation to the task completion is also stronger (r=-0.198, p=0.01) than sentence error rate (r=-0.139) or word error rate (r=-0.032). These observations may signify its usefulness on system performance evaluation.[4]

3.2 Analysis of User Survey Data

Users' judgments on the system usability at the end of a dialogue session are based on the Likert paradigm [10] in which a subject expresses the degree of agreement with each of five statements related to the system performance. The degree of agreement is expressed using a numeric value ranging from 1 (disagree) to 5 (agree).

Table II displays the mean Likert scores for five user survey questions, as well as an averaged score, as a function of task completion. All subjective scores are higher when the task is completed; ANOVA analysis shows that differences between the two groups of dialogues are significant ($p < 0.01$) except for the 3rd question ("Know What to Say"). It seems that the second and third questions are less affected by task completion. The first, fourth, and fifth statements explain 94% of variance in user satisfaction.

Correlations between the system usability rating and the objective dialogue metrics were examined for task-completed dialogues. As a representative value of system usability, the sum of five user survey scores is used. All the correlations given below are significant (p=0.01). Interestingly, the best (although not strong) correlation is obtained for total number of user words (r=-0.549), followed by the number of user turns (r=-0.495) and the concept error rate at the sentence level (r=-0.458). However, the correlation between the number of user turns and the word error rate is relatively weak (r=0.229). This suggests that longer dialogue duration or the larger number of user turns is not necessarily due to poor recognition performance; users prefer shorter interactions.

Considering both task-completed and task-incomplete dialogues, the best correlation to user satisfaction is still obtained for the total number of user words(r=-0.458), followed by the concept error rate at the word level (r=-0.425), the concept error rate at the sentence level (r=-0.417), and the number of user turns (r=-0.411), as shown in Table III. It is worth noting that the error correction metric shows a higher correlation to the user satisfaction (r=-.405, p=.01) than the sentence error rate does (r=-.336, p=.01). In order to identify relatively important objective dialogue metrics for predicting user satisfaction, multiple linear regression analysis was performed. The number of user words in dialogue and the recognition accuracy at the "concept" level were found to be the best predictors of user satisfaction among objective dialogue metrics tested in the study. The number of user words alone can explain 19.9% of variance in the user satisfaction and the two variables combined can explain about 27.2% of the variation. The effectiveness of the number of user words in the prediction of user satisfaction results from the

[4] Although monthly change of user satisfaction during the period of evaluation is roughly inversely correlated with the error correction metric, the degree of correlation was not strong enough to make any conclusion against other competitive variables such as the number of user turns.

TABLE II: AVERAGE SUBJECTIVE EVALUATION SCORES WITH AND WITHOUT TASK-COMPLETION

	Task Comp.		No Comp.	
Question	mean	std	mean	std
Easy to Get Info	3.61	1.37	1.62	1.05
Easy to Understand	4.02	1.09	3.10	1.42
Know What to Say	3.56	1.27	2.97	1.47
Know What to Expect	3.55	1.29	1.98	1.30
Future Use	3.31	1.50	1.69	1.04
Overall	3.61	1.15	2.23	0.90

Summary of responses to five questions:

1. "In this conversation, it was easy to get the information that I wanted" **(Easy to Get Info)**,
2. "I found the system easy to understand in this conversation" **(Easy to understand)**,
3. "In this conversation, I knew what I could say or do at each point of the dialogue" **(Know What to Say)**,
4. "The system worked the way I expected it to in this conversation" **(Know What to Expect)**, and
5. "Based on my experience in this conversation using this system to get travel information, I would like to use this system again" **(Future Use)**.

TABLE III: CORRELATION BETWEEN USER SATISFACTION AND OBJECTIVE METRICS

Rank	Objective Metric	Pearson Correlation
1	Number of User Words	-.458
2	Concept WER	-.425
3	Concept SER	-.417
4	Number of User Turns	-.411
5	Error Correction Metric	-.403
6	Total Number of Turns	-.370
7	Duration	-.359
8	Sentence Error Rate (SER)	-.336
9	Word Error Rate (WER)	-.278

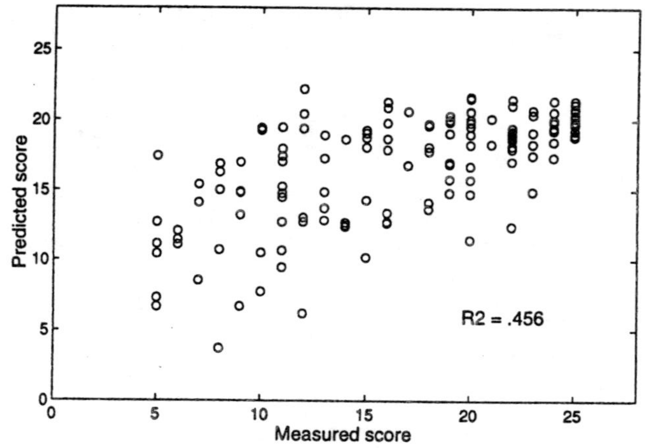

Figure 1: Distribution of the measured user satisfaction scores and predicted scores using the number of user words, concept word error rate, and task completion judgment

fact that the single variable is highly correlated with not only user satisfaction but also important objective metrics such as on-task dialogue duration, total number of turns, and recognition accuracy at the sentence levels.

When the perceived task completion judgment by users is added as another variable in the regression, about 45.6% of variation in the user satisfaction can be explained.[5] Adding other metrics such as dialogue duration show only marginal effects. A scatter plot of measured scores and predicted scores is shown in Figure 1. In [9] it was reported that 38% of variation in the user satisfaction data collected from 9 different sites can be explained by combining task completion judgment, sentence accuracy, ontask dialogue duration, and systemturn duration. The result of this study indicates that it may be possible to get more prediction power by substituting the sentence accuracy with the accuracy in the concept level and the system turn duration with the number of user words, respectively. A comparative study of the two user survey data sets may be needed to verify this assumption.

4. SYSTEM EVALUATION USING SUBJECTIVE METRICS AT EACH DIALOGUE TURN

We would like to locate "hot spots" in the spoken dialogue, i.e., system responses that are judged to be poor by the user. The possible causes of such problematic dialogue turns can be poor prompt wording, misrecognitions, or other semantic errors. In order to find these "hot spots", one must examine the dialogue turn-by-turn. However, it is not clear that post-hoc analyses can reproduce the subjective opinions of the original caller. Therefore, in these experiments, we also measured the inter-rater robustness of subjective metrics.

4.1 Method

Twenty dialogues (14 complete and 6 incomplete) were randomly selected from the 139 dialogues analyzed previously. Three naive subjects with no prior interaction with the Communicator system and three expert subjects, who have had experience designing and implementing one or more components of the Communicator system, were independently asked to evaluate each dialogue using the Likert questions of Table II. As opposed to the user survey, the questions were asked for every pair of the transcribed user utterance and the corresponding system response. Upon completion of a dialogue, the subjects then assigned the overall usability scores as the Communicator callers did. Most of subjects processed all twenty dialogues in a single session.

4.2 Analysis

In Figure 2, averaged scores of individual system response rating and overall rating assigned at the end of each dialogue are plotted for the two groups of dialogues. Each point is the averaged value across five question and dialogues in each group. Positive correlation and the linear tendency of data point distribution indicates that all subjects assign lower ratings to incomplete dialogues, indicating a general consensus on judging system usability. However, as is apparent from the ratings by subject 1 and subject 5, large inter-subject variability exists in terms of the magnitude of assigned values: Note that subject 1 used an extremely narrow range of scores.

The above observations suggest that subjects apply individual standards or criteria in assigning values to the system usability judgment. It thus may be difficult to reproduce human judgments in general. In fact, correlations of the overall scores among the subjects in the study including the Communicator callers are not strong and vary widely ($r_{\min} = 0.232$, $r_{\max} = 0.727$, p=0.01).

One of the major aims of the experiment was to isolate hot spots of the system determined as follows: the mean and standard deviation of the individual prompt scores are computed for each participant in the rating experiment. Outliers whose sum of scores are more than one standard deviation below the mean value are regarded as hot-spots determined by the subject. This procedure was repeated for each subject and hot spots which got four or five votes from 5 subjects were regarded as system's hot spots. Of 570 system responses presented, about 10.0% were regarded as the system's hot spots by the five subjects.

On average task-incomplete dialogues show a larger number of the hot spots (34.3 vs. 25.9) but it is not statistically significant. Examination of the system's hot spots also indicates that subject ratings are largely biased by speech recognition/understanding errors and vague system responses (e.g., "tell me what to change", "Thursday, July nineteenth is in the past. Would you like to continue on to another destination?"), which may or may not reflect system flaws.

5. CONCLUSION

We have presented some initial analyses of dialogues with our Communicator system, confirming and extending some of the results that have been previously shown for other systems. Specifically, we found that the error correction metric introduced in this study could be an effective objective metric for system performance evaluation. It is also better correlated with both user satisfaction and task completion than the recognition accuracy at the word or sentence level. More importantly, multiple regression analysis revealed that the total number of user words in dialogue and recognition accuracy at the concept level are the best predictors of user satisfaction among objective dialogue metrics tested in the study. The two variables explain about 27.2% of variation in user satisfaction. By adding perceived task completion judged by users as another variable in the regression, about 45.6% of variation in user satisfaction can be explained. Adding more variables such as dialogue duration was found to have marginal or negative effects.

We have also shown that it is difficult for independent human

[5]The task completion judgment alone can explain 23% of the variance in user satisfaction. However, it is not clear whether it can be regarded as an objective metric or not.

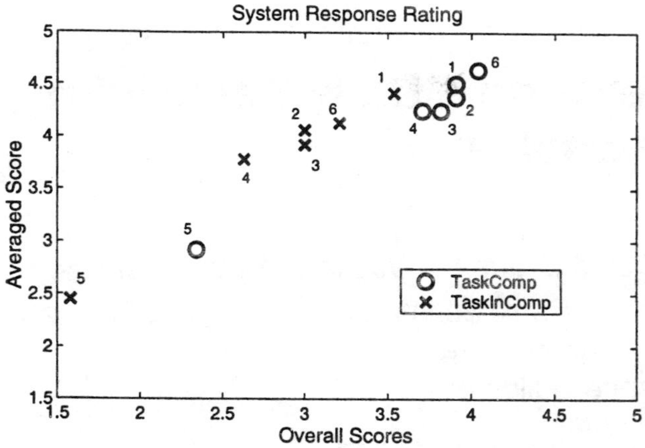

Figure 2: Averaged score vs. overall score obtained from the individual system response rating experiment.

raters to reproduce the Likert ratings given initially by the Communicator callers. Given the noisy nature of subjective metrics it is not surprising that there is little correlation between subjective and objective evaluation metrics, and between objective metrics and overall user satisfaction. The dependency of evaluation metrics on task completion and quality of service (e.g., fare price) makes dialogue evaluation an even harder task. From our experiments we conclude that objective measures (concept accuracy, error correction metric) can often be a better judge of the quality of the spoken dialogue interface than subjective measures. However, subjective measures and especially user satisfaction is the ultimate judge of service quality and should also be used (with care) when designing spoken dialogue systems.

6. ACKNOWLEDGMENTS

This work was funded by DARPA under the auspices of the Communicator project. The authors would like to express their sincere appreciation to NIST and the Communicator Evaluation Committee for designing and organizing the data collection and providing the user survey.

7. REFERENCES

[1] E. Ammicht, A. Potamianos, E. Fosler-Lussier, "Ambiguity Representation and Resolution in Spoken Dialogue Systems," in *Eurospeech*, (Aalborg, Denmark), Sep. 2001.

[2] J. Chu-Carroll, "Form-based reasoning for mixed-initiative dialogue management in information-query systems," in *Proc. Eurospeech*, (Budapest, Hungary), pp. 1519–1522, Sept. 1999.

[3] Larsen, L.B., "Combining objective and subjective data in evaluation of spoken dialogues," In ESCA Workshop on Interactive Dialogue in Multi-Modal Systems", 1999.

[4] Boros, M. et al, "Toward Understanding Spontaneous Speech: Word Accuracy vs. Semantic Accuracy," Proc. of ICSLP, 1996

[5] A. Potamianos, H.-K. J. Kuo, A. N. Pargellis, A. Saad, and Q. Zhou, "Design principles and tools for multimodal dialog systems," in *Proc. ESCA Workshop Interact. Dialog. Multi-Modal Syst.*, (Kloster Irsee, Germany), June 1999.

[6] A. Potamianos, E. Ammicht, and H.-K. Kuo, "Dialogue management in the Bell Labs communicator system," in *ICSLP*, (Beijing, China), Oct. 2000.

[7] A. Rudnicky and W. Xu, "An agenda-based dialog management architecture for spoken language systems," in *Proc. Workshop on Automatic Speech Recognition and Understanding*, (Keystone, Colorado), Dec. 1999.

[8] S. Seneff, E. Hurley, R. Lau, C. Pao, P. Schmid, and V. Zue, "Galaxy-II: A reference architecture for conversational system development," in *Proc. ICSLP'98*, (Sydney, Australia), Dec. 1998.

[9] M. Walker *et al.*, "DARPA Communicator Dialog Travel Planning Systems: The June 2000 Data Collection," in *Eurospeech*, (Aalborg, Denmark), Sep. 2001.

[10] M. Walker, L. Hirschman, and J. Aberdeen, "Evaluation for DRAPA Communicator Dialog Systems," Proc. Language Resources and Evaluation Conference, LREC-2000.

[11] M. Walker, C. Kamm, and D. Litman, "Towards developing general models of usability with PARADISE," Natural Language Engineering: Special Issue on Best Practice in Spoken Dialogue Systems, 2000.

[12] W. Ward and B. Pellom, "The CU Communicator system," in *Proc. Workshop on Automatic Speech Recognition and Understanding*, (Keystone, Colorado), Dec. 1999.

Tracking and Summarizing News on a Daily Basis with Columbia's Newsblaster

Kathleen R. McKeown   Regina Barzilay   David Evans   Vasileios Hatzivassiloglou
Judith L. Klavans   Ani Nenkova   Carl Sable   Barry Schiffman   Sergey Sigelman
Department of Computer Science
450 Computer Science Building
Columbia University
1214 Amsterdam Avenue, New York, N.Y. 10027
{kathy, regina, devans, vh, klavans, ani, sable, bschiff, ss1792} @cs.columbia.edu

ABSTRACT

Recently, there have been significant advances in several areas of language technology, including clustering, text categorization, and summarization. However, efforts to combine technology from these areas in a practical system for information access have been limited. In this paper, we present Columbia's Newsblaster system for online news summarization. Many of the tools developed at Columbia over the years are combined together to produce a system that crawls the web for news articles, clusters them on specific topics and produces multidocument summaries for each cluster.

General Terms

Multidocument summarization

Keywords

clustering, topic detection and tracking, Columbia Newsblaster

1. INTRODUCTION

Current technology in summarization and topic detection and tracking is mature enough to be used reliably in a live, online environment. Newsblaster is a system developed at Columbia to provide news updates on a daily basis; it crawls news sites, filters out news from non-news (e.g., ads), groups news into stories on the same event, and generates a summary of each event. Summaries are generated using the Columbia Summarizer [8, 7, 13], which was evaluated in the Document Understanding Conference (DUC) in 2001. News is grouped into stories on the same event using a Topic Detection and Tracking (TDT) style system developed at Columbia [4]. Unlike other TDT systems, Columbia's uses a learned, weighted combination of features to determine similarity of stories, grouping articles on the same event. Newsblaster (`http://www.cs.columbia.edu/nlp/newsblaster`) typically generates summaries on clusters of between five and 30 news stories, but in cases where an event generates a lot of interest, we may find a much larger cluster; for example, on November 23rd, Newsblaster generated a summary of 75 articles all describing the advance of troops towards Kunduz. We began running Newsblaster on September 16th, 2001, when the summarization system was robust enough to run on a daily basis. We were also interested in archiving news on the September 11th events. The archives (see the bottom of the Newsblaster web page) show the progress on the interface since that time, as we have moved from very rudimentary classification of events to a three-level hierarchical classification in the current version.

Newsblaster is unique in its integration of TDT and summarization to provide a system for daily browsing of news. Integration of the separate components, for which papers have previously been published, introduced a number of unexpected research issues. First, one of our summarizers had been designed to generate summaries on a single event. Current TDT approaches produce clusters that are topically related, but not necessarily on a single event. We needed to create fine-grained clustering that could produce the kind of input needed by the summarizer. Second, given the wide variety in news that we find in an online environment, we needed multiple strategies to allow us to summarize different kinds of news clusters. This led to our use of multiple summarization systems within one architecture, with a router which automatically determines which summarization system should be invoked. Third, the user interface needs inherent in displaying large quantities of information each day created demands on the clustering and summarization process. For example, in our early implementation, we used a single level of clustering to feed document sets to the summarizer. However, the results did not provide a very useful breakdown of large quantities of news for browsing. This led to our interleaving of categorization with clustering to create a hierarchical view of the news along with a new approach to generating labels of clusters.

In this paper, we overview the system, discussing the gathering of news, the organization into events, subsequent summarization of events, and the integration of related images.

Proceedings of HLT 2002, Second International Conference on Human Language Technology Research, M. Marcus, ed., Morgan Kaufmann, San Francisco, 2002.

2. SYSTEM DESCRIPTION

Newsblaster follows a pipeline architecture. First, the system crawls the web for news articles, followed by a pre-processing phase which normalizes the text into a standard form and extracts images. The news articles are clustered into event clusters, then these clusters are grouped at a higher level, putting together related

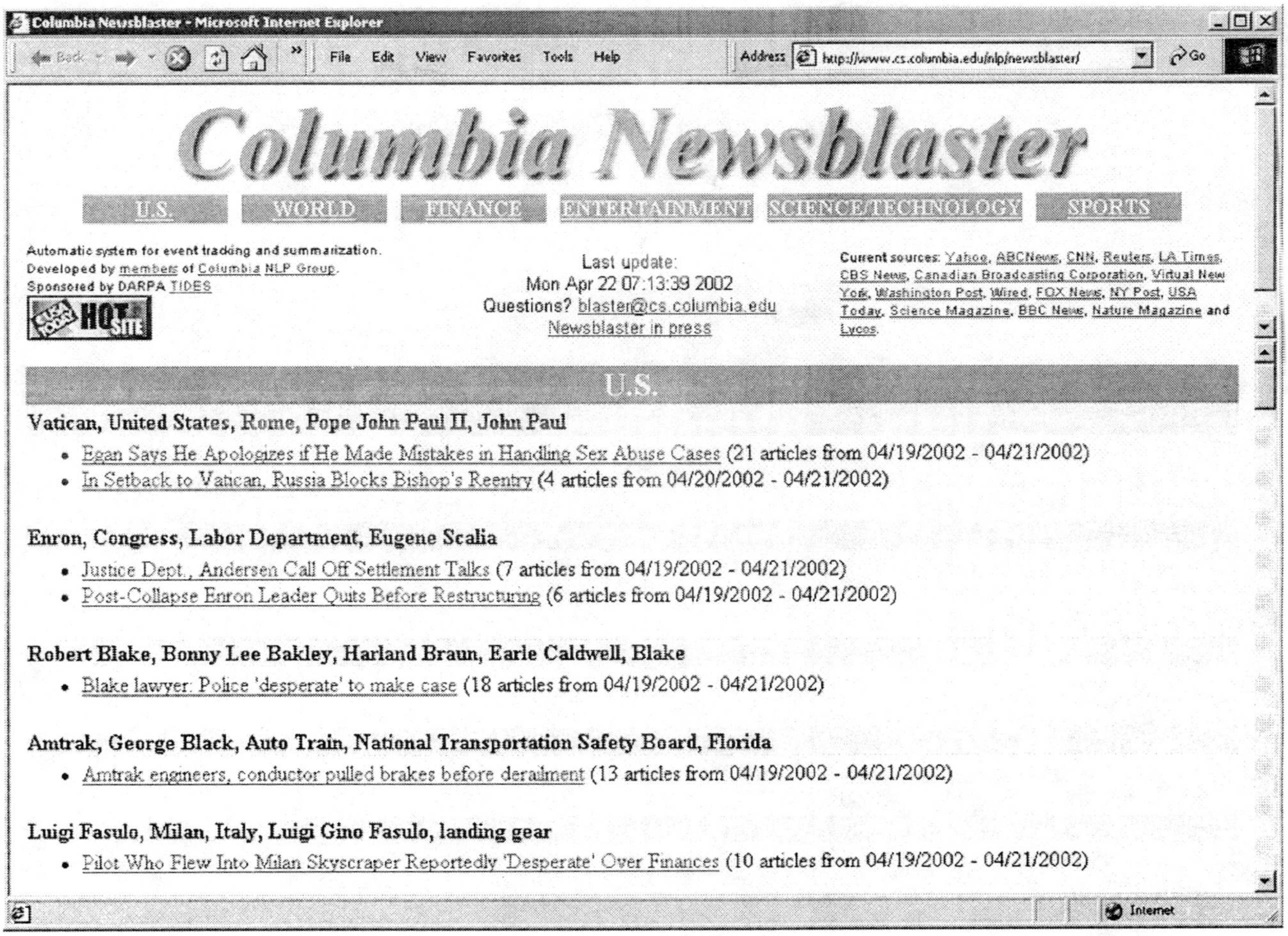

Figure 1: Newsblaster frontpage

events. Events are also categorized into one of the six top-level categories. A multidocument summary is created for each event cluster and augmented with pictures extracted from the articles.

3. GATHERING NEWS

Newsblaster currently crawls 17 news sites including those of CNN, Reuters, Fox News, NY Post, and USA Today, among others. The list of sites is stored in a text file and may change over time. Each site is traversed up to a maximum depth (currently 4) and only links within the site are considered. For each page examined, if the amount of text in the largest cell of the page (after stripping tags and links) is greater than some particular constant (currently 512 characters), it is assumed to be a news article, and this text is extracted. Note that tables are used in many web sites to format the page and the largest table cell usually contains the body text of the article.

4. ORGANIZATION OF STORIES

Newsblaster hierarchically classifies the news stories gathered by the crawler into three levels. At the top level, it uses text categorization to determine whether the story falls into one of six predetermined categories: US, International, Financial, Entertainment, Science and Technology, or Sports. We calculate category TF*IDF vectors for each category, and compare the TF*IDF vector for each article in a given cluster to all categories. In this manner, articles are assigned to the closest (most similar with a cosine measure) category. Then we classify the cluster into the category to which the largest number of articles in the cluster are assigned. During these calculations, we smooth estimated frequencies in the articles using smoothing bins [10]. These categories are shown in large orange bands on the main Newsblaster front page, shown for the US category on April 22nd, 2002 in Figure 1.

Within each broad category of articles, Newsblaster further organizes the news stories into two hierarchical levels. The lowest level corresponds to articles on the same event (see the underlined text as in "*Egan Says He Apologizes if He Made Mistakes in Handling Sex Abuse Cases*", Figure 1), while the higher level groups together related events (shown in bold, heading each group of events as in "*Vatican, United States, Rome, Pope John Paul II*", Figure 1). For both of these, we use a hierarchical clustering system developed at Columbia [4]. On this particular day, there were two specific events related to the Vatican and the United States. While related, each of the clusters is a different event which has its own summary page containing the articles about the event.

The system uses agglomerative clustering with a groupwise average similarity function. It is distinguished by its use of not only the usual TF*IDF weighted words, but also linguistically motivated features, such as terms, noun phrase heads and proper nouns, likely to correlate with events and not simply topically related stories.

It also incorporates a log-linear statistical model for automatically adjusting the relative weights of the different features. We

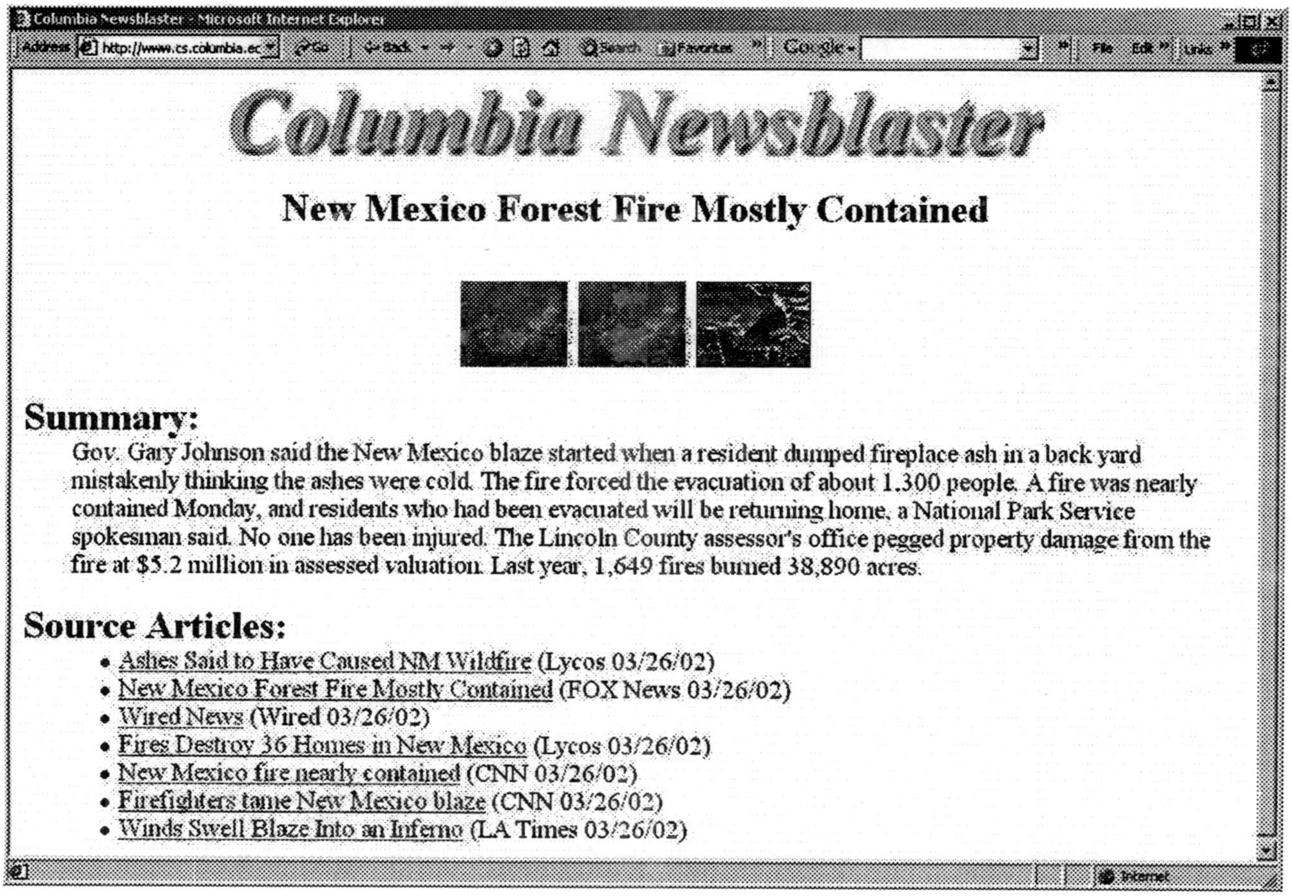

Figure 2: A MultiGen Summary

have evaluated our news clustering system using TDT-2 data. Our system performs comparably to the top TDT-2 participants under most measures, and outperforms them in macro-averaged detection cost [4]. For its use within Newsblaster, we have empirically determined two thresholds for the clustering at each of the two levels (single event and group of related events).

To facilitate the user's interaction with the categorized stories, we also provide labels for each cluster. For the lowest (event) level, where the articles are closely related in content, we use heuristics to select the article that is most related to the other articles in each cluster, and label the entire cluster with that article's title (shown in blue on the main page). For the second level (related events) we extract from all articles in the cluster all proper names and terms, then weigh those according to their total frequency and inverse document frequency, and select up to five such terms that are most representative of the related events (shown in black, heading each group of events).

5. SUMMARIZING EVENTS

All sets of clustered articles corresponding to the lowest event level are sent to the Columbia Summarizer to generate summaries of events. The Columbia Summarizer is a composite summarization system that uses different summarization strategies dependent on the type of documents in each cluster; this contrasts with other systems which typically perform one type of summarization only [3]. A router automatically determines the type of documents in each cluster and invokes the appropriate summarization subcomponent.

Using the training corpus provided for DUC, we manually derived a typology of document sets. *Single-event* documents center around one single event happening at one place and at roughly the same time, involving the same agents and actions. *Person-centered* (or "biography") documents deal with one event concerning one person and include background information about that person. *Multi-event* documents describe several events occurring at different places and times, and usually with different protagonists, are reported together. There is a common theme to these events, e.g., a cluster might collect many fire incidents on unrelated cruise ships. The time span covered is unpredictable, but longer than in the single-event case. *Other* clusters contain even more loosely related documents and do not fit any of the categories above.

To summarize documents on the same event, the Columbia summarizer uses an enhanced version of MultiGen [2, 8]. MultiGen integrates machine learning and statistical techniques to identify similar sentences (set set of similar sentences is called a *themes*) across the input articles [5, 6]. It then uses an alignment of parse trees to find the intersection of similar phrases within sentences [2]. It orders the selected themes [1] and uses language generation to cut and paste together similar phrases from the theme sentences. Each theme corresponds to roughly one sentence of the summary.

For biographical documents, it uses an alternate system, DEMS (Dissimilarity Engine for Multidocument Summarization) [13], tuned to the biographical task; and for sets of loosely similar documents, it uses DEMS with a more general configuration. DEMS selects

Figure 3: A DEMS summary

sentences that contain information that is important or interesting enough to be included in a summary. It uses a combination of several features that are critical for new-information detection with some traditional heuristics used in single-document summarization [13]. For example, it uses frequencies of concepts (or sets of synonyms) as opposed to individual words, combined with global information about what words are likely to appear in a lead sentence, to determine whether an article sentence should be included in the summary. For biographies, it also incorporates techniques used in the BioGen system, developed jointly by Mitre and Columbia [12]. Since there were no sets of similar sentences in the input, the generation strategy that we used in MultiGen was not applicable in DUC. We have investigated some ways to rewrite the summary [13] and are continuing to explore techniques.

While all clusters in Newsblaster are more closely related than in DUC, we still needed a summarizer to handle clusters that are not as closely related as most single event descriptions. For example, Figure 3 shows a summary of a loosely connected set of articles related to Afghanistan, Pakistani borders with Afghanistan and a recent visit by Cheney to the area. DEMS has selected different important facts from the articles, which are not necessarily sequentially or strongly linked to each other (Figure 3. In this case, the summary provides an overview of the different topics touched on in the articles.

Figure 2 shows a MultiGen summary on a single event, a fire that grew out of control in New Mexico. In this summary, all sentences relate different stages in the sequence of events, with the exception of the sentence on fires last year. These sentences are ordered chronologically in the summary. Individual summary sentences have been drawn from pieces of several article sentences. Figure 6 shows how the first sentence of the summary was generated from pieces of similar phrases in the theme from which it was produced. Here, the third theme sentence provides the summary wording on how the blaze was started. Note that while the exact wording from the third sentence is used, this information is repeated across the different sentences of the theme. The second sentence of the theme contributes the clause *"mistakenly thinking the ashes were cold."*. This information is repeated across two sentences of the theme.

6. ADDING RELATED IMAGES

Newsblaster selects and displays thumbnails of images that are related to an event on the same page where the summary of events is displayed. During the web crawling phase, in addition to looking for news articles, Newsblaster also looks for embedded images in the articles. Since articles are taken from many different sources on the web, and these sources might change over time, it is important that the rules used by the system to find such images are general, and can be applied to multiple sites. The rules must extract most of the appropriate images without also taking advertisements and other inappropriate images. We weighted precision higher than recall, since users will not notice if certain images are not found, but inappropriate images would be visible. Some patterns we noticed when manually examining news sites were: (1) Images are almost always in the same cell as the article or an embedded cell. (2) Images that are jpeg's tend to be appropriate, but other formats are more likely advertisements or link related. (3) Images with a word like "ad" or "advertisement" in the URL are probably not appropriate. By combining such rules, our system seems to achieve nearly perfect precision while still recalling the high majority of appropriate images.

We are currently working on rules to retrieve corresponding captions to the images that have them. In prior research, we have developed techniques for categorizing images based on their captions [11] as well as image features [9]. In current, ongoing research, we are exploring the categorization of images into sub-categories of news categories based on shallow parsing of captions and simple word similarity metrics. For example, for news concerning disasters, we have found that the main subject and verb from the first sentence of an image caption is often enough to determine if the image likely focuses on victims, workers responding, or wreckage. This research can be incorporated in Newsblaster by displaying images with similar content together, allowing users to further browse or search the group.

Figure 4: Theme for the first sentence of the MultiGen summary

<Gov. Gary Johnson said> <the New Mexico blaze> <started when a resident dumped fireplace ash in a back yard> <mistakenly thinking the ashes were cold.>

<THEME 11>

<Art 1 Par 1 (global para num: P1) >
Fireplace ashes dumped in a back yard sparked a grass and timber wildfire that burned 28 homes in an affluent neighborhood in the mountains of southern New Me xico, authorities said Sunday.

<Art 2 Par 14 (global para num: P50) >
Gov. Gary Johnson, who toured the fire zone Sunday, said the blaze started Saturday when a resident dumped fireplace ash in the back yard, **<mistakenly thinking the ashes were cold.>**

<Art 3 Par 7 (global para num: P72) >
<Gov. Gary Johnson said> the south - central **<New Mexico blaze>**, which charred about 960 acres, **<started when a resident dumped fireplace ash in a back yard>** in the mistaken belief the ashes were cold.

<Art 7 Par 11 (global para num: P140) >
Gov. Gary Johnson said Sunday the fire was sparked when a local homeowner dumped what he believed were harmless fireplace ashes into his backyard.

7. CONCLUSIONS AND CURRENT DIRECTIONS

This paper summarizes innovative contributions in the areas of multilevel document clustering and categorization, multidocument summarization using data driven routing to different summarizers and image retrieval linked to text categorization. These research achievements are incorporated into Newsblaster, a deployed prototype which demonstrates the robustness of summarization and TDT technology today. We have begun a large scale online evaluation measuring usage and preferences. Newsblaster is an ongoing project; we are exploring linking summary text phrases directly to the context from which they were drawn, tracking events across days, and incorporating our work on summarizing new information. We are also exploring personalization of Newsblaster, restricting it to user preferred topics or questions. Our vision is the development of system that can provide true updates on current events morning, noon, and night.

Acknowledgements

The work reported here was supported in part by the National Science Foundation under STIMULATE grant IRI-96-18797 and by the Defense Advanced Research Projects Agency under TIDES grant NUU01-00-1-8919. Any opinions, findings, or recommendations are those of the authors and do not necessarily reflect the views of the funding agencies.

8. REFERENCES

[1] R. Barzilay, N. Elhadad, and K. R. McKeown. Sentence ordering in multidocument summarization. In *Proceedings of the 1st Human Language Technology Conference*, San Diego, California, 2001.

[2] R. Barzilay, K. McKeown, and M. Elhadad. Information fusion in the context of multi-document summarization. In *Proc. of the 37th Annual Meeting of the Assoc. of Computational Linguistics*, 1999.

[3] Document understanding conference, 2001.

[4] V. Hatzivassiloglou, L. Gravano, and A. Maganti. An investigation of linguistic features and clustering algorithms for topical document clustering. In *Proceedings of the 23rd Annual ACM SIGIR Conference on Research and Development in Information Retrieval (SIGIR-00)*, pages 224–231, Athens, Greece, July 2000.

[5] V. Hatzivassiloglou, J. L. Klavans, and E. Eskin. Detecting text similarity over short passages: Exploring linguistic feature combinations via machine learning. In *Proceedings of the 1999 Joint SIGDAT Conference on Empirical Methods in Natural Language Processing and Very Large Corpora*, pages 203–212, College Park, Maryland, June 1999. Association for Computational Linguistics.

[6] V. Hatzivassiloglou, J. L. Klavans, M. L. Holcombe, R. Barzilay, M.-Y. Kan, and K. R. McKeown. SIMFINDER: A flexible clustering tool for summarization. In *NAACL Workshop on Automatic Summarization*, pages 41–49. Association for Computational Linguistics, 2001.

[7] K. McKeown, R. Barzilay, D. Evans, V. Hatzivassiloglou, M. Kan, B. Schiffman, and S. Teufel. Columbia multi-document summarization: Approach and evaluation. In *Proceedings of the Document Understanding Workshop (DUC)*, 2001.

[8] K. McKeown, J. Klavans, V. Hatzivassiloglou, R. Barzilay, and E. Eskin. Towards multidocument summarization by reformulatin: Progress and prospects. In *Proceedings of the Seventeenth National Conference on Artificial Intelligence*, 1999.

[9] S. Paek, C. Sable, V. Hatzivassiloglou, A. Jaimes, B. Schiffman, S. Chang, and K. McKeown. Integration of visual and text-based approaches for the content labeling and classification of photographs. In *ACM SIGIR Workshop on Multimedia Indexing and Retrieval (SIGIR-99)*, 1999.

[10] C. Sable and K. W. Church. Using bins to empirically estimate term weights for text categorization. In *Proceedings of the 2001 Conference on Empirical Methods in Natural Language Processing (EMNLP)*, 2001.

[11] C. Sable and V. Hatzivassiloglou. Text-based approaches for non-topical image categorization. *International Journal of Digital Libraries*, **3**(3):261–275, 2000.

[12] B. Schiffman, I. Mani, and K. J. Concepcion. Producing biographical summaries: Combining linguistic knowledge with corpus statistics. In *Proceedings European Association for Computational Linguistics 2001*, 2001.

[13] B. Schiffman, A. Nenkova, and K. McKeown. Experiments in multi-document summarization. In *HLT 2002*, 2002.

XML Tag Information Management System – A Workbench for Ontology-based Knowledge Acquisition and Integration

Hideki Mima[1], Sophia Ananiadou[2], Goran Nenadic[2], Junichi Tsujii[1]

[1]Dept. of Information Science, University of Tokyo
Hongo 7-3-1, Bunkyo-ku, Tokyo 113-0033, Japan
{mima, tsujii}@is.s.u-tokyo.ac.jp

[2]Computer Science, University of Salford
Newton Building, Salford M5 4WT, UK
{S.Ananiadou, G.Nenadic}@salford.ac.uk

Abstract

In this paper, we propose an integrated information management system in which ontology-based knowledge integration and XML-based text/data retrieval are combined using tag information and ontology management tools. The main purpose of the system is to implement a query answering system for XML-based documents in the domain of molecular biology. The aim is to provide efficient access to heterogeneous biological and genomic textual data and databases, enabling users to use a wide range of textual and non-textual resources effortlessly. Our system includes automatic term recognition, context-based automatic term clustering, ontology-based inference, and intelligent tag information retrieval. Through further description of the implementation and architecture of the system, we will demonstrate how the system can accelerate knowledge integration on the textual and non-textual resources even for novice users of the field.

Keywords
knowledge acquisition, automatic term recognition, term clustering, interval operation, ontology

1. Introduction

With the recent dramatic increase of importance of electronic communication and data-sharing over the Internet, there exists an increasingly growing number and amount of publicly accessible knowledge sources, both in the form of documents and fact data bases.

Proceedings of HLT 2002, Second International Conference on Human Language Technology Research, M. Marcus, ed., Morgan Kaufmann, San Francisco, 2002.

These knowledge sources (KSs) are intrinsically heterogeneous and dynamic. They are *heterogeneous* since they are autonomously developed and maintained by independent organizations with different purposes in mind. They are *dynamic* since constantly new information is being revised, added and removed. Such heterogeneous and dynamic nature of KSs imposes challenges on systems that help users to locate information relevant to their needs.

In attempt to handle such dynamic nature of knowledge sources efficiently, several efforts have been proposed based on knowledge acquisition (KA) [13] and knowledge integration (KI) framework [17]. Further, the Semantic Web framework [1] has been proposed in order to link relevant Web resources using Resource Description Framework (RDF) [2] and an ontology. However, although the semantic web framework is powerful in expressing content of resources to be semantically retrieved, some manual description is expected using the RDF/ontology. In addition, no further answer to the ontology conflictions/mismatches [16] is provided.

An additional problem for efficient and consistent knowledge acquisition and integration is the lack of clear naming conventions in the domain of molecular biology, which necessitates the automated handling of terminological variations. However, recent solutions such as [8] cover only syntactic and morpho-syntactic variations. Currently, there are no proposals for the proper handling of semantic variations.

In this paper, we propose an integrated information management system in which ontology-based knowledge integration and XML-based text/data retrieval are combined using tag information and ontology management tools. The management of knowledge resources, similarly to the Semantic Web, is based on XML, RDF, and ontology-based inference.

However, our aim is to facilitate the KA and KI tasks not only by using manually defined resource descriptions, but also by exploiting NLP techniques such as automatic term recognition (ATR) and automatic term clustering (ATC). ATR and ATC can be used for semantic term variation by automatically and uniformly organizing knowledge resources.

The ideas that will be presented are implemented in the domain of molecular biology. Currently, the size of knowledge in that domain is increasing so rapidly that it is impossible for any domain expert to assimilate the new knowledge without automated help. Vast amounts of knowledge still remain unexplored and this poses a major handicap to this knowledge intensive discipline. Our system aims to help biologists to systematically gather data crucial for their research.

The paper is organized as follows: in the next section, we present the overall architecture of the system and briefly describe the components incorporated in the system, while section 3 presents the proposed method for knowledge integration and management. In section 4 we present some results and evaluation, while section 5 concludes the paper.

2. TIMS – system architecture

In order to facilitate an efficient integration and organization of KSs, we have developed an XML-based Tag Information Management System (TIMS). The main purpose of the TIMS workbench is to implement a knowledge integration tool and a query answering system for XML-based documents in the domain of molecular biology. TIMS integrates the following modules via XML-based communication: the JTAG annotation tool, the ATRACT automatic term recognition/clustering tool and the LiLFeS abstract machine. Figure 1 shows the system architecture.

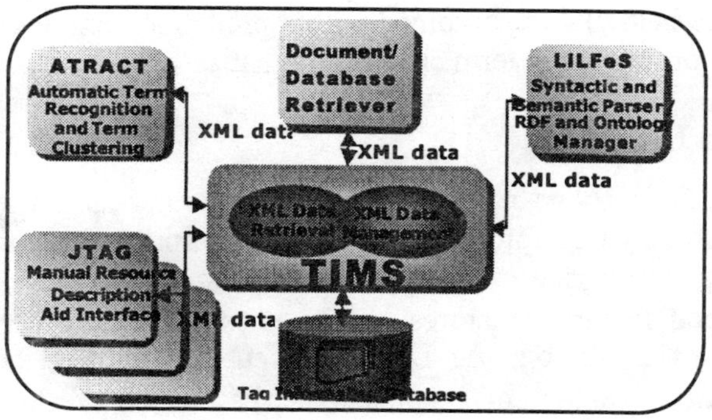

Figure 1. System architecture of TIMS

2.1 JTAG

JTAG is an XML-based manual annotation and resource description aid tool. A purpose of the tool is to support manual annotation, such as tagging, adjusting term recognition results, developing RDF logic, etc. All the annotation can be achieved via GUI. In addition, ontology information described in XML can also be developed and modified using the tool.

2.2 ATRACT : A Terminology Workbench

In the domain of molecular biology, there is an increasing amount of new terms that represent newly created concepts. Existing term dictionaries cannot cover the needs of specialists, and therefore automatic term extraction tools are important for consistent term discovery. ATRACT [11] is a terminology workbench that integrates automatic term recognition (ATR) and automatic term clustering (ATC). Its main aim is to help biologist to gather and organize terminology in the domain.

Our ATR method is based on the *C/NC-value* method [3]. It dynamically recognizes terms in texts, which often include unknown, unregistered words and/or new term candidates. This method is a hybrid approach, combining linguistic knowledge (term formation patterns) and statistics (frequency of occurrence, term length, etc). Also, acronym acquisition and resolution are incorporated in the ATR process. The ATR module retrieves terms on the fly and sends the results as XML tag information to the TIMS workbench.

Besides term recognition, term clustering is an indispensable component in a knowledge organization process. In molecular biology, terminological opacity and variation are very common. Therefore, term clustering is essential for semantic integration of terms, construction of domain ontology and for choosing appropriate semantic tag information. The automatic term clustering (ATC) method is based on Ushioda's AMI (Average Mutual Information)- hierarchical clustering method [18]. Our implementation uses parallel symmetric processing for high speed clustering and is built on the *C/NC-value* results. As input, we use co-occurrences of automatically recognized terms and their contexts and the output is a dendrogram of hierarchical term clusters (like thesaurus). The calculated term cluster information is stored in LiLFeS (see below) and combined with a predefined ontology according to the term classes automatically assigned.

2.3 LiLFeS

LiLFeS [14] is a Prolog-like programming language and language processor used for defining definite clause programs with typed feature structures. Since typed feature structures can be used like first order terms in Prolog, the LiLFeS language can describe various kinds of applications based on feature structures. Examples include HPSG parsers, HPSG-based grammars and compilers from HPSG to CFG. Furthermore, other NLP systems can be easily developed because feature structure processing can be directly written in the LiLFeS language. In the TIMS workbench, LiLFeS is used to 1) infer relevance between terms using type hierarchy processing, and 2) parse sentences using HPSG-based parsers and convert the results into an XML-based formalism.

Figure 2 shows the model of knowledge integration using TIMS and LiLFeS. LiLFeS plays a central role in ontology-based inference, such as logic inference and hierarchical matching of classes using term ontology information.

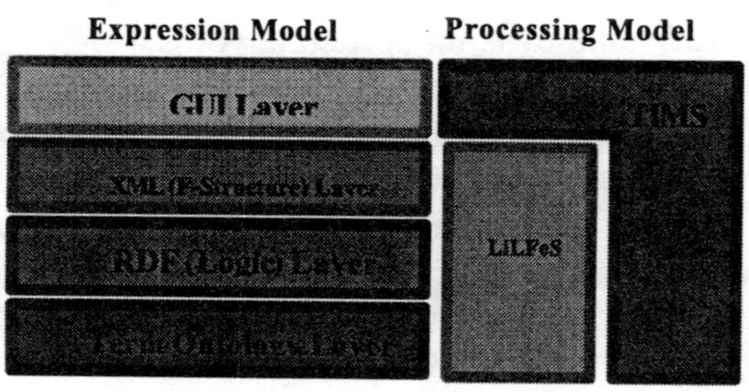

Figure 2. Model of knowledge integration in TIMS workbench

3. Knowledge Integration and Management in TIMS

The knowledge integration and management in TIMS are organized by integrating XML-data management and tag- and ontology-based information retrieval.

3.1 The XML tag data management

In an attempt to accumulate a large amount of linguistic information for accelerating language processing, several linguistic tag systems have been proposed, such

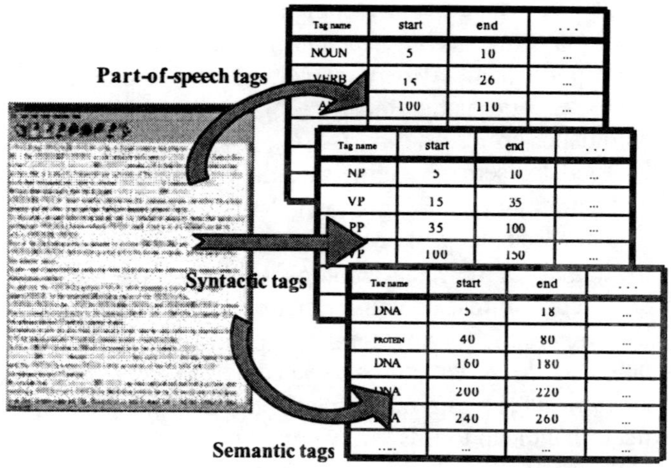

Figure 3. Tag data management in TIMS

as GDA [5], GENIA [6] or GATE [4]. In general, since tagged information is embedded in texts using HTML-like tags, multiple tag information can reduce the visual transparency of the tagged documents. In addition, when we allow the tagging scheme to include structural complexity (e.g. nesting, candidate combinations of syntax and semantic structure, etc.), the overhead of processing the tag information causes inefficient corpus processing.

Communication within the TIMS workbench is based on XML-data exchange. TIMS initially parses the XML documents and de-tags them. Then, like in TIPSTER architecture [7], each tag information is stored separately from the original documents and managed by an external database software. This facility allows, as shown in figure 3, different types of tags for the same document to be added.

3.2 Tag- and ontology-based information retrieval

Another key feature of TIMS is its facility to search logically for tags, which is implemented via 'interval operations'. Interval operations (IO) are XML specific text/data retrieval operations, which can be performed over TIMS documents. These operations can be performed over the specified documents and/or tag sets (e.g. syntactic tags, semantic tags, etc.) simultaneously or in batch mode, selecting the documents/tag sets from a list. This accelerates the process of KA, as users are able to retrieve information from multiple KSs simultaneously.

The main notion of interval operations is that the XML tags are assumed as information that specifies certain *intervals* in documents. Each interval operation takes two sets of intervals as input and returns a set of intervals according to the specified logical operations. Currently, we define four types of logical operations:

- **Intersection** '⊗' returns intersected intervals of all the intervals given.
- **Union** '⊕' returns merged intervals of all the intersected intervals.
- **Subtraction** '⊖' returns differences in intervals of all the intersected intervals.
- **Concatenation** '+' returns concatenated intervals of all the continuous intervals.

For example, suppose X denotes a set of intervals of manually annotated tags for a document and Y denotes a set of intervals of automatically annotated tags for the same document. The interval operation [1] $((X \otimes Y) \oplus \{X \cup Y\})$ results in the differences between human and machine annotations (see figure 4).

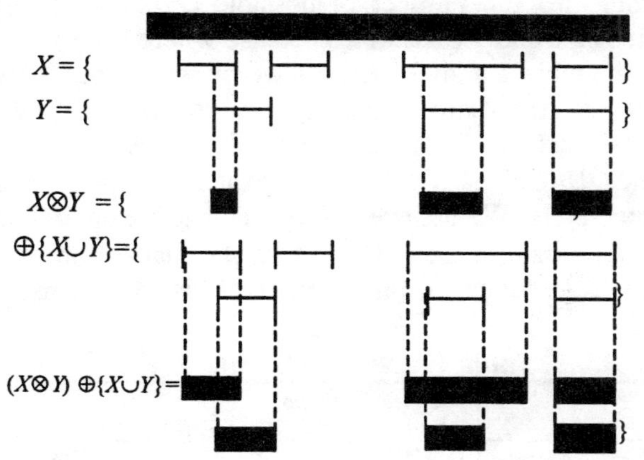

Figure 4. $(X \otimes Y) \oplus \{X \cup Y\}$

Interval operations are powerful means for data mining from different sources using tag information. In addition, LiLFeS enables tag (interval) retrieval to process not only regular pattern/string matching, but also ontological hierarchy matching to subordinate classes using either predefined or automatically derived term ontology. Thus, **semantic** similarity based tag information retrieval is achieved.

In order to integrate and expand the above components, we have developed a tag information query language (TIQL). Using this language, a user can specify the interval operations to be performed on selected documents. The basic expression in TIQL has the following form:

```
SELECT [n-tuple variables]
   FROM [XML document(s)]
      WHERE [interval operation]
  FROM [XML document(s)]
      WHERE [interval operation]
  ......
```

where, `[n-tuple variables]` specifies table format as output, `[XML document(s)]` denotes a document to be operated on, and `[interval operation]` denotes an interval operation to be performed over the corresponding document with variables of each interval to be bound.

For example, a typical KA task in our system is achieved by specifying an expression like the following:[2]

```
SELECT x1, x2
  FROM "paper-1.xml"
    WHERE <VP>⊗{x1:<EVENT*>∪x2:<nucleic_acid*>}
  FROM "paper-2.xml"
    WHERE <VP>⊗{x1:<EVENT*>∪x2:<nucleic_acid*>}
```

In this example, TIMS, as shown in figure 5, extracts all the hierarchically subordinate classes matched to

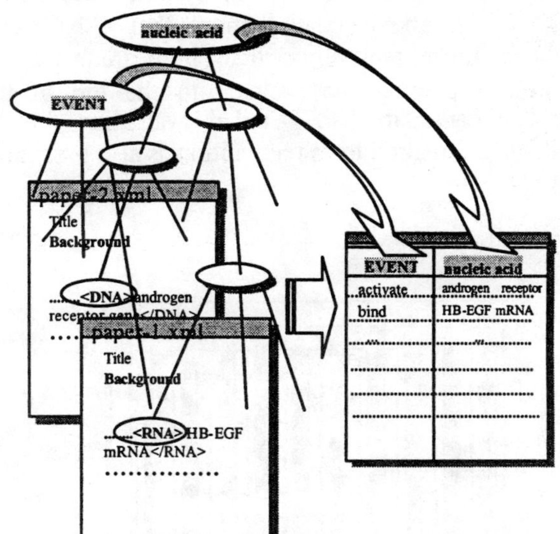

Figure 5. Ontology-based Tagged Information Retrieval

[1] '∪' denotes a merged set of all the elements.

[2] '* ' denotes hierarchical matching.

(<EVENT>, <nucleic_acid>) pair from specified KSs, and then automatically builds a table according to n-tuple order to display the results.

4. Evaluation

We conducted preliminary experiments on the proposed workbench design. In this paper, we focus on the quality of automatic term recognition and similarity measure calculation via automatically clustered terms to show the feasibility of our proposed term-oriented KA. In addition, we examine the performance of tag manipulation in TIMS compared to string-based XML tag manipulation to show the advantage of the tag information management scheme. The evaluation was performed on the NACSIS AI-domain corpus [9], which includes 1800 abstracts for term recognition. For term clustering and tag manipulation performance, we used GENIA corpus [6] which includes 1,000 MEDLINE abstracts [10], with overall 40,000 (16,000 distinct) semantic tags annotated for terms in the domain of nuclear receptors.

We have examined the performance of the C/NC-value method with respect to its precision. The results are shown in figure 6 In the results, we have observed that C-value increases the precision for the first 3 intervals by 5 %, and NC-value by 7 %. They are noteworthy that the precisions of the top 100 interval are more than 93 % for both methods, which are high in quality. The above results show that C/NC-value produces more real terms than pure frequency of occurrence placing them closer to the top of the extracted candidate list. Detailed evaluation for the C/NC-value method term recognition is also presented in [12].

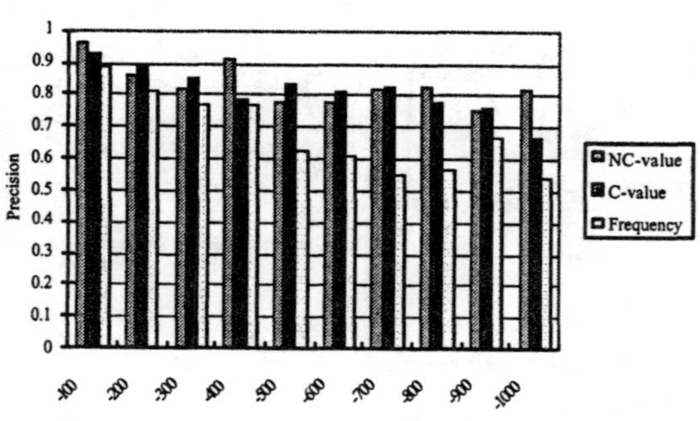

Figure 6. NC-value vs. C-value vs. Freq.

We have used the similarity measure calculation as the central computing mechanism for inferring relevance between XML tags and tags specified in TIQL/interval operation, determining the most relevant tags in the XML-based KS(s). The clustered terms were obtained by using Ushioda's AMI-based hierarchical clustering algorithm [18]. As training data, we have used 1,000 MEDLINE abstracts. Similarities between terms were calculated according to the hierarchy of the clustered terms. In this experiment, we have adopted a semantic similarity calculation method for measuring the similarity between terms described in [15]. Three major sets of classes (namely, *nucleic_acid*, *amino_acid, SOURCE*) of manually classified terms from GENIA corpus [6] were used to calculate the average similarities (AS) of the elements with every possible combination of the sets, that is,

$$AS(X,Y) = \frac{1}{n} \sum_{x\in X,\, y\in Y,\, x\neq y} sim(x,y)$$

where X, Y indicate each set of the classified terms, $sim(x,y)$ indicates similarity between terms x and y, and n indicates the number of possible combinations of terms in X and Y (except in the case where $x = y$). As the table 1 shows, and as we expected, each AS between the same classes, i.e. AS(*nucleic_acid, nucleic_acid*), AS(*amino_acid, amino_acid*), AS(*SOURCE, SOURCE*), was greater than the others respectively. We believe that this is feasible enough to use automatic clustered terms as the main source of knowledge for calculating similarities between terms.

Table 1. Average Similarities

	nucleic acid	*amino acid*	*SOURCE*	*#. of terms*
nucleic_acid	**0.498**	-	-	3108
amino_acid	0.396	**0.492**	-	4284
SOURCE	0.390	0.388	**0.480**	3302

In order to examine tag manipulation performance of TIMS, we measured the processing times consumed for executing an interval operation in TIMS compared to time needed by using string-based regular expression matching (REM). We focused on measuring the interval operation '⊗' with intervals (tags) '`<title>`' and '`<term>`' (cf. [6]). The average TIMS processing was about 40-80% faster (depending on number of tags and corpus length) than that of REM. Therefore, we assume that the TIMS tag information management scheme can be seen as an efficient mechanism to facilitate knowledge acquisition process.

5. Conclusion

In this paper, we examined some problems dealing with IR over large KSs. We have proposed an XML-based integrated KA aid system where we combined tag data management and ontology-based information retrieval. The TIMS workbench allows users to search and combine information from various sources. An important source of information in the system is derived from terminological knowledge; this is provided automatically in XML format where we extract potential terms and term clusters from running text. The system has been tested on 1,000 abstracts of MEDLINE [10]. Additionally, we are conducting experiments using GENIA project's tag information and ontology.

Important areas of future research for the system will involve expanding the scalability of the system to real WWW knowledge acquisition tasks to test and improve the functionality of the system.

References

[1] Barners-Lee, T. 1998. *The Semantic Web as a longuage of logic*, http://www.w3.org/DesignIssues/Logic.html

[2] Bricklet, D. and Guha, R. 2000. *Resource Description Framework (RDF) Schema Specification 1.0*, W3C Candidate Recommendation, available at http://www.w3.org/TR/rdf-schema.

[3] Frantzi, K. T., Ananiadou, S. and Mima, H. 2000. *Automatic Recognition of Multi-Word Terms: the C-value/NC-value method*, in International Journal on Digital Libraries, Vol. 3, No. 2, 115—130.

[4] GATE, 2001. *General Architecture for Text Engineering*, http://www.dcs.shef.ac.uk/research/groups/nlp/gate/.

[5] GDA, 2001, *Global Document Annotation*, available at http://www.i-content.org/GDA.

[6] GENIA corpus, 2001. GENIA project home page. http://www-tsujii.is.s.u-tokyo.ac.jp/GENIA/

[7] Grishman, R. 1995. *TIPSTER Phase II Architecture Design Document*, New York University, available at http://www.tipster.org/arch.htm.

[8] Jacquemin, C., Tzoukermann, E. 1999. *NLP for Term Variant Extraction: A Synergy of Morphology, Lexicon and Syntax.* In T. Strzalkowski, editor, Natural Language Information Retrieval, pages 25-74, Kluwer, Boston, M.

[9] Koyama, T., Yoshioka, M. and Kageura, K. 1998. *The Construction of a Lexically Motivated Corpus - The Problem with Defining Lexical Units.* In Proceedings of First International Conference on Language Resources and Evaluation, 1015—1019. Granada, Spain.

[10] MEDLINE 2001. National Library of Medicine, http://www.ncbi.nlm.nih.gov/PubMed/

[11] Mima, H., Ananiadou, S., Nenadic, G. 2001a. *ATRACT Workbench: An Automatic Term Recognition and Clustering of Terms,* in Text, Speech and Dialogue - TSD2001,Lecture Notes in AI 2166, Springer Verlag

[12] Mima, H. and Ananiadou, S., 2001b. *An Application and Evaluation of the C/NC-value Approach for the Automatic term Recognition of Multi-Word units in Japanese,* in International Journal on Terminology, Vol. 6(2) pp 175-194.

[13] Mima, H., Ananiadou, S. and Tsujii, J. 1999. *A Web-based integrated knowledge mining aid system using term-oriented natural language processing.* In Proceedings of The 5th Natural Language Processing Pacific Rim Symposium, NLPRS'99, pp. 13—18

[14] Miyao, Y., Makino, T., Torisawa, K. and Tsujii, J. 2000. *The LiLFeS abstract machine and its evaluation with the LinGO grammar.* Journal of Natural Language Engineering, Cambridge University Press, Vol. 6(1),

[15] Oi K., Sumita E. and Iida H. 1997. *Document Retrieval Method Using Semantic Similarity and Word Sense Disambiguation* (in Japanese). Journal of Natural Language Processing, Vol.4, No.3, pp.51-70.

[16] Visser, P.R.S., Jones, D.M., Bench-Capon, T.J.M. and Shave, M.J.R. 1997. *An Analysis of Ontology Mismatches; Heterogeneity versus Interoperability*, AAAI 1997 Spring Symposium on Ontological Engineering, Stanford University, California, USA.

[17] Uramoto N. and Takeda K. 1998. *Recent Trends in Information Description and Exchange on the Internet,* Journal of Japanese Society for Artificial Intelligence, Vol. 13, No. 4.

[18] Ushioda A. 1996. *Hierarchical Clustering of Words*, In Proc. of COLING '96, Copenhagen.

Maximum Entropy Estimation for Feature Forests

MIYAO Yusuke
Department of Computer Science,
University of Tokyo
Hongo 7-3-1, Bunkyo-ku, Tokyo 113-0033 Japan
yusuke@is.s.u-tokyo.ac.jp

TSUJII Jun'ichi
Department of Computer Science,
University of Tokyo
Hongo 7-3-1, Bunkyo-ku, Tokyo 113-0033 Japan
CREST, JST
(Japan Science and Technology Corporation)
tsujii@is.s.u-tokyo.ac.jp

ABSTRACT

An algorithm is proposed for maximum entropy modeling. It enables probabilistic modeling of complete structures, such as transition sequences in Markov models and parse trees, without dividing them into independent sub-events. A probabilistic event is represented by *a feature forest*, which is a packed representation of features with ambiguities. The parameters are efficiently estimated by traversing each node in a feature forest by dynamic programming. Experiments showed the algorithm worked efficiently even when ambiguities in a feature forest cause an exponential explosion of unpacked structures.

1. INTRODUCTION

Maximum entropy models [2] are widely used for probabilistic modeling of various tasks, such as part-of-speech tagging [9, 5] and parsing [10], because they achieve higher accuracy. However, studies so far have merely applied maximum entropy models to traditional, chain-rule-based models, such as n-grams and lexicalized versions of a probabilistic context-free grammar (PCFG). That is, an event is divided into *independent* sub-events, and the probability of the event is defined as the product of the probabilities of the sub-events. Such studies inherently restrict flexibility by independence assumption, which is not required for maximum entropy modeling.

The algorithm proposed in this paper enables probabilistic modeling of complete structures, such as transition sequences in Markov models and parse trees, without dividing them into *independent* sub-events. In general, complete structures have exponentially many possibilities, which is problematic in estimating parameters of a maximum entropy model. Our algorithm avoids an exponential explosion by representing an event by *a feature forest*, which is a packed representation of trees (or directed acyclic graphs). If a complete structure is represented by a feature forest of a tractable size, the parameters are efficiently estimated by dynamic programming similar to *the inside/outside algorithm* without unpacking the feature forest.

The proposed algorithm enables a more flexible model for various NLP tasks because it allows incorporating various overlapping features of a complete structure, not only of sub-events, into the model. Moreover, it can be applied to a probabilistic model of events that are difficult to divide into independent sub-events, such as a probabilistic model of feature structures [1].

Rosenfeld's study of a whole sentence maximum entropy model [11] had a similar motivation. However, the model was basically a sequence model, so it could not produce a solution for complex structures like our model can. Johnson et al. applied a maximum entropy model to a lexical functional grammar (LFG) [4], but they ignored the problem of an exponential explosion of unpacked parse results. We argue that the exponential explosion is inevitable, especially with large-scale wide-coverage grammars. In such cases, their method does not work. The forthcoming work of Johnson has the same motivation as ours [3]. The solution is similar to our approach, while their method is designed for directly traversing parse results with conditional disjunctions. We should also mention the work of Lafferty et al. in solving a similar problem in the context of maximum entropy Markov models [6]. Their solution was an algorithm similar to *the forward-backward algorithm*, and it is a special case of our algorithm in which each conjunctive node has only one daughter. This fact shows that our algorithm is applicable to various tasks, not only to parsing.

Section 2 overviews maximum entropy models and its applications. Section 3 discusses the problem with conventional maximum entropy modeling. Section 4 describes our algorithm for solving the problem. Section 5 discusses the evaluation of our algorithm using a parsing experiment.

2. MAXIMUM ENTROPY MODEL

Maximum entropy models [2] are widely used for probabilistic modeling of various NLP tasks, such as part-of-speech tagging [9, 5] and sentence parsing [10]. They do not require independence assumption to divide a probabilistic event into sub-events, enabling flexible modeling with many overlapping features. When modeling a probabilistic distribution of event $e = \langle t, h \rangle$, where t is *a target event* and h *a history event*, e is represented by a bundle of *feature functions* (or *features* for short) $f_i(e)$. A feature function represents the existence of a certain characteristic in event e, and a set of *activated* features, i.e., $f_i(e) \neq 0$, is considered to be an abstracted representation of an event.

Figure 1 shows an example of features in a simple maximum entropy bigram model for part-of-speech tagging[1]. As in conventional tagging models, an individual event is an assignment of a tag to a word, given previous words and tags as a context. The target event is a part-of-speech tag to be assigned, and the history event is

[1]Part-of-speech tags are of the Penn Treebank [7].

Proceedings of HLT 2002, Second International Conference on Human Language Technology Research, M. Marcus, ed., Morgan Kaufmann, San Francisco, 2002.

sentence	He	gave	books	to	his	sister .
part-of-speech	PRP	VBD	?			

feature	*target*	*current word*	*prev. word*	*prev. tag*
f_0	NNS	books	gave	-
f_1	VBZ	books	gave	-
f_2	NNS	books	gave	VBD
f_3	NNS	books	-	VBD
f_4	NNS	*ends_with_"s"*	-	-
f_5	VBZ	*ends_with_"s"*	-	-

Figure 1: Maximum entropy bigram model for part-of-speech tagging

a tuple ⟨*current word, previous word, previous tag*⟩. Each feature function represents a certain characteristic of the target and history events, and in particular, a maximum entropy model enables incorporating features that are not statistically independent, such as f_0, f_2 and f_3 in Figure 1. This enables flexible modeling with various kinds of overlapping features.

Formally, maximum entropy model p_M is a log-linear model that gives a conditional probability of event $e = \langle t, h\rangle$, where $\tau(h)$ is a set of targets observable with history h [2]:

$$p_M(t|h) = \frac{1}{Z_h}\prod_i \alpha_i^{f_i(t,h)}$$

$$\textit{where}\quad Z_h = \sum_{t'\in\tau(h)}\prod_i \alpha_i^{f_i(t',h)}$$

A feature function is an indicator for a certain characteristic of an event, and *model parameter* α_i corresponding to f_i is its weight. A maximum entropy model assigns a probability to an event by multiplying weights α_i when the corresponding features are activated, i.e., $f_i(e) \neq 0$. A maximum entropy model yields a probability distribution that maximizes the likelihood of the training data given a set of feature functions [2].

Note that the above model does not require independence of feature functions. It yields a maximum likelihood estimation even when the features are not independent, which is unattainable when using relative frequency estimation, as in traditional probabilistic models. This advantage enables flexible modeling with various kinds of overlapping feature functions, as described above. In addition, maximum entropy models can consistently model complex structures such as feature structures, which are difficult to decompose into independent events [1].

The improved iterative scaling (IIS) algorithm [8] (Figure 2) finds the model parameters that maximize the likelihood of the training data, $\tilde{p}(t,h)$, which is an observed distribution of events. The parameters are iteratively updated: $\alpha_i \leftarrow \alpha_i\Delta\alpha_i$, where $\Delta\alpha_i$ is the solution to the following equation.

$$\begin{aligned}\sum_{t,h}\tilde{p}(t,h)f_i(t,h) &= \sum_{t,h}\tilde{p}(h)p_M(t|h)f_i(t,h)\Delta\alpha_i^{f^{\#}(t,h)}\\ &= \sum_{f^{\#}}\Delta\alpha_i^{f^{\#}}\mu_{\langle i,f^{\#}\rangle}\end{aligned}$$

$$\textit{where}\quad f^{\#}(t,h) = \sum_i f_i(t,h)$$

The algorithm shown in Figure 2 implements this. Note that the algorithm is optimized by factoring the terms having the same $f^{\#}(t,h)$. The main part of the algorithm is the computation of *a factored model expectation* $\mu_{\langle i,f^{\#}\rangle}$, which is the expectation of feature f_i given by the model.

```
Input:  training data p̃(t, h),
  feature functions f_i(t, h), initial parameters α_i
Output:  optimal parameters α_i

E_i ← Σ p̃(t, h) f_i(t, h)
loop until α_i converges
  foreach e = ⟨t, h⟩
    foreach t' ∈ τ(h)
      foreach i such that f_i(t', h) ≠ 0
        μ_⟨i,f#(t',h)⟩ ← μ_⟨i,f#(t',h)⟩ + p̃(h) f_i(t', h) (1/Z_h) Π_k α_k^{f_k(t',h)}
      end_foreach
    end_foreach
  end_foreach
  foreach f_i
    Let Δα_i be the solution to the following equation:
      Σ_k μ_⟨i,k⟩ Δα_i^k = E_i
    α_i ← α_i Δα_i
  end_foreach
end_loop
```

Figure 2: Parameter estimation algorithm based on improved iterative scaling

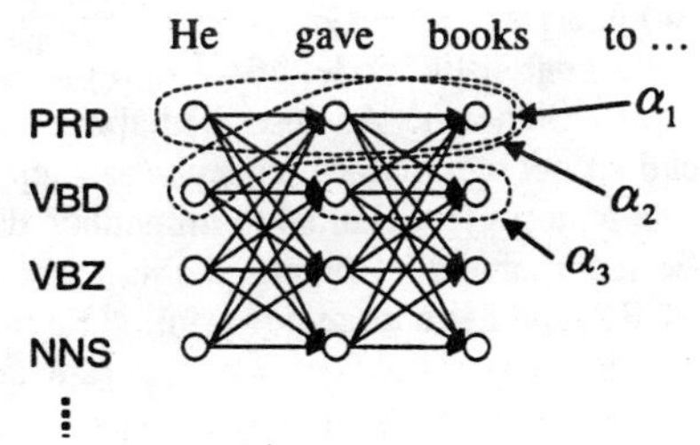

Figure 3: Maximum entropy tagging model without independence assumption

$$\mu_{\langle i,f^{\#}\rangle} = \sum_h \tilde{p}(h)\sum_{t'\in\tau(h)} f_i(t',h)p_M(t'|h)$$

The computational complexity of each iteration is $O(|\mathcal{T}||\mathcal{E}||F|)$, where $|\mathcal{T}|$, $|\mathcal{E}|$, and $|F|$ are the number of targets and events, and the average number of activated features, respectively. The algorithm is sufficiently efficient for various applications, such as part-of-speech tagging, because $|\mathcal{T}|$ and $|F|$ are usually small (more or less than 100), while $|\mathcal{E}|$ is large, as in other statistical models.

However, this model/algorithm still cannot be applied in some cases due to the problem described in the next section.

3. PROBLEM

Let us consider the maximum entropy modeling of tagging tasks. Conventional models divide a tagging sequence into a tagging event for each word [9, 5]. That is, the models incorporate independence assumption, which is not required in maximum entropy models. Figure 3 shows a tagging model without independence assumption, where the complete tag sequence for a sentence is considered to be a target event. The model chooses the most probable tag sequence from the set of all possible tag sequences. We can incorporate various dependent features such as bigram/trigram/n-gram features as in the figure. This model is an extension of conventional models, and it has a more powerful modeling scheme [6].

A similar argument can be made for the maximum entropy modeling of parsing. In conventional parsing models, similar to PCFGs, each branching is assumed to be an independent event, and the

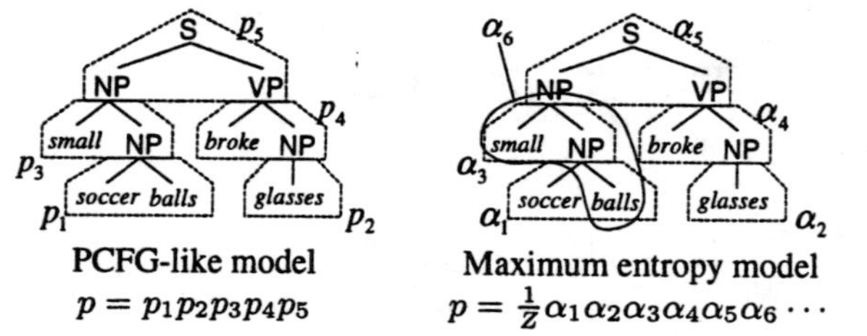

Figure 4: Probabilistic models for parsing

probability of the complete parse tree is defined as the product of the probabilities assigned to the branchings (left-hand side of Figure 4). On the other hand, we can consider a maximum entropy model that assigns a probability to the complete parse tree without independence assumption (right-hand side of Figure 4). Feature functions correspond to the branchings (or other characteristics such as α_6) in a parse tree. Given such features, the model is formulated as a probabilistic model of selecting parse tree t from a parse forest for sentence h. As described above, the maximum entropy model does not require independence assumption, and various overlapping features (not limited to immediate dominance relations) can be incorporated. Obviously, this model is a natural extension of PCFG, and has a more powerful modeling scheme.

The remaining issue we should consider is parameter estimation. The problem arises here: the number of targets t, (i.e., the number of possible tag sequences or parse trees for a sentence), is quite large in general. This is because local ambiguities in a tag sequence or a parse tree result in exponential growth in the number of structures, resulting in billions of structures. This is quite a problem, because, as described in Section 2, the complexity of parameter estimation is proportional to the number of targets. While a similar problem arises when using a PCFG to compute the probability of each parse tree, it can be avoided by using *the inside/outside algorithm*, which efficiently computes the probability of each parse tree by dynamic programming. Why don't we use the same approach?

This idea yields a new algorithm for parameter estimation, as described in the next section.

4. SOLUTION

Our solution to the problem is an efficient algorithm for parameter estimation using *the inside/outside α-product*. Similar to the inside/outside algorithm, we can compute the product of α_i for each node in tree structure. *An inside α-product* is the summation of each product of α_i in one of the daughter sub-trees. This value is incrementally computed by multiplying the inside α-products of the daughter nodes. *An outside α-product* is the summation of each product of α_i in the upper part of the trees. Given the inside α-products, this value is also incrementally computed by multiplying the outside α-product of the mother node and the inside α-products of the sister nodes. Given all inside/outside α-products, the model expectation, $\mu_{\langle i, f\# \rangle}$, is easily computed by multiplying them for each node.

To describe the algorithm, we first define *a feature forest*, a generalized representation of features in packed forest structure. Feature forests are used for enumerating possible structures of target events, that is, they correspond to $\tau(h)$ in conventional models described in Section 2.

DEFINITION 1 (FEATURE FOREST). *Feature forest Φ is a tuple $\langle C, D, r, \gamma, \delta \rangle$, where*

- *C is a set of conjunctive nodes*
- *D is a set of disjunctive nodes*
- *r is the root node: $r \in C$*
- *$\gamma : D \mapsto 2^C$ is a conjunctive daughter function*
- *$\delta : C \mapsto 2^D$ is a disjunctive daughter function*

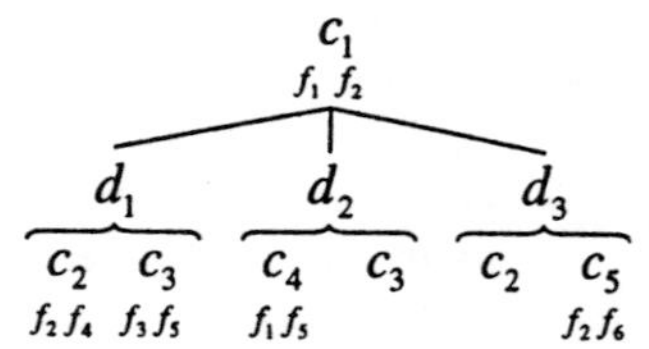

$$C = \{c_1, c_2, c_3, c_4, c_5\}$$
$$D = \{d_1, d_2, d_3\}$$
$$r = c_1$$
$$\gamma(d_1) = \{c_2, c_3\},\ \gamma(d_2) = \cdots$$
$$\delta(c_1) = \{d_1, d_2, d_3\},\ \delta(c_2) = \cdots$$

Figure 5: A feature forest

Feature functions are defined over conjunctive nodes[2], and thus a feature forest represents a set of trees of features, which are associated to conjunctive nodes. We denote a feature forest for history h (for a CFG, the activated features of a parse forest for a sentence) as $\Phi(h)$. We assume that a feature forest is acyclic and can be a directed acyclic graph. It is evident that the models introduced in Section 3 can be represented with this structure.

Figure 5 shows an example feature forest. Each disjunctive node has alternative nodes, which are conjunctive nodes. Each conjunctive node has activated features, i.e., $f_i(c) \neq 0$; it also has disjunctive nodes as daughters. A feature forest can include a reentrant structure, that is, a node can appear more than once in a feature forest, such as c_3 in d_1 and d_2.

Since Figure 5 resembles a parse forest of a PCFG, it might be asserted that a feature forest can represent only immediate dominance relations in each node, as in a PCFG, resulting in only a slight, trivial extension of the PCFG. However, a feature forest is a generalized representation of an ambiguous structure, and each node in a feature forest does not need to correspond to a node in a parse forest. That is, a node in a feature forest can represent any linguistic entity, including a fragment of a syntactic/semantic structure and other sentence-level information. Instances of a node can thus be neglected in the following discussion, and our algorithm is applicable whenever the feature forest is of a tractable size. However, a feature forest might be sometimes too large due to incorporating sentence-level features. In those cases, an approximation method to reduce the computational cost might be required [11].

As mentioned, a feature forest is a packed representation of feature sets, and each feature set is extracted by using the following function.

DEFINITION 2 (UNPACKING). Unpacking function σ *is a function*

- σ: $C \mapsto 2^C$

such that

$$\sigma(c) = \bigcup_{d_i \in \delta(c)} \{c_i\} \quad \textit{where} \quad c_i \in \gamma(d_i)$$

[2]While feature functions can also depend on history events, we omit the histories in the following discussion for simplicity.

We extend function σ to take set C as an argument:

$$\sigma(C) = \bigcup_{c \in C} \sigma(c)$$

Intuitively, unpacking function σ selects one conjunctive node for each disjunctive node. By applying this function to each node, we can extract the set of conjunctive nodes. Let us denote multiple applications of σ as σ^n, and a tree extracted from a feature forest is defined as follows.

DEFINITION 3 (UNPACKED TREE). *An unpacked tree rooted at conjunctive node $c \in C$ is defined as*

$$\sigma^*(c) = \bigcup_i \sigma^i(\{c\})$$

Each unpacked tree is then represented by $\sigma^*(r)$, and each function σ corresponds to each unpacked tree. Note that an unpacked tree is equivalent to a set of conjunctive nodes because our concern is only the set of features associated to each conjunctive node; the shape of the tree structure is irrelevant to probabilistic models. In this paper, we do not distinguish an unpacked tree from a set of conjunctive nodes.

The feature forest in Figure 5 represents a set of $2 \times 2 \times 2 = 8$ unpacked trees. For example, if we select the left-most conjunctive node at each disjunctive node, we extract tree $\{c_1, c_2, c_4, c_2\}$. Generally, a feature forest can represent an exponential number of trees with a polynomial number of nodes. Thus, a complete structure, such as tag sequences and parse trees with ambiguities, can be represented compactly.

Given the above formalization, a feature function for an unpacked tree is

$$f_i(\sigma^*(r)) = \sum_{c \in \sigma^*(r)} f_i(c)$$

Once a feature function for an unpacked tree is given, a factored model expectation can be defined as in the traditional model described in Section 2.

DEFINITION 4 (MODEL EXPECTATION). *Factored model expectation μ for a feature forest is defined as*

$$\mu_{\langle i, f^\# \rangle} = \sum_h \tilde{p}(h) \frac{1}{Z_h} \sum_\sigma f_i(\sigma^*(r)) \prod_{c \in \sigma^*(r)} \prod_{f_j} \alpha_j^{f_j(c)}$$

It is evident that the naive computation of factored model expectations requires exponential time complexity since the number of unpacked trees (i.e., σ) is exponentially related to the number of nodes in the feature forest. We thus need an algorithm for computing factored model expectations without unpacking a feature forest.

To efficiently compute the factored model expectations, we incorporate an approach similar to the inside/outside algorithm of a PCFG. We first define the notion of inside/outside for a feature forest.

DEFINITION 5 (INSIDE/OUTSIDE). *We define the* inside, *$\iota(c)$, of a feature forest at conjunctive node $c \in C$ as a set of unpacked trees:*

$$\iota(c) = \{C_i | C_i = \sigma_i^*(c)\}$$

The outside, *$o(c)$, is defined as*

$$o(c) = \{C_i \backslash \sigma_i^*(c) | C_i = \sigma_i^*(r)\}$$

Figure 6 illustrates this concept, which is similar to that of a PCFG. Inside denotes a set of partial trees (conjunctive nodes) derived from node c. Outside denotes the complement of the inside trees.

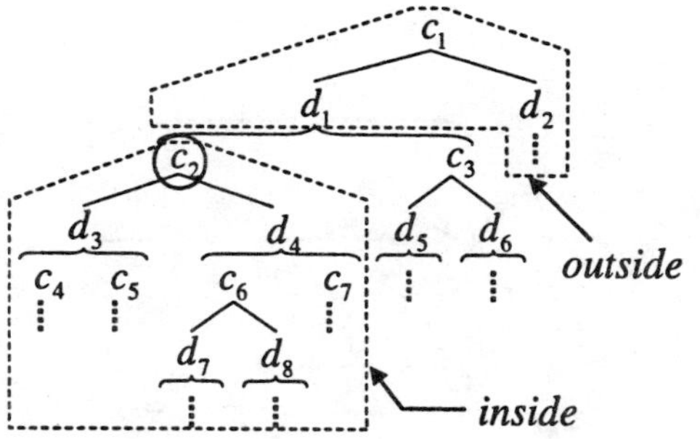

Figure 6: Inside/outside at node c_5 in a feature forest

An inside/outside α-product is then defined for each conjunctive/disjunctive node. The inside/outside α-products are the summation of the products of α in the inside/outside trees.

DEFINITION 6 (INSIDE/OUTSIDE α-PRODUCT). *An inside α-product at conjunctive node $c \in C$ is*

$$\phi_{\langle c, f^\# \rangle} = \sum_{C' \in \iota(c)} \prod_{c' \in C'} \prod_{f_i} \alpha_i^{f_i(c')}$$

$$\text{such that} \quad f^\# = \sum_{c' \in C'} \sum_{f_i} f_i(c')$$

An outside α-product is

$$\psi_{\langle c, f^\# \rangle} = \sum_{C' \in o(c)} \prod_{c' \in C'} \prod_{f_i} \alpha_i^{f_i(c')}$$

$$\text{such that} \quad f^\# = \sum_{c' \in C'} \sum_{f_i} f_i(c')$$

We can also define inside/outside α-products for disjunctive nodes:

$$\phi_{\langle d, f^\# \rangle} = \sum_{c \in \gamma(d)} \phi_{\langle c, f^\# \rangle}$$

$$\psi_{\langle d, f^\# \rangle} = \sum_{\{c | d \in \delta(c)\}} \psi_{\langle c, f^\# \rangle}$$

We can derive that the factored model expectation of a feature forest is defined as the product of the inside and outside α-products.

$$\mu_{\langle i, f^{\#_\phi} + f^{\#_\psi} \rangle} = \sum_h \tilde{p}(h) \frac{1}{Z_h} \sum_{c \in C} f_i(c) \phi_{\langle c, f^{\#_\phi} \rangle} \psi_{\langle c, f^{\#_\psi} \rangle}$$

This equation shows a method for efficiently computing the factored model expectation by traversing conjunctive nodes without unpacking the forest, if the inside/outside α-products are given. The remaining issue is how to efficiently compute the inside/outside α-products.

Fortunately, the inside/outside α-products can be incrementally computed by dynamic programming without unpacking the feature forest. Figure 7 shows the process of computing an inside α-product at a conjunctive node from the inside α-products of its daughter nodes. Since an inside α-product is the product of all α_i of its descendants, it is computed by multiplying the α-products of the daughter trees. We should take care of the computation of an index $f^\#$, and the following equation is derived.

$$\phi_{\langle c, f^\# \rangle} = \prod_{d \in \delta(c)} \phi_{\langle d, f^{\#_d} \rangle} \prod_{f_i} \alpha_i^{f_i(c)}$$

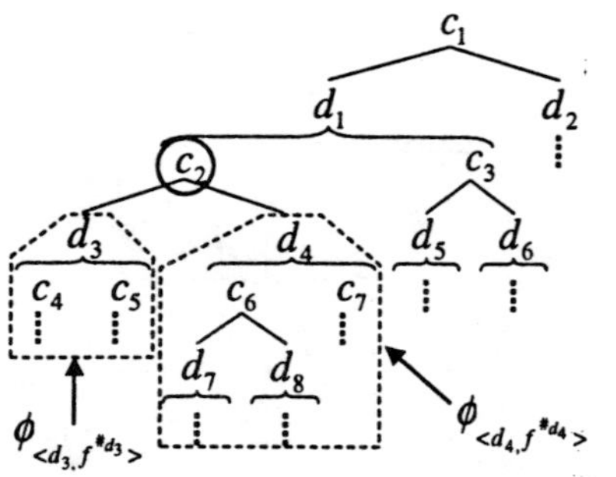

$$\phi_{\langle c_2, f^{\#d_3} + f^{\#d_4} + f^{\#} \rangle} = \phi_{\langle d_3, f^{\#d_3} \rangle} \phi_{\langle d_4, f^{\#d_4} \rangle} \prod_{f_i} \alpha_i^{f_i(c_2)}$$

Figure 7: Incremental computation of inside α-products at conjunctive node c_2

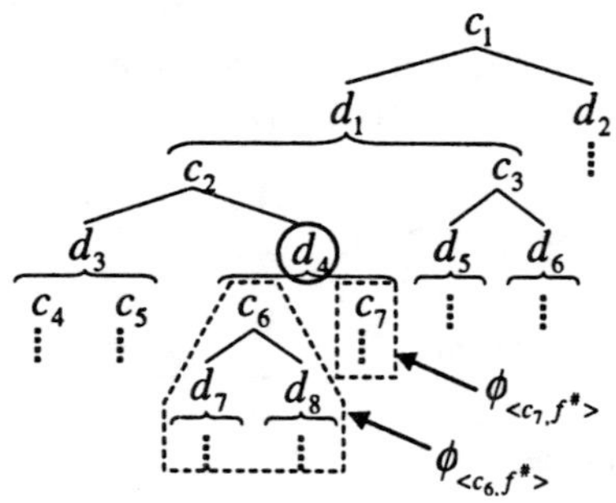

$$\phi_{\langle d_4, f^{\#} \rangle} = \phi_{\langle c_6, f^{\#} \rangle} + \phi_{\langle c_7, f^{\#} \rangle}$$

Figure 8: Incremental computation of inside α-products at disjunctive node d_4

$$\text{such that} \quad f^{\#} = \sum_d f^{\#d} + \sum_i f_i$$

The inside of a disjunctive node is the collection of the inside trees of its daughter nodes. Hence, the inside α-product at disjunctive node $d \in D$ is computed as follows (Figure 8).

$$\phi_{\langle d, f^{\#} \rangle} = \sum_{c \in \gamma(d)} \phi_{\langle c, f^{\#} \rangle}$$

The outside of a disjunctive node is equivalent to the outside of its daughter nodes, and the outside α-product of a disjunctive node is propagated to its daughter conjunctive nodes (Figure 9).

$$\psi_{\langle c, f^{\#} \rangle} = \sum_{\{d | c \in \gamma(d)\}} \psi_{\langle d, f^{\#} \rangle}$$

The computation of an outside α-product of a disjunctive node is a little more complicated. The outside trees of a disjunctive node are all combinations of (Figure 10)

- the outside trees of the mother nodes and
- the inside trees of the sister nodes.

From this, we get

$$\psi_{\langle d, f^{\#} \rangle} = \sum_{\{c | d \in \delta(c)\}} \left\{ \psi_{\langle c, f^{\#c} \rangle} \prod_{\{d' | d' \in \delta(c), d' \neq d\}} \phi_{\langle d', f^{\#d'} \rangle} \right\}$$

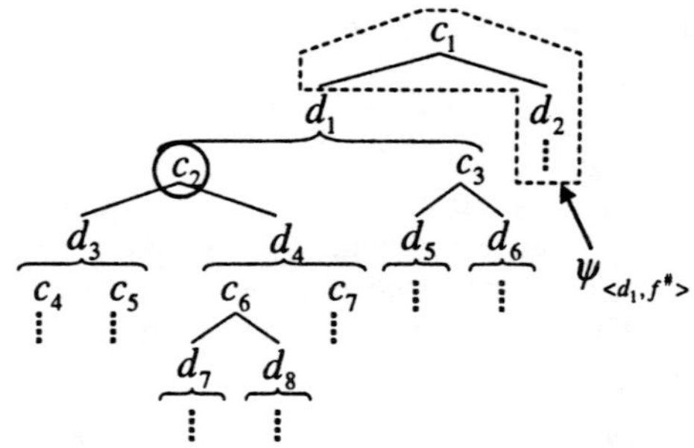

$$\psi_{\langle c_2, f^{\#} \rangle} = \psi_{\langle d_1, f^{\#} \rangle}$$

Figure 9: Incremental computation of outside α-products at conjunctive node c_2

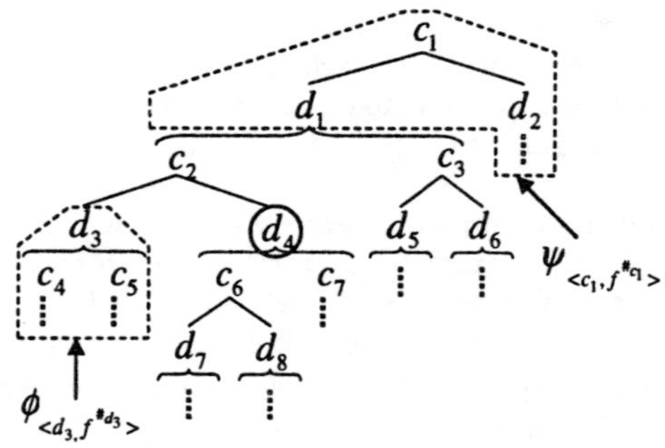

$$\psi_{\langle d_4, f^{\#c_2} + f^{\#d_3} \rangle} = \psi_{\langle c_2, f^{\#c_2} \rangle} \phi_{\langle d_3, f^{\#d_3} \rangle}$$

Figure 10: Incremental computation of outside α-products at disjunctive node d_4

$$\text{such that} \quad f^{\#} = f^{\#c} + \sum_{d'} f^{\#d'}$$

Figure 11 shows the overall algorithm for estimating the parameters, given a set of feature forests. The key point of the algorithm is to compute inside α-products ϕ and outside α-products ψ for each node in C, not for all unpacked trees. The functions `inside_product` and `outside_product` compute ϕ and ψ efficiently by dynamic programming. Note that the order of traversing nodes is important for incremental computation, although it is not shown in Figure 11. The computation for the daughter nodes and mother nodes must be finished before computing the inside and outside α-products, respectively. This constraint is easily solved using a topological sort.

The complexity of this algorithm is $O((|C|+|D|)|\mathcal{E}||F|)$, which is tractable when $|C|$ and $|D|$ are of a reasonable size. As noted in this section, the number of nodes in a feature forest is usually a polynomial even when that of the unpacked trees is exponential. This result shows that we can efficiently compute factored model expectations with polynomial computational complexity.

5. EVALUATION

The proposed algorithm was implemented in a maximum entropy estimator, and its correctness was tested experimentally by comparing the output of the original IIS with that of our algorithm. We also evaluated the efficiency and applicability of the algorithm by using a probabilistic model of an automatically extracted lexicalized tree adjoining grammar (LTAG).

```
Input:  training data p̃(t, h), feature forests Φ(h)
   feature functions f_i(c), initial parameters α_i
Output:  optimal parameters α_i

E_i ← Σ p̃(t, h) f_i(t, h)
loop until α_i converges
  foreach e = ⟨t, h⟩
    {φ} ← inside_product(Φ(h))
    {ψ} ← outside_product(Φ(h))
    foreach c ∈ C(Φ(h))
      foreach f_i(c) ≠ 0
        μ⟨i, f#φ + f#ψ⟩ ← μ⟨i, f#φ + f#ψ⟩
                          + (1/Z_h) f_i φ⟨c, f#φ⟩ ψ⟨c, f#ψ⟩
      end_foreach
    end_foreach
  end_foreach
  foreach f_i
    Let Δα_i be the solution to the following equation:
      Σ_k μ⟨i,k⟩ Δα_i^k = E_i
    α_i ← α_i Δα_i
  end_foreach
end_loop

function inside_product(Φ(h))
  foreach c ∈ C(Φ(h)), d ∈ D(Φ(h))
    φ⟨c, f#c⟩ ← Π_{d' ∈ δ(c)} φ⟨d', f#d'⟩ Π_{f_i} α_i^{f_i(c)}
        s.t.  f#c = Σ_{d'} f#d' + Σ_i f_i
    φ⟨d, f#⟩ ← Σ_{c' ∈ γ(d)} φ⟨c', f#⟩
  end_foreach
  return {φ}

function outside_product(Φ(h))
  foreach c ∈ C(Φ(h)), d ∈ D(Φ(h))
    ψ⟨c, f#⟩ ← Σ_{d' | c ∈ γ(d')} ψ⟨d', f#⟩
    ψ⟨d, f#⟩ ← Σ_{c' | d ∈ δ(c')} { ψ⟨c', f#c'⟩ Π_{d' ∈ δ(c'), d' ≠ d} φ⟨d', f#d'⟩ }
        s.t.  f# = f#c' + Σ_{d'} f#d'
  end_foreach
  return {ψ}
```

Figure 11: Parameter estimation algorithm for feature forests

Table 1: Experimental results

number of features	5715
number of sentences	868
avg. number of nodes	17412
required memory	1532 MB
required time	547 min.

The LTAG grammar we used was extracted from Section 00 of the Penn Treebank [7]. This section consists of 1603 sentences. The grammar was consistently extracted from about a half of the sentences (868 sentences), and consisted of 826 elementary tree templates for 3275 words. We parsed the sentences used for the grammar extraction and extracted the feature forests from the parse results. The parse trees were lexicalized; that is, each node in each tree was lexicalized using its head word. Each lexicalized parse forest consisted of 17,412 nodes on average; the number of unpacked parse trees could not be counted because it reached the limit for the `int` type (i.e., $> 2^{32}$).

Table 1 shows the results of estimating parameters using 100 iterations on a Pentium III 550-MHz CPU. In spite of the exponential growth in the number of unpacked parse trees, the estimator worked with a tractable cost. The results also show the algorithm costs somewhat more than traditional maximum entropy models. This is mainly because $|C| + |D|$ is much larger (17,412 on average, and more than 1,000,000 at the maximum) than with conventional models (100 or so). Although the proposed algorithm is more costly than conventional ones, it provides more flexibility and applicability with a tractable cost.

6. CONCLUSION

A new algorithm was presented for maximum entropy modeling and shown to be applicable to probabilistic parsing. Experimental results showed that it enables parameter estimation of probabilistic models of complete structures without independence assumption. It provides a more flexible modeling scheme than conventional algorithms, and furthermore, it is applicable to more complex structures where an event is difficult to decompose into independent sub-events, such as probabilistic modeling of feature structures.

Future work includes precise comparison of parsing models based on our algorithm with conventional ones. Furthermore, the model should be applicable to more complex representations, such as derivation trees in LTAG, feature structures, and predicate-argument structures. The algorithm described in this paper provides a consistent solution for probabilistic modeling of complex structures.

7. ACKNOWLEDGMENTS

We are very grateful to Dr. Takashi Ninomiya for his useful suggestions and encouragement. We would also like to thank the anonymous reviewers for their helpful comments.

8. REFERENCES

[1] S. P. Abney. Stochastic attribute-value grammars. *Computational Linguistics*, 23(4), 1997.

[2] A. L. Berger, S. A. D. Pietra, and V. J. D. Pietra. A maximum entropy approach to natural language processing. *Computational Linguistics*, 22(1):39–71, 1996.

[3] M. Johnson. Dynamic programming for parsing and estimation of stochastic unification-based grammars. To appear in Proc. 40th ACL, 2002.

[4] M. Johnson, S. Geman, S. Canon, Z. Chi, and S. Riezler. Estimators for stochastic "unification-based" grammars. In *Proc. ACL '99*, pages 535–541, 1999.

[5] J. Kazama, Y. Miyao, and J. Tsujii. A maximum entropy tagger with unsupervised hidden Markov models. In *Proc. NLPRS2001*, 2001.

[6] J. Lafferty, A. McCallum, and F. Pereira. Conditional random fields: Probabilistic models for segmenting and labeling sequence data. In *International Conference on Machine Learning 2001*, 2001.

[7] M. Marcus, G. Kim, M. A. Marcinkiewicz, R. MacIntyre, A. Bies, M. Ferguson, K. Katz, and B. Schasberger. The Penn Treebank: Annotating predicate argument structure. In *Proc. AAI '94*, 1994.

[8] S. D. Pietra, V. D. Pietra, and J. Lafferty. Inducing features of random fields. *IEEE Transactions on Pattern Analysis and Machine Intelligence*, 19(4):380–393, 1997.

[9] A. Ratnaparkhi. A maximum entropy model for part-of-speech tagging. In *Proc. Empirical Methods in Natural Language Processing Conference*, 1996.

[10] A. Ratnaparkhi. A linear observed time statistical parser based on maximum entropy models. In *Proc. Empirical Methods in Natural Language Processing Conference*, 1997.

[11] R. Rosenfeld. A whole sentence maximum entropy language model. In *Proc. IEEE Workshop on Automatic Speech Recognition and Understanding*, 1997.

DialogXML: Extending VoiceXML for Dynamic Dialog Management

Eric Nyberg, Teruko Mitamura,
Paul Placeway and Michael Duggan
Language Technologies Institute
Carnegie Mellon University
Pittsburgh, PA 15213
ehn,teruko,pwp,md5i@cs.cmu.edu

Nobuo Hataoka
Central Research Laboratory
Hitachi Ltd.
Kokubunji, Tokyo, Japan
hataoka@crl.hitachi.co.jp

ABSTRACT

The characteristics of VoiceXML make it an attractive choice for the implementation of embedded dialog systems on networked hardware. Nevertheless, VoiceXML lacks some important features found in existing proprietary approaches. It is difficult to build a complex, multi-dialog system directly in VoiceXML. This paper describes DialogXML, an extension to VoiceXML that supports a more implicitly declarative language for dialog scenarios, and ScenarioXML, a straightforward combination of DialogXML with the template-filling mechanism of Java Server Pages. The paper describes an initial prototype system, which extends the OpenVXI VoiceXML interpreter for DialogXML, implements a web server for ScenarioXML, and utilizes the KANTOO natural language analyzer for understanding user inputs.

1. INTRODUCTION

Depending on the nature of the task, a dialog system might utilize different dialog representations of varying degrees of complexity. The simplest approach involves the use of a hierarchy of menus or state transition graphs, which restrict the user to a fixed set of pre-defined dialog turns. More sophisticated systems support mixed initiative, where the precise number and sequence of dialog turns are not pre-defined. Some tasks (e.g. navigation or route planning) require dynamic creation of dialog turns at run time, based on access to a remote database or information service [7, 2, 3, 11, 9].

The proposed W3C standard for VoiceXML [13] provides a representation for flexible form-filling in a dialog scenario. A single VoiceXML element can contain several form elements, which correspond to dialog states. A form can invoke multiple grammars in order to recognize the user's input. The system's response depends on which context variables have been set as a result of input matching. Through the use of conditional expressions and goto statements, the VoiceXML interpreter may transition to a different form in the current VoiceXML structure, or to a new VoiceXML structure. Transitions within the current structure are local to the VoiceXML interpreter; transitions from one VoiceXML structure to another are triggered by URLs which are retrieved via HTTP/CGI (see Figures 6 and 7).

The characteristics of VoiceXML make it an attractive choice for the implementation of embedded dialog systems on networked hardware. The VoiceXML interpreter may rely on remote server(s) to provide the sequence of dialog scenarios to be presented to the user. Nevertheless, VoiceXML lacks some important features found in existing proprietary approaches, such as the HDDL description language supported by Philips SpeechMania [2, 3]. While the form-filling action of the VoiceXML interpreter does not impose a particular dialog ordering upon the user, and could be thought of as a simple agenda or plan-based dialog manager, it is difficult to build a complex, multi-dialog system directly in VoiceXML. If an application requires several related dialogs, and flexible switching between dialogs and subdialogs, all possible transitions from a given state must be coded exhaustively by hand. This is less preferable than the more declarative approach taken in HDDL, where dialogs are defined as separate scenarios and the system automatically handles transitions between dialogs.

Our goal is to extend VoiceXML to make it more practical for large-scale dialog systems. We envision a mobile application environment (e.g. a mobile information system) where an embedded speech recognizer and VoiceXML interpreter are connected to remote servers that support a variety of information-seeking tasks (car navigation, restaurant information, voice-activated control, etc.). While we prefer the simplicity of VoiceXML for run-time processing, a more supportive representation is required for creation of the dialog scenarios. It should be possible for different developers to write dialog scenarios independently – a given developer should not need to know the names of the other dialogs, their states, etc. in advance in order to write his or her own dialogs. It should also be possible to integrate the VoiceXML interpreter with more sophisticated natural language analyzers, to take advantage of the broader coverage and deeper linguistic analysis provided by unification grammar-based systems [6].

This paper describes DialogXML, an extension to VoiceXML that supports a more implicitly declarative language for dialog scenarios. We also introduce ScenarioXML, a straightforward combination of DialogXML with the template-filling mechanism of Java Server Pages (JSP) [12]. ScenarioXML provides an easy way to dynamically generate content (e.g. navigation directions accessed from a remote database). Dialog scenarios in ScenarioXML are also JSP pages. Dynamic content creation and compilation of DialogXML to VoiceXML are handled automatically at run time through the invocation of JSP filters by the web server. We also describe the integration of the OpenVXI VoiceXML interpreter with

Proceedings of HLT 2002, Second International Conference on Human Language Technology Research, M. Marcus, ed., Morgan Kaufmann, San Francisco, 2002.

the unification grammar and pattern matching components of the KANTOO natural language analyzer [6] (see Figure 1).

We have constructed an initial prototype system that handles text input. The next phase of our research will address the integration of the dialog management system with speech recognition and understanding. Therefore this paper does not address an important set of issues related to robustness at the speech recognition / NLP interface. The proposed architecture is independent of and neutral with respect to speech recognition; any approach which can be integrated via the `grammar` mechanism in VoiceXML can be utilized.

In Section 2, we introduce DialogXML and ScenarioXML. In Section 3, we present the details of the architecture and the current implementation. In Section 4, we summarize the current status of the system and discuss our planned research activities for the future.

2. DIALOG XML AND SCENARIO XML

The use of VoiceXML with a suitable interpreter has generated substantial interest as an effective way to develop simple command and control systems [13]. However, in order to use an existing VoiceXML interpreter in more complex environments with dynamic context and context switching, some enhancements to the VoiceXML representation and interpretation process are desirable.

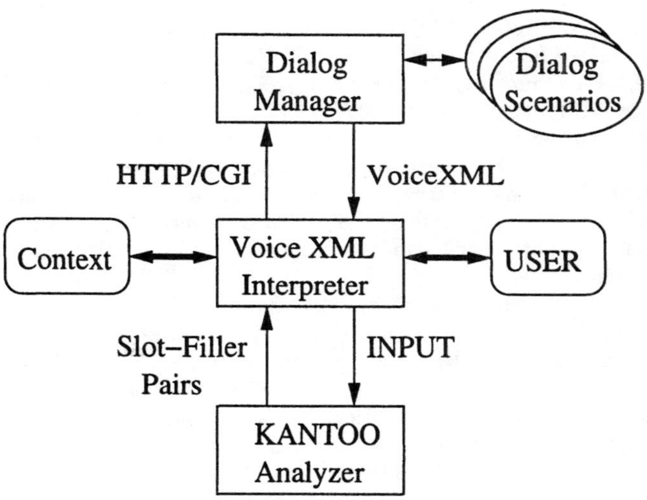

Figure 1: Modular Architecture

Most VoiceXML dialog systems use simple context-free language models for user utterances. In order to support full natural language parsing (e.g., with a unification grammar), the VoiceXML interpreter must be extended to handle `grammar` elements that contain references to more sophisticated grammar modules.

Natural dialog has a notion of state, and dialog designers often think in terms of state-transition networks. VoiceXML supports simple form and action pairs, but does not explicitly model states and transitions among states. Although it is possible to author and maintain a set of large-scale dialogs directly using VoiceXML, it would be tedious and time-consuming to do so.

2.1 Dialog XML

To address these issues, we have formulated a new level of representation, called Dialog XML (DXML), which clearly expresses the notion of states and transitions. Furthermore, each element in Dialog XML has an unambiguous mapping to a corresponding set of VoiceXML elements, so that Dialog XML can be automatically compiled to VoiceXML. An example Dialog XML structure is shown in Figure 5. The corresponding (compiled) VoiceXML structure is shown in Figures 6 and 7.

In Dialog XML, transitions between states in a dialog are clearly represented by `arc` elements which contain `grammar` and destination (`dest`) elements. This makes the structure of the resulting dialog much easier to follow visually. Note that the corresponding VoiceXML structure does not directly link or encapsulate the grammar and destination together. In VoiceXML 1.0, the `form` element allows its `grammar` and `filled` tags to appear anywhere. By enforcing a more dialog-centric structure, Dialog XML provides a more convenient notation for the dialog designer.

Transitions in Dialog XML include `dest` and `push`. The `dest` element is directly mapped to the `filled` element in Voice XML. However, the `push` element cannot be directly mapped to a corresponding VoiceXML element. Instead, each `push` is mapped into a specially constructed `form` element which invokes a subdialog and returns to the current state. For example, the single, concise `push` in the second arc in state `s1` in Figure 5 corresponds to the (much more complicated) third `form` element in Figure 6.

2.2 Scenario XML

An independent consideration is how the system will handle dynamic content and linking between dialogs. In a system with a wide variety of possible interactions or information exchanges, it becomes necessary to work with templates rather than static, hard-wired states and transitions. Since our goal is to use VoiceXML interpretation at run-time, some higher-level representation must be provided to represent dynamic content in a more abstract manner.

To address this need, Dialog XML is combined with a template-filling system (Java Server Pages [12]), deriving a higher-level representation we refer to as Scenario XML. Java Server Pages are used to express dynamic content (see Figure 4). In the example, the arcs which follow the `prompt` element are filled in by invoking a filter (`common-arcs.jspf`) that will derive the possible set of transitions by examining the available set of dialogs for triggering grammars. The four arcs generated by this call in the current system follow the `prompt` in Figure 5. The process of gathering the triggering conditions for a set of dialogs into a set of arcs is visually represented n Figure 2.

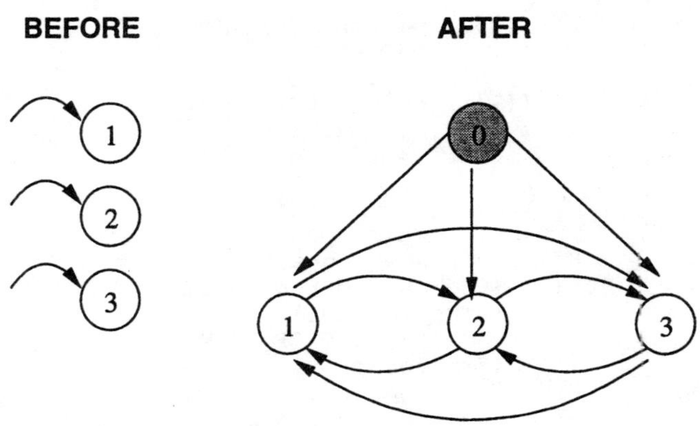

Figure 2: Arc Compilation

The Scenario XML example illustrates two important characteristics of our approach: a) when dialogs share a considerable amount of content and/or structure, this can be written once in a shared template; b) dialogs can be constructed independently of one another, since the system will insert global transitions to other dialogs automatically. This is important because requiring the human developer to maintain a correct and consistent treatment of global transitions across a large set of dialogs with many states is cumbersome and error-prone.

3. ARCHITECTURE AND DATA FLOW

The architecture shown in Figure 1 illustrates how the Dialog Manager component interacts with the VoiceXML Interpreter and KANTOO Analyzer. The system is started by calling the VoiceXML Interpreter on the JSP page that represents the top-level dialog scenario (`main.jsp`, see Figure 4). The JSP URL is fetched from the Dialog Manager (web browser), which invokes the appropriate JSP calls to fill in the dynamic information. The Dialog Manager also invokes a JSP filter which converts the higher-order DialogXML constructs into their low-level VoiceXML forms[1]. The resulting VoiceXML page is passed back to the VoiceXML interpreter, which the prints the prompt and initiates the dialog with the user.

Once the user has entered some input, the system will test all of the `grammar` elements in the current `form`; these correspond to the arcs in a particular dialog state in the original DialogXML. In order to integrate the use of full NL analysis, we extended the `grammar` interpretation mechanism in VoiceXML by defining a new grammar type, `kantoo/patrick`. This involves creation of a new type-to-class mapping, and coding of a new class that implements the abstract `grammar` interface (these are straightforward extensions, which are directly supported by the VoiceXML implementation).

The KANTOO Analyzer processes the user input to produce an interlingua expression (semantic frame). The individual `grammar` elements in VoiceXML refer to pattern-matching rules which are unified with the interlingua, possibly setting slot-filler values in a context variable as a side-effect (see Figure 3). The main advantage of this approach is that multiple variations of the same utterance can be recognized by a single semantic pattern rule, a useful improvement over simpler context-free or regular-expression grammars.

```
;; This PATRICK rule file handles the
;; top-level switch to the directions module.
;; It accepts an optional location and
;; destination.
(node DIRECTIONS :rules
  ((*TRY*
    ((*OR* ((%(ir patient CONCEPT)
             =c *O-DIRECTION)
            (%dir <= %(ir patient)))
           ((%(ir object CONCEPT)
             =c *O-DIRECTION)
            (%dir <= %(ir object)))
           )
     ;; This is our convention for
     ;; reporting which pattern matched
     (%(x "directions_request") = "accept")
     (*TRY* ((%pp <= %(dir q-modifier))
             (%(pp CONCEPT)
               =c "*Q-SOURCE_FROM")
             (%(x location)
               = %(pp object CONCEPT))))
     (*TRY* ((%pp <= %(dir q-modifier))
             (%(pp CONCEPT) =c "*Q-GOAL_TO")
             (%(x destination)
               = %(pp object CONCEPT))))))
  )
```

Figure 3: Sample Context Rule

[1] A full description of the DXML to VoiceXML compiler is beyond the scope of this document.

In the standard VoiceXML interpreter, subdialogs can only influence the outcome of a parent dialog through their return value. Since the parsing of a complex NL input might provide several important pieces of information about the context (current location, destination, etc.), it was necessary to extend the context-handling capabilities of VoiceXML. The new grammar type can return a set of slot-filler context variables to the VoiceXML interpreter, which merges this information with the existing dialog context.

Another feature of standard VoiceXML is that the context of a particular dialog does not persist when a new dialog is invoked. Since we require the ability to maintain context across two sequential dialogs (e.g., if the user asks about parking at a location following a navigation scenario), it was necessary to modify the VoiceXML interpreter to maintain context across dialogs unless an explicit reset is encountered.

While implementing these features did involve modifications to the VoiceXML Interpreter itself (and should be considered a proposed extension to the 1.0 standard), the modifications were minor, involving less than 20 lines of source code. As a result, the VoiceXML interpreter becomes a "stateful" rather than "stateless" client in the architecture.

4. CURRENT STATUS AND FUTURE WORK

The first prototype of this system has been implemented using the Speechworks VXML Interpreter [10], Tomcat web server [5] and KANTOO Analyzer [6]. The Dialog Manager (Tomcat) and KANTOO run on a single server machine, which is accessed by the VXML Interpreter via HTTP/CGI (Tomcat) and TCP/IP (KANTOO). A set of simple navigational dialogs have been implemented in English, which feature information about directions and parking that are dynamically accessed from a separate database. The compilation of ScenarioXML and DialogXML to VoiceXML is carried out in real time, and requires at most only a few seconds per invocation.

Our next steps include: a) extending the system to Japanese; b) adding other information-seeking tasks (e.g. restaurant information) and control tasks (car systems interface); c) integration with real-time speech recognition. We believe that DialogXML and the proposed extensions to VoiceXML will provide a useful open-source system that is much more suitable for dialog management in large-scale practical applications than VoiceXML alone.

```
<DialogXML>
<dialog name="main">
  <state name="s0">
    <arc>
      <dest state="s1"/>
    </arc>
  </state>
  <state name="s1">
    <action><prompt>
      How can I help you?
    </prompt></action>
<%@ include
  file="dxml-templates/common-arcs.jspf" %>
    <arc>
      <dest state="s0"/>
    </arc>
  </state>
</dialog>
</DialogXML>
```

Figure 4: Sample ScenarioXML

```
<DialogXML>
<dialog name="main">
  <state name="s0">
    <arc>
      <dest state="s1"/>
    </arc>
  </state>
  <state name="s1">
    <action><prompt>
      How can I help you?
    </prompt></action>
    <arc>
      <grammar src="directions_help.pat"
               type="kantoo/patrick"/>
      <push dialog="directions-help.jsp" />
    </arc>
    <arc>
      <grammar src="directions_request.pat"
               type="kantoo/patrick"/>
      <push dialog="directions-request.jsp"/>
    </arc>
    <arc>
      <grammar src="parking_request.pat"
               type="kantoo/patrick"/>
      <push dialog="parking-request.jsp"/>
    </arc>
    <arc>
     <grammar src="top_level_no_context.pat"
              type="kantoo/patrick"/>
     <dest dialog="main.jsp"/>
    </arc>
    <arc>
      <dest state="s0"/>
    </arc>
  </state>
</dialog>
</DialogXML>
```

Figure 5: Sample DialogXML

```
<vxml version="1.0">
  <form id="main.s0">
      <block>
        <if cond="delete DMEnv.topic"/>
        <goto next="#main.s1"/>
      </block>
  </form>
  <form id="main.s1">
    <grammar src="top_level_no_context.pat"
             type="kantoo/patrick"/>
    <grammar src="park_req.pat"
             type="kantoo/patrick"/>
    <grammar src="dir_req.pat"
             type="kantoo/patrick"/>
    <grammar src="dir_help.pat"
             type="kantoo/patrick"/>
    <block>
      <prompt>How can I help you?</prompt>
    </block>
    <block cond="DMEnv.top_level_no_context
                != undefined">
      <goto next="main.jsp"/>
    </block>
    <field expr="DMEnv.top_level_no_context"
           name="top_level_no_context"/>
    <block cond="DMEnv.park_req
                != undefined">
      <if cond="delete DMEnv.park_req"/>
      <goto next="#main.s1.arc2"/>
    </block>
    <field expr="DMEnv.park_req"
           name="park_req"/>
    <block cond="DMEnv.dir_req
                != undefined">
      <if cond="delete DMEnv.dir_req"/>
      <goto next="#main.s1.arc1"/>
    </block>
    <field expr="DMEnv.dir_req"
           name="dir_req"/>
    <block cond="DMEnv.dir_help
                != undefined">
      <if cond="delete DMEnv.dir_help"/>
      <goto next="#main.s1.arc0"/>
    </block>
    <field expr="DMEnv.dir_help"
           name="dir_help"/>
    <filled namelist="dir_help">
      <if cond="delete DMEnv.dir_help"/>
      <goto next="#main.s1.arc0"/>
    </filled>
    <filled namelist="dir_req">
      <if cond="delete DMEnv.dir_req"/>
      <goto next="#main.s1.arc1"/>
    </filled>
    <filled namelist="park_req">
      <if cond="delete DMEnv.park_req"/>
      <goto next="#main.s1.arc2"/>
    </filled>
    <filled namelist="top_level_no_context">
      <goto next="main.jsp"/>
    </filled>
    <block>
      <goto next="#main.s0"/>
    </block>
  </form>
```

Figure 6: Sample VoiceXML (Part I)

```
  <form id="main.s1.arc0">
      <subdialog name="retval"
                 src="directions-help.jsp">
          <filled>
              <if cond="retval.retval">
                  <goto next="#main.s1"/>
                  <else/>
                  <goto next="#main.s1"/>
              </if>
          </filled>
      </subdialog>
  </form>
  <form id="main.s1.arc1">
      <subdialog name="retval"
                 src="directions-request.jsp">
          <filled>
              <if cond="retval.retval">
                  <goto next="#main.s1"/>
                  <else/>
                  <goto next="#main.s1"/>
              </if>
          </filled>
      </subdialog>
  </form>
  <form id="main.s1.arc2">
      <subdialog name="retval"
                 src="parking-request.jsp">
          <filled>
              <if cond="retval.retval">
                  <goto next="#main.s1"/>
                  <else/>
                  <goto next="#main.s1"/>
              </if>
          </filled>
      </subdialog>
  </form>
</vxml>
```

Figure 7: Sample VoiceXML (Part II)

Acknowledgements

The authors thank Denso Corporation and Hitachi Ltd. for their support of this research.

5. REFERENCES

[1] Araki, M., K. Ueda, T. Nishimoto and Y. Y. Niimi (2001). "Dialogue scenario generation from XML-based database", Proceedings of the 1st NLP and XML Workshop, held at the Sixth Natural Language Processing Pacific Rim Symposium, Nov. 27-30, Tokyo, Japan, http://www.afnlp.org/nlprs2001

[2] Aust, Harald and Olaf Schröer (1998). "An Overview of the Philips Dialog System", Proceedings of the DARPA Broadcast News Transcription and Understanding Workshop February 8-11, 1998, Lansdowne, Virginia.

[3] Baum, M., G. Erbach, M. Kommenda, G. Niklfeld and E. Puig-Waldmüller (2001). "Speech and Multimodal Dialogue Systems for Telephony Applications Based on a Speech Database of Austrian German", ÖGAI Journal 20/1, pp.29-34, 2001. http://www.ftw.at

[4] Belvin, R., *et al.*, "Development of the HRL Route Navigation Dialogue System", *Proc. HLT 2001*, pp. 74–78.

[5] Jakarta Tomcat, http://jakarta.apache.org/tomcat.

[6] Nyberg, E. and T. Mitamura (2000). "The KANTOO Machine Translation Environment", *Proceedings of AMTA 2000.*

[7] Price, P. (1990). "Evaluation of Spoken Language Systems : The ATIS domain", *Proc. 3rd DARPA Workshop on Speech and Natural Language*.

[8] Ramakrishnan, N., *et al.*, "Mixed-Initiative Interaction = Mixed Computation", *Proc. ACM SIGPLAN Workshop PEPM'02*, January 2002

[9] Seneff, S., *et al.*, "Organization, Communication, and Control in the Galaxy-II Conversational System", *Proc. Eurospeech 99.*

[10] SpeechWorks OpenVXI 2.0.1, http://www.speech.cs.cmu.edu/openvxi

[11] David Stallard, "Talk-n-Travel: A Conversational System for Air Travel Planning," in Proceedings of the Association for Computational Linguistics 6th Applied Natural Language Processing Conference (ANLP 2000), Seattle, Washington, April 29 - May 4, 2000, pp. 68-75.

[12] Sun Microsystems (2002). "Java Server Pages", http://java.sun.com/products/jsp.

[13] VXML 1.0, 03/07/00, http://www.w3.org

MeetingLogger: Rich Transcription of Courtroom Speech*

Rohit Prasad, Long Nguyen, Richard Schwartz, John Makhoul
BBN Technologies, Cambridge MA 02138.
{rprasad,ln,schwartz,makhoul}@bbn.com

ABSTRACT

In this paper we describe our on-going effort in developing a speech recognition system for transcribing courtroom hearings. Court hearings are a rich source of naturally occurring speech data, much of which is in public domain. The presence of multiple microphones coupled with presence of noise and reverberation makes the problem simultaneously rich and challenging. We have exploited the availability of multiple channels to mitigate, to some extent, the severe noise problem prevalent in courtroom speech. By using a novel technique for channel change detection, domain-specific language modeling, and unsupervised channel adaptation we have been able to achieve a word error rate (WER) of 36% with an acoustic model trained on 150 hours of broadcast news data. We also report on our preliminary acoustic modeling experiments with the "legal" transcripts provided with 120 hours of courtroom speech training data.

1. INTRODUCTION

The benefits of having a system that can automatically record, transcribe, index, and archive minutes of court hearings are many and obvious. Court hearings challenge existing speech and language technologies in a number of dimensions, including the presence of various types of noise, reverberation, simultaneous speakers, and multiple distant microphones. In this paper we describe our exploratory work in developing a speech recognition system that will provide rich transcription of courtroom hearings.

To develop an understanding for the problems posed by courtroom speech, we started acquiring a corpus of real-world court hearings. In particular, we have partnered with FTR Pty Ltd., a leading supplier of court and hearing room digital recording systems, to supply us with digital speech data and the corresponding "legal" transcripts. Till date, we have received 165 hours of audio data for 125 courtroom sessions.

In section 2, we describe the audio data collection process and the various characteristics of the data. In Section 3, we present our initial recognition results with a small amount of supervised acoustic training and domain-specific language modeling. In Section 4, we report recognition accuracy improvements with an acoustic model trained on broadcast news data, which have resulted in a word error rate (WER) of 36% on this difficult task. In Section 5, we present recognition results with acoustic models trained on large amount of court hearings in lightly supervised mode using the legal transcripts.

*This work was sponsored by the Defense Advanced Research Projects Agency under Contract No. N66001-99-D-8615 and monitored by SPAWAR.

Proceedings of HLT 2002, Second International Conference on Human Language Technology Research, M. Marcus, ed., Morgan Kaufmann, San Francisco, 2002.

2. COURTROOM CORPUS

2.1 Courtroom Speech Data

When recording a courtroom proceeding digitally, typically multiple microphones are placed in different positions in the courtroom: one for the judge, one for the witness, one on each of the two attorneys' desks, and the others are located next to the jury and other locations. It is not unusual to have as many as eight microphones in a courtroom. The digital audio signals from the different microphones are then mixed and recorded over either 2 or 4 channels. A person in the courtroom monitors the recording and enters *log notes*, which include timestamps and the names of the people speaking in the courtroom. Later, a human transcriber prepares a transcript of the session by listening to the recording and typing the transcript into a computer. The final legal transcript is a cleaned-up version of what was spoken and it includes the name of the speaker at each speaker turn, and other data taken from the log notes.

The data we have received from FTR includes the audio data, the log notes, as well as the legal transcript. Most of the audio files are 4-channel audio with a sampling frequency of 22.05 KHz. The files are time-stamped and are of 5 min. duration each. The legal transcripts, however, are in a single document per session and mostly do not contain any timestamps. So, we do not have a direct or simple correspondence between the transcripts and the audio data.

Our study has indicated that the quality of the audio data is highly variable. The microphones around the courtroom pick up various types of background noise and non-speech events like coughing, laughing, whispering, paper rustling, etc. We have also observed that the speaking style in the courtroom is very spontaneous. This is illustrated in the following passage from a judge.

```
I also appreciate uh Mr. uh, uh, Jessup's
um uh willingness to go forward and uh be
uh as forthcoming as uh he uh can. But I,
I, I still think we're on a little bit of
a precipice here, Mr. Kennedy.
```

Besides the quality of speech mentioned above, the legal transcripts presented a number of problems for our work. One problem was the lack of timestamps in the transcripts, so it is not easy to match the transcripts to the speech. Another problem is that some audio segments were never transcribed, while in other cases there was text with no corresponding audio. Moreover, these transcripts were generated to provide content rather than providing faithful annotation for training acoustic models. So, they lack most of the non-speech events and do not include hesitations and restarts.

2.2 Test and Training data

The criterion we used for selecting the test data was the session duration. We chose the 8 smallest sessions as our test set, which totaled 6 hours of audio. The remainder of the data we planned to use for acoustic and language training. On the average there are 5 speakers per test session and tend to be primarily male speakers. The test sessions covered topics such as, corporate bankruptcy, insurance coverage, driving under influence, and car accident.

Since the legal transcripts are not accurate enough for evaluation purposes, we decided to have the entire test set transcribed, i.e., each of the 5 min. audio chunks had an accurate transcription associated with it. The transcripts were prepared by a commercial transcription company. For controlled acoustic modeling experiments, we also had 8 hours from 5 sessions transcribed accurately. We found that the mismatch, in terms of WER, between accurate transcriptions (AT) and the legal transcripts (LT) from FTR was 25%, as illustrated in the alignment result below.

```
AT: I I I appreciate uh very much um
LT: * * I appreciate ** very much **
```

This means that we can not use the legal transcripts as-is for acoustic modeling.

3. INITIAL EXPERIMENT

3.1 Data Pre-processing

First for both 8 hours training and 6 hours test data, we separated the multiple data streams from the 4-channel FTR audio. Then, for convenience, we added the four different streams to form a single signal. We also down-sampled the signal to 16KHz for compatibility with the other audio data we already had. The resulting 5-min. audio files were segmented into smaller chunks by using Broadcast News [1] acoustic models for Viterbi alignment of the transcript with the audio. And then, segmenting during silence segments of at least 200 ms.

3.2 Supervised Acoustic Modeling

We trained speaker and gender independent acoustic models on 8 hours of manually transcribed data. The training audio segments were analyzed to extract the conventional 45-dimensional feature vector comprising 14 mel-frequency cepstral coefficients (MFCCs), energy, and their first and second derivatives. To enhance robustness to channel variations, the features extracted from the speech signal were normalized using RASTA [2] processing. We estimated triphone models using Phonetically-Tied Mixtures (PTM) and State-Clustered Tied Mixtures (SCTM). The PTM models used a set of 256 Gaussians for all the states of triphone models for each center phoneme, for a total of 13K Gaussians, and 7K sets of mixture weights. The SCTM models used about 500 distinct sets of 64 Gaussians for a total of 32K Gaussians, also with 7K sets of mixture weights.

3.3 Language Modeling

Domain-specific language modeling is critical for achieving the best recognition performance. After selecting the test and training data, we had legal transcripts for 28 sessions remaining. These 28 sessions had around 400K words, which is not sufficient training data for language modeling. Therefore, we surfed the Web for sources of text from court proceedings. Thus far, we have downloaded 22M words of such text. Even though this type of text did not correspond exactly to the acoustics of what was said in the actual proceedings, we felt it should be helpful nonetheless since the domain is at least the same.

We trained both bigram and trigram language models with a simplified backoff strategy [3] using both language data sources. The lexicon size for this language model was 52K words, and the out-of-vocabulary (OOV) rate was 1.1%.

3.4 Recognition Results

The recognition system used was a simple configuration of the BBN BYBLOS system [1, 4]. The first pass uses a single-phonetic-tree fast-match algorithm with PTM models and a bigram grammar [5] to constrain the acoustic search space. In the second pass, the decoder uses the SCTM non-crossword models and a trigram grammar to generate the N-best hypotheses. The N-best hypotheses are rescored using SCTM crossword models and reordered to output the top-1 hypothesis as the final recognition result.

We decoded the entire 6 hours test set with the acoustic models trained on the 8 hours of court hearings and language model trained above. The resulting WER was 61.4% as shown in Table 1. Since we knew that 8 hours of training was very small for a task of this size, we decided to perform recognition with acoustic models trained on 150 hours of broadcast news (BN) data [1]. The BN acoustic models employed quinphones, instead of just triphones as above. Again using the same language model, the WER on the test set was 58.4%.

Acoustic Source	Amount	#Gaussians	WER
Court Hearings	8 hrs	32K	61.4%
Broadcast News	150 hrs	277K	58.4%

Table 1: Initial recognition results using domain-specific and broadcast news models

The high WER of these initial recognition experiments clearly shows that transcription of courtroom speech is a challenging task, largely due to reasons mentioned in Section 2. An obvious strategy for reducing the WER on this task would be to train acoustic models on more than 100 hours of courtroom speech from different hearings. But, as mentioned earlier the legal transcripts made available to us from FTR can not be used for acoustic training as-is. Therefore, we decided to first focus on exploiting certain characteristics of the courtroom data to significantly reduce the WER using the broadcast news acoustic models, and then develop strategies for utilizing the legal transcripts to train better acoustic models on the in-domain data.

4. ACCURACY IMPROVEMENTS

First, we split the 6 hours test set into 2 sets of approximately the same duration. One set we plan to use as a development set, and the other as a validation set. We report recognition improvements on the 3 hour development set using the BN acoustic models.

4.1 Channel Change Detection

In the experiments described in Section 3, for convenience we had summed the channels to form a single signal. It became clear by subjective listening, that summing the channels had introduced significant distortion in the speech signal. We observed that in the courtroom corpus, most of the time, the speaker is dominant on a single channel. Rest of the channels for a speaker turn do pick up some speech, but are primarily a source of noise and other non-speech events. Therefore, we decided to investigate recognition on individual channels for improving the WER.

Under the assumption that speakers are dominant on a single channel, we developed a channel change detection procedure. First, we detect speaker changes on the summed channel signal. Next, for each speaker turn we select the channel with the highest signal-to-noise ratio (SNR). We define SNR(dB) as the difference between the 80th and 20th percentile log energy over the entire speaker turn. For speaker change detection, we used the novel 2-stage approach developed for transcribing broadcast news [6, 7]. In this approach, the first stage detects speech/non-speech boundaries using a coarse gender-independent phoneme recognition. We used an 8-class phone model trained on 20 hours of broadcast news: three broad phonetic classes (vowels, fricatives, and obstruents) and five models for non-speech phenomena (silence/noise, laughter, breadth, lip-smack, and music). The second stage performs the actual speaker segmentation by hypothesizing a speaker change boundary at every phone boundary that was located in the first stage using a penalized likelihood ratio criterion.

The WER when decoding the highest SNR channel for each speaker turn was 43.0%, as shown in Table 2. The corresponding WER for decoding on the summed channel was 59.6%. Therefore, by detecting channel changes and performing recognition on individual channels, the WER reduced by more than 16% absolute.

We also investigated the quality of SNR as a criterion for channel selection. To get the lower bound on the WER for channel selection, we decoded all 4 individual channels for each speaker turn, and then selected the hypothesis with the least WER. The overall WER was 42.4%. Assuming there were no errors in the detection of the speaker changes, this 0.6% absolute difference clearly shows that SNR is a good criterion for selecting the best channel.

4.2 Improved Language Model

As mentioned in Section 3, we had trained a language model on legal transcripts from 28 FTR sessions and 22M words of text downloaded from the Web. Both these sources do not correspond to the actual acoustics of the court proceedings. Therefore, we added the text of the 8 hour manually transcribed data to our language modeling data. This particular data set had a faithful annotation of phenomenas like false starts, hesitation, pause fillers, etc. We also added legal transcripts for another 27 FTR sessions that were made available to us recently. Decoding the same segments as in Section 4.1, with BN acoustic models and the new language model reduced the WER to 42.1%.

4.3 Unsupervised Channel Adaptation

The channel characteristics for courtroom speech is significantly different from broadcast news data. The recording conditions may vary from one session to the other. Moreover, each hearing has a few dominant speakers, primarily the attorneys who speak for a long duration. Therefore, adapting the BN speaker independent (SI) acoustic models to courtroom speakers or channels seems very appropriate in this cross-domain recognition task.

For adapting to individual channels, we first decode the highest-SNR channel for each speaker turn as in Section 4.2. We then group all the audio segments and corresponding recognition hypotheses for each of the individual channels. Finally, we use the recognition hypotheses to adapt the mixture densities' parameters of the broadcast news acoustic models using maximum likelihood linear regression (MLLR) [8].

Improvement	WER
Summed Channel (Baseline)	59.6%
Channel Change Detection	43.0%
Improved Language Model	42.1%
MLLR Channel Adaptation	36.2%

Table 2: Summary of recognition improvements using broadcast news acoustic models

We decoded the same test set with channel-adapted mixture densities and the improved language model. The resulting WER was 36.2% as shown in Table 2 - a 14% relative reduction in comparison to using BN-SI acoustic models.

To develop an understanding for the acoustic and language characteristics for individual sessions and how they affect the WER, we analyzed each session in detail. In Table 3, we present various features, such as, number of speakers, number of words, perplexity, SNR, and WER for each of the test sessions. Our study shows that there is very little correlation between any of the above mentioned features and the WER for the session.

Ses	#Spkrs	#Words	Perp.	SNR(dB)	WER
S1	8	8.2K	328	20.4	31.4%
S2	3	4.3K	276	19.4	32.6%
S3	13	7.8K	335	12.8	35.9%
S4	4	4.8K	317	17.3	47.7%
All	28	25.1K	317	17.3	36.2%

Table 3: Acoustic and language characteristics of the individual test sessions

5. IN-DOMAIN ACOUSTIC MODELING

Since supervised training requires an accurate orthographic transcription of the audio, and since obtaining such accurate transcriptions is very costly and time consuming, we decided to investigate methods that could take advantage of the legal transcripts that are being provided to us along with the audio data, similar to those described in [9, 10].

5.1 Training with Channel Change Detection

The first experiment we performed was to incorporate channel change detection in our acoustic modeling paradigm to train a model on 8 hours of accurately transcribed data. For each of the 5 min. transcript, we derived timestamps for the reference words by Viterbi alignment of the transcript with the summed channel signal. Next, as in Section 4.1, we detect speaker changes on the summed signal and select the highest-SNR channel for each speaker turn. We made a reference for all speaker turns by using the timestamps for the reference words obtained earlier.

We trained speaker and gender independent triphone models with the highest-SNR channel segment and the corresponding transcript. The PTM models used a total of 13K Gaussians, and 9K sets of mixture weights. The SCTM models used about 800 distinct sets of at-most 64 Gaussians for a total of 40K Gaussians, also with a set of 9K mixture weights. Using this acoustic model, we decoded the same test set as in Section 4, with the language model in Section 4.2. After channel adaptation, the resulting WER was 44.4% as shown in Table 4, which is 8.2% absolute worse than using the broadcast news acoustic models.

Acoustic Source	Amount	#Gaussians	WER
Broadcast News	150 hrs	277K	36.2%
Court Hearings	8 hrs	40K	44.4%

Table 4: Recognition results with acoustic models trained on 8 hours of accurately transcribed courtroom data, using channel change detection

5.2 Training with Legal Transcripts

In this section we describe our strategy for training acoustic models on 120 hours of raw courtroom data using the legal transcripts and the BN acoustic models as bootstrap models. In [10] it was demonstrated that for broadcast news data the approximate transcripts in the form of closed-captions can be used for training a powerful language model. Decoding results with this language model can be used for training acoustic models that result in about the same recognition accuracy as the acoustic models trained with accurate transcripts.

In our strategy, for each session we train a session-specific language model using the legal transcript. This language model is obtained by merging the N-gram counts from the legal transcript for the session with the counts used in training the language model in Section 4.2. Next, we apply the channel change detection procedure on the audio data to select the highest-SNR channel for each speaker turn. The highest-SNR channel for each speaker turn is decoded with BN acoustic models and the session-specific language model. The decoding result is used for unsupervised channel adaptation, and speech segments are decoded again with adapted parameters. The recognition results from channel adapted decoding are used as transcripts for training acoustic models.

We processed entire 120 hours of raw audio corresponding to 88 sessions according to the procedure described above. Since courtroom speech has significant amount of silence and non-speech events, in reality, we had decoding results for 100 hours of speech segments. We discarded about 25 hours of data by using heuristics such as percentage of noise words and SNR. Therefore, we ended up with 75 hours of speech segments with approximate transcripts.

We estimated triphone models using PTM and quinphone models using SCTM on 75 hours of speech segments resulting from above processing, in addition to 8 hours of accurately transcribed data from Section 5.1. Using this acoustic model, we decoded the test set in Section 4 with the language model in Section 4.2. After channel adaptation, the resulting WER was 38.7% as shown in Table 5. Therefore, by adding 75 hours of automatically processed courtroom speech to 8 hours of accurately transcribed data, we have improved the WER from 44.4% to 38.7%, but the BN acoustic models are still 2.5% absolute better.

Acoustic Source	Amount	#Gaussians	WER
Broadcast News (BN)	150 hrs	277K	36.2%
Court Hearings (CH)	83 hrs	244K	38.7%
BN + CH	233 hrs	277K	37.1%

Table 5: Recognition results with acoustic models trained on court hearings using legal transcripts and another set of models trained on union of broadcast news data and court hearings

Since acoustic models trained on 150 hours of accurately transcribed BN data performed better than models trained on 83 hours of courtroom speech, we decided to train acoustic models on the union of these two acoustic sources. We estimated triphone models using PTM and quinphone models using SCTM on 233 hours of audio data. After channel adapted decoding, the resulting WER was 37.1% as shown in Table 5. It seems that adding *in-domain* data, but with *approximate* transcripts, into the BN acoustic models does not improve recognition accuracy at all.

6. CONCLUSIONS AND FUTURE WORK

We have succeeded in establishing an initial corpus of courtroom hearings. In our exploratory work we have achieved a WER of 36% on actual courtroom hearings, primarily due to channel change detection and channel adaptation. In addition, we have demonstrated that the legal transcripts provided with the audio data can be used to obtain reasonable recognition accuracy. We are still receiving data from FTR which will be used for improving the acoustic models as well as the language model. We will also explore speaker adaptation with speaker adaptive training (SAT). Once the WER is reduced to below 30%, we will focus on metadata extraction for providing a rich transcription.

Acknowledgments

The authors would like to thank FTR Pty Ltd., especially Steve Townsend, for providing the courtroom data and information regarding courtroom proceedings.

7. REFERENCES

[1] L. Nguyen, S. Matsoukas, J. Davenport, J. Billa, R. Schwartz, and J. Makhoul, "The 1999 BBN BYBLOS 10xRT Broadcast News Transcription System," *Proc. NIST 2000 Speech Transcription Workshop.*

[2] H. Hermansky and N. Morgan, "RASTA Processing of Speech," *IEEE Trans. Speech and Audio Proc.,* Vol. 2, No. 4, pp. 478-489, Oct. 1994.

[3] P. Placeway, R. Schwartz, P. Fung, and L. Nguyen, "The Estimation of Powerful Language Models from Small and Large Corpora," *IEEE ICASSP,* Minneapolis, MN, pp. 33-36, Apr. 1993.

[4] L. Nguyen and R. Schwartz, "Efficient 2-Pass N-Best Decoder," *Proc. EuroSpeech '97,* Rhodes, Greece, pp. 167-170, Sep. 1997.

[5] L. Nguyen and R. Schwartz, "Single-Tree Method for Grammar-Directed Search," *Proc. IEEE ICASSP '99,* Phoenix, AZ., pp. 613-616, Mar. 1999.

[6] D. Liu and F. Kubala, "Fast Speaker Change Detection for Broadcast News Transcription and Indexing," *Proc. Eurospeech'99,* Budapest, Hungary, pp. 1031-1034, Sept. 1999.

[7] J. Makhoul, F. Kubala, T. Leek, D. Liu, L. Nguyen, R. Schwartz, and A. Srivastava, "Speech and Language Technologies for Audio Indexing and Retrieval," *Proc. IEEE,* Vol. 88, No. 8, pp. 1338-1353, Aug. 2000.

[8] C. J. Leggetter, and P. C. Woodland, "Flexible Speaker Adaptation Using Maximum Likelihood Linear Regression," *Proc. Spoken Language Systems Technology Workshop,* Austin TX, pp. 110-115, Jan. 1995.

[9] G. Zavaliagkos, M. Siu, T. Colthurst, and J. Billa, "Using Untranscribed Training Data to Improve Performance," *Proc. ICSLP-98,* Sydney, Australia, Nov. 1998.

[10] L. Lamel, J.L. Gauvain, and G. Adda, "Investigating Lightly Supervised Acoustic Model Training," *Proc. IEEE ICASSP-01,* Salt Lake City, UT, May 2001.

An Efficient Incremental Architecture for Robust Interpretation

Carolyn P. Rosé
LRDC, University of Pittsburgh
3939 Ohara St.
Pittsburgh, PA 15260 USA
rosecp@pitt.edu

Antonio Roque
LRDC, University of Pittsburgh
3939 Ohara St.
Pittsburgh, PA 15260 USA
roque@pitt.edu

Dumisizwe Bhembe
LRDC, University of Pittsburgh
3939 Ohara St.
Pittsburgh, PA 15260 USA
bhembe@pitt.edu

ABSTRACT

In this paper we describe ROSENHEIM, the RObust SENtence level arcHitecture for Efficient Incremental Multi-sentence interpretation. Its efficiency is the result of its novel layered scheduling algorithm. This scheduling algorithm makes it possible to ensure that when edits are made to already processed portions of text, only the minimum changes are made to the chart. Thus, it allows the parser to take advantage of the user's typing or speaking time so that it can complete the majority of the work of parsing an input text before the user enters the last word. Our evaluation demonstrates that this layered architecture makes the parser's response time almost imperceptible. We also show that our incremental parser performs more efficiently than other well known incremental parsers [34] [20]. An implementation of the ROSENHEIM architecture is currently part of the WHY Conceptual Physics Tutoring System [28], one of several recent dialogue based tutoring systems [23] [1] [7] [11].

General Terms

robust incremental interpretation

Keywords

robust sentence level interpretation, incremental parsing

1. INTRODUCTION

In this paper we describe ROSENHEIM, the RObust SENtence level arcHitecture for Efficient Incremental Multi-sentence interpretation. An implementation of the ROSENHEIM architecture is currently part of the WHY-Atlas Conceptual Physics Tutoring System [28], one of several recent dialogue based tutoring systems [23] [1] [7] [11]. The WHY-Atlas system assists students in creating and revising multi-sentence, typed physics explanations while receiving feedback from the system during each revision cycle.

One obstacle that currently makes it impractical for dialogue systems to make use of sophisticated natural language understanding technology, such as deep syntactic and semantic analysis, and discourse level analysis, is the tremendous computational expense involved, especially for long input texts. This type of processing is desirable, however, for applications like intelligent tutoring where the goal is to detect the subtle ways in which student misconceptions are encoded in their explanations. The ROSENHEIM architecture overcomes this obstacle by processing the users' utterances as they are being spoken or typed, thus hiding as much of the necessary processing time as possible, and drastically reducing the time in between when the user's turn is finished and when the system can respond.

The ROSENHEIM architecture is general purpose for applications with natural language input, whether typed or spoken. ROSENHEIM's incremental parser has been demonstrated to complete parsing input texts within a third of a second of when they have been finished being entered even at a word input rate of 180 words per minute, which is roughly the average rate of human speech. It has also been demonstrated to perform more efficiently than other well known incremental parsers [34] [20]. Our goal is to achieve a good balance between the preciseness of symbolic approaches and the imperviousness of text classification approaches. In particular we make use of both a version of the previously introduced LCFLEX robust parser [24] for symbolic processing that we have incrementalized as well as Rainbow [18], a Bayesian text classification package, as a fail-soft fall-back strategy when the parser fails. Additionally, this architecture has provided us with a test bed for developing an effective hybrid approach, which outperforms both the symbolic and the statistical approach alone [22]. In all cases, ROSENHEIM's target representation is a set of one or more first order propositions. The form of the output representation is easily adaptable, however, for use in other systems.

2. THE WHY-ATLAS CONCEPTUAL PHYSICS TUTORING SYSTEM

Recent studies of human tutoring suggest that a productive activity for teaching is to have students explain physical systems qualitatively [5]. The goal of the WHY-Atlas project [28] is to coach students as they explain physics systems in natural language in response to short essay questions such as, "Suppose you are running in a straight line at constant speed. You throw a pumpkin straight up. Where will it land? Explain." The WHY-Atlas system has at its disposal a library of knowledge construction dialogues (KCDs), i.e., interactive directed lines of reasoning, each of which is designed either to elicit a specific idea (i.e., an elicitation KCD) or to remediate a specific misconception (i.e., a remediation KCD) [23].

Students interact with WHY-Atlas through a GUI interface with an essay input area, a dialogue input area, and a dialogue history display. The student is presented with an essay question. After reading the essay question, the student types in an initial essay in the

Proceedings of HLT 2002, Second International Conference on Human Language Technology Research, M. Marcus, ed., Morgan Kaufmann, San Francisco, 2002.

essay input area. The system then analyzes the student's essay in order to detect the presence of misconceptions and required concepts, which are determined when each of WHY-Atlas's problems are designed. The system then uses KCDs both for coaching students to insert missing required concepts (elicitation KCDs) and to remove the expression of misconceptions (remediation KCDs). KCDs are conducted through the dialogue input area and displayed in the dialogue history display.

ROSENHEIM is responsible only for sentence level analysis. We use the CARMEL grammar and semantic interpretation framework [21] along with the COMLEX lexicon [12] for sentence level analysis. It takes natural language as input and produces a set of first order logical forms to pass on to the discourse language understanding (DLU) module [13]. The LCFLEX parser using the CARMEL grammar builds a deep syntactic functional analysis of input texts. Syntactic feature structures produced by the CARMEL grammar factor out those aspects of syntax that modify the surface realization of a sentence but do not change its deep functional analysis. These aspects include tense, negation, mood, modality, and syntactic transformations such as passivization and extraction. In order to do this reliably, the component of the grammar that performs the deep syntactic analysis of verb argument functional relationships was generated automatically from a feature representation for each of COMLEX's verb subcategorization tags.

We verified that the 91 verb subcategorization tags documented in the COMLEX manual were covered by the encodings, and thus by the resulting grammar rules. These tags cover a wide range of patterns of syntactic control and predication relationships. Each tag corresponds to one or more case frames. Each case frame corresponds to a number of different surface realizations due to passivization, relative clause extraction, and wh-movement. Altogether there are 519 syntactic patterns covered by the 91 subcategorization tags, all of which are covered by the CARMEL grammar.

Rainbow [18], our naive Bayes classifier, assigns sentences to statistical classes that correspond to lists of logical forms in the same representation language as CARMEL produces. Additionally, a hybrid classification approach, CarmelTC [22], performs a similar classification making use both of the symbolic analysis as well as the Rainbow classification. Since in both the purely symbolic approach as well as the classification approach, the result is in the same format, the output from either source is appropriate input for the DLU module. However, the classification approach has the drawback that it embodies the underlying simplifying assumption that students always express required points in a single sentence, which is normally true, but not always the case.

3. MOTIVATION

At the heart of ROSENHEIM is a new incremental version of the LCFLEX robust parser [24]. LCFLEX is a flexible left-corner parser designed for efficient, robust interpretation. Its basic parsing algorithm is similar to that of other left corner parsers described previously [25, 4, 24]. It uses the reflexive and transitive closure of the left-corner relation [27] both for top-down filtering and bottom-up prediction in order to limit ambiguity and thus enhance efficiency. The underlying graph representation of LCFLEX's chart allows words to be easily inserted or deleted at any point in the chart. The underlying grammar formalism used by LCFLEX is a unification-augmented context-free grammar formalism originally developed for the GLR Parser/Compiler [26]. It is a similar formalism to that used for LFG and PATR-II. However, it is not limited to cycle-free context free grammars as is the preliminary work adapting PATR-II to incremental parsing described in [34].

From an efficiency standpoint, it is the fine grained incrementality of this new version of LCFLEX that makes it uniquely appropriate for the ROSENHEIM architecture. Here we use incrementality to refer to the process of parsing text as it is entered and edited rather than waiting to begin processing until it has been typed in its final form. As the text is progressively revised, only minimal changes are made to the chart. The challenge of fully incremental parsing of text as it is being typed and revised is effectively coordinating the parallel tasks of keeping the lexical edges in the chart consistent with the text as it is being entered and modified at the interface, detecting when edges in the chart become invalid and removing them, and proceeding with the analysis of the lexical edges currently in the chart. If these tasks are not managed effectively, then the parser may inadvertently build analyses using invalid edges that have not been identified yet as invalid.

Some previous incremental parsers are described in [30] [31] [29]. However, these parsers are only weakly incremental. Although they revise their internal representations on successive analyses as their input is revised, they do not process their input as it is being entered. Instead they process their input text as a whole when an explicit command is given. Thus, they do not have to solve the problem of avoiding building analyses using invalid edges. But this simplification of the problem comes with a computational expense. In particular, they waste the time the user spends entering text, time that could be used to absorb the majority of the processing time.

Two previously described incremental parsers claim to be fully incremental [20] [34]. The approach described in [20] adds two operations to standard bottom-up chart parsing in order to project complete, albeit underspecified, syntactic structures from initial segments of input sentences. These two operations include (1) applying grammar rules to active edges, and (2) replacing the leftmost undecided term of a rule with an active edge. This approach is only feasible with very small, purely context free grammars. For example, because the algorithm applies grammar rules to active edges, it would get into an infinite loop with recursive rules.

Furthermore, let us consider what would happen if we used this algorithm with the CARMEL grammar. As mentioned above, the 91 COMLEX verb subcategorization tags cover 519 configurations of a verb in relation to its arguments. Considering also that it is common for nouns and verbs to be indistinguishable out of context (i.e., take as in "take an apple in your lunch" and take in "what's your take on that?"), a huge number of useless junk edges would be routinely created for each parse. Most of these junk analyses are not produced in the course of ordinary chart parsing since edges are only created where grammar rules match up with completed edges as their children and where the unification augmentation does not fail. Thus, only the configurations that are both appropriate for a verb, based on the subcategorization tags found for it in the lexicon, and that match the completed edges found in the sentence would be built. Another drawback of the [20] approach is that it makes the simplifying assumption that all words in the input stream are included in the final parse. This is an invalid simplifying assumption where robustness techniques are used such as those described in [24]. Robustness techniques, most notably skipping over some unparsable portions of input, have been demonstrated to significantly improve the performance of parsers over speech input, which may contain many ungrammaticalities and disfluencies.

Wirén's incremental parsing approach in [34] claims to be fully incremental. However, the degree of incrementality of that algorithm is evaluated only in terms of the percentage of chart edges that are invalidated by a single macro edit operation, i.e., inserting or deleting n contiguous words in the chart. What this measure does not take into account is the interaction between separate macro edit operations. In Wirén's algorithm, whenever one or more consecutive words are insert into or deleted from a position p in the chart, after all of the invalidated edges are removed, every chart position from p until the end of the chart is reprocessed. If at any time after the edit operation at position p occurs an edit operation is performed at a position $p+x$ in the chart, then any resources having been spent reprocessing chart positions greater than or equal to $p+x$ for the edit operation at p will have been wasted since those positions will now have to be recomputed again. The layered ROSENHEIM approach addresses this problem by checking for new edit operations after each chart position is processed. All performed edit operations are processed on the lexical level before the next chart position is fully processed. What this means is that all lexical insertions and deletions are performed, and all invalid edges are removed. The Wirén algorithm and the ROSENHEIM algorithm are indistinguishable in the case where the parser will have finished reprocessing the whole chart before the next edit operation is performed. But in the case that one or more new edit operations are performed before a previous edit operation is completely processed, the ROSENHEIM algorithm creates fewer new edges. In particular, our evaluation demonstrates that in practice the layered ROSENHEIM approach is at least 12% more efficient than the Wirén approach. More details about this comparison are described in the Evaluation section of this paper.

The advantage of the ROSENHEIM architecture is that it was designed to uniquely avoid inadvertently building analyses using invalid edges that have not yet been identified as invalid or unnecessarily redundantly reprocessing chart positions as in [34] while also avoiding building the unnecessary junk edges required by [20]. Additionally, it is not constrained to purely context free rules with no recursion. Our evaluation demonstrates that it behaves efficiently even with the large scale CARMEL grammar.

Furthermore, the new incrementalized version of LCFLEX is also unique among incremental parsers in that it has been enhanced with robustness techniques in order to address the major types of disfluencies that plague spontaneously produced language input. These robustness techniques give it the ability to skip words, the ability to consider insertion of missing words and categories, which can also be thought of as partial rule matching, and finally the ability to relax grammatical constraints expressed within the parser's unification augmentations. All of these robustness techniques are controlled by thresholds that limit how much flexibility is allowed at parse time. For example, a `skip beam` controls how many words from the input are allowed to be skipped within an analysis. Very few modifications to the original LCFLEX robustness techniques described in [24] were necessary in order to adapt them for the new incremental version, full description beyond the scope of this short paper. Our evaluation demonstrates that these robustness techniques, because they necessarily create more ambiguity in the parser's analysis, make the difference between the ROSENHEIM approach and the Wirén approach even more striking.

4. SCHEDULING

Let us first consider what is involved in analyzing an input text. After that we will divide this task into sub-tasks and lay out an efficient scheduling algorithm for them. Figure 1 contains an inventory of the sub-tasks that are involved.

The interface collects edit operations as they are either typed or spoken. An edit operation consists of (1) the name, i.e., either *add* or *delete*, (2) the position in the input buffer, and (3) in the case of an *add*, the lexical item added. To process an edit operation, first the chart is modified at the lexical level. For an *add* operation, a lexical edge is inserted into the indicated position. For a *delete* operation, a lexical edge is deleted. Whenever one or more edges are deleted,

- Cheap Operations:
  - Insert a Lexical Edge
  - Delete a Lexical Edge
  - Delete Invalid Edges
- Semi-Expensive Operations:
  - Perform Chart Parsing Algorithm at One Chart Position
- Very Expensive Operations:
  - Statistical Disambiguation
  - Discourse Level Processing
- Region Level Operations:
  - Bayesian Classification

Figure 1: Inventory of Sentence Level Interpretation Tasks

each dependent edge, i.e., such that one or more of the deleted edges were used in the derivation of that edge, must also be deleted. As indicated in Figure 1, the time it takes to perform these very cheap tasks is negligible.

Next, at each position in the chart, the chart parsing algorithm must be applied so that any edge that can be created that does not duplicate an edge already in the chart is created and inserted into the chart. Edit cycle markers on edges and chart positions make it very quick to determine which, if any, new edges must be created at each chart position. When this process is finished, a complete all-paths parse for the entire input buffer will have been computed. In line with Figure 1, the bulk of parse time is spent on these Semi-Expensive tasks.

The input buffer is automatically divided into regions roughly at sentence boundaries. After a region is parsed, it is disambiguated using LCFLEX's statistical disambiguation algorithm. At this point, a parse quality heuristic [17] can be applied to that parse to determine whether it is an acceptable analysis. If an acceptable analysis is found, it is reformatted into a set of first order propositions. The Rainbow statistical text classification program [18] or CarmelTC [22] are used to deal with cases where the parser fails to construct a full analysis. Rainbow uses a statistical word model trained on a corpus of tutoring dialogues to classify text using a Naive Bayes classification method with Laplace smoothing and a unigram event model. Input sentences are assigned by Rainbow to semantic classes that have been paired with sets of first order propositions. Thus, the result is in the same form regardless of whether it comes from the parser or the statistical classifier. Applying the Bayesian Classifier is very cheap. It is classified as a Region Level task in Figure 1 because it is only applied after a region has been fully parsed and disambiguated. CarmelTC is a rule learning approach where rules for classifying units of text rely on features extracted from CARMEL's syntactic analysis of that text as well as on the Rainbow "Bag of Words" classification of that text. Similar to Rainbow, it is trained over hand classified example texts. In the initial version of CarmelTC, we have used a simple decision tree learning algorithm [19] with excellent results.

The interface is continually available for the user to manipulate. As a separate process, ROSENHEIM's scheduling algorithm loops continuously until the student's turn is complete and all of the edit operations have been fully processed at all levels. On each loop, it retrieves all of the new edit operations from the interface and performs all the tasks classified as Cheap in Figure 1. Next the one Semi-Expensive task is performed at the next chart position where it is necessary. If there is a region that has been fully parsed but not disambiguated, then the Very Expensive tasks as well as the Region Level task if necessary are performed for that region. Whenever an edit operation is performed in a region that had been fully parsed, it loses the status of being fully parsed. Thus, when it becomes fully-parsed again, the region will be disambiguated again to keep the result consistent with the user's text.

5. HYBRID UNDERSTANDING APPROACHES

As mentioned, the ROSENHEIM architecture employed by the WHY-Atlas tutoring system uses both a symbolic (i.e., CARMEL) and a "Bag of Words" statistical (i.e., Rainbow) approach to sentence level language understanding, as well as the hybrid CarmelTC approach. Many successful tutoring systems that accept natural language input employ shallow approaches to language understanding. For example, CIRCSIM-TUTOR [10] and Andes-Atlas [23] parse student answers using shallow semantic grammars to identify key concepts embedded therein. The AUTO-TUTOR [32] system uses Latent Semantic Analysis (LSA) to process lengthy student answers. "Bag of Words" approaches such as LSA [16, 15], HAL [2, 3], and Rainbow [18], have enjoyed a great deal of success in a wide range of applications. Recently a number of dialogue based tutoring systems have begun to employ more linguistically sophisticated techniques for analyzing student language input, namely the Geometry tutor [1], and BEETLE [7]. Each approach has its own unique strengths and weaknesses. "Bag of Words" approaches require relatively little development time, are totally impervious to ungrammatical input, and tend to perform well because much can be inferred about student knowledge just from the words they use. On the other hand, symbolic, knowledge based approaches require a great deal of development time and tend to be more brittle than superficial "Bag of Words" types of approaches, although robustness techniques can increase their level of imperviousness [24, 21]. To their credit, linguistic knowledge based approaches are more precise and capture nuances that "Bag of Words" approaches miss. For example, they capture key aspects of meaning that are communicated structurally through scope and subordination and do not ignore common, but nevertheless crucial, function words such as 'not'.

Let us consider some shortcomings of a pure "Bag of Words" approach for our application that CarmelTC overcomes. Using our text classification approach, in order to compute which set of key points, i.e., "correct answer aspects", are included in a student essay, we first segment the essay at sentence boundaries. Note that run-on sentences are broken up. Once an essay is segmented, each segment is classified as corresponding to one of the set of key points or "nothing" if it does not include any key point. We then take an inventory of the classifications other than "nothing" that were assigned to at least one segment. As an example, let us consider essays collected from students interacting with our tutoring system in response to the question "Suppose you are running in a straight line at constant speed. You throw a pumpkin straight up. Where will it land? Explain.", which we refer to as the Pumpkin Problem. Thus, there are a total of six alternative classifications for each segment:

Class 1 Sentence expresses the idea that after the release the only force acting on the pumpkin is the downward force of gravity.

Class 2 Sentence expresses the idea that the pumpkin continues to have a constant horizontal velocity after it is released.

Class 3 Sentence expresses the idea that the horizontal velocity of the pumpkin continues to be equal to the horizontal velocity of the man.

Class 4 Sentence expresses the idea that the pumpkin and runner cover the same distance over the same time.

Class 5 Sentence expresses the idea that the pumpkin will land on the runner.

Class 6 Sentence does not adequately express any of the above specified key points.

Note that this classification task is strikingly different from those typically used for evaluating text classification systems. First, these classifications represent specific whole propositions rather than general topics, such as those used for classifying web pages [8], namely "student", "faculty", "staff", etc. Secondly, the texts are much shorter, i.e., one sentence in comparison with a whole web page, which is a disadvantage for "bag of words" approaches.

In some cases what distinguishes sentences from one class and sentences from another class is very subtle. For example, "Thus, the pumpkin's horizontal velocity, which is equal to that of the man when he released it, will remain constant." belongs to Class 2 although it could easily be mistaken for Class 3. Similarly, "So long as no other horizontal force acts upon the pumpkin while it is in the air, this velocity will stay the same.", belongs to Class 2 although looks similar on the surface to either Class 1 or 3. A related problem is that sentences that should be classified as "nothing" may look very similar on the surface to sentences belonging to one or more of the other classes. For example, "It will land on the ground where the runner threw it up." contains all of the words required to correctly express the idea corresponding to Class 5, although it does not express this idea, and in fact expresses a wrong idea.

Recent work demonstrates that symbolic and "Bag of Words" approaches can be productively combined. For example, syntactic information can be used to modify the LSA space of a verb in order to make LSA sensitive to different word senses [14]. Along similar lines, syntactic information can be used, as in Structured Latent Semantic Analysis (SLSA), to improve the results obtained by LSA over single sentences [33]. CarmelTC makes use of features extracted from CARMEL's syntactic analysis of the text [21]. These features encode functional relationships between syntactic heads (e.g., (subj-throw man)), tense information (e.g., (tense-throw past)), and information about passivization and negation (e.g., (negation-throw +) or (passive-throw -)). Like [9], we also extract word features that indicate the presence or absence of a root form of a word from the text. Additionally, for CarmelTC one of the features for each training text that is made available to the rule learning algorithm is the classification obtained using the Rainbow naive bayes classifier [18]. Because the texts classified with CarmelTC are so much shorter than those of [9], the feature set provided to the learning algorithm was small enough that it was not necessary to use a learning algorithm as sophisticated as RIPPER [6]. Thus, we used ID3 [19] instead with excellent results. In a 50 fold cross validation evaluation over 126 previously unseen student essays, CarmelTC achieves an 80% recall and 90% precision, where recall for an essay was computed by dividing the number of correctly identified required points over the total number of required points present in the essay, and precision was computed by dividing the total number of correctly identified required points in the essay by the total number of identified required points. The syntactic features make CarmelTC sensitive to those features of student input that tend to be glossed over by purely "Bag of Words" approaches.

6. EVALUATION

To evaluate the overall effectiveness of the ROSENHEIM scheduling algorithm and the LCFLEX incremental parsing algorithm, we ran two separate evaluations. In the first evaluation we demonstrate that the ROSENHEIM approach creates fewer edges than the Wirén

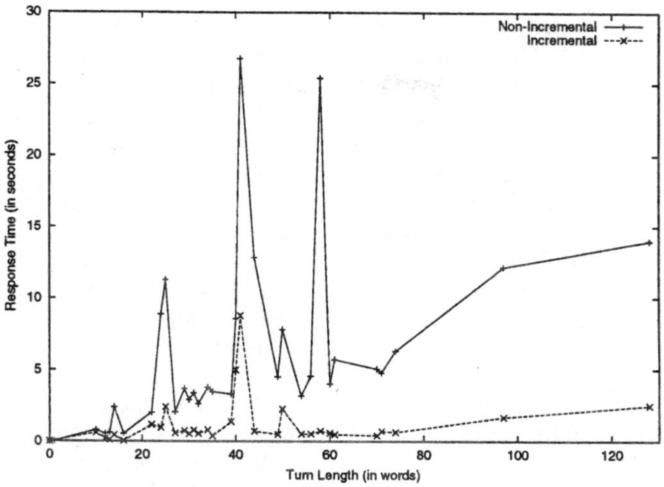

Figure 2: Response Time

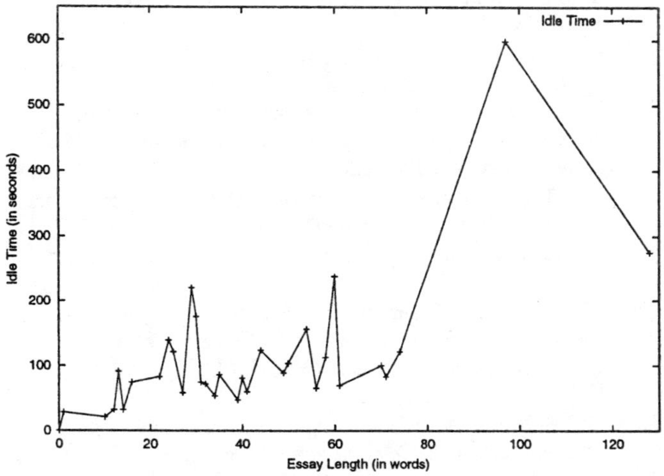

Figure 3: Idle Time

approach, thus demonstrating the advantage of its more fine grained incremental approach. Secondly, we evaluated the response time of ROSENHEIM between the time when a student finishes typing and when the system has completed its analysis in order to demonstrate its ability to keep up with the student's typing, thus hiding the majority of the processing time in the student's typing time.

6.1 Comparison with Wirén Algorithm

To compare the efficiency of the Wirén approach with the more finely incremental ROSENHEIM approach, we compared the total number of edges generated in to process of parsing 200 student essays collected during their interaction with the WHY-Atlas system. The essays were parsed using the CARMEL syntactic grammar (with 419 rules) and the COMLEX lexicon [12] (with 40,000 lexical entries). Note that in this evaluation only a syntactic analysis was constructed. Each individual edit operation (i.e., insertion or deletion of a single word at the interface) was recorded along with the time at which the edit operation was performed so that the student's typing could be simulated realistically during the evaluation. On average the essays used in the evaluation contained 87.7 individual edit operations, or 19.4 macro edit operations, where a macro edit operation is defined as the insertion or deletion of n contiguous words. When the two algorithms were run over this corpus with the parsers in non-robust mode, the Wirén algorithm generated 1,806,763 edges altogether, while the ROSENHEIM algorithm generated only 1,589,070, a savings of 12%. In robust mode, the savings is quite a bit larger. For example, even with the parser's skip limit set only to allow skipping of at most two words, the Wirén algorithm generates a total of 3,480,989 edges while the ROSENHEIM algorithm generates only 2,789,558, a savings of 20%. On the majority of essays, the difference between the two algorithms was very small. However, in cases where there were multiple macro edit operations in quick succession, the difference was very significant, thus leading to a noticeable overall advantage for the ROSENHEIM approach.

6.2 Evaluation of Parser Response Time

We ran an additional evaluation over 44 student essays to measure the time in between when students finish typing and when the parser is finished parsing a student's sentence. These results confirm that ROSENHEIM is able to keep up with student's typing time in the context of a realistic system. As in the previous evaluation, each edit operation had been previously recorded in a log file along with a time stamp so that the log file could be replayed in order to simulate the student's typing. The essays were parsed using the CARMEL syntactic grammar (with 419 rules), the COMLEX lexicon [12] (with 40,000 lexical entries), and the WHY ontology (with 123 semantic concepts).

We compared the ROSENHEIM approach with a serial processing approach using the non-incremental version of LCFLEX. In each case, we measured the time in seconds in between when the student finished typing and when WHY completed its sentence level processing of the input (including statistical disambiguation and classification where necessary). The results are displayed in Figure 2. Note that since LCFLEX using the CARMEL grammar constructs the syntactic and semantic analysis for a text in parallel, parse times on essays of similar length can vary widely depending upon how much uninterpretable text the student types. However, the ROSENHEIM architecture is a clear win, often responding almost 6 times faster than the serial approach. The test set is small, but the difference even with this small test set is quite striking.

In order to isolate the performance of our sentence level understanding approach, we did not pass the results from sentence level understanding on to our discourse level understanding module. However, we did evaluate how much of student typing time is used by ROSENHEIM for building a sentence level analysis, and thus how much time is left over for discourse level processing. Figure 3 demonstrates that only a very small part of the student's typing time is being used for ROSENHEIM's incremental sentence level understanding, which leaves a great deal of time, even up to 5 or 10 minutes on longer essays, to absorb a large amount of discourse level processing time as well.

7. ACKNOWLEDGEMENTS

This research was supported by the Office of Naval Research, Cognitive Science Division under grant number N00014-0-1-0600 and by NSF grant number 9720359 to CIRCLE, the Center for Interdisciplinary Research on Constructive Learning Environments at the University of Pittsburgh and Carnegie-Mellon University.

The first author would like to dedicate this paper to her maternal grandmother, Olive Rosenheim, whose industriousness and strength have always been so inspirational.

8. ADDITIONAL AUTHORS

Additional authors: Kurt VanLehn, University of Pittsburgh, email: vanlehn@pitt.edu

9. REFERENCES

[1] V. Aleven, O. Popescu, and K. Koedinger. Pedagogical content knowledge in a tutorial dialogue system to support self-explanation. In *Papers of the AIED-2001 Workshop on Tutorial Dialogue Systems*, 2001.

[2] C. Burgess, K. Livesay, and K. Lund. Explorations in context space: Words, sentences, discourse. *Discourse Processes*, 25(2):211–257, 1998.

[3] C. Burgess and K. Lund. Modeling parsing constraints with high-dimensional context space. *Language and Cognitive Processes*, 12(2):177–210, 1997.

[4] J. A. Carroll. *Practical Unification-Based Parsing of Natural Language*. PhD thesis, University of Cambridge, Computer Laboratory, 1993.

[5] M. Chi, N. de Leeuw, M. Chiu, and C. LaVancher. Eliciting self-exsplanations improves understanding. *Cognitive Science*, 18(3), 1981.

[6] W. W. Cohen. Fast effective rule induction. In *Proceedings of the 12th International Conference on Machine Learning*, 1995.

[7] M. G. Core, J. D. Moore, and C. Zinn. Initiative management for tutorial dialogue. In *Proceedings of the NAACL Workshop Adaption in Dialogue Systems*, 2001.

[8] M. Craven, D. DiPasquio, D. Freitag, A. McCallum, T. Mitchell, K. Nigam, and S. Slattery. Learning to extract symbolic knowledge from the world wide web. In *Proceedings of the 15th National Conference on Artificial Intelligence*, 1998.

[9] J. Furnkranz, T. M. Mitchell, and E. Riloff. A case study in using linguistic phrases for text categorization on the www. In *Proceedings from the AAAI/ICML Workshop on Learning for Text Categorization*, 1998.

[10] M. S. Glass. *Broadening Input Understanding in an Intelligent Tutoring System*. PhD thesis, Illinois Institute of Technology, 1999.

[11] A. Graesser, K. Wiemer-Hastings, P. Wiemer-Hastings, R. Kreuz, and the Tutoring Research Group. Autotutor: A simulation of a human tutor. *Journal of Cognitive Systems Research*, 1(1):35–51, 1999.

[12] R. Grishman, C. Macleod, and A. Meyers. COMLEX syntax: Building a computational lexicon. In *Proceedings of the 15th International Conference on Computational Linguistics (COLING-94)*, 1994.

[13] P. W. Jordan, M. Makatchev, M. Ringenberg, and K. VanLehn. Engineering the Tacitus-lite weighted abductive inference engine for use in the Why-Atlas qualitative physics tutoring system. submitted, 2002.

[14] W. Kintsch. Predication. to appear in the Cognitive Science Journal, 2002.

[15] D. Laham. Latent semantic analysis approaches to categorization. In *Proceedings of the Cognitive Science Society*, 1997.

[16] T. K. Landauer, P. W. Foltz, and D. Laham. Introduction to latent semantic analysis, 1998. To Appear in *Discourse Processes*.

[17] A. Lavie. *A Grammar Based Robust Parser For Spontaneous Speech*. PhD thesis, School of Computer Science, Carnegie Mellon University, 1995.

[18] A. K. McCallum. Bow: A toolkit for statistical language modeling, text retrieval, classification and clustering. http://www.cs.cmu.edu/ mccallum/bow, 1996.

[19] T. M. Mitchell. *Machine Learning*. McGraw Hill, 1997.

[20] D. Mori, S. Matsubara, and Y. Inagaki. Incremental parsing for interactive natural language interface. In *Proceedings of the 2001 IEEE International Conference of Systems, Man, and Cybernetics*, 2001.

[21] C. P. Rosé. A framework for robust sentence level interpretation. In *Proceedings of the First Meeting of the North American Chapter of t he Association for Computational Lingusitics*, 2000.

[22] C. P. Rosé, D. Bhembe, A. Roque, S. Siler, R. Srivastava, and K. VanLehn. A hybrid language understanding approach for robust selection of tutoring goals. In *Proceedings of the Intelligent Tutoring Systems Conference*, 2002.

[23] C. P. Rosé, P. Jordan, M. Ringenberg, S. Siler, K. VanLehn, and A. Weinstein. Interactive conceptual tutoring in atlas-andes. In *Proceedings of Artificial Intelligence in Education*, 2001.

[24] C. P. Rosé and A. Lavie. Balancing robustness and efficiency in unification augmented context-free parsers for large practical applications. In J. C. Junqua and G. V. Noord, editors, *Robustness in Language and Speech Technologies*. Kluwer Academic Press, 2001.

[25] D. J. Rosenkrantz and P. M. Lewis. Deterministic left corner parsing. In *Procedings of the IEEE Conferenc eof the 11th Annual Symposium on Switching and Automata Theory*, 1970.

[26] M. Tomita. The Generalized LR Parser/Compiler - Version 8.4. In *Proceedings of International Conference on Computational Linguistics (COLING'90)*, pages 59–63, Helsinki, Finland, 1990.

[27] G. Van Noord. An efficient implementation of the head-corner parser. *Computational Linguistics*, 23(3), 1997.

[28] K. VanLehn, P. Jordan, C. P. Rosé, and The Natural Language Tutoring Group. The architecture of why2-atlas: a coach for qualitative physics essay writing. submitted, 2002.

[29] M. Vilares Ferro and M. A. Alonso Pardo. Exploring interactive chart parsing. *Procesamiento del Lenguaje Natural*, 17:158–170, 1995.

[30] M. Vilares Ferro and B. A. Dion. Efficient incremental parsing for context-free languages. In *Proceedings of the 5th IEEE International Conference on Computer Languages (ICCL'94)*, 1994.

[31] T. A. Wagner and S. L. Graham. History sensitive incremental parsing. In *ACM Transations on Programming Languages and Systems*, 1995.

[32] P. Wiemer-Hastings, A. Graesser, D. Harter, and the Tutoring Research Group. The foundations and architecture of autotutor. In B. Goettl, H. Halff, C. Redfield, and V. Shute, editors, *Intelligent Tutoring Systems: 4th International Conference (ITS '98)*, pages 334–343. Springer Verlag, 1998.

[33] P. Wiemer-Hastings and I. Zipitria. Rules for syntax, vectors for semantics. In *Proceedings of the Twenty-third Annual Conference of the Cognitive Science Society*, 2001.

[34] M. Wirén. *Studies in Incremental Natural Language Analysis*. PhD thesis, Linkoping University, S-581 83 Linkoping, Sweden. ISBN 91-7870-027-8, 1992.

Automatic Paraphrase Acquisition from News Articles

Yusuke Shinyama
Department of Computer Science
New York University
715 Broadway, 7th floor, New York, NY, 10003
yusuke@cs.nyu.edu

Satoshi Sekine
Department of Computer Science
New York University
715 Broadway, 7th floor, New York, NY, 10003
sekine@cs.nyu.edu

Kiyoshi Sudo
Department of Computer Science
New York University
715 Broadway, 7th floor, New York, NY, 10003
sudo@cs.nyu.edu

ABSTRACT

Paraphrases play an important role in the variety and complexity of natural language documents. However, they add to the difficulty of natural language processing. Here we describe a procedure for obtaining paraphrases from news articles. Articles derived from different newspapers can contain paraphrases if they report the same event on the same day. We exploit this feature by using Named Entity recognition. Our approach is based on the assumption that Named Entities are preserved across paraphrases. We applied our method to articles of two domains and obtained notable examples. Although this is our initial attempt at automatically extracting paraphrases from a corpus, the results are promising.

1. INTRODUCTION

Expressing one thing in other words, or "paraphrasing", plays an important role in the variety and complexity of natural language documents. One can express a single event in thousands of ways in natural language sentences. A creative writer uses lots of paraphrases to state a single fact. This greatly adds to the difficulty of natural language processing.

Table 1 shows how the headlines differ in several newspapers. Although every expression reports the same event – Bush's decision for government funding for people in New York – each expression differs considerably from the others.

Many natural language applications, such as Information Retrieval, Machine Translation, Question Answering, Text Summarization, or Information Extraction, need to handle these expressions correctly. Because analyzing these expressions at semantic level is a rather difficult task, we hope to build a paraphrase database to find expressions which have the same meaning. However, building such databases by hand is still difficult. There are two reasons: the first reason is that there are too many possible language expressions for someone to come up with. Even if several people work on this task, it is still laborious to cover many common expressions. The second reason is that expressions considered as paraphrases are different from domain to domain. Even if two expressions can be regarded as having the same meaning in a certain domain, it is not possible to generalize them to other domains.

So we are trying to create a system that automatically acquires paraphrases from given corpora of a specific domain. Even though their usage is limited to a certain domain, it is still useful for many applications. In this paper, we describe an approach to automatic paraphrase acquisition from corpora. Our main focus is Information Extraction (IE). In an IE application, a system uses patterns to capture events which are relevant to a certain domain. Although there have been several efforts to obtain such patterns automatically, little work has addressed the problem of capturing the semantic knowledge of such patterns, which is crucial for IE. Using a paraphrase database, we can connect one pattern to another. We expect this will reduce the cost of creating IE knowledge by hand. Although our approach aims to collect paraphrases for IE applications, our method can be applied to other purposes also.

Proceedings of HLT 2002, Second International Conference on Human Language Technology Research, M. Marcus, ed., Morgan Kaufmann, San Francisco, 2002.

2. CHALLENGES

To acquire paraphrases automatically, we focused on news articles that describe the same event. Take a look at the examples in Table 1. These headlines are taken from several news articles on the same day. If we can find these articles in different newspapers on a certain day, it is likely that they contain similar expressions; i.e. paraphrases.

However, the difficulty of paraphrase acquisition is to recognize that one sentence has the same meaning as another. These expressions may differ from the others not only in lexical properties, but also in syntactic features. By looking at Table 1, one can easily observe that a simple criterion is not enough to find paraphrases.

Our basic concept is to use Named Entity (NE) to find such expressions reporting the same event. NE is a proper expression such as names of organizations, persons, locations, dates, or numerical expressions [2]. In Table 1, "Bush", "New York" and "$20 billion" are regarded as NEs. Since they are indispensable to report an event, NEs are often preserved across different newspapers. Therefore we can expect that if two sentences share several comparable NEs, it is likely that they are reporting the same event. This likelihood increases as the number of NEs shared by two sentences increases. Here, using NE recognition techniques, headlines 2. and 3. can be generalized as follows:

- Bush, in New York, Affirms $20 Billion Aid Pledge
  ⇒ $PERSON_1$, in $LOCATION_1$, affirms $MONEY_1$ Aid Pledge
- Bush Reassures New York of $20 Billion
  ⇒ $PERSON_1$ Reassures $LOCATION_1$ of $MONEY_1$

This way, we can find the comparable expressions, or paraphrases from corpora by using NEs. So far we have applied our method to

No	Newspaper	Headline
1.	CNN	Bush says he'll deliver $20 billion to NY
2.	New York Times	Bush, in New York, Affirms $20 Billion Aid Pledge
3.	Washington Post	Bush Reassures New York of $20 Billion

Table 1: Expressions of the same event

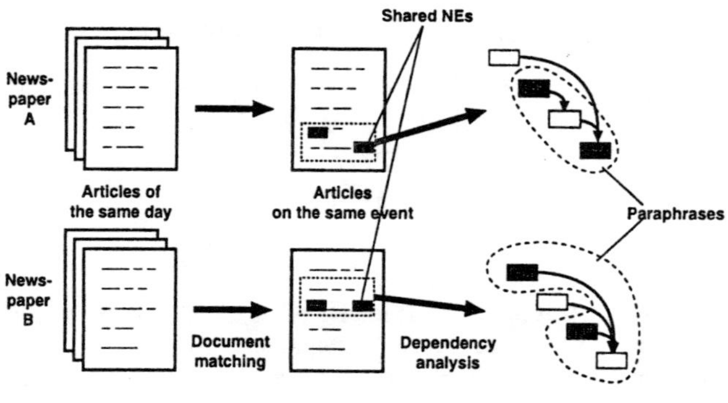

Figure 1: Overall method of paraphrase acquisition

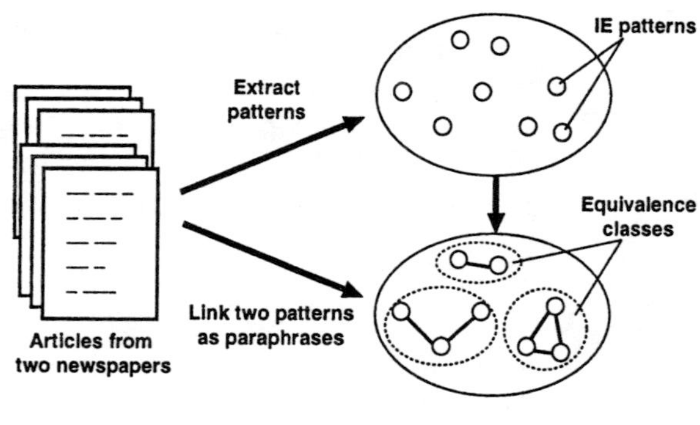

Figure 3: Actual experiment using IE patterns

two domains in Japanese newspapers and obtained some notable examples.

There are a few approaches for obtaining paraphrases automatically. Barzilay et al. used parallel translations derived from one original document [1]. They targeted literary works and used word alignment techniques developed for MT. However the syntactic variety of the resultant expressions is limited since they used only part-of-speech tags to identify the syntactic properties. In addition, compared with our method using newspapers, their resources are relatively scarce. Torisawa et al. proposed a learning method for automatic paraphrasing of Japanese noun phrases [6]. But this is also limited to a certain type of noun phrases.

3. ALGORITHM

3.1 Overview

As we stated in the previous section, our approach is based on the following assumption: NEs are preserved across paraphrases. So if the portions of each sentence in the articles share several comparable NEs, they are likely to be expressing the same meaning; in other words, they are paraphrases. The expectation increases as the number of NEs shared by the portions increases.

Paraphrase acquisition goes as follows. First we find articles in a certain domain from two newspapers. We use an existing IR system to obtain articles from a given class of events, such as murders or personnel affairs. Then we find pairs of articles which report the same event. In this stage we use a TF/IDF based method developed for Topic Detection and Tracking (TDT). Next we compare all the sentences in each article to find pairs of sentences sharing comparable NEs. Then we extract appropriate portions of sentences using a dependency tree. A dependency tree can be used later to reconstruct a original phrase. If the number of comparable NEs which both portions contain exceeds a certain threshold, we adopt them as paraphrases. Finally we generalize an NE as a variable in retrieved phrases so that these phrases can be applied to other sentences. The overall process is illustrated in Figure 1.

Additionally, we need to consider the domain of the expressions. Otherwise our method yields a lot of noise. For example, two expressions "*Bush has expressed his confidence in Koizumi's reforms*" and "*Bush and Koizumi watched a demonstration of horseback archery*" are both found in the articles from the same day and both contain the comparable NEs (*Bush* and *Koizumi*), but they are not paraphrases. So we try to filter out such noise using a set of IE patterns obtained from the same articles in advance. In this way we can limit our patterns to only those concerning a certain domain.

Sudo et al. described a procedure for automatically gathering common patterns appearing frequently in a set of articles about a given topic [5]. Each IE pattern has slots which can be filled by NEs. For example, the sentence "*Vice President Osamu Kuroda of Nihon Yamamura Glass Corp. was promoted to President.*" contains four patterns found for the personnel domain, as shown in Figure 2. NEs in these patterns are generalized into slots which hold the types of the NEs and the case roles of each node are preserved. We apply these obtained patterns to the articles itself, and then find paraphrases only among those which match any of the patterns. This means we find paraphrases among these IE patterns. Actually this is done by linking two IE patterns as paraphrases. These links form a set of equivalence classes, in which each pattern conveys the same meaning (See Figure 3).

3.2 Details

Now we describe the details. Our method can be divided into 4 stages:

1) Preprocessing articles

First we obtain pairs of articles of a certain domain from two newspapers, as a source of both IE patterns and paraphrases. First we obtain relevant articles for a domain from one newspaper, and then we find articles which report the same event from the other newspaper. In this experiment, we used a stochastic-based IR system by Murata et al. [3] to get articles of a specified domain. We pick up the most relevant 300 articles for a domain. For each relevant article from one of the newspapers, we search for an article corresponding to the first article from the other newspaper. This is done by calculating the similarity between two articles and taking the one whose similarity is the best. Since this task is very similar to the task defined in TDT [8], we used a technique developed in TDT. We implemented this part based on the University of Massachusetts system, which worked the best for our purpose [4]. The similarity $S_a(a_1, a_2)$ of two articles a_1 and a_2 is defined as follows:

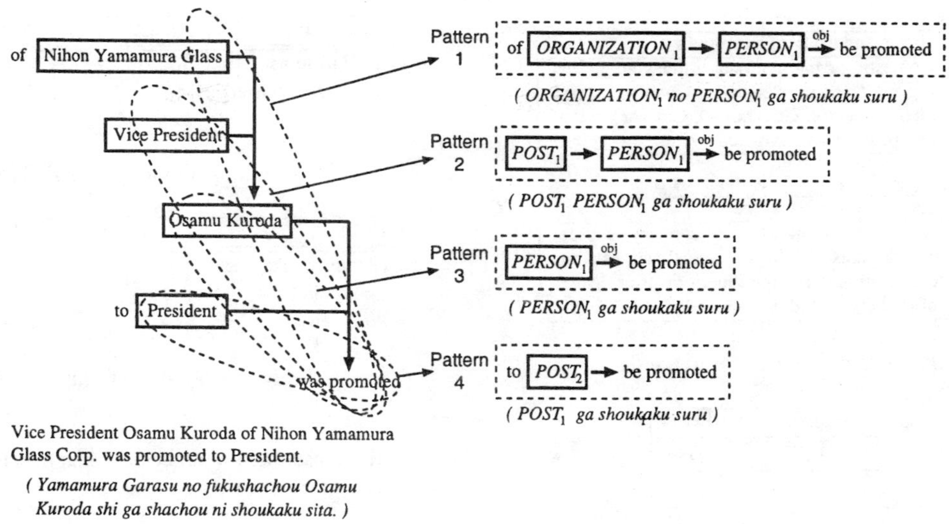

Figure 2: IE Pattern Extraction

$$S_a(a_1, a_2) = \cos(W_1, W_2) \quad (1)$$

$$W^i = TF(w_i) * IDF(w_i) \quad (2)$$

$$TF(w_i) = \frac{f(w_i)}{f(w_i) + 0.5 + 1.5 * \frac{dl}{avgdl}} \quad (3)$$

$$IDF(w_i) = \frac{\log(\frac{C+0.5}{df(w_i)})}{\log(C+1)} \quad (4)$$

Here W_1 and W_2 are vectors with elements W_1^i and W_2^i for article a_1 and a_2, with dimension equal to the number of NEs in the corpus. $f(w_i)$ is the number of times NE w_i occurs in the article. $df(w_i)$ is the document (article) frequency, which is the number of articles containing the NE w_i. dl is the document length. C is the number of articles, and $avgdl$ is the average article length.

We apply this metric to the NEs appearing in an article and adopt the article pairs whose similarity is above a certain threshold. In this stage we use a simple dictionary-based NE tagging system to pick up NEs, instead of the one used in later stage. This system picks up only words which are not contained in a common noun dictionary and doesn't recognize the type of NEs.

2) Acquiring IE patterns

Next we run the IE pattern acquisition system for the pairs of articles [5]. This system performs NE tagging and dependency analysis, and picks several paths of nodes in a dependency tree as IE patterns. In this experiment, we use IE patterns which appear more then once in the corpus and contain at lease one NE.

3) Preprocessing sentences

Now we take a closer look at a pair of articles which report the same event. We mark all NEs using an statistical NE tagging system [7]. Next we apply a dependency analyzer to the sentences. Here Juman and KNP were used as the morphological analyzer and dependency analyzer respectively. Thus we have a set of NE-tagged dependency trees for each article. Here we apply the obtained IE patterns to the sentences. We drop a sentence that doesn't match any of the patterns. For sentences which do match one or more patterns, an instance of each pattern is created and attached to the sentence. The variables in these patterns are filled with the actual NEs.

This stage is illustrated in Figure 4. Suppose sentences A and B contain paraphrases. Sentence A matches pattern 1 and sentence B matches pattern 2. These patterns are attached to the sentences and each slot in the patterns is filled with the actual NE (here, $POST_1$ slot is filled with the actual NE *"President"*).

4) Extracting paraphrases

Now we can get paraphrases. First we take pairs of similar sentences. To penalize frequently occurring NEs, this is done by calculating TF/IDF based similarity in terms of comparable NEs for all possible pairs of sentences. Sentence similarity $S_s(s_1, s_2)$ of sentence s_1 and s_2 is defined as follows:

$$S_s(s_1, s_2) = \cos(W_1, W_2) \quad (5)$$

$$W^i = TF(w_i) * IDF(w_i) \quad (6)$$

$$TF(w_i) = f(w_i) \quad (7)$$

$$IDF(w_i) = \log(\frac{C}{df(w_i)}) \quad (8)$$

Here W_1 and W_2 are vectors with elements W_1^i and W_2^i for article s_1 and s_2. $f(w_i)$ is the number of NEs which are comparable to w_i in the sentence. $df(w_i)$ is the number of sentences in the article which contain NEs that is comparable to w_i. C is the number of NEs in the article.

We use substring matching to compare two NEs. This is because several NEs referring to one entity can take various forms, such as "Bush", "George W. Bush", or "Mr. Bush". Since we use Japanese newspapers for this experiment, we regard two NEs as comparable if one begins with the half of the beginning string of the other. [1]

Then we take pairs of sentences whose similarity is above a certain threshold. If two IE pattern attached to the two sentences share

[1] In Japanese, a name of a person can take the following forms: "Koizumi", "Koizumi Jun'ichirou", "Koizumi-san" etc.

Arrest Events:

Description	Hiring and firing of executives
Narrative	Domestic or international articles about hiring and firing of executives. Chairman, President, Director, CEO, COO, CFO or equivalent positions are targeted.

Personnel Affairs:

Description	Arresting robbery suspects
Narrative	Articles reporting arrest of robbery suspects or criminals. Multiple crimes such as murder accompanied by robbery or prior crimes of robbers should be included.

Table 2: Query Used for Article Retrieval

Newspaper	Mainichi	Nikkei
Articles	111373	181086

Table 3: Articles Used for the Experiment

the same number of comparable NEs, we link the two patterns as paraphrases.

In Figure 4, each sentence in the pair shares four comparable NEs (*"Nihon Yamamura Glass"*, *"President"*, *"Vice President"*, and *"Osamu Kuroda"*). Moreover, the variables in pattern 1 and 2 also have the same type ($POST_1$) and content (*"President"*). So we can conclude these two patterns are paraphrases.

4. EXPERIMENTS

We used one year of two Japanese newspapers (Mainichi and Nikkei) in this experiment. First we obtained the most relevant 300 articles from Mainichi newspaper (total of 111373 articles) for two domains, arrest events and personnel affairs (hiring and firing of executives). The descriptions and narratives we gave to the IR system are shown in Table 2. Next we find the corresponding articles of Nikkei newspaper from 181086 articles (See Table 3). The pairs whose similarity is below a certain threshold were dropped at this time. We got 294 pairs of articles in arrest events, and 289 pairs of articles in personnel affairs. Next we ran an IE pattern acquisition system for those articles. After dropping the patterns which appear only once, we got 725 patterns and 157 patterns respectively. Then we ran the paraphrase acquisition system for each pair or articles, and finally got total 136 pairs of paraphrases (a link between two IE patterns). The number of article pairs, obtained IE patterns and obtained paraphrases pairs are shown in Table 4.

5. EVALUATION

We evaluated our results in two respects: precision and coverage. To measure them, first we need to prepare the answer data. This is done by manually classifying the IE patterns for each domain. The criteria of classification are the following:

1. Do they describe the same event?

Domain	Arrest events	Personnel affairs
Article pairs	294	289
Sentences	4445	5962
Obtained IE patterns	725	157
Obtained paraphrase links	53	83

Table 4: Article pairs and IE patterns

Domain	Arrest events	Personnel affairs
IE patterns (forms a cluster)	363	129
Clusters	111	20

Table 5: Manually Classified Patterns

Domain	Arrest events	Personnel affairs
Obtained links (yield)	53	83
Correct links	26	78
Precision	49%	94%

Table 6: Precision of paraphrase links

2. If we use them in an actual IE application, do they capture the same information?

For example, the following two patterns are regarded as the same class [2] :

- $ORGANIZATION_1$ decides ϕ.
  ($ORGANIZATION_1$ *ha kettei suru.*)
- $ORGANIZATION_1$ confirms ϕ.
  ($ORGANIZATION_1$ *ha katameru.*)

In the above example, both describe the same event (decision) and the information captured by them is the same (which organization decides).

However, the following two patterns are not in the same class:

- ϕ is promoted to $POST_1$.
  ($POST_1$ *ni shoukaku suru*)
- $POST_1$ is promoted.
  ($POST_1$ *ha shoukaku suru*)

Although these patterns describe the same event (promotion), the information they capture is different. The former pattern captures the new post someone is promoted *to*. However the latter captures the old post someone is promoted *from*. So we put these patterns in different classes. This way, we get several clusters of patterns for each domain. We take only patterns which form a cluster and drop single-element patterns which do not have a paraphrase among the patterns. The result of manual classification in this experiment is shown in Table 5. We got 111 distinct clusters for arrest events and 20 for personnel affairs.

Now we describe how to measure precision and coverage. If the two patterns linked by our procedure are both in the same cluster, it is correct; otherwise, it is incorrect. Thus we measured the precision by counting how many paraphrase links are correct. The results are shown in Table 6. In arrest events domain, we got correct 26 out of 53 links and the precision was 49%. In the personnel affairs domain, we got correct 78 out of 83 links and the precision was 94%. We got quite high precision in personnel affairs, although it is not so high in the arrest domain. We will discuss the difference in the later section. Some examples of obtained correct and incorrect paraphrases are shown in Figure 6.

Next we define the coverage, how well the system obtains all the necessary links. This is done by calculating how many additional links are necessary to connect all the patterns in every cluster. See Figure 5. In this figure, cluster 1 has four obtained links. But the

[2]Note that these patterns are originally written in Japanese and include zero pronouns, which are shown as ϕ.

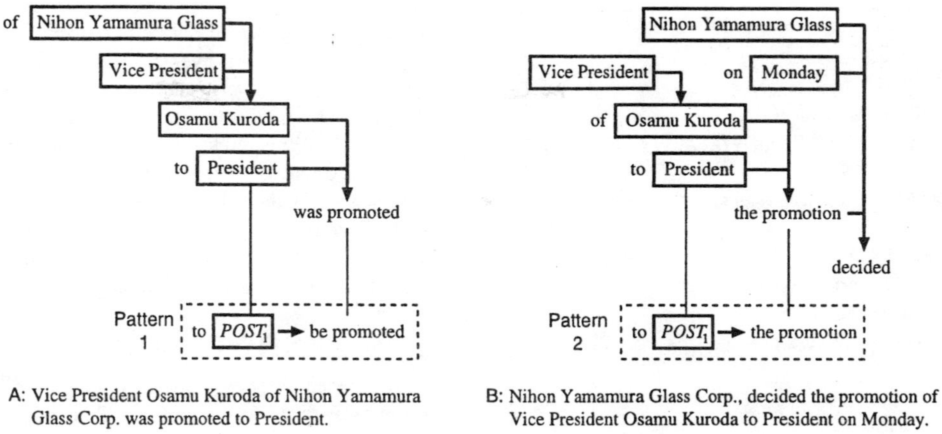

Figure 4: Sample Paraphrase Extraction

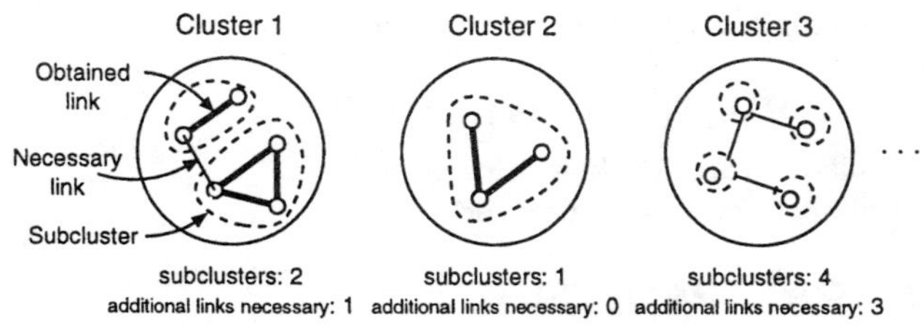

Figure 5: Evaluation of Coverage

Domain	Arrest events	Personnel affairs
Clusters Obtained	6	5
Additional links necessary L	230	57
Total necessary links M	252	109
Coverage	9%	47%

Table 7: Coverage over paraphrase links

cluster is split into two subclusters. So we need at least one additional link to unify these subclusters. Therefore, the number of additional links necessary in cluster 1 is 1. In cluster 2, all the patterns form one cluster, so no further link is needed. In cluster 3, there are four unconnected subclusters. So we need at least three additional links to unify these subclusters. In this way we can calculate the total number of additional links necessary L as:

$$L = \sum^{n} (s_i - 1) \tag{9}$$

Here s_i is the number of subclusters in cluster i. n is the number of clusters.

The smaller the value of L, the more coverage we get, which means the clusters obtained are properly formed. To normalize this value, we use the total number of the necessary links M to make the manually created clusters. This is calculated by summing the number of the links necessary to connect all the patterns in each cluster. So the definition of the coverage C is:

$$C = 1 - \frac{L}{M} \tag{10}$$

Here M is calculated as

$$M = \sum^{n} (p_i - 1) \tag{11}$$

where p_i is the number of the patterns in cluster i.

The results are shown in Table 7. In the arrest domain, links were discovered in 6 of the 111 clusters. 230 additional links would be needed to connect the patterns within all the clusters. The coverage in the arrest domain was 9%, which is not high and we will also discuss this problem in the next section. In the personnel affairs domain, links were discovered in 5 of the 20 clusters. 57 additional links would be needed to connect the patterns within all the clusters. The coverage in the personnel affairs domain was 47%.

6. DISCUSSION

Although this is our initial attempt at automatically extracting paraphrases from a corpus, the results are promising. In particular, we obtained expressions which are different in structure such as "ϕ was promoted to $POST_1$" and "the promotion to $POST_1$ was decided". We also obtained expressions which can be regarded as paraphrases not in general, but in this particular domain. For example, *to admit (mitomeru)* and *to testify (kyoujutsu suru)* are generally not regarded as synonyms. But this semantic relationship is quite useful in this domain.

However, many problems remain. We reviewed our results in terms of the precision and the coverage:

Precision

Currently the precision in arrest events is not high. The main reason is that the average number of NEs in arrest events is low. This makes the obtained IE patterns short. Generally the more NEs contained in a pair of patterns, the more likely that they are paraphrases. However, only 41 patterns out of 725 patterns in arrest events domain contained two or more NEs. Additionally, the expressions used in this domain vary widely in meaning. This makes the obtained IE patterns equally varied. For example, there are 206 patterns in arrest events that contain only one *PERSON* NE. These expressions have varied predicates like *murder, die, run, abduct, rob, testify*, and so on. Since our method only considers the NEs contained in these patterns, a wrong pair of patterns can be paired as paraphrases in this domain.

The lack of NEs raises another problem in the calculation of the sentence similarity. Since we use only NEs for the calculation currently, sentences which contains fewer NEs are likely to be misidentified. So it is important to consider other words in calculating sentence similarity. A possible solution for this problem is to

Arrest events
Correct:

- $ORGANIZATION_1$ arrests ϕ.
  ($ORGANIZATION_1$ ha taiho suru.)
- the investigation authority of $ORGANIZATION_1$ arrests ϕ.
  ($ORGANIZATION_1$ sousa toukyoku ha taiho suru.)

- $PERSON_1$ admits ϕ.
  ($PERSON_1$ ha mitomeru.)
- $PERSON_1$ testifies ϕ.
  ($PERSON_1$ ha kyoujutsu suru.)

Incorrect:

- $PERSON_1$ is arrested.
  ($PERSON_1$ ha taiho sareru.)
- $PERSON_1$ conspires.
  ($PERSON_1$ ha kyoubou suru.)

Personnel affairs
Correct:

- ϕ is promoted to $POST_1$.
  ($POST_1$ ni shoukaku suru.)
- the promotion to $POST_1$ is decided.
  ($POST_1$ no shoukaku wo kettei suru.)

- $ORGANIZATION_1$ decides ϕ.
  ($ORGANIZATION_1$ ha kettei suru.)
- $ORGANIZATION_1$ confirms ϕ.
  ($ORGANIZATION_1$ ha katameru.)

Incorrect:

- $PERSON_1$ is promoted.
  ($PERSON_1$ ha shoukaku suru.)
- $PERSON_1$ hold successively ϕ.
  ($PERSON_1$ ha rekinin suru.)

Figure 6: Examples of obtained paraphrases
(Note that these patterns are originally written in Japanese and include zero pronouns.)

use not only NEs but also common nouns to find similar sentences.

Coverage

In this experiment, the coverage of obtained paraphrases is still low. However, we can expect that we will finally obtain a sufficient number of paraphrases, because the variety of paraphrases in a certain domain can saturate as we use a sufficient number of articles. Instead, the number of potentially obtainable paraphrases is more important because we want to be able to capture as wide a range of paraphrases as possible. So the problem is how to create a system that can handle such varied phrases. Our current IE patterns are limited to a single path in a dependency tree because of the limitation of the IE pattern extraction system we used [5]. For example, we cannot obtain a pattern like "$PERSON_1$ is promoted to $POST_1$", since the dependency tree of this expression has two branches. Now we are independently trying to extend them to include several branches to represent more complicated patterns, which would enable us to obtain more varied paraphrases.

Another possible problem is that not all sentences can be cleanly divided. A phrase used in one sentence may have inherently composite meanings and describe two events at once, whereas the expressions of the two events are separated in the other sentence. These patterns may reduce the overall coverage. For example, a pattern "$PERSON_1$ strangle ϕ" can be regarded as reporting two events: throttling and killing. This is one aspect of our future work.

Moreover, it is natural that comparable NEs appear in several forms which cannot be covered by current NE matching method, like "New York City", "NYC", or "the city". To solve this problem, we may need to consider co-reference information also. We are planning to refine the NE matching method in future.

7. ACKNOWLEDGMENTS

This research is supported by the Defense Advanced Research Projects Agency as part of the Translingual Information Detection, Extraction and Summarization (TIDES) program, under Grant N66001-001-1-8917 from the Space and Naval Warfare Systems Center San Diego, and by the National Science Foundation under Grant IIS-0081962. This paper does not necessarily reflect the position or the policy of the U.S. Government.

8. ADDITIONAL AUTHORS

Additional authors: Ralph Grishman
email: grishman@cs.nyu.edu

9. REFERENCES

[1] R. Barzilay and K. R. McKeown. Extracting Paraphrases from a Parallel Corpus. In *Proceedings of the ACL/EACL*, 2001.

[2] R. Grishman and B. Sundheim. Message Understanding Conference - 6: A Brief History. In *Proceedings of the COLING*, 1996.

[3] M. Murata, K. Uchimoto, H. Ozaku, and Q. Ma. Information Retrieval Based on Stochastic Models in IREX. In *Proceedings of the IREX Workshop*, 1994.

[4] R. Papka, J. Allen, and V. Lavrenko. UMASS Approaches to Detection and Tracking at TDT2. In *DARPA: Broadcast News Workshop*, 1999.

[5] K. Sudo and S. Sekine. Automatic Pattern Acquisition for Japanese Information Extraction. In *Proceedings of the HLT*, 2001.

[6] K. Torisawa. A Nearly Unsupervised Learning Method for Automatic Paraphrasing of Japanese Noun Phrases. In *Proceedings of the Sixth Natural Language Processing Pacific Rim*, 2001.

[7] K. Uchimoto, M. Murata, Q. Ma, H. Ozaku, and H. Isahara. Named Entity Extraction Based on A Maximum Entropy Model and Transformation Rules. In *Proceedings of the 38th Annual Meeting of the Association for Computational Linguistics (ACL)*, pages 326–335, 2000.

[8] C. L. Wayne. Topic Detection & Tracking: A Case Study in Corpus Creation & Evaluation Methodologies. In *Proceedings of the LREC*, 1998.

Resources to Facilitate Progress in Place Name Identification and Reference Resolution

Beth Sundheim
SPAWAR Systems Center
53560 Hull St., Code 244207
San Diego, CA 92152-5001, USA
+1-619-553-4145
sundheim@spawar.navy.mil

Abstract

This paper addresses the issue of enabling improved system performance on analyzing place names in text, especially with respect to resolving place name homonyms, and determining the unique physical location referenced by a name. The utility of reference gazetteers is discussed, and some major characteristics of three broad-coverage ones are described. Ideas are outlined for a community resource comprising one or more reference gazetteers and a variety of algorithms that take named entity tags and gazetteer entry information as input and seek to identify the "location focus/foci" of a document for use by downstream NLP system components and -- via a feedback loop -- by a named entity recognizer. Input from the human language technology community is sought concerning the ideas presented in the paper.

Keywords

gazetteer, toponym, lexical resource, named entity recognition

1. Challenges

Given a reference to "Santiago," how confident would a state-of-the-art name recognizer be about its decision to label the string a geopolitical location name versus a personal name versus some other type of name or a non-name? If it has identified the string in some context correctly as a location name, can the recognizer or a downstream component successfully associate that name with the intended, specific geographical location?

One gazetteer identifies about one million distinct named places [12]. It records "Santiago" as the citation form of the name of 18 different "inhabited places" in the world (in 10 different countries), and also as a "cape," "province," "mine," "deserted settlement," and "river." "Santiago" is also listed as an accepted variant name for 5 additional places. Thus, the homonym "Santiago" can be viewed as having 23 distinct senses, according to this gazetteer.[1] There are larger gazetteers that list even more references for Santiago. What resources do NLP systems need that will permit them to take advantage of such rich reference materials in a way that they won't bog down in excessive name ambiguity?

This paper explores ways to address challenges that NLP systems face in the analysis of named entities that have a geospatial dimension to them:

- **Categorization of place names.** Fine-grained named entity recognition requires the ability to distinguish among at least three major subclasses: politically defined places such as cities and countries, physically defined places (natural features) such as mountain ranges and rivers, and places that are defined by human-built structures and socially-oriented activities, such as airports and parks. In the case of "Santiago," categorization at that level would require distinguishing references to the river and the region (which are both categorized as natural features in the gazetteer used) from references to the province and inhabited places. The ability to do even finer-grained categorization may be necessary to enable complete resolution of homonyms such as "Santiago."
- **Resolution of place name homonyms.** The ability to do such things as distinguish among the many politically defined places known as "Santiago" is especially important when the results of analyzing multiple documents must be merged, as when building a unified database of facts extracted from a large collection of documents, summarizing information gleaned from multiple sources, or answering questions from a large text database.
- **Association of place names with geospatial location.** A geospatial location can be in the form of an absolute location (e.g., coordinates – defining a single, central point, or better yet, defining the entire area) or a relative location (position in a containment hierarchy). Containment information is particularly useful in text analysis, and can generally be derived from coordinate information. However, in general text, coordinate information is seldom given.

1.1 Categorization of Place Names

In the field of information extraction, detailed work has been done on defining terms, including the definition of what

[1] This count disregards multiword citation and variant names in which "Santiago" appears, unless "Santiago" by itself is included as an acceptable variant. However, the gazetteer may not account for all variants that are in common use. Thus, this count may significantly underestimate the true ambiguity of the name.

constitutes a *location*. Recent work in the U.S. Department of Defense's Automatic Content Extraction (ACE) program has included defining criteria for distinguishing a *location*, in the sense of a physically defined place, from the concepts of *geopolitical entity* and *facility* [2]. Actually, the target distinctions made in ACE are more complicated than that, as systems are expected to recognize metonymies (e.g., of an organization as a facility, as in "He visited General Motors.") and to distinguish "roles" of geopolitical entities (e.g., to distinguish "China" as a nation (pure geopolitical entity) from "China" as a physical place (a true location)).

The ability to categorize place names may also play a critical role in a question-answering context. These examples are from the TREC-8 question-answering track [5]:

- **"Which city has the oldest relationship as sister-city with Los Angeles?"** If the system thinks it has evidence from the documents for both "Japan" and "Rio de Janeiro", it needs to realize that "Japan" is not a city and therefore not really a potential answer.
- **"Name a country that is developing a magnetic levitation railway system."** If the system finds text evidence for both "Tokyo" and "Japan", it needs to know to filter out the city "Tokyo".

1.2 Homonym Resolution

The coreference phenomenon underlies the information extraction task of aggregating text references to distinct entities. For this task, it is not enough to determine that two instances of "Santiago" are both references to cities; the system must decide if the references are to the *same* city or not.

In an information extraction application, the need for merging multiple text references to a place into a single database-type record is clear. It is also necessary that references to distinct places be kept separate in the database. In a question-answering application, both needs are also clear. An example from TREC-8 is, "Who is the mayor of Marbella?" If the system finds text evidence for more than one person (mayor), it needs to know if Marbella is the name of more than one city in the world. If there is only one city named Marbella, the system should return information about just one person (the current mayor). If there is more than one such city, then the system could be correct in returning information about more than one person.

Within a single document, one may encounter variant names of a single place (e.g., both "Los Angeles" and "L.A.", both "New York City" and "The Big Apple", or both "Yosemite National Park" and "Yosemite") or mentions of more than one place that happen to have the same name (e.g., "San Diego" appearing in one context as the name of a city and in another context as the name of the county that contains the city). The problem of resolving place name homonyms becomes more salient and more difficult when we extend the coreference task to require the identification of equivalence classes across many documents.

1.3 Association with Geospatial Location

Information on a place's absolute or relative location is potentially useful to a system in the course of analysis. A question-answering example of the potential utility of relative location (containment) information from TREC-8 is, "Where is the Taj Mahal?" If the system is headed in the right direction in its interpretation of "Taj Mahal," and it finds answer evidence for "Agra" in one document and "India" in another, it needs to realize that there is a containment relationship between the places that will allow "Agra, India" to be composed as a single answer. It may or may not be reasonable to assume that systems have this sort of information in their lexicon for major places in the world. However, it is probably not reasonable to assume that they would have such information for all the lesser-known places, and it is certainly the case that state-of-the-art name recognizers, which are statistically-based, avoid the use of long lists of names.

There may also be times when text interpretation requires knowledge of absolute location (geospatial coordinate) information. Consider, for example, a case where the phrase, "These two neighboring cities..." appears in a context where it's not clear which pair of some set of previously mentioned cities is intended. In such a case, containment information would not necessarily help to resolve the ambiguity, but comparison of precise coordinates for the various cities could yield the correct analysis.

In a situation where natural language is being used as a front-end interface to non-text databases, knowledge of the geospatial coordinates of a named location may be critical. An example in [8] is "What satellite images cover the area of Lisbon?", where the coordinates for Lisbon must be discovered before the query can be answered by the backend system. And, of course, in geospatial information system applications where information gleaned from text sources is to be linked to a point displayed on a map, knowledge of coordinates is essential for end-to-end functionality. The Mitre GeoNode system [9] is an example of this sort of application.

2. Reference Gazetteers

One resource that can help systems to identify more location names and to understand them in greater depth is a next-generation gazetteer, tuned to the needs of NLP. We consider a gazetteer to be a geographical dictionary that contains the name(s), type, location and perhaps other attributes of politically and physically defined places. A gazetteer can be used to find the geographic location of a named place, and conversely, to find all named places within a certain geographic area.

Usually, a gazetteer is organized around a "standard" version of the name, with alternative names identified as variants (possibly including foreign-language versions of the standard name). A next-generation gazetteer would come off the shelf with algorithms that do more than just dictionary lookup. They would also manage the ambiguity that results from the lookup and would offer alternative, coherent analyses of the set of location names found in a given text. The analyses would indicate which gazetteer entries correspond to which names, and would associate a ranking or likelihood score to each overall analysis.

For the DARPA-sponsored Tipster Text program some years ago, a gazetteer was distilled from primary sources and made available to information extraction system developers [4]. This was used to support the "scenario" (event-related) informtion extraction task requirements of MUC-5 and MUC-6. A gazetteer also supported the broadcast news (HUB) named entity evaluations, but only as reference for the annotators, who had to label location names in the monocase transcripts. In that case, the gazetteer was a commercial, hardcopy one, and its main function was to enable improved interannotator agreement on tag assignment [10].

Under the auspices of DARPA's Translingual Detection, Extraction and Summarization (TIDES) program, the Space and Naval Warfare Systems Center, San Diego is currently exploring ways to enable the language technology community to directly address the challenges outlined earlier in this paper. One aspect of this effort is to survey existing world gazetteers and to gauge the necessity, advisability and feasibility of selecting one or more to support development of a community resource. Three candidate gazetteers that are more comprehensive and more highly-organized than the Tipster one are the Alexandria Digital Library gazetteer at the University of California, Santa Barbara [1], the Thesaurus of Geographic Names (TGN) produced by the Getty Museum [12], and the GEOnet Names Server database (GNDB) of the National Imagery and Mapping Agency [7]. All except the Tipster gazetteer are available in relational database format, as well as via web server. ADL's design is based on their Gazetteer Content Standard, which is intended to facilitate incorporation of data from multiple sources and mapping among sources.

The Tipster, ADL, and TGN gazetteers all draw heavily from GNDB. They also draw from a second government source, the US Geological Survey's Geographic Names Information System (GNIS) Digital Gazetteer, for coverage of places in the United States [6]. Each contains contributions from other sources as well; for example, the Tipster gazetteer also draws from open-source CIA materials. Bibliographic source information is not recorded in the Tipster gazetteer entries. Many TGN entries reference multiple bibliographic sources, including a number of commercial ones, while ADL sources are generally limited to GNIS and GNDB. Both ADL and TGN record the contributor of information contained in each entry. The Getty's own Vocabulary Program is one TGN contributor, and it has provided such useful information as nationality names (as variants of country names).

The Tipster gazetteer (v4.0) contains entries for around 240,000 different places. The TGN, which has entries for approximately 1 million places, is intended to meet the needs of organizations with an interest in art and architecture and therefore does not necessarily include smaller places that are not somehow important in the art world. ADL, which was built primarily from the 3.81-million entry GNDB (as of February 2002) and the 2 million-entry GNIS, has almost 4.44 million entries (as of April 2001).

With the exception of the Tipster gazetteer, all the gazetteers discussed include coordinate information in one or more formats, along with other descriptive information. Coordinate data is generally limited to a single point reference; however, for a small number of entries for places in the US, ADL records multiple coordinate pairs (linear points for rivers, bounding boxes for administrative areas).

The Tipster gazetteer includes a type attribute for each entry, which identifies the place as a city, province, or country. This is recorded together with containment information, e.g., Santiago (CITY) is contained in Santiago (PROVINCE), which is contained in Chile (COUNTRY). The other gazetteers mentioned cover a broader range of location types and have a correspondingly broader set of types.

Places in TGN are identified explicitly as being either physical or political. Physical features are children of politically-defined places, attaching as low in the politically-defined hierarchy as the "county" level (for places in the U.S.) or the "populated places" level (for places outside the U.S.). A place may have may have both a physical and a political parent. Bermuda, for example, is a "dependent state" that is physically in North/Central America and politically part of the United Kingdom. Containment relations in ADL are generally not explicit; however, certain types of containment relations (*in-state-of*, *in-province-of*, *in-country-of*, *in-region-of*) are recorded in some cases, and in other cases a *part-of* relationship is recorded. The former is handy when there exists a political (administrative) containment relationship, but not a physical (spatial) containment relationship, as in the Bermuda case mentioned above. The latter is used for recording other geospatial containment relationships than those that are specifically defined, and for recording the place's absolute location in coordinate systems other than latitude and longitude.

Along with the type attribute, the Tipster gazetteer entries for cities, ports, provinces and islands include an accompanying numeric value to indicate the relative size/population or general importance of the place (within a given type). There is an attribute for this sort of ranking in GNDB, but it is only sparsely populated. (GNIS also has an attribute that is defined to contain either population information or elevation, but currently it is not used for population.) Size/population information is not explicitly given in the TGN; however, it is often possible to gauge the relative significance of a place by the number of bibliographic sources cited. In both TGN and ADL, national capital cities can be distinguished from other cities.

3. Algorithms for Gazetteer Exploitation

The next-generation gazetteer resource would include algorithms to enable NLP systems to exploit the gazetteer effectively. The results of the effort to build such a resource would not only enable the systems to better understand isolated location references in a document, but would also provide the foundation for them to obtain a spatially grounded understanding of the whole document. We see these algorithms being invoked early during system processing, perhaps on the output of a statistically-based name recognition component.

Given the location names identified by the name recognition component, the algorithms would provide answers to the following questions:

- What names are unambiguous, and where are those named locations? That is, which specific gazetteer entry corresponds to each unambiguous name?
- Of the ambiguous names, are there any that are ambiguous only within a certain country?
- Do all the names in the document bear some containment relationship to each other, if we assume the ambiguities are resolved in a certain way?
- Can some common level of granularity be found among all or most of the names, and can that

granularity information help resolve any of the name ambiguities?

The answers to these questions would be synthesized into a set of alternative hypotheses about the *location focus* or *location foci* of a document. Each hypothesis would account for all the location names in the text. These hypotheses would be preserved in some ranked form on the basis of their relative likelihood. Downstream components of the system could consider one or more of them in their analysis.

We believe that some of the same sorts of enriched gazetteer information can help the performance of the name recognition component itself. The concept is to assist the component by feeding information back to it about the coherence of the place names it believes it correctly recognized. The gazetteer algorithms would also examine person and organization names identified by the component, and would attempt to evaluate whether some of those should be recategorized as locations, given the hypothesized location focus. For example, if "Santiago" were identified as a person by the component, these algorithms might suggest that it be considered a likely location if they had determined that the location focus of the document was probably Chile. In other words, the algorithms' top-down view of the document could supplement the bottom-up type of bigram information that the name recognizer might depend on. If the name recognizer knew that it had had only weak statistical evidence to support its original analysis, it might then actually be able to assign new weightings and rerun its analysis.

3.1 Testing the Ideas

In order to gauge the feasibility of our ideas, we have conducted a very small study in which we have run BBN's IdentiFinder name tagger system [3] on ten texts from Chilean news sources on Latin American terrorism. These texts were taken from the corpus used in an evaluation of information extraction systems [11]. We have analyzed IdentiFinder's output and done manual gazetteer lookup of location names found in the ten texts, focusing primarily on the TGN as our gazetteer. We have then attempted to characterize the types of evidence that would lead to a correct resolution of the place name references made in each text.

IdentiFinder is delivered off-the-shelf with a location word list of 3,718 entries. Each entry is just an isolated name; there is no information about the type of the referenced location, its containment relations, or its coordinates. The system uses the list as a supplement to its statistical model. The system has no idea that the name "Modesto" is on its default location word list because of its significance as a California city. Given a news article about Chile, it has no way of knowing that a mention of Modesto in that context is unlikely to be a location (i.e., more likely to be a person). In the absence of training data, however, it can make no better decision than to identify Modesto as a place name.

On the ten news articles from Chile, IdentiFinder correctly tagged many of the location names (28 out of 42 ground-truth tags), but it also made a total of about 16 errors (16 out of 44 system-generated tags). Informally stated, there were 9 errors of commission: incorrect categorization as person (5) or organization (2) rather than as location, or incorrect categorization as location (2) rather than as person. The latter 2 errors account for the higher denominator in the error ratio. In addition, there were 7 errors of omission, i.e., failure to identify a location name as a name at all. In addition, in one case a location name that appeared twice in a document was correctly identified once and incorrectly identified once.

In the next sections, we will analyze two of the ten texts used in the experiment after having run the texts through IdentiFinder and having manually looked up names in the TGN. The names that were looked up included all those that IdentiFinder categorized as locations, plus all other names that the human reader believed to be locations, including those that were tagged by IdentiFinder as organization or person.

The examples show how gazetteer information might be exploited to gain one or more coherent, document-level interpretations of place names, and how the information might feed back to a location name recognizer. In these examples, IdentiFinder was configured to run using its default location name word list. IdentiFinder's tags for persons and organizations are shown in addition to those for locations; tags for dates have been removed. The ground-truth location names appear in boldface, including ones that are not tagged by IdentiFinder.

3.2 Example of Location Focus Based on Political/Physical Containment Data

Figure 1 shows an article about terrorist acts that have taken place in various locales in Chile. TGN contains just one entry for Melipilla, a populated place in Chile. Rapel also exists only in Chile, and can refer to either a river or a reservoir. These two places are in a different province from the one that contains Melipilla. Although we may not be able to determine which of the entries for Rapel is the correct one, the fact that Rapel is a known location could be used to refine IdentiFinder's tagging of "Melipilla-Rapel" as a single location.

The unambiguous country location of Melipilla and Rapel can be used as evidence that if the document has an overall location focus, it could be Chile. This hypothesis is further strengthened by the names Copiapó and Carrizal Bajo, which are listed as places in a third province in Chile. (Copiapó can be either an inhabited place or a river in Chile; there is also a mine called Copiapo Mine in the US, but "Copiapo" alone is not listed as a variant form of that name.) This strong evidence could then be used to bias the interpretation of the name Santiago, i.e., toward one of three entries -- the capital city of Chile, the containing region, and the South American river. The fact that the name appears in the dateline would further bias the interpretation toward the city.

Unfortunately, the names Maitenes, Itahua and Alto Jahuel do not appear in TGN. A search in NIMA's GNDB yields at least 14 exact matches on "Maitenes", all in Chile, plus 11 matches on Maitenes as head word in a multiword name of a place in Chile and 3 similar matches in Argentina. There are no exact matches on Itahua. There is just one match on Alto Jahuel, and it is for a place in Chile. It could be interesting to use TGN as a first source of information, supplemented by lookup in GNDB of just the names that are not found in TGN. Since our implementation plan would limit our lookup to just those strings that a name recognizer had tagged as location, person or organization, the number of separate lookups would be limited.

In the current example, IdentiFinder mistakenly categorized Itahua-Alto Jahuel as a (single) person. The GNDB information on Alto Jahuel and the document location focus hypothesis provided by our gazetteer exploitation algorithms could provide feedback to the name recognition process. If the tag on Alto Jahuel could be corrected, the recognizer could perhaps also correct the tagging of Itahua, despite the fact that that name does not appear in the gazetteer.

<ID TYPE=LOCATION>**Santiago**</ID>, 3 Oct 88 (<ID TYPE=ORGANIZATION>Domestic Service</ID>) -- [Text] A terrorist attack, in which Czechoslovak bombs were used, has destroyed four high tension towers in the central region. This attack has cut the electricity supply to a vast region between <ID TYPE=LOCATION>**Copiapo**</ID> and <ID TYPE= LOCATION>**Santiago**</ID>. The blackout occurred on Saturday night, 1 October, and lasted for approximately one-half hour in the metropolitan region.

According to <ID TYPE=ORGANIZATION>ENDESA </ID> [<ID TYPE=ORGANIZATION>National Electric Power, Inc.</ID>], one of the towers knocked down was located on km 24 of the <ID TYPE=LOCATION>**Melipilla-Rapel**</ID> highway.

The tower, located in the **Maitenes** sector, is one of the main towers of the high tension network.

Another tower destroyed by the terrorists was tower No 430 in the <ID TYPE=PERSON>**Itahua-Alto Jahuel**</ID> sector, which is connected to the main electricity network.

In addition to these four destroyed towers, other explosions were heard that same night in <ID TYPE=LOCATION> **Santiago**</ID>. They were caused by bombs planted by terrorists who seek to frighten the population.

According to police sources, the bombs used to cause so much damage are powerful Czechoslovak-made plastic bombs, of the same type that were found among the clandestine arsenals smuggled into the country by the Marxist leftists at <ID TYPE=ORGANIZATION>**Carrizal Bajo**</ID>. [...]

Figure 1. News article about terrorist acts in Chile

3.3 Example of Location Focus Based on Granularity Data

Figure 2 shows an article about international travel made by Chilean terrorists.

If we approach the analysis the same way as before, looking at commonalities in geographic location among the location names in the article, then

1. Santiago, Cuba, and Angola have USA in common (where each could be one of any number of different places in a variety of US states);
2. Santiago, Cuba and Europe have Europe in common (where Santiago is in Spain, Cuba is in Portugal, and Europe is the continent);
3. Santiago and Angola have Africa in common (where Santiago is in Cape Verde and Angola is the African nation).

However, none of the above commonalities in geographic location leads to the correct analysis of the location focus of the document. The document, in fact, has more than one location focus.

If we look instead at commonalities in granularity, then we note that all but one of the location references could be to a nation or a continent:

1. Cuba and Angola have nation granularity in common;
2. Europe is a continent (and unambiguous).

Further evidence for an interpretation based on coarse granularity comes from the nationality names that appear in the text: "Angolan", "Chilean", "Cuban" and "Cubans". With the exception of the plural form "Cubans", all of these appear in the TGN as variant names for the nation.

The only anomaly in the granularity-based analysis is "Santiago", then, which would have to undergo special datelin analysis, as in the previous example. The presence of "Chilean" in the article gives weight to Santiago being a place in Chile.

<ID TYPE=LOCATION>**Santiago**</ID>, 22 Aug 88 (EL MERCURIO) -- [Excerpt] Very reliable security sources have reported that the clandestine entry of FPMR [<ID TYPE= PERSON>Manuel Rodriguez</ID> <ID TYPE= ORGANIZATION>Patriotic Front</ID>] members, who fought alongside the Marxist Angolan Government, has recently been detected in the country.

The extremists, all Chilean nationals selected from <ID TYPE=ORGANIZATION>FPMR</ID> members, first completed their theoretical training in guerrilla warfare in <ID TYPE=LOCATION>**Cuba**</ID> before traveling to <ID TYPE=LOCATION>**Angola**</ID> with Cuban troops. The Cubans were assigned to the defense of the Marxist government that is fighting against the <ID TYPE=ORGANIZATION> UNITA</ID> rebels. Having finished their practical training in a country where approximately 50,000 troops are stationed, these <ID TYPE=ORGANIZATION>FPMR</ID> terrorists returned to <ID TYPE=LOCATION>**Cuba**</ID>, from where they traveled to <ID TYPE=LOCATION>**Europe**</ID>, before finally returning to Chilean territory. [...]

Figure 2. News article about Chilean terrorist movements internationally

3.4 Evaluation Plans

To evaluate the end-to-end concept outlined in this paper after the exploitation algorithms have been developed, we currently expect to carry out a study that includes three configurations of IdentiFinder and that entails manual review of the output of the gazetteer exploitation algorithms.

1. IdentiFinder will be set up to use different word lists during evaluation, e.g., there will be a run in which its off-the-shelf word list is used, one in which a gazetteer-derived list drawn from all the words in the test corpus is used, and one in which no word list is used.
2. The gazetteer exploitation algorithms will be applied to IdentiFinder's output. The results will be analyzed quantitatively to determine where the correct location focus solution for a document is found in the ranked

output (or if it is not found in the output at all), how often it correctly and incorrectly concluded that an IdentiFinder category assignment was in error, etc.

4. Conclusion

Perhaps the biggest overall challenge in developing exploitation algorithms on top of broad-coverage gazetteers is to avoid overwhelmin systems with potential ambiguity. As part of a general strategy to manage the ambiguity issue, we propose to

1. use the output of a statistically-based name recognizer as input to the gazetteer lookup, rather than looking up all the terms in a document;
2. do the initial lookup in a smaller gazetteer such as the TGN, and resort to a larger one such as ADL only in cases where no entry exists in the smaller one;
3. develop algorithms that seek to identify the most probable location focus/foci of a document, based on political/geographical containment data and granularity data, and that rank the results in order of likelihood.

We invite the human language technology research community to provide feedback to the goals and ideas expressed in this paper.

5. REFERENCES

[1] Alexandria Digital Library gazetteer website. http://www.alexandria.ucsb.edu/adl.html.

[2] Automatic Content Extraction program website. http://www.itl.nist.gov/iaui/894.01/tests/ace/phase1/doc/index.htm.

[3] D. Bikel, S. Miller, R. Schwartz, and R. Weischedel. 1997. "Nymbel: a High-Performance Learning Name-finder," in *Fifth Conference on Applied Natural Language Processing*, Association for Computational Linguistics, pp. 194-201.

[4] L. Carlson, B. Onyshkevych, M.E. Okurowski. 1993. "Corpora and Data Preparation," in *Proceedings of the Fifth Message Understanding Conference*, Morgan Kaufmann Publishers, pp. 1-5.

[5] Eighth Text Retrieval Conference website. http://trec.nist.gov/pubs/trec8/t8_proceedings.html

[6] Geographic Names Information System. http://nsdi.usgs.gov/products/gnis.html.

[7] GEOnet Names Server website. http://164.214.2.59/gns/html/index.html.

[8] L. Hill. 2000. "Core elements of digital gazetteers: placenames, categories, and footprints," in J. Borbinha & T. Baker (Eds.), *Research and Advanced Technology for Digital Libraries: Proceedings of the 4th European Conference, ECDL 2000.* Berlin: Springer, pp. 280-290.

[9] R. Hyland, C. Clifton, R. Holland. 1999. "GeoNODE: Visualizing News in a Geospatial Context," Federal Data Mining Symposium and Exposition '99, AFCEA, March 9-10, 1999, Washington, D.C.

[10] P. Robinson, E. Brown, J. Burger, N. Chinchor, A. Douthat, L. Ferro, L. Hirschman. 1999. "Overview: Information Extraction from Broadcast News," in *Proceedings of DARPA Broadcast News Workshop*, Morgan Kaufmann Publishers, pp. 27-30.

[11] B. Sundheim. 1992. "Overview of the Fourth Message Understanding Evaluation and Conference," in *Proceedings of the Fourth Message Understanding Conference*, Morgan Kaufmann Publishers, pp. 3-21.

[12] Thesaurus of Geographic Names website. http://www.getty.edu/research/tools/vocabulary/tgn/.

Infrastructure for Open-Domain Information Extraction

Mihai Surdeanu
Language Computer Corporation
6440 North Central Expressway
Dallas TX 75206
mihai@languagecomputer.com

Sanda M. Harabagiu
Language Computer Corporation
6440 North Central Expressway
Dallas TX 75206
sanda@languagecomputer.com

ABSTRACT

The problem of performing open-domain Information Extraction (IE) was historically tied to the problem of ad-hoc acquisition of extraction patterns. In this paper we show that this requirement is not sufficient and that we also need to build new IE architectures that combine the role of linguistic patterns with coreference knowledge and ambiguous syntactic and semantic information. We present the implementation of a novel IE architecture, namely the CICERO system and show how (1) both high precision and high recall results were obtained for a variety of extraction domains; and (2) how textual information can be extracted for virtually any domain in a precise and reliable way. The evaluation of CICERO's performance shows a significant improvement over MUC IE systems.

1. INTRODUCTION

In the 90s, the Message Understanding Conferences (MUCs) and the TIPSTER programs gave great impetus to research in information extraction (IE). The systems that participated in the MUCs have been quite successful at extracting information from newswire messages and filling templates with the information pertaining to the events of interest. Typically, the templates model queries regarding *who* did *what* to *whom*, *when* and *where*, and eventually *why*. The most remarkable results concerned the performance of some of the IE subtasks that has reached near-human precision. For example, current Named Entities were recognized with over 90% precision. Not as successful was the broader task of event recognition (i.e. filling in scenario templates) which resulted in at most 60% recall and 70% precision. For a while, this was believed to be a de-facto performance barrier of IE systems. The rationale of this belief is partly explained by the converging results of different IE systems performing scenario template extractions. The other explanation stems from the similar architectures of IE systems that participated in the last MUC evaluations.

In todays' world the need for Information Extraction is more pervasive than ever. In fact, we need to be able to operate open-domain IE, in which the domain of interest results from several interactions with the user, in quest of capturing novel data trends from massive text collections. Successful open-domain IE cannot be achieved only by automatically learning linguistic patterns that encode the domain knowledge. We also need to reliably recognize corefering entities or events of interest and we need to disambiguate precisely syntactic and semantic information pertaining to the topic of interest, regardless of domain. Moreover, in this paper we claim that open-domain IE systems need to extract scenario templates with better performance than the typical systems evaluated in MUC. For this reason we have developed the infrastructure that surpassed the 70% F-score ceiling, and thus provides high-performance IE for any possible domain. This infrastructure is best illustrated by the architecture of CICERO, the IE system developed by Language Computer Corporation and represented in Figure 1. In order to emphasize the novelties introduced by our information extraction system, we separated CICERO's modules in two categories: modules seen in traditional IE systems, and novel modules introduced in CICERO.

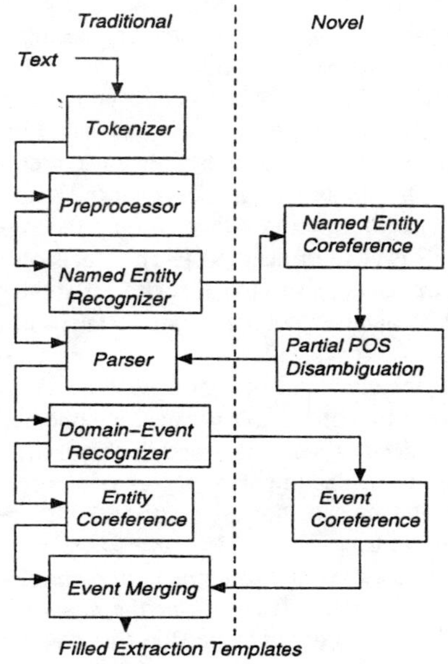

Figure 1: The architecture of the CICERO IE system.

CICERO's first module is the *tokenizer*, whose task is to break the message into lexical entities or tokens. A lexical recognizer identifies tokens or groups of tokens that are entries in dictionaries or gazetteers[1]. The *preprocessor* patterns identify simple numerical lexical entities, such as *money*, *percents*, *dates*, or *times*. The next

[1]Gazetteers are long lists of location or person names.

Proceedings of HLT 2002, Second International Conference on Human Language Technology Research, M. Marcus, ed., Morgan Kaufmann, San Francisco, 2002.

module recognizes named-entities like *persons*, *organizations*, or *locations*. The *named-entity coreference* is the first novel module introduced by CICERO. Its task is to help disambiguate incomplete or ambiguous named entities. For example, given the name *Austin*, it is classified either as a *person* or a *location* depending on possible reference to previous entities from the text. This module is described in more detail in the next section. The *partial part of speech (POS) disambiguation* module is another CICERO novelty. We use this module to enhance the precision of POS tagging. This feature is important for the resolution of nominal anaphorae in texts, which in turn greatly influences the overall performance of IE, as we will show throughout this paper. We implemented the POS disambiguation module using voting between our lexicons and an external POS tagger (Eric Brill's POS tagger [2]). The next module is a *phrasal parser*, used to identify noun, verb and particle phrases. As reported in [4], successful IE systems can be implemented by relying only on phrasal parsers and by cascading Finite-State Automata (FSAs) that recognize patterns corresponding to (1) named entities; (2) simple and complex phrases and (3) information relevant to the domain of interest. Such traditional IE architectures (cf. [1], [3], or [5]) prefer finite-state models over full natural language processing because they would rather do only the *right* language processing for IE instead of deep NLP. This decision was largely inspired by the tremendous success in MUC-3 that the group at the University of Massachusetts obtained with a fairly simple system [6].

Anaphoric expressions hinder the process of matching event patterns. To resolve pronominal and nominal anaphorae, we use an *open-domain coreference* resolution module that generates coreference links between each noun phrase and antecedents that agree in number, gender and are semantically consistent with the anaphora. Coreference resolution enables the *domain event recognizer* to match text against event patterns and to populate the corresponding domain templates/templettes[2]. The task of the *domain coreference* module is to fill template or templette slots that could not be filled using domain patterns. The *merging* module is used to combine templates/templettes that refer to the same event. It gives precedence to templates found inside the same sentence.

The novel IE architecture implemented in CICERO generates impressive extraction results. For example, on the *"management succession"* domain tested in the MUC-6 evaluations, it obtains an F-score of 83%. The F-score is defined as $F = \frac{P \times R}{R+R}$ where P is precision and R is recall.

2. IMPROVING EXTRACTION RESULTS

After the MUC-6 evaluations it was believed that the performance of an IE system is directly proportional with the number of rules available. The ACCELERATE program analyzed this claim and showed that it is not valid. Thus, before creating any open-domain IE infra-structure, we need to analyze in depth the conditions that enable the best performing IE system. We have found that two factors are determinant for obtaining high-performance IE:

1. *Coreference* plays an important role. In fact coreference resolution is an engineering bottleneck in IE systems because (1) it influences *merging* of information referring to same entity or event, and (2) it participates in the *disambiguation* of incompletely defined entities/events. We identified three forms of coreference useful for IE:

   (a) Coreference is first used by the *named-entity recognizer* to classify named entities. For example, the named-entity "Michigan" can be either a location name, or an organization abbreviation. A coreference chain linking this entity to "Michigan Corp." disambiguates this entity to a not-so-intuitive organization name. To evaluate the impact of coreference on the named entity recognizer (NER) we evaluated the performance of CICERO's NER on the MUC-6 test data, with and without coreference information[3]. Our experiments indicated that, for the NE task alone, the coreference determines over 5% increase in F-measure: the NER F-measure without coreference information is 87.81, whereas the F-measure after coreference information is available is 93.64.

   (b) An open-domain *entity coreference* algorithm is used to resolve nominal and pronominal anaphors. Similar approaches were taken by other IE systems, hence we do not focus on this issue.

   (c) *Event coreference* is used to fill template or templette slots that can not be filled using pattern matching rules. The domain coreference uses the same candidate retrieval strategy as any open-domain coreference module, but each semantic filter is adapted for the type of entity that is compatible with the corresponding missing slot. Consider the following text from the "natural disasters" domain:

   > ... flooding has become a way of life in Guerneville in the last several years. This gas station along the Russian River gets hit nearly every time. ...

   CICERO's domain event recognizer successfully recognizes the text "This gas station along the Russian River gets hit" as part of the `<DISASTER DESTROYS ARTIFACT>`, but it fails to identify "flooding" as the disaster type. Event coreference fills the empty templette slot with the disaster entity closest to the recognized pattern (.e.g. "flooding").

   To evaluate the impact of coreference on the rest of IE system, we used as baseline the system with the entity and event coreference modules disabled, and compared the baseline against a system with entity coreference enabled, and against a system with all coreference modules enabled. Figure 2 plots CICERO's performance for the MUC-6 domain and the three configurations, when the number of meta-rules increases from 1 to 26. Figure 2 shows two important ideas: first, it indicates that coreference almost doubles the performance of an IE system, a radical result different from previous IE system performance analysis reports. As Figure 2 indicates, CICERO without coreference barely approaches the 50% F-measure range, while with coreference enabled it reaches the upper 70% range.

2. The usage of *non-deterministic finite state automata (FSA)*, which can handle ambiguous input and can generate ambiguous output is vital for the handling of natural language ambiguities. The non-deterministic FSAs are used to postpone the decision taking for ambiguous output until sufficient contextual information (i.e. coreference chains or do-

[2]For each extraction task a domain template is defined, as an interface to database entries. The TIPSTER MUC evaluations used predefined templates. The population of templates required cumbersome rules for filling and scoring. In an attempt to simplify the template processing, the Hub-4 Event99 introduced the "templettes", consisting of just a few slots representing basic information such as main event participants, event outcome, time and location.

[3]Throughout this paper we use MUC-6 dry run documents as training data, when not mentioned otherwise.

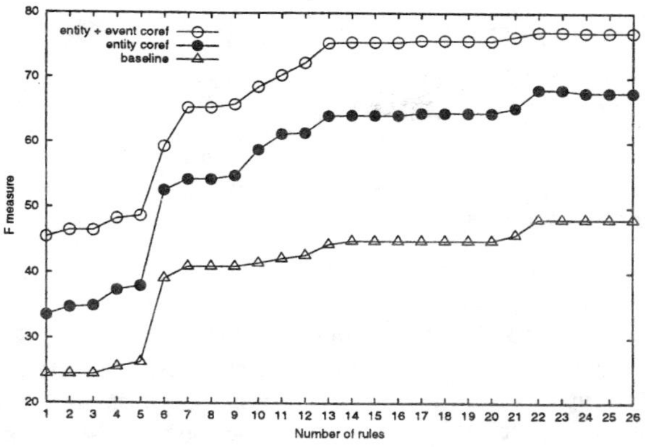

Figure 2: The impact of entity and event coreference on the performance of the CICERO IE system.

main patterns) exists to eliminate ambiguities. For example, our named entity recognizer is able to associate multiple semantic tags to named entity, leaving the task of tag disambiguation to the named-entity coreference module, which has access to increased context because it uses textual information from the whole document. Our novel non-deterministic pattern matching technique reduces the propagation of errors between IE modules, because we propagate all possible solutions, which increases the probability that we identify the correct solution. In other words, we maximize the *recall* of the initial FSA-based modules (i.e. preprocessor, named-entity recognizer and parser) and use the domain-event recognizer and the coreference modules to increase *precision* due to their better understanding of the processed text.

Nevertheless non-deterministic FSAs need to be controlled to avoid the generation of spurious input objects for the next processing stage. This observation is implemented in CICERO with a series of additional filters. For example the "Partial POS disambiguation" module is used to control the phrasal parser output. If POS disambiguation is not enabled, the phrasal parser generates different syntactic phrases for each POS tag combination that matches a grammar rule. For example, the word "seek" can be both a noun and a verb phrase if additional constraints are not present in the text. Allowing the phrasal parser to generate all possible phrases complicates significantly the task of the entity coreference module, which attempts to build coreference chains for all noun phrases. That is why in the current CICERO implementation we have added the POS disambiguation stage, which uses a voting algorithm between our internal lexicon and Eric Brill's POS tagger to reduce the number of noun phrases constructed by the parser. Similarly, named-entity coreference can be regarded as a filtering stage for the spurious entries generated by the named-entity module.

3. THE ROLE OF COREFERENCE IN IE

This section describes the novel coreference resolution mechanisms implemented in CICERO. We noticed five different situations where coreference resolution is important. The first three situations are handled by the named-entity coreference module, and the last two by the open-domain coreference and the domain coreference correspondingly.

1] Disambiguate incomplete named-entities
This task disambiguates entities that are likely to be part of a name, but can not be identified as such due to incomplete information. For example, the second occurrence of the string "Michigan National" in the text:

> "Michigan National Corp. said it will eliminate some senior management jobs... Michigan National said the restructuring..."

can not be identified as a named entity, but it can be safely associated with an organization name because the string "Michigan National Corp." appears as a coreference candidate in the same context.

2] Disambiguate named-entities
This task disambiguates entities which have either ambiguous length or ambiguous type. For example, the type of the named entity "Michigan" will be changed from location to organization if the string "Michigan Corp." appears in the same context. The second issue addresses the disambiguation of named entities with ambiguous length: if no NE pattern is matched, the string "Young's" may correspond either to the organization named entity "Young's" or to another named entity of shorter length: "Young". Our solution to the above problem is to construct both entities in the named-entity recognizer. In the named-entity coreference module we maintain only the entity that is consistent with its context. For example, if the context surrounding the ambiguous entities contains the organization "Young's Corp.", the shorter length entity "Young" is deleted and "Young's" is disambiguated to an organization named entity.

3] Recognize headline named-entities
The headline named entity recognition is considered to be a more complicated problem than the recognition of named entities located in the message body, because headline words are typically all capitalized or start with capitalized letters and case is a very important feature in named entity grammars. As an alternative to case-insensitive grammars, we proposed a coreference-based approach for the headline NE recognition. We initially delay the processing of headline named entities until after the message body is processed. Then we use a longest match approach to match the headline sequence of tokens against entity names recognized in the first message paragraph. For example, in the headline "McDermott Completes Sale" only the string "McDermott" is disambiguated to an organization named-entity because "McDermott International Inc." appears in the first message paragraph. Note that our case sensitive grammar would have matched the whole headline as a potential named-entity. By using coreference we are able to achieve better results with a simpler approach.

4] Resolution of nominal/pronominal anaphors
The resolution of nominal and pronominal references increases significantly the recall of the pattern recognition mechanism implemented in the domain event recognizer. For example, if a domain pattern expects to see an organization name in a certain position, it will not match over the "it" pronoun, unless the pronoun refers to an organization name. The coreference algorithm is implemented in two steps: a *candidate retrieval* step which identifies possible candidates for the current coreference link, and a *semantic consistency filtering* step, which selects the first candidate that is semantically consistent with the anaphor. For semantic filtering we employ dedicated filters for pronoun, person name, organization name, and common noun candidates. For example, a common noun candidate is considered consistent with the anaphor if the two entities agree in number and gender and the anaphor is a hypernym or synonym of the candidate in WordNet.

5] Fill in missing template/templette slots
Following the domain event recognizer the domain coreference fills

the template or templette slots that could not be filled by the previous module using patterns, which are represented as Finite State Automata (FSA). Due to the inherent complexity of the natural language, there are many situations when relevant information is not expressed in a form that can be captured by a reasonable pattern, hence the importance of domain coreference. The following example from a "natural disaster" message illustrates the problem:

> ... Although warmer temperatures have helped out Montreal today, and ice has come crashing down nearly everywhere, public utilities here are still a mess. Overnight, massive power outages knocked out a water filtration plant, ...

For the above text, CICERO's domain event recognizer partially matches the `<DISASTER DESTROYS ARTIFACT>` pattern over the text "knocked out a water filtration plant". Due to the incomplete match, the constructed templette lacks the type of disaster that caused the event, and the location and date of the event, which, even though present in the text, can not be extracted with an acceptable pattern. The domain-dependent coreference module is used in such situations to search the pattern context for entities that match the missing slots. In the above example, using domain coreference we are able the retrieve the disaster type ("ice"), the event location ("Montreal") and the event date ("today").

4. NON-DETERMINISTIC FSA

The addition of non-deterministic FSAs is another contributing factor in CICERO's performance. The following examples show how non-deterministic FSAs are used to accommodate the natural language ambiguities. For example, in the text:

> "... the storm hit Lincoln ..."

the named-entity recognizer generates both location and person named-entities for the string "Lincoln" due to scarcity of semantic information. This ambiguity propagates through CICERO's modules up to the domain event recognizer which disambiguates "Lincoln" as a location named-entity with the pattern `<DISASTER HAPPENED-IN LOCATION>`. Another example was presented in the previous section, where coreference is used to disambiguate ambiguous named-entities. If non-deterministic FSAs were not used, the construction of ambiguous output, either of different type like "Michigan" as both location and organization name, or of different length like "Young" and "Young's" would not be possible. The last example presented shows the application of non-deterministic FSAs to parsing. One of the problems we encountered during the implementation of the deterministic parser was the treatment of "that", which can be both a determiner and a particle. The correct parsing of "that" is extremely important because it affects all domain patterns that contain nouns with this determiner, and also all the domain patterns expressed in relative form. For example, the pattern `<LOCATION CONTAINED DISASTER>` can not be matched over the text:

> "... the flood that Florida saw today ..."

if "that" is parsed as a determiner part of the "that Florida" noun group. Our relative object pattern macro matches over forms like `<OBJECT THAT SUBJECT VERB>`, hence the recognition of "that" as a particle is crucial. Because the distinction between determiner and particle is extremely difficult for a FSA-grammar parser, we allowed both forms of "that" to be generated with equal priority.

In order to implement non-determinism in CICERO we had to provide solutions for the following issues:

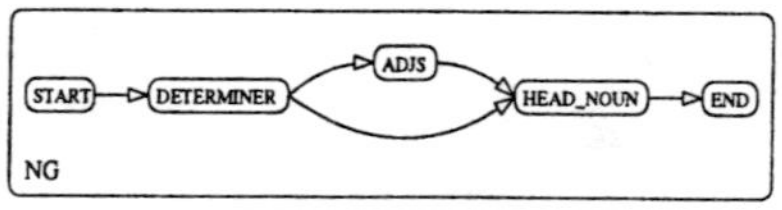

Figure 3: FSA for the pattern: `NG ==> DETERMINER ADJS? HEAD_NOUN`

1] Allow ambiguous input
Because CICERO's backbone is implemented as a sequence of FSAs, one module's ambiguous output becomes the next module's ambiguous input. For example, if the named-entity recognizer could not decide between an organization or a person named-entity, both entities are passed as ambiguous input to the next FSA module, the parser. The solution we adopted in CICERO was to implement the interface between FSAs as a lattice of objects instead of a linear vector. Our lattice implementation allows for multiple objects to start at the same position, and for objects that start at the same position to end at different positions. The search algorithms were modified to scan all alternative lattice entries.

2] Allow the generation of ambiguous output
The generation of ambiguous output is implemented by allowing the search process to continue after the first match, in one of the following two conditions:

- The solution path contains OR alternatives. For example, one of the first rules in the parser grammar is `START ==> VG | NG`. In this situations, CICERO's run-time search system investigates all the other alternatives in the OR constructs, even if the first one (e.g. VG) has been already matched.
- There are grammar rules with equal priority as the rules used to obtain the first solution path. CICERO's grammar rules are prioritized and rules with higher priority are always preferred over rules with lower priority. Ambiguities are allowed in the search process by investigating all rules with similar priority as the rules used to obtain the first solution.

3] Optimize the search on non-deterministic FSAs
In Cicero all grammar patterns are implemented as FSA. Figure 3 shows a sample FSA generated by CICERO's compiler. The pattern above implements a noun group grammar rule, where the noun consists of a determiner, followed by an optional sequence of adjectives, followed by a head noun. Figure 3 shows that this grammar rule is translated into a FSA, with all states and transitions stored in between two control nodes: START and END. Each grammar regular expression construct yields a different sequence of transitions. For example, the optionality construct "?" yields two possible transitions, one through ADJS, and an empty one linking DETERMINER with HEAD_NOUN directly. Note that CICERO's FSA allow recursive constructs. For example, the DETERMINER construct shown in Figure 3 is actually a link to the automaton that implements the DETERMINER grammar rules. The DETERMINER constructor is traversed successfully only if there is match from START to END in the corresponding automaton.

The main problem we encountered in the implementation of searching non-deterministic FSA was the high backtracking cost. In CICERO, each grammar rule can be associated with a C/C++ function executed upon successful matching. The execution of rule actions during the search process has not only a high cost but is also useless considering that actions should be committed only when a full search solution is found. Our solution to this problem is to implement the search algorithm as a *two-step process*: the first phase

```
expand {
  ActiveBase | ActiveRelativeSubj | PassiveBase | ...
} with {
  SUBJECT = in.B("isCompany")
  VERB = $REMOVE_WORD
  OBJECT = in.B("isPerson")
  PREP1 = "as" | "from"
  OBJECT1 = in.B("isPosition")
  SEMANTICS = makeRemove(...)
}
```

Figure 4: Domain pattern implemented as an expansion of domain-independent meta rules.

performs a graph search on the grammar FSAs. This step is a read-only process: solution search stacks containing all visited automaton nodes are constructed, but no actions are executed. The second phase of the search algorithm traverses the search stacks and executes all actions encountered. This approach provides the fastest search algorithm because it guarantees that only the actions associated with solution paths are executed.

5. PERFORMING OPEN-DOMAIN IE

A key issue that simplifies CICERO's porting to new domains is the fact that CICERO cleanly separates the rule construction into domain-independent and domain-dependent parts. CICERO facilitates this separation with *meta rules*. A meta rule expands upon domain-independent *syntactic patterns* with domain-dependent *semantic constraints*. For clarification Figure 4 shows the implementation of a domain Subject-Verb-Object (SVO) pattern as an expansion of domain-independent meta rules. Note that while SVO patterns have by far the biggest contribution of all patterns in CICERO (i.e. SVO patterns plus coreference account for over 96% CICERO's score for the MUC-6 domain), meta rules are not limited to SVO patterns: the same concept is used for the implementation of complex noun groups. Figure 4 shows the implementation of the "REMOVE" pattern, which matches over text constructs such as:

> Artisoft Inc. said it fired its chairman...

or

> Artisoft ousts Schoof from top two posts...

What is significant in this example is that the domain-dependent part of the rule is contained in the "with { ... }" construct, which defines the semantic constraints to be applied on the elements part of the SVO pattern: subject, verb, and object. The domain-independent meta rules, shown within the "expand { ... }" construct define the way SVO patterns can be expressed in the current development language (in this case English). We currently have implemented 35 meta rules that implement domain-independent syntactic constructs for the English language, for example the active SVO pattern, where the subject precedes the verb in active form.

The previous example indicates that there are at least two relevant things that have to be learned for a new domain: first and most importantly, one needs to detect the semantic constraints to be imposed on meta rules (i.e. the second part of Figure 4). Second, each syntactic pattern must be expanded with other applicable meta rules to increase the pattern coverage. It is however important to keep the meta rules associated with each syntactic pattern to a minimum, because too many meta rules may not only introduce spurious entries due to incorrect matches, but also slow down the system significantly due to the exponential number of patterns generated.

The open-domain IE platform implemented in CICERO allows the implementation of supervised machine-learning mechanisms capable of learning new rules for new domains, given a set of training texts and templettes. The meta-rule framework and the usage of coreference algorithms guarantee large coverage of the learned rules. Below we present the infrastructure of such a rule learning algorithm.

---

1. Learn strict rule instances
2. Generalize learned rules with meta-rules
3. Learn templette slots that can be filled with event coreference

---

For the clarity of the presentation we describe the algorithm behavior on a simple example. The algorithm input is two-fold: the first item is CICERO's lattice after the the full parsing and the entity coreference steps. The lattice consists of a sequence of possibly overlapping noun, verb, and particle groups. Noun and verb groups may be tagged with semantic information, such as named-entity tags or WordNet information pre-tagged as domain-relevant (e.g. nouns such as "flood" and "tornado" are relevant for the "natural disasters" domain). The second input item for this algorithm step is the sequence of training templettes. Consider the following training text "natural disasters" domain as example:

> ... flooding has become a way of life in Guerneville in the last several years. This gas station along the Russian River gets hit nearly every time. ...

and the corresponding pre-tagged templette:

```
<NATURAL_DISASTER> :=
     DISASTER: "flooding"
     AMOUNT_DAMAGE: "this gas station"
     LOCATION: "Russian River"
```

During the first algorithm step all possible SVO patterns are generated and matched over the training text. Some validation algorithm must be used to preserve only the patterns that have a positive contribution to the overall score. During this step the following SVO pattern will be generated:

```
expand {
  PassiveBase
} with{
  VERB = "hit"
  OBJECT = has facility feature
  SEMANTICS =
    set amount damage = object;
    set location = event adjunct location (if any);
}
```

The output of the first algorithm step is a set of simple rules, which in CICERO are implemented as syntactic pattern that expand a single meta rule. However, the derivation of meta-rules of extraction does not solve the sparse data problem. The remaining two algorithm steps address this specific issue, first by increasing the coverage of the learned patterns, and then by using event coreference to include information that cannot be retrieved using pattern matching.

The second algorithm step expands the rules learned in the first step with additional meta-rules, and semantically equivalent words, such as WordNet synonyms. This step expans the rule generated in the previous example as follows:

```
expand {
  ActiveBase|ActiveRelativeObject|PassiveBase|...
} with{
  VERB = "hit" | "strike" | ...
```

```
    OBJECT = has facility feature
    SEMANTICS =
      set amount damage = object;
      set location = event adjunct location (if any);
}
```

The above example shows how the previous rule is expanded by increasing the number of syntactic patterns covered. The rule coverage is further increased by expanding the head verb constraints with synonym verbs such as "strike".

As our previous analysis of the CICERO IE system indicates, successful pattern matching rules are only half of the extraction process. Coreference, in the form of domain-independent entity coreference and domain-dependent event coreference, is responsible for the other half. Hence, a successful automatic domain customization algorithm must address the implementation of event coreference.

The task of event coreference is to fill in the slots missing in the templettes constructed by the previously learned meta-rules. Missing slots occur both due to incomplete matches and because most patterns are not designed anyway to fill all slots. It is important to note that not all missing slots should be filled using event coreference. Depending on the currently matched rule, some slots should be left empty because event coreference might introduce incorrect fills from the rule context.

We exemplify the use of the event coreference learning mechanism on the same example used throughout this section. When the "natural disaster" meta-rule learned in the previous step is applied on the training text it will fill in the slots corresponding to the artifact damaged ("this gas station") and the disaster location ("Russian River"). Nevertheless, two important fields are missing: disaster type and disaster date. Filling the disaster type slot using coreference is beneficial because it successfully identifies "flooding" as the disaster type, but it fails on the disaster date slot. In this example, event coreference fills the event date slot with "last several years", which is a spurious entry. Hence, the learning algorithm eventually marks the date slot in the templette generated by the above meta-rule as "not to be filled" by event coreference. The final learned templette has the following form:

```
expand {
  ActiveBase|ActiveRelativeObject|PassiveBase|...
} with{
  VERB = "hit" | "strike" | ...
  OBJECT = has facility feature
  SEMANTICS =
    set amount damage = object;
    disaster type = fill using coreference;
    set location = event adjunct location (if any);
}
```

6. EXPERIMENTAL RESULTS

CICERO has currently been evaluated on three domains part of the Message Understanding Conference (MUC) competition: MUC-5, MUC-6, and MUC-7. For all domains the system has been trained on the "dry run" messages and tested on the formal test messages.

Table 1 shows a detailed analysis of the system modules. We present a series of average numbers per message document, where the average MUC message size is 2.25 KB. The values presented in Table 1 are: the average number of patterns matched per message, the average number of entity coreference links per message, and the average number of event coreference links per message. The relative small number of event coreference links versus entity coreference links is somewhat surprising considering the large contribution of event coreference to the system performance. The explanation is that all event coreference links have an influence on the final score, while the entity coreference links influence the system performance only if the corresponding entities are caught in a pattern. Nonetheless, Table 1 sustains the conclusions drawn from Figure 2 that coreference is indeed a significantly active module of an IE system.

Domain	Pattern #	Entity Coref Links	Event Coref Links
MUC-6	18	34	4
MUC-5	12	22	3
MUC-7	25	47	6

Table 1: Analysis on various domains

Domain	Results with non-deterministic FSA	Results with deterministic FSA
MUC-6	77%	72.55%
MUC-5	79.1%	74.26%
MUC-7	75.25%	70.73%

Table 2: Deterministic versus non-deterministic FSA

Figure 2 indicates that coreference is the single most important module of an IE system. This result is the first significant architectural novelty introduced in CICERO. The second novel issue introduced in this paper claims that non-deterministic FSA are important for a high-performance IE system. Table 2 supports this claim. We present the overall F-measures obtained by CICERO when non-deterministic FSA are enabled and then disabled. The results presented indicate that non-deterministic FSA are responsible for approximately 5% increase in system performance.

7. ACKNOWLEDGMENTS

This work was partially supported by the ARDA contract ARDA#2001*H238400*000 and by the "ARP:Knowledge Mining for Open-Domain Information Extraction" grant from the Advanced Research Program of the Texas Higher Education Coordinating Board.

8. REFERENCES

[1] D. E. Appelt, J. R. Hobbs, J. Bear, D. Israel, M. Kameyama, A. Kehler, D. Martin, K. Myers, and M. Tyson. Description of the fastus system used for muc-6. In *Proceedings of the Sixth Message Understanding Conference (MUC-6)*, pages 237–248. Morgan Kaufmann, 1995.

[2] E. Brill. A simple rule-based part of speech tagger. In *Proceedings of the Third Conference on Applied Natural Language Processing*, pages 152–155, 1992.

[3] R. Grishman and R. Yangarber. Nyu: Description of the proteus/pet system as used for muc-7 st. In *Proceedings of the Seventh Message Understanding Conference (MUC-7)*. Morgan Kaufmann, 1998.

[4] J. R. Hobbs, D. E. Appelt, J. Bear, D. Israel, M. Kameyama, M. Stickel, and M. Tyson. Fastus: A cascaded finite-state transducer for extracting information from natural-language text. *Finite State Language Processing*, page edited by Emmanuel Roche and Yves Schabes, MIT Press 1997.

[5] G. Krupka. Sra: Description of the sra system used for muc-6. In *Proceedings of the Sixth Message Understanding Conference (MUC-6)*. Morgan Kaufmann, 1995.

[6] W. Lehnert, C. Cardie, D. Fisher, E. Riloff, , and R. Williams. Description of the circus system as used for muc-3. In *Proceedings of the Third Message Understanding Conference (MUC-3)*, pages 223–233. Morgan Kaufmann, 1991.

AGORA: A GUI APPROACH TO MULTIMODAL USER INTERFACES

Manolis M. Tsangaris and Alexandros Potamianos

Bell Laboratories, Lucent Technologies, 600 Mountain Ave., Murray Hill, NJ 07074, U.S.A.

ABSTRACT

Multi-modal user interfaces bring the best of the two worlds to the user; the navigational aspect of graphical user interfaces and the declarative aspect of voice interfaces. The user can move around forms providing a concrete visual representation, while speech input allows natural form filling and form navigation. Unlike the unimodal speech interfaces, the visual interface efficiently reflects the state of the dialog as well as the speech recognition and understanding results. Agora uses a hierarchical form flow motivated from the traditional GUI design philosophy and is loosely based on VoiceXML. Agora also brings up several design issues including: ambiguity resolution, modality synchronization, focus representation, preferred modality for input and output.

1. INTRODUCTION

After several decades of speech processing research we have mature technology that is being used today in real world applications and services. More than two decades of work on graphical user interfaces has also enabled us to effectively design user friendly applications.

Mobile terminals present new interface design challenges that can be addressed by a combination of speech and visual interfaces [2, 7]. Limited screen real estate, the absence of keyboard, and their usage in unpredictable mobile environments, set new constraints. Thus, multimodal interfaces have emerged, as systems supporting speech input and output, as well as visual input and output.

A fundamental issue when designing multimodal systems is the choice, integration and appropriate mix of input and output modes in the user interface [6, 8]. Few guidelines exist for selecting the appropriate mix of modalities [2, 4], however, it is clear that a spoken language interface is not always the best choice. This is especially true for system output, where speech plays a secondary role to visual input (with the exception of hand-free applications). It is often the case when designing multimodal user interfaces, that the developer is biased either towards the voice or the visual modalities. This is especially true if the developer is voice-enabling an existing GUI-based application or building a GUI for an existing voice-only service. Our goal is to follow an approach that respects both modalities, creating an interface that is both *natural* and *efficient*. The first step towards the seamless integration of the input and output modalities is a *consistent* user interface: the GUI represents system state and possible actions (including state and actions that are specific to the voice-modality). A second important step towards a truly multimodal experience is creating a user interface that utilizes the *synergies* between the input and output modalities, e.g., using visual feedback from the recognizer (including possible ambiguities).

This paper, represents a new philosophy in building such interfaces; in our system, the visual interface offers a concise task oriented procedural style interface, while the speech part, facilitates easier input and navigation. No attempt is made to make the two modalities equivalent in terms of what they can do to the state of the system; the user can choose the appropriate modality for the given task. In this paper, we built on the extensive literature and experience on graphical user interfaces (GUIs) design and on voice user interfaces (VUIs) design. Web standards such as HTML and VoiceXML have also influenced our approach [10, 1].

The organization of the paper is as follows: First the system architecture is discussed. A modular client-server architecture is used; a thin client is run on the mobile device and the bulk of the processing is happening at the server side. In Section 3, the Agora Multimodal Service Language (AMSL) is introduced for building multimodal interfaces. AMSL defines the voice interface semantics, the visual form semantics and then binds the two semantic spaces; arbitrary TCL code can be executed before or after the form is loaded. The form flow model and the GUI approach to multimodal interface design, is described in Section 4. Next we present an example application from the travel reservation domain. Implementation issues for different parts of the application (form-filling, result presentation and navigation) are presented. Issues such as ambiguity resolution, focus changes and interface consistency between the two input modalities are also mentioned. We conclude in Section 6.

2. MULTIMODAL SYSTEM ARCHITECTURE

The multimodal interaction model defines the communication between two actors: the user and the (multimodal) terminal. The multimodal Agora terminal, is a device capable of

1. visual input (using pen, buttons and possibly keyboard),
2. speech input (via an attached or a lapel microphone),
3. visual output (using a color or black and white high resolution screen),
4. speech output (using a headset or the attached speaker).

We have implemented Agora, a prototype to study some of the multimodal user interface issues, as a three level architecture. The multimodal terminal (MMT) is a Compaq IPAQ running a thin client; it collects audio from its microphone, it plays audio, and displays a local graphical user interface using a TCL/TK engine. It connects to the Agora multimedia presentation server (MMPS) using either a wireless LAN (802.11) or a GPRS/GSM link. MMPS is a collection of Unix server processes including a GUI engine written in TCL, a Lucent ASR/TTS engine for performing speech recognition and synthesis, and an AMSL engine for fetching and interpreting multimodal scripts from the Service Back-end servers.

AMSL is a simple form language we have developed that can express all service logic (forms and spoken I/O) declaratively (using an XML like syntax) and procedurally (using TCL scripts).

3. AMSL: THE INTERFACE DEFINITION LANGUAGE

AMSL stands for the Agora Multimodal Service Language, and it is currently under development. AMSL is the UI engine part of the classic three tier service architecture. Like VoiceXML for voice [1], AMSL is a multimodal service definition language. But more like JavaSpeech and unlike VoiceXML, AMSL does not rely on external logic in order to interact with the user and handle visual/voice input/output. As it happens with graphical user interfaces, a service specific computational back-end provides the user interface engine with the proper data services, in order for the entire service to be implemented.

AMSL is partly based on VoiceXML, a standard followed by much of the spoken dialogue services community. AMSL adds multimodal support, inheritance, and full-scripting capabilities. We feel that the multimodal interface language needs to include both declarative syntactic structure (that could be expressed using XML) as well as procedural behavioral constructs. In the development of our system we heavily borrow concepts and practices from the WEB and (Voice)XML worlds, and similarities are not accidental.

Next, we illustrate Agora in a step by step process through our standard air travel reservation example.

The Agora user needs to download and install the Agora browser (AMUI) on the mobile terminal. When accessed for the first time, the user will be automatically registered to the Agora server; any appropriate transport (IP over WLAN or IP over GPRS) could be utilized, provided that it can support the necessary Quality of Service (i.e. adequate bit rate and delay).

The service author writes the AMSL code and stores it on one or more AMSL code pages on a standard HTTP server. For example:

```
http://air-travel.com/reserve.amsl
```

When the above URL is registered with the the Agora server it will appear next time a user logs in to the Agora server as new services to try. A general service discovery method has been suggested, but it is out of the scope of this paper. The user may decide to subscribe to the service, and in that case the corresponding icon will be available at the top level menu.

The file reserve.amsl contains TCL code defining the form(s) needed by this application:

```
form toplevel -title "Trips" {
  grammar {
    city    -> "athens" | "rome" | "milan" : {T $1}
    sfcity  -> "from"       <city> : {city $city.T}
    stcity  -> "to"         <city> : {city $city.T}
    sdepart -> "departing" <date> : {date $date.T}
  }
  fields {
    departure.city      "From" city
    arrival.city          "To" city
    departure.date "Departing" date
  }
  bind {
    sfcity  -> departure.city
    stcity  -> arrival.city
    sdepart -> departure.date
  }
  # -- insert user specific TCL code here
  code {

  }
```

The form encapsulates grammars, fields, event bindings, and TCL code:

- The *grammar* is expressed as BNF definitions with tag extensions, as it is the case within the speech community. In the example, a city is simply defined as either "athens" or "rome" or "milan", and once parsed, it will generate an event tagged as `city` and the name of the city. For example, when the user says: "from athens" the following tagged event record will be generated:
  `event grammar sfcity city "athens"`
- The form may contain *fields*, which is currently a list of slots with tag, name, and type. Fields will be intelligently laid on screen automatically, but that could be overridden by the user.
- *Binding* enables speech events to be associated to form actions. For example, if the user says "from athens" the generated event (`sfcity`) will be bound to the "city" field and the value of city will be assigned to the field "departure.city". If the user says "from athens to rome" two events will be generated:
  `event grammar sfcity city "athens"`
  `event grammar stcity city "rome"`
  causing two assignments to the corresponding from and to fields. Any events that do not match the binding rules are currently rejected.
- Arbitrary TCL *code* can be executed before or after a form is loaded, and event handling could be passed to the code as well.

A major design decision was to use a flat name space for forms, and to make URLs have nothing to do with naming. As a result, an application or a service can be conveniently stored on one or more AMSL pages and it will be incrementally loaded as needed using the standard HTTP protocol. This was mostly motivated by the Java Applets architecture [REFERENCE?].

On the client side, each different service will be given its own "thread of control", and will run in its own protected namespace; there is no direct possibility to interact with other services that happen to be active on the user terminal.

4. FORM FLOW

As a GUI approach to multimodal interfaces, AMSL is heavily based on the GUI form flow model. Forms structure the user interaction, making each step simpler and more effective. At each step, only one form is active; visual and speech events are mostly processed by the active form. The user navigates the form hierarchy, visually or via speech, and the visual context concisely represents the form hierarchy.

Forms structure the user interaction, making each step simpler and more effective. Each form represents a logical step of the user-machine interaction, used for gathering information (input fields/form filling), for displaying information (output fields/results), for controlling other forms, or for a combination of the three. In the example above, the first one is a control form, the subsequent forms are mostly input forms, and the last one is an output only form.

A form may define and activate one or more sub-forms; at each step, only one form is active, visual and speech events are mostly processed by the active form. The child form is given the visual and speech focus, which remains there until the form explicitly finishes. During this time, the user cannot access any other form visually or via speech. This restriction allows the service designer to structure the user interaction as a sequence or a hierarchy of simpler steps.

As the user navigates the form hierarchy, visually or via speech, the visual context concisely represents the form hierarchy. When the form is completed, it is removed from the display and its parent form receives the result; that is, a standard (TCL) exception, or a set of tagged values (exactly as the grammar does when parsing succeeds). Those values can be used by the parent of the form, thus, making the form a unit of modularity and re-usability.

Forms are object oriented, and as such, their behavior is a affected by inheritance. All forms inherit by default from the `baseform`, which defines many standard aspects of the form behavior. For example, form cancellation or confirmation are properties of the `baseform`. Form objects also encapsulate the procedural behavior, which can be hidden or exposed at the interface level.

5. AN EXAMPLE: AIR TRAVEL RESERVATION

Next, we will illustrate the proposed model, using a sequence of examples from the classic application of air travel reservation. The sequence of forms is shown in Fig. 1.

5.1. Simple Forms

As the user enters the service (say by dialing the service or clicking a button, or even automatically as the terminal is switched on), a top level screen is displayed. In our case, the screen is click sensitive, so "Trips", "Weather" or "Taxis" can be selected visually; a reasonable spoken command is also accepted.

Notice here one of the most important aspects of multimodal interfaces. The visual part can serve as a cue card reminding the user of possible choices as well as voice commands to make those choices. The visual part will also highlight the choice before an action is taken, thus serving as a precise feedback mechanism.

5.2. Forms with fields

As soon as the "Trips" choice is made, the user is transferred to the reservation screen. That screen also exploits the cue-card philosophy, inviting the user to explore it both phonetically and visually.

The user can select the departing and arriving cities in a variety of ways. Sentences like: "from athens", "from athens to rome", "from athens greece to rome italy" are all accepted. As soon as a choice is spoken and it is accurately recognized, the form will be updated to indicate the choice made.

5.3. Subordinate Forms

Since the departure time was not specified precisely, the system brought up a calendar form in order to help the user make a selection easier. The calendar can accept visual choices of specific dates, it can "scroll" through the year, and can accept speech commands like: "august sixth", "next month please", "september" etc. In response to those commands, the calendar reacts, and when appropriate, it highlights the user's choice. The form will not go away, until the choice is committed visually or via speech.

The form is cascaded (not shown in Fig. 1), as a standard way to indicate context. If the user touches the parent form, or if "back" is said, the calendar choice will be canceled and the parent form will become active again.

5.4. Rendering the Results

Once the input form is filled a query is made to the database back-end which may return flight results. In our case, the user specified flight schedule produced three different ticketing possibilities. As the page is being displayed, a brief TTS synthesized sentence informs us about the aggregated result and also reconfirms our query: "there are three flights from athens to rome". We will not attempt to read the entire page to the user. The spoken sentence is just a feedback mechanism and a summary of the result. The flight query results form can be further rendered by the user via speech or pen input.

5.5. Navigating forms

If the user now wants to return to the reservation form, it can readily do so visually by clicking on the cascaded par-

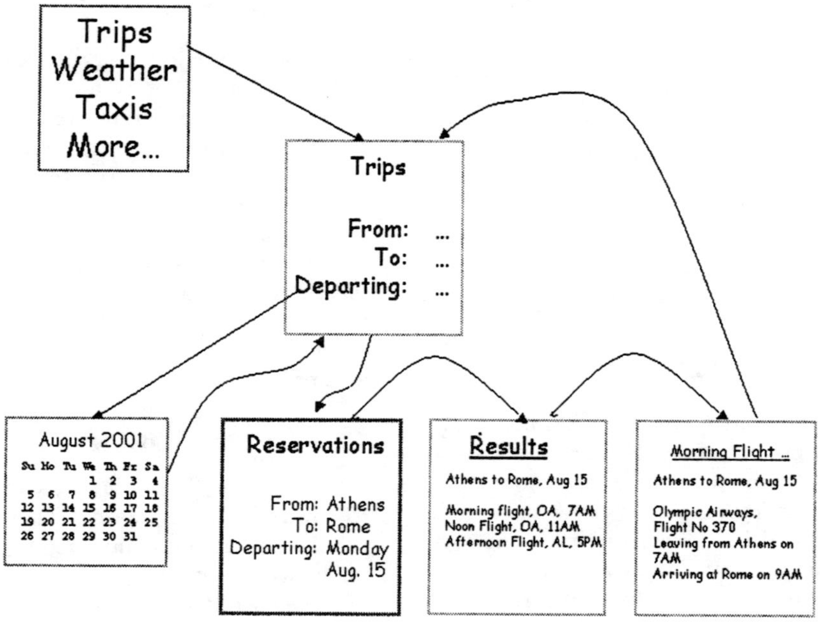

Figure 1: Form flow for the air travel reservation example.

ent form or by simply saying: "Reservations again please" or simply "Reservations". A spoken sentence confirms the return and the form is now ready to be changed. Indeed, the user now could say: "to Milan" thus, changing the destination city. The form is updated to reflect the correction.

5.6. Handling Ambiguity

Ambiguity is probably the major difference between GUIs and VUIs (Voice Interfaces) and Agora does not encourage semantic ambiguities.

In general, GUIs have precise and clean semantics, and there are no major ambiguity issues. User actions are very specific to the graphical widget, leaving no room for further interpretation; very often, this is achieved at the cost of increased user effort. For example, a typical form filling application requires different physical fields, one for each input item, like destination and departure city, and departure date. It is very rare to allow a free text form interface, accepting a sentence like:

"travel from Athens to Rome tomorrow night"

In the case of VUI ambiguity could result from recognition errors or from loose semantic context or imprecise user phrase; saying "Athens" in the above example raises the ambiguity of which field Athens was intended to.

Some multimodal systems have proposed specific "click to speak" gesture to resolve those issues; click to speak on a destination field could make obvious that Athens is a destination city for example. We are not in favor of such capability, simply because the user effort required to perform the correct click to speak gesture is simply too much for the achieved gain (of not saying departing from .. athens). We believe that the visible form and the context it implies, in addition to the names of the fields provide adequate context for a natural dialogue.

Some forms of ambiguity could be handled on the event mapping phase; in anticipation of such ambiguity the form author could write a new binding to much "city" only phrases, and then post a choice subdialog so the user can resolve the ambiguity. Currently, the default action is that the phrase will be ignored with a brief audio gesture (a feedback rejection tone).

5.7. Preferred input modalities

As we have indicated previously, we do not want to go the extra mile to make both modalities fully equivalent to what they can express. This will create a cumbersome interface which will combine too many complexities from both modalities.

The issue is more evident on the calendar form posted when a date needs to be selected; we make no attempt not interpret all possible voice commands to express a date, but rather the ones to navigate the calendar and select a currently visible date. We hope that the GUI will offer enough visual cues to guide the user on the style of language accepted as input.

As a result, the user can say "1", "13" or any number to select a day; "February", "March", or the name of a month to go to any month; and "Next month", "Last Month" to move relative to the currently displayed month. Although it is possible to click on the arrows, or to click on the given date, real estate limitations make it quite tricky. In this case as in many other situations, voice is the preferred in-

Figure 2: Calendar navigation form.

put modality, whereas the display is definitely the preferred output modality.

The exact level of priority between the two modalities is subject of further research and more experimentation.

5.8. Handling Focus

Agora forms are mostly visual and the focus semantics have been adopted to the philosophy of GUIs and PDAs.

When it comes to interactions, only one form at the time "talks" to the user. Other forms are partially visible, just to remind us the context and the tasks that have been suspended temporarily, until the current forms have been filled.

Unlike windows systems, and much like the PDAs, Agora does not allow multiple services to share the screen at the same time. Once the user switches to a different service, the former service forms disappear from the screen. As a result, inter-service focus switching is very easy.

The only exceptions is that some voice commands allow the focus to move to a different service temporarily suspending the current service; or to return to a previously posted toplevel form, thus, canceling all subordinate forms. In the case of the travel reservations example, the user could say "go to taxis" at any point during the navigation of travel forms to cancel any reservation work and explore the "taxis" options.

The Agora system is fully capable of alternative focus policies, but this is also subject of further research.

6. CONCLUSIONS

We have presented Agora, a simple framework for defining and building multimodal applications, where the visual part dictates the flow and speech is mostly used as a convenient mechanism for input. A simple interface creation language (AMSL) is defined that explicitly defines the voice interface and visual interface semantics, along with possible binding between the two. This approach has been demonstrated in a working multimodal travel reservation prototype. Further work is required to evaluate this approach and compare it with existing descriptive and procedural multimodal interface languages. We have tried to define a simple, consistent, and intuitive paradigm, which once accepted by the user it will generate the same amount of familiarity and productivity, GUI constructs like pull-down menus have achieved.

7. REFERENCES

[1] R. Beasley et al, *Voice Application with VoiceXML*, Sams, 2001.

[2] N.O. Bernsen and L. Dybkjaer, "Is speech the right thing for your application?," in *Internat. Conf. Speech Language Processing*, (Australia), Oct. 1998.

[3] P. Cohen, M. Johnston, D. M. and S. Oviatt, J. Clow, and J. Smith, "The efficiency of multimodal interaction: A case study," in *Proc. ICSLP 98*, (Sydney, Australia), 1998.

[4] V. Bilici, E. Krahmer, S. te Riele, R. Veldhuis, "Preferred Modalities in Dialogue Systems," in *Proc. ICSLP'2000*, (Beijing, China), Oct. 2000.

[5] X. Huang et al,"MIPAD: a next generation PDA prototype," in *Proc. ICSLP'2000*, (Beijing, China), Oct. 2000.

[6] S. Narayanan, A. Potamianos, and H. Wang, "Multimodal systems for children: Building a prototype," in *Proc. European Conf. on Speech Communication and Technology*, (Budapest, Hungary), Sept. 1999.

[7] S.L. Oviatt et al, "Designing the user interface for multimodal speech and gesture applications: State-of-the-art systems and research directions," Human Computer Interaction, 2000, vol. 15, no. 4, 263-322.

[8] A. Potamianos et al, "Design principles and tools for multimodal dialog systems," in *Proc. ESCA Workshop Interact. Dialog. Multi-Modal Syst.*, (Kloster Irsee, Germany), June 1999.

[9] R. Sharma, V. Pavlovic, and T. Huang, "Toward multimodal human computer interface," *Proceedings of the IEEE*, vol. 86, no. 5, pp. 853–869, 1998.

[10] XHTML, *http://www.w3c.org/MarkUp/*

Detecting Discrepancies in Numeric Estimates Using Multidocument Hypertext Summaries

Michael White
CoGenTex, Inc.
840 Hanshaw Road
Ithaca, NY 14850, USA
mike@cogentex.com

Claire Cardie
Dept. of Computer Science
Cornell University
Ithaca, NY 14850, USA
cardie@cs.cornell.edu

Vincent Ng
Dept. of Computer Science
Cornell University
Ithaca, NY 14850, USA
yung@cs.cornell.edu

ABSTRACT

To aid analysts in detecting discrepancies in numeric estimates in news articles from multiple sources, we propose the automatic generation of hypertext summaries that include a high-level textual overview; tables of all *comparable* numeric estimates, organized to highlight discrepancies; and targeted access to supporting information from the original articles. The RIPTIDES system, which exemplifies the more flexible human-computer interface we propose, combines information extraction and multidocument summarization techniques to produce such hypertext summaries. In evaluating the system's ability to facilitate discrepancy detection, we find that, on average, the hypertext summaries provide a significantly more complete picture of the available information than the latest article.

1. INTRODUCTION

Previous work in multidocument summarization has pointed to the importance of identifying differences and discrepancies in the information that is reported across multiple news sources [9, 12]. To our knowledge, however, this problem has not yet been systematically or thoroughly investigated. Radev and McKeown [9], for example, identify discrepancy detection as a potential problem for multidocument summarizers via anecdotal evidence, but provide no empirical evidence to indicate how often such differences actually represent significant discrepancies in the available information, vs. simple updates in what is known. In particular, it is unclear whether readers may usually find a complete and accurate picture of the available information by simply looking at the latest article.

Similarly, our recent case study in the domain of natural disasters as part of the DUC summarization evaluation only begins to investigate issues of discrepancy detection [12]. The study attempted to (1) quantify the need for detecting discrepancies in numeric estimates of injury and death tolls, and (2) evaluate the ability of automatically generated summaries to deal with discrepancies and provide a more complete and accurate picture of an ongoing event than is available in the latest article. The study confirmed our impression that although the estimates do usually converge, they change rapidly at first and are often dropped from later articles, making the latest article an unreliable source for this information. We also found that manually scanning articles from multiple news sources for the latest death and injury estimates is exceedingly tedious. Further details from this case study are presented in the next section.

While our case study indicated that discrepancy detection, at least in the domain of natural disasters, is a task that could certainly benefit from automation, we unfortunately also found that the previous version of our RIPTIDES summarizer [12, 13] could not help identify such discrepancies more reliably than the latest article, on average. The conclusion we drew from this study was that length-limited, generic textual summaries necessarily preclude the inclusion of a complete and detailed assessment of discrepancies, while simultaneously making it difficult for the end-user to identify any inaccurate estimates in the summary.

We hypothesize here, therefore, that complete, accurate, and easily absorbed numeric estimates would be better conveyed to analysts in multidocument summaries that espoused a more flexible human-computer interface. For this, we propose the automatic generation of hypertext summaries that include a high-level textual overview; tables of all *comparable* numeric estimates, organized to highlight discrepancies; and targeted access to supporting information from the original articles.

In the sections below, we present and evaluate the new and improved RIPTIDES system and its hypertext summarization capability, which exemplifies the proposed more flexible human-computer interface. Our evaluation shows that, on average, the hypertext summaries provide a significantly more complete picture of the available information than the latest article. Most strikingly, when compared to a subset of 10 articles with incomplete reporting of the available information on the death toll, the RIPTIDES summarizer scores 4.55 on a 5-point scale in its completeness of death toll reporting, vs. only 2.05 for the selected articles.

2. CASE STUDY

In contrast to many available document collections that have been used in multidocument summarization research (e.g. the DUC and TDT corpora [7]), which consist of relatively small sets of articles about a given topic, our study instead required a fairly complete set of news articles about a single, evolving event. As a result, we created a corpus of as many articles from the web as we could easily find during the first week after the January 2001 earthquake in Central America: 132 articles from five news sources — AP, Reuters, CNN, BBC and the Washington Post. We then examined articles from days one through four of the quake to see how often the most recent article gave a signficantly different picture of the death toll than one would obtain from reading all the articles up

Proceedings of HLT 2002, Second International Conference on Human Language Technology Research, M. Marcus, ed., Morgan Kaufmann, San Francisco, 2002.

to that point. We found that 20% (22/107) of the articles failed to provide an accurate picture of what was known about the death toll at the time, containing either a significant discrepancy or no information on the overall death toll whatsoever (half of the 22 articles). For example, a BBC article on the second day reported a death toll of at least 80, which was consistent with the latest confirmed estimates from CNN and Reuters, but conflicted with another BBC article (posted one minute earlier) that gave an estimate of hundreds, as well as with the latest AP estimate of at least 122, and a quote from a police agency in the same AP article of 234.

We also examined the leading two paragraphs of all articles, and found significant variation in the facts reported, suggesting that there is considerable opportunity for a multidocument summarizer to surface key facts that may be missing from the most recent article leads. For example, while the death toll was mentioned in the first two paragraphs in 72% of the articles (95/132), the number missing appeared in only 41% (54/132), and the number injured in only 10% (13/132). In contrast, upon examining the full text of the articles, we found that the death toll was mentioned in about 92% of the articles, and both the number missing and injured in around 60% of the articles.

3. SYSTEM DESCRIPTION

RIPTIDES combines information extraction (IE) and multidocument summarization techniques to produce its domain-specific hypertext summaries. First, the system requires (1) the selection of one or more scenario templates (extraction domains), and (2) a set of documents in which to search for information. Our current study uses the domain of natural disasters and the Central American Quake (CAQ) corpus described above, respectively. RIPTIDES then applies its IE subsystem to generate a database of extracted events for the selected domain and invokes the Summarizer to generate a hypertext summary of the extracted information. The next subsection walks through sample hypertext summaries, pointing out the key features of the RIPTIDES interface. It is followed by descriptions of the IE and Summarizer system components.

3.1 Examples

The hypertext summaries consist of a high-level textual overview plus an indexed set of tables of all extracted information. Figure 1 shows a textual overview of the first dozen or so articles in the CAQ corpus. The 200-word overview contains sentences extracted from the original articles. The selection of sentences to extract is designed to favor adjacent sentences, in order to improve the intelligibility of the resulting summary; in figure 1, three blocks of adjacent sentences are shown. Clicking on the magnifying glass icon brings up the original article in the right frame, with the extracted sentences highlighted.

The index to the hypertext summary appears in the left frame of figure 1. Links to the overview and lead sentence of each article are followed by links to summary information organized according to the base level extraction slots for the main event (here, an earthquake) including its description, date, location, epicenter and magnitude. Access to overall damage estimates appear next, with separate tables for types of human effects (e.g. dead, missing) and for object types (e.g. villages, bridges, houses) with physical effects.

Figure 2 shows the extracted estimates of the overall death toll. In order to help identify discrepancies, the high and low current estimates are shown at the top, followed by other current estimates and then all extracted estimates. Heuristics are used to determine which estimates to consider current, taking into account the source (either news source or attributed source), specificity (e.g. *hundreds* vs. *at least 200*) and confidence level, as indicated by the presence of hedge words such as *perhaps* or *assumed*. The tables also provide links to the original articles, allowing the user to quickly and directly determine the accuracy of any estimate in the table. By following the high-low estimate links in figure 2, for example, one would discover that the lower estimates (of at least two dead) appear to only take the Guatemala estimates into account, whereas the higher estimates also include the reported death toll from Las Colinas, near San Salvador.

Figure 3 shows a more substantial index of tables. The input articles for this example are from topic 89 of the TDT2 corpus, a set of newswires that describe the May 1998 earthquake in Afghanistan. As above, the index begins with the overview, the article leads, entries for each extraction slot in the main event, and overall damage estimates. Here, however, the overall estimates are followed by estimates for specific locations, such as Shari Basurkh or Rustaq. The same indexing pattern is then followed for any related events mentioned in the articles, such as aftershocks, landslides, or previous quakes in the same area.

3.2 IE System

The RIPTIDES IE system combines existing language technology components in a traditional system architecture [2]: named entity identification via BBN's Identifinder [1]; sentence boundary detection and date normalization via Mitre's Alembic Workbench [4]; syntactic parsing via the Charniak [3] parser; WordNet-based [5] selectional restrictions; and linguistic annotation management via an in-house implementation of the TIPSTER architecture [6]. Unique features of the system include a weakly supervised extraction pattern-learning component, Autoslog-XML, which is based on Autoslog-TS [10], but operates in an XML framework and acquires patterns for extracting text elements beyond noun phrases, e.g. verb groups, adjectives, adverbs, and single-noun modifiers. In addition, a heuristic-based clustering algorithm organizes the extracted concepts into output templates specifically designed to support multi-document summarization [13]: the IE system, for example, distinguishes different reports or views of the same event from multiple sources.

Figure 4 shows the output (on the left) of the information extraction system given a sample input text from topic 89 of the TDT2 corpus (on the right). Output templates from the IE system for each text to be covered in the multi-document summary are provided as input to the summarization component along with all linguistic annotations accrued in the IE phase.

3.3 Summarizer

The Summarizer operates in three main stages. In the first stage, the IE output templates are merged into an event-oriented structure where comparable facts are semantically grouped. Towards the same objective, surface-oriented clustering is used to group sentences from different documents into clusters that are likely to report similar content. In the second stage, importance scores are assigned to the sentences based on the following indicators: position in document, document recency, presence of quotes, average sentence overlap, headline overlap, size of cluster (if any), size of semantic groups (if any), specificity of numeric estimates, and whether these estimates are deemed current. In the third and final stage, the hypertext summary is generated from the resulting content pool. A stochastic search procedure is used to select the highest ranking set of sentences for the overview summary; in this search, the inclusion of adjacent sentences is favored and the selection of repetitive material is penalized, in order to improve intelligibility. Further details on each stage follow in the paragraphs below.

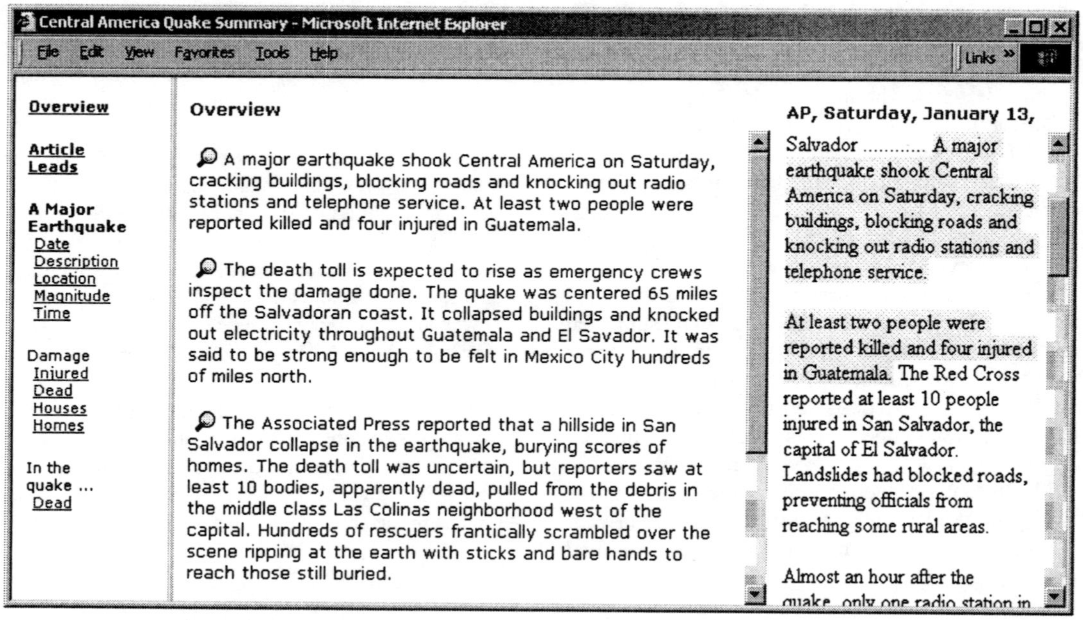

Figure 1: Example Multidocument Hypertext Summary Overview

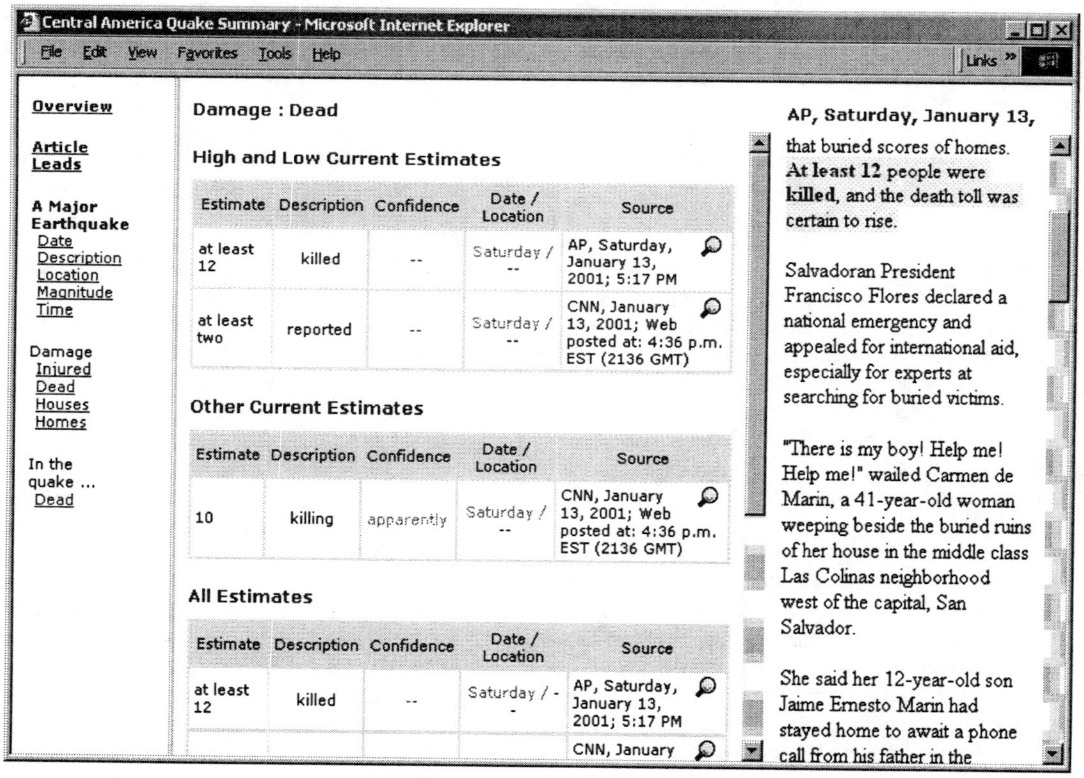

Figure 2: Example Tables of Death Toll Estimates

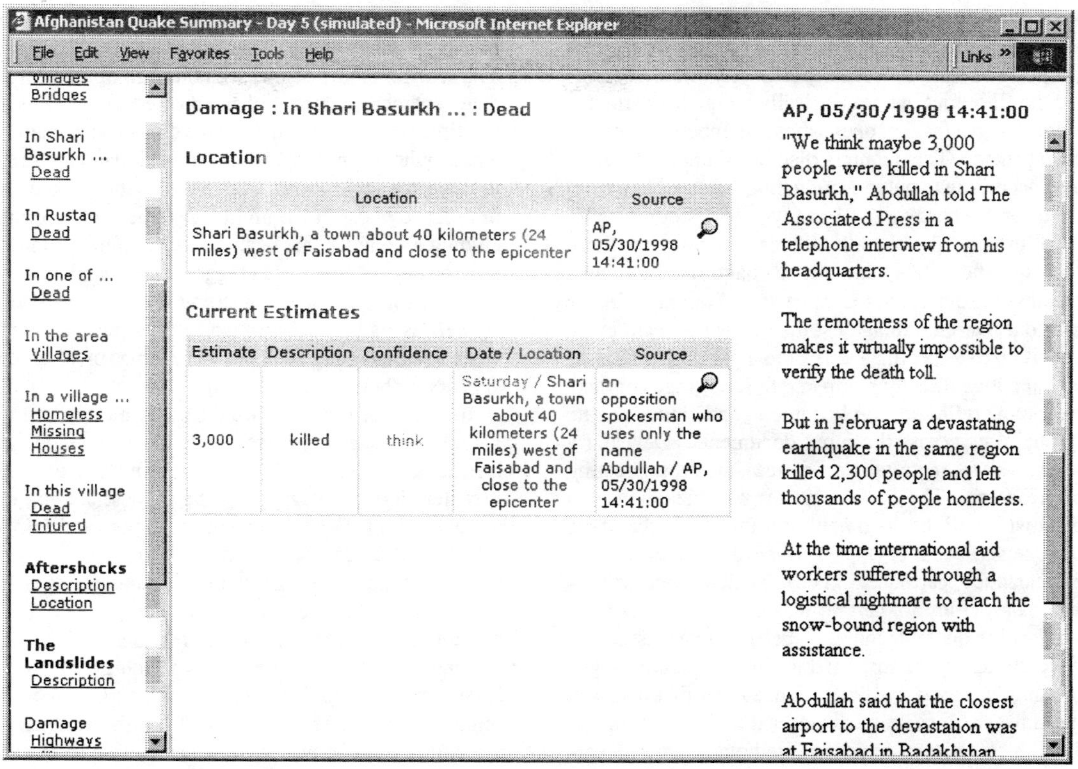

Figure 3: Example Index With Groupings by Type, Location and Related Event

Document no.: ABC19980530.1830.0342
Date/time: 05/30/1998 18:35:42.49

Output	Input

Disaster Type: earthquake
•description: *a powerful earthquake*
•location: *Afghanistan*
•date: *today*
•magnitude: *6.9*
•magnitude-confidence: high
•epicenter: *a remote part of the country*
•damage:
  •human-effect:
    •victim: *Thousands of people*
    •number: *Thousands*
    •outcome: dead
    •description: *dead*
    •confidence-marker: *feared*
    •confidence: medium
  •physical-effect:
    •object: *entire villages*
    •outcome: damaged
    •description: *buried*
    •confidence: medium
    •confidence-marker: *Details now hard to come by / reports say*
	PAKISTAN MAY BE PREPARING FOR ANOTHER TEST
	Thousands of people are feared dead following... (voice-over) ...a powerful earthquake that hit Afghanistan today. The quake registered 6.9 on the Richter scale, centered in a remote part of the country. (on camera) Details now hard to come by, but reports say entire villages were buried by the quake.

Figure 4: Information Extraction in the Domain of Natural Disasters. Output of the system is shown on the left; input, on the right.

In the analysis stage, we use Columbia's SimFinder tool [8] to obtain surface-oriented similarity measures and clusters for the sentences in the input articles. To obtain potentially more accurate partitions using the IE output, we semantically merge the extracted slots into *comparable* groups, i.e. ones whose members can be examined for discrepancies. This requires distinguishing (i) different types of damage, according to outcome (e.g. injured, dead, missing) for human effects, and according to object type (e.g. houses, vehicles) for physical effects; (ii) overall damage estimates vs. those that pertain to a specific locale; and (iii) damage due to related events, such as previous quakes in the same area. For example, we want to separate out overall damage estimates for the main event from ones that pertain to a specific locale or to a previous quake, as these estimates cannot be directly compared to see if they conflict.

The merging routine relies on simple domain- and genre-specific heuristics to group slots across the input documents. Devising a more accurate and robust merging routine remains an interesting topic for future research. The current routine assumes there is a single main event which all the documents are about, and that there is no more than one sub-event or related event for each event type (i.e. landslide, aftershock, earthquake, etc.). To determine when a damage estimate is specific to a certain locale, we ran a decision tree induction algorithm on the manually labeled damage estimates from TDT2 topic 89, and were surprised to find that sentence position is a surprisingly strong predictor; indeed, on this data set, classifying an estimate as localized whenever it had a location and appeared in the fifth sentence or beyond turned out to be 99% correct on the training data.

During the analysis stage, we also analyze the numeric estimates for specificity, using a small set of patterns over POS tags. Three levels of specificity are identified: rough estimates (e.g. *hundreds*), ranges and exact figures. Some numeric estimates, such as percentages, remain unanalyzed. The patterns identify the magnitude of the rough estimates and the lower and upper bounds of the ranges, so that the high and low estimates in a group can be identified. After the numeric estimates have been analyzed and confidence levels assigned, the current estimates are identified. In determining when to consider an estimate current, a later report from the same source (news agency or attributed source) is assumed to supercede an earlier one when it is at least as specific or higher, and has at least the same confidence level.

In the scoring stage, SimFinder's similarity measures and clusters are combined with the semantic groupings obtained from merging the IE templates in order to score the input sentences. The scoring of the clusters and semantic groups is based on their size, and the scores are combined at the sentence level by including the score of all semantic groups that contain a phrase extracted from a given sentence. More precisely, the scores are assigned in two phases, according to a set of hand-tuned parameter weights. First, a base score is assigned to each sentence according to a weighted sum of the position in document, document recency, presence of quotes, average sentence overlap, and headline overlap. The average sentence overlap is the average of all pairwise sentence similarity measures; we have found this measure to be a useful counterpart to sentence position in reliably identifying salient sentences, with the other factors playing a lesser role. In the second scoring phase, the clusters and semantic groups are assigned a score according to the sum of the base sentence scores. After normalization, the weighted cluster and group scores are used to boost the base scores, thereby favoring sentences from the more important clusters and semantic groups. Finally, a small boost is applied for current and more specific numeric estimates.

In the generation stage, the overview is constructed by selecting a set of sentences in a context-sensitive fashion, then ordering the blocks of adjacent sentences according to their importance scores. The scoring model begins with the sum of the scores for the candidate sentences, which is then adjusted to penalize the inclusion of multiple sentences from the same cluster or semantic group, or sentences whose similarity measure is above a certain threshold, and to favor the inclusion of adjacent sentences from the same article, in order to boost intelligibility. A larger bonus is applied when including a sentence that begins with an initial pronoun as well as the previous one, and an even bigger bonus is added when including a sentence that begins with a strong rhetorical marker (e.g. *however*) as well as its predecessor; corresponding penalties are also used when the preceding sentence is missing, or when a short sentence appears without an adjacent one.

To select the sentences for the overview according to this scoring model, we use a simple stochastic search method, namely randomized local search from multiple starting points (cf. [11]). For the first iteration, we begin with the highest scoring sentences up to the word limit. For subsequent iterations, we begin with randomly selected sentences, weighted according to their scores, up to the word limit. During each iteration, a random step or a greedy step is repeatedly performed until a greedy step fails to improve upon the current set of sentences. In each random step, a randomly selected sentence is added to collection. In each greedy step, one sentence is chosen to add to the summary, and zero or more (typically one) sentences are chosen to remove from the summary, such that the word limit is still met, and this combination of sentences represents the best swap available according to the scoring model. The search continues for a predetermined number of iterations, keeping track of the best combination of sentences found so far; we have found that 10 iterations often suffices to find a reasonable collection.

Once the overview sentences have been selected, the hypertext summary is generated as a collection of HTML files, using a series of XSLT transformations.

3.4 Training and Tuning

For the evaluation below, the IE system was trained on 12 of 25 texts from topic 89 of the TDT2 corpus. It achieves 42% recall and 61% precision when evaluated on the remaining 13 topic 89 texts. The parameters of the Summarizer were chosen by hand using the TDT2 topic 89 document set.

4. EVALUATION METHOD AND RESULTS

To determine the inputs for the evaluation, we selected 10 of the first 22 articles in the CAQ corpus that failed to completely and accurately report the available information on the overall death toll, since these represent some of the more interesting cases where automatic support for detecting discrepancies would be most useful. For each article, we then ran the RIPTIDES system on the articles up to and including that article (with a limit of 20), producing overview summaries of 200 words or less, as well as a series of hyperlinked tables of damage estimates. Next we had two judges[1] rate each selected article and its corresponding hypertext summary on the completeness of its reporting of both the overall death toll and the overall number injured. The ratings were given on a five point scale, where 1 = 'not at all,' 2 = 'somewhat,' 3 = 'fairly,' 4 = 'mostly,' and 5 = 'entirely.'

Table 5 shows the results averaged across the two judges. The 200-word overviews scored significantly better than the selected articles in their death toll reporting, with an average completeness score of 3.85 vs. 2.05 ($p < 0.001$, two-tailed paired t-test). The

[1] The first two authors were the judges.

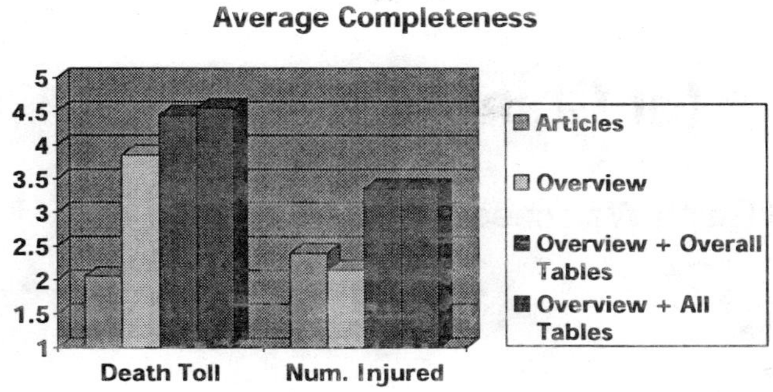

	Death Toll	Num. Injured
Articles	2.05	2.40
Overview	3.85	2.15
Overview + Overall Tables	4.45	3.35
Overview + All Tables	4.55	3.35

Figure 5: Results of Discrepancy Detection Evaluation

overviews scored slightly worse on their reporting of the number injured (2.15 vs. 2.40), but this difference was not significant. When we looked at the overviews in combination with the tables of extracted estimates for the overall death toll and the overall number injured, the system fared even better, scoring 4.45 (vs. 2.05) for the death toll, and 3.35 (vs. 2.40) for the number injured ($p = 0.011$). Looking further to all the death toll tables raised the system's score another notch to 4.55, as these tables contained a few current estimates that were mistakenly grouped with reports for specific locations or previous disasters.

We consider these results to be quite promising, as they show that the system is able to identify discrepancies in numeric estimates reasonably well even on hard cases. While the information analyst must examine the hypertext tables carefully in order to separate out the best available estimates from those that have been superceded or are incorrectly classified, we have found that it is still much easier to scan the tables for this information than to scan the full text of the original articles.

5. ACKNOWLEDGMENTS

This work was supported in part by DARPA TIDES contract N66001-00-C-8009.

6. ADDITIONAL AUTHORS

Daryl McCullough, CoGenTex, Inc., daryl@cogentex.com.

7. REFERENCES

[1] D. Bikel, S. Miller, R. Schwartz, and R. Weischedel. Nymble: A High-Performance Learning Name-Finder. In *Proceedings of the Fifth Conference on Applied Natural Language Processing*, pages 194–201, San Francisco, CA, 1997. Morgan Kaufmann.

[2] C. Cardie. Empirical Methods in Information Extraction. *AI Magazine*, 18(4):65–79, 1997.

[3] E. Charniak. A maximum-entropy-inspired parser. Technical Report CS99-12, Brown University, 1999.

[4] D. Day, J. Aberdeen, L. Hirschman, R. Kozierok, P. Robinson, and M. Vilain. Mixed-Initiative Development of Language Processing Systems. In *Proceedings of the Fifth Conference on Applied Natural Language Processing*. Association for Computational Linguistics, 1997.

[5] C. Fellbaum. *WordNet: An Electronic Lexical Database*. MIT Press, Cambridge, MA, 1998.

[6] R. Grishman. TIPSTER Architecture Design Document Version 2.2. Technical report, DARPA, 1996. Available at `http://www.tipster.org/`.

[7] D. Harman. *Proceedings of the 2001 Document Understanding Conference (DUC-2001)*. NIST, 2001.

[8] V. Hatzivassiloglou, J. L. Klavans, M. L. Holcombe, R. Barzilay, M.-Y. Kan, and K. R. McKeown. Simfinder: A flexible clustering tool for summarization. In *Proceedings of the NAACL 2001 Workshop on Automatic Summarization*, Pittsburgh, PA, 2001.

[9] D. R. Radev and K. R. McKeown. Generating natural language summaries from multiple on-line sources. *Computational Linguistics*, 24(3):469–500, 1988.

[10] E. Riloff. Automatically Generating Extraction Patterns from Untagged Text. In *Proceedings of the Thirteenth National Conference on Artificial Intelligence*, pages 1044–1049, Portland, OR, 1996. AAAI Press / MIT Press.

[11] B. Selman and H. Kautz. Noise Strategies for Improving Local Search. In *Proceedings of AAAI-94*, 1994.

[12] M. White, C. Cardie, V. Ng, K. Wagstaff, and D. McCullough. Detecting discrepancies and improving intelligibility: Two preliminary evaluations of RIPTIDES. In *Proceedings of the 2001 Document Understanding Conference (DUC-2001)*, 2001.

[13] M. White, T. Korelsky, C. Cardie, V. Ng, D. Pierce, and K. Wagstaff. Multidocument Summarization via Information Extraction. In *Proceedings of the First International Conference on Human Language Technology Research*, San Diego, CA, 2001.

A Statistical Parser for Chinese

Jinxi Xu, Scott Miller and Ralph Weischedel
BBN Technologies
50 Moulton Street
Cambridge
MA 02138
{jxu,szmiller,weisched}@bbn.com

ABSTRACT

This work describes how a statistical parser which was originally designed to parse English was adapted to parse Chinese with little human effort. The only modifications were a head table for Chinese and a set of automatically derived word features for dealing with unknown Chinese words. When trained on the Chinese Treebank, the resulting parser achieves state of art performance on parsing tokenized Chinese sentences.

1. INTRODUCTION

Effective parsing of natural language text is essential to many natural language processing applications. In recent years, the adoption of statistical parsing models in modern parsers has greatly improved parsing accuracy. However, most studies so far have focused on parsing English text. We will demonstrate that a statistical parser that was originally designed to parse English can be easily adapted to parse Chinese. The parser which was used as the basis for this work, BBN's SIFT parser (Miller et al 2000), is a state of art parser that achieves precision and recall of 88% for English newswire texts using the standard Penn Treebank training (Marcus et al., 1993) and PARSEVAL measures (Black et al., 1991). The only changes made to the system were a head-table for determining Chinese head-modifier relationships and a set of word features for handling out of vocabulary Chinese words. Since the creation of the head-table takes little manual work, and the word features can be automatically induced, the amount of work required is very small. Chinese word endings that have a low perplexity of parts of speech, computed from a training corpus, were chosen as word features. The resulting parser works surprisingly well using the Chinese Treebank (http://www.ldc.upenn.edu/Catalog/LDC2000T48.html) as training data. Given the same amount of training data, it rivals the original SIFT parser on parsing English sentences, suggesting the model is language independent. The parser also compares favorably with state of art results in Chinese parsing (Bikel and Chiang 2000).

Proceedings of HLT 2002, Second International Conference on Human Language Technology Research, M. Marcus, ed., Morgan Kaufmann, San Francisco, 2002.

2. THE SIFT PARSING MODEL

The SIFT parsing model is based on the Lexicalized Probabilistic Context Free Grammar (LPCFG) framework, similar to that of (Collins, 1997). In this framework, a parse tree for an input sentence is generated by probabilistically applying a series of lexicalized CFG production rules. The probability of generating the parse tree is the product of the probability scores for the production rules applied during the derivation. To overcome the problem of data sparseness, each production rule is broken down into a number of smaller steps, whose probability estimates are multiplied to give the probability for the entire rule. Specifically, the head of each parse constituent is produced first, then its right modifiers, and finally its left modifiers. The modifiers are generated one at a time, from the head outward. Details of this formulation and the associated model structure are given in (Collins 1997 and Miller 2000).

3. A HEAD TABLE FOR CHINESE

Obviously, to train the above parsing model, we need to know the head constituent for each non-terminal in the parse trees in the training corpus. That information will tell us the head word and its tag for each node. In the original SIFT parser, as well as in many other parsers, this is achieved by associating each non-terminal symbol with a search routine that looks for the head constituent from the expansion list (i.e. the right hand side of a production rule).

A problem with the above approach is that coding the search routines correctly for a new language is a painstaking effort and is error-prone. The alternative adopted in this work is to create a table of production rules with marked head constituent. Our table contains about 300 most frequently applied production rules (un-lexicalised) in the Chinese Treebank. For each rule, we manually marked the head constituent based on the linguistic interpretation of the rule. Since most rules have an obvious linguistic interpretation, the task is very easy. For example, a common rule in Chinese is "IP→NP VP NP", meaning that a clause (IP) can be expressed as a noun phrase (NP) followed by a verb phrase (VP) and then another noun phrase. In this case we marked VP as the head because the verb is more informative in predicting other constituents of the clause than either the subject or the object. With the head table, identifying the head constituent requires simply finding a matched rule. Nodes not covered by the head table were handled by a small number of default rules. Figure 1 shows a few rules in our head table. The resulting head table covers over 97% of all non-terminal node-expansions in the Chinese Treebank.

ADJP-> (JJ)
ADVP-> (AD)
CLP-> (M)
IP-> NP (VP)
IP-> (VP)
IP-> NP (VP) PU
IP-> IP PU (IP) PU
IP-> IP PU (IP)
IP-> NP NP (VP)
LCP-> NP (LC)

Figure 1: Example rules in Chinese table. Constituents in () are heads.

4. WORD-FEATURES FOR CHINESE

Word features allow us to group words with similar grammatical roles into equivalence classes. They are an effective mechanism for dealing with unknown words during parsing. For example, a good feature in English may be the suffix "-or": An unknown word with this ending has a good chance of being an animate noun. In the original SIFT parser, word features are linguistically motivated. In fact, most of the features are simply common English word endings.

In Chinese, such features are harder to come by because word affixes in Chinese are not widely documented. Since compiling Chinese word features by hand is costly, we used an automated solution. We automatically induced about 200 Chinese features by using a Chinese corpus with manual part of speech labeling, Academia Sinica Balanced Corpus (ASBC corpus, http://godel.iis.sinica.edu.tw/ROCLING/). We used this corpus because it has 5 million words, far larger than the Chinese Treebank. Since word derivation in Chinese is mainly through word-endings, our features are based on the suffixes. Since Chinese words usually contain 2 or three characters, we define the suffix of a word as the last character of that word. All Chinese words in the ASBC corpus were binned by suffix and suffixes were sorted by perplexity over the parts of speech. Our assumption is that words with the same part of speech shall have similar grammatical roles. Suffixes with the lowest perplexities are chosen as features. Suppose a suffix s is shared by the set of words $\{w_1, w_2, \ldots w_n\}$:

$$Perplexity(s)=2^{-\Sigma p(t|s) \log p(t|s)}$$
$$P(t|s)=\Sigma p(t|w_i)/n$$

where $p(t|w_i)$ is the probability that word w_i was assigned the tag t in the ASBC corpus. Note that in perplexity computing we give equal probability to all words sharing the same suffix. This prevents frequent words from dominating infrequent ones. The perplexity of a suffix tells us the average number of parts of speech for words that have the suffix. For example, Chinese words with the ending -者 (roughly translates to "-or" or "-er") have 1.7 parts of speech on average. Figure 2 shows some of the features, their perplexities and gloss translations.

社	1.37	(agency, organization)
百	1.38	(hundred)
员	1.38	(member, employee)
额	1.41	(amount)
院	1.42	(ministry, department)
千	1.49	(thousand)
物	1.49	(product)
费	1.58	(cost)

Figure 2: Example Chinese features

5. PERFORMANCE

We measured the performance of our parser by holding out part of the Chinese Treebank as testing data. Two partitions of training/testing of the Chinese Treebank were used. The first used the first 5% of the sentences for testing and the next 95% for training. In order to compare with the results in Bikel and Chiang 2000, the second partition used the first 80% for training, the next 10% for test and the last 10% for development (unused in this work).

Table 1 shows the performance of our parser on the first data set. If we used the unmodified SIFT English parser (without a Chinese-specific head table and the Chinese word features) to parse Chinese sentences, the labeled recall and precision are around 68% for sentences with no more than 40 words. If we used the Chinese word features, the performance was improved to around 75%. Using the Chinese head table in addition to the Chinese word features improved performance to around 80%. As expected, longer sentences are harder to parse than shorter ones.

The Chinese Treebank has around 100 K words, which is about 10% of the English Treebank. The performance of the SIFT English parser using 10% of English Treebank is around 81%, suggesting the parsing model is largely language independent.

Table 1: The impact of head table and word features on Chinese parsing. LR=labeled recall, LP=labeled precision.

	Sentences ≤40 words long		All sentences	
	LR	LP	LR	LP
English System	68%	68.4%	67.6%	68.1%
Chinese word features	75.4%	75.8%	71.5%	72%
Chinese head table and word features	80.4%	79.7%	77.1%	77.4%

Table 2 compares the performance of our parser with the best result reported in Bikel and Chiang 2000. Both systems used the second data set. Our parser achieved slightly better results than theirs.

Table 2: A comparison of our parser with the results in Bikel and Chiang 2000

	Sentences ≤40 words long		All sentences	
	LR	LP	LR	LP
Bikel & Chiang	76.8%	77.8%	NA	NA
Our parser	78.6%	78.7%	75.1%	75.4%

6. CONCLUSIONS AND FUTURE WORK

We demonstrated how a statistical parser for English can be easily adapted to effectively parse Chinese. The changes made include a Chinese head table and a set of automatically induced word features. Given the same amount of training data, the resulting parser rivals the original parser in parsing English. It also competes favorably against state of art results in parsing Chinese.

Our parser assumes that the input sentences are segmented. An area for future work is to parse un-segmented text. While we can conveniently treat word segmentation as a preprocessing step, differences in segmentation criteria can be a problem. For example, the parser and the segmentor may deal with compound words differently. This problem can result in sub-optimal parsing. We believe a better solution is to have an integrated model for both segmentation and parsing. After all, the goal of both tasks is to bracket strings. Another area is to apply our parsing algorithm to other languages. Although English and Chinese are two very different languages, both have strong requirements on word orders. It would be interesting to see how well our algorithm will work for languages with less stringent word orders (e.g. German).

7. REFERENCES

[1] Bikel D. and Chiang D.. 2000. Two Statistical Parsing Models Applied to the Chinese Treebank. In *Proceedings of the Second Chinese Language Processing Workshop,* (Hong Kong, October 2000), pages 1-6.

[2] Black E. et al. 1991. A Procedure for Quantitatively Comparing the Syntactic Coverage of English Grammars. In *Proceedings of the DARPA Speech and Natural Language Workshop*

[3] Collins M.. 1997. Three Generative Lexicalized Models for Statistical Parsing. In *Proceedings of the Association for Computational Linguistics.*

[4] Marcus M., Santorini, B. and Marcinkiewicz M.. 1993. Building a Large Annotated Corpus of English: the Penn Treebank. In *Computational Linguistics* 19(2):313-330.

[5] Miller S., Fox H., Ramshaw L., and Weischedel R. 2000. A Novel Use of Statistical Parsing to Extract Information from Text. In *Proceedings of the North American Association for Computational Linguistics..*

DEMONSTRATIONS
(in alphabetical order)

Rapid Response Translingual Information Access in the Alias-i Interface

Breck Baldwin
alias-i inc.
1500 Walnut St
8th Floor
267 970 4305
breck@alias-i.com

Aaron Ross
alias-i inc.
1500 Walnut St
8th Floor
267 970 4305
ross@alias-i.com

Michael Moore
alias-i inc.
1500 Walnut St
8th Floor
267 970 4305
moore@alias-i.com

Dipen Shah
DigiNexus, Inc
1500 Walnut St
8th Floor
dshah@diginexus.com

ABSTRACT

Our alias-i interface provides a limited class of translingual information access for English speakers in very short period of time. Alias-i consists of three components: An interface for bootstrapping recognition algorithms, a backend indexing and annotation algorithm that processes data, and an information access interface for end users. The system is built upon the linguistic phenomenon of coreference. Essentially, coreference abstracts over superficial differences in how a person, place, concept or event is represented in text, e.g. coreference recognizes that 'Mulla Omar', 'Omar', 'he', his name in Somali all refer to the same person. Coreference is a cognitively natural organizing principle which is an advancement over traditional information access approaches like keyword indexed data (i.e. search engines).

Keywords

Search, coreference, anaphora, information access.

1. Description of Demo

The alias-i system provides rapid response information access in foreign languages that are not in the current scope of machine translation systems and other tools. Alias-i breaks down into three components, 1) RETT, a rapid translation access tool for entities, 2) BEAD, a backend annotation engine and data base of information about entities, and 3) FEEB, an information access interface based on the principles behind the trinity system.

2. RETT

The goal of RETT is to quickly map from English realizations of entities like 'Mullah Omar' to their foreign language representations. The RETT interface supports several approaches to recovering this relationship, they are:

Proceedings of HLT 2002, Second International Conference on Human Language Technology Research, M. Marcus, ed., Morgan Kaufmann, San Francisco, 2002.

Brute Force: A list of English names/aliases is translated by hand into the desired languages. Alternate means of referring to the entity are included as well, phrases such as pronouns, honorifics or aliases.

Phonetic Mapping: If a phonetic mapping exists between English and the foreign language, RETT can speculatively guess likely matches with human oversight.

A one time translation of Omar to its Arabic counterpart immediately links an English speaking analyst to every sentence in the Arabic corpus about that individual. RETT allows a linguist to spend a few hours linking key individuals, events and concepts in English to their foreign language counterparts with the immediate effect that English analysts can request specific sentences to be translated rather than documents or entire corpora.

3. Backend Entity Annotation and Database (BEAD):

BEAD takes the descriptive variations of a set of entities, annotates a document collection for mentions of each entity. The annotation engine is sensitive to context and can carry out pronoun resolution in both English and Foreign languages if they are specified. It recognizes and manages issues of string variation and has active components to prevent incorrect merging of entities just because they have the same name. BEAD is very much like a search engine's reverse word lookup data structure with the important advancement that BEAD provides a mapping from 'entities to mentions' rather than 'words to documents'. BEAD also records relationships between entities, for example the fact that two entities were in the same sentence.

Front End Entity Browser (FEEB):

FEEB allows an analyst to quickly examine all information in a data collection irrespective of language. While on the face of it the utility of seeing 47 sentences in Farsi about 'Mullah Omar' appears limited, there are immediate benefits. The analyst can direct a translator to focus on just those sentences.

A second benefit is that the English speaking analyst can find relationships between entities in the foreign language materials, i.e. Mulla Omar is mentioned in the same sentence as Yassar Arafat. An Arabic sentence about these two individuals would be well worth getting translated. The analyst is in a position to recognize that fact and act upon it.

Below is a snapshot of the alias-i front end which shows the 'entity' view of the person named President Mohammad Khatami in both English and Romanized Somali in the right frame.

In the left bar we see high lev topic descriptions for Africa, Asia and the Middle East. Each high level topic has entity names below which correspond to individuals that the user wants to track over time.

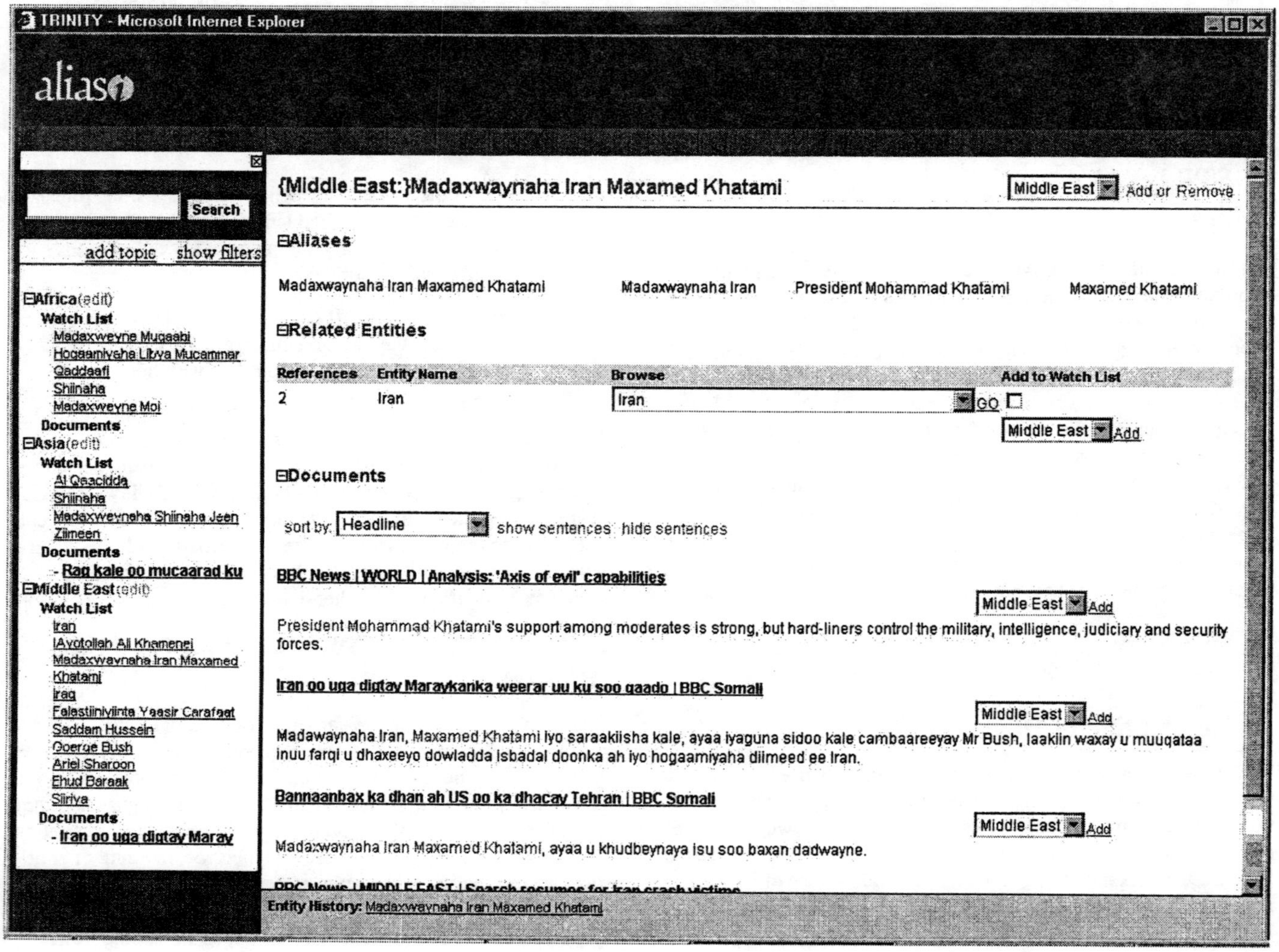

Implicit Speech Recognition: Making Speech a First Class Object on Computers

Eric Chang
Microsoft Research Asia
Beijing Sigma Center, Beijing, PRC, 100080
echang@microsoft.com

Chengyuan Ma
Microsoft Research Asia
Beijing Sigma Center, Beijing, PRC, 100080
i-chenma@microsoft.com

ABSTRACT

This paper introduces implicit speech recognition, where we focus on extracting features such as speaker identities, speaking rate, emotion and transcriptions from utterance spoken between people. Such technologies can increase one's productivity, especially in enhancing the efficiency of meetings and education. We have incorporated this technology into Microsoft Outlook to assist the processing of voicemails.

Keywords

Implicit Speech Recognition, Speaking Rate Estimation, Emotion Detection, Speaker Identification

1. INTRODUCTION

Traditional focus for speech recognition research has been using speech recognition to improve the computer human interface. Successful application examples can be found in dictation, command and control, and dialog systems over the telephone. However, from our experience in including dictation into actual products (Microsoft OfficeXP, Chinese edition), we have learned that most people find it difficult to learn to speak to the computer in a "dictation" style with a headset microphone. Furthermore, while dictation for text input can improve input speed for frequent users of Mandarin speech dictation software compared to using a keyboard, for English users, in the foreseeable future, keyboard entry would still be faster than keyboard due to the amount of time spent on error correction [1].

Our current research focus is thus on extracting information from casually spoken speech, which we call implicit speech recognition. The difference in implicit speech recognition is that the speaker is primarily speaking to other people while they are speaking as opposed to knowing that they are explicitly speaking to a machine. Since the speaker is not explicitly speaking to a machine, many traditional strategies such as requiring the speakers to enunciate clearly, using dialogs to clarify speaker intent, and performing long term speaker adaptation can not be applied. However, we believe that equipping computers with robust ability to extract information from voice signal is critical in making sure that voice can be processed as simply as other data types. Modern computers are quite capable of processing numbers and texts. Other media types such as images, video, and music are gradually being stored and organized on computers and the ability to retrieve them have improved over time [2]. Currently there is also a great deal of effort surrounding other data types such as ink to make them easily searchable on the computer. Our goal in implicit speech recognition is to make speech processing easier on the computer, allowing users to search, edit, and transmit speech signals easily.

Proceedings of HLT 2002, Second International Conference on Human Language Technology Research, M. Marcus, ed., Morgan Kaufmann, San Francisco, 2002.

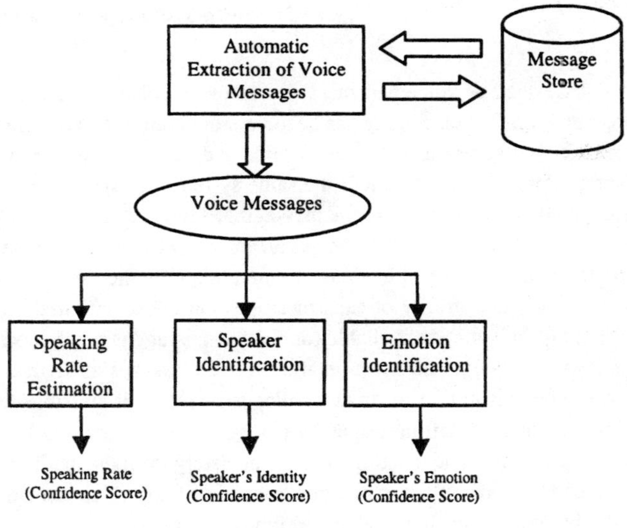

Figure 1: block diagram of the voice mail processing system.

2. CONCEPT DEMONSTRATION: VOICE MESSAGE PROCESSING

We hear speech in a variety of context in our daily lives. The different contexts can be casual conversations between friends, formal meetings or lectures, or broadcast programs heard through radios or television. We have chosen the context of voice message processing for our first application of implicit speech recognition.

People are now inundated with many types of messages in modern life. It is not uncommon to return to office from a vacation

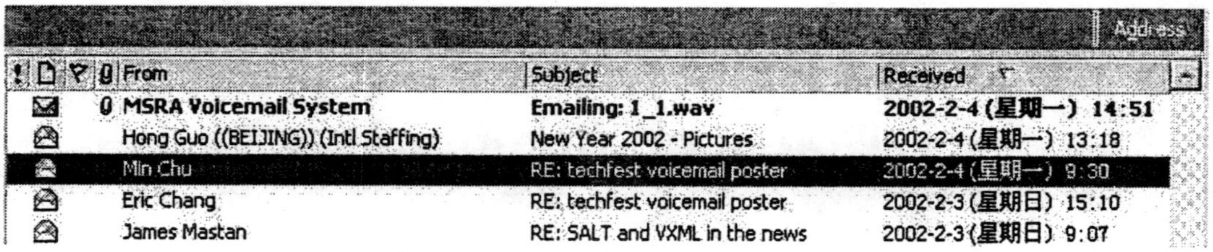

(a) Received a voicemail

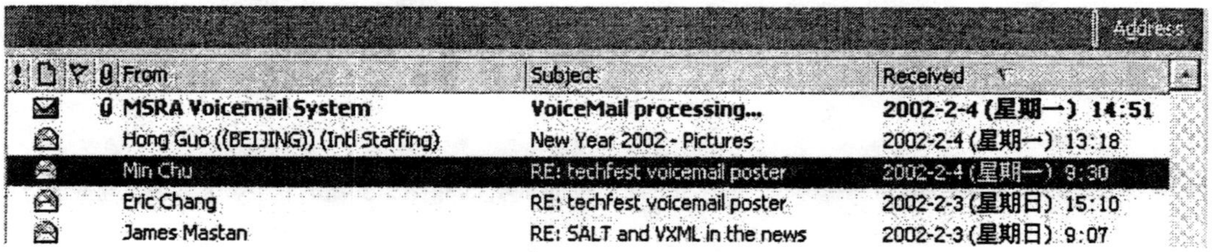

(b) Voicemail in processing

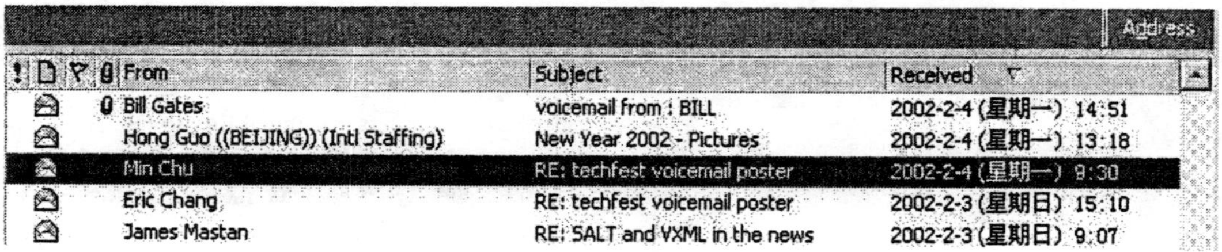

(c) Voicemail processed

Figure 2: Screen shot for voicemail system incorporated into Microsoft Outlook.

and have tens of voicemail messages in one's voicemail system. Recently, unified messaging has become more common, where the creation and access of voice, email, fax, and instant messages are being seamlessly united under the same system [3] [4]. However, compared to email and instant messaging, the types of information associated with voice messages are very limited. For example, for an email message, it is not uncommon to know the sender, the subject, and the priority of each message. On the other hand, the amount of information available for a voice message is much more limited. The lack of information about voice messages make them more time consuming to process. For example, it is possible to eliminate many email messages by just skimming the subject line or the sender line and deleting them immediately from the mailbox. This can be done either automatically by specifying rules or manually by quickly scanning the email inbox list. However, for scanning voice mail messages, one would typically spend a lot more time listening to each message just to extract the basic information such as the sender and the subject of the voice message. It is also not possible to automatically create rules to pre-organize the voice mail messages (for example, to rank them by sender or urgency.)

In our system, a program periodically surveys the user's messaging system and look for voice messages. After the voice messages are found, the program automatically scans the voice message and extracts information that will help the user to more efficiently process the voicemail message. Examples of information extracted from the voice message include the speaker's identity, his speaking rate, his emotion state, and the content of his message. This will allow the user to set rules to filter messages. Similarly, the user can sort messages by sender ID or search for information by message content.

2.1 Speaker detection

Each waveform is processed by the speaker identification system which classifies each sentence as being from one of the previously known message senders, with a confidence score associated and displayed as a part of the user interface. The user can then utilize the confidence score to determine whether to believe in the speaker identification result. The user can also choose to confirm the speaker identity hypothesized by the speaker. If the system makes a mistake, the user can type the correct name in the window and commands the system to automatically train up a new speaker model for the speaker. The user can choose to update the model so that speaker identification becomes more accurate in the future. Conversely, it is also possible for the system to incrementally update the speaker model in an unsupervised fashion. For example, the system can decide to update the model if the confidence score on the hypothesis is high and the user didn't actively correct the system. A discriminative training approach can be incorporated to make the automatic adjustment of system parameters more efficient [5].

2.2 Speaking rate detection

The speaking rate of the message is automatically evaluated using an energy based approach [6]. Once the speaking rate has been determined, that knowledge can be used to normalize the speaking rate of the message when it is played back. In our implementation, the user can pre-select a preferred speaking rate. The system will then automatically evaluate the speaking rate of the incoming sentence and adjust the speaking rate of the sentence with a time scale modification algorithm. The system can also automatically reduce the length of silence and pause within the waveform for more efficient listening. Our experiments on speaking rate detection have shown that this method is effective. We first modified the speaking rate of a message using Time Scale Modification (TSM) method, then we detect the speaking rate using energy based method for each message after time scale modification. Here we show the detected speaking rate and the corresponding TSM factor for 3 different messages.

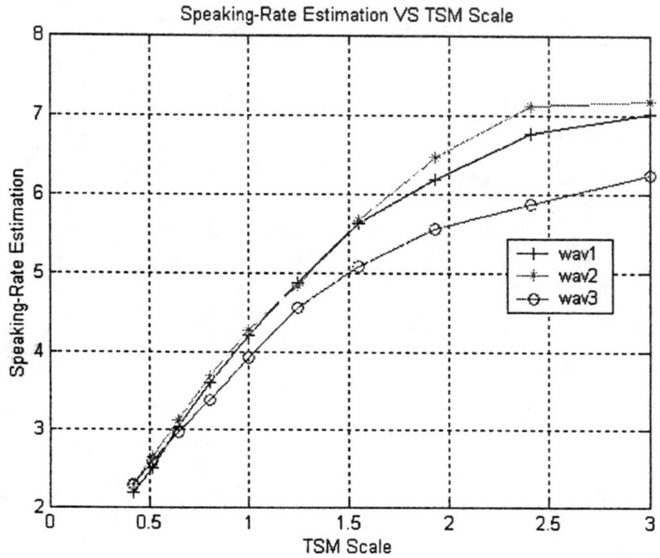

Figure 3: Speaking rate estimation versus Time Scale Modification factor.

2.3 Emotion detection

Much information is embedded into a voice message. In the past year, we have worked on a feature extraction system which can classify the emotional state of the speaker [7]. The system can classify emotions into general categories such as anger, happiness, and neutral. By using such information, the system can classify the urgency of the message based on the sender and the emotional state of the sender. In our implementation, we are extracting the pitch of the incoming speech and using several derivatives of the pitch signal as basic features. The features are then sent to a support vector machine which categorizes each sentence as being happy, sad, or angry. Since each support vector machine is a binary classifier, the system can decide that multiple emotions exist in each sentence with varying weights. This corresponds to the fact that multiple emotions can exist in the same sentence.

2.4 Meaning extraction

We have also incorporated Microsoft's SAPI 5.1 speech recognition engine into the system. Once a voice mail is transcribed, the content can be added to the message. Currently, accurate transcription of voice mail messages is still a very challenging task [8]. As transcription accuracy improves over time, we plan to incorporate automatic text pre-processors to tag certain portions of message, for example, meeting time, phone numbers, etc.

Table 1: close-set experiment results.

Number of Speakers	Error Rate (%)
5	3.96
10	7.15
15	8.32
20	9.17
25	10.64
30	11.52
35	11.11
40	12.23
45	13.60

3. EXPERIMENTAL RESULTS

We have evaluated the speaker detection and speaking rate detection portions of our system. We are currently enlisting trial users of our system to obtain feedback on the interface and will perform evaluation on other portions of system in the future.

3.1 Database

We are using the database from NIST's 1996 speaker recognition benchmark. There are 88 speakers in this database. For each speaker, there are about 4 minutes of training utterance (2 minutes from the same session, 1 minute from different session but the same handset, 1 minute from different handset). There are 315 files with different session, channel and handset used for testing. Additionally, 150 files from the NIST'97 database were selected to train the UBM model. In our closed set experiment, all the test files come from the in-group speakers. We used 2 minutes of training data from the same session to train each speaker model. We then used 30 seconds of utterance from different session, different channel and different handsets for testing.

MFCCs are used as acoustic features for speaker verification. All utterances are pre-emphasized with a factor of 0.97. A Hamming window with 32ms window length and 16ms window shift is used for each frame. Each feature frame consists of 10 MFCC coefficients and 10 delta MFCC coefficients. Finally, the relative spectral (RASTA) filter and cepstral mean subtraction (CMS) are used to remove linear channel convolutional effects on the cepstral features.

3.2 Evaluation result

Table 1 lists the current speaker identification results with our system. As the number of speaker models increase in the system, the probability of error increases. The state of the art GMM-UBM model methods described in [5] was used. In all our experiments, we change the number of in-group speakers from 5 to 45. For each experimental condition, 50 experiments were carried out to get average accuracy and error rates.

4. CONCLUSION AND FUTURE WORK

An important use of speech technologies will be the use of implicit speech recognition. While currently our work focus on extracting a variety of meanings from spontaneous voice messages deposited to a voicemail system, we believe that there is also much potential in other scenarios, such as lecture transcription, meeting recording transcription, and ordinary daily conversation transcription. In all these domains, absolutely perfect transcription is not critical, since we believe that the computer power is best applied in helping to identify meaningful segments of speech that can be listened to by the user. In other words, retrieval precision and recall is a better measure of the system's effectiveness. We are currently working on combining speech recognition with information retrieval in a unified framework to improve retrieval performance overall.

5. REFERENCES

[1] C. Karat, C. Halverson, D. Horn, and J. Karat, "Patterns of entry and correction in large vocabulary continuous speech recognition systems," in *Proc. ACM CHI'99*, 1999.

[2] Z. Chen, W.-Y. Liu, C.-H. Hu, M.-J. Li, and H.-J. Zhang, "ifind: A web image search engine," in *Proc. SIGIR 2001*, 2001.

[3] J. Hirschberg, M. Bacchiani, D. Hindle, P. Isenhour, A. Rosenberg, L. Stark, L. Stead, S. Whittaker, and G. Zamchick, "Scanmail, browsing and searching speech data by content," in *Proc. Eurospeech 2001*, Aalborg, Denmark, September 2001.

[4] M. Bacchiani, J. Hirschberg, A. Rosenberg, S. Whittaker, D. Hindle, P. Isenhour, M. Jones, L. Stark, and G. Zamchick, "Scanmail: Audio navegation in the voicemail domain," in *Proc. HLT 2001*, 2001.

[5] X.-H. Li, E. Chang, and B.-Q. Dai, "Improving speaker verification with figure of merit training," in *Proc. ICASSP 2002*, Orlando, May 2002.

[6] N. Morgan and E. Fosler-Lussier, "Combining multiple estimators of speaking rate," in *Proc. ICASSP 1998*, 1998.

[7] F. Yu, E. Chang, Y.-Q. Xu, and H.-Y. Shum, "Emotion detection from speech to enrich multimedia content," in *Proc. 2nd IEEE Pacific-Rim Conference on Multimedia*, Beijing, 2001.

[8] M. Padmanabhan, G. Saon, S. Basu, J. Huang, and G. Zweig, "Recent improvements in voicemail transcription," in *Proc. 10th Hub 5 Conversational Speech Understanding Workshop*, 1999.

Biologically Inspired Lexicon Structuring Technique

Angelo Dalli
University of Malta
417, Department of CS & AI
University of Malta, Msida, Malta
+356 79646464, +356 32902507
adall@cs.um.edu.mt

ABSTRACT

This paper describes a machine learning technique that applies bioinformatics concepts from genome sequencing and data mining to learn the lexical structure of a language during the lexicon building process. Human linguists are fully integrated in the learning process. Phonetic mapping of input data ensures the universal applicability of the technique including application in reverse to obtain a linguistic treatment of biological data.

Keywords
Lexicon Building, Bioinformatics, LST, Phonetic Mapping, Weakly-Supervised Learning, Clustering.

1. INTRODUCTION

A novel technique that reduces the amount of work on the part of linguists by utilising bioinformatics techniques is presented. Aided by human effort, the technique allows the system to learn the lexical structure of a language during the building process. The technique also permits related words to be clustered together and a suitable headword to be extracted automatically from any list of words without any prior knowledge of the source language grammar or morphology, using only weak human supervision..

Computational lexicon building is a labour intensive process that involves linguists at all stages. Linguists are presented with a list of word forms extracted from some corpus and these word forms are then grouped together under a headword to form a smaller set of lemmas. Lemmas in this sense consist of a headword together with related word forms or variants of the same word. Additional information can then be added to every lemma entry manually or through some other system.

The objectives behind the development of the Lexicon Structuring Technique (LST) are twofold. The first was to have a method that would automatically identify lemmas in a list of words without having any predefined rules that cater for morphological and syntactical processes. Thus no a priori knowledge of the language and its grammar is used by the system.

Proceedings of HLT 2002, Second International Conference on Human Language Technology Research, M. Marcus, ed., Morgan Kaufmann, San Francisco, 2002.

The second was to seamlessly integrate human expert knowledge to increase the accuracy of the automated discovery of lemmas by the system. Instead of having linguists enter formal rules explicitly it was desirable to have linguists teach the system by example.

LST was developed as part of the Maltilex Project, that has the creation of the first computational lexicon for Maltese as its primary aim [4].

2. BIOINFORMATICS AND NLP

The first objective was achieved through the application of bioinformatics algorithms – that are usually used to sequence and structure genome data – to linguistics. The ultimate aim of bioinformatics algorithms is generally to sequence and find groups of related or similar proteins and then utilise these results to find likely genes in the genome. The basic idea was to apply slightly modified versions of these algorithms to computational linguistics in a manner that makes it possible to apply any resulting improvements back in reverse to biological data. This novel cross-fertilization of ideas from bioinformatics and computational linguistics proved to be very productive since improvements in one discipline could be almost directly applied to the other.

LST is based upon a variety of bioinformatics algorithms that aim to sequence and find groups of related or similar proteins in order to find likely genes in the genome [2]. LST aims to reduce the amount of manual work in computational lexicon building by identifying lemmas in a list of words automatically. Since no a priori knowledge of the language and its grammar is used, LST can apply universally to all natural languages.

2.1 Phonetic Transcription

Data from different source languages is mapped to a universal phonetic representation utilising the International Phonetic Alphabet using language-dependent phonetic transforms that map orthographic forms into their IPA equivalent. IPA is a language-independent format that ensures universal applicability of the LST algorithms regardless of the source language. The web-based LST implementation also caters for interoperability between different language resources as discussed in [1]. Figure 1 shows the main interface of the web-based LST implementation as part of the Maltilex Computational Lexicon for Maltese. Language-independent representation would also help in applying LST to the modeling of biological data since only two language systems would need to be handled – IPA on the linguistics side and DNA on the bioinformatics side.

Figure 1 LST System Web Interface

A main problem that had to be overcome is to find some universal way of mapping linguistic data originating from different source languages, so that the developed system would only need to cater for two language systems – a universal human language representation on the linguistics side and DNA on the bioinformatics side. For this reason a phonetical, rather than orthographic, representation of the word forms is utilised.

Untagged input word lists are processed through a source language-dependent phonetic transform that maps orthographic forms into their International Phonetic Alphabet (IPA) equivalent. The phonetic transform is initially defined manually by phoneticians.

Once the word form data is in IPA form, the same algorithms can be employed to any natural language that is represented in the IPA. Figure 2 shows the web interface to the automated transcription facility that has been implemented for the Maltese language.

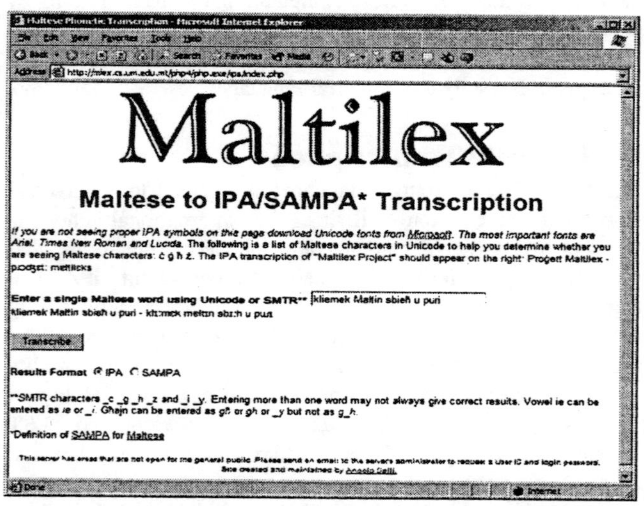

Figure 2 Automated Maltese-IPA Transcription Facility

A set of language-independent scoring matrices, analogous to the PAM and BLOSUM matrices in bioinformatics [5, 6], are used in the creation of a non-linear phonetically based distance function, which takes care of gap lengths and similarity matching, just as bioinformatics algorithms do for protein sequencing and alignment.

The scoring matrix tries to define a measure of the phonetic distance between two words by comparing the similarity between different phonemes. The scoring matrix was computed using data from various feature-based models, taking into account principles from the sonority hierarchy [9].

The distance function is defined on sequences rather than strings of phonemes in order to cater for morphological or other processes that might change the expression of a particular word [2]. Simple functions like the Levenshtein string edit distance algorithms were not found suitable since they do not cater for things like gap lengths and local alignments adequately [10, 12].

2.2 Alignment and Clustering

Alignment algorithms suffer from a variety of computational complexity problems that can be partly alleviated through intelligent implementations including techniques like the Four-Russians speedup [13]. A reduction in the computational effort needed to cluster the word form lists was achieved through the use of clustering techniques adopted from data mining.

Clusters are initially formed quickly using approximate matching algorithms coupled with the Not-Yet lazy buffering strategy described in [3] and illustrated in Figure 3. The cluster contents are then processed with the same alignment algorithms that are used for protein alignment, modified to work with IPA data. Cluster re-alignment occurs every time a new word is added or removed from the cluster but other clusters are unaffected. An extension to the standard alignment algorithms based on the Minimum Description Length principle is then used to identify cluster members that do not conform to the general data distribution within the cluster.

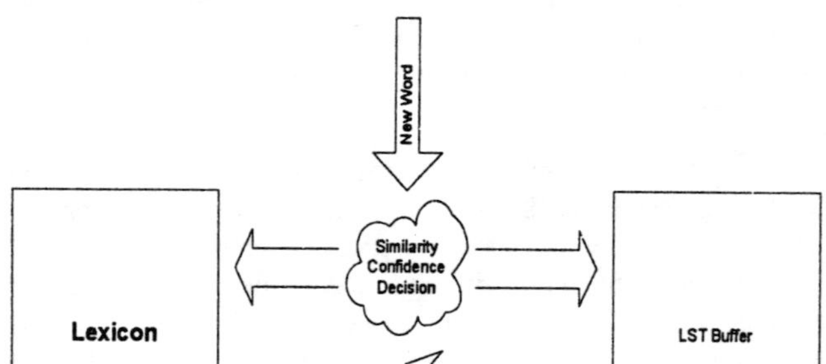

Figure 3 Addition of new words to the lexicon using LST

The number of gaps and gap lengths are used as a measure of the quality of a particular alignment. Gaps are used to modify the phonetic distance by preferring words that align against each other with the minimal amount of gaps. The constant, affine, convex and arbitrary weighting models were all considered for their suitability and practicality in implementation with the convex weighting model providing the best trade-off [8, 14].

Local alignment techniques were extensively compared against global alignment techniques, generally giving better results. Since local alignments may be found through random chances a threshold value was incorporated into the model. This is analogous to the k-tuple parameters found in FASTA and BLAST [7, 15]. A threshold value of around 3 seems to give the optimal results for IPA data.

Every cluster is assigned a representative member – which does not need to be a member of the cluster itself – to aid in the calculation of intra-cluster distance. The representative member is actually a vector determined from a statistical analysis of the alignment inside the cluster. A threshold value is used to display the representative member at a specific level of detail. The intra-cluster distance is a measure of the phonological similarity between different lemmas and can also be used to calculate the similarity of a word form to a cluster quickly. In languages of Semitic origin, like Maltese, the representative member generally corresponds closely to the word's root pattern as illustrated in Figure 4. Figure 4 shows part of the word cluster for the word `kelma` (literally, word) and its representative member `kelm` that closely corresponds to its Semitic root `klm`.

```
_ _ _ k e l _ _  m a  _ _
_ _ _ k _ l _ ie m _  _ _
_ _ _ k e l _ _  m ie t _
_ _ t k e l l e  m _  _ _
_ _ t k e l l _  m u  _ _
_ _ t k e l l _  m e  t _
_ _ t k e l l i  m _  t u
m i t k e l l e  m _  _ _
```

Figure 4 Typical Aligned Word Form Cluster obtained by LST with the Representative Member highlighted

LST ideally needs an adequately large sample of word forms to extract a high quality representative member. Initial testing on English and Italian shows that the system is capable of identifying the common subset of character sequences shared by most related word forms. Although this effect is more pronounced in Semitic languages, this data can still be utilized for a variety of uses including approximate matching and morphological analysis.

The ability of the system to distinguish between word forms pertaining to different lemmas depends on the degree to which the principle of sufficient perceptual separation holds. It would be interesting to investigate whether this principle applies as strongly in biological systems as in natural languages.

3. WEAK HUMAN SUPERVISION

In certain ambiguous cases, alignment and approximate distance measurement functions are not enough to distinguish between word forms pertaining to different clusters. In this case weak supervision by human experts is needed. Experts can decide to split a cluster into two or join two clusters together. The system then tries to generalize this action by creating a formal rule that accounts for the split or join event. These rules are retained together with every cluster making the system's accuracy increase over time. When a splitting action is done the system compares the new representative members together against the old representative member. A discriminant rule that identifies the differences in the representative members of the new sets is automatically generated. Any existing rules will be re-assigned to any of the two new clusters accordingly. When a joining action is done a joining rule is created in a similar fashion to a discriminant rule, but instead all new and existing rules are automatically associated with the new cluster.

Generated rules are represented by a modified probabilistic context sensitive rule notation. Rules are readily understood by human experts and help to keep the underlying system more transparent. Using this system there is less scope for errors in writing formal rules since the system generates the rules by itself without sacrificing human expert control over the final lexicon structure. Additionally, new words that are added will also be subject to these rules, ensuring that classification accuracy is maintained at an acceptable level by the algorithm.

The LST system has been tested on Maltese, which is a Semitic based language with a strong Romance influence and a Latin script, together with limited testing on English and Italian. LST is capable of handling any natural language and find likely lemmas without any predefined knowledge about the language. Current tests indicate that the system consistently achieves lemma identification accuracy levels of around 80%-90% when compared to the results obtained by average linguists.

LST is one of the few existing examples of an extensive application of bioinformatics to computational linguistics. It draws upon a large number of analogies between biological and linguistical problems to achieve results that can be applied as easily to natural languages as to DNA. The minimal amount of bias in the learning component together with the full integration of human experts as part of the learning process make this technique attractive both for computational linguists as well as for bioinformaticians. It is hoped that the improvements incorporated into LST from a linguistics perspective will be applied to bioinformatics tasks. A highly promising area for the technique might be the identification of genes and related protein sequences in large amounts of data and aiding with phylogeny studies.

4. ACKNOWLEDGMENTS

My thanks goes to Mike Rosner for providing me with helpful advice and to the University of Malta for its support.

5. REFERENCES

[1] Dalli, Angelo. Interoperable Extensible Linguistic Databases. *IRCS Workshop on Linguistics Databases,* University of Pennsylvania, Philadelphia, 2001.

[2] Gusfield, Dan. *Algorithms on Strings, Trees, and Sequences.* Cambridge University Press, Cambridge, UK, 1999.

[3] Roure, Josep. Talavera, Luis. Robust incremental clustering with bad instance ordering. Catalonia, Spain, 1998.

[4] Rosner, Michael et. al. Linguistic and Computational Aspects of Maltilex. *Proc. of the ATLAS Symposium,* Tunis, 1999.

[5] Dayhoff, M. Schwarz, R. Matrices for detecting distant relationships. *Atlas of Protein Sequences,* 353-58, 1979.

[6] Henikoff, S. Henikoff, J. G. Amino acid substitution matrices from protein blocks. *Proc. Natl. Academy Science,* 89(10):915-19, 1992.

[7] Myers, E. Algorithmic advances for searching biosequence databases. *Computational Methods in Genome Research*, 121-35. Plenum Press, New York, 1994.

[8] Waterman, M. S. Efficient sequence alignment algorithms. *Journal of Theoretical Biology,* 108: 333-37, 1984.

[9] Ladefoged, Peter. Maddieson, Ian. *The Sounds of the World's Languages*. Blackwells, 1996.

[10] Mitchell, Tom. *Machine Learning*. McGraw-Hill, Singapore, 1997.

[11] Barnett, Vic. Lewis, Toby. *Outliers in statistical data.* 3rd. ed. John Wiley & Sons, West Sussex, UK, 1995.

[12] Levenshtein, V. I. Binary codes capable of correcting insertions and reversals. *Soviet Phys. Dokl.,* 10:707-10, 1966.

[13] Arlazarov, V. L. et. al. On economic construction of the transitive closure of a directed graph. *Dokl. Acad. Nauk SSSR,* 194:487-88, 1970.

[14] Pearson, W. R. Effective protein sequence comparison. *Computer Methods for Macromolecular Sequence Analysis*, 266:227-58. Academic Press, New York, 1996.

[15] Pearson, W. R. Lipman, D. J. Improved tools for biological sequence comparison. *Proc. Natl. Academy Science*, 85:2444-48, 1988.

Real Users, Real Data, Real Problems: The MiTAP System for Monitoring Bio Events

Laurie Damianos[*], Steve Wohlever[*], Jay Ponte[*], George Wilson[†], Florence Reeder[†], Tom McEntee[†], Robyn Kozierok*, Lynette Hirschman[*], David Day[*]

[*]The MITRE Corporation
202 Burlington Road
Bedford, MA 01730
+1.781.271.2000

[†]The MITRE Corporation
7798 Old Springhouse Road
McLean, VA 22102
+1.703.883.6000

{laurie, wohlever, ponte, gwilson, freeder, tmcentee, robyn, lynette, day}@mitre.org

ABSTRACT

The MiTAP (MITRE Text and Audio Processing) system [13] is a prototype for monitoring infectious disease outbreaks and other global threats. MiTAP focuses on providing timely, multi-lingual, global information access to analysts, medical experts and individuals involved in humanitarian assistance and relief work. Multiple information sources in multiple languages are automatically captured, filtered, translated, summarized, and categorized into searchable newsgroups. Critical information is automatically extracted and tagged to facilitate browsing, searching, and sorting.

The demonstration highlights how different users cull different kinds of information from the MiTAP system. Some use it in order to track disease outbreak; others have been using it to monitor economic and political situations worldwide.

Keywords

Biological threats, terrorism, infectious disease outbreaks, extraction, translation, summarization

1. INTRODUCTION

Over the years, greatly expanded trade and travel have increased the potential economic and political impacts of major disease outbreaks, given their ability to move rapidly across national borders. These diseases can affect people (West Nile virus, HIV, Ebola, Bovine Spongiform Encephalitis), animals (foot-and-mouth disease) and plants (citrus canker in Florida). More recently, the potential of biological terrorism has become a very real threat. On September 11th, 2001, the Center for Disease Control alerted states and local public health agencies to monitor for any unusual disease patterns, including chemical and biological agents. In addition to possible disruption and loss of life, bioterrorism could foment political instability, given the panic that fast-moving plagues have historically engendered.

Appropriate response to disease outbreaks and emerging threats depends on obtaining reliable and up-to-date information, which often means monitoring many news sources, particularly local news sources, in many languages worldwide. Analysts cannot feasibly acquire, manage, and digest the vast amount of information available 24 hours a day, seven days a week. In addition, access to foreign language documents and the local news of other countries is generally limited. Even when foreign language news is available, it is usually no longer current by the time it is translated and reaches the hands of an analyst. This is a very real problem that raises a very urgent need to develop automated support for global tracking of infectious disease outbreaks and emerging biological threats.

The MiTAP system was created to explore the integration of synergistic TIDES[1] language processing technologies: translation, information detection, extraction, and summarization. TIDES aims to revolutionize the way that information is obtained from human language by enabling people to find and interpret needed information quickly and effectively, regardless of language or medium. The component TIDES technologies were integrated and adapted to support an Integrated Feasibility Experiment in Bio-Security (IFE-Bio). The IFE-Bio experiment was intended to provide real users, such as medical professionals and analysts, with access to live, global information for monitoring epidemiological events in the geopolitical contexts of interest. By applying current natural language processing technology to bio-security problems, MiTAP could provide the end user with timely, accurate information and present it in a way that would allow the analyst to spend more time on analysis and less time on finding, translating, distilling and presenting information.

Since September 11th, 2001, the research prototype system, designed to support the IFE-Bio experiment, has been providing real data to real users for real problems.

Proceedings of HLT 2002, Second International Conference on Human Language Technology Research, M. Marcus, ed., Morgan Kaufmann, San Francisco, 2002.

[1] TIDES is a program in human language technology funded by the Defense Advanced Research Projects Agency (DARPA).

2. TEXT AND AUDIO PROCESSING

2.1 System Overview

MiTAP currently captures between 3500 and 6000 articles a day from over 90 global information sources (e.g., epidemiological reports, newswire feeds, email, online news, television news, and radio news) in multiple languages (i.e., English, Chinese, French, German, Italian, Portuguese, Russian, and Spanish). Figure 1 represents a graphical overview of the services provided.

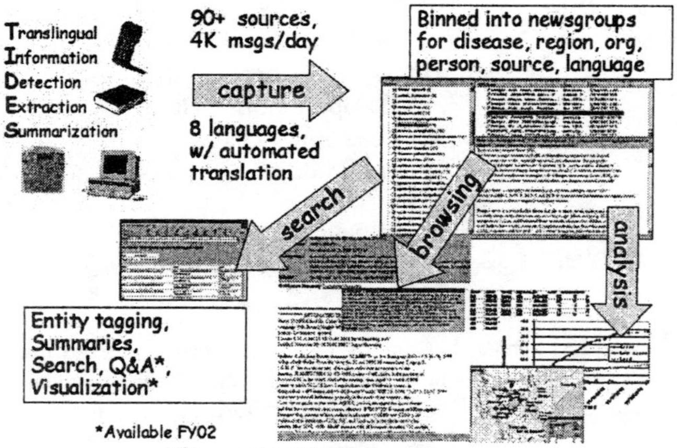

Figure 1 MiTAP Overview

The captured data are automatically filtered, translated, summarized, and categorized into searchable newsgroups based on disease, region, information source, person, organization, and language. Critical information is automatically extracted and tagged to facilitate browsing, searching, and sorting. Extracted named entities are color-coded, making scanning of documents easier. Pop-up keyword lists and automatic summarization show useful information at a glance. An additional component, a web-based search engine, provides a source-specific, full-text search capability.

The architecture of the MiTAP system consists of three major phases: information capture, information processing, and user interface. See the illustration in figure 2.

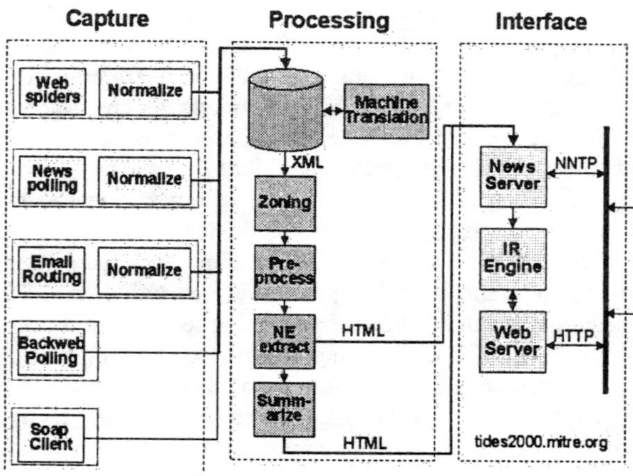

Figure 2 MiTAP Architecture

2.2 Information Capture

The capture process supports sources from the web, electronic mailing lists, newsgroups, news feeds and audio/video data. The first four of these source types are automatically harvested and filtered, and the resulting information is normalized prior to processing. The ViTAP system [9], captures and transcribes TV news broadcasts, making the text transcriptions available to MiTAP via a SOAP-based interface [16]. The data from all of these sources are then sent on to the next major phase, information processing, where the individual TIDES component technologies are employed.

2.3 Information Processing

Each normalized message is passed through a zoner that identifies the source, original date, and other fields such as headline or title, article body, etc. The zoned messages are preprocessed to identify paragraph boundaries, sentence boundaries, word boundaries and part-of-speech tags. This preprocessing is carried out by the Alembic natural language analyzer [1, 2, 19, 20]. The preprocessed messages are then fed into the named entity recognizer, another component of Alembic, which identifies person, organization and location names, as well as dates, diseases, and victim descriptions. This extended set of "named entities" is critical in routing the messages to the appropriate newsgroups and is also used to color-code the message contents so users can quickly scan the relevant information. Lists of top named entities are compiled and made available through pop-ups and tables. Finally, the document is automatically summarized using WebSumm [7]. WebSumm depends on the TempEx normalizing time expression tagger [8] which identifies and normalizes the time expressions [3, 4]. TempEx will normalize relative time expressions such as 'yesterday' to the correct date. For non-English sources, the CyberTrans machine translation system [12], which "wraps" either commercial or research translation engines and presents a common set of interfaces, is used to translate the messages automatically into English. The translated messages are then processed as the English sources are. In spite of translation errors, the translated messages have been judged by users to be useful. There is generally enough information for users to determine the relevance of a given message, and the original, foreign language documents remain available for more accurate human translation, if desired. Without the machine translation, these articles would effectively be invisible to analysts and other users.

2.4 User Interface

The final phase consists of the user interface and related processing. The processed messages are converted to HTML, with color-coded named entities, and routed to newsgroups hosted by a Network News Transport Protocol (NNTP) server, InterNetNews (INN) [5]. See Figure 3 for a view of MiTAP as seen through a typical newsreader. The newsgroups are organized by category (i.e., source, disease, region, language, person, and organization) to allow analysts with specific information needs to locate material quickly. The article summaries are included via a web link and JavaScript code embedded in the HTML that displays a pop-up summary when the mouse is positioned over the link.

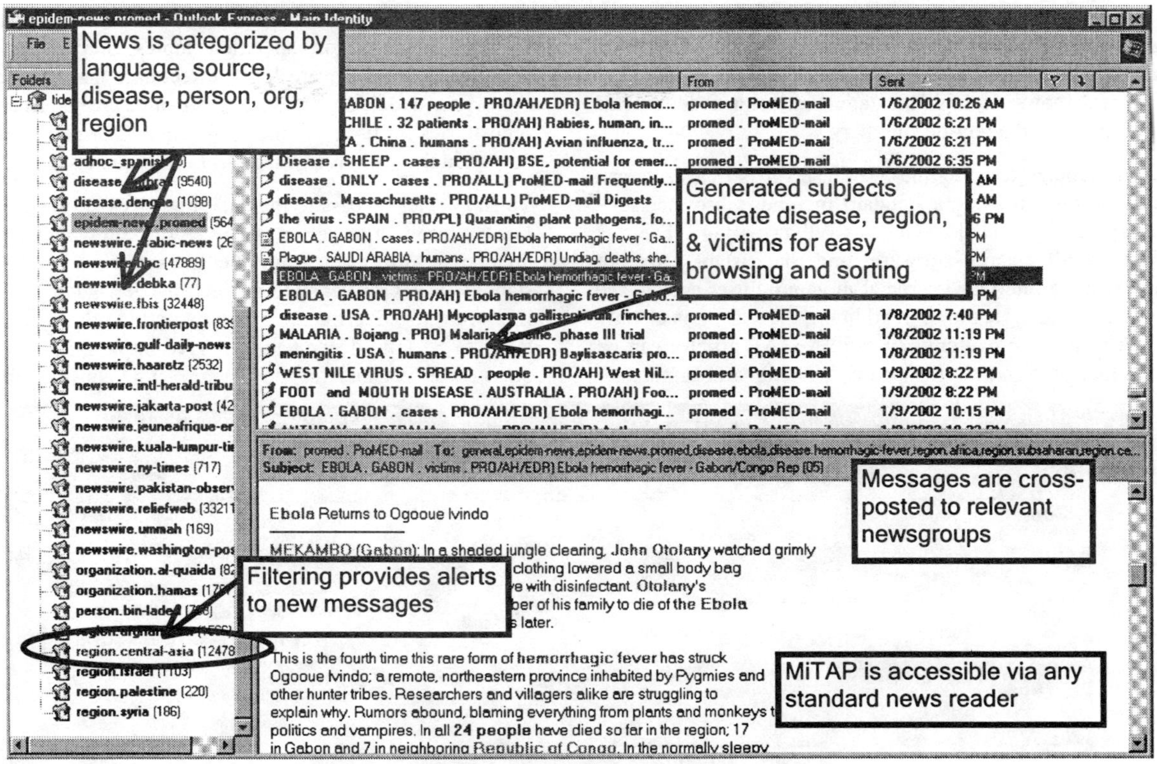

Figure 3 MiTAP viewed through a newsreader

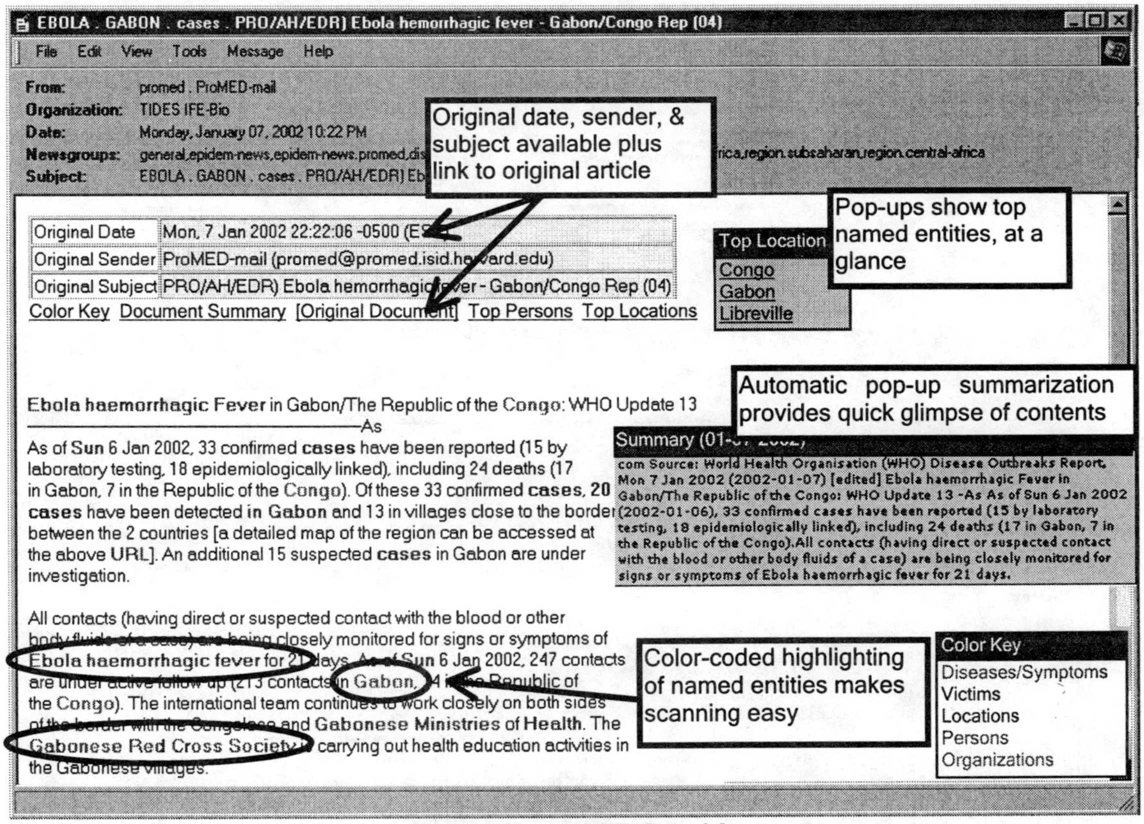

Figure 4 Sample MiTAP Article

Another type of summary, pop-up tables, show categorized lists of top named entities found in the document. Machine-translated documents contain a web link to the original foreign language article. Figure 4 shows a sample message with color-coded named entity highlighting and a pop-up summary.

One major advantage to using the NNTP server is that users can access the information using a standard mail/news browser such as Netscape Messenger [14] or Outlook® Express [11]. There is no need to install custom software, and the instant sense of familiarity with the interface is crucial in gaining user acceptance - little to no training is required. In addition, the system is already integrated with users' email environment; MiTAP articles can be treated as email and saved, forwarded, printed, and annotated. Mail readers also provide additional functionality such as alerting to new messages on specified topics, flagging messages of significance, and private local, directories that can be used as a workspace. Additional newsgroups can be created as collaborative repositories for users to share collective information. (Read about *hotbox* in the section on usage and utility, below.)

To supplement access to the data, messages are indexed using the Lucene information retrieval system [6], allowing users to do full text, source-specific queries over the entire set of messages via a standard web browser such as Netscape Navigator [15] or Internet Explorer [10]. See figures 5 and 6. As the relevance of messages tends to be time dependent, we have implemented an optimized query mechanism to do faster time-constrained searches.

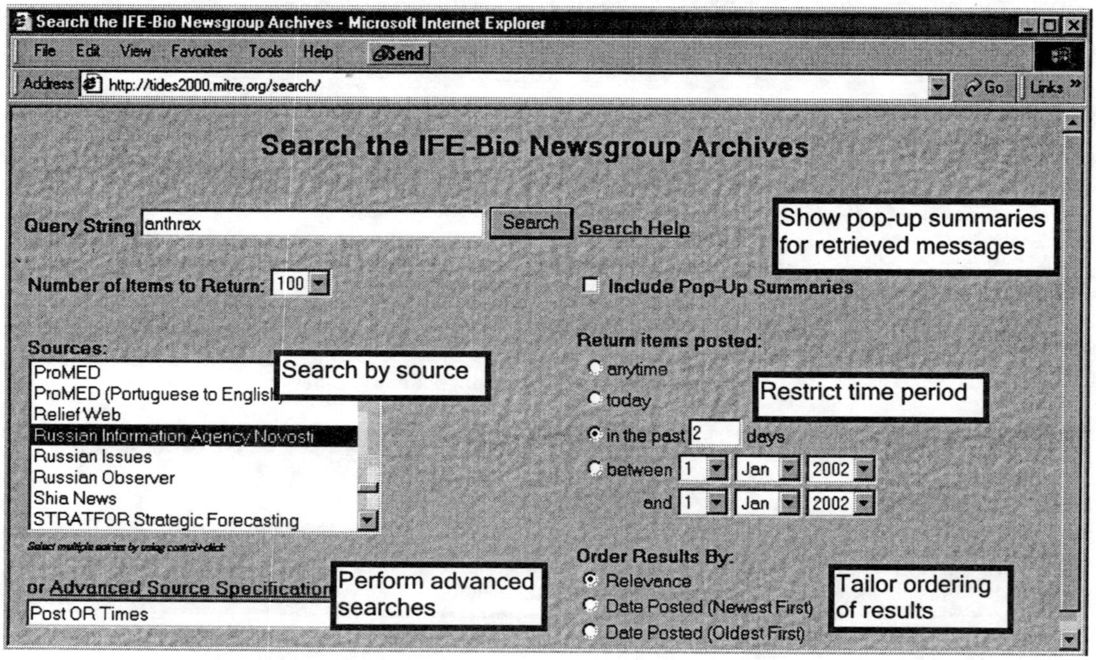

Figure 5 Web-based search engine to MiTAP

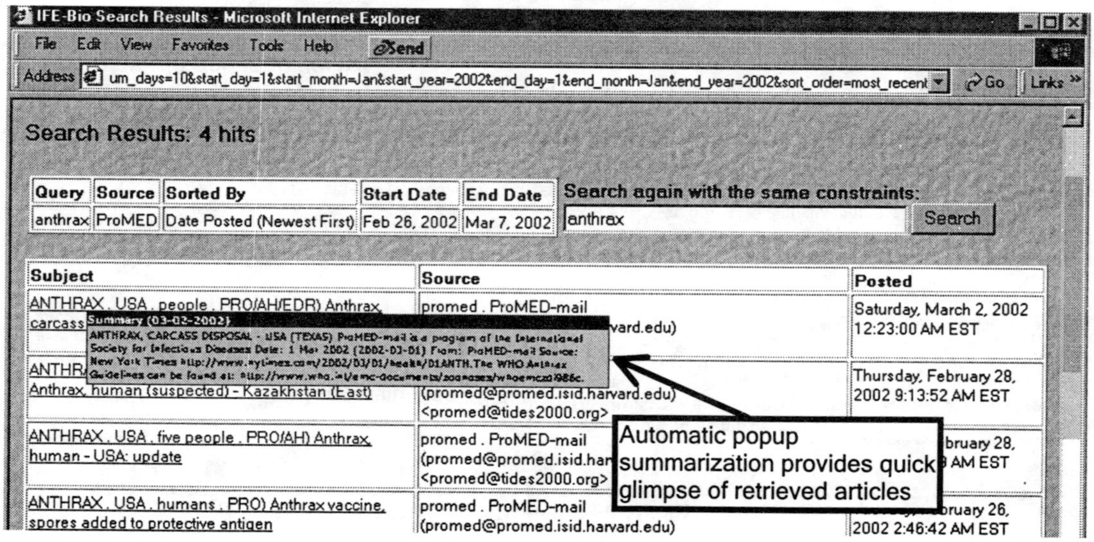

Figure 6 View of retrieved documents

3. MiTAP Usage and Utility

3.1 Usage

MiTAP has been accessible to users since June 2001. Originally, access was permitted via IP filtering or domain name, but this posed a problem for people with dynamic IP addresses and limited our users to specific machines. It was a potential security risk, as well, since it was impossible to control access if the system was open to an entire domain in order for a single user to get to MiTAP. As the demand for access, and more flexible access, continued to grow, we added user accounts, a feature that has provided more freedom to our users and improved security for us.

MiTAP data can be accessed in two ways: via newsgroups or through our web-based search engine. No special software is needed - just a standard news reader [14, 11] or web browser [15, 10]. The number of users that the system can support at one time is limited only by the loads that can be handled by the web and news servers. At the time of this writing, we have over 60 individual user accounts. Almost 20 people have used the system on any particular day, with a daily average of 8 regular users, including weekends. Our user base includes medical analysts, doctors, government and military officials, members of non-governmental organizations, and members of humanitarian assistance/disaster relief organizations. They access the system for updates on disease outbreaks as well as to read current news from around the world. Not only is the system being used for research and business purposes, but many of our users have also expressed personal interest in perusing the news in MiTAP.

To support collaborative work, there is a newsgroup, called *hotbox*, to which users can submit news and messages of current interest. Personal opinions and annotations can be included as well. Almost all of our subscribers read the contents of *hotbox* every time they login to the system.

One regular user, in particular, is a paid consultant of an organization of medical professionals. This user spends one to two hours a day reading 800 to 1000 MiTAP articles from over 30 international sources. He is able to isolate between 20 and 50 articles of significance and five to 15 articles of high importance. These selected articles are used to create the *TIDES World Press Update* [17], a daily newsletter available to users of MiTAP (through *hotbox*) and distributed to an internationally-wide list of readers. (See figure 7.) The consultant considers MiTAP a "*labor-saving and intelligence gathering tool*" and credits the accurate headline extraction and color-coded highlighting of named entities for his ability to extract critical information quickly.

3.2 Utility

The popularity of MiTAP and the *TIDES World Press Update* is growing monthly by word of mouth. Users request additional news sources, coverage of other areas, and more languages. The dynamic nature of the system has allowed it to become broader in scope and richer in detail over time. Most of our users (89%) are repeat users, with 63% logging in to the system at least once a week. We measure the success of the MiTAP system by the ever-increasing number of accounts requested, the 89% repeat user rate, the popularity of the *TIDES World Press Update* (read by MiTAP account-holders as well as 120+ subscribers, many of whom re-distribute the newsletter), and the overwhelmingly positive user feedback. An additional measure of success is the number of immediate complaints we receive the few times we have had temporary access or network problems.

Although MiTAP contains only open-source information, much of it is sensitive, as are its usage and the identity of our users. Below are several quotes from government users, decision makers on whom MiTAP and the *TIDES World Press Update*, a product of MiTAP, have made a major impact.

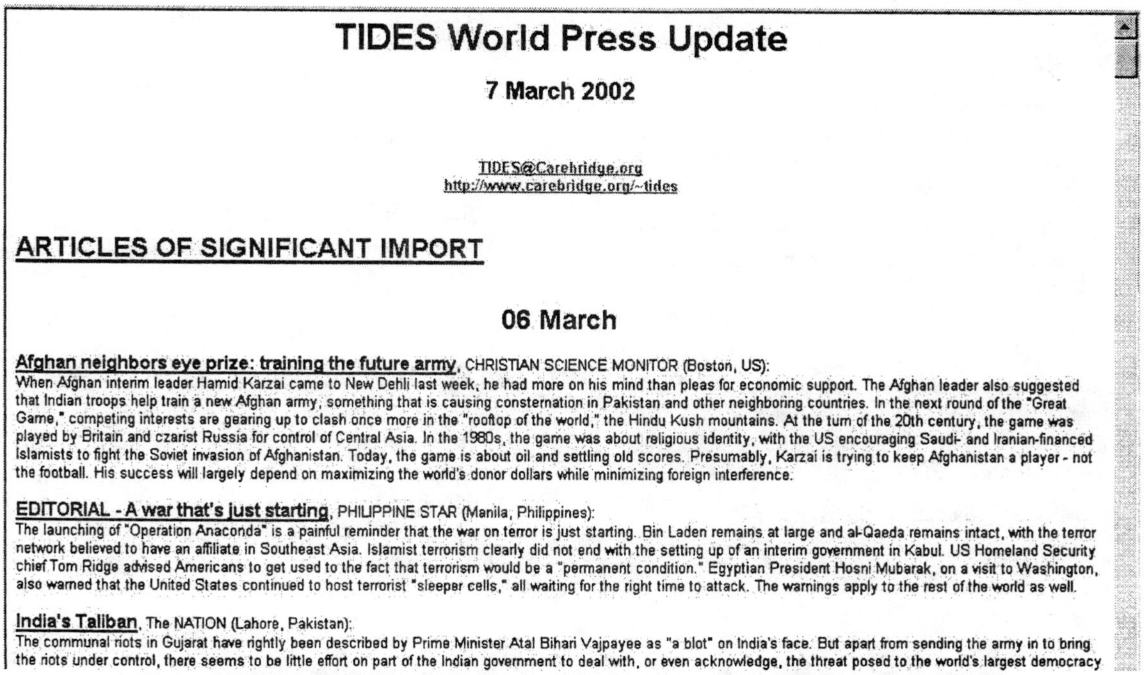

TIDES World Press Update

7 March 2002

TIDES@Carebridge.org
http://www.carebridge.org/~tides

ARTICLES OF SIGNIFICANT IMPORT

06 March

Afghan neighbors eye prize: training the future army, CHRISTIAN SCIENCE MONITOR (Boston, US):
When Afghan interim leader Hamid Karzai came to New Dehli last week, he had more on his mind than pleas for economic support. The Afghan leader also suggested that Indian troops help train a new Afghan army, something that is causing consternation in Pakistan and other neighboring countries. In the next round of the "Great Game," competing interests are gearing up to clash once more in the "rooftop of the world," the Hindu Kush mountains. At the turn of the 20th century, the game was played by Britain and czarist Russia for control of Central Asia. In the 1980s, the game was about religious identity, with the US encouraging Saudi- and Iranian-financed Islamists to fight the Soviet invasion of Afghanistan. Today, the game is about oil and settling old scores. Presumably, Karzai is trying to keep Afghanistan a player - not the football. His success will largely depend on maximizing the world's donor dollars while minimizing foreign interference.

EDITORIAL - A war that's just starting, PHILIPPINE STAR (Manila, Philippines):
The launching of "Operation Anaconda" is a painful reminder that the war on terror is just starting. Bin Laden remains at large and al-Qaeda remains intact, with the terror network believed to have an affiliate in Southeast Asia. Islamist terrorism clearly did not end with the setting up of an interim government in Kabul. US Homeland Security chief Tom Ridge advised Americans to get used to the fact that terrorism would be a "permanent condition." Egyptian President Hosni Mubarak, on a visit to Washington, also warned that the United States continued to host terrorist "sleeper cells," all waiting for the right time to attack. The warnings apply to the rest of the world as well.

India's Taliban, The NATION (Lahore, Pakistan):
The communal riots in Gujarat have rightly been described by Prime Minister Atal Bihari Vajpayee as "a blot" on India's face. But apart from sending the army in to bring the riots under control, there seems to be little effort on part of the Indian government to deal with, or even acknowledge, the threat posed to the world's largest democracy

Figure 7 TIDES World Press Update, a daily newsletter produced from MiTAP data

"I look it over each day and consider it a tool in the war on terrorism."

"I use it to improve my understanding of opinions that affect our Nation's safety."

"Superb work and an asset to the new war in which information sometimes trumps fire and steel. My staff uses it daily."

"This is a war, like all others, decided by information, but the opposition is obscure, affecting, and affected by, voices we cannot hear unless something like MiTAP amplifies and illuminates them."

"The Update is used here every day and at the [College] in several classes. It has deepened our understanding of the problems we now face, and we've noted that the questions to guest lecturers are better informed."

"As the lines between technology research and the application of that research to real world problems is blurred, access to read world information becomes critical to understanding the problems we're trying to address, if not solve...The MiTAP news server has provided me with original, and in many cases, first hand information... Though clearly otherwise available, it would require far more time than available to find, organize, and filter the critical information items. As it is, simple searches are recovering information from vastly different sources and providing me with ongoing opportunities to round out [my] understanding."

4. ACKNOWLEDGMENTS

This work is supported, in part, under DARPA contract number DAAB07-01-C-C201.

5. REFERENCES

[1] Aberdeen, J., Burger, J., Day, D., Hirschman, L., Palmer, D., Robinson, P., Vilain, M. "MITRE: Description of the Alembic System as Used in MET". In *Proceedings of the TIPSTER 24-Month Workshop*, May 5-8, 1996.

[2] Aberdeen, J., Burger, J., Day, D., Hirschman, L., Robinson, P., and Vilain, M. "MITRE: Description of the Alembic System as Used for MUC-6". In *Proceedings of the Sixth Message Understanding Conference* (MUC-6), November 1995.

[3] Ferro, L, Mani, I, Sundheim, B, and Wilson, G. "TIDES Temporal Annotation Guidelines: Version 1.0.2", *MITRE Technical Report* MTR 01W0000041. McLean, Virginia: The MITRE Corporation, 2001.

[4] Ferro, L. "Instruction Manual for the Annotation of

[5] Temporal Expressions." *MITRE Technical Report* MTR 01W0000046. McLean, Virginia: The MITRE Corporation, 2001.

[6] INN: InterNetNews, Internet Software Consortium, http://www.isc.org/products/INN, 2001.

[7] The Jakarta Project, http://jakarta.apache.org/lucene/docs/index.html, 2001.

[8] Mani, I. and Bloedorn, E. "Summarizing Similarities and Differences Among Related Documents". *Information Retrieval* 1(1), 35-67, 1999.

[9] Mani, I. and Wilson, G. "Robust Temporal Processing of News". In Proceedings of the 38th Annual Meeting of the Association for Computational Linguistics (ACL'2000), 69-76, 2000.

[10] Merlino, A. "ViTAP Demonstration," submitted to HLT2002.

[11] Microsoft® Internet Explorer Web Site http://www.microsoft.com/windows/ie/default.asp, 2002.

[12] Microsoft® Outlook® Express Web Site, http://www.microsoft.com/windows/oe, February 2002.

[13] Miller, K., Reeder, F., Hirschman, L., Palmer, D. (2001). "Multilingual Processing for Operational Users", *NATO Workshop on Multilingual Processing at EUROSPEECH*, September 2001.

[14] MiTAP (MITRE Text and Audio Processing) System, http://tides2000.mitre.org/, 2001.

[15] Netscape Messenger, http://www.netscape.com/communicator/messenger/v4.0, 2000.

[16] Netscape Navigator, http://browsers.netscape.com/browsers/main.tmpl, 2002.

[17] SOAP Version 1.2 Part 1: Messaging Framework. Eds. Gudgin, M., Hadley, M., Moreau, J., Nielsen, H., http://www.w3.org/TR/soap12-part1/ (work in progress), December 2001.

[18] TIDES World Press Update, http://www.carebridge.org/~tides/, 2001.

[19] Vilain, M. "Inferential Information Extraction", in Pazienza, M., ed., "Information Extraction", *Lecture notes of the 1999 SCIE Summer School on Information Extraction.* Springer Verlag, 1999.

[20] Vilain, M. and Day, D. "Finite-state phrase parsing by rule sequences". *In Proceedings of the 1996 International Conference on Computational Linguistics* (COLING-96), Copenhagen, Denmark, 1996.

Demonstration of a Spoken Dialogue Interface for Planning Activities of a Semi-autonomous Robot

John Dowding†, Jeremy Frank‡, Beth Ann Hockey†,
Ari Jónsson† , Gregory Aist†
†Research Institute for Advanced Computer Science
‡NASA Ames Research Center
Moffett Field, CA 94035
{jdowding,bahockey,aist}@riacs.edu
{frank,jonsson}@ptolemy.arc.nasa.gov

ABSTRACT

Planning and scheduling in the face of uncertainty and change pushes the capabilities of both planning and dialogue technologies by requiring complex negotiation to arrive at a workable plan. Planning for use of semi-autonomous robots involves negotiation among multiple participants with competing scientific and engineering goals to co-construct a complex plan. In NASA applications this plan construction is done under severe time pressure so having a dialogue interface to the plan construction tools can aid rapid completion of the process. But, this will put significant demands on spoken dialogue technology, particularly in the areas of dialogue management and generation. The dialogue interface will need to be able to handle the complex dialogue strategies that occur in negotiation dialogues, including hypotheticals and revisions, and the generation component will require an ability to summarize complex plans.

This demonstration will describe a work in progress towards building a spoken dialogue interface to the EUROPA planner for the purposes of planning and scheduling the activities of a semi-autonomous robot. A prototype interface has been built for planning the schedule of the Personal Satellite Assistant (PSA)[12], a mobile robot designed for micro-gravity environments that is intended for use on the Space Shuttle and International Space Station. The spoken dialogue interface gives the user the capability to ask for a description of the plan, ask specific questions about the plan, and update or modify the plan. We anticipate that a spoken dialogue interface to the planner will provide a natural augmentation or alternative to the visualization interface, in situations in which the user needs very targeted information about the plan, in situations where natural language can express complex ideas more concisely than GUI actions, or in situations in which a graphical user interface is not appropriate.

Keywords

spoken dialogue systems, mobile robots, constraint-based planning

Proceedings of HLT 2002, Second International Conference on Human Language Technology Research, M. Marcus, ed., Morgan Kaufmann, San Francisco, 2002.

1. MOTIVATION

The Mars Pathfinder mission landed a semi-autonomous robot, Sojourner, on the surface of Mars which operated for 85 days, from July 4, 1997 to Sept 27, 1997[1]. At the end of each day, Sojourner would broadcast data back to earth, and hibernate for the Mars night. On Earth, teams of scientists and engineers would engage in marathon planning sessions each night to plan the next day's activities. This planning contended for time against analysis of recently collected data; as one of the Pathfinder participants reported in her field journal, "[The scientists] have all this wonderful data coming down and they barely have time to look at it, because they have to be preparing for the next day's experiments. It's driving them nuts. They still want to make every bit count, but some data are better than no data, and we will only have this firehose to drink from for a short while."[8] This planning needed to be completed, formalized, and approved in time to be broadcast to Sojourner at the start of the next Mars day. Unfortunately, sometimes the generated plans were fragile, and a day or more could be lost diagnosing and fixing the problems[15]. Also, occasionally the planning was not completed on time, which would result in the Pathfinder being dormant for that day. These factors taken together make planning an important area for research into enabling more effective mobile robotics for aerospace applications – to reduce the time and cost to create the plan, and reduce the risk of failing to find a plan or finding an inappropriate plan.

If human planners were able to correctly and completely specify all the constraints and priorities on a planning problem of this magnitude at the outset, then this would just be a very hard planning problem. But, human planners do not work that way. They can come up with an initial estimate of the constraints, but that may not be satisfiable, in which case they are faced with choices of which constraints to consider removing. Even when the set of constraints is satisfiable, when the human planners are given a description of the current plan, they may come up with additional constraints and priorities in an attempt to improve the plan. Thus, constraint and priority generation is a process that proceeds iteratively with planning, and requires increased sophistication in the planner interface.

Spoken dialogue systems offer opportunity to interface to planners. The capabilities of natural language allow talking about the future, discussing complicated structures and concisely describing time and location constraints. The combination of planning and spoken dialogue technologies is thus a natural match for addressing co-construction of complex plans for NASA applications.

2. EUROPA PLANNER

Researchers at NASA's Ames Research Center, together with colleagues at the Jet Propulsion Laboratory, are developing new planning technology to address this problem: EUROPA. EUROPA is a system for representing and reasoning about complex temporal plans involving constraints on time, resources, and routes. EUROPA is the descendent of the Remote Agent Planner (RAP)[7]. RAP was deployed as part of the control system for the Deep Space One spacecraft in May of 1999. EUROPA has been combined with APGEN, a mission operations planning tool[9], to provide a plan visualization interface for EUROPA plans. APGEN has been deployed to help automate and visualize the planning for the Cassini mission to Saturn and Titan.

The Extensible Universal Remote Operations Planning Architecture (EUROPA)[5] is based on an interval representation of time. EUROPA consists of the following components: A *predicate* is a uniform representation of actions and states, and an *interval* is the period during which a predicate holds. Each interval is defined by constraints on the interval's start, end and duration, as well as other parameters which further elaborate on the predicate. For instance, a `thrust` predicate may have a parameter describing the thrust level, which can be either `low`, `medium` or `high`. The planning domain is described by *planning schemata* which specify, for each interval, other intervals that must exist (e.g. pre and post conditions), and how the intervals are related to each other. Schemata can specify conditional effects and disjunctions of required tokens. Planning schemata can also include constraints on the parameters of the token. EUROPA schemata are described using *attributes*. An attribute is a subsystem or component of a planning domain. Attributes permit more intuitive modeling of planning domains, and enable the enforcement of mutual exclusion. A timeline represents a sequence of actions or states on a single attribute. Timelines represent how an attribute changes during the course of a plan. Using intervals and attributes adds powerful constraints to the planning problem, which make it possible to eliminate a large number of candidate solutions.

EUROPA manages plans by continuously reformulating the planning problem as a Dynamic Constraint Satisfaction Problem (DCSP). This reformulation is done by mapping each partial plan to a CSP. The temporal constraints form a Simple Temporal Network, which can be efficiently solved[3], while the rest of the constraints form a general, non-binary CSP represented by procedural constraints[6]. Planners may interact with the EUROPA interface by modifying plans, asking whether a plan is consistent, and asking whether any more work must be done to complete the plan.

3. PSA PROTOTYPE

The PSA is a mobile robot designed for a micro-gravity environments such as the International Space Station, and is being developed at Ames Research Center. It is designed to be equipped with a variety of sensors, cameras, and microphones, and is intended to carry out remote sensensing, monitoring, and video conferencing tasks. The PSA is an initial target for this work in that we can build on earlier work on a spoken dialogue interface to a simulation of the PSA[13], and focus for this work on the specific problems that arise when interfacing a spoken dialogue system with a planner. Plans for activities to be carried out by the PSA are sufficiently complex to require sophisticated planning technology.

The demonstration scenario for the PSA prototype is as follows:

> *You are an astronaut on the International Space Station, having just completed a long day's work, with the assistance of your Personal Satellite Assistant (PSA). Before quitting for the day, you want to review the schedule for tomorrow with the PSA. Unknown to you, scientific teams on Earth have been uploading requests to the PSA for help in monitoring experiments also planned for the next day. You will need to talk with the PSA to investigate it's current plan, and to update and modify that plan to make it consistent with your own demands on the PSA's time.*

The demonstration prototype can engage in dialogues like this:

A: Describe your plan.
PSA: I will be at the mid deck at 15:00, followed by the commander's seat, followed by the flight deck, followed by the storage lockers until 17:00.
A: Why will you at the mid deck?
PSA: I will be measuring the carbon dioxide level at the mid deck at 15:00.
A: Can you be at the flight deck at 16:30?
PSA: Yes, I will be at the flight deck starting at sometime between 15:22 and 16:47 and continuing until sometime between 15:24 and 16:49.
A: When will you be at lower deck?
PSA: I will not be at the lower deck.
A: Be at the flight deck at 16:30.
PSA: Okay, I will be at the flight deck at 16:30.
A: Can you be at storage lockers at 16:30?
PSA: No, I will not be at the storage lockers at 16:30.
A: Be at storage lockers at 16:30.
PSA: Sorry, I can not be at the storage lockers at 16:30.
A: How about 15:30?
PSA: Okay, I will be at the storage lockers at 15:30.
A: Describe your plan now.
PSA: I will be at the mid deck at 15:00, followed by the commander's seat until 15:20, followed by the storage lockers from 15:30 until 16:20, followed by the flight deck at 16:30, followed by the storage lockers until 17:00.

The language and dialogue capability in this prototype is largely the same as the previously demonstrated PSA Dialogue System[13], that controlled a simulated PSA robot in a simulation of the Space Shuttle. This features an asynchronus dialogue manager[2], combined with the Nuance Speech Recognizer[11], the Gemini language understanding system[4] , and the Festival Speech Synthesizer[14]. The components are integrated using SRI's Open Agent Architecture (OAA)[10]. The extensions to the language used in this system are largely to expand the grammar and lexicon with words and phrases for temporal expressions for time points and durations. The majority of the effort to date has been in building an OAA interface to EUROPA, modifying the dialogue manager to interact with EUROPA, and to generate summaries of EUROPA plans.

4. CHALLENGES

Creating effective spoken dialogue interfaces to state-of-the-art planners provides several significant challenges to the underlying components, particularly the dialogue manager, the generator, and the planner itself.

The dialogue manager will need to be augmented with dialogue moves for a richer variety of dialogue moves than have been supported by existing dialogue systems. Some of these moves include:

- Summary - Provide a high-level description of the current plan

- Review - Provide a description of the changes made to the plan
- Dive-down - Provide a more detailed description of a restricted segment of a plan
- Explanation - Describe the causal relationship between plan components

The ability to describe, summarize, and review plans will place added emphasis on the generation capabilities. In particular, adding a new constraint to a plan may have difficult to predict perturbations throughout the plan. For instance, adding a new constraint like "Be at the flight deck at 15:30" might require a response summarizing the difference between two complex plans, such as "Okay, I can do that, but I will need to leave the flight deck by 15:45, and relocate the video conference at the commander's seat to 13:00".

The advantages of a constraint-based planner that produces underspecified plans may be a disadvantage when using the planner in a dialogue system. For instance, given N constraints, and adding a new constraint may yield a very different plan than using all $N+1$ constraints initially. Similarly, adding a constraint, and then removing that constraint may not lead back to the plan that was started with. Users speaking with the planning system may expect a continuity of plans that current systems do not provide.

5. FUTURE WORK

Future robotic missions will place even greater demands on planning capabilities. The Mars Exploratory Rover (MER) mission, scheduled to launch in 2003, involves 2 rovers operated concurrently over 90+ days with a very ambitious science plan to explore multiple sites that are far apart. This makes it essential that each day be productive which means generating complex plans each and every day.

We have access to video-taped training sessions of human planners practicing planning for the Mars Exploratory Rover mission. We plan to analyze these video-tapes to uncover what kinds of language and dialogue strategies people employ as they are negotiating a complex plan, and to take advantage of these strategies in our own interface to make interacting with the planner as natural as possible. We intend to incorporate such language and dialogue strategies into the PSA prototype.

6. REFERENCES

[1] *Mars Pathfinder Fact Sheet.* http://www.jpl.nasa.gov/news/fact_sheets/mpf.pdf, 1997.

[2] J. Boye, B. Hockey, and M. Rayner. Asynchronous dialogue management: Two case-studies. In *Gotalog: Fourth Workshop on the Semantics and Pragmatics of Dialogue*, 2000.

[3] R. Dechter, I. Meiri, and J. Pearl. Temporal constraint networks. *Artificial Intelligence*, 49:61–94, 1991.

[4] J. Dowding, M. Gawron, D. Appelt, L. Cherny, R. Moore, and D. Moran. Gemini: A natural language system for spoken language understanding. In *Proceedings of the Thirty-First Annual Meeting of the Association for Computational Linguistics*, 1993.

[5] J. Frank, A. Jónsson, and P. Morris. On reformulating planning as dynamic constraint satisfaction. *Symposium on Abstraction, Reformulation and Approximation*, 2000.

[6] A. Jónsson and J. Frank. A framework for dynamic constraint reasoning using procedural constraints. *Euopean Conference on Artificial Intelligence*, 2000.

[7] A. Jónsson, P. Morris, N. Muscettola, K. Rajan, and B. Smith. Planning in interplanetary space: Theory and practice. In *Proceedings of the Fifth International Conference on Artificial Intelligence Planning and Scheduling*, 2000.

[8] B. Landry. *Much more than ever expected.* http://quest.arc.nasa.gov/mars/team/journals/landry/11.html, 1997.

[9] P. Maldague, A. Ko, D. Page, and T. Starbird. Apgen: A multi-mission semi-automated planning tool. 1997.

[10] D. Martin, A. Cheyer, and D. Moran. Building distributed software systems with the open agent architecture. In *Proceedings of the Third International Conference on the Practical Application of Intelligent Agents and Multi-Agent Technology*, 1998.

[11] Nuance. http://www.nuance.com, 2001. As of 1 April 2001.

[12] PSA. *Personal Satellite Assistant (PSA) Project.* http://ic.arc.nasa.gov/ic/psa/, 1999. As of 1 April 2000.

[13] M. Rayner, B. Hockey, and F. James. A compact architecture for dialogue management based on scripts and meta-outputs. In *Proceedings of ANLP 2000*, 2000.

[14] T. F. S. S. Systems. http://www.cstr.ed.ac.uk/projects/festival, 2001. As of 28 February 2001.

[15] R. Washington, K. Golden, J. Bresina, D. Smith, C. Anderson, and T. Smith. *Autonomous Rovers for Mars Exploration.* http://ic.arc.nasa.gov/publications/pdf/1999-0078.pdf, 1999.

Real-Time Event Extraction for Infectious Disease Outbreaks

Ralph Grishman Silja Huttunen Roman Yangarber

Computer Science Department
New York University
New York, NY 10003

grishman@cs.nyu.edu silja@cs.nyu.edu roman@cs.nyu.edu

ABSTRACT

We describe a system for creating and automatically updating a data base of information on infectious disease outbreaks. A web crawler is used to retrieve current news stories; potentially relevant stories are fed to an information extraction engine, whose output is used to update the data base. A web-based browser allows users to examine the data base and select records based on date, disease, location, and other fields. The browser can also display the source text from which the data base information is derived.

The data base provides an alternative to conventional search engines for retrieving documents in this domain; the advantages and disadvantages of this approach are discussed.

1. INTRODUCTION

New York University has developed a system, Proteus BIO, for maintaining, in real time, a data base of information on infectious disease outbreaks, linked back to the reports from which they are derived. This system has been developed under the TIDES program as an offshoot of the IFE-BIO Integrated Feasibility Experiment [3].

The goal of our system is to provide a simple but rich index structure for access to both current and historical reports on infectious disease outbreaks. The tool is intended to allow retrospective summaries to be quickly prepared by analysts in response to current events. Searches can be performed using any combination of date, location, and disease information. The data base (event index) is automatically updated on a daily basis from on-line news reports.

Proceedings of HLT 2002, Second International Conference on Human Language Technology Research, M. Marcus, ed., Morgan Kaufmann, San Francisco, 2002.

The system consists of

1. a Web crawler and mail reader
2. a text zoner
3. an information extraction system
4. an interface to a relational data base
5. a Web-based data base viewer, linked to the original texts

We describe each of these briefly in turn.

2. WEB CRAWLER / MAIL READER

The web crawler gathers daily news from multiple sources, including general news sources (such as newspapers) and medical sources such as the communicable disease reports from the World Health Organization and ProMed, a moderated electronic forum where medical professionals exchange reports on the spread of infectious diseases. For added coverage, the crawler also invokes a news search engine, using a small set of keywords that are relevant to epidemics of diseases. In addition, the system incorporates a mail reader interface, so that information from mailing lists can be added to the data base as it is received.

For general news sources, the system applies a keyword filter, requiring that one of a set of keywords (derived from the event patterns used by the extraction system, as described in section 5) be present before the document is sent to the extraction engine. This is done for efficiency purposes, to avoid further processing of totally irrelevant articles. The final discrimination between relevant and irrelevant is made by the extraction engine, using the full event patterns.

3. TEXT ZONER

The text zoner divides the incoming documents into zones for use by the information extraction engine. The zones include headline, source, date, and text body. For documents incorporating multiple stories, story boundaries are marked, for separate processing by the extraction engine (to block incorrect use of contextual information across stories.)

The zoner is rule-based. For HTML text, we parse the HTML and rely primarily on the mark-up for identifying zones. For plain text (such as the ProMed mailing list input), the rules make use of layout and appearance (such as blank lines, underscores, all-cap lines) as well as keywords.

4. STRUCTURE OF EVENT DATA BASE

To record the information on disease outbreaks, we have developed a relatively simple event structure, whose primary components are the range of dates, the location, the name of the disease, the number and type of organisms affected, and whether the organisms died. A disease report may give rise to a substantial number of such elementary events [4]. For example, "7 people were infected and 2 died" generates two events in the data base; so does "15 people were infected last week, bringing the total for 1999 to 100". Events may contain other (sub-) events, either geographically or temporally (as in the last example). The data base includes linking fields which are intended to capture such containment relations.

Normalization of data is critical to support effective retrieval of information. Dates and date expressions (including dates relative to the report time, such as "last week") are normalized to a standard form, with explicit day, month, and year ranges. City and area names are tagged with the country, using both a gazetteer (for major cities) and information from elsewhere in the document. Disease names are normalized using a list of disease synonyms.

The events are stored in a relational data base, implemented using mysql.

5. EXTRACTION ENGINE

The extraction engine is a multi-phase finite-state transducer, previously used on several MUC evaluations and other extraction tasks. Processing begins with tokenization and lexical look-up. This is followed by finite-state pattern matching to recognize names (of people, locations, organizations, and diseases), noun and verb groups, select noun phrases, and finally select clause structures. Event recognition (in this case, finding reports about the incidence of infectious diseases) occurs at both the noun phrase ("outbreak of ...") and clause ("people died from ...") levels. Reference resolution is used to resolve anaphoric noun phrases, and event merging rules combine information about a single event from several clauses or sentences. Links back to the original text are maintained throughout the processing. The events extracted from the document, along with the links to specific phrases, are used to update the data base.

To monitor the combined performance of the text zoner and extraction engine, we maintain test corpora derived from the ProMed and WHO sources. Our current performance on these corpora is F=0.54, which is comparable to the best performance on MUC tasks, but this performance is continuing to improve as we enlarge our knowledge sources and training corpora

Customization of this system to the domain of infectious-disease outbreaks — primarily, the development of the domain-specific concept hierarchy and patterns — was done using our example-based customization tool [1]. Additional patterns have been found using the ExDisco pattern-discovery procedure [2].

6. INTERFACE

To provide access to the data base, we use a Web-based interface which provides a spreadsheet-like presentation of data base records. Users can select subsets based on any combination of attributes, including date, location, and disease type. Each event is linked back to the corresponding text record; selecting an event on the spreadsheet brings up the text and highlights the event, with the components (date, location, disease) suitably color-coded. This allows for rapid validation of the extracted information and review of associated information.

A snapshot of the interface is shown below. The main window shows the data base itself, with one record highlighted, along with the record selection criteria (in this case, either 'anthrax' or 'smallpox' in the disease name field). The window in lower left shows the selected record in more detail. The window at lower right shows the text from which the record is derived, with the text used for specific fields (date, location, disease name, case descriptor) color-coded.

Our original interface was implemented as a client-side Java applet. Because this interface required a browser supporting Java Swing, we have recently completed an alternative interface implemented on the server side using JavaServer Pages (JSP), which can operate with all standard browsers.[1]

7. STATUS AND PLANS

The current data base incorporates

- all of ProMed (11,471 reports, 17,899 disease outbreak events)
- all of the WHO Infectious Disease reports

In addition, we are currently accumulating events reported by the Chicago Sun-Times, and from various sources retrieved through the Northern Light news search engine, and plan to add several other news sources.

Access to documents through the event data base created by information extraction has some significant advantages over keyword-based browsing. Requiring disease names to be in the context of outbreaks excludes incidental mentions, descriptions of treatments, etc. Having normalized dates allows searches over date ranges which would not be possible with the original documents; associating countries with city and area names similarly allows search in geographical regions. For example, a query such as "Which countries have reported anthrax outbreaks in the past year?", which could be answered quickly from the event data base, would be difficult to answer efficiently with a keyword-based search. In addition, the tabular structures provide a compact summary of outbreaks in a particular region or involving a particular disease. An informal evaluation we conducted in September 2001 (using a task designed by MITRE, which required us to prepare a report in a 2-hour period) indicated to us the benefit of such tabular structures for the rapid creation of summaries.

On the other hand, the set of extraction patterns will be incomplete and so will miss some instances of disease outbreaks. In circumstances where one can exhaustively review the documents returned by a keyword-based search for a disease, the results can be more comprehensive. Since a user may not always have time for such an exhaustive review, the combination of

[1] The client-side interface was based on an earlier version written by Troy Straszheim; the server-side interface was written by Joshua Rosenblatt.

keyword-based and extraction-based search can offer the user the most flexibility. This will be one avenue of development as we continue to work with MITRE, the lead IFE-BIO contractor, to integrate our event extraction technology with their keyword-based routing and retrieval system.

As we add more sources to our system, we are seeing multiple reports of the same outbreaks. These present both a problem and a potential strength. If the event entries from individual documents are kept separate, the user will be presented with redundant entries reporting the same event, a potential distraction. However, combining compatible entries can yield multiple benefits. Extraction patterns are likely to miss some events, but the chance of missing an event if stated differently in two sources is considerably reduced, so the data base will be more complete. Data which is successfully extracted from two sources can be reported with improved confidence. This will be one area we will focus on as we continue our development.

One other important direction for extension involves linking infectious disease reports to other news events for which we have developed an information extraction capability, such as "natural disasters" (hurricanes, floods, earthquakes). Natural disasters often have repercussions involving disease outbreaks. Linked data bases with common formatted fields (location, date) will allow for event search and summary along multiple dimensions.

8. ACKNOWLEDGMENTS

This research was supported by the Defense Advanced Research Projects Agency as part of the Translingual Information Detection, Extraction and Summarization (TIDES) program, under Grant N66001-001-1-8917 from the Space and Naval Warfare Systems Center San Diego, and by the National Science Foundation under Grant IIS-0081962.

This paper does not necessarily reflect the position or the policy of the U.S. Government.

9. REFERENCES

[1] Roman Yangarber and Ralph Grishman. Customization of Information Extraction Systems. *Proceedings of International Workshop on Lexically Driven Information Extraction*, Frascati, Italy, July 16, 1997.

[2] Roman Yangarber, Ralph Grishman, Pasi Tapanainen, and Silja Huttunen. Automatic Acquisition of Domain Knowledge for Information Extraction. *Proc. 18th Int'l Conf. on Computational Linguistics (COLING 2000)*, Saarbrücken, Germany, July-August 2000, 940-946.

[3] L. Hirschman, K. Concepcion, L. Damianos, D. Day, J. Delmore, L. Ferro, J. Griffith, J. Henderson, J. Kurtz, I. Mani, S. Mardis, T. McEntee, K. Miller, B. Nunam, J. Ponte, F. Reeder, B. Wellner, G. Wilson, A. Yeh. Integrated Feasibility Experiment for Bio-Security: IFE-Bio, A TIDES Demonstration. *Proceedings of HLT 2001, First International Conference on Human Language Technology Research*, Morgan Kaufmann, San Francisco, 2001.

[4] Silja Huttunen, Roman Yangarber, and Ralph Grishman. Diversity of Scenarios in Information Extraction. To appear in *Proceedings of the Third International Conference On Language Resources And Evaluation*, Las Palmas, May 2002.

Snapshot of the Proteus-BIO Data Base Interface

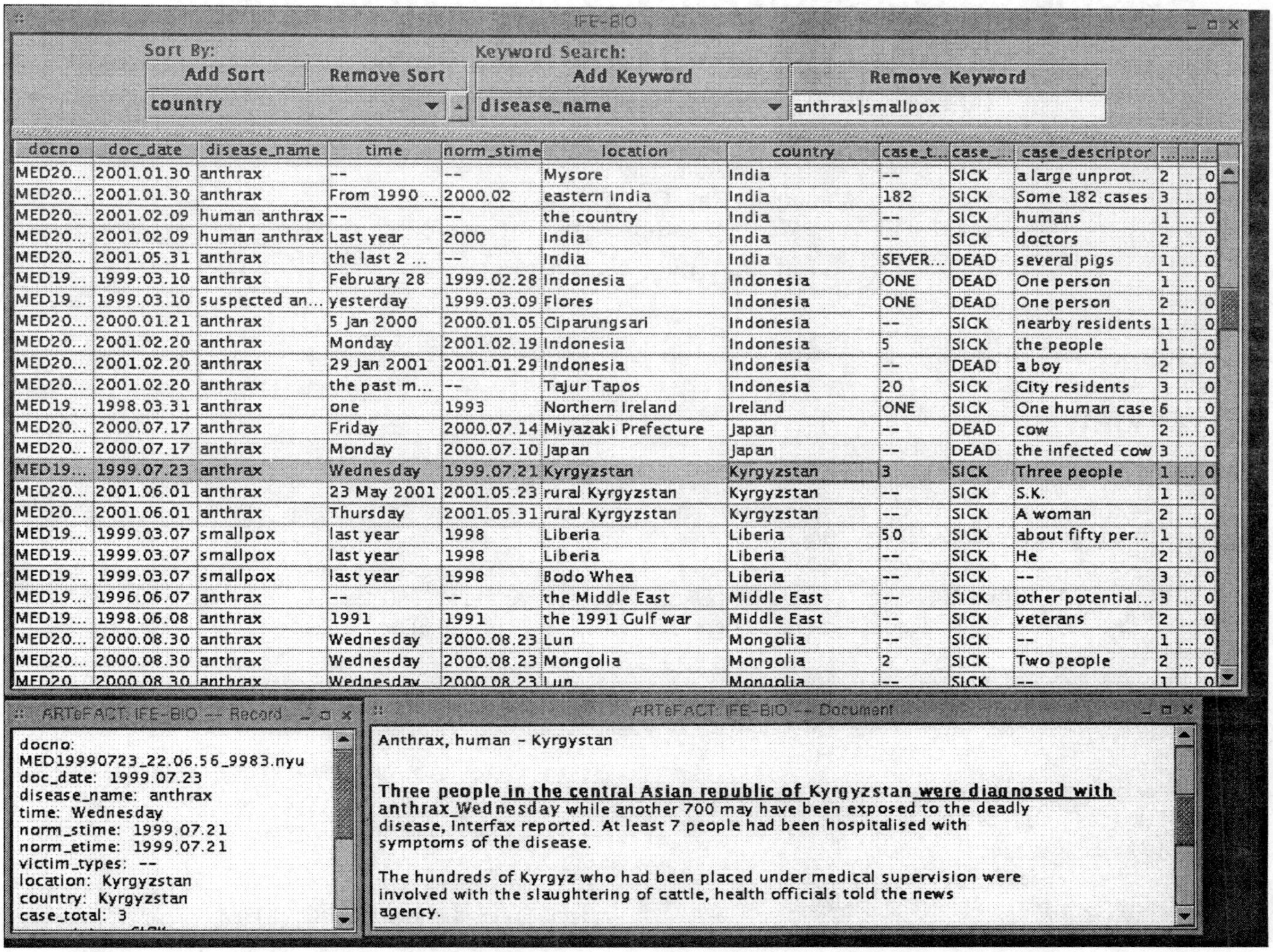

Automated Question Answering in Webclopedia: A Demonstration

Ulf Hermjakob, Eduard Hovy and Chin-Yew Lin
USC Information Sciences Institute
4676 Admiralty Way
Marina del Rey, CA 90292-6695
Tel: 310-448-8476, 310-448-8731 and 310-448-8711
{ulf,hovy,cyl}@isi.edu

1. OVERVIEW

In this demonstration we present work in our Webclopedia (Hovy et al. 2000, 2001) project on semantics-based answer pinpointing. Through a live interface, users can type in their questions in the query window or select a TREC10 question (Figure 1). The system will then parse the question and return the top 5 answers (Figure 1).

Webclopedia achieved 31% in MRR (mean reciprocal rank) score in TREC9 Q&A track and 45% in TREC10 Q&A track. The architecture includes:

- Question parsing: Using BBN's IdentiFinder (Bikel et al., 1999), the CONTEX parser produces a syntactic-semantic analysis of the question and determines the QA type.
- Query formation: Single- and multi-word units (content words) are extracted from the analysis, and WordNet synsets are used for query expansion. A series of Boolean queries is formed.
- IR: The IR engine MG (Witten et al., 1994) returns the top-ranked N documents.
- Selecting and ranking sentences: For each document, the most promising K<<N sentences are located and scored using a formula that rewards word and phrase overlap with the question and its expanded query words. Results are ranked.
- Parsing segments: CONTEX parses the top-ranked 300 sentences.
- Pinpointing: Each candidate answer sentence parse tree is matched against the parse of the question. It sometimes also considers the preceding sentence. As a fallback the window method is used.
- Ranking of answers: The candidate answers' scores are computed and the topmost 5 are output as final answers.

Webclopedia classifies desired answers by their semantic type, using the approx. 180 classes. These types include common semantic classes such as PROPER-PERSON, EMAIL-ADDRESS, LOCATION, and PROPER-ORGANIZATION, but also classes particular to QA such as WHY-FAMOUS, YES:NO, and ABBREVIATION-EXPANSION. They have been taxonomized as the Webclopedia QA Typology (Hermjakob el al. 2002).
The system increasingly makes use of syntactic and semantic (world) knowledge to improve the accuracy of its results. We will identify the strength and weakness of our approach during the demonstration with examples.

Proceedings of HLT 2002, Second International Conference on Human Language Technology Research, M. Marcus, ed., Morgan Kaufmann, San Francisco, 2002.

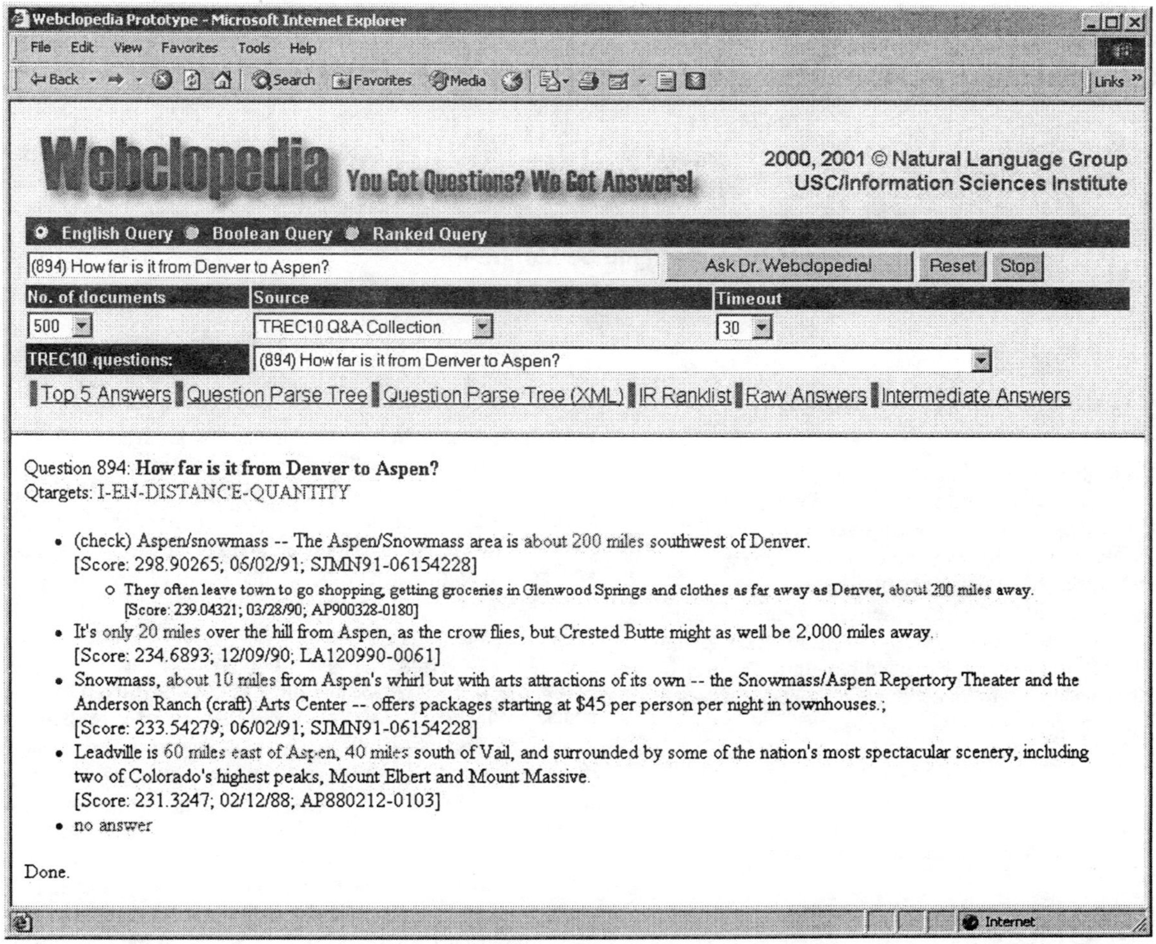

Figure 1. Webclopedia web interface.

2. REFERENCES

Hermjakob, U. 1997. *Learning Parse and Translation Decisions from Examples with Rich Context.* Ph.D. dissertation, University of Texas at Austin. file://ftp.cs.utexas.edu/pub/~mooney/papers/hermjakob-dissertation-97.ps.gz.

Hermjakob, U., E. Hovy and D. Ravichandran 2002. *A Question/Answer Typology with Surface Text Patterns.* Submitted to Human Language Technology Conference 2002.

Hovy, E.H., L. Gerber, U. Hermjakob, M. Junk, and C.-Y. Lin. 2000. Question Answering in Webclopedia. *Proceedings of the TREC-9 Conference.* NIST, Gaithersburg, MD. November 2000.

Hovy, E.H., L. Gerber, U. Hermjakob, C.-Y. Lin, and D. Ravichandran. 2001. Toward Semantics-Based Answer Pinpointing. *Proceedings of the DARPA Human Language Technology Conference (HLT).* San Diego, CA. March 2001.

Witten, I. H. and A. Moffat and T. Bell 1994. Managing Gigabytes. New York: Van Nostrand Reinhold.

TransType: Text Prediction for Translators

George Foster Philippe Langlais Guy Lapalme

RALI, Université de Montréal

{foster,felipe,lapalme}@iro.umontreal.ca

ABSTRACT

Text prediction is a novel form of interactive machine translation that is well suited to skilled translators. It has the potential to assist in several ways: speeding typing, suggesting possible translations, and averting translator errors. However, recent evaluations of a prototype prediction system showed that predictions can also distract and hinder translators if made indiscriminately. We demonstrate an experimental prototype intended to address this problem by selecting the prediction that has maximal expected benefit to the user in any given context. This leads it to make longer predictions where it is more certain and shorter ones—or none at all—in contexts where it is less certain.

Keywords

text prediction, interactive machine translation, user modeling, statistical translation models

1. INTRODUCTION

The idea of using text prediction as a tool for translators was first introduced by Church and Hovy as one of many possible applications for "crummy" machine translation technology [2]. Text prediction can be seen as a form of interactive MT that is well suited to skilled translators. Compared to the traditional form of IMT based on Kay's original work [5]—in which the user's role is to help disambiguate the source text—prediction is less obtrusive and more natural, allowing the translator to focus on and directly control the contents of the target text. Predictions can benefit a translator in several ways: by accelerating typing, by suggesting translations, and by serving as an implicit check against errors.

The TransType project at the Université de Montréal [6] was set up to explore the idea of a predictive tool for translators. It resulted in a prototype system for English to French translation that displays a short pop-up menu of completions for the next word or lexicalized multi-word unit after each character the translator types, as shown in figure 1. Although TransType is capable of correctly anticipating over 70% of the characters in a freely-typed translation, this does not mean that users can translate in 70% less time when using the tool. In fact, in a trial with skilled translators, the users' rate of text production *declined* by an average of 17% as a result of using the tool [7]. There are two main reasons for this. First, it takes time to read the system's proposals, so that in cases where they are wrong or too short, the net effect will be to slow the translator down. Second, translators do not always act "rationally" when confronted with a proposal; that is, they do not always accept correct proposals and they occasionally accept incorrect ones.

The system we are demonstrating is intended to address these problems by making proposals that maximize the expected benefit to the user in each context. Benefit is estimated from two components: a statistical translation model that gives the probability that a candidate prediction will be correct or incorrect, and a user model that determines the benefit to the translator in either case. The user model takes into account the cost of reading a proposal, as well as the random nature of the decision to accept it or not. This approach results in longer predictions in contexts where the translation model is confident, shorter ones where it is less so, and no predictions at all where it is very uncertain. In addition to taking user benefit into account, our new prototype also improves on the previous one by using more accurate translation models, and by using a decoder to predict arbitrary amounts of upcoming text, rather than just the next word or lexicalized unit. The user interface remains the same, except that at most one prediction is made in any context, rather than a menu of alternate predictions.

As implied above, the predictive tool consists of two main components: a graphical user interface to make predictions available to the translator, and a predictor to generate them. These are described in the following sections.

Proceedings of HLT 2002, Second International Conference on Human Language Technology Research, M. Marcus, ed., Morgan Kaufmann, San Francisco, 2002.

2. USER INTERFACE

As shown in figure 1, the user interface is similar to that of a commercial translator's workstation, with a split screen for simultaneous display of source and target texts, and standard editing capabilities. The current interface is implemented in TCL/TK. To use it, a translator selects a sentence in the source text and begins typing its translation. After each character is typed, the system may display a prediction for one or more upcoming words (only one proposal, not a menu as shown in figure 1). These suggestions are continually adapted to conform to the translator's input. At any point, the translator has the option of incorporating a suggestion into the target text with a special keystroke or mouse action, or ignoring the proposals and continuing to type normally.

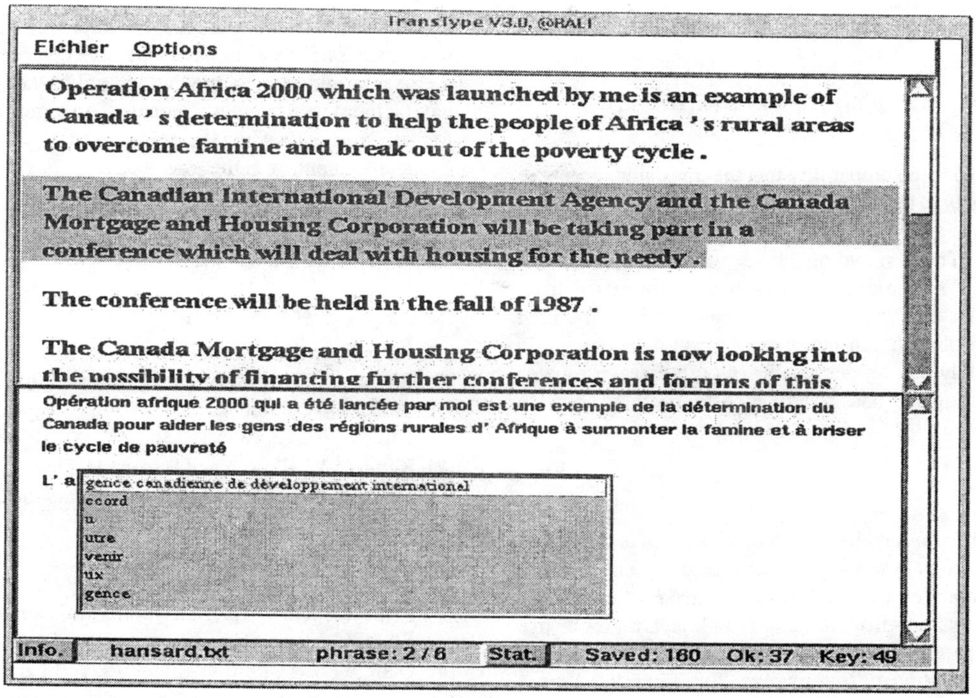

Figure 1: Screen dump for the TransType prototype. The source text is shown in the top half of the screen, and the target text is typed in the bottom half, with suggestions given by the menu at the cursor position.

3. PREDICTOR

In this section, we briefly outline how the predictor works; further details are available in [4]. The basic task is to find the prediction $\hat{\mathbf{x}}$ that maximizes the expected benefit to the user:

$$\hat{\mathbf{x}} = \operatorname*{argmax}_{\mathbf{x}} B(\mathbf{x}, \mathbf{h}, \mathbf{s}), \tag{1}$$

where $B(\mathbf{x}, \mathbf{h}, \mathbf{s})$ measures typing time saved, $\mathbf{s}$ is a source sentence, and $\mathbf{h}$ is a prefix of its translation (the target text before the current cursor position). Figure 2 gives an example.

To model $B(\mathbf{x}, \mathbf{h}, \mathbf{s})$, we begin with the major simplifying assumption that the user edits only by erasing wrong characters from the end of a proposal. Given a TransType-style interface where acceptance places the cursor at the end of a proposal, this is the most common editing method, and it gives a conservative estimate of the cost attainable by other methods. With this assumption, the key determinant of benefit is the length of the correct prefix of $\mathbf{x}$, so the expected benefit can be written as:

$$B(\mathbf{x}, \mathbf{h}, \mathbf{s}) = \sum_{k=0}^{l} p(k|\mathbf{x}, \mathbf{h}, \mathbf{s})\, B(\mathbf{x}, \mathbf{h}, \mathbf{s}, k), \tag{2}$$

where $p(k|\mathbf{x}, \mathbf{h}, \mathbf{s})$ is the probability that exactly k characters from the beginning of $\mathbf{x}$ are correct, l is the length of $\mathbf{x}$, and $B(\mathbf{x}, \mathbf{h}, \mathbf{s}, k)$ is the benefit to the user given that the first k characters of $\mathbf{x}$ are correct.

Equations (1) and (2) define three main problems: estimating the prefix probabilities $p(k|\mathbf{x}, \mathbf{h}, \mathbf{s})$, estimating the user benefit function $B(\mathbf{x}, \mathbf{h}, \mathbf{s}, k)$, and searching for $\hat{\mathbf{x}}$. The following three sections describe our solutions to these.

3.1 Translation Model

The prefix probabilities $p(k|\mathbf{x}, \mathbf{h}, \mathbf{s})$ come from a maximum-entropy translation model for $p(w|\mathbf{h}, \mathbf{s})$, where w is a word that follows $\mathbf{h}$ in the translation of $\mathbf{s}$. This model is essentially a maximum-entropy analog of a linear combination of a trigram language model for $p(w|\mathbf{h})$ and the classical IBM model 2 [1] for $p(w|\mathbf{s})$. It was shown in [3] to have significantly lower test corpus perplexity than an equivalent linear combination used in the previous TransType prototype. It also supports very rapid searches for upcoming text, chiefly by virtue of the fact that it completely ignores the relation between $\mathbf{h}$ and $\mathbf{s}$.

s: Let us return to serious matters.

t: $\overbrace{\text{On va r}}^{\mathbf{h}}\overbrace{\textit{evenir aux choses sérieuses.}}^{\mathbf{x}^*}$

x: *evenir à*

Figure 2: Example of a prediction for English to French translation. s is the source sentence, h is the part of its translation that has already been typed, x* is what the translator wants to type, and x is the prediction.

The technique for deriving the required probabilities $p(k|\mathbf{x}, \mathbf{h}, \mathbf{s})$ from the model $p(w|\mathbf{h}, \mathbf{s})$ is straightforward but rather tedious to describe. Briefly, it involves first expressing $p(k|\mathbf{x}, \mathbf{h}, \mathbf{s})$ in terms of string probabilities $p(\mathbf{x}'|\mathbf{h}, \mathbf{s})$, then calculating the string probabilities by summing over all compatible token sequences. Further details are given in [4].

3.2 User Model

The purpose of the user model is to determine the expected benefit $B(\mathbf{x}, \mathbf{h}, \mathbf{s}, k)$ to the translator of a prediction $\mathbf{x}$ whose first k characters match the text that the translator wishes to type. This will depend heavily on whether the translator decides to accept or reject the prediction, so the first step in our model is the following expansion:

$$B(\mathbf{x}, \mathbf{h}, \mathbf{s}, k) = \sum_{a \in \{0,1\}} p(a|\mathbf{x}, \mathbf{h}, \mathbf{s}, k)\, B(\mathbf{x}, \mathbf{h}, \mathbf{s}, k, a),$$

where $p(a|\mathbf{x}, \mathbf{h}, \mathbf{s}, k)$ is the probability that the translator accepts or rejects $\mathbf{x}$, $B(\mathbf{x}, \mathbf{h}, \mathbf{s}, k, a)$ is the benefit they derive from doing so, and a is a random variable that takes on the values 1 for acceptance and 0 for rejection. The first two quantities are the main elements in the user model. The parameters of both were estimated from data collected during the TransType trial described in [7], which involved nine accomplished translators using a prototype prediction tool for approximately half an hour each. In both cases, estimates were made by pooling the data for all nine translators, so as to reflect as accurately as possible the characteristics of an average translator.

3.3 Search

Searching directly through all character strings $\mathbf{x}$ in order to find $\hat{\mathbf{x}}$ according to equation (1) would be very expensive. The fact that $B(\mathbf{x}, \mathbf{h}, \mathbf{s})$ is non-monotonic in the length of $\mathbf{x}$ makes it difficult to organize efficient dynamic-programming search techniques or use heuristics to prune partial hypotheses. Because of this, we adopted a fairly radical search strategy that involves first finding the most likely sequence of words of each length, then calculating the benefit of each of these sequences to determine the best proposal. The algorithm is:

1. For each length $m = 1 \ldots M$, find the best word sequence of that length:
$$\hat{\mathbf{w}}_m = \operatorname*{argmax}_{\mathbf{w}_m} p(\mathbf{w}_m|\mathbf{h}, \mathbf{s}),$$
2. Convert each $\hat{\mathbf{w}}_m$ to a corresponding character string $\hat{\mathbf{x}}_m$.
3. Output $\hat{\mathbf{x}} = \operatorname{argmax}_m B(\hat{\mathbf{x}}_m, \mathbf{h}, \mathbf{s})$, or the empty string if all $B(\hat{\mathbf{x}}_m, \mathbf{h}, \mathbf{s})$ are non-positive.

Step 1 is carried out using a Viterbi beam search with the translation model $p(w|\mathbf{h}, \mathbf{s})$. To speed this up, the search is limited to an *active vocabulary* of target words likely to appear in translations of $\mathbf{s}$, defined as the set of all words connected by some word-pair feature in our translation model to some word in $\mathbf{s}$. Step 2 is a trivial deterministic procedure that mainly involves deciding whether or not to introduce blanks between adjacent words (eg yes in the case of *la* + *vie*, no in the case of *l'* + *an*). Step 3 involves a straightforward evaluation of m strings according to equation (2). With this algorithm, the average time to make predictions with $M = 5$ is less than .02 seconds on a 1.2GHz processor. This does not cause a perceptible delay to users of our prototype.

4. FUTURE WORK

Each of the components of the predictor described in the previous sections offers some fairly obvious possibilities for improvement. The translation model could be made to capture some of the dependence between $\mathbf{h}$ and $\mathbf{s}$, ideally in such a way as to preserve its efficient search properties. It could also be made to adapt to the translator's previous input, which should be a valuable source of information about what translations are appropriate in the current context. The user model could also be made adaptive, to conform to the preferences and characteristics of the current user. Finally, there are numerous possibilities for improving the search for $\hat{\mathbf{x}}$, for instance using the n best word sequences of each length (rather than just one) as input to steps 2 and 3 of the algorithm above.

The user interface could also be improved in various ways. One obvious possibility is to have a passive completion mode in which the user would request predictions only when desired rather than having them be made automatically. An extension to this would be to make proposals when the user paused, signalling possible receptiveness to input from the tool.

We look forward to pursuing these and other research avenues in the TransType 2 project, due to begin this year under the auspices of the European Commission's 5th Framework programme.

5. REFERENCES

[1] Peter F. Brown, Stephen A. Della Pietra, Vincent Della J. Pietra, and Robert L. Mercer. The mathematics of Machine Translation: Parameter estimation. *Computational Linguistics*, 19(2):263–312, June 1993.

[2] Kenneth W. Church and Eduard H. Hovy. Good applications for crummy machine translation. *Machine Translation*, 8:239–258, 1993.

[3] George Foster. A Maximum Entropy / Minimum Divergence translation model. In *Proceedings of the 38th Annual Meeting of the Association for Computational Linguistics (ACL)*, Hong Kong, October 2000.

[4] George Foster, Philippe Langlais, and Guy Lapalme. User-friendly text prediction for translators. In *Proceedings of the 2002 Conference on Empirical Methods in Natural Language Processing (EMNLP)*, Philadelphia, PA, 2002. Submitted.

[5] Martin Kay. The MIND system. In R. Rustin, editor, *Natural Language Processing*, pages 155–188. Algorithmics Press, New York, 1973.

[6] Philippe Langlais, George Foster, and Guy Lapalme. Unit completion for a computer-aided translation typing system. *Machine Translation*, 15(4):267–294, December 2000.

[7] Philippe Langlais, Guy Lapalme, and Marie Loranger. Transtype: From an idea to a system. *Machine Translation*, 2002. To Appear.

ViTAP Demonstration

Andrew Merlino
Virage
600 Unicorn Park Drive
Woburn, MA 01801
781.938.9761
andy@virage.com

ABSTRACT

Automatically processing US English broadcast news such that a Government data analyst can efficiently and accurately discover points of interest is a challenge. Performing this task on a new language without understanding the language makes the task near impossible. But with a little knowledge of broadcast news and state of the art audio, video and textual processing technologies at hand, we have built a system built that processes US English and Arabic broadcast News. Also, the collected data is programmatically shared to researchers.

INTRODUCTION

VITAP (Video, Text and Audio Processing) is a system that is built using Virage's commercial software foundation and SDK to integrate DARPA research technologies to detect observations. The observations are used to query for points of interest or reused by the system to perform a higher level of understanding (e.g., story segmentation, topic identification).

VITAP consists of three software components (diagram 1). For each signal, there is a VideoLogger and Advanced Audio Indexer. The Videologger contains the following detection and extraction plug-ins most initially funded by DARPA:

- Apptek – Machine Translation
- Cobion – Logo Detection
- BBN, IBM – Automatic speech recognition, speaker identification
- SRI – Optical character recognition
- Visionics – Face recognition
- Virage – Encoding, segmentation, shot change analysis, shot classification

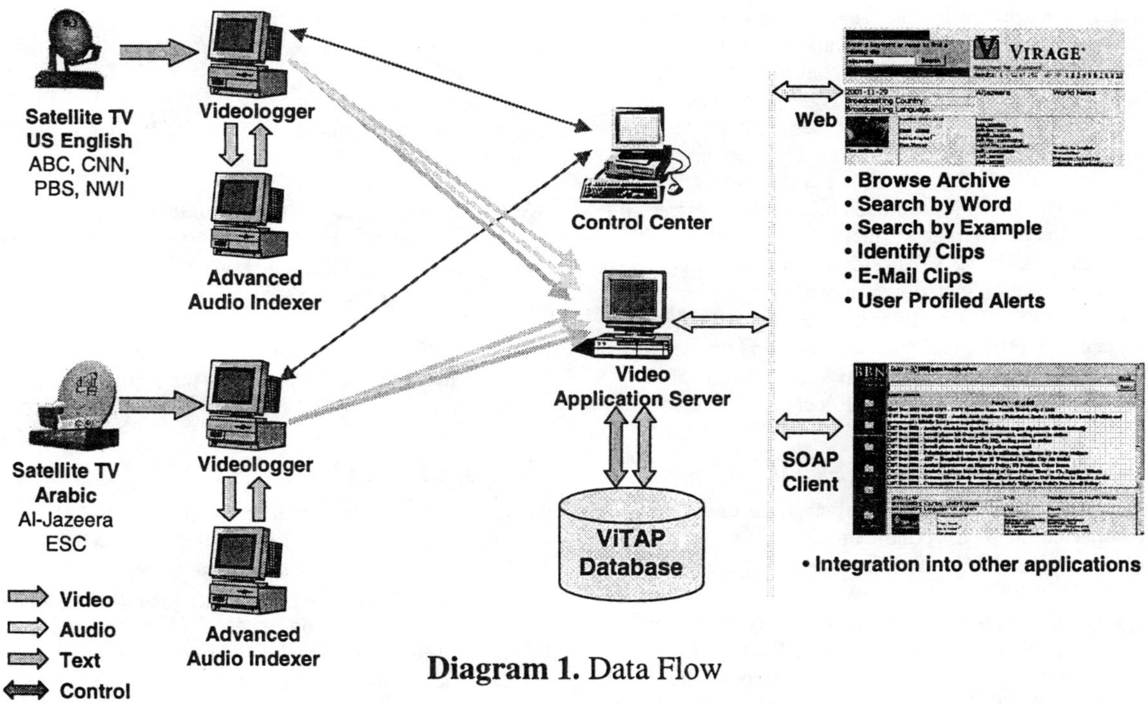

Diagram 1. Data Flow

One of the plug-ins, Advanced Audio Indexer, from BBN Technologies, performs the following analysis: US English and Arabic automatic speech recognition, named extraction, audio classification, speaker turn detection and speaker identification and US English topic identification. These detections are viewed as tracks in the VideoLogger.

Diagram 2. Video Solutions Server Presentation with Arabic

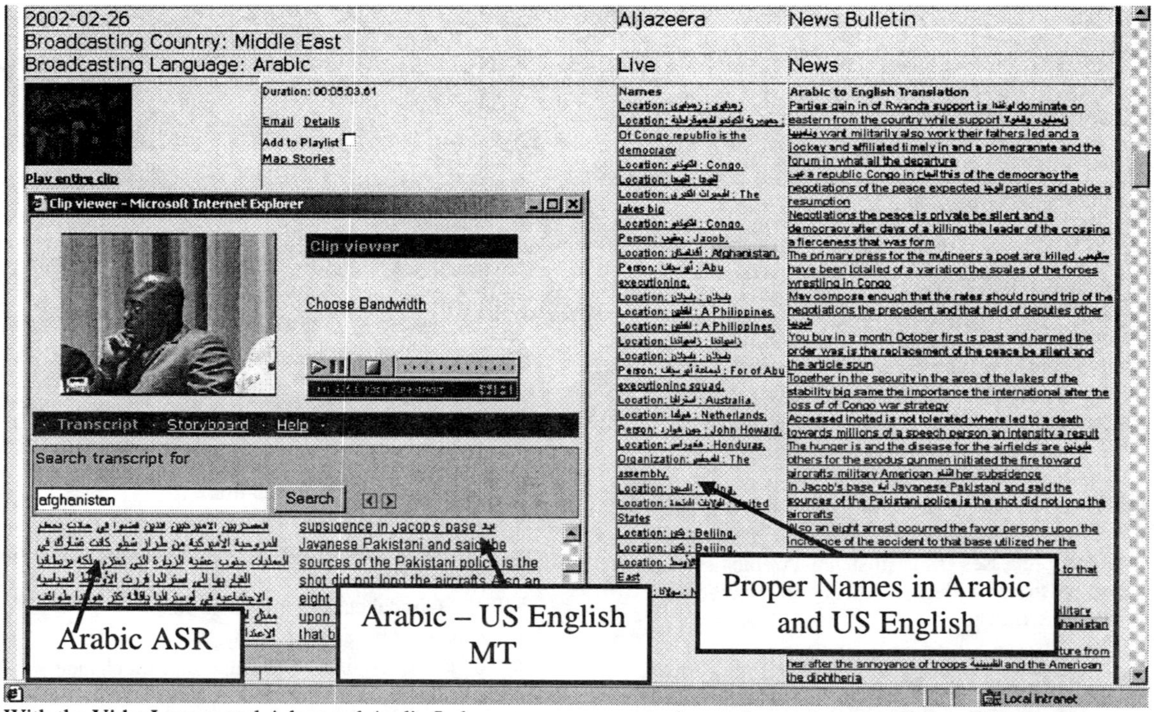

With the VideoLogger and Advanced Audio Indexer configured appropriately, Virage's Control Center is used to automatically setup capture events much like you would setup a VCR. With control center, every capture is automated. Note many programs have their own specific configurations such as face libraries, logos, speaker voices and story clipping models.

When an event is automatically captured, the extracted data is stored in Virage's Video Solutions Server (VSS) (Diagram 2). VSS is a data storage and a web based software solution that allows user to view the extracted data. The ViTAP server has been configured for news on demand retrieval templates. User clip bins have also been added to allow users to save query results of interest in their own or shared folders.

RAPID CHANGE IN SCOPE

Due to 9/11, the focus of VITAP changed to automatically process Arabic broadcast news (Aljazeera and ESC). To automate this process there were only a few changes that were made to the overall system. One of the most important changes was the addition of BBN's Arabic Automatic Speech Recognition System. This change occurred on the Advanced Audio Indexer only. Next, plug-in libraries were modified to work with the new news formats. This entailed training new broadcast agency logos, capturing anchor and reporter speaker libraries and capturing anchor and reporter faces. With the new detections and manually marked up story segments, we trained the segmentation system to automatically detect story segments.

While this occurred, we recognized that not all data analysts spoke Arabic. Using the VideoLoggers Media Analysis API, we integrated Apptek's machine translation software into the system.

Because all Virage products support UTF-8, we didn't have to make any changes to view the Arabic font (diagram 2).

TIDES PARTICIPANT ACCESS

Due to Integrated Feasibility Experiments, the TIDES architecture participants (i.e. BBN- OnTAP, MITRE-MITAP) desired direct access to the detections. We rapidly gave them access by writing VAS code to allow SOAP (Simple Operation Access Protocol) access. This allowed the participants to programmatically access and use the data on an as need basis (Diagram 3).

CONCLUSIONS

Multi-modal applications are in their infancy. In order for them to work properly, rapid integration of appropriate detection, extraction and analysis technology is required. With the correct technologies and environment, rapid application development and integrations are feasible.

ACKNOWLEDGEMENTS

The work reported here was supported in part by the Defense Research Project Agency under contract number (N0001400C0456). The views and conclusions contained in this document are those of the authors and should not be interpreted as necessarily representing the official policies, either expressed or implied, of the Defense Advanced Research Projects Agency or the United States Government.

Diagram 3. BBN TIDES OnTAP System

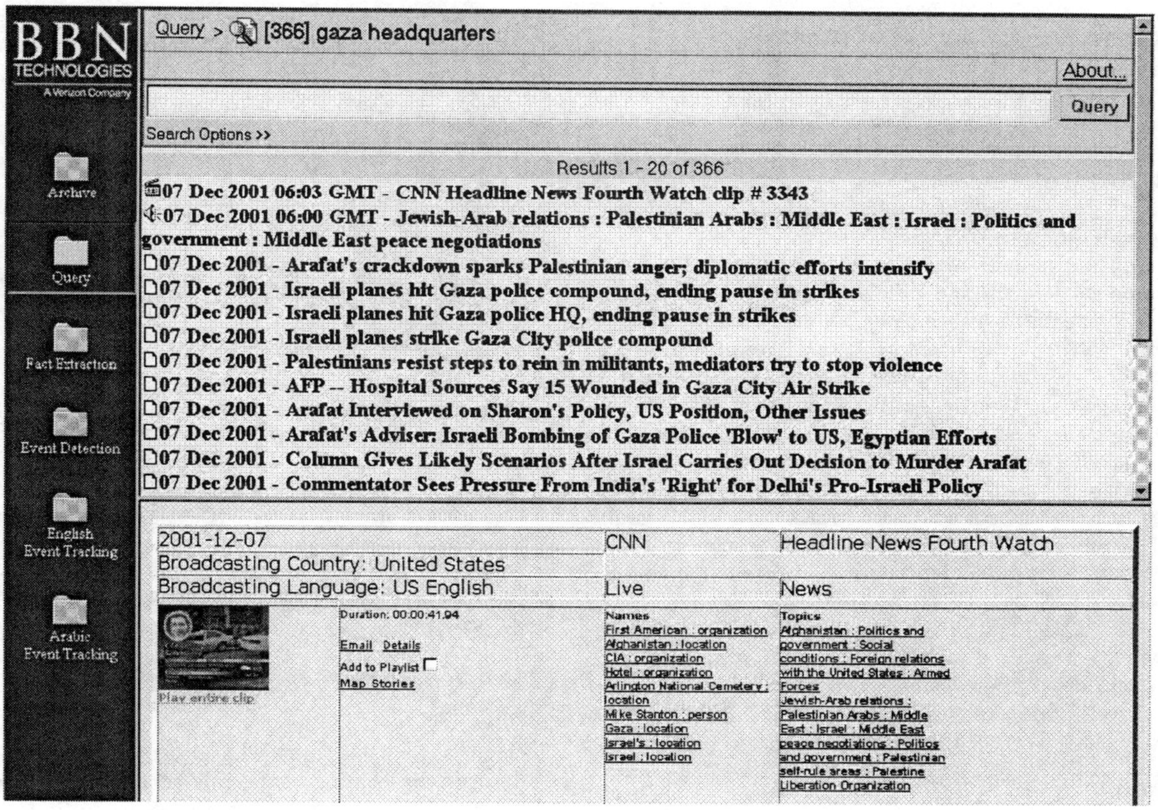

The NESPOLE! Speech-to-Speech Translation System

F. Metze, J. McDonough, H. Soltau, and A. Waibel*
Interactive Systems Laboratories
Universität Karlsruhe (TH)
Karlsruhe, Germany
{metze|jmcd|soltau|waibel}@ira.uka.de

A. Lavie, S. Burger, C. Langley, K. Laskowski, L. Levin, and T. Schultz
Carnegie Mellon University
Pittsburgh, PA, USA
{alavie|sburger|clangley|kornel|lsl|tanja+}@cs.cmu.edu

F. Pianesi, R. Cattoni, G. Lazzari, N. Mana, and E. Pianta
ITC-irst
Trento, Italy
{pianesi|cattoni|lazzari|mana|pianta}@itc.it

1. INTRODUCTION

This paper describes the first showcase of the NESPOLE![1] system. NESPOLE! is a speech-to-speech machine translation system designed to provide fully functional speech-to-speech capabilities within real-world settings of common users involved in e-commerce applications. The project is a collaboration between three European research laboratories (IRST in Trento, Italy; ISL at Universität Karlsruhe (TH) in Germany; and CLIPS at Université Joseph Fourier in Grenoble, France), one US research group (ISL at Carnegie Mellon University in Pittsburgh, PA) and two industrial partners (APT; Trento, Italy – the Trentino provincial tourism board, and Aethra; Ancona, Italy – a tele-communications company). The project is funded jointly by the European Commission and the US' NSF.

The main goal of NESPOLE! is to advance the state-of-the-art of speech-to-speech translation in realistic scenarios and involving naive users. The first showcase presented in this demonstration involves an English–, French–, or German–speaking client enquiring about winter-sports possibilities in the Trentino region of the Italian Alps via a NetMeeting® connection. His or her questions are answered by an Italian-speaking agent at APT, while the NESPOLE! system provides speech-to-speech translation and a multimodal Whiteboard, which users can use to point to shared web-sites or draw on shared maps, therefore enhancing the oral communication with extra capabilities.

This paper is organized as follows: we will first present a general system description which covers the current hardware setup as well as the design principles of the NESPOLE! system in general. We will then present the user interface, and the results from two system evaluations, one with respect to system performance under different network conditions and an end-to-end evaluation. The references at the end of this paper serve as pointers to further information about the NESPOLE! system.

[1]NESPOLE! – NEgotiation through SPOken Language in E-commerce.
*Also at Carnegie Mellon University, Pittsburgh, PA.

Proceedings of HLT 2002, Second International Conference on Human Language Technology Research, M. Marcus, ed., Morgan Kaufmann, San Francisco, 2002.

Figure 1: A user during a NESPOLE! video-conferencing session.

2. SYSTEM DESCRIPTION

The NESPOLE! system uses a client-server architecture to allow a common user, who is browsing web-pages on the Internet, to connect seamlessly to a speech-to-speech translation service using for example Microsoft's NetMeeting® software. In the current showcase, a user browses the web-pages of the Trentino region in Italy for winter-sports possibilities and, as he doesn't find all the information he wants, clicks on a button provided on the web-page to establish a video-conferencing[2] connection to a human "agent" of the Trentino tourist board (see figure 1). He can then ask natural-language questions to the agent, which the NESPOLE! server will translate and vice-versa. Currently, the

[2]The use of the video-conferencing feature is optional and can be dropped to reduce bandwidth, as the system functionality is fulfilled entirely by the data and audio streams.

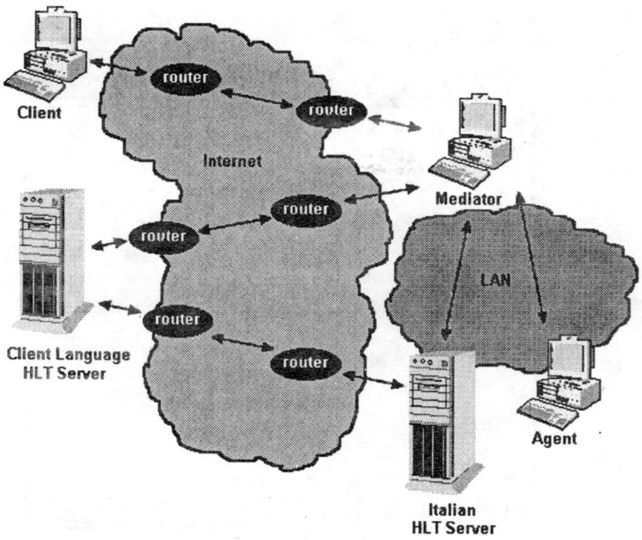

Figure 2: The distributed NESPOLE! system architecture.

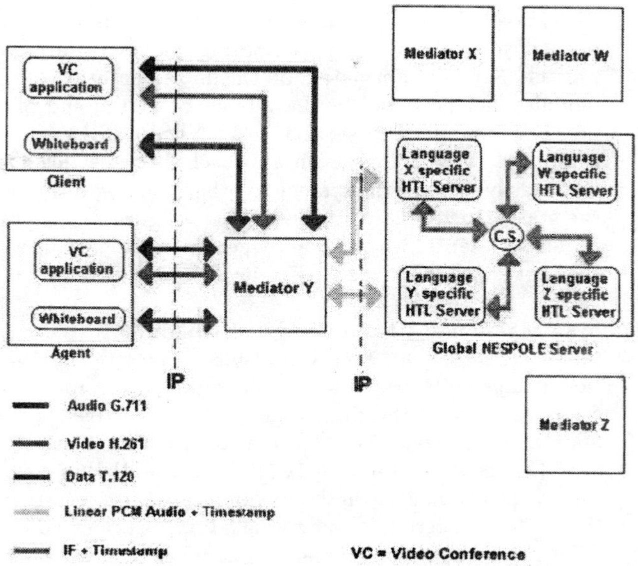

Figure 3: The logical view of the NESPOLE! system.

agent speaks Italian, while the client can speak either English, French or German.

The Interlingua-based translation system covers the activities of planning and scheduling winter holidays and similar activities in the Trentino region. By using NESPOLE!, customers can be served in several languages without the need to employ agents capable of speaking all of them. Additionally, the NESPOLE! system incorporates a special Whiteboard with multi-modal capabilities, allowing the agent and the client to share maps or web-pages.

2.1 Hardware requirements

The system requires no special hardware on the client's side, except a standard PC or portable device with microphone and loudspeakers or headsets as well as an Internet connection with a bandwidth of about 64kbit/s. We have for example demonstrated the system on a laptop running Windows 2000, connected to the Internet via a wireless LAN link.

The hardware setup used within the NESPOLE! system is shown in figure 2. The client connects to a special server, the so-called "Mediator" machine, which then in turn establishes connections to the so-called "HLT-servers", which provide the ASR and MT capabilities. The Mediator also runs under Windows, while the HLT servers run on different flavours of Linux on Intel PCs or Unix workstations. The IP connections between the Mediator computer and the agent and client use the H323 video-conferencing standard, which is based on UDP for the audio stream. Data is transmitted via TCP. This means that there will be little time delay during transmission, which is important for human-to-human communication, but short segments of speech can be lost during transmission. The links between the Mediator and the HLT servers use TCP. The effect of packet-loss on the demo will be discussed in the system evaluation section. The logical system design is shown in figure 3.

The system complexity is hidden from the user, as he only communicates with the Mediator computer. Currently, we usually run the Mediator at IRST in Trento, while the agent is being called at APT, also in Trento. The HLT servers, which provide speech recognition, translation and synthesis, run at the locations of the participating partners, i.e. at the Universities in Trento, Pittsburgh, Grenoble and Karlsruhe.

The chosen design allows for maximum flexibility during usage: Mediators and HLT-servers can be run in several locations, so that the optimal configuration given the current user location and network traffic can be chosen at runtime. The computationally intensive part of speech recognition and translation is done on dedicated server machines. The client machine can therefore be very "thin", so that the service is available nearly everywhere and to everyone, including mobile devices and public information kiosks.

2.2 Software

A complete call through the system starts by a client requesting a NetMeeting connection with the Mediator. The Mediator identifies the client's native language by an entry in the "Name" field, which is transmitted during calls and will then contact the HLT server for the client's language, the HLT server for the agent's language (currently Italian), to check the availability of translation services and try to establish a NetMeeting connection to an agent. It will only accept the call from the client, once these three required connections have been established. Speech from the client will be received by the Mediator, forwarded to the respective HLT server, which will in turn perform speech recognition and analysis into a language-independent "Interchange Format" (IF) [6], which is then transmitted to the HLT server associated with the agent, where text will be generated from the IF. This text string will then be synthesized and the resulting audio is transmitted to the agent via the Mediator. Multi-modal gestures, such as drawing on a map or video data is transmitted directly between the communication partners.

The speech recognition and translation components have been developed by the participating partners during the project. Further information on the implementation of these modules can be found in the references at the end of this paper, summarized in section 5. In NESPOLE! we use an Interlingua-based translation approach, because this allows us to easily expand the system to other languages thanks to the star-shaped architecture evident in figure 3, and incorporate an user feed-back loop by generating a paraphrase in the user's own language (useful for error correction).

System response time is highly variable due to the uncertain and varying network conditions. The speech recognition components use run-on recognition, i.e. recognition starts as soon as the first packets of data arrive, and run approximately real-time (German) or less than 3 times real-time (English) on standard 1GHz Pentium-III PCs running Linux. Depending on network conditions, text representations of speech recognition or translation, as discussed in the following section on the user interface, can be available in less than one second after a subject stopped speaking. Under bad network conditions, the same process can however take several seconds, too.

3. USER INTERFACE

Significant attention was therefore devoted to designing an appropriate front-end user interface for the system, that allows both clients and agents an intuitive and relatively simple control over their communication process. The user interface display is Windows®-based and consists of four windows:

- the Microsoft®Internet Explorer
- the Microsoft®Windows NetMeeting
- the AeWhiteboard
- the Nespole Monitor

These windows can be seen in figure 4. Using Internet Explorer, the user activates the audio and video call with an agent who can help him and give him the answers and the details he needs: all the user has to do is to click a button on the browser page and automatically Microsoft Windows NetMeeting is opened and the audio and video connection goes up.

We found it important to visually present aspects of the speech-translation process to the end user. This is accomplished via the Nespole Monitor display. Three textual representations are displayed in clearly identified fields, shown in figure 5:

1. a transcript of the spoken utterance (the output from the speech recognizer);
2. a paraphrase of the utterance – the result of translating the recognized input back into the client's own language;
3. the textual translation of the utterance spoken by the other party.

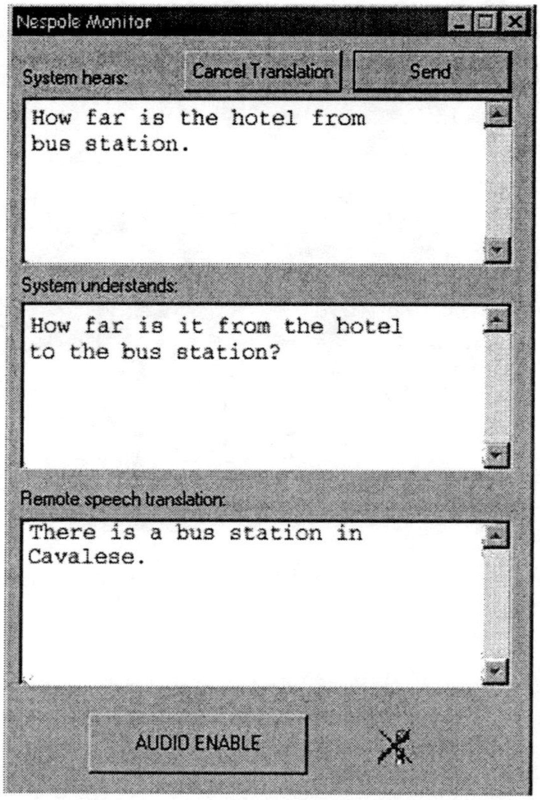

Figure 5: The NESPOLE! monitor window.

These textual representations provide the users with the capability to identify wrong translations and indicate errors to the other party. A bad paraphrase is often a good indicator of a significant error in the translation process. When an inaccurate translation is detected, the user can press a dedicated button that informs the other party to ignore the translation being displayed, by highlighting the textual translation in red on the monitor display of the other party. The user can then repeat the turn. The current system also allows the participants to correct speech recognition and translation errors via keyboard input, a feature which is very effective when bandwidth limitations degrade the system performance. The "Monitor" window, which allows such interaction, is shown in detail in figure 5.

The AeWhiteboard is provided to improve the quality and the clarity of the conversation through multi-modal tools: it gives to the user the possibility to share with his remote interlocutor an image or a user's free-hand drawing; this is realized in a very simple and intuitive way through a user interface that follows the standards of Windows applications: there is a menu, a tool-bar, and a status bar where the user can read system, state, and button functionality explanations.

The functionalities provided by the AeWhiteboard include: image loading, free-hand drawing, area selecting, color choosing, scrolling the image loaded, zooming the image loaded, URL opening, and Nespole! Monitor activation. The most important feature is that each operation the user does is shared with his remote interlocutor, so they can com-

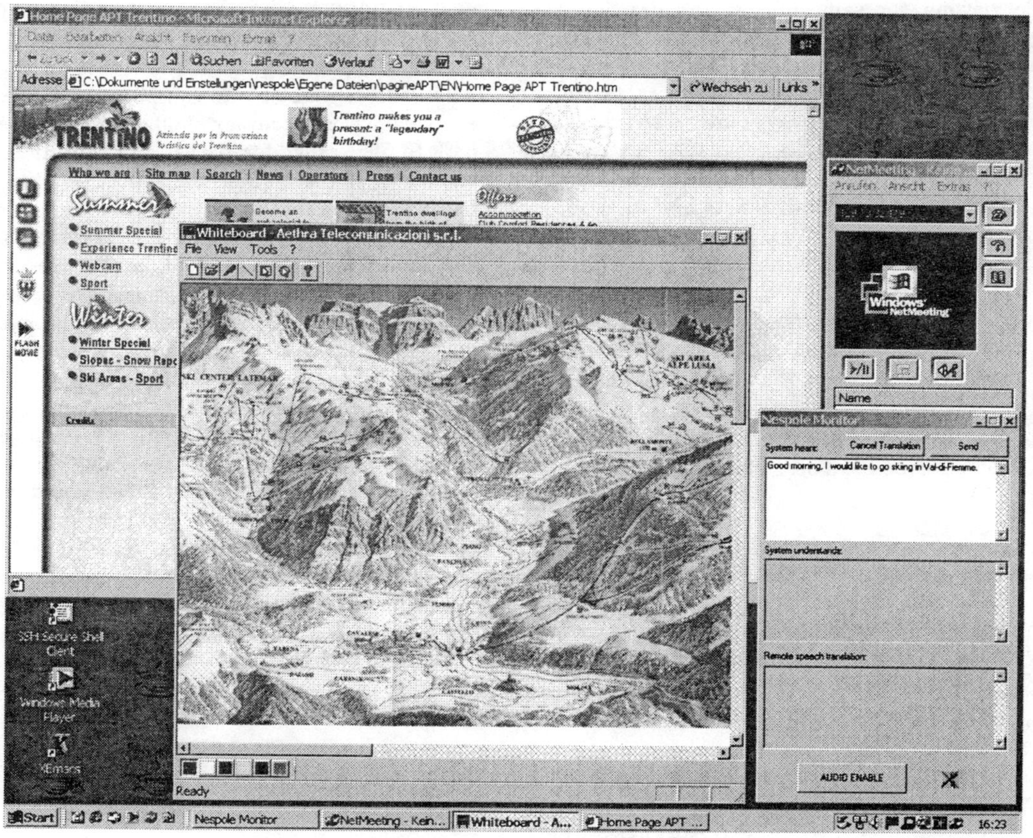

Figure 4: The user's view of the NESPOLE! system.

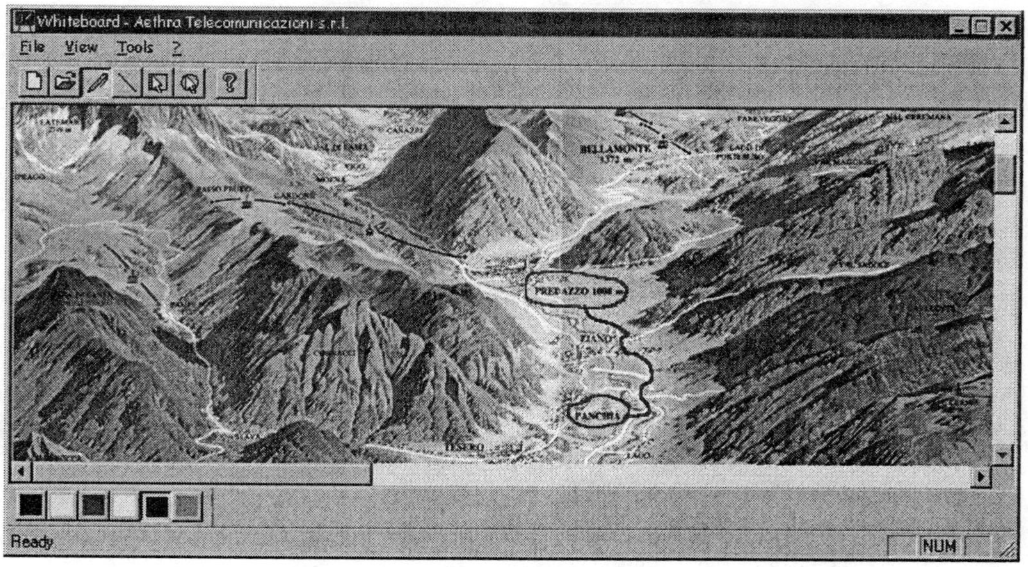

Figure 6: The AeWhiteboard in use.

municate while viewing the same images and drawing on identical-image whiteboards. An example of the AeWhiteboard being used to highlight two towns and hiking path between them is shown in figure 6. This figure is taken from an extension of the system, which we currently develop, that can also handle summer activities.

Typically, the client would ask for distances and directions from a proposed location, say a hotel, to another, e.g., ski slopes. By using the White-Board, the agent can indicate the locations and draw routes on the map, accompanying gestures with verbal explanations. The front-end of the NESPOLE! system allows the participants to communicate entirely with speech and use gestures whenever they want.

4. SYSTEM EVALUATION

Different evaluation sessions have been conducted, targeting different aspects:

1. the impact and usability of multi-modality;
2. experiments for assessing the impact of network traffic and the consequences of real packet-loss, on the system's performance; and
3. end-to-end performance evaluations.

The database collected during the project and which is being used in the various evaluations is described in [2]. The evaluation concerning Multi-Modality is presented in the accompanying HLT2002 poster presentation [4]. In this work we will present the results from Network Traffic impact and the End-to-End evaluation.

4.1 Network traffic impact

In our various user studies and demonstrations, we have been forced to deal with the detrimental effects of network congestion on the transmission of VoIP in our system. The critical network paths are the H323 connections between the Mediator and the Client and Agent, which rely on the UDP protocol, in order to guarantee real-time human-to-human communication. For demonstration purposes, we can of course circumvent the problem by positioning the three components involved (client, agent, mediator) within close proximity, this is however not a realistic scenario.

To quantify the influence of UDP packet-loss on real-world system performance, we ran a number of tests between German client installations in the USA (CMU at Pittsburgh) and Germany (UKA at Karlsruhe) calling a Mediator in Italy (IRST), which in turns contacted the German HLT server located in Karlsruhe. The tests were conducted by feeding a high-quality recording of the German development-test set collected at the beginning of the project into a computer set-up for a video-conference, i.e. we replaced the microphone by a DAT recorder (or a computer) playing a tape, while leaving everything else as it would be for sessions with real subjects. In particular, segmentation was automatically performed by NetMeeting. The thus produced segments were recognized separately by the HLT servers and the hypotheses concatenated to calculate the WER over the whole dialogue. These tests (a total of more than 16 hours) were conducted at different times of the day on different days of the week.

All in all, we were able to run 16 complete tests, resulting in an average word accuracy of 60.4%,[3] with single values in the 63% to 59% range for packet-loss conditions between 0.1% and 5.2%. Higher packet-loss ratios, resulting from generally bad network conditions, usually led to a breakdown of the Client-Mediator or Mediator-HLT server link due to timeout conditions being reached, or the inability to establish a connection at all. These results are presented in graphical from in figure 7. We were however able to record one dialogue with 21.0% packet loss, which resulted in a word accuracy of 50.3%. This dialogue is very difficult to understand even for humans. From the recorded statistics, which we present in a paper describing the Nespole! demo also in these proceedings, we conclude that at least for packet-loss ratios below 5%, this number alone is not sufficient to predict word-error rate. For 20% packet-loss, the loss in WER is significant, but we still observe less degradation than reported in [8] on synthetic data. In practical use, one is, according to our experience, likely to deal with packet-loss ratios below 5%, where there is no clear correlation between packet-loss and word-error rate.

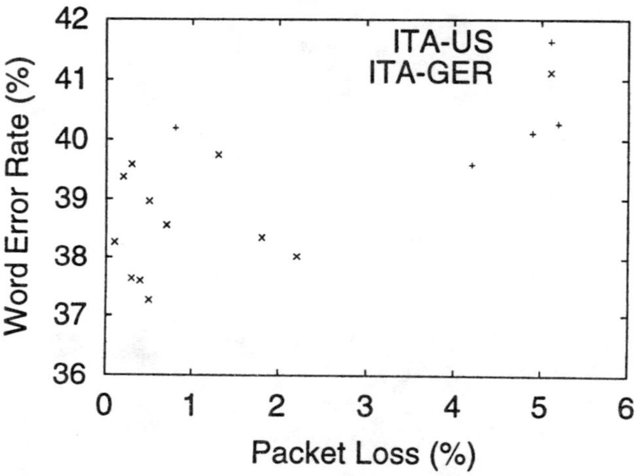

Figure 7: Influence of packet-loss on word accuracy of the German Nespole! recognizer.

Generally, we conclude from these experiments, that packet-loss influences the performance of the system, but there is no clear and drastic influence of packet-loss on ASR performance for the conditions we observed on our experiments. However, because lost packets can also occur during the transmission of synthesized voice, and the original voice is also transmitted between Agent and Client, the user is easily disturbed by the chirping associated with lost packets. A full End-to-End evaluation under all types of network conditions however is beyond the scope of the presented work.

4.2 End-to-End evaluation

In December 2001, we conducted a large scale multilingual end-to-end translation evaluation of the Nespole first-showcase system. For each of the three language pairs

[3]The word accuracy on the clean 16kHz recording is 71.2%.

(English-Italian, German-Italian and French-Italian), four unseen test dialogues that were not previously seen by the system developers were used to evaluate the performance of the translation system. The dialogues included two scenarios: one covering winter ski vacations, the other about summer resorts. One or two of the dialogues for each language contained multi-modal expressions. The dialogues included a mixture of dialogues that were collected mono-lingually prior to system development (both client and agent spoke the same language), and data collected bilingually (during the July 2001 MM experiment), using the actual translation system. This mixture of data conditions was intended primarily for comprehensiveness and not for comparison of the different conditions. The evaluation was conducted by human graders, who manually segmented the dialogues into "Semantic Dialogue Units" (SDUs) and then assigned scores to every SDU present in the utterance. This scoring scheme is discussed in [6].

Language	Transcribed	ASR hypotheses
English-to-Italian	55%	43%
German-to-Italian	32%	27%
French-to-Italian	44%	34%
Italian-to-English	47%	37%
Italian-to-German	47%	31%
Italian-to-French	40%	27%

Table 1: Cross-lingual End-to-End Translation Results ("Fraction of Acceptable SDUs (Interlingua Units)") on Transcribed Input and Hypotheses from Speech Recognition.

The results of the cross-lingual evaluation are summarized in table 1. Our results indicate that between 27% and 43% of Interlingua Units (i.e. translation concepts such as "Request to reserve 1 room for 2 persons and 1 week" or "Enquire distance between hotel and bus-stop") have been translated correctly. While this level of translation accuracy cannot be considered impressive, our user studies and system demonstrations indicate that it is already sufficient for achieving effective communication between real users, especially with the multi-modal capabilities of the present system.

5. FURTHER INFORMATION

The NESPOLE! project [5] has already lead to a number of publications on speech recognition [7, 10, 1] and Interlingua-based speech-to-speech translation [6, 3, 9]. The NESPOLE! database is described in [2]; as the system is currently regularly demonstrated we are still collecting data under a number of different conditions. An accompanying poster presentation is also appearing in these proceedings [4]. The project web-site can be found at `http://nespole.itc.it`.

6. ACKNOWLEDGMENTS

The research work reported here was supported by the National Science Foundation under Grant number 9982227 and the European Union under Grant number IST 1999-11562 as part of the joint EU/ NSF MLIAM research initiative. Any opinions, findings and conclusions or recommendations expressed in this material are those of the author(s) and do not necessarily reflect the views of the EU or the NSF.

7. ADDITIONAL AUTHORS

L. Besacier, H. Blanchon, and D. Vaufreydaz (CLIPS; Grenoble, France; e-mail: `{Laurent.Besacier|Herve.Blanchon|Dominique.Vaufreydaz}@imag.fr`), and L. Taddei (AETHRA; Ancona, Italy; e-mail: `l.taddei@aethra.it`).

8. REFERENCES

[1] L. Besacier, H. Blanchon, Y. Fouquet, J. Guilbaud, S. Helme, S. Mazenot, D. Moraru, and D. Vaufreydaz. Speech Translation for French in the NESPOLE! European Project. In *Proc. EuroSpeech 2001*, Aalborg, Denmark, 2001. ISCA.

[2] S. Burger, L. Besacier, P. Coletti, F. Metze, and C. Morel. The NESPOLE! VoIP Dialogue Database. In *Proc. EuroSpeech 2001*, Aalborg, Denmark, 2001. ISCA.

[3] R. Cattoni, M. Federico, and A. Lavie. Robust Analysis of Spoken Input combining Statistical and Knowledge-based Information Sources. In *Proceedings of the 2001 IEEE Workshop on Automatic Speech Recognition and Understanding (ASRU 2001)*, Madonna di Campiglio, Italy, 12 2001.

[4] A. Lavie, L. Besacier, F. Metze, F. Pianesi, and al. Enhancing the Usability and Performance of NESPOLE! - a Real-World Speech-to-Speech Translation System. In *Proc. HLT 2002*, San Diego, CA, 3 2002.

[5] A. Lavie, F. Pianesi, and al. Architecture and Design Considerations in NESPOLE!: a Speech Translation System for E-Commerce Applications. In *Proc. of the HLT2001*, San Diego, CA, 2001. ACM.

[6] L. Levin, D. Gates, F. Pianesi, D. Wallace, T. Watanabe, and M. Woszczyna. Evaluation of a Practical Interlingua for Task-Oriented Dialogues. In *Proc. AMTA-SIG-IL Workshop On Interlinguas and Interlingual Approaches*, Seattle, WA, 2000. AMTA.

[7] F. Metze, J. McDonough, and H. Soltau. Speech Recognition over NetMeeting Connections. In *Proc. EuroSpeech 2001*, Aalborg, Denmark, 2001. ISCA.

[8] B. Milner and S. Semnani. Robust Speech Recognition over IP Networks. In *Proc. ICASSP 2001*, Salt Lake City, USA, 5 2001.

[9] S. Rossato, H. Blanchon, and L. Besacier. Evaluation of a Speech to Speech Translation System: French Experience in the NESPOLE! Project. In *Submitted to: Proc. 19th International Conference on Computational Linguistics (COLING 2002)*, Taipei, Taiwan, 8 2002.

[10] D. Vaufreydaz, L. Besacier, C. Bergamini, and R. Lamy. From generic to task-oriented speech recognition: French experience in the NESPOLE! European project. In *Proc. ITRW Workshop on Adaptation Methods for Speech Recognition*, Sophia Antipolis, France, 2001. ITRW.

JAPANESE BROADCAST NEWS TRANSCRIPTION DEMONSTRATION

Long Nguyen, Xuefeng Guo, Richard Schwartz, John Makhoul
Toru Imai†, Akio Kobayashi†, Atsushi Matsui†, Akio Ando†

BBN Technologies
10 Moulton Street, Cambridge, MA 02138, USA

†NHK Science and Technical Research Laboratories
1-10-11 Kinuta, Setagaya-ku, Tokyo 157-8510, Japan

ln@bbn.com imai.t-mq@nhk.or.jp

ABSTRACT

In this demonstration, we show a real-time transcription of TV broadcast news in Japanese using a very large vocabulary speech recognition system developed at BBN Technologies. Both signal processing and speech recognition are run on a commodity notebook computer. Transcription word error rate is about 1.5% with average word latency less than 2 seconds. The high recognition accuracy in real time is achieved by a fast, and with low latency, 2-pass Byblos recognizer utilizing good acoustic and language models trained on the NHK Broadcast News Corpus.

1. INTRODUCTION

Television live captioning – the concurrent display of text of what has just been spoken – has become a wide-spread necessity for the hearing-impaired audience. For broadcast program in English, live caption can be provided through some hybrid system utilizing pre-scripted material and stenographers. For language such as Japanese, providing live caption through typing is rather difficult. Since 1999, BBN has been assisting NHK (or Japan Broadcasting Corporation) in using automatic speech recognition to provide live caption for NHK's TV news programs. A system (*separately developed by NHK*) has been put in use since March 2000 at NHK broadcast centers in Japan to automatically provide live caption for the anchors' read news segments of the daily Evening News programs. Since then, the collaboration effort has been geared towards improving transcription accuracy and speeding up processing time for the remaining parts of NHK's news programs.

Live broadcast news transcription is a very challenging speech recognition problem. A successful system is required not only to have a very low word error rate (WER), but also to produce results within a very short time delay. These two requirements must be satisfied to allow minimal manual error correction to achieve close to 100% accurate caption in real-time. For live captioning of Japanese broadcast news, NHK empirically determined that the automatic transcription word error rate has to be less than 5% and the average word latency has to be less than 2 seconds [1].

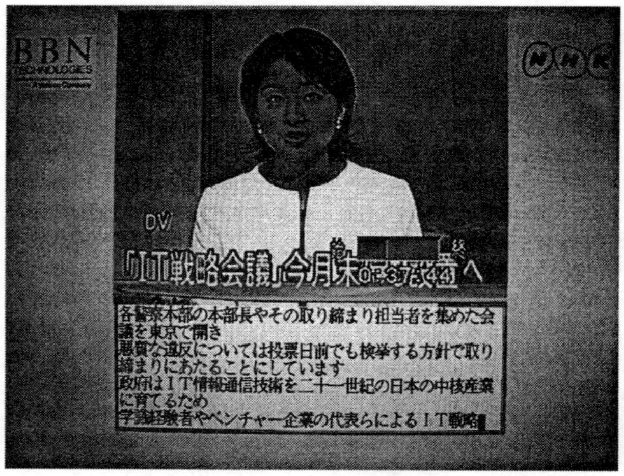

Figure 1: A screenshot of the demonstration system

In this demonstration, we show a *live* transcription of some recorded NHK broadcast news segments (spoken by anchors) using the BBN Byblos speech recognition system running on a commodity notebook computer. The overall WER of this demonstration system for anchors' speech is around 1.5% and the average word latency is 1 second. Figure 1 displays a screenshot of the demonstration system.

2. DEMONSTRATION CONFIGURATION

In the real captioning system, speech signal is directed to a front-end module for signal processing and feature extraction. Extracted feature vectors are then sent to a speech recognition engine to be *converted* into text. The hypothesized texts are then sent to a manual error-correction system so that a few speech recognition errors, if any, can be corrected. The corrected texts are then processed (such as being formated to fit the limited display, etc.) and encoded to be broadcast with the TV signal. However, in this demonstration system, we show only the transcription stage.

2.1. Equipment

The transcription system to be demonstrated consists of only portable hardware as listed below.

- A portable mini-DV player (Canon ZR25) to play back the recorded TV program. Its audio output is hooked up to the hardware that runs the Byblos speech recognition system.
- A notebook computer (Dell Latitude C400) where both the signal processing and feature extraction and the speech recognition engine run. Despite its light and thin look, this notebook computer sports a Mobil Intel Pentium III 1.2GHz CPU and is equipped with 1GB SDRAM memory. We chose to run RedHat Linux 7.2 operating system on this notebook computer.
- An optional multi-function LCD monitor (Samsung SyncMaster 170MP) to display both the video playback and transcription result.

2.2. On-Line Recognizer

The transcription engine used in this demonstration is a two-pass 1-best recognizer developed at BBN. (The recognizer fielded at NHK broadcast centers was developed separately at NHK [2].) The first pass is a fast-match utilizing only a single phonetic tree to produce scores for word endings using a coarse phonetically tied-mixture (PTM) acoustic model and a bigram language model [3]. Next, a state-clustered tied-mixture (SCTM) acoustic model and a trigram language model are used to generate the best hypothesis, similar to the algorithm described in [4]. However, instead of delaying until the first pass finishes (as in the original algorithm), the second pass is executed periodically at fixed 25-frame intervals. Hypothesized words are output if they occur in two consecutive runs of the second pass.

3. NHK BROADCAST NEWS CORPUS

The NHK Broadcast News Corpus consists of well-designed collections of acoustic and language data to be used in training Japanese speech recognition system's models and for performing speech recognition experiments.

3.1. Acoustic Training Data

The acoustic training data set consists of about 800 hours of speech selected from NHK news programs (*Good Morning Japan, News at Noon, and News at 7pm*) in the 1996-2000 period. Approximately, 600 hours were from male speakers, and 200 hours from female speakers. The speech was manually segmented into sentences with corresponding orthographic transcripts. The transcript of each sentence is written in a combination of *Kanji* and *Kana* characters according to NHK's *New Characters and Words Dictionary* [5]. In addition, there are two phonetic transcripts for each sentence: a sequence of phonetic symbols corresponding to the Kanji-Kana transcript, and another sequence of phonetic symbols manually transcribed by carefully listening to the audio. Each sentence is annotated with tags describing the gender of the speaker (male or female), type of speaker (anchor or reporter), and background noise level (clean or noisy), etc.

3.2. Language Modeling Data

The text corpus for *general* broadcast news language modeling consists of about 74M words of NHK's broadcast news manuscripts produced in the 1991-2000 period. In addition, daily manuscripts available before broadcast time are used as *adaptation* data. For practical purpose of an operational system, the language models are always re-estimated before broadcast time to take advantage of pre-scripted materials. All data from 1991 up to 12 hours before broadcast time are used to generate the base trigrams counts. Manuscripts prepared within the 12 hours before broadcast time are used to generate the adaptation counts which are then added into the base counts with a large weight. The final trigram models are then estimated from the pooled counts [1]. In other words, language models in the corpus are date-dependent and show-specific (DDLMs).

Several lexicons and dictionaries are also available in the Corpus. For each show on each day, a lexicon is constructed by selecting the most frequent words from the base material. All new words from the adaptation text before the show, typically less than 100 words, are also added into the lexicons.

To facilitate research towards *micro-domain* systems, there are two domain-specific language models in the corpus. For weather forecast, there is a 5K-word lexicon and a 166K-trigram language model. For sports news, a 46K-word lexicon and a 3M-trigram language model are available.

3.3. Development Test Set

The development test set is a collection of 3 hours of speech selected from the same NHK news shows (*Good Morning Japan, News at Noon, and News at 7pm*) broadcast on June 1-7, 2000 (1-7jun00d). The inclusion of programs broadcast in seven contiguous days is on purpose so that both weekday's and weekend's newscast are included in the test set. The entire test set is manually segmented into 1830 sentences and categorized into 7 narrow focus conditions: Studio News (C1), Studio Reports (C2), Spontaneous Speech (C3), Weather Forecast (C4), Sports News (C5), Noisy News (C6), and Field Reports (C7).

The division into narrow conditions was designed to focus

research effort to improve transcription accuracy for one condition at a time. As mentioned earlier, to have acceptable live captioning for a focus condition, the overall WER for that condition has to be less than 5% and the average word latency less than 2 seconds.

4. BBN TRANSCRIPTION SYSTEM

Within the collaboration to develop the multi-stage live closed-captioning system, BBN's effort has been focused only in improving the speech recognition engine such that:

1. Transcription result is accurate enough. Specifically, average word error rate is required to be below 5%.
2. Transcription result is delivered quickly enough. Specifically, average word latency is required to be below 2 seconds.

4.1. Off-Line Recognizer

The speech recognition system used in this collaboration effort at BBN is a special configuration of the BYBLOS English Broadcast News Transcription System [6]. The BYBLOS multi-pass decoder first does a fast match of the data to produce scores for numerous word endings using a coarse phonetically tied-mixture (PTM) acoustic model and a bigram language model (forward pass) [3]. Next, a state-clustered tied-mixture (SCTM) acoustic model and an approximate trigram language model are used to generate N-best hypotheses (backward pass) [4]. N-best hypotheses are then re-scored and re-ranked using an SCTM acoustic model and an exact trigram language model. The top-1 of the re-ranked N-best hypotheses is the recognition result.

4.2. Acoustic Models

Acoustic models in BYBLOS are based on the modeling of context-dependent phonemes using hidden Markov models (HMM). Mixture densities are used to model the output probabilities in the HMM states. The models used in our Japanese transcription system are speaker-independent and gender-dependent.

In the PTM model, all HMM states of all triphones having the same center phoneme share a 256-Gaussian mixture density (i.e. phonetically tied) [7]. The model consists of about 10K Gaussians ($41phone * 256Gaussian/phone$). However, the corresponding HMM states are clustered to share sets of mixture weights. There are approximately 14K of such mixture weights clusters.

The SCTM model extends the PTM model further by grouping the corresponding triphone HMM states into state clusters to share sets of Gaussians [7]. In our Japanese broadcast news transcription system, there are typically 4K or more clusters sharing sets of 64 Gaussians each (i.e. about 250K Gaussians). As in the PTM model, there are roughly 14K mixture weight clusters.

C1	C2	C3	C4	C5	C6	C7
410	57	175	599	314	152	123
<10	20-30	100+	60-90	60-90	<10	20-30

Table 1: Test material separated into focus conditions. Top row: number of sentences; Bottom row: perplexity range.

4.3. Language Models

BBN transcription system uses statistical N-Gram language models. A tree bigram language model [3] is used in the first fast-match decoding pass, while a word trigram language model is used in both the backward decoding and N-Best rescoring passes. Both N-Gram language models are estimated from the trigram counts available in the NHK Corpus. Typically, with a 62K-word lexicon, a general Japanese broadcast news language model contains about 3M bigrams and 14M trigrams.

For general news, we use 62K-word date-dependent lexicons. For each show on each day, the lexicon was made up by selecting the top 62K most frequent words from the base material. New words from the adaptation text before the show are always included in the lexicons.

5. EXPERIMENTAL RESULTS

The testing material used in the experiments reported here is the *1-7jun00d* development test set (briefly described in Section 3). The test set consists of 196 minutes of speech for 1830 sentences with 37250 words. Roughly, 2 hours are from male speakers and 1 hour from female speakers. When measured against the general broadcast news, date-dependent, 62K-word lexicons and N-Gram language models, this test set exhibits interesting values! Overall out-of-vocabulary (OOV) rate is 0.5% for all conditions, while just 0.1% for Studio News (C1). Trigram perplexities are remarkably low: less than 10 for read news (C1 and C6), 20-30 for reports (C2 and C7), 60-90 for weather forecast and sports news (C4 and C5), and a little more than 100 for spontaneous speech (C3). The separation of numbers of sentences and their trigram perplexities into focus conditions (C1-C7) are tabulated in Table 1.

In terms of computation, these off-line recognition experiments typically run at 4.8 times real-time. Timing was measured on PCs equipped with Intel Pentium III 1GHz CPU, 2GB RAM, and RedHat Linux 7.2 OS.

	C1	C2	C3	C4	C5	C6	C7	All
male	0.8	4.5	15.3	10.4	6.1	1.5	2.8	**4.4**
female	0.9	5.8	12.7	3.4	15.4	2.3	3.2	**4.8**

Table 2: Transcription WERs when using general Japanese broadcast news date-dependent language models

LM	OOV	perplex.	%WER		
			male	female	both
General 62K	0.5%	72	10.4	3.4	7.6
Weather 5K	1.8%	22	4.7	2.7	**3.8**
% relative			-54	-20	-50

Table 3: Comparison of WERs for the Weather Forecast condition (C4) when using different language models

5.1. General Broadcast News System

Table 2 shows the results of a recent experiment. Acoustic models were trained on all 800 hours of speech available. Language models, used for all focus conditions, were the general broadcast news date-dependent trigram models. WERs for Studio News (C1), Noisy News (C6), and Field Reports (C7), for both genders, are well below the 5% target, ranging from 0.8% to 3.2%.

It is surprising to see that the WER for Studio Reports (C2) is significantly higher than that of Field Reports (C7), while their trigram perplexities are within the same 20-30 range. In general, speech from field reports tends to contain more background noise than speech from studio reports. Nevertheless, our acoustic models seem to be quite robust to background noise (even though we haven't yet incorporated any explicit noise compensation algorithms into the system).

There are no significant differences in WERs between male and female speakers for focus conditions C1, C2, C6, and C7. These four conditions mostly contain read speech. For conditions C4 and C5, the WER difference between the two genders are quite alarming. However, since there are only a few speakers in these two focus conditions, it's probably inappropriate to generalize system performance at the gender level. Recall that the test set is real data selected from broadcast programs in 7 contiguous days from *one* TV network. That means there are probably only two meteorologists and two sports reporters. Specifically, for the sports news, there is only one female reporter, and her speech is quite animated: spontaneous, emotional, and full of excitement related to the sports footage. Note that, even though there are 800 hours of speech in the acoustic training data set, neither sports news nor spontaneous speech are well represented.

As shown in Table 2, spontaneous speech (C3) is the most difficult condition, with WERs about three times higher than the average (12.7% and 15.3% vs. 4.8% and 4.4%). As pointed out above, both the acoustic model and language model are not quite well-equipped for spontaneous speech: lack of a reasonable amount of spontaneous speech in the acoustic training data, and the language training data is dominated by prepared manuscripts. Trigram perplexity for the spontaneous speech condition (C3) is 100+ while prepared speech (C1, C2, C6, and C7) are in the 10-30 range.

5.2. Micro-Domain Systems

We also explored the possibility of using micro-domain language models for weather forecast and sports news. In general, it is not very difficult to switch recognition systems during broadcast time in the broadcast studio since weather forecast and sports news are scheduled at fixed slots of a regular news program.

For the Weather Forecast Condition (C4), the WER is still high (7.6%) when using the general broadcast news language model. However, when using the weather-specific 5K-word lexicon and the 166K-trigram language model, the overall WER is 3.8%, a 50% relative reduction, as shown in Table 3. However, if taking into account the higher OOV rate (1.8% vs. 0.5%) when using the small 5K-word weather-specific lexicon, the actual relative improvement must be much higher. In general, an OOV word causes at least 1 error. That means, the WER can be brought down to 2% or less by increasing vocabulary coverage.

For the Sports News Condition (C5), for both genders, we achieved a 32% relative reduction in WER, as shown in Table 4, by using sports-specific language models. The date-dependent sports-specific language models were estimated from 7M words of NHK sports news manuscripts in the 1991-2000 period (described in full details in [8]). The sports-specific 46K-word lexicon include all unique words occur in that 7M-word training data. However, the WER for the female sports reporter is still too high (11.2%).

In contrast to other general news announcers and reporters whose speech are included in the acoustic training data set, the female sports reporter is not one of the speakers observed in the training data. To overcome this difference, we attempted to use speaker batch adaptation to improve the acoustic model for this speaker. We managed to identify 30 minutes of her speech without transcripts from programs broadcast in May 2000 (i.e. before the time epoch of the test set). We decoded this 30-minute speech and

LM	OOV	perplex.	%WER		
			male	female	both
General 62K	0.7%	66	6.1	15.4	10.2
Sports 46K	0.5%	42	3.7	11.2	**6.9**
% relative			-39	-27	-32

Table 4: Comparison of WERs for the Sports News Condition when using different language models

then used the recognition hypotheses as *truth* for a *quasi*-supervised MLLR adaptation. Recognition results for this female sports reporter when using the adapted acoustic model are shown in Table 5. When adapting only the means of the mixture densities, the WER is 9.3%. When the variances are also adapted, the WER is 9.0%, a 20% relative improvement when compared to the result obtained by using the speaker-independent acoustic model. [If comparing against the 15.4% obtained by the general broadcast news language model, the relative reduction in WER for the female Sports News condition is 42%.]

6. DISCUSSION

Anyone who is familiar with the DARPA Hub-4 Broadcast News Transcription task would be curious to know why the recognition accuracy for NHK TV broadcast news is much higher than that for American Network TV or Cable news used in the Hub-4 Benchmark Evaluations. In most recent Hub-4 evaluations in 1998 and 1999, the WER for best systems was around 15% for all focus conditions and 8-10% for the clean speech condition [9]. We think we have some valid answers that might explain the better recognition accuracy for NHK TV news programs.

First of all, the Hub-4 acoustic training data were collected from several sources, including both TV and radio programs. Test data mostly comes from different shows or different TV broadcasters. While on the other hand, the NHK acoustic training data were collected from the same source as the test data. Most of the speakers in the test set, especially the anchors and key reporters, have significant amount of speech in the training data. It could be said that, this is a multi-speaker speech recognition mode. Meanwhile, in the Hub-4 task, it is a speaker-independent mode.

Model	adapted-means	adapted-vars.	%WER
SI	NA	NA	11.2
Adapted	yes	no	9.3
Adapted	yes	yes	**9.0**

Table 5: Comparison of WERs for the female Sports News subset when using *quasi*-unsupervised speaker adaptation

Secondly, the NHK language modeling corpus consists of mainly manuscripts written exclusively for broadcast news. A clear evidence of better language models is the low perplexity, as reported in Section 5. Whereas, the Hub-4 language modeling data are mostly written text from newspapers, and newswire sources.

7. CONCLUSION

The BBN Byblos speech recognition system has been successfully applied to the Japanese broadcast news transcription task. Transcription results for the Studio News, Noisy News, and Field Reports conditions are well below the 5% WER target, ranging from 0.8% to 3.2%. Micro-domain language models were used effectively to reduce WER for Weather Forecast and Sports News conditions by 30-50% relative. We have also described briefly a low-latency recognizer used in this real-time transcription demonstration. However, further work is needed to lower transcription word error rate for all other conditions.

References

1. A. Ando, T. Imai, A. Kobayashi, H. Isono, K. Nakabayashi, "Real-Time transcription system for simultaneous subtitling of Japanese broadcast news programs," *IEEE Trans. on Broadcasting*, Vol. 46, No. 3, Sep. 2000, pp. 189-196.
2. T. Imai, A. Kobayashi, S. Sato, H. Tanaka, A. Ando, "Progressive 2-pass decoder for real-time broadcast news captioning," in *Proc. IEEE ICASSP '00*, Istanbul, Turkey, May 2000, pp. 1559-1562.
3. L. Nguyen and R. Schwartz, "Single-Tree method for grammar-directed search," in *Proc. IEEE ICASSP '99*, Phoenix, AZ., Mar. 1999, pp. 613-616.
4. L. Nguyen and R. Schwartz, "Efficient 2-pass N-Best decoder," in *Proc. EuroSpeech '97*, Rhodes, Greece, Sep. 1997, pp. 167-170.
5. *NHK: New Characters and Words Dictionary*, Japan Broadcasting Publishing Association, 1981.
6. L. Nguyen, S. Matsoukas, J. Davenport, J. Billa, R. Schwartz, J. Makhoul, "The 1999 BBN Byblos 10xRT broadcast news transcription system," in *Proc. NIST 2000 Speech Transcription Workshop*, http://www.nist.gov/speech/publications/tw00/pdf/bn20.pdf
7. L. Nguyen, T. Anastasakos, F. Kubala, C. LaPre, J. Makhoul, R. Schwartz, N. Yuan, G. Zavaliagkos, Y. Zhao, "The 1994 BBN/Byblos speech recognition system," in *Proc. ARPA Spoken Language Systems Technology Workshop*, Austin, TX, Jan. 1995, pp. 77-81.
8. A. Matsui, H. Segi, A. Kobayashi, T. Imai, A. Ando, "Speech recognition of broadcast sports news," in *Proc. EuroSpeech '00*, Aalborg, Denmark, Sep. 2000, pp. 709-712.
9. http://www.nist.gov/speech/publications/tw00/

Oasis Translator's Aide

Scott Shepard, Sean Colbath, Dr. Kathleen Egan[1]*, Francis Kubala*

BBN Technologies, Cambridge, MA 02138
sshepard@bbn.com

[1] Department of Defense

1. INTRODUCTION

The Oasis Translator's Aide is a tool that increases the productivity of a human translator as they create English transcriptions from Arabic radio and TV broadcasts. The Oasis Translator's Aide is an extension of BBN's Oasis system that performs real-time indexing for browsing of broadcast news in English and Arabic. Oasis utilizes five speech and language technologies to automatically create a rich-content transcription of audio: speech recognition, speaker change detection, speaker clustering, speaker identification, and named entity extraction. This system operates in a streaming mode, recording broadcast news data off the air, performing recognition and indexing in real-time and storing the results in a database for later browsing over the Web. In this demo, we show a real-word application of an Oasis system that was deployed into the field in November 2001 as an aid for human translation of Arabic audio and video broadcasts.

2. HUMAN TRANSLATION WITHOUT THE OASIS TRANSLATOR'S AIDE

The translators' finished products are English translations of selected Arabic audio broadcasts. There are typically three major tasks in developing these products: selection, translation, and publication. Selection is the process of choosing a segment of audio or video to translate. Since human translation is a time consuming task, only important portions of a broadcast are translated. This makes selection a critical step in the human translation process for audio and video sources. A translator will often work from recorded audio broadcasts saved in a digital format. The translator "skims" the complete digital audio broadcast listening for segments that are suitable for translation. The translator then replays selected segments, translating the speech while transcribing with a word processor. This transcription stage typically requires much iteration through the audio segment, where the transcriber is "rewinding" the audio stream repeatedly to keep the translation and playback in synch. Only after the translator feels that the translated audio segment is accurate and complete is the document published.

3. OASIS TRANSLATOR'S AIDE

The Oasis Translator's Aide improves the translator's productivity by incorporating BBN Oasis human language technologies into the translator's working environment. The Oasis Translator's Aide architecture consists of one or more BBN Oasis Audio Indexers and a Translator's Aide server, as shown in Figure 1. The Translator's Aide server is a Microsoft Windows web server that is visible to the user's desktop machine. The user's desktop is only required to have a supported browser (IE 5.0+), Real Networks RealPlayer for Audio playback, Microsoft Word (2000 or XP), and a Translator's Aide Microsoft Word macro file.

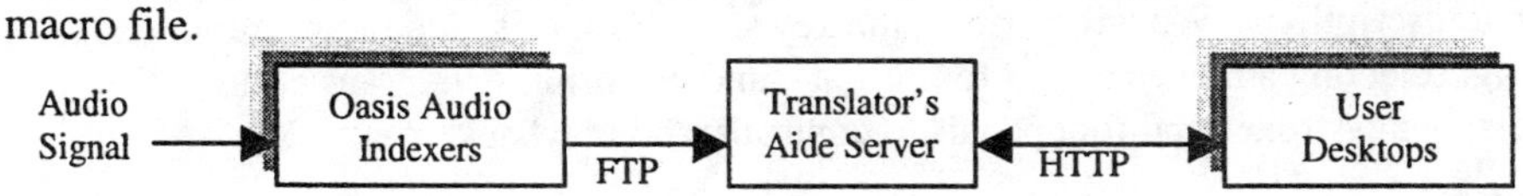

Figure 1: Conceptual System diagram

The Oasis Translator's Aide improves the selection process by automatically transcribing a complete audio broadcast while marking all named-entities and speaker turns. This changes the translator's task from one of listening (foreign language interpretation) to reading (foreign language translation). The Oasis Audio Indexers produce transcriptions of the complete audio broadcasts and publishes them to the

Translator's Aide Server. The translator uses a web browser to view the Oasis transcriptions. The translator is able to skim the Oasis transcriptions with accompanying audio faster than using the audio signal alone. Named-entity detection and speaker identification provide the translator many helpful visual cues within a transcription that serve to focus attention on terms that may be important to him. When the translator is viewing an Oasis transcription, he can mark segments for immediate translation or for future review, as shown in Figure 2.

Once a segment has been marked for translation, a single-mouse click presents the original transcription as well as an area for translation in Microsoft Word (2000 or XP), as shown in Figure 2. In this view, the translator is free to transcribe in Microsoft Word while controlling the playback of the audio segment using keystrokes or foot pedals. During audio playback, the transcription pane will highlight the word that is currently being spoken. This gives the translator the ability to follow the transcription visually while listening to the original audio broadcast. The Translator's Aide also provides the ability to easily select the starting point of audio playback from any word within the audio segment. The translator can pause and resume audio playback as well as rewind a user definable amount of time. At any time, the translator can save the translation for future modifications or for publishing.

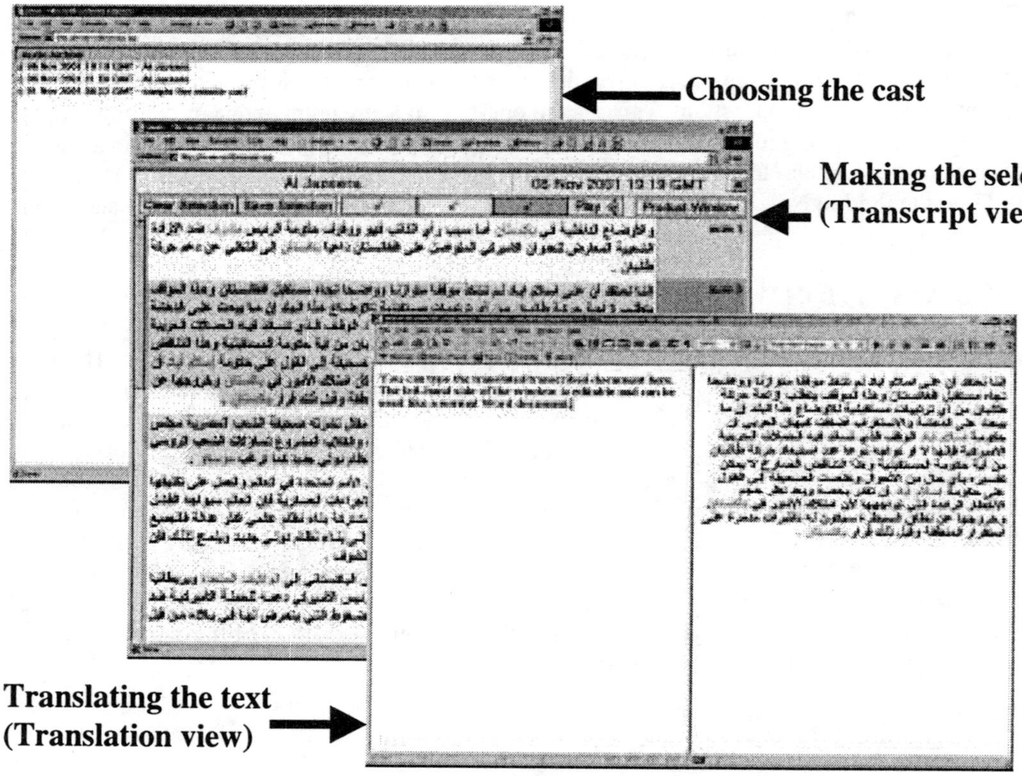

Figure 2: Oasis Translator's Aide

4. DEMONSTRATION

This demo will show the advantages of using the Oasis Translator's Aide when translating Arabic audio broadcasts into English transcriptions. We will perform the key steps for Oasis aided translation: choosing a Oasis cast for browsing, selecting a ranges of text to translate, and performing the translation in the translator editor while using keystrokes and foot pedals to control audio playback.

Newsroom OnTAP – Real-time alerting from streaming audio

Scott Shepard, Sean Colbath, Dr. Kathleen Egan[1]*, Francis Kubala*

BBN Technologies, Cambridge, MA 02138
sshepard@bbn.com

[1] Department of Defense

1. INTRODUCTION

The Newsroom OnTAP system is an operational system that permits automatic monitoring of several continuous data streams for detection of speech passages that match user-defined profiles. The Newsroom OnTAP system is an example of an OnTAP system which means that it employs a diverse set of human language technologies for processing a large and continuous stream of speech and text data from diverse media sources.

BBN's OnTAP system, which stands for *Online Text and Audio Processing*, is an experimental system under development in the DARPA TIDES program. The Newsroom OnTAP system is to be fielded in stages beginning in February 2002. In this demo, we show the capabilities of the Newsroom OnTAP system that provide real-time alerting of user-defined subjects and events from continuous data streams.

2. REAL-TIME ALERTING

Real-time alerting is the process of notifying a user that data related to specific profiles, or user-defined criteria, has been detected. The time between the presence of the data and the user notification is critical and should be minimized. There are two forms of profile specifications: keyword and event. A keyword profile enables the user to query the continuous data streams for specific combinations of keywords, similar to a typical search engine query but a keyword profile persists and is applied continuously to incoming data. Event based profiles enable the user to define a target event by one or more example documents. By combining these two forms of real-time alerting, the system provides the user with a flexible way of defining data of interest while providing real-time notification when relevant data has arrived.

3. NEWSROOM ONTAP

The Newsroom OnTAP system provides the user with a means of monitoring more data streams than previously possible. By automatically monitoring multiple data streams in the background and only notifying the user when data of particular interest is detected, the user can focus his attention on only data that is of particular interest to him.

The Newsroom OnTAP system architecture consists of one or more BBN Oasis Audio Indexers, one or more Event Trackers, and the Newsroom Server, as shown in Figure 1. The user's desktop is only required to have a supported browser (IE 5.0+) and Real Networks RealPlayer installed. The Newsroom OnTAP system handles speech and text interchangeably.

The Oasis Audio Indexers produce real-time transcriptions of data from the continuous data streams. They publish these transcriptions to the Event Trackers and the Alerting Service. The Event Trackers perform an incremental tracking operation on the data provided by the Oasis Audio Indexers and report the results to the Alerting Service. The Alerting Service compares the data provided by the Oasis Audio Indexers and Event Trackers to the user-defined alerting criteria. If the data satisfies the alerting criteria, the data is stored in the alerting database and the user is prompted with an alert via the web. The alert will appear in the users web browser without any user interactions, it is not necessary for the user to refresh the web page.

All user interactions with the Newsroom OnTAP system are accomplished via a Web browser. The user can create new alert criteria as well as receive alert notifications via the web. When the user receives an alert notification, they have the ability to view the relevant data immediately. If the data stream was an audio broadcast, the user will see a transcription of the broadcast with the relevant words highlighted. The user has the ability to replay the audio for the relevant portion of the broadcast directly from their web browser. If the data stream is text, the user will see the complete document with all of the relevant words highlighted in the web browser.

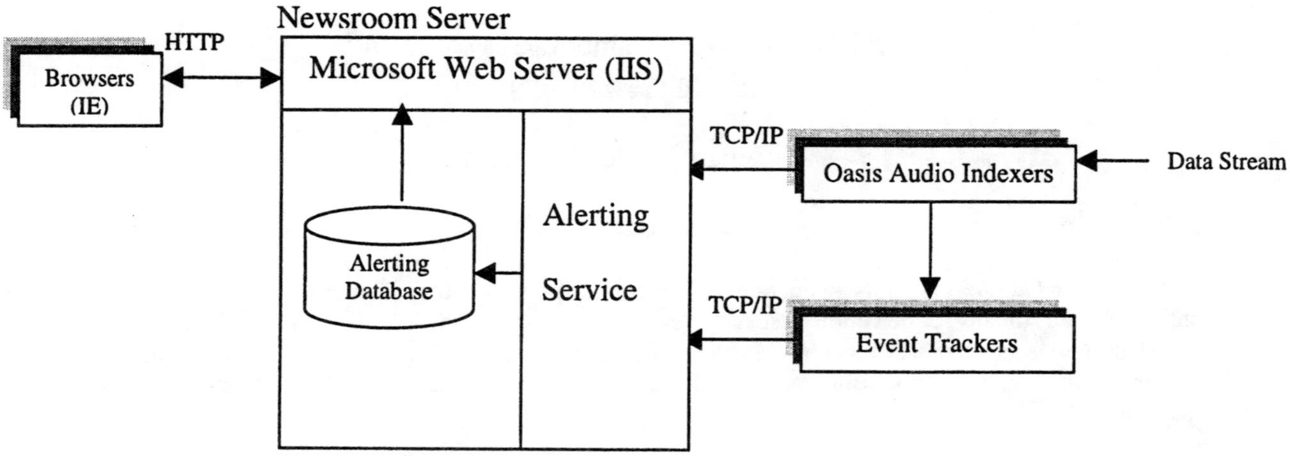

Figure 1: Newsroom OnTAP System diagram

4. DEMONSTRATION

The HLT demonstration system will monitor one continuous data stream throughout the demonstration period for real-time alerting. The audience will be encouraged to set up profiles throughout the conference and experience the technologies offered by Newsroom OnTap.

TExtractor: a multilingual terminology extraction tool

Antonio S. Valderrábanos
SchlumbergerSema Spain
Albarracín 25
28037 Madrid, Spain
+34 91 440 88 00
antonio.valderrabanos@sema.es

Alexander Belskis
SchlumbergerSema Spain
Albarracín 25
28037 Madrid, Spain
+34 91 440 88 00
alexander.belskis@sema.es

Luis Iraola
SchlumbergerSema Spain
Albarracín 25
28037 Madrid, Spain
+34 91 440 88 00
luis.iraola@sema.es

ABSTRACT

This demonstration presents a tool (TExtractor) employed for enriching terminology sets in four languages: English, French, German and Spanish. We present the associated linguistic resources and the experimental results obtained in the medical domain. TExtractor has been developed within project LIQUID (IST-2000-25324), which aims at developing a cost-effective solution for the problem of cross-language information retrieval (CLIR) in multilingual document bases in technical and scientific domains.

Keywords

Natural language processing; content-based indexing and retrieval; cross-language information retrieval; terminology extraction; medical texts; gastroenterology.

1. INTRODUCTION

LIQUID aims at providing solutions to CLIR from unstructured, multilingual document bases that belong to highly specialized domains within the medical field (e.g. gastroenterology). LIQUID focuses on specialized terminology as indexing terms for two main reasons:

- terms bear most of the semantic content
- compared to general language vocabulary, terms tend to be monosemic

According to [1] terms represent best quality descriptors for document indexing due to their high informational content.

In this context, the following requirements were defined:

- affordable and feasible, i.e. the development process should be as streamlined as possible
- domain independent, i.e. portable to other domains (initially medical domains)
- language neutral, i.e. portable to other (initially Western European) languages with a reasonable effort
- complementary with existing IR systems, so it can be seamlessly integrated with them.

Proceedings of HLT 2002, Second International Conference on Human Language Technology Research, M. Marcus, ed., Morgan Kaufmann, San Francisco, 2002.

2. THE LIQUID APPROACH TO CLIR

LIQUID uses a query translation strategy in order to ensure affordability and feasibility. Using a document-translation approach requires either human or machine translation, which is expensive (in time or money) for large document collections. The main components of LIQUID are:

a) *The document base*: it contains the documents that will be accessed through the CLIR system.

b) *The term sets*: they provide the link between the documents and the queries, while connected to the concepts present in the domain ontology.

c) *The domain ontology*: it serves to structure the terminology according to its meaning and to represent the domain knowledge.

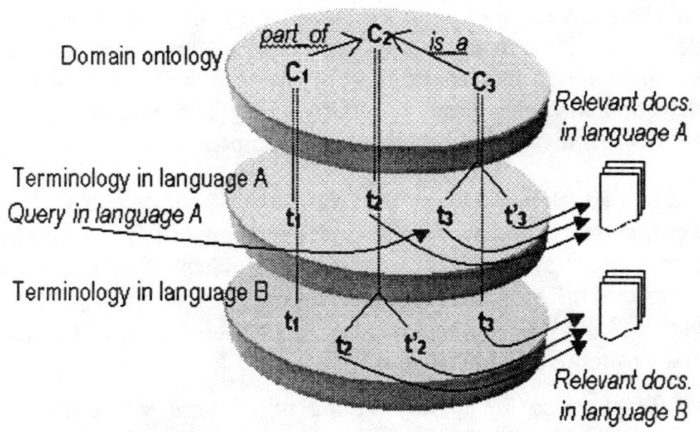

Figure 1. CLIR using a domain ontology

As a result of the combination of these three components we can link every document in the document base to the domain ontology through the set of indexing terms it contains, thus obtaining a semantic organisation of the documents. The linkage will be based on the presence of particular terms in both the semantic network and in the document. Since the semantic network is mapped to terminological resources in several languages, it is possible to make the document database available across languages.

3. TERM EXTRACTION

According to the resources used, CLIR systems can be classified in two main groups [2, 3, 4]:

- knowledge based approaches, that use multilingual glossaries and dictionaries;

- corpus based approaches, that use parallel or comparable multilingual corpora.

Examples of the first are [5] or [6]; and of the second [7]. Currently there is a tendency to combine the two approaches. The major problem for knowledge based approaches is that technical terminology is not normally present in reference works and it grows at a fast pace. Reference works hardly keep up with these new terms and then lack the necessary exhaustiveness. For corpus based approaches the problem is exactly the opposite: lack of broadness or generality. Since they are based in a particular set of texts, they are very sensitive to domain changes.

Statistical approaches can cope with high frequency terms but tend to miss low frequency terms [8], generating what's called "silence". Conversely, linguistic approaches are more efficient at identifying infrequent terms [9]. However, strategies based on linguistic knowledge tend to produce "noise" and identify as terms word combinations that are not. TExtractor uses linguistic knowledge, in the form of rules, to identify potential terms, and statistical knowledge to validate them.

Furthermore, CLIR systems need to cope with the term variation problem, i.e. the same concept can be expressed in different ways (e.g. "vaccine against HIV" and "HIV vaccine").

Our term extraction strategy is based on statistical evidence and driven by linguistic data. Linguistic analysis is based on identifying phrase delimiters and on very shallow parsing. As already stated, expensive resources like general dictionaries or full-fledged parsers, as used by [10] or [11], will not be part of our strategy in order to ensure feasibility and portability.

We will not start building new term sets from scratch, but from previously existing resources. Reusing previous efforts and ensuring coverage of most common terms are two reasons for doing so. Other researchers, like [12, 13], stress the fact that starting with a reference set improves the results of automatic term detection strategies. Since we start with a set of initial terms, the study of term variation becomes a key component [14].

3.1 Variant and New Terms

Term variation negatively affects the performance of information management systems that are unable to identify as synonyms terms that differ in their morpho-syntactic realisation (e.g. "polio vaccine" and "vaccine against polio"). The ability to detect variant and new terms will have two main benefits:

- To increase the quality of the initial term sets (which is particularly necessary when these sets do not have a wide coverage of the domain), and
- To facilitate the task of keeping the whole system (text databases and semantic networks) synchronised and updated as new documents are added.

Variant terms are terms that express the same concept as the term they derive from. They include the following types of changes or variations:

1. Morphological variations, identifying the root and its forms, like in: "X-ray therapy" and "X-ray therapies"
2. Syntactic variations in the construction of terms, like in: "HIV vaccine" and "vaccine against HIV"
3. Formal variations, like abbreviations or acronyms, like in: "PAHO" and "Pan-American Health Organization"

New terms are terms that express a different concept than the one expressed by the term they derive from. Different strategies and linguistic knowledge are employed:

1. Using known terms as a source, like extracting "common bile duct obstruction", based on "common bile duct"
2. Using suffixes, like "-itis": "diverticulitis"
3. Analysing other linguistic phenomena like co-ordination, as in the derivation of: "stomach ulcer" and "duodenal ulcer" from "stomach and duodenal ulcer"

Variant and new term generation patterns have been expressed in derivation rules. These, together with bits of linguistic knowledge, are applied by TExtractor over an initial set of seed terms in order to produce the variant and new terms.

4. TEXTRACTOR

TExtractor is a Java-based console application that allows users to produce automatically a set of new terms that are valid indexing items for a given domain. In order to achieve this goal, the tool must be provided with:

1. *Linguistic knowledge*: elementary morphological rules (stemming) plus lists of function words for each of the languages tested.
2. *Initial term sets* containing known terms for the domain and language of choice[1].
3. *Derivation rules*. Applied over known terms, they produce candidate new terms. Because of the approach followed, derivation rules are highly re-usable among languages. French and Spanish rules are almost identical, the same happens with the English and German rule sets.
4. *Validating document base* containing documents for the domain and language of choice.

All these resources are provided to TExtractor as plain text files. The results are generated also as plain text files but in order to ease their inspection, they are imported into a database (MS-Access) in which pre-defined forms and queries help users to inspect the generated terms and trace how input data has been used to produce them.

4.1 Generation and Validation

TExtractor works in two phases: generation and validation. As shown in Figure 2, the generation phase depends on two resources: an initial term set and a set of derivation rules that, applied over them, generates new terms. The initial term set is built by reusing existing glossaries; they are used as seeds or examples in order to enrich the initial term set.

The heuristic nature of the morphological derivations, the limited scope of the syntactic information (reduced to the knowledge of function words) and the absence of any semantic or contextual information, provokes over-generation. This is by no means an unexpected result, and in fact the whole approach can be viewed as an instance of the generate-and-test paradigm. Although produced according to linguistically motivated rules, many of the

[1] In the medical domain, MeSH (Medical Subject Index), SNOMED (Systematized Nomenclature of Medicine) and ICD (International Classification of Diseases) are very valuable terminological resources.

newly generated terms are not good indexing terms and should be discarded afterwards during the validation process.

Every generated term is validated against a document base that contains a substantial amount of domain-related documents. As a first validation criterion, a term is considered valid if it occurs in at least one of the documents of the base. This initial criterion can be modulated afterwards considering the frequency of appearance of the new term in the collection and/or usability constraints. For our current purposes, the criterion provides us with a reliable indication of the potential usefulness of the new term.

In order to implement the validation process, we have employed Lucene, an open source tool that provides extensive search and

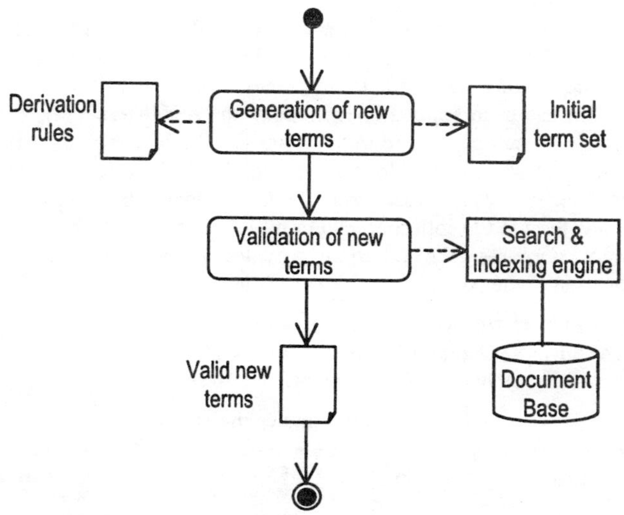

Figure 2. UML activity diagram of the term extraction and validation process

indexing capabilities over text files. Lucene [15] offers a well-documented interface for accessing its capabilities and we have coupled TExtractor to Lucene for checking the presence of candidate terms in our document base. Figure 3 shows the dependencies between these components:

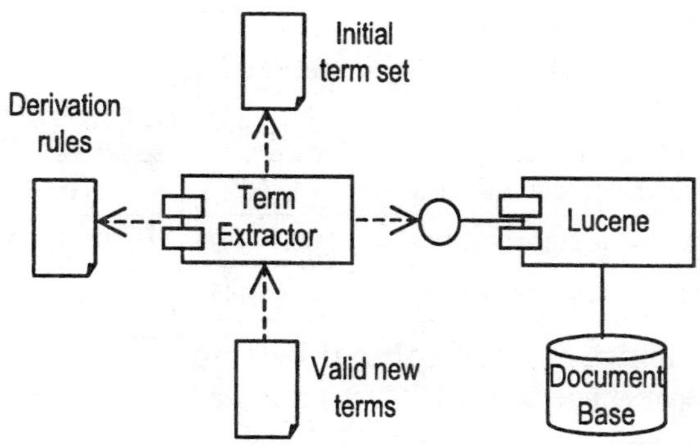

Figure 3. UML diagram of the components involved in the extraction and validation process

4.2 Derivation Rules

Rules for deriving new indexing terms conform to the classical conditional structure:

IF Antecedent Conditions THEN Consequent Actions

Antecedent conditions are checked on a singular term (a member of the set of initial terms) and, if fulfilled, applying the sequence of consequent actions over it produces a newly generated term. Both conditions and actions apply over the individual tokens that compose a typical multi-word term.

4.2.1 Rule syntax

Derivation rules consist of three clearly differentiated parts:

1. *Rule identifier.* Typically a brief phrase describing the derivation pattern implemented in the rule. It is used for tracking which rule has been applied for deriving a particular term. The rule identifier is separated from the rule proper by a colon sign.
2. *Antecedent.* A sequence of blank-separated token identifiers. Each token identifier is represented by the characters "tr" plus an ordering number that identifies each of the tokens that appear in a single rule. Bounded and unbounded repetition operators (+, *, ?) can be added to token identifiers, thus allowing the codification of highly flexible input term patterns. The antecedent ends with the greater than (">") symbol, that separates it from the consequent.
3. *Consequent.* A sequence of blank-separated token identifiers (a subset of the tokens mentioned in the antecedent) and/or actions over those tokens.

4.2.2 Antecedent conditions

The kind of conditions that can be imposed over any individual token fall under one of the following categories:

1. Typographical, such as the presence of a hyphen or an initial capital in the token.
2. Morphological, such as the property of number for nouns.
3. Syntactic, such as the part-of-speech of function words.

Morphological properties are determined by means of simple suffix checking and applying highly productive heuristics. Because of their simplicity and quick development, these mechanisms are cost-effective and scalable to most European languages. Although cases of over-generation do occur, they are discarded in the subsequent validation phase. This approach could also be described as a form of stemming [16].

As an example of the kind of morphological processing done in TExtractor, what follows is an excerpt of the singular-plural Spanish morphology:

```
#Singular; Plural for Spanish
DEFINITION_BEGIN
#casa;casas
a;as
#tahalí;tahalíes
í;íes
#verdad;verdades
d;des
#vez;veces
z;ces
#análisis;análisis
sis;sis
```

The second example is taken from the set of English suffixes employed for deriving medical terminology:

```
#Suffixed; Resuffixed for English
# anaesthesia ; anaesthetic
esia ; etic
etic ; esia
# cardiography ; cardiogram
graphy ; gram
gram ; graphy
# microscope ; microscopy
scope ; scopy
scopy ; scope
...
```

Regarding part-of-speech determination, and following the general approach towards cost-effectiveness and scalability, only function words (closed categories) are considered. Conditions imposing the membership to an open POS category are automatically granted, as in the following rule that derives a new term if the initial one is a singular noun:

```
plural: tr1[Noun, Singular] > MakePlural(tr1)
lobotomy > lobotomies
```

Given that TExtractor does not have in its current state any means for tagging "lobotomy" as a noun, the rule fires anyway and the plural form is derived. POS tagging of open categories has been included in the rules mainly to improve their readability, since no wide coverage mechanism for POS determination has been incorporated. On the other hand, words belonging to closed categories have been compiled in lists and are available for checking tokens in rules:

```
conjunction_right_part:
tr1+ tr2[Class:ConjunctionCopulative] tr3+ > tr3
Head and neck neoplasms > neck neoplasms
```

4.2.3 Consequent actions

Consequent actions apply over individual tokens identified in the antecedent, as in the previous example where the action "MakePlural" is applied over token number one.

Consequent actions may affect to several tokens of the term, such as when:

1. Re-ordering the token sequence.
2. Joining two tokens in a single one.

Or may affect to an individual token, such as when:

3. Removing/inserting a certain token.
4. Modifying the typographical, morphological and/or syntactic properties of a certain token.

4.3 Experimental Results

As an initial test of TExtractor, we have taken the ELCANO document base, a publicly available collection of clinical cases in the domain of gastroenterology (http://www.imim.es/elcano). This base includes medical articles belonging to that domain and written in English and Spanish[2]. Each article is provided with several indexing terms (keywords) also in English and Spanish. We have written 67 derivation rules for English and the same number of rules for Spanish. Most of the rules are identical for both languages and the differences when exist are mostly due to syntactic differences between both languages in the structure of noun phrases.

Table 1. Initial resources employed

Language	# documents	# initial terms	# rules
English	563	1222	67
Spanish	563	1226	67

Newly generated terms have been automatically validated against the ELCANO document base, thus considering valid new terms to those new terms that occur in at least one document. The same criterion has been applied for validating the initial term sets, so producing a subset of valid initial terms (i.e. those keywords that do occur in at least one document). This initial criterion can be modulated afterwards considering the frequency of appearance of the new term in the collection and/or usability constraints. For our current purposes, the criterion provides us with a reliable indication of the potential usefulness of the new term.

Our main performance metric is the ratio between valid new terms and valid initial terms. It gives us a quantitative measure of how successfully we have enriched the initial term set.

Table 2. Performance metric

Language	# valid initial terms	# valid new terms	enrichment ratio
English	874	525	60%
Spanish	888	800	90%

In order to verify the quality of the automatic validation process, the set of valid new terms has been manually checked. New terms in both languages have been reviewed, looking for *spurious terms* (syntactically ill-formed terms, such as *"infection in surgical"*) and *irrelevant terms* (generic non-medical terms such as *"History" or "expert"*).

Table 3. Quality inspection results

	English	Spanish
Number of spurious terms	13 (3%)	8 (0,94%)
Number of irrelevant terms	8 (1,14%)	27 (3,19%)
Spurious plus irrelevant terms	21 (4,14%)	35 (4,13%)

4.4 TExtractor Graphical Interface

The graphical interface of TExtractor responds to the necessity of easily demonstrating its capabilities and also to allow users unfamiliar with the intricacies of the application to run it and inspect its results.

[2] Work on French and German is ongoing: while results are still preliminary, enrichment percentages are encouraging. We are in the process of incorporating the most prestigious multilingual terminological resource for our domain: *The International Wordbook of Gastroenterology*, Pounder, R. & M. Hudson, Radcliffe Medical Press, 1994.

Given that TExtractor is a Java-based console application that takes as input many text files and produces as output several others, its use requires a certain degree of familiarity with its operation parameters and specially with the location and name of all its input and output files. The graphical interface attempts to hide all those details from its demonstrator or its occasional user, allowing them to focus on the design and performance of the tool instead of on the minute details of its operation.

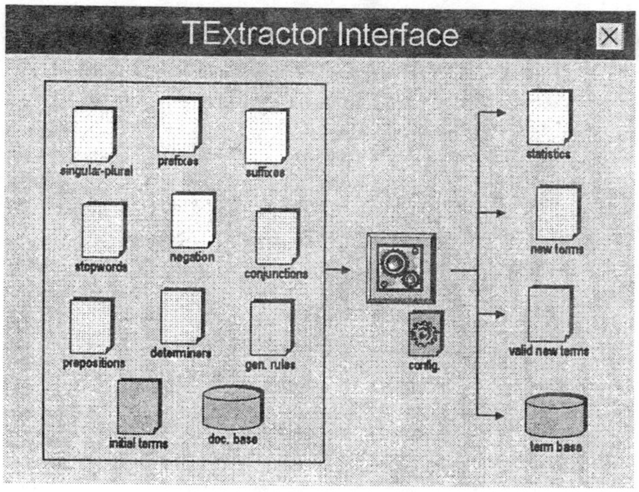

Figure 4. Screenshot of the TExtractor graphical interface

Input and output text files are represented as document icons. Each icon can be activated by clicking onto it. When activated, a text editor is invoked and the represented text file loaded in it. The user may then view, edit and save the file contents.

The TExtractor application is represented as a central button. Pressing it opens a system console were the Java application runs. When the application ends the console is also closed and the user may then inspect the output files. The document and term bases can also be accessed in the same way as text files, except that instead of a text editor, MS Access is used to view them.

Variants_Intersection_Valid : Consulta de selección

Generated Term	Rule Name	Initial Term
Tumor markers	choose_adj_in_coord	Colorectal cancer Tumor markers
carcinoma	isolate_noun_after_adj	Colorectal carcinoma
stenosis	isolate_noun_after_adj	Colorectal stenosis
surgery	isolate_noun_after_adj	Colorectal surgery
clamshell	isolate_noun_1st_mod_in_PP	Complications of the clamshell
clamshell	isolate_PP	Complications of the clamshell
Complications	isolate_noun_before_prep	Complications of the clamshell
biomaterials	isolate_noun_after_adj	Composite biomaterials
tomography	isolate_noun_after_adj	Computed tomography
system	isolate_noun_after_adj	Computer-based clinical decision supp
support system	choose_adj_in_coord	Computer-based clinical decision supp
support system	choose_adj_in_coord	Computer-based, clinical decision supp
system	isolate_noun_after_adj	Computer-based, clinical decision supp
hernia	isolate_noun_after_adj	Congenital diaphragmatic hernia
diaphragmatic hernia	choose_adj_in_coord	Congenital diaphragmatic hernia
surgery	isolate_noun_after_adj	Conservative surgery
treatment	isolate_noun_after_adj	Conservative treatment
Conversions	pluralize_noun	Conversion
fistulectomy	isolate_noun_after_adj	Core fistulectomy
vasculopathy	isolate_noun_after_adj	Coronary vasculopathy
Costs	pluralize_noun	Cost
pancreatitis Cost	reverse_PP	Cost of pancreatitis
pancreatitis	isolate_noun_1st_mod_in_PP	Cost of pancreatitis
pancreatitis	isolate_PP	Cost of pancreatitis
Cost	isolate_noun_before_prep	Cost of pancreatitis
disease	isolate_noun_after_adj	Crohn's disease

Figure 5. Excerpt from a list of new valid terms along with the rule names and initial terms that generated them.

5. CONCLUSIONS AND FURTHER WORK

We have presented TExtractor, a solution to the problem of cross-lingual access to multilingual document bases in specific domains. The solution involves a language independent domain ontology and a terminology extraction tool that provides to the ontology linguistic realisations of domain concepts in four languages: English, French, German and Spanish.

In this paper we have focussed on the terminology extraction tool, Textractor. We have shown that it is possible to enrich substantially an initial set of indexing terms applying a generate-and-test framework. Our approach to term extraction can be characterised by:

- Very low dependency on linguistic resources.
- Small set of linguistically motivated derivation rules.
- Incorporation of publicly available software tools.
- Exhaustive validation of the newly generated terms against a domain document base.

This approach has been tested in the domain of gastroenterology with a collection of documents and an initial set of indexing terms, both in English and Spanish. In further work, we will pay attention to issues such as:

- Re-use of derivation rules. Attempting to capture language independent derivation phenomena.
- Incorporation of publicly available, wide coverage linguistic resources that will enhance the derivation capabilities while maintaining the overall cost-effectiveness and scalability.
- Incorporation of publicly available terminological resources in the medical domain and for the languages considered in the project.

6. REFERENCES

[1] Lewis, D. and Croft, W. "Term clustering of syntactic phrases". In ACM SIGIR-90, 385-404. 1990.

[2] Gonzalo, J., F. Verdejo and I. Chugur. "Using EuroWordNet in a Concept-Based Approach to Cross-Language Text Retrieval". Applied Artificial Intelligence Special Issue on Multilinguality in the Software Industry: the AI contribution. 1999.

[3] L. Ballesteros and W.B. Croft. "Phrasal Translation and Query Expansion Techniques for Cross-Language Information Retrieval", in Proceedings of ACM SIGIR Conference, 20: 84-91. 1997.

[4] Jacquemin, C., Bourigault, D. "Term Extraction and Automatic Indexing". In R. Mitkov, editor, Handbook of Computational Linguistics. Oxford University Press, Oxford. 2000.

[5] Hull, D., and Grefenstette G. "Experiments in Multilingual Information Retrieval". Proceedings of ACM, SIGIR'96. Zurich. 1996.

[6] L. Ballesteros and W.B. Croft. "Phrasal Translation and Query Expansion Techniques for Cross-Language

Information Retrieval", in Proceedings of ACM SIGIR Conference, 20: 84-91. 1997.

[7] Sheridan, P. and Ballerini, J. P.. "Experiments in multilingual information retrieval using the spider system". In Proceedings of ACM/SIGIR. 1996.

[8] Evans, D., and Chengxiang Zhai. "Noun-Phrase Analysis in Unrestricted Text for Information Retrieval". Proceedings, 34th Annual Meeting of the Association for Computational Linguistics, 17-24. 1996.

[9] Bourigault D.. "An endogenous corpus-based method for structural noun phrase disambiguation". In Proceedings of the 6th Conference of the European Chapter of the Association for Computational Linguistics (EACL'93). Utrecht, The Neederlands. 1993.

[10] Arppe, Antti. "Term Extraction from Unrestricted Text". Paper presented at NODALIDA-95, Helsinki (Available at http://www.lingsoft.fi/doc/nptool/term-extraction.html - 20-12-00). 1995.

[11] Justeson, J. and Katz, S. (1995) "Technical Terminology: Some Linguistic Properties and an Algorithm for Identification in Text", in Natural Language Engineering, Vol. 1, No 1: 9-27

[12] Jacquemin, C., Klavans, J., Tzoukermann, E. "Expansion of multi-word terms for indexing and retrieval using morphology and syntax". Proceedings, 35th Annual Meeting of the Association for Computational Linguistics and 8th Conference of the European Chapter of the Association for Computational Linguistics (ACL-EACL 97), 24-31. Madrid. 1997.

[13] Jacquemin, C., and Tzoukermann, E. "NLP for Term Variation Extraction: a Synergy of Morphology, Lexicon and Syntax". In T. Strzalkowsky, editor, Natural Language Information Retrieval, 25-74. Kluwer. Boston, MA. 1999.

[14] Daille, B., Habert, B., Jacquemin, C., and Royauté, J.. Empirical observation of term variations and principles for their description. Terminology, 3(2), 197-258. 2000.

[15] Goetz, Brian. "The Lucene search engine", Java World. The official Lucene web site is located at: http://jakarta.apache.org/lucene. 2000.

[16] M.F.Porter. "An algorithm for suffix stripping", Program, 14(3):130--137. 1980.

AnswerBus Question Answering System

Zhiping Zheng

School of Information
University of Michigan
Ann Arbor, MI 48109
zzheng@umich.edu

ABSTRACT

AnswerBus[1] is an open-domain question answering system based on sentence level Web information retrieval. It accepts users' natural-language questions in English, German, French, Spanish, Italian and Portuguese and provides answers in English. Five search engines and directories are used to retrieve Web pages that are relevant to user questions. From the Web pages, AnswerBus extracts sentences that are determined to contain answers. Its current rate of correct answers to TREC-8's 200 questions is 70.5% with the average response time to the questions being seven seconds. The performance of AnswerBus in terms of accuracy and response time is better than other similar systems.

Keywords

open-domain question answering,, QA specific dictionary, information retrieval

1. INTRODUCTION

Automated question answering (QA) research can be dated back to the 1960s, nevertheless has often been confined to domain-specific expert systems ([12], [9]). Researchers have experimented with QA systems based on closed, pre-tagged corpora (e.g., [8], [13], [3]), or knowledge bases (e.g. [11], [5], [4]). Many of these systems focus on Text REtrieval Conference (TREC) tasks. Researchers also have attempted to build QA systems on large collections of documents on the Web by combining information extraction and most advanced information retrieval technology (e.g., [7], [12], [1]). Recently, researchers have been attracted to the task of developing open-domain QA systems based on collections of real world documents, especially the World Wide Web. Examples of such systems include LCC[2]([7]), QuASM[3], IONAUT[4]([1]), START[5]([11]) and Webclopedia[6]([10]). At the current stage, these systems seem to typically have long response times and/or accuracy rates that may not be acceptable to users.

AnswerBus is an open-domain question answering system based on sentence level information retrieval. It accepts users' natural-language questions in English, German, French, Spanish, Italian and Portuguese and extracts possible answers from the Web. It can respond to users' questions within several seconds. Five search engines and directories (Google, Yahoo, WiseNut, AltaVista, and Yahoo News) are used to retrieve Web pages that potentially contain answers. From the Web pages, AnswerBus extracts sentences that are determined to contain answers. The current rate of correct answers to TREC-8's 200 questions is 70.5%. AnswerBus demonstrates that practical question answering on the Web is highly feasible.

Figure 1 describes the working process of AnswerBus. AnswerBus takes a user question in natural language. A simple language recognition module will determine

Proceedings of HLT 2002, Second International Conference on Human Language Technology Research, M. Marcus, ed., Morgan Kaufmann, San Francisco, 2002.

[1] http://www.answerbus.com/

[2] http://www2.languagecomputer.com/qa/head.html

[3] http://ciir.cs.umass.edu/~reu2/

[4] http://www.ionaut.com:8400/

[5] http://www.ai.mit.edu/projects/infolab/

[6] http://www.isi.edu/natural-language/projects/webclopedia/research.html#QUESTION

whether the question is in English, or any of the other five languages. If the question language is not English, AnswerBus will send the original question and language information about the question to AltaVista's translation tool BabelFish[7], and obtain the question that has been translated into English.

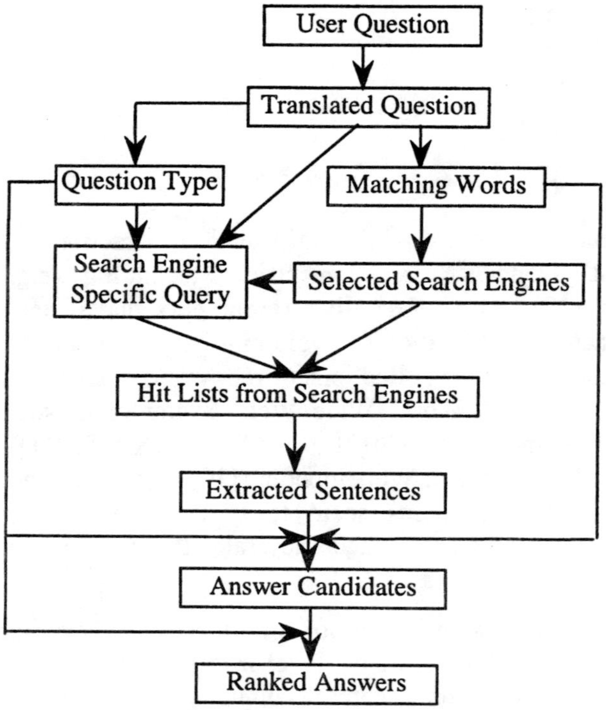

Figure 1 Working process of AnswerBus

The rest of the process is comprised of mainly four steps: 1) select two or three search engines among five for information retrieval and form search engine specific queries based on the question; 2) contact the search engines and retrieve documents referred at the top of the hit lists; 3) extract sentences that potentially contain answers from the documents; 4) rank the answers and return the top choices with contextual URL links to the user. Instead of returning a snippet of fixed length of text, AnswerBus returns sentences, which can provide users with some contextual information for the answers.

2. RELEVANT DOCUMENTS RETRIEVAL

AnswerBus aims to retrieve enough relevant documents from search engines within a response time that is acceptable to users. The main tasks in this stage are to select one or more appropriate search engines for a specific user question, and then form queries that are tailored to the question as well as the selected search engines. The formation of the queries is an essential procedure because it can largely influence the recall and accuracy of question answering and the speed of the system operation.

[7] http://babel.altavista.com/

2.1 Search engine selection

Different search engines or directories may suit different types of questions. For example, for questions about current events, Yahoo News may be a better choice than Google. Thus, for a specific question, AnswerBus chooses to use two to three most appropriate search engines among the five ones.

In order to determine which search engines are best suited for a specific question, AnswerBus pre-answered 2000 sample questions, including TREC 8 and TREC 9 questions, and also questions typed in by testing users. It sent the queries based on these questions to all of the five search engines. For each question, it recorded the number of possible answers that came from the different search engines. All the words used in queries are indexed. For example, for Word 1, Google may return 8 answers, AltaVista returns 4 answers, and Yahoo returns 7 answers; for Word 2, Google 6 answers, AltaVista 6 answers and Yahoo 5 answers. For a query with Word 1 and Word 2, AnswerBus will choose to use Google (8+6) and Yahoo (7+5). If a query contains words not included in the indexed list, AnswerBus uses the search engines' average returns for all the indexed words to determine which search engines are most appropriate.

2.2 Search engine specific query formation

Most search engines are not designed for natural language questions. [2] shows that QA systems using good queries will significantly outperform the underlying web search engines and a commercial search engine specializing in question answering. [6] argues that using extra information to direct the search process provides more valuable results than by considering only the query.

Search engine specific query here refers to the query formed from a user's natural- language question that tailed to particular search engines, and will generate optimal search outcomes. "Optimal" does not necessarily mean recall of the largest number of relevant documents. Instead, it means the best outcomes in terms of both recall of documents and time to retrieve the documents for a QA system. For example, a user wants to find out "How tall is Mount

Everest." If a full question is sent to a commercial search engine like Google, normally the user will be able to harvest the documents that contain the answer. Nevertheless, more web pages in the returned hit list will be irrelevant to the question, thus leads to lower precision. It certainly takes a much longer time to retrieve and process the documents. Thus it is necessary to form a *search engine specific query*, in this case, "Mount Everest", that will best fit the search engine and yield optimal search results.

However, the task of forming the search engine specific query is not always as simple as this example, given that each question has its unique structure and content while different search engines have different rules about the queries they accept.

Some approaches expand one query to several queries, for example, by adding synonyms, then either concatenate these queries together with operator "OR" or keep them as separate queries. These approaches can increase the possibility of getting the correct answers, however, may also make the search more complicated and significantly prolong the search response time, and overall may be detrimental to the QA outcomes.

The computing speed has been regarded as very important throughout the development of AnswerBus. For a scalable Web-based QA system, trade-offs need to be made between speed and recall of answers. Thus AnswerBus does not try to find the best query; instead, it tries to locate the good enough query that will conduct the search task very fast. The focus has been laid on generating one simple query instead of an expanded one.

Several approaches are combined to form queries, including functional words deletion, use of word frequency table, special words deletion, and word form modification.

Functional words deletion

Functional words include prepositions, determiners/ pronouns, conjunctions, interjections, and discourse particles. Functional words deletion, which often can make the query short enough, can be used as a baseline of search engine specific query formation.

Some words are not functional words but are acting as functional words either logically or structurally for example, "kind of," "name the designer of" can also be deleted from the query:

For long questions, the query made by this step is still too long. For example, after deleting all the functional words in question "*What is the name of the rare neurological disease with symptoms such as: involuntary movements (tics), swearing, and incoherent vocalizations (grunts, shouts, etc.)?*", we get "*name rare neurological disease symptoms involuntary movements tics swearing incoherent vocalizations grunts shouts*". The length of this query is 13 words and is not good enough to be a query for QA tasks.

Use of word frequency table

Another way to make a query shorter is to delete frequently used words in the query. The basic idea is that the more frequently a word is used in a language, the less discriminating the word is. Thus AnswerBus implements a word frequency table. For a long query, AnswerBus sorts all the words in the query and deletes one or more words that are identified as frequently used by the frequency table.

Word form modification

Some words in the original question are converted to another form then put in the query. Usually they are verbs, for example,

> *end* → *ended* in question "When did the Jurassic Period end?"
>
> *have* → *has* in question "How many hearts does an octopus have?"

3. CANDIDATE ANSWER EXTRACTION

At this stage, AnswerBus downloads and processes the documents referred at the top of search results returned by different search engines. It first parses the documents into sentences and then determines whether a sentence is an answer candidate through a process of word matching.

The sentence segmentation tool used in AnswerBus is designed to process complicated Web documents. In addition to deleting HTML tags, it excludes non-contextual content; regards some special HTML tags as sentence boundary indications; and takes different formatting exceptions into consideration.

In order to determine whether a retrieved sentence is potentially an answer to the question, AnswerBus classifies all words in the original question or sentences in retrieved documents into two categories: matching words and non-matching words. All words that are used to form the search engine specific query are matching words. The rest are non-matching words.

The following formula is used to filter retrieved sentences.

$$q \geq \left\lfloor \sqrt{Q-1} \right\rfloor + 1$$

In this formula, q is the number of matching words in the sentence; Q is the total number of matching words in the query. For example, if a query contains three words, then an answer candidate sentence should have at least two of them. When a sentence meets the condition as indicated by the above formula, it will receive a primary score based on the number of matching words it contains. Otherwise, it will receive a score of "0."

4. ANSWER RANKING

After the extraction of answer candidate sentences, each sentence has received a primary score. Those sentences with a score of "0" are dropped. Nevertheless, the primary scores are not robust enough for the judgment whether a sentence is a real answer. AnswerBus uses several techniques to refine the primary scores, including the determination of question type, use of a QA specific dictionary, named entities extraction, coreference resolution. The final score that is used to determine the rank of an answer is a combination of the primary score and the influence of all the different factors.

4.1 Question type and QA specific dictionary

Almost all QA systems use question type to judge the answer. They classify the question types on the basis of types of answers users are expecting. For example, a "*Who is ...?*" will be assigned a "PERSON/ORGANIZATION" type; while "*When did ... happen?*" will be classified as "DATE/TIME" question.

AnswerBus also uses question type as an important piece of information to judge whether a sentence can be an answer to a question. AnswerBus classifies questions into different question types together with some parameters. For example, AnswerBus classifies both of "*How far ...?*" and "*How close ...?*" questions as DISTANCE question, but it also differentiate these two types of questions: the unit of the answer to "*How far ...?*" most likely will be "mile," "kilometer," "light year" and other related bigger unit, it has small chance to be "inch," "centimeter" etc. For "*How close ...?*" question, the unit of the answer to this question could be any of above, depending on the context in the question, it even could be "nanometer" or others.

AnswerBus uses a QA specific dictionary, a database containing this kind of information about the relationship of words between questions and answers. For example, for the entry of word "far," the definition provided in the dictionary contains "miles," "kilometers," "light years;" for the word of "high," the definition contains "feet," "meters." The dictionary is used to distinguish question types, and determine whether a sentence is the right answer.

4.2 Dynamic basic named entities extraction

Named entities extraction has been widely used in closed QA systems to provide support for answer selection. It is achieved through pre-tagging of the corpus or knowledge base on which a QA system is based. According to [13], the speed of tagging is approximately 100M/hour. With the assumption that, for one question, a Web-based QA system needs to process 50 HTML documents of average length, with the total size of 1M bytes, the time needs to be extended for tagging these documents will be 36 seconds. For such a system, there are still other time cost such as network response, network transfer, and other textual processing. Thus, normal tagging techniques are not unfeasible for real-time QA systems.

AnswerBus conducts dynamic named entities extraction while processing sentences from Web documents. AnswerBus only extracts the named entities that match question types. For example, when a question is asking about "how much money", a sentence with the entity of "CURRENCY" will receive a higher rank.

4.3 Coreference resolution

Some sentences contain words, such as "he," "they," that coreference to other objects described in the document. They are not as good as a real noun phrase to be answers to the questions, but they can direct users to the contextual URL links that contain the full answers. Thus, AnswerBus gives lower but still valid scores to these sentences. Coreference resolution is also a heavy NLP task like named entities extraction. Instead of using full coreference resolution, AnswerBus only solves the coreferences in the adjacent sentences. When this type of coreference is detected, the later sentence receives part of score from its previous sentence.

4.4 Hit position and search engine confidence

The ranking score of a sentence can also be related to the position that its source document is located in the hit list returned by a search engine. A sentence extracted from the first hit receives the highest score associated with hit positions and the score decreases as the position moves down. Documents returned by different search engines may also receive different scores.

4.5 Redundancy

Different search engines can retrieve a same document for a question. Same or very similar sentences can be extracted from either a same document or different documents. This leads to candidate answer sentence redundancy.

To detect the sentence redundancy, AnswerBus compares so-far highly ranked sentences against one another. However, punctuations, spaces, other special characters, and the words with very high frequency are not considered in order to make comparisons among the sentences.

5. EVALUATION

TREC 8's 200 questions were used to evaluate AnswerBus's question answering performance and also compare its performance to that of four other similar systems. A computer program was written to send questions one by one to AnswerBus, START[11], LCC, IONAUT, and QuASM; and also retrieve the answers from the systems. After the answer to a question was received, a time interval of 10 seconds was provided before next question was sent to ensure that a system's performance would not be affected by its work on the previous one. The response times to each question by the systems and the lengths of the returned answers were recorded. In order to minimize the impact of network performance on the variations of the systems' response time, the answers from these systems were retrieved at the same time using a same computer.

Except for IONAUT, the top five answers to each question from the systems were then evaluated manually to determine the answers' accuracy. IONAUT returned long passages of information as the answers to the questions. The evaluation of the information was beyond the resources of this project. Thus, for the rest of the systems, the answers were first compared to answer keys provided by TREC. Since these systems are based on the Web, which is different from the large corpus of newswires on which the TREC questions are based, some answers that were different from answer keys were also judged as being correct. The answers were also carefully examined to ensure contextually correct answers are located.

Table 1 presents the performance of AnswerBus and other four systems. It provides the numbers of correct answers in the systems' top five and top one answers, the standard NIST scores, the maximal, minimal and average response times measured in seconds, standard deviation of response times, and the average lengths of returned answers.

Table 1 demonstrates that AnswerBus outperforms other similar systems, in terms of both accuracy and response time. AnswerBus also returned more concise answers than other systems.

Table 1 The Performance of Online Question Answering Systems

Systems	Correct TOP 5	Correct TOP 1	NIST Score	*Tmax (s)*	*Tmin (s)*	*Tmean (s)*	*Tstd dev*	*Lmean (byte)*
AnswerBus	141	120	64.18%	15.06	3.79	7.20	3.07	141
IONAUT				44.88	2.78	12.51	6.81	1312
LCC	97	75	41.73%	342.52	4.30	44.24	32.63	178
QuASM	13	7	4.45%	284.29	2.61	20.72	33.92	1766
START	29	29	14.50%	62.07	2.02	9.84	7.45	

Table 2 Performance of AnswerBus As Compared to Mulder

Systems	Correct Top 5 Answers	Correct Top 1 Answers	NIST Score
AnswerBus	70.5%	60%	64.2%
Muldera		34%	

Note: [a] Source [12].

No similar data for other two famous QA systems, Mulder and Webclopedia, were obtained because of their off-line status when the experiment was taken. According to [12], Mulder correctly answered 34% of TREC-8 questions. Table 2 gives some comparison between AnswerBus and Mulder.

References

[1] Steven Abney, Michael Collins, and Amit Singhal. Answer Extraction. *Proceedings of ANLP 2000.* Seattle, WA. April 29 - May 3, 2000.

[2] Eugene Agichtei, Steve Lawrence, Luis Gravano. Learning Search Engine Specific Query Transformations for Question Answering. *Tenth World Wide Web Conference.* May 1-5, 2001, Hong Kong, China.

[3] Eric Breck, John Burger, Lisa Ferro, David House, Marc Light, and Inderjeet Mani. A sys called Qanda. *Eighth Text REtrieval Conference (TREC-8).* Gaithersburg, MD. November 17-19, 1999.

[4] Jay Budzik and Kristian J. Hammond. Learning for Question Answering and Text Classification: Integrating Knowledge-Based and Statistical Techniques. *AAAI Workshop on Text Classification.* Menlo Park, CA, 1998

[5] Peter Clark, John Thompson, and Bruce Porter. A knowledge-based approach to question-answering. *AAAI'99 Fall Symposium on Question-Answering Systems.* Orlando, Florida. 1999.

[6] E. J. Glover, S. Lawrence, M. D. Gordon, W. P. Birmingham, and C. L. Giles, "Web Search -- Your Way," *Communications of the ACM*, To appear.

[7] Sanda Harabagiu, Dan Moldovan, Marius Paşca, Mihai Surdeanu, Rada Mihalcea, Roxana Girju, Vasile Rus, Finley Lacatusu, Paul Morarescu and Razvan Bunescu. Answering Complex, List and Context Questions with LCC's Question-Answering Server. *Tenth Text REtrieval Conference (TREC-10).* Gaithersburg, MD. November 13-16, 2001.

[8] Sanda Harabagiu, Marius Pasca, and Steven Maiorano. *Experiments with open-domain textual question answering. COLING-2000. Association for Computational Linguistics/Morgan Kaufmann*, Aug 2000.

[9] Lynette Hirschman and Robert Gaizauskas. Natural Language Question Answering: The View from Here. *Natural Language Engineering,* 2001.

[10] Eduard Hovy, Laurie Gerber, Ulf Hermjakob, Michael Junk and Chin-Yew Lin. Question Answering in Webclopedia. Ninth Text REtrieval Conference(TREC-9). Gaithersburg, MD. November 13-16, 2000.

[11] Boris Katz, From Sentence Processing to Information Access on the World Wide Web. *AAAI Spring Symposium on Natural Language Processing for the World Wide Web.* Stanford, California. 1997.

[12] Cody C. T. Kwok, Oren Etzioni and Daniel S. Weld. Scaling Question Answeringto the Web. *Tenth World Wide Web Conference.* Hong Kong, China. May 1-5, 2001.

[13] Rohini Srihari and Wei Li. Information Extraction Supported Question Answering. *Eighth Text REtrieval Conference (TREC-8).* Gaithersburg, MD. November 17-19, 1999.

PLENARY DEMONSTRATIONS

(in alphabetical order)

A Statistical Mixed-initiative Dialog System for 401k Management

Rajesh Balchandran, Linda Boyer, Mark Epstein, Robert Krewson, Margaret Marler, Howard Page

IBM, T.J. Watson Research Center
Route 134, Yorktown Heights, NY 10598, (914) 945 1326
rajeshb@us.ibm.com

Thomas Kazmierczak, Edward Kemp

T. Rowe Price
Owings Mills, MD

ABSTRACT
In this paper, we describe a statistical mixed-initiative dialog management system that was developed by IBM for T. Rowe Price. A live version of this system was demonstrated at the HLT 2002 conference.

Keywords
IBM, T. Rowe Price, NLU, natural language understanding, mixed-initiative, dialog system, 401k, statistical

1. INTRODUCTION
This demonstration will highlight an application of IBM's mixed-initiative, Natural Language Understanding (NLU) technology developed for T. Rowe Price. Participants in 401k plans serviced by T. Rowe Price can now manage their accounts by speaking naturally to an automated telephony system, powered by IBM's speech recognition and NLU technologies. Working with IBM, T. Rowe Price is the first company to test and deploy this technology for financial applications, making retirement account management quicker and easier.

2. DIALOG SYSTEMS
Dialog systems can be classified as:

- Limited vocabulary, directed dialog
- Natural language, directed dialog
- Natural language, mixed-initiative dialog

In a *limited vocabulary directed dialog system*, the system controls the dialog through structured menu choices and prompting for one item at a time. The caller must respond directly to the prompts without any variation. For example, if the system asks for a fund, it would only accept a fund name, and not allow variations like 'I want the growth fund'. It cannot accept additional information like 'Buy $500 of the growth fund', or requests outside the on-going transaction like, 'What funds are available?'.

A *natural language directed dialog system* is similar, except that it can handle a finite set of 'natural language' responses, typically from a pre-defined grammar.

The IBM-T. Rowe Price 401k application is a *natural language mixed-initiative dialog system.* It allows the caller to take control of the dialog if desired; otherwise, the dialog flows in a pre-defined manner. The system allows the caller to phrase requests in a natural way, providing as much or as little information as they want, just as they would with a human operator. If the user chooses, a transaction that would take several turns in a directed dialog system could be completed in just one turn.

Additionally, the system can respond to requests that are outside the on-going transaction and then continue with the original transaction. This is a very powerful feature, which humans employ often and quite naturally when communicating with a live operator.

IBM's natural language, mixed-initiative technology provides the user with a high degree of flexibility and freedom, satisfying both the novice and the power user as illustrated in Figure 1.

3. TECHNICAL OVERVIEW
Mixed-initiative NLU dialog processing consists of three tasks – recognizing *natural language* requests, interpreting them and managing the dialog flow.

The speech recognition component recognizes context-free natural language requests at every turn in the dialog, in addition to thousands of fund names, plan names etc. This is particularly challenging as the system cannot rely on context specific grammars as in a directed dialog system.

Natural language interpretation is based on a statistical model derived from collected training data. Unlike complex grammars, the statistical approach is more robust to variations in user input and speech recognition errors.

The dialog flow is controlled by a dedicated dialog manager that determines the next step in the dialog based on the current user response. The dialog is not bound by a pre-defined flow, but is tailored to satisfy user requests.

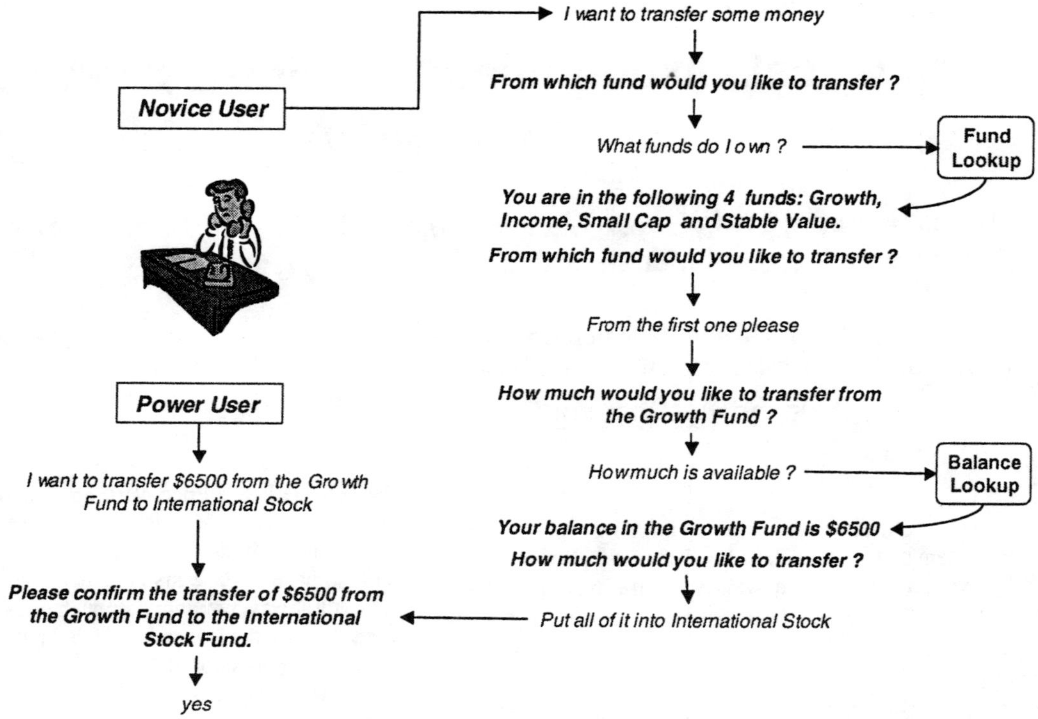

Figure 1: NLU Mixed-Initiative Sample Dialog

4. THE T. ROWE PRICE 401K SYSTEM

The system deployed at T. Rowe Price supports over a million participants across numerous 401k plans. The system currently supports:

- Signing on by speaking an SSN and PIN
- Information Requests
    - Fund/Account balance
    - Price/performance/objective of a fund
    - Current market update
- Transactions
    - Transfer money between funds
    - Set up/change future investment allocation
    - Change PIN
    - Request statements
- Transfer Requests
    - To a representative or other systems

OnTAP: Mixed-media Multi-lingual Language Processing

Sean Colbath, Scott Shepard, Daben Liu, Amit Srivastava, Jay Billa, James Gugerty, Daniel Kiecza, Mohammed Noamany, Dr. Kathleen Egan[1], Francis Kubala

BBN Technologies, Cambridge, MA 02138
scolbath@bbn.com

[1] Department of Defense

OnTAP (Online Text and Audio Processing) is a fully automatic language processing demonstration system for processing human-language data in mixed media and multiple languages. Created under the DARPA TIDES program, OnTAP acts as a technology test bed for the program. The core technologies that comprise OnTAP include: automatic speech recognition in multiple languages, speaker change detection, speaker clustering, speaker identification, named entity extraction, topic identification, story segmentation, fact extraction, event detection, and event tracking. OnTAP includes the Oasis Audio Indexing system for processing audio from radio and TV.

The goal of OnTAP is to provide a user with an advanced set of tools for manipulating human-language data. To that end, OnTAP has a web-based user interface that allows a user to query the document database, browse the enriched documents, play back audio or view the original source of a document, search extracted data, set up profiles (by giving example documents) that will track future documents entering the system, and look at visualizations of document clusters. Users can search the archive of documents retrospectively, looking back in time for important information, or can set up alerts and traps for desired names, keyword strings, and events.

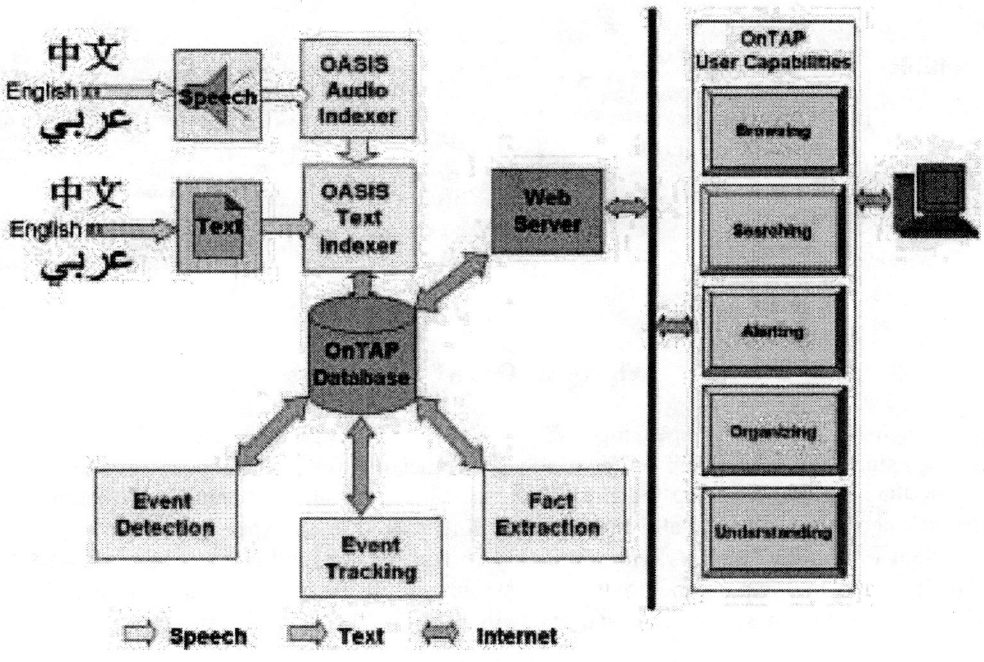

Figure 1: OnTAP Conceptual Architecture

OnTAP collects human language data in both audio and text form from a wide variety of sources in both English and Arabic. Data is collected in real-time, and is automatically processed to extract rich-content metadata. Documents are annotated with topic labels and named entity classes, and audio documents are further annotated with speaker names, speaker turns, and story boundaries. They are then distributed to a number of downstream human language technologies.

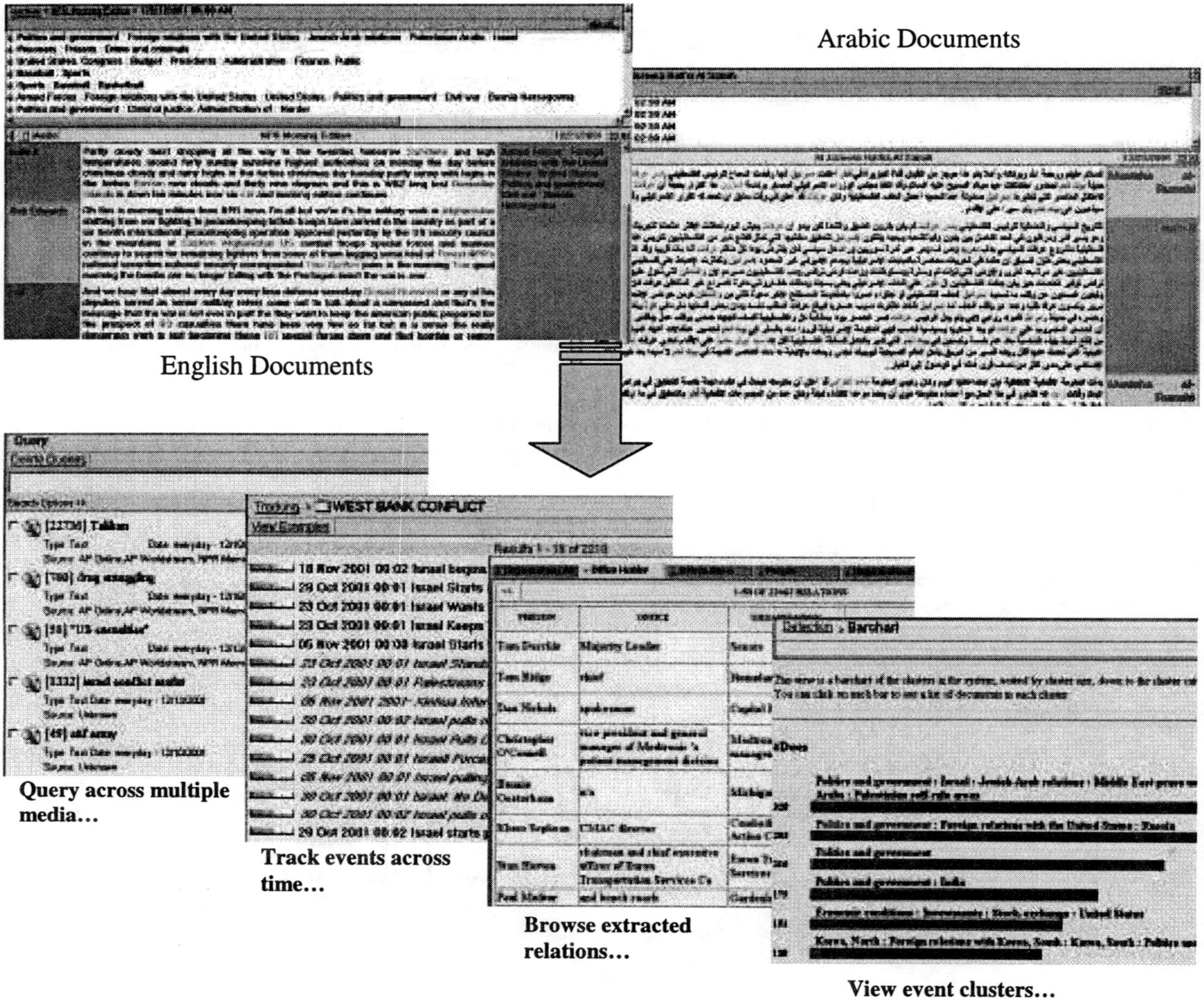

Figure 2: OnTAP Capabilities

Multiple English- and Arabic-speaking users are currently evaluating the OnTAP system. A live experiment using the system took place during December of 2001, with repeat experiments to occur in March and June of 2002. During the December experiment, the user community worked on a real-world problem, taking the role of an intelligence analyst. The goal of these experiments is to appraise the ability of the system to provide its users with the ability to search, sort, and classify large quantities of human language data, and to compare and contrast the system's abilities in English and Arabic. OnTAP will be expanded to include Chinese broadcast and newswire news in 2002.

The OnTAP demo will show the audience the basic capabilities of the OnTAP system, both in English and Arabic. It will show the variety of sources processed by the system across all available media and language, as well as the query function and its features, the process of setting up a tracking profile (in English and Arabic) using document sources from within OnTAP and elsewhere, the relations extracted from the document flow, and the visualization of the document clusters.

An Automatic Speech Translation System for Travel Conversation

Akitoshi Okumura, Ken-ichi Iso, Shin-ichi Doi, Kiyoshi Yamabana,
Ken Hanazawa, Takao Watanabe
Multimedia Research Laboratories, NEC
4-1-1 Miyazaki, Miyamae-ku, Kawasaki 216-8555, Japan
{okumura, iso, s-doi, yamabana, hanazawa, watanabe}@ccm.cl.nec.co.jp

ABSTRACT

We present a speech-to-speech translation system for notebook PC's that helps oral communication between Japanese and English speakers in the various situations in the travel abroad. Due to the high accuracy of the compact continuous speech recognition engine and our lexicalized grammar approach to machine translation that utilizes corpus but is oriented to model general linguistic phenomena as well as word-specific ones, a versatile speech-to-speech translation system for travel abroad is achieved, which is with much larger vocabulary (50,000 Japanese words and 10,000 English words) and capable of translating spoken conversations in more situations compared to previous work [1].

Keywords

automatic interpretation system, speech recognition, machine translation.

1. INTRODUCTION

We present a speech-to-speech translation system for notebook PC's that helps oral communication between Japanese and English speakers in the various situations in the travel abroad. Due to the high accuracy of the compact continuous speech recognition engine and our lexicalized grammar approach to machine translation that utilizes corpus but is oriented to model general linguistic phenomena as well as word-specific ones, a versatile speech-to-speech translation system for travel abroad is achieved, which is with much larger vocabulary (50,000 Japanese words and 10,000 English words) and capable of translating spoken conversations in more situations compared to previous work [1].

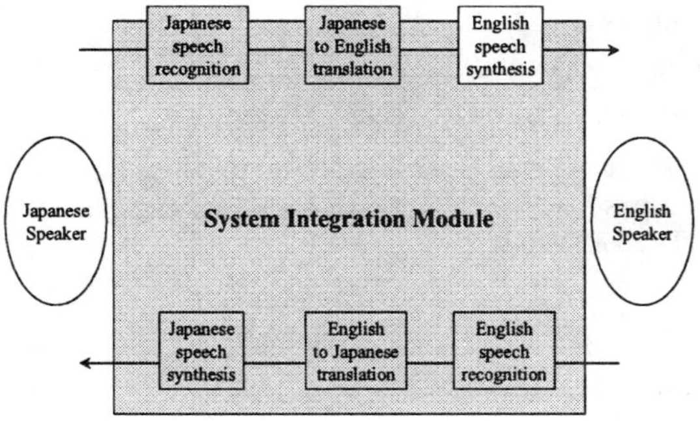

Figure 1. Configuration of the automatic interpretation system.

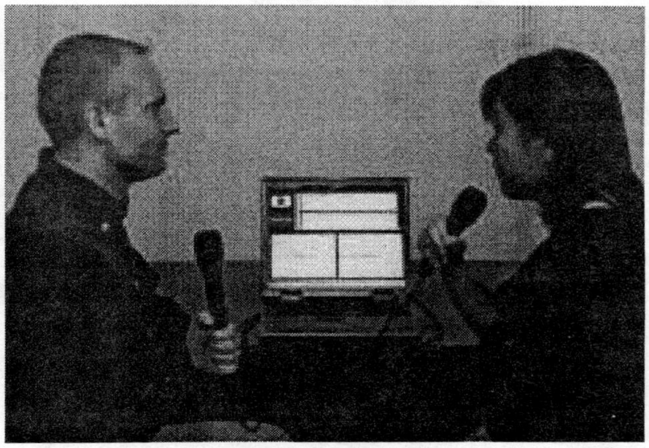

Figure 2. System demonstration.

2. SYSTEM OVERVIEW

The system consists of four modules: speech recognition, translation, speech synthesis and system integration as is shown in Figure 1. Users can have their speech simultaneously translated in real-time by a mobile PC from either Japanese or English to the other, as shown in Figure 2, 3.

To reduce misunderstanding in the conversation between users talking with each other through the system and to avoid the halt in the conversation, the system accepts input of any utterance unit other than a sentence, namely a fragment of a sentence, a phrase, or a word. For each utterance, translated result is obtained in real-time. System requirements for the software include a mobile PC with a Pentium II-class processor (400MHz) running either Windows 98/NT/2000/Me and 128MB of RAM.

3. MODULES

3.1 Speech Recognition

Speech recognition module performs speaker-independent large-vocabulary continuous speech recognition of conversational Japanese and English. The module consists of an acoustic model, a language model, a word dictionary and a search engine. For domain independent acoustic model, triphone HMM was adopted and trained with a large speech corpus. The language model was designed for travel conversation. It contains a bigram and a trigram. The search engine performs two-stage processing. On the first stage, Viterbi beam search is performed to decode input speech to generate a word candidate graph using the acoustic model and the bigram language model. On the second stage, the

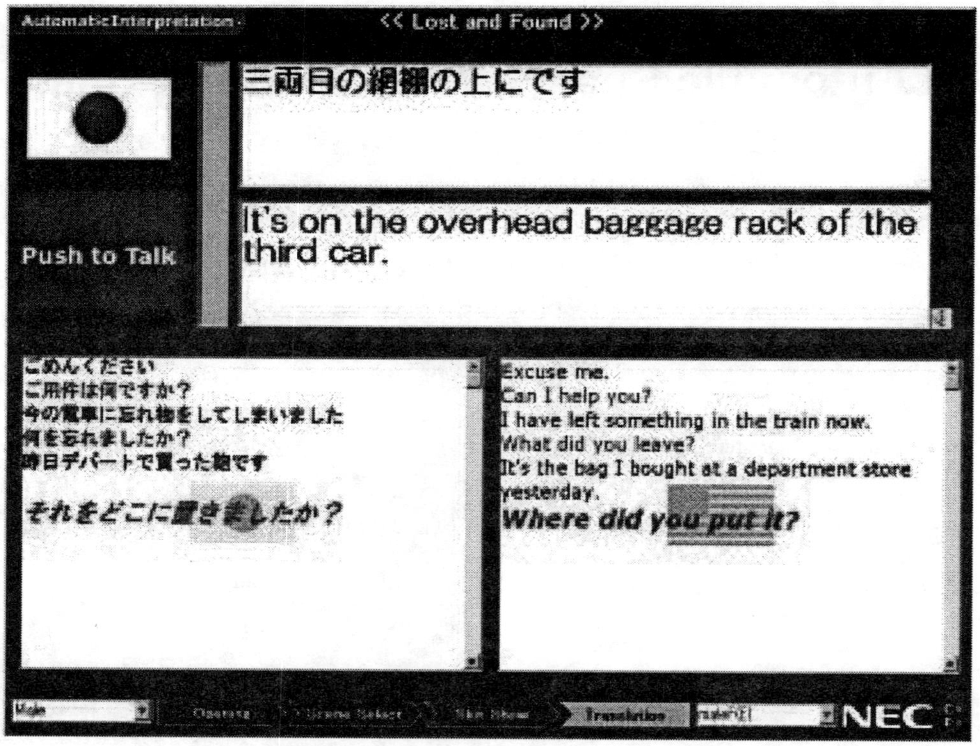

Figure 3. Example of a display

engine performs a search to find the optimal word sequence using the trigram language model. The recognition module also has a speaker adaptation capability. It is possible to adapt the acoustic models efficiently to the speaker just using as few as five utterances.

3.2 Translation

In translation of conversations, a translation module is required to cope with highly word-specific phenomena, including various colloquial and idiomatic expressions. Handling idiosyncratic word behavior is also important to improve the translation quality for the target domain. In addition, translation module is required to cover a wide range of input sentences.

To achieve both broad coverage for general input and high quality for the target domain, we employed a rule-based method that allows writing of both general abstract rules and example-like concrete patterns in a unified framework. Precisely we adopted the Lexicalized Tree AutoMata-based Grammar (LTAMG)[3]. This method is in line with strong-lexicalization approach to the grammar [2], where each grammar rule (tree) is associated with at least one word, making all the rules lexical. An advantage of the LTAMG to other strongly-lexicalized grammars is use of a simple bottom-up chart-parsing algorithm, which is a straightforward extension of the context-free grammar case.

4. EVALUATION

For the preliminary evaluation for relative short and clean sentences, a word accuracy of 85 - 96% for speech recognition and a sentence understanding rate of 83 - 87% for translation were obtained as a result. We expect that the performance will be further improved by expanding the grammar with regard to domain-specific or colloquial expressions, which were not yet described in the grammar and caused the incorrect translation. We will also evaluate the usability of the system as aids for cross lingual communication.

5. REFERENCES

[1] Watanabe, T et al., An experimental automatic interpretation system: INTERTALKER, Proc. of Acoustic Soc. of Japan, (Spring 1992), 101-102 (In Japanese).

[2] Schabes , Y. et al., Parsing Strategies with `Lexicalized' Grammars, COLING'88, (1988) 578-583.

[3] Yamabana, K. et al. Lexicalized Tree Automata-based Grammars for Translating Conversational Texts, COLING 2000, (2000) 926-932.

MEDSTRACT: Natural Language Tools for Mining the Biobibliome

James Pustejovsky
Computer Science Department
Brandeis University
Waltham, MA 02254
jamesp@cs.brandeis.edu

Brent Cochran
Department of Physiology
Tufts University
136 Harrison Ave., Boston MA
University School of Medicine
cochran@opal.tufts.edu

Jose Castaño
Computer Science Department
Brandeis University
Waltham, MA 02254
jcastano@cs.brandeis.edu

ABSTRACT

We have been developing robust natural language tools for the automated extraction of structured information from biomedical texts as part of a project we call MEDSTRACT. Here we will present demonstrations of two biological literature database servers, the *Bio-Relation Server* and the Bio-Acronym server, *Acromed*, both derived automatically from robust natural language processing of Medline text. Visualization tools for navigating the databases and exploring the results of a search are also demonstrated. The presentation consists of four distinct demos over these two databases, demonstrating the extraction results, presented in both tabular form and graphically, as well as a live illustration of how the text coherence and anaphora resolution module improves overall performance of the database results.

1. INTRODUCTION

The automatic extraction of information from Medline articles and abstracts (the biobibliome) promises to play an increasingly critical role in aiding research while speeding up the discovery process. We have been developing robust natural language tools for the automated extraction of structured information from biomedical texts as part of a project we call MEDSTRACT (www.medstract.org). Here we will present demonstrations of two biological literature database servers, the *Bio-Relation Server* and the Bio-Acronym server, *Acromed*, both derived automatically from robust natural language processing of Medline text. Visualization tools for navigating the databases and exploring the results of a search are also demonstrated. The presentation consists of four distinct demos over these two databases, demonstrating the extraction results, presented in both tabular form and graphically, as well as a live illustration of how the text coherence and anaphora resolution module improves overall performance of the database results. It is hoped that this set of applications will allow for organized rapid access to relevant information on individual genes by biologists over the web. One further goal is that the automatic analysis of biological abstracts will eventually be combined with information derived from sequence databases to provide an up-to-date and comprehensive biobibliome of information regarding individual known genes and proteins.

We will have 2-3 machines with large displays running programs from remote servers.

Proceedings of HLT 2002, Second International Conference on Human Language Technology Research, M. Marcus, ed., Morgan Kaufmann, San Francisco, 2002.

2. BIORELATION SERVER

We have populated a bio-relational database using a a robust parser for identifying and extracting biomolecular relations from the biomedical literature (Medline) (e.g., *A inhibits B*, *X regulates Y*). We have measured the system at a performance of 90% precision, 59% recall, and 22% partial recall, as reported in Pustejovsky et al. (2002). The Bio-Relation server provides the ability to search the Medstract relational database, which contains various regulatory and inhibitory relations of bio-entities (proteins, cellular processes, etc) extracted from six months of Medline data (250,000 abstracts). The user can select the type of relation to be searched (i.e.,*inhibit*, *regulate*, etc.) as well as the UMLS type (e.g. *gene*, *amino acid*) or name of the bio-entities which are the arguments of the relation. As a result of the search, all biological relations relevant to the specified bio-entities are returned in either the form of a database table or a navigable hyperbolic graph. Both forms link directly to the citations from the abstracts.

3. COHERENCE AND ANAPHORA RESOLUTION IN MEDLINE

Identifying the arguments of the relations may not be enough for identifying the actual entities involved in the relation. Often anaphors, both pronominal (e.g. *it*, *they*) and sortal (e.g. *the protein*, *both enzymes*) are the actual arguments to a relation, but are not specific enough to establish a unique reference to an entity or process. We found that the use of anaphors, especially sortal anaphors, is quite prevalent in Medline abstracts. For example, out of the 62 anaphors identified in a set of 35-40 Medline documents, approximately 60% are sortal anaphors. The Coherence and Anaphora Resolution Application (CARA) labels the biologically relevant anaphors within Medline abstracts and assigns each anaphor a pointer to the sentence which contains its antecedent, while binding it to the antecendent in that sentence. Importantly, CARA focuses on the resolution of sortal anaphors as well as pronominal anaphors. Antecedent matching for an anaphor of either type

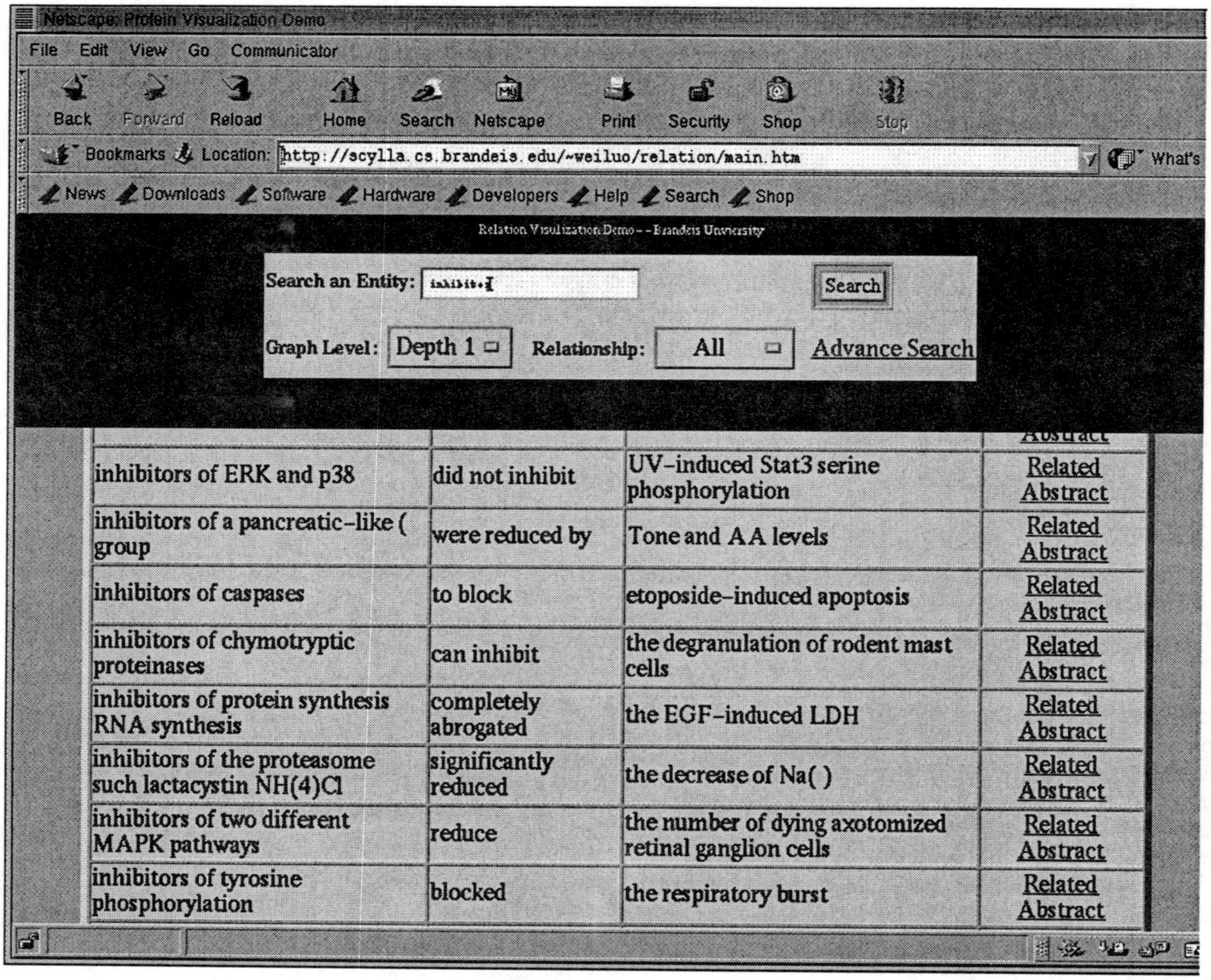

Figure 1: Relations table

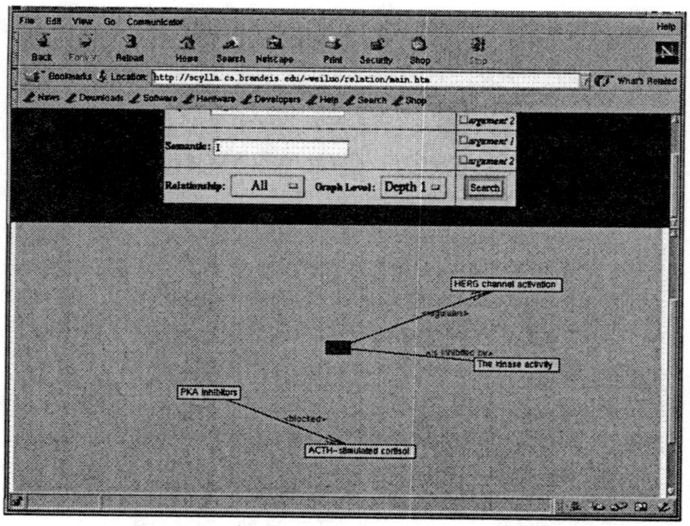

Figure 2: Relations graph

is determined by finding the NP that has the highest compatibility, which is determined by matching syntactic and semantic features of the candidate NP with that of the anaphor, along with measures of textual and thematic salience. By utilizing the anaphora resolution algorithm, the performance of the relational extraction module improve by 15-20% (cf. Zhang et al, (forthcoming)).

4. BIOACRONYM DEMO

The Bio-Acronym Server (*AcroMed*) will also be demonstrated. This system is an automatically generated searchable database of over 121,000 biomedical acronyms and their associated normalized long-forms extracted from one year of Medline abstracts (2001). The process of normalization groups equivalent long forms together, which form a single meaning sense. Those acronyms (*polynyms*) which have more than one non equivalent long form are displayed with the corresponding set of senses.

Each acronym-long form pair in the database is linked to the abstracts in which it was discovered, and the set of equivalent long forms corresponding to a single sense can be submitted directly to PubMed as searches by a single click as a query reformulation. Furthermore, Acromed also attempts to classify each acronym-long form pair by its semantic type, using an ontology comprised of both UMLS and Go taxonomic terms.

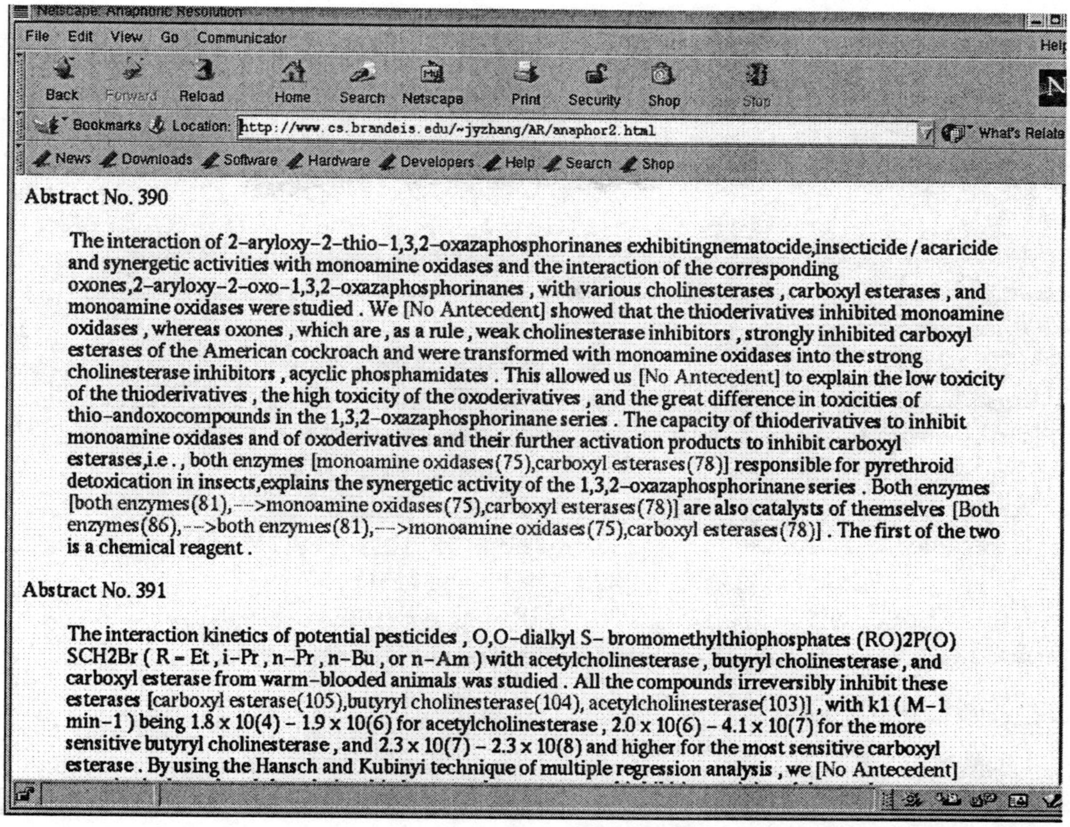

Figure 3: Anaphor resolution

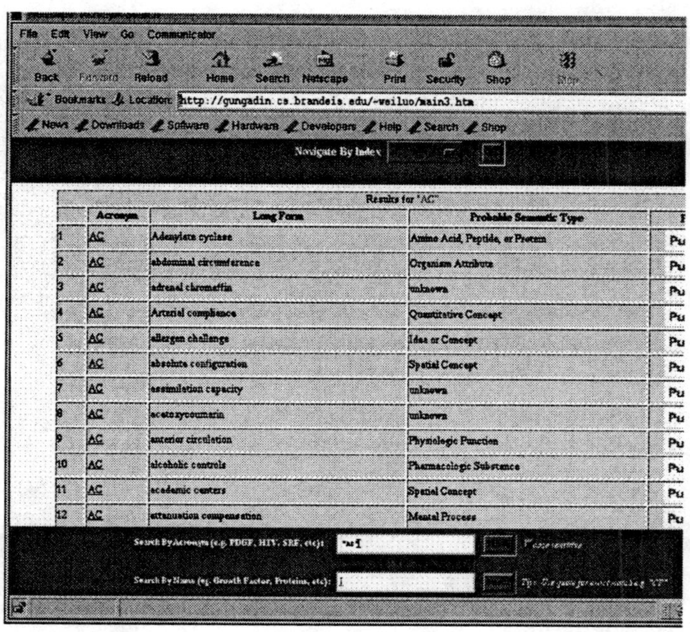

Figure 4: Acronym server

5. ADDITIONAL AUTHORS

Jason Zhang (email: `jyzhang@cs.brandeis.edu`)
Roser Saurí (email: `roser@cs.brandeis.edu`)
Michael Morrell (email: `mmorrell@argus.cs.brandeis.edu`)
Wei Luo (email: `weiluo@argus.cs.brandeis.edu`)

Computer Science Department
Brandeis University
Walthem, MA 02254

6. REFERENCES

Pustejovsky, J., J. Castaño, B. Cochran, M. Kotecki, M. Morrell, A. Rumshisky (2001) "Extraction and Disambiguation of Acronym-Meaning Pairs in Medline." An updated version of the paper presented at Medinfo 2001, London.

Pustejovsky, J., J. Castaño, J. Zhang, B. Cochran, M. Kotecki (2002) "Robust Relational Parsing over Biomedical Literature: Extracting Inhibit Relations." Pacific Symposium on Biocomputing, 2002.

Zhang, J., J. Castaño, and J. Pustejovsky (forthcoming), "Coherence and Anaphora Resolution in Biomedical Literature", submission to EMNLP 2002.

Author Index